Till The Trumpet Sounds Again – The Scots Guards 1914-19 in their own words

Volume 1: 'Great Shadows', August 1914 – July 1916

Randall Nicol

Helion & Company Limited

Helion & Company Limited
26 Willow Road
Solihull
West Midlands
B91 1UE
England
Tel. 0121 705 3393
Fax 0121 711 4075
Email: info@helion.co.uk
Website: www.helion.co.uk
Twitter: @helionbooks
Visit our blog http://blog.helion.co.uk/

Published by Helion & Company 2016
Designed and typeset by Mach 3 Solutions Ltd, Bussage, Gloucestershire
Cover designed by Paul Hewitt, Battlefield Design (www.battlefield-design.co.uk)
Printed by Gutenberg Press Limited, Tarxien, Malta

Text © Randall Nicol 2016
Images © as individually credited
Maps drawn by George Anderson © Helion & Company Ltd 2016

The right of Randall Nicol to be identified as the author of this work has been asserted by him in accordance with the Copyright Designs and Patents Act 1988.

Every reasonable effort has been made to trace copyright holders and to obtain their permission for the use of copyright material. The author and publisher apologise for any errors or omissions in this work, and would be grateful if notified of any corrections that should be incorporated in future reprints or editions of this book.

Front cover: Lieutenant Arthur Mervyn Jones with 3 Platoon Right Flank 1st Battalion in the tannery, Richebourg-St Vaast, May 1915 [Courtesy of the Regimental Trustees Scots Guards]. Rear cover: 2nd Battalion marching out of the Tower of London on 16 September 1914 [Courtesy of Lord de Saumarez].

ISBN 978-1-911096-06-1

British Library Cataloguing-in-Publication Data.
A catalogue record for this book is available from the British Library.

All rights reserved. No part of this publication may be reproduced, stored in a retrieval system, or transmitted, in any form, or by any means, electronic, mechanical, photocopying, recording or otherwise, without the express written consent of Helion & Company Limited.

For details of other military history titles published by Helion & Company Limited contact the above address, or visit our website: http://www.helion.co.uk.

We always welcome receiving book proposals from prospective authors.

Contents

List of Photographs		iv
List of Maps		ix
Foreword		x
Preface		xiii
Acknowledgements		xvii
1	The Regimental Background	19
2	The Retreat from Mons – 1st Battalion	36
3	The Battles of the Marne and the Aisne – 1st Battalion	62
4	The First Battle of Ypres – 2nd Battalion	91
5	The First Battle of Ypres – 1st Battalion	141
6	The Prisoners of War	183
7	The Rouges Bancs Trenches and the Winter 1914-1915 – 2nd Battalion	225
8	The La Bassée Canal and the Winter 1914-1915 – 1st Battalion	284
9	The Battles of Neuve Chapelle and Festubert and the Summer 1916 – 2nd Battalion	322
10	The Battles of Neuve Chapelle and Aubers and the Summer 1915 – 1st Battalion	363
11	The Battle of Loos – 1st Battalion	403
12	The Battle of Loos – 2nd Battalion	440
13	The Laventie and Neuve Chapelle Trenches and the Winter 1915-16 – 1st Battalion	456
14	The Laventie and Neuve Chapelle Trenches and the Winter 1915-16 – 2nd Battalion	482
15	The Ypres Salient 1916 – 2nd Battalion	496
16	The Ypres Salient 1916 – 1st Battalion	519
Alphabetical List of Other Ranks Showing Their Ranks, Substantive or Acting, When First Mentioned in the Text		569
Select Bibliography		584
Index		593

List of Photographs

1	Officers Mess Staff 1st Battalion 1914, left to right, front to back, K King [untraced], Privates David Turner, Joseph McLoone, Lance Sergeant Alfred Burgess, Privates George Whitney, Richard Dennis, Hugo Kershaw [Courtesy of the Regimental Trustees Scots Guards]	i
2	Drawing of front line on the Chemin des Dames, Battle of the Aisne [Letters of Captain Sir Edward Hulse, Bt]	i
3	2nd Battalion marching out of the Tower of London on 16 September 1914 [Courtesy of Lord de Saumarez]	ii
4	F Company 2nd Battalion on SS *Lake Michigan* to Zeebrugge on 6 October 1914 [Courtesy of Lord de Saumarez]	ii
5	2nd Battalion train leaving Zeebrugge for Bruges on 7 October 1914 with well-wisher waving from top of railway signal [Courtesy of Lord de Saumarez]	iii
6	2nd Battalion Transport en route from Ostend to Ghent on 9 October 1914 [Courtesy of Lord de Saumarez]	iii
7	Refugees near Ghent [Courtesy of Lord de Saumarez]	iv
8	Lieutenant Edward Warner with G Company digging in among sugar beet near Ghent on 10 October 1914 [Courtesy of Lord de Saumarez]	iv
9	2nd Battalion halt on road from Thielt to Roulers on 13 October 1914 [Courtesy of Lord de Saumarez]	v
10	Lieutenant Colonel Pat Bolton with 2nd Battalion digging in at Zandvoorde on 16 October 1914 [Courtesy of Lord de Saumarez]	v
11	The 2nd Battalion advance towards Gheluwe on 20 October 1914 when Drummer Charles Steer was killed [Courtesy of Lord de Saumarez]	vi
12	Sergeant William Young with men of the 2nd Oxfordshire and Buckinghamshire Light Infantry at west side of Polygon Wood on or just after 22 October 1914 [Courtesy of Lord de Saumarez]	vi
13	Shrapnel exploding around Kruiseecke but far enough away from the men on left of picture [Courtesy of Lord de Saumarez]	vii
14	Transport going west down the Menin Road through Hooge [Courtesy of Lord de Saumarez]	vii
15	The Menin Road [Courtesy of Lord de Saumarez]	viii
16	2nd Battalion Roll Call at Hooge on 28 October 1914 with Sergeant Major Jimmy Moncur in the centre [Courtesy of Lord de Saumarez]	viii

List of Photographs v

17	2nd Battalion men breakfasting in woods at Hooge [Courtesy of Lord de Saumarez]	ix
18	2nd Battalion Transport on the Menin Road with shelling not far off [Courtesy of Lord de Saumarez]	ix
19	2nd Battalion drafts at Méteren, November 1914 [Courtesy of Lord de Saumarez]	x
20	Clearing out a communication trench behind front line at Rouges Bancs, early Winter 1914 [Courtesy of Lord de Saumarez]	x
21	Breakfast in the front line opposite Rouges Bancs [Courtesy of Lord de Saumarez]	xi
22	Cartoon by Major Alby Cator of a soldier coming out of the line [Courtesy of Christopher Cator]	xi
23	Lieutenant Tom Ross, who, with Company Quartermaster Sergeant Horace Crabtree, second right, was in the 2nd Battalion throughout [Courtesy of Lord de Saumarez]	xii
24	Regimental Aid Post at Rue Pétillon [Courtesy of Lord de Saumarez]	xii
25	Captain The Honourable Dick Coke, Lieutenant Geoffrey Ottley and Captain George Paynter [Courtesy of Lord de Saumarez]	xiii
26	Cartoon by Major Alby Cator of himself and Brigadier General Frederick Heyworth setting off to visit the line [Courtesy of Christopher Cator]	xiii
27	Graves at Rue Pétillon [Courtesy of Lord de Saumarez]	xiv
28	Lieutenant Sir Edward Hulse and four of his raiding party on 26 November 1914, Private Leonard Dolley on left [Courtesy of Lord de Saumarez]	xiv
29	One German soldier [Courtesy of Lord de Saumarez]	xv
30	Meerschaum pipe given by a German soldier to a Scots Guards sergeant during the Christmas Truce [Courtesy of the Regimental Trustees Scots Guards]	xv
31	Lieutenant Alan Swinton in the Rouges Bancs trenches on Christmas Day 1914 [Courtesy of Major General Sir John Swinton]	xvi
32	1st Battalion, one man wearing a Teddy Bear coat, with mountain gun in The Keep built from the brickstacks at Cuinchy, January 1915 [Courtesy of the Regimental Trustees Scots Guards]	xvi
33	1st Battalion behind primitive breastworks probably near Festubert, early 1915 [Courtesy of the Regimental Trustees Scots Guards]	xvii
34	Lieutenant Neil Fergusson with Lieutenant Merton Beckwith Smith and Lieutenant Colonel John Ponsonby, both 1st Coldstream, and Captain Arthur "Nipper" Poynter and Lieutenant Lionel Norman, Spring 1915 [Courtesy of the Regimental Trustees Scots Guards]	xvii
35	1st Battalion billets at Gonnehem, late April 1915 [Courtesy of the Regimental Trustees Scots Guards]	xviii
36	Lieutenant Arthur Mervyn Jones with 3 Platoon Right Flank 1st Battalion in the tannery, Richebourg-St Vaast, May 1915 [Courtesy of the Regimental Trustees Scots Guards]	xviii
37	Member of Right Flank 1st Battalion hit by shrapnel during Battle of Aubers on 9 May 1915 [Courtesy of the Regimental Trustees Scots Guards]	xix

38	Waiting behind breastworks north of Rue du Bois during Battle of Aubers, Lieutenant Mervyn Jones at the back on right [Courtesy of the Regimental Trustees Scots Guards]	xix
39	1st Cameron Highlanders going into action on afternoon of 9 May 1915 [RT]	xx
40	Company Sergeant Major Arthur Burrough, Right Flank 2nd Battalion, killed at Battle of Festubert on 16 May 1915 [Courtesy of the Regimental Trustees Scots Guards]	xx
41	1st Battalion trench at Le Rutoire just taken over from the French 296e Regiment, late May 1915 [Courtesy of the Regimental Trustees Scots Guards]	xxi
42	1st Battalion rough front line trench at Le Rutoire soon after taking over [Courtesy of the Regimental Trustees Scots Guards]	xxi
43	Captain Harold Cuthbert outside Some Hut at Le Rutoire [Courtesy of the Regimental Trustees Scots Guards]	xxii
44	1st Battalion company cooker at Vermelles [Courtesy of the Regimental Trustees Scots Guards]	xxii
45	1st Battalion billets at Sailly-Labourse where they were first in late May 1915 [Courtesy of the Regimental Trustees Scots Guards]	xxiii
46	Captain Miles Barne [Courtesy of Miles Barne]	xxiii
47	1st Battalion reading letters in the front line at Cuinchy, Summer 1915 [Courtesy of the Regimental Trustees Scots Guards]	xxiv
48	1st Battalion in front line at Cuinchy [Courtesy of the Regimental Trustees Scots Guards]	xxiv
49	Corporal George Stewart, Right Flank 1st Battalion, firing a rifle grenade during a tour from 25-28 July 1915, days before his death on the 31st [Courtesy of the Regimental Trustees Scots Guards]	xxv
50	1st Battalion sniperscope in front line at Cuinchy [Courtesy of the Regimental Trustees Scots Guards]	xxv
51	Lance Sergeant James Blair's cover for the July Spasm of the *Left Flank Magazine* [Courtesy of the Regimental Trustees Scots Guards]	xxvi
52	Cartoon by Lance Corporal Paul Anderton of the Kaiser and Crown Prince and darkening cloud of Doom [Courtesy of the Regimental Trustees Scots Guards]	xxvi
53	Cartoon by Lance Corporal Paul Anderton of Smiling by Numbers, following order when entering St Omer "When we march through the town I want you all to look happy, even if you don't feel that way." [Courtesy of the Regimental Trustees Scots Guards]	xxvii
54	Cartoon by Lance Corporal Anderton of the march to St Omer [Courtesy of the Regimental Trustees Scots Guards]	xxvii
55	2nd Battalion sentry in sap beside trench block at Big Willie after 17 October 1915 [Courtesy of the Regimental Trustees Scots Guards]	xxviii
56	Hole through Lieutenant Tom Ross' tent at the Transport Lines from shell 60 yards away, which caused no casualties, but others did that day in October 1915 [Courtesy of the Regimental Trustees Scots Guards]	xxviii

List of Photographs vii

57	A bombing post at the head of a sap in the Hohenzollern, October 1915 [Courtesy of the Regimental Trustees Scots Guards]	xxix
58	B Company 1st Battalion in Big Willie October 1915, grenade boxes on right [Courtesy of the Regimental Trustees Scots Guards]	xxix
59	After a relief at the Hohenzollern pipers playing the 2nd Battalion back to billets at Vermelles, October 1915 [Courtesy of the Regimental Trustees Scots Guards]	xxx
60	Left Flank 2nd Battalion in Big Willie before the bombing attack on 17 October 1915 [Courtesy of the Regimental Trustees Scots Guards]	xxx
61	Michael, the 2nd Battalion's illicit car, acquired by Lieutenant The Honourable Charlie Mills [Courtesy of the Regimental Trustees Scots Guards]	xxxi
62	2nd Battalion Lewis gunner, Neuve Chapelle area, December 1915 [Courtesy of the Regimental Trustees Scots Guards]	xxxi
63	2nd Battalion in front line breastworks, Neuve Chapelle area, late 1915, with Captain "Monty" Hill standing to the left of the duckboard [Courtesy of the Regimental Trustees Scots Guards]	xxxii
64	The Reverend Alexander MacRae visiting men in the line, Neuve Chapelle area, December 1915 [Courtesy of the Regimental Trustees Scots Guards]	xxxii
65	Member of 2nd Battalion pumping water from behind breastworks, Neuve Chapelle area, December 1915 [Courtesy of the Regimental Trustees Scots Guards]	xxxiii
66	Sergeants of Right Flank 2nd Battalion in front line breastworks, Neuve Chapelle area, late 1915 [Courtesy of the Regimental Trustees Scots Guards]	xxxiii
67	2nd Battalion Lewis Gun team, Neuve Chapelle area, December 1915 [Courtesy of the Regimental Trustees Scots Guards]	xxxiv
68	2nd Battalion water cart at front line, Neuve Chapelle area, December 1915 [Courtesy of the Regimental Trustees Scots Guards]	xxxiv
69	Lieutenant Colonel Alby Cator and Lieutenant Jimmy Lumsden with ratting pack at Laventie, December 1915 [Courtesy of the Regimental Trustees Scots Guards]	xxxv
70	Miniature Fort Tickler, Neuve Chapelle area, December 1915 [Courtesy of the Regimental Trustees Scots Guards]	xxxv
71	Christmas tree given to a Scots Guards corporal by a German soldier during the brief truce on 25 December 1915 [Courtesy of the Regimental Trustees Scots Guards]	xxxvi
72	2nd Battalion snowballing near Poperinghe, March 1916 [Courtesy of the Regimental Trustees Scots Guards]	xxxvi
73	The 2nd Battalion camp at Poperinghe, March 1916 [Courtesy of the Regimental Trustees Scots Guards]	xxxvii
74	The First Calais Spring Meeting on 12 March 1916, with two 2nd Irish Guards bookmakers in bowler hats prominent [Courtesy of the Regimental Trustees Scots Guards]	xxxvii
75	Lieutenant Calverley Bewicke winning a race [Courtesy of the Regimental Trustees Scots Guards]	xxxviii

76	The Snow Lady built by Captain Hugh Ross and Sir Iain Colquhoun [Courtesy of the Regimental Trustees Scots Guards]	xxxviii
77	2nd Battalion in The Gully, Ypres Salient, looking towards an advanced bombing post, Spring 1916 [Courtesy of the Regimental Trustees Scots Guards]	xxxix
78	2nd Battalion in The Gully [Courtesy of the Regimental Trustees Scots Guards]	xxxix
79	2nd Battalion in front line on right of The Gully [Courtesy of the Regimental Trustees Scots Guards]	xl
80	2nd Battalion in The Gully [Courtesy of the Regimental Trustees Scots Guards]	xl
81	The Reverend Alexander MacRae at the Transport Lines near Poperinghe, Spring 1916 [Courtesy of the Regimental Trustees Scots Guards]	xli
82	2nd Battalion having a quiet game of nap along the Canal Bank, Ypres Salient, Spring 1916 [Courtesy of the Regimental Trustees Scots Guards]	xli
83	2nd Battalion on the Canal Bank [Courtesy of the Regimental Trustees Scots Guards]	xlii
84	Mary of Ypres, born to one of the cows, near Poperinghe, Spring 1916 [Courtesy of the Regimental Trustees Scots Guards]	xlii
85	Company Sergeant Major John Shields, B Company 1st Battalion, Spring 1916 [Courtesy of the Regimental Trustees Scots Guards]	xliii
86	1st Battalion in the line, Ypres Salient, early Summer 1916 [Courtesy of the Regimental Trustees Scots Guards]	xliii
87	1st Battalion probably in reserve position, Ypres [Courtesy of the Regimental Trustees Scots Guards]	xliv
88	Sanctuary Wood in June 1916 [Courtesy of the Regimental Trustees Scots Guards]	xliv
89	Lieutenant Gordon Stirling, 2nd Guards Brigade Machine Gun Company, and his dog Wipers, late Spring 1916 [Courtesy of the Regimental Trustees Scots Guards]	xlv
90	2nd Lieutenant Grey Leach, 1st Battalion, early Summer 1916 [Courtesy of the Regimental Trustees Scots Guards]	xlv
91	Blighty Bridge, Ypres Salient, early Summer 1916 [Courtesy of the Regimental Trustees Scots Guards]	xlvi
92	Captain Jimmy Lumsden and Lieutenant David Chapman, 2nd Battalion, wading between platoon positions, Ypres Salient, early Summer 1916 [Courtesy of the Regimental Trustees Scots Guards]	xlvi
93	Lieutenant Bobbie Abercromby, 1st Battalion, early Summer 1916 [Courtesy of the Regimental Trustees Scots Guards]	xlvii
94	Drill Sergeant Charlie Kitchen, 1st Battalion, early Summer 1916 [Courtesy of the Regimental Trustees Scots Guards]	xlvii
95	Lieutenants Eric Miller and Henry Dundas, 1st Battalion, in the support company line next to the French at Boesinghe, July 1916 [Courtesy of the Regimental Trustees Scots Guards]	xlviii
96	Posed photograph of British, Russian and French prisoners at Schneidemühl, Lance Corporal Alexander Cairns standing in the middle at the back, Summer 1916, [Courtesy of the Regimental Trustees Scots Guards]	xlviii

List of Maps

In colour section

1.	The Retreat from Mons and Advance to the Aisne	a
2.	The Battle of the Aisne	b
3.	The First Battle of Ypres – The Menin Road	c
4.	The First Battle of Ypres – Langemarck 21-24 October 1914	d
5.	The First Battle of Ypres – Kruiseecke 25-26 October 1914	e
6.	The First Battle of Ypres – Gheluvelt 29 October 1914	f
7.	The First Battle of Ypres – Nonne Bosschen 3-11 November 1914	g
8.	The Rouges Bancs Trenches – Winter 1914-15	h
9.	The Actions at Givenchy, the Railway Triangle and the Cuinchy brickstacks	i
10.	The Battles of Neuve Chapelle, Aubers and Festubert	j
11.	The Béthune area before the Battle of Loos	k
12.	The Battle of Loos – Puits 14 Bis and Hill 70 27 September 1915	l
13.	The Battle of Loos – The Hohenzollern Redoubt and Line 17 October 1915	m
14.	The Neuve Chapelle Trenches – Winter 1915-16	n
15.	The XIV Corps Sector of the Ypres Salient – Spring and Summer 1916	o
16.	The Poperinghe area behind the Ypres Salient	p

Foreword

When W.A. "Archie" Elliott joined the 2nd Battalion Scots Guards as a new subaltern in Tunisia in August 1943, he found them very ready to go home. They had been abroad for four years, had fought through the North African campaign and had suffered heavy losses. Their mood when they heard they were to form part of the second front in Europe was not good. "After a few days with the Battalion, however, it became apparent that they were settling down to the prospect of fresh action and steeling themselves to the likelihood of more heavy casualties. *Esprit de corps* demanded that the name of *the* Battalion and *the* Regiment be maintained in the face not only of the enemy but also of rival regiments."

Esprit de Corps was the title that Archie Elliott gave to his account of active service in Italy and North-West Europe over the next two years. It came to mind as I read Randall Nicol's exhaustive account of the same regiment's experience of a previous war, precisely because he explains, albeit in a different way from Archie Elliott, how the Scots Guards coped with loss and tribulation, with triumph and disappointment. For those on the outside the reputation of the Foot Guards is stamped on the drill square and is manifest in their immaculate turnout and firm discipline. Their officers, warrant officers and senior non-commissioned officers are the custodians of those standards, but they know – or should know – that they are means to an end, not ends in themselves.

There is not much drill in Randall Nicol's history, but there is a lot of fighting and there are many deaths. His empathy for his subject explains how a distinguished regiment works, how it holds together in adversity, and how it generates bonds which cross class, region, religion and education – and which persist. He writes well, and with a wry sense of humour – one which would have been as much appreciated by those whose doings he describes as it will be by today's readers. Indeed a sense of humour is an enduring element of any *esprit de corps*, but so too is an awareness of when the joke must stop and professionalism take its place.

Randall Nicol lets his men have their own voices as often as possible. By the end the reader will have become caught up in the fates of those officers and men who are regularly quoted in these pages. Some of their vocabulary reminds us that the past is indeed another place, where things were done differently. We no longer describe those who are physically afflicted by illness or wounds as looking 'seedy', but we should not fool ourselves into thinking that somehow they possessed a stoicism which could amount to insensitivity and with which we today cannot sympathise. Private John Osborne remarked, as he struggled with the impact of casualties on the Marne in 1914, that "to hide one's emotions is considered an accomplishment in our present state of civilization, yet, whether it is or not, we only partially deceive others – never ourselves".

So this is the story of many individuals, not just the history of a regiment. It is also the story of the animals they adopted on the way: the cows who returned to retirement in Britain despite quarantine regulations, the lion cub which grew into a lion but stayed in the care of Tom Bridges, and the parrots to whom the Scots Guards taught some new words after the Armistice. What accent the parrots spoke as a result is not recorded but it was almost as likely to be Lancashire as Scots, or North American rather than English. The Scots Guards drew their recruits from across Britain, for all their Scottish identity, and by the war's end boasted university graduates in their ranks and promoted rankers in the officers' mess.

Unlike the infantry of the line, the Foot Guards in the First World War did not form 'Service' battalions as part of Kitchener's New Armies, nor had they raised Territorial battalions before the War. Outwardly, therefore, they remained purely regular regiments, and externally that was how they were seen, not least by those alongside whom they served. And yet we can too easily overstate what that meant. Randall Nicol points out that when war broke out few were grizzled veterans of the Boer War. Most had about three years' service. Across the channel French conscripts served as long. By the year's end the First Battle of Ypres, which all but destroyed the original British Expeditionary Force, had reshaped both battalions of the Scots Guards as did no other battle – including the Somme and Third Ypres. The last four months of 1914 were proportionately their bloodiest of the War, and immediately afterwards, in 1915, they suffered their greatest absolute losses in a single year.

However, to describe the passage from the Somme in 1916 to the Armistice in 1918, the phase of the War in which the British Army shouldered an increasing burden, as 'easier' for the Scots Guards would not only be insulting, it would also be wrong. The First World War was a world war, and the battalions of many infantry regiments fought against the Ottoman army, or in Macedonia or Italy. From first to last, the entire experience of the Scots Guards was enfolded within the Western Front, the epicentre of Britain's, France's and, in due course, America's war. That meant that they – unlike those in far-flung theatres in the First World War or those whom Archie Elliott joined in Tunisia in the Second World War – were able to go home on leave, but it also meant constant rotation, as new drafts arrived and those who had recovered from wounds or sickness returned. Outwardly the Scots Guards of 1918 looked more like their 1914 former self than many other regiments of the British Army; inwardly they – like the rest of the Army – had been changed by an industrialised war, whose relentless intensity bore scant comparison with anything experienced before.

As did other regiments, the Scots Guards set about recording that experience. They had two distinguished authors in their ranks, Stephen Graham and his friend and mentor, Wilfrid Ewart, both of whom bulk large in these pages. Both were improbable soldiers: Graham had been writing pro-Russian propaganda for a sceptical British audience before he joined the Scots Guards as a private, and Ewart, blind in one eye and myopic in the other, made an unlikely and somewhat inefficient officer, albeit brave and humane. Graham's *A Private in the Guards* was published in 1919 and reprinted twice in the same year. Ewart's war novel, *Way of Revelation*, appeared in 1921 and sold 30,000 copies within months. As middle-brow fiction with a taste for melodrama, it has never joined the canon of First World War literature, although it certainly remains worth reading. It is as striking for its portrayal of louche life in wartime London as it is for its evocation of the Western Front on which Ewart served between 1915 and 1918. "War is not merciful" Ewart wrote in *Way of Revelation*. "It recks neither of place nor circumstance nor time. It recks nought of the love of the human body, of the love of women, of the claims of human pity, of the warmth that life once held and that death alone can destroy and that no earthly power can give back. It does not laugh, it does not weep, it cannot make beautiful or make good; neither can it destroy the immortal soul.'

The Scots Guards gave Ewart the task of writing their wartime history, a brave decision which might have produced a regimental record like no other. But Ewart, having survived the War, died in absurd and accidental circumstances in Mexico on New Year's Eve 1922. He left a brief and posthumously published memoir, *Scots Guard*, as well as the opening chapters of the regimental history on which he had been working. Thereafter, the project struggled to regain its footing, despite the involvement of two proven military historians, F. Loraine Petre, who also died in harness, and Major General Sir Frederick Maurice, who wrote the Regiment's history up to 1914. Whatever their input none of the three appear to have influenced the end result published in 1925. Randall Nicol is too modest to say so, but his book can claim to be the history of their service in the First World War for which the Scots Guards have been waiting for a hundred years.

Hew Strachan
Professor of International Relations,
University of St Andrews
Broughton, February 2016

To the memory of the Scots Guardsmen of the Great War,
of those whom they loved and of those who loved them
and to those who love them still

Preface

> The Muse of History must not be fastidious. She must see everything, touch everything, and, if possible, smell everything.
>
> Winston Churchill: *Great Contemporaries*

Rather than being a military or a regimental history or an academic analysis, this is a story. The story is of soldiers at war, as much as practical by themselves, which happens to have as its background the two Battalions of the Scots Guards who served in Belgium and France from 1914 to 1918. My purpose is not to look at and examine them from the outside but to display to the best of my ability by, so to speak, getting in amongst them, what they knew, saw, heard, felt and experienced and who they were. I have looked at and listened to what happened mostly through these men's eyes and ears and sometimes through the eyes and ears of others who watched and listened nearby. I have tried to convey how the War appeared to them and I have not sought to achieve any wider view, nor otherwise to explain more than what is essential. What went on when they were not in the trenches or fighting a battle holds just as much interest as when they were. There are, even in simple circumstances, differing accounts and what follows reflects that. In more complex circumstances, far from unique to the Great War, everything usually became very quickly very confused once battle was joined and afterwards it was nearly always very difficult to assess, at least beyond the balance of probability, what had taken place, when and where. The experiences of the 2nd Scots Guards at Neuve Chapelle are a very good example.

These officers and men were ordinary human beings who experienced extraordinary events. In all other ways they behaved as soldiers do, did what they had to do, often misbehaved out of the line, but rarely in it, enjoyed what there was to enjoy and grumbled about much else. Among themselves they had their personal likes and dislikes, but all had to depend on and work together with the comrades around them. Because of that comradeship borne of the shared experience at close quarters they got to know each other very well indeed. One cannot but be humbled and moved by their resilience amid dire adversity, not least in the winter conditions of 1916-17. It is extremely important when reading to remember that they had no idea how long the War would continue and it is not surprising how unexpected and unreal the announcement of the Armistice was for many.

The Scots Guardsmen's understanding of what others were doing at any time was limited to what they saw and heard, very rarely anywhere near the whole story, often inaccurate and sometimes also, however unintentionally, unfair. However, they made fewer disparaging remarks than one might expect about other front line units, given the tribal nature of human beings, accentuated by the tribalism of all regimental loyalties. They, and particularly officers, were more likely to abuse the Staff, those in such comparatively safe and comfortable roles as the Army Service Corps or in jobs such as Railway Transport Officers, to say nothing of their attitudes to politicians, the press and those at home other than their own families and friends. In short, they were most likely to be unsympathetic to anyone who did not have the same type of experiences as they did.

The central characters are therefore the individuals who by the chances of fate, including, before conscription, mostly their own choices, served in the two Battalions. Many others, men, women and children appear, some by name, some not, some soldiers, some not, some British, some not. It is generally easier to identify and find out more about those who died rather than those who survived and often there is more to find out recorded about the former. A soldier of any rank who went to war at any time, who survived fit and unhurt, and otherwise unnamed by anybody, without distinction or even disciplinary record, left much less trace and sometimes virtually none. If someone is mentioned without, relatively, much detail it is because it has not been possible to find out more about them.

Those British soldiers who took part in the Retreat from Mons saw and were well aware of the plight of refugees and they could see behind them the fires as the advancing Germans burnt the farms and villages. Those who landed at Ostend and Zeebrugge early in October 1914 were similarly well aware of the plight of refugees. Those in the area east of the Somme battlefields after the Germans withdrew to the Hindenburg Line in March 1917 saw the scale of calculated destruction. Those in the last weeks of the War who advanced across largely unfought over Belgian and French territory, in the case of the Scots Guards east of Cambrai, first met pathetically grateful civilians. Whatever else the War was about it was also about liberation.

I have written in chronological, narrative form, using as bones the War Diaries of the Battalions, supplemented from August 1915 by the two volumes of Cuthbert Headlam's *History of the Guards Division in the Great War 1915-1918*. The Scots Guards history, *The Scots Guards in the Great War 1914-1919*, is an unsatisfactory work containing some useful pieces of information, but mainly comprising a summary of the War Diaries. It had a bad start when Wilfrid Ewart began working on it and was shot dead accidentally on his hotel balcony during a fiesta in Mexico City. F Loraine Petre, an established military history writer, took over and then died. After that it was written by a committee under Major General Sir Cecil Lowther's chairmanship.

The flesh, muscles, senses, emotions, spirit and ideas come from diaries, letters, notes, occasional pieces of verse, military documents and reports, here and there press cuttings and some published works. Most important are officers' and soldiers' files. Officers are listed in the main index. In a separate schedule appear alphabetically all other ranks with their regimental numbers and the ranks they held when first mentioned in the text. Unless there is definite information otherwise I have had to assume that a person's first given name was the one used. Officers' nicknames are much more frequently known and identifiable than those of most of the men.

In the case of a few words spelled in several different ways, such as whizz-bang, I have standardised them both in text and quotations and, sparingly, I have added or adjusted punctuation in some quotations to make them more readable or consistent. Otherwise quotations are set out exactly as they were written. Where there is an unattributed quotation in the text it comes from the applicable battalion war diary.

At the end of each chapter I have summarised the sources used, but not itemised the origin of each piece of information. Once a source has been mentioned after the chapter in which it first appears, for example the Cator Papers, though referred to in subsequent chapters, it will not be mentioned again, unless it is not self evident. The Cator Papers illustrate the widespread practice of the recipient of a letter from the BEF typing up copies and circulating them among family and friends. There is a bibliography and list of sources at the end of the book. There is sometimes more than one copy of a document or set of documents and so it is in more than one collection. I have referred, with very occasional exceptions, only to where I have seen the copy that I have used. Copies of divisional operation orders from August 1915 onwards, from which detail is drawn, appear as appendices in the Cuthbert Headlam volumes, along with operation orders, instructions, reports and narratives in the War Diaries of the 2nd and 3rd Guards Brigades.

I refer to all regiments by their full names the first time that they appear and, if short, such as The Rifle Brigade, continuously, but otherwise abbreviated to a form then in use. The 1st Gloucestershire Regiment thus becomes the 1st Gloucesters. A regiment such as The King's Shropshire Light Infantry, is given its full name the first time it appears with its abbreviation in square brackets [KSLI], as used subsequently, provided in such a case that that abbreviation would have been in common use at the time. However, in order to maintain the flow of language I do not use contemporary official abbreviations for battalions and regiments and so refer to the 1st Battalion Scots Guards in the text as the 1st Scots Guards and not 1/S.G., then the military usage.

Otherwise I have generally followed the historic military conventions. So, while it is usually clear from the text whether a village or hamlet is on the Allied or German side of the line, where reference is made to roads in static situations they are set out from west to east e.g. from Ypres to Zonnebeke. Also, generally, unless the context makes it inappropriate, I have set out locations occupied by Allied and German forces from right to left as they respectively looked at them. A standard convention is to refer to Allied formations as First Army, IV Corps, 7th Division and 20th Brigade, and clearly indicate whether British or not. The first time a British division appears the full name is given e.g. the 46th (North Midland) Division, Territorial Force, called thereafter simply the 46th Division. At the time the number of a British artillery brigade, now called an artillery regiment, typically with three or more gun batteries, was shown in Roman numerals, but I have not followed that. German formations are always in italics, e.g. *16th Bavarian Reserve Infantry Regiment*. German words, but not proper names or places, are also in italics, unless the word was one in common British use, such as minenwerfer, a trench mortar.

Very broadly speaking, something described as being of strategic importance means that political objectives required military resources e.g. the German offensive at Verdun in February 1916. Operational importance means large scale military significance e.g. the fighting in Bourlon Wood in November 1917 during the Battle of Cambrai. Tactical importance means a matter for a division or less, typically the seizure or defence of higher ground or the capture of an intact bridge. However, these terms are fluid and a successful tactical operation could have a far wider effect, as did the 2nd Australian Division's capture of Mont St Quentin, outside Péronne, beginning on 31 August 1918.

Place names in Belgium are in French as then used. The maps show the detail of individual areas and battlefield events, but modern road maps will show the routes travelled described in the text, such as the train journey of the 1st Scots Guards from the Ypres hinterland to the Somme in 1916.

I am well aware that I have not explored beyond many of the doors that I have opened and glanced behind, but to have done so would have gone beyond what this story is about.

Those who read I ask to think, to reflect and not to judge.

Acknowledgements

What led to the start of this book was when Ella McLeod brought me the medals and papers of her uncle Lance Corporal Alexander Cairns and I set out to find out about him and his service in the 1st Scots Guards, followed by four years captivity at Schneidemühl after First Ypres. From then on I have had great help from very many, all of whom have contributed to the whole. They include Anthony Leask, David Hawson for his advice and commentary on medical issues, the late Richard Holmes, Wendy Maynard, Jean Menage, Malcolm Nicol, Michael Orr, Edward Crofton, Martin Snow, Mike Scott, Philip Wright, Meriel Balston, Jamie Crookenden, Martin Haldane, Nick Knollys, Mark Laing, John Purves, Richard Stirling-Aird, Kevin Gorman, formerly, and Leighton Platt, currently, of the Scots Guards Archives, the Regimental Archivists of the Grenadier, Coldstream, Irish and Welsh Guards, Pete Starling of the Army Medical Services Museum, David Blake of the Museum of Army Chaplaincy, Andrew Parsons, Curator The London Scottish Museum, Tom Smythe, formerly Archivist of The Black Watch Museum, Staff and Volunteers at The Highlanders Museum, the Staffs of the Commonwealth War Graves Commission, Imperial War Museum, Liddle Collection, Brotherton Library, University of Leeds, National Army Museum, National Library of Scotland, and The National Archives, Mrs F Hooper of George Watsons's College and the Committee of Managers of the New Club.

I am most grateful to all those who have lent me, let me study and granted me permission to quote from family letters, diaries and other material and to reproduce photographs and drawings.

The Asquith Papers: The Earl of Oxford and Asquith
The Balfour Papers (for Captain RF Balfour): The late Peter Balfour and Hew Balfour
The Barne Papers: Miles Barne
The Cator Papers: Christopher Cator
The Colquhoun Papers: Sir Malcolm Colquhoun of Luss, Bt, and James Colquhoun
The Cuthbert Papers: Aidan Cuthbert
The Dundas Papers: Benjamin Carey
The Kinnaird Papers: The Honourable Caroline Best
The Ross Papers: James Hepburne Scott
The Saumarez Papers: Lord de Saumarez
The Warner Papers: Sir Philip Warner, Bt
Others who wish to remain anonymous

I am similarly most grateful to those who have granted me copyright permission for papers held in the Imperial War Museum
Captain Dougan Chater: Simon Chater
Brigadier EC Craig Brown: John Martin
Lance Corporal Charles Green: Tom Green
Brigadier Lord Kindersley: Lord Kindersley
Major General Sir Cecil Lowther: Caroline Countess of Lowther
Private Ernest Mellor: Dave Mellor
Major Clive Morrison Bell: David Moore
Rifleman Reginald Prew: Brian Prew
Brigadier General Hubert Rees: Diana Stockford
General Sir Andrew Thorne: Lady Anne Thorne

Further I am most grateful to:
Lieutenant General Jonathon Riley, Chairman of Trustees of the Royal Welch Fusiliers Museum, and Miles Stockwell for permission to quote from Major CH Dudley Ward, Historical Records of The Royal Welch Fusiliers, Volume III, including quotation from Captain Clifton Stockwell.
The Trustees of The Highlanders Museum for permission to quote from the Historical Records of The Queen's Own Cameron Highlanders, Volume III, and from the Papers assembled by Brigadier EC Craig Brown held at The Highlanders Museum.
Brigadier Harry Nickerson, Regimental Lieutenant Colonel and Chairman of the Regimental Trustees Scots Guards, for permission to quote from and use all material held in the Scots Guards Archives.
Lucy Mackenzie Pannizon, separately, for permission to quote from the duplicate of The Mackenzie Papers held in the Scots Guards Archives.
Ipswich Record Office for permission to quote from the small file of letters to Captain The Hon J St V B Saumarez from serving officers, soldiers and others in the de Saumarez Family Archive, accepted by HM Government in Lieu of Inheritance Tax and allocated to Suffolk County Council, 2007.
University of Birmingham Special Collections for permission to quote from the letters of Lieutenant F Pretyman to Lady Cynthia Curzon.
Talbot House Museum Poperinghe for details of individuals.
Clare Ajenusi for permission to quote from Donald Boyd, *Salute of Guns* (London: Jonathan Cape Ltd 1930)
Tom Clayton for permission to quote from The Reverend PB Clayton, *Tales of Talbot House in Poperinghe & Ypres* (London: Chatto & Windus 1919)

Every reasonable effort has been made to identify and trace copyright holders, but in many cases it has proved impossible. Should any copyright holder wish to make contact and seek an acknowledgement that would be appreciated.

Hew Strachan has been an interested supporter over a long period and I am most grateful to him for writing the foreword and for his constructive suggestions about the text. I pay warm tribute to Duncan Rogers for his courage and enterprise in taking on the publication by Helion of what I have written, with thanks also to others at Helion and to George Anderson for the significant collection of maps.

Finally, my grateful thanks to Filly, my wife.

1

The Regimental Background

> Never in our whole history as a nation has a struggle been entered into with greater suddenness. Never perhaps has there been a war, the necessity and importance of which – for our national existence – has been less appreciated by the general public.
>
> Private William Luck, 1st Scots Guards

In the House of Lords on 24 July 1924 Lord Grey of Falloden said "Practically every nation in Europe was afraid of Germany, and the use which Germany might make of her armaments. Germany was not afraid, because she believed her army to be invincible, but she was afraid that a few years hence she might be afraid…. In 1914 Europe had arrived at a point in which every country except Germany was afraid of the present, and Germany was afraid of the future." GM Trevelyan's 1937 biography of Lord Grey, Foreign Minister in 1914, sets out very clearly the shifting diplomatic rivalries and pressures among the European powers from after the Franco-Prussian War in 1870 to the outbreak of the War in 1914. The influences and strains reached right round the world. For example, territorial rivalry in Europe might not have led to war between Britain and France, but territorial rivalry over colonial interests might have, though the terms of the Entente Cordiale of 1904 had cleared up several areas of possible conflict. After the turn of the century there was grave British apprehension about German naval expansion and the implications for maritime trade, though most British were relatively sanguine about German military power. France, humiliated in 1870 and morally undermined since, was beginning to regain her self respect and put her military house in order, which gave Germany a sense of rising apprehension. This increased as Russia recovered from the defeats of the Russo-Japanese War of 1904-05 and, in addition to other reforms and modernisation, started to develop the railway systems beyond Germany's eastern borders. France and Russia had entered into a treaty of mutual defence in 1894 as a counter to the existing treaty between Germany, the Austro-Hungarian Empire and Italy and this raised the tension when the Germans found out about it. Their solution was to continue to enhance their military preparedness and fine tune their operational procedures for a preemptive strike on the outbreak of war. Since the Entente Cordiale there had been informal but detailed military discussions between the British and French about what each might do if Germany invaded France, which in practice meant almost certainly through Belgium. Staff plans were drawn up but there was no formal obligation on either country to do anything, whatever the French may have thought about having an understanding with the British.

When on 28 June 1914 the Austro-Hungarian heir apparent, Archduke Franz Ferdinand, was assassinated with his wife at Sarajevo in Bosnia-Herzegovina, then part of the Austro-Hungarian Empire, there was nothing to suggest that a major war was going to break out five weeks later. Germany could have restrained the Austro-Hungarian government's demands on neighbouring Serbia for redress, not issued till over three weeks after the murders, but did not do so. The Serbian government response then was as quick, reasonable and conciliatory as practicable, though the nature and tone of the demands looked like a pretext for the war declared on them on 28 July. Thereafter events moved very quickly. Russia began to mobilise to support Serbia, so drawing France in closer. Germany displayed public and diplomatic alarm, but was militarily very well prepared for this eventuality. German mobilization was certain to lead to war, which they intended to be short and sharp. It had always been English and later British policy to ensure that a hostile power was not in occupation of all the Channel ports and that had been a prime consideration after Napoleon's defeat in 1815. Initially a new state of the Netherlands was created but this split along religious affiliations after fifteen years. What became Belgium, the Catholic part with the most sensitive seaboard, was set up as a buffer state with international guarantees of neutrality. Most of the British population still did not see any reason on 28 July 1914 for concern, let alone for involvement on the European mainland. Germany having declared war on Russia on 1 August, France, while doing nothing otherwise to provoke Germany, mobilised that day, but there was great apprehension that Britain would not come to help. Henry Asquith was Prime Minister, heading a Liberal Cabinet in which the atmosphere was unsettled. None of them wanted to go to war with Germany, though Winston Churchill, First Lord of the Admiralty, who saw the threat very clearly, had mobilised the Fleet on 28 July as part of a training exercise. However, as events unrolled on the Continent, most of the Cabinet, with the backing of the Conservative Opposition, became convinced that Britain was going to have to fight to prevent a French defeat. Bringing public opinion round would be difficult, if not impossible, unless the Germans invaded Belgium, which they then did, at the same time attacking over the French border. The British ultimatum to Germany to stay out of Belgium expired at 11pm on 4 August. Once at war, for every European nation directly involved it would turn out to be to the death, however long it lasted, and for the British it was recognised that victory was a matter of national survival, in which preservation of the British Empire was an important factor. Just as the influences and strains beforehand reached right round the world what struck in 1914 was felt and experienced right round the world.

However, though some individuals served elsewhere, for the Scots Guards the War that followed concentrated on France and Flanders. They had three Battalions, the 1st and 2nd being operational ones serving with the British Expeditionary Force on the Western Front and the 3rd (Reserve) Battalion being in London at Wellington Barracks, predominantly training and preparing officers and men to go out in reinforcement drafts. Regimentally, above all of them were Regimental Headquarters at Buckingham Gate, close to Wellington Barracks. The structure of the Scots Guards reflected their historical origins and were of the same pattern as that of the other Foot Guards and similar historically to all the cavalry and infantry regiments in the Regular Army. In 1642 the Marquis of Argyll raised Argyll's Regiment and became their first Colonel, but he was no soldier and appointed his kinsman Sir Duncan Campbell of Auchinbreck as his Lieutenant Colonel. Over the course of time the Regiment that in 1877 became known permanently as the Scots Guards continued to have Colonels, sometimes senior military officers, sometimes senior members of the Royal Family, but it was the regular officer holding the appointment of Lieutenant Colonel Commanding Scots Guards who did precisely that in all matters affecting the Regiment, other than military training and operations. In 1914 the Colonel of the Regiment was Field Marshal Lord Methuen and the Lieutenant Colonel Commanding was Colonel Frederick Heyworth. However, soon after war was declared Colonel Henry Fludyer, retired from the Army but having previously held the appointment, returned in order to release Colonel Heyworth to attend full time to his other peacetime appointment commanding a brigade of London Territorials. It would fall to Colonel Fludyer and his staff, his principal assistant being the Regimental Adjutant, to organise the recruiting of men and the selection of new officers. Crucially, it was his responsibility and from 1916 that of his successor Colonel James Smith Neill to make permanent appointments of Commanding Officers and other senior ranks, commissioned or not, within the Battalions to replace those who had been promoted or become casualties. This depended on suitability as seen in London and then seniority within the serving Regular Army. The main flaw was that some of these senior appointees, invariably keen to go abroad, appearing to be medically sound and having been passed fit, turned out to be unable to bear the physical or mental strain. In the cases particularly of those who had already been severely wounded or shell shocked it was a gamble to let them go.

An infantry battalion of the 1914 Regular Army had a wartime establishment of thirty officers and just over one thousand men. There were Battalion Headquarters, which included signallers, clerks, medical staff and stretcher bearers, including many pipers and drummers, and orderlies, who carried messages and were also trained horsemen. The two Maxim machine guns, with teams of six men each, under an officer and a sergeant, were also with Battalion Headquarters. The four rifle companies consisted of a company headquarters and four platoons each, total strength six officers and about two hundred and twenty men, and each platoon, an officer and about fifty men, had four sections. They were supported administratively by the Transport, over whom the Quartermaster presided. Here were the storemen, drivers of horses, cooks, shoeing smiths, grooms, farriers, bootmakers, tailors, pioneers [carpenters], and postmen, all of whom tended to be trained men of longer service or else with preexisting specialist skills. After the First Battle of Ypres in October and November 1914 it became clear that the strain on the Quartermaster of not only indenting for stores and running every aspect of his department as well as ensuring the resupply of his Battalion was too much. So the post of Transport Officer came into being. This was often an older rejoined officer, who worked with the Quartermaster and was responsible for the physical delivery of supplies to the Battalion. This was no soft option, required determination and skill, was often subject to shelling and therefore casualties, quite apart from traffic congestion and bad road conditions, and had to be got right; otherwise everyone suffered. The Transport Officer needed to be familiar with horses.

The Commanding Officer was a Lieutenant Colonel, his deputy holding the appointment of Senior Major, which in the Scots Guards during the War quickly became known instead as Second in Command. Apart from the Commanding Officer, customarily called "Sir" by all officers at all times, the others were all on first names, other than on parade. They might and did at times during the War refer to the Commanding Officer as "The Colonel". Towards the end there was one whose very junior Second in Command was on first name terms with him. At the start of the War there might be another major in Battalion Headquarters with a somewhat nebulous role, as happened with the 1st Battalion, but companies had captains, and only occasionally majors, commanding them. Until 1913 all infantry battalions worked on an eight company basis, but when this changed by doubling them up so that there were only four companies, the company commander, whether a major or a captain by rank, continued to be known as the Captain of that company and his immediate subordinate, a captain, became known initially as the Second Captain. The War soon changed that in the Scots Guards too. Each platoon commander was by rank a lieutenant, known as a subaltern, or a 2nd lieutenant, known as an ensign, but casualties quickly put NCOs into command of platoons. Subalterns and ensigns were called subaltern officers collectively and individually addressed formally, for example, as Mr Picquet, not as Lieutenant Picquet, and verbally that was how the men also referred to them. All officers were addressed as "Sir" by the men, as were the senior non commissioned ranks down to Colour Sergeant and Company Quartermaster Sergeant by their subordinates. The Quartermaster, invariably having come up through the ranks, held a different type of commission from the other officers and would be, for example, Quartermaster and Honorary Lieutenant Hardtack. The Adjutant, either a captain or a senior subaltern, was the Commanding Officer's staff officer, as well as being directly responsible to him for the Battalion's discipline. There were some specialist roles, such as machine gun officer. Later new specialist officer roles emerged, such as signal officer, bombing officer, sometimes combined with intelligence officer, assistant adjutant and sniping officer.

The senior non commissioned officer was the only person with the rank of Warrant Officer and he held the appointment of Sergeant Major, addressed as such by the officers and referred to simply as "The Sergeant Major" and not as the RSM or any variant. While there were other appointments, such as Regimental Quartermaster Sergeant, the Quartermaster's right hand man, Drill Sergeant, of whom there were two, the Sergeant Major's key subordinates and senior to all others except the Regimental Quartermaster Sergeant, and the Company Sergeant Majors, all these held the ranks of Colour Sergeant or Sergeant. The rank of Warrant Officer Class II was first introduced early in 1915 for those appointed Company Sergeant Majors and above once they had proved themselves. Here and there in Scots Guards individual accounts there is reference to a "Sergeant Major" where the subject is a Company Sergeant Major, but it is rare. There were strict rules applied out of the line about the relationships between the ranks. Lance corporals were not to socialise in any way with privates and so on, though it is evident from the individual accounts that there was more familiarity when closer to the enemy.

Unlike the other regiments of Foot Guards, who numbered their companies, the Scots Guards used letters, but with another variation. In the others all companies were numbered one to four within the battalions, with the exceptions of the senior company in the 1st Grenadier Guards, The King's Company, containing the tallest men in the Regiment, and of the senior company in the 1st Welsh Guards when they were raised in the spring of 1915, The Prince of Wales's Company. Each Scots Guards Battalion's senior company was known as Right Flank, formally Right Flank Company, with the tallest men, whose origins derived from the grenadier companies formed in the 18th Century. The next two companies in the 1st Battalion were B and C Companies and then came Left Flank, or Left Flank Company, whose origins lay with the light companies of long before. In the 2nd Battalion there were Right Flank, F and G Companies and Left Flank.

Of the officers serving in 1914, there were many whose homes were in Scotland, more who were on the face of it completely English, the occasional one from Ireland and Wales and, mixed in, a very strong strain of family connections in the Regiment. Many had been to university at Oxford or Cambridge, predominantly at Oxford and most of them at Christ Church or Magdalen College. More had come from The Royal Military College, Sandhurst, some had transferred from other regiments and a few had joined through the Territorial Force and its predecessors, at that time a recognised method of obtaining a commission in the Regular Army. The War Office realised from the start that very many more officers were going to be required. There was a pre-war category of officers commission in the Special Reserve, intended to provide a back up in the event of general war and the Scots Guards had a small number of officers in it. They did basic officer training in a Battalion and then a moderate amount of training annually, but were otherwise civilians. The Special Reserve was now broadened to include wartime volunteer officers, while Sandhurst continued to train cadets for regular commissions, though these were only a small proportion of the total. A lot of pre-war officers rejoined, some of whom had been out of the Army for a long time, and hardly had time to familiarise themselves in some cases before they found themselves in action. Most who joined had no military experience from before 1914, some straight from school and some much older and usually university educated, having then progressed into very varied professions. Others transferred from elsewhere in the Army as the War went on. Regimental and family connections continued strongly throughout, but there were relatively few officers from Scotland itself. Later, here and there, men were commissioned into the Scots Guards from the ranks, but for these and soon for almost everybody else granted wartime commissions there was intensive training, notably, but not exclusively, in the ranks of the Household Brigade Officer Cadet Battalion at Bushey, Hertfordshire.

The oldest man in 1914 to serve in a Scots Guards Battalion on the Western Front was Major Baden Baden Powell, for a short time in the 2nd Scots Guards as Second in Command before being put in charge of the Guards Division Bombing School, training officers and men in grenade throwing and tactics. He was born in 1860, the younger brother of the founder of the Scout Movement. Running him close was Captain Henry Beaumont, who rejoined aged fifty. He had left the Regiment in 1892 and next served in the Boer War, for the last six months of which he was with the locally recruited Thorneycroft's Mounted Infantry, where he reached the rank of Lieutenant Colonel. Very soon after the start of the War all the cadets at Sandhurst were commissioned early, those who had only completed one term staying only for the early weeks of the next term before they too went to their regiments. This accounted for the youngest Scots Guards officer to lose his life, Lieutenant Geoffrey Ottley, but soon the War Office brought in a regulation that officers must be nineteen before going overseas and it was easier to verify an officer's age than a soldier's, subject in theory to the same restriction.

Just as among the officers there were many sets of brothers and others who were related to each other, so also among the men. The Scots Guardsmen of 1914, serving and reservists, came from all over Scotland, but predominantly from around Glasgow, and also from all over England. There was strong representation from Yorkshire and North Lancashire, while, of the cities, both Leeds and Liverpool were prominent. There were men from London and the Southeast, a surprising number from Dorset, Hampshire, Herefordshire and Shropshire, together with the occasional Welshman and a few, mostly former seamen, whose lives had begun in the Dominions or in one or two cases in the USA. Most surprising of all, however, on first appearances, was the large number of men originally from Ireland, but almost all had enlisted in the Glasgow area or Liverpool. Most of the soldiers were from urban backgrounds and occupations and of those born in the country few had had rural jobs before they joined.

Before the War only occasionally was a Scots Guards recruit accepted who was under five foot eight inches, but it was reckoned that physical training and the military diet could add half an inch or more to a man's height and it was evident from comparing men's original enlistment papers with later medical reports if they extended their service that this indeed happened. Even then not many were over six foot tall. Men were accepted who had flat feet or were even quite badly knock kneed. Teeth were often an issue, though not a critical one if all else was medically sound. A significant number of those who had served before the War and were still serving or were called up as reservists had been treated for syphilis or gonorrhoea or both contracted in the Army. Private James Mackenzie, in 1914 very brave when it came to it, had had such a bad case of gonorrhoea that part of the treatment involved circumcision. Venereal disease continued to be significant, particularly in the London area, through the War, and several men returning to the Battalions in the BEF off UK leave were found to have it, but fewer than might be expected caught it on the other side of the Channel.

The standard term of service in the Foot Guards was three years with the Colours and nine on the Reserve, though there were variations within this twelve year term and a man might serve all twelve years with the Colours and leave without any Reserve commitment. Provided that someone was suitable he could extend his service beyond twelve years, but only very occasionally beyond twenty one unless he was a senior Non Commissioned Officer. This also applied to those on twelve year terms who had gone onto the Reserve, some of whom voluntarily added four more years to their commitment. Not that many of those serving with the Battalions immediately before the War broke out had been in the Scots Guards for more than three years at the time. In theory, drummers and others with specialist skills enlisted as boy soldiers once over eighteen excepted, no one known to be under nineteen was permitted to be sent on active service. Sometimes this was respected and sometimes it was not, notably in the period after mid November 1914.

After mobilization was announced on 4 August reservists began to report, mostly very promptly. Very few failed to do so. Volunteers quickly began to enlist and among these were many former soldiers whose time on the Reserve had expired. Those with previous service who reenlisted, mostly Scots Guardsmen previously, would be the first into reinforcement drafts once there were no more fit reservists and serving soldiers. A new wartime Short Service category came into being whereby men signed on for three years or for the duration of the War, the enlistment paper stating that if the War lasted less than three years every effort would be made to discharge them as quickly as possible. How old the volunteers were was difficult to verify. If they were under nineteen, but stated that they were over, then the ages that they gave appeared on their enlistment papers. Only later and then usually because they had been killed did other figures for their ages appear, though some were quickly discharged soon after enlistment for misstating their ages. When what was then the Imperial War Graves Commission were recording details of the dead after the War they attempted to contact the families, asking for information, wishes for any special inscriptions on identified graves and other personal details. In many cases nothing was forthcoming, but in a lot the relatives did, amongst other information, give soldiers' ages. The Commission could not verify what they were told and so what appeared in their records and on the headstones of the dead was the best that they could do. That many men were apparently so young when they died was emotive, but there were elements of doubt, without there having been any wish or intention to mislead. In the case of men definitely well into their twenties there were frequent disparities between the ages they gave on enlistment and those provided later by their families to the Commission. Those who insisted that they were definitely under nineteen, but over eighteen, were likely to be signed up on regular twelve year engagements. One of the strangest stories, but not unique, was that of Private Robert Daisley from Ibrox in Glasgow, who joined up in mid August 1914, giving his age as nineteen years and ten months. He went to France in November and joined the 1st Scots Guards. During the fighting at Givenchy-lez-La Bassée, "lez" having the same meaning as "by" in English, as in the Suffolk village of Stoke by Nayland, just before Christmas he was sent down the line with a bruised back, later diagnosed as lumbago. After a second bout in July 1915 he was evacuated to England, where his much younger true age came to light and he was then discharged for misstating his age on enlistment. If some were very young, others were into their forties, and, provided that they stated that they were under forty two on enlistment or under forty six if they had previous service, they were accepted.

The volunteers came from all over Scotland and England and many, to begin with, were still originally from Ireland. As time went by there were changes. While the Glasgow area and Liverpool continued to be prominent, Leeds and Yorkshire became less so. There was still a steady flow of Londoners, but fewer from elsewhere in England, except the North. However, particularly from North Lancashire, distinctively from Preston and remarkably from nearby Leyland very many became Scots Guardsmen. In Scotland, apart from Glasgow and its surrounding area, which predominated, the other cities provided a steady flow. In the country certain parts stood out, Banffshire, Buchan and Donside in Aberdeenshire, the Mearns and Strathmore in Kincardineshire and Angus, the mining villages of Fife, Kirkcudbrightshire and Wigtownshire. Others came back from overseas and a group of emigrants to the USA, not yet American citizens, appeared in July 1917.

Most of those who served with the Battalions in Belgium and France were volunteers in one form or another, including those who put their names forward under the Derby Scheme. All serving soldiers and reservists in 1914 were enlisted as such in the first place. How many of them there were is beyond determination. When it came to wartime volunteers the allocation of regimental numbers did not work entirely chronologically by date of enlistment but roughly eight hundred men volunteered from 5 August till the end of the month. When news came of the Retreat from Mons and then Field Marshal Earl Kitchener, Minister of War, appealed for men in his recruiting poster published on 5 September there was a surge. Men of all trades, occupations and professions came forward, but, at the start two stood out, miners and policemen. There were quickly scores of both. Captain The Honourable Archibald Campbell Douglas, himself called up from the Reserve of Officers, was Regimental Adjutant from soon after the start of the War. He wrote on 30 September to Brigadier General Gerald "Cupid" Cuthbert that "we have had 2500 recruits since mobilization, all good men nearly, about 200 Glasgow Police who should make first class NCOs. My record day I posted 304 men to the Regiment." There had been single years since the Boer War when less than three hundred men had been recruited, while two and a half thousand represented an aggregate for approximately six years of peacetime recruits, a proportion of whom each year having soon been discharged as unsuitable. Through the later autumn of 1914 the pace of voluntary enlistment began to slacken, but there were still more Glasgow policemen, still more miners and the total of Scots Guards war volunteers at the end of December stood at just short of four thousand. So many policemen enlisted from Glasgow that in October at the Guards Depot at Caterham, Surrey, sixty eight of them formed a training squad of their own, along with a lone sixty ninth man. The Glasgow Police Squad became immediately famous. What, however, they were not was Glaswegians, with occasional exceptions. They were from all over Scotland, a few were Irish, one or two English. One feature immediately became apparent at Caterham, nicknamed "Little Sparta". Several recruits were either not physically fit enough or else did not have the aptitude. Others were injured in training, some deserted and a very few were discharged for specific disciplinary reasons.

Recruiting gradually fell off through 1915, during the first nine months of which slightly under one thousand seven hundred men volunteered for the Scots Guards. Then, when the Earl of Derby became Minister of Recruitment on 11 October he published what became known as the Derby Scheme five days later. This was a half way measure towards conscription, by which men could either volunteer in the normal way or else register by 15 December, join the Army Reserve and wait until called up. These were known as Derby Men and were issued with grey armbands with red crowns to indicate their status. The Derby Scheme did not achieve its object, it being found that less than half of the men not classified as engaged in essential wartime civilian occupations had either volunteered or registered. The Government then accepted the need for full conscription and introduced the first Military Service Act in the middle of January 1916. It came into force on 10 February and was adjusted and tightened later on. Up to 2 March men were still encouraged to volunteer and they could alternatively register as reservists. The combined effect of the Derby Scheme and the initial phase of the Military Service Act to 2 March 1916 brought another thousand men into the Scots Guards. After that volunteering virtually ended as conscription made everyone liable to call up unless they could show an acceptable reason why not, but men could still volunteer as regulars. Formally, a conscript no longer had any choice over which part of the Army he joined. Most Scots Guards conscripts continued to come from the usual places, but it became much more haphazard as conscripts for the Foot Guards were sent to the Guards Depot and allocated there. So it was that in 1917 several dozen men from Scotland were enlisted into the Coldstream Guards and only later transferred to the Scots Guards. From 2 March 1916 anybody identified as liable for call up was automatically deemed to be an army reservist. They were divided into year groups, single and married, the younger year groups of single conscripts and Derby Men being the first called up. Some of the older Derby Men were not mobilised for eighteen months. It was not till 1917 that Derby Men and conscripts became significant numerically in the two Scots Guards Battalions abroad. About three and a half thousand men were called up into the Scots Guards after 2 March 1916, but many conscripts in the later stages of the War were never in the Battalions before the Armistice.

The rapid expansion of the Army in 1914 and the problems and challenges were mirrored in the Scots Guards. Training and equipping these numbers of men was not easy and was made worse once First Ypres left the 1st Scots Guards needing to be rebuilt from scratch and the 2nd Scots Guards in only slightly better shape. The last of the fit reservists, men who had recovered from sickness or lesser wounds already incurred and many of the reenlisted former soldiers were rushed out but the first of the volunteers without any pre-war military experience also started to go out to France in November 1914. By the turn of the year they constituted the majority of the men in both Battalions. It was then that the BEF was at its weakest, very short of experience at all ranks and inadequately equipped for what was in hand. It was from then that the serving soldiers, reservists, reenlisted men and early volunteers bore the brunt in the Scots Guards. Of these some perished, were disabled or captured very early. Many of the Fife miners and Glasgow policemen were casualties by the end of January 1915, but there were also serving soldiers or reservists at the start of the War who lost their lives or were irreversibly injured in the closing weeks.

A few, but more than one might expect, were there from start to finish unhit, but for those who were involved from the very beginning there was more occasion of being wounded, recovering and returning once more to the War, in some cases several times. Private Charles Hendrick, whose father was a Scots Guardsman in the 1890s, enlisted in his home town of Preston in April 1913, where he was a labourer, and went out with the 1st Scots Guards at the start of the War. Between 1914 and 1917 he was wounded on four separate occasions requiring hospital treatment, twice in the UK, at First Ypres, Loos, the Somme and Third Ypres, the last probably from shelling while on a working party. On 9 October 1917 during the Battle of Poelcapelle, also Third Ypres, he was hit for the fifth time and disabled because of the injury to his arm. By contrast Lance Sergeant Ernest Evans, once a hairdresser from Whitchurch, Shropshire, had been serving for over two years by August 1914. He was a signaller with the 1st Scots Guards from start to finish unwounded.

A stable feature of the Foot Guards was that any soldier sent to the BEF in a draft would always serve with a Battalion of his own Regiment, though possibly not always the one with whom he had started, so that once he had enlisted and been trained he had a strong sense of identity from then on. Once he arrived in a Scots Guards Battalion abroad that did not mean that he was there in a rifle company until death, wounds, illness or captivity claimed him. There were a variety of other avenues available. Some of these were internal, such as at Battalion Headquarters and the Transport. As communications became more sophisticated more men were needed as signallers, both at battalion level and, from August 1915, up to and including the Guards Division Signal Company. The Maxim machine guns, evolving into the Vickers, initially inadequately limited to two per battalion, started to be concentrated in brigade machine gun companies and from later 1915 the lighter and more easily deployed Lewis Gun became the main infantry support weapon. Experienced and suitable men moved on to become machine gunners with the Vickers Guns. Over time the brigade machine gun companies were themselves more closely integrated and out of this process eventually came the 4th (Foot Guards) Battalion Guards Machine Gun Regiment. None of these and other activities were safe, but they were different. As the Army expanded and as the system began to function more efficiently much more training went on in the UK. So men arriving in drafts for the BEF were already trained as Lewis gunners, as bombers equipped to use the hand grenade known as the Mills Bomb and how to take the latest precautions against gas. Notably, the ablest were selected and trained as signallers, Vickers machine gunners or specialist instructors.

Further away, but still in France, was the Base Camp at Harfleur near Le Havre, apart from a short time in the autumn of 1914. This became the Guards Division Base Depot. Officers and men from all the Foot Guards provided the training and administrative staff. This provided another good method of giving a break to those who needed it. The same was true of the 7th (Guards) Entrenching Battalion and later and to a lesser degree the Guards Reinforcement Battalion, an intermittent appendage of the Guards Division. It was preferable for men waiting to go to the Battalions in the line to be definitely occupied, rather than waiting at the Base Depot. So the Entrenching Battalion formed on 1 December 1915 at Chipilly on the River Somme upstream from Amiens, in which general area they worked until the spring of 1917, before being finally disbanded that October. They dug reserve trenches, built gun and machine gun emplacements, constructed and repaired roads, cut brushwood for revetting trenches and found carrying parties. Among their recorded activities were preparations for the Battle of the Somme, repairing roads at Fricourt in July 1916 after it began, building up the defences of Ginchy and Combles further east in January 1917, construction work at Havrincourt Wood in April 1917 after the German withdrawal to the Hindenburg Line west of Cambrai and digging a trench line from Épehy, in the same area, south to three miles from St Quentin. At one time in 1917 there were over two thousand men in the Entrenching Battalion from all five regiments of Foot Guards. 2nd Lieutenant Henry Dundas was with them in the spring of 1916 and called them "the Diggers". They were never completely safe and there were occasional casualties from shells. On the other side of the Channel were the Guards Depot at Caterham, other training establishments and ranges, the 3rd Battalion at Wellington Barracks, Regimental Headquarters nearby in Buckingham Gate, and the recruiting offices. All needed staffing.

Longer serving and older reenlisted men were sometimes discharged or conditionally released into reserved occupations such as munitions and the mines, the arrangement being dependent on their having a definite job to go to and staying in it. Men also moved on from the Battalions permanently for other reasons. A significant number were commissioned, most, but not all, either pre-war soldiers of various ranks or wartime volunteers. While there was a wide spread, many went to Lowland Scottish regiments. To begin with it was very much the custom throughout the Army, as it had been before the War, that someone should not be commissioned from the ranks within their own regiment.

Another alternative was transferring to a different part of the Army, in the case of the Labour Corps often compulsory and a means of moving on a man who was not up to it or simply too old. The Labour Corps activities immediately behind the line included salvage and often the burial of the dead. Some went to the Military Foot Police, as opposed to the Military Mounted Police, the Royal Army Medical Corps and others, but much the most frequent destination was the Royal Engineers. Many, often miners, transferred to the Tunnelling Companies, to an existence at least partly familiar to them, to shift work and better pay, but also dangerous. They did not spend all their time digging shafts to place explosives under enemy positions, because they were also active in constructing bunkers, underground headquarters, dressing stations for the RAMC and stores, rest and assembly areas. The Royal Engineers were also responsible for army signals, another specialist requirement, while their Field Companies worked on everything connected with roads, bridging, drainage, water supplies, explosives disposal, demolitions and the whole panoply of trench system works. There were also Royal Engineers railway and inland waterway sections.

The battles and trench tours apart, what went on in the Battalions had three notable elements, marching, fatigues and drill. The distances marched, particularly to begin with, mostly with full equipment, including packs, were substantial. Some narrow gauge lines developed in the summer of 1915 and as time went by there was more movement by narrow or broad gauge railway and by motor transport. Fatigues featured very largely and were one of the most significant elements of existence on the Western Front. As much as possible went up towards the front line trenches by railway, by mule, by horse transport and, in due course, lorry. At a certain point, however, only men could carry those stores forward, whether over open ground in the dark or up communication trenches, also usually in the dark. Ration parties carried up food, mail, messages, items of equipment and, most awkwardly, petrol cans of water. Ammunition parties carried just that. Carrying parties brought up defence stores, which included coils of barbed wire and razor or concertina wire, known as "French wire", stakes, hurdles with which to revet the sides of trenches and bind the earth, sandbags, corrugated iron for dug-out roofs and coke for braziers, among much else. Under Royal Engineer direction large digging parties worked on new trenches, built strong points and cleared and improved ditches. There was road construction and repair in all forms, which was likely, as in the Ypres Salient in 1917, to involve carrying up and laying railway sleepers to form a firm base. This had its effect on the military efficiency of the infantry. It made it very difficult to find sufficient time in which to train and in any event a battalion well used to life in and out of the trench systems was likely to be rusty when it had to start marching again and inadequately prepared for any different phase of warfare. It is noticeable too that bad weather frequently caused the cancellation of training, which, considering how frequently men had to fight in it, was unfortunate. The principal reason was that at any time a soldier only had one suit of uniform.

Drill went on regularly and systematically in the Foot Guards when out of the line, to the amusement and amazement of many others. However, there was good reason for it. First of all drill was a team effort and for it to be done well required everybody to do their best and work together. It was therefore a natural way of achieving cohesion, including immediately involving new arrivals. Next, as everyone was familiar with it, drill had a steadying effect on shaken and tired men because of its normality, which also, from the point of view of keeping them occupied, did not require much space. Underlying it all was the relationship between discipline, self-discipline, respect, self-respect, confidence and self-confidence.

Private Stephen Graham, in 1917 a somewhat surprising Scots Guards conscript, was an established author and travel writer with the education, but not the inclination, to be commissioned. In "*A Private In The Guards*", published in 1919, he mentioned being told by a former Sergeant Major of the 2nd Scots Guards whom he did not name, but can hardly have been anyone but Captain Tom Ross, the Quartermaster, that "A correct discipline must be obtained, and you cannot get it without absolute obedience. But a fine discipline needs a warm glowing esprit de corps, and to get that you must win the men's hearts." The Scots Guards had two nicknames, one used by officers of other regiments, "The Kiddies", believed to derive from when their ancestors joined those of the Grenadier and Coldstream Guards on Hounslow Heath for the first time in James II's reign. Among the rank and file, completely irrespective of their homes and origins, they took pride in and referred to themselves by the nickname by which they were also known to the rest of the Foot Guards, exemplified by an early volunteer in 1914, whose verses appeared through the War, Private George Morris.

> It's queer hoo every Guardsman thinks nae regiment like his ain.
> The "Bill Broons", "Colies", "Micks", an' "Taffys" think they staund alane.
> An' yet, what are they at their best? A lot o' wooden blocks,
> When up against the Scots Guards; MY Regiment – "The Jocks".

The Grenadiers' nickname at that time was the "Bill Browns", the "Colies", "Micks" and "Taffys" being those of the Coldstream, Irish and Welsh Guards.

Discipline was very rigidly enforced on active service. Minor offences would lead to punishments consisting of a few extra fatigues, extra drill or extra parades at which kit had to be shown. More serious breaches, such as absence, drunkenness, insubordination and gambling, let alone theft, would result in varying sentences of Field Punishment Numbers One and Two, the active service equivalent of military detention. A man "under sentence" might have it commuted if he did well in the trenches, as time spent in the line, which he had to do as normal, counted as part of the sentence. Someone undergoing FP No 2 had a stiff programme of extra fatigues and parades out of the line, often including "pack drill" at a fast pace while in Field Service Marching Order, i.e. wearing and carrying full equipment, but no rifle. The only difference between FP No 2 and FP No 1 was that the latter had another element. That was the tying of the man under sentence to a fixed object or a wagon wheel or similar, depending on what was available, in the open air, for up to two hours a day in one hour sessions on not more three days out of four. Until prohibited later in the War there was still provision for the man to be tied up spreadeagled. Sentences could be long. Private Peter Baird, a miner, originally from Carnwath, Lanarkshire, and a reservist mobilised in 1914, arrived in the 1st Scots Guards with a very bad previous disciplinary record. On 25 January 1915 he was wounded in the hand in the battle at the Cuinchy brickstacks near the La Bassée Canal. When he came back he was posted to the 2nd Scots Guards with whom he sprained an ankle on 16 September 1916 near Ginchy during the Battle of the Somme. In July 1917 he was charged not only with drunkenness, not for the first time, but also with theft of an officer's property. A court martial found him guilty and sentenced him to three months FP No 1 and to forfeit his 1914 Star. He was still in the Battalion as the War entered its final phase until severely wounded in the left leg on 4 September 1918 near the Canal du Nord at Moeuvres.

The machine gun was not a constant threat, the fall of shells, which later on might be gas ones, and minenwerfer bombs was. Once the technology of trench warfare became sophisticated, being in a trench knowing that the enemy had the precise range and could bring down shells and minenwerfer bombs accurately at any time and then have it happen continuously for three or four hours or more, with or without intervals to increase tension, was as hard as anything to endure. The longer the War went on the more sophisticated and frequent bombing from the air became and that added another very frightening unpredictable element, the more so at night. There was terrible fear of being buried alive and dread of drowning in mud or shellholes.

Right from the very start of the War what was misleadingly called "shock" or "shell shock" was a recognised reality among all ranks doing the fighting. Instantaneous shock was recorded as a wound, but it included both concussion and also immediate mental trauma. What that was medically and how to treat it was another matter. Some recovered sufficiently to return, others never, and those who came back frequently succumbed again. Those who had reached the limit of exposure to the strain of the fighting and the environment near and at the front could often do other necessary military tasks away from it and many did so for the rest of the War. Anybody suffering from shock in any way was a liability to himself and to everyone else.

Shock from exposure to strain and exhaustion, sometimes extended, sometimes brief, but not instantaneous, was covered by the then medically recognised condition of neurasthenia. The symptoms collectively amounted to lethargy, lassitude and poor responses, constituting inability to function. Again, some diagnosed with this reappeared later and others did not. There was also "debility" to which some degree of shock could be a contributing factor, but where rest was normally sufficient. The concept of the "nervous breakdown" was known and understood too. Wherever symptoms suggested neurasthenia the medical system scrutinised the patient very thoroughly because instantaneous shock as a wound was clear cut, whereas what was cumulative was easier to simulate. Someone apparently uninjured in any way might turn up in a casualty clearing station without any recollection of how he got there, but with some account of a nearby explosion and no memory of anything else. Strain, possibly shell shock related, but manifesting itself as heart strain, featured frequently and the letters DAH, Disordered Action of the Heart, appeared often on medical records. Again, sometimes the effects were permanent, sometimes not.

For some weeks during the summer of 1916 Captain Hugh Bayly was Medical Officer of the 1st Scots Guards until wounded on 15 September on the Somme during the Guards Division attack from Ginchy towards Lesboeufs. Much later he wrote that "The term "shell shock" was far too loose a term as used during the war to cover: (1) Shell concussion, with a more or less prolonged period of unconsciousness and almost certain damage to brain substance. (2) Shell neurasthenia, the result of nerve exhaustion after a prolonged period of strain and tension and lack of sleep. (3) Abnormal nerve reaction to the stimuli of explosions owing to a sensitive and highly strung nervous system. (4) A lack of normal nerve control in the face of danger, to which the ugly name of 'cowardice' is sometimes, but only sometimes, rightly given.

All gallant men dread shell shock more than any other wound, for the simple reason that an extremely small percentage of the men returned with this disability may possibly include a few poltroons. There is no form of casualty that has my greater sympathy.

The time funk is most likely to grip a man is when he is under shelter and his duty is to move out of shelter. When one is under fire one feels that it is a matter of luck, and is more or less philosophical, but moving out of cover is not a matter of luck, it is a matter of one's own decision." He felt exactly that "on leaving my shellhole dressing station at Ginchy to move forward, and…it left me when I was in the open."

One of the most prevalent medical problems was trench foot. To begin with it was not identified for what it was and, because the very painful symptoms and indeed the consequences, if untreated, gangrene, leading to loss of limbs and ultimately death, were the same, frostbite was what it was thought to be. It first appeared as a serious issue once the lines became static in trenches dug in the late autumn of 1914 after First Ypres and after the fighting further south at the same time, known later as the Battle of Armentières. Fairly soon tightly fastened puttees and tight fitting boots were identified as part of the problem, but the cold and the wet were believed to be the culprits, rather than the aggravating factors that they were. By early 1915 there began to be rubber Wellington boots and thigh waders, known as trench waders. There was also whale oil which the men rubbed over their feet and which could have provided some degree of insulation. This was still going on in the winter of 1917-18, but the real problem was circulation. Provided that men could move about and keep their legs and feet moving they should not get trench foot, but where they were standing in mud or water and movement was badly impeded, then it was likely to result.

The life of the infantryman is never that comfortable whether on a peacetime exercise or on operations. The soldier has to make the best of where he has to be and either mud is his habitual companion or else dust, usually augmented by flies. The experience of the infantry on the Western Front, leaving aside the principal battles, was not one of constant, unrelieved, physical misery. The front line trenches, particularly in the Ypres Salient, were always potentially and often actually dangerous, but even there a trench tour could often pass without any incidents at all. If there was a lot of rain or snow things could be very uncomfortable indeed, but that too was not always the case. During the winter of 1916-17 weather conditions on the Somme were so bad that sometimes it was impossible to put troops into the forward trenches for more than forty eight hours at a time and this made it almost equally impossible for troops rotating with them to get themselves clean and dry in the interval in rest areas not far back. Out of the line the administrative arrangements for soldiers' welfare were crude and limited to begin with, but an enormous amount of effort went into improving them and to good effect.

However bad the physical experiences on the Western Front, these were at least equalled in other parts of the world where British, Dominion and Colonial troops fought, Italy, Gallipoli, Mesopotamia, Palestine, Salonika, to name only some, and, as bad as anywhere, East Africa.

There are also the comparisons with the Second World War in which Burma stands out, along with the heat and dust and the cold of the Western Desert and along too with the gruelling Italian campaign. Finally, there is the fighting from Normandy till the German surrender in 1945, an experience just as physically demanding and mentally intense. That the First World War went on so long, to nearly the end of 1918 as far as the British and French were concerned on the Western Front, while not forgetting that war persisted elsewhere for some years afterwards, was inevitable considering the war aims of the participants and the even balances of their forces. Simply for the British to carry on the War to a conclusion required the industrialization of the economy to operate the military machine and this process in varying degrees affected every nation fighting in it. That the Western Front was largely static until the very end, a prolonged and gigantic siege, was a further dehumanising factor, but had there been four years and more of a major war of movement the costs of all types could hardly have been less. The Reverend PB "Tubby" Clayton, one of the founders of Talbot House in Poperinghe and of the Christian movement known by the House's nickname, Toc H, remarked afterwards that "Hideous and detestable as trench warfare was, a war of movement, so glibly desired by the critics on both sides, has for the civilian population the terrors of a tornado, and tenfold its precipitancy and power."

It did take over four years to weaken Germany to the stage where the War was won. The experience of the Union in the American Civil War showed the way towards what the United Kingdom had to do from 1914 onwards, militarily, industrially, politically and diplomatically. While there were different influences and other factors at work, in the American Civil War it took the Union slightly over four years to defeat the Confederacy. In the Second World War it took the Russians just under four years to defeat the Germans and it took the Americans, with the Atomic Bomb, not far short of four years to defeat the Japanese. In each case there was no scope for a negotiated peace. In each case the fighting was intense. In each case the casualties among those doing the fighting reflected that and in the Second World War, particularly, there was a huge toll of civilian casualties.

Way beyond all others the battle that marked the Scots Guards in the Great War was the First Battle of Ypres. Taking the Commonwealth War Graves Commission figures for the Scots Guards dead from all causes there were 672 from September to December 1914, but none in August, 817 in 1915, 528 in 1916, 456 in 1917 and 423 in 1918. Of the 1914 deaths 421 occurred in Belgium between 18 October and 15 November, plus 17 in France at Base hospitals on the Channel coast likely to be attributable to First Ypres, and 4 in England of whom 2 were definitely from that battle. That is without counting any who died after 15 November of wounds during Ypres or who, captured there, died of wounds as prisoners once they reached Germany, while several more died there as prisoners from other causes. The First Ypres total exceeds that for the whole of 1918, which included a number who died of Spanish Flu, some of them First Ypres prisoners, and would exceed that for 1917 if the First Ypres subsequent deaths are taken into account.

Where Scots Guardsmen who died are now buried or commemorated in Belgium or France is usually a good indicator of where they fell, but not necessarily. After the War the battlefields were carefully and thoroughly cleared and considering the circumstances it was remarkable that so many recovered then were identifiable. There were many small cemeteries and known individual graves all along the Western Front and these were mostly consolidated. One of the consequences was the large number of Scots Guardsmen reburied in the Cabaret-Rouge British

Cemetery, Souchez, between Arras and Loos, some miles from either and well away from where either Battalion ever fought. A second and very strange particular consequence was the burial of several, apparently completely without any method to it, in places a very long way from where they died. An example was the group of twelve men from the 2nd Scots Guards, including Company Sergeant Major Charles Lilley of F Company, the only one identified, among the many killed on the evening of 18 December 1914 at Rouges Bancs, between Armentières and Neuve Chapelle. When their group grave was found they were reburied very far away in the London Cemetery and Extension, Longueval, in the middle of the Somme battlefield beside High Wood.

Very many of the wounded died. The chances of someone surviving if badly hit in the stomach were negligible, a head wound, unless superficial, was usually fatal and many did not survive amputations, whether from previous loss of blood, the condition the wounded man was in otherwise on being operated on or what was generally put down to the shock of the amputation, but could easily have been infection. Where the casualty clearing stations were there are war cemeteries, as at Méaulte, on the Somme, where the hospitals were, further back, there are war cemeteries, as at Doullens, southwest of Arras, and where the Base hospitals were there are war cemeteries, as at Boulogne.

Soldiers were often posted as missing when it was known that they were dead, but not formally recorded as such, and so "missing" came also to be a euphemism for those known to be dead, but unburied. Missing could also mean just that, particularly when there was nothing left to pick up and bury. However, it could also hold out the chance, however remote, of someone turning up, most likely as a prisoner of war, news of which might take months. If, after time had passed and there was no further information or trace of an individual the War Office would determine, normally not less than six months later, that for official purposes the soldier was deemed to have died on the last date on which he was known to have been alive or the first date on which it was evident from a roll call that he was missing. There was sometimes a difference later between what appeared on one of the Memorials to the Missing and how a casualty was first reported. In many instances men were killed, reported correctly as such, with the burial of their bodies in specific locations recorded by description and map reference. Later, however, their graves were lost, whether by shellfire, mining, or other disturbance of the ground, such as the digging of fresh trenches, and as there was no sign of them their names were later shown on the Memorials to the Missing.

Amid all the contemporary letters and diaries there was confidence that the War would be won, with albeit much understandably optimistic wishful thinking about when. There were also some very astute observations, such as the recognition in 1915 that the War would go on until the Germans ran out of men, which, though not the whole answer, turned out to be very close to the mark, though it took a long time, and some much less astute ones, such as the belief that heavy artillery fire in sufficient volume brought on rain. At first sight it might appear odd that there was so much that was found very funny, even at close quarters with the enemy, but those who could see a funny side when there was one were those who were most likely to be able to cope with the strain.

There were men who did not attract attention then or later because, air raids apart, they were physically out of danger and their work meant that they were in London. They were those, taking just the needs of the Scots Guards, both in the War Office and at Regimental Headquarters, who handled the notification of casualties and had to live day in and day out with awareness of the pain that the notifications of death would cause, of the distress and the clinging, elusive hopes of the families of the missing, of the anguish and uncertainty of the relatives of the badly wounded and maimed. Thereafter there were the requests for more details, often when there would never and could never be any and sometimes when what did come to light might be worse than knowing nothing. The forwarding of personal effects might only be upsetting for the recipients, but there could be no exercise of discretion. Everything that was available had to be passed on in whatever state it was in, sometimes coming to light long after the end of the War. The complete absence of any effects or of particular items, notably watches, could be worse.

Though it only appears in the second volume of the Official History, dealing in particular with First Ypres, Brigadier General Sir James Edmonds wrote "As so often in its history the British Army had been launched into a great enterprise with wholly insufficient means."

Notes on Chapter Sources

Diary-style account of Pte W Luck is in three forms, the original and a cleaned up typed version as of an unnamed Scots Guardsman, both in the National Army Museum ("NAM"), and a third slightly different typed version, used here, under his name, 1968 *Scots Guards Magazine* ("SGM").
GM Trevelyan, *Grey of Falloden* (London: Longmans, Green and Co Ltd 1937).
Standing Orders of the Scots Guards 1901.
Officers' files at The National Archives ("TNA"), mostly in TNA/WO339 and a few in TNA/WO374.
Officers' Records, Scots Guards Archives ("SGA").
For officers who died before 30 June 1915, Colonel AL Clutterbuck and Others, *The Bond of Sacrifice, Volume 1, August to December 1914 and Volume 2, January to June 1915* (London: The Anglo-African Publishing Contractors 1916).
For individuals who were already or became during the War VC holders or, in the case of officers, DSO holders, Gen Sir O'Moore Creagh and EM Humphris (Eds), *The V.C. and D.S.O.* in three volumes (London: The Standard Art Book Co Ltd, undated).
Soldiers' files, by regimental number, in which are everything currently known about them officially and unofficially, unless another source is obvious from the text, with abbreviated information in the Enlistment Books, all SGA, enlistment forms of Scots Guardsmen held on behalf of TNA.
Charles Messenger, *Call to Arms: The British Army 1914-1918* (London: Weidenfeld & Nicolson 2005).
All correspondence to or from any member of the Cuthbert Family, Cuthbert Papers, Private Collection.
Summary of activities of the 7th (Guards) Entrenching Battalion, Appendix VIIII, Cuthbert Headlam, *History of the Guards Division in the Great War 1915-1918 Volume II* (London: John Murray 1924).
Stephen Graham, *A Private in the Guards* (London: Macmillan and Co Ltd 1919).
LCpl George Morris, 'Extracts from a Notebook of World War I', 1959 SGM.
Dr Hugh Wansey Bayly: *Triple Challenge: Or, War, Whirligigs and Windmills* (London: Hutchinson & Co 1933).
Rev PB Clayton, *Tales of Talbot House in Poperinghe & Ypres* (London: Chatto & Windus 1919).

The Commonwealth War Graves Commission website www.cwgc.org, with reliable regimental numbers.

History of the Great War based on Official Documents by direction of the Historical Section of the Committee of Imperial Defence.

Brig Gen Sir JE Edmonds, *Military Operations France and Belgium, 1914:* Volume II: *Antwerp, La Bassée, Armentières, Messines, and Ypres, October-November 1914* (London: Macmillan and Co Ltd 1925).

2

The Retreat from Mons – 1st Battalion

It was not part of French thinking to start a war with Germany. If war came, as they expected it to do sometime, they appreciated that the Germans were likely to attack them through Belgium, but assumed that they could knock such a move off balance by attacking along the mutual border. Their military doctrine required an attack immediately to recover Alsace and those parts of Lorraine taken by the Germans in 1871 after the Franco-Prussian War, but there was no intention of invading Germany. They were also unwilling to prepare to take a defensive stance or to protect their frontier with Belgium. This had most to do with the perceived need to reassert national self-confidence by being aggressive from the outset.

The emphasis of German military planning was on a short, sharp war and the conclusive defeat of France, followed by the containment of Russia to whatever extent necessary. It was thought unlikely that Russia would persist for long after France had been knocked out. However, the contingency that when a war came it would not be short, sharp and conclusive had received much attention. The outcome of these discussions about both military and industrial systems meant that decisions could be taken quickly after war broke out so Germany could fight a long one if that would ultimately achieve their desired results of going to war in the first place. It was far from the preferred option. The decision to strike first against France, derived from many years of planning, was because they considered that Russia would take longer to deploy and attack German soil, though East Prussia would be vulnerable from the outset. Because of the French defensive systems along the mutual border, the German operational plan, depending on their railways and subsequently on those of others, was for a very heavily weighted right wing attack to break through and round the left of the French armies. There were the advantages that the landscape and communications lent themselves to the purpose, but the only way of doing it was by breaching Belgian neutrality on a large scale. Once through and behind the French left, the German right wing armies were to swing round onto the rear of the French armies, push them eastwards and destroy them. Meanwhile, their intention was that the French armies opposite them along the mutual frontier in the south were to be held there by sufficient operations to keep them occupied and so prevent any redeployment to meet the northern thrust. The French military planners did not anticipate the scale, let alone the purpose, of the German move through Belgium, having also ignored the pre-war pointers. The main reason that they seriously underestimated the size of the German Armies was that they had not realised that these would include reserve corps, whose identification numerals were the same as the regular ones.

Aldershot

By August 1914 the 1st Scots Guards had been two years at Ramillies Barracks, Aldershot, and before that in Egypt. They, the 1st Coldstream, alongside whom they would fight throughout the War, the 1st Black Watch and the 2nd Royal Munster Fusiliers were in the 1st (Guards) Brigade, under the command of Brigadier General Ivor Maxse, a Coldstreamer. Major Charles Corkran, the Brigade Major, and Captain Andrew "Bulgy" Thorne, the Staff Captain, were both Grenadiers. The 1st (Guards), 2nd and 3rd Brigades formed the 1st Division, under Major General Samuel Lomax. This and the 2nd Division comprised Aldershot Command which would, on mobilization, metamorphose directly into I Corps, the Army's only fully operational such formation, complete with staff officers. Lieutenant General Sir Douglas Haig, who commanded Aldershot Command, would become Corps Commander.

One of the subalterns was Lieutenant Sir Edward Hulse, Bt, known to his brother officers as "Teddy", but invariably signing himself "Ted" in his letters home to his widowed mother at Breamore, Hampshire. Edith Hulse was the sister of Lord Burnham, who had served in the Scots Guards. Lord and Lady Burnham's home was in Buckinghamshire, near Beaconsfield, and their son, 2nd Lieutenant The Honourable William "Bill" Lawson, commissioned in 1912 after Eton and Sandhurst, was also in the Battalion. Sir Edward Hulse had also been at Eton before Balliol College, Oxford, and then in 1912 trained with the Coldstream before joining the Scots Guards in March 1913. In the late afternoon on Sunday 2 August 1914 he wrote to his mother from London, having gone there for lunch and then on to visit the 2nd Battalion at the Tower of London, "where I found them very busy, and mobilization machinery complete and ready to be set in motion at moment's notice." Preparations for mobilization of the Army had begun on 28 July "the precautionary period", so when it was ordered everything went very smoothly. All Scots Guards reservists were to report to the Tower to be passed medically fit and kitted out. Each man's Reserve Certificate, printed on parchment, included instructions about what to do on receipt of a mobilization notice which "should reach you within two days of Mobilization being ordered" with details of where to report. It stated that "The notice will have attached to it a free pass for your journey and a postal order for three shillings advance of pay." Sir Edward Hulse noted the "Overwhelming opinion amongst "the man in the street" that we must help France. It is not a question of national honour any longer, but of national welfare and actual life in the future." He saw the British Empire as part of that future but also remarked that "As far as the French authorities are concerned, they want our fleet, and would like a force also; they don't want numbers; ten Boy Scouts and British flag is all that is wanted. The whole thing lies in the moral support and the fact of the British flag on French soil. As a matter of fact, 120,000 or 160,000 troops from us at Maubeuge would mean a very real help to France, although people talk about our army as a drop in the ocean." There was no doubt in his mind that the Germans would violate Belgian neutrality and that every British soldier in France would be valuable to the French. That he picked the fortress town of Maubeuge, just on the French side of the border with Belgium and roughly equidistant south of Mons and southwest of Charleroi, as the point of concentration for the BEF was quite correct. How he did not explain.

The Monday was a Bank Holiday and Lieutenant James "Jamie" Balfour's parents went to see him at Aldershot on their way back to London from Devon, their home being at Newton Don, Berwickshire. Charles Balfour, who had been in the Scots Guards himself, found "Everything was in apple pie order – and ready for instant action in case of war. There was nothing to do

– and Jamie and "Meat" Lowther (the Colonel) and others were playing tennis – like Drake's historic game of bowls." Lieutenant Colonel Cecil "Meat" Lowther, the bachelor Commanding Officer, had been at Charterhouse and Sandhurst and had a DSO from the Boer War. On 4 August Lieutenant Sir Iain Colquhoun of Luss, Bt, known as "Luss" to his brother officers, wrote to Geraldine "Dinah" Tennant "This place is seething with quite unbelievable excitement and every hour sees a whole crop of new and ridiculous rumours started. They all think we shall be ordered to Belgium this week, and I've just completed bets of 250 to 300 pounds that we don't leave England." The outcome of the bets was never recorded. He ended his letter "Well Dinah I told you we shouldn't meet for some time and it don't look much like it." Lieutenant Edward Tennant, Dinah's brother, in the Scots Guards but a pilot attached to the Royal Flying Corps, was disappointed and frustrated at not being allowed to be back with the Battalion. He served with the RFC, later transferring to the RAF, throughout the War and survived. Sir Iain Colquhoun's home was at Rossdhu on Loch Lomond. He had been to school at Fettes, was commissioned in 1908 and five years later was Lightweight Boxing Champion of the Army in the officers' competition.

At six on the evening of the 4th they received the order to mobilise. The following day three parties of reservists arrived, "magnificent, clean steady men." One was Private John Osborne, who reported at the Tower, from where, passed fit, he was sent straight on with his new uniform and equipment. He was in York when he enlisted in 1905, having previously been a glass beveller, and had a rose, thistle and shamrock tattooed on his right arm and clasped hands and a star on his right wrist. By 1914 he was a London tram driver, living with his wife Kate in Lower Edmonton. Private James Kendall was another reservist, whose father's business in Liverpool was Bell Brothers & Thomson, Ship Store and Provision Merchants Ship Chandlers and Sailmakers. He, a tall man at just under six foot four, had worked there before joining the Army, which was not wholly to his liking as he was absent without leave both in 1910 and 1911. In order to draw reserve pay reservists were required to check in annually to confirm that they were alive and where they were living, as well as carrying out twelve days' training in some years, but soon after he went to the Reserve after Christmas 1912 he set off for Melbourne without telling the authorities that he was going to Australia. When this came to light there was firm correspondence on the risk of his forfeiting his reserve pay. By then, however, he was back in Liverpool, where James and Ellen Kendall lived in Huyton, working again with his father. Lance Corporal Eric Leary, from Halifax, was promoted Sergeant immediately he reported and sent to the Guards Depot. Five weeks later he was commissioned into the 1st Royal Irish Regiment, with whom he was killed in 1915. Private John Gargan left for the Reserve in the autumn of 1910, then disappeared for more than half of the interval before mobilization and only reported in again in March 1914. He had been working as a caulker in Glasgow when he enlisted, but came originally from near Carrickmacross, County Monaghan. On mobilization he failed medically and was discharged from the Army two weeks later.

By the 6th the 1st Scots Guards were complete to their war establishment of men and by midnight on the 7th ready to move. The next four days were taken up with training and route marching. In Sir Edward Hulse's letter home on the 12th he wrote "We start tonight, about midnight, but do not know destination or anything yet…I have delivered myself of three 'eavy lectures to my platoon, on everything from the general situation, no quarter and discipline down to French money, etc. The Colonel's instructions as to behaviour for the battalion are "Towards all inhabitants kindness and a helping hand, towards all womankind, courtesy, but no intimacy." This, including the wording, reflected directions from higher up the chain of command, Lord Kitchener having ordered that his words were to be put into every soldier's field service pay book.

On the 13th Lieutenant Balfour, with five years service, started a diary. Inside the front cover, written up later, he listed the officers, with nicknames, who left for France, twenty nine, including the Quartermaster, Lieutenant David Kinlay. Of the other twenty eight, eighteen were killed, most in 1914 and the rest early in 1915. Two of these had previously been wounded in September during the Battle of the Aisne, returned and then lost their lives. One, unwounded, was taken prisoner on 29 October during First Ypres and two days later another, wounded and unable to be moved, was also captured. With the exception of Colonel Lowther, who was only wounded once, but not seriously, and promoted very soon after he came back, all the others were physically wounded at least twice in the War, without counting gas or shell shock. The only brothers, Captain Sir Victor Mackenzie, Bt, and 2nd Lieutenant Eric Mackenzie, neither of them married, both survived. Their home was outside Ballater, Aberdeenshire, where their widowed mother was living. Lieutenant Kinlay had been serving since 1888, married Florence Rossiter four years later and had a son and a daughter with her. He was with the 1st Scots Guards until late August 1918 and was three times mentioned in despatches, as well as winning the Military Cross, but there was a price. He contracted a serious chest complaint and that was why he went home. It led to his early retirement in March 1919 and he never recovered his health.

In 1914 a photograph was taken of seven members of the Officers Mess Staff at Aldershot. They were wearing smart, dark waiter's suits. All were named in the caption, but some of the initials attributed were incorrect and hence the identity of one, shown as "K King", was lost, because many other men called King were serving at the time and none had K as an initial. The fates of the other six are known.

Going Abroad

They breakfasted in barracks at half past two in the morning on the 13th, marched down to Farnborough Station and left in two trains, at an hour's interval, for Southampton. Colonel Lowther, who likewise started writing that day, noticed how "A black kitten walked under my horse's nose as we marched off. Is it my luck or the battalion. Train loaded and away well on time and in perfect order." Private Osborne in B Company, another to start a diary, wrote that "we stole silently away from North Camp to Farnboro Station. No talking or smoking allowed. Everything was carried out in such a hush hush manner that some of us expected to be in action at Frimley or Camberley." Private William Luck, in the same company, a thirty year old reservist from Cross-in-Hand, Sussex, where he lived with Lizzie, his wife of three years, and their daughter born in 1912, remarked in his later account, probably from a diary, that "To myself, who looked upon the departure of a Battalion for war as something to be accompanied by bands playing, flags waving and crowds cheering, it was something of a shock to crawl out of Aldershot at 3.15 on the foggy morning of August 13th 1914, bound for an unknown destination." No one knew where they were going, but once at Southampton they guessed Le Havre. Lord Methuen, Colonel of the Regiment, was among those at Farnborough to see them off. By eight o'clock the second train had arrived in Southampton. At once they went aboard the SS *Dunvegan Castle*.

Private Thomas Hutchison, a groom before he joined the Army in 1909, had two tattoos on his left forearm, a tombstone and a girl with a heart. He was with them as they left Aldershot and, apart from a very slight head wound in June 1917 near Ypres, was in France, Belgium and eventually Germany till he went home in January 1919. He was awarded the Military Medal in May 1918. His father David Hutchison lived in the New Town, Edinburgh. Private John Menzies' story was similar. When the War broke out he had been serving for nearly two years, before that having been a farm worker. He too was there as they left Aldershot and, so slightly wounded on 29 March 1918 during the German Spring Offensives that he did not have to leave for treatment at all, was otherwise present and unscathed, from start to finish, till he went home in March 1919. His MM came after the War. His parents Archibald and Jane Menzies lived near Aberfoyle, Perthshire.

Headquarters 1st (Guards) Brigade had signed a contract on 3 August with Fortnum & Mason to provide "Mobilisation Provision Boxes as scheduled" to Aldershot within twenty four hours of notice to do so and "a suitable chef" at a rate of £5 per week plus expenses. Captain Thorne noted all this and that at Southampton the chef "had difficulty in getting onto quayside, name Jasinski rather against him." The *Dunvegan Castle* sailed at noon with Brigade Headquarters, the Coldstream, Scots Guards and Munsters and their transport wagons. Captain Thorne told his wife Margaret that it was "a Donald Currie ship, which is in a horrible state of filth." Colonel Lowther noted being "Packed like sardines, over 3,000, about 8 lifeboats and 300 belts, an accident would have made the "*Titanic*" disaster look like 30 cents. Intricate exit from the Solent through minefields. Minesweepers cruising off, otherwise little military shipping. A delay at Sandown for examination and then a perfectly smooth crossing. Havre about 3.0am or later, bad night as the Munsters were singing and making a noise all the time." The horses travelled separately in a tramp steamer, the SS *Orange Prince*. Lance Corporal Charles Green, a former clerk, another Liverpudlian, the son of Charles and Elenor Green of Walton and a serving soldier since 1910, remembered their departure from Southampton "with great cheers etc. from the quayside." Private Luck noticed the final messages semaphored from the Royal Marines posted on floats guarding the approaches. There was very sound reason for the secrecy. So effective was British and French security that the arrival of the BEF in France remained unknown to anybody who had not physically seen the British soldiers on French soil. The possibility that there were British troops somewhere in the area of the nearest Channel ports, with one such as Calais as their base, was a consideration for General Alexander von Kluck, in command of the German *First Army* on the right wing of the swing through Belgium into northern France, and was to waste much of his cavalry's time. Not until there was a public announcement from Lord Kitchener on 20 August in London that the BEF were in France was it known generally. Where they were still remained unspecified and General von Kluck had no inkling until the first cavalry skirmish in front of his line of advance.

The *Dunvegan Castle* reached Le Havre well after midnight, where they disembarked at once. In spite of the time Private Osborne saw how "The people gave us a hearty welcome. All was excitement, we were "Vive L'Anglais" at every step, and when we halted en route a lady sang "The Marseillaise" from the balcony of a house. The voice of the singer was wonderfully sweet. It was a fitting song for a fitting occasion." Corporal Green remarked their disembarkation "amidst great cries of "Vive la Angleterre"." He went on "Many French soldiers were present dressed in flaring red trousers, blue caps and jacket." There followed a very trying two hours march steeply uphill to a camp six miles away, between Granville and Harfleur, where there were bell tents, ten men to each. This was where Henry V's army camped to besiege Harfleur in 1415 at the start of the campaign which led to the Battle of Agincourt. They were left to sleep until eleven on the 14th when there was breakfast of tea, bully beef and biscuits. Colonel Lowther noted "Only territorial French soldiers to be seen, many of them busy harvesting. A good camping ground on stubble. But little washing water and no fuel." The water problem resolved itself and the Adjutant, Captain Albert Stephen, found some fuel.

The steamer bringing the transport and the horses was delayed and so baggage parties, including Private Luck, were left to wait for them. Not till the sun was well up and hot could they leave the docks, much attended by French well wishers handing them wine and fruit on the way. Later Colonel Lowther went to Le Havre "and poured with perspiration…had a bad lunch and a good bath and shave and changed a lot of money. Men none the better from sudden cessation of green food. None to be had, got them some bread and cigarettes in Harfleur…Official news limited to a few minor French successes…I see that the orders issued for landing and for rest camps are dated three years back. Most creditable staff work. There are no alterations in them." Lieutenant Balfour also went to Harfleur for lunch and a shave and to make some purchases. On their way back he and Lieutenant Hugh Ross, who would feature frequently, stopped to swim in a little river.

Captain Thorne wrote home on the 15th "The thunder & lightning effects were very fine and until the rain descended, we thought it was a naval battle." At the end of his letter he added "Our censor is very hard hearted, so rumour has it and will probably delete most of this letter." The censor added "No I am not" and sent it on. The heavy rain from eleven the previous night till mid afternoon on the 15th, prevented any training. The Scots Guards paraded at nine that evening "deep mud, torrents of rain, wet through" and, once on their way to entrain for an unknown destination, the 1st Lincolnshire Regiment of the 3rd Division marched straight across their front at a crossroads and held them up. Then there was a broken down wagon blocking the road, which meant that all theirs had to go another way. Next the Medical Officer, Captain Alban Meaden RAMC, got lost with his cart but eventually turned up. While the companies got to Le Havre station on time at midnight, it was not until an hour later that the Transport arrived after a terrible time with the mud and steep descents. Corporal Green, in their escort, wrote "We marched along a cart track up to our knees in mud, but quite contented. We could not see where we were going, it was so dark." At the station they "slept on the hard stones." It was now the morning of Sunday 16 August. With their wagons and sixty horses they boarded a train at three o'clock, forty men in a horse box or ten in a third class carriage compartment, and left just over an hour later. To Corporal Green "to judge by the way we were packed, I thought it was Stamford Bridge, and not a troop train, our destination was unknown, but what mattered?" Colonel Lowther noted "Just as we left a thunderous noise in a horse truck, horse with broken leg, pitched out onto platform to be executed by the local powers."

Lieutenant Balfour recorded "Reached Rouen 11am where we stopped for a half of an hour and had a wash at a pump, destination unknown. From Rouen onwards we were cheered at every level crossing and at every town we stopped the Colonel being given a bouquet and the men apples, chocolate, cigarettes, flags, etc. the people asking for "souvenirs"… At Arras about 10,000 old men women children turned out to cheer us and the town guard turned out on the platform and presented arms to us. The whole country for miles here is nothing but corn in stooks: it seems a horrible waste for there are only old men women and children and no horses so it can't be got in. I have not seen a single man between the age of 16 and 40." Sir Edward

Hulse wrote up some brief notes about this period after he lost his own diary subsequently. He mentioned "Tremendous reception. Embrace particularly good looking girls, who load us with sweets, smokes, coffee, and souvenirs. Army arrives at detraining point without any badges, all given as souvenirs." Private Luck observed that at Rouen "the inhabitants tried to make hay while the sun shone by selling small meat sandwiches at 5d each. We soon entrained again and on our way up country were greeted most enthusiastically and treated most kindly by the population. At every station where the train slowed down fruit, cider, tea and cigarettes were thrust on the troops, the only payment demanded being a cap star or button as a souvenir. It was rather pleasant to have a button begged by a little French girl, although there was a deuce of a row in the Battalion next day when we formed up, mostly without cap stars, shoulder numerals or buttons. The largest crowd was at Cambrai where there must have been a French garrison. Amongst others in the station was a Dundee girl, who distributed a box of bonbons amongst the troops. It was like giving strawberries to a donkey." Colonel Lowther found the "reception all along the line very flattering, cheers, bouquets, flags, (but few Union Jacks, not much used in ordinary times in France!) Stephen had to kiss a small boy, as proxy for me. Reception flattering but tiresome as it gave one no peace and quiet at all. Men very annoying, giving away their badges, cap stars, etc." He spoke to all the section commanders about this next day and added "These trifles are very vexing when the men are so willing and work so well." Their cap badge was the Star of the Order of the Thistle and hence a cap star.

From Cambrai the railway wound southeast and when, later that evening, the train came into Busigny, south of Le Cateau, Lieutenant Balfour was told by the French Commandant there "that two days ago they did not even know themselves that British troops were coming." On leaving Busigny the train went east, crossed the Sambre and Oise Canal at Etreux and continued to Le Nouvion, arriving at eleven that night. Sir Edward Hulse recorded that forty eight trains carrying the BEF had arrived there on time, only one being late. Lieutenant Balfour went with a French officer to arrange billets but, on reaching a large school, which was to take three companies, found it locked. The town had to be searched for the schoolmaster. The rest were to occupy indifferent accommodation in a cider factory. Starting at one in the morning, he had everyone settled in by half past two. He then had to ride off at four on horseback with the four Company Quartermaster Sergeants on bicycles and go seven miles west to Boué, their next destination and close to the Canal. He got there just before six from when it took him two and a half hours to arrange billets. This involved visiting each house and trying to organise everything so as to keep each company together as much as possible. He wrote "They were beautiful billets all with straw and decorated with flowers. Ofrs had rooms to themselves with beds, basins. Everybody delighted to see me giving one coffee and cider at every house." Then he had the first opportunity to change and have a wash and shave since Le Havre. Also, apart from nodding off on the train, he had not had much sleep, but "Have got a dear old lady whose house I am in who has got two little grandchildren about 7 and 9. The old lady brings me coffee when I get up and looks after me like an old nurse."

He must have had a close call with his billeting arrangements for Corporal Green wrote of the Battalion arriving at eight. "Here we were split up into small parties…Everything was commandeered in the way of barns, outhouses, lofts etc. according to the size of the house, barn, or loft." He, a sergeant and eight men were in an old stable "but everything had been made ready for us." Boué was not a big place, but there was an hotel, an estaminet and one or two confectioners and others. "We were all very eager to sample the eggs, butter, and bread of the French. Quite a change from our own daily ration of one lb bully beef, four dog biscuits, two oz cheese, a spot of bacon, and a pound of jam (?) for five or seven men." Sir Edward Hulse recorded that they "Lived in extreme luxury, and people did everything in their power for us" and Private Luck's section were "lucky in being billeted in a hayshed, where we were very kindly treated. The next three days, the 18th, 19th and 20th, were spent route marching in the district and drinking all the beer in the village, and we decided then that campaigning came a long way before manoeuvres." Colonel Lowther remarked "Boué is only a village of less than 1,000 and to have 4,000 strangers suddenly thrust on it is rather a strain. Great foraging for vegetables, eggs and tobacco in all forms. Sanitation is none of the best, as there are no drains. Water all from wells and therefore vitiated. Bakeries and dairies are things to make one shudder."

He noted on the 18th "News patchy and unreliable. It is said that poor Jimmy Grierson has dropped dead; always a friend of mine and of the Scots Guards. Route march of about 11 miles, very hot, but not much falling out. As yesterday I went round our area and the men all seemed cheery. But as they have only one shirt and socks they are not very comfortable." In the same section as Corporal Green was Private Ernest "Bill" Mellor, who recorded in his sparse diary that on the 19th they received their first pay and the first mail from home and that there was an issue of tobacco the day after. He, a reservist who had only left the year before after eight years service, had formerly been a miner in Derbyshire, where his father James Mellor was living in Hasland. Lieutenant General Sir James Grierson, commanding II Corps, an able officer with a sound knowledge of the German Army, had a heart attack and died in a train after arriving in France. Lord Kitchener appointed Lieutenant General Sir Horace Smith Dorrien to replace him when General Sir John French, Commander in Chief of the BEF, who did not like him, had particularly asked for Lieutenant General Sir Herbert Plumer. II Corps had assembled on mobilization and consisted of the 3rd and 5th Divisions.

Deployment

Lieutenant Balfour, the Machine Gun Officer, had the two Maxims painted green so that they did not stand out so much and practised his teams in their gun drills. It was very hot and he revelled "in a delicious bath in the reservoir before tea" on the 20th, noting also that during that day's route march the 1st Coldstream had met the 2nd and 3rd Coldstream from the 4th (Guards) Brigade, the first time on record that the whole Regiment had met on active service. He heard of a move next day. On the 21st he "said goodbye to all the old people who had looked after us: the old lady at my billet insisting on my kissing her." Once all four battalions were at Boué their Brigade had become operational. The Scots Guards left at eight to march ten miles northeast to Cartignies, taking five hours, Colonel Lowther noting that "a few men lagging from sore feet due to badly fitting boots (Reservists). News of Belgians being driven back and no wonder! They have done well to do as much as they have. Great shortage of oats, – The French Government having requisitioned everything nearly. Supply folk only got about 1/5 of the necessary amount. Another mail yesterday and papers up to 17th. Field Paymaster produced £500 for us so the men are full of money, but there is very little indeed to be bought in this little place. All the young overeaten Officers well again now; at Boué I find many of the men subscribed various sums as tips for the people where they lodged. Most of the latter refused them, very kind and nice of the men. They have earned golden opinions by their conduct in billets." However, just afterwards "we heard of bad behaviour, men taking things out of a small shop at Cartignies." Private Luck watched as "A French infantry battalion marched past singing the Marseillaise, and I must admit it evoked greater enthusiasm amongst them than "Get out and get under" or "Ragtime Cowboy Joe" did with us." On 22 August Reveille was at three before they left at five. Soon, once they were out onto the Avesnes-Maubeuge road heading north, General Maxse told Colonel Lowther "some of our own and the French dispositions, also that our Cavalry had been engaged North of Mons and had located 30,000 Germans there, and had also found their right." He commented "Marching through the country gives a strange effect of Sunday morning, as there is no one working in the fields, the villages seem quite dead with every able bodied soul at the war or employed away from home in some capacity." The skirmish that day was between C Squadron 4th Dragoon Guards, commanded by Major Tom Bridges, and German cavalry at Soignies, northeast of Mons. Only after that was General von Kluck aware that the BEF were in front of him.

While resting in a field near Beaufort, five miles from Maubeuge, and having lunch, waiting for orders and trying to sleep, the Scots Guards saw their first German aeroplane which, Lieutenant Balfour wrote, "came and had a look at us about 2pm. All our artillery have branches all over them, to hide them from the aeroplanes." He then went foraging for eggs in the village of Limont-Fontaine, just to the west, where they were now starting to go into billets, and came back with one hundred and fifty, which he handed over to a mess cart. When Major Corkran came to tell Colonel Lowther that the 1st Division were going to move on again billeting stopped and they gathered and lay down to wait in a stubble field. They marched off north at half past five and, later, around ten that evening, suddenly there was the sound of demolition explosions, initially thought to be guns. They were now approaching Maubeuge, south of which they crossed the River Sambre. Lieutenant Balfour described the change as "The Bn suddenly become serious; the war previously having been more like a picnic. We march right through Maubeuge in the dark being cheered by the whole population chiefly composed of soldiers (50,000 reservists who have been digging terrific earthworks since war was declared). Just as we were going out we met some of our flying corps. One had been up this morning: he got 9 shots thro' his plane and 1 grazed his petrol tank. He says, "He saw the Germans advancing in such thick masses that they could hardly get along." What a chance for MGs! Our cavalry bagged the German aeroplane that came and had a look at us this morning (rifle fire)." Right from the start air reconnaissance was very valuable and British intelligence was one of two parts of Sir John French's Headquarters that functioned well, but was largely ignored or wilfully misinterpreted higher up.

Throughout the day's march there had been repeated interruptions and consequent standing around, all very wearing. Colonel Lowther wrote that "we flopped down pretty well exhausted in our billets." Corporal Green remembered how at two in the morning on the 23rd "we came to the little village of Grand Reng. The whole of our company was sent into the huge barn, very warm and plenty of straw." Grand Reng was just over the Belgian frontier. As Private Luck marched through Maubeuge at about quarter past eleven at night "Some of us were lucky enough to get our water bottles filled, which we could well do with. After passing the town we received orders to march in silence and soon knew we were getting near the Belgian frontier because we were continually passing French outposts, with wire entanglements guarding the road against any Uhlan patrols." All German cavalry carried lances and the British called them all Uhlans, whereas only those wearing the four pointed headdress, very similar to the Full Dress cap of British lancers, were technically Uhlans. They had marched well over twenty miles from Boué north to Grand Reng. Expecting to be able to sleep for six hours from when they got there at two o'clock, they were instead woken at three thirty and ordered to stand to arms at four. Standing to arms went back a long way in British military history, could occur at any time of day or night in the event of alert or alarm or by procedure, which, later, in trench routine, meant invariably before and during dusk and dawn. They stood to for an hour and a half and were then told they could sleep, but at ten minutes notice to move. After breakfast they again lay down, undisturbed till noon, but all four commanding officers and adjutants had to go on a reconnaissance with General Maxse to Peissant. The afternoon and night followed the same pattern with the warning that they might have to fight imminently. At Grand Reng Private Luck "found the inhabitants eagerly awaiting us, as the Germans were expected any minute and they were deluded into believing that our arrival meant the end of their trouble. They tried, if possible, to outdo the French in kindness, everything in their houses being at our disposal. For myself, a corner of a hayshed and a bundle of straw felt the most comfortable bed I had been in, for the previous marching and being on guard I had been on the "go" for 45 hours." For Corporal Green "The day passed very peacefully, although in the distance we could hear the boom of artillery very plainly…I went into an orchard behind our billet, and could, by listening very intently, hear the ping! ping! of bullets, although a fairly good way off." Afterwards they learned that the sound of the guns, not demolitions, that day was the Battle of Mons. The Brigade, out on the right of I Corps, got little news when the *First Army* collided with II Corps of the BEF. Both sides' operational plans required them to reach the line of the Mons-Condé Canal that day, the BEF still complying with the French offensive concept. Colonel Lowther heard only that there had been a cavalry skirmish involving the Royal Scots Greys near Binche, further east down the road towards Charleroi, and that two battalions of II Corps had been badly mauled near Mons. In the afternoon he got three hours badly needed sleep and then had to ride out with General Maxse to look at the ground between Mons and Binche.

Not until three in the morning on the 24th, still without any other information beyond their immediate orders, did the Scots Guards march a mile and a quarter to the north, to get ready to dig in between the sixteenth and seventeenth kilometre stones on the side of the Mons-Binche road. This was their furthest point of advance. They could see and hear heavy shelling to the east and north without knowing what it was. To the east General Charles Lanrezac's French Fifth Army were fighting and losing the Battle of Charleroi, having failed to hold their defensive positions along the River Sambre against General Karl von Bulow's *Second Army*. General Lanrezac broke off the battle and withdrew. To the north II Corps were still fighting and breaking contact with the Germans at Mons, the firing from that direction dying down at one that afternoon. Unknown to the Scots Guards, the pressure of the *Second Army* on the Fifth Army was completely exposing the right flank of I Corps. During the day all that reached Colonel Lowther was that the Germans "were advancing on Erquelinnes and Jeumont which are held by two French reserve divisions. By about 2.0 the last of the troops were pretty well past us, all giving the same accounts of the bad shooting of the German guns." Erquelinnes was immediately southeast of Grand Reng in Belgium and Jeumont due south of it on the other side of the Sambre in France. Colonel Lowther's information was consistent with the pressure on the Fifth Army, but of the BEF's growing vulnerability he was unaware. Relations between Sir John French and General Lanrezac got off to a bad start and never improved. There were several factors, but General Lanrezac, correctly very apprehensive about his left flank because of the German pressure, if still unaware of the full scale of what they were attempting, became very dubious about the BEF's commitment, not least because they had never been forward anywhere close to his left flank. General Lanrezac reported his interpretations of what the Fifth Army, the only French one not to have carried out an attack, were facing to General Joseph Joffre, the French Commander in Chief. When he was correct in his assessments General Joffre repeatedly told him that he was wrong. His reaction was rising resentment and among his own staff publicly aired disloyalty. General Joffre soon had similar concerns about Sir John French, who had been initially very optimistic, but was by this time the very opposite, but General Joffre could only coax and encourage, not issue orders, to the British. Sir John French did little to direct the BEF and ignored intelligence reports, even his own, while communications between I and II Corps themselves also left much to be desired. What, in particular, Headquarters BEF did not realise as the Retreat developed was in what good condition the troops were, albeit gradually more and more tired and footsore.

Fortunately for the BEF and for the French, four of whose armies had by this date been heavily defeated while attacking in Alsace, Lorraine and the Ardennes, the Germans had their problems. These included lack of determined overall command and control, poor and lengthy communications between formations and inadequate gathering and interpretation of intelligence. Further, the Belgians had done a better delaying job than expected, including demolitions, and at the highest German level there was apprehension about the Russian armies in the east, already, surprisingly early, well into East Prussia. Large bodies of German troops were needed and detached to mask the Belgians in Antwerp and the French garrison in Maubeuge and now, at a very critical moment, the German Supreme Command removed two corps from the right wing to reinforce their forces in East Prussia. On top of all this there was wishful thinking that in the west the War was over with a comprehensive and complete defeat of the French Armies, the wishful thinking growing in scale as each day passed and the further it went up the German chain of command.

The Start of the Retreat

On 24 August it was the dawning awareness of both the BEF and the Fifth Army, just in time, of just how powerful the German right wing was that forced retreat to avoid envelopment. During the days following Mons General von Kluck tried to work round the left of the BEF, but was not good at keeping contact with them and so failed to follow. Instead of making their way towards the coast, as he was inclined to expect, the BEF were heading south.

At six on the morning of the 24th, when digging was just about to start, General Maxse summoned Colonel Lowther and told him that a general retirement had been ordered and that the Scots Guards and Munsters were to move back to a line west of Villers-Sire-Nicole, just north of Maubeuge, and hold it while the rest of the 1st Division withdrew through them, keeping clear of Maubeuge itself. Colonel Lowther was glad that he had arranged for breakfast to be brought up to the men at the main road, so that they had eaten before they had to start moving. While eating they saw a German plane come over and watched German shrapnel bursting in little puffs of smoke all around a British one, but without any sign of hitting it. Private Luck noticed for the first time the British guns shelling what he took to be the German advance guard. Lieutenant Balfour wrote sadly "The whole road is full of refugees, poor people: it makes one almost weep to see them: they don't know where to go and point excitedly to the shells. They have only the things they stand up in and a small bundle, women with little children crying and ringing their hands, having seen their homes burnt behind them." On reaching their temporary defence line just across the border they then dug for seven hours in the bright sunshine "a more beautiful position cannot be imagined one could see for about 10,000 yards: our trenches were also a work of art the men putting all they knew into it. One field in which we had dug the stooks had been taken in so the men went ... and fetched up bundles of corn and put them about in stooks to hide the trenches more effectively. I made a pictorial range card. At 5pm we are told the plan has been changed and we are going to move off W of Maubeuge. Fearful grousing at having to leave our beautiful trenches and not getting a fight. We march round Maubeuge to Longueville arriving at 9.30pm. Fall on food as we have had nothing since breakfast. Everybody dead beat and men very disheartened at not getting their fight. Lie down on stone floor in the back parlour hope we may get some rest. Hear Middlesex have lost 15 officers and 500 killed and wounded at Mons." Those figures for the 4th Middlesex Regiment's casualties were not far wrong. The order to march to La Longueville came "suddenly and unexpectedly" to Colonel Lowther where "The people not very pleased to see us and think we are running away as we were seen going North a few days ago. Slept on one bed with Garnier and we were both too tired to be disturbed by the other. The men were too beat to have their dinners, so these were kept over for breakfast the next day." Apart from the digging they had also marched eighteen miles. It had been very hot. Major Jack "Chips" Carpenter Garnier was the Senior Major.

The timings and the distances, possibly exaggerated, recorded during the Retreat varied because of differing individual accounts, but their variances impaired neither the effect nor the picture of the experience. As a sample, Private Luck gave the typical average timings as "Reveille 4am, march off 4.30, halt at 9 (with half an hour for breakfast), midday halt from 1 to 3, get to billets between 10pm and midnight." 25 August was hard. They paraded at four and had to march without breakfast "in rather a tangle" so Colonel Lowther put it. It was very hot, close and very dusty, so bad indeed that it was difficult for the men in one section to see those in that marching in front. It did not help that many were sunburnt from working the day before with their shirts off. All were footsore and, Colonel Lowther added, "disappointed at not getting a crack at the Germans. Never saw so much falling out in my life, 17 had not rejoined when we sent in the return. At one time there must have been 300 out in the Brigade…Even the Officers were many of them tired out, and the men are feeling the weight of the packs." Lieutenant Balfour noted that some forty Scots Guardsmen fell out altogether, but all rejoined in the evening. For Private Osborne it had been a "Most awful march, many fell out because of intense heat and dust." They had marched eighteen miles from La Longueville, including recrossing the Sambre, to Taisnières, where they eventually billeted at three in the afternoon and where food was ready. During the morning Colonel Lowther had met Major Toby Long of the Greys with his squadron, whose grey horses had been smeared to make them look brown and so less conspicuous. At seven that evening there was firing from the outposts, only a false alarm, later very heavy rain and then the sound of heavy firing, including machine guns. This went on all night to the west from Landrecies. Sir Edward Hulse recorded that at Taisnières, when only he, his billeting party and some of the Transport had arrived, two Frenchmen told them of German cavalry close by to the north in Noyelles. He set his small group to fight it out, but nothing happened and refugees told them later that the enemy were too busy with the liquor they found to do anything else.

From now on Sir John French's lack of control of the BEF became a political and military liability. On 25 August it had been decided, so as to reduce congestion on the limited roads, that I Corps should march south down the east side of the Forest of Mormal, while II Corps withdrew to the west of it, currently only just ahead of pursuing Germans. Sir Douglas Haig and his headquarters had halted for the night at Landrecies on the southeast of the Forest. Here the 4th (Guards) Brigade outposts were suddenly attacked in the dark and there was a sharp skirmish. Sir Douglas Haig, who had had diarrhoea on the 24th, though feeling better the next morning, was badly shaken by this surprise and his early report on this indicated a degree of disruption to I Corps that was very far from the case. Once he was himself clear of Landrecies early on the 26th and at Le Grand Fayt he received a message from Sir John French giving him completely free reign as to how he continued to retreat. So he directed I Corps south by the most direct route, without further reference to Sir John French and without telling Sir Horace Smith Dorrien, who had understood that I Corps would come in on his right flank from the south end of the Forest. Instead they were soon marching further away. During that same night Sir John French had no influence on Sir Horace Smith Dorrien's decision, on getting reports from his subordinates and assessing the implications, that the best, probably only, option open to him was for II Corps to fight where they were. The enemy exposed and exploited his now open right flank, but in a very severe battle at and around Le Cateau II Corps checked them significantly. When General von Kluck did follow up it was southwest, in the wrong direction, in the belief that he had engaged and defeated the whole BEF.

One person who had shed most of his illusions, if not about the fundamental flaw in the offensive strategy, the crux of the matter, but about the results of the French armies' operations so far, was General Joffre. There had been massive casualties, though the Germans had suffered very severely too. General Joffre, who kept calm throughout from now on, was all the same very concerned about what was being reported to him from Headquarters BEF and about the BEF. He realised that he needed to have French troops under his command out to the left if he was to have any control over events. Three French Territorial divisions were already there, with whom the *First Army* collided next after Le Cateau. These Territorials consisted of older men beyond the age of reserve commitment, but with previous military service, whose role was supposed to be only local home defence, though that ceased to be adhered to as the War gathered momentum. Also, General Sordêt's Cavalry Corps had by this time passed north across the British II Corps' line of retreat, with difficulty and inconvenience for all concerned. Later on during the 26th General Joffre met Sir John French and General Lanrezac together. It led to his further forebodings about both, Sir John French being demoralised and fevered about the situation in which he and his men had been placed, General Lanrezac truculently silent on the one opportunity he had left to reason how matters stood to both the others together. General Joffre had also taken note that General Lanrezac had yet to show any signs of using attack as a means of defence.

Because of all the uncertainty through the night the Scots Guards were woken at half past three on 26 August at Taisnières, stood to arms till five and then breakfasted. They could not move off, however, with the road blocked by a French Territorial brigade, among whom Lieutenant Balfour found an officer who had a cigarette case with a Scots Guards star engraved on it, given to him as a keepsake by the widow of an old friend, Bob Finnie, according to Colonel Lowther, who had been in the Regiment. The day's march finally began at eight but the twelve miles, mostly as the brigade rearguard, southwest to Rejet-de-Beaulieu, again on the other side of the river, here again the Sambre and Oise Canal, took twelve hours with many hold ups. At one stage during the morning they "occupied another line to cover the passage of the 3rd

Brigade who are pretty well done up. At a nice farm we bought butter, eggs, beer, poultry etc., and the men had teas. We had saved a bit of meat so we were able also to give them some soup on reaching billets at night. An awful walk with halts and crowds and reached Rejet-de-Beaulieu in pitch darkness and brisk rain at about 10. The place almost deserted by terrified inhabitants." Everyone had apparently left in a hurry when German cavalry came through during the morning. Lieutenant Balfour heard that Boué close by to the southeast on the other side of the Canal "is in flames my poor old lady wonder if she has gone or is a cinder." However, he and other officers found in their billet a hundred and four eggs, pounds of butter and a cellar and left a note for the absent owner to say what they had taken and whom to contact after the War for payment. Colonel Lowther recorded her name as Mme Fernand Fournier and in 1920 went back to find her and pay for everything, but there was no trace. Again it poured in the night. He also mentioned hearing heavy fighting going on to the northwest, without knowing anything about the Battle of Le Cateau.

Etreux

There were no orders until daylight on the 27th. These were to move at once. They set off without breakfast to dig in nearby, just southwest of Cambrésis, itself just on the west side of the Sambre and Oise Canal, to cover I Corps' further withdrawal down the main road which ran from Landrecies south towards Guise. Shortly afterwards the 2nd Brigade, till then the rearguard, marched back through their positions. Colonel Lowther remarked "All this retirement is very disappointing and disgusting as my Brigade has not yet fired a shot, and I myself have literally not set eyes on a German." There were reports of small bodies of the enemy being seen to the north and of larger ones, allegedly to the southwest, "seen by two men who were taken prisoner, stripped, and escaped last night." He thought that "The stripping of prisoners means of course that the enemy are adopting Boer methods and using our uniform to get up to our lines." When the time came for the Brigade to start to withdraw the Scots Guards had dug trenches in open country out at the left rear of the Brigade's positions, with the Coldstream forward of them but to the right, just west of the main road at Oisy. The Black Watch, further forward still, were in covering positions around the canal bridge at Cambrésis. Only the Munsters were still on the east side of the Canal, centred on the village of Fesmy, separated from but roughly level with the Black Watch. To rejoin the Brigade involved their either crossing the Canal by the bridge at Oisy or by the railway bridge further south and just east of Etreux.

To begin with Colonel Lowther "Spent some hours in the morning close to a beautiful farm belonging to the Mayor of Oisy. He and his had gone but we requisitioned a bullock, forage and potatoes, by order. But I was sorry to notice that some of the Artillery were simply stealing chickens and other produce. The Artillery are terrible looters as a general rule. At 11.0 a terrific rainstorm, all more or less wet through and filthy from being out in the ploughed fields. About 2pm, saw us retiring through Etreux on Guise. The retirement was too long delayed. (I was nearly shot by an Uhlan 100 yards off). I think there was a mess up, the Munsters in Fesmy being cut off and disappearing (except for 2 Officers and 150 men) with 2 guns into thin air. This let in the German Cavalry rather and we found them nosing into Etreux as we came through it. Just South of that place is a high plateau a mile or so in length; this we crossed in "Artillery formation". Were left in peace till all but two of my Companies and the Black Watch were over when a battery and 2 howitzers opened on us from the East and there was also some rifle fire from the same side, but at long range and harmless. German gunnery poor, tho' an easy target and one they had been on for some time before. They made a couple of good shots with howitzers all among the gun teams, but hit no one. My casualties were two very slightly wounded, but I had an anxious time with nearly 2 Companies far in rear and looking like being hung up; the rest of the Brigade slipping further and further away as dusk fell. Much relieved when all my men were finally marching down the Guise road, although it was dark by now and 2 regiments of German cavalry were messing about on our flank. We could hear a mysterious fight going on in Etreux." The enemy were the *Second Army*.

"Artillery formation" for infantry crossing open country owed its direct origins to the Boer War, but was an evolution of methods recognisable from much earlier. The first stage for a battalion was four company columns of men in fours either marching abreast or one behind the other, or as four points of a diamond or of a square, or in echelon. All were normal when completely out of contact with the enemy. The next stage, a little more spread out, saw each company split up into four separate columns of platoons, still in fours. In the third stage each platoon split down into four sections, these being commonly known as "blobs". Finally, if approaching an enemy position, depending on what was required on the spot, the sections would deploy into line, with the leading ones then making their way forward using fire and movement. Fire and movement was a well understood skill practised by the pre-war Regular Army.

Lieutenant Balfour "Started off 4am eat 34 raw eggs. Go to a place 2 miles W of Oisy and dig ourselves in. Hear shooting 1 mile SE of us. Awful thunderstorm about 9am and tropical rain and soaked to the skin and lying in the trench up to my neck in water…Hear we have shot a bullock (requisitioned) so we shall get some fresh meat for dinners. We were told we should probably retire at 12 noon. Orders arrived retire at 2pm on Guise." They started pulling back two companies at a time, leapfrogging to fire positions from which to cover the withdrawal, but, as Colonel Lowther had noted, it did not go smoothly.

At noon General Maxse had personally issued written orders for that day's withdrawal to officers of all four battalions, including Major Francis Day, the Second in Command of the Munsters, leaving only the time of withdrawal blank. The Black Watch were to move back, leapfrogging the Coldstream, and take up rearguard positions at Etreux until everyone else was safely past them. It can be inferred that the Munsters were to move back at the same time with the Coldstream protecting the crossing at Oisy until they were over. Headquarters 1st Division sent a message timed twenty past twelve that Etreux was now clear of all other troops and transport and at quarter to one General Maxse sent the time for withdrawal as "At once". The Black Watch withdrew to the next blocking position at the canal road bridge south of Etreux as soon as they had that order, but the Munsters bicycle orderly could not get through owing to the weight of fire and never reached them, only turning up at three with the Coldstream at Oisy. The Coldstream hung on for another hour, very worried about the Munsters, patrols having failed to find any sign of them. They waited for as long as they dared and then went back through Etreux, the Scots Guards following them. Villages were ablaze, German troops seen and several German corps reported close behind. The withdrawal had to continue. Once all the Scots Guards were through Etreux, Lieutenant Balfour and his machine gunners stayed behind to be near the Black Watch, where "We dig in like furies." He and two platoons of B Company covered the Black Watch withdrawal from Etreux and then went on through the unexpectedly named hamlet of Jérusalem. "Nobody seems to have heard anything of Munsters. Hear tremendous firing going on from direction of where they were this morning so suppose they are cut off."

The Germans had approached the Munsters positions driving cattle in front of them for cover and distraction. Until the end the Munsters had managed effectively, but they were spread out in very thick country with a lot of hedges and there was what turned out to be a fatal delay when the others were waiting for one company to rejoin. When Fesmy became untenable they had moved back south through Oisy, where they must have crossed the Canal, but had then been trapped. The Germans had got round behind them and occupied buildings on the north side of Etreux, cutting off their line of retreat. Apart from the rear company, they were surrounded and fighting it out with an estimated six German battalions. Firing could still be heard at six in the evening. They had with them a section of two eighteen pounders from the 118th Battery RFA, also lost with their officers and gunners. The two troops of C Squadron 15th Hussars, part of the 1st Division's Mounted Troops, who had been shielding their eastern flank, mostly managed to get away.

Shells started falling, initially without effect, as Lieutenant Balfour's machine guns and the B Company platoons headed down the road to Guise with the Black Watch. The British infantry were well spaced out in section groups of twenty men. There was then a shower of bullets at long range as well. He got his machine guns out onto the top of a six foot bank, surveyed the scene and, unable to spot anything, concluded that the source was probably a turnip field eight hundred yards away. He had the machine gunners spray it, with the desired effect of enemy fire almost ceasing. There had been reports variously of a German cavalry brigade or division that had got into the Forest of Nouvion over to the east. However, by then shells were bursting on the line of the road at a rate of about twenty a minute, one of which, according to Lieutenant Balfour, killed a Black Watch soldier just in front of him, so that he had to jump over the body to reach his pony. "Got to pony with great difficulty as she was terrified and would not stand still: then saw driver of SAA cart fall off and horses running away, dashed after them and caught them and managed to stop them ½ mile further on. Waited for team to collect: All very hot; but all present." By ten o'clock they were all at Jonqueuse on the St Quentin road to the southwest of Guise, exhausted. Two Scots Guardsmen were recorded as slightly wounded that day and two of the Black Watch as wounded, but none dead. For both it was their first day in action and the first casualties. They had also marched twenty two miles. One of the wounded Scots Guardsmen was the reservist Private William Davies, a labourer when he enlisted in 1908 in Leeds, who had a bullet wound in his left calf. He recovered and not long before he came out again to France a year later, this time to the 2nd Battalion, he married Ethel Naysmith, a widow with two children, in London. She continued to live in Fulham and later they had a son of their own. Private Davies was back in France for three weeks in September 1915 before being evacuated with an abscess in his back. He returned once more to the BEF.

Private Osborne was probably in a B Company platoon at Etreux. German cavalry charged them as soon as they started to withdraw, but he wrote that they wiped them out. Then "Our Brigade was ordered to act as rearguard. We were soon in action. After fighting for a few hours it became obvious that we were up against an overwhelming horde. Enemy nearly succeeded in cutting us off from the main body. The noise was awful. Shells and bullets were coming our way from seemingly all directions. A most unhealthy spot." News of the Munsters came through and he saw "a very pathetic sight when the survivors – one officer (Major Day) and 120 rank and file – were seen to be marching wearily and sadly along the road leading to the main body. What a day!" The Munsters eventually gathered five officers and one hundred and ninety six men. Until the Retreat ended they were attached to the Coldstream. This disaster was the worst, but not the only one of its type, to affect I Corps. In II Corps there were more incidents where whole battalions were cut off, notably during Le Cateau.

Private Luck, also in a platoon with the machine gun teams, recalled "It was… about 4pm, that we got the first intimation that something was wrong with the Munsters…when one or two stragglers came back… they could not tell a proper story, except that the Battalion was engaged," while his own company had enough of its own to think about. They had the distraction of an enemy plane overhead and "were more engaged in admiring the eagle shaped wings than in thinking of the harm it could do us." As they started to pull back from Jérusalem with the machine gunners, he mentioned the firing from the east and inaccurate shelling with shrapnel. While the machine guns were getting into position at the top of the bank he and the men with him got into a deep ditch along the road side and moved quickly along it until they reached the same bank. They and the machine gunners opened fire, while a British battery "had turned back and with marvellous quickness had come into action." Colonel Lowther placed C Company to give supporting fire and cover their withdrawal.

Private Luck thought that the German plane had alerted their cavalry about where to go in order to take them in the flank. He added "This, of course, was my first experience of being under fire and I must say I was surprised at my own coolness as well as that of the whole Company. We came into action as if it had been an Aldershot Field Day, and at this time, as we had no covering fire at all, the bullets were pretty thick. Directly we opened fire, however, their's slackened, and as soon as our artillery and C Company got going we were able to retire. We were under fire altogether for about three quarters of an hour, and got out of it with two men slightly wounded." The loss of the Munsters made the Retreat all the harder. Each day one battalion had to do advance guard and one rearguard for the Brigade and so with only three they only had one day off. All the same, he remembered, "The men by this time, however, were in the pink of condition, except for the most important part, the feet, which were in a few cases very bad indeed. The march discipline of the Battalion was all this time very strict."

Colonel Lowther recorded "It was nearly eleven when we got to Jonqueuse 3 miles down the La Fère road and the Battalion flopped down in an orchard dead tired and footsore. I slept(?) in a barn, which was very cold and draughty, for a short time and soon after 3 on the 28th we roused the men with great difficulty and started off breakfastless towards La Fère: cold and foggy early, it soon grew terribly hot and the march was most trying. Most Battalions falling out freely, but mine behaved well and I felt very proud of them when they marched into St Gobain at dusk, after being about 36 hours out of 48 under arms and mostly on the march. These days have been very hard and officers and men are weary; there has been no fighting to amuse and cheer us up and it is vexing to be always retiring, but we know there is a good reason for it…The men are well fed and will soon recover their fatigue. On the road we had 1¼ hours rest for dinners near Brissay and there were several other longish halts." The route they had taken from Jonqueuse was down the road towards St Quentin before turning south down the east side of the Canal.

That day they were free from contact with the enemy. The War Diary recorded "Roused Battn with difficulty and left at 4am. A most trying march, very hot, and constantly impeded by the 2nd Division. 1¼ hr halt near Brissay for dinners helped us along, and we reached St Gobain at dusk, with the loss of relatively few men." Lieutenant Balfour wrote of the "march to St Gobain: terrific march 31 miles and terrific heat." When they were seven miles from it he went on ahead to find food but, with no billets, the only alternative was bivouacking in a field. He managed to "get plenty of eggs and chickens fruit and wine and Bn arrives at 8pm (just crawling)." Private

Osborne "Marched off at 4am and, with the usual half hour halts, kept on the move until 7pm. A most exhausting march. When a halt was called it was not unusual to see men throw off their packs and lie down on the roadside, utterly worn out and unable to resume the march: these, unfortunately, had to be left to the mercy of the enemy. Considering that we had to carry a rifle, bayonet, 350 rounds of ammunition, and overcoat, waterproof groundsheet, a change of under-clothing, a full water bottle, a holdall, complete with knife, fork, spoon, razor, comb, lather brush and button stick, 3 day's rations and an entrenching tool, making a total of not less than 70 pounds, it's not surprising that some of the men could not stick it. I used to wonder how long it would be before I packed it up." Colonel Lowther described how "At St Gobain the Battalion bivouacked in a field, as quarters were few and bad, Battalion Headquarters in an unfinished house and slept on a tiled floor. Had no sleep to speak of as Stephen was dead beat and I had messages brought to myself and did the little work that would have disturbed him; then he walked in his sleep and came and stood over me and babbled. We were disappointed in our hope of a long night as we had to "stand to arms" at 4.30am. But soon after 6am on the 29th we got the order that we were to have a day of rest and right thankful we were to hear it. Last night I had my first complete wash since Boué and changed my clothes. Two much needed events!" On their way into St Gobain, near the northern edge of the large Forest of St Gobain, they passed the 4th (Guards) Brigade and heard something of the fighting at Landrecies. They had also passed Sir Douglas Haig on the line of march, who "was pleased with the look of the Battalion."

General Joffre was preparing a counterstroke, but had two worries. The first was his continuing apprehension about Sir John French's commitment and therefore whether the BEF were capable either of fighting or of being in the right place to do so. There was little that he could do about the British, other than seeking to cajole and invigorate, but to little effect as, by the 29th, the BEF were well back to the left rear of the Fifth Army. Also, though Sir Douglas Haig had recognised the opportunity and told General Lanrezac that he would join in if Sir John French agreed, he refused to allow I Corps to participate in the French operations that day, which they could certainly have done. Meanwhile, southeast of Amiens, out to the west of the BEF and well clear of them, General Michel-Joseph Maunoury was assembling the new French Sixth Army, partly from those troops out to the left of the BEF all along, but more from others moved by train from eastern France, where the situation was stabilising, and from the Paris Garrison. The purpose was to attack the right flank of the *First Army*. General Joffre's second worry was General Lanrezac. The Fifth Army, the defensive Battle of Charleroi apart, in which they had been badly mauled, had done little but withdraw as the *Second Army* advanced. This was something that General Joffre could do something about. He went to see General Lanrezac, ordered counterattacks westwards across the River Oise and then stayed while these were put into effect. The first towards St Quentin was repulsed, but the second, later in the day, by General Louis Franchet d'Esperey's I Corps, striking at Guise, was a resounding local success, though the full import and consequences, that General von Kluck would turn his attention towards the southeast and the Fifth Army, were not yet apparent.

The Retreat continues

The BEF simply rested on 29 August and Private Osborne wrote "My birthday! Rested at St Gobain, got permission to indulge in the luxury of a bath. The only time I have taken off my clothes since leaving Aldershot" while Private Luck "had the chance of a bath and a swim in a lake about half a mile away from our camping ground, and this was taken full advantage of by the Battalion." Colonel Lowther noted "For some days up to yesterday the thunder of guns has been virtually incessant from dawn till long after dark; yesterday it was less insistent and more distant, which looks as if the French advance were in progress. The whole of the roads are littered with refugees in wagons, carts, bicycles and on foot, with bundles of pitiful and incongruous belongings. The poor creatures are afraid to stay and fools to go, for they may easily be worse off than at home. But we cannot wonder at their fear when one sees on all sides the flames rising from burning farms and villages and hears the stories of things done by the enemy. Lots of good official news kept coming in all morning from all sides. Most satisfactory after what looked like an unsatisfactory week's performance. But one wonders whether things are really very gaudy. One thing is quite certain and that is that the English force has got safely – so far and to a certain extent – out of a very, very nasty place, almost in the grip of an overwhelming force. An entire day of rest was of course too good to be true. At 11.40pm we got orders to move "at once" to Terny 5 miles North of Soissons: and at 12.30am, August 30th, we left. A horse had got lost in the night so I had to leave a tool cart behind. I walked till 7.20am and got pretty tired, through the Forest of St Gobain, under the great arch of Coucy le Château. Got water for the men at about 6 and at 8 we halted in a field at Terny for breakfasts and a little rest. After an early mist the day became terrifically hot, quite still too, in fact a model bad marching day. The whole road was crowded with transport and the march was therefore a hard one. Heard some explosions at about 3am, probably the French destroying bridges." Private Luck described how "Although we did not actually get in touch with the enemy we could see their trail all round us at night as the sky was lit up by the burning towns and villages so they must have been very close on our heels."

In spite of the success at Guise on the 29th the Fifth Army were now completely exposed, both the BEF on their left and the Fourth Army on their right being a day's withdrawal march ahead of them. General Lanrezac was not going to take responsibility for ordering a withdrawal of his own, taking the line that General Joffre had ordered him into this position of great danger. So he would not move without General Joffre's express order, which did not get through to him till early on the 30th. Fortunately the *Second Army* did not close up before or follow the Fifth Army's withdrawal. Out to the northwest a part of the *First Army* were fighting General Manoury's Sixth Army, who were also having to withdraw from around Amiens. The situation was very black. Paris was threatened, though General Joffre was quite prepared to turn it into a battleground. The non-participation of the BEF was a great liability and, mercifully unknown to General Joffre, Sir John French composed and sent a despatch on the 30th to London stating his intention of withdrawing west of Paris to regroup, which caused consternation. Then information came of the Russian annihilation at Tannenberg in East Prussia. The only ray of light was other intelligence of the two German corps travelling east by train through Berlin as it was correctly interpreted that they could only have been withdrawn from the west. In spite of this General Joffre went on withdrawing troops from the other armies both to build up the Sixth Army and also to form the force under General Ferdinand Foch which would become the Ninth Army, between the Fourth and Fifth Armies. The First and Second Armies were successfully holding out against very heavy German pressure along the line from Belfort to Verdun and it was critical that they did so.

Having marched eighteen miles before breakfast on the 30th the Scots Guards rested till five that evening before going a little further east to Allemant, to Colonel Lowther "a little village of 200 inhabitants" where he "spent a comfortable night on straw in a little shed." The 31st was relatively quiet but "a baking hot day." They left early and marched down the road to Soissons. After a halt caused by a report of the *II Cavalry Corps* of the *First Army*, being close, they marched through Soissons, crossing the River Aisne, and then going up the steep hill beyond to Vauxbuin. They had taken up rearguard and outpost positions as necessary, including for a time deploying two companies to protect bridges at Soissons and guard demolition charges, but the enemy did not appear. On arriving at Vauxbuin at half past six, just before dark, they had to bivouac in a field. There were more explosions in the night as the Aisne bridges were blown. Private Mellor recorded the issue of double rations and, for the first time, rum.

Exasperated, and with the full support of several appalled fellow members of the Cabinet, there having been further telegram exchanges and an unsuccessful attempt by the British Ambassador in Paris to intervene with Sir John French, Lord Kitchener set off there in the small hours on 1 September. He allowed Sir John French to choose the British Embassy for that day's meeting. It did nothing to improve their relations, left Sir John French bad tempered and no more motivated, but did keep the BEF in the field.

In the meantime there had been a dramatic development. By 30 August General von Kluck was under the impression that his contacts with the Sixth Army had been conclusive and that the BEF, whom he had failed to catch, were beaten. He deduced that there was no longer a viable threat to his right flank and that there was the opportunity to complete the larger envelopment operation by taking the Fifth Army in the flank, which would also close the gap with the *Second Army*. He did not seek prior approval from higher authority, though once he had started he informed them and they did not stop him, so tacitly concurring. Instead, using as confirmation of his ideas a request on the evening of the 30th from General von Bülow for assistance, which he took to be for the same purpose, General von Kluck changed direction. The purpose was to cut off the Fifth Army's retreat. Hitherto the *First Army* had most recently been advancing generally southwest towards Amiens on the right and Montdidier on the left. Now, starting on 31 August, they went southeast towards Compiègne on the right and Noyon on the left, the River Oise between them. They had a surprise next day.

Colonel Lowther noted on the morning of 1 September, when there was a heavy dew, that the Brigade had set off along the road, dropping off battalions at intervals to cover the retirement of the remainder. They were heading southwest from Soissons and entered the northern part of the Forest of Retz, in the middle of which was the village of Villers-Cotterêts. To begin with he remarked on the "lovely road through the forest with a high avenue of poplars. All went quietly with us as far as Villers-Cotterêts where we stopped…at about 1. Also each battalion had five wagons sent to it to carry the men's coats and thus lighten them for marching. There was sharp firing as our rearguard reached Villers-Cotterêts and this turned out to be the 4th Brigade who had got into a mess and had many of our friends killed and wounded. Our Divisional Staff was obviously anxious as we passed through the forest en route to La Ferté-Milon." The 4th (Guards) Brigade, then the I Corps rearguard, were attacked in the Forest by the *First Army* approaching southeast in search of the French. There was nothing about the British resistance to suggest that they were beaten at all.

Corporal Green noted that artillery wagons from the 26th Brigade RFA carried their packs. Lieutenant Balfour's entry for 1 September began "Started at 4am, went about 4 miles and dig ourselves in for ¾ hour and then told we are to prepare ourselves for a great march (probably 35 miles more (it was!!))." They had been unable to stop for breakfast until about one o'clock and were just settling down to it when they "were told to dash off at once towards the woods to cover retirement of 4th (Guards) Brigade who are heavily engaged in the woods. We take up a splendid position but the Germans would not follow up near us. Saw Scott Kerr coming out of the wood so I went down and had a small talk. He was looking like an old warrior hanging out of his saddle with his arms through an orderly (mounted) his grey hair flying in the wind and his clothes on his left leg cut away and his left thigh bandaged and dripping blood." Brigadier General Robert Scott Kerr, a Grenadier commanding the 4th (Guards) Brigade, was badly wounded. Private Osborne wrote of the halt at Villers-Cotterêts, that "the place was deserted, so the boys helped themselves to whatever they could find, that is in the way of food and drink, in the belief, I suppose, that "God helps the man who helps himself." However, the Colonel didn't help them much, for those caught looting – ugly word – were punished very severely. I wasn't caught." The Brigade then withdrew towards La Ferté-Milon, nine miles through the southern part of the Forest. The Scots Guards, at the rear, marched with fixed bayonets. When they came out of the woodland Lieutenant Balfour set up his machine guns along alternate rides with those of the Black Watch. The others reached La Ferté-Milon at seven o'clock and could hear heavy firing to the northwest, the 4th (Guards) Brigade's battle in the middle of the Forest, much more serious than Landrecies. By contrast, Colonel Lowther wrote of La Ferté-Milon that "We found the town deserted almost, and went into bivouac for an hour in an orchard behind the old castle. It did the men great credit that they did not so much as touch a single apple. Then at dusk we hustled back to the hilltop and started to dig a position. I guessed that we should have to move and did not let the men do much digging. By 7.30 came orders for a move at night, so we slept a while in a stubble field and dug no more." Lieutenant Balfour continued "At 7.30pm Brigadier tells us to dig ourselves in on high ground as we may be attacked at dawn. Dig till 11.30pm and we are then told we move off at 1.30am. Have dinners and move off at 1.30am walking in our sleep." Corporal Green noted "In the distance could be seen great fires – the work of the Germans. Our engineers were forced to blow up every bridge immediately we were the other side."

Colonel Lowther heard that enemy cavalry had come up to the I Corps outposts in the night, but were not to be seen from dawn on the 2nd. He wrote of "A tiring march…very slow at first down the Meaux road. Not too hot and a breeze. Stopped 8 to 10.45 …for rest and breakfast. When we started again the heat was very great, even to those riding, and the men needed water badly." They went on till they arrived around three at Chambry, immediately north of Meaux, where there were billets. There had been a welcome halt six miles north of it for breakfast for over two hours during the morning. They had covered forty one miles with a single halt of six hours, all of which was spent digging in. By this time Lieutenant Balfour "Don't think I could walk another mile if the Germans drove us with their lances." Colonel Lowther found "Nearly all the population had flown from the villages and the few left were almost hostile in their manner, and it needed some tact to get anything out of them. Doors had to be broken to put the troops into billets, and when they began to break, keys began to appear in the possession of the remainder of the natives. They seem to regard us as a beaten army, whereas, as a matter of fact, it has required some skill not to be beaten! Heard of a success of the 4th Division and capture of guns… A little distant shooting to the west in the afternoon but we were not bothered. A shave in an inch of tea at breakfast time and a complete wash in the afternoon made a new man of me." He could not change his clothes as the Transport were nowhere close by. "The people have left the beasts tied up in the farms and if we had not turned up numbers of them would have died of thirst and hunger. Comfortable bed, but interrupted night, orders being late and frequent." The 4th Division arrived from England as the Retreat started, were at Le Cateau and had just become part of the newly formed III Corps. The success, however, was not their's but the 1st Cavalry Brigade's rout of *First Army* cavalry and capture of guns that morning at Néry, south of Compiègne, another indicator that the BEF were still very much in the field. The performance of the British cavalry throughout was a major contributor to General von Kluck's failure to locate and close with the BEF.

On 3 September General Joffre dismissed General Lanrezac and put General Franchet d'Esperey, known to the British as "Desperate Frankie", in command of the Fifth Army, by then across the River Marne to the south of Château-Thierry. Further east General Foch's troops were deploying into a gap south of the Marne, well back from the line of the river in the neighbourhood of Châlons. However, as General Joffre, still positive and resourceful, was maturing his preparations for the coming battle, whose potential was becoming clear to him, the BEF still went on retreating.

Early that day the Scots Guards paraded and took up rearguard positions, but, with the 3rd Cavalry Brigade in front and no evidence of the enemy, they had a quiet time before marching on again at half past seven a short way east to cross the Marne at Germigny and get water for horses and men. Then after many delays and a long hot march east, mainly through forests and woods, with a halt for dinners, they arrived at Jouarre at seven in the evening. The billets were in the old Abbaye de Jouarre, in Sir Edward Hulse's description an erstwhile Benedictine monastery with room for two and a half thousand men. Lieutenant Balfour "spent night at a house belonging to a Padre who had dinner with us. He produced some filthy white wine which tasted like bad honey. Hear we may have a long night's rest. As we are retiring to bed at 10pm hear we are to start at 3am. Shall we ever get any sleep!!!" This will also have been where Colonel Lowther found himself. "I, for my sins, in the curé's house, where I lay on an uncomfortable bed, smothered in fleas till 2.0 and soon after, when I could bear it no longer and went and sat in the garden with my forehead on a window sill till it was time to leave... Was full of fleas all day." Captain Thorne wrote home that "We are completely out of touch with all news – about 2 miles outside our own immediate surroundings is the extreme limit of our information. " He added, referring to his own horses which he had brought out, "The fact that both Punch & Judy had to be reshod after 12 days work shows what they are getting."

The Scots Guards marched out of Jouarre at four that morning to go on south to Coulommiers, arriving four hours later. There, Colonel Lowther noted, they were "to begin with bedded down in the stone paved "Place du Marché" but found them billets of sorts in course of time. My headquarters in the ignoble little Hotel la Nouvelle. Most of the shops shut but many of them opened after we had been in for a little while. English papers – and a – for me – scant mail. I fear many of our letters were lost with the supplies at Le Cateau." Corporal Green "Halted in the market square whilst accommodation was found for us. My company were sent into a school. Sisters of Mercy gave us eggs and fruit amongst us." They were allowed to walk out into the town which was "duly taken advantage of by "our school" – Bill Mellor, Joe Holroyd, Bill Stride, Bill Shaw and myself. All four belonged to my section... Money was fairly plentiful with us all, but everything was very cheap. Fruit, eggs, bread, jam, underclothing, etc. all found their way to our pockets. A large number of the inhabitants had left... The news came of our guns giving the enemy a reverse just outside the town." This was not so, but there had been events to bring an end to the Retreat. They could hear some shelling and rifle fire from the north but nowhere near them. Lieutenant Balfour slept till noon that day and after lunch found a table with sides to it, which, turned upside down, lined with a waterproof sheet and filled with five buckets of water, gave him a fine bath. He was followed by Colonel Lowther, Major Carpenter Garnier, Captain Stephen and, finally, by Lieutenant Nigel Gipps. He was also able to change his shirt for the first time since leaving Boué. Colonel Lowther "Caught most of the fleas, but a small breeding stock was still left over." They were initially warned to march on at seven that evening, but that was cancelled and replaced with a likely move very early next morning, so almost everyone had the chance of several hours sleep. 4 September had turned out to be a quiet day. Private Osborne was "Billeted in a large house that stood in its own grounds. A lovely stream ran through the estate, so took advantage of another bath: also washed a shirt, towel and socks, then following the example set by the lizard, basked in the sun, at the same time keeping a sharp lookout on the articles I had washed – in case the wind blew them away Ahem!" Colonel Lowther regretted that "Sorry to say a Sergeant and 3 men got drunk, the first such offences since we left home."

Meanwhile, Lieutenant Balfour was ordered to go out to cover a bridge over a stream on the Coulommiers-Boissy road during the night with his machine guns to support B Company of the Black Watch. There were reports of German cavalry patrols. At the bridge he pointed out to the Royal Engineers sent to help that blocking it with a tree would provide the enemy with cover and obstruct his own field of fire and that a few strands of wire would be better. The sappers still went ahead, felled a tree and wired it up. While the machine guns were sited back from the bridge, around it was a Black Watch picquet under a corporal whose company commander and Lieutenant Balfour told him to fetch Lieutenant Balfour to deal with any refugees who appeared. Further, if he had to pull back from the bridge, he was to go through the fields, not back down the road as that would mask the machine guns. At eleven one of the men at the bridge came to tell Lieutenant Balfour that a car full of French women had crashed into the barrier and asked him to deal with it. The women, all weeping and shaken, were otherwise unhurt. He arranged to help them over the obstacle and had the car pushed into the ditch. An hour later another Black Watch soldier came back to tell him that there were male refugees stopped some twenty yards on the far side of the bridge, who would neither come forward nor go back. He went to investigate and saw nothing. The bridge sentry had apparently watched the other man going to report to Lieutenant Balfour so, when he turned round and looked again across the bridge, the men had disappeared. Lieutenant Balfour took eight of the bridge picquet with him to investigate. Having seen nothing after a hundred and fifty yards up the road, he concluded that these men were unlikely to be refugees and decided to return. He had not gone thirty yards when he noticed a man on a bicycle about thirty yards away up a side road talking to someone behind a bank, so he realised shortly afterwards, very close to where he was standing. It was not till the Black Watch soldiers challenged the cyclist that Lieutenant Balfour first saw the German uniform and helmet. At this the cyclist leapt on his bike and rode off as six other Germans dashed away into the woods without a shot fired at them. Lieutenant Balfour only had a revolver and went back to his machine guns. Half an hour later there was a fresh alarm. Though he never saw them himself, he heard that thirty Uhlans had charged along the road from Boissy to within thirty yards of the bridge and halted. The Black Watch picquet fired a few shots at them and then bolted up the road, making it impossible for the machine guns to fire for at least forty five seconds, after which they fired off eighty rounds each, by then too late. Sir Edward Hulse heard that four Germans had been captured and three killed, Colonel Lowther that the figures were five and three respectively and that the "prisoners were apparently scared to death as they went on their knees and begged that they might be neither mutilated nor shot!" The rest of the night was quiet.

The end of the Retreat

At five next morning, the 5th, Lieutenant Balfour went back twelve miles with the machine guns through Coulommiers and rejoined the rest of the Scots Guards, whom he found at ten o'clock bivouacking in a field at Nesles. They had marched out of Coulommiers six hours earlier. Going southwest by Pézarches and then Ormeaux, they arrived at Nesles, from where Colonel Lowther had to send out three companies as overnight outposts covering three miles of open country. Later he rode round and found them well and comfortably dug in, but he had some difficulty locating the 3rd Brigade to their right. It was a much cooler day with a good breeze. Nesles marked the end of the Retreat. Lieutenant Balfour wrote next "Hear we are going to retire no more cheers! Advance at last!!" The first reinforcement draft, an officer and ninety one men, joined them in the afternoon, after "knocking about Northern France in the train trying to get to us for about a fortnight," in Colonel Lowther's words.

Other than the small identified figure for slightly wounded, how many men were lost otherwise during the Retreat was not recorded, but Private Luck referred to the arrival of that draft as bringing the Battalion to proper establishment. He added that "out of my section three men had been sent to hospital suffering from bad feet. It is marvellous how well the men had stuck it, as at one time we looked more like Chelsea pensioners than Guardsmen going along the road, but still everyone stuck it like a hero." Those officers and men sent back sick were, depending on what was wrong, either treated in hospitals in France or evacuated to England. Private Edwin Hawkins, a former machinist from Newport, Shropshire, had served for three years and left in 1913. He was a reservist who had difficulties on the Retreat and was evacuated home on 1 September with a "sprain and flat feet". On the 5th Private Fredrick Eccles was admitted to hospital, sent on from a field ambulance with sore feet. He came from Blackburn and was a farm worker until he joined up two years earlier. The doctor who examined him noted that he was slightly pigeon chested but that he was "A likely looking recruit, will fill out." Both would reappear. Someone who either fell out on the line of march or got lost was Private Sidney Swanson, a footman who enlisted in 1909 in London, served for three years and was called up as a reservist. The Germans buried him in the cemetery at Guise, but there was no news of this for a year and it came first through the American Embassy in Berlin. He was later presumed to have died on or about 4 September, the only fatality. Charles and Lucy Swanson, his parents, lived in Newnham, Cambridge, A bizarre casualty elsewhere was Private James Jarvis, stone mason and reservist from Aberdeen, not originally passed fit on mobilization. Waiting as a reinforcement at St Nazaire, he was shot on 30 August in a scuffle with the French Police and died two weeks later on a hospital ship to Southampton.

Before the first clash at Mons Major General Sir William Robertson, Quartermaster General of the BEF, had anticipated the possibility of a major withdrawal and so also of a threat developing to the initial supply lines. He laid plans and implemented them accordingly for and during the Retreat. St Nazaire on the Atlantic coast became the port used for a few weeks by the BEF and Le Mans, halfway between there and Paris, the main advanced base. It was owing to his foresight and flexible thinking that the men of the BEF were resupplied during the Retreat. It was a major and essential achievement.

At eight on the evening of 5 September, while many of the officers were having dinner at Battalion Headquarters, there was the sound of about fifty rounds being fired by Right Flank. A message came by lamp that they had shot a German officer, who was wounded, as well as the horse of another. Colonel Lowther observed that this captured officer "had the cheek to send and ask for his field glasses back." An hour later Captain Frederick "Father" Campbell in B Company saw some cavalry approaching, whom he thought were British. He sent a corporal out to warn them about barbed wire. They were Germans, who fled at once, so that, when B Company did fire, it was too late. Private Osborne wrote "It is rumoured we are in touch with the French Army, so from today it is hoped that the chased will become the chasers. I am in a small trench as I write this, and expecting an attack from German cavalry. No doubt we'll give a good account of ourselves. We did!" Colonel Lowther thought that "Campbell of B Company had played the silly ass and when he heard the patrol coming sent out a corporal to stop them as he thought they were our own Cavalry!! Intolerable fool!" He noted that in another part of B Company's position bicyclists came up, who stopped when challenged, and that Captain Robert "Jack" Balfour, a cousin of Lieutenant Jamie Balfour's, and his servant had gone out and wrestled with a man who escaped. However they recovered his and two other bicycles, which were useful. Colonel Lowther suspected that in this instance the owners were Frenchmen, not Germans, but "All quiet the rest of the night, except for continuous messages making sleep difficult."

Colonel Lowther wrote to Captain Campbell Douglas at Regimental Headquarters a few weeks later of the Retreat "But all the time the men were very cheerful though dog tired; what helped them to be merry was that we always had full rations, with a lot of extras such as bacon, cheese, jam, tobacco and rum. What they felt most was the lack of opportunity to wash. I made all officers shave, and the rank and file – without being ordered to – followed suit, so we look far more respectable than most battalions."

Notes on Chapter Sources

Background derived from John Terraine, *Mons* (London: B.T. Batsford 1960), Barbara W Tuchman, *August 1914* (London: Constable & Co 1962) and *History of the Great War based on Official Documents* by direction of the Historical Section of the Committee of Imperial Defence.
Brig Gen Sir JE Edmonds, *Military Operations France and Belgium, 1914: Volume I: Mons, the Retreat to the Seine, the Marne and the Aisne, August – October 1914* (London: Macmillan, 1922).
Capt Sir Edward Hamilton Westrow Hulse, Bt, *Letters Written from the English Front in France between September 1914 and March 1915* (Privately published, 1916).
Diary of Capt CJ Balfour, SGA.
Letters of Lt Col Sir Iain Colquhoun of Luss, Bt, Private Collection.
Copy Diary of Maj Gen Sir Cecil Lowther, Imperial Museum ("IWM"): IWM/Documents 6388.
Reprinted diary of Pte J Osborne, 1954 SGM.
Letters of Capt AFAN Thorne and other papers, NAM/1987-03-31 and IWM/Documents 5583.

Diary-style account and diary of LCpl CE Green, Liddle Collection ("Liddle"), Brotherton Library, University of Leeds, Liddle/WW1/GS/0657 G and IWM/Documents 4303.

Diary of Pte E Mellor, IWM/07/1/1.

Sir John Ross of Bladensburg, *The Coldstream Guards 1914-1918, Volume I* (Oxford University Press, London: Humphrey Milford 1928).

Capt S McCance, *History of the Royal Munster Fusiliers, Volume II* (Aldershot: Gale & Polden Ltd 1927).

Papers of Gen Sir Ivor Maxse with reference to the 2nd Royal Munster Fusiliers, IWM/Documents 3255.

Copy letter of Lt Col HC Lowther to Capt The Hon A Campbell Douglas, Cator Papers, Private Collection.

War Diaries: 1st Division TNA/WO95/1227, 1st (Guards) Brigade TNA/WO95/1261, 26th Brigade RFA TNA/WO95/1250, 1st Coldstream Guards TNA/WO95/ 1263/1, 1st Scots Guards TNA/WO95/1263/2, 1st Black Watch TNA/WO95/1263/3 and 2nd Royal Munster Fusiliers TNA/WO95/1279/1.

3

The Battles of the Marne and the Aisne – 1st Battalion

The opportunity for what became the first stage of the Battle of the Marne arose from General von Kluck's turn southeast away from Paris and became definite when the German Supreme Command implicitly confirmed their approval by changing the main plan. As at 4 September a fifteen mile gap, covered only by cavalry, had appeared between the Fifth Army and the BEF and that day the German *First Army* were still advancing towards the Fifth Army. Nevertheless, the last day of the BEF's retreat, 5 September, not only unnecessary but also unhelpful for the immediate future, was the product of confused communications and hence misunderstandings between the British and French about future moves onto the offensive. That Sir John French was out that day visiting troops and that the Chief of Staff, General Sir Archibald Murray, was ultra cautious and pessimistic were exacerbating factors. While the BEF were still moving back, from the west the Sixth Army attacked the *IV Reserve Corps* of the *First Army* on the right bank of the River Ourcq, a large tributary of the Marne, which it joined near Meaux. The move to the battle of the French IV Corps, recently arrived from the Third Army after heavy losses in the Ardennes, was mainly on foot. General Joseph Galliéni, Commander of the Paris Garrison, was an officer of great resolution and energy, who, though he did not see fully eye to eye with General Joffre, once his subordinate, was a major contributor to the success of the Marne. Quite apart from anything else, the Sixth Army attack from an unexpected direction threatened German communications more widely. While the Germans successfully defended themselves, General von Kluck was badly disturbed and disobeyed the orders he had just been given to keep his two left hand corps close to the right flank of the *Second Army*. Instead he sent them to reinforce his own right flank. So, immediately in front of the BEF, the gap opened, lightly held by *First Army* cavalry divisions.

The Battle of the Marne

The next part of the counteroffensive was the attack by General Foch's Ninth Army against the left flank of the *Second Army* from the St Gond Marsh, south of Épernay. When this started on 6 September it distracted General von Bülow's attention and so the gap between the *First* and *Second Armies* widened. The Fifth Army and the BEF, Sir John French finally being willing to engage following a face to face appeal by General Joffre on the afternoon of 5 September, all other approaches having been rejected, were to attack simultaneously to their front, but both were now a day's march further back than they needed to be to go over immediately to the offensive. Sir John French did not convey any sense of urgency in his orders and when the BEF did advance progress was not quick. It was generally wet, the terrain was hilly and thickly wooded and the small rearguards from supporting units of the German cavalry divisions were allowed to fight well, instead of being bypassed and isolated. A German cavalry division included at least one battalion of *Jäger*, riflemen who travelled by lorry, a cyclist company, a section of six machine guns and three horse artillery batteries of four guns each. Also, once they fully appreciated what was going on Generals von Kluck and von Bülow reacted sensibly, withdrew northeast and were never close to a severe defeat. Strategically, however, this halting of the German right wing meant the failure of the grand plan for rapid and conclusive victory by which they had set so much store.

Meanwhile at Nesles the 1st Queen's Own Cameron Highlanders began to arrive to replace the Munsters, whose survivors left to become General Headquarters troops, to reorganise and be brought back up to strength. The Camerons had till now been GHQ troops themselves with two companies acting as escort to Sir John French and one each to the Corps Commanders. The companies with Sir John French had had a fairly easy time of it during the Retreat, travelling mostly by train, but those with the Corps Commanders had had the same marching as everyone else, as well as contact with the enemy, respectively at Landrecies and Le Cateau. The Scots Guards, having received orders during the night, were ready to draw in their outposts at seven on 6 September and move off. Colonel Lowther described a long delay in getting away, so, by the time, having left Nesles, they were heading along a road east, they heard that the Coldstream, in the lead, had already become involved in severe fighting beyond Voinsles. Lieutenant Balfour "suddenly heard heavy firing down the road…machine guns ordered up and we prepare to get into action. We have to leave limbers and crawl into action 800x through a hail of bullets." There was then a report of the Coldstream having been heavily shelled as they moved northeast and losing quite a number of men at Le Plessis, partly because they had advanced too far ahead without guns up close enough to support them. They and the Black Watch had to withdraw temporarily, so Lieutenant Balfour's machine guns were forced to turn round too, without any of their crews being hit. The Scots Guards, in reserve all day, had to move back half a mile in their turn and were then hard at work digging in among a field of turnips. They were also shelled, but once the British guns fired back that settled matters. Sir Edward Hulse was having lunch with the other B Company officers when a shell burst on the road quite close to them and Captain William "Peckham" Wickham "was hard at it with the vin rouge, and did not even remove bottle from his mouth." Private Osborne observed "For coolness in a perilous position I would award the palm to one of the Black Watch. He was leading an ammunition mule when a high explosive (a Jack Johnson) shell burst not many yards behind him. All he did was to cast a disdainful glance at the enormous crater, then taking a little black pipe from his mouth, he spat contemptuously and carried on. He was just a rugged-looking old soldier, unkempt and covered in mud like the rest of us, but at that moment he was an object of admiration by all who witnessed the incident." Sir Edward Hulse "First saw German infantry in motor lorries at distance of about three miles. We shelled them, also shelled farm with howitzers; first shell landed in farm and about 50 German cyclists came rushing out and started peddling down road for all they were worth." At half past four they were told to advance at once and found their supporting gunners having tea a mile up the road. That was reassuring. There was no further opposition and no sign of the Germans in Voinsles. They bivouacked for the night behind a barn to the north of Le Plessis, having gone forward nine miles. Colonel Lowther was in "Bed not till close on 11 as it was long after dark when we got in. Lay on and under straw very comfortably and were not disturbed till nearly 5; not a message of any kind all night. The first such night of the war."

Early the following morning, the 7th, a patrol found and brought in two German ammunition wagons and "a cart full of junk of all sorts, rifles, a sword, wallets, medical equipment, some food and a bottle of Eau de Cologne. Latter very refreshing and good for flea bites!" he added. The leader of this patrol was Lieutenant Geoffrey Monckton, whose elder brother, Francis, was on his way to join them with a reinforcement draft. At six o'clock Lieutenant Balfour breakfasted on kidneys, some sheep having been killed the day before for the men's dinners. There was a lull to begin with and they did not move off till after half past ten, continuing then without interruption. Private Osborne mentioned that "they had marched all day in intense heat", Lieutenant Balfour that "we went through several villages which the Germans had pillaged." After fifteen miles march northeast they billeted that night, again a quiet one, in La Frenois, a hamlet just outside Choisy-en-Brie. Beyond the line of hills to their north was the valley of the River Petit Morin with a steep slope down to the river.

With the Black Watch and Camerons in the lead, the Scots Guards, still in reserve, moved on hurriedly at half past five on the 8th. Two companies had not had breakfast. Some distance on and approaching the Petit Morin, Colonel Lowther described "At Bellot an unpleasant surprise. The two leading Battns had got into B when the Germans from a hill NE of Bellot opened on our artillery on the road in close formation. They made good shooting and the guns bolted uphill towards us. I moved the Companies off the road to such cover as I could find, and 10 seconds later came a shell on the exact spot where Stephen and I had been standing; it killed 5 and wounded about 7 of the Coldstream stretcher bearers and finished off the poor chap lying wounded on the stretcher." Sir Edward Hulse blamed poor French cavalry screening for this shelling while part of their Brigade were moving downhill through Bellot in close order. He and six other officers were sitting beside the road when this shell landed fifteen yards away. None of them were touched, which he wrongly ascribed to a faulty burst. The man on the stretcher, badly wounded by one of the first German shells and killed by this one, was probably a gunner. Coldstream stretcher bearers had carried him back four hundred yards and then set the stretcher down in the road, while a medical officer tried to help. Private Osborne saw as "A party of stretcher bearers, together with a Captain-Surgeon, were on the road above about 25 yards from where I stood, when an enemy shell burst in their midst. It was a horrible sight to see a group of dead and dying where a moment before stood a party of vigorous young men. The surgeon was badly wounded: his horse killed. One poor fellow who was carried near my section, and who had only a few minutes to live, asked for his mother. In his semi conscious state his thoughts wandered to the one who had first place in his affection. The orderly trying to make his last moments as easy as possible looked up to me with tears in his eyes and said apologetically, "One cannot get used to this." I feel that way myself too, but for some reason was glad I didn't show it… To hide one's emotions is considered an accomplishment in our present state of civilization, yet, whether it is or not, we only partially deceive others – never ourselves." Lieutenant Balfour was told to get off the road after three shells, which he had seen, landed ahead. Then he received a message "to say I was to go forward with my machine guns so I rode on ahead and found the road blocked by a horrible mess. 15 dying horses, 4 dead Frenchmen, 3 dead British and a dying doctor who was lying across the middle of the road. We cleared and killed the horses and I then approached the doctor: he was just about done, poor fellow, shot through both legs. He said,

"Turn me on my back" so we turned him and his legs remained behind. He then said "Oh my God I thought I knew something about death but for my sake finish my end quickly for it takes so long to die." I then put some morphia under his tongue and about 5 minutes later he died and so we carried him and put him in the ditch by the side of the road and went on." In the Communal Cemetery at Bellot nine British soldiers were buried, Captain Thomas Scatchard RAMC, attached to the 26th Brigade RFA, Gunner George Canton, 117th Battery RFA, part of the 26th Brigade, Lance Corporal Albert Lintott and Privates Herbert Bartlett, Frederick Macey, Wilfred Norman and Peter Stenson, all Coldstreamers, and two unidentified men. The only Scots Guards casualty was Lance Corporal David "Davy" Thomson, a Glaswegian with twenty four years service, which included the Boer War, who got only a slight wound from a shell splinter in his right wrist. He, a regimental policeman at the time, was permitted in 1911 to stay on in the Army beyond twenty one years.

From here onwards, Sir Edward Hulse noted, "We now began to see real signs of retreat. Dead horses and men (German, French and English) and abandoned limbers. All villages looted, and most noticeable thing was enormous quantity of broken bottles." Around midday they moved into Bellot which, Colonel Lowther wrote, was "full of French troops, who seemed a bit sticky. A comfortable halt near water for teas at noon. Badly wanted, but the men now relieved of their greatcoats step along well." "Sticky" suggested poor morale. From Bellot they went a short distance west, halting about a mile south of Sablonnières and moving into position on the left of the main road from Coulommiers. The Black Watch were next to them and the Camerons on the other side of the road. As they approached Lieutenant Balfour's machine gunners saw a wounded German. One of them said "I don't like the way yon German looks at us. I'm thinking he'll have a shot at us." So he went over himself, broke the German's rifle and dragged him behind the British firing line. Then he spotted some Germans twelve hundred yards away, had the machine guns fire two hundred rounds and saw them disappear. Hearing that the Camerons had had casualties, he moved across the road with his machine guns, which they were very pleased to see. Some enemy bullets were coming in, but no sign of where from, so he set off up the road, accompanied also by the Black Watch machine gunners, taking advantage of the cover of a high bank on the right side. He concluded that the firing was probably from a thick clump nearby, so they sprayed it from one side to the other, whereupon six Germans ran out of the north corner. "We let them go 20x and knocked them over and then 12 more came out and over they went. We finally killed 15, wounded 12 and took 15 prisoners (quite a good bag). We then bandaged up the wounded Germans: one man held up his watch and offered it to me for his life." He told Lieutenant Balfour that he had heard that the 1st (Guards) Brigade killed all their wounded and prisoners and was "much relieved when he was allowed to keep his watch and his life was spared." Having given water to the wounded Germans, Lieutenant Balfour and his men then settled down to brew up tea. The rest of the Battalion came up past them on the road and Colonel Lowther told them to follow when they were ready. To Colonel Lowther the German withdrawal had "all the outward signs of a rout. Evidently many of them just halted and bivouacked by the roadsides." While resistance in front appeared to have reduced there was fighting until dark to the west as well as gunfire, probably French, far to the right. They billeted near the south bank of the Marne at Basseville, "a quiet night, but very cold for those who slept out. Yarns are many and one cannot believe more than about 1 per cent. Some rain before dark, which helped to lay the intolerable dust we had suffered from for the past days." That day there was no British effort to secure the river crossings. Lieutenant Francis Monckton brought up a second draft of ninety three men, putting the fighting strength about one hundred over establishment. The other notable event at Bassevelle, described by Private Osborne, was that each man of his platoon received a pound of soap given by the manufacturers of Watson's Matchless Cleanser. Colonel Lowther dined with Brigadier General Henry de Beauvoir de Lisle of the 2nd Cavalry Brigade, later a corps commander, one of those who recognised at the very start that the War would be a long, hard one. Major Tom Bridges, 4th Dragoon Guards, recorded him saying so at a conference before they left Ireland. Later Major General Tom Bridges commanded the 19th (Western) Division, New Army. He, a formidable, but most positive and inspirational character, among other things acquired a young male lion cub from a British friend who won it in a raffle in Paris. Called Poilu, it became the divisional mascot. When awaiting surgery in the autumn of 1917 to amputate his leg after a shell splinter hit him on his way back after visiting his brigadiers in the Ypres Salient and taking bottles of champagne to them, he told a nurse that he wanted the leg fed to the lion afterwards.

In a letter to Dinah Tennant posted on 9 September Sir Iain Colquhoun wrote "Only two letters from home have reached me up to now, I expect Kaiser Bill has the rest and much good may they do him. So far this war has been the biggest picnic you ever been on, wonderful weather, glorious country, hard exercise and heaps to eat and what more can one want; the men are hardening up splendidly and are in fine form. We've been in action 3 times now but mostly at long range so our casualties are few…I don't know when we'll be back but I've an idea we'll have these swine beat by 4 months and those of us who are coming will be back by Christmas. That would be splendid it would suit me as I haven't had nearly enough of this game yet…I wear your mascot on my sword always."

They left Bassevelle at seven and marched some fourteen miles without incident, crossing the Marne at Nogent-l'Artaud, their main event on the 9th. A report of a large force of Germans between seven and eight miles to the north around Château-Thierry, moving northeast, came from a British pilot. This wasted several hours until it was established that it was only a German cavalry division withdrawing. There was wider caution in the BEF because the Fifth Army were not up with them on the right and they knew that the Sixth Army were blocked on the Ourcq by the *First Army*. Meanwhile, however, British cavalry reported no enemy in front. Lieutenant Balfour heard heavy firing from the direction of Château-Thierry "where the French are giving the Germans a hard time. An old German "Taube" came and had a look at us. Nigel [Gipps] and I went out and picked blackberries and we had a glorious compot for dinner. Had a very good night's sleep under a hedge." He was lucky. The bivouac was in a stubble field at a farm called La Marette and the War Diary recorded its starting to rain from midnight. Colonel Lowther heard the "Interesting report of the landing of 70,000 Russians at Ostende. A very unexpected move I must say." It was a complete rumour, but not without its benefit as a distraction for the Germans. It had been widely accepted as fact back in Britain. Alan Swinton, a Sandhurst cadet, writing to his father on 30 August about the state of the War, mentioned that "Reports have come in that Russians shipped from Archangel to Scotland have come down by rail & are now at Ostend also that Canadians have landed at Liverpool & sent via Lichfield, Reading to Southampton whence they have left for an unknown destination. This is not all rumour, but reports that are fully credited by at least half the officers here."

The Advance to the Aisne

It was still raining when they left at seven next morning, 10 September, as reserve to the 2nd Brigade, out in front and being shelled around Licy-Clignon. Lieutenant Balfour heard that the 2nd Royal Sussex Regiment were losing heavily and so went forward with his machine guns to see if he could help. He was very lucky when a German shell landed within ten yards of him, bowling him over two or three times and blowing a man nearby to bits. From a point a little further on he saw what turned into a heavy artillery duel while German infantry withdrew and French troops advanced. British shells were "plastering the Germans retiring at Vichel and Nanteuil" just west of the main road north from Château-Thierry to Soissons. Colonel Lowther was grateful that, following the rain, they had a fairly quiet day and "a chance to dry off while we watched the shelling of our artillery with high explosive shell. They made a tremendous blow up and hole in the ground, but have to be lucky to kill many men." The BEF had little HE ammunition and were mainly equipped with shrapnel, designed for and effective against troops in the open. The significance of HE, available to the German guns in large quantities, would become apparent when movement ceased and the BEF had to dig trenches from which to fight defensively. Colonel Lowther was cautiously optimistic at this stage "At 3.30 moved on to Latilly and got into billets long before dark. This pursuing business is relatively easy work, and the accounts of the haste and confusion among the Germans are pleasant to hear of. It is a month since we left. Our total casualties from the enemy's fire are so far 3 very slightly wounded, and we are 2 officers and about 100 men over strength. Thank God for it; but it is too good to last. Got my socks off for the first time since the 4th, it was quite time!" There were reports of French armies closing in from either side on the Germans to the BEF's front and that "the French have won a victory at Châlons against the German Crown Prince's army." There were other reports of the capture of a lot of prisoners but, on the debit side, the British guns had shelled the 1st Loyal North Lancashire Regiment [Loyals] of the 2nd Brigade, killing their colonel amongst others, after mistaking them for Germans, as well as firing on the French "as they had not informed us of their somewhat rapid and unexpected advance." Again, there was no sense of urgency to keep up the pressure on the withdrawing enemy.

As Captain Stephen had a bad headache, Colonel Lowther let him rest and himself received a variety of orders during the night after it was decided that the BEF were to leave the enemy in front of them for the Fifth and Sixth Armies to deal with and head eastwards to link up with General Foch's Ninth Army. So, after breakfast at half past four on 11 September, the Scots Guards left Latilly at five. They marched northeast for four hours and at nine arrived at Bruyères-sur-Fère, the Fère being a small tributary of the Ourcq. There they bivouacked in another wood, all day and on through the night. When they halted after eleven miles Corporal Green "was glad. It was pouring with rain, and so it came we had to stay out in it. Our company was taken behind a high wall, where a big heap of straw lay – wet through. Search was made, and everything burnable was placed in a heap and fired. One small comfort was had anyway." Lieutenant Balfour and his men "collected wood and logs and made fires to try and keep ourselves dry. I got stung by a hornet at 5pm was rather bad swelling up all over and was too miserable to eat any dinner." At nine in the evening the rain stopped. There was initially no sound of artillery while they were in the wood, which, to Colonel Lowther, made "a pleasant change from the noise of yesterday and the pitiful wounded bloodstained figures crawling rearward. Not that casualties were many, but when one is unoccupied they strike the men's imagination. A good camp up to a certain point, with cover and lots of wood, but several hours rain all pm did not help to make it more agreeable. Most of us had built shelters which kept off the worst of the rain, but by the time I had collected enough logs for a fire my boots were full of water, which meant a rather sleepless night with cold feet." In the afternoon he heard "shelling away to the West, which went on in rain and fog till long after dark. Convoy and troops passing our camp nearly all day." He had little news otherwise. Sir Edward Hulse noted that the Fifth Army passed across in front from right to left, a process which went on for some time and into the night. He understood that the BEF's easterly move was "to tap the right of a German Army which had been heavily hammered by the French at Châlons. But they fell back too quickly for us." As it became clear during the day that the Germans had reorganised and that there was now no such open flank to attack, the BEF resumed their northwards march towards the River Aisne.

Sergeant William "Bill" Shepherd, whose father of the same name lived in Forfar, had been a soldier since 1907 and a clerk before that. At Battalion Headquarters he saw and heard virtually everything that occurred. "I went to France, a sergeant, as "Commanding Officer's Field Clerk", an innovation, I believe, of General Maxse, our Brigadier. The job was a sort of Orderly Room Sergeant in the front line, and my presence was marked by a small flag by day, and a lamp by night, for the guidance of messengers, orderlies, etc." He related how "I was supposed to destroy daily, by fire preferably, my redundant paper matter. By fire was not always possible in the Retreat from Mons, as the Germans were usually too hot on our trail, and then burial had to be resorted to. Sometime after the Retreat, Captain Stephen, the Adjutant, called me over and said, "Look at that". "That" was a message from Army to which was attached a bundle of my messages, now mud-covered, which had been taken from a German prisoner. Then Army demanded to know how, when and where, and by whom, etc. "Now read that", said the Adjutant, and I read Colonel Lowther's reply which was to the effect that he personally was responsible for everything which happened in his Battalion. Neither officer ever mentioned the matter to me again, but ever afterwards I made sure that no snooping jerry would have the chance to go through my waste paper basket." That day Captain Thorne observed to his wife "I am afraid a great many convalescent homes will be required before this war is over."

On 12 September the Scots Guards were the rear battalion of the Division, not moving off till nine. To begin with they went east for a short distance "a dragging walk on muddy roads broken by days of heavy work, much of it in heavy rain. Cavalry divisions all out in front and severe fighting going on in the direction of Soissons." This was British infantry approaching the Aisne at Venizel, close to Soissons, where the enemy were well dug in. From Fère-en-Tardenois the Scots Guards turned north again over the next ridge and then down the other side to Bazoches, on the River Vesle, which ran into the Aisne upstream of Venizel. At two in the afternoon they stopped in a field for teas. Colonel Lowther found "Jamie Balfour quite seedy from his hornet's sting of yesterday and poisoned all over. When we moved on it began to rain and continued to do so. Wet through we reached Bazoches at dusk. Only one Company billeted, the other 3 in the open. Found the French, who lost some men here this morning, in possession of the billets we should have had. Battalion staff crowded into a little cottage, and we were more or less comfortable; but the men had a miserable night, most of them standing all the time by the fires. At 2am a regular tornado and after that it was a shade better, but it was an awful night. Felt something like lumbago or rheumatism myself and some of the younger officers were rather out of sorts." Lieutenant Balfour, in pouring rain, did manage to find a cellar for his machine gunners, fortunately for them.

Sir Edward Hulse remarked "From here we found ground foul, doorsteps and even inside of houses fouled on purpose by Germans… all this time battle of Aisne was preparing, but we did not know whether Germans were only preparing rearguard action, in order to save their supplies at Soissons… or whether it was a big position." There was still an unfilled gap of eighteen miles in the German line, covered only by their cavalry, along the Aisne between the left of the *First Army* at Vailly, to the east of Soissons, and the right of the *Second Army* at Berry-au-Bac, northwest of Reims. The Germans decided to stand and fight on the river line, but to do so they had to fill the gap. On 8 September the French garrison in Maubeuge surrendered. That released General Johann von Zwehl's *VII Reserve Corps* from the siege and they started a forced march south towards Laon. From there they were to go up to the left of the *First Army* onto the higher ridges between Laon and the Aisne, the area known as the Chemin des Dames. Another German formation, *XV Corps*, were on the move towards the right of the *Second Army*. Early in the morning of 13 September, having marched forty miles in twenty four hours, the *VII Reserve Corps* arrived five miles south of Laon and bivouacked briefly.

Crossing the Aisne

At much the same time on the same day, no rations having come up, the Scots Guards were breakfasting as best they could at Bazoches. Colonel Lowther noted "we were ordered to eat the "iron" reserve ration. I fancy many of the men have already eaten theirs. This will be a lesson to be more provident. They are quite reckless about water too, drinking up their bottles at once, forgetting that any day may find them in action from sunrise to sunset with no chance of refilling." With the 3rd Brigade ahead of them the 1st (Guards) Brigade continued north steeply uphill through Vauxcéré and over the ridge beyond, then steeply downhill to Longueval, heading for Bourg on the far bank of the Aisne. There they were to cross that evening. Lieutenant Balfour heard that the enemy had only left that morning. Between them the French and the Germans had blown up almost all the bridges. So the 1st Division had to make their way carefully, with their guns, first over the road bridges of the Aisne Lateral Canal, running south of the river for most of its length as far as Soissons, and then over the Oise and Aisne Canal, which met the Aisne Lateral a little further east. To cross the river they turned left off the main road, northwest along the canal towpath, continuously under repair by the Royal Engineers, and then along the damaged viaduct carrying the Canal over the river. This was under fire from the German heavy guns, though, when the Scots Guards went over, the shells were landing well short. All the same Sir Edward Hulse saw two holes through it already. Later on the German observers corrected the ranging and the British infantry then had to get across in rushes. He wrote afterwards "So little did our senior officers suspect what was in front that we had orders to march to a place behind the present German position, which we have not yet got to!" They went on along the towpath on the far side until they reached the main road and turned right into Bourg. As they marched through the village Colonel Lowther was told to move east "to cover a battery said to be exposed near Pargnan, so up we went, to find two British and one French batteries, a Cavalry Bde, a platoon of Cyclists on the hill, and the Household Cavalry on the way up. No more room on the hill!" First they had to go to Oeuilly, just up river from Bourg at the foot of a long spur leading up to the main ridge of the Chemin des Dames, Pargnan being the next hamlet up the spur. Lieutenant Balfour recorded how as they followed the line of a road uphill towards Pargnan "we advanced over the high ground among Turcos and Spahis above

Oeuilly in artillery formation about 6pm under shrapnel fire." On their right they now had the French 35th Colonial Division, Fifth Army, of whom Zouaves, Algerian infantry, were the main component. Turcos were French colonial tirailleurs [riflemen] from Algeria and Spahis colonial light cavalry from south of the Sahara. At Paissy, another hamlet some three miles to the north further up the spur, the Zouaves, having fought hard, had cleared a wood and so, near Pargnan, the Scots Guards were told to continue up the spur to join them. From now on they were under fire, mainly shrapnel. Private Osborne saw Captain Jack Astley Corbett have his pack shot off his back. "I was curious to see how he would react to this, and I saw that he was more surprised than alarmed, and, wondering for the moment what he should do about it, he lit a cigarette. I picked up a German officer's helmet, but dropped it quickly. There was part of the officer's head inside." Captain Astley Corbett, an Etonian, had been in the Scots Guards since 1903. On 23 September he went down with acute diarrhoea and was sent back to England for the time being.

Corporal Green saw French 75mm field guns, commented that the German gunners' aim was "very erratic", but mentioned casualties caused by shells as they moved in artillery formation behind the French guns. Waiting for his machine gun limbers to come up, Lieutenant Balfour could see about forty miles to his right and twenty to his left. Nearby an area half a mile wide, including the wood that the Zouaves had cleared, was being thoroughly shelled by the enemy. Further on he could see where British gunners were doing the same to the Germans. When his limbers arrived he went forward himself. Then two shells landed, neither causing any damage to the limber he was with. However, his pony, hit by some thirty shrapnel bullets, "went down stone dead." He was hit by a single bullet in his upper thigh, a flesh wound, and five of his machine gunners were also wounded, one of them, Private Robert Brown, a signaller with seven years service, "hopelessly" with shrapnel in the head. He died on 20 September in a clearing hospital [later called a casualty clearing station] at Braine, in the Vesle valley. Private Brown was the son of Robert and Isabella Brown of Glasgow, but his wife Lizzie and their child lived in Tottenhall, Wolverhampton.

As the Medical Officer, Captain Meaden, was with them he looked after the wounded behind the crest of the ridge where they had been hit. Lieutenant Balfour sent the machine gun teams on to Paissy, while his servant Private Dan Allison looked out for stretcher bearers. Later on some Zouaves came along and Captain Meaden and Private Allison persuaded them to get stretchers and carry the British wounded back to their bivouac at a farm. A French doctor there put them up in a loft where "after ½ an hour I felt the man next to me very chilly and with the help of my electric torch found we were with dead Zouaves. So I said to the man who was with me "Are you comfortable. We are in the dead loft." He said, "I was comfortable but I am no so comfortable the noo." They shouted and were moved to another loft with only wounded men. At midnight a horse drawn ambulance arrived and took them, surprisingly, forward to a British dressing station at Paissy. On the 14th he and fourteen other wounded "were put into a room on mattresses and got some beef tea which was very acceptable." At three that afternoon another ambulance took them to a dressing station at Vendresse, itself under shellfire, not least because British field guns were firing from only forty yards away. Lieutenant Balfour was lying helplessly in bed wondering if the place was going to be blown to bits. The shelling stopped when darkness fell but he knew it would start again after dawn on the 15th. It did. Three hours later a medical orderly came to say that they were going to try to get the wounded down to the railway, though it would be difficult, because for the first two miles the road was being shelled. Those who were unable to cope with this journey were put in the cellar of the dressing station, but a shell soon afterwards took the roof off and flattened the building. Two hundred yards further back there was another dressing station, where ambulances were congregating. Lieutenant Alwyn Holt of the Black Watch, also wounded, later told Lieutenant Balfour that he was making his way across the courtyard when a shell landed twenty yards behind him. When told to get into an ambulance he made his way towards it only for another shell to blow the ambulance into the air, killing all the wounded and decapitating two orderlies as they put the last man in. Lieutenant Holt recovered and survived the War. Lieutenant Balfour continued "We then started off and 1200 German prisoners walked alongside ambulance. We were under shellfire for 2 miles and then peace. On reaching 2 miles S of Oeuilly we were put into motor lorries and went down to railhead 20 miles to Fère-en-Tardenois. Awfully jolty and very painful. Had slept on stretcher at railhead and was well looked after." On the evening of the 16th they got into a "very comfortable train: we were lucky because most people only get cattle trucks." Sir John French "came along the train and had a personal chat with everybody." Late the following afternoon the train stopped "and I suddenly saw another train stop about 5 yards off us and saw the glint of a London Scottish kilt. I shouted for Duncan and we had a 2 minute talk. An extraordinary coincidence. Arrived Versailles at 7pm having taken 25 hours to go 80 miles." His brother Private Duncan Balfour was in the 1/14th London Regiment, London Scottish, Territorials. Lieutenant Balfour spent five days at the Trianon Palace Hotel, converted into a hospital, before being evacuated uncomfortably and slowly to England.

On 13 September the first Scots Guardsmen of the War were killed in action, Private James Newlands, a reservist living with his wife Elizabeth in Glasgow, and Private Walter Pickard, a single man whose parents lived off Bishopthorpe Road in York. Previously a confectioner's labourer, he had enlisted a year before. Private Newlands had military "form" and when he left after his initial three years service in 1910 his conduct was described as "Indifferent on account of numerous regimental entries & acts of drunkenness". Both men's personal effects, for Private Newlands an identity disc, a picture postcard and three letters and for Private Pickard an identity disc, a permanent pass and an Army 3rd Class Certificate of Education, were recovered and sent to their families. Anything of more immediate use or value was likely to go straight into the pockets of others, which was even more likely to happen when those who dealt with the dead were not from the same regiment. A third Scots Guardsman, unidentifiable because of the many casualties next day, was stated in the War Diary as having been killed, probably having been fatally wounded on the 13th, but not dying immediately and, if so, quite possibly Private Robert Brown. 2nd Lieutenant William Houldsworth, hit in the head and unconscious, was successfully evacuated and lingered on till 23 September, when he died in Paris. When Lieutenant Balfour was in the dressing station at Paissy "Houldsworth is lying next to me, he is wounded through the head. I don't think he will live till tomorrow, but he is completely paralyzed and has no pain." His parents Thomas and Eulalie "Lilly" Houldsworth lived in London, where his father was a Church of England clergyman, but they also had a house at Cranston, North Berwick. After Eton and Magdalen College, Oxford, he had his probationary commission confirmed on 4 August 1914. Lieutenant Geoffrey Monckton, the younger brother, had a bullet wound in his thigh. A few days earlier he had led the patrol that brought in the German wagons. Eleven men were wounded altogether. One of them, hit by bullets in his left hand and right wrist, was Private Hugh Wright, a serving soldier since 1904, originally from Galston, Ayrshire, and a miner before he joined up. He had thistles tattooed on his right forearm. Clara

Wright, a Londoner, and their three children were living in Camden Town. A fourth child was born on 18 September. Two days after that Private Wright was evacuated home in a hospital ship, not badly hurt and only spending just over two weeks in hospital in England. He came back out later.

Colonel Lowther described that night's arrangements in Paissy with "2 whole Companies being put into one farm, which had limestone caves like churches. Battalions of tirailleurs and zouaves were crowded up against us (we being the right of the British line), but none the less I had a company out on outpost, as the "savage Turco" is in my opinion rather an overrated fighting man." By this time the BEF were across the Aisne in all places, but, owing partly to enemy activity further west and partly to geography, only I Corps on the right had a potentially workable footing, across on the north bank with their guns. Broadly speaking, looking from the Allied positions, the French XVIII Corps and other formations had the right half of the gap in the German line in front of them and I Corps of the BEF and the newly formed Cavalry Corps to their west the left half. When darkness fell on 13 September nothing was known of what the Germans were doing in front.

Battle on the Chemin des Dames

A long ridge ran along the south side of the Chemin des Dames feature, four miles north of the Aisne, parallel to it and just over six hundred metres at its highest. North of the ridge was a plateau along the middle of which ran the road, the Chemin des Dames, and beyond that was another ridge. The road started in the east at Craonne, from where it went westwards for about sixteen miles, before turning southwest to go down the hill to Soissons. Smaller ridges, including, in particular, the one that jutted out south towards Vendresse, on the main road from Bourg to Laon, and spurs with steep banks projected on either side. Late on the afternoon of 13 September the *VII Reserve Corps* began to move into position primarily opposite the British and the *XV Corps* began to arrive opposite the French at Craonne. They had filled the gap and were firmly in occupation of the northern ridge line but, at least to begin with, apparently without occupying the village of Cerny, set back from where the Bourg-Laon road crossed the Chemin des Dames. Cerny would become, with these crossroads just south and a nearby sugar beet factory, if unintentionally, central to the 1st (Guards) Brigade's operations on 14 September. The British plan was, in conjunction with the French, to drive the enemy off the Chemin des Dames ridges, the 1st Division's task being to secure Cerny and Courtecon, further to the west, and the lines of two roads north towards Laon. There was nothing to suggest any material difference from the pattern since the advance began, but the weather the day before had made aerial reconnaissance virtually impossible.

2nd Brigade patrols during the night found German positions next to the Chemin des Dames road around the crossroads and sugar beet factory south of Cerny. On hearing this Brigadier General Edward Bulfin sent the 2nd Royal Sussex and the 2nd King's Royal Rifle Corps [KRRC] at three in the morning up beyond Vendresse, through the hamlet of Troyon and on to occupy the ridge line on the spur just above it. An hour later he sent the 1st Northamptonshire Regiment up the next spur east to secure the right flank. This was without opposition but when around five they advanced with Cerny as their left hand objective they came under fire straight away. They reached the Chemin des Dames road and fought hard there, but could not take it, though they had some success in suppressing the enemy in front, including driving them back from the crossroads and sugar beet factory. They captured about three hundred prisoners, whom the Camerons saw coming past them later in the morning, as well as, according to Corporal Green, "twelve big guns". In rain and thick mist in unknown country there was loss of control from the start and men and units became mixed up, which soon became worse. In addition, the British infantry had no artillery support because the gunners were fearful of firing blind and did not know exactly where the infantry had got to, observers being unable to reach any point from where they could see properly. The German gunners had used the time available to prepare and to measure distances and generally knew where their own troops were. Once all their reinforcements were in place the German orders were to attack all along the line.

Nevertheless Corporal Green's recollection was how "The tremendous thunder of the artillery, combined with rifle fire, woke us at daybreak." Their Brigade started the day at the right of the 1st Division, with French Colonials still their immediate neighbours. However, they moved across westwards from Paissy once the 2nd Brigade were on the ridge line above them, then on through Moulins and Vendresse. The Coldstream led, next came the Camerons and then the Black Watch, with two companies of the Scots Guards as reserve, in the rear. At Vendresse they were to cross the Bourg-Laon road, deploy onto the spur of high ground beyond, head up it and then advance over the Chemin des Dames and on to the villages of Cerny and Courtecon, coming up to do so on the 2nd Brigade's left. Colonel Lowther noted that they "stood to arms before daylight, and when we left soon after it was evident that a good sized battle was in progress. I had only two companies with me, the other two having been sent to Tour de Paissy as escorts to 5 batteries." As the Brigade reached the spur they began deploying, the Camerons on the left, the Black Watch in the centre and the Coldstream on the right. The first two had a relatively clear approach and it would seem that both skirted round the southern end of the spur and lined up initially facing northeast in the narrow valley above the hamlet of Chivy. However it subsequently occurred, when they advanced seven Black Watch platoons ended up immediately south of Cerny, far further to the right than they should have been, in the area of the sugar beet factory. Another five Black Watch platoons reached a point almost a mile away behind the forward left hand positions to which the Camerons eventually moved later. These were just to the south of the wooded area called Le Blanc Mont, from which the Chivy stream flowed towards the hamlet. Meanwhile half of each of the two right hand Camerons companies also arrived near the sugar beet factory. Some even managed to get over the Chemin des Dames road at the crossroads, but at considerable cost. The Coldstream, though closest to Vendresse to begin with and having the least distance to cover, had to make their way uphill through a very steep and thick wood onto the top of the spur, were delayed as a result, started to advance in a direction which would have taken them diagonally across the line of advance of their neighbours on the left and then had to readjust to their right and find space for themselves next to the 2nd Royal Sussex. Most of them ended up in the area of the sugar beet factory and crossroads as well.

The left hand Camerons companies, who came out onto open stubble at the top of the ridge and thus into view and under fire of the Germans earlier, because their route brought them sooner out of the cover of the woods above Chivy, veered to cover their left flank and return enemy fire from that direction. While it was intended that the 3rd Brigade would attack later on their left, until they did so the Camerons were very exposed and German resistance was stiffening. It became apparent at half past seven that the first counterattack was developing from the direction of Le Blanc Mont, enemy infantry having crossed the road from out of their firing line.

Both the Scots Guards and Camerons machine guns started off near some stacks a quarter of a mile south of the crossroads, but the Camerons guns were moved across because of the threat on the left. There were German counterattacks of increasing severity over the next three hours. When the mist then lifted the struggle intensified. It was about now that the *VII Reserve Corps* became fully deployed on the Chemin des Dames. Sometime in the morning Colonel Lowther and Captain Stephen found large numbers of Camerons and Black Watch "in full retirement across the valley in rear, saying retirement had been ordered, but they were soon reorganised and the line strengthened again." Soon after one o'clock a heavy German counterattack from all along the line dislodged the Black Watch and Coldstream around the sugar beet factory. This exposed the right of the Camerons and the enemy pushed them back. It was into the gap opened between the Camerons and the Black Watch near the sugar beet factory that Right Flank of the Scots Guards, on the left, and Left Flank, on the right, advanced from behind the ridge at Troyon. As each moved off, with two platoons forward and two in support, a few men were hit by shellfire before crossing the ridge. Once they were beyond it the enemy machine gun and rifle fire became intense and with shrapnel as well. They went on, well spread out, in rushes. Nevertheless, one shell killed and wounded a number of men in a Right Flank platoon, including 2nd Lieutenant Eric Mackenzie, hit in two places and wounded, but not seriously, for the first time in the War, while another killed Sergeant Robert Royall and seven other men in another platoon. Sergeant Royall, a bachelor and Boer War veteran had been in the Army since 1897, when he gave up being a French polisher in Stepney in the East End of London. One of those wounded was Private Peter Murker, a former moulder and brass finisher from Bainsford, Stirlingshire, who, although a serving soldier for eighteen months, had not gone out initially, but came up in a draft after the Retreat. He had a fair amount of military "form" for missing parades and drunkenness. He was hit in the left shoulder, but it was not a serious wound and he was treated in France.

It was at once apparent on reaching the gap they were to fill that there was no chance of going any further forward. Sir Victor Mackenzie sent a runner back to report this, who, unwittingly, passed another coming up to tell him not to go beyond where they already were. There they helped beat off the counterattacks, which died out after three o'clock before everything quietened down at dusk. All the same the 1st Division had to pull back into cover and dig in behind the Vendresse ridge because any positions forward of it were untenable, without cover and in very open country. The casualties had been heavy, those of the Camerons particularly severe, there had been problems with ammunition resupply and several men's rifles had become too clogged with mud to function. Colonel Lowther wrote "At first there was rain and mist and the artillery could not get to work, therefore, we had everywhere all the best of it; but as the weather cleared our situation became worse. The German side had all the artillery positions and we had none; so all day continued a diabolical shelling with infrequent lulls…As the cover was good it was only in the open that we lost men."

Corporal Green's experience in Right Flank was "Very little progress made on either side. The weather was cold and foggy. Many wounded passed by, evidence of the violence of German fire. My company was in reserve, ready to reinforce where necessary. The casualty lists on both sides were large. We knew that from our observers. Sgt Brown, No 1 Platoon ordered to reinforce the front line. The Huns, as we could see, were strongly entrenched on the near side of a wood, two or three hundred yards away. Brown forced to rejoin the Battalion on the quarry, as he was unable to take his platoon into the front line. He had advanced some distance, but could go no further. A Highlander came up to us and dropped, utterly exhausted. But he was only there a few minutes before he was killed by a piece of shrapnel…At dusk we took over trenches, and we could see, or rather hear, Fritz, at no great distance." Lance Sergeant Frederick Brown came from Windleshaw, Lancashire, and had been serving for eight and a half years. He was invalided to England early in October and discharged medically unfit in April 1917.

The 113th Battery RFA noted that it had been a wet day and that they "came into action E of Vendresse with orders to "fire anywhere" to hearten the infantry. Left fruitless task to go to Chivy valley on urgent call. Arrived just in time to swing into action in open against heavy counterattack on Beaulne ridge at about 2000x open sights. Repulsed. Seemed as if no German lived." They had fired about ninety five rounds per gun in the day.

In hospital at the Trianon Lieutenant Colonel John Ponsonby, the Coldstream Commanding Officer, later told Lieutenant Balfour about his adventures. He went along to his right hand forward company, by then just on the south side of the Chemin des Dames road near the sugar beet factory. The German guns brought down the factory chimney soon after he got there. Realising that there might be scope to move forward, he led the company on, together with a separate mixed party of fifty, consisting of a Camerons officer and ten men, nine Black Watch, a few other Coldstreamers and some Scots Guardsmen. Telling the company to go ahead down the main road to Laon, he led the mixed party into Cerny where, having sent two men to scout ahead, they were able to shoot up two German battalions whom they surprised eating in the main street and took five machine guns from them. A senior German officer, covered with decorations, whom he thought was General von Zwehl himself, emerged from a house with a Red Cross brassard on his arm, accompanied by some forty other officers, pleading for mercy for the one thousand wounded he said were in the house. It may have been complete bluff, yet Colonel Ponsonby undertook not to do anything to the house. It was quickly clear that his party were in a very tight spot and they headed for a wood, where there was a ditch with a hedge in front of it. Surrounded on three sides by Germans, they gave all their ammunition, bar ten rounds each, to a marksman. While they were fired at continuously they were not attacked because whenever a German showed himself the marksman shot him. This went on for seven hours. Colonel Ponsonby was the only one of the party hit, with a small bone in his leg broken by a bullet as he reached the ditch. The Germans stopped firing once it got dark. His party next saw carts carrying German dead and wounded before a large number of enemy arrived, bivouacked on the other side of the hedge and posted sentries. Keeping very quiet they waited until a gale blew up around midnight and covered any sound they then made while crawling along the ditch past the German sentries, a process made the harder by the need for four men to carry him. They all safely reached the British line. Colonel Ponsonby recovered quickly and returned to the Coldstream a few weeks later.

Throughout 14 September B and C Companies were protecting the guns at the Tour de Paissy, a farm uphill from Paissy. Private Osborne had this to say "We have been fighting all day. High explosive shells and shrapnel are bursting in all directions. The attacking part of the business has ceased. One of the French Algerian soldiers was blown up in the air for about thirty yards." Private Luck wrote "Rain was falling heavily and there was a thick fog. B and C Companies were escort for the artillery, so we did not have far to march but spent a miserable day lying just in front of the guns with nothing to do, after we had dug what shelter we could from the shrapnel which had begun to fall all around us, as the enemy tried to find our guns to put them out of action. We also experienced the effect of the Jack Johnson or Coal Boxes. At last a rather a nerve racking day ended." Jack Johnsons or Coal Boxes or Black Marias, were the German HE shells fired by 150mm howitzers, known to the British as 5.9 inch howitzers. The shells' nicknames were from the black smoke and violence of their explosions.

During the 14th and 15th three officers and sixteen men were killed, including Major Carpenter Garnier, who died later after being hit in the head by shrapnel at Battalion Headquarters just behind the ridge near Troyon. He was unmarried and his parents lived at Rookesbury Park, near Fareham, Hampshire. After Harrow and Christ Church, Oxford, he was commissioned and had served in the Boer War. Another of the dead was Lieutenant Henry "Young Bones" Inigo Jones, educated at Eton and Magdalen College, Oxford, whose home was in London and whose parents were Major General Richmond Inigo Jones, a retired Scots Guards officer, and Elinor Inigo Jones. 2nd Lieutenant James Stirling Stuart was hit, not badly, in both knees and was not long away. Eighty six men were wounded and twelve missing. Private John Thomson, a ploughman from Alyth before he enlisted just after New Year 1910, had served only two years before becoming a reservist and joining the police in Glasgow. He did not come out at the beginning and so missed the Retreat. After the War he described how he and Private McCabe, who, he said, was later killed on the Aisne, carried Lieutenant Mackenzie back to the quarries after he was wounded. Private Hugh McCabe, a miner and reservist from Kilmarnock, was hit in the head later the same day, but not killed. The wound was not a serious one and he was treated in Base hospitals before returning to the Battalion the following January. Private Patrick Hastings was dead, but never found. He had just completed three years in the 2nd Battalion and became a reservist only three weeks before mobilization. During the course of the three years he had grown two inches from just under five foot eight and he had a completely clear disciplinary record. His parents George and Catherine Hastings lived in Portobello on the Firth of Forth outside Edinburgh, and he was their only son, though he had three elder sisters. Private William Hall, a reservist from Wakefield, left in 1911 after eight years service, just after the end of which he married Nellie Payne at Caterham. They had two daughters. Nellie and her girls were in Wakefield with Private Hall's parents. He was killed on 14 September and, although his body was known to have been buried near Vendresse, the grave was lost. He had tattoos of an anchor and a horn on his left forearm. Private Oscar Price, another reservist, the son of William Price of Bromyard, Herefordshire, was missing on the 14th. A clerk previously, he left the Colours after ten years only a few months before. In unexplained circumstances some of his belongings appeared in 1917 and were sent to another member of his family, Elizabeth Price. Private Thomas Hampton, a baker, was born in Dublin, but enlisted in Glasgow in 1904 and served for three years before returning there. In 1912 he married Daisy Macpherson, a widow with a three year old son. Called up in August 1914, he was killed a month later. Daisy Hampton only received the basic war widow's pension, because no allowance was made for step-children. Lance Corporal David MacLennan was a farmworker at Avoch, Easter Ross, before he enlisted at Inverness in 1906 and served seven years, becoming a Lance Corporal. When he left the Army his first job was as a River Tweed Water Bailiff, before he moved on in March 1914 to Northumberland County Constabulary at Wallsend. The same month he and Elizabeth Millar married in Galashiels. Mobilised in August as a Private, he was soon restored to his rank as a NCO and was killed on the 14th. Private John Pretswell, a reservist like so many others, was also killed the same day. He had been a butcher in Biggar, Lanarkshire, served for seven years from 1907 and so had only been a reservist for a few months. His wife Annie, whom he married in 1912 at Upton-cum-Chalvey, Buckinghamshire, was living in Biggar with their son, an eight month old baby. Private Hugo Kershaw, a serving soldier for three years, born in Bremerhaven on the German North Sea coast, but whose home was in Dartford, Kent, was Captain Reginald "Reggie" Stracey's servant and was in the Officers Mess Staff photograph just before the War. Hit in the head and stomach, he died on 15 September at a field ambulance at Vendresse. Captain Stracey commanded C Company and was the nephew of Major General Henry Stracey, another retired Scots Guardsman.

After dark all the Camerons were very scattered and men gradually trickled back by various ways and routes. By midnight on the 14th they had managed to collect a total of six officers and about two hundred men. Earlier on some Germans had discovered Captain Alexander Horne, who had served in both the Omdurman campaign in the Sudan and in the Boer War, lying in a hollow near Le Blanc Mont with a very clearly visible bandage on his wounded left leg. They shot and killed him as well as Private William Finnie, who was helping him, but took Company Sergeant Major W Gordon and Lance Corporal Willis Swithenbank prisoner. Both contrived, separately, to escape later that night, managed to find the 2nd Welsh Regiment of the 3rd Brigade and told them what had happened to the others. When he was captured during the evening of the 14th Private Arthur Burgess and two other prisoners saw a German NCO use his revolver, presumably because, so Private Burgess thought, his victim could not walk, to kill 2nd Lieutenant Hector Cameron, lying on a waterproof sheet, badly wounded in the shoulder and both legs and unable to stand. During the fighting that day Private Ross Tollerton was lying on the small spur at the head of the Chivy valley next to Lieutenant James Matheson, who was then hit and badly wounded. With the assistance of Lance Sergeant George Geddes, who was killed helping to lift him up, Private Tollerton carried Lieutenant Matheson some distance to shelter and then went back to the firing line, although by this time wounded himself in the head and hand. When the rest of the men he was with retired down the valley, Private Tollerton returned to Lieutenant Matheson and stayed with him for three days until they were both rescued. He won the VC.

Of later on the 14th Colonel Lowther wrote "Night came, and with it rain; the most unpleasant night I've had all the war. Lying in white mud in a limestone quarry, shelling going on till after dark. But we got up the cookers with hot tea for the men, at least for as many of them as we could collect, and made the best of it. About once an hour all through the night a shell from a big German gun went singing overhead, landing 2 or 3 miles to the SW with what object it is impossible to conjecture." B and C Companies were still away with the guns. At dawn he "had a bit of trench dug facing NE to hold about 50 men, no room for more. At daylight all was fairly quiet but things soon livened up…I went over to report to the Brigadier and sent Stephen away to fetch in our two missing Companies…Guns had been put in the quarry where I had the Battalion reserve, reducing the space available for my men…Tried to sleep, but as the whole country was being searched by shells this was hard to do. The whole place seemed alive with bursting shrapnel and high explosive shell. One burst a few feet over the crest line, hitting gun horses and my own poor horse. I had just time to call to the gunner drivers that it was no use running about, when another 5.9 HE shell came just right for us. It struck a little tree about 12 foot up its trunk and exploded. I felt something hit me in the left breast and on right instep, no pain and did not think I was wounded. I looked up and heard Corpl Jack saying his leg was broken, and the lad lying next to me looked pitifully round and I saw he was practically disembowelled by the base of the shell. Then I opened my shirt, found a fair hole about 4 inches long above the left nipple, and a lot of blood flowing, foot only bruised, but very painful, and end of spur shot away. The bullet, or shell fragment, had gone through my medal ribbons. Did not feel sick and was not spitting blood, so concluded it was not serious, but as well to clear out; picked up my kit, got out the field dressing and stepped off down the road. Clancy of the machine gun detachment helped me unpack the FFD [First Field Dressing] which I held on the wound. Half way down the hill found B & C Companies just arrived with Stephen; also my poor horse lying dead. Stephen had finished him off. Secured my sword, on which the horse had fallen, bending it to scythe shape, and offered it to the advanced dressing station at Vendresse. There Meaden diagnosed my trouble as a superficial injury; he was wrong, as I know the bullet if not in me will be in my trousers. Got a dressing put on, felt fine, and asked if I might return to the battalion. This was refused, and quite right, as I soon felt groggy with loss of blood, and pain and stiffness increased. At about one I drove off on the box of a horsed ambulance to Villers 4 to 5 miles back, and beyond the Aisne, where a fresh dressing was put on, and the missile was found lying on my breastbone. I decide not to have it out then as I had had enough interesting incidents for one day."

Lance Corporal Alexander Jack, from Govan, served an apprenticeship as a ship's joiner on the Clyde before enlisting at the end of 1904. He had been a regular soldier ever since. In 1907 he was convicted by magistrates in Lambeth of "Indecency in the Streets" in that he did "aid and abet one Lily Smith, a common prostitute to wander in a public street there, and then and there behave in an indecent manner." He was fined twenty shillings and lost his first military good conduct badge. That apart, he matched up to his company officers' assessment in 1913 of being an "exceptionally good man in every way". He never recovered and died on 6 December 1914 at Brighton. Private Joseph Clancy was from Manorhamilton, County Leitrim, and had also been serving since 1904 after enlisting in Glasgow, where one of his brothers was living in Bridgeton. He was described in 1913 by a company officer as "A very good man, but needs watching" and had qualified as a 1st Class Machine Gunner that year. Corporal John Buchan, yet another reservist, had left the 2nd Battalion two years before. Originally working as an engineer in Edinburgh, his home town, he had been in the Army for nine years, qualifying as a 1st Class Signaller and also passing his 1st Class Army Education Certificate, an obligatory requirement for higher promotion. Corporal Buchan was killed on 15 September. He had married Janette Millar, a Londoner, in Lambeth on Christmas Day 1909, and she, with their small daughter, born in 1911, was in Hounslow.

Colonel Lowther was very lucky to be taken back to Fère-en-Tardenois in a motor ambulance belonging to the RFC, which he understood was one of only two such ambulances in the BEF at the time. Because of the number of wounded the church had been taken over to help accommodate them and he was put there. Next day "Soon after dawn the Curé came in and celebrated Mass, a very strange sight with the early sun shining in through the stained glass windows of the well proportioned church, the little congregation with a few Highlanders taking the Sacrament at the altar rails, and behind them along each side of the nave and aisles a double row of tired, injured and bandaged figures." He was sent back later that day in an American ambulance to Paris, under the directions of Robert Bacon, from 1909 to 1912 the US Ambassador to France, who had come up to Fère. It meant sitting up for six hours in a seat without a back, but the journey could have been far worse. When he was wounded the diary was with his kit and there it stayed. He did not get it back until much later. He did not make any corrections in the light of later knowledge and, as for the worst inaccuracies, "I have let them stand and send the diary home to show how little – when engaged in big operations – one knows of what is going on all round and how hard it is, with the best intentions, to ascertain the truth….It may also indicate the very calm nature of the British soldier, for, in all the long retreat from Maubeuge there was never the slightest evidence, among any of the troops I saw, of anxiety as to results or lack of confidence in our leaders French or British."

Meanwhile, Private Osborne recorded on 15 September "The enemy still hold the same position and the fighting has become fast and furious. Shells cut up the ground in front and behind us. Mutilated bodies of men and horses are lying about everywhere. Yesterday and today have been hell. A lot of my old comrades have been killed today. The Colonel was wounded in the chest and the left forearm. I saw blood staining his medal ribbons: his horse was so badly wounded that it had to be shot. One of the orders issued on the Retreat from Mons was that men should not leave the ranks to look after wounded men. The Colonel, after saying goodbye to his charger, abided by that order and would not let anyone assist him to the dressing station. I saw one of the French Algerians with a most gruesome souvenir – a German's head – he seemed very pleased with it." Private Luck's section had their first casualty when Private George Cossey, from South Town, near Great Yarmouth, Norfolk, was hit by shrapnel in the leg and back, but not badly. He was an unmarried reservist who had left eight years before, having started his military career in 1903 by first enlisting into and being paid and equipped by the RFA, before reappearing at a recruiting office in Southampton purporting to be a civilian and joining the Scots Guards. This practice, known to the military as "fraudulent enlistment", led to a civil conviction for theft. Those who did it would usually be held to their second regiment and so he served with the Scots Guards. Private Luck, marching up with B Company to the ridge, heard that Colonel Lowther had been hit and then passed him on the road, which was disheartening for all of them. "From the greyness of his face it was evident that he had been badly hit but he made light of it when passing the Company and tried to persuade us he would soon be back." He did return, but not until 17 November. In the meantime, Major Carpenter Garnier having been killed, command devolved to the next senior officer, Major Bates Van der Weyer. In reality, as would become apparent, Captain Stephen ran the Battalion.

Stalemate on the Chemin des Dames

Though the concept and practice of digging in was well understood before the War and acted upon right from the start at Mons, from 15 September onwards came the first British experience of trench warfare amid constant daytime shelling and intermittent German infantry attacks. Private Mellor noted going up into position at night, spending all day in a quarry and digging trenches and the next two days making dug-outs. Where they were from the 15th to the 19th there were about a thousand yards between the front lines, unpleasant and uncomfortable. Private Osborne wrote on the 17th "The weather is cold, and it is a dull cheerless day with drizzling rain. My clothes are wet, covered with mud, and other things. The trench is not roomy enough to stretch my legs, and I ache all over. There isn't a match in the whole platoon, therefore I cannot comfort myself with a smoke. What a life!" while he continued next day "The difference between yesterday and today is that the weather is much colder and there is more rain. I am trussed up in a trench, cold, wet, hungry and thirsty, with rain trickling down my back. A few of our boys have been killed: the Company Sergeant Major severely wounded. During the night the Germans made an attack, and what with machine gun and rifle fire of both the enemy and our own, the noise was deafening. Owing to the darkness we could not see the effect of our fire, but judging by the huge number of dead on the field next morning it was evidently disastrous for Fritz." Company Sergeant Major Albert Pettit was hit by shrapnel in his back and right thigh. He recovered and served with the 3rd Scots Guards in London, becoming a Drill Sergeant, before returning to France and being appointed Sergeant Major of the Battalion early in July 1917. On enlistment in 1897 as an eighteen year old he gave his occupation as a baker and shortly afterwards served in the Boer War. He married Mary Williams in Pimlico in 1908 and they had a daughter in 1914. Private Luck's experience was that "We had been worried all day with shellfire which upset our nerves more than anything else, but the night was worse, as there was rain, rifle shooting and the call of stand to arms. It was a case of praying all night for morning to come. As far as casualties were concerned we escaped very lightly having only one killed and about half a dozen injured."

In the notes he wrote to replace the lost diary Sir Edward Hulse described the rain starting on the 10th and being "practically ceaseless up to 20th. Trenches one to seven or eight inches deep in mud and water; very cold at night. Practically ceaseless bombardment from 13th onwards, with frequent day and night attacks, especially latter. Germans wasted hundreds of men in these attacks. Prisoners very thin and haggard, and complained of hunger and fatigue." He noted not just the shrapnel but the big howitzer shells as well. The most exposed place was at the bottom of the slope behind the ridge, the trenches being at the top. A number of horses pulling the Black Watch field cookers were killed from being too far out from the bottom of the slope. He estimated that from top to bottom there was a height difference of about two hundred and fifty feet, the slope itself being steep and thickly wooded. It was therefore more likely that a howitzer shell would fall at the bottom of the slope, or further back still, than somewhere on the side of it and, unless the trench line, a very narrow target, got a direct hit, the men were safe from shrapnel because they scraped out burrows at the front of the trench and crouched in them. The top of the ridge consisted of sand and gravel and looked out over turf or stubble. The support line was a bit further back down the slope and quite safe from the howitzers. Wherever there were caves in among the limestone quarries these were used for cover, likewise safe except if there was a direct hit. The German lines across the plateau were in three rows of trenches in tiers on the far ridge. The Scots Guards observed by day from a haystack just in front of their trenches. At night they sent out posts about one hundred and fifty to two hundred yards forward to overlook the slope towards the enemy. Parties went down to fill up bottles after dusk, when the shelling slackened, from the only water supply in Vendresse, at one time put out of action for six hours after a shell hit it. All rationing had to be at night because movement in most trenches in daylight was too dangerous. The British guns were on a spur south of Vendresse, it and its valley being where most of the shells landed. Apart from the incident on 15 September the dressing station was fortunately never hit. Typical of a night in the line was Corporal Green's account of 18 September "At eleven pm, we were ordered, by Captain Stracey to "Stand To", as an attack was expected. After a long weary wait, a heavy rifle fire started from the enemy in front. Our guns soon picked up the challenge, and so it lasted the whole night."

On the 17th Captain Thorne told his wife that news had come that General Maxse was being promoted Major General, but, more down to earth, "we haven't seen our baggage for some days & my pockets are filled with maps & food – 2 essentials that can't be done without." Sir Edward Hulse had managed previously to write short letters to his mother, three out of five eventually reaching her. However, his first long letter was on the 18th from a cave, part of an old limestone quarry behind Vendresse. He thanked her for sending out foot grease, pipes, tobacco and cigarettes, which arrived at just the right moment, when the two hundred men of B Company had nothing left and one box of matches between them "We split open cartridges and use the cordite as matches now." He was careful not to go into any military details but said "The most unpleasant work I have had so far is being escort to our guns, which of course draws all fire, including that of the German heavy siege gun, which was meant for the siege of Paris, which they were so certain of reaching! I have acted throughout as officers' cook and messman for my company, and on the few occasions when we have been able to get both eggs and milk the result of my cooking has been praised to the skies! I have also (owing to knowledge of French, as the Colonel told me) acted as billeting officer since the fourth day of our arrival. It entails going on ahead of the Brigade and seeing to the lodging or bivouacking of the Battalion, and commandeering all eggs, butter, milk, etc., possible. It is no easy matter, and when one arrives about 11pm dead tired and pitch dark, with rain, it requires an inordinate control of temper! The most welcome presents are cigarettes and chocolate, none of which exist any longer in NE France. Please send me out another pair of regulation puttees…mine are in shreds now. We all look very sweet sights and have not seen water, except to drink, for 7 days, but the rain has done a good deal; no clothes off for the last 10 days, and of course no billeting, and no sleeping bags, etc. The German atrocities cannot be exaggerated, there is nothing they will not descend to." What he was thinking of particularly came out in his next letter on the 21st, after receiving two batches of letters from her, which arrived together with all the parcels she had sent him. "The great thing in sending welcome little parcels is that they should be small and frequent rather than large at long intervals, as we have all we can carry as regards weight on our backs. Please send one thick vest and one pair short drawers (thick, and only down to above the knee) at once; also same a fortnight afterwards." He summarised events in general terms, the previous few days having been far more intense than anything before. He told her that mail was coming through frequently now that they were advancing, as they thought, "and letters are appreciated more than anything, and waited for with feverish anxiety." Next he turned to atrocities "People think the German atrocities are exaggerated, I believe. I will now give you an absolutely authentic instance of what they do. This is a true story of Dick Compton Thornhill's death. He was wounded, and together with some of our men and the Black Watch, and, I believe, a few Coldstream, had crawled into a pit to avoid further fire. The Germans came up and fired on this party of our men (35-40 in all) and all wounded. Dick Compton Thornhill and a Black Watch officer put up a handkerchief as a signal to them, upon which the Germans walked in and shot the lot point blank. Two men escaped, – and one of them was our's, – by feinting to be dead and crawling back by night to our lines; they had two wounds each. The rest, as I say, were butchered, although already incapacitated completely." On the 22nd Sir Edward Hulse collapsed and had to be sent back sick. He told his mother how he had had bad dysentery for nine days and that his right leg, in which he had had rheumatism when he was much younger, had seized up completely. He was evacuated to Nantes to recuperate. Corporal Green mentioned that on the 17th "Word arrived of Huns shooting some of our wounded with Red Cross flag showing." Lieutenant Richard Compton Thornhill, in the Battalion two years following Eton and Sandhurst, was missing on 14 September. His parents Sir Anthony and Lady Compton Thornhill lived near Ipswich and he was engaged to Mary Pollen, who would appear later in the story.

On 19 September, as their Brigade came out of the line for three days rest at Oeuilly, the Scots Guards handed over to the 2nd Sherwood Foresters of the 6th Division, just arrived in France and going into the front line for the first time. To Corporal Green "Very pleased we were too, as our short sojourn had been a great nerve wracking experience." On the way to Oeuilly "The enemy shelled us the whole journey." Private Osborne described how Captains Balfour and Wickham in B Company "marched us across field in zigzag fashion to dodge the shells, but they had us in range all the time. About thirty men just ahead of me were killed. A piece of shell struck my rifle and staggered me a little, otherwise I was unhurt. It occurred to us that the fire was being deliberately directed." It would seem that the men he described as being killed were from another regiment. On the 20th he recorded "A spy has been caught and brought to the village. The house of this despicable creature occupied a very high position, from which he directed the German artillery by telephone. He was shot the same day." There were a lot of other alarms of one sort and another at Oeuilly, all passing Private Luck by as he was comfortably billeted in a hayloft. After only thirty hours out of the line on the evening of the 21st the Brigade were on their way two miles west to take over from the 5th Brigade of the 2nd Division, who had been badly knocked in an unsuccessful attack. Private Osborne was correct that they relieved the 2nd Worcestershire Regiment.

They moved in the dark over previously unseen ground into what was described as "a difficult position" at Canal Post amid thick woods where the Oise and Aisne Canal went into a tunnel that began near Braye and ran northwest under the Chemin des Dames. The nearest village in British hands was Moussy. The relief was not completed till midnight. Private William McLennan was killed when a trench collapsed and suffocated him. He was working as a fitter's helper in Glasgow when he enlisted in February 1909, following which he served for three years before going onto the Reserve. He had married Annie Campbell in Glasgow in April 1914. They already had a son in 1910 and their daughter was born on 7 January 1915. Annie McLennan wrote to Regimental Headquarters on 20 March 1915 "I received Her Royal Highness Princess Mary's Gift I must thank her kindly for allowing me to have it as it is always a remembrance of my Husband Pte W McLennan 7387 who was killed in action as my little baby never saw him I will always keep Princess Mary's Gift to show her when she become a girl to understand meaning of gift." Princess Mary was the daughter of King George V and Queen Mary and first proposed to pay out of her own pocket for small Christmas gift boxes for soldiers and sailors of all ranks serving overseas or in the Fleet. This was not practical and so a national fund opened in November 1914. While there were variants, a folder of writing materials for non-smokers for example, the standard gift consisted of a rectangular brass box embossed with Princess Mary's head in profile. Those distributed in time for Christmas 1914 contained a Christmas card, a photograph of Princess Mary, a pipe, tobacco, cigarettes and a lighter. The next of kin of those who had been killed received them on their behalf, often much later, and the wounded did so too, whether they were still abroad or not.

Later on that evening Private Osborne noted "About midnight Captain RF Balfour took over our section on reconnoitring patrol. We hadn't gone far before rapid fire was directed on us from a wood on our right front. Owing to the darkness the bullets flew wide. As per arrangement we laid flat on the ground for a couple of minutes, then the firing ceased, so we crawled away and found excellent cover in a natural trench. This turn of events did not suit the Captain and he decided to push on again. To avoid risking the lives of all the section he asked for a volunteer; several volunteered. I was selected. Then we went straight towards the wood, but this time all was silent, which meant that the outpost, or whatever they were, had retired to the main body. Being satisfied on this point, the Captain sent me back for the remainder of the patrol, and then we all pushed through the wood. We were all getting a little war weary and on this occasion

I say quite frankly I was filled with apprehension. In Army language I "had the ruddy wind up." We were lucky enough to find a narrow path, the surface of which was clay, very wet and slippery owing to its having been much used by the enemy. I was leading file with the Captain just behind, and after travelling about ¾ of a mile we were challenged by a German sentry. I nearly bumped into him and my nerves being a bit frayed I shot him instead of going for him and taking him prisoner. I don't know whether I killed him or not. I didn't stop to feel his pulse. It was a great mistake to shoot this sentry, what was done couldn't be undone, so the captain ordered us to retire as quickly as possible. Dawn found us skirting the edge of the field on which severe fighting had taken place the previous day. Corpses, German and our's, were strewn all over the field. Some had died on their hands and knees and remained in that position. One body I saw, one of our's, was standing; the left shoulder was pressed against the trunk of a small tree, the hands grasping the rifle with the bayonet fixed as in the charge: the bayonet was buried in the ground. We did what we could to remove the ghastliness by placing the body in a trench, then made our way back to our own lines."

23 September was fairly quiet. That night the Coldstream relieved the Scots Guards who went into reserve trenches at Verneuil, behind Moussy. Captain Thorne told his wife next day of the departure of their Signal Officer back to his battalion and that "Hugh Ross in the Scots Gds has taken his place. The latter has often been up to Lossie and we have been great friends for years. He is the fellow who draws so well. Do you remember the ladies dressing room at Maidenhead & his drawings there?" At quarter past seven on the morning of the 25th, perhaps partly because there was a British battery just to the south, the Germans started shelling the hill to the west of Beaulne, the next spur off the main ridge. Here the Camerons were in the front line trenches. Corporal Green wrote of "Heavy shelling on both sides opened the day. Moved back into shelter of the high wall." They first knew of something serious when "A Cameron Highlander came up and asked for Headquarters. He said his battalion had been wiped out." After a quarter of an hour of shelling two howitzer shells scored simultaneous direct hits, one just outside the entrance and the other on top of a limestone cave, demolishing it. Inside were the Camerons Battalion Headquarters. Rescuers, including Royal Engineers and Scots Guardsmen, were very much hampered by the continuing shellfire. When they did finally manage to clear a way in, they found four Camerons still alive, one very seriously crushed, two injured and one, remarkably, untouched. Five officers were killed, the Commanding Officer, Adjutant, the Medical Officer, Lieutenant John Crocket RAMC, and two company commanders, one of whom, Lieutenant Napier Cameron, had been fortunate on 14 September above Chivy to get away by successfully feigning death as German soldiers cut off his revolver and binoculars. Killed also were the Sergeant Major, a Company Sergeant Major and twenty two others, including almost all the clerks, medical orderlies and stretcher bearers. After dark Sir John French came to visit the Camerons and look at the scene. Captain Thorne did not mention this, nor could he, but he did tell his wife that "You would laugh if you saw my coiffure. I had a Sergeant of the Scots Gds in, who is a barber at home, and he ran the clippers right over my head. The fateful result of it is that now all my head gear is miles too big and it all flops about."

On the 26th the Scots Guards marched back under heavy shellfire to Oeuilly where Private Osborne observed "We had no rest or comfort during the few hours' respite from the trenches, what with the enemy shelling village and orders continually coming in about being ready to move at a moment's notice. We are heartily glad to get away to the trenches again. Remained in trenches for a week. Under fire day and night." One shell knocked over both Sir Victor Mackenzie and Captain Charles "Pash" de la Pasture, without injuring them, while another killed three reservists, blowing them to bits. The first was a Liverpudlian, Private George Browne, a shoemaker from Everton, who had started in the 2nd Life Guards, but bought himself out. Then in 1909 he joined the Scots Guards instead, serving three years. He and his wife Elizabeth married on Christmas Day 1913 and were living in Bishop Auckland, County Durham. Just after he reported on mobilization their daughter was born on 9 August. The second was Private Robert McGill, originally from Troon on the Ayrshire coast, who collected a long string of disciplinary entries in the three years he served from the end of 1902. He married Charlotte Innes in 1912 and they had a little girl born five weeks before mobilization. Private Patrick Corcoran, the third, was a farmer from Mountmellick, Queen's County, who joined up at Chester in 1904. He had a "slight tendency to flat feet" on enlistment, when he was also described as "very stiffly built". He had a very good disciplinary record during his three years. He was unmarried and when Margaret Corcoran received his 1914 Star she wrote when she sent back the receipt after some delay that "I beg to acknowledge Medal for my son. For which I am most grateful & I highly esteem. The Paper got misled on me and that leaves me so late."

On the 27th Brigadier General Charles FitzClarence VC arrived to take command of the Brigade and General Maxse, already promoted, was posted to England to command and form the 18th (Eastern) Division, New Army. In the aftermath of the Retreat from Mons he was not the only brigade commander to go home, but others never reappeared in the BEF, though Sir Douglas Haig was not at all pleased about the Munsters at Etreux. General FitzClarence was originally in the Royal Fusiliers, but early in the Boer War had been a prime mover in raising and training locally recruited horsemen in South Africa into an effective force of mounted infantry. They, the Protectorate Regiment, became part of the besieged garrison at Mafeking. For three separate acts of exceptional courage and ingenuity during the Defence of Mafeking he won his VC, where his men nicknamed him "The Demon". He transferred to the Irish Guards in 1900.

The procedure continued that the front line was fully manned at night and that in the daytime most men were back in the dug-outs just behind the ridge. On the 28th Corporal Green was in a dug-out and "The enemy tried very hard to shell us out of our cover behind the hill, but it was too steep for them. Bodies of English and Germans could be seen in abundance, lying just outside our barbed wire entanglements. A Burial party went out, but were forced to return. The Hun had turned his machine guns on them." Again they had to remain awake and alert all night. Next day "The tops of our trenches completely blown away and we were very much exposed to enemy fire. Rations had been issued under fire." Several more men were hit. Private Donald Wood, a reservist from Falkirk, where he lived with his wife Elizabeth and their three children, had been out in the BEF from the start. That day he was severely wounded in the left forearm, his left hand was amputated and he was discharged "No longer physically fit for war service" as early as 13 November. The same day Private Martin Dohney, an Irishman from Waterford and another reservist, but a later arrival in France, was hit in the chest by shrapnel and evacuated. He died of a secondary haemorrhage at home on 31 October 1915, leaving his wife Catherine and their two small daughters, the younger one of whom had had her first birthday a week earlier. Corporal William "Billie" Watson, a qualified physical training instructor, was killed on the 29th. He was a Fife miner, served eight years to 1912 and was called up from the Reserve. His wife Sarah was a Londoner and they married in West Ham towards the end of 1912, their daughter being born in 1913. Also killed was Lance Sergeant Angus Wilkinson, whose parents' home and his birthplace was Fort William. He, formerly a railway fireman in Glasgow, had also left for the Reserve after eight years in 1912. His wife Henrietta, whom he married early in 1911, and their son born the same year, were living in Bermondsey, South London.

Private Wilfred Crossfield, the son of John and Esther Crossfield of Headingley, Leeds, had been a soldier since early 1909 and was described in a report signed by Sir Victor Mackenzie and Sir Iain Colquhoun in 1913, by which time he was an officer's servant, as "A very good valet. Has a good knowledge of cookery." He was shot through the buttock into the pelvis on the 30th near Vendresse. The open wound was very serious and, though he was quickly on his way home by hospital ship, there was little that the doctors could do with a punctured bladder and "matted intestines". To these was soon added peritonitis and he died on 8 October near Southampton. Also on the 30th Private Richard Vine, a warehouseman in London until he joined up in 1899, was shot in the head and died next day in the dressing station at Vendresse. By this time he had signed on for twenty one years. Before the War he had had a chequered career, being promoted and then reduced to the ranks more than once, drink being involved each time. While stationed in Cairo in 1911 he had to go to hospital to recover from alcoholic poisoning from "native spirit", but he soon got over it. He had a sister living in Watford.

On the 29th Captain Thorne wrote home "This battle is never ending, it started on the 14th or rather afternoon of 13th and looks like lasting into the New Year." He added that there was a tale doing the rounds of a Turco with a German head in a haversack as a present for his fiancée. Then he remarked "(Our new Brigadier is a great man, we are jolly lucky to have got him)". Next day he went on that the "Brigadier goes out at 5am to 7am each morning and 5.45 to 7pm each evening". As Captain Thorne accompanied him he worked up a fair appetite, but "There must come a limit. The nation that can hang on long enough will then be certain to win." On 1 October, commenting on the battle he could "see no prospect of anything in our near neighbourhood to end it for many a long day." Later on in the same letter "I am more and more sure that we have made a good exchange in our Generals. The present one is much fitter, more solid and very much a gentleman."

The Brigade were shortly back in the line above Vendresse, along the spur running southwest from Troyon and facing the Chemin des Dames obliquely, and were to stay there until 16 October. To begin with the Scots Guards were on the left nearest to Chivy, the Coldstream on the right south of Cerny, physically closest to the German line, with French troops next to them on the east. On the face of it matters had degenerated into the routine. There were few significant incidents, but nevertheless a trickle of casualties from shellfire, repeated and prolonged periods of being on the alert against surprise night attacks, together with rifle fire, usually nocturnal, and sniping. Quite apart from patrols at night, that was also the main time for improvement of fire and communication trenches and for digging saps out in front for observation. Significantly, Royal Engineers were bringing up and erecting sufficient barbed wire to strengthen the positions. The main challenges were survival and trying to achieve some degree of comfort. On 4 October Corporal Green mentioned "Socks, shirts, tobacco, etc. issued, and not before time." The day before Captain Thorne commented to his wife that "(It does annoy me so much to hear them called "Kitchener" Army! Why His Majesty is not permitted to own them I don't know.)"

There having been reconnaissance previously, after dark that night 2nd Lieutenant Merton Beckwith Smith of the Coldstream led his platoon in a silent attack to rush two lines of forward German trenches near the sugar beet factory. These, probably sapped forward for artillery observation, were only a hundred yards away. However, the Germans in the third line behind opened fire. While certain that they had inflicted significant casualties, the Coldstream suffered too. What they could not do in the dark under fire was fill in the enemy trenches and they had to withdraw. General FitzClarence reported to Headquarters 1st Division that he had told the Coldstream to develop and push out their own sap to "make the enemy's advanced trenches as uncomfortable as possible. A supply of rifle grenades is urgently required for this purpose as also iron or steel plates for strengthening loopholes – the ordinary sandbags at close range not being of much use." Early on commanders like General FitzClarence recognised the kinds of equipment that the infantry needed. It would be some time before they became available. Much else had to be improvised. On the 5th Captain Thorne wrote of how "The men were given a blanket apiece last night and you can't imagine what a glorious picture they made this morning when we had our early morning constitutional. The blankets are of every colour, procured from goodness knows where Joseph would have been extremely jealous."

On 6 October Private Adam Hogg, a reservist, was killed. He enlisted in 1904 in Hamilton with the judicious reference from Mr Downie, the station master at Lanark, that he was "Quite a respectable man". After serving three years he became a railway policeman at Tyne Dock, South Shields, and married Mary Sales there in April 1909, their first son being born five weeks later. Three more children followed, the last a girl born on 29 August 1914, whose father never saw her. The same day Private George Maudsley was shot in the head. Originally from Southport, Lancashire, his parents' home, he had been a signal fitter before enlisting in August 1908 and serving three years. The day after he was hit he died in the dressing station at Vendresse. Not long after he left the Colours in 1911 he married Harriett Finney at Biddulph, Cheshire, where she was now and where she gave birth to their son on 29 October. On 7 October Lance Corporal John "Harry" Holden, described as a confectioner when enlisting on 9 October 1908 as a fifteen year old boy soldier in his home town of Grimsby, was wounded in the right leg and sent home. He did not serve abroad again during the War, but gradually worked his way up the ranks in the 3rd Scots Guards. He had completed his 1st Class Army Certificate of Education in 1912 and already begun to show his skill as an instructor. Ten years after the War ended he returned to this part of France. On 8 October after being hit in the side Company Sergeant Major William Fowler died of wounds at the clearing hospital at Braine. His parents were John and Maria Fowler of Landport, Hampshire, and his wife Florence was living in Aldershot. They had two small boys. From 1907 to 1914 he was an instructor with the Army Gymnastics Staff, but at once rejoined the Battalion when the War started.

That day at least three Privates were promoted Lance Corporal, one of whom was a pal of Corporal Green's from Coulommiers, Private George "Joe" Holroyd, a reservist. He served for three years from 1903 and then joined the police in Bradford, his home town. He and Ethel Holroyd married there in 1911 and had one son. Another, Private Alexander Cairns, was a painter's labourer in Leith before he joined up in 1913. A third was Private Alexander McPherson, born in Cardross, Dunbartonshire, whose first job had been as a railway porter. He completed seven years service with the Battalion on 25 July 1914 and left for the Reserve, only to be called back on mobilization. All three would feature later. Corporal Green was very pleased on 9 October by the issue of new boots and clothing. He observed that enemy planes were overhead marking their positions by dropping what he thought was white powder, but could have been smoke grenades. At the start of the War the German aircraft were more geared to artillery spotting than the British. This method was rudimentary, but worked.

Sir Iain Colquhoun wrote that day to Dinah Tennant "We've been here now with never a move for nearly a fortnight and mighty tired of it I am; one day's much the same as another… The part of the allied entrenched line my battalion holds runs right across a glen (valley in England) and up the slopes on either side with German position 1500 yds away. The majority of the trenches we evacuate at dawn as the German shellfire makes them unusable and we go into shrapnel proof shelters behind the shoulder of the hill where they shell us all day; it amuses them and doesn't do us much harm beyond doing away with all movement. We have of course advanced posts of a few men up the glen to give us warning of any advance and as our guns cover it, and we are at hand to get to our trenches at a moment's notice it makes any movement either German or British impractical. At dusk when the gunners cannot see to shoot we line our trenches and stand by for night attacks which come about twice a week. The Germans creep up to about 80 yds and fire volleys at our trenches, the gunners join in by firing "Star Shells" which light up the whole countryside, our men loose off at anything they see, often at our own troops, men get caught in our barbed wire entanglements, rockets go off in all directions, no one knows what's happening. Pitch darkness and all hell let loose then suddenly the whole thing fades away and in the morning you'll be damned unlucky you've three men hit. The whole thing is one big joke. For the last week they have left us entirely alone as "MacFarlane's Lamp" has been sailing into a cloudless sky and turning night into day. The glen is thickly wooded in parts and these woods are infested with snipers who fire at our men if they show a head. The colonel sends me out nearly every day at 3.30am with three men to snipe them in return and there is scarcely one left in the whole wood now. We got too careless however and they got two of my men yesterday but I'll get them tomorrow all right, as I saw the way they've been coming down. There is a little village midway between the Germans and ourselves, all in ruins from shellfire, and going through that by moonlight is about the most exciting thing I know as there are nearly always one or two hanging about there as it's sort of debatable land. It's the best fun this snipering… How awful England must be, all tears and drilling and black I could stand most things except patriotic songs they always have me beat…If you like to send fifty pairs of socks they would be awfully appreciated by the men I'll tell them they're from Edward's people…I can't describe a battle by day it's beyond me but it ain't much fun Dinah not very much." He was referring to her brother Lieutenant Edward Tennant, the pilot with the RFC.

On 9 October Captain Thorne was reflecting that if the Allies could turn the German right flank they would "have to go back all along the line & then thank goodness we ought to get some more exercise again." Then "Hugh Ross came back with a beaming face this morning, we asked him why and discovered that he had put in ½ hours practice in the pipes with the Camerons Pipe Major." The Coldstream had reported that afternoon "that they could hear a German band playing in the enemy's lines." By this time he knew that the British and Germans were exchanging lists of prisoners but advertisements were in the newspapers asking for news of the missing, in this instance in The Times Annie Charrier was trying to find out about her husband Major Paul Charrier, commanding the Munsters at Etreux. Then "Yesterday Hugh Ross got some acid drops so we all had a rare good tuck in." A little to the west next day Captain Hubert Rees was resting near Beaulne with his company of the 2nd Welsh, having just come out of the line after eight days. It was a bright, clear and completely still day. Suddenly there was a great roar of cheering from the German trenches all along the Chemin des Dames. He knew that they had heard that the Belgians had surrendered at Antwerp, expected for some days. "A man sitting in the trench near me sat up and listened, temporarily suspending his efforts to open a tin of bully beef, & shouted down the trench "those blokes must 'ave 'ad an issue of fresh meat." This set me chuckling, but the real spice of the evening was yet to come. The Germans, having finished cheering, sang with great patriotic fervour "*Deutschland, Deutschland über alles*" followed by the Austrian national anthem. It was really magnificent, & very impressive." There was then "another intense silence which was broken after the lapse of some couple of minutes by a single cockney voice from our lines up on the Vendresse ridge singing "Come, come, come and 'ave tea with me down at the old Bull and Bush." After Antwerp fell Captain Thorne could see that outflanking would be more difficult and estimated the end of the War as by March 1915.

The Camerons uniform did not lend itself to the conditions. Where they could get them, they were starting to wear boots and short puttees. However, many men still only had shoes, the issue brogues, known as Shoes Highland, but had mostly ditched spats as wholly unpractical. No one was using a sporran and, similarly disliked and abandoned was the khaki apron worn over the kilt, the material of which was found to work well as tinder in the absence of matches. Cap badges, worn on their plain dark blue glengarries, were hidden as they presented too visible an aiming mark, but most had already been handed to the French as souvenirs. Many of the soldiers took to wearing knitted woollen "leg mittens" to cover their knees, but were told to stop this. Each man carried a greatcoat and a waterproof sheet. Many officers and men had started, with permission, to grow beards.

Private Osborne wrote on 11 October "We are still taking up same positions in trenches and the usual non-stop bombardment is kept up everyday. To break the monotony we have an occasional night attack. It is evident we are playing a waiting game and that when the time comes our commanders will hold the trump cards. Sometimes we manage to do a little cooking (what is known among the troops as "drumming up"). This is no easy matter for the first thing is to get water, which may be ½ mile or indeed a mile distant it may be nearer of course: so near has it been at times that I have stood in it, sat in it and even slept in it: but the close contact water was, for various reasons, quite unfit for culinary purposes. The next thing to get is dry wood, and as in the case of water it may be found close handy or a long way off. Now considering that all this is done under heavy fire the game is scarcely worth the candle, still the majority of the boys are all for it, working in pairs to minimize risk and trouble. Last night, I went under cover of darkness to a small lake about 4 mile distant and filled some water bottles for the section: this morning I went to the same place to fill some more and found to my horror two partly decomposed bodies half immersed in the water. I kept the gruesome fact to myself and filled the bottles – "where ignorance is bliss." It is a crime to dig up potatoes. Woe betide the wretch caught digging: still there are ways and means of adding to the meagre issue, but the addition must be made surreptitiously. Last night we took up new positions – always done when dark – my chum and I, having charge of the rifle grenades, were placed in a small trench by ourselves. At 3.30am when the stand to arms was passed along we could see several figures crawling about very stealthily, but couldn't see what was going on: suddenly a voice rang out, "Return to your trench you fellows, and leave those ruddy spuds alone." What a pair of fools my chum and I felt! We had been on a potato field all night and didn't know it. The cooking was worth the trouble shortly afterwards. (By the way, a potato field cannot be distinguished from any other field because the potatoes should have been dug long ago; the haulms are withered, and so trampled in the soil as to be almost obliterated.) My section commander seems to think I like going on reconnoitring patrol every night. I have been selected for this hazardous job for six consecutive nights. It is far from pleasant creeping along in the darkness not knowing that at any moment I might be clubbed, bayoneted or shot, so I told him this morning that although I greatly appreciated his confidence in me, my feelings would be somewhat relieved if he gave some of the others a chance to distinguish themselves, and I mentioned quite casually that I was not on a VC hunting expedition. After this protest each man had to do his bit." Captain Thorne told his wife on the 12th that, the Germans having drunk all the wine, "we have become perforce teetotallers." He had heard of Germans taking food and drink to wounded British, after being shot at when trying to carry them in. Of these fifteen were eventually recovered by the British, probably owing their lives to the enemy.

Their time on the Chemin des Dames was coming to an end, but remained dangerous. Private George Wilson, a Londoner and a reservist, had been a plumber's mate before becoming a soldier in 1904, but worked for the Post Office after he left the Colours. His wife Bessie, whom he married in Marylebone in 1908, was living in Kilburn with their daughter. On 13 October Private Wilson was wounded by shrapnel in his left side and back and died three days later from his wound and from pneumonia on an ambulance train at Braine. Bessie Wilson received an identity disc, a pocket knife and some letters. Private Richard Dennis was born in Wrotham, Kent, but, when he enlisted in Edinburgh in 1908, his only relative was an elder brother, whereabouts unknown. So there was no one to notify when he died on the 13th of wounds in the groin and abdomen received the day before. In 1913 he was an officer's servant, probably Sir Victor Mackenzie's, and may still have been at the time of his death. He was another in the Officers Mess Staff photograph. Eventually in 1921, Mrs Kate Henderson received the few personal effects "belonging to my dear friend Richard Dennis…as I am his only friend known." On the 15th Private William McIver was killed. He had been born in Aultbea, Wester Ross, and joined up in Glasgow in 1906, having been a barman. He served seven years and had only become a reservist eighteen months before the War. He was in a draft which joined on the Aisne. The last known address for his mother was in Inverness, there was said to be an uncle in Campbeltown, Argyll, and there were details for a female cousin in West Kilbride, Ayrshire. However, with him too, it proved impossible to tell anyone. The Battle of the Aisne cost the Scots Guards four officers and thirty seven men killed, five officers and one hundred and fifty seven men wounded and twelve men missing. Relatively, they had been fortunate and, for a short time later in October, relatively, they would continue to be. The Camerons had had two hundred and six officers and men killed and died of wounds and very many more than that wounded.

I Corps were the last British troops to be withdrawn from the Aisne, the 1st Division not coming out of the line till the 16th. All the rest of the BEF had already gone to Flanders. The first reason for this was the reopening of their original lines of communication through Le Havre and Rouen, up to where the River Seine was navigable to ocean going ships, now augmented by Boulogne and Calais. The other reason was that, with solidifying trench lines by now as far north as Lens in Artois, the British and French commanders planned to attack the Germans round their northern flank, at the same time aiming to secure the Channel ports. By the middle of October the options were narrowing. From Lens north to the Aire-La Bassée Canal the French were ceasing to make any more progress. Also, both II and III Corps of the BEF, as well as the French, were involved in heavy fighting from La Bassée up to Armentières, being gradually pushed back, after initial advances, onto the flat, low-lying and wet ground below and to the west of what the British came to know as the Aubers Ridge. Here too the front line solidified in October. North of Armentières, however, there was still what appeared to be open space for an outflanking offensive against the Germans to the east of an old mediaeval town, whose historical prosperity derived from the cloth trade, Ypres.

The night of 16 October was wet with thick mist. The relief was delayed by casualties to the incoming French 32nd Division from shelling, by the sticky wet clay over which they had to make their approach uphill and, lastly, by the shortage of interpreters, but, by good fortune, the whole of the 1st Division got away early on the 17th without interference. The 1st (Guards) Brigade marched from Vendresse, back over the river at Bourg and then via Longueval to Blanzy-lez-Fismes. The Scots Guards and both Highland battalions arrived at nine that morning. Corporal Green found the march "very trying, owing to being so long in the trenches. Three days rations issued. Enjoyed good sleep." The Historical Records of the Cameron Highlanders described everyone's feelings "The relief experienced in being out of range and sound of the artillery, and the reduction of mental strain, were remarked on by everybody. The day was spent in making up for lost sleep and in washing. The men of all three battalions washed together in the village pond, the local washerwomen continuing their work at the same time, so before long the entire pond had a layer of soapsuds from edge to edge." On the morning of the 18th the Coldstream left Blanzy at half past eight and marched two miles to Fismes station. At three hour intervals the Scots Guards followed, then the Black Watch and then the Camerons. There would appear to have been quite a lot of waiting at Fismes, because the Camerons arrived in time to see the Black Watch train leaving. They did not board their's until nine that night and had to be quick because it left only twenty minutes later. The railway plan itself was faultless. The destination was not published, but there was a general understanding that they were going up towards the left of the Allied front and nearer the Channel. Forty men were put into each horse box on the train which Corporal Green found "Too crowded to sleep." They went via Paris and Boulogne to Hazebrouck, taking about twenty six hours. Many thought at first that they were at Arras.

Notes on Chapter Sources

Sgt W Shepherd, 'Fifty, or more, years ago', SGM 1958.
Historical Records of the Queen's Own Cameron Highlanders, Volume III (Edinburgh and London: William Blackwood & Sons, Ltd 1931).
War Diaries: 1st Cameron Highlanders TNA/WO95/1264/1 and 25th Brigade RFA, including 113th Battery, TNA/WO95/1248.
Details of officers of the 1st Black Watch, The Black Watch Museum.
Everard Wyrall, *The Gloucestershire Regiment in the War 1914-1918* (London: Methuen & Co Ltd 1931).
Letters to or from members of the Swinton family and other material relating to them, Swinton Papers, Private Collection.
Interview of Pte A Burgess 1st Camerons, among Interviews of former Prisoners of War, repatriated to UK before the Armistice on grounds of sickness or injury or escapers, series TNA/WO161.
Diary of Brig Gen C FitzClarence with Thorne Papers, NAM/1987-03-31.
Copy of Capt The Hon A Campbell Douglas letter, Cuthbert Papers.
Papers of Brig Gen HC Rees, IWM/77/179/1.

4

The First Battle of Ypres – 2nd Battalion

In 1914 the 2nd Scots Guards were in barracks at the Tower of London. Lieutenant Colonel Richard "Pat" Bolton was Commanding Officer and Major The Honourable Hugh "Bosun" Fraser the Senior Major. Neither was married. Colonel Bolton had been at both Eton and Cheltenham and was commissioned in 1887. His mother lived in South Kensington, London. Major Fraser was the son of Simon Fraser, 13th Lord Lovat, who died before the War, and of Alice, Dowager Lady Lovat. He went to The Abbey School, Fort Augustus, and had been twenty years in the Scots Guards. Until eighteen months earlier he was Aide de Camp to the Viceroy of India.

Captain The Honourable Douglas Kinnaird, The Master of Kinnaird, eldest son of Lord and Lady Kinnaird, of Rossie Priory, Perthshire, was commissioned in 1901 after Eton and Trinity College, Cambridge. On 29 July he, the Second Captain of F Company, wrote to his mother "Still we have not mobilised yet, and everything seems to depend on Russia: if she will keep the peace I hope European war may be avoided." Two days later "The position of affairs seems to be going from bad to worse, and this morning it is difficult to see how European war can be avoided." They were out training on the ranges at Purfleet, down the Thames on the Essex bank, when suddenly called back to the Tower. "I don't think the country realise what a crisis there is…This tension cannot last much longer and personally I think it will inevitably end in war: it's too awful to contemplate the whole of Europe being dragged in." As events moved on his letter of 2 August was very much in favour of supporting the French "It is hardly possible to speak calmly of what appears to be our policy in this terrible crisis! It really looks during the last 24 hours as if Great Britain was going to stand aside, and not go to the help of France: it seems to all of us the most insane action, whether we have or have not given a promise to France." He was then sent with a detachment to guard the London docks "in this awful part of London, I think it is called the Isle of Dogs."

Lieutenant The Honourable Vincent Saumarez was from a prominent Guernsey family and, after Harrow and Trinity College, Cambridge, was commissioned in 1909. He served with the 1st Battalion in London and Egypt and became a close friend of Sir Iain Colquhoun with whom he went down to take part in boxing contests in the East End. In March 1914, having become engaged to Gunhild Balck, he resigned his commission but was still liable to recall. They married in Stockholm on 30 April and by the end of July were beginning to settle into a house on Guernsey. Gunhild Saumarez recorded that "And then the blow suddenly fell. "Report immediately to Barracks." Did England's honour demand war after the invasion of Belgium? We were soon to learn. We got ready at once and caught the boat next morning. During our passage we experienced our first feeling of the possible approach of war, when our ship was stopped by a torpedo boat. The sea was rough and a young officer in oilskins stood on the heaving deck, washed over by the waves. He shouted an order through a megaphone, making us change our course to another port than the usual Southampton. After landing we caught the first possible train to London, watching with secret apprehension the flaming sunset. The whole sky seemed to be on fire, but London seemed as calm as ever." Owing apparently to his having resigned Lieutenant Saumarez was now posted to the 2nd Scots Guards and "not to be sent to the front yet awhile. He was so desperately keen to go; so anxious lest the war might be over before his turn came. His soldier servant – Orchard – who had come with him to Sweden, and whom he had bought out of the army to become our butler, was now with him again. Orchard had served in the South African War as a drummer boy, and did not expect the new war would be half as severe as the one he knew." Private Arthur Orchard, from Godalming, Surrey, enlisted as a boy soldier in London in February 1898, training as a drummer, served in The Boer War and but reverted to Private at his own request in 1909, leaving as described in April 1914. Called up on mobilization, he was posted to the 2nd Scots Guards once it was decided that Lieutenant Saumarez would go there. He and Jessie Giles married in Chobham, Surrey, in April 1908 and had two daughters.

On 4 August a court martial tried Private Reginald Spencer for desertion. He was a shoemaker and machinist in Leeds before joining up in April 1913, but from mid April 1914 absent without leave until apprehended on 22 July. Though found guilty and sentenced to twenty eight days detention, that part of his sentence was rescinded because of the War, but what stood was forfeiture of all his previous Army service so that he had to start his initial three years with the Colours all over again.

Back at the Tower on 9 August Captain Kinnaird, amid all manner of rumours, told his mother that as far as they knew "no soldiers have at present left for the continent…it is impossible to know what to believe, but one can be sure that with Lord Kitchener at the War Office, we shall not be allowed to know a word more than he intends us to do." However, by the 12th "Now that it is no longer a dead secret, I am able to tell you about the movements of British troops, by the end of this week I believe the whole of our 6 Divisions will be on the way to France…before the war ends Britain will have to send many more men I expect." For the time being, even if there had been a slight leak, the security blanket was rapidly tucked in again tightly. So, by the 14th, though he knew that troops had left, their destination was hidden. "There is no news today from the war: one has so often talked about the "fog of war" but had no idea that secrets could be kept by the papers as they have been."

In complete ignorance of what was happening, apart from General Grierson's sudden death, a great blow as Captain Kinnaird knew him well and liked and admired him, he wrote again on the 18th "We have 500 reservists who have returned to the battalion and are just as regulars now…our peace strength is so small that we actually require all that to bring us up to war strength: it is rather depressing from the officers' point to view as they are practically strangers to us, and many of them have not trained for 4 or 5 years." However, the War had also brought back former officers whom he knew, such as Major The Viscount "Jack" Dalrymple and Captain The Honourable John "Jack" Coke, both old friends. Lord Dalrymple was the eldest son of the Earl and Countess of Stair, had served with the Scots Guards in the Boer War and was MP for Wigtownshire. He and Violet Dalrymple had five children by this time. Captain Coke was one of a very large family. His father was the then Earl of Leicester, whose children by his first wife ran into double figures, though some had not survived childhood. When she died Lord Leicester married again and fathered several more children. Captain Coke, who had also been in the Boer War, was one of the second family and through his wife Dorothy was related to Lieutenants Sir Edward Hulse and Lawson in the 1st Battalion.

There continued to be little definite news till the first casualty lists were published with reports of the Retreat up to 29 August. Captain Kinnaird wrote on 6 September "as it is, though our soldiers must be disheartened by this continuous retreating, the German plans must miscarry, as long as we can keep unbroken armies in the field." On the 12th he went on "the Scots Guards have now 1600 magnificent recruits at the Depot – many of them have joined us from the Glasgow police." The night before he was asked to dinner with Captain Malcolm "Flossie" Romer and his wife Evelyn, whose brother Lieutenant Gipps was with the 1st Battalion. When war was declared the Romers had been in St Moritz because of his health and had a very difficult time getting back to England, eventually travelling for a week by train via Genoa. Captain Romer was "quite miserable that he is not fit yet to go out."

Private Hugh Quinn, previously a riveter in Glasgow, had been a reservist for five years when called up. Between 23 August and 7 September he was twice convicted of absence without leave, then confined to barracks for three days for gambling outside the canteen and next awarded fourteen days detention for breaking out of barracks when confined as a defaulter and remaining away for nearly four full days and nights. He was the son of John Quinn, of Stewartstown, County Tyrone. After the Battalion left London Private Quinn was absent for short periods twice more before they went abroad. On 13 September it became likely that they would soon move to somewhere near Southampton. Captain Kinnaird was bothered about what personal kit he should take, the permitted weight being thirty five pounds "with the prospect of seeing it only once a week."

When orders arrived to move Gunhild Saumarez "went to the Tower to see the Battalion off, and met with an unexpected and happy surprise. Going past me, he just had time to whisper: "There is a rumour that we may have to wait a while for troops to arrive from overseas at Lyndhurst in the New Forest. There is a comfortable hotel close by at Brockenhurst. It may be worth while to get rooms." Overjoyed at the prospect, I saw the Battalion march out, and then hurried to Victoria Station to wave my farewell. The cheering soldiers were very excited and shouted lustily; "We are going to the Kaiser's tea party!" I saw the crowded train move slowly out of the station." In fact it was Waterloo that they left from on the 16th to go to Southampton and then on to Beaulieu for a day or two in tents. In anticipation of being sent on active service, probably at the instigation of Lieutenant Tom Ross, the Quartermaster, a keen amateur, they had approached a capable professional photographer, Sergeant Christopher Pilkington of the 1/28th London Regiment, Artists Rifles, Territorials, and invited him to go with them. Not only did he take photographs, the first being of them marching out of the Tower, but also wrote a somewhat disorganised diary. Moving on to Lyndhurst on the 20th they joined the 7th Division, forming up from scratch under Major General Thompson Capper into three infantry brigades and supporting arms. The 2nd Scots Guards were in the 20th Infantry Brigade commanded by Brigadier General Henry Ruggles Brise, a Grenadier, together with the 1st Grenadier Guards, 2nd Border Regiment and 2nd Gordon Highlanders. Major Albemarle "Alby" Cator, a Scots Guardsman, was the Brigade Major. Of the twelve battalions in the Division, only four, including the Grenadiers, Scots Guards, and Borders, had been in

England and were operationally ready after mobilization. The other eight were brought back from garrisons in South Africa, Malta, Gibraltar and Egypt and needed time to travel home, the Gordons, the last, only arriving back on 25 September from Cairo. The overseas battalions had more serving soldiers and were not predominantly made up from reservists. From Lyndhurst onwards the 1st Grenadiers and 2nd Scots Guards served together continuously till the early spring of 1919 when they went home from Cologne. Gunhild Saumarez acted on her husband's suggestion and moved to the New Forest too, where the Balmer Lawn Hotel "proved to be very welcoming and pleased to see me, as it was almost empty except for a few old ladies. We had the choice of excellent rooms. A sitting room, bedroom and maid's room next door. We were only just installed when Vincent came, very pleased with me for having acted promptly. Dinner was served by the fire in the little sitting room, and we spent a lovely evening until a late hour. This was the beginning of three happy September weeks, when a warm sun shone from a clear sky nearly every day. Next day the hotel was flooded out with relatives of the departing soldiers, and every nook and corner was filled."

In an undated letter, probably sent on the 26th, Captain Kinnaird thanked his mother for two pairs of mittens, but would give a pair away as he had only asked for one. He remarked "Either the open air or billets will be our fate: I imagine the latter during the winter months will be almost essential if any of us are to be fit for fighting." Casualty lists had come from the Aisne and on 23 September he told her "How terrible the strain of fighting for a fortnight on the Aisne must be. The Germans are in a strong position, and I don't see how the Allies are going to turn them out." That same day Sergeant Clement Irons, a signaller with sixteen years service, married Ethel Miles in the church at Lyndhurst, she having come down from London. Both were Londoners, he originally from Southgate, while she was living in Haringey and did so through the War. On 1 October all further leave was cancelled, though officers were allowed to go not more than an hour's drive away, contactable by telephone, and everyone made ready to go abroad. Captain Kinnaird told his mother this, adding that they had no idea where they were going, though he mentioned the BEF, Ostend or Antwerp as possibilities. They had been issued with French maps. As for luxuries to send out, he told her that chocolate from Fortnum & Mason was very popular, adding that he would like "a pair of socks, a refill for my Orilux electric torch, a cake of coal tar soap, every month, and occasionally a towel, silk handkerchiefs." On the 4th Captain Horace Kemble, Captain Kinnaird, Lieutenant Giles Loder and Lieutenant Ronald Steuart Menzies, the Adjutant, drove over for the afternoon to Stratton Park, just north of Winchester, the home of Lord and Lady Northbrook. Nina Northbrook, who had remarried after her first husband died, was Captain Kemble's mother in law. She took photographs of them with her elder son Captain Sir George Abercromby, Bt, previously in the Scots Guards, now a Territorial in the Black Watch, whose 8th Battalion he would later command, surviving the War. While they were having tea the telephone rang and they all got up and left, called back to camp.

They had their first casualty that day. Private John Devan, a reservist for six years, was initially found unfit for active service when he reported, but had since been passed fit. He went absent for six days on 15 September and was given fourteen days FP No 2 for that, which he was still serving as their departure approached. It had been noticed that he was behaving in a very strange way and so he was put under observation in the Guard Tent. In spite of that he killed himself with his service rifle on 4 October. His wife Mary and their daughter were in Cashel, County Tipperary. The War Office accepted that his death was caused by the War and she was given a pension.

That evening while Gunhild Saumarez was "by the fire waiting for Vincent, he did not come, and when at last the door opened, it was not he who entered, but Orchard, his soldier servant. "We are marching tonight, and I have a taxi waiting to take you to the camp at once." The sight that met me was the most unforgettable one of my life. The Seventh Division was at last complete…The huge camp was lit by great fires flaming ever higher, as fuel of every sort was thrown on them. Dark figures were moving hurriedly, tents were taken down, carts loaded and horses put to gun carriages. All transport was horse drawn in those days. Loud orders rang out in the still autumn air, fires crackled and noise and the tumult were awe inspiring, of soldiers going to war. Vincent was not easily found, but at last he came. By that time his mind was already far away with his battling brethren, and our farewell was necessarily short." On the 4th he wrote her a brief note, which presumably Private Orchard delivered, "I do not know yet whether I am going off with the battalion or not, but in case I do will you take the bag which is in the motor (in your charge), they are things I do not want, and come on here as soon as you conveniently can in the motor. Please bring my thick socks and "British warm Great coat" with you. The Battalion may be off tonight or early tomorrow morning. But of course I may not go with them." He did. It was from that evening that he kept a notebook recording very briefly events and times. In his first entry he noted that half the Battalion departed that evening at quarter to nine and the other half at ten.

Zeebrugge and the Belgian Coast

At Southampton they started embarking at half past midnight. There were 31 officers, 1 warrant officer, 43 sergeants, 30 corporals, 20 drummers and 879 privates, a total of 1002. Among them was Private Robert Thompson, aged nineteen, a soldier for a year and before that a clock maker in Leeds. When he enlisted it was noted that he was a "Smart lad, desires Scots Guards only." William and Mary Thompson lived in Headingley. On 23 February 1919 he was posted home from Cologne, having not been wounded once, and completed his twelve years service in 1925. Sergeant Horace Crabtree, from Bradford, was a labourer until he enlisted in 1904, serving continuously since. Promoted to Colour Sergeant and appointed Company Quartermaster Sergeant soon after the Battle of Festubert in May 1915, he continued in that role until made up to Company Sergeant Major soon after the Armistice. He and his wife Helen, who married in 1908, had had four daughters before the War. A son was born in 1919. He was another never wounded. Private William Lamb, the son of James Lamb of New Lanark, was a farm worker until he enlisted in April 1914. He was with them from now to when they went home from Cologne, by then a Sergeant, and was only wounded once, shot in the shoulder, not seriously, at the Battle of Neuve Chapelle. He recovered at Rouen and rejoined immediately after Festubert, away for just over two months. Lieutenant Edward Warner, the son of Sir Courtenay and Lady Leucha Warner of Brettenham, Suffolk, had been to Eton and Christ Church, Oxford, where he coxed the Oxford Eight in the 1904 Boat Race. He was commissioned in 1905. Though not with either Battalion all the time, he was on the Western Front throughout the War unwounded and went home from Cologne. At Southampton embarkation was relatively simple but there was also a great deal of loading to be done which took up all day on the 5th. Lieutenant Saumarez was working on that, managing to send a telegram before midday "Think am off after all am still at Southampton. All well Vincent"

Half the Scots Guards were on the SS *Lake Michigan*, the Canadian Pacific Railways ship on which Sergeant Pilkington was travelling and on which he took a lot of photographs, and the other half on the SS *Cestrian*. Captain Kenneth Bruce of the Gordons found the *Lake Michigan* "an inconceivably dirty… boat, with no washing and hardly any sanitary arrangements." They sailed at seven in the morning on the 6th to Dover, off which they spent most of the day, apparently because of a submarine scare. Major Cator noted their destroyer escort not only reporting the presence of submarines, but also a claim that one had been sunk. Captain Kinnaird later posted a card to his mother written on board ship, thinking then that they were likely to go to Ostend or Dunkirk, but not knowing and "I'm afraid we shall have another very uncomfortable night on board, no blankets or mattresses." Sergeant Pilkington photographed Scots Guards officers eating a meal on deck and Captains Bruce and Kinnaird sitting talking to each other. They had been at Eton together. On the SS *Cestrian* Lieutenant Warner recorded that before sailing from Dover they took on a pilot to guide them through the minefields. Nobody knew anything definite. After dark they sailed on, arriving off Zeebrugge at half past three. As they waited Major Cator "could plainly hear the Guns booming round Antwerp. At 6am the transports were ordered to come alongside of the Quay & commence disembarking." The immediate orders were for their Brigade to go on to Bruges, eight miles away, by train. Lieutenant Warner wrote down "English Marines are said to be in Antwerp." At Bruges Major Cator found "The population seemed very pleased to see the British & the troops were welcomed everywhere. Antwerp apparently on its last legs & the role of the 7th Division is to draw off the German Army besieging it & enable the Belgian Army to clear out of Antwerp unmolested." With him was his groom, Private Harry Clarke from Huddersfield, a soldier for over three years and trained as a groom before that, who had crossed flags tattooed on his left forearm and clasped hands on his right. The Scots Guards were in one of the earlier trains and, on arriving at eleven o'clock at Bruges, marched four miles southwest to Varssenere. Lieutenant Warner saw British planes overhead. Next, following reports of Germans about sixteen miles away, two companies were sent at once as outposts on the roads towards Ostend and Thourout. The others were in unsatisfactory and scattered billets at Varssenere, G Company being in a school, with straw to sleep on. The officers were comfortable in a château. All were now fully aware that they were to assist the Belgian withdrawal from Antwerp. As far as Lieutenant Warner could understand the 20th and 22nd Brigades were in a semi circle facing southwest with Belgians out in front of them. Before leaving Zeebrugge, but unable to say where they were, Lieutenant Saumarez managed to write to Gunhild in which he mentioned that there were a lot of people out in the villages watching and cheering as they marched to Southampton and then their hard work in loading everything. Now, however, "At last one thing is certain, and that is that we have got across the water all right after crossing the mine area, or a part of it last night…The battalion has just entrained up country and I am following on horseback in about an hour with the transport and a party of 40 men. I have been unloading hard all morning and am very hungry!…A destroyer and a submarine have just come in. The country here looks horribly flat. Have just had an interesting talk with a foreign officer who gave me 3 very good maps, extraordinary luck as they are scarce…He gave me his card and his name is Lieut. A. Clesse of the Gendarmerie Nationale…I think we shall be into it pretty soon – all is well."

For all the Scots Guards officers 8 October began with their being given breakfast by what Lieutenant Saumarez called the "occupant" of the château and his family before the Battalion assembled at Varssenere but for Major Cator "The day began by a real jumble." The Division were suddenly ordered to Ostend, each Brigade by a different road. "The start was ordered for 7am but orders were only received at 6.30am & it was impossible to get units collected…to make a punctual start." Not till two hours later were they "on the move more or less in their proper order." They were now to occupy the line of the Bruges-Nieuport Canal to cover the landing of the 3rd Cavalry Division, some of whose regiments had also only just got back from overseas postings. So the Scots Guards had a march of fourteen miles, arriving well on that afternoon at Steene, two miles south of Ostend, in reserve. Lieutenant Warner found the "billets very comfortable…hoped for a good night's rest." They, unlike some others, had had a relatively unbothered day in spite of Lieutenant Saumarez noting "Long march, bad paved roads". After all the battalions were already on their way, as Major Cator was aware, orders came from above for changes to the plan. This meant that some arrived where they were first told to go and then had to move elsewhere. So some never had any rations. As a whole the Division were not in place till ten that night after what he noted had been "a long and tiring day for the troops much fatigue of which could have been avoided by getting orders out earlier & not altering the dispositions in the middle of the march." There had been no physical contact with the Germans but "one of their aeroplanes a Taube… was flying over us the greater part of the afternoon only disappearing on a British Aeroplane appearing from Ostend. We passed on the road this day many hundreds of Belgian refugees all looking too miserable & frightened for words. With them were often disorganized parties of the Belgian Army." He noticed that there had been some preparation of trenches, but as far as he could see no organised defence lines, though railway and canal bridges were guarded.

Overnight there were fresh orders for the Division to go by train to Ghent, with only 1st Line Transport to bring up each unit's immediate resupply and each man carrying two days' rations. The 20th Brigade were to go first at six on the 9th. So Lieutenant Warner and everyone else found themselves woken suddenly at four and ordered to parade in half an hour. Extra ammunition was issued before they left Steene and marched into Ostend. To Major Cator "It all sounded very simple & plain sailing but words cannot describe the chaos which we found in Ostend. Antwerp apparently has fallen or just about to, in addition to 2000 wounded Belgians arriving from there at Ostend were many thousands of refugees all terror stricken wandering aimlessly about making the streets almost impassable. The Ostend railways staff were quite unable to cope with the abnormal irregular traffic, in addition they now had demands made on them to entrain and despatch our 7th Division to Ghent." Each train, at fifteen minute intervals, was supposed to carry one battalion, but the process was very awkward, not helped by the absence of any loading ramps for horses and vehicles. One had to be constructed in the station goods yard. The Scots Guards were in the first train, which left reasonably promptly at seven, taking three and a half hours to reach Ghent. They bivouacked in the town and waited for the rest of the Brigade, a long wait. Here Lieutenant Saumarez was able to write briefly to Gunhild "Last night we slept in a farm house 6 in a room quite comfortable, but night before we were in outpost up all night. Marching is hard on cobbled stones which are on nearly every road. My torch has got out of order already could I have another. Hostile aeroplane came over us yesterday a blue one called Taube class with wings back." In his notebook that day he jotted down that there was a rumour that Antwerp had fallen, that at Ghent the inhabitants were very generous to them and that they were stopping refugees and helping identify passports.

While the Gordons had got onto their train in a hurry at much the same time as them, it did not move for five hours. Once all battalions were at Ghent they deployed east to outposts for five miles along a railway embankment. Lieutenant Warner saw "Belgian cavalry, Infantry and Artillery in retreat. Belgian cavalryman told me that Germans were about 3 miles away. 3 Battns Belgian Infantry were evacuating village of Loochristy, 7 kilos from Ghent and we were put straight on outpost to cover their retreat, with no troops between us and the Germans. We entrenched until midnight. I got about 2 hours sleep between 1am and 4am." It had been a very long drawn out day, of which the Scots Guards had had the best. Major Cator observed "after a long and weary day, by dint of much badgering in bad French, the last man of our Brigade arrived in Ghent at 1am on Oct 10th the remainder of the Division following throughout the night & the following day." It was as well that the 21st Brigade stayed at Bruges and had not had to travel as well. By now most of the defenders of Antwerp, including surplus sailors of the Royal Navy deployed as infantry, as well as Royal Marines, had either withdrawn down the coast, been evacuated or crossed the Dutch border to internment for the rest of the War.

After Antwerp's formal surrender on 10 October the 7th Division's role, with French troops, was purely to assist the Belgian withdrawal, but most of their guns were still at Ostend. The Scots Guards noted of the Belgian soldiers "They appeared to have had enough" while "Ghent was full of German spies" adding that "The people seemed pleased to see the British troops." Those in Ghent were particularly welcoming and gave them food and tobacco. Major Cator heard reports of strong enemy patrols being seen from time to time and next day refugees told the Scots Guards that the Germans were only a few miles away. Again heavy firing was audible from the Antwerp direction. In between the 20th and 22nd Brigades there was one of French Marines [Fusiliers Marins], whom Major Cator thought "very jumpy & not at all bucked up by beating off an attack by some German infantry in which action they did very well killing some 200 of the enemy." While those in the main positions were not involved with the enemy on the 10th and 11th and so went on digging themselves in, those at outposts and on patrols were. Major Cator noted his appreciation of Lieutenant Edward Joicey's troop of the Northumberland Hussars, attached to the Brigade, who had obtained "very useful information." There were reports of German snipers and patrols from all along the Brigade frontage and of "the Scots Guards claiming first blood one of their scouts Private Rae reporting a patrol near Loochristy which he avowed had lost one of their men on his opening fire on it." Private John Rae, a reenlisted Scots Guardsman, originally from the Aberdeen area, whose wife Irene and two children were on Guernsey, was one of the very first men through the door of any recruiting office after war was declared. He had left the Colours in 1903. Lieutenant Warner was told by a Northumberland Hussar on the 10th that "they had two men missing, but these turned up having had horses shot. Stood to arms 12 midnight so got 3 hours sleep. Heavy firing on our right." The Northumberland Hussars, Territorials, were the 7th Division cavalry.

There was no purpose in their staying near Ghent after most of the Belgian Army had withdrawn. All the indications were that the Germans were approaching the British and French and not concentrating on the Belgians, which Major Cator remarked "is just what is required of them." He was apprehensive about what might happen if the enemy shelled Ghent, in particular the "Hotel de Ville... a most beautiful building." 11 October was generally quiet until at nine at night the Scots Guards suddenly got orders to withdraw at once into Ghent, where two hours later the Brigade were to assemble. Just as they headed off, heavy firing started up to their right and they saw the flashes of the French guns close by, in reply to these first German shells fired towards them. Some struck the 22nd Brigade Transport without causing much damage.

This sudden move came as a shock to Sergeant John Burke and Privates James O'Halloran and Harry Wood. When they deployed two days before these three battalion scouts set up an observation post a mile and a half forward of Right Flank's position, coming back to report each evening. After dark on the 11th Sergeant Burke sent Private O'Halloran to report to Captain Charles Fox, then temporarily the company commander. Private O'Halloran left at seven to return to the outpost. When Sergeant Burke went back himself early the following morning there was no sign of anyone. A civilian told him that they had gone at ten the night before. While the dates he gave afterwards were out by a day "I immediately returned to my two men who I found coming towards me with a report that large force of the enemy was advancing on the main road from Antwerp to Ghent. Just before I reached my men I was fired on by Uhlans. Before my two men fell back they hid themselves in a ditch and watched German forces marching along the road. While in the ditch, a dog which was with the Germans on the road came up to them, smelt them, and went off again…My men took details of numbers and gradually crawled back…and then met me. This was about 10am on the morning of 11th Oct. We then proceeded backward hiding until we met a railwayman who beckoned us to his hut and told us to change our uniforms for civilian clothing which we now have on. We changed and carried our uniforms and equipments to a farmhouse and buried it in a large hole made by the farmers to hide in. We remained there the night of 11th October when we met this gentleman, (a nurseryman) M. Engels Louis Camiel now with us. He told us the place was surrounded by Germans and that we had better remain till he saw a favourable opportunity to escape. On the 12th Oct. this man's schoolmaster friend came and said that we should have to have passports if we wished to get out of the hands of the Germans. So between them they managed to get us passports made out in false names which we have. On the 13th Oct. we started across country accompanied by M. Camiel and another gentleman who cycled ahead of us to see if all was clear till we came to Loochristy, where the gentleman left us." They then made their way northwards carefully keeping clear of Germans, the local people being very helpful in telling where the enemy were. Skirting round the village of Selzate "we were pulled up by a German cyclist who said we were all Englishmen. He shouted, "Stop", and barred our way. M. Camiel told him we were Belgians and not Englishmen and he asked us for our passports which satisfied him (he was half drunk and asked us to come and have a drink, but we declined on the grounds that we were teetotallers), and he allowed us to pass." They managed to get past German and Dutch soldiers at the frontier unnoticed, caught a train to Terneuzen and reported to the British Consul there. He gave all four of them papers and arranged their passage as tourists on the SS *Lagen*, a British steamer, on which they arrived at Gravesend, Kent, on the morning of the 16th. Sergeant Burke concluded "We owe our escape entirely to M. Camiel." Sergeant Burke was born in Poona of Irish extraction and enlisted in 1906. He and his wife Lily married in Kensington in 1913 and had a son in June 1914. Sergeant Burke developed a serious mental condition, classified as hysteria, soon after this and was discharged with a disability pension in 1915. Private O'Halloran, another Irishman, who had been working as a maltman in Edinburgh when he joined up, also in 1906, went back to the Battalion soon afterwards. He had married Florence Batchelor in Wrexham in April 1914. Early in 1917 he became a Guards Division Vickers machine gunner and then, in the spring of 1918, joined the RAMC. He survived the War and emigrated to Canada. Private Wood, the son of John and Marie Wood, was from York, where he had been a labourer until 1903 and then served eight years. He too was soon back with the Battalion, with whom he was for much, but not all, of the War.

The march inland and the early stages at Kruiseecke

As the Belgian Army were lining up from the coast at Nieuport inland along the River Yser and its canalised continuation, the Ypres-Yser Canal, the 7th Division were to go to Ypres to join French troops and the British 3rd Cavalry Division already there, shortly to be joined by I Corps from the Aisne. Having left Ghent and marched sixteen miles southwest through the night the Scots Guards reached Somerghem at six on 12 October after several delays on the road, blocked by artillery and transport. The War Diary recorded "the men were very tired after the long march… The night was bitterly cold and their feet were very sore from marching on the paved roads." For a short time they were billeted nearby to rest and sleep and then marched on west at two in the afternoon to Thielt, arriving at nine, having again had a lot of inconvenience from roads blocked by transport. "The Headquarter wagon broke down and QMSgt Heffer brought on the contents in a farm cart." Quartermaster Sergeant Herbert Heffer was in Glasgow when he enlisted in 1900. He had been a shorthand writer and was described by Colonel Bolton as "far above the average QrMaster sergeant. He is very capable and hardworking, and has every detail of his duties at his fingerends." He, almost certainly in the role of a military chief clerk, served with the Battalion until 5 November, when he was posted back to Wellington Barracks for a year until commissioned into the 4th Middlesex. His wife Alice and their son were living in Wandsworth. Since leaving the positions east of Ghent they had covered thirty two miles on the cobbled roads, the "pavé", very awkward to march on in hobnailed boots, and that evening Right Flank still had a further five miles to go onto outpost duty. The others stayed that night at Thielt, where there were by then a lot of troops. Sergeant Burke was reported missing and presumably Privates O'Halloran and Wood also. The Gordons had also had to move so quickly in the dark that they could not locate all their men. Of these a party of fifteen managed to make their way, directed by Belgian villagers, to rejoin them at Thielt. Major Cator heard reports that the Germans had occupied Ghent, but had not tried to follow the 7th Division or the French closely. He was unimpressed by that day's march as "The staff arrangements for getting into Thielt were very bad. The roads were blocked for miles by guns & wagons & it was not until 10pm we got our very tired Infantry into their billets." There were strong outposts all round the town and "all roads entering Thielt blocked by felling large trees across them to prevent any possible rush being made by the Germans in large numbers." He liked Thielt, a "pretty old town with an old church in the market place having a quaint old clock & chimes striking every half hour. The chimes are very old & sound very like a musical box." He had heard that the Germans were in Somerghem and there were reports that they were closing in, but nothing happened.

At some stage recently a letter reached Lieutenant Saumarez from Gunhild to which his reply was dated 11 October, though his dates were currently a day behind the War Diary and everyone else's. She had indicated to him that she was pregnant, which in these circumstances he found difficult to think out "as my mind is not in good enough working order to fathom the problem which you have put before me… Well to tell the truth I have dined too well to think it out as a draft of 250 men and 7 officers have just joined us and there was luckily plenty of rum! Therefore I will end and bid you good night." As a postscript he asked her for a balaclava. There was no mention by anyone else of the arrival of a draft. Early the following morning, the 13th, the combination of rifle fire from British infantry and of a French battalion passing through Thielt brought down a low flying German plane. Captain Bruce of the Gordons "was awakened from a very comfortable bed by loud shots just outside the window, and found that some Belgians and Scots Guards had just brought down a German Taube." The Scots Guards did not claim it formally, though Lieutenant Warner, who had also had a good night's sleep, did record their firing at it and Lieutenant Saumarez inferred that it was them in his notebook. They heard that British cavalry found it later, crashed with its pilot and observer dead. The Brigade marched on west at ten that morning, when it was very wet, en route for Roulers, arriving nine hours later. Major Cator wrote again of troubles from poor and conflicting movement planning, but that it had been "not quite such chaos as last night at Thielt. The late hours getting the troops in are making them very tired. However they are all in good spirits." At Roulers there were comfortable billets, Lieutenant Saumarez being in a "padres house". The Gordons received particular attention in St Joseph's Convent, Captain Bruce writing how "the good nuns gave us unlimited hot water and cooking facilities, and spent the whole night dressing and bandaging the men's sore feet. The shoes were found to be in a dreadful condition, long night marching on the hard Belgian causeways having swollen the feet, and the constant wet and mud having shrunk the shoes so that most of the men had slit, or even cut off the uppers." During the day there had been more alarms over the Germans, reported from various directions, but again nothing happened.

At eight on 14 October the Scots Guards were on the move, arriving in Ypres after a five hours march. There they saw the 3rd Cavalry Division, who had been in action the day before to the southwest, and heard that the enemy had occupied Thielt soon after they left. Major Cator wrote "We have had no fighting but it has been a hard time on the troops, a good deal of marching, outpost work at night and they have had very little sleep." Captain Bruce described the Gordons seeing cavalry skirmishes and one company firing at "stray Uhlans." He heard too that a patrol from the Borders had killed seven German cavalrymen in a village. Figures for such events varied and Major Cator noted "The Borders scouts under Lt Lamb doing very good work accounting for some twenty over-curious Teutons." Two Scots Guards companies went out at once two miles from Ypres to outposts at Haalte, near Zillebeke, and for some there was soon their first sight of the enemy when German cavalry backed off after firing a few shots. Lieutenant Warner heard of "A German Column of all arms, reported to be advancing close on us. The Battalion ordered to entrench rapidly at about 7pm. This force turned out to be our own Cavalry." At some stage on the 14th Lieutenant David Drummond caught Private John Laurence smoking on outpost duty instead of concentrating on watching for the enemy. This led to a sentence of ten days confined to camp, irrelevant in the circumstances. Private Laurence had a bit more than two years service and was a miner with the Middleton Estate & Colliery Company before that. His home was at Beeston Hill, Leeds. Lieutenant Saumarez and his platoon were also on outpost duty. He noted the "skirmish" with Uhlans, that they waited unsuccessfully for French troops to relieve them and that he, having borrowed a lady's bicycle, managed to acquire a spare torch from a footman. He had also found food at possibly more than one château for his men.

After French infantry relieved the companies at Haalte next morning the Scots Guards all moved south beyond Zillebeke and spent 15 October in reserve at Verbrandenmolen. Lieutenant Saumarez' platoon were in a painter's shop, but the Battalion dug in, while, well spread out, the rest of the Brigade covered the southern approaches to Ypres. An Uhlan, badly wounded in the legs, was brought into Battalion Headquarters. In a postcard that day Captain Kinnaird wrote "We were delighted to get our first mail last night, two letters from you. I have at last managed to have my first bath, and actually slept in a bed, such a luxury... We have brought down 2 German aeroplanes." Lieutenant Warner recorded another enemy plane being shot down nearby the day before and now, after a bad night in a farmhouse with only three hours sleep, "Heavy firing not far away…Got some shoemakers to repair men's boots, also oil. Slept in straw shelter." On the 15th it would appear that two letters, one with a parcel, reached Lieutenant Saumarez from Gunhild because he wrote two very brief replies, dated that day. In the first he thanked her for cigarettes and tobacco. Then "Please send skiing boots and socks. We are marching hard all day on outpost all night it rains occasionally which is not pleasant." In the second "Could you get me another pack i.e. nap sack as mine is wearing out. News is hard to give. I am afraid my letters contain nothing but wants!! Compressed cocoa is very welcome."

During the afternoon of the 15th orders came for the Division to move out east to occupy a line from Zandvoorde, then northwards gradually uphill to the east of Gheluvelt, past the east side of Polygon Wood at Reutel and on swinging northwest to Zonnebeke, in practice to Broodseinde, in the north. The 20th Brigade would be responsible from Zandvoorde to immediately south of the road from Ypres to Menin at the Gheluvelt Crossroads, downhill about one and a half kilometres east of the village and nine east of Ypres. The Scots Guards, told that they were to go to Zandvoorde and dig in between there and Gheluvelt, set off at five on the 16th in the thick mist before it was light and established themselves, with the Grenadiers on their right at Zandvoorde itself. The Gordons, who had started from further west and had further to march, were delayed because the French troops due to relieve them at dawn were late. These Captain Bruce described as "funny old reservists with guns dated 1880, and fine black beards." He heard that the 2nd Yorkshire Regiment, officially renamed The Green Howards after the War, were bringing in nine prisoners. They, the right hand battalion of the 21st Brigade, had advanced early that morning along the Menin Road and were now around the Gheluvelt Crossroads and on the immediate left of the Scots Guards. The other three battalions of the 21st Brigade were lined up northwards to beyond Reutel, which was at about the middle point of a ridge, with Polygon Wood running west behind and Becelaere out in front at the ridge's east end. The 22nd Brigade were from just north of Reutel to Broodseinde, with Polygon Wood behind them to the south. Over to the right of the 20th Brigade dismounted British cavalrymen held the line beyond Zandvoorde on west towards Messines. Currently it was still intended to take Menin, believed to be lightly held, seven kilometres southeast of the Gheluvelt Crossroads. Not for some days would it dawn on both General Joffre and Sir John French that an outflanking movement round the German right wing was unachievable.

On 16 October Captain Kinnaird had a letter taken home by an officer going back on duty. This bypassed the censor and so he was able to tell his mother what was going on in broad terms, including that they were now with Sir John French and "Expecting a battle at any moment with a retiring German force…So far I have been able to buy chocolate." So far too there had been minimal contact with the enemy, but a staff officer from Headquarters 20th Brigade went out along the road from Zandvoorde to Gheluvelt to keep in touch with the 21st Brigade and Major Cator wrote "A few minutes before he arrived a cyclist scout of the Bedfords had been surprised by an Uhlan patrol who kicked a certain soft spot of his anatomy, took his rifle & bike & told him to go back to his command." Lieutenant Saumarez noted a Belgian, captured by the Germans but released, reporting that there were twenty five guns in position at Gheluwe, further along the Menin Road. He acquired sixty loaves, dates and honey for seventy francs.

The 21st Brigade, the 2nd Bedfordshire Regiment being one of their battalions, were attacked during the night north of the Menin Road. That led to two Scots Guards companies being ordered at three in the morning to move forward to occupy Kruiseecke, the next village southeast of the Gheluvelt Crossroads and a bit more than a kilometre away. Major Fraser led them to the unoccupied village and they dug in beyond, now right out on their own. First they saw a German cavalry patrol some distance off and then another appeared almost behind them. This they fired at and drove off. Refugees said that the Germans were themselves digging in thoroughly to the east and south from Menin to Wervicq and on to Comines on the River Lys. They learned for themselves that there were enemy at a windmill half a mile away and also in the hamlet of America, downhill and south of Kruiseecke towards Wervicq. At around four in the afternoon the Germans appeared to be setting fire to everything that they could in the Comines direction. There was trouble from enemy snipers and patrols and when Captain Thomas "Tommy" Rivers Bulkeley led a patrol forward to clear the wood in front of the new trenches they had to withdraw because of shelling from a German cavalry gun. This wood, about six hundred yards away, was a source of trouble from then on. Major Fraser reported back that there were German cavalry around Wervicq, that the two companies beyond Kruiseecke were not enough to hold the ground and that the village was extremely difficult to defend. The significance of Kruiseecke, on a slight rise above but not high enough to dominate the ground to its east and south, was that by holding it the British could prevent enemy artillery observers from having a clear view of the south side of Gheluvelt, the plateau running westwards from it and, also, towards Zandvoorde.

Following Major Fraser's report, on the morning of 18 October the other two companies moved forward to Kruiseecke. According to the Scots Guards War Diary, though no one else, except Lieutenant Saumarez who noted that they lost forty men, mentioned this and the 2nd Bedfords' War Diary suggests that they were north of the Menin Road at the time, the 2nd Bedfords were sent to clear the wood out to the east, did so and, though very heavily shelled, not otherwise shot at as they came out beyond onto the open ground sloping towards Gheluwe, the next village east on the Menin Road. Having lost a number of men in a few minutes they had to withdraw. A party from Right Flank under 2nd Lieutenant Billy Wynne Finch went out to help them and brought in some of their wounded. No Scots Guardsmen were hit. As part of a larger operation the Scots Guards all then moved out slightly further east from Kruiseecke and dug deep, narrow trenches with traverses every six or seven yards. When the Gordons came up on the right they did likewise, extending the line on this slight rise of ground down towards America, with a sharp right angled salient from where the Borders, facing south as far along as Zandvoorde, came in to link up on the right of the Gordons. Throughout the day there was light shelling, the Brigade's first proper experience of it, Captain Bruce noting "Shellfire very terrifying, but not very dangerous in finished trenches." It was, however, the Gordons who were on the receiving end from when they moved to their new positions and some were hit. This line had major defects which concerned Major Cator. It was far too long for a brigade to hold and trying to do so meant using all the infantry, without reserves. Next, it was close to many woods from which the enemy could harass them and also, without being seen, prepare attacks on the most vulnerable points, of which he identified the salient as most vulnerable of all. Further, unless America itself could be firmly held, the enemy could assemble and manoeuvre in the dead ground downhill beyond it towards Wervicq, similarly unobserved. He also noted that the German guns were "extraordinarily accurate" firing on the Kruiseecke-Wervicq road.

The countryside, one of small fields, hedges, ditches, orchards, spinneys, small villages, farmhouses and a few large woods, was difficult for attackers, but for defenders very short of men it posed serious problems of observation and coordination. The trenches were nowhere continuous and individual platoon positions often out of sight of their neighbours. Because next day, the 19th, the German shelling of the forward positions towards America became heavy it was decided to give them up and revert to the previous arrangement at Kruiseecke in spite of its limitations, including its salient. Then the Division were ordered to capture Menin, though this was halted soon after the 22nd Brigade, starting the advance from the left, met stiff opposition from German infantry dug in east of Becelaere. Also several columns of enemy were seen approaching from the northeast. South of the Menin Road the 20th Brigade now had only the Grenadiers and the Borders in the line at Kruiseecke, while the others became the divisional reserve after the attack on Menin was called off. So the Scots Guards, whose part in the capture of Menin would have required them to advance along the north side of the Menin Road, instead went on north up the hill to Becelaere. There they and the Gordons bivouacked in a field while there was still daylight, waiting to hear what they were to do next. Nothing affected them, but there was heavy firing from the German guns until dark. Then it died down and they both marched back south four miles to Zandvoorde. As the Scots Guards left first Captain Bruce watched them go by and "Douglas Kinnaird shouted out as he passed me "Well, Kenneth, we might be in different hemispheres for all we see of one another."" They never met again. Back at Zandvoorde Lieutenant Saumarez was able to "sleep in small room with stove very hot."

These activities contributed to the Scots Guards' first fatal casualty abroad when Company Sergeant Major Sidney Wilson, having apparently lost his way while visiting trenches in the dark and got in front of them, was shot by a sentry. He was buried first near the farm at America, with Private Peter Riddle as witness, who reported the precise location, and his body was found and identified after the War. The Company Sergeant Major, a Londoner from Rotherhithe, had been serving since the end of 1899. He married Margaret James from South Lambeth in August 1914. In terms of his will set out in his Active Service Pay Book all his effects went to his wife, who received sixpence halfpenny in French and Belgian money, an electric pocket lamp, an Ingersoll watch and chain, two sets of brass Scots Guards shoulder letters and plates, a shaving brush, two razors in a leather case, one pair of socks, one cap comforter, a tooth brush, two boxes of pills, a letter and a telegram, a towel and a woollen cap. Private Riddle, a pottery worker on joining up in 1904, but a miner when mobilised as a reservist, had a long, colourful and varied history of disciplinary offences. He was wounded in the arm on 24 October and after recovering in England returned in the spring of 1915 after the Battle of Neuve Chapelle. On 19 September that year he was given twenty one days FP No 1 for being drunk on active service and on 4 November 1917 eight days for striking a military policeman. Wounded slightly in the left leg three weeks later at Bourlon Wood during the Battle of Cambrai, he was discharged in August 1918 to Class P of the Army Reserve as a miner. This required him to comply with the order to report to and continue to work at the Niddrie & Behar Coal Company, near his birthplace and home at Portobello. His wife Alice, whom he married in 1905, was there with their four children. Company Sergeant Major Wilson's death was not the only incident of this kind as Lieutenant Philip Egerton of the Borders was severely wounded by his own platoon when he appeared in front of their trench early on the morning of 16 October, dying next day.

The events of the 19th still did not alter faith in an offensive to work round the German flank. So the Division received orders to make a reconnaissance in force next day. For this the Scots Guards were leading their Brigade. Starting from Zandvoorde, they advanced through the forward positions at Kruiseecke towards Gheluwe and had gone a mile and a half before German shelling from the Wervicq direction made further progress impossible. They were told to withdraw. There was only one casualty when Drummer Charles Steer, son of Regimental Sergeant Major Sidney Steer of the King's Own Yorkshire Light Infantry [KOYLI], previously a Scots Guards Sergeant, and Gertrude Steer of Caterham, was hit by a dud shell and killed outright. Four years before he had joined as a boy soldier when he was fourteen. On returning to Zandvoorde they reoccupied their trenches, exposed to enemy observation from the southeast, particularly on the right. Two shells hit the church tower without stopping the clock. Zandvoorde stood on its own small hill, with low lying fields to the east across to Kruiseecke and also to the south. The Gordons were on their left as far as Kruiseecke, the Borders between there and Gheluvelt and the Grenadiers in the trenches which the Scots Guards had originally dug on the east side of Kruiseecke. Later during the 20th a few more Scots Guardsmen were killed, of whom one was Corporal Theophilus Newman, a former railway labourer from Sturminster Newton, Dorset, where his widowed mother Martha was living. He had been in the Army for more than three years, was, amongst other things, a 1st Class Machine Gunner and had been promoted within days of the start of the War. Another was Private Charles Whitley, a Yorkshireman, the son of Charles and Annie Whitley of Keighley and a blacksmith's striker before he enlisted two years before. That night both were known to have been wounded, both were missing, but both were dead and both were found and buried by the enemy. After the War a German anonymously handed in Private Whitley's Soldier's Small Book to the British Consulate in Hamburg. Private Herbert Dare, the son of Edmund and Ada Dare of Hampstead, was also wounded and missing, but there was no more news of him. He had been an outdoor porter in London until he enlisted just before Christmas 1912. In 1921 Ada Dare sent a letter asking about his medals, reporting also that her husband had recently died, and wrote how "my dear son who went out full of courage if I could have only been there to hold his aching head or closed his weary eyes my poor heart I think would not have felt the bitter tears now shed." She added that his fellow soldiers had nicknamed him "Phyllis" after the actress Phyllis Dare.

During the afternoon the 5th Cavalry Brigade of the 2nd Cavalry Division sent a message that they had been ordered to withdraw from around Tenbrielen, south of Zandvoorde, which was going to leave the 20th Brigade completely exposed on the right until the 3rd Cavalry Brigade, of the same cavalry division, arrived at Houthem and Kortewilde, though that was three miles from Zandvoorde. All that could be done was to send Lieutenant Joicey and his Northumberland Hussars to screen the gap and make direct contact with the 3rd Cavalry Brigade beyond. Next the Grenadiers and Borders reported opening fire at eight hundred yards on a large enemy force, who, apart from permanently occupying America for the first time, appeared to be reconnoitring rather than attacking.

The Scots Guards began 21 October at Zandvoorde, but two companies soon went to Gheluvelt as the divisional reserve. Meanwhile F Company were in trenches out on the right towards Kortewilde. With no idea when he might be able to post it, Captain Kinnaird managed to start a letter home about how "yesterday we had our first experience of advancing under heavy shrapnel fire. It was most exciting to see pits being dug in the ground all round one by the shells but it is quite as exciting to see pits being dug in the ground all around as I write, I am sitting at the bottom of a trench while the shells are literally bursting all round us, but the trenches are very safe: we had a bad dose an hour ago, but no casualties. I thought the Germans had forgotten us, when I began writing to you, but they have just started again, one just has to sneak down at the bottom." He was unable to write any more because the shelling got worse and several men were hit. Next they were heavily attacked at half past ten and Major Lord Esmé Gordon Lennox, his company commander, was badly wounded, among many other casualties.

Right Flank, temporarily under Lieutenant Warner, had a very busy day. To begin with they were sent east to reinforce the Gordons at Kruiseecke, who were under a lot of pressure and once had to clear Germans out of some forward trenches with the bayonet. There was shelling as Right Flank advanced but it all went over their heads, destroying a farm behind them. When the situation quietened down they were next sent out west towards Hollebeke to hold about a mile of line because of the gap on the right. As if that was not enough, Lieutenant Warner heard at half past three that the British cavalry at Hollebeke Château were in difficulties, so he sent two platoons across to help. They succeeded in driving out the Germans, but British artillery fire prevented their exploiting it. Meanwhile the Gordons reported that they had been attacked and from everywhere there were reports of enemy approaching Tenbrielen. It was that day that their main attacks began towards Ypres, everything earlier having been preliminary. Merely taking the rest of the 7th Division's frontage, there were heavy attacks from Gheluvelt to Reutel and around Zonnebeke. To the right was the sustained pressure on the British cavalry across to Hollebeke. The Gordons began to report being under machine gun fire from buildings opposite. Next, they and the Borders had heavy attacks on them. Though the enemy did not press these home, they were now too close in places for the British guns to fire for fear of hitting their own men. The Grenadiers and beyond them the Yorkshires at the Gheluvelt Crossroads were facing repeated attacks. The heavy shelling, starting later on during 21 October and a major feature from then on, was to cause three persistent problems for the British and French, which they could do nothing about throughout the battle. All were caused by the accurate observed fire of the German artillery, well supplied with HE shells. The first was that the more the enemy shelled the trenches the more unstable the light sandy soil became and so the more difficult it became to maintain them. The second was that the sand itself, settling after shells landed, fell on rifles and machine guns and often quickly jammed the working parts. The third was the steadily increasing incidence of men being buried by shell explosions, those going to dig them out then being shot at.

A casualty on 21 October, hit, but not seriously, in the head, was Private Orchard. He sailed a few days later for England and was in hospital in Wandsworth for two months. Private Temple Sinclair, another reservist, became Lieutenant Saumarez' servant. He was from Latheron, Caithness, and was a railway signalman before enlisting at Forres in May 1905. After three years he left the Colours and he and Maud Norris married in Newington, London, a year later.

Polygon Wood

Apart from shelling, nothing significant affected the Scots Guards at Zandvoorde until at about ten that evening dismounted cavalry of the 1st Royal Dragoons and the 10th Hussars from the 6th Cavalry Brigade, who had now appeared immediately to the right, took over all their trenches as well. They were then told to march to Veldhoek, which, one way and another, took up all the rest of the night till five in the morning on the 22nd, although Veldhoek, on the Menin Road west of Gheluvelt, was not far away. For a time they were again in reserve, resting beside the road. Lieutenant Warner had an hour's sleep in a field until "woken about 6am by shellfire." They then began digging in. The German guns having opened up, shortly afterwards their infantry attacked the 21st Brigade generally from the east of Polygon Wood and the 22nd

Brigade from beyond the north of it. The latter, already driven back first from Broodseinde and then from Zonnebeke, were now on a line running northwest from the top right hand corner of Polygon Wood. In order to be ready to help, at eight o'clock the Scots Guards were sent across the farmland north of Veldhoek under heavy shellfire which wounded seven of F Company. Although not yet directly drawn into the fighting, they next dug support trenches near the eastern end of Polygon Wood. However, at three in the afternoon word came that the Grenadiers and Gordons were under heavy pressure too around Zandvoorde and Kruiseecke and so Major Fraser took Right Flank and G Company back to Headquarters 20th Brigade and into a reserve position between Zandvoorde and Kruiseecke, three more men being wounded in re-crossing the Menin Road. Somehow on the 22nd at Polygon Wood Captain Kinnaird was able to continue the letter, which had been interrupted "by the most awful shelling, and we suffered the most irreparable loss in having our Captain Esmé Gordon Lennox wounded: I helped him out of the trenches and as far as I could to the rear: this morning I heard that he had a good night and with any luck he may get over the shock of the wounds." Captain Fox took command of F Company, very briefly as it turned out. The reference to Major Lord Esmé Gordon Lennox, a son of the Duke and Duchess of Richmond and Gordon, as "our Captain" reflected the custom that a company commander was known as the captain of the company.

Colonel Bolton and Battalion Headquarters were in a farm on the western edge of Polygon Wood, thick pines and dense hardwood scrub. For the two companies with him the situation soon became very fluid. By this time a gap of some six hundred yards, threatened by German machine and field guns, had developed around the northeast edge of the Wood between the 2nd Wiltshire Regiment's trenches on the left of the 21st Brigade facing towards Reutel and the 1st South Staffordshire Regiment's on the right of the 22nd Brigade facing northeast. Any available men were put into this gap. While leading them there and when well ahead of the rest of Left Flank, reconnoitring with a patrol of only six men, Captain Tommy Rivers Bulkeley was killed by a shell. He had joined from the Oxfordshire Militia in 1899 and served in many actions during the Boer War, including being wounded at the Battle of Belmont. He and his wife Evelyn married in 1913 and had a son early in 1914. Captain Fox, bringing up F Company behind, moved across to command Left Flank and Captain Kinnaird replaced him. Otherwise that day was fairly uneventful at Polygon Wood, but back on the other side of the Menin Road, Right Flank, who went up in the dark behind the Grenadiers in Kruiseecke, and G Company had little rest, as there were frequent alarms to their front, while behind them Zandvoorde was ablaze from shells. Lieutenant Warner was "Billeted in a farm, a bad night as it was cold and there were several alarms." At dawn on the 23rd he brought Right Flank back to Zandvoorde and they dug in again. By this time it was known that it was the *53rd* and *54th Divisions* of the *XXVII Reserve Corps* attacking them.

Left Flank were not involved, but F Company were sent to the east end of Polygon Wood during the night of the 22nd under command of the Wiltshires, who were in trenches on the Reutel Ridge back from the far edge of the plateau, but outside the Wood. The village hindered visibility to their immediate right front and they could not see further over to the right where the 2nd Royal Scots Fusiliers were downhill around the hamlet at Poezelhoek. Three platoons of F Company were deployed separately among the Wiltshires, with the fourth back in reserve. The positions had, at best, only two to three hundred yards fields of fire on the plateau and were roughly the same distance from the Wood. The layout and location of the trenches were unsuitable, particularly when the German artillery got the range, in what was already a poor position in a very exposed salient. This was exacerbated when, to their right, the Germans captured Poezelhoek from the left hand company of the Royal Scots Fusiliers, unknown to the rest of that battalion, and also got into the buildings in Reutel from which they sniped and observed the Wiltshires. Then, using dead ground, they penetrated through the new gap at Poezelhoek and into a reentrant behind the Wiltshires right flank. The Wiltshires did not know about the loss of Poezelhoek and had orders not to withdraw. Consequently, following more heavy shelling and infantry attacks from in front, when an attack came in on them from behind their right flank they were badly "cut up". Colonel James Forbes and four hundred and fifty of his officers and men were captured. Most of F Company with them were killed, buried alive or taken prisoner. What had also contributed to the fate of the Wiltshires was rifles unserviceable because of sand thrown up by shells. Captain Kinnaird, further back, had gone on with his letter "We are sheltering now in small Scots fir woods and the men are digging for all they are worth and we are told we may be here for several days…Would you sometimes give me news of the war in your letters as we hear absolutely nothing here." There had been no more mail and only one tiny delivery of parcels, including three pairs of socks for him. "Will you please send me as soon as possible a pair of warm khaki gloves."

Lieutenant Ronald Gibbs, also of F Company, told his mother in a letter sent on 25 October, but written the day before, "Yesterday was our worst day as my Company 220 men strong has now only 77 men left…F Company was sent for by the Wilts Line Regt to reinforce them as they had suffered 3 days continuous shelling. We had the greatest difficulty in getting to their position, and, when we did, found their trenches untenable and had to dig new ones at 1am with no spades, only our entrenching tools. In the morning we were heavily shelled, which was perfectly beastly, a few men being buried under the parapet, and suddenly found that the Wilts had run, and the Germans were charging." The first attempt to halt the enemy after they broke through the Wiltshires was a joint effort between the 2nd Royal Warwickshire Regiment of the 22nd Brigade and about fifty of F Company on their right. Sergaent John Bell wrote how, as they moved through the Wood the F Company men found in front of them a turnip patch surrounded by woodland. Though their left was secure, their front and right were not and, once they were well out into the open, there was an ambush, particularly from their right rear, and they were trapped. Turning round to deal with this, in spite of losing a number of men, they fought back and started to extricate themselves. They were then fired at from behind as well and during this an English speaking German stood up, wearing British uniform, and called out "The French are on our right." Captain Kinnaird raised himself to look round and began to call back "Cease fire behind, we are the Scots G…" The last word never came out. Sergeant Bell, beside him, felt as "He dropped his left shoulder against my right shoulder, and with the faintest 'Oh' was dead." A bullet had entered at the breast and gone through to the hip. The survivors fought their way out. Lieutenant Alastair "Daisy" Orr, who had survived from the overrunning of the Wiltshires, was quite badly wounded and sent back to England.

The Germans then got deeper into Polygon Wood with only the thinnest defence left to hold them back, but lost cohesion and control. The 5th Brigade of the 2nd Division, recently arrived from the Aisne, were sent to drive them out. The 2nd Highland Light Infantry [HLI] on the right and the 2nd Worcesters on the left were ordered only to use the bayonet because it was known that there were still British troops in the Wood, whereabouts unknown. Though control was very difficult, they succeeded in clearing it out to the east completely, but were stopped at the far edge, the Germans beyond alerted by the sound of the cheering coming towards them.

Near the top northeast corner the Worcesters came upon Scots Guardsmen dug in, presumably Left Flank. The experiences of the Wiltshires and of F Company were shortly replicated for others in unsuitable, but important positions, without sufficient men to ensure properly linked and mutually supporting observation and fire and without adequate artillery support, partly owing to the lack of ammunition and partly because of poor fields of observation.

Sergeant Bell told how on the 23rd "At night a search party under Lieut Gibbs…went out for the captain's body which was found, and early on the morning of the next day…he was buried, alongside the grave of the late Major Bulkeley. The funeral was carried out with all available military honours, 4 Sergeants (of whom I was one) bore the body to and lowered him in his grave." Colonel Bolton said a prayer of committal and everyone then said the Lord's Prayer. After the grave had been filled in rough wooden crosses were put up at either end and Sergeant Pilkington took photographs in daylight. This was to the west of the Wood near the Battalion Headquarters farm, where Captain Kinnaird's body was found after the War, but not Captain Rivers Bulkeley's.

Captain Kinnaird's servant, called "Nelson", probably a nickname as no soldier of that surname was recorded as then in the Battalion, had recovered from his pocket the unfinished letter home, his mother's last letter to him and goodbye telegram, as well as his watch, and he took these back for her when he went to England on 1 November. Some weeks later, on 22 December, by which time hardly anyone in F Company was left of those few still fit to fight when darkness fell on 24 October, Lance Corporal George Fairbank wrote to Lord Kinnaird "on behalf of the remainder of the rank and file" of the Company about his son who "died, as he had lived, a God fearing, brave, and great hearted man. He fell leading his company in a charge we made after vacating some improvised trenches which were literally blown in by the enemy's artillery, and in which we lost several men buried alive." Corporal Fairbank, a Boer War veteran, was an old soldier from London, where his father Robert Fairbank lived in Tufnell Park, and had been serving since 1898. Before that he was a cigar maker. Lady Northbrook sent Lady Kinnaird a letter of sympathy, enclosing copies of the photographs she had taken at Stratton on 4 October, in which she described the afternoon and how they had all got up and left after the telephone call. "It is all so sad and sorrowful. It is a glorious death to die for your country, but it's very hard for those who are left behind."

Not till 28 October could a Battalion roll call establish who was present and what was known about those who were not but Lieutenant Gibbs' figure for F Company at the end of these two days was likely to have been correct. His platoon, though involved in the fight in the turnip patch, was still fairly strong, but only twenty six had got back from the other three unhurt. He was still confident and went on "I think that now however we have the Germans on the run, and we have now joined up with all the other divisions…The Germans are absolutely rotten shots but their artillery is excellent. It is not pleasant to have Black Marias and Lyddite turned on one, but the artillery is the only thing to fear. Individual Germans have been surrendering for lack of food and they seem thoroughly afraid of us. As a Belgian officer said to me "Ils tirent comme des cochons, mais leur artillerie, ça c'est quelque chose." We are making a general advance today."

Lance Corporal Harry Gaunt, a soldier for a year and promoted soon after the War began, was a warehouseman in Leeds before that. Though reported missing as at 6 November, when it was first possible to start to find out full details from 20 October onwards, there was then sound evidence from two other soldiers, one of whom was Sergeant Bell, that he was killed outright on 23 October. Such definite information was unusual. In 1913 George and Mary

Jane Gaunt were apparently living in Germany, but were untraceable after his death. Private James Peebles was missing on 24 October. He was a baker when he joined up in 1905 and his family lived in Broughty Ferry, east of Dundee. When he had his medical examination he was passed fit subject to an undertaking that "I James Peebles do hereby certify that I am willing to provide myself with Artificial Teeth to an amount not exceeding £3, and further, that I am willing to maintain them in good repair during my period of Service in the Army." He left for the Reserve in 1908 and got married in 1910, he and Nellie Peebles having a daughter the year after. His parents managed to make contact some months later with Private John Tattershall, a prisoner of war, who replied on 30 June 1915 "Dear Friends I received your letter and I am very sorry at the news which I have got to give you. Your son James was killed on the 24th October at six am near YPRES. I can tell you his death was painless as he was shot through the brain and never spoke. I straightened him out in Trenches. I was wounded then and got captured at 6.30am and brought here. Your son was one of the best soldiers and never grumbled as we got it very hard. I am yours sincerely J Tattershall." Because Private Tattershall was recorded as being taken prisoner on the 24th he and Private Peebles were likely to have been in F Company. He, though born in Liverpool, was a miner and had settled in North Lanarkshire before enlisting in 1903. After he went onto the Reserve he returned to the mines, married in 1908 and by the start of the War he and Mary Tattershall had two daughters and a son. She was pregnant with their fourth child, born in 1915, whom her father saw for the first time after he was repatriated in January 1919. Back in Ypres on 24 October Private John McLinden died of his wounds. A reservist for eight years, he had been living with his wife Nappy and their two small children, in West Calder, Midlothian, her home village. She received a broken rosary, two medallions, a pocket knife, a pocket book, three one penny stamps, a prayer book and some letters.

Kruiseecke

Meanwhile, away to the south of the Menin Road on 23 October the other two companies were ordered to dig themselves into shallow trenches in a second defensive line behind Kruiseecke, the Gordons being under heavy attack in front of them. Lieutenant Warner, back with G Company, wrote of "A good deal of fire but only a few stray bullets coming this way." Next the Borders reported several of their trenches having been blown in, being heavily attacked by infantry and machine guns and, further, the enemy being through the breach where their trenches had been. This was not so, but because of this at half past one both Scots Guards companies were called forward to support the Gordons in closing the non-existent breach. Brigade Headquarters had had to react when "the report was brought through by one or two faint hearted 'gentlemen' who in a moment of intense terror had rushed back to Headquarters." Lieutenant Warner "Went up to our outpost trenches through a wood under shellfire and found them occupied. A good deal mixed up but men behaved well." So they were told to go back, but General Ruggles Brise stopped Lieutenant Warner and his men on the way so they "Remained near farm for about an hour, very heavy shrapnel, luckily no one hit." The companies later returned to their trenches but had needlessly lost some fifty men in the open. Nevertheless, there was no doubt about the proximity of the German infantry. At dusk three platoons of Right Flank took over trenches from The King's Company of the Grenadiers on the east side of Kruiseecke. The Grenadiers, under heavy pressure all day, had just managed by courageous counterattacks to prevent a breach in their line, suffering unavoidable casualties. In the evening Lieutenant Warner and G Company were "Taken out to dig in front line. Lying in a ditch waiting for orders when our own troops opened heavy rifle fire on us from left. A few men wounded before we carried out retirement as ordered." Through the night there was little chance of rest and twice both companies had to turn out ready to fight when there was heavy rifle fire at the outpost positions. Lieutenant Warner was aware of "Plenty of bullets flying but mostly high. G Coy lost about 20 men today." Captain Bruce and the Gordons had an unanticipated further distraction as "all the night we felt dropping, either like the quality of mercy, or with a large flop, frogs between 1 and 4 inches long, which fell in the trench on their way." Major Cator, as Brigade Major, had wider knowledge than most. Already on the 23rd he was writing that "at times the situation is most critical, & it is as much as we can do to hold on." All reports on the 24th were of the enemy digging in along the Brigade's south boundary and in front of Kruiseecke. Then he heard of the 21st Brigade's having had their line broken, followed by a message from the 7th Division that they were organizing a counterattack and "ordering us to hold on to the last gasp." This presumably referred to the destruction of the Wiltshires and the counterattack by the Worcesters and HLI. However, while throughout the day the shelling again went on heavily around the 20th Brigade, the closest German infantry attacks were on and around the Gheluvelt Crossroads, with the left of the Grenadiers being drawn in. The Brigade lost some two hundred men and Major Cator commented on the "great difficulty experienced in getting them removed." The Scots Guards companies still had a fairly quiet day. After dark on the 24th G Company and 4 Platoon of Right Flank under Lieutenant William "Willie" Holbech, went to replace the other three Right Flank platoons in Kruiseecke, Lieutenant Warner noting "Had to lie by roadside because of firing on way up. Quiet night."

Meanwhile Colonel Bolton was told to bring back Left Flank and the remains of F Company once the 4th (Guards) Brigade of the 2nd Division had taken over the north and east sides of Polygon Wood. Lieutenant Saumarez recorded Left Flank being relieved by the 2nd Oxfordshire and Buckinghamshire Light Infantry of the 5th Brigade, after which he had his first wash and shave for five days. At about this time Sergeant Pilkington took a photograph of Sergeant William Young and a group of soldiers from the Oxford and Bucks LI sheltering from shrapnel behind a wall. Sergeant Young, a railway servant, joined up in Glasgow in January 1895 and had been serving ever since, including the later stages of the Boer War, and was a signalling instructor. He and Alice Maude's wedding in July 1903 was in Battersea, where she was living now. They did not have children.

As Colonel Bolton led them to rejoin the others "Gheluvelt was being badly shelled at the time, so I took my Battn by another route across fields to the South, on my way we met Major General Capper with Staff, who congratulated me on the excellent work done by my Battn in Polygon Wood. It was later in the day when we arrived and I reported to Brig Gen Ruggles Brise, and told him that all ranks were much exhausted from want of sleep etc. I saw my men billeted in a Barn and outhouses." Captain Bruce noted German planes dropping smoke bombs as markers for their guns.

When dawn broke on 25 October the Grenadiers, whose left had been in another tough battle around sunset the evening before, were still on the left of the Brigade between the Menin Road and Kruiseecke, facing east. 4 Platoon of Right Flank were next to them, with G Company on their right, also facing east. For Lieutenant Warner it was a "Quiet morning. We shot at some Germans 550 yards and got an Officer." On their right the Borders were round from the point of the salient at the southeast of Kruiseecke with the Gordons next to them on the right also facing south. Captain Bruce recorded German sniping becoming more accurate, four enemy machine guns permanently positioned in houses in front and some German trenches only one hundred and twenty yards away. The Gordons had been unable to do any cooking for three nights. Next orders were suddenly received to be acted on in the event of a general retirement, which came as a surprise because "we had had no hint that the bloodiest battle of the war was in progress." Still at the Gheluvelt Crossroads and to the north were the 21st Brigade, but the 22nd Brigade had moved down to the south of the Menin Road.

In this area the main German effort on the 25th was along the line of the Menin Road and at three in the afternoon the Grenadiers reported that they and the Yorkshires were under heavy attack from infantry and machine guns, but that the Yorkshires had had a very successful shoot down the road with one of their's. The Brigade line was intact but heavy shelling with HE, as elsewhere, had by now badly damaged many trenches. Apart from those at Kruiseecke, the Scots Guards were still in reserve near Zandvoorde, but an unnamed officer, presumably at Kruiseecke, wrote "Never have I been through such a day as it was. It was a veritable hell on earth. There was an incessant shower of shells from 7.30am to 6pm. Luckily, the majority of shells fell well in rear of the trenches, and, therefore, did little or no damage. However, two shells struck the edge of my trench, knocked over the four of us who were sitting there, and broke down all the loopholes of that section. No one was hurt beyond bruises."

Lord Dalrymple, commanding Right Flank, wrote that the Germans had a machine gun position on a knoll one hundred and fifty yards away from and completely dominating the 4 Platoon trench and that three other machine gun positions, each about six hundred yards away, enfiladed the rest of the trenches at Kruiseecke. "There were no communication trenches between trenches or with the rear. The ground round the trenches was so pulverised by artillery that it would not stand when any improvements were attempted. There was no head cover and no wire entanglement." Later that night under cover of darkness and in heavy rain the Germans launched a major attack and managed to rush 4 Platoon's trench. Lieutenant Holbech rallied the survivors, charged their former position, failed to retake it and lost almost all his men. The enemy were repulsed elsewhere, but parties did penetrate into the village. Lieutenant Warner noted "Soon after dark, about 6.30pm, we heard cheering on our right, and word was passed down that a counterattack was taking place. Then we saw a considerable body of men advancing towards us. Three came right onto the traverse of my trench, and I saw the German helmet. We at once opened fire. I shot the first with my revolver, the second was bayoneted and the third dropped and we afterwards took him prisoner. We kept up a steady fire for about fifteen minutes." Because there were Germans in the village "It was awkward knowing that some were behind us, as we did not like to fire for fear of hitting our reinforcements. In my trench I and one man looked out behind, the remainder watching in front." Private Rae, the battalion scout, brought the news of 4 Platoon and of the Germans entering Kruiseecke in strength to Major Fraser at Battalion Headquarters. Meanwhile, separately, Lance Corporal John McLean from 4 Platoon, who does not seem to have been believed initially, brought the same news at eight that evening to Lord Dalrymple. This was confirmed when Lieutenant Holbech arrived an hour later. Corporal McLean, with a butterfly tattooed on his right wrist, a former Scots Guardsman who reenlisted at the end of the first week of the War, became a Lance Corporal ten days later. He and Margaret McLean had been married for eight years and were living with their four children in Falkirk, where he was a labourer. Major Fraser took Private Rae to explain what he had seen to General Ruggles Brise, who ordered a counterattack, Major Cator noting that

Lieutenant Giles Loder had also come to explain the situation. Word of what was wanted had already gone back by some other means because Lord Dalrymple was starting off before Major Fraser came back. There were about three hundred men available altogether, the rest of Right Flank, Left Flank and the remnants of F Company. Colonel Bolton recounted how "late in the evening Major Hon Fraser (my second in command) told me he had just been ordered by Brig Gen Ruggles Brise to take command of two companies (RF and LF), to retake a trench which had been lost; I saw them start, and then went to my HQ with Lieut Steuart Menzies, my Adjutant, and being absolutely beat, lay down." Lieutenant Ronald Steuart Menzies' family home was at Arndilly on the River Spey near Craigellachie. He and Olivia Steuart Menzies married in 1912 and their daughter was born the next year. He had joined soon after the Boer War.

Once Lieutenant Saumarez with Left Flank were back from Polygon Wood they heard that a trench had been lost and "I was told off to take back this bit of trench with my platoon when we reached headquarters which was in a farmhouse just behind the line. Subsequently it was found to be a more serious job than they thought and they said that half the battalion would attack. We threw off our greatcoats and took off our packs and left them behind and we marched into Kruisiec at dusk with fixed bayonets. This place was very badly ruined, broken glass and slates lying about everywhere. The terrific noise made by our marching over these attracted the attention of snipers in the village who fired on us. We could not make out where these shots came from. We were continually halting and watching certain houses and every man tried to tread as quietly as possible despite the glass and slates scattered everywhere."

When Major Fraser caught up he took command of the counterattack before Lieutenant Holbech with three men met them and explained where the Germans were in the northeast of the village. He then turned into the southern end and halted his men along the main street. As they approached they had had to pause while a large force of Germans marched in from the direction of the captured trench and headed off the other way up the main street towards the Gheluvelt Crossroads, but these they had to leave unhindered. They then searched each house they came to and, on reaching the first turning to the right, while the rest waited, Major Fraser and two men went up it to find out from Captain George Paynter, commanding G Company, how much of the line was intact. Captain Paynter told him of some casualties but that they had held and would continue to hold their ground. He did not know what had happened on his left. The Germans seemed to have infiltrated through the gaps in some places and so been able to isolate and surround the 4 Platoon trench. Having satisfied himself that that was the only one which the enemy had captured, Major Fraser went back to his men and they all moved up the street, keeping carefully to either side, to get into position for the counterattack. At this point they saw a house with a light in it just off the street and next to a cinder track leading east towards the lost trench, along which the large force of Germans, estimated, they thought, at a thousand men, had come shortly before. They found the house full of British wounded, mostly South Staffords of the 22nd Brigade, a company of whom had been under command of the Grenadiers. Major Fraser set off down the cinder track towards the lost trench with forty men, Lieutenant Holbech guiding them. When they were twenty or thirty yards away he gave the order to charge, but the Germans opened fire as he did so. He was killed, Lieutenant Holbech severely wounded in the thigh and every man a casualty apart from Sergeant Thomas Mitchell and four others. Half an hour later these five came back and found Lord Dalrymple, who took command in Kruiseecke.

In Captain Paynter's recollection of the 25th to half past eleven at night "Our trenches were tremendously shelled all day, some of the trenches being blown in; Drummond and Kemble, being buried in their trench, had to be dug out. A lot of cheering was heard in the distance when it became dark, and it was passed down the trenches that the French were attacking on our right. Then we noticed masses of troops advancing on our trenches. It was extremely dark and raining in torrents. Some got as far as our trenches and were shot down, others lay down in front calling out "We surrender," and "Don't shoot; we are Allies," "Where is Captain Paynter "G" Company?" Parties got through the line on my right and left and commenced firing at us from behind, others got into houses. We shot at and silenced all these. Fresh lots kept coming on; but, as our fire was pretty heavy, they seemed to make for the places where others had got through. After a couple of hours all was quiet. I was very relieved to hear Major Fraser's voice, about 11.30pm, calling to me we would be relieved…at dawn on October 26th." Captain Paynter, a bachelor regular officer, had, after Eton, joined in 1899 from the 4th Lincolns and been through the Boer War. Both his parents were dead, his mother having died when he was very young. A very capable horseman, he had twice won the Grand Military Gold Cup, most recently in 1914. Captain Kemble and Lieutenant Drummond were buried, but dug out. G Company were certain that from daylight onwards their trenches would be untenable because the Germans had the range exactly. This, as Lieutenant Warner noted, they reported. Not much more could be done.

While the unsuccessful attempt was going on to recapture the lost trench, another platoon, deployed off the village street to give cover and lined up along the north of the cinder track, spotted a light in another house, the one which Lieutenant Saumarez said was the school, set well back from the street in a field further north. There were Germans in it. Lord Dalrymple and Captain Fox made a plan for Right Flank to attack and surround the house from the south and for Left Flank to cover it from the west. As he was just coming up to the platoon along the cinder track the Germans in the house fired at Lord Dalrymple, who immediately charged it with that platoon. Having killed any Germans outside, he called on those inside to surrender. While they were coming out and being passed over to Left Flank other Germans appeared and opened fire, killing Sergeant Mitchell and several others. Sergeant Mitchell had been standing beside Lord Dalrymple, who immediately seized two German prisoners and, shielding his own men with them, made them call out to their comrades that they had surrendered. This had the unexpected, but desired, effect. Firing ceased at once and a large number of Germans emerged and gave themselves up, to be led away to Brigade Headquarters by Captain Fox and most of Left Flank, who were told to come back at once. There were at least five officers and one hundred and eighty seven men, Captain Fox' figures being eight and two hundred and four. Most were from the *233rd Reserve Regiment*. After daybreak on the 26th, back down the Menin Road towards Ypres, Sergeant Pilkington, with Lieutenant Ross, the Quartermaster, and the Battalion Transport on the roadside, saw Northumberland Hussars escorting them towards Ypres.

Sergeant Mitchell, son of Stephen and Anne Mitchell of Romsey, Hampshire, had been serving for nine years after giving up being a brewery labourer in Southampton and then extended his service to twenty one years just before they left the Tower. Private Joseph Ogden also died on the 25th. He came from Bardsley, Staffordshire, and his father William Ogden was there. Private Ogden enlisted in February 1914 in Liverpool. Before that he was a steeplejack. Private Albert Doody was last known to have been alive on the 25th. He was a reservist from

Shropshire, where his family were at Edgmond Marsh, and where Maggie, his wife of just nine months, lived in Wellington. Private George Dorrins, previously a hammerman in Glasgow, but whose parents George and Helen Dorrins were in Irvine, Ayrshire, had left the Colours at the end of 1911 with a lot of convictions for drunkenness and gone to the Reserve. When he was mobilised he was sent to the 2nd Scots Guards at the Tower where he was given fourteen days detention for insubordination on 2 September. Though initially reported missing as at 6 November, later there was firm information that he was killed on 24 October.

Pending Left Flank's return Lord Dalrymple posted pickets at the eastern approaches and organised a search of the houses for snipers. Lieutenant Saumarez, his platoon not in the prisoner escort, wrote of "entering every house in pitch darkness all the time except for our flash lamps, but we were unsuccessful in discovering any snipers." At this point Lieutenant George Hope of the Grenadiers appeared. His platoon trench was their right hand one and next to the Scots Guards lost one, though he, too, did not seem to know this until then. He did, however, know where it was and offered to point out a position from which to enfilade it once it became light, for which Lieutenant Wynne Finch's platoon were detailed. Lord Dalrymple then went back to the junction of the cinder track and the street "to see Lieutenant Holbech who had crawled back with a broken thigh from Major Fraser's party. When I had sent Lieutenant Holbech back on a door, Lieut Hope returned and reported that he had placed the platoon, but that Lieut Wynne Finch had been severely wounded from another house that they had examined on the way." So Lord Dalrymple went himself to this platoon, moved them closer to the lost trench "and gave them orders to charge at once if they heard a shout from me, and, crawled myself right into trench AB, in which I found nothing but dead and wounded men, both Germans and my Company, mostly with bayonet wounds. I occupied trench with platoon, and informed Capt Paynter trench was recovered." While waiting in the village for the rest of Left Flank Lieutenant Saumarez and his men then "stumbled upon a horrifying scene before the rest of the force came back. In searching the houses I came across an estaminet in the village which was full of wounded men. It was a terrible sight; every other man had expired. They had been there for days with nobody to look after them." He said he found Lieutenant Holbech there as well, possibly after only a short time, perhaps carried in, because to have covered the distance of two hundred and fifty yards or so entirely on his own with a shattered thigh was improbable. This house may have been a different one from the first one described and Lord Dalrymple mentioned their finding two houses with British wounded in them. Evacuated home to hospital in Woolwich, Lieutenant Holbech died there on 1 November. He had been on the Reserve since 1907. His widowed mother Mary Holbech lived at Farnborough, Oxfordshire.

While it was still dark Lord Dalrymple, having put in hand the removal of the dead and wounded from the recaptured trench, ordered Captain Fox on his return to make sure that the village was completely clear of the enemy and then to relieve all the G Company trenches with men from Left Flank. He went himself with Lieutenant Ralph Fane Gladwin and a machine gun team to take over from Grenadier machine gunners in the trench at the southeast corner of the village, the point of the salient. He then returned to the recaptured trench, where he directed as much improvement as possible as dawn approached. Captain Fox wrote that, after taking the prisoners to Brigade Headquarters, Left Flank returned to Kruiseecke, their next task being to move a large number of British wounded from the houses. An ambulance wagon was got up in order to evacuate them, but it was difficult owing to the volume of shellfire, which demolished almost every house then still standing. By dawn, about seven o'clock, the Flank Companies, both badly depleted, had taken over from G Company in the trenches.

Through the night of the 25th Major Cator had heard news at intervals at Brigade Headquarters, much of it very worrying. In a letter home on 27 October "It was a most awfully anxious night, but by morning we had the line restored." At some stage Colonel Bolton "was roused by the arrival of Brig Gen Ruggles Brise who was accompanied by his Brigade Major. He told me that my Battn had taken 200 Prisoners of War but that the trench was still untaken, and that it must be taken at all costs. I told him I would arrange to take it and asked him what reinforcements he had at his disposal in case of a strong attack, he told me he had none. I went out immediately accompanied by my Adjutant and guided by Lieut G Loder, the ground being new to me, on our way we met Lieut Hope, Grenadier Guards, who informed me he knew the trench had been retaken, and then guided us to the trench, it was then dawn, and Major Lord Dalrymple was busy directing the clearing of the trench which was full of dead and wounded men, our own and the enemy." Colonel Bolton "then proceeded to inspect the other trenches, and came to the conclusion the most vulnerable point of attack was opposite the trench taken before, and the one on the right of it, there being a Wood about 600 to 700 yards to the immediate front and also in dead ground. I could see Germans concentrating in the Wood. Just about this time Lieut Loder brought me a statement from a wounded German Officer saying we would not be there long as there would be an attack in force presently: I sent him back with this information to Brigade HQ: and then having regard to Major General Capper's repeated Divisional Orders that trenches were to be held at all costs and that no retirement was to be made on any excuse I decided to remain in the trenches with my men, and sent a message to them saying so. I then sent a runner with a written message to Brig Gen Ruggles Brise saying I considered it my duty to remain in the trenches unless he wished me to return to HQ, also asking for more ammunition, which was badly wanted. Later on through my glasses I located an enemy battery taking up a position on the high ground NE of Gheluvelt, and sent another runner with this information, and also a rough map of position. During all this time there was much movement in the Wood to my front, and advances from it were kept in check by our fire. Here I may state our trenches were poor, there was no communication between them, or with the rear, there was no wire entanglement and no head cover, and no telephone; everything that was possible was done to improve them in the morning, my own trench, like others, was partly broken down by shellfire, and later on was more so." Colonel Bolton was on the east side of the village in the next trench to the south of the recaptured one. Lieutenant Wynne Finch's platoon were occupying it, but after his wound he had been sent back. Because of the rain in the night there was the fresh problem of keeping weapons clear of mud, worse, if anything, than keeping them clear of dry earth and grit.

At some stage Colonel Bolton and Lord Dalrymple went in different directions. Lord Dalrymple next received a message that Colonel Bolton intended to stay in the front line, partly from his erroneous impression that the whole Battalion was there, as he did not realise that G Company had been relieved and gone back. Just as Lord Dalrymple was about to reply and ask whether he should therefore go back to take command of those not at Kruiseecke rifle fire opened from their right rear.

Lieutenant Saumarez' platoon had taken over the first Scots Guards trench facing south, round the corner from the machine gunners on his immediate left. Lieutenant Clement Cottrell Dormer's platoon were next on the right. The Borders were beyond on either side of the road to America and Wervicq and had the South Staffords supporting them. What Lieutenant Saumarez saw in the first light of dawn was "corpses strewn over the front of the trenches as far as the eye could see among whom were a number of wounded who were crying out for water. Some of these Germans we brought into the trench and gave them water. We spent the intervening time trying to improve our trenches which were exceedingly bad. They did not communicate with each other and in some places were merely scratches in the ground about four feet deep and they were at the point of the salient in a circle on the forward slope of the hill so that the enemy's guns could be sighted directed full on these trenches."

Captain Fox stated that artillery and rifle fire began at seven in the morning and that there was a breakthrough on the right almost immediately, which fitted the accounts about firing from the right rear, though in the light of what the Borders recorded it could have been a bit later. When the Germans started firing Lord Dalrymple, Company Sergeant Major William Edwards and four men got into a small trench together. "The Germans then opened a very heavy bombardment, first on the village, then on the trenches. Shortly after this began a party of about fifty Germans doubled across our rear from right to left, disappearing behind houses at X. We shot several as they passed." He noted that while they had been bringing in German wounded earlier the Germans did not seem to be occupying the knoll in front of his trench, beyond which was the dead ground in which they could move unobserved. They brought a machine gun up to the knoll during the morning, but it then appeared to become a victim of the next German artillery bombardment. At the height of this he and Company Sergeant Major Edwards between them counted over a hundred and twenty shells within a radius of a hundred yards in a timed two minute period. "It consisted mainly of shrapnel, burst in salvos of eight at a time, bursting directly over trench, and doing no harm, but the other shells knocked the trench about a good deal."

Lieutenant Saumarez thought that the German artillery observers "Apparently… surmised that we were in the trench behind as there was a kind of support trench a few yards behind us and they demolished this trench completely. At first we only received the shells which fell short but eventually they discovered their mistake and they shelled our line very heavily. I was in a small emplacement about six yards behind the rest of my platoon in between these two trenches together with my platoon sergeant James. We did not seem to be in touch with anybody except the platoon on our right commanded by Lieutenant Dormer. Later in the afternoon a wounded corporal staggered into my emplacement announcing that they were all buried in the portion of the trench where he was, in front, so Sergeant James and myself ran out with spades and dug out several men and it seemed that the Germans had found the exact range all along the line. The whole of my platoon was buried, there being no supports to keep the trench secure and the sides simply fell in burying everybody who was in them. I instructed my platoon sergeant to get the men into whatever cover he could, either in what remained of the trench or in the support trench a few yards in the rear as I have already explained and I told him of my intention to run along to Lieutenant Gladwin…and then to Lieutenant Dormer with a view to seeing what was on the right as a great many bombs kept coming from that direction and enfilading us from the right. I then ran across to Lieutenant Gladwin and had a talk with him and he was certain, as I was myself that there was a gap on the right. I then ran across the exposed ground to Lieutenant Dormer's trench…and found Sergeant Ross the platoon sergeant who informed me that a shell had recently struck Lieutenant Dormer and blown him to atoms and he further informed me that he was not in touch with anybody on his right and that a lot of firing was coming from that direction. I then proceeded along his bit of trench which was not blown in to the extent that ours had been, and was in a much better condition, and when I reached the end of the trench I took another man from this platoon with me and we ran across the open space to a piece of brick wall evidently the ruins of some cottage that had once stood there and as the wall made an angle it offered good protection on two sides. From this point of vantage I was trying to see if I could discover signs of anybody whom we could get in touch with on our right, when a shell struck the wall and knocked us both unconscious into a ditch running along the side of the wall." Sergeant Alfred James was a twenty two year soldier with three years service. Walter and Janet James lived in Walton, Liverpool, where their son had been a labourer before enlisting. The other platoon sergeant was probably Lance Sergeant William Ross, in the Battalion at that time. He had five years service and before that was an engineer in Glasgow, where his widowed mother, or possibly stepmother, Jeannie Ross was living in Jordanhill.

Lieutenant Saumarez put in his notebook for that day that they found the trenches they took over from G Company "littered with dead" though he was in a "good trench with Sgt James" and they had bottles and provisions. The first name he jotted down was that of Private Edward McGowan, without adding more. Private McGowan, a reservist, came from Glenfarne, County Leitrim, and was a warder when he enlisted at Dumbarton in February 1904, it being noted that he was "A very fine recruit", and served for three years. He and Margaret Grimes married in Wishaw in July 1911 and she was now pregnant with the only child they would have, a daughter born at the beginning of May 1915. Her husband was never heard of again. The time Lieutenant Saumarez gave for the start of the really heavy shelling was seven and then at ten "our trenches all blown in with Jack Johnson/Cpl Corlet drops in my trench wounded/dig out all I could who were buried/tell remainder to move up and take wounded into other trenches." There followed Lieutenant Saumarez' visit to Lieutenant Dormer's trench and he named the soldier with him next to the wall and then unconscious in the ditch as "Sgt Isset", Lance Sergeant Harry Issott, of whom more later. He referred to German machine guns behind a hedge. Lance Corporal Robert Corlett, from Edge Hill, Liverpool, was a butcher when he enlisted there in March 1911 and may therefore have become a reservist. He was discharged medically unfit in July 1915.

At about noon Lord Dalrymple received word from his left that those there were withdrawing, but could not get confirmation and did not pass it on. Next he heard that reinforcements were coming up on the left and there was the sound of apparently increased firing from the line of the Menin Road, likely to have been the 1st Coldstream and 1st Scots Guards advancing that day from Gheluvelt. At about half past one he saw Lieutenant Saumarez, but it may have been someone else, retiring slowly across his rear. "After this there was very heavy firing in south end of village until a MG appeared to be firing somewhere about the main street or further side of it." Again the houses at the junction of the cinder track and the village street contained British wounded, but by this time they also contained unwounded Germans and when Lieutenant Lord Gerald Grosvenor went to one of them at about one o'clock to have his wounds dressed he was immediately captured.

The Scots Guardsmen in Kruiseecke were completely isolated. Lord Dalrymple learned subsequently from a Borders subaltern and from Captain Henry de Trafford of the South Staffords that the Germans broke through the Borders at nine o'clock and worked their way into the village from there, restrained from pressing on, so it seemed, primarily by their own artillery. The breakthrough came as a result of their massing in the woods to the Borders front, attacking up the Wervicq road and then breaking their B and C Companies in the front line. Only about seventy men altogether got away. While the remainder of the Borders, assisted by the South Staffords, managed to prevent any further German exploitation westwards, it was only a matter of time before the Scots Guards in the village were surrounded and overwhelmed. Lieutenant Fane Gladwin's machine gunners and their gun were knocked out around midday. Captain Fox wrote "At 1.40pm I had just crawled into my Colonel's trench, to ask what he was going to do when I saw one British "Tommy" with his hands up – Germans were coming along the trenches from our right and from the village behind. We had no field of fire to the right owing to a hedge and none to the rear owing to the houses. We had had no sleep for five nights, and had shot away all our ammunition…Just before the end, I got out of my trench to try to crawl to a house in rear which was held by a German machine gun. Six men followed me out, four were shot dead, Lce Corpl Dodd was severely wounded…and Pte Farrell was wounded. I received two slight wounds myself. I dragged Pte Farrell into a trench where I found only one man alive. I was bandaging Pte Farrell when a bullet passed through the flesh of my shoulder, killing Pte Farrell instantly." Private James Farrell was a former shale miner, called up as a reservist. His personal effects were sent to Mrs Ann Farrell in Dalkeith, Midlothian. Corporal Dodd's fate became known later, but now he was missing.

Captain Fox next found Colonel Bolton fighting with a rifle and telling him "My orders are to stay in the trenches" but very soon afterwards "Quicker than I can write it some 20 of our men were standing up surrounded by Germans. A last salvo was fired at our trench; when we put our heads up again, the Germans were standing over us with their rifles. We were prisoners." Lord Dalrymple thought it was a bit later. "I was expecting attack from dead ground in front all the morning, but none came from there until about three pm, when we were heavily fired at from the village to our right rear, and the shelling stopped. We tried to occupy right end and right face of trench, but trench had no command that way, and we had thrown most of the earth out in rear in remaking the trench, and we could see nothing, owing to hedges and ruined houses in that direction. We could have got away then by retiring to our left, but our orders were definite to hold all trench to the last. From our trench we never saw the actual attacking Germans until they were all mixed up with our people in next trench. While we were waiting for them to get clear of their prisoners and give us a chance of firing when they should come on, enemy in considerable numbers got right up to rear of our trench, quite unseen through gardens and ruined houses. There appeared to be nothing I could do, with only five men within hearing, against such numbers, and the trench, with South Staffords on my left appeared to be already surrendering, so I told the five to smash their rifles, and surrender." Colonel Bolton mentioned at the end of his report particularly how well Lieutenant Fane Gladwin had done until he was killed and that "when taken to the German lines through his zone of fire I found the ground strewn with dead."

Lieutenant Fane Gladwin was the son of Hamilton Fane Gladwin of Seven Springs, Gloucestershire. In 1911 he and his wife Isabelle were married at Broughty Ferry and they had a son in 1912. When her husband returned to the Scots Guards from the Reserve she went to live with her parents outside Dundee. She was pregnant with her second son, born in February 1915. Initially her husband was reported missing, though there was an informal private report that he was dead. Then his name was among the wounded in the casualty list published on 11 November and she immediately sent a telegram to the War Office for confirmation and details of his whereabouts. There were none and official confirmation of his death came through the American Consul General in Berlin, as well as in a letter which reached her from Colonel

Bolton. 2nd Lieutenant Clement Cottrell Dormer, an Etonian, was twenty three when he died and his brother, Charles, a year younger, died on 8 February 1915 at Béthune of wounds incurred just before at the Cuinchy brickstacks, with the 3rd Coldstream. Captain Charles and Mrs Ursula Cottrell Dormer lived at Rousham, Oxfordshire.

Company Sergeant Major Herbert Wilford, who joined as a boy soldier in 1901, lost his life on 26 October. He came from Waltham, Leicestershire, where Jesse and Keturiah Wilford lived. He married Lilla Weedon at Caterham in June 1913, their only child, a daughter, being born on 12 November 1914. Also killed that day was Lance Corporal Thomas McKim, another former boy soldier, born in Chelsea, but of Scottish extraction and educated at the Royal Caledonian Asylum. He was a piper. His mother Alice McKim lived at the Duke of York's School, Shenfield. Private William McPherson was known to have been wounded, but was missing. Born in Leith, where John and Jessie McPherson were living, he had served with the Royal Scots in the Boer War before joining the Scots Guards for three years in 1903. A tall man at six foot two inches, he became a policeman in Winchester and was called up as a reservist in August. His wife Alice came from Boscombe, Bournemouth. Corporal Bernard Kelly was another of the dead. He had two brothers in Letterkenny, County Donegal, but had settled in Glasgow and was working in a life assurance office there when he enlisted in 1907. After five years without a single conduct sheet entry he went back to life assurance, this time in London, having married Mabel Richens at Staines early in 1912, their son being born the year after. Corporal Kelly was a Private when mobilised, was promoted Lance Corporal at the end of August and Corporal at the end of September. Private Walter Fudge was a reenlisted former Scots Guardsman who rejoined on 8 September in Bournemouth, where he and Mildred Fudge had their home and where he worked as a market gardener. He had tattoos of a bowl and an orange tree on his right forearm and of a female figure on his left. On 3 October he was posted to the 2nd Scots Guards and went out with them two days later. He was killed on 26 October. Some postcards and letters reached his widow. When he was hit was unknown, but Private Bernard McNally, originally a dock labourer and the son of Hugh and Susan McNally of Leith, was admitted to hospital in Boulogne on 28 October with a bullet wound in his skull. He had served for eight years before leaving for the Reserve in 1912. At quarter to seven on the evening of 30 October he died. His belongings which arrived with his family were a rosary, a cap star, a pipe, a prayer manual, a medallion, a combined knife, fork and spoon, a farthing coin, three brass Scots Guards title letters and three pendants.

On the south side of Kruiseecke as the afternoon of 26 October wore on Lieutenant Saumarez was still lying unconscious in the ditch near the village street. "When I came to my senses there was a badly wounded man lying on me and above this wounded man lay a dead one. In this position I was unable to move as a great many bricks had fallen in the ditch all round us and we could only just breathe through the debris. Here I remained unable to move with a rifle underneath me, until dusk. During the latter part of the time I could hear shells coming from our direction, which puzzled me very much as it seemed we were being shelled by our own side and then I heard German being spoken in undertones. Eventually at dusk a man who was lying behind me in the ditch succeeded in extricating me and crawling back along the ditch I reached the outskirts of the village where I saw several of the enemy. Leaving the village on my right, I made for the direction in which I could hear our guns shelling the village. Coming to a little wood I saw a private (one of our men) who was carrying, one by one, four wounded men back to our line. He was almost completely exhausted by the time I came up to him and I assisted him until I also was exhausted when we were picked up by some gunners who spotted our approach." The gunners told him about the withdrawal from Kruiseecke and Lieutenant Saumarez stayed with them until he set off the following morning on a borrowed horse to rejoin the Battalion, by then at Hooge. He sent Gunhild two cards, one dated the 27th, "You might see in the papers that I was missing or something as we had a bad time yesterday and I have got separated from my batt and am with some gunners who are being generosity itself to me. Do not worry."

In his notebook he named the badly wounded man lying on him when he came round in the ditch at Kruiseecke as "Corpl Mackenzie wounded in head on me and man killed on him". Lance Corporal Alexander Mackenzie came from Urray, Easter Ross, and was an ironmonger when he enlisted in Glasgow in March 1905. After eight years he left for the Reserve in March 1913 and became a policeman. He was captured and in camps at Göttingen, Saxony, and Niederzwehren, Hesse, until he went for internment at The Hague in March 1918. He was, like very many other former prisoners, discharged early in 1919 medically unfit, in his case because of debility and insomnia. With no known relatives he had listed friends as next of kin, Ellen Stewart at Killearnan Manse, Easter Ross, and Miss D Nichols, Kitchen Department, Buckingham Palace.

Also in his notebook on the subject of helping the wounded Lieutenant Saumarez was the name "Finlayson". Private James Finlayson, a reservist, originally from Hamilton, Lanarkshire, enlisted in 1905, the same year that he married Julia McDonald in Aldershot. Immediately before the War he was a policeman in Hamilton, Ontario, and was called up from there. A few days after the battle at Kruiseecke he was hit in the left forearm by shrapnel and sent home. Early in 1915 he was in hospital at Sheringham, Norfolk, where Private Orchard contacted him and suggested that he write to Lieutenant Saumarez, by that time also in England, wounded in several places, including his right hand. Private Finlayson in a dictated letter on 12 February told Lieutenant Saumarez that after leaving his first hospital at Colchester he had a very bad time with tetanus setting into his wound, but very quick action by a doctor at Sheringham saved both his arm and his life. He was worried that the damage to his arm might prevent his being accepted back by the police in Ontario. He then described what he remembered of Kruiseecke "With regard to other events before I saw you that morning I had cleared some of our wounded also three German wounded out of a house the Germans had shelled and fired also Lieut [Dudley] Twiss of the South Staffords. The Lieut & 2 men as you are aware I got to hospital safely but I see by the papers the stretcher bearers & the other wounded whom I could not move have been reported missing." Private Finlayson responded to Lieutenant Saumarez' reply in another dictated letter on 23 February "I must thank you for writing the two reports about what I did but as you state it is mostly luck coupled with a little pluck which obtains such medals. I was very pleased to see that I was mentioned in Sir J French's dispatches for conspicuous conduct on the field which in itself is a great honour though a DCM would have been far greater." There had been another attack of tetanus and another operation to remove a small piece of bone, the cause of all the trouble. He ended by congratulating Lieutenant Saumarez "on your left hand writing". The announcement of Private Finlayson's DCM was published in the London Gazette on 15 September 1915. He did not serve abroad again and returned to the police in Ontario after he left the Army.

G Company were not involved at Kruiseecke on the 26th. Lieutenant Warner's summary was "About 8am Germans were seen in Kruiseecke and rifle fire was opened on the Scots Guards' trenches from the rear. From 9am to 10am the salient was subjected to a violent bombardment of all calibres up to 8 inch howitzers. Most of the trenches of the Borders, South Staffords and Scots Guards were destroyed, and soon after 10am the Germans launched fifteen battalions in the attack. By noon the south face of the salient had been definitely broken. Two companies of the Border Regiment had been overwhelmed and the Germans were in full possession of the village. Between 12 and 2.30pm the Scots Guards, assailed on three sides, were gradually destroyed, being killed or captured in small parties, fighting independently. There was now a serious gap in the line and little to stop an advance on Gheluvelt from the southeast except small isolated reserves whose commanders had no knowledge of the situation. Beyond occupying the high ground west of Kruiseecke, however, the enemy made little forward movement.

The 1st (Guards) Brigade moved the Black Watch forward to the spur southeast of Gheluvelt. In the meantime to return to the salient, the Grenadier Guards, who had easily withstood minor infantry attacks on their front, were ignorant of the disasters which had occurred on their right; but about 2.30pm, when they saw Germans collecting wounded east of the village, they realised that the line was no longer intact. This spectacle, combined with the complete cessation of all fighting in their vicinity, decided the company commander to endeavour to clear up the situation. He therefore dispatched Lieut Pilcher to battalion headquarters for information and orders. As Pilcher approached the village he was fired on at close quarters by Germans from the houses. Their aim was ineffective, presumably deflected by astonishment at the sight of a British officer strolling into a village which they had captured three hours before. Pilcher took to his heels expedited by a scattered but fortunately harmless machine gun and rifle fusillade. He reached battalion headquarters to find that they had been withdrawn and, stopping only to collect his letters from the mail which had arrived that morning, started to rejoin his company. Near Oude Kruiseecke crossroads, however, he met Captain Fortune of the Black Watch with his company, accompanied by Lieut Hope, and they made a plan to extricate the Grenadiers from their untenable position. Fortune agreed to make a demonstration towards Kruiseecke, while the Grenadiers were to cut their way through the Germans in their rear to join him. The plan entailed Pilcher's return to his company through the Germans. He went back by the same route through the northern end of the village, making use of such cover as a ditch by the side of the road afforded and not lingering on the way. He was again saluted by the Germans and again escaped unscathed. Word was passed down to fix bayonets and charge westwards on the company commander blowing his whistle and leaving the trenches. The manoeuvre, supported by "Fortune", was a complete success as well as a complete surprise to the Germans. It is indeed probable that a counterattack against Kruiseecke village from the north during the afternoon would have met with little resistance, as the Germans do not seem to have done much to consolidate their position." The 1st Black Watch, Captain Victor Fortune being one of the company commanders, had come up the Menin Road that morning with the 1st (Guards) Brigade and they were directly and the 1st Cameron Highlanders indirectly drawn into salvaging the broken line as best as possible. The two officers of The King's Company were Captain The Honourable Arthur Weld Forester and Lieutenant William Pilcher.

Also in his letter on the 27th Major Cator described how the day before on "Sunday morning about 7am they began to bombard us with big guns and high explosive shells, you can't imagine what a perfect hell it was like, any battle in South Africa was a mere skirmish to it. These big shells make a hole big enough to bury a wagon, and absolutely blow the trenches clean away. About 12 noon we had in places no trenches left, so I and Brooke organized a second line in rear, and collected all the survivors from everywhere to hold it, we both galloped our horses to a standstill. About 3pm we had quite a respectable line to hold on to, which we held till 10pm when we retired to the main line of the army." Captain Bertram "Boy" Brooke, a Grenadier, was the Staff Captain. In his diary account Major Cator described "the shells repeatedly blowing in the trenches & burying five and six men at one time each of whom had to be got out with shovels in some cases as much as three feet of earth being on top of them. Many being suffocated before they could be extricated." This fragile defence line from Gheluvelt to Zandvoorde was formed by Major Cator and Captain Brooke from those who remained or could be assembled of the Scots Guards, South Staffords and Borders. Over to their right were the then still fairly intact 2nd Gordons. This line was, however, too isolated and thinly held if seriously attacked, though the Germans did not try to, and it was therefore decided after dark to go further back onto a better position in the woods beside the Bassevillebeck, a stream to the east of Herenthage Wood and south of Veldhoek. The Grenadiers, relieved first, had gone back there in the middle of the afternoon at the same time as the guns. Soon after the decision was taken to withdraw everyone the others went back, without hindrance, by way of Zandvoorde and bivouacked a mile and a half further north near the Bassevillebeek. Zandvoorde was still in British hands and further over to the left the 1st (Guards) Brigade had taken the place of the 21st Brigade from the Gheluvelt Crossroads northwards. By the end of the 26th Major Cator assessed that the 20th Brigade had lost half their men, though it had not yet been possible to hold roll calls. It was not quite that bad, but he was not far wrong. So far the Gordons were in fairly good shape, the Grenadiers reasonably so, but the Borders had suffered heavily and the Scots Guards most of all. Captain Paynter now commanded the Battalion and Lieutenant Loder became Adjutant. His home was at Slaugham, Sussex, though his parents were dead and his brothers in London were his next of kin. He had been at Eton and Sandhurst before being commissioned in 1903.

On the 27th the 7th Division came under Sir Douglas Haig's command in I Corps and the 20th Brigade were withdrawn down the Menin Road to Hooge. There, in reserve, there was at last an opportunity for some rest till late afternoon on the 28th. When the Scots Guards held a roll call, which Sergeant Pilkington photographed, twelve officers, including the Medical Officer, Captain Davis RAMC, and the Quartermaster and four hundred and sixty other ranks, including the Transport men, answered their names. Many who did not were prisoners, though news of them might take weeks or months to come through. Some men were known to be dead, more were missing and were never heard of again, but some of the missing were likely to be wounded and in the medical system, unknown to the Battalion. Others may have become genuinely lost and would reappear later and more than one was missing in dubious circumstances. Sir Douglas Haig came to visit them.

Sergeant Robert McConnell was killed on the 26th. His home was in Milngavie, just north of Glasgow, and he was the middle son of Alexander and Jane McConnell. A soldier for four years, he had previously worked as a clerk. After qualifying in 1913 at the School of Musketry, Hythe, when he was a Lance Corporal, early in 1914 he was promoted to Lance Sergeant and then within a week of the outbreak of war to Sergeant. He was twenty two when he died. At the roll call at Hooge among the missing was Sergeant Arthur Stuart from Preston, where he had been a weaver. He had been serving two years longer and was two years older than Sergeant McConnell. He had been to Hythe early in 1914 when already a Lance Sergeant and was made a Sergeant immediately the War began. His next of kin was his aunt Sarah Breeze in Preston. Sergeant Hugh Smith was slightly younger than Sergeant McConnell and had joined up a few months after him. His promotion to Sergeant was on 1 September. His home, where Robert and

Catherine Smith lived, was in Abbeyhill, Edinburgh. His father was the Church Officer of St Michaels' Parish Church, Slateford, and later became Acting Mess Sergeant of the 2/8th Argyll and Sutherland Highlanders, Territorials, in Berts Hotel, Montrose. At the roll call Sergeant Smith was also missing. Before enlisting towards the end of February 1911 he had been a telegraph messenger in Edinburgh. So had Private George Plant, who enlisted the same day. Both qualified as 1st Class Signallers in 1913, but when three years were up they went different ways. Lance Sergeant Smith stayed in the Battalion and Private Plant went to the Reserve till mobilization. Private Plant was hit in the stomach on the 29th, but it was a treatable wound, from which he recovered, though it was eighteen months before he returned to the BEF. His parents George and Mary Plant lived near Holyrood Park.

The Menin Road

Major Cator continued his letter on the 27th "I am very tired as I have not slept for five nights except for about an hour each night. I couldn't help laughing, on Friday a big Black Maria shell burst just outside the house, to see all the servants coming out through the window as fast as they could, fat little Alfred was bungling his body through when the window sash came down and pinned him by the foot, his frantic endeavours to escape made us all roar with laughter. I sent the horses to the rear every day before daylight, and have still got them safe and sound. I keep the Belgian horse for the battles. I was very lucky yesterday and never got touched. Just the last shell of the day though, wounded my poor Belgian, but only slight. I had galloped across to get some men into a position and two shells came, one burst just to the right and the other right under my horse. It knocked us both over and marvellous to say the only result was a small flesh wound on the horse. I suppose luckily, it was a bad burst on soft ground. I am very well and only sleepy. It was an awful strain the last four days but I don't feel it in the least. Ruggles Brise is wonderful and never gets rattled and it has been a trying time….Water is very scarce here, but Alfred managed half a bucket for me and I got an all over wash today." "Alfred" can only have been his servant's first or nickname, but who he was is not known.

Lieutenant Saumarez wrote to Gunhild on 28 October "We have just been through rather a fearful day and night and have lost 17 officers killed wounded or missing and nearly 500 men. I got separated from my batt and was picked up by some gunners who put me on a limber and carried me along with them. Yesterday I borrowed a horse from them and trekked off in search of my battalion or the remains of it rather. I found them about 2:00 at this place and almighty glad I was to see them again, although it was very terrible to see. How decimated we were. Everyone was greatly surprised to see me turn up as I had been reported as killed, severely wounded, 1/2 my head blown off and a prisoner! However whatever happened which I have not time or space to tell you here, I am now quite well only very stiff and sore. Our batt did a very big coup just before the disaster and captured over 200 Germans including 7 officers. We rounded them up at night in a ruined town where they had just broken through our lines. After sending the prisoners back to Head Qts we charged the lost trench 3 times losing several men and 3 officers, and took it the 3rd time. We then occupied it again but the next morning when dawn appeared they shelled our line so accurately that nearly all our poor fellows were buried in their trenches. I managed to dig out several under fire from 2 machine guns and then retired with all the men I could get together which were not many then came a very bleak 5 hours which I will tell you about some time and then I found myself on a gun limber." He listed those of the officer casualties he could think of, identifying with a star all he knew to be dead, nothing definite being then known about the rest, wounded or not. Then he continued "Orchard was wounded in the head some days ago and went to hospital since which I have heard nothing. My next servant an excellent fellow called Sinclair had disappeared and I fear he was struck with a shell when our Head Qts was shelled 2 days ago. I must now be off. By the way I hear the first batt is somewhere quite close and young Lawson is killed. Heaps of love to yourself and do send some chocolate and meat lozenges. 2 boxes of meat lozenges were all mouldy pea green in colour! from Fortnum and Mason. Cocoa is also welcome. Heaps of love to Mother Father and sisters and the socks and Burberry lining 1 shirt and tobacco and cigarettes have arrived, got them last night. George Paynter is commanding the batt no one could be better."

At half past three that afternoon a message arrived at Headquarters 7th Division of reliable information, later confirmed as a wireless intercept, that the *XXVII Reserve Corps* were going to attack the Gheluvelt Crossroads at dawn on 29 October. An hour later the 20th Brigade were told to send two battalions towards the Crossroads, held by this time by B Company of the 1st Black Watch under command of the depleted 1st Coldstream on the right of the 1st (Guards) Brigade. As the Grenadiers and the Gordons were the strongest, they were chosen to occupy the line from the Crossroads southwest towards Zandvoorde. Soon afterwards the Borders and Scots Guards were sent up in the dark to be ready to support them as necessary by occupying the buildings on the south of Gheluvelt and guarding the approaches. However, as there was no prepared position for them there, once it was daylight they were to withdraw so as not to be out in the open and exposed to shelling. As the Scots Guards marched up the Menin Road two shells fell suddenly, one causing no damage. The other landed between the rear of Right Flank and the head of the remainder of F Company killing Lieutenant Gibbs, their only surviving officer, six men and two pack animals and wounding two officers and another eight men. Lieutenant Gibbs, born in Australia near Melbourne, his third Christian name, was an Etonian who had joined in September 1913 for training as a Special Reserve officer. He was called up on mobilization and sent on to them at Lyndhurst. His widowed mother Alice Gibbs lived in Chelsea, her brother being Major General Sir Charles Crutchley, a Scots Guardsman who had been Lieutenant Governor of The Royal Hospital, Chelsea, since 1909. Captain Kemble had shell fragments in his left arm, which destroyed his elbow joint, through the back of his right knee and into the calf and through the flesh of his left ankle. He had been serving since 1901, left in 1912 and returned when the War began. The knee wound was minor, the ankle one went on troubling him and the arm never healed, even stiffly, and had to be amputated in 1918. Lieutenant Saumarez noted on the 28th that Left Flank, with only sixty men left, were amalgamated with the few left of F Company and that after the shelling on the Menin Road the Battalion were "separated temporarily – bad night getting batt together & wait in ditch on road."

One example of the confusion of all kinds by now affecting the BEF at Ypres and would become worse was over promotions in the field. One morning, probably on 19 October, because that was eventually decided on as the effective date, Colonel Bolton made Private William Vaughan of F Company a Lance Corporal when he became a section commander. Afterwards there was no record of this happening. Corporal Vaughan was then hit in the head on 28 October and evacuated, his platoon commander, Lieutenant Orr, who recommended him for promotion, having been wounded already at Polygon Wood. Not until after Corporal Vaughan had come back out again, been wounded a second time on 27 September 1915 in the knee and left arm with the

1st Battalion at Puits 14 Bis during the Battle of Loos and returned to England to recover was the matter properly investigated and witnesses found who could vouch for his initial promotion. He came out a third time in September 1916 just after the attacks at Ginchy and Lesboeufs on the Somme and very quickly became a Sergeant, back again in the 2nd Scots Guards. He went home finally in March 1917 and ended the War as a Company Sergeant Major. His home was in Kirkdale, Liverpool, and he had nearly finished three years as a soldier in August 1914. He and May Vaughan married in Liverpool in July 1917.

Hit on 28 October by a bullet in the thigh was Private William Rose, in the Army for four and a half years and before that a clerk in Edinburgh, following school at George Watson's. He was given two days confined to barracks in April 1913 for "Loitering in Birdcage Walk in company with a female about 1.15am contrary to Brigade of Guards Standing Orders Para 80". In January 1914 he married Katherine Summers in Islington and she continued to live there. Private Rose reached Alexandra Hospital, Cosham, Portsmouth on 9 November, was described as "Dangerously Ill" next day and died on 3 December. His funeral was on 7 December at Portsdown, the day that his and Katherine's four month old son died of septicaemia in Great Ormond Street Hospital, London.

Gheluvelt

Notwithstanding everything in this part of the battlefield so far, 29 October saw the biggest attack yet by the Germans, down the Menin Road itself, with more attacks from Kruiseecke towards the south side of Gheluvelt and between there and Zandvoorde, completely exposed to German artillery observers at Kruiseecke. All of the weakened 7th Division were south of the Menin Road, the 20th Brigade responsible for the sector nearest to it. Although the main attack started at half past five that morning, just as the intercepted wireless message had indicated, in silence in the mist, as soon as it became light the German guns began a fierce bombardment, shelling both the Veldhoek area, from which British reinforcements and resupply had to come, as well as the forward trenches. At half past seven, so Major Cator recorded, the Scots Guards and the Borders were withdrawn from the south side of Gheluvelt to Veldhoek. Then, because the Grenadiers and the Gordons had got into difficulties from ten o'clock onwards, if not earlier, and the Grenadiers were being driven back up the slope on which Gheluvelt stood, the Borders were first sent up to help. Then the Scots Guards, along with the 2nd Queen's Royal West Surrey Regiment [Queen's] from the 22nd Brigade, were ordered forward. The situation to the north was very serious, the enemy having broken through at the Crossroads, veered to their right, destroyed the 1st Coldstream and the two Black Watch companies they had under command, as well as a company and a half of the 1st Scots Guards next up the line. To begin with the 2nd Scots Guards and the 2nd Queen's helped to hold the village, very exposed after the destruction of the 1st Coldstream. Then at four in the afternoon, about the time that the 3rd Brigade arrived up the Menin Road to drive the Germans back towards the Crossroads, they counterattacked the weakened area to the south side of it, while other 7th Division battalions bolstered the defence towards Zandvoorde. Along the line of the Menin Road the 3rd Brigade recovered the Crossroads and the Scots Guards and Queen's were also successful as the evening drew on. The Scots Guards had captured two machine guns and drawn level with a trench in which were a company of the Gordons who had held their ground throughout and, Major Cator noted, "inflicted a terrible punishment on the Germans." Broadly speaking, when night fell the 20th

Brigade were back holding the ground where they had been at dawn, but the Grenadiers, at the start of the day with twenty officers and six hundred and seventy men, had five officers and about two hundred men left. At nightfall orders went out to establish an outpost line from Gheluvelt towards Kruiseecke and then bending back round to Zandvoorde. Behind this everyone was to withdraw. Lieutenant Saumarez noted that, having moved back early on, at half past nine they were ready to go forward again, but waited for two hours by the roadside, seeing great numbers of wounded men coming down it. At about eleven they headed off towards Gheluvelt and were under shrapnel fire all day. He had Lieutenant Drummond with him for most of the time, the Queen's on their left and the Gordons and some Grenadiers without an officer on their right. There was confusion in the dark, rain, lots of firing and alarms and after Lieutenant Loder went for orders they were told to withdraw back to Gheluvelt. Lieutenant Saumarez, with Sergeants James and Ross and about fifty men, mostly from Right Flank, got detached from the rest of the Battalion and were directed by the Commanding Officer of the 2nd KRRC, by mistake, to Battalion Headquarters of the 1st Battalion in the stables at Gheluvelt Château, where were Major Van der Weyer and Captain Stracey. Lieutenant Saumarez had something to eat, slept for three hours and at half past four in the morning relieved the 1st Gloucesters in the trenches.

When, as ordered, the rest of the 2nd Scots Guards, who had penetrated further east than anyone else realised, came back towards the new outpost line, which Lieutenant Saumarez party missed, there was a disaster. In the darkness and rain the Queen's mistook them for enemy, shot at them heavily, killing and wounding many and contributing grievously to their day's total of a further thirty one killed and one hundred and four wounded. Those who could be found after this, some one hundred and fifty altogether, went into billets at a farm behind the outpost line. "The night was pitch dark, and it rained in torrents, the men being wet through. The transport did not come up this night" wrote Lieutenant Loder in the War Diary. So on top of everything else they did not have any food. Gradually about fifty more found their way back, possibly in addition to those with Lieutenant Saumarez, who were still near Gheluvelt Château.

After all this Private Clifford Keay, a reservist, was missing. He was a Londoner, whose parents Walter and Eliza Jane Keay were in Streatham, and had left the Colours after three years in March 1914. The Germans reported that they captured him, badly wounded, and that he died on 4 November. Very unusually, the German Foreign Office forwarded an identity disc. On 29 October Piper Charles Maguire was hit in the spine by a bullet, removed the same day at a field ambulance. He was moved first to Boulogne and then to England, paralyzed completely, but able occasionally to feel lightning pain in his legs and feet. He died in hospital in London at twenty five to nine on 12 July 1915. His family, a large one as he was one of four brothers and four sisters, lived at Inner Leven, Fife. When he was hit was not recorded, but Sergeant Bertie Chaddock, wounded in the head, died at half past twelve on the afternoon of 1 December in hospital in Boulogne. He was a regular soldier, having given up being a baker in Leek, Staffordshire, in 1904, when, on enlistment, it was noted that he had a large mole four inches below his right nipple. Unusually for a serving soldier, he qualified as a chiropodist in 1907. Though their son was born the year before, he and Ethel Hesketh married in August 1914 at Caterham.

Lieutenant Loder wrote that on 30 October "The Germans shelled Zandvoorde till the sky became as black as a London Fog." At noon the Scots Guards were sent back temporarily to give protection to the guns in the woods. There they met the Gordons, who had been sent further over to the right and who had been having a very hot time. "Their wounded were going back in streams. There was also a Battery in a field which was silenced by the Germans – with dead gunners lying all round, one gun being turned upside down." The Germans captured Zandvoorde during the day after dismounted Household Cavalrymen, heavily outnumbered, did their best to hold it. As it got dark the 20th Brigade, with very scant resources and still not including the Gordons, were withdrawn to Veldhoek and able to rest for a few hours. The other two Brigades were on a spur a bit further on towards Gheluvelt, from beside the Menin Road down to five hundred yards north of Zandvoorde. Gheluvelt itself and its surroundings, but not as far as the Crossroads, were now held by the 3rd Brigade of the 1st Division, who during the next day would become linked to the left of the 21st Brigade to begin with.

Lieutenant Saumarez' party spent all day in the trenches, good ones, with the 1st Battalion, who, he noted, at that time had nine officers and seven hundred men. He also noted Black Maria shelling throughout. At four in the afternoon he received a message to rejoin the 2nd Scots Guards when "Germans in trenches opposite shouting for *wasser*." They followed the railway track back to the Provost Marshal's hut at or near Veldhoek and went on to what appears to have been Headquarters 20th Brigade because he mentioned seeing Major Cator, having a meal and then being led to the Battalion by General Ruggles Brise. At ten o'clock that night, as Major Cator recorded, a message came down from Headquarters 7th Division with the outlines for an attack by the 1st and 2nd Divisions, both of whom had brigades in the Klein Zillebeke area, plus all available British cavalry, at half past six the following morning between Zandvoorde and the Ypres-Comines Canal. Nothing more was heard of that. At one next morning the Scots Guards and the Borders went up close behind the left of the 21st Brigade so that they were on a reverse slope on the eastern edge of the thick wood which ran down from Veldhoek towards Zandvoorde. There they dug in for the night, Lieutenant Saumarez noting that this went on all night, the men very tired, on the edge of a wood, well concealed by the trees in front. At dawn the German guns opened up again. During 31 October the Scots Guards remained in these trenches and were not involved in the intense fighting in and around Gheluvelt, but very heavily shelled throughout.

Major Cator described what they missed on the 31st. From pre-war usage the Regular Army used "shell" as both a single and plural noun, which explained his next use of it, but "shells" for plural soon became usual. "As soon as day broke the Germans began a terrific shellfire all along the line – by 8am the bombardment became so terrific that shell were bursting over and on the line in one unceasing flow, towards noon word came in to say that the 21st & 22nd Brigades had been shelled out of their position and had been forced to retire. The Scots Guards & Borders still held their line in rear of the 21st Brigade, & the Grenadiers were led up in prolongation of this line by their Brigadier in hopes of stemming the German advance, on gaining the ridge through the woods it was found that in order to be of any use it was necessary to push them forward & occupy the empty trenches of the 21st Brigade, this was effected with some difficulty owing to the very heavy shellfire, and three or four of the most forward trenches on the right of the 21st & left of the 22nd Brigade were occupied just in time to meet a portion of the main German attack which was now being delivered on the Gheluvelt-Zandvoorde frontage. The small portion of Grenadiers were now confronting some thousands of Germans, their right being exposed as the 22nd Brigade trenches were unoccupied. Luckily brave men though the Germans were their attack appeared to be utterly disjointed and unorganised. Nowhere could Officers be seen leading their men, who advancing in dense masses up to within three hundred yards of the trenches were simply mown down by the fire of the Grenadiers. All seemed going on well to our front when the right hand trench reported the Germans to be streaming through a wood & crossing the Veldhoek-Zandvoorde road working their way into the large wood immediately on our rear, matters were looking ugly." An officer from Headquarters 20th Brigade, whom he did not name and could have been him, crawled down to find out exactly what was happening in this wood, saw large numbers of Germans massing there and crawled back to report. There were no troops available to drive them out, so all they could do was try to hang on till dark and warn Headquarters 7th Division. The same officer, after "finding a loose horse… galloped off & found Maj Gen Capper," who took immediate action to find troops. However, once he did, a counterattack by the 2nd Brigade and 4th (Guards) Brigade was already starting.

The 3rd Brigade were almost completely destroyed on 31 October, but the 1st Division, with assistance, had just held and eventually restored the line at Gheluvelt and north of the Menin Road. On the other side of it, however, the Germans had penetrated past the village to the south and disrupted the 7th Division there. The fragile situation from south of the Menin Road across to Klein Zillebeke was the principal reason for the complete withdrawal from Gheluvelt during the night. In conforming with this the Grenadiers were brought back after dark and the 21st Brigade were ordered to take over the trenches where the Scots Guards and the Borders were. Major Cator recorded "Two guns… had been left out in rear of the left of the 22nd Brigade trenches. A party of forty men from the Scots Guards & some Bedfords were taken out & manhandled them back behind our trenches." He felt that after dark "the situation remained very much as when we started as far as our Brigade were concerned," but he was very unimpressed with the German tactics as though "the shelling was the worst we had so far experienced, nearly all our casualties had been caused by shellfire, their Infantry can neither shoot nor make any use of the ground over which they manoeuvre. Had they been of any use at all they must have wiped us out by sheer weight of numbers & advanced into Ypres." He was aware of a new defence line which they might have to withdraw to, from a mile east of Zillebeke up to the five kilometre post on the Menin Road, which meant along the highest ground from Hill 62 north to where many roads met on the Menin Road, later called Clapham Junction.

Herenthage Château Wood

In the evening Lieutenant Saumarez noted that General Capper came round about seven, that they moved off with entrenching tools an hour later and assembled on the road at nine to collect rations, though the War Diaries indicate that not till midnight did the 21st Brigade take over from the Scots Guards and the Borders. Lieutenant Saumarez and his men "dig all night. LF advanced post – nasty position…found 3 dead spies in farm. Farm on fire." In this context "spies" probably meant men from a German reconnaissance patrol.

The three 20th Brigade battalions, less the Gordons, took up a line along the east edge of the Herenthage Château Wood, too weak to hold more than between three and four hundred yards. They dug in again, the Scots Guards on the left and the Borders on the right, with the Grenadiers behind the other two in reserve. On their right the Borders were to link up with the 2nd Brigade, but where they were was anyone's guess until Colonel Hugh Montgomery, GSO 1 of the 7th Division, the most senior staff officer, at considerable risk of meeting Germans, rode off through the woods himself and found them. Strangely, Major Cator noted, the Grenadiers "were reinforced by 175 French Cavalry on foot, their Captain informing us they were unable to obtain any more horses in France." There had been little or no news of the Gordons for some time, but on the 1 November they heard that the Gordons had been "fiercely engaged all day yesterday and only three officers and 200 men were left of them." The four battalions in the Brigade had a total of eighteen officers and a little over nine hundred men, fairly evenly spread. These numbers were better than those of many others at Ypres. Missing on 1 November was Lance Sergeant Issott, mentioned by Lieutenant Saumarez at Kruiseecke on the 26th, a reservist from Leeds who had left the Colours eighteen months before. While not married, he had a daughter with an affiliation order against him for four shillings per week earlier in 1914 at Newmarket, Suffolk, for the child born in 1911 to Lucy Hogg. Lieutenant Saumarez recorded being shelled all day by both British and German guns in their "bad position – 4.30 hear German entrenching and talking 150 yds in wood in front." He mentioned Royal Engineers bringing up wire after dark, that there was a gun in the wood, a bright moon in their faces, that they pulled back further about midnight and again dug all night, "some trenches under water."

On the 1st the next development Major Cator commented on was "terrific shellfire" on Herenthage Château, where Brigade Headquarters were, with "one shell…stripping the entire back off the house." They all decamped after this into nearby dug-outs near the Grenadiers and the French cavalry, but the shelling became so bad that it was thought better to move the soldiers further back into better cover near the road from Clapham Junction to Klein Zillebeke. This and the next four days were characterised by shelling, making it impossible to leave the trenches until after dark, when everything possible was done to strengthen them, including putting out wire. Meanwhile, the Germans continued to try to push their way up the Menin Road, as well as pressing hard to the south of it, but, apart from the shelling, the Scots Guards had little involvement and few casualties. However, to Lieutenant Saumarez, 2 November was "Bad day. Shelled. Water rising in all trenches – clear the stream – dig fresh trenches – lost 9 men – attack at night repulsed." On their right the Borders, however, had a very tricky day. Halfway through the morning there was a message from the 2nd Brigade that their left hand battalion, the 1st Northamptons, were unable to hold their left hand trenches any more. This completely exposed the Borders' right and they were badly enfiladed after the Germans got through the resulting gap. However, they stood their ground and held on until a composite counterattack organised by the 2nd Brigade drove the enemy back and closed it. General Capper was very pleased with the Borders and made it widely known. While his Headquarters were in the woods near the Grenadiers after being shelled out of Herenthage Château General Ruggles Brise was hit by a shell in both arms and the shoulder blade. Having listened all day to the sounds of very heavy fighting the other side of the Menin Road, Major Cator was now commanding the Brigade.

He wrote an unaddressed note on 2 November, most likely to Violet Cator, "Just a hurried line to say I am all right. The battle is still raging. Just as I had written these 2 lines word came in to say a trench had been taken by the Germans. Have just returned from finding out what was up & have sent 40 men down to stop up a hole in the line. Today is the 13th we have been fighting. I think we shall hold them alright – though once or twice it has been anxious work…Their infantry are rotten and the only way they ever make us retire is by their shellfire directed from some five miles off. About 3 days ago we lost some trenches & I got hold of some Grenadiers & we reoccupied same, their infantry were swarming towards us & could easily have walked over us – but the fire from our few men caused the whole lot to stop & we killed a lot of them." Continuing next day "We were attacked four different times by the Germans & each time I had to go off to the trenches with reinforcements, & stay there to report on how things were going. We beat them off every time thank God. They had a tremendous hard try to get in the last thing about 6pm & the whole line came on cheering very feebly & blowing things which sound like toy trumpets." Early on the 3rd Lieutenant Saumarez managed to write to Gunhild, having received a letter from her dated 28 October the previous evening "We have been on the go continually ever since our big smash, no time even to find out who is missing properly. There are now 5 of us left to look after the 350 men [probably an overestimate], which remain of the batt…I am feeling rather sad at the minute as poor David Drummond was shot just 10 minutes ago at my side by a sniper through the head. We have been working together through some ugly times during the last few days. Please find out where his poor wife is and go and see her. We had arranged that if one of us was knocked out and got away the other would go and see the others wife and do what one could. He was a real good friend and a really brave man. I feel his loss more than anyone. I know you will keep your spirits up darling and have faith that everything will be for the best. Paynter now commands. Taylor, Loder, Warner and FitzWygram are all that remain. Thank you ever so much for all your letters which have been a real comfort to me the parcels have also come all in the last 3 days with boots shirts socks and 1 parcel of chocolate and butter. We have had no milk for 5 days, but otherwise have done fairly well in the food line…The French are coming up I hear so we still keep smiling. My trench is very nice but the water comes up from below periodically!…You can't think how delightful it is to get news from home and distract one's thoughts a bit. I have to choose my time to read them though, as there is something doing all day and most of the night. Lots of work for 5 poor officers! By the way do write a letter to poor young Gibbs' people and say that I wrote to you saying what a plucky young fellow he was. He was killed 10 yards from me by a shell as we were walking with the batt in fours down a road at 11.00 at night." He added as a postscript that the Battalion's censor's stamp had been in Lieutenant Steuart Menzies' pocket as Adjutant. "It is believed that he was captured by the Germans with our C.O. and several others. The Germans might do a lot of damage with this stamp so try and make it known to someone in authority." In his notebook he recorded Lieutenant Drummond's death, losing fourteen men, worse shelling and repulsing two attacks in the night. Lieutenant Drummond joined from the Black Watch Militia in 1903, transferring to the Special Reserve in 1911. Hilda Drummond and their three small girls were living in Bexley, Kent. On 7 May 1915 Lieutenant Saumarez met her and next day she wrote asking further questions, hitherto avoided, and to thank him for all he had told her. She asked "Do you think David suffered after he was shot; & how long afterwards did he live? Was he very disfigured afterwards? & do you know whether he ever spoke again after being shot?"

Later, during the afternoon of the 3rd the Scots Guards reported Germans massing in the woods in front of them and there were signs of movement towards the right of the Borders, but no attack seemed imminent and when the British guns opened fire that appeared to disperse any enemy activity. The 4th was very similar, with more shelling. In spite of everything normal disciplinary procedures continued. Private John Wells had served in the Army first as Private John Lancaster of the 2nd Yorkshires. He deserted from them on 14 May 1911 and applied to enlist two days later in Birmingham and was accepted for the Scots Guards, giving his age as twenty one and his occupation as blacksmith and brickworks labourer. He was soon found out, punished for fraudulent enlistment and stayed in the Scots Guards. He had tattoos of Buffalo Bill, clasped hands and scrolled L.O.V.E. on his right forearm and the Crucifixion, a woman's head and "Ethel" on his left forearm. He was also nicknamed "Bombardier" after the British heavyweight boxing champion. On 4 November he was charged with "Not digging the trench when ordered by the company officer" for which he got seven days Confined to Barracks, which was irrelevant. Lieutenant Warner recorded hearing a message from General Capper that reliefs were expected soon. The night was a very wet one and Royal Engineers came in the dark to drain the trenches. Lieutenant Saumarez recorded a few men being hit. At dawn on the 5th Lieutenant Warner went out with three men to hunt for a sniper, finding a rifle and firing point, but no sniper. By this time there were adequate dug-outs and as far as possible men went into them during shelling, ready to come out quickly if an infantry attack developed. Company Sergeant Major Edmund O'Connor, a former iron turner and the son of HJ O'Connor of Preston, who had been serving since 1905, was promoted and appointed only a week before he was hit by a shell and had his right leg broken that day. He never recovered and died at Norwich, aged twenty eight, on 5 April 1915. Lieutenant Saumarez noted "Sgt O Connor hit thigh by shell. Fired at point blank but not much damage except setting small farm alight. Scorching heat from shells overhead / several aeroplanes over us."

Relief

On 5 November, as Sir Douglas Haig had recommended and requested, Sir John French agreed that the 7th Division should be relieved to rest, refit and be quickly brought back up to strength as far as practicable. The first of two good reasons was that they were reaching the stage of no longer being capable of fighting. The second was that the infantry of the 6th Division to the south of Armentières had been in the front line in a very wet area continuously for over two weeks already, with minimal reserves, and needed to be replaced as soon as it could be arranged. This was to be the 7th Division's next destination, not that they would learn about it till the last moment before they went. At noon on the 5th there was a message that the 20th Brigade would be relieved at nightfall and leave the battlefield. It was not till eleven that it took place and they all marched away through the night.

Major Cator wrote another letter home, referring to the arrival of his younger brother Lieutenant Kit Cator with a draft of a hundred Scots Guardsmen. "Here we are still in the same spot, living very much the life of a rabbit i.e. underground all day and coming out in the night. I think we all feel pleased with ourselves – as our small force has driven off the repeated attacks of three German Army Corps, under the personal direction of the Kaiser – who meant having us if he possibly could – we have given them hell every time they have come up to us…old Kit arrived in the night, but I have not seen him yet, as they turned him and his men to dig about a mile back. He is to come on at 3.30pm this afternoon…We are in a large plantation, which has more the appearance of a very exaggerated stubble field than a wood, high explosive shells whiz in and fairly level everything. Another German attack had just begun, so I had to stop this letter, it is still going on but does not seem to be going to worry us much. A message has just come in to say we are to be relieved so I suppose tonight we shall be sent off to a safe place to refit, it will be a rest. The strain on the men who are left here has been very severe – they are wonderful chaps – and it's been awful at times when they have kept appealing for help, and there has been none to give them. Several times they have just hung on with a thin firing line and no reinforcements behind them. We are all right now as a French Army Corps has come up, but it's been anxious work."

Two days later Lieutenant Cator first wrote to his mother describing his arrival at half past one that afternoon at a station near Ypres. He had been in charge of a draft of four hundred men for four battalions of the 7th Division. They left Le Havre on 2 November, the officers travelling in 1st Class and the men in 2nd and 3rd Class carriages "in which they were very lucky, because as a rule the troops travel in converted cattle trucks. I am sorry to say that it is strictly forbidden to mention any places in our letters, and one has to be very careful what one says. On arrival at railhead we detrained and I marched the men off to an open space near the station where we waited for orders, and the men cooked some tea etc. raining heavily. All the time we could hear the thunder of Artillery all round us but some miles off. My orders never came so we got off about 5pm in the dark to try and find the division. It was drenching rain and after we had gone three miles we came to the town of ***** (which half the world have been talking about lately). There I managed to get some orders which were to put the men for that night in the town hall November 4th, and one of the Staff Officers took me off to Divisional Headquarters in a motor some four miles from the town. The Chief Staff Officer there told me I was to take the men into some trenches in a certain wood the next morning, and to be there by 7am and I should then get further orders. We then returned to the town and had a more or less exciting drive as the Germans shelled the road and the town at intervals through day and night. The men were most comfortable in the Town Hall sleeping on straw and fortunately no shell hit the place that night, so all was well. Some of the Staff gave me dinner and rum and I have never enjoyed a meal more, as I was pretty tired and I slept in a convent that night, and oddly enough I have slept each of the three nights that I have been at the front in Convents, which are delightful places, beautifully clean, and the beloved old sisters cannot do enough for me. Well we paraded the next morning November 5th at 5.30am and went off to the wood four miles, and not a single shell came on the road, and got the men in the trenches in the wood by 7am and went off to see the General whose headquarters were also in the wood. General Capper was too charming and walked up and down talking to me for ten minutes." This was the Herenthage Château Wood. He was quite surprised to find that his brother was commanding the Brigade and Captain Paynter the Battalion, but General Capper had "seemed delighted with Alby" and he soon saw that Captain Paynter was excellent.

"Well we then had to go through the wood and dig a line of supporting trenches between the Worcesters and the Gordons. Before we started one of the Staff Officers took us to see how they were dug. They are like long subterranean passages and all the men are underground when anywhere near the firing line to avoid as much as possible the intense shelling which goes on incessantly. We dug hard till 4pm except when German aircraft was sighted (which was continuously hovering over our line to give direction to the German guns) when three whistles are blown and every man in the line lies flat on his face perfectly still as it is then more difficult for the airmen to see you. We were right up against some of our own guns and the continuous din of our guns and the Germans was absolutely deafening, with rifle fire going off from the trenches in bursts. There was a continuous stream of wounded being carried and walking past us down to the field hospital on the road, poor chaps. That day and the one previous when we arrived I must have seen 2000 wounded and oddly enough it does not make me feel sick and one takes it all as a matter of course, though fearfully sorry for all the poor things. We had no shells burst very near to us but it is an unpleasant feeling having them flying round and overhead. They make a roar like 50 wild ducks would who were sweeping down into a place with wings spread." At the time he knew that the Battalion were about half a mile forward of where he was with his draft and understood that they were to go forward after dark. However, the order then came for the withdrawal of the Brigade and so, when the battalions gradually assembled on the Menin Road after dark, Lieutenant Cator took his men there. He told his mother "The men were completely dead beat and we had the most awful job to get them along. I have never been so tired in my life."

His draft had been up since half past five that morning and digging hard all day. At eleven at night the 1st Gordons of the 3rd Division relieved the 2nd Scots Guards, who left the First Battle of Ypres with further casualties since 27 October of four officers and one hundred and thirty six men. The 20th Brigade marched fifteen "extremely trying" miles through the night of 5 November, mostly over the pavé, via Ypres, where they turned southwest towards Dickebush and then on to that night's destination at Locre, behind Kemmel Hill. They passed artillery and wagons almost continuously, also going back to refit. On arriving at six next morning, they found "the whole village was filled with French troops and no billets were available. The Grenadiers were put up in the Church and Scots Guards into the Convent. The Gordon Hrs and Border Regiment had to bivouac in the open." In Lieutenant Saumarez' notebook was "Long nights march to Locre / shelled while passing through Ypres 2 shells in 12 bursts – lucky – men very done. Ride some of the way / billet /near church Locre /b[r]ead & coffee. Inhospitable host / men very crowded up / bad billets." He slept from six to eleven, then had breakfast, followed by a wash at midday. He observed again "host very unpleasant". During the afternoon the Brigade marched further southwest from Locre, the Scots Guards heading through Bailleul and on to Méteren, arriving five hours later, the others to villages nearby, where, for only a few days, they all stayed. Their Division were gradually withdrawn from the battle between 5 and 7 November.

On the 6th Major Cator wrote his next letter "Last night I slept between sheets and got my boots off which had been on since October 20th. I have had two bathes and feel as fit as a flea. I also slept from 8.30 last night till 8 this morning…When we got to the place we were told to billet, we found 20,000 French men, and no billets, so we asked the Padre to open his Church and got most of the men in there. Kit came and shared our food and blankets at a convent where there were some charming old Sisters. The Germans were shelling Ypres as we came through. Such a lovely old town built by Flemish weavers in 1400; an awful shame to shell it." Only occasionally a long range shell came anywhere near them, but "We have not heard a gun today. Crowds of French have been coming up for the last two days. They are not pleasant troops to be alongside of, they are too dirty, and never make any sanitary arrangements at all. You ask me for news of everyone. Many who are missing we know nothing about, they may be killed, missing or wounded. The hardest part about the fighting is the wounded. One is not allowed to have them taken out of the battle except by stretcher bearers. The fighting men are not allowed to go back, of course they do, but we are supposed to stop it." In the Brigade he was the senior officer and there were only three captains, Captain Paynter, Captain Guy Rasch of the Grenadiers and Captain Stephen Worrall of the Borders. A subaltern was commanding the Gordons. Captain Bruce was wounded towards the end and evacuated. He survived the War.

Major Cator had a visit that afternoon from Lieutenant General Sir William "Putty" Pulteney, a Scots Guards officer commanding III Corps, who sent a car in the evening to take him and Captain Paynter over to dinner at his headquarters. He ended his letter "Capper is a most splendid chap, the Germans would have been in Ypres but for him. He pushed everyone up against the Germans, leading them personally himself. The Scots Guards under George are wonderful, and have done most awfully well."

There was a roll call on 7 November at Méteren when among the missing was a young soldier called Lance Corporal John Bucknell. His father had been a Scots Guardsman and John Bucknell had been born at Victoria Barracks, Windsor. Aged just over fifteen when he enlisted as a boy soldier in 1911, he trained as a drummer and was with F Company when he was last seen, some three months short of his nineteenth birthday. William and Louisa Bucknell were by then at the Oxford Colliery Institute, Bolsover, Derbyshire. Private John Gibson from Dalton-in-Furness was another reservist called up in August. On 27 October he had sent Isaac and Hannah Gibson a field postcard to say that he was all right. So they were shocked to be notified that he had been killed between 20 and 26 October and wrote to Regimental Headquarters hoping that there was a mistake. If Private Gibson was alive on 27 October, soon afterwards he was not, but no one knew anything when he missed the 7 November roll call. Many could only be recorded as having been missing over quite a long period, with no one left able to say when they had last been seen or what had happened to them. Jeannie Thomson, whose husband was Lance Corporal Alexander Thomson, a reservist, was living with her two small daughters in Aberdeen. He was from Strichen originally, but had a job as an asylum attendant in Glasgow when he joined up in 1906, having previously bought himself out of the Gordons. When he enlisted he had a blue scar between his eyebrows and two tattoos, one of which, on his right forearm, was a full length figure of "a woman in kilts" and the other, on the back of his left forearm, consisted of a horseshoe, heart and "Lizzie" with a thistle on each side. He had worked as a clerk in the Battalion Pay Office and left in January 1914 after eight years service. He and Jeannie Anderson married in Auchterless in January 1910. Jeannie Thomson was told officially on 27 November that her husband had gone missing between 20 and 26 October, but, having received two field post cards from him dated 27 and 28 October, she asked for definite information. When this was investigated the Battalion reported that they believed that Corporal Thomson had been killed on or about 6 November. It had to have been before.

On 5 November Lieutenant Ross, the Quartermaster, wrote to Regimental Headquarters "to give you a few more details, which is strictly private as the information was got from the men, and may, or may not, be reliable." He knew the details of Captains Kinnaird's and Rivers Bulkeley's deaths and stated that Major Fraser had been killed "shot by a German officer, (Revolver) whilst rounding up German prisoners. He was buried but not by us, and the ground is now held by the enemy." He also knew correctly that Lieutenants Cottrell Dormer, Drummond and Gibbs were dead. "Those who are missing may be killed or wounded or prisoners; it is impossible to say." He continued that Colonel Bolton, Captain Fox and Lieutenant Steuart Menzies were seen in the trenches at Kruiseecke. He had no information on the other missing officers as "I cannot find any man who saw them." He went on "I pass the 1st Bn every evening on my way to the trenches, but have not got the nerve to ask their casualties. The less one knows the better it is."

Then "You would be surprised to know how cheerful the men are in the trenches." At Méteren Lieutenant Saumarez was pleased with the accommodation "good billets at Convent dormitory". Next day he noted a pay parade in conjunction with the roll call. They soon found that most men were very short of equipment, but new boots were issued and there was fresh meat and wine, as well as a large amount of mail. It was "very foggy." Then he wrote to Gunhild "Last night I slept in a BED. Think of it, the first one since Lyndhurst!! Our Brigade has been marched back here just out of shell range (I hope!!) to reorganise ourselves and we want a bit of reorganising I tell you! It seems quite a queer sensation not to be under shellfire as we have been in that state continuously for over a fortnight – and the reaction of it all is too much for me. We arrived here late last night dined like dukes slept like hogs and here we are reorganising and making nuisances of ourselves to everybody round us." Major Cator wrote "The morning was spent in reorganising the Battns, companies were equalised & commanders of platoons appointed. The rifles were thoroughly gone through & cleaned many of them having got into a very bad state in the trenches."

In a letter on Sunday 8 November Major Cator told his mother that the Brigade then had twenty officers and nine hundred men altogether. "Today we had a church service parade, there being no parson I officiated. I read them the 91st Psalm which old Cuthbert always used to read to the men on Sundays in S Africa. We sang "Onward Christian Soldiers" and "Jesu lover of my soul" finishing up with "God Save the King". I am always thinking of you all at home." The Catholics had gone to Méteren Church. In the same letter Major Cator told his mother that General Capper had been round to inspect them that day "and told me our Brigade was the best he had got and he is going to have the men on parade tomorrow to thank them and compliment them on the work they have done." Separately he told Violet that "My poor Belgian mare had to go to hospital as I got three bullets in her – the casualties among the horses have been very heavy…I think we have got all the Scots Guards casualties in up to date. The Grenadiers never will get in – all their staff were killed & the only thing we could do was to send the names of those who were present in…I hope they will have conscription…we want quite a million men over here to do any good it's uphill work always being so fearfully outnumbered…Later on perhaps you might be able to get out & see me, as I expect there will be lulls in the winter campaign."

In the morning on 8 November there was more tidying up, but also, Major Cator recorded, each battalion "did one hour's steady drill." In the afternoon the Brigade assembled in a hollow square and General Capper spoke to each battalion individually and then to the Brigade as a whole and "expressed his approval & admiration for the way in which they had fought round Ypres." The same day his brother wrote that "This war when one is up at the front does fairly open one's eyes. One sees so much horror – that you get to take no notice of it. I have not yet been in the front trenches, though we were digging some more on Thursday night in rear of the front line & were under fire most of the time – in fact you are always under fire anywhere within 5 miles of the firing line." Captain Paynter immediately impressed him, "d****d good he is too though ill I knows – but he won't own it."

Before they first reached Ypres the 7th Division had been continuously on the move since 12 October. They, along with the 3rd Cavalry Division, had been the first British troops to make contact with the Germans there and since 21 October had been fighting intensely on too wide a frontage, albeit one that was gradually reduced after, first, the 2nd Division arrived to take over the north and east sides of Polygon Wood and later the 1st Division took over from the Menin Road to Polygon Wood. The 7th Division's total casualties were three hundred and sixty four officers and nine thousand three hundred and two men, the worst of all the British divisions, after being the strongest at the start of the battle. Of the individual battalions the Gordons had had the fewest casualties, thirty officers and five hundred and thirty eight men, while the 1st Royal Welsh Fusiliers ["Welch" replacing "Welsh" after the War] had had the most, thirty seven officers and one thousand and twenty four men. Because of the Division's next task all available officers and men, either already at the Base camps in France or coming out from home as reinforcements for their regiments, were sent up to their battalions in villages to the west of Bailleul. These had to be completely reconstituted, as well as reequipped. For example, only three of them still had a single machine gun. Most of the men coming up as reinforcements were new to active service in France and there was no opportunity to prepare them. Apart from some recovered sick and wounded, they were predominantly either men who had just joined up and had had only eight to ten weeks basic training or veterans outside their reserve commitment, who had reenlisted. Sir Edward Hulse, fit again after being sent back sick from the trenches on the Aisne, had been at Le Havre waiting to return to the 1st Battalion. Now all available reinforcements in two drafts, who arrived on 11 and 12 November, fourteen officers, including him, and about five hundred and fifty men, went to the 2nd Scots Guards at Méteren. Their casualties had been twenty two officers and seven hundred and seventy four men, two thirds currently posted as missing. Sir Edward Hulse wrote "we are hard at it mixing up the "remains" with the two reinforcements in due proportion, and finding NCOs, etc. We are pretty short of the latter, and they are different from the fine lot I had under me before!" Among the new arrivals were 2nd Lieutenants Geoffrey Ottley, educated at Harrow, and Alan Swinton, at University College School, then in Gower Street, London, who knew each other's families well and had both been commissioned on 1 October after only completing one full term at Sandhurst and part of the next. Lieutenant Swinton told how a Boer War veteran in their draft had asked Captain Paynter whether he might grow a beard. He was turned down flat.

On 10 November Nina Campbell wrote from St Andrews to Elsie Swinton, Lieutenant Swinton's mother, in London, to sympathise with her about his going out to the BEF "God help us all; we are poor mothers! (<u>proud</u> mothers, as well, though!) to bear all that may come – the awful anxiety will be almost unbearable…Life seems a sort of nightmare just now – which, alas, we <u>don't make up</u>." The main topic of Lieutenant Saumarez' letters and cards to Gunhild from Méteren was the baby, preparations to be made and when to tell others, also thanking her for everything she had sent him. In a card on the 9th "Ever so many thanks for letter of the 2nd arrived today. Letters evidently take exactly a week to come. We are still here organising and getting fat. No news especially – heaps of thanks also for parcel with all sorts of good things. I hate acid drops! but luckily my new servant Sinclair a very good fellow is very fond of them. We all like plum puddings!"

On 10 November Major Cator told Violet that he "had a most disagreeable job this morning. I was president of a court of inquiry on a Commanding Officer who had bolted out of action. I suppose he will now be tried by court martial & either be shot or cashiered." Next day a Field General Court Martial heard a charge of cowardice against Corporal Carl Rosenthal from Upper Parkstone, Dorset, who had been in the 2nd Scots Guards for three and a half years. What occurred was not recorded afterwards but he was convicted and sentenced to be reduced to the ranks and to undergo two months FP No 2. Over the course of time he redeemed himself completely, surviving the War.

Writing to his mother again on the 13th Major Cator described Sir John French's visit when he "was very pleased with the work the Brigade had done and went round and saw them in their billets, to thank them personally. I had lunch with him. He is full of confidence, and said he thought the Germans had really made their supreme effort and failed. Ypres is the one place they were bent on having. It is still ours, although it has cost thousands of our men. He said the German casualties had been simply terrific. We are off again tomorrow, but where we do not know. Gen Heyworth is coming out to take command of this Brigade, I shall be very sorry to give it up…Kit is very flourishing, and has got Capt Romer in command of his Company, who I think will not last long, as he gets bad rheumatics." Speaking to soldiers was something that Sir John French was very good at and he was going round throughout the BEF. Continuing the letter to his mother "Yesterday, I had a grand view of the battle from the top of a very big hill near here, and one could see it going on in one continuous line for miles. All the towns were on fire, and every house. It was a grand sight, but truly awful. It is simply extraordinary, but every house one comes across in Belgium has shellholes in it, and most are reduced to powder. Poor wretched Nation. I don't see how she will ever get over it." He knew about the Prussian Guards attack on 11 November, which had "gained some ground in places, but were repulsed." He knew also that General FitzClarence, commanding the 1st (Guards) Brigade, had been killed and he had heard that that Brigade only had four officers and four hundred men left "but I don't know if it is true."

Lieutenant Cator also wrote to their mother that day, telling her about the two large drafts that had arrived, so that they now had twenty two officers and about eleven hundred men. The Grenadiers had also been heavily reinforced but the other two battalions, though they had received drafts, were still short. Captain Romer had now joined them "but poor chap he should never have come out as he has lately had rheumatic fever badly, and he is far from right now and it is quite impossible for him to go into the trenches now with all this cold weather which seems to be settling in." Captain Paynter had sorted this problem by leaving Captain Romer nominally in command of G Company, while also appointing him Transport Officer, but putting Lieutenant Cator in executive command, which got round the problem that there were other officers senior to him.

Lieutenant Swinton wrote home on 13 November and listed what he would like sent out "50 cigs, Isherwoods if possible, ¼ pound of tobacco, these only once a fortnight. Once a week two boxes of matches, one box of beef tea lozenges, any amount of choc of all kinds, socks and underclothes once a fortnight. A tinned plum pudding or cake is very acceptable to the men, as we pool all our goods. Also you might send me a small gunmetal cig. Case. I have got an entire man's equipment, which I shall wear when we do any fighting. We can hear the guns at intervals by day and night…Another thing we want badly here is papers, illustrated and otherwise. The papers do publish such rot, that it is interesting to read them. This is a typical example, the papers say "Great Allied Victory, Great Results", the real thing being a German advance of five miles…Two more things I want, a chamois leather waistcoat and a pair of pants to match."

Though not published in the London Gazette until some time later, there were five DCMs, in addition to Private Finlayson's. One was to Private Peter Burns from Edinburgh, an electro plater before he enlisted. He was a signaller and his citation mentioned particularly his mending of telephone wires several times while under fire. He was killed on 1 November and his medal was sent to his father in the 4th Royal Scots. A second recipient was Private Alexander Clark, a London reservist, whose mother lived in Hackney. He was also a signaller and his citation was for gallantry in conveying messages under fire. He later joined the Guards Division Signal Company on formation, was wounded and then gassed at Loos the following autumn and discharged. The third was Private Hugh Russell, originally from Inverkeithing, Fife, where his father worked in the shipyard, but whose wife Florence was living at Stoke Heath, near Coventry. His citation was identical to Private Clark's. He survived unhurt until 28 September 1915 when he was badly wounded in the trenches on Hill 70 at Loos and discharged a few months later. The fourth was, yet again, involved in repairing telephone wire and carrying a message under heavy fire. This was Private George Urquhart from Inverness, formerly a lithographer, a regular soldier up and down the ranks before the War, but up them continuously after it started. He became a Sergeant at the end of May 1915, married his wife Elizabeth in December that year in Inverness and in June 1916 was badly wounded in the chest and left armpit in the Ypres Salient. He returned to France at the end of March 1918 and was appointed Company Sergeant

Major a month later. The Spanish Flu epidemic laid him low for a month after the Armistice but he served on, eventually leaving the Army in 1929. Unlike the other four citations which all mentioned Kruiseecke, the fifth did not but instead read "For gallantry and resource under fire during operations before Ypres". The recipient was Lance Corporal Alexander Mavor from Aberdeen, a labourer when he enlisted at Caterham in 1909. Unwounded throughout, though gassed once, but otherwise with the Battalion all the time, he became Company Sergeant Major of Right Flank in 1916 and in 1918 won a second DCM, one of only two Scots Guardsmen to do so, and also became a Drill Sergeant. He finally left the Army in 1931. DSOs were awarded to Captain Paynter and to Captain Fox, his being for escorting back the German prisoners of war, no easy matter in the dark with the number of men available to him. It would appear from Colonel Bolton's later statement that Captain Fox was at pains to make clear that it was because of Lord Dalrymple that the Germans were captured in the first place and Lord Dalrymple, by then Earl of Stair, was awarded a DSO in 1920.

It was after Sir John French's visit on 13 November that new orders came to move off next day to trenches in the neighbourhood of Fleurbaix, south of Armentières. Major Cator gave no indication of having known earlier. The 20th Brigade were to replace the 19th Brigade of the 6th Division in the line immediately.

Note on Chapter Sources

History of the Great War based on Official Documents by direction of the Historical Section of the Committee of Imperial Defence.
Brig Gen Sir JE Edmonds, *Military Operations France and Belgium, 1914:* Volume II: *Antwerp, La Bassée, Armentières, Messines, and Ypres, October-November 1914* (London: Macmillan and Co Ltd 1925).
CT Atkinson, *The Seventh Division 1914-1918* (London: John Murray 1927) for background, including final casualty figures.
Letters of Capt The Master of Kinnaird and letters about him and F Company at Polygon Wood, Kinnaird Papers, Private Collection.
Letters of Maj ABE Cator and other documents and Letters of Lt CH Cator, Cator Papers, Private Collection.
War Diaries: 20th Infantry Brigade (written by Maj Cator) TNA/WO95/1650, 1st Grenadier Guards TNA/WO95/1657/2, 2nd Scots Guards TNA/WO95/1657/3, 2nd Bedfordshire Regiment WO 95/1658/2, 2nd Yorkshire Regiment WO95/1659/4, 2nd Border Regiment TNA/WO95/1655/1, 2nd Worcestershire Regiment TNA/WO95/1351/1, 2nd Wiltshire Regiment TNA/WO 95/1659/3 and 2nd Gordon Highlanders WO 95/1656/2.
Diary of Capt KH Bruce, Gordon Highlanders, IWM/Documents 12125.
Diary of Maj ECT Warner, Private Collection.
Col ECT Warner, 'Kruiseecke, October 25th-26th 1914', Winter Number 1931-32, *Household Brigade Magazine*.
Account of Sgt J Burke escape, SGA.
Col HC Wylly, *The Border Regiment in the Great War* (Aldershot: Gale & Polden Ltd 1924).
Col NCE Kenrick, *The Wiltshire Regiment* (Aldershot: Gale & Polden Ltd 1963).
Capt H FitzM Stacke, *The Worcestershire Regiment in the Great War* (Kidderminster: GT Cheshire & Sons Ltd 1928).

Quotations by unnamed officer on 25 October and by Capt GCB Paynter, Wilfrid Ewart, F Loraine Petre, Cecil Lowther (Eds), *The Scots Guards in the Great War 1914-1918* (London: John Murray 1925).

Lt Col RG Bolton report after release from captivity in 1918, Maj The Lord Dalrymple report in a POW camp, smuggled when sent for internment in Switzerland, and Captain Fox report after his escape, War Diary 2nd Scots Guards.

Lt J StV B Saumarez (a) account of Kruiseecke, Liddle/WW1/GS/0454, (b) letters to and from his wife, her notes and his war notebook, Saumarez Papers, Private Collection, and (c) letters to him and to his wife from Scots Guards officers and men, Suffolk Record Office, Ipswich, as part of HA93/SA/3/1/27.

Letters of Lt AHC Swinton, other material and documents and all other letters to or from the Swinton family, Swinton Papers, Private Collection. Also three articles, SGM 1957, 1958 and 1970.

Copy letter of Lt TA Ross about casualties, Cuthbert Papers.

5

The First Battle of Ypres – 1st Battalion

On arriving at Hazebrouck on 18 October the 1st Scots Guards went into billets nearby. Corporal Green and Right Flank were in a farm on the edge of the town, some two miles away, but could get plenty of bread, jam, eggs, butter and wine there. The day after was very quiet and each section was allowed to send one man into the town. On the 20th their Brigade marched twelve miles to Poperinghe, saw many refugees going the other way and got in after dark for a quiet, undisturbed night. Private Luck was in "an excellent billet that night in a convent. The room in which my section was, was lovely, having some beautiful figures of the Crucifix. At this billet we received a mail, our luck was in; my word parcels by the dozen. As for myself I was particularly lucky as I had a parcel from the Men's Club Cross-in-Hand." Corporal Green, in probably the same convent, mentioned that socks and "smokes" had been issued.

The Battle of Langemarck

On the 21st I Corps took over from the French northeast of Ypres, from near Zonnebeke through St Julien, Langemarck and Bixschoote to the Ypres-Yser Canal at Steenstraat. The 2nd Division held from Zonnebeke, with the 22nd Brigade of the 7th Division next to them on their right, across to Langemarck and the 1st Division from Langemarck to Steenstraat. The 1st (Guards) Brigade marched out of Poperinghe at half past five that morning, taking the most direct route through Elverdinghe to cross the Canal at Boesinghe. They realised, as Private Luck remembered, that the sound of the guns meant getting closer to the action. At some point along the same road that led on through Pilckem and then to Langemarck Battalion Headquarters and two companies turned off northwards to the extreme left of the new British line, from just south of Bixschoote across to Steenstraat. There they found a brigade of French Territorials, as well as "several regiments of Cuirassiers", French heavy cavalry, still wearing ceremonial helmets and breastplates which, as the Camerons noted, were showing signs of rust. Meanwhile B Company and Left Flank were sent forward from Pilckem to north of Langemarck to help cover the withdrawing 1st Gloucestershire Regiment of the 3rd Brigade around Koekuit, Private Luck commenting that the Gloucesters "had suffered considerably from shrapnel fire and were now threatened with an attack from the German Infantry." After dark both companies rejoined by marching along the Langemarck–Bixschoote road.

At Koekuit four Scots Guardsmen were killed and five wounded. Private Osborne was in the thick of the fighting "21 Oct. ... My God, what a battle! All the fighting is done in the open.

The noise is deafening. You must shout in the next man's ear to make yourself heard… We lost a lot of men, amongst whom was my friend Jack Frampton. I saw a Captain staggering about, at first I thought he had had a good swig of rum, but when he turned his face towards me I saw that he was blind. A bullet had struck him sideways and pierced both eyes. I do not know to which Regiment he belonged – most likely the Gloucesters. A sergeant of ours who had his jaw shattered led the officer away to the dressing station." Lance Corporal Jack Frampton was originally from Sandown on the Isle of Wight and a gardener on enlisting at Portsmouth in 1904. He served three years, was called up on mobilization and had already been slightly wounded on 7 October on the Aisne. His wife Clara was living in Edgware, North London, and wrote on the receipt for the Princess Mary's Christmas Gift sent to her "Thank you for which I shall prise for my Husband sake." Another, also a reservist, was Lance Sergeant James Carnighan, a Liverpudlian by birth and a general labourer who enlisted at Hereford, also in 1904, and served eight years. Margaret Carnighan was living with their three children in Pimlico, London. The third was Private James Murray, a soldier for a year and once a vanman in Glasgow, where his brother Daniel Murray lived in the Gallowgate. Private Michael Screeney, former farm worker from Foxford, County Mayo, was the fourth. He had been serving for almost a year longer than Private Murray, but it took some time after he joined before anybody discovered that he was an absentee from the Connaught Rangers. For that he got fifty six days detention for fraudulent enlistment, but remained with the Scots Guards. His mother Margaret Slurkin in Middlesbrough received personal effects consisting of postcards, a purse and an identity disc. Private Edward Page, a former Cockney labourer who completed three years with the Colours at the end of January, only to be called up from the Reserve, was very badly wounded in the stomach and died next day in a field ambulance. He had been removed from the Battalion towards the end of the Retreat from Mons when he developed gonorrhoea and was away for three weeks. Only an identity disc reached Edward and Alice Page at their home in Bow. Private William Clark, the son of William and Elizabeth Clark of Gorgie, Edinburgh, was a railwayman until he enlisted in August 1902, served for three years and was therefore close to the expiry of his reserve commitment when mobilised. On 21 October he was severely wounded in the back and died at Boulogne on the afternoon of 8 November. He married Helen Mason in Edinburgh in 1908 and they had two daughters and a son, who, born in April 1914, only survived his father by two weeks. Helen Clark received her husband's possessions of one farthing, a silver ring, a matchbox, a shoulder knot with regimental numerals, a letter, his identity disc and a French dictionary.

The Camerons were to the right of the Scots Guards near Bixschoote, but initially there was a gap, not sorted out until General FitzClarence went that night with one of the Camerons company commanders, Major George Sorel Cameron, to make sure there was proper liaison. Behind where the Camerons first dug in, facing roughly east, a minor road crossed the Langemarck-Bixschoote road and an inn, the Kortekeer Cabaret, stood at the junction. This was their Battalion Headquarters. Beyond their right, however, there was a gap of about three quarters of a mile without any British troops at all until the Coldstream immediately west of Langemarck. The Black Watch were in reserve south of the road, roughly in line with the gap, but half a mile back from it. German attacks were likely to form up from the Staden direction and under cover of the Forest of Houthulst to the northeast, but, quite apart from that, because of folds in the ground and woodland there was plenty of other cover and the Germans were already in most of Bixschoote. The Camerons watched and protected the likely approaches over two streams between the Forest and their main positions. As the afternoon wore on there was more enemy harassing fire and they and some French Territorials with them also took casualties from French guns firing short. During the night they saw some enemy movement, including patrols, but there was nothing significant until after dawn on the 22nd. Then the main force of French Territorials, still on the left at Steenstraat, moved across the front of the Scots Guards and attacked the Germans in Bixschoote, unsuccessfully, and withdrew afterwards to the west bank of the Canal. Lieutenant Lawson, Sir Edward Hulse's cousin and Corporal Green's platoon commander, tried to direct the French and was killed by a sniper.

The Scots Guards were having a fairly quiet time. At one stage Captain Stracey and C Company were supporting the Camerons and then later supporting a counterattack at the Kortekeer Cabaret by the 2nd Brigade at six in the morning of the 23rd. There was only a single German attack on the Scots Guards, at one that afternoon, which they drove off with heavy losses. Corporal Green mentioned digging trenches on the 22nd, then being held up by fighting going on in front, presumably the unsuccessful French attack on Bixschoote, then a move leftwards and more digging. The day after that they moved into still deeper trenches and there was more enemy artillery fire. He wrote of very heavy fighting on the 24th. Generally it was a period of incoming shellfire and a lot of sniping, mingled with persistent apprehension that they were or might very soon become cut off from the rest of the Brigade because, to their right, matters were much more serious. Private Osborne wrote on the 22nd that "between the Germans and ourselves is an Inn, a solitary guesthouse…The possession of which is costing thousands of lives. German and British. This is no exaggeration: it is a plain statement of fact."

For the Camerons the fighting began at about nine that morning, from when German infantry attacks closed in, increased in numbers and intensity and were conducted quite imperviously to losses. Later on, to great effect to begin with, a Black Watch machine gun was carried up and installed in the upper storey of a derelict windmill on the roadside just to the east. However, because of the pressure, the Camerons had to give ground and were forced back to the south of the road, including having to abandon the Inn. At half past four that afternoon three enemy battalions attacked their left from the north with two colours flying, a band playing and all their soldiers singing. These, from German reserve divisions, had some regular soldiers, but predominantly consisted of out of time reservists, reservists and newly joined men, ill equipped, with varying levels of individual military training and almost none together in their companies.

Earlier in the afternoon a mass of Germans had poured through the gap between their right and the Coldstream left. As the light began to fail an ammunition resupply reached the windmill, still in the Camerons' hands, together with the welcome news that the Black Watch were counterattacking the gap. This succeeded and from the windmill the Camerons could see the enemy withdrawing across the road by the light of a burning farmhouse. In the subsequent confusion and not knowing where anyone else was, Major Sorel Cameron, four other officers and seventy five men of the Camerons set out down the road to join the Coldstream, successfully. There they stayed for the next two days. The remainder of the Camerons joined up and formed a trench line in front of a farm some three hundred yards southeast of the inn. More troops came up during the night, so that at dawn on the 23rd the British line was significantly reinforced by 2nd and 3rd Brigade battalions. During the morning there was a sharp and successful British counterattack, which recovered much of the old line, while the 1st Queen's recaptured the Inn, took many prisoners and recovered several wounded Camerons. There were enormous numbers of German dead, whose equipment lay all around, with here and there a body in a Cameron kilt. However, the Germans were only routed temporarily and, because of their subsequent sniping and ever increasing shelling, it was decided to consolidate again at dusk to the south of the road, the Camerons going back into their trench line at the farm. On the 24th they got some respite as the Queen's took over the firing line but "Nobody had washed since leaving Hazebrouck on the 20th, and there was no chance yet to break the spell. Meals, too, were difficult of attainment, as the mess cart had been temporarily in the hands of the Germans at the inn, and officers could be seen sitting behind a haystack eating fids of meat with their fingers. The men were disposed in ditches and what cover could be found: they were all dead tired and preferred sleep to safety."

By nightfall on the 24th the Camerons had lost three officers dead and eleven wounded and approximately seventy six men dead or fatally injured, plus forty seven more wounded. Among those who died of wounds was Lieutenant George Chisnall RAMC, the second doctor to lose his life with them in a month. Others were missing, among them Lance Corporal Richard Law, who was captured. "The evening I was taken prisoner at Langemarck about 8pm I saw to the left of a farm near the crossroads, where there were some haystacks on fire, the German troops throwing our men into the burning haystacks. I could see the men who were being thrown into the fire wore kilts; I could plainly see the kilt as they were being swung into the fire. I am not sure whether they were dead or not." He listed the names of four other Camerons, all prisoners at Göttingen, Saxony, who could confirm this. The Scots Guards had an officer killed and another wounded, eight men killed and twenty five wounded, including those at Koekuit, and five more missing. Private Roderick McDonald was wounded dangerously on the 24th, with a bullet in his stomach, and died of wounds in Ypres. He was born near Dingwall, Easter Ross, and had been a farm worker. After serving three years he left in 1906 for the Reserve, with an accumulated disciplinary record long and varied, and apparently went back to the land. He left no next of kin and a letter addressed to "Miss Mary McDonald, Strathpeffer", believed to be his sister, to tell her of his death, came back undelivered. Private William Kennett, born in Chicago, Illinois, where his father still was, and a plumber's mate on enlisting in Brighton in 1904, had been a reservist for two years. On 24 October he was severely wounded in the right thigh and died three days afterwards in Boulogne. He married Beatrice Wilson in London in November 1910 and she was in Deptford with their son and daughter. An identity disc and her husband's prayer book were all that were recovered.

One issue was becoming ever more stark. On 24 October Sir John French wrote, far from the only telegram which he sent on the subject, to Lord Kitchener to the effect that the BEF would have to fight without artillery unless there was a more constant supply of ammunition. The response requested him to see that economy was practised. The BEF only had one hundred and fifty rounds per gun still in reserve, unissued to the ammunition parks in the field. The rate of resupply from across the Channel was no more than seven rounds per gun per day. The effect on the capacity of the British infantry and dismounted cavalrymen to defend their positions, when already very stretched for numbers, was very serious. Despite this Sir John French still thought that offensive operations were going to deliver results. As it was becoming apparent that the 7th Division would not be able to do this on their own on the east side of the Gheluvelt Plateau, he decided to redeploy I Corps to take over on the north side of the Menin Road, provided that French troops replaced them between Zonnebeke and the Canal. This was arranged with General Joffre for after dark on the 24th. It proved to be a long drawn out affair for the 1st Division, assisted neither by the early disappearance of the more senior French officers taking over from them, nor by the fact that the French commander "had to be fetched from his bed in Chateau Boesinghe at 1am in the morning before anything could be accomplished."

The Coldstream experience, as Captain St Andrew Warde-Aldam described it, was typical. Very soon after dark a message reached him that the French were to relieve them. He stopped his company from working on their fire trenches and put them to getting their kit and ammunition together. Then, as he was setting off to Battalion Headquarters for further orders, the Germans opened up with their heaviest yet rapid rifle fire, machine guns and artillery and there was just time to dive into a trench. "I made all the men keep down, except one to watch but they all wanted to stand up and shoot." The fire died down and nothing more happened so he went back for orders. "It was about 7.30 and the French 73rd Regiment (Territorial) had arrived: at least a battalion, 1100 strong, had arrived some distance in the rear, where it had halted: somehow it had lost all its officers, except the Commandant and one other: Granville had met the battalion and brought the Commandant to our Headquarters. When I arrived, the latter was shrugging his shoulders and explaining to Leslie that he had no idea that the fire was so bad; that his men had never been under fire and that he did not feel justified in relieving us until he had informed his Colonel of the situation, Leslie was extremely polite, said he quite understood, and that we would wait until he had seen his Colonel, so off he went accompanied by Granville. We expected them back in an hour, but they did not get back till 10, when the Commandant shrugged his shoulders more than ever and was more than ever profuse in his polite apologies, but the long and short of it was, he did not intend to go into the trenches." The Commandant went off, again accompanied by Lieutenant Granville Smith, the Machine Gun Officer, and the Coldstream prepared themselves for another twenty four hours where they were. However, at half past two in the morning word came that the relief would take place after all, so they packed up and prepared to move. When Captain Warde-Aldam then returned to Battalion Headquarters "It appeared, though I cannot guarantee the truth of the story, that Granville had told the one lie of his life, having informed the French that he was a special messenger from Lord Kitchener and that Kitchener would take away the whole Expeditionary Force, if the French did not relieve us. Anyway, there was the Commandant and, shortly afterwards, the Colonel himself arrived: somehow Granville was responsible for this." However, that was not the end of it. More French officers had to be found and their companies brought up and allotted to companies of the Coldstream, Camerons and Gloucesters. As they waited "It was a curious scene, the kitchen of this small farm, dimly lighted by two candles. Every crack was carefully covered so that no light should be shown: whenever anyone entered, he was only allowed to half open the door and to slip hurriedly in. There was a big kitchen table, on which were the remains of a meal: at one end sat Leslie, patient but anxious, occasionally talking to the Colonel: opposite was the Commandant, his elbows on the table, his face buried in his hands." Officers, mostly Coldstreamers, but including Captain Archibald McLeod of the Gloucesters and Major Sorel Cameron, sat waiting. Captain Sir Gordon Hargreaves Brown, Bt, was sound asleep in a hard kitchen chair with his head hanging over the back. Four orderlies slept on the floor in the corner, but often one or two were away taking messages, while "the party was completed by a fox terrier, which had been left in the farm and which Geoffrey had befriended. Just before we had all collected in this kitchen, a high explosive shell had burst over the barn on the other side of the farmyard, where the men of the Headquarters' section were, and had wounded several, two of whom were now dying: occasionally we could hear a scream." Major The Honourable Leslie Hamilton had been commanding since Colonel Ponsonby was wounded, Sir Gordon Hargreaves Brown commanded No 1 Company and Lieutenant Geoffrey Campbell was Adjutant.

When the French soldiers did start to appear there were delays whenever the Germans opened fire. Captain Warde-Aldam became increasingly worried that his company would not be relieved before daylight. As the ground behind was completely open, all movement would then become impossible. "I got hold of a French NCO and made him, and the French on the right, follow me, and told an English machine gunner to keep passing along until he had counted 150. I then rushed along the line of trenches, saying "suivez, suivez" and putting them into my trenches, as fast as my men could evacuate them." He found that the French soldiers themselves, from Brittany, immediately did exactly what he told them and showed complete confidence in him, but he was apprehensive for them. "I do not think that they had any tools and they had only 88 rounds of ammunition per man. I saw no reserve ammunition nor rations." The French NCO was disappointed that none of the Coldstream were going to stay to help them. "I found the Company ready to march off. We started at once, across country to Pilckem, followed by the remains of Battalion Headquarters and two goats from the farm. It was now practically daylight. The Germans were dropping high explosive shells near the railway, but none fell near us. The Battalion assembled on the road where we had halted so long three days before. We were kept there some time as the relief of the Gloucesters had not been finished, and we were told we might have to go back and help them." This railway from Ypres went north to Boesinghe, crossed the Canal there and ran on northeast past Pilckem and Langemarck to Staden. When the Coldstream heard that the Gloucesters had moved by a different road they marched on, going south through St Jean, where they saw an accidentally crashed British plane, and reached Zillebeke, southeast of Ypres, about ten o'clock.

The Scots Guards had had an easier time getting away. Corporal Green noted "At 7pm the French took over our position, and we retired to Pillein [Pilckem]." Next day "The enemy during last night, made three very desperate attempts to force their way through our line…I have never heard such a fusillade of bullets as while I lay the whole night on that hard road." Sergeant John Macdonald of C Company had been a clerk before he enlisted in Stockport in 1903, but had some family link with Forfar, Angus. He recorded that they marched through St Jean around daybreak en route for Zillebeke, where they arrived at about eleven and "got rations, post and had a decent wash and shave, also a long sleep." Corporal Green was "billeted in a brick field. A big mailbag arrived, and was distributed. Two days rations issued." The rest of the Brigade were at Zillebeke, but they had gone on to Klein Zillebeke, further southeast.

The Advance to Gheluvelt on 26 October

Sir John French had now put the 7th Division under the command of I Corps and Sir Douglas Haig began rearranging them. The 22nd Brigade had already been relieved by the 4th (Guards) Brigade in Polygon Wood, but the heaviest German pressure was currently along and to the south of the Menin Road and was becoming too much for the 20th Brigade, where they were soon to fail to hold Kruiseecke. On 26 October the 1st (Guards) Brigade were told to go up the Menin Road as far as Veldhoek, two kilometres west of Gheluvelt, as the Corps Reserve. They left with the Coldstream leading, followed by the Scots Guards, Black Watch, Camerons and 26th Brigade RFA. By the time they reached Veldhoek, Sir Douglas Haig's latest orders for them had reached General FitzClarence as the 4th (Guards) Brigade were preparing to attack Reutel.

These were to move forward in the general direction of Poezelhoek alongside the 4th (Guards) Brigade. In orders issued at 8.20am General FitzClarence detailed the Coldstream to advance behind the right of the Scots Guards with the woods south of Poezelhoek and the Gheluvelt Crossroads-Becelaere road as their objective and the Scots Guards to advance with Poezelhoek and German trenches in front of it as their objective. There was nothing to suggest that anyone had a clear idea of where the enemy were, while knowledge of the whereabouts of the British infantry in front was sketchy at best. The 21st Brigade of the 7th Division were still responsible for the line from the Gheluvelt Crossroads up to the southeast corner of Polygon Wood. So, as the Coldstream and Scots Guards advanced, there were, dug in somewhere in front of them, on the right the 2nd Yorkshires at and to the north of the Gheluvelt Crossroads, in the centre the 2nd Bedfords, forward of Gheluvelt Château, and on the left, short of Poezelhoek, which the Germans had taken from one of their companies three days before, the 2nd Royal Scots Fusiliers. The day's operations would lead to the 1st (Guards) Brigade taking over all of this line. In the orders the 57th (Howitzer) Battery RFA were to support the Coldstream and Scots Guards and the 26th Brigade RFA to be ready to act as instructed including sending up individual gun teams as required. None of the subsequent individual accounts mentioned any artillery support. Sergeant Shepherd described their being billeted at Klein Zillebeke on the 25th and leaving very early next day to join the rest of the Brigade. Then they went by the "secondary road from Zillebeke to Menin-Ypres road just west of 3km milestone & then along road towards Gheluvelt (passed Tam Ross & Jimmy Moncur of 2nd Battn at roadside) until just W of Xrds at Veldhoek when Bde went into wood on right of road here we received our orders for attack." Those he mentioned were the Quartermaster and Sergeant Major of their 2nd Battalion.

What the Coldstream on the right and the Scots Guards on the left had to do was an advance to contact. Lieutenant Gerald Jolliffe of Right Flank remembered that there was neither reconnaissance by officers nor contact with the 2nd Bedfords beforehand. He had no recollection of any gunner officer with the Battalion. The objective was the "clearly visible" hamlet of Poezelhoek and, Sergeant Shepherd went on, the advance was over "the open country between the woods surrounding Gheluvelt chateau on the Right & those surrounding Polderhoek chateau on the Left." Although there had been one or two incoming shells, the Germans, who, Sergeant Shepherd thought, must have been able to see them long before, did not open heavy fire with rifles, machine guns and field artillery until they were level with Gheluvelt Château. From then on "the advance was continued in rushes by sections, & latterly by individuals, until within 200 yds of the German position." After that "A message was sent back to Bde HQ (about 11am) asking for more artillery support & saying attack held up. Only answer received was about an hour later saying to hang on to position gained." He stated that the line of trenches they subsequently formed during that night was back slightly from the furthest point reached and that he thought that the enemy firing line was west of Poezelhoek.

Corporal Green said little, but noted that Private Kennedy and Drummer Bradford were killed by a shell. Private Harold "Ginger" Kennedy had been in the Battalion since 1909. Originally from Inverness, where his father lived at Muirtown, he was something of a character. While described in a September 1913 report as "A hard working, honest and trustworthy man. Clean & smart" less than a month later he had a conduct sheet entry for "Improper conduct in Birdcage Walk about 1.15am (indecent conduct in the streets)" for which he received eight days confined to barracks. He was slightly flat footed. It was also recorded that he had five teeth removed at Aldershot in February 1912 at Government expense of nine shillings, followed in

July 1913 by the extraction of a further five with gas at a cost of twelve shillings and sixpence. Drummer Frederick Bradford joined as a five foot tall boy soldier, aged fourteen, at Lichfield in 1909. John and Sarah Bradford lived in Sutton Coldfield, Warwickshire. On the same date in September 1913 as they had reported on Private Kennedy, the same officers described Private Bradford as "A very good hard working honest sober & reliable man. A good shoemaker. Very clean & smart." Sadly, though there was no doubt about his death, his brother heard that a sergeant in the 1st Scots Guards had seen him on 30 October. This led to a letter on 1 February 1915 from his father, Sergeant John Bradford of the 8th South Staffords, asking for confirmation that his son was now a prisoner, which he was not. In March 1908 Private James Dobson joined up in Edinburgh and had been serving since then. Before that he was a cellarman for six years at the Fountain Brewery, working for William McEwan & Co Ltd. On the front of his left forearm he had a tattoo of a sailor's bust and on the back of it clasped hands and a heart. On 26 October he was hit in the forehead and badly wounded, dying two days later in an ambulance train to the coast. The family lived in Musselburgh and his mother Joan Dobson was still there, but his father William Dobson may have been dead by this time. Private Dobson's effects consisted of an identity disc, a letter and a stamp case.

Sir Iain Colquhoun was now first mentioned by an eye witness, Sergeant Macdonald, who began his account of the day with "Off at 4am in the direction of Gheluvelt where we passed lot of prisoners taken by 2 Scots Guards. We halted by the road leading into Gheluvelt where it was very woody, from about 6am to 9am." C Company, having crossed over it, followed Left Flank up the line of the tramway, Gheluvelt Church being off to their right. The Ypres tramway ran beside the Menin Road to west of Gheluvelt and then diverged towards Becelaere. "My Platoon No 9 was last over, we were getting shelled very heavily – then down through some gardens with a pond at the back of the Chateau where there were a lot of Bedfords dug in all over the place. We went on to the further hedge, East, I think, of the Chateau. LF bore to the left and C settled down behind that hedge, where the Bedfords had been. We were overlooking a road running N to Becelaere, Sir I Colquhoun with No 10 went on down the slope and took over a trench that was almost on the above road on his right were a haystack and a large wood. RF and B were I believe, in front of that wood and to the right." His platoon were probably on the slight rise in the ground on the south side of a stream, the Scherriabeck, with to his right, on the far side of the tramline, the pond north of Gheluvelt Château. The large wood he mentioned was Poezelhoek Wood, well away from the hamlet itself, to the south of the Gheluvelt-Becelaere side road. Though moved at one stage to some farm buildings to their right, Sergeant Macdonald and his men were later sent back to their first position. There was shelling and machine gun fire for the rest of the day. When darkness fell he was told to move forward to join Sir Iain Colquhoun's platoon and return to his daytime trench before dawn. His mention of the 2nd Bedfords being dug in around Gheluvelt Château was in line with Sergeant Shepherd's sketch map, which showed their firing line between the northwest of the Château grounds and the southeast corner of Polderhoek Wood, but some were further forward on the right.

Sir Victor Mackenzie wrote of the Bedfords how "We attacked over ground already occupied by them. I don't think anybody knew they were there." He was now with Left Flank who had to advance with their left exposed and unsupported, there being no link with the 4th (Guards) Brigade in Polygon Wood, and, when enfilade fire came at them, presumably from north of Poezelhoek, they lost direction. Captain Cecil Pryce Hamilton, the company commander, sent a message to Battalion Headquarters that he and twelve men were one hundred and fifty yards from the German trenches at the hamlet. Soon after that he was very badly wounded and, though successfully evacuated, died next day in Ypres. A Boer War veteran, he joined the Scots Guards from the Militia in 1901. He and his wife Iris had lived in London, just off Piccadilly.

Private Osborne described how "Captain Balfour, who was near me, said he thought we were too far advanced, and that we were almost surrounded. Losses on both sides were staggering. During one of the attacks I saw one of our fellows (Charles Burtenshaw) make a right lunge at a big German's throat, and as the bayonet was entering the fellow's neck, Charles, to make sure of his man, shot him – as a sort of makeweight." When asked later, while they were resting, why he had done it Lance Corporal Burtenshaw could not remember anything at all. Private Osborne commented that, ordinarily, he had "a gentle disposition". Corporal Burtenshaw was another reservist, a carman until 1906 when he enlisted in Brighton, whose mother lived at Ardingly, Sussex. Right Flank and B Company, south of the tramway, found themselves on their own in a very sharp salient.

When Private Richard Lumb, born in Burley in Wharfedale, Yorkshire, and a boilermaker before enlisting, left at the end of his three years service with the Colours in 1913 an officer wrote that he "Could not recommend this man for civil employment". Whether that affected Private Lumb's prospects was unknown, but he returned on mobilization, was seriously wounded in the jaw and arm on the 26th and quickly sent back to England. His younger brother Private Fred Lumb, who had joined up a year later, went onto the Reserve in April 1914. He was admitted to hospital with rheumatic fever early on during the Battle of the Aisne, recovered and was now back. Private William Miller, a riveter born in Dumbarton, joined up for three years just after New Year 1904. Called up as a reservist, on the 26th he was badly wounded in the left leg and died next day. He and Mary McGregor married in Partick, Glasgow, in July 1910 and had a young daughter and a younger son. His personal effects consisted of his identity disc, a knife, some letters and a money bag. Corporal Green put the casualties that day at 50% from what he saw, his own section being reduced from fifteen to five, including himself, Privates Mellor, Stride and Shaw. The fifth was Private John Friars, the son of John Friars of Bo'ness, West Lothian, and a labourer in a chemical works until the year before, who was later officially recorded as having died on the 26th. As he was not captured it is unlikely that he was still alive after 29 October. Corporal Holroyd, first named at Coulommiers, but since promoted, would therefore have been with another section.

Private Edward King, a gardener, joined up in London in May 1910, served with the 2nd Battalion and left three years later. Called up on mobilization, he was sent to the 1st Scots Guards and went to France immediately. On 14 September he was hit in the arm and left thigh on the Aisne and sent down the line to hospital at Le Mans, but must have returned to the Battalion before the fighting began at Ypres. On 26 October he was hit six times by shrapnel, three of his wounds going septic. By the time he reached the 3rd London General Hospital, Wandsworth, he had "haemorrhage, ligature femoral artery, gangrene of foot and leg". He died on 16 November. His stepmother, Mrs James King, in Cranfield, Bedfordshire, was his next of kin. Lance Sergeant Donald King, also a reservist, had been an engine cleaner in Bradford, enlisted in May 1903 and served eight years. In August 1913 he married Mary Ann Purcell at Mexborough, Yorkshire. He, too, went to France at the start. No date was recorded for the bullet wound to his head but on 27 October he was admitted to an unnamed hospital with a depressed fracture producing paralysis. By 30 October he was in Boulogne and on 13 December arrived in London. Discharged from the 2nd London General Hospital, Chelsea, on 3 April

1915, he was sent two forms to sign in June pending medical discharge from the Army in July. His wife returned them and wrote "Sir I think you will find all correct on the paper as my Husband is not well yet it bothers is Head is left Hand is not right he suffers with very bad Head akes at times he never be fit to do any work again I have to give him salts evry morning to move is bowels since he as been wounded & if he stoops down or gets writhing [writing] he as Headakes I think he done is Duty in the Army all the years & at the front I think you ought to look in to the case we have no children not at present & the food so Dear one hardly no How to live he is good man & good Husband to me & I Hope & trust the War will soon come to End & that we shall win. Yours Obedient Mrs DC King"

Private Sidney Curtis, a baker, enlisted in Hereford in July 1908 and had been serving since then. He was posted missing as at 29 October. He gave the names of William and Rose Curtis in Gloucester as his next of kin. While William probably was his father his relationship with Rose Curtis turned out to be something else. On 17 May 1915 Regimental Headquarters received a letter from her in which she said that she had been asking around among fellow soldiers and named Private Walter Teale as having provided some information. She continued "Dear Sir as I am his wife in every way but <u>one</u> & the mother of his child you can understand what the suspence is to me not to know one way or the other I should be very grateful." Private Teale had by this time recovered from a wound in his right forearm on 26 October and was with the 3rd Battalion at Wellington Barracks. He gave a statement that after being hit "while lying in a house in the vicinity, waiting for a conveyance to take me to Hospital, I heard the name "Curtis" mentioned as being the name of a man killed in action that morning." He did not know him and had no direct knowledge. Born in Paris where Thomas Teale, his father was still living in 1902, Private Teale was a clerk in Leeds when he joined up on New Year's Eve and served nearly four years before becoming a reservist. After being wounded he married Emily Carwell in Leeds that December and she moved to Pimlico. He remained in England until 1918, became a Lance Sergeant immediately he returned to France at the beginning of April and a Sergeant in June and was with the Battalion till they went home. Both he and Private Curtis had sailed to France at the very start.

Next to the Menin Road the Coldstream had been told to advance on a frontage of about a thousand yards, with No 2 Company, under Captain Warde-Aldam, on the right and No 1 Company on the left, both being warned that they would "have to go through some very thick wood." From Gheluvelt they were to go about one and a half kilometres up to and across the road from the Gheluvelt Crossroads to Poezelhoek. He continued "The whole Battalion marched to the eastern edge of Gheluvelt, where a small lane turned northwards into the fields. Leslie Hamilton, Brown and his platoon commanders, myself and my platoon commanders went down this and had a thorough inspection of the ground. We were standing on a hill looking northeast; below us stretched a broad, green valley, covered with green fields and plantations. About 1,500 yards away, there ran across our front a straight line of poplars, evidently the Poezelhoek-Kruiseik road: just beyond was another line of trees – our first objective: in the distance, on another hill was Becelaere, whose church spire was a feature of the landscape… There was a plantation about 500 yards from where we started: No 1 Company went round this: No 2 Company had to go through the southeastern corner of it, where we were delayed, partly owing to the thickness of the plantation and the fence round it, partly owing to a nasty fire which the enemy opened at this time. Several men were shot in the plantation…We then advanced in extended order, over a big field, partly stubble and partly beetroot, to another plantation consisting of very thick, young trees. Just as I got my platoon lying down behind this plantation, two men of the Bedfordshire Regiment without kits came running up to me from my right front: they stated that "thousands of Germans" had broken through on our right and the British were all retiring. I pulled out my glasses and could see large numbers of khaki-clad figures retiring west on the Menin-Ypres road. This meant that we and the Scots Guards would get cut off." This plantation of thick, young trees was Poezelhoek Wood and extended right up to the road. Captain Warde-Aldam had already sent two platoons forward, one of which was mostly across the road. There was increasingly heavy enemy fire and a lot of Coldstream casualties. Captain Warde-Aldam found Sir Gordon Hargreaves Brown off to the left about four hundred yards from Poezelhoek, told him what he had seen and heard and asked him to tell both Major Hamilton and the Scots Guards. He then went to see his two leading platoons, finding most of the men now just short of the road. He learned that the platoon which had crossed into a narrow plantation beyond had been badly shot up. The Germans were at Poezelhoek in strength and could fire down the road and into the narrow plantation, triangular in shape, from about two hundred yards. In spite of this "On the far side of the road was a British trench, in which were a few odd men of the Bedfords who told Sergeant Johnson [untraced] the astounding story that they had seen no officers nor rations since last Wednesday."

It was impossible to make any further progress with the enemy at Poezelhoek commanding the road, as well as a machine gun to their right front, which opened up accurately whenever there was a target. The threat from the right along the Menin Road, however, had fizzled out. It was about midday. "During parts of the day De La Pasture, Victor Mackenzie and Reggie Stracey of the Scots Guards joined us. De La Pasture had been knocked down by a shell earlier in the day and had a large hole in his cap. We all agreed that we… could not get on until the Scots Guards captured Poezelhoek and that they could not do this without reinforcements or a preliminary artillery bombardment, neither of which we could get… During the afternoon I ran across the road myself and crawled up to the Bedford trenches but could see nothing. All this time the German infantry kept shooting through the wood and we had several casualties but their shells were going well over us." That there were no reinforcements was because soon after they started General FitzClarence had to send the Black Watch and later most of the Camerons to support the 20th Brigade south of the Menin Road. While the Black Watch became actively engaged helping the 1st Grenadiers, the Camerons were not and spent most of the day marching first towards the 20th Brigade and then back and ultimately round behind the Scots Guards to Polderhoek Château Wood.

Around midday Lieutenant Cyril Hosking and Captain Theodore Crean of No 4 Squadron RFC were flying below low cloud on artillery reconnaissance when their plane fell in flames, shot down by British infantry at a height of about a thousand feet. Both were killed. General FitzClarence wrote in his diary that "By great misfortune we fired on & destroyed an aeroplane (British)." It would appear that he himself mistook it for a German one and ordered the 2nd Worcesters, bivouacking near Veldhoek, to fire at it. The Camerons recorded being ordered to fire at it too and did so. Particularly in poor light the Union Jack markings on a plane could easily be mistaken for German black crosses. The French had already adopted roundels for aircraft identification. The British were soon to do so too. Corporal Green swallowed a rumour that it had been a British plane with German officers flying it. Sergeant Shepherd marked on his sketch plan where he saw it fall, a bit to the north of the point where the tramway first turned away northeast towards Becelaere.

The Coldstream reorganised in the evening. They concluded that their most suitable line was along the east side of the first plantation which they had gone through giving a field of fire of a few hundred yards. They moved back just as it was getting dark and began digging. A little afterwards Captain Warde-Aldam was wounded and evacuated home. Exactly where the Scots Guards established themselves was not clear, but they pulled their firing line back slightly, according to Sergeant Shepherd, and, on the right at least, there were still Bedfords out in front of them. At least initially there could have been quite a wide gap between No 1 Company of the Coldstream and Right Flank, who were closest to the Poezelhoek-Gheluvelt Crossroads road. Next to the left were half of B Company up to the tramway, the other half being in reserve, C Company were beyond that and Left Flank met the Camerons at the southeast of Polderhoek Château Wood. Company Sergeant Major Joe Barwick of C Company described two lines of trenches beyond Gheluvelt Château, two of his platoons being in the firing line about eight hundred yards away, where Sir Iain Colquhoun was, and the other two in a support line about two hundred yards away, where Sergeant Macdonald was. They were covering the low ground northeast of Gheluvelt, which Captain Warde-Aldam had looked out over earlier in the day. Sometime after dark the rest of the Bedfords were withdrawn. Corporal Green moved forward in the middle of the night "To get there we had to go round a corner, on which stood a farmhouse. Immediately we got to the front of the farm nearest the trench, flames were seen to burst out all over the house. This naturally shewed us plainly to the Hun. A fusillade of bullets came over, and we were forced to lie down until nearly dawn. When all was again quiet, we relieved the Bedfords, and kept low owing to the sniping from all sides. We could see the German infantry, eight hundred yards away to half right." Sergeant Shepherd at Battalion Headquarters "spent the night in a farmhouse near the tramlines opposite Gheluvelt chateau wood. When we went there at dusk we found the buildings full of a mixed lot of stragglers. They were sorted out, & cursed at, by Capt Stephen & despatched to their units. During the night we were under constant rifle fire from the direction of Polderhoek chateau wood but not from enemy facing us (It was a very clear night – moonlight I believe)." Since the Camerons were in that wood the firing must have come from somewhere to the east. In spite of this random shooting in the dark it was only then that resupply, the evacuation of the wounded and the burial of the dead could take place in comparative safety and undisturbed by observed artillery fire. There was still the noise of firing, near and far, and that was disturbing. An advantage for those in the firing line and elsewhere was the thick autumn mist on many mornings, sometimes for quite a while. As long as it lasted they could move about outside the trenches, but it could clear quite suddenly. Otherwise, movement above ground in daylight was very hazardous.

On the night of 27 October the 1st (Guards) Brigade, the forward brigade, fully took over the 1st Division's new front line from the nine kilometre stone at the Gheluvelt Crossroads on the Menin Road up to the east edge of the woods opposite Reutel. The Black Watch, less two companies, had their left on the Reutel–Polygon Wood road beside the Camerons who were along the east side of Polderhoek Château Wood. Major Hamilton had immediately informed General FitzClarence that the Coldstream did not have enough men, a rifle strength by now of about five hundred and fifty, only just over half of war establishment, to hold the line given to him from the Gheluvelt Crossroads up to the northwest corner of Poezelhoek Wood. General FitzClarence concentrated his attention on the Crossroads, as all the indications were that there would be a major German thrust along the Menin Road and allocated two Black Watch companies, B and C, to the Coldstream. After dark on the 28th he obtained seventy men from the

1st Gloucesters, under Lieutenant Henry Wetherall, and the machine gun teams both of the Gloucesters and of the 1st South Wales Borderers, also from the 3rd Brigade, to bolster the defence. Captain Thorne noted that "Lt Wetherall himself was North of Menin road but his party was extended over a front of some 500 yds & was on both sides of the road, acting chiefly as a connection between 1st & 20th Bde. One mg was posted about 200 yds N of the road while the other was practically on the road itself, sited to fire down it." The rest of the Gloucesters were brought up to dig in to the east of Veldhoek, as reserve for the 1st (Guards) Brigade. General FitzClarence had ordered the siting of the machine guns, either so as to fire down the road or to fire "down the lane leading from a hamlet south of Becelaere", presumably the lane from Zuidhoek which came in just north of the Crossroads. At this period little imagination was applied to siting machine guns. In the background of Fortunino Matania's post-war painting of the 2nd Yorkshires on 22 October at the Gheluvelt Crossroads their two were depicted in sandbagged positions on either side of the Menin Road sited to fire directly down it, without any concealment. Had they been sited in defilade there would have been the element of surprise as well as giving the machine gunners more protection. Altogether there were far too few men and company positions were frequently out of sight of each other, particularly because of woods and hedges. Runners were the only means of communication below a battalion headquarters. No battalion could spare more than two platoons in reserve. Some men managed to get some rest from time to time out of the firing line itself, even if not far from it and always likely to be called upon at short notice. Others had no respite at all.

Most likely soon after dark on the 27th, the Coldstream moved further east from where they had first been outside Gheluvelt on the 26th when the Yorkshires were still at the Crossroads. All their companies thereafter had their main positions on the east side of the Poezelhoek-Gheluvelt Crossroads road. B Company of the Black Watch under Captain Percy Moubray, were dug in immediately forward of the Crossroads. No 1 Company of the Coldstream were about three hundred yards further north and No 2 Company four hundred yards beyond that. Nos 3 and 4 Companies, combined together, were another four hundred yards further on around the southeastern corner of the narrow triangular plantation on the east side of the road. C Company of the Black Watch under Major Axel Campbell Krook occupied some former trenches of the Bedfords three hundred yards further up the side of it. This was the same narrow plantation where one of Captain Warde-Aldam's platoons got into difficulties on the 26th. Major Campbell Krook wrote that the German trenches were about two hundred yards away to the east. What he found on the night of the 27th and what followed next day was that "We had very little ammunition and very few tools. We found some perfectly useless overhead cover, which, while making the trench conspicuous, was no protection whatever. Some of this we managed to remove, but any noise brought a burst of fire, and such improvements as were possible were carried out before daybreak. On the 28th we were heavily shelled all day, and mutual sniping went on. A number of men were buried by heavy shells and owing to the lack of tools many were dug out too late. Such ammunition as we had was marked "For Practice Only"." While it was not clear when it took place Right Flank of the Scots Guards moved forward, either very early on the 27th, if Corporal Green was right, or, possibly more likely, after dark in the course of the wider reorganisation. This would explain how it came about that from now on 1 Platoon, on their extreme right, were at the northern apex of this narrow triangular plantation, a further three hundred yards along. They were commanded by Lance Sergeant John Shields, also known as "Sam" and "Sammy", born and initially brought up in Edinburgh, where he went to school at

George Watson's. Later the family must have moved north because he continued his education at Inverness College, but by the time that their son enlisted in March 1909, giving his occupation as a clerk, William and Isabella Shields were in Hillhead, Glasgow. Sergeant Shields had a lot of tattoos, including a VC on his right forearm.

Unfortunately nobody at Brigade Headquarters and therefore no one at a higher headquarters knew that they had men in the narrow plantation, nor that a company and a half of the Scots Guards were equally far forward south of the tramway. Contemporary operational maps showed the deployment as running west of Poezelhoek Wood across to the corner of Polderhoek Château Wood. General FitzClarence's report from Veldhoek on 4 November covering the period 27 October to 2 November stated "The line ran east of the 9th kilo stone – Poezelhoek road crossing the latter road just behind a large wood – thence west of Poezelhoek and east of the Chateau woods touching the right of 2nd Division on the Reutel Road." The Coldstream Battalion Headquarters were well forward on higher ground about five hundred yards northwest of the Gheluvelt Crossroads. Only subsequently did it become known what degree of contact there was within the Scots Guards positions and the Coldstream battalion area. At Right Flank's salient Sergeant Shields did not know where the other three platoons were, though at least one was in line to his left. He could not see anything of the Black Watch company to his right, but added that at the edge of the wood where it met the road "I had a field of fire of about 300 yds to my right, a little more to my front, but less than 100 yds to my left so what happened outside that area I have no idea." Major Campbell Krook had visited his position and knew where it was, but could not see it. C Company could not see what was going on to their right, though they later solved that problem. The Camerons were able to see to C Company's right from their slightly higher ground, which did become useful. Left Flank were in contact with the Camerons but could not see C Company because of a hedge.

On the 27th the Scots Guards Battalion Headquarters moved to the northwest corner of Gheluvelt Château Wood and stayed there until the evening of the 29th. Sergeant Shepherd wrote "Our cyclist despatch riders were posted in the village & we had runners between them & Bn HQ. B Coy were ordered to dig a trench along footpath between NW corner of Gheluvelt Chateau wood & Polderhoek Wood but were so heavily shelled in doing so that they were ordered to desist & were then put into the Gheluvelt Chateau wood in front of Battn HQ. The Coy hdqrs were in the stable. During the 27th Gheluvelt village was heavily shelled. HE shells of large calibre being much used. Our firing line had constant & heavy losses from shellfire during this & the following day although no actual attack (enemy) was made." It was the reserve half of B Company who were told to dig. Lieutenant James Stewart RAMC was at Veldhoek with No 1 Field Ambulance of the 1st Division. He came from Aberdeen, where his father was the Minister of the North United Free Church. On the 27th he noted that he had been up with the field ambulance stretcher bearers to the Scots Guards at Gheluvelt Château and had brought in about eighty five wounded. They had gone there after dark and were back at half past four in the morning. At this stage the Château was a reasonably safe and secure place for the wounded. Those that they carried back were probably from several battalions.

On that morning of the 27th Corporal Green saw as "About 9am my great colleague Bill Stride sniped. He suffered agonies that day, until he passed away 5pm (RIP) One of the best fellows I have ever known. With darkness falling, the enemy artillery commenced their activity again. Very little peace we got that night. Continual alarms." Private William Stride was in his fourth year as a soldier. His widowed mother Annie Stride lived at Portswood, Southampton, where her son had once been a baker's porter. Then on the 28th "CSM Dilworth was sniped under one of his armpits, and died in the evening. The Platoon Sergeant told me to get hold of his kit and rifle. I might as well say I, looking over the contents, came across about three pounds of tobacco, and nearly the same of cheese. I put them into my overcoat pocket, as I was in need of tobacco." Company Sergeant Major William Dilworth, a Londoner born in Woolwich, had joined up in 1898 and served in the Boer War. He had already been slightly wounded on 22 September on the Aisne. He left his widow Alice in Battersea. From Brigade Headquarters Captain Thorne told his wife "We have another glorious sunny day and the bursts of shrapnel look so pretty in the sunshine – it is the only pleasant thing about them." Further on in the same letter "Unfortunately you get 2 very stubborn and obstinate nations, both thinking they are entirely in the right, and both feeling that the best solution is a fight to the finish." Meanwhile, Sergeant Macdonald remembered how "at daybreak a crowd of German Cavalry came round by the wood on Sir Iain's right and prepared to charge, but we stopped them and what were left turned about and went. After that bit, I trooped off to the hedge again. Here we heard from Captain Stracey that there was to be a big attack about 5am tomorrow 29th, so we collected wire, etc. pulling down fences from the near farms." This, from the intercept of the German radio message that the *XXVII Reserve Corps* were to attack in the direction of Kruiseecke-Gheluvelt at half past five next morning, was telephoned to Sir Douglas Haig at about three that afternoon. Initially the British brigades were told about this confidentially, but all battalions were warned at once to take particular care that all rifles were free of dust and grit. The message that reached the Camerons about an attack on Gheluvelt from the directions of Menin and Kruiseecke at the stated time was sent from Brigade Headquarters at 9.27pm. It included the instruction that all transport was to be clear of Gheluvelt by 3am. Sergeant Shepherd continued "On the 28th the shelling of Gheluvelt continued & the village was rapidly reduced to ruins. On this day we received information from Bde HQ that the Kaiser was to be present on the 29th & that a determined attack was to be made to reach Ypres & that the point of attack was to be the road itself. In the afternoon of the 28th an attack was made by the enemy on the CGs on our right (for what reason wasn't apparent) unless it was to secure a better jumping off place for the following day) & our RF Coy & MG team had a glorious afternoon's shooting as from their position they were able to enfilade the attackers who came on in close formation. We had constant appeals for more & more ammunition & had difficulty in supplying the firing line quickly enough. An officer mounted on a white horse was very prominent leading the attack until he was shot down. The attackers never got near their objective. LF also had a good deal of shooting as troops kept passing along behind the Poezelhoek position evidently going towards the scene of the attack. Strangely enough during this attack the enemy in the position facing us gave us little trouble & did not seem to make any effort to support their attack by keeping our fire down. The Germans' movements & conduct this afternoon mystified us all. They seemed to offer us targets & suffer very heavy losses for no object."

At about eight that evening Captains de la Pasture and Balfour were standing somewhere near the Gheluvelt Crossroads-Poezelhoek road, having finished going round checking their trenches. A sudden volley was fired from the German trenches and a bullet hit Captain Balfour in the side of the head. Captain de la Pasture sent an urgent message to Captain Meaden, who hurried down with stretcher bearers, but he was dead when they got there and could not have been saved. Some of his men carried his body up to Gheluvelt Château. When a grave was ready a small party gathered round it and Captain Meaden described the scene in a later letter to Captain Balfour's father. "We buried him about midnight. We had no prayer book, and it was arranged that Captain Stephen should say what he knew of the burial service, but he broke down and was only able to say, "Good Bye Jack Old Man, We all loved you," after that he asked me to carry on, and I did my best with the burial service as far as I remembered it." The others whom Captain Meaden mentioned as being there were the B Company stretcher bearers, one or two wounded men and Sergeant Turner, in charge of the battalion stretcher bearers. Sergeant Shepherd was there too.

29 October at Gheluvelt

29 October's events were finally to dispel the Allied illusion of turning the German right wing. General Erich von Falkenhayn, Chief of the German General Staff, had arrived at *Headquarters Sixth Army* on 27 October to issue orders for a general attack two days later, for which all the available heavy artillery and later all the ammunition from that army were assembled. Quite apart from heavy attacks elsewhere, out of very thick mist infantry from the *XXVII Reserve Corps* attacked the 1st (Guards) Brigade at half past five on the 29th from the Gheluvelt Crossroads as far up as the right front of the Camerons. They approached in silence without artillery support as the German observers could not see until the mist cleared about three hours later. There was no serious activity in front of the Black Watch companies on the left, though they were shelled later. At 7.50 Major Sorel Cameron sent a message to his Battalion Headquarters "German attack developing in front of D Coy trenches" but there was no direct attack on the Camerons. Their right hand companies were able to help beat off the attacks on the Scots Guards, but later the German guns also shelled them throughout the day and there were casualties.

Sir Victor Mackenzie wrote that the initial attack at half past five was stopped two hundred yards away. It came southwest down the road from Becelaere to Poezelhoek heading for the centre of the Scots Guards positions. Sergeant Macdonald's platoon must have gone back to their daytime trench before this. He recalled a "Fairly quiet night and then it did start about 5.30am." He added that there was "plenty of rifle fire onto LF on my left and also my right rear but saw no Germans over my front. Sir Iain was still in his forward trench about 500 yards in front of me." The firing from the right could only have been later on. Corporal Green remembered "At dawn the enemy came over, en masse, but were repulsed with heavy losses. Seven times they came with only a short interval, but every time they were beaten back. It was impossible to miss a target, they came in such dense mass." Sergeant Shields' platoon were not in the direct line of this, but he saw Germans advancing towards the Coldstream and his right hand section fired into their flank to stop them. He was wounded by a bullet in the face at about nine o'clock and made his way back, being evacuated to England very rapidly. He returned in the spring. At some stage a piece of shrapnel hit Private Luck through his instep. He got into a shellhole from where he crawled to Battalion Headquarters. With his wound dressed he "started off on my hands and knees the best I could for half a mile and then I saw the stretcher bearers very busy with bad cases in the village that had been destroyed by German shellfire, so I waited behind a wall, thinking it was safe for a time." It was about half a mile from where Battalion Headquarters were in the northwest corner of the Château Wood down its west side to the Menin Road.

At the Gheluvelt Crossroads it was different. There, when the attack started, the three battalions of the *16th Bavarian Reserve Infantry Regiment*, among whom was a company runner called

Adolf Hitler, managed to approach without being detected until too late, perhaps fifty yards away, and in such numbers that they almost immediately swamped B Company of the Black Watch, though some of the rear platoon got back. Captain Moubray was killed. Pressure on the 1st Grenadiers, on the left of the 20th Brigade and next to the road on its south side, and on the 2nd Gordons, beyond them, was also intense. On the north side the Coldstream Battalion Headquarters now fought it out with everything they could. The attackers, starting to head to their right and away from the line of the road, attacked Major Hamilton's position and that of No 1 Company. In turn thereafter from the south each Coldstream position was demolished by weight of numbers.

Major Campbell Krook described what gradually happened between half past five and half past eleven on the 29th. "Sound of rifle firing on the right of the Coldstream. The firing runs along the line to me, and past me. It is foggy, and difficult to see any distance. As the fog clears my left is attacked three times in succession." These attacks were also on the Scots Guards. Then a few survivors of B Company of the Black Watch from the Crossroads somehow managed to reach him but they were "much too hot & bothered to have any coherent story in the short time that I had in which to question them, so that I could not find out from them where the breakthrough had occurred." Then "Bullets begin to kill men from behind. I meet Evelyn Gibbs and we realize that Nos 1 & 2 Coys of the Coldstream cease to exist, and the Germans occupy their trenches. We sent three sections to occupy a ditch…in order to prevent Germans from entering the wood behind us without our knowing it. We decide to stay where we are, especially as we expect a counterattack." This was because a message about a possible counterattack by the 3rd Brigade relating to operations two days earlier had only just reached him. "Firing is difficult as faulty cartridges burst in the chambers and rifles jam. We have no machine guns. The men holding the ditch are wiped out, so that we get no report of the entry into the wood by the Germans. Our own artillery start to shell us – thinking that the whole line is occupied by the Germans. Casualties occasioned by this artillery fire. Many messengers sent out … no result. No messages received. I have not many men left. I am engaged in writing out another message, notebook in one hand, pencil in the other, when there is a burst of fire from behind, and a charge of Germans from the wood behind me into the trench. I just remember seeing the butt end of a rifle coming down; and I remember nothing more until I find myself a prisoner. As a prisoner I was taken along with 2 men of my company and about 10 from Moubray's company who had joined me, to the Coldstream line, where I met Evie Gibbs." Captain Evelyn Gibbs commanded the combined Nos 3 and 4 Companies. About half of the rear Black Watch platoon managed to fight their way out. Major Campbell Krook's lament about being shelled by the British guns was significant and went back to the ignorance at Brigade Headquarters about where the companies were. Directing fire onto these target locations was logical as they were precisely where German attacks would form up or be developing from. Also, British observers could not get a good field of view.

In response to the breakthrough at the Crossroads, just before seven General FitzClarence ordered Lieutenant Colonel Alfred Lovett, commanding the Gloucesters at Veldhoek, to counterattack at once. Colonel Lovett decided to send in his companies as soon as each was ready to go, rather than pausing until he could attack with them all together. They were not sent in as part of a coherent plan and quite a lot of men lost all sense of direction. While the arrival of the right hand company on the eastern side of Gheluvelt contributed to stabilising the situation on the Menin Road that was as much as was achieved. How much, if anything, that the Scots

Guards Battalion Headquarters knew of what was happening, even at this stage, was unclear. Throughout there was no contact between Right Flank and Major Campbell Krook's company, even allowing for both being very actively engaged, while no one from Battalion Headquarters was keeping a lookout for what was happening to their east or indeed curious about it initially. All that was needed was to place an observer or two to watch from somewhere up the bank to the south of the first plantation Captain Warde-Aldam mentioned on the 26th. Having eliminated the Coldstream and Black Watch companies the Germans continued northwards. The time Lieutenant Jolliffe of Right Flank gave of before six o'clock was far too early, but sometime in the morning Captain de la Pasture "sent me to the Coldstream trenches to see what was going on and they were then occupied by the Germans and I believe Krook and Evie Gibbs were scuppered together." Whenever he went it was too late. He continued "I never met or heard of an Art[illery] Officer with the Battn, if there was one, I should like to meet him, as on the morning on the 29th he shelled my trench to pieces and killed as many men, including Father Campbell, as the Germans did. I had to send three men on different occasions whom I could ill spare, to try to get back to headquarters with messages to stop the guns, as they were killing all my men. If it had not been for those guns the position would not have been as desperate, but with their kindly aid the position became impossible. Very few Gloucesters reached us, about 15 men under an ensign, whose name I forget. Not one man left the trenches occupied by RF until the Germans were in our trenches, when I tried to collect the few men surviving to retire on C Coy. But by that time innumerable Germans had got round behind us." "Father" was Captain Colin Campbell, who had exasperated Colonel Lowther at the end of the Retreat from Mons. He had originally been in the Camerons and transferred in 1905. He and his wife Helen Stewart had only got married in June 1914. Lieutenant Ronald FitzRoy, a Reserve officer who had served in the Boer War, arrived on the night of 26 October, but only reached Right Flank on the evening of the 28th. Next morning he saw as the "Enemy attacked at dawn on 29th October 1914 and was easily repulsed, leaving considerable numbers of dead in front of our positions. Later on, about 10am a very heavy rifle and artillery fire was opened upon us from all sides, which ceased suddenly: The enemy rushed our rear through the wood, and captured the position. Every rifle in my vicinity had been put out of action by the enemy fire. There was no surrender, my sword and revolver were forcibly taken from me." He heard that Captain de la Pasture, who must have been somewhere towards the right of the company position, had been killed. "I also saw Capt [Lt] Jolliffe second in command of Right Flank Co with a few men out in the open in the most gallant manner & under a very heavy fire, trying to bring rifle fire to bear on the enemy enfilading our position."

The scene at Gheluvelt Château was described by Sergeant Shepherd. "The morning of the 29th opened with the heaviest shellfire we had yet experienced. It was directed on the line where it crossed the Menin-Ypres road & for some considerable distance on each side of it & to a depth which included Gheluvelt village. Very early (about 10am I think) we received reports from our RF Coy that the troops on their right … had been literally blown out of their trenches & were retiring to Gheluvelt & that the enemy were advancing down the road towards the village. (This was the last message we received from Capt de la Pasture. I learned afterwards from prisoners that 2 or 3 platoons of RF were captured from the rear by the enemy that had advanced towards Gheluvelt & that Capt de la Pasture refused to surrender & was killed). Capt Stephen left Battn Hdqrs to see the situation for himself." Significantly and characteristically it was he who did so. Captain Charles de la Pasture had been to school at Downside, served first as a trooper in

Plumer's Force prior to the Relief of Mafeking in the Boer War and was commissioned into the Sherwood Foresters in April 1900, before transferring in September that year. He and Agatha, his wife, had married in April 1914. His father was the Marquis de la Pasture, who lived at Usk, Monmouthshire.

C Company had also started to wonder what was going on to their right, since it would appear that till then they thought that since everything had gone quiet all was in order, and Sergeant Macdonald at "About 10am Barwick and I went out to the farmhouses and got up into the roof and pushed out a few slates. Through the hole we were able to see further afield. After a time we spotted a line of Germans advancing in extended order over high ground towards us, on their right of the Menin road. Barwick went back to the Chateau and reported to Stracey and then came back again for me. We had nobody to meet that lot on our right. Stracey told me to go to LF and tell Sir Victor and then down to Sir Iain, which I did. Sir Iain came back with his Platoon and with a crowd from LF we all lined the hedge facing the attack and S of the Chateau. The Germans came on, but we managed to keep them off. They seemed to be all over the place, trying, I thought, to get back again. Of course when anything moved, we let drive. I recollect that morning Barwick came along to see how we were and gave me a drink (Red Wine) and Captain Stracey sent the sections of my Platoon under Sergeant Graham and Corporal Bruce out to the wood where RF and B were supposed to be and I never saw them again." Both were captured, Corporal Bruce also being wounded.

Meanwhile at Left Flank Sir Victor Mackenzie "We heard that the Germans had broken through the BW. We expected to get enfiladed. About 1pm a coy of Glosters came doubling through my company in disorder. I collected a few and also a few Coldstreamers. We hear that the CG and BW have been cut up, leaving our right flank exposed. Soon seen to be true. Poor RF coy surrounded absolutely and cut off. They hung on splendidly. C Coy took up fresh position about 100 yds in rear and faced half right. LF remained where they were. C Coy were being heavily pressed right and front. I ran to Reggie and found out where I could best help him. I brought up a platoon of LF and some stragglers on C's right and after a bit the Germans began to withdraw. They were within a hundred yards and God knows how many we killed. I got wounded here and got help back to the dressing station at the Chateau. We heard that the 3rd Bde were now at hand to help us....the other half of B also came to C's support." He was taken to Ypres in an ambulance and evacuated to England, recovered from his wounds and returned next summer.

At 10.55am Major Sorel Cameron sent back a message "S Gds retiring on right. Strong German advance on our right". This was forwarded to Brigade Headquarters who replied in a message timed 11.18am "3rd Brigade counter stroke now coming in AAA Stay on for all you are worth".

Captain Stephen, now fully aware, took a decisive hand. Although the Germans were pressing towards Gheluvelt, a significant number were being deflected towards the Château because of British fire from the south. Sergeant Shepherd continued about how Captain Stephen, with Captain Stracey's assistance, "energetically set about altering the dispositions of the battalion to meet this attack. First of all the machine guns came into action, then he took two platoons from Left Flank, pulled back the two front platoons of C Company to face southeast, lined the southern fence of the chateau grounds with these two platoons from Left Flank and those of B Company from reserve, and, having satisfied himself that the attack was checked, he started off to find more troops with which to counterattack and drive the enemy back." Knowing that Sir Douglas Haig had ordered the 3rd Brigade up to retake the Crossroads, Captain Stephen went to hurry them on their way. Company Sergeant Major Barwick was discreet in saying that "The conduct of Capt Stephen during the whole of this period he was the live wire directing operations and from all accounts he was responsible for getting up every available officer and man he could lay hands on." Sergeant Shepherd, however, did not hold back. "From the time we lost Col Lowther & Maj Carpenter Garnier on the Aisne Capt Stephen had been acting as CO, Second in Command & Adjutant. The nominal CO – Maj Van der Weyer – was an utterly inefficient fool. I regret to say this but it is the truth. I was never out of their company for 7 weeks & heard the arguments & quarrels they had & know what Capt Stephen had to put up with through the CO's timidity & inability to make up his mind & give definite orders on any question which had to be dealt with. Capt Stephen ran the Battn & there wasn't an officer in France put in the amount of work he did. He was the brains behind everything the Battn did & the previous week had received the personal thanks of Gen Bulfin for the work he had done near Pilkem. I read the message myself & it was accompanied by the gift of cake for his tea. To get back to the subject – after Capt Stephen left to see the situation Maj Van der Weyer, who had remained at Battn HQ, which were still at the corner of the wood, received a message from the firing line that the gap on the right was wider than ever. Maj v d Weyer then ordered me to take Battn Hdqrs back down the tramlines to the main road & to await him there as he was going to retire. I suggested waiting until Capt Stephen returned but was told to go at once. I reached the main road which was being heavily shelled & under some rifle fire from the direction of Gheluvelt. I waited near a cottage on the S side of the road just opposite where the tramline came on to the road. A Battn of Infantry (I believe SWB [South Wales Borderers]) was lying in a ditch on the other side of the road. I hadn't been there long when I saw Capt Stephen come striding up the road from Ypres direction at the head of two companies of infantry…He was cursing & swearing & evidently wasn't on the best of terms with the officer in charge of the companies who wasn't rushing up quickly enough to suit him (the coys were then in fours). When he saw me he said "What the bloody hell are you doing here?" I told him that the CO had sent me there & was coming to join me. He told me to get back where I came from or he would put a bullet through my head & that I was to tell the CO that he would put one through his head as well when he saw him. He asked me if I knew what the CO intended doing & I said I thought he meant retiring. He said "No bugger in this Army is retiring so long as I am here." He went off up the road to Gheluvelt at the head of the coys. I didn't see him again until sunset when he came round the SW corner of the chateau & just as I caught sight of him an 18pdr shrapnel shell burst behind him & a bullet went in his back just under the right shoulder blade. Capt Stracey was with him & supported him whilst he walked into the chateau & lay in the hall."

The ambulance with Sir Victor Mackenzie also took Captain Stephen to hospital in Ypres, where he died two days later. Sergeant Pilkington, on one of his errands there from the 2nd Battalion, saw his body and those of three other officers awaiting burial in Ypres Town Cemetery. Captain Stephen's parents were both dead, his elder brother Captain Douglas Stephen of the 2nd Grenadiers had died of wounds on 10 September and his only close relation was his married sister Dulcie Dalglish, of Sundorne Castle, Shrewsbury. It was to her that the telegram was sent on 5 November, the standard printed words on the form in italics, which read "Deeply *regret to inform you that* Captain AAL Stephen Scots Guards died from wounds received in action 31 October Lord Kitchener expresses his sympathy." Captain Stephen was educated both at

Westminster and Eton, had fought in the Boer War, where he won his DSO, and from 1906 served with the Ottoman Gendarmerie, but resigned while in Smyrna in 1911. One of his awards from the Turks was the Liakat Medal for his services "in suppression of brigand bands in Macedonia". He had a thorough knowledge of French, essential for the Turkish service, and a fair knowledge of German.

On the Menin Road about noon a man came upon Private Luck sheltering behind his wall and tried to help him, but could not because he was unable to walk. Then the man found a wheelbarrow. "He got me on this, and off we went to the dressing station…about half a mile down the road…and, my word, it was a ride over those cobble stones (if you have not tried it, don't!)" This would have been at Veldhoek from where he was taken away by ambulance. Next day he went by train to Boulogne and left soon afterwards for England. He returned to France in the middle of February 1915 and served with the 2nd Battalion for nearly a year before joining the 3rd Guards Brigade Machine Gun Company. He was a Vickers gunner for the rest of the War, became a Sergeant just after the end of it and was awarded the MM. He then went back to his family in East Sussex, including the son born in 1915.

In the late afternoon Lieutenant John Boyd, the Coldstream Quartermaster, came up with the resupply wagons to about a mile west of Veldhoek. When he heard there that "something desperate had happened to the Battalion, I at once rode forward to Brigade Headquarters, which were at Veldhoek. Brig General FitzClarence told me what had happened to the Battalion & that I was the only Officer left. The survivors of the Battalion (32 NCOs & men) were collected in a barn near Brigade Headquarters. I posted a Sergt at the crossroads to collect any stragglers of the Battalion who might come along, during the night he collected 30." Early next morning he was told to occupy some reserve trenches nearby. "That evening 60 men belonging mostly to No 1 Company joined me from the front line, they had been fighting alongside the 1st Bn Scots Guards since the smash up of the Battalion the day before." Every one of the Coldstream officers who had sat waiting for the French with Captain Warde-Aldam in the farmhouse near Pilckem was missing and would remain so. On 2 November Captain McLeod of the Gloucesters, who had also been there, was posted missing and on 11 November Major Sorel Cameron of the Camerons was captured. Nothing was ever heard again of the machine gunners of the Gloucesters and South Wales Borderers.

Sergeant Shepherd continued "From this time until I was hit Capt Stracey took Capt Stephen's place as the brains & directing power of the Battn, the CO continuing to be as ineffective as ever. We were lucky to have two such officers as Stephen & Stracey. Without them I don't know where we should have been. During the evening of the 29th Capt Stracey told me he was very proud of what the Battn had done that day, as, besides breaking up several attacks on our own lines we had been very largely instrumental in reestablishing the position on our right by the enfilading fire we had kept up against the enemy who were attacking that portion of the line. (He specially mentioned the MG team & Ptes Clancey & Deignan for the work they had done.)" All the same the casualties had been heavy. Sergeant Shepherd went on "I shouldn't think we had more than 150-160 in the firing line with about 60 or 70 in reserve." Private Clancy had helped Colonel Lowther when he was wounded on the Aisne and Private Patrick Deignan was another Irishman serving when the War broke out. He, formerly a farm labourer from Moyvoughty, County Westmeath, had joined seven years earlier and, like Private Clancy, was a 1st Class Machine Gunner. After dark Battalion Headquarters moved into the stables west of the Château, which itself was filling with badly wounded men. Back at No 1 Field

Ambulance Lieutenant Stewart had been the Orderly Medical Officer, or duty doctor, since six in the morning. By the time he was relieved twelve hours later he had treated six hundred cases.

That evening the Scots Guards were still from slightly beyond the northeast corner of the Gheluvelt Château Wood up to the southeast corner of Polderhoek Château Wood. Their right, a small party of survivors from Right Flank, was on the side road leading from Gheluvelt village to Poezelhoek. They were very stretched and, if not then, shortly afterwards, the Camerons moved to take over part of their ground. Meanwhile, to their right, the 1st South Wales Borderers were in a firing line, roughly dug by the Royal Engineers, on the slightly higher ground immediately northeast of the village about seventy yards out from the Château Wood. Starting at about two in the afternoon the 3rd Brigade had successfully counterattacked and recaptured the lost and now very exposed trenches around the Crossroads. Since the Germans had a complete view after pushing back the 7th Division it was decided that these trenches were no longer defensible and a new line was formed on the edge of the Plateau just east of Gheluvelt. The 3rd Brigade had the 2nd KRRC, borrowed from the 2nd Brigade, on their right to the south of the Menin Road, on ground previously held by the 7th Division. Next to them, also south of the road, but further forward overlooking the Crossroads, were the 2nd Welsh and, to their left on the north side of the road, the 1st Queen's. The South Wales Borderers were between the Queen's and the Scots Guards. Repeatedly over the next two weeks a different battalion appeared on the Scots Guards right, but on their left they had the Camerons throughout. At the end of his report on the fighting between 27 October and 2 November General FitzClarence wrote "I should like to say that in the foregoing operations the right of the 1st Bn Scots Guards was on each occasion uncovered by the retirement of the troops on their right. The Battalion however maintained perfect steadiness on every occasion and inflicted loss on the enemy." While stating that the Battalion was commanded by Major van der Weyer, General FitzClarence added that he was "greatly assisted by Captain A Stephen."

Many Scots Guardsmen missing on 29 October were prisoners, though that took time, in some cases months, to clarify, but more were dead. Not that many of the missing who were dead were ever definitely known to have disappeared on a particular day, then or later during the War, and presumptive dates had to be determined. Sergeant Thomas Mackenzie, who, after giving up being a law clerk in Inverness, had been serving for ten years and working very successfully as a clerk, including in the Headquarters of the Egyptian Army, was one of the missing who were dead. His next of kin was his brother Alex Mackenzie at Muir of Ord, Easter Ross. Another was Private Charles Blackshaw, a former boot packer and warehouseman, who had been a soldier for three years and whose father Joseph Blackshaw lived at St Anne's-on-Sea, Lancashire. However, Private Stride was recorded as wounded on 26 October and later as missing as at 11 November, when Corporal Green, who knew the facts, was a prisoner. Also missing after 29 October and never seen again was another reservist, Private Archibald McAffer, born in King Williamstown, South Africa, near where all his family lived. He was working as a butcher in Glasgow when he enlisted in 1910 and served for three years. Soon after he left the Army and settled back in Glasgow he married Flora Corbett, a widow with a daughter. They also adopted Flora's orphaned nephew and niece. Because these three children, who were totally dependent on him, were not his own children, Flora McAffer only received the basic war widow's pension of ten shillings per week, though, as an act of compassionate stretching of the regulations, separation allowance for the children, for which they were eligible, was extended to the end of September 1915. Another who was missing and dead was Private Mandy Devir, "Diver" being his real name, previously a blacksmith's labourer in Glasgow and a soldier for a year, from Carrigart, County Donegal, where his father Neil Diver lived. Private Peter Lambe had been working as a railway fireman in Glasgow until he joined up in the autumn of 1911 and thereafter attracted a number of drink connected and other charges in the Army, all of them pre-war. It was probably on 29 October that he was wounded in the right arm, badly, and from complications he died on 17 November in hospital in Boulogne. Bernard Lambe, his father, lived in Broadstone, Dublin.

Soon after this Captain Thorne's letters to his wife contained attempted reassurances about missing officers, who, he said, were most likely to be prisoners, in response to her pressing requests for information. Her father had been the 2nd Lord Penrhyn and she was a daughter of his second marriage. She was particularly worried about her half brother Lieutenant The Honourable Charles Douglas Pennant, a reserve officer, by 29 October commanding No 2 Company of the Coldstream, and her nephew Lieutenant The Honourable Alan Douglas Pennant of the 1st Grenadiers, son of her eldest half brother, the 3rd Lord Penrhyn. Both uncle and nephew were missing that day, both of them dead.

31 October at Gheluvelt

At Gheluvelt, apart from shelling, which was heavy, and sniping from the woods to the east, 30 October was otherwise without significant incident north of the Menin Road. Sergeant Shepherd recorded their reconnecting the telephone with Brigade Headquarters using the equipment Colonel Lowther had obtained personally and given to the Battalion on the Aisne. Initially Lieutenant Colonel Burleigh Leach had the South Wales Borderers Battalion Headquarters upstairs in the stables, the Scots Guards being below. When the German shelling became too intense he moved to a dug-out nearer the Château. He very much regretted not having his machine gun teams, lost with the Coldstream two days before. Then "In the early hours of the morning of the 31st it became evident that the Germans contemplated a renewal of their attack. The whole of the ground from the village to the Chateau was subjected to a violent and searching bombardment by guns of all calibres – the large majority of the houses in the village including the church were reduced to ruins and it became increasingly difficult even for men to move about singly." Understandably, he concentrated on what directly affected him, describing the trenches as "practically untenable", though they had to hold them in spite of the heavy loss of men. What he could not know was that the Queen's and the Welsh had been shelled almost completely out of their trenches and then completely overrun. The Queen's ended the day with two officers and forty men. Captain Hubert Rees, who on that autumn day on the Aisne listened to the Germans celebrating the fall of Antwerp, now one of only two surviving officers, described the Welsh as "annihilated". He went on fighting from further back on the south side of the road in command of a small combined group of survivors from both battalions. The 2nd KRRC, further to the right, and the already battered battalions of the 7th Division beyond, had been further battered as well.

Colonel Leach went on "From this stage the fighting was practically continuous and often hand to hand…There seemed little chance of any assistance being within reach and the situation grew exceedingly critical." However, there was then an incident which "instilled new life into everyone." Sergeant Macdonald with his platoon was not far from the northeast corner of Gheluvelt Château Wood. Apparently in a pause following the beating off of another mass attack, sometime between seven and eight in the morning according to Colonel Leach, he noticed that Germans were making their way forward along a ditch which approached his position at right angles. "I told Stracey and a Machine Gun was brought along from somewhere, with Clancy working it. We let the ditch get full up and then Clancy, with Stracey watching, let them have it – those that could put up their hands and came trooping in through a gap in our hedge." Some were hit by their own shellfire. Captain Thorne recorded that fifty eight were captured originally. Because the Scots Guards were so short of men the South Wales Borderers took over the forty one surviving prisoners and escorted them to the rear, a very dangerous task. Three of the escort and one prisoner were killed.

Sergeant Shepherd stated that the first attack on the 31st was at six, that reports of the breakthrough on the right started to come through about nine or ten and that shortly afterwards they heard that the enemy were in Gheluvelt. He went on that this led Captain Stracey to move Left Flank and the remaining half of B Company nearer the Château. Meanwhile the telephone line to Brigade Headquarters continued to work at least from time to time, but in the middle of the morning General FitzClarence told Captain Thorne, who was again writing home, to ride to the Scots Guards and find out precisely what was happening. When he got to the stables Captain Thorne heard from Colonel Leach and Captain Stracey that, unless the situation in the village was restored, their own positions were untenable because, after crushing the other 3rd Brigade battalions, the Germans were in Gheluvelt. The pressure along the southeast side of the Château Wood was now intense and the enemy were beginning to break through the South Wales Borderers firing line. In this crisis Captain Stracey quickly gathered most of Left Flank and the B Company men from north of the Wood, brought them round behind it and lined them up among the trees on the west side of the drive near the Château. When the Germans, having got past the South Wales Borderers, emerged from the east side of the drive Captain Stracey charged them and drove them all back. When, after being reinforced, the Germans tried again an hour later Captain Stracey repeated the process, this time with his men starting from further forward. Colonel Leach wrote "Captain Stracey and a Quartermaster Sergeant of 1st Scots Guards together with many Non Commissioned Officers and men of the same Battalion added most materially to the enemy confusion. Many Germans were either bayoneted or shot at close quarters. Others fled leaving their arms and equipment in their flight. The Chateau grounds were littered with bodies and debris of equipment, rifles, caps and helmets of the discomfited enemy and the line of the South Eastern edge of the chateau grounds restored." Sergeant Shepherd thought that the first charge was about eleven o'clock. He watched it from just in front of the steps of the Château while trying, unsuccessfully that time, to get through to Brigade Headquarters on the telephone. He also saw the second charge. Then he was wounded at about two and carried into the Château. He wrote "If it had not been for Capt Stracey's conduct on this day there is no doubt that our line would have been rolled up from the right. It was brilliant leadership I think to anticipate exactly the enemy move as he did & to get the troops ready lined up to charge the Germans the minute they came into the open, when the only information he then had was that Gheluvelt was occupied." The "Quartermaster Sergeant" was most likely Sergeant Major Thomas Tate or else Company Sergeant Major Barwick.

The South Wales Borderers tried for some time to find out what was happening in the village but none who went to look came back. Eventually Lieutenant Vincent Ramsden was successful and returned to say that, while the village was heavily occupied, the Germans were showing little sign of continuing their attacks and appeared to be more concerned with finding water.

Colonel Leach sent this information back to Headquarters 3rd Brigade. Meanwhile, after Captain Thorne had returned and reported to General FitzClarence he quickly went back to writing to his wife. "I had to break this letter off to take a message through to the Scots Gds it was most exciting and uncomfortable and I am very glad to be back here again…We are having a pretty warm time today and this letter's style is likely to suffer." Then next "I must finish this off as we have to make a counterattack." General FitzClarence had obtained the 2nd Worcesters as a temporary reserve. Earlier, after news came of the destruction of the battalions east of the village, he placed one company of Worcesters in a blocking position on the tramway west of Gheluvelt to cover the Menin Road. That helped to prevent the enemy from working their way further along the north side. The rest of the Worcesters were further back, waiting in Polygon Wood. Acting on what Captain Thorne had said, General FitzClarence sent him at one o'clock with orders to Major Edward Hankey, commanding the Worcesters, to counterattack the village. He also told Captain Thorne to guide them by the most unobserved route, which served them well until they came over a low rise about half a mile to the west, after which there was no concealment. Having got to the Château Wood they stormed Gheluvelt and cleared it up to the Menin Road, completely saving the situation. Their casualties were one hundred and eighty seven killed and wounded, out of some three hundred and seventy. Both Major Hankey and Captain Thorne gave the credit to General FitzClarence.

The decision was taken, nevertheless, to pull back after dark about half a mile west into a new line prepared by the Royal Engineers running north–south through Polderhoek Château. This was mainly because of the fragile situation to the south of the Menin Road all the way to Klein Zillebeke. The Germans had partly penetrated into the woods behind the forward positions of the 7th Division and the cavalrymen dug in beyond were very much under pressure. Orders to withdraw reached the South Wales Borderers at five that evening and they began to move an hour later. The Worcesters had gone first to rejoin the 5th Brigade, then the South Wales Borderers moved back and finally the Scots Guards. Colonel Leach described that "This was carried out with complete success, and apparently without arousing the suspicion of the enemy. In position on new line by 9pm." There was then a roll call and Colonel Leach recorded "The numbers, which speak for themselves, were as follows:- 1st Scots Guards 105 1st South Wales Borderers 224." Captain William Wickham, described as continuing his picnic nonchalantly under shellfire during the Retreat from Mons, had been commanding the remaining half of B Company. He was killed that day and buried in front of the Château, though his body was never found afterwards. Captain Henry and The Honourable Mrs Teresa Wickham lived at Wootton Hall, Warwickshire, and their son had been at Eton and Trinity Hall, Cambridge.

Company Sergeant Major Barwick recorded "Up to the time I was wounded Captain Stracey set the finest example possible. He organised the withdrawal of the battn from the positions held in front of and around the Chateau. He gave me instructions to personally collect every man wounded or otherwise who could walk and get them away from the Chateau. I collected about 40 men all told…We left a party of about 40 German prisoners fastened up in the stables." Captain Stracey told him to have the now badly wounded Major van der Weyer carried back, but Captain Meaden would not permit it, staying behind himself with the one hundred and twenty men too badly wounded to move. Captain Stracey came to say goodbye to Sergeant Shepherd, who was one of them. Colonel Leach described Captain Meaden saving the lives of many men, single handed and wounded himself. The Germans did not come anywhere near the Château till five the next morning. Captain Meaden was, as a doctor, repatriated from Germany quite quickly. He returned to the Western Front and had been mentioned in dispatches four times by the end of the War, as well as being awarded the DSO in 1916 for Gheluvelt, most likely on Colonel Leach's recommendation.

Sergeant Shepherd, posted wounded and missing, was a prisoner at Güstrow in Mecklenburg, the first information of this coming from Major van der Weyer's wife. When arrangements were agreed for long term prisoners who were Officers and NCOs to be interned in the Netherlands from March 1918 onwards he went to The Hague. He landed back in England on 18 November 1918 and married Mary Massingham at Petersfield on 3 December. He was discharged from the Army in January 1919, medically unfit, which did not stop him making a successful career in the Kent Police and becoming a Superintendent in Tonbridge. One of the most lightly, though awkwardly, wounded at Gheluvelt was Private William Schmidt, a reservist, who had been a barman in Liverpool, with a dragon tattooed on his right forearm and a bird on his left when he enlisted in 1910. He was hit in the finger and evacuated to England, where he remained with the 3rd Scots Guards for the rest of the War, becoming a Sergeant. He changed his name to Smith. More seriously wounded and possibly one of those left behind at the Château was Private Evan Barnett, a miner from Treherbert in the Rhondda, one of the few Welshmen in the Scots Guards, who had been on the Reserve for six years. He had a lively disciplinary record while serving, which included being absent from parade for Trooping the Colour in 1906. He was wounded near Vendresse on 14 September and evacuated, but returned from hospital in Le Mans, only to be wounded badly in the leg at Gheluvelt and captured. He died on 8 November in the German *XV Corps Field Hospital* at Werwicq.

Colonel Leach wrote long afterwards "I can only repeat that what they did that day & previously has never been adequately recognised. I had them under me & know – it made me angry – & still does – that all and sundry [have] been referred to – but not the Scots Guards – they – or what remained of them were simply splendid." When matters were looking very dire, probably before the Worcesters' charge, Lieutenant Mascevell "Max" Salmon of the South Wales Borderers was with a Company Sergeant Major of the Scots Guards discussing what was to be done. A Scots Guardsman "interrupted by saying to the CSM "Sir, the Germans are behind us." To which he received a barking reply, "What's it got to do with you? Look to your front!"

The Battle of Nonne Boschen

During the night of the 31st the Scots Guards worked on the new line, now with the Gloucesters on their right. At 10.33pm Brigade Headquarters sent a message to the Battalions "Brigadier again directs that trenches be dug really deep and narrow AAA Some barbed wire and a very few picks and shovels are available at Bde Head Quarters AAA". 1 November was fairly quiet and after dark the Gloucesters left. The Coldstream came back, brought up to a strength of two hundred, took charge of a barricade across the Menin Road and dug in on either side of it, with the 2nd KRRC to their south. On the 2nd there was very heavy shelling and a heavy German attack swamped the Coldstream, most of whom were casualties, before moving on south and rolling up the KRRC. Again Lieutenant Boyd had to take command and rally the survivors, who went to join the 2nd and 3rd Coldstream with the 4th (Guards) Brigade in Polygon Wood, but he insisted on their maintaining their own identity. The immediate consequence for the Scots Guards was that the Germans started firing from the former Coldstream positions on the road. C Company moved back partially, so as to face that way, but there were still casualties from enemy machine guns firing at their rear and also from enfilade shellfire. About 2.15pm a message, roughly written on a torn scrap of paper, reached B Company of the Camerons from Sir Iain Colquhoun "Position on the Right appears excellent. There are only few Germans and our men have forced them to retire leaving a few in one of the Houses who cannot get away. The French are pressing forward on our extreme right." Later that day he was hit in the backside and evacuated home. The Camerons recorded one of the few remaining Scots Guards officers, unnamed, as saying that it was "a period of intense boredom punctuated by paroxysms of fear". Captain Stracey was buried in a trench by shelling, but dug out unhurt. Many other trenches were blown in. Private Thomas Bruce, formerly a groom and a soldier for six and a half years, was very badly wounded in the right knee and just above it. On 26 November he left France and had his leg amputated next day in London, but died six days later of heart failure. Richard and Janet Bruce in Lauder, Berwickshire, received four packets of cigarettes, twenty four coins, an identity disc, a tin of tobacco, his pipe, a cardigan, a handkerchief, a sock, a belt, a razor and Army 2nd and 3rd Class Certificates of Education. His elder brother Private George Bruce was in the Battalion. Private John Goodread, born and brought up in St Helier, Jersey, was a bicycle mechanic until he joined up in 1904, serving slightly less than the standard three years. Called up from the Reserve, he had been out since the start until he was killed on 2 November. He married Elizabeth Burkill in March 1910 in London and she was in Battersea with their daughter. When he was hit in the hip was not recorded but Private Joseph McLoone, sometime asylum attendant in Glasgow, without named family, but from Glenties, County Donegal, and serving soldier for three years, was evacuated home on 9 November, never returned and was medically discharged because of neurasthenia in February 1916. He was in the Officers Mess Staff photograph.

In order to try to restore the situation General FitzClarence assembled a scratch force from six battalions, including Captain Rees and his band from the Welsh, slightly reinforced, and charged the Germans in the darkness with the bayonet. It did not work owing to the lack of coordination and the shortage of officers. Telling his wife about General FitzClarence, Captain Thorne wrote "last night about 6pm he led an attack personally up to the German trenches. How he escaped I don't know; I missed the charge (I am cowardly enough to say) fortunately owing to Judy being killed & to having to complete a longish distance on foot." Judy, his own horse, had to be shot after being hit by a shell splinter. That day, the 3rd, Lieutenant Ross, the Signal Officer at Brigade Headquarters, was wounded and evacuated home where he would be till early 1916. Later the three remaining much thinned out battalions in the Brigade moved back a further three hundred yards, so that they were on a roughly south-north line from near the Menin Road just west of Veldhoek to the southwest corner of Polygon Wood. Sir Douglas Haig had anticipated the possible need for a defence line here several days before and instructed Colonel Spring Robert Rice, his Commander Royal Engineers, to select suitable positions for strong points, then known as "pivot points" or, from the French, to whom the concept was already familiar, as "points d'appui", to which were delivered initially all barbed wire available. It was for this reason that, whereas wire, in small quantities, was beginning to reach the British trench lines elsewhere, it was not available to the infantry of the 1st (Guards) Brigade for their trenches, though the Camerons seem to have had a little. The Scots Guards and Black Watch started work on two strong points on the night of 3 November. All went on digging themselves in further.

The Scots Guards, on the right, were partly in and around an orchard, with some buildings, later known as Northampton Farm, and also had a trench line angled slightly back towards, but not as far as Veldhoek Château Wood on the north side of the Menin Road. Just forward of them and to their right up to the Menin Road were now a Zouave battalion. To the south of the Zouaves, on the far side of the road, along the forward edge of Herenthage Château Wood were the 1st Loyals of the 2nd Brigade. The Scots Guards Battalion Headquarters, such as they were, were probably somewhere near Brigade Headquarters in farm buildings, later called FitzClarence Farm, due west of the orchard. Their strong point was around a burnt out farmhouse between their main position around the buildings and orchard and Brigade Headquarters. Lieutenant Stewart was sent up to replace Captain Meaden as the Scots Guards Medical Officer, but was unable to find anybody. He did find them on the 3rd. He arranged to evacuate the wounded and slept where he was in the dressing station beside the Menin Road. A Scots Guardsman hit about now for the first time was Private Charles Hendrick. His head wound was not bad and he reached hospital in Rouen on 10 November. He worked as a general labourer in Preston before enlisting in 1913 and had been out in the BEF from the beginning. His father Charles Hendrick served in the Scots Guards in the 1890s and he and Jane Hendrick had settled in Preston.

The Camerons, in the centre, the strongest battalion and still with both their machine guns, had a longer length of line from the edge of the orchard occupied by the Scots Guards up to north of a stream, the Reutelbeck. Both the Black Watch and the Camerons Battalion Headquarters were at Verbeck Farm near the northeast corner of what was later known as Glencorse Wood. Both had forward and support trenches. The Black Watch, on the left, held the line from north of the Reutelbeck up to the southwest corner of Polygon Wood. Their strong point was behind their firing line in the garden of a cottage some three hundred and fifty yards to the southwest of the Wood and was occupied by Lieutenant Francis Anderson with forty men.

Major Ernest Craig Brown, who arrived on the Aisne, was commanding A Company of the Camerons, immediately next to the Scots Guards. "We all went in turns to our Bn HQ for meals having breakfast before 5am while it was safe to walk abroad (i.e. before it got daylight) & dinner after 7pm, or as soon as it could be prepared. Fires could not be lit by day on account of the smoke. Our lines & supports were shelled every day by the Germans with varying severity so, during our 8 days occupation of these trenches, we accepted it as the normal state of affairs & had many casualties daily who were buried, or carried off by the stretcher bearers after dark. It was impossible to move about by daylight, except for orderlies who had to take their lives in their hands & crawl from one bit of cover to another. There were no telephones from Bn HQ to the trenches. The Col & Adjt came round to inspect after dark each evening. Misty mornings were greatly appreciated as, until the mist cleared, officers & men could walk about & stretch their legs unseen by the Germans. As regards moving about by day, a certain amount could be done by means of communication trenches wh[ich] were being improved by working parties at night, & I could, from my dug-out, cut over to the garden & houses which were the boundary between the Camerons & the Scots Guards. This latter was, however, rather a risky thing to do & I did not do it oftener than I could help." The garden was the Scots Guards orchard.

On the 4th General FitzClarence noted in his diary that Sir John French "promises to relieve us", news he passed on to the Camerons. It was not to be and so he added next day "Fairly quiet. 1st Div cannot be relieved." The 7th Division were the priority and left the battle. Captain Thorne told his wife that his new pair of boots, which had just arrived, were destroyed when a shell hit the kitchen of the building they had been using, fortunately with no casualties. The Scots Guards recorded a fairly quiet day during which they went on constructing their strong point.

Apart from those there, about half the rest, including Private Clancy and the sole remaining machine gun, were in the orchard, and the other half in the firing line leading down towards the northeast edge of Veldhoek Château Wood. On the 5th there was heavy shelling, but reinforcements consisting of Sergeant Frank Howson and fifty men arrived. Sergeant Howson, from Lancaster, previously a labourer in a cotton factory, had been serving since 1904. When he was hit in the spine was not recorded but Piper James Mackenzie died at Boulogne because of it on 5 November. He was, apparently, without a job as a motor driver when he enlisted in Inverness in February 1913. He was not with the Battalion at the start but arrived in a draft while they were on the Aisne. Murdo and Johann Mackenzie had been at the Station Hotel, Muir of Ord, but by this time Murdo Mackenzie was in his other role of Pioneer Sergeant of the 4th Seaforth Highlanders, Territorials.

They were followed the day after by Lieutenant Bernard Winthrop Smith and sixty more men. Lieutenant Winthrop Smith had been at Eton and Trinity College, Cambridge, where he won a Rowing Blue in 1905. He was six foot five inches and broad in proportion and had been in the Scots Guards since 1907. In 1913 he went out to be ADC to the Governor and Commander-in-Chief of the East African Protectorate and had some difficulty in extricating himself when the War began. In this second draft was Private Donald Stewart, originally from Ullapool, Wester Ross, who had served for three years before leaving in 1908. He spent five years with the police in the South of Scotland before deciding in 1913 to emigrate and become a railway policeman with the Canadian Pacific Railway Company. Called up out there, he reported with other army reservists at Quebec, as instructed, and reached London at the end of August. The draft left St Nazaire by train on 3 November under Lieutenant Winthrop Smith, to Private Stewart "an excellent officer", and arrived near Ypres on the evening of the 5th. They marched to and through Ypres, fairly intact but deserted except for the military, and to the accompaniment of the sound of the guns marched on "along the main road in the dark… We halted for a rest about a couple of miles from the firing line and lay down on each side of the road." At this point he described a group of walking wounded going the other way, whom he thought were from the 2nd Battalion. "I knew many of them. Their clothes were torn and muddy, some had rifles and some had not, and they all looked pale and haggard, as if they had awakened from a ghastly nightmare. They informed us that the British army was losing heavily, that the Germans were greatly superior in artillery and men, and that the draft which joined the 1st Scots Guards only that morning, was wiped out almost to a man. They wished us luck and proceeded on their way." His draft went into the line early on the 6th where "We found shallow temporary trenches which had apparently been dug under most unfavourable conditions, and which were not even connected. Some were six to ten feet in length, about three feet wide, and barely deep enough to protect a man when sitting or kneeling. We were so crowded in the holes that we could not stretch our legs. Consequently we soon began to suffer from cramp. We all had to keep the sharpest possible lookout, as the Germans were only about two hundred yards away, and they were continually sniping at our parapet. When daylight appeared on the morning of 6th [7th] November, I saw that we were situated in a field adjacent to the ruins of either a farmhouse, or a barn, on our right. The country appeared flat and there were tall trees standing to our front and left. There was an unoccupied farm building, partly demolished by artillery fire, about a hundred yards to our left front, and I afterwards found it was necessary to go to this farm building under cover of darkness, for our drinking water." This could only have been the buildings at the orchard. Private Stewart's account suggested that he was in the trench line in the fields between the orchard and Veldhoek Château Wood. During the daytime they also had to keep their heads down because of the very accurate and heavy German artillery fire, the more so when it was concentrated on them as at two that afternoon. "When night began to fall, the firing subsided, and those of us who escaped injury had to get busy, digging graves to bury the dead, and removing the wounded. Our dead were much in excess of our wounded, in those days. One of my draft, named Cockburn, a native of Edinburgh, who was next to me in the trench, suddenly stood up rigid, with his eyes staring, and a deathlike grip on his rifle. He appeared to have gone mad under the strain of the day. I helped to have him removed to the stretcher bearers." No one called Cockburn fitted Private Stewart's description but Private Patrick Docherty, an iron worker from Coatbridge who enlisted two weeks before the War, was evacuated with shell shock on the 8th. He was wounded twice more during the War. At four in the afternoon the Camerons recorded that two platoons of B Company had left their trenches. Of one there were no details but of the twenty four men by this time in the other "14 were recovered, 2 were dead, 2 wounded, 6 missing." There were other instances of those unable to stand the strain of which the largest recorded was when Major General Herman Landon, now commanding the 1st Division, wrote on 7 November to Major General Frederick Wing of the 3rd Division listing the names of two men of the 1st Cheshire Regiment, nine of the 1st Northumberland Fusiliers and twenty three, including a sergeant, of the 1st Bedfords, all apprehended on the Menin Road without arms or equipment on 7 November. Later on the 7th Private Stewart "was ordered with several others to go on a very risky mission – to go back in the open, about a thousand yards or more, for rations…our party returned safely with rations for our platoon, and these had to be distributed by us to the men in the trenches. The rations consisted of dry bread and cheese and tins of bully beef. Hot tea or coffee were a luxury which we were unable to get."

Writing home again on the 8th Captain Thorne reflected "The battle is not yet over but the crisis is shortly to be and we all pray for success. Both sides are making tremendous efforts and the decision sways to and fro." There was heavy shelling again and at about half past two that afternoon the Germans, following this up, successfully routed the Zouaves out of their trenches to the right front of the Scots Guards and drove them onto the forward companies of the Loyals behind them both in Veldhoek Château Wood and Herenthage Château Wood, so pushing them back as well. The rest of the Loyals counterattacked with partial success. Again the Scots Guards were exposed to enemy flanking fire, now from the trenches that the Zouaves had lost and from the wood behind, though the enemy were unable to get far into it and were fiercely and successfully resisted by the French occupants, from another regiment, in a strong point close to Veldhoek Château. An attempt was made to eject the enemy with machine gun fire, followed by a further counterattack, ultimately successful in recovering the Loyals trenches and stabilising the line between the Scots Guards and the Menin Road. This owed most to the efforts of the Brigade reserve of Captain Fortune with seventy men of the Black Watch and to a single howitzer. There was a 4.5 inch howitzer close to Brigade Headquarters, the use of which General FitzClarence obtained in order to shell the Zouaves' former trenches. However, on 7 and 8 November the Scots Guards lost fifty men, twenty of them killed.

Six officers were hit, of whom five died, one was evacuated home and recovered, leaving Captain Stracey as the last survivor. Two died of wounds, one being Lieutenant Winthrop Smith, hit by a shrapnel ball at the base of the skull, causing a compound fracture. He was taken to Boulogne on the 11th and his parents Francis and Constance Smith came out to see him, but he was unconscious till his death on the 15th. They took his body back home to Wingfield Park, Ambergate, Derbyshire, for burial. Repatriating the dead occurred occasionally early in the War, mostly at the family's expense. Then, unless sanctioned officially, the practice was banned from April 1915. The other officer who died of his wounds on 9 November was Lieutenant James Stirling Stuart, who, after Eton, had been at Christ Church, Oxford. He joined from unspecified Territorials when war was declared and went straight out with the 1st Scots Guards to France. He had only returned on 28 October after recovering from being wounded on the Aisne. There was a long family history at Castlemilk, Lanarkshire, but William and Constance Stirling Stuart were now living in Reigate, Surrey. Three officers were killed. One was Lieutenant Francis Monckton, commissioned two years before, after Eton and Christ Church, who arrived on the Aisne, though since away sick, and whose younger brother had been wounded there. They were the sons of Francis and Evelyn Monckton of Stretton, Staffordshire. Another was Lieutenant Nigel Gipps, commissioned early in 1911 after Wellington and Sandhurst. Both his parents were dead, his father, a Lieutenant General when his son was born, having served with the Scots Fusilier Guards in the Crimean War. His only sister was married to Captain Romer, unfit to come out with the BEF at the start. Lieutenant Stewart, the Medical Officer, noted Lieutenant Gipps' death on the 7th and that he had been buried at Hooge. The third was Lieutenant Archibald Douglas Dick, not seen after 8 November, initially reported missing and of whom there was never any further word. He had been educated at Beaumont and was commissioned in 1909. Colonel Archibald Douglas Dick and his wife Edith lived at Pitkerro House, outside Dundee. Staying with them was their daughter Isabelle Fane Gladwin, whose husband Ralph had just been killed with the 2nd Battalion at Kruiseecke. She had now lost her brother as well. In the daylight it was impossible for Lieutenant Stewart to do anything to help the wounded. He wrote of 8 November "Nothing doing all day." At night he went to the trenches.

Because the Germans were still in the Zouaves' former trench forty yards in front of and to the right of where Captain Fortune's men had got to during the day the Black Watch machine gun teams went down again to enfilade them in the dark. Twenty three German dead were found the following morning. The rest had gone. However, the Zouaves refused to reoccupy the trenches. Generously the Camerons noted "The Scots Guards behaved splendidly throughout the day, sticking to their line under a merciless fire of shells and rifle bullets. They had many casualties." Captain Stracey, from then on, if not before, based himself in the orchard. On the 9th it was again fairly quiet but this was followed next by heavy shelling once more.

The Loyals, having got back into their positions on 8 November after the counterattacks, started handing over in Veldhoek Château Wood after dusk on the 10th to the 2nd Duke of Wellington's West Riding Regiment in a relief completed at two next morning. These were from II Corps, who, after the Aisne, had been in the La Bassée area and had now been replaced by the Indian Corps. So it became possible to feed II Corps into Ypres. The Duke of Wellington's had when they first arrived been put into trenches on the Menin Road, apparently near the Loyals, early on the 5th, going back into dug-outs near Hooge late on the 8th. However, they were generally unfamiliar with the positions and had had no opportunity to make contact with the Scots Guards on their left. There was, as well, a gap between them. The final point was that their forward trenches at the eastern edge of the wood, as well as on the other side of the Menin Road on the forward edge of Herenthage Wood, were in a salient, rather forward of the right hand Scots Guards trenches in the field to their north. They were the left hand battalion of the

3rd Division, now south of the Menin Road instead of the 7th Division. The Scots Guards were therefore on a divisional boundary. Many of Private Stewart's recollections of the twenty four hours starting after dark on the 10th, though improbable, were not impossible. He described the men in his trench line being told to go back about three hundred yards and dig in there, which they did. If correct, it could either have been a reserve or communication trench. While this was going on "I had an opportunity…of meeting men of my battalion, the survivors till then, and who admitted to me courageously and calmly, that they felt they would all be wiped out in a very few hours." This may have had something to do with the gap because Lieutenant Michael Abraham, 57th Howitzer Battery RFA, part of the 1st Division artillery, noted on the afternoon of the 10th when sent up as an observation officer, that there were the beginnings of a communication trench to be dug that night out from Veldhoek Château Wood to join up with the Scots Guards. This confirmed that there was then a gap. He returned after dark and, while going out again early the next morning to his post, miscalculated and walked straight into a German trench.

Captain Thorne told Margaret "This battle is never going to end until both sides are finished, I believe now. It is twice as strenuous as the B of the Aisne… I am writing this in the one remaining room of the farmhouse where we repair for dinner and breakfast in fact between 5.30pm and 6.30am except that we sleep in the dug-out. I have just finished my breakfast and have had a short run round a paddock outside – this was terminated rather suddenly by a toss into a new shellhole which I had not marked down before dark last night…The weather is still fine by day but the mist at night is very heavy and damp."

Major Henry Rochfort Boyd, commanding the 9th Battery RFA, had been to speak to the Camerons Battalion Headquarters about fire support for the Scots Guards in the orchard and for D Company of the Camerons to the north of the Reutelbeck and in particular about bringing his fire down closer to the British infantry. As a result of that Major Craig Brown sent a message at 3.30pm to "The NCO in command of the Scots Guards detachment in the garden. The artillery officer is going to shorten his range by 100 yards but fears for your own trenches if he shortens it more. He hopes infantry fire will be opened on the German trenches after he has fired." The reply came back "Sir, The last five shots fired just now resulted as follows, 1st Two, wants 50x up. 3, 4, 5, correct. J Macdonald Sgt".

The Prussian Guards

Matters stood as set out in the Historical Records of The Queen's Own Cameron Highlanders "Let us now take stock of the situation on the night 10th-11th November 1914. Since the 1st Brigade went into the battle of the Aisne on 14th September fifty eight days had passed and during this period there had been no rest for the troops. It is true that from the hour at which they reached Blanzy-lez-Fismes on 16th October to that on which they left Poperinghe early on the 21st they were out of range of the German guns, and the same applies to about twenty hours spent at Zillebeke on the night 25th-26th October; but these breaks, amounting in all to six days out of the fifty eight, were largely spent in marching or on the train. For fifty two days out of the fifty eight they had been in close proximity to the enemy and under an artillery fire to which our own artillery was not in a position to reply effectively…In addition to what has been stated above the troops had begun to suffer from exposure to the weather, which had been distinctly autumnal for several weeks." The Brigade now had about eight hundred men altogether to hold about a thousand yards. Those who had been at Ypres all along were very weary and the others had been pitched into the battle without preparation. A week earlier the 1st Division had figures of about two hundred and forty men each for the Scots Guards and Black Watch and about three hundred and fifty for the Camerons. By the night of the 10th the Camerons were still the strongest. The Black Watch had somewhere over two hundred. The Scots Guards had had one hundred and five at the roll call on 31 October and reinforcements of one hundred and ten since, but casualties of fifty on 7 and 8 November. That left Captain Stracey with a maximum of one hundred and sixty five but it can only have been fewer.

As soon as it began to get light at around six on 11 November, a grey, overcast day, the German artillery started the heaviest bombardment yet. It continued for three hours and became heaviest in its final hour. There was also mist and a slight breeze blowing from the west and so the smoke from the exploding shells drifting past the British trenches further obscured their observation, but mattered not to the German gunners who had the ranges from earlier. Significantly for the defence, dug into a series of foxholes, partly linked by shallow communication trenches, along the south side of Polygon Wood at right angles to the Black Watch were four hundred and fifty men of the 1st King's Liverpool Regiment [King's] of the 2nd Division. Significantly also, the guns of the 16th Battery RFA, part of the 41st Brigade RFA, the other batteries being the 9th and 17th, also of the 2nd Division, situated down the slope to the west of Nonne Boschen [Nuns Copse] were trained on their "Night Lines" to fire shrapnel immediately to the east of the Black Watch strong point and south of the line of Polygon Wood. There was something of a dip in the ground in front that the King's could not see into.

Major Rochfort Boyd of the 9th Battery started the morning in his observation post at a building called Lone House behind the Camerons' trenches, but went forward, apparently leaving his two signallers behind, to a trench he had used before some fifty yards further out in front of the Scots Guards orchard. His battery's "Night Line" was as adjusted the previous afternoon.

What the Germans were preparing was a broad fronted attack all along the Gheluvelt Plateau, though its emphasis was on an assault, with the Menin Road as its axis, by a specially assembled corps, commanded by General Karl Freiherr von Plettenberg, consisting of two divisions, each of twelve battalions, comprising the *4th Division* and Lieutenant General Arnold von Winckler's composite *Guards Division*, formed of Prussian Guards regiments from different formations near Arras. It was therefore immediately north and south of the Menin Road that the German artillery fire was most heavily concentrated. When nine o'clock came everything developed very quickly. The first person to see the Prussian Guards advancing towards the 1st (Guards) Brigade was almost certainly Major Rochfort Boyd observing from his trench forward of the Scots Guards orchard. The first German infantry he saw were to the south, almost level with him, in an unbroken line moving forward at a jog in complete silence through the mist. They did not fire but used the bayonet. He noticed that there was one gap in the enemy line, possibly caused by his battery's now firing on their Night Line in front of the Scots Guards orchard. There was little British resistance and he did not think that the Scots Guards had seen them coming. Unnoticed by the enemy, he then made his way carefully northwards up the line of the lost British front line trenches towards Polygon Wood, which he reached safely.

The *4th Division* attacked further south of the Menin Road, coming up behind the bombardment, but, apart from some initial success against the forward British trenches, were held and beaten off. Along the road itself and to its immediate south the two regiments of the *4th Guard*

Infantry Brigade attacked and made some progress, also capturing the 3rd Division forward trenches, but not getting any further. However, what started to unhinge the situation was when part of the right hand regiment, the *2nd (Emperor Franz) Guard Grenadier Regiment,* succeeded in overrunning both the firing line and support trenches of the Duke of Wellington's at the east of Veldhoek Château Wood. Those of them who kept going straight were stopped and driven back, but by then the damage had been done. The Scots Guards in their trench in the open field nearby could see this, as well as what had suddenly appeared to their front. There was also still the gap on their right.

Major Craig Brown was in a support line dug-out just north of the Scots Guards orchard. "At about 6am the Germans began to shell our lines, but there was nothing unusual about that. The shelling, however, went on & on, & got heavier & heavier, so we all, except sentries on lookout took cover in our trenches. Luckily for "A" coy where I was the shells all went over our heads, though most of them burst fairly close. We could tell however, that the Scots Gds on our right & the three other coys of the 79th on the left of "A" coy were having a pretty bad time of it. Shortly before 9 o'clock it became obvious that something more than a mere shelling was on foot, so I passed the word down the lines as loud as I could shout that all must stand to arms in their trenches & keep a very sharp lookout. There was a light breeze from the west, so that the smoke of the German shells blew slowly from us towards the enemy, and we could just see our own barbed wire & no more…I was standing at the door of my dug-out from where I could overlook all the trenches of "A" coy when suddenly through the smoke crowds of Germans in pickelhaubes appeared at our barbed wire fence next the garden hedge." This barbed wire ran along the front of the Camerons down to the northeast corner of the orchard occupied by part of the Scots Guards, who had none. It would seem that the barbed wire deflected some of the attackers round the south side of the orchard. When he saw the Germans in front Major Craig Brown "shouted to our front trench to open fire on them, but it was throat racking work trying to make oneself heard above the noise of the shelling. As I was shouting, Coy Serjt Maj Grant who was standing beside me suddenly told me to look round to my right rear. The sight I saw through the smoke was the Scots Guards leaving their trench & running back across the open in a Northern direction. Round the corner of the houses came a dense mass of Prussian Guards marching slowly, their officers in front with their swords drawn. There was no hurry, they did not charge or move out of a walk, only a few leading men fired occasionally at the retreating Scots Guards. They swung round to the N & NW in full view across the open. These were the only Germans I could see, as the smoke prevented me seeing far to the right or left. When I again turned to my coy. I saw, to my dismay, that they were hurriedly scrambling out of their trenches both in the firing line & in the support & following the Scots Guards in a confused & undisciplined crowd. I shouted to them to turn & open fire, but I might just as well have shouted to the winds. A few men & NCOs did fire one or two shots, but it was only a few seconds before I found myself standing there alone with the Prussians only 30 or 40 yards away." He hid away at the back of his dug-out to wait until dark in the company of Lance Corporal Douglas [untraced], who appeared five minutes later. A German did casually investigate and concluded that Corporal Douglas' protruding foot was that of a corpse, but otherwise the only enemy they could see was a sentry further up where B Company had been, beyond the Reutelbeck. During the afternoon they were joined by Private Robert McLagan of the Camerons, wounded by a bullet in the throat, bleeding profusely and gulping up frothy blood from time to time. They bandaged him as best they could, but still he bled. They had to wait for darkness and meanwhile promised that they would take care of him and go slowly for him when they tried to make their way back. While it was still light Major Craig Brown had a look outside very carefully. Apart from the dead there was nothing.

The Scots Guards in the orchard appear to have stayed and fought it out and then kept quiet, when there was nothing more that the survivors could do, but the Prussians made little effort to clear the positions. The strong point to the west of the orchard was right in the path of the left of the *1st Foot Guard Regiment*, whom Major Craig Brown saw coming round the southwest corner of the orchard, and they overran it. Captain Thorne wrote that the Prussians' undetected approach had the consequence that, of the two machine guns, one of which must have been a Camerons gun, at the east end of the orchard, one managed to fire two belts at point blank range, the other only one, "before they were swamped by the oncoming masses." He mentioned that an unnamed sergeant in charge of one of these teams managed to get away by the same route as Major Rochfort Boyd. A machine gun at Brigade Headquarters had a clear field of fire at the enemy approaching south of Polygon Wood, the right of whose attack was concealed from the King's by the fold in the ground.

The Prussian Guards had already started to lose cohesion. The *2nd (Emperor Franz) Guard Grenadier Regiment* began to veer off to the right under fire from the woods and shortly also from Brigade Headquarters in the farm buildings. Next to them the *1st Foot Guard Regiment*, possibly disrupted by shrapnel fired by the 9th Battery RFA on its "Night Line" through which they had to advance, had gone through the Camerons trenches, but could do nothing about the fierce resistance of the Black Watch and Camerons Battalion Headquarters in Verbeck Farm, who beat them off and deflected them, also to their right. The *3rd Foot Guard Regiment*, advancing between the Reutelbeck and Polygon Wood, were not only fired on effectively by the King's, though partly masked by the fold in the ground, but also shelled by the 16th Battery RFA on its Night Lines on precisely that line of advance. Lieutenant Anderson and his men in the Black Watch strong point did not see the Germans at all until they were past them, but then fired into their backs as they closed on the woods, which was when the German guns generally stopped firing. Lieutenant Anderson, badly wounded, and his men succeeded in holding on all through the day and inflicted very significant casualties, as well as disrupting the Prussian advance. Though the Prussians were milling around his strong point, they made no serious effort to attack it. Otherwise the Black Watch suffered severely and were largely overwhelmed. The Prussian losses were very heavy because, quite apart from anything else, this time the British gunners were not given any restriction on ammunition expenditure. The 16th and 17th Batteries fired 662 and 682 rounds respectively in the day, the 9th Battery rather fewer. For part of the time the gunners were firing over open sights and afterwards one dead German was found only three hundred yards in front. Further, the French IX Corps artillery also shelled the Prussians from further to the northwest and there was a French 75mm battery close to the 2nd Division's gun lines. The French guns were more difficult to manage and, while helpful to begin with, became a hindrance to the British once they contained the attack.

As had already occurred often and was to be a recurrent problem throughout the War it was difficult for any headquarters to learn what was happening. Major Corkran, the Brigade Major, wrote that the first news they had was when a private from the Scots Guards arrived at half past eight, but likely to have been later, to say that the Germans had got through on their right. This was followed at quarter past nine, probably more accurate, when a mixed party of Black Watch and Camerons with the Camerons Adjutant, Captain Ewen Brodie, killed later in the day, came to report that the enemy had broken through the centre and left and were in Nonne Boschen. This was correct. Though serious, the situation was not as bad as it could then have seemed. When some of the Prussians headed for Nonne Boschen others followed. The direction and control of the attack was lost. Even part of the *2nd (Emperor Franz) Guard Grenadier Regiment* went off that way. Some, not many, appear to have got into what became Glencorse Wood, just to the southwest, but most stopped in Nonne Boschen, though several lined up on the northwest edge. Only a very few went on through it and tried to advance through the gap between there and Polygon Wood, but there was some sniping at the British batteries beyond. The 1st Northamptons, in the wood later known as Inverness Copse, immediately west of Veldhoek Château Wood, and the by now very under strength Gloucesters, further back as I Corps reserve, were put under General FitzClarence's command. He ordered the Northamptons to clear the woods as far as and including the southern part of Nonne Boschen, which they achieved, and then they set about recovering the lost 1st (Guards) Brigade trenches to the east of there, generally those of the Black Watch north of the Reutelbeck. This was stopped immediately by both German and French artillery fire. The Gloucesters, as best they could, reinforced the line between where the Northamptons had got to and the Duke of Wellington's further back in Veldhoek Château Wood, the line otherwise being held by Brigade Headquarters on the edge of Glencorse Wood, the remaining Black Watch and Camerons at Verbeck Farm, any other available men from whatever source and survivors from the three battalions.

The British artillery, firing freely, prevented any German efforts to bring forward reinforcements, so it was now a case of dealing with the Prussian Guards in the northern part of the Nonne Boschen, steadily being shelled by the 16th and 17th Batteries RFA and by the French. This meant bringing up the 2nd Division's reserves, the nearest being the 2nd Oxford and Bucks LI. They formed up near Westhoek and, approaching from the northwest with two companies in front and two behind, at three o'clock made their way uphill into and through the Nonne Boschen, their counterattack perhaps partly concealed by trees and branches broken by shellfire, though the trees themselves were well grown and there was little undergrowth. In the wood they charged the Prussians, variously estimated at between five hundred and a thousand and routed them. It was a complete success, with support from the Northamptons on the south and from the 5th Field Company Royal Engineers and others on the north. The Prussians who survived fled, only to be mown down by French guns and British rifles when they came into the open. The Oxford and Bucks LI's losses were remarkably light, but, again, it was French guns which stopped further immediate pursuit of the enemy and immediate recovery of the lost northern trenches. It was about this time that the Northamptons relieved the Black Watch strong point. Lieutenant Anderson survived the War, winning two DSOs and a MC.

Further south, once the light went those who were still in the Camerons and Scots Guards positions, undetected and able to move, started off. Two more Camerons appeared and Major Craig Brown explained his plan, the most risky part being crossing the road immediately behind. This they decided to do by crawling across it one at a time at short intervals. All would meet up in the field of long wet grass beyond the hedge along the far side of the road and then work their way along a ditch which ran westwards towards Glencorse Wood. It was all very uncertain. Just before they started a Prussian stalked past going south but did not see them. The first obstacle turned out to be a pig killed in the morning, which they had to move round. Almost as soon as they started one of the men who had recently appeared went off on his own, but Major Craig Brown, Corporal Douglas, Private McLagan and the other soldier all managed to get to the ditch, which they could move along crouching. Major Craig Brown then stood on a body which moved, a Cameron bandsman, who had been lying there all day. So he came too. The ditch had been partly widened and deepened as a communication trench towards Verbeck Farm and that helped. Then they saw a building with a light. Major Craig Brown cautiously approached it on his own and found Brigade Headquarters. He confirmed to Major Corkran that the Germans were occupying their lost trenches of that morning. Then Regimental Sergeant Major Sydney Axten of the Camerons, who was there, took him to their Battalion Headquarters. At Verbeck Farm there were signs of a fierce struggle where the Prussians had come right up to it. Though they had been successfully beaten off, leaving many dead, there were also many dead Black Watch and Camerons. The body of Private John Grant, the Camerons Officers Mess Cook, was lying on the dug-out floor. Of Major Craig Brown's Company Sergeant Major, Donald Grant, there was no trace. Private McLagan stated later that the other soldier with them was Private Turner, a pioneer, [untraced] and that when Sergeant Major Axten met them he asked if there were any Camerons wounded. Private McLagan was unable to speak and Private Turner had a speech impediment, so, without an answer, the Sergeant Major went off. Later they reached the Camerons dressing station but there were no dressings left and so they went to be treated by the Scots Guards.

Just as a number of Camerons got back after dark, so too did several of the Scots Guards, whether they used the ditch or made their way straight across the field. Captain Stracey must have reached the British lines that way. From his account it is impossible to deduce where Private Stewart was, though, surprising as it may seem, he may have been or got himself close to the orchard and he may have stayed on and kept quiet in the firing line trenches when others left them. He mentioned having been buried by a shell and having dug himself out with difficulty. However, assuming that he was somewhere nearby, then it would figure that at some stage after dark Captain Stracey managed to pass the word to get back as best they could, though Private Stewart described him improbably as shouting out "Every man for himself" and Private Stewart ran for it, with his rifle and bayonet. Heading northwest he found the ground was "literally furrowed with shellholes into which I was falling every few minutes." He could see several others coming back with him and he reached a line of men, probably on the edge of Glencorse Wood, the remnants of several battalions, lying in extended order in the open. Lieutenant Stewart, the Medical Officer, noted "Heavy shelling – shrapnel bursting very close. Horrible night…out at trenches twice Bed 3.30." He was up at six in the morning to go round again.

By the later afternoon of the 11th the weather changed, it started to rain and after dark it was coming down hard. A plan was made to attack the Prussians in the old British front line later in the evening but various changes, doubt about precisely where they were, possibly in a new trench line dug slightly back from the lost British trenches, and the problems of assembling the infantry in the right place led to postponements and ultimately to a failure to make any positive move. Finally, General FitzClarence himself led forward the 2nd Grenadiers and 1st Irish Guards of the 4th (Guards) Brigade, along with a company of the 2nd Munsters. When they were two hundred yards from Polygon Wood an Irish Guardsman lost control and fired his rifle, Germans fired out of the darkness and General FitzClarence was killed. That ended counterattacks. To his wife Captain Thorne wrote "The poor old 1st Bde had a baddish day yesterday from the Germans. They finished up killing our Brigadier at 3am this morning while leading a night attack. Charles [Corkran] and I are nearly heartbroken, he was such a splendid man to serve & a glorious one to follow. I hadn't known him intimately for long but he was a man one would follow directly he came along and gave you the order he was so splendid. We were taken out of the firing line for a rest after the attack and well we have earned it…I wasn't with him when he was shot but just a little way behind taking a message for him. He died at once & I think without any suffering at all." General FitzClarence was buried near where he fell, but his grave was lost. Captain Thorne, who willingly mocked his own misadventures, provided that they did not affect anyone else, noted separately that at two that morning he had missed the path at Brigade Headquarters and fallen into the farm midden.

The effect of the Prussian Guards attack was a British loss of ground of some three hundred yards depth on a front of about one thousand yards. It took some time to clear Nonne Boschen and its vicinity of dead and wounded Prussians and a figure of about five hundred was given for the wood itself. Some three hundred wounded, of whom only about a dozen were British, were passed through the 41st Brigade RFA dressing station over the next three days, almost all suffering from shrapnel wounds. There was an unlooked for additional problem in the enormous height of the Prussians, awkward for stretcher bearers and sometimes making it impossible to shut ambulance doors.

Captain Fortune, who had been with the BEF throughout, was the only Black Watch officer left, with one hundred and nine men. He had a successful career until June 1940 when he had to implement the order to surrender when commanding the 51st (Highland) Division at St Valéry. The Camerons had three officers and one hundred and forty men, Major Craig Brown being one of the officers. He survived the War. In the two and a half weeks beginning with the advance towards Poezelhoek on 26 October the Scots Guards lost nine officers killed, seven wounded and five missing, of whom four, including Captain Meaden, were prisoners. One hundred and five men were known to have been killed, one hundred and fifty one had been wounded and four hundred and thirty were missing. Generally, little was known of when and where individuals had been hit, if that was what had happened. Company Sergeant Major Barwick, with wounds to his left elbow and to one of his hips, was sent back at the end of November to hospital in Leeds, where he was treated for four months. Later in 1915 he became a Drill Sergeant in the 3rd Battalion before going to the Guards Depot as Sergeant Major in April 1916, remaining there for the rest of the War. He married Eliza Watkins in Camden Town in 1905 and they had two sons. Sergeant Howson, having arrived on 6 November, was on his way back to England with a gunshot wound in his left shoulder on 10 November. He would have a lot of future medical problems, including recurrence of trouble from this wound, chose to revert to Private at his own request at the end of 1916, being required to sign a certificate that he was not doing so to avoid a court martial, but survived the War and became a policeman in Wigan. Of the two machine gunners mentioned at Gheluvelt Château, Private Clancy, who was posthumously mentioned in despatches, was posted missing after 11 November and Private Deignan was taken prisoner, probably that day.

Wounded in the right breast and shoulder on 11 November, Sergeant Major Tate was captured and remained in German hands, at least for part of the time at Nürnberg, until the March 1918 agreement, after which he was interned in Holland. He and Ellen Tate married in Sutton, Surrey, in 1903 and she was there with their son and daughter. A grocer's assistant when he enlisted in 1897, he had been serving ever since, but without being involved in the Boer War.

Posted missing was Private Dan Allison, the son of William and Maria Allison of Rawburgh, Norfolk, and Lieutenant Jamie Balfour's servant, who, when he was wounded on the Aisne, had helped to persuade the Zouaves to carry him to their dressing station near Vendresse. Previously a labourer, he had been serving since 1908. Lance Corporal David Thomson, the old soldier and regimental policeman wounded in the wrist on the Aisne, was missing and somehow his family were not told formally. A letter dated 26 December 1914 came from them at Bannockburn, which included "As there has been no letter from him since 8th Oct we are at a loss to understand his not writing, and no official notic of his being wounded or missing."

Some of the missing had close links. Privates Gilbert Ivall and Albert Turton, both born in Upton-cum-Chalvey, joined up together at nearby Slough in 1903 and both served for four years before going to the Reserve. Private Ivall had been slightly wounded on the Aisne, no details being recorded. He, a labourer, married Alice Jupp in Pimlico, in August 1913 and she was now living in South Lambeth. She wrote from London to ask if any of his possessions had been recovered, but there were none. Private Turton, a bricklayer, married Alice Stephens in Upton-cum-Chalvey in August 1911 and their son was born a year later. Their home was on the Chalvey side of Slough. Privates Alfred and Walter Purver were also reservists, the sons of Elijah and Clarah Purver of Sutton Scotney, Hampshire. They, a year apart in age, had joined up on the same day in 1906 at Winchester and each had served three years. Walter, who was not married, was missing and already dead, but Alfred, whose wife Ethel was living with his parents, was a prisoner. Another pair of brothers James and Thomas Freemantle, the sons of William and Sarah Freemantle, of Easton, near Winchester, both of them reservists and both with seven years previous service, were never seen again. James had married Grace Hoare at Cobham in May 1914, Thomas was unmarried. There were other Freemantles in the Scots Guards from the same part of Hampshire. One of them, Private Percy Freemantle, whose family lived at Bishopstoke, Winchester, enlisted in 1910, having been a plumber's mate. He served as a pioneer, which included being a plumber, in the 2nd Battalion throughout the War, apart from a few days in hospital with influenza at the beginning of November 1918, from which he quickly recovered. Privates James McNab and John Thomson were both from Alyth and gave their occupations as ploughmen when they enlisted together at Blairgowrie in 1910. After three years Private McNab extended his service with the Colours, but Private Thomson left for the Reserve, joining the police in Glasgow and coming back on mobilization. During the Battle of the Aisne he had helped rescuing and bringing in Lieutenant Eric Mackenzie when he was wounded. Both were prisoners by 11 November, though Private Thomson was wounded and captured earlier at Gheluvelt, with a gash six inches by two in his back. Both survived captivity.

There were false hopes that some had survived. The reservist Private Frank Fay, originally from Mottisfont, Hampshire, had served for eight years as a signaller from 1905. While the Battalion were in Egypt he was admitted to hospital in Cairo after accidentally swallowing a pebble, but the "Pebble was not seen in motions." He was posted missing on 11 November but, to begin with, mistakenly reported from Germany to be a prisoner, which had to be formally corrected when known in 1916. His body was found after the War, buried in the lawn in front of Gheluvelt Château. His widowed mother Mary Fay lived in London, at Twickenham. At the same time Captain Jack Balfour's body was found there too. Private Lenord Bird's home with his parents Thomas and Sarah Bird was in Portobello. He was a tram conductor in Edinburgh before enlisting for three years in July 1911, which meant that he had been a reservist for just under four weeks when mobilised and sent straight out to France. He was missing on 11 November, reported initially to be wounded and in a German field hospital at Ledinghem, but never confirmed. Another man missing was Private James Kendall, the tall Liverpudlian reservist, who worked with his father in the ship's chandlers business. Private John Harrison from Dundee served for seven years from 1899, including the Boer War, and completed his time on the Reserve in 1911, but signed on for another four years. He had a job as a pipe layer for the Dundee Gas Commissioners. Soon after he left the Army he and Mary Harrison got married, she being a widow with three children. They had five children of their own, the youngest being less than a year. Mary Harrison heard quite soon after it happened that her brother Leading Stoker John May, a Royal Navy reservist, had died when the battle cruiser *HMS Bulwark* blew up on 26 November off Sheerness in the Thames Estuary. Private Harrison had gone out to France in September to join the Battalion. It would be not till mid December that Mary Harrison heard that he was dead, killed sometime between 4 and 11 November. His identity discs and some postcards were all that were recovered. Private Fred Lumb, born in Leeds, was working as a carter when in 1911 he decided to enlist, but unlike his brother, Private Richard Lumb, by this time back, badly wounded, but otherwise safe, in England, Private Fred Lumb was now missing, never seen or heard of again. Sergeant Henry Arrowsmith from Walton, Liverpool, had been serving since the end of 1908 and held that rank at the start of the War. He had been married before he joined up, but his wife Clara had obtained a separation order in April 1914 on the grounds that he had deserted her, pregnant with their son, since two days before he enlisted. He was sent home to hospital on 20 November and continued being treated until September 1915, eventually being discharged unfit owing to neurasthenia in May 1917. He went to live in the Union Jack Club near Waterloo Station.

Private Peter Paton from Paisley had been out of the Army since 1902, soon after he came back from the Boer War. When his reserve commitment expired in 1910 he volunteered for four more years and was called up in August with only weeks to go. He was missing on 11 November and after a while word came that he had been shot through the left eye and captured, dying on 3 December in a war hospital in Courtrai. As happened with others, the Belgian staff in those hospitals tried to recover and hide dead British soldiers' possessions, even if very little, and so it was that Private Paton's identity discs reached his widow Catherine after the War. Private James Lacey had ceased to be a reservist some time before and been a brickworker in Cumbernauld before he reenlisted on 1 September. He arrived in France twelve days later, but almost certainly waited at the Base at St Nazaire to begin with and there was no record of when he joined the Battalion. He was missing as at 11 November. There was no one to tell. He had said that he had a brother in the USA, but did not know where, and gave no name. Private Harry Clarke was a miner in the Fife coalfield when he enlisted eight years earlier in Lochgelly and served three years. On mobilization he joined the Battalion immediately and had been in the BEF from the start. When he went sick was not recorded but on 29 November he was sent home. A spell in hospital in Sheffield made little ultimate difference, but next came his marriage just after New Year to Sarah Ann Redhead, a widow living in Sunderland with her three young daughters. A month later he was in hospital again and he left the Army at the end of January 1916 owing to "Disability caused by military service". He was insane.

It became very difficult to know when most individual casualties occurred from 29 October onwards, and often from earlier, unless there was clear evidence. Consequently, many men were posted missing as at 11 November, the last day when they could still have been with the Battalion. Apart from the roll call on 31 October, which only established who was then present, there was no complete roll call till 12 November and no earlier opportunity to ask about those not there. The survivors consisted of Captain Stracey and sixty nine men, though another four rejoined soon afterwards. Only five survived from the fire trench on the Battalion's right that morning, thirty from the orchard, four from the strong point, so the others must have been at Battalion Headquarters. Captain Stracey and Sergeant Macdonald were both mentioned in dispatches. Sergeant Macdonald, awarded the DCM in 1916 for consistent good work, rather than for any specific action, was never wounded and retired in 1924 as a Drill Sergeant. The Military Cross was instituted at the end of December for warrant officers and officers up to the rank of captain. The only Scots Guardsman awarded it in the first list was Sergeant Major Tate. In the second, not long afterwards, was Company Sergeant Major Barwick. Private Thomas Rickman, originally from Winchester, wounded in the right leg by a bullet on 1 November, won the DCM for reconnaissance. He had married Brigid Meaner in Dublin in 1909 and they had two children.

From 12 to 15 November the Scots Guards survivors, joined shortly by those of the Black Watch and Camerons, originally left holding part of the line near Nonne Boschen, stayed in dug-outs they had made near Hooge Château. Snow and rain fell heavily on the 15th, turning everywhere to mud. Next morning they marched west, initially down the Menin Road to Ypres, through it to Vlamertinghe and on southwest to Westoutre for the night.

Notes on Chapter Sources

Interviews of Pte R Law, 1st Camerons, and of Lt M Abraham RFA, TNA/WO161.
Contemporary documents, orders and messages sent to or among the 1st Camerons and personal accounts, including Pte R McLagan's statement, Craig Brown Papers, The Highlanders Museum.
Account of Capt StA Warde-Aldam, TNA/CAB45/141.
Diary of Capt J Stewart RAMC and papers, SGA.
Letter of Capt AA Meaden, Balfour Papers, Private Collection.
All other material relating to the events at Gheluvelt, all eyewitness accounts and correspondence (Sgt J Macdonald, Lt BG Jolliffe, Sgt W Shepherd, Sir Victor Mackenzie, CSM J Barwick, Maj AW Campbell Krook, LSgt J Shields and Lt Col B Leach), Thorne Papers, NAM, obtained during research into 'Gheluvelt Cross Roads, October 29th, 1914', Summer Number 1932, *Household Brigade Magazine*.
Those educated at George Watson's College and some of the other material about them, Watson's War Records on www.gwc.org.uk.
Account of Lt RH FitzRoy, TNA/CAB45/140.
Letter of Lt J Boyd, TNA/CAB45/140.
Lt M Salmon story of the Scots Guardsman told to look to his front, letter from his cousin, Capt CAB Young, a survivor of the 2nd Welsh at Gheluvelt, SGM 1965.
Statement of Capt EG Christie Miller, TNA/CAB45/141.
Brig Gen C FitzClarence reports on 27 October to 2 November and on 8 November and Maj C Corkran report on 11 November, 1st Division War Diary TNA/WO95/1227.
Diary of Maj E Craig Brown, IWM/Documents 1862.

Pte D Stewart, *"With the "Old Contemptibles" in 1914 against Germany's formidable War Machine"* 1938 New Westminster, British Columbia, SGA.

Maj Gen H Landon letter of 7 November to Maj Gen F Wing, TNA/WO154/18.

War Diaries: 41 Brigade RFA TNA/WO95/1326 and other material TNA/CAB45/141, 2nd Duke of Wellington's Regiment TNA/WO95/1552.

Two accounts of Maj H Rochfort Boyd, TNA/CAB45/141 and 143.

Account of Capt AFAN Thorne, TNA/CAB45/143.

6

The Prisoners of War

Most Scots Guardsmen taken prisoner during the War were captured in five events during First Ypres. The first two, affecting the 2nd Scots Guards, were the overwhelming of two thirds of F Company on 23 October with the 2nd Wiltshires between Polygon Wood and Reutel and three days later both Right and Left Flank at Kruiseecke. The other three, affecting the 1st Scots Guards, were, first, on 29 October the capture of about eighty men, but it may have been more, from Right Flank and B Company just northeast of Gheluvelt, next, the loss of the wounded who had to be left behind on the evening of 31 October at Gheluvelt Château and lastly, further back west, those captured during the days leading up to and in particular on 11 November during the Prussian Guards attack. What happened on the spot varied depending on who the immediate captors were, their standard of self control and their frame of mind.

The same variations applied in the prison camps and the hospitals, but living conditions were usually very harsh, there was never enough food, which was why food parcels were so important, generally, but far from always, respected by the Germans, though, again generally, they did not permit matches, British newspapers or pepper, which they believed and apparently was used to put tracker dogs off the scent of escapers. Work included coercion into coal, salt and other mines, munitions factories and, in the case of many British and other prisoners, but no recorded Scots Guardsmen, the immediate rear areas behind the German front line. The disciplinary regime, always severe and more often than not arbitrary and unfair, included punishing prisoners by tying them by wire to posts, sometimes with their feet off the ground, but this was also a military punishment administered to German soldiers and the British FP No 1 was similar. There were, however, several incidents with varying consequences for the recipients which could not be attributed to any recognised proper exercise of military discipline. The other factor threatening prisoners was disease, notably typhus, not in all camps, but serious in some, and a killer, though most of the British who caught it recovered, TB, which several developed, a slow, lingering killer, and in 1918 Spanish Flu, widely prevalent and a widespread killer. Further, there were industrial accidents, most frequently in the mines. A few, usually wounded men, who chanced to be sent initially to military hospitals in unusual places and so had very few other British with them, later reported favourably on how they were treated. For most, however, it was a rough, sparse and frequently cruel existence in camps all over Germany and that theme runs through account after account. Thirty seven Scots Guardsmen were recorded as having died as prisoners in Germany, mostly the victims of disease. Several others died of wounds in Belgium and France after capture.

During the War interviews took place with prisoners returning to the UK, either escaped or exchanged because of disabling illness or wounds, and the more worthwhile responses were collated and printed. The same applied to those later on during the War sent from Germany for internment in Switzerland and Holland. The questions included circumstances of capture, treatment of all sorts, compulsion to work, particularly in munitions factories, visits by neutral observers, the internal situation in Germany and approaches on subversion.

The 2nd Scots Guards at Reutel and Kruiseecke

Considering what happened shortly afterwards to many wounded prisoners unable to walk, those of F Company badly wounded and captured to the east side of Polygon Wood were very fortunate in being relatively well treated when the Germans came upon them on 23 October and immediately afterwards. Lance Corporal Oliver Blaze was one. James and Clara Blaze were in London, living in Pimlico, and their son was a tobacconist's assistant. Then he joined up at the end of 1911, soon afterwards becoming a clerk in the Battalion Orderly Room. He was captured with a bullet wound in his right arm, which a German doctor amputated almost immediately. Corporal Blaze was then carried on a stretcher to a field hospital at Zonnebeke where he remained, well treated, till 7 November, before being sent to Münster, Westphalia. While there he noted that once, when the prisoners played the German camp guards at football and won, the guards took the ball away for three days. Exchanged in August 1915, he was discharged in February 1916. Private David Milne, a reservist, came from the fishing village of Gourdon, south of Aberdeen, though he had been in a wagon works before he enlisted in Hamilton in 1904 and served for eight years. The Germans who captured him took him first to Zonnebeke with shrapnel wounds in his left ankle and right shin, which led to the immediate amputation of his left foot. He was reported as a prisoner while in hospital in Brussels. Just over a year later he was exchanged and soon sent to Queen Mary's Convalescent Hospital, Roehampton, Surrey, to be fitted with an artificial limb. Almost at once he married his long term girlfriend Ethel Beck with whom he already had a five year old son. He was discharged in April 1916 and seems to have gone back to Gourdon. Private Herbert Helstrip, a soldier with two years service, was recorded as captured on 24 October [but likely to have been in F Company on the 23rd]. Like others he was taken first to Göttingen. In late 1917 he was in a camp near Soest, Westphalia, and it was in hospital there that he died on 21 December. Two days before he had been riding in a cart when, frightened that the horse was about to bolt, he jumped off, lost his balance as he fell and hit his head on the ground, fracturing his skull. He did not regain consciousness. Previously he had been a porter in Leeds, where Walter and Clara Helstrip lived in Armley. The experience of the unwounded was not smooth and Private Thomas Bradshaw described how "I was …stripped of all pack and kit, and would have been "done in" but for a German sentry who claimed me as his prisoner" and how he was fortunate to manage to hold on to his jacket. Private Bradshaw, a labourer until 1904, had been a reservist for seven years. His father Harry Bradshaw lived in Burnley. In captivity Private Bradshaw developed a tubercular lung, was exchanged in May 1916 and discharged medically unfit. Private Vincent Howard told how he had been taken prisoner with about a hundred other men, some of them wounded, when the Germans surrounded them. The Germans did bandage their wounds. "We were not allowed to speak to each other. We were taken prisoners about 7 o'clock in the morning, and were taken to the grounds of a large house, where we remained all day in the open air…As soon as we were captured we were stripped of our overcoats, tunics, helmets and jerseys. About midday we each got a small bag of biscuits and a piece of fat bacon." Private Howard, blacksmith and shoeing smith and the son of Kathleen Howard of Liverpool, served for three years from 1908, left briefly and then returned to the Colours. He had a different future as a prisoner.

Three days after the events at Polygon Wood Bavarians overwhelmed most of the defenders of Kruiseecke. Private Alexander Beattie, a labourer till 1907 and a reservist since 1910, had been married for a year to Barbara Beattie of Fountainbridge, Edinburgh. In his case "We were captured at 3 o'clock in the afternoon of 26th October 1914 – about 70 of us altogether. The first thing the enemy did after we were captured was to kill the wounded lying about, all those who could not walk. They then took us over to their headquarters to the east. They formed us into a ring and left us in the danger zone of our own shells and told us that if we were killed by our own shells they could not help it. Our officers were taken to the headquarters, but the men were left in that ring. We remained there about an hour. They then searched us and took away all our personal possessions such as money, knives, letters, &c. Some got all their money taken while others were left with it. Personally I had no money on me. Officers as well as privates searched us and the men were best treated by the officers. We were then marched further east perhaps about half a mile. We were left there with a lot of cavalry round us. Privates then came up to us, and I think I was about the first man to get stripped of my overcoat and my tunic. The clothes they took off us they donned themselves, and if they did not fit they interchanged the garments amongst themselves. The only men left with their coats were those who had been wounded but could walk. They had mercy on them. I felt very cold without my tunic and coat." By contrast, Lance Corporal Jack Gill, a reservist, who had become a Durham policeman, was kindly treated by the German sergeant who dressed his badly wounded right leg, broken in two places by machine gun bullets, which later had to be amputated in a military hospital at Wesel, Lower Rhineland. At the beginning of February 1915 he was sent to the camp nearby at Friedrichsfeld but, because no reports of his being alive had reached England for four months, he never received any food parcels until May that year. Exchanged in August 1915, he was discharged the following March. He was a Lancashire man from St Helens, but his wife Barbara came from South Shields. They married there two weeks after he went onto the Reserve in 1912 and there they settled down. The first information which reached Regimental Headquarters of his being a prisoner at Friedrichsfeld came from a fellow Scots Guardsman and reservist, Private William Blackburn, who, wounded in the thigh and captured on 26 October at Kruiseecke, had been in hospital in Düsseldorf before being sent on. He was originally from Halifax and an engine cleaner before becoming a soldier. He and Kate Millett got married in 1913 in Pontefract and she was there with their daughter. Private Thomas Cowan, the son of John and Elizabeth Cowan of Kelty, was a Fife miner who served three years and became a reservist in March 1914. He and Margaret Murray married two weeks before war was declared and she became pregnant at once. When he reported on mobilization she stayed in Lumphinnans. At Kruiseecke Private Cowan was hit in the left arm and side and taken prisoner, dying of his wounds on 19 November in hospital at Courtrai. The Belgian staff saved his identity disc and that was sent to Margaret Cowan on 14 May 1919.

Captain Charles Fox, from Milltown, County Dublin, was brought up there and then went to Oxford, where he excelled as an oarsman, notably sculling, and joined the Scots Guards in 1900. In the same year he won the Wingfield Sculls at the British Championships and the next year the Diamond Sculls at Henley Royal Regatta. He spent most of the time between then and

1912 attached to the West African Frontier Force before going to the Sudan. There, amongst other activities, he successfully conducted an elephant poacher hunt, was himself captured and then escaped. In 1912, fighting at middleweight, he was runner up in the officers competition of the Army Boxing Championships. During the Balkans War in 1913 he was a Special War Correspondent with the Turkish Army. The words in brackets are an informed guess at the ones missing from the text of the 2nd Scots Guards War Diary copy of Captain Fox's letter of 8 January 1918 to the Commanding Officer 3rd Scots Guards describing his capture at Kruiseecke. "I could not keep up with the other prisoners, and a wounded man asked me by name not to leave him. I was trying to carry him [when a] German bayoneted him. I was making my best pace towards [the others when a] group of Germans seized me, and stripped me of [all my equip]ment, money and valuables. The Officer came up [and then sent some of] my own men to help me back. I was taken along the line of our trenches. I saw no man come out of them alive. In front of Lieut Fane Gladwin's machine gun was a pile of dead Germans, which I estimated at 240. The nearest dead German was lying on the parapet itself of the gun pit. Our orders were to hold on at all costs. I think we obeyed those orders. We fought a superior force to a standstill. We paid all the costs ourselves – three awful years of prison, of insult, of brutality." Captain Fox counted a total of eighty four prisoners of all ranks from the 2nd Scots Guards, 1st South Staffords and 2nd Borders, including six Scots Guards officers. He stated that there were a number of men whom he would like to see recognised for what they had done at Kruiseecke. Separately Captain Fox described how he also had his greatcoat and tunic removed by the Germans before, wounded in the right shoulder and left leg, he was bundled into a car with Lieutenant Lord Gerald "Gerry" Grosvenor, who had a shrapnel wound in the head. They were then put on a train to the officers camp at Crefeld. Lord Gerald Grosvenor was the youngest son of the 1st Duke and Duchess of Westminster. An Etonian, he was commissioned in 1899, served in the Boer War, where he was slightly wounded in the thigh at Bethlehem in October 1900, and left the Army in 1905. After rejoining at the start of the War, he was hit in the right eye at Kruiseecke and, though he did not lose it, his sight was permanently affected.

In 1907 Private Frank Dodd, from Toxteth, Liverpool, enlisted and served for three years, after which he joined the police in Liverpool. He and his wife Ethel got married in 1912. Having reported on mobilization, Private Dodd became a Lance Corporal on 5 October, the day the Battalion embarked. He was wounded on the 26th while with Captain Fox and lay out all night, very cold and in great pain from a wound in his right groin, until found and brought in by the Germans next morning. Exposure led to pneumonia and he was handed over to the Belgian run Nôtre Dame Hospital in Courtrai. Meanwhile, Ethel Dodd had been officially notified that he was missing, believed killed. However, he managed to write to her twice, on 30 October and 18 November, and she then wrote on 21 December to Regimental Headquarters to say that he was alive and "getting on much better now." The next report dated 23 April 1915 that reached the British authorities was that Corporal Dodd had died in captivity. In great distress Ethel Dodd wrote on the 26th "I was deeply greived at receiving the report stating my Husband's Death but I can Hardly belive it to be true as I only recived a letter from him on Thursday morning saying he had fully recovered from his wounds and was now getting about on crutches. He is still in the same hospital where he was first taken Prisoner of War since the 26th of Oct 1914 trusting the Report is not true." This second report of Corporal Dodd's death was finally dispelled when Ethel Dodd forwarded his letter of 10 May, with a photograph of him in hospital. Shortly after this he was exchanged, convalescing in London and later at the Police

Convalescent Home in Harrogate, before being discharged from the Army. He went back to Liverpool and became a police sergeant. On 30 January 1920 the London Gazette published the award to him of the DCM. There was no citation, but Major Charles Fox must have been involved. Even this did not go smoothly, for it was a Long Service and Good Conduct Medal that Police Sergeant Dodd received by post and had to send back, requesting his DCM instead. At Kruiseecke the Germans also captured Company Sergeant Major William Edwards, who enlisted at the end of 1899, another Liverpudlian. Immediately before the War he spent a year as a Colour Sergeant with the 4th Nigeria Regiment, West African Frontier Force, before he and Phoebe Fry got married in June 1914 at Horningsham, Wiltshire. He survived four years in captivity, but his health was so broken, made worse by malaria contracted in West Africa, that he left the Army as soon as he got back to England and went to live off Wandsworth Common in South London. Private John Duffy, a reservist, was very lucky to get away with his life when taken prisoner on 26 October. He had been bayoneted in the right cheek. Before he enlisted in 1908 for three years he was a labourer and gas stoker in Bradford, where William and Kate Duffy lived. He survived captivity and left the Army with a medical discharge after the War.

Captain John Rose Troup of the 1st Queen's, who could speak German and understood it perfectly, was captured on 31 October 1914 by Bavarians at Gheluvelt. He and about forty men were then beaten about the back and head with rifle butts and sworn at. Though wounded, he was able to walk and once his party were in the hands of German doctors they were well treated. Then he walked back to a German field hospital in a convent, where two young German doctors invited him to see a seriously wounded British officer. This turned out to be Lieutenant Colonel Maxwell Earle of the 1st Grenadiers "who told me that he had been well cared for there. I was given a cup of coffee and a sandwich. All the wounded were evacuated from the hospital at about 7pm, and were sent to Courtrai in a steam train. On arrival at Courtrai the more seriously wounded were placed in the waiting room. The others, including myself, slept on benches in the booking hall." A German civilian Red Cross worker befriended him and lent him his blanket for the night of the 31st. The next afternoon they were all loaded onto a train of German wounded, the accommodation for the British being a couple of bare trucks with plenty of straw but nothing else. In one were Captain Rose Troup and sixteen men. "Some of them were badly wounded, especially No 3353 Cpl Higgins, Scots Guards…At every station during the journey the door was opened and soldiers and civilians shook their fists at us, cursed us, and in some cases spat at us. The language of the soldiers was extremely violent and filthy. During the whole journey which lasted a little over 48 hours, we were given no opportunity of relieving ourselves although I complained several times. During the night of November 1/2, while the train was at rest in a station, two men entered the truck and kicked us and spat on us. On the morning of November 2nd, the German doctor i/c the train, a lieutenant in the medical corps, came in to see us. He said that he had no time to do any bandaging. He used abusive language at me and then turned to the crowd on the platform and urged them to curse and spit at us. At one station during the morning we were given coffee and bread. In the evening when a Red Cross orderly was giving us a sandwich, a Red Cross sister tried to stop him and said "They must not be given anything to eat; they are accursed English pigs." This was the last food we had until 5.30pm next day. On 3/11/14 at about midday, as we had had nothing to eat that morning, I asked a Red Cross orderly to get us something at a station. The only thing he could get was a very small slab of chocolate, for which he paid out of his own pocket. During the afternoon, while the train was in the station at Minden, a German soldier entered the truck and took a greatcoat which was covering one of the seriously wounded men. At about 5.30 pm we arrived at Hanover. We were taken to the Red Cross waiting room where we were given coffee and bread. The seriously wounded British were taken to hospital. The doctor refused to let them have anything to eat before they got to hospital…only three of the worst cases were sent to hospital." Lance Corporal Albert Huggins [not Higgins] gave his occupation as a labourer when enlisting in April 1900 in London. From there he went on to serve in the Boer War and during his eight years with the Colours before becoming a reservist was awarded ten days Confined to Barracks in March 1902 for "Creating a disturbance and using obscene language in a brothel in Eton." In May 1909 he married Agnes Bloomfield in Shoreditch and they had two daughters and a son, the younger girl, the youngest of the family, being born in 1914. When his reserve commitment ended in 1912 he volunteered to extend it for four years. Reported wounded and missing on 28 October, he died on 15 November in the Reserve Hospital at Hameln, Saxony, news of this coming through the American Embassy in Berlin over two months later. A direct contemporary of his was Private William McHugh, a Northern Irishman and a farm worker before he enlisted at Hamilton the day after Corporal Huggins. Apart from serving a year less with the Colours his military career was identical. He and Mary McHugh, though he also used the surname Boal, married in Newtonards, County Down, in 1902 and had four sons and a daughter, the youngest son being born in 1915. Private McHugh, also missing as at 28 October, died on 18 May 1916 of heart failure while on a working party from the main camp at Göttingen. A week later a fellow Scots Guardsman, Sergeant James Huston, wrote from the main camp reporting this to Regimental Headquarters and added "we could not go to the Funeral from here, but I made a subscription from the Camp for a wreath which was sent on to the remainder of the men who are working at the same place. I cannot communicate with his relatives as I have not the address, but will take the opportunity of the first letter that arrives for him." Sergeant Huston had been a regular soldier since enlisting in 1904 at Southampton, where he was a fishmonger. He was probably captured at Reutel. Martha Huston, his mother, lived at St Helier, Jersey. He survived.

Private Reginald Spencer, the man who, after five months absence, had been convicted of desertion on 4 August 1914 in London, was another prisoner. After starting at Göttingen he was moved and it was in the camp hospital at Hameln that he died of peritonitis on 10 November 1916. William and Elizabeth Spencer lived in Halton, Leeds. Unusually quickly, a report that he was a prisoner came on 19 November 1914 and quicker still was that on 12 November about Private Frederick Smith, who was known as "Corporal Smith" in captivity and may have been one of the men promoted in the field in October of which there was no subsequent record. He was a Londoner, a time expired former Scots Guardsman and a packer by occupation, who reenlisted on 13 August. By the spring of 1917 Corporal Smith was at Friedrichsfeld, but he was out in a working party in a coal mine when on 11 March he was killed falling down a mineshaft. Three weeks later the Reverend AG Wilkin, a very recently repatriated chaplain, not British, but possibly Canadian, wrote of "one of the bravest soldiers I have ever come across, Corporal Smith of the Scots Guards, killed through gross carelessness. He was sent to work in an old disused shaft where there was a gallery which crossed round the shaft and on the side of the gallery was an open shaft without any railing or protection. One night in the darkness the first night he was sent along this gallery, he fell down the shaft and was killed. He was a fine man. When young soldiers came in from the Somme he made them look after themselves and keep themselves clean and he was the life and soul of the camp, much beloved by the men." Corporal Smith was also known as Frederick Packman. His wife Mabel, whom he had married on Boxing Day 1912, lived under that name in Lavender Hill, London.

Private Joseph Barry was reported missing on 28 October 1914. On 18 January 1918 a guard at Sennelager, Westphalia, shot him dead. News of the murder got out very quickly and there were prolonged attempts by the Foreign Office, through the Dutch Government, to make representations to the Germans, who were not having any of it. There was overwhelmingly consistent second hand evidence from Australian, British and Belgian prisoners. However, not till the autumn could an eyewitness statement be obtained from Private Walter Palmer of the 2nd Royal Warwicks, though the account put together by Company Quartermaster Sergeant Patrick Nolan of the 2nd South Lancashire Regiment by interviewing witnesses put it most clearly of all. The practice was that those being sent out on working parties spent the night before at the bathhouse, where they were also deloused. At about half past four in the morning on 18 January a guard with a rifle came into the room at the bathhouse where were some sixty three prisoners, Private Barry being one of six British. He called for men to fetch coffee and seven Frenchmen stepped forward, but he wanted a British man as well, Private Barry being the first he saw. On being told to fetch coffee Private Barry explained quite politely that he would not, because the British did not like the coffee and never drank it. It seems that the guard then, probably in order to force Private Barry towards the door, tried to strike him with his rifle. Private Barry attempted to ward off the blow, whereupon the German walked to the door himself, motioned three Frenchmen to step aside and deliberately shot him dead. The camp authorities held an inquiry but failed to get any evidence to back up the guard, whom they nevertheless permitted to continue his duties, while taking great care to keep his name concealed. Private Barry was from Kirkdale, Liverpool, where his mother Sarah was living and where he was a casual labourer before enlisting in April 1914.

Private Hugh Quinn, habitual absentee at the Tower of London and later at Lyndhurst, was another missing at 28 October. He started at Göttingen, but when the Germans identified him as a Roman Catholic they sent him to Limburg and later to Giessen, respectively northeast and north of Frankfurt. He survived captivity and was discharged medically unfit soon after being repatriated. Limburg was used for Catholic Irish prisoners, whether in Irish regiments or not, as well as other Catholics and it was here that Private Patrick Deignan, the 1st Scots Guards machine gunner from County Westmeath, probably captured on 11 November, died in the military hospital on 7 March 1915. The reasoning was that they might be attracted to the Irish Brigade, for which Sir Roger Casement was trying to recruit. The take up for this was insignificant, but a few agreed to join, were housed in a much better camp close by and dressed in green uniforms. Two were involved in Sir Roger Casement's landing in the west of Ireland just before the Easter Rising in April 1916. Apart from when trying to recruit, the Irish Brigade men were kept away from the prisoners. Subsequently, those interviewing former prisoners sometimes questioned them about any approaches they had had to join the Irish Brigade. Most knew nothing about it.

The 1st Scots Guards at Gheluvelt and Nonne Boschen

Schneidemühl in West Prussia, on the main Berlin-Königsberg railway, already held a very large number of Russians captured at the Battles of Tannenberg and the Masurian Lakes earlier in the autumn. This was the destination for British other ranks taken prisoner unwounded on

29 October to the north of the Menin Road, though there were some others. The train stopped at Schneidemühl station on 6 November. They, the first British arrivals, then had two miles march to the camp.

Private James McGinlay, a reservist, was captured on 29 October. He had been a miner before enlisting in Hamilton in 1908 but by 1914 was working again as a miner. He had married while he was serving and he and Ethel McGinlay had since had three boys. They were living at King's Norton, near Birmingham. Once he returned home he said that he did not see "any breach of the rules of fair warfare" while fighting, but that when captured he had his overcoat, tunic, cap, all papers and money taken off him. His description of going to Schneidemühl mirrored that of others, except that he added that at stations the guards sometimes opened the doors of the cattle trucks "to show us to the people." He was involved in doing fatigues at the camp, mainly clearing latrines and cookhouse slops, which after a month led to an issue of additional bread to those doing this work. There was also the detail that after they had been there a week all the British prisoners were made to hand in their boots and were issued with wooden clogs with leather toecaps. Corporal Benjamin Guy of the 1st Coldstream, from Northfleet, Kent, was captured the same day and sent to Schneidemühl. He described how the Germans, whom he thought were Bavarians, had come along the line of the trench as others stood overlooking it and deliberately killed all the wounded lying there. "Before we left the battlefield we were stripped of everything except our shirts, trousers and boots. I am speaking of the majority of us." He said that these soldiers seemed to be doing so without orders. While, quite apart from the Bavarians killing the wounded who could not walk, the plight of the prisoners was bad enough, Corporal Guy did not suffer an experience which he heard about soon afterwards. This was the imminent killing of unwounded prisoners as "my own chum, Private Kewell, of the Scots Guards…told me that he was one of a party of five which was lined up in this way to be shot and that this party was saved by the intervention of the German officers." Other British prisoners he spoke to at Schneidemühl confirmed this. Private Frederick Kewell was from near Bognor, Sussex, served for three years from 1902 and then became a reservist. He and his wife Sarah married at Angmering in 1906 and had two daughters. He went out of his mind in captivity, possibly because of the effects of typhus, and was sent back to England, where he arrived at the beginning of October 1915. After two and a half months in hospital in Wandsworth, he was discharged from the Army on account of "chronic mania", his future address the Milton Asylum, Portsmouth. Private Edward Fegan, a reservist since 1912, whose parents Matthew and Annie Fegan lived in Edinburgh, was a van driver in Glasgow before being mobilised. Word that he was at Schneidemühl came first through a letter from a relative to Regimental Headquarters. He caught typhus but recovered. Later on he developed TB, possibly not until after he left Schneidemühl, because it was from Neuhammer in Silesia, when he already had the disease, that he was sent down a coal mine for two weeks. He refused all payment for this work and so was punished by being sent to live on his own with Russian prisoners for three months. Because of the TB he was passed in May 1916 to go to Switzerland under the disabled prisoners internment scheme.

Corporal Green described how later in the morning on 29 October "disaster came to us – news arrived they had broken through on our right. Finally they completely encircled us, and about 11am we were forced to throw down our arms." He was close by when Captain de la Pasture fell wounded "and died with the words "Tell my wife I died fighting" (He was a born gentleman, and an excellent officer). About 170 Scots Guardsmen were captured – few indeed when considering the losses we had inflicted." The numbers of men taken prisoner varied significantly in the different accounts. "I shall never forget the ensuing hours as long as I live. They brought us to our knees, and we should have been dead men if a German Officer had not intervened. They took away everything – money, smokes, pipes, etc. But my luck was in. The Hun who searched me was a decent fellow – one in a million. He told me to put everything back in my pockets, which I gladly did. All of us, however, were ordered to discard our greatcoats. We felt the loss too, the weather was cold. The fellows who suffered most were those on whom German money, etc. were found. We now commenced to march back to the enemy's Headquarters. They forced us to march hands above heads the whole way. We stopped at a farm, and left our wounded, also all our small books, photographs. On restarting, some of our escort were so kind enough as to give our fellows their packs to carry. Fighting had evidently been going on all around. We passed many wounded who made motions they would dearly like to cut our throats. After a very uncomfortable journey, we reached Becelaere. For an hour or two, we were confined in a church. A German Officer, speaking excellent English, came up and asked for Colonel Lowther, whom he had known in Berlin some years before. He asked other questions – but he would have had better results in asking a brick wall. Lieut Jolliffe and Captain FitzRoy said nothing. About 4pm they packed us into tram cars, and took us to Courtrai, a large town and that particular army's headquarters. At the railway station, they packed and securely locked in cattle trucks." Next day "We did not appreciate the existing circumstances – our "bed" was very hard, and the "inner man" was beginning tell the tale. However, we were given a bit of black bread to appease our hunger, but couldn't bring ourselves to tackle it. The smell of it was quite sufficient. Later in the day the train halted, and we politely enquired for a drink of water. A pompous railway official attired in a resplendent and glittering uniform, went away, and shortly returned with a bucketful. But he was kind enough to throw it over us with the remark "*Das ist gut trink*." The train then moved off." Next day "Although our train halted several times it was 3am this morning before we received any more food. Then it was only a slice of black bread again. On the resuming of our journey, the train soon afterwards passed through the ruined town of Louvain. At 8pm that evening we again halted, and ordered to get out. Our escort marched us into a wooden hut, where we received a basin of barley soup and a piece of sausage (don't call it a name)." On 1 November "Onwards again at the usual pace of a snail. Sometime later in the day we halted and received another decoction of soup. Then we had to run back to the train, or else a rifle butt dropped across our shoulders. Surprise again at 7pm by halting for more soup, raw bacon, black bread and coffee. This proved to be the last during our journey." On 2 November the train arrived at Schneidemühl and they got off at eight o'clock in the morning "and very glad we were, too." They did not see the camp until close to it, which was "then in the course of erection. Arriving inside the barbed wire, and notwithstanding the bitterly cold weather, they made us stand there for three hours. We felt it all the more, because we had received no food and hot drink, besides only wearing the regimental Khaki. Then a move was made, and in parties of fifty, were all inoculated. Before I go further, I have to write of the cruelty with which the camp Adjutant treated three old Belgian women. These old people had been brought with us – what for, I cannot tell. But at any rate, they suffered exactly the same way we did, and finally fell to the ground exhausted. The camp Adjutant brutally kicked them, but they absolutely beyond human aid. We never saw them afterwards, I believe the Hun got rid of them by some means. Then we were issued with basins, spoons, and blankets. Proceeded to the cookhouse and some sort of brown meal soup was given out. But a pig couldn't eat it, never mind human beings. And we all suffered from the same complaint – hunger. The Russians benefited by this soup. They could put away as much as you liked to give them. Our next thing was to find shelter, very easy done. They had already had holes dug in the ground, and banked with straw, [and] this is [where] we found ourselves that evening." Of Corporal Green's three pals from Coulommiers the one he referred to as Private Bill Shaw could have been one of two men. It was initially thought that Private John William Shaw, a boot finisher and the son of John and Alice Shaw of Leeds, had been captured and sent to Schneidemühl. He was not there, but missing. As no one knew where and when, the official date for his death, as with that of many others, was later set as 11 November. He had been serving for two years and trained as a stretcher bearer the year before. Alternatively, it could have been Private William Henry Shaw, who was a prisoner at Schneidemühl, as were the other two, Private Mellor and Corporal Holroyd. This Private Shaw, once a plasterer from Portsmouth, where his father Edmund Shaw was living, had served for three years from 1905 and then become a policeman in Kettering, Northamptonshire. When he was called up from the Reserve on mobilization there were details that any casualty was to be reported to the Superintendent of Police, Kettering, and also to Miss E Sampson at an address in Pont Street, London.

Also taken prisoner was Corporal Alexander Cairns, the former painter's labourer from Leith promoted on the same day on the Aisne as Corporal Holroyd. He subsequently wrote a poem about Gheluvelt on 29 October, of which this was the last verse:

> Of the brave lads who fell in the field, Sir
> May the sod on their heads lightly rest
> For they all fell bravely fighting
> Doing their own level best

Corporal Cairns stayed at Schneidemühl till the end of the War. So did Private Frank Mills, general labourer and packer until he enlisted in 1904, serving for eight years before going to the Reserve and returning to his home town of Chelmsford, where his widowed mother Susie Mills was living. Private George Whitney, a Londoner, whose mother Susan Whitney lived at West Norwood, was a chauffeur until he joined up in 1911. Just before the War he too was in the photograph of the Officers Mess Staff at Aldershot and he was another at Schneidemühl throughout. All three had been in France from the start, all were on the ship home that docked on 18 December 1918 at Leith and all left the Army in the spring. Private Harry Morris was also at Schneidemühl all along, but only returned from Germany later and was discharged in March 1919, suffering from debility and anaemia. When the War broke out he had been a soldier for just over a year, described on enlisting as a "Smart young fellow, anxious for Scots Guards." William and Emily Morris lived in Hunslet, Leeds, and he had been both a barman and a glass blower there beforehand. The NCOs leading the two sections from C Company sent across on 29 October to help B Company were both captured. Sergeant Harry Graham, a cabinet maker from Edinburgh with a capital H tattooed on his right arm, had been in the Army since 1906. In July 1914 he married Harriett Parkwood, who was living in Oxford and as soon as war was declared he became a Sergeant. Unwounded, he survived imprisonment at Schneidemühl, though he was very ill with typhus. Lance Corporal Gilbert Bruce's family were living in Northwood, Middlesex. He was a clerk with the Metropolitan Railway Company when he joined up early in 1911 and worked subsequently as a clerk in the Battalion. The army doctor who examined him when he enlisted noted "Back teeth defective but likely to be sufficient." He was wounded, but tetanus killed him on 10 November at a German field hospital in a Roulers convent. It was not until the very end of August 1915 that confirmation of this, with the certificate, was received from the Red Cross in Geneva and Colonel Fludyer could write to George Bruce to give definite news of his son's death.

Sergeant William Chapman, a single man whose father William Chapman lived at Long Eaton, between Derby and Nottingham, was the most senior Scots Guards NCO captured at Gheluvelt. Previously a waiter in Leeds, he had been in the Army since just after New Year 1905. Once it was set up he was put in charge of British Lager No 1 and that would appear to have been where Corporal Green and Private McGinlay were. After being exchanged in the autumn of 1915 Sergeant Chapman said that there were a total of two hundred and eighty one British prisoners on the train to Schneidemühl and that no more appeared until July when just over four hundred came from two other camps. He thought that there were four thousand French there, forty eight Belgians and somewhere between thirty five and forty thousand Russians, a figure that his interviewer considered could be an overestimate, while accepting everything else that Sergeant Chapman stated. When they arrived they were "Turned into a compound, given a blanket, spoon and basin. After a few days turned into the shell of a barrack…No heating. Only method of getting warm at night was by getting into dug-outs. In December stoves. No fuel; practically none. Prisoners had to get it as they could…No facilities for washing for months. Soap given about December, and then bucket, towel and mattresses served out…In the compound no sanitary arrangements to start with. Latrines put out after a fortnight. Not cleared sufficiently often."

The 1st Grenadiers had a very difficult day on 29 October to the south of the Menin Road, none of them more so than Colonel Earle. He was wounded in the head and fainted. When he came round he found his head was being bandaged by Lieutenant John Butt, the twenty four year old Medical Officer from Dunfermline. At just this moment German soldiers approached. They shot Lieutenant Butt dead and also killed a wounded Grenadier who was lying across Colonel Earle's legs, wounding him in the leg as well in doing so. The Germans dragged him away and then stripped him of his greatcoat, jacket, shirt, vest and most of his possessions. His saviour was Private Sydney Venton of the 1st Coldstream, who appeared and then stayed with him, preventing the Germans from taking his watch and some money, though he would lose them later. A German nurse at the field hospital found Colonel Earle a flannel shirt and Private Venton gave him his cardigan. Between them they then found an old jacket in an abandoned farm and a piece of dirty old carpet, which was all that he had to wear from then on from the waist up. He suffered very much from the cold and Private Venton and he "lay very close together on the ground for mutual warmth." Private Venton came from Heavitree, near Exeter, and was a farmworker before he joined the Coldstream for three years in 1907. On enlistment he was five foot nine and three quarter inches, but after six months service and a gymnastic course five foot eleven inches. This was not unusual. When he left in 1910 he went to Canada, returning on mobilization. He survived captivity.

One of the wounded left on 31 October at Gheluvelt Château, hit that day in the left thigh, was Private George Bell, a coal miner and reservist, the son of George Bell of Ormiston, East Lothian. He described their all being left lying for two days after capture. Next they lay for two days in a convent school, though he did not know where, and then spent two days en route to Germany, on straw in a closed cattle truck. The doors were rarely opened and they only had one opportunity to relieve themselves properly. At Halberstadt, Saxony, where they arrived on 6 or 7 November German civilians gave them food, but throughout there were neither medical treatment nor change of dressings until they reached the military hospital. In this, a converted theatre, all the patients were prisoners and the medical and general treatment was fairly good. "I did not think that they had much love for the English, but they toned down towards the finish… letters and parcels were received alright. My own were sent and received and not one was lost." There was plenty of food, of indifferent quality, but the bedclothes were rarely changed and he only once had a bath there. Very briefly he went to another camp ahead of being exchanged in August 1915. Then his leg was amputated well up the thigh and after being fitted with an artificial limb at Roehampton he was discharged from the Army in April 1916. Another of those too badly wounded to move and so left behind was Sergeant John Turner, hit in the left testicle and right buttock. He had been a butcher in Preston till he enlisted in 1898. Next he and Mildred Turner married in London in 1899 before he left for the Boer War. Captain Meaden wrote later "He was the Scots Guards sergeant working under me in charge of the stretcher bearers…he is one of the best and most intelligent NCOs I have ever met." Captain Meaden kept in touch while Sergeant Turner was in a camp near Cologne and it was most probably at his instance that on 16 February 1915 Sergeant Turner was mentioned in despatches, followed on 11 January 1916 by the DCM.

Private Fredrick Eccles, sent down the line with sore feet near the end of the Retreat from Mons, was back in the Battalion after treatment and reported missing as at 11 November. Not till the middle of February did information arrive through the American Embassy in Berlin and the Red Cross in Geneva that he had been wounded and captured and was in hospital in Cassel, Hesse. On 20 June 1915 he died of typhus. News of this was likewise slow and it was not until 30 September that Samuel and Elizabeth Eccles heard in Blackburn.

Officers Camps at Crefeld, Clausthal and Heidelberg

Crefeld, west of the Rhine and surprisingly close to the Dutch border for an officers camp, was the first destination for many British officers captured in 1914. Answers about the 2nd Scots Guards officers who were prisoners, all but one captured at Kruiseecke, came from Crefeld once Colonel Bolton's letter of 12 November reached Regimental Headquarters. He, Viscount Dalrymple, Captains Coke and Fox (slightly wounded) and Lieutenants Lord Garlies, Steuart Menzies and Trafford were at the Hussaren Kaserne, Crefeld, and Lord Gerald Grosvenor was in hospital wounded. He knew that Lieutenants Cottrell Dormer and Fane Gladwin were dead and thought that Lieutenant Saumarez was too. He summarised what happened when the Germans got round behind them and went on "It is dreadful to think so many of us (I do not know the number of men taken alive, about 85 or 90) have now to be useless to the Regiment during this stage of the War, My Brigadier knows my reason for going into the Trenches after Fraser was killed and his conscience is clear, but I cannot help my ever present wish that one was left buried in them….We are only allowed to write two letters a month here, but may receive any written to us." Lord Garlies had been commissioned in 1913 after Harrow and Sandhurst. He was the eldest son of the Earl and Countess of Galloway, of Newton Stewart, Wigtownshire. Captured when F Company were overrun with the 2nd Wiltshires, he remained in Germany until late 1917 and was then interned in Switzerland. Lieutenant Edward Trafford was commissioned in 1905 after school at The Oratory, Edgbaston. Most recently he had been with the

Sierra Leone Battalion, West African Frontier Force, but was back in England in time to join the Battalion on 4 August. His parents were dead and his next of kin was his eldest brother, Captain Sigismund William Joseph Trafford, of Wroxham Hall, Norwich.

In his later report on his captivity Colonel Bolton stated that, apart from indignity briefly at point of capture, he had been well treated at the German local headquarters, though he refused to answer questions. Notwithstanding Captain Fox's description of going in a car to a station, Colonel Bolton also wrote of going in one with Lord Gerald Grosvenor. There, while he was waiting, he saw Germans taking greatcoats away from some of his men. When he protested they said they had orders to do so to give the greatcoats to the Red Cross. All the 2nd Scots Guards officers went in a second class carriage on a journey lasting over two nights. During this each only had a bowl of soup. Overall Colonel Bolton rated the treatment until arriving at Crefeld as "fair". Officers from other regiments he then met told of far worse experiences. Colonel Bolton was allocated a single room five feet by nine feet. More junior officers, Belgian, British, French and, later, Russian as well, were all mixed together in large rooms, on average with eight or nine in each. The British tended to determine the ventilation arrangements. Only the top windows would open which the British did as much as possible, deliberately taking meals at different times in order to enjoy the fresh air while the others were away eating. Colonel Bolton had nothing to compare it with but heard later that the food at Crefeld was generally better than in other camps. There was a large shower room with adequate hot and cold water and the latrines were kept clean by orderlies. Letters from home took anything between five days and a month to arrive and parcels, which rarely disappeared altogether, generally arrived without having been pilfered. There were language classes, lectures on many subjects not touching on the War, and all nationalities participated in the camp theatre. Three times a day there was a roll call. As soon as he arrived Colonel Bolton sought out a German Protestant clergyman to come to take Sunday services, but after the second the clergyman made a disparaging remark about Great Britain and Colonel Bolton made sure he never came back. For a long time he took the services himself. About every three months in 1915, however, the Reverend Williams, Vicar of the Dowager Empress's Church in Berlin, came to take a Communion Service. Later he was not allowed to speak to the British officers without a German interpreter being present. At the end of all services they sang "God Save The King" without asking to do so, but no one stopped them. To begin with the only exercise was on the barrack square, there being supervised physical training classes, football also being played in the winter, tennis in the summer, but soon walks were allowed outside and, initially, supervision was not conducted with rigour. Lieutenant Colonel Crofton Vandeleur was a Cameronians officer captured when commanding the 1st Cheshire Regiment a few weeks earlier. He picked his moment when on a walk in the town and escaped altogether, using fluent German to talk his way past any hindrance. He was the first British officer to escape home from a POW camp.

Towards the end of May 1917 the Germans suddenly closed Crefeld down and dispersed the prisoners. A large group of the more senior, including Colonel Bolton, went to Clausthal in the Harz Mountains, Saxony. This was overcrowded and uncomfortable, with inadequate facilities for the numbers. Unlike Crefeld, where the German officers and guards had been courteous and firm, but fair, he found the officers at Clausthal insulting, incompetent in executing their duties and unreasonable in the rules they imposed. Symptomatic of the tone of the place, mail for the prisoners was censored elsewhere and in Colonel Bolton's view, deliberately held up. Some mail sent to him from home in May did not arrive till September. Ultimately responsible for this state of affairs, in his opinion, was Major General Karl von Hänisch, who commanded the *10th (Hanoverian) Army Corps* area. Colonel Bolton recorded that because the General was known to the Germans as "The Pig of Hanover" this had inevitably percolated to the British. Apparently, he had been dismissed from a command appointment for an unsatisfactory performance against the British and so gave British prisoners as hard a time as he could. Major General Hurdis Ravenshaw, the Senior British Officer, made a complaint direct to General von Hänisch about their treatment, and was put into the punishment cells for eight days. At the beginning of October Colonel Bolton arrived at Heidelberg, another overcrowded camp, with fair conditions, but good overall because the German commandant made it his business to do his best for those there.

The 1st Scots Guards at the Cuinchy brickstacks

The only other time apart from First Ypres when a significant number of Scots Guardsmen were captured was during the German attack on 25 January 1915 in front of the Cuinchy brickstacks, just south of the Aire-La Bassée Canal. Two officers and thirty three men of Right Flank were prisoners and about two dozen of Left Flank. There may have been others captured who were wounded and survived and there were a few wounded, who died almost immediately. Apart from the officers, the most senior was Sergeant James Young, a grocer before he enlisted in 1900 and now a reservist, having left the Colours in 1907. When called up he was immediately promoted Sergeant, but only came to France with the January drafts. Starting at Giessen, where he and most, if not all, of the unwounded and slightly wounded went first, he spent the next three years in several different camps before going with other long term NCO prisoners and some others to Holland for internment in March 1918. His wife Florence was living in Aldershot.

One prisoner was Private William Beeby, a shop assistant in Bedford and early September volunteer. He had a slight shrapnel wound in his left knee, for which he does not seem to have received any initial medical treatment, though he said that the Germans had behaved correctly. En route to the first camp at Giessen, where he was briefly, he and the others were crammed into cattle wagons without room to sit down and given very little to eat, but got as much water as they needed. There was a lot of abuse from German civilians. When towards the end of 1915 he developed heart trouble while at Merseburg, his second camp, just south of Halle, Saxony, and could not work, he was thereafter moved round a lot of camps. Conditions varied considerably. He mentioned guards pricking prisoners with bayonets, very variable food, shirts and socks being issued when needed and wooden clogs provided when boots wore out. He noticed that the Germans treated the French best and the Russians worst, with the British somewhere in between. At Soltau, to the immediate north of Lüneburg Heath, he said that on average one Russian died every day from starvation. On 27 July 1916 he was sent to Switzerland for internment and spent just over a year at Mürren in the Bernese Oberland before being repatriated and discharged unfit. He ended his account by saying "In my early years of captivity the German guards were middle aged men who had not been to the front. As time went on men who had been wounded took their place, both young and old. Those who had seen fighting treated us more sympathetically than our first guards." Percy and Edith Beeby, his brother and sister, were living in Bedford. Private John Hipkin, a comb and brush maker in South Ealing, Middlesex, and early September volunteer, was unwounded when captured and was probably also in Sergeant Young's group. He and his wife Daisy married in Walthamstow in 1907 and had a daughter a year and a half later. He described how, as they were being marched back, some women tried to give them food, only to have Uhlans ride at them with their lances down to drive them indoors. The Uhlans pricked women with the points of their lances, which led to screams. From Merseburg Private Hipkin was sent to work in a coalmine. After a year and a half he developed asthma from the coal dust, though he said his treatment was good and the accommodation quite good. He was the only British soldier among twenty or so French and Russians. After hospital treatment back at Merseburg, which achieved little in spite of the best efforts of a Russian doctor, Private Hipkin was classified by the German camp doctor as Category 4, unfit for work or parades. He still had asthma, with attendant breathing difficulties, as well as bronchitis, when four German military doctors from Magdeburg came to the camp. One of them reclassified him as Category 1, fully fit, immediately on hearing he was British, without any examination. This led to very rough treatment for most of 1917 in coal mines before he was eventually returned to Merseburg. In March 1918 he was sent for internment in Holland, where he stayed until July before being repatriated and discharged because of asthma.

Private Alexander Allan, a clerk and another early September volunteer, whose father Robert Allan lived in Dennistoun, Glasgow, was hit by shrapnel in the back and right arm, and his hand was paralysed. When the Germans found him they treated him well, first at a dressing station and later in military hospitals. Then he went to a large camp at Würzburg, where were very few other British prisoners. Later on he was sent further north in Bavaria to Hammelburg, which he described as filthy, with insufficient food supplied, though the prisoners could buy lemonade, sausages and tobacco at the canteen. However, his parcels from home arrived in good condition, being opened by the guards in his presence. As elsewhere, only matches and newspapers were not allowed. He could write two letters and four cards home each month. Football was the only form of exercise. Smoking indoors was a punishable offence. Because of his injuries he qualified later for internment in Switzerland and left for Château D'Oex in July 1916. Lance Corporal Alexander Taylor, an Edinburgh policeman and also an early September volunteer, whose mother Isabella Taylor lived at Forgue, Aberdeenshire, was shot both through the right shoulder and the right hip, and lay out for two days before the Germans found him. They looked after him well and sent him to the main French run hospital in Lille, where he stayed for four months, well fed, including wine and beer, and nursed, but, strangely, not allowed to write to his family. At the end of May he was sent to Germany and his account of the journey was another mentioning the very hostile attitude of civilians. From a military hospital at Wesel, where he spent six weeks being very well looked after, he was at last able to send a card home. Thereafter he was at Friedrichsfeld, in and out of what he described as the comfortable camp hospital, until mid November 1916, when he started the process for internment in Switzerland. Once approved, he went to Mürren and remained there until March 1919. He mentioned the shooting of two British soldiers who tried to escape from a working party at Friedrichsfeld and were killed and, like others, the very rough treatment of the Russian prisoners. Private Cecil Kennedy, the son of William Kennedy of Dunoon, Argyll, was an at least partly trained electrician when he joined up in Glasgow in April 1910, serving for three years. He then went to New Zealand, duly reported to the British military representatives on mobilization and sailed for the UK on 10 August 1914. At the brickstacks he was shot in the right hand and captured. Unlike most, he did not mind working in mines because, as an electrician, he was employed as such. However, captivity and working conditions left their mark and he was discharged after the War disabled because of debility and bronchitis. Mobilised the same day in Auckland, because that was his home, was Private Benjamin Good, a seaman by occupation who had served for three years after enlisting in Liverpool in 1908 and then gone back to New Zealand. He had several tattoos, a ship, clasped hands and two flags on his right forearm and an American flag, an eagle, and "liberty" on his left forearm. When he joined up it was noted that he had a slight squint in his left eye. He spent the rest of the War at Merseburg. His real name was Kenneth Cook Whistler. Lance Sergeant John Reid was an older man, aged thirty five when he reenlisted in September, his reserve commitment expired. He had been a Lance Sergeant before and was immediately reappointed. When he left the Army previously he became a butler and he and his wife Louisa and their daughter were living at Egham Wick, Surrey. He arrived in France on 13 January 1915, twelve days before he was taken prisoner. He was sent to Holland for internment in March 1918 and, after being discharged in 1919, went to live in a lodge at Mentmore, Buckinghamshire, presumably working for the Earl of Rosebery.

Lance Corporal William Martin, the son of Margaret Martin of Perth, was a student in Edinburgh when he enlisted on 5 August 1914. Three months later he landed in France, but not in time for First Ypres. Wounded in the head and left arm, he was captured at the brickstacks and kept till April in hospital in Lille before being sent on to Germany. He spent the rest of the War in camps at Celle, northeast of Hanover, and later Soltau.

The living conditions at Göttingen

It was to the main camp at Göttingen that many of the 2nd Scots Guards prisoners were taken from the Ypres battlefields and that included Privates Beattie, captured at Kruiseecke, and Howard, captured east of Polygon Wood. There were only minor differences in their accounts. They were on different trains a day apart, probably from Courtrai, Private Howard being on the earlier one which after three days and nights arrived on 28 October. Their experiences were very similar to those who went to Schneidemühl. From capture to arrival at the camp they had almost nothing to eat or drink, were very cramped in cattle trucks and without any sanitary facilities, though Private Howard said that the train did stop once and they were all let out for that purpose. There was the usual abuse from German civilians. Private Beattie told how once at the camp they were given a pail of soup and nothing else till some sort of coffee concoction in the evening. The next day was one of more coffee or a substitute and soup, but nothing else and no bread. On the third day there was more of the same but each man was also given a three pound loaf to last him for three days. "This went on for about two months at Göttingen, then they substituted a pail of soup at night for the coffee. They gave us a loaf of black bread a day among five men. That was the diet right through to the end. The soup was sometimes carrot, sometimes potato, turnip, chestnut, or cherry – always very thin and very little sustenance. Occasionally a piece of meat, just a fragment, could be seen in the soup, but otherwise we never saw butchers' meat the whole time." On arrival Private Beattie was allowed to write to his wife and then not again for two months, but after that two letters were allowed each month and a postcard once a week. All incoming mail came regularly and, though parcels were opened in a prisoner's presence, he was satisfied that nothing, other than newspapers, was removed. Private Beattie "was fortunate enough at once to be put into a hut along with about 60. Others had to go under canvas. But, speaking generally, the arrangements at Göttingen were good. The camp was only in its initial stage when we went there and the huts had to be built up." Private Howard was less lucky. "For the first two months we had to sleep under canvas tents raised about 4 feet from the ground. There were about 50 men in each tent, and we slept on straw. The only clothing supplied was one blanket apiece. It was impossible for us to keep ourselves warm, and in the daytime we walked about with the blankets over us trying to keep warm." In the huts it was no better to begin with, but a bucket of coal was issued after New Year, barely enough to keep the two stoves going for a day at a time, though supplemented by wood shavings and chips left over from building huts until that was complete. The washing facilities, Private Beattie described, "were simply at three pumps in the camp, and we had two basins, one large for washing, one small for soup. The sanitary arrangements were at first only a trench, but later they were splendid, when the camp got made." His wife sent him a civilian jacket in April 1915, but otherwise he only had the single issue blanket and what he had left after his captors had stripped him at Kruiseecke. When he asked the Germans for clothing he was told to ask for it from England and Private Howard confirmed that that was the only source. There was no change of underclothing, so when they washed it, in cold water without soap, they had to wait until it dried to put it on again. The only pair of boots that Private Beattie had was that issued to him on mobilization and a year later all that was left was the uppers.

Prisoners could supplement the food by purchasing from the German canteen, but only if they had any money. Then after four months the first food parcels came, subsequently regularly, and that effectively made the canteen redundant. Private Beattie told how there was no recreation of any sort, indoors or outdoors, till May 1915 "when the Americans put up a YMCA hut, and we were allowed to go there about once a week. No football or any outdoor recreation was permitted. There was no card playing in the hut. There were no cards, and we had no light until the month of February, when an electric lamp was put in." Later Private Howard referred to cards, as well as books, sent from home. Smoking was not allowed until New Year and then only from two to four in the afternoon, but tobacco, poor at that, could only be got from the canteen and Private Beattie had no money. Once the YMCA hut was up a German Protestant clergyman came to take a service for an hour, usually on weekdays "always the same German clergyman. He preached well enough." There were alternately French and British concerts each week. The work at Göttingen was road building and expanding the camp, for which they were not paid. Private Beattie did not recall any of them being "asked to make munitions, but we were asked to volunteer for mines. None volunteered to my knowledge." The discipline was strict, with placards setting out the camp rules in French, English and Russian. The main offences were refusing to work, irrespective of the justification, insubordination, smoking in the huts and not saluting, including not saluting German private soldiers. The punishments included binding men to posts, in the case of refusals to work making a man stand facing a wooden wall from six in the morning till nine at night, with quarter of an hour's break for soup, and there was also solitary confinement on bread and water. Once there was a guardroom, so Private Howard said, the tying to posts stopped. Private Beattie was once given five days in the cells for refusing to work because it was wet and his boots had disintegrated. He mentioned generally some "minor acts of cruelty for very minor offences, and arms and shoulders cut with swords… The Germans treated the French and Belgians best and the Russians and British worst – the English worse than any nationality. They were decidedly the most hated nation." According to Private Howard, the commandant, Oberst Bogen, "was rather an old man and at first treated the English soldiers very harshly but afterwards improved very much."

Private Beattie did mention "The only cruelty that I saw at Göttingen" and Private Howard was in the working party concerned. On 1 December 1914 Private Thomas Bolwell of the 2nd

Wiltshires was washing at the pump at about eight o'clock in the morning when "I saw a party of… British being marched along a road through the camp by the Germans, about 50 yards from me. About 20 yards behind them one of them was following by himself. He seemed so ill that he could hardly walk. A German sentry was kicking him along and hitting him with the butt of his rifle. I saw a German officer approach then, and spoke to him, the two Germans were laughing. After the officer had left them, the treatment continued. The British prisoner turned and spoke to the sentry apparently perfectly quietly. The sentry hit him again across the back with the butt of his rifle, then brought the rifle to the ready position at his side, and fired. The man fell face downwards and did not move again. Several British soldiers who were not far from the scene ran up, but the sentry prevented them from approaching, and the body was left there. A few minutes later some Belgians from the cook house picked him up and carried him to the hospital. I heard next morning that he had died in hospital the previous day. I did not know the man personally but learnt that he was Pte McEwan of the Scots Guards." Private Charles McEwan had a wound in his foot from when he was captured. It was reported by the German authorities that he had died of wounds, but his recorded cause of death was later found to be a gunshot to the heart. He was the son of William and Mary McEwan of Leyton, Essex, and had been a machinist in a piano factory when he enlisted in April 1914 at Stratford, it being noted that he had a tendency to flat feet. He was posted missing after the roll call on 28 October. Private Howard stated that the German guard was sent away, but as far as he knew there was no inquiry and certainly none of the prisoner witnesses were asked by the Germans to give statements.

When the American Ambassador's representative visited the camp Private Beattie told how "we were warned by the Germans that any complaint to him would be punished after he went away. He was not allowed to speak to the prisoners except in the presence of a German officer. The day of his visit the soup was made specially good, and there were sausages hung up in the cookhouse, but they were not supplied to the prisoners. We did not notice any special improvements after the visit." In July 1915 about two hundred British prisoners left Göttingen by train, en route for Münster, this time well supplied by the contents of food parcels. Two on board were Privates Beattie and Howard.

Schneidemühl at the start and during the 1914-15 typhus epidemic

Sergeant Chapman told his interviewer that at first the food at Schneidemühl was inedible. "Prisoners very hungry. After two or three days it improved; fair amount of bread. Mostly soups. Recently the allowance of bread has become less. Not always enough to go round." When the British first arrived there were no stated regulations, no stated offences beyond disobedience to superiors, which meant any camp guard and the senior national NCOs, but no system of military discipline either. So there was "Kicking, striking, and flogging." Later ordinary military law was applied. "At the beginning the general treatment was vile kicks and insults. An officer, name unknown, ran a sword into a man called Stimson for no reason. He died. The men were constantly struck with rifles and hit and kicked." At this stage Sergeant Chapman reckoned that the camp guards of all ranks treated the British worst. On 26 January 1915 a German officer stabbed Private William Stimpson of the 1st Coldstream with his sword. He died a little later from blood poisoning, according to Corporal Guy, though the official cause of death was typhus.

Only two days after Private Henry Bolam, also of the 1st Coldstream, captured on 29 October at Gheluvelt, arrived at Schneidemühl, he got into an altercation with a camp guard, who hit him on the back of the head with his rifle butt. In the scuffle that followed the guard lost his balance and fell over. On being picked out at an identity parade, Private Bolam was beaten so badly by a number of guards with thick batons or truncheons that he could not stand and was then hit across the face by a German officer with the flat of his sword, drawing blood. Unconscious, he was next tied to a post with wire. Private McGinlay told how the Germans made the British prisoners watch their "punishment" of Private Bolam and forced them to continue to do so. "Pte Devlin was struck across the face with a baton of wood for turning his head while the punishment was going on. He was struck a heavy blow right on the jaw." Private Bolam died a few weeks later after he caught typhus. Corporal Green's account was that "Whilst still dark, we heard the bugle blowing, calling us to fall in for breakfast (savour the name). There was a terrible crush going on outside the cookhouse. This resulted in Private Bolam…being struck by a sentry. Bolam got hold of the sentry's rifle, and kept it for a few minutes, then ran away. A search party, and the Hun identified his assailant, who was escorted away by the order of the camp Adjutant. The latter was ingenious the way he thought of punishing people. He ordered an ordinary barrel be brought, over which they threw Bolam, face downwards. The Hun officer was given a thonged whip, and he beat Bolam until the latter was unconscious. He was taken to hospital, where he died – his brain had been injured." Corporal Green understood that, following representations by the British Government through the American Embassy in Berlin, a German court of inquiry had condemned the German officer, who wrote what amounted to an apology before he left the camp, presumably for the front. Private James Devlin, a reservist for four years, was the son of Thomas and Margaret Devlin of Birkenhead. Before he enlisted in 1906 he was a driver, but more recently he gave his occupation as a dock labourer. He was captured at Gheluvelt, posted missing as at 11 November. The first news of his being a prisoner was in a letter to his mother. He survived captivity at Schneidemühl, where he spent the whole of the rest of the War, but was discharged soon afterwards no longer physically fit.

Corporal Green recorded the normal daily rations as a pound of black bread with coffee made from burnt barley at breakfast, soup at half past eleven and coffee on its own at five in the evening. Twice a week raw herrings were issued at the same time as the soup, but the British did not care for these and usually sold them for five pfennig each. On 12 November they "were shifted into huts, a welcome change. The dug-outs in which we had been kept since our arrival here were absolutely walking away with lice. These huts were divided in two parts, with a small part partitioned off for the chief non commissioned officers. We English were placed five or six to each room so that we could not cause any trouble. The Russians numbered about sixty to every five English, and welcomed us as *"Kameraden"* (comrades). There was little room space… in fact you were nearly on top of each other at nights." On the 15th "German field post cards sold, and we all sent one away, just to let them at home know we were still alive, but no more." Corporal Green wrote that on 13 December "A bundle of letters arrived, with a few parcels. I was lucky enough to have a letter. But our luck then finished. All English were paraded, boots taken away, and given big wooden ones in their stead. My feet suffered, I can tell you." Sergeant Chapman described parcels starting to arrive at the end of November in good condition and that it was in that month that "the boots were taken from British prisoners and kept for three weeks. No clothing issued until January, and then a few cotton shirts given out. Not enough for all. Later on – May or June a uniform issued to those whose clothes were worn out."

A camp where large numbers of men were cooped up in limited space, with poor living conditions and in very cold weather, so that it was doubly difficult to keep themselves and their clothes clean, was a likely venue for typhus. This fever, with rashes, headaches and muscle pains, once started, would travel because of lice. The lice were not themselves infected but once a louse had bitten and sucked the blood of an infected man, its faeces would contain the typhus bacterium. A man who had not caught the disease until then would succumb if the louse faeces entered his blood stream through an open wound or from his scratching a louse bite. If untreated or poorly treated typhus could be fatal. It was not understood at the time that it could not be transmitted from one man to another, though it was understood that lice were involved. The typhus epidemic in the winter of 1914-15 killed fewer of the British prisoners than it might have done, the dates of the British victims' deaths being then generally only approximate, though Sergeant Chapman wrote to Regimental Headquarters with as accurate information as he could if a Scots Guardsman died. Corporal Green put the start of it as mid December and he had it on 15 January. "While I waited to see the doctor, I fell down twice – my legs were so weak. On my forehead they marked three crosses – meaning for hospital in camp. A straight line across the forehead meant for Schneidemühl civilian hospital." Sergeant Chapman gave near enough the same start date, continuing till mid May 1915. He caught it himself and did not go to the camp hospital, entirely staffed by Russians, but he mentioned that a German hospital became available from later December once the epidemic took hold. In one of the Russian sections of the camp he said that there was cholera.

Among the dead from typhus was Private Alexander, but known as "Donald", Ross, captured during the advance on Poezelhoek on 26 October. After being in the Lovat Scouts for the Boer War he served for seven years from 1902 in the Scots Guards and was called up as a reservist. George Ross, his father, was a blacksmith who had gone to Canada and was living in Brooks, Alberta, but his mother was still in Brora, Sutherland. Corporal Green was in hospital at the time, about the middle of February. "I woke up one morning and found my two mates, one on either side, both dead. One was a very decent Russian, the other Donald Ross…in his day a famous Army Footballer." Another who died around the same time was Private David Cuthill, a serving soldier in 1914 and former blacksmith's labourer from Glasgow with tattoos of a girls' head, a tombstone and a sailor's head on the back of his left arm. He had not gone out with the Battalion to begin with, but was in an early reinforcement draft. His brother Robert Cuthill wrote on 8 December from his home in the South Side asking whether he "is still in the land of the living or wounded as we are very anxious to know we were getting letters from him every week since he went away but we have never heard from him this last six weeks we have sent on letters & cigarettes 3 & 4 time & has had no answer."

Private Alex Borland, the son of Daniel Borland of Greenock, was a spirit salesman until he enlisted in October 1913, just over a year before he was captured at Gheluvelt. He recovered from typhus, at a price. After a prisoner caught it, if he came out of delirium, he was simply carried outside into the open air and left to fend for himself, a very rough quarantine at that time of year. They could only burrow down wherever they could in the early dug-outs and holes they had made when they first arrived, before there were any huts. Private Borland lost every toe to frostbite and then spent almost six months in a German hospital, after which he was only briefly back in the camp before being exchanged in October 1915. He said that by then the British were living off their food parcels and giving their rations to the Russians in return for doing washing and generally cleaning up. At that point Private Borland was issued with prison uniform of a blue jacket and trousers with a yellow stripe down the seams. He spoke of football being played and "The Germans wanted to take photo of us playing football, and ordered us to play. Some went, but others had their doubts and would not: and then they stopped football for a long while. There was also trouble because the football broke a window." They had visits from an English chaplain once every six weeks and there was an English-speaking German Protestant minister. The prisoners also held services of their own in a barrack room. Refusal to work led to being put in the punishment cells, in which the majority at any time would be British. There were arrangements where neutral diplomats were supposed to inspect camps and some did. Private Borland said that an ambassador of some country did come once and spent all his time with the Russians. Before he arrived the Germans provided clothing for some of the Russians and let out those of them in the cells. After he left they removed the clothing and replaced them in the cells. His interviewer described Private Borland as a "Bright Scotch youngster." In the spring of 1916, medically downgraded and serving in London, Private Borland disappeared and was away for six months, for which he was sentenced to one hundred and twelve days detention for desertion, as well as forfeiting all his previous service. He was also discharged almost immediately as unfit for war service. Lance Corporal William Forster of the 1st Coldstream, from Durham, lost seven toes and reckoned that a hundred and seventy British prisoners had had typhus. Surprisingly few, something over twenty he thought, had died of it, a figure borne out by Corporal Guy and others. Deaths among the Russians, however, were far more numerous. Corporal Guy put them at seven thousand.

When Corporal Green was over the worst of it he was one of the first to have to live for three days in the dug-outs or holes. One of his Coulommiers pals, Private Mellor, had already died on or about 6 January 1915 and Private Shaw, the Kettering policeman, died on or about 10 March, also probably from typhus. Only one of his pals survived the War, Corporal Holroyd. He was a reservist, who, after three years service ending in 1906, became a policeman in Bradford, where he lived with Ethel, his wife since 1911, and their son.

The living conditions from January 1915 at Schneidemühl

Once huts were built in another part of the camp most of the British went to live there. Corporal Green was one of the small number who remained behind, now in huts too, as a working party under Sergeant Chapman with responsibility for the cleanliness of the camp. The British prisoners and the others, of whom the first were Belgians, had generally a much better time of it than the Russians. Corporal Green wrote that they were ordered to go for an exercise walk for an hour each morning and each afternoon, whatever the weather "several times with a blanket over shoulders, whilst our pants were being fumigated." Sergeant Chapman confirmed this. So far as the British were concerned there was another distinct further improvement from soon after New Year when the Camp Adjutant, Hauptmann von Heinrich, was returned to active duty, a man Sergeant Chapman said was "Bombastic. Spoke good English and made a speech to the British that Expeditionary Force wiped out and he would soon have all British there." By contrast he rated his successor, Hauptmann Bohn, as "Very good" and, what was more, "he prevented blows and kicks and insults." Sergeant Chapman spoke of "very few letters and parcels at the start. After December postal arrangements were very good; some complaints of missing parcels, but there were not many." German censors opened the parcels but did not take anything out as far as he saw and he was in charge of the postal department for all the British. The items prohibited were alcohol, knives, razors, newspapers, civilian clothing and firearms. He added that at the beginning there was no restriction on outgoing letters but from mid February each man was limited to sending a postcard weekly and a letter fortnightly. A prisoner might receive as many letters and cards as were sent to him. Footballs arrived first in March. Corporal Green remembered that from then onwards parcels, money and letters came regularly "making us all a little better towards each other."

Private Peter Lawson, a slater until he enlisted in Paisley and served for seven years, had been on the Reserve for nearly a year when he was mobilised. Captured on 29 October at Gheluvelt like almost everyone else then at Schneidemühl, he spent the rest of the War there. He married Emily Chapman in October 1910 in London and she was currently living in West Kensington with their daughter. Sometime in May 1915, according to Corporal Green, two men, one of them Private Lawson, were court martialed and given twenty eight days in the cells for insubordination, not to a German, but to Drill Sergeant William Hogan of the 1st Grenadiers, the senior British soldier in the camp. Corporal Green recorded that "A German officer visited the English rooms and found the two men there instead of on the exercise parade. The entire English lost their midday soup that day, with the exception of Hogan & Co., and a few men who had washed the floors that morning. The food issued to the prisoners consisted of two days bread and water then a day only soup, and so on." He went on "This same Hogan was a proper rotter to us, and safeguarded his own interests by reporting several trivial matters to the Germans." The Germans expected the senior British NCOs to keep order among the prisoners, but their only authority was German military discipline. Some soldiers were very aggrieved and Private Harry Barker of the 1st Coldstream, captured at Gheluvelt, said on his return to England that "CSM Hogan, Grenadier Guards, often tied men to the post in the snow and also stopped their bread ration. This man was treated well by the Germans. Sergeant Chapman, Scots Guards, was in charge of the parcel office; he has often sold Britishers' parcels to the Russians, and has also taken postal orders from their parcels. Both these NCOs got back to England as stretcher bearers." Private Barker, by that time suffering from "debility", was sent for internment in Switzerland in August 1916 and spent the rest of the War at Mürren. By the time Sergeant Chapman, a trained stretcher bearer, left in the autumn of 1915 he said that there was not much to complain about as conditions had improved so much under Hauptmann Bohn "except that the food was very short." He added that there had been fourteen working parties or *"Kommandos"* out on farms and a hundred and forty six British, of whom only two were volunteers, had been sent to the mines. After spending some time in hospital on returning to England he became a Company Sergeant Major in the 3rd Scots Guards before being commissioned in June 1917 into the 17th Cameronians. The allegation about selling parcels arose because British prisoners thought that they should have any which arrived for those who had died and, by extension, those who had been moved to other camps. Instead the Germans ordered them to be sold inside the camp.

Corporal Ralph Charman, whose mother lived in Crawley, Sussex, had been serving since 1905 when he gave up being a bricklayer's labourer. He too was captured at Gheluvelt. When all the other NCOs left for The Hague on 15 March 1918 he was not included and he wrote on 27 March to Regimental Headquarters "I hope you will not be offended at my taking the liberty of writing to you. I have been a prisoner of war since the 29th October 1914, and all Non Commissioned Officers captured with me and after that date have been exchanged to Holland. Unfortunately I am the only one left behind which came as a great surprise & disappointment to me. I favourably ask your assistance in this matter sir, for it seems the only means I have of establishing my rank." On 19 April a certificate was sent to him stating that Corporal Charman had held the substantive rank of Corporal since 23 February 1911 and so, in terms of the agreement, he was "eligible for internment in a neutral country." On 30 April he arrived in Holland.

Münster

The train in which Privates Beattie and Howard went to Münster, where there was more than one camp, took nine hours. What they found, Private Beattie described, was "not so clean as Göttingen Camp. The sanitary arrangements were poorer and the huts more crowded, but the food was better and the treatment of the sentries far nicer, and things were a lot better there. They supplied the prisoners with old clothes to take the place of worn out ones, boots and stockings, but they were all second hand." Once a week they got a small piece of meat, but otherwise everything was much the same. Private Beattie finally received a new pair of boots sent from home. There was one principal difference they noticed at Münster in that, apart from work at the camp, working parties were sent out elsewhere, but usually they did not know where to, nor what they were going to do until they got there. Hence some found themselves in mines or munitions factories. Initially there was resistance, but eventually they were forced to give in. When Private Beattie was picked for a working party in September he was fortunate to find himself on a farm till just after New Year 1916. Soon after that he was sent to work in a quarry, briefly. While on farm work he was paid thirty pfennig a day. Private Howard, who had hitherto been working only on land drainage, was picked to go to work in a coal mine, but he and other British and French prisoners found out and refused to leave Münster. For this they were all put into the guardroom for a week, their parcels from home withheld. The Russians, who received no parcels, needed the extra food issued for mining work and so were easier to coerce.

On 15 March 1916 Privates Beattie and Howard, passed fit for the purpose by the camp doctor, found themselves detailed for a working party of some thirty British. They went from Münster by train to Wettringen, a large village to the north, much closer to the Dutch border, where they lived in some sort of school building or children's asylum, where, as Private Howard put it, "Beds were provided for us, but they were filthy and lousy with vermin. There was only a small yard where we could walk about. The food supplied was just the same as in camp, and our parcels were sent on to us." It was pretty cramped. There were some British and French there already, who told them that they would be working in the fields. They were paid at the same rate of thirty pfennig a week, but the Germans deducted two pfennig as a delivery charge for every parcel and also made them pay ten pfennig for a weekly bath. Private Beattie mentioned there being no fire provided and so they "carried in sticks from the fields to light a fire to make our tea when we got home at night." The work lasted twelve hours a day, mainly to dig a wide drainage ditch or small canal. They had an hour off half way through each day. Another man in the party was Private James Badams of the 1st Royal Welsh Fusiliers, well travelled and before the War farming in Canada, from where he returned on mobilization. He had been captured northeast of Ypres on 21 October 1914.

Lechfeld, Altengrabow and Beienrode

Sergeant Francis Stedman had started off as a tailor's cutter in Leeds, then served for eight years and transferred to the Reserve as a Lance Sergeant in 1913, when he became a postman.

Immediately he reported on mobilization he was made up to Sergeant and went out to the 1st Scots Guards in mid September 1914. He was captured on 11 November after being shot below the right knee during the Prussian Guards attack. Ethel Stedman, his wife of just over two years, and their son were living in Altofts, Yorkshire. Before being sent to Holland Sergeant Stedman was in the Bavarian camp at Lechfeld, west of Munich, where "there practically exists a system of peculation of all medicines, drugs, bandages etc., sent by Mrs Bromley Davenport of the British Red Cross, for the use of British prisoners of war. The parcels in which these are sent also contain articles of food, such as condensed milk, Oxo, Bovril etc. All these latter are given to the prisoners of war, but the Germans retain all the medicines and medical appliance alleging that they are for use in the infirmary. I know for a fact that beyond an occasional aspirin tabloid, which is apparently given for every complaint, none of these medicines are ever given to the prisoners of war...Thefts of parcels are rife in Germany. Lechfeld is particularly bad in this respect. As a case in point I may mention that from June 1917 onwards, I should have received 1 parcel of tobacco a fortnight, but up to the time of my leaving the camp on 15/3/18, I only received 4 of these parcels."

When there was an opportunity the Germans attempted to exploit racial and cultural differences among their prisoners. This occurred at Altengrabow, northeast of Magdeburg. Once in Holland Sergeant David Walshe of the 1st Irish Guards made a statement, corroborated by Lance Corporal John Gall of the 1st Scots Guards, that Altengrabow "was a Belgian Camp, and I should say it contained about 6000 Belgians and about 200 British NCOs and men. There was a school in this camp for the Belgian prisoners of war but about July 1917 the Germans prohibited the French speaking Belgians from using this and only allowed the Flemish to use it. The Flemish were all put in one Company together and received preferential treatment." Further he heard from a Belgian NCO who worked in the camp office "that orders had been issued by the Germans that when the Flemish were sent on *Arbeit Kommandos* they were to be treated as "BROTHERS."" Later, he said, the French speaking Belgians were all sent elsewhere. He added that "the parcels for the Flemish came from England and they lost no opportunity of abusing them and I myself have seen them selling their cigarettes to other nationalities." Corporal Gall was a reservist working as a railway shunter in London in 1914. Not long before he went onto the Reserve he married Nellie Mullins in December 1910 and they had three small girls. The family were living in Harlesden. Corporal Gall was wounded in the left side and thigh and taken prisoner on 29 October 1914 at Gheluvelt.

In a statement, also in Holland, Lance Corporal Andrew Jones of the 48th Canadian Battalion, Highlanders, described how on 27 June 1915 he was one of a hundred and fifteen British prisoners sent away by train from a camp at Celle. They did not know where they were going. About midday they arrived at Beienrode, not far east from Brunswick. It was a potash mine. There were already about a hundred French prisoners and one Belgian, with a hundred and fifty German civilian mineworkers and the same number in the accompanying factory. As time went by some Russians joined them, plus a few more Belgians and just over two dozen deported Belgian civilians, while the number of German civilians dropped significantly. Corporal Jones was at Beienrode continuously until sent to Holland in 1918. He described the mine manager, Herr Stark, and the engineer, Herr Schwarz, as "nothing more or less than "SLAVE DRIVERS." Stark spoke a little English and Schwarz only German. The latter knew every man in the mine by name." From September 1915 each man in the morning shift had to fill fifteen wagons and each man in the afternoon shift twenty. The number went on escalating until from September 1916 it was thirty wagons per man per shift and anyone failing to fulfil his task was made to stay until he had. The Germans working underground were doing the blasting and boring and had an easier time than the prisoners. "Filling and pushing wagons… is the hardest work in the mine. The salt is blasted into large heaps and it is very sharp and hard, the result is the men, when working cut their hands and bodies. It is so poisonous and any man getting it into a cut or abrasion gets terribly swollen and inflamed…salt flying about after the blasting and during the boring with compressed air drills got into the eyes of many men who as a consequence suffer most acutely from eye trouble." He spoke of men "who on reaching the surface have to be led back to the barrack…as they could not see at all." Among several additional incidents "about February 1918, was that of Pte Peter Lyon, Scots Guards, who had quarrelled with a Russian soldier. The Russian reported it to the German sentry (called Storm, *42nd Regiment*) who came to the barrack and took Pte Lyon away to the so called *Lazarett* (which was a bare room where prisoners did their punishment) and with the aid of a *Landsturm* man, Wilkie, *42nd Regiment*, thrashed him, Pte Lyon, with insulated rubber packing for about 10 minutes. I saw Pte Lyon afterwards and his body was one mass of weals and his blood was coming through the skin. He was returned to work the same day although not in a condition to do it and on the following day he was taken away again, by the same soldiers, and given a second thrashing in a similar manner." He described "Morning Shift. Reveille 4am (1 bowl of *Ersatz* Coffee) Parade 4.45 Descend 5.30 Work 6-9.30 Breakfast about one cupful of Cold Thin Meal Soup saved from the previous evening's supper Work 10-1.45 Surface and bath house and to barrack room about 2.45" The afternoon shift was similar. Private Lyon was a wartime volunteer, a miner who joined up in Dunfermline within a week of the outbreak of War. Which Battalion he was in and where and how he was captured are unknown. Afterwards he went back to Lassodie, Fife.

The captured U-Boat crews in 1915 and the German retaliation

The Royal Navy captured thirty nine survivors of two U-boat crews early in 1915. Winston Churchill, as First Lord of the Admiralty, himself directed that the German submariners should not be treated as prisoners of war on account of their attacking unarmed merchant ships without warning and all that followed from that. Instead he had these crews shut up in the Naval Detention Barracks at Chatham and Devonport respectively. The officers and men, thirty nine altogether, were segregated, but not separated individually. The Germans retaliated by placing thirty nine British officers in solitary confinement in civilian prisons or "arrest barracks". Six were Scots Guardsmen, four, Captain Coke and Lieutenants Trafford, Steuart Menzies and Lord Garlies going from Crefeld to prison at Cologne and two, Lieutenants Jolliffe and FitzRoy, from Villingen in the Black Forest to prison at Rastatt well to the north. They were encouraged to write home and describe their treatment and so apply pressure. On 21 April 1915 Lieutenant FitzRoy wrote to Colonel Fludyer about the move to Rastatt on 15 April and how he was "in a cell, deprived of smoking, etc., and locked up for twenty three hours out of twenty four as Germany's reply to Sir Edward Grey's answer concerning the treatment of German Submarine Prisoners of War…I can hear Jolliffe's step and voice in the corridor outside but am not allowed to see or speak to him. No doubt he is another hostage." The stand off continued until the end of June when the Admiralty were persuaded to hand the submariners over to the War Office, who had responsibility for all enemy prisoners of war.

Escapers

Privates Badams, Beattie and Howard had been discussing escape for several months and when they got to Wettringen they saw their chance, not hiding what they were up to from the others there. They made their break after dark on 22 March 1916. Another prisoner distracted a German sentry by playing the mouth organ and others created diversions to mask any noise made while the escapers forced open an exit through the wooden panelling of a latrine block, Private Badams applying the craftsmanship. Outside was a road past the camp. They got out, the rather stout Private Beattie having to be eased through the hole. While Private Badams carefully replaced and nailed back the panelling, the other two hurried off across the road and into the fields beyond to wait for him. They knew that they were lucky that no one had seen them because the road was lit up outside, though they could watch the sentries both inside and outside the compound. Private Beattie reckoned that they covered between fifteen and twenty miles that night, a Wednesday, but not so far on Thursday night, as they had to go very cautiously. They hid during daylight on Thursday and rested, having had to wade every river they came to. They only had chocolate, saved from food parcels, to keep them going. It was fairly cold, but clear, until early on Friday morning when it started to snow hard. They were by then lying up in a hollow in a thick part of a wood, all very wet. Private Badams' legs were so numb and cold that he could not stand up when darkness fell and it was time to move on. He was frightened that the others would leave him as both had spare, dry pairs of socks in their pockets and he did not, but they massaged his legs and feet and got him going, though he was very weak. There were soon further excitements. First, on the far side of the wood was a railway line that they had to get over. Two shots were fired in their direction down it and soon after they saw Germans searching the wood they had just been in. Next a soldier passed fifteen yards away on a bicycle. Then there was another river to cross, more fields, a final river to wade and finally the apprehension of disclosing themselves to people who might not to be Dutch, though Private Beattie knew from their map when they had reached Holland. They walked on, continuing in daylight until midday on Friday when, too tired to go further, they went to a farm and asked the farmer to prove that they were in Holland by showing them Dutch coins. He did and then he and his wife and daughters gave them some coffee and a meal and they handed over to their hosts the rest of their chocolate. This was on the edge of the village of Losser. A week later they sailed from Rotterdam to Tilbury on a Dutch steamer. In common with all successful other ranks escapers they were awarded the Military Medal in a list published in 1920.

There was a main camp called Heuberg in the Black Forest, not far from the Danube. On 5 March 1918 a working party left there for a farm at the very small village of Ippingen, further west and much closer to the Swiss frontier. One of those in it was a 2nd Scots Guards reservist, Private Henry Butler, taken prisoner on 23 October 1914 during First Ypres, most likely with F Company near Reutel. He was working as a draper before he enlisted in 1904 in Edinburgh and served for eight years. During the War his wife Ada and their daughter were living in Kensington. A second man was a Territorial, Lance Corporal George Carlé of the 1/5th London Regiment, London Rifle Brigade, captured near Hébuterne on 1 July 1916, the first day of the Battle of the Somme, very slightly wounded in the left foot, but able to walk. By the spring of 1918 he had been in a number of camps and had made three escape attempts. At the farm those who had parcels from home fed that way, but the farmers were required to feed those without. Corporal Carlé and the others thought that their employers "have a dreadful way of eating, and we preferred to have nothing to do with them, but to live on our parcels." However, they were more comfortable than anywhere else they had been because the farmers provided beds with sheets. "There was one guard over this party, a *Landsturmer*, who lived in the village and used to return to the barrack at night. He treated us properly, and did not interfere with us." A third man in the party, another Territorial, was Private Richard Thompson of the London Scottish, also captured on 1 July 1916 near Hébuterne, unwounded. He had been at Heuberg almost all the last eighteen months, had escaped twice and only just failed to cross the frontier the second time. He was not meant to be in a working party because of this history but somehow contrived to join this one. After his most recent escape the Germans failed to find either the small compass he had acquired or the map of the neighbourhood he discovered in a schoolboy's atlas. Since then he had managed to barter a better compass in return for some soap. At Ippingen he, Corporal Carlé and Private Butler "walked out in our prison clothes on the 12th March, with as much food as we could carry. We did about sixty miles in two nights, and crossed the frontier at Stühlingen, as we now knew the habits of the sentries." It was there he had been caught the previous time. "We went to Schleitheim, where the Swiss Hotel proprietor gave us a good meal and would not allow us to pay." On 15 March 1918 John Cameron, the British Vice Consul in Schaffhausen, wrote to Percy Bennett, the Consul General in Zurich, that three escaped British prisoners had reported to him that day, adding that at Schleitheim "they were treated with great kindness by the landlady of the Gasthaus zum Post. I am writing to this lady to thank her." Private Butler was back at Wellington Barracks on 26 March.

Later on in the War, by which time Corporal Guy of the 1st Coldstream, previously at Schneidemühl, was at Friedrichsfeld, he escaped and reached Holland. Another Coldstream escaper, also taken prisoner on 29 October at Gheluvelt, was Lance Corporal Henry Wilson, a reservist, who had become a policeman in his home town of Hull. In July 1917 he was at Heuberg and also managed to get away from a working party on a farm before making his way through the hills and woods of the Black Forest to the Rhine opposite the Swiss frontier. There he lay up and watched the German patrols before stealing down to the river bank at three in the morning, throwing away his boots and jacket and slipping into the water. Although a strong swimmer, once he was in the river he quickly realised that he was going to have to get rid of his trousers too. He reckoned that the current had carried him a mile downstream before he reached the Swiss bank, near which, dripping, in only his shirt, he found a local man, who directed him to the nearest police station. From there he was quickly collected by officials from the British Legation in Berne.

Private Osborne's diary ended because it was taken away when he was captured on 29 October 1914 at Gheluvelt. An unknown German eventually returned it to him through the British Legation at The Hague in 1920. Corporal Burtenshaw was captured with him and both were at Schneidemühl and later at Friedrichsfeld. From there Private Osborne was sent to Ossenberg, a small working camp near Wesel. Amongst others there were two Australians, Private George Reed of the 54th Battalion, Australian Imperial Force, captured wounded on 20 July 1916 during the 5th Australian Division's attack on Fromelles and Private Percy Cooke of the 15th Battalion, wounded in three places on 9 August 1916 near Pozières on the Somme and captured three days later when he stumbled into the German lines in a thick mist. From Ossenberg they were sent to work on farms, Private Cooke at a different one from the others. The three of them had decided to escape and waited for the moonless night of 5 April. Privates Osborne and Reed stole away at eight that evening and met up with Private Cooke as planned. They crossed the

Dutch border about half past eight on the morning of 7 April. Private Osborne's treatment as a prisoner had damaged his health and he was discharged from the Army in August.

Although not technically an escaper, Private James McGinlay developed and then practised a ruse for a long time to be repatriated. In August 1915 he saw Private Borland leave Schneidemühl to start the process of exchange, but it was from another Scots Guardsman, who had gone out of his mind there, whose name he could not remember, but must have been Private Kewell, that Private McGinlay later got an idea. Then, because he was a Catholic, on 27 October he was taken to Limburg, but he had no interest in the Irish Brigade. He was not long there, which he found a much better camp than Schneidemühl, but very crowded, though "the numbers helped to keep it warm." Next he was sent out to work in a silver mine, from where he made an escape, remaining on the run for three days before being caught in Halle. While awaiting trial, which never took place, he broke out in a rash and that was the start. Not long afterwards there was another working party, a very arduous one in an iron ore mine, and Private McGinlay was so continuously and persistently sick that in May 1916 he was sent back to the camp hospital at Limburg. Here he was very well looked after. "The food was exceptionally good; we had eggs and fish besides other things, and for any bad case whisky and wine were ordered. When I was taken away from Limburg it was because I was supposed to be queer in the head; but I was "bluffing". I had had a bad scalp disease; I had running sores all over my head and all my hair came off. I was suffering much from this cause, and I got moody and depressed. I noticed I was being watched, so when I wrote to my wife I always wrote a lot of nonsense, as I knew my letters would be censored." In September he was removed to a civilian mental hospital and after four months sent to Aachen, where the exchange cases were finally assessed, only after ten weeks to be sent very briefly to Langensalza, Saxony, one of the worst camps of the lot, and thence to the camp hospital at Cassel, where he was for the last eight months of 1917. Then he went again to Aachen and this time he was sent back to England, arriving on 7 January 1918. There was nothing wrong with him mentally.

Captain Charles Fox

The train which took Captain Fox and the others to Crefeld took two days. None of them had anything to eat, though he considered that the guards treated them quite well. A German Red Cross nurse, bringing soup along the train at a station, opened their carriage door and asked if there were any British officers there. On finding there were, she paused, slammed the door and left. The first time he had his wounds dressed was by British officers when he reached Crefeld on 29 October. He was in a barrack room with three other British, three French and three Russians, where he had a straw mattress, a pillow and a double sheet, changed, he thought, monthly, but no blanket. It was very crowded, but good, accommodation and there were coal stoves and satisfactory washing facilities. Sanitary arrangements were insufficient. Captain Fox described the food as very good and the exercise facilities satisfactory once the prisoners had made them so. Smoking was allowed unless everyone was being punished collectively, such as after Colonel Vandeleur escaped, when all smoking was stopped for a fortnight. For the first six months of 1915 Captain Fox was at a very bad camp at Werl, out to the east of the Ruhr beyond Dortmund, from where he made his first escape attempt, failed and was sent back to Crefeld for court martial. Of the Irish Brigade he knew nothing, but this was when a German asked him if he would say he was a Home Ruler and an admirer of Sir Roger Casement. When

Captain Fox queried this the reply was that it might help him. By now he had the impression that at Crefeld the British officers had the upper hand. He then discovered that a member of the Merchant Navy in the camp was about to be transferred to the camp at Brandenburg, where naval and merchant seamen were held. He swapped places and, disguised as the Third Engineer of the SS *Voltaire* of the Lamport & Holt Line, Liverpool, sunk the previous December by the German commerce raider *SMS Möwe*, was put on a train to Berlin. He jumped off this, badly hurting himself. The two German soldiers who found him forty eight hours later beat him up and he was otherwise very badly handled until a doctor appeared and patched him up. Then he was put back onto a train, allowed to take a tram, for which he paid himself, to get towards the camp at Brandenburg, but still had a long walk. It was a very bad camp and he said that all the men there looked very ill. Captain Fox knew that it was much easier to get out of an other ranks camp, such as Brandenburg, but after a few weeks his cover was blown and he was sent to the officers camp at Schwarmstedt, on Lüneburg Heath. All the officers, some four hundred, were British and had been sent there a few weeks before when Crefeld closed. Though the German commandant and his subordinate were decent, the camp was badly constructed and the conditions poor, attributable to it too being in the corps area of General von Hänisch. There was no kitchen in the camp and officers had to collect firewood on walks in order to cook tinned food sent from England. The baths were outside the camp and could be used four times a week if an officer gave his parole not to escape, failing which it meant queuing twice a week. There were queues for almost everything. It was very dusty, with thick black dust penetrating everywhere, and the flies, probably horse flies as well as mosquitoes, were very troublesome. Parcels were received regularly but there was a suggestion that clothing and footwear sent from Britain were sometimes tampered with at the British end. Lieutenant Trafford, also now at Schwarmstedt, received a pair of old worn out boots in a box purporting to contain new ones. Captain Fox was soon preparing for another escape and after three weeks he left on 21 June with an unnamed lieutenant after they bribed two British orderlies to let them take their places in a working party cutting trees outside the perimeter wire. They slipped off. Captain Fox had previously buried a rucksack seven kilometres away, in which were supplies, including civilian clothes, a map and compass. They went to dig it up and headed west. Officer prisoners, provided that they gave their parole not to escape while doing so, but undertaking not to prepare an escape was apparently not covered, were generally permitted to go for walks away from their camps and there was no other explanation for his means of prepositioning his escape kit. Two days after they started out they met, completely by chance, Captain John Caunter of the 1st Gloucesters, captured on 31 October 1914 at Gheluvelt, who escaped from Schwarmstedt the day before them. They knew he had done so when they left. The three travelled together towards Holland, moving by night and lying up by day, the crossing of rivers being the trickiest part. When they had got most of the way the unnamed officer went off on his own and the other two heard no more of him. They could both swim well and he could not. Then on the last day before they got across the frontier German border guards saw them. Captain Fox ran off across country before hiding undetected in some rough pasture. The guards ran after and then lost him. He and Captain Caunter continued on their way together, shortly afterwards splitting up to cross the canal on the frontier on 5 July, quickly meeting up beyond and then identifying themselves to two Dutch soldiers. They were directed to and then most kindly treated by a policeman and his family before he accompanied them to the British Consul in Rotterdam. On returning to England Captain Fox was received by King George V, as were many other escaped officers, and elected

President of the Escapers. He was promoted to Major and spent the remainder of the War in the Ministry of Munitions. What he was up to there was continued involvement with escaping. He and a group of others, in close consultation with the families of officer prisoners who were trying to get home, contrived to send a very significant amount of contraband material to them concealed in food parcels, notably maps of routes from individual camps to the Swiss or Dutch borders, tiny luminous compasses, German money, very small torches, details of frontier patrols and restrictions and much else. Enough was sent to one officer per camp for him to equip several others. Such parcels sometimes arrived ahead of the advance letter containing hints of what was coming. This required quick thinking by the recipient if, for example, there was a tube of toothpaste of a different make from what he usually used. Among those who benefited was Captain Henry Cartwright of the 4th Middlesex, captured at Mons among their very heavy casualties. He was an inveterate escaper ever after and most witty and observant cartoonist until, after many attempts, he finally reached Holland in August 1918. His future wife, whom he married very soon after he was back in England, had materially assisted his escape efforts by carefully following his coded instructions, such as for the easily adaptable clothes she made for him.

The mines in Upper Silesia

Corporal Green recorded that on 27 August 1915 at Schneidemühl "All the English for strict doctors inspection, and some names taken, what for we knew not then." Two days later all those named were told that they were to work in a coal mine and left in a train that morning, joined by some British and French prisoners from another camp. They had no idea where they were going, got out of the train next day at a place called Borsigwerk, from where they were marched two miles west to Miechowitz. Their accommodation from then on was in a building at the bottom of the Kronprinzstrasse. They were in Upper Silesia and, apart from three months later in 1918, Corporal Green was living in Miechowitz, two and a half miles west of Beuthen, and working at the nearby Preussengrube coal mine. Here he started his diary account on 10 January 1916, writing it up from the outbreak of war.

On 31 August 1915 they were all marched to Preussengrube and issued with working clothes and boots. Until their arrival those working in the mine were either civilians, German and Polish, or Russian prisoners. On 1 September they had their first eight hour shift from three in the afternoon till eleven at night, after which they bathed and changed their clothes before going back to Miechowitz. Corporal Green was sent down a shaft eight hundred yards deep with another man to lay lines for coal wagons, an easy first shift for him. On 6 September he was in trouble allegedly "for refusing to work on Tuesday afternoon." He was tied to a post. "It poured hard with rain, and I was wet through in a very short time." It did not help that Private George Hudson of the 1st Coldstream shouted out to him "Buck up Jimmy. We'll have you released in a bit." The German guards thought that a mutiny was starting and brought all the British prisoners out into the yard at bayonet point, confiscating any knives and razors that they had. They then decided that Private John Long of the 1st Scots Guards was the ringleader and punished him. Private Long's father Bernard Long was living in Hamilton, but died during the War. He enlisted at the beginning of 1912, having been a railway platelayer in Perth before that. Captured on 29 October 1914 at Gheluvelt he too had been at Schneidemühl. Although only a Private it was noted on his file that for the purposes of addressing parcels he should have the rank of Corporal and so it came about that in March 1918 he was sent for internment in Holland.

For the next six months Corporal Green recorded little, other than that several prisoners, too weak for the heavy work in the mine, had been sent to a neighbouring camp at Lamsdorf, while others were in hospital in Beuthen, one of whom, Private WM "Napper" Davis of the 1st Gloucesters, died on 1 January 1916. In February a new detachment of prison guards arrived, most of them Poles and more considerate. Parcels and letters were coming through in good condition and fairly regularly. Then on 22 March "I think this was the luckiest day of my life. We happened to be on days, and consequently home about 3.45pm. The ensuing shift came on as usual at 3pm, and two hours later the pit was torn by a terrific explosion. It occurred in the same place I had been working for some time – "*Pochhammer*" 600 metres level. The death toll numbered twenty two…All available men were set to work looking for the bodies. First one was a Russian lying stone dead – a large lump of coal had fallen on him. Three shifts of eight hours were hard at it." This part of the mine shaft system was wrecked and the last two bodies were not found till 4 April. An inquiry established that the coal "hewer had bored a hole, filled it with powder, fired it, and it had penetrated a gassy seam in the coal." Two British soldiers on this shift were unhurt.

On 30 April they read in a special edition of the local paper that Major General Charles Townshend had surrendered to the Turks at Kut el Amara on the River Tigris with 13,300 men. There was so much of this sort of thing in the German press that it was some time before they would believe it. That same day, because there were threats of strikes in Silesia, the Polish guards were relieved, replaced by Prussians and Saxons mostly, it being supposed that the Poles would side with the strikers. There was a strike at the mine on 2 May for a minimum wage of ten marks per shift, with an additional half mark and half a pound extra pork for working ten hours. Most did go on strike that day and those who did not were the ones likely to be called up for military service as, if they did not comply with the mine owners' wishes, they could expect to be sent to the Army, whether they were Poles or Germans. The strike went on till 9 May, ending with better conditions for the miners. Confirmation of the surrender at Kut came in an English paper sent in a parcel to one of the prisoners, something that normally would not have got through, with newspapers not permitted. Corporal Green wrote "It was a great blow to us, and gave the ignorant Pole no end of joy." Worse was soon to follow in German reports of the Battle of Jutland, though the British prisoners "accepted it with the usual pinch of salt, and waited till we got one of our own papers through." Most demoralizing of all was the special edition of the local paper published on 6 June reporting the death of Lord Kitchener after HMS *Hampshire* struck a mine off Orkney. "I need not remark on the utter consternation this news gave us. I know a lot of our fellows, including myself, thought now the Germans had the war in their own hands. But of course we did not know what was happening at home. That made it all different. Of course the civilians were now more domineering than ever. If they were in mortal dread of one man, that man was Kitchener. We could quite understand their present jubilant spirits." What surprised them was that soon afterwards the German papers were printing accounts of Russian successes against the Austrians in Galicia. On 18 June another English paper arrived with news of the trial of the leaders of the Easter Rebellion in Dublin, but "Otherwise no special news."

Through the summer of 1916 Corporal Green noted a number of fatal accidents in the mine, all to civilians. There were few unusual events but he commented on 23 September that they had just come to the end of "a very rough fortnight" during which very few parcels had arrived from home. The reason given to them was that there was no available rail transport as troop movements had to come first. The date could have been significant because it was during September

1916 that the pressure on the German Army during the Battle of the Somme was at its most intense. The prisoners were paid three marks a week and were surprised on 2 October to find themselves deducted a mark or two each. Two days later they found out why. Corporal Green recorded on 4 October that "The German Reichstag was applying for another "Victory War Loan", as they were all so named. The civilians, very rightly too, were extremely doubtful about the "Victory" part of it. However, if they refused to give voluntarily, the authorities simply mentioned one word, "*eingezogen*" or call up, and the man paid up. A list was published, giving the amounts subscribed by prisoners on working parties. Ours came to two thousand marks (£100), another pit three thousand six hundred (£180), and so on. It fairly enraged the Poles, who quite believed it." During the week beginning 9 October "On our way home from work just after midnight, we saw the people making raids upon the potato fields…the penalty was a great one if found out." Later in the month it became very cold. There were some new arrivals, mostly Russians, some of whom escaped. Prisoners deemed to have been idle working down the mine were punished by being put to work on the surface and six of the British started in the timber yard on 6 October. Corporal Green described this as "very heavy work…But it was better than below." Two of these men were reservists from the 1st Scots Guards, Private Charlie Unsted and Private Thomas Walmsley, both captured at Gheluvelt. Private Unsted was a gardener from Herstmonceux, Sussex, who had served four years and left for the Reserve in 1908. Two years later he married Maud Ister in Eastbourne and they had two sons and a daughter. Private Walmsley was a butcher when he enlisted in Liverpool in 1904, three weeks after Private Unsted joined up. He married Mary Keane, a widow, in 1909 in Salford and they had two young daughters. Their home was in Bootle.

There were two physical attacks on British prisoners down the mine in January, but the repeated feature which Corporal Green noted was accidents, steadily, often fatally, and predominantly in the *Pochhammer* 600 metre level gallery. The worst incident nearby, on 20 January, did not involve the British and was not in a mine. This was a "Tremendous boiler explosion at a works at Borsigwerk…Twenty young women were killed, also several Russian prisoners. A large number were severely burnt." There was more difficulty over parcels that month with the same explanation about trains as previously, though some bread arrived through the Red Cross in Berne, and on 5 March Corporal Green wrote "About this time I was faring badly for parcels from England. Since the Regiment took it over last December, I had three parcels from them. But I'm not blaming them – the parcels would all arrive in a batch some day. I know I couldn't tackle the Berne bread without anything with it." There were about one hundred and thirty British at Miechowitz at this period. On 15 March another war loan was announced so, when the papers stated next day that the Russian Revolution had broken out in St Petersburg and that the Tsar had disappeared with thousands of Russian troops going over to the rebels, the British prisoners thought that this was a stunt to encourage the German civilians to subscribe.

On 28 March there was another fatal accident at the *Pochhammer* 600 gallery. Private Frank Johnson of the 1st Scots Guards was filling pit wagons with coal in the gallery, which Corporal Green then pulled along to the mine shaft, bringing back empty wagons to be filled. "Everything went smoothly until ten o'clock. I was returning with an empty wagon, when a civilian came up and told me Johnson was hurt. I left the wagon, took my lamp, and ran to give any help that I could. It was over seventy feet high, but we finally got him below. A lump of stone had dropped from the roof, and caught him behind the head. The blood was streaming down his back, but he fully understood me when I spoke to him." They carried him out on a stretcher and quickly found the pit doctor, who sent the badly injured man to the Reserve Hospital in Beuthen. At the time the British prisoners' official interpreter was Lance Corporal William Galloway of the 1st Coldstream who went to the hospital next day to find out how Private Johnson was. A German orderly told him that he was unconscious and had not long to live. "Such proved to be the case, for poor old Frank died at seven o'clock this evening. (He was a very nice fellow. Belonged to the same platoon as myself. Owned a large butcher's business in Bradford, his native town.)" Private Johnson, from Burley-in-Wharfedale, Yorkshire, first joined up in 1904 only five weeks after Private Walmsley. He married his wife Mary at Ilkley in 1907. Called up from the Reserve in August 1914, he went out to France at the start and had been with Corporal Green throughout. Mary Johnson was living in Burley, which was also the home of her parents in law, Fred and Winifred Johnson. Private William Craine, probably captured on 29 October 1914, because he had first been at Schneidemühl, wrote from Miechowitz to Regimental Headquarters to report Private Johnson's death. He had served for nearly five years by the start of the War. Before that he was a blacksmith in the Isle of Man where William and Ann Craine lived at Andreas. Corporal Green heard that there was an inquiry on 2 April into the cause of the accident, "but we have not heard the result." On 6 April "Good Friday, and we have to work! The body of Johnson was buried in Beuthen Cemetery. A funeral party, comprising all the Englishmen working on the pit head, and a number of "below" men finished work at one pm. They returned to the house, cleaned up, and marched to the hospital. We all saw the body lying in the coffin, and wrapped in a pure white shroud. He was buried soon after three o'clock and about five we arrived back at our residence."

From this time on he wrote repeatedly about parcels. They were certainly coming through, but often a box was empty or some of the contents, particularly tins, were no longer there. It turned out that this was, at least partly, deliberate German policy, as retaliation for alleged sabotage of the agricultural and industrial war effort. On 20 May Corporal Green wrote that the boxes "now contain only a quarter pound of tea, half pound of biscuits, fifty cigarettes or one ounce of tobacco, and an occasional pound tin of syrup." Without the parcels the men were losing weight and becoming weaker. Miechowitz was a subsidiary of Lamsdorf, a main camp, but for administration a satellite of Neuhammer, some way away in Lower Silesia, All at Miechowitz were formally recorded as being at Neuhammer and so that was where parcels for them arrived first. Corporal Green mentioned that before 1 May there appeared to be "great prospects of a general strike throughout the country" for that day, but made no further comment about strikes until 1 July when he heard that "Five pits near here are out on strike for more food. During the week, the Uhlans have been called out. But they refused to fire and the infantry were next sent to the scene. The latter fired on the cavalry, who returned it. In the end, eighteen horsemen and seven foot soldiers were killed, together with many civilians. A large number were also wounded." On 2 July the civilians at Preussengrube went on strike for more money and food and also demanded an end to rationing. More money was paid, but they were told that any change to food arrangements was impossible. At another mine nearby, so Corporal Green heard two days later, an underground mine manager had been shot dead by strikers, and a strike breaker killed. There would be more unrest, more mine accidents, more trouble with parcels, which sometimes arrived consisting only of the wrappings of parcels unpacked elsewhere. On 16 August "A large number of boots and shoes (taken previously from our parcels) arrived from Neuhammer. I received a pair." They had been complaining about the parcel situation in letters home and the censor at Neuhammer returned some of these on 22 August. Locally the food was very poor and on 9 August "Today they served up "preserved vegetables" (dried turnips) for sale at midday."

Through the spring and summer some British had gone to Lamsdorf and a few others arrived, including three men of the Duke of Cornwall's Light Infantry captured by the Bulgarians near Salonika. More Russians appeared, several of whom continued to escape. There were also new civilian workers who were discharged soldiers, one of whom, only recently back from serving in France, was killed on 18 August in the same place that Private Johnson was fatally injured. Corporal Green noted on 29 August that "Five hundred newly captured English and French prisoners have arrived in the locality, for work." One of the worst jobs at the mine was clearing the burnt coal ash from the boiler house and filling wagons with it to be taken away. It was therefore often used as a punishment. On 2 September Private Unsted was sent to work there for giving a French prisoner a black eye. Two days later the locals were celebrating again. In spite of the Revolution the Russians were still fighting and continued to do so until the Bolsheviks seized power in October. In what was a very well planned and executed operation the Germans captured Riga and so on 4 September their flags were flying at Miechowitz. A hundred parcels arrived on 6 September, of which Corporal Green had one. It was the first proper batch for some time. Three days after that a civilian was shot for stealing potatoes. On 16 September he noticed "Big transport of troops to Italy, as the Hun is about to take up an offensive on that front." This was the substantial German supported offensive from the mountains northeast of Venice along the border between Austro-Hungary and Italy, where there had been tactical stalemate along the River Isonzo since Italy joined the War in May 1915 on the side of the British and French. General Otto von Below led a very successful attack on the Italians starting on 24 October, causing a collapse and inflicting very large losses on them in the Battle of Caporetto. Corporal Green heard of this on 27 October. However, the initial victories were not exploitable and the Italians, bolstered by British and French troops sent from the Western Front, dug in again on the River Piave to the southwest. On 18 September more parcels arrived "this time with cigarettes present – greatly to our surprise." On 9 October "eleven large cases of tins arrived." Both times they had been warned shortly beforehand that they were not to write in their letters complaining of the cigarettes having been taken out nor of their tinned food being stolen. The cases with the tins were held back until a senior German NCO came over from Beuthen to administer their issue and before this happened on 29 October another smaller delivery arrived. Corporal Green's share of these was six pounds of corned beef, six tins of milk, one of sausage, and five tins of pâté. "I am on the committee, so I had my pick." Over the next few weeks the flow of parcels improved considerably.

The war news, besides Caporetto, consisted of a report on 24 October of a Zeppelin raid on London. Three airships were said to have been shot down while six got lost. On 4 November the Prussian lance corporal whom they called "Bullet Chest" stopped Corporal Galloway from holding a prayer meeting. Private Frederick Bodsworth of the KOYLI ran the prisoners band who had a rehearsal the same day. "Bullet Chest" stopped that too because Private Sillence of the Hampshire Regiment would not let him have a go on the trombone. The next day Private Sillence was sent off on his own to work with a party of Russians as a punishment.

Until the United States entered the War against Germany the Americans had been the protecting power for British prisoners, but thereafter the role passed to the Dutch. Meeting prisoners and discussing conditions without the Germans present was difficult but on 8 January 1918 Corporal Green wrote "Our place was visited by the Dutch Ambassador's deputy. He caused great excitement amongst the Germans in charge of us, and departed absolutely loaded with complaints from us, composed mainly on the subject of Sunday work, parcels, and also the amount of work we were daily compelled to perform. He enquired of Scoular how many wagons one man filled, and was told anything from eighteen to twenty two (each of sixteen cwts). It surprised him a little. But he should have gone underground to obtain proper information." Private James Scoular, an iron moulder and the son of William and Margaret Scoular of Newmains, Lanarkshire, had been in the 1st Scots Guards for nearly three years when the War began. Although hit in the right knee and left thigh on 29 October 1914 at Gheluvelt, where he was captured, his wounds must have been slight ones as otherwise he would not have been sent at once to Schneidemühl. A week later Corporal Galloway was sent as interpreter to another group of prisoners working at the mine and his place with Corporal Green's group was taken by Private Alexander Forbes, one of the youngest Scots Guardsmen at Miechowitz, aged nineteen and a half when captured at Gheluvelt. He too was wounded, in the right thigh, but he too went straight to Schneidemühl. He was the youngest of the five sons of James and Jane Forbes of Macduff, Banffshire, and had been a hairdresser before he enlisted in 1913.

There had been rumours and speculation for some time that long term prisoners might be exchanged in some form and the hope that this would happen was a constant theme of Corporal Green's. When it did it was limited and so disappointing for almost all. From Miechowitz only Sergeant Sidney Blackman of the 1st Scots Guards, Corporal Galloway and Lance Corporal Pitt of the 2nd KRRC left on the 15th to be interned at The Hague and three others, at least one of whom was not even a NCO, on the 19th. Corporal Green wondered "Is my turn coming?" He, a substantive Lance Corporal from before the War, was eligible and unlucky not to be listed. However, he did not do anything about it. Sergeant Sidney Blackman came from Arundel, Sussex, and had been serving since 1905. He and Annie Blackman, who married in 1909, had a son and a daughter. He was captured at Gheluvelt and was in charge of the Schneidemühl party in August 1915 for Miechowitz. Soon after he reached Holland he made a statement. He arrived at Miechowitz on 28 August 1915 with about one hundred and fifty eight British prisoners, having been told beforehand that his role was to look after the men and organise their parcels. However, on arrival the Germans informed him that he was to work like all the others. When he complained he was punished by being sent off on his own to work with Russians. "The food and accommodation were as good as could be expected, but the work was very heavy and the treatment bad." While the shifts were nominally ones of eight hours the early shift had to get up at three in the morning and were not back till four in the afternoon and the late shift left at one in the afternoon, not returning till quarter to two in the morning. He told the Court of Enquiry at The Hague that the German NCOs and camp guards never went down the mine themselves which meant that the prisoners of all nationalities were completely at the mercy of the civilian mine foreman, who with his assistants frequently struck them with coal hammers or beat them otherwise. By the time he left Miechowitz he said that there were still some one hundred and twenty five British there. A few days after Sergeant Blackman left Corporal Green noted that the local papers were making much of the successes of the German attacks on the Somme which began on 21 March. Then, on 1 April the British prisoners "promoted a concert party, performing in Bobrek, a small town near here. It was an unqualified success, too."

On 25 April they heard of a fresh agreement between the British and Germans for all prisoners over forty five to be exchanged, as well as all over forty with three children. There were four beneficiaries of this at Miechowitz. By 1 June the delivery of parcels was once again "slack" and

Corporal Green recorded "The enemy still on the offensive, and claim to have captured 45,000 Allied troops – English, French, Americans, and Portuguese." On 5 June late in the evening there was news of "a big explosion occurred at Farnowitz forty kilometres away [untraced]. It was in Krupp's second largest munition works in the country, and the employees numbered well over nine thousand, men and women." A special edition of the local paper two days later stated that two workers had been killed and six injured. Corporal Green was told by a civilian miner who worked with him that he had lost four daughters in the explosion. He also heard that forty newly captured British soldiers were now at a nearby mine. More and more Russians were escaping, but on 6 July a hundred new French prisoners from the recent German offensive on the Chemin des Dames and Reims arrived. Throughout his time at Miechowitz Corporal Green had been in generally good health though off work from time to time with minor ailments, including once hurting his foot. Frequently the German doctors took the view that anyone could work even if not fully fit to do so. A new threat was imminent and on 17 July Corporal Green wrote of "Five men suffering from Spanish influenza." Two days later he had it himself and had to stop work early, but his attack was a mild one and he was back to normal by the 21st, a Sunday, when all was quiet and everyone was resting. Hitherto there had almost always been work on Sundays.

To his surprise, he and nine other British prisoners were assembled next day and sent to another mine, Myslowitz, just east of Kattowitz. Two in his party were from the 1st Scots Guards, both captured on 29 October 1914 at Gheluvelt and both previously at Schneidemühl. One, Private Matthew Dowd, a former labourer with a year's service on the outbreak of War, had been wounded in the right arm when he was captured. John Dowd, his brother, lived in Niddrie, Edinburgh. The other was Private Albert Ingham, reservist and former mill hand from Milnsbridge, Huddersfield, whose mother Charlotte Ingham was there. They found themselves in a working party of about six hundred British, Italian, Roumanian and Russian prisoners. Corporal Green described these British as "the queerest lot of fellows I've ever seen. There is a certain amount of excuse for them, as so far they have never received no parcels from home. All of them were taken in the recent great push of the enemy on the west." At two next morning four of Corporal Green's party had to get up and help because there had been an accident to two of the newcomers in the mine. One was gassed, dying two days later, and another had hurt his leg. On 27 July Corporal Green wrote "I believe there are a lot of these newly captured Englishmen around this part of the country, and large numbers are dying of hunger, dropsy (caused by filthy food), fever etc. One died today, from pure starvation." On the 30th one tried four times to cut his throat, explaining later "That although he always worked until he dropped exhausted, the civilians thrashed him unmercifully." Corporal Green observed that he was seeing a lot of this kind of thing, these men being too weak to stand up for themselves. A few Miechowitz men had already been for a few days at Myslowitz when Corporal Green arrived. One was Private William Crowe, whom Corporal Green frequently mentioned at Miechowitz. He, eldest of the seven sons of William Crowe of Alexandria, Dunbartonshire, was a shipyard worker on the Clyde until he enlisted in January 1913. He had a flag tattoo on his right leg. Like Corporal Green a Gheluvelt prisoner, Private Crowe had been with him at Miechowitz all along. He was demobilised in April 1919 and married soon afterwards but, still held to his twelve year engagement, continued to be liable for mobilization. This occurred in April 1921 because of industrial unrest in the British mines. Private Crowe got into serious trouble while back in uniform, was convicted by a criminal court in London of drunkenness and assault and sent to Wandsworth Prison. This led to disciplinary discharge from the Army and forfeiture of his war medals.

Back at Miechowitz Corporal Green heard that Spanish Flu had taken a firm hold and some eighty of the British had it, of whom two were already dead. At Myslowitz there was another British death from gas poisoning, then one from pneumonia. On 19 August sixty parcels were forwarded to the former Miechowitz men, of which he received six. On the 25th he recorded that more than twenty Russians had escaped that week and that eighty boxes of biscuits had been issued to the new arrivals "and they deserved it." Generally the delivery of parcels had become very erratic. Another twenty Russians disappeared the following week and more than sixty over the next ten days. Four very sick British were sent to Lamsdorf on 11 September. Private Dowd followed on the 24th. The conditions had affected him and when he was repatriated at the end of December he was found to be partially paralysed on the right side of his face and also diagnosed with neurasthenia, in this sense more general debility than cumulative shell shock.

On 9 October a German sergeant sent Corporal Green across to another mine two miles away called Giescha Grube to interpret. There had been a party of about ninety British there but he found only forty, the rest being dead or "returned as unfit for the heavy work. Their rooms are more like pig sties, and the food is only fit for swine." He went back to Miechowitz on the 11th to the news that the British had taken Cambrai and that Allied troops were in charge of all the railways in Bulgaria. There was again some prospect of long serving prisoners being sent away and there was word of going to Minden in Westphalia, but nothing happened. On the 30th he was sent again to Giescha for three days and heard that Austria-Hungary was asking for peace. On 10 November his entry read "Sunday, and no parcels have come up during the past week. But the war news is good. Austria, Bulgaria and Turkey have finished, whilst Germany is looking for an armistice. In Russian Poland great rioting, finding out all the rich Jews who have been hoarding up food, and murdering them. I think now that the exchange of prisoners will be at the conclusion of hostilities. The German delegates have gone to Versailles, to consult with the Allies." On the 11th "At eleven am this morning, French time, the Armistice will commence, provided our terms are accepted by the Huns. Doctor ordered me to stay at home for a few days. I went to the post office to see if any parcels had arrived. On the way, I bought a paper, and read of our terms being accepted. All the soldiers and sailors have torn off their badges etc., and in their place can be seen Republican (red) ribbon. Our sentries have come under the mine owners who pay them eight marks a day."

For the time being the deal was that the prisoners would continue to work at the pre-war rate of pay for civilian mineworkers and it was not until 17 December that they were finally paid off. Corporal Green received thirty two marks and spent the evening in Miechowitz celebrating with Private Walter Keeler of the 1st Coldstream and Private Hudson of the Yorkshires [untraced]. The next day all the British headed northwest in a train of cattle trucks, which stopped at several other places to pick up more. In the evening they got out at Lamsdorf and marched for two hours to the camp. Almost all these men had been captured during the past few months and only eighty six had been prisoners for four years.

Internment in Switzerland

From the spring of 1916 there was an agreement that seriously wounded or sick British and German officers and men who were prisoners of war in each other's hands might be interned in Switzerland, subject to the Swiss authorities being satisfied that individuals' medical conditions justified it and subject to undertakings being given by other governments that in the highly unlikely event of any internee escaping and being apprehended, in Italy, for example, he would be returned to Switzerland. The internees were subject to Swiss military discipline, exercised when it arose by Swiss Army doctors. The first British parties from Germany, totalling thirty two officers and four hundred and twenty other ranks, arrived by train at the end of May 1916. They were settled initially at Château D'Oex or, if they had TB, at Leysin. From 13 August Mürren also started to take those who were badly injured. All were Alpine villages beginning to be known as resorts. Wives were allowed to come out for limited visits, limited because of the shortage of suitable accommodation, fifty at a time at Château D'Oex, ten at Leysin, none at Mürren. Colonel Earle of the 1st Grenadiers was the Senior Officer at Château D'Oex and wrote in November 1916 asking for two or three women to be sent out to start and run a tea place, his reasoning being that this would keep the soldiers from drinking in the long winter evenings. There was no record of anything resulting.

Private George Pollock of the 1st Scots Guards had a bullet wound in his right temple and eye when he was captured on 29 October 1914 at Gheluvelt. He came from Darvel, Ayrshire, and was a baker before joining up in 1912. The Germans put him into a hospital at Courtrai to begin with and when he could be moved he went to Giessen and later Merseburg. With that kind of injury and unable to work he was an early candidate for the internment scheme and was among those who travelled between 28 and 30 May 1916 to Switzerland, where he lived at the Hotel Berthold, Château D'Oex. In June 1918 he was repatriated, being discharged two months later "No longer physically fit for war service." To try to improve the effects of the wound to his head the doctors trepanned it and issued him with a skullcap. In January 1924 Lord Stair, whom George Pollock had known in Switzerland, wrote to Regimental Headquarters, sending on a request from him for some kind of reference or certificate in connection with a job application. In his letter Lord Stair recommended this, stating "he was badly knocked about, & suffered a good deal from what was left of his head. Can you send him what he requires. He deserves to get on if he can."

Private Edward Fegan, originally at Schneidemühl, was invalided to Leysin because of his TB. He wrote to the Regimental Prisoners Committee on 5 June 1916 from the Grand Hotel "Just a few lines to let you know of my change of address and also to discontinue sending the parcel of food which has been my main support for over a year. I hope you will excuse my saying more than seems necessary here, just my change of address, but I cannot let this go without telling you how really grateful we feel about the parcels, which came so regularly. In all four Lagers which I was in our chaps spoke highly of the Regimental parcel as being their principal means of keeping body and soul together. The parcels started arriving at Schneidemühl early in 1915 when the majority of us were just recovering from typhus. The nourishing food helped many of us to scrape thro'. Right on since that the parcels came regularly and seemed to improve, till now, there is not a better Regimental parcel going into Germany, than the Scots Guards. Without it one could not live, far less maintain good health on the German food allowance." He was repatriated in June 1918 and almost immediately discharged. He died in June 1923.

Private George Farries, a reservist in the 2nd Scots Guards, had his right arm badly damaged at Kruiseecke and was captured. He was a millworker from Hawick, where his family lived, but had served in the Boer War with the Northumberland Hussars and joined the Scots Guards afterwards. He had a Northumberland Hussars cap badge tattoo on his left forearm, along with one of a dancing girl. He served three years with the Colours and among other disciplinary entries was awarded two days confined to barracks on 23 September 1905 by Lieutenant

Colonel William Pulteney for "Obtaining beer on the line of march" at West Wycombe, Buckinghamshire. He travelled to Switzerland at the end of May 1916 and spent the rest of the War at the Hotel Beausejour at Château D'Oex. Twice he was in trouble with the Swiss authorities. The first time, on 24 June 1917, he was sent to the cells for five days by Leutnant Mayer for "1. Insulting married women in Café Three Suisses 2. Threatening two NCOs 3. Drunk". The second occasion on 31 May 1918 for absence from work, roll call and the hotel, initially led Leutnant Mayer to punish him with eight days in the cells, but this was commuted to four days confinement in his hotel. He came back to England on 9 December 1918.

Because he was partially disabled, Sergeant Turner, the medical sergeant wounded and left behind on 31 October 1914 at Gheluvelt Château, was also sent to Switzerland, arriving in August 1916 and staying at Mürren for the rest of the War. For three months after the Armistice he helped at the British Consulate at Geneva with repatriated and escaped British prisoners of war, receiving an excellent testimonial for this. On return to England he had to be discharged from the Army because of his injuries. At the start of the Second World War John Turner was appointed Senior Air Raid Precaution Warden in Mayfair, a post he held until he was bombed and trapped in debris in 1941. He had to give up. The bombing caused insomnia and increasing pain in his right leg from aggravation of his 1914 wound. Another at Mürren was Lance Corporal William Fraser, a reservist mobilised in Western Australia, captured at the Cuinchy brickstacks on 25 January 1915. He arrived in Switzerland on 12 August 1916, after first being at Merseburg and then other camps. When he was discharged after the War he had partial disabilities, heart strain and weakness in his left leg, but was not classed as medically unfit. Drill Sergeant David Ingham arrived at the same time at Mürren, where he lived in the Hotel Regina. He was a clerk in Leeds until 1900 and had been serving ever since. He was missing from the 1st Scots Guards in the trenches between Gheluvelt and Veldhoek as at 6 November 1914. The Germans found him with a shell wound in the back of his head which temporarily blinded him completely for between three and four days. Gradually over the same number of weeks his sight began to come back, but never more than to about two thirds of what it had been. For some weeks after he was captured he was in hospital, then he was sent to camps at Gardelegen, north of Magdeburg, then nearby Stendal, then hospital again, and lastly Mannheim. He was repatriated in September 1917 and left the Army early in 1918. He had married Edith Matthewman ten years before in Horbury, Yorkshire, and she was living in Pimlico with their son and the daughter born in September 1914 after her father had been in France for a month.

As Mürren and other places filled up Interlaken, on the low ground between Lakes Thun and Brienz, was added to the list. That was where Private William Roff arrived on 27 November 1917. He had one wound in his left arm but the second in his throat when he was captured on 29 October 1914 at Gheluvelt was more than a flesh wound. It caused traumatic epileptic fits, hence his approval for internment. Then on 24 March 1918 he was sent back to England and left the Army, no longer physically fit for war service, in July. George and Hannah Roff lived at Upper Parkstone, Dorset, and William was the third of their family of five sons. He was just over eighteen when he enlisted at Poole exactly a year before the start of the War. Another arrival at Interlaken was Private William Miller, accommodated in the Hotel du Nord. He was a miner, living in Hamilton with Jane, his wife of twenty years, and their five children when the War broke out. He went to reenlist three weeks later, aged forty one and a half, previously having served in the Scots Guards from 1890 to 1902. Less than four weeks after rejoining he was in the BEF and was sent to the 2nd Scots Guards after First Ypres. He took part in the night attack on 18 December at Rouges Bancs and was captured unwounded. Subsequently he developed heart disease and bronchitis and so was approved as an internee. On an unrecorded date early in 1918 the Swiss authorities charged him with being I. Absent from Dinner at 12 noon until found in his room Drunk and having II. Untidy room at Interlaken, punishing him with "20 days cells" to be served during March. However, he left Switzerland for repatriation on the same day as Private Roff and was discharged, likewise no longer physically fit for war service, also in July and only three days later.

Some who could have been sent to Switzerland never left Germany. Private William Forbes of the 1st Scots Guards was a wartime volunteer, a crane man, who joined up in Glasgow in September 1914. After the Cuinchy brickstacks on 25 January 1915 he was missing, having only landed in France twelve days before. His sister Annie Sinclair wrote on 22 February from her home in Kelvinhaugh Road, Glasgow, to say that she had had a card from him that morning giving his address at Giessen. Later he was moved to Merseburg and at half past eleven on the morning of 23 July 1918 he died in the camp hospital there of an abscess on the lung and TB.

Internment in Holland

The effect of the other agreement that came into effect in March 1918 that unwounded long term prisoners who were officers and NCOs, but including some private soldiers, should be interned in neutral countries led to a concentration of former British prisoners at Scheveningen on the Dutch coast, most of them arriving very soon afterwards. No 9 (Guards) Group were there and one of the places where they lived was the Hotel des Galeries. Among the Scots Guardsmen was Sergeant Clement Irons, the signaller from the 2nd Scots Guards who had married Ethel Miles at Lyndhurst in the New Forest ten days before leaving for Zeebrugge in 1914. He was captured unwounded at Kruiseecke and was in the camps at Göttingen and later Dülmen before being sent for internment. Lance Corporal William Bland of the 1st Scots Guards, recommended, without result, for gallantry after the Railway Triangle counterattack on New Year's Day 1915 and captured unwounded on 25 January at the Cuinchy brickstacks, had been through the camps at Merseburg, Friedrichsfeld, Cottbus and Frankfurt am Oder before going to Holland. Not long before the end of the War he applied to marry a Dutch girl, Antonia Schavers. It was suggested that this should be held over until he returned to London. On his records he had asked that in the event of his being a casualty not only should his mother Anne Hayhurst be informed in Grayrigg, Westmorland, but also a friend Mary Ann Fletcher, in Brixton. On 18 November 1918 Corporal Bland went back to England and on 1 January 1919 he married Mary Ann Fletcher. In mid July 1914 Company Quartermaster Sergeant William Goddard of the 2nd Scots Guards went absent for ten days and was reduced to Corporal. Soon afterwards he was restored to Lance Sergeant, then went out with the Battalion to Zeebrugge, was captured during First Ypres and sent to Göttingen. Later he was at Langensalza and then Soltau before internment in Holland. At about five o'clock in the morning on 7 May 1918 he was accidentally killed. No one saw what happened, but none of the witnesses thought that he had been behaving oddly in any way. The conclusion was that he had mistaken the window he fell through for the latrine door and that it broke when he pushed against it. James Goddard lived at Hampton on Thames, and his son had been a telegraphist before he joined up in 1902. The internees at Scheveningen were the first POWs to reach home after the Armistice.

The Spanish Flu epidemic in 1918

Apart from typhus in the winter of 1914-15, relatively few prisoners died between then and 1917. It was 1918 which was fatal for most of the British who died in captivity, from one main cause. By then conditions were becoming harsher than ever, partly because, following the German spring offensives, there were more prisoners for them to feed, but mostly because there was less and less for the German civilian population. This was partly because of the success of the Royal Navy's blockade, applied with vigour after the United States entered the War, but more because of the German Government's inability to organise and then direct food production and distribution. Then came the Spanish Flu epidemic. Just as it did worldwide, it killed the vulnerable, as well as the fit, in large numbers in Germany. Among several other Scots Guardsmen who died of it in captivity in 1918, three members of the 1st Scots Guards, all of them having gone out on 13 August 1914 to France and all of them captured during First Ypres, died over three days in the last ten days of the War. Private John McRae, his real name, but serving under the alias of Douglas Hughes, a reservist, died on 2 November in the hospital at Schneidemühl. He had been a town carter in Liverpool and only left for the Reserve seven weeks before the War began. The year before a report had noted that he was "A very good boxer". He was wounded and after being taken prisoner, almost certainly at Gheluvelt as he was recorded as being in a hospital in Brussels on 1 November 1914, went quickly on to Germany. Thomas and Sarah MacRae lived in Tranmere, Birkenhead. Private Thomas Craig died of Spanish Flu on 3 November, also in the hospital at Schneidemühl. He was a reservist from Edinburgh, where he had been a golf ball maker and where David and Mary Craig lived in the New Town. Posted missing after 11 November 1914, he was probably captured at Gheluvelt. Private Alexander Young died of Spanish Flu on 4 November at a Merseburg satellite camp. The family lived in Partick, Glasgow, where his father David Young was a journeyman blacksmith and his son followed in the same trade until he enlisted in November 1913. He was slightly wounded early in October in the trenches on the Aisne and wounded again and captured, possibly during the fighting beside the Menin Road on 2 November, though no one knew what had happened to him and he was simply missing. News that he was alive as a prisoner only came to the British authorities in March 1915 and then, surprisingly, from a list passed to the French naming their prisoners in Germany. That Private Young was dead from flu and that neglect had also contributed was in a report which Private James Birss, a Glasgow policeman, made when he was repatriated. Private Young's mother Elizabeth died of cancer of the tongue in February 1918.

Repatriation

Corporal Green left Lamsdorf in a party of four hundred and seventy five former prisoners on the afternoon of the 23 December in a train of cattle trucks heading for Danzig, arriving at seven in the morning on Christmas Eve. A Royal Navy officer greeted them, billeted them in a schoolhouse and issued them with tea and tobacco. After dark on Christmas Day they were told to pack up and move to the quayside to embark on two destroyers, HMS *Concord* and HMS *Wessex*. The crews welcomed them warmly and provide all the food, drink and tobacco that they asked for. At noon next day they landed at Copenhagen and were accommodated in a cold warehouse for the night. On the 27th they were told initially that they were to embark at once on an American steamer, but this was cancelled to their mortification. Instead they went by train to a camp at Sandholm, north of Copenhagen. Here on the 28th two small parties were selected "to entertain some Danish people on our experiences", as the British adjutant of the camp told them. The first party of three men from the 1st Coldstream went to one house, while Corporal Green and Private Walmsley went "to a Field Marshal's widow, with her son and daughter. Had a splendid time, and have to return again tomorrow." On the 29th "We two returned as promised, but earlier in the day. They took us to have a big dinner elsewhere, and I had to help two ladies in to dinner. I shan't forget that experience for a while. They were very homely people. Telephoned to camp asking if we could stop for a few days, and go over to Helsinki for a short holiday. But we were for home tomorrow, so it is impossible."

On 30 December they went back to Copenhagen and embarked on the SS *Huntsend*, formerly the German steamer *Lützow* captured during the War. Corporal Green noted that since the British had had her she had been twice torpedoed, "but is still good." They sailed at four in the afternoon. "The ship is forced to travel slowly, on account of floating mines, of which we can see plenty. Ordered to wear life belt night and day, so great is the danger." On New Year's Day a "Terrible gale started to blow, and the majority of us were soon sea sick." By the morning of the 2nd they could see lights along the English coast, but still did not know their destination. "However, we sailed up opposite Leith, and anchored at four pm we disembarked, no words can describe our reaction. Issued with stamped post cards, soap, cigarettes, chocolate, meat pie, handkerchief, matches, biscuits, and cheese." They were at once put on a train which arrived at Ripon, Yorkshire, just before midnight. There next morning they were issued with clothing and such kit as they required when in uniform and given fifty shillings. Doctors inspected each of them twice. On 4 January Corporal Green left Ripon for two months leave. There was a heavy fall of snow and it took the train four hours from Leeds to Manchester before he went on to Liverpool "and it was about half past eight in the evening when I finally reached Fountains Road, tired out."

Notes on Chapter Sources

Interviews of former Prisoners of War, either repatriated for reasons of sickness or injury or escapers (not all were printed), back in the UK before the end of the War, series TNA/WO161.
Interviews of those sent to Holland for internment early in 1918 (not all) at courts of enquiry from March to June 1918 at The Hague in eight files of sworn statements and other documents sent to the Government Committee on the Treatment by the Germans of British Prisoners of War, series NAM/2001-07-703.
Material about prisoner of war camp conditions, escapes, reports on treatment of prisoners, including compulsion to work, subversion, deaths in captivity, the transfer of sick and badly injured to Switzerland and events there and the handling of captured German submariners in 1915 and consequences, series TNA/FO383.
Account of LCpl H Wilson, 1st Coldstream, LIDDLE/WW1/POW/070.
Account of Capt Fox augmented by entry in Gen Sir O'Moore Creagh and EM Humphris (Eds), *The V.C. and D.S.O.* Volume II (London: The Standard Art Book Co Ltd, undated) and, subsequent to his escape, also reference in Maj MCC Harrison and Capt HA Cartwright, *Within Four Walls* (London: Edward Arnold & Co 1930).

7

The Rouges Bancs Trenches and the Winter 1914-1915 – 2nd Battalion

On 14 November Brigadier General Frederick "Pa" Heyworth arrived to command the 20th Brigade. A very different phase began that day as all the 7th Division infantry were marching south through Bailleul and Steenwerck and over the River Lys. The 2nd Scots Guards crossed at Bac-St Maur and waited there till after dark, Sailly-sur-la-Lys being the next village upstream. The Division became responsible for some seven thousand yards of the line facing east from, on the right, opposite Rouges Bancs, a hamlet in German hands on the Sailly-Fromelles road to, on the left, Bois Grenier, south of Armentières. The 20th Brigade went to the line at Rouges Bancs, Major Cator recording that initially the 1st Grenadiers were on the right, the 2nd Scots Guards in the middle and the 2nd Borders on the left. He was not impressed. "The trenches taken over by the Grenadiers an absolute disgrace to any British Regt a Battn of the… Royal Fusiliers had been in occupation of the ground for three weeks & apparently have done no digging or entanglements to speak of at all. All the trenches had been kept in a very dirty state." He got the name of the regiment wrong as it was the 2nd Royal Welsh Fusiliers, who, with the rest of the 19th Brigade, had been in this line without relief at all for over three weeks. Private Frank Richards, author of *Old Soldiers Never Die*, with some help from the poet and writer Robert Graves, an officer with whom he served later on, described how "By this time we were as lousy as rooks. No man had washed or shaved for nearly a month, and with our beards and mud we looked a proper ragtime band of brigands." Private Richards, called up as a reservist, had gone out at the very start with the BEF, remained with them throughout the War, refused all promotion and postings, won the DCM and MM and was never hit once.

Compared with Ypres there had not, relatively, been that much fighting, but trench warfare with its routines and hazards had started. It was remarked that had the line been established a mile further back it would not have prejudiced the military situation, while making it far harder for the Germans to observe and snipe. They had secured the best of the ground tactically, overlooking the British from the Aubers Ridge, which rose very gradually up behind Rouges Bancs by only ninety feet. Fromelles was on its lower slopes. The Royal Welsh Fusiliers were at one stage in Fromelles, but had to withdraw when neighbouring French cavalry went back and left them on their own. The 19th Brigade were then ordered to begin a line of trenches on the flat ground just to the west of Rouges Bancs. Keeping a wary eye out across No Man's Land the Royal Welsh Fusiliers had started digging in by sections, then they linked the section posts together into platoon trenches and finally formed a continuous line. To begin with the Sailly-Fromelles road, the Rue Delvas, was the 7th Division's right boundary.

La Cordonnerie Farm, a few hundred yards back from the front line, became the Scots Guards Battalion Headquarters for this trench tour and others. Lieutenant Swinton was on his way forward when he first tried to eat a tin of the issue tinned stew known as a Maconochie Ration, which exploded in his face. They halted in the Rue Pétillon, a side road off the Rue Delvas about two thirds of a mile behind the Farm, and waited to go up to take over the line for the first time. Later he remembered "the sinking feeling as the bullets whined and cracked overhead." He gave his first impressions in a letter home next day. "We entered this celestial abode last night as soon as it got dark. We are not in a very bad place as they have only just started shelling and it is 9am they usually start at daybreak. They are just getting the Jack Johnsons to work; they shake the whole ground and blow a hole large enough to bury a horse. The snipers are the worst of this place, if you put your head up for an instant they let fly at you, both by day and by night. One only missed me by about a foot this morning…This is a very dull and boring life, you sleep all day and the best part of the night, and in the interval you eat and dodge shells and bullets." In his next letter, written later the same day or the next, he asked his mother to send food only sparingly and clothes only if he asked for them. "I spotted a captive balloon this morning and reported it to the gunner officer. He was quite interested." He had gone out to see what the British guns were firing at and was back under cover when "Damned if one of those snipers of their's didn't see me; he's just put 4 shots just over the place where I was standing a minute ago." Already the conditions were dire as in "part of the bit I control we have nice smelly mud like breadsauce up to your knees."

Major Cator, an accomplished cartoonist, recorded "the distances from the German trenches vary from 5 or 6 hundred yards to one hundred and fifty." Here and there they were to get closer as the Germans sapped their way forward and by the 16th in one place opposite the right of the Scots Guards they were less than a hundred yards away. Down to the south towards Neuve Chapelle were the Indian Corps, "who keep up an incessant roar of musketry all night. They are shortly to be relieved by the 8th Division." He went on that on 15 November "Inhabitants in neighbourhood of trenches being removed. Snipers & spies reported to be plentiful in rear of the trenches." Next day he told his wife that "the fighting in these parts is very meek and mild compared to what we were having round Ypres. The cold is getting horrible yesterday we had snow…Their "snipers" are busy but beyond that there is not much to worry about. The German trenches vary from 80 to 200 yards in front of our's. They do a lot of digging at night. Like we do. Kit crawled out last night to find out how they were progressing, and sent us in a very good report this morning…Old Pa arrived here the day before yesterday…he left London Friday morning and we had him under fire Saturday evening. I took him round the trenches."

To begin with, the Brigade did not man the trenches by a set system and battalions were not regularly in and out of the same part of the line, in which, because of the shortage of men, they could expect to spend seven days, followed by three in billets. A very cold spell began on the 17th, snow falling that day and the next. Major Cator first noted, both on the 18th and 20th, that there had been cases of what he called frostbite, but was almost certainly trench foot, and there would be many more. He mentioned the collection and issue of braziers in the trenches, but it was not them but carrying forward fuel that was the problem, along with everything else in these conditions, exacerbated by how the trenches had been formed in the first place. Lieutenant Swinton described how "the original inhabitants of our line had dug in along the ditches, and it was not long before we realized the error of their ways in this flat and, to be, waterlogged country. We started by digging down, each man, six feet, so as to enable him to stand up without being seen; then the individual holes were joined up to form a trench and, finally, a firing step formed so that each man could use his rifle through, or over, the parapet. All this excavation was thrown over the parapet which, in time, became bulletproof. At first we all slept on the firing step, covered with a waterproof sheet, but within a few days it began to snow, with a sharp frost at night. So we dug into the back of the trench and formed little bays where two or three men could sleep in greater comfort. After a bit we had an issue of charcoal and this we put, each man, in a discarded bully beef tin, suitably punctured and, after much blowing, we were able to get some benefit by crouching over the glowing tin. There was some trouble over using this charcoal in the little dug-outs until it was realized how poisonous the fumes could be in a confined space." Washing was impossible, but the Scots Guards always managed to shave.

From the very start there were casualties, mostly from sniping, sometimes from shells or minenwerfer bombs. Major Cator told Violet on the 18th "The snipers here are devilish good shots. They killed five yesterday and wounded seven the day before, nearly all through the trap holes, the latter are rotten things and we are having them all blocked up…There are still quite a lot of dead Germans lying in front of our trenches, who were killed a fortnight ago – before we arrived." The recorded date of the deaths of five Scots Guardsmen was the 16th. One was Private John Malarkie, a six foot tall East Lothian coal miner, who had only enlisted in May and whose mother Ellen Malarkie was then living in Leith. Private James Douglas, a reservist, was mortally wounded and died soon afterwards the same day. His family lived at Castleblaney, County Monaghan, though he had settled in Glasgow, where he and Jessie Douglas were living in Dennistoun. Their elder son, born in 1913, died two years later, their younger one only being born ten days before his father's death. Private Peter Campbell, another six footer, also killed, an iron moulder from Falkirk and reenlisted former Scots Guardsman, left behind his wife Jane and two sons and a daughter. They had another son born in 1915. Private Campbell had reenlisted on 22 August in Stirling, reached France on 20 September as a reinforcement and was sent up the line on 12 November. Until the War came, when he enlisted later on in August, Private John Hull had been a labourer in Liverpool. On 8 November he arrived in France and now he was dead. His father Thomas Hull was dead, but his mother Annie Hull was living in Walton, Liverpool. Private John Hacking was the fifth man killed. His reserve commitment had expired and he reenlisted at the beginning of September in Blackburn, where he and his wife Sarah lived and he had a job as a driver, probably for a grocer. It was noted that he had varicose veins in both legs. He too arrived in France on 8 November and died eight days later.

Sergeant Pilkington, the photographer, went on the 19th with Corporal Mavor, the DCM winner, up to a support line trench. "The bottom of the trench was a mass of slush and also very slippery. The top and surrounding country white with freezing snow. There was a lot of sniping going on but so far as I could judge no bullets came very near us. After some time we left the trenches with orders to look for a cow. It was rather creepy as the snow showed up our black figures, but we found a herd and selected a cow and brought her back along to furnish milk for the officers." At the time there were still many abandoned farm animals about. After another cow was caught and brought to La Cordonnerie Farm they were christened Bella and Bertha. Though he never took any credit for it Lieutenant Ross, the Quartermaster, was the likeliest initiator. Lieutenant Swinton wrote that "in no time we had an officially appointed cowman; he was on my payroll, and for the rest of the war the officers had fresh milk." The officers paid for the cows' upkeep during the winter months and during the rest of the year they grazed. Later it would appear that the Medical Officer had first call on the milk. The cows would go everywhere with the Battalion for the rest of the War, often by train, and were shod for longer marches. One at a time was in calf and so the supply of milk proceeded steadily.

That day Lieutenant Cator started his next letter, telling his mother that his company "has a front of about 450 yards. I have three Subalterns under me and about 250 men. So it is a nice command, but there is a great deal to do and think about, and naturally the responsibility is heavy. The Germans are about 180 yards from my line at the nearest places and 300 in others. There has not been any very heavy shelling along here…but there is continual sniping with rifles going on and you are safe enough from that as long as you keep your head down as much as possible below the parapet. I have only had one man killed and one wounded in my company so far…Our life here is a pretty hard one I must confess and resembles that of a rabbit more than a human being." Because of the snow and the way that dark uniforms showed up against it there was an issue of white smocks for patrolling, as his brother noted that day. Major Cator sent their mother his news on 20 November and was waiting for an early start the next morning because General Capper was coming round the trenches, intending to set off at half past five. He had to get him back and out of the line before dawn because of the snipers. "Capper is much too fond of risking himself for a General, and we can't afford to lose him, but we are constantly trying to stop him going there, the fire is too hot, but as often as not he takes no notice and goes just the same." He reflected on the "Stale Mate" of the Germans having been stopped in their attacks and the British not wanting to mount attacks themselves, so his projected outcome was that the Germans should wear themselves out. He then told her that "I don't think I should have got through one or two of the days of the fighting unless one has faith in Christ, to help one through." Particularly when going into shelling "I think one just surrenders oneself to Christ, and one goes on determined to win if you stand up. Have you ever jumped into icy water from a warm bath? It's just the first plunge that is disagreeable, and after that it is not too bad. Well going into a shell swept zone is like that. A short prayer and you feel alright or nearly so. It isn't a comfy feeling at any time."

Sir Edward Hulse, knowing how long the previous occupants had been there and hoping that it was not to be repeated, wrote home the same day. "It has been snowing hard, after two nights' sharp frost, and it is lying about two inches deep, except in the foot of the trenches, where by the continual passage of men up and down, it has become a freezing cold slush of mud, and chills one's boots or socks even, and far and away the worst part is the cold in one's feet at night, which makes sleep impossible for more than half an hour at a time. Otherwise we are keeping pretty warm in our dug-outs, and are gradually getting a bit of straw into them, where it keeps dry and is warm to lie on. We get a certain amount of charcoal served out, but not much, and with old mess tins, with holes punched in all over them, get the charcoal going, spread two or three oilsheets over the trench, and with three or four men sitting around, they can get quite a degree of warmth out of it. I believe blankets are coming up, but we must get them into the trenches *dry*, or they will be no good at all; even so, they can only come in by driblets, as so few men are allowed to leave the trenches at a time, and of course only by night. The three quarters of a mile or so of slush, across churned up ploughed fields with deep ditches and well sprinkled with dead cattle, etc., is a trying journey, and none too easy on a dark night. The first night ration parties and watering parties on their way back got lost, were sniped at by the enemy and promptly "panicoed". Instead of crouching and keeping stock still, they dropped the rations and doubled about the place like lost sheep, and finally arrived in helter-skelter, by twos and threes, into the trenches without any food and water; and the result was we went hungry for the next twenty hours. I cursed them to heaps, and had all the NCOs up and explained everything all over again and took them out and back the next night myself. At last they cooled down, and are working properly each night, and with less hubbub and pandemonium and talk than at first."

Private Alexander Sutherland, a miner from Musselburgh, was a Territorial soldier before the War but had no other military training. Notwithstanding that he was in France within two months of enlisting, leaving behind Agnes, his wife of four years, and their daughter, born some years earlier. He lost his life on the 20th. When he enlisted he said that he was forty two, but Agnes Sutherland stated to the Imperial War Graves Commission after the War that he was forty six when he died, in which case he underdeclared his age in order to get into the Army.

Lieutenant Cator had not been able to finish the letter he began on 19 November until they were back in billets three days later. His men were sleeping on the straw in barns and the four officers shared two small cottages. In one of these he had to share a bed with Lieutenant Viscount Clive, eldest son of the Earl and Countess of Powis, of Powis Castle, Welshpool, who after Eton and Sandhurst had been commissioned the year before. He had been at Ypres. Lieutenant Cator went on "You can't imagine what heaven it is to be in a house, however rough it may be, after the trenches and near a nice fire. I had eight hours good sleep which I wanted badly and never moved a muscle. Today is Sunday and we all went to church parade and General Heyworth… read the service… A few shells burst about 100 yards off us but did no damage. I had a real good wash this morning and a bath in my canvas bath, the first wash and shave I have had for eight days as it is quite impossible to wash in the trenches as water is very difficult to get and wanted for drinking. One never takes one's clothes or boots off there either, not that one wants to as it is much too cold. I had no idea one could be so cold as one is sometimes, as there has been a fall of snow and now a hard frost has set in, and when we first got there it was very wet. Anything is better than rain though, as when wet you walk in mud and water nearly up to your knees and your feet are always wet. Several of the men have gone sick with frostbitten feet, as the frost came so suddenly on top of the wet." He did not want his mother to think he was complaining, simply describing how they were living, and, apart from a cough, he was feeling very well. "One good thing is we are all fed like fighting cocks and the supplies for the Army have been run in the most wonderful way. The ordinary rations for the men which they get every day are 1¼ lbs of meat, half fresh and half tinned, ½ a loaf of bread or biscuits (1 lb) bacon, cheese, potatoes, jam, groceries (tea, sugar, salt, mustard and pepper) sometimes butter and rum."

Then he went on about the trenches "open about 2ft wide and 5ft deep, dug straight down into the ground and in rear of the line of trenches various passages lead off to deep holes called dug-outs or shellproof shelters and they are roofed over with earth on the top and are places where men can get into and sit and rest, filled with straw. We officers have our meals in one of these dug-outs and we have a regular little mess there, which we call Piccadilly Circus, as various connecting trenches lead off from there, and I have my own headquarters there. Three Artillery Officers mess there with us, such nice chaps and I was horrified yesterday morning when a sergeant came running back for a stretcher bearer and told me one of them Scott, had been shot, he had only been talking to me a few minutes before and had gone up to one of my trenches to observe the fire of his guns, he was killed instantaneously I am glad to say, as one of their beastly snipers got him right through the head. I said a prayer over him and made the sign of the cross on his chest and that was all one could do. It is impossible to move the wounded or dead until night time. This trench fighting is such a horrible, cold blooded form of warfare as our casualties are all from either snipers or shellfire, and there you sit and watch each other and whether our game is just to hold the Germans or whether we shall attack their line later on I don't know, but what I mean is, in an attack in the open you get your blood up and feel that if you get killed or wounded you have some excitement and a fair run for your money as it were." Lieutenant Edward Scott, Royal Garrison Artillery, from Winchester, was killed on 21 November. Besides the casualties a number of men had gone sick and several officers too.

However, Lieutenant Cator had been able to vary his time in the trenches. "I have been out scouting and observing two or three times with a trained scout and have been able to gain a certain amount of useful information. It is exciting work and rather amusing. Two days ago I was on top of a thatched roof observing, and four shells came and burst within a few yards of us which was too close to be pleasant as we felt the rush of air on our faces from the concussion so we left our peephole and decamped, and having caught two chickens on our way back returned to supper. All the farms and houses near the firing line are all demolished from shells and it is all a very sad sight and you see a poor dog sometimes remaining in the ruins having been left behind, and cows too, often wounded but then we shoot the poor beasts." Meanwhile "We have lost three out of the four Captains who came out with the drafts, namely Tom Coke, Appendicitis, Bagot Chester, Piles, and Romer, rheumatic fever. I expect they have all gone home…I doubt if this war will end for some time and I feel sure it will go on for another year anyway. Please send me out some chocolate and peppermints and writing paper as I have got none, and am writing this in my field service note book." Captain Viscount Coke was the eldest son of the eldest half brother of the other Cokes who served in the Scots Guards during the War. Like two of them, but not the third, he had been in the Regiment previously, including the Boer War. He never served again with one of the Battalions. Because of his father's age and his grandfather's second marriage he was the same generation as his half uncles. Captain Greville "Bubbles" Bagot Chester, born in 1865, had served for more than twenty years, including the Boer War, before becoming a member of the London Stock Exchange in 1910 and rejoining as soon as war broke out. When he was younger he had been a very fit and athletic man and had once won a £100 bet when he rode a mile, ran a mile and walked a mile inside twenty minutes. Both he and Captain Romer would reappear. As Lieutenant Saumarez continued his notebook there was little of significance other than his remarking on the 18th of hearing that in the 1st Battalion there were only Captain Stracey and seventy men left. On 22 November he wrote to Gunhild "We are just back from the trenches where we have spent just a week in the same place. It was the dry bed of a river with small 'dug outs' on the near side of it. The first day was all right – then it rained – and then the water began running in and by the next morning we were well under water…Well it rained merrily for 2 days then 2 days of hard frost and then 2 days hard snow. We have even had a few cases of frost bite. Casualties however have been comparatively few and things have been much quieter, neither side feeling much inclined to do much fighting under these circumstances. Our only hope was that the Germans were worse off than we were!! -: Nice kindly feeling -: Have just returned from Church Parade and were under shellfire all through the service. Nobody was hit, but curiously enough it only went on as long as the service lasted! When we stopped, they stopped – We are now in Reserve for 2 days and then we go off back to our ditch again. Thank you most awfully for your 2 letters of the 14th and 15th which arrived this morning early. I was asleep in some straw in a farm kitchen here when the orderly came in with them, a very pleasant start for the day. It is so nice to know what you are thinking about and have your views about things. I wish all English people were endued with the same real patriotism as the Swedish people. If we had just that one thing as strong in us as you have it, I really think we should be a very great nation, but this one most important thing of all seems to be lacking in the great majority of the people I am ashamed to say —As to whether this confounded government would risk having conscription brought in during their term of office, I don't know – of course its a damned scandal and they ought to be kicked out, if they don't bring it in at once, after what the army has done for them." Next day he wrote again "1000's of thanks for the nice watch it looks a beauty. You really must not go on ruining yourself in this way. Last night piles and piles of parcels arrived for me all sorts of good things from waistcoats and plum pudding down to boots and Keatings powder. You really are most noble, but as I said before you must not ruin yourself: as I don't want to find a poor bankrupt wife when I return!! The Left Flank mess is now well replenished in fact we are doing ourselves so well that you can scarcely hear yourselves speak in this kitchen. We are a very cheery crowd in the company. Dick Coke in command a very nice fellow and good sportsman in spite of his age… and a Sandhurst cadet called Ottley who is young and rather a well meaning fool…I was just thinking that the last time I saw snow was under very different circumstances. Well here's to the time when we find ourselves skiing in Sweden again." Then at the end "We are rather short of cocoa. I have already got a fur coat thanks ever so much all the same." Captain The Honourable Richard "Dick" Coke was the eldest of the three brothers and had, like his half nephew, arrived at Méteren. He had been in the Scots Guards from 1897 to 1905 and served in the Boer War. He and Doreen Coke were living at Weasenham, Norfolk, and by this time had two daughters. The middle brother, Captain Jack Coke, was captured at Kruiseecke.

Major Cator noted the same day the trench reports of machine guns and rifle oil freezing up and of the poor quality of the new boots, made of very indifferent leather with soles coming away from the uppers. Lieutenant Swinton was writing home "Please have a pair of boots made for me large enough to wear two pairs of thick socks with and also well nailed." He had worked out that this was likely to be the best way of keeping his feet warm. The snow did not last more than a few days and thawed slowly. The effect was instantly to turn the trenches into "a stream of liquid mud." Then there was more and more rain, often very heavy. Conditions in the trenches and, more particularly, in the communication trenches were very wet, the latter being mostly over a foot deep in water and thick and clogging clay mud and in places far more. It was hardly surprising in winter in country only sixteen feet above sea level, almost entirely flat west of Aubers Ridge. The whole area was riddled with ditch systems, with a stream running north to the River Lys called the Rivière des Layes, known as the Layes Brook, into which the ditches drained. To the south of Rouges Bancs this stream was behind the German line, then it crossed No Man's Land and entered the British line at the point where it ran under the Sailly-Fromelles road. There were some abandoned farm buildings, while willows were very much a feature of the landscape. It was land hitherto intensively farmed, there had been a lot of cattle and pigs and the fields were well manured wherever crops were cultivated. Much was down to root crops, such as turnips, unlifted. Sir Edward Hulse wrote "Every single farm and homestead near our trenches, four miles from here, is knocked to atoms and blown to pieces, and a few poor old cows are wandering about with nothing to eat, ground frozen and no shed to go to at night. We shot one, and portioned her out among the Battalion, and also a stray pig found wandering down a hedge." Not far back there was more farming activity going on than he thought, but the buildings were always at risk of shelling.

Animal waste added to the hazards. If wounds came into contact with it and were not treated they would go septic, likely to lead to gas gangrene. Tetanus was also a problem until inoculation started later. In addition, to make things worse, the bodies of in many cases long dead men and animals were lying where they had fallen, burial being only a partial solution. Further, the men on both sides had to use latrines, getting to which was initially hazardous by day. Sir Edward Hulse was well aware of the need for strict sanitary discipline. Private Richards of the Royal Welsh Fusiliers considered that the German pickelhaube helmet was better used as a receptacle when one was caught short than kept for eventual display as a souvenir provided that one survived. Lieutenant Swinton described the Battalion's billets in Sailly as being still occupied and farmed by their owners. "Our's was the typical French farmstead, square, with the farmhouse on one side and farm buildings on the other three, the centre being occupied by one large midden. The officers had the parlour of the house and the men slept in a big barn, half full of straw, which occupied one side of the square. During the winter, on each occasion that we returned to this farm, we had a battalion concert or a boxing show in our barn." On 25 November Lieutenant Saumarez, having told Gunhild that they were well off for food and clothing of all sorts and that "The only want really is cocoa and perhaps a cake or two!" went on to drink. Rum was the only alcohol available at the time and he was anxious to have some wine and port. "I think only 3 bottles at a time would be safe well wrapped up and labelled medicine or something! 3 of port and then 3 of Burgundy – I was only remarking this morning, to my brother officers that we would be fit to qualify as parsons soon after all this time of abstinence – no ladies no wine and no song!"

On the night of 26 November Sir Edward Hulse was detailed to raid the enemy trenches with one NCO and eight men. This was the first raid by the 7th Division, though night reconnaissance in No Man's Land by scouts was commonplace. After the moon went down his patrol of volunteers crawled out at half past one with orders to get right up to the German trenches, peep over if not spotted, select targets, fire two rounds rapid, kill as many enemy as possible and then make their own way back individually. It had been very quiet opposite for several days and so the British had the impression that the Germans were only occupying the front line with snipers and building it up with working parties by day, with all of them going back to their second line at night. The patrol were equipped with a "trench bomb", a rifle grenade which none of them had ever seen before, let alone had any training with, six of these Hale's grenades having simply come up to the trenches four days before with the rations. The first surprise was to find how easy it was to get through the British wire. Putting wire obstacles up was still only a Royal Engineers role, maintaining them that of the infantry. Both would become a mutual responsibility. Sir Edward Hulse wrote that normally it should have been possible to carry out the operation as prescribed because of the light manning of German trenches and the tendency for sentries to be sleepy. However, when his patrol was about halfway across there was some firing further to the right and this put the enemy on the alert. He then suspected that the German trenches were fully manned. "A little further on I made certain of this, as I saw five fires, or rather the reflections of them (as they were in dug-outs and bomb-proofs and one could just see the reflection on bits of smoke which penetrated through) within a space of 50 or 60 yards! These were charcoal fires with a bit of wood burning probably. The fire I was making for was a proper wood fire, showing a lot of smoke, and it was there that I hoped to be able to peep over and find a little group of men to polish off. Progress was very slow indeed, as it was all crawling on hands and knees over turnips, and only four or five yards at a time, and then "lie doggo" and listen. Their sentries to our front were firing every now and then at our trenches but all bullets passed over us, and we could locate them by the flash of the rifle. All went well up to about 15 yards, when I extended from single file, to the right towards this fire. We did another 5 yards and I had given instructions that directly I loosed off my rifle, we should double forward, select marks, do all damage possible, and make off. I had seen where the sentry in front of me was, and told the scout to fire at the top of the parapet, in case he had his head over, and that I would fire at the place where the flash of the rifle appeared. We could only just make out the line of the top of the parapet at ten yards' distance. We were just advancing again when the swine called out in King's English, quite well pronounced, "Halt, who goes there," and fired straight between the scout and myself; he immediately fired at the point of the flash of the rifle, and there was a high pitched groan; at the same time we all doubled up to the foot of the parapet, saw dim figures down in the trenches, bustling about, standing to arms, and my NCO fired the trench bomb right into the little party by the fire. The other fellows all loosed off two rounds rapid; there were various groans audible in the general hubbub, and we then ran like hares. The minute the alarm was given they threw something on the fire which made it flare up, and the machine gun, which we knew nothing about, opened just to my left. I had time to see that it was in a little shelter, with a light inside, visible through the slit (for traversing) and they had evidently just lighted it up to set the gun going. They had already stood to arms by the time we had turned tail, and they and the machine gun opened a very hot fire on us. I ran about 30 yards, and then took a "heavy" into the mud and slush of the ploughed field and lay still for a minute to find out where the machine gun bullets were going. They were just over me and to the right, so when I got up again and turned half left instead of half right, as I had been going originally, and did another 30 yards or so, I found that the bullets were all round me, so fell flat and waited another half minute or so, until they seemed to alter the direction of their fire a bit. Then another run, and a heavy fall bang into our barbed wire, which was quite invisible, and which I thought was further off. These short sprints were no easy matter, as one carried about an acre of wet clay and mud on each foot. I had to lie flat and disentangle myself, and at that moment their machine gun swerved round and plastered away directly over my head not more than 2 or 3 feet. I waited again until it changed, and then ran like the devil for our trenches. I had lost direction a bit, and came on them sooner than I expected, and took a flying leap right over the parapet down about 9 or 10 feet into the trench."

He had landed up over 50 yards to the right of the ditch up which his patrol had started and fell into trenches occupied by the Borders. Apart from banging his head on his rifle when he did so and finding a bullet hole in his coat he was untouched. The NCO and six of his men made it back untouched to the British line, two finishing up 400 yards from where they had started, but two were missing and, in spite of scouts going out later, there was no trace. He thought that they might have accidentally stumbled into the German trenches during the assault. Private John McNeil, a serving soldier when the War started, but held back initially because he was too young, was sent to the Battalion after Ypres and so had been with them for just a fortnight. He was reported killed the next day. Before he became a soldier he was a plumber's mate and his father, also John McNeil, lived in Rutherglen. If he was on that patrol he would not have had any personal possessions on him and a few of these including a cigarette case were sent to his home. Private William Linthwaite, a former wire drawer from Preston had been in the Army since 1907. However, after serving two and a half years he went absent for a prolonged period and as a result forfeited all his previous service and had to start again as at 8 June 1910. He then completed three years, was mobilised as a reservist and also sent to the Battalion after Ypres. On

1 August he and Alice Tongue married in Fulham, but when he returned to the Army she went to live in Lillingstone Lovell, Buckinghamshire. There their son was born on 5 December, his father having been posted missing a week before.

The main result of this patrol was a very different and now accurate picture of the German trenches. There were no obstacles in front of them, their steel loopholes were sited very low down in the parapet and obliquely and there was some suggestion that the German sentries were not that alert. Sir Edward Hulse was very pleased with how quietly his men had moved over No Man's Land in spite of everybody's having coughs and colds. There had not been a sound. General Heyworth asked for a list of their names and complimented them, but unfortunately there was no record kept. Sergeant Pilkington took a photograph a few days later of four of the patrol with Sir Edward Hulse, who sent a copy to his mother on 5 January and identified the tall man on the left as Private Dolley, "a grand, great fellow," noting that, sadly, he was killed shortly afterwards. Private Leonard Dolley was born in Hertingfordbury, Hertfordshire, and was an eighteen year old labourer at the Asphalt Works, Letchworth, when he joined up in March 1911. He served three years and left in March 1914. On mobilization he was not passed fit for active service to begin with, but sailed from Southampton on 20 September, was sent up the line on 12 November and killed on 7 December. His personal effects consisted of a pocket book, letter, photographs and two postal orders totalling fourteen shillings, all of which were forwarded to Christina Peterson in Shadwell, in the London Docks. Also sent to her later was his Princess Mary's Christmas Gift and later still, after the War, his medals.

On 27 November Lieutenant Saumarez wrote to his father "We are still in our river, but it becomes more watery every day and I fear we shall have to move from our happy home very soon into trenches which we have been digging by night in front. We ourselves i.e. the officers live in a culvert with one side closed up to prevent the draft. We have rigged up a kitchen next door and have 2 chefs, so we do not do ourselves badly in the food line. Drink is rather a question however as there is no wine so we have to have tea every meal and a tot of rum occasionally to wash it down. We are having quite a peaceful time at present as regards fighting the enemy, but other enemies are assailing us now such as damp, cold and bad smells. Our own battalion is fairly all right but these damned line regiments rear all over the place, and our doctor says enteric or something will very soon break out if they are not more careful – our casualties are low but fairly regular about 3 or 4 every day – from snipers who are a perfect curse. They say the Germans are bad shots, but their snipers certainly are not, they hit our men plum in the head every time. Am now commanding my company in Left Flank. A fellow called Dick Nugent has just joined the company he left about 2 years ago, and he says lots of fellows are getting 4 days leave to go home, however I don't suppose I have much chance. I am luckily keeping extraordinarily fit and the old trouble has not bothered me since the first week I landed. Everybody else however seems to be getting it as well as bleeding piles poor fellows. One officer Granger has got frost bitten feet…We have to do most of our work at night other[wise] they shell us at once if they see any movement. They must have observation posts everywhere – what I really want is a pair of waders as these ditches are up to your knees is some places." After school at The Oratory, Edgbaston, Lieutenant Richard "Dick" Nugent joined on probation in 1906, an attack of typhoid having prevented him taking the Sandhurst entrance exam, and went onto the Special Reserve in 1911. By this time his father was dead, but Anne Nugent was still at Ballymacoll, County Meath. Lieutenant Henry "Fat Boy" Liddell Grainger, whose mother lived at Ayton Castle, Berwickshire, had also been at The Oratory, Edgbaston, and served with the Scots Guards for two and a half years from 1905. He rejoined in September 1914 and arrived at Méteren.

Patrols were also going out by day. On the 28th Private John Rae, the scout, first mentioned when he claimed to have inflicted the first 20th Brigade casualty on the Germans, and who, during the period here when there was snow on the ground, had got close to the German trenches, partly camouflaged in a white nightshirt he had found, went out during the afternoon with Privates John Ferguson and John Robertson. They started from the left hand end of the Battalion's trenches. Private Rae was almost up to the German parapet when they noticed and shot him dead as he crawled back. Men from the Gordons recovered his body later and buried him. In the list of gallantry awards published on 2 February 1915 Private Rae received the DCM. Irene Rae could not bring herself to sign and return the receipt for it or that for her husband's Princess Mary's Christmas Gift until 26 June 1916. Private Ferguson was born in New Pitsligo, Aberdeenshire, but was in Glasgow when he enlisted in 1913. Private Robertson was a former ship's carpenter from Glasgow, who had also joined up in 1913. Lieutenant Cator, their company commander, wrote home on 3 December, telling how the three men had tried "to get into the German trenches in broad daylight which they reported to me to be quite possible after having carefully reconnoitred the ground the day before. They crawled up a ditch at a spot where the Germans are only 80 yards from ours and I think that they must have made a little noise, anyway when they got right into the trenches they found about 20 Germans waiting ready for them instead of being engaged in digging (which they expected) and Rae was shot through the head, after waiting till his two pals had got back first and the other two fortunately got off safely." He rated Private Rae as the best scout in the Battalion.

Following on from Major Cator's observations about the state of the British wire and also the ease with which Sir Edward Hulse's patrol had negotiated it, the 55th Field Company Royal Engineers were ordered to remedy matters on the night of the 28th. The following day Major Cator recorded that Captain Launcelot Rose, their company commander, "was killed last night putting up the wire outside the trenches, a great loss. Neither he nor his company had spared themselves in helping us with our trenches and wire entanglements the whole war. He was a man full of resource and courage." His wife Wendela Rose lived at Hartford Bridge, Hampshire. Two of his men died with him.

Meanwhile the biggest problem for all battalions who had been at Ypres continued to be rebuilding with newly arrived men and very inexperienced NCOs. There were very few officers and those fit became fewer. Many with the 2nd Scots Guards had to be sent back sick, suffering most commonly from temperatures, fever, rheumatism and "frostbite", while two were wounded. Sir Edward Hulse wrote on 2 December that "the NCOs are improving; we have been promoting men from the ranks, and corporals to sergeants, to replace the absolute stumers that came out with the drafts…As usual, the long and short of it is, that whether it is a serious matter, or only digging latrines, or cleaning up the whole thing devolves upon the officer, and one has to stand there and see it done oneself, and even show the NCOs how to do the simplest things oneself. The other night, after two hours' sleep, I woke up and thought I had better go down the trenches to see that everything was all right. Of course I found one whole platoon in the most hectic state ever seen. Not a sentry on the alert, the NCO on duty sitting down instead of patrolling his lines, and 100 other things. Any enterprising 20 or 30 Huns could have simply walked right in; unless one is at it day and night, nothing is done. There are individuals, scouts, etc., volunteers and picked men, who are priceless, and worth a platoon in themselves, but, by

Jove, one has to work at the rest. The unfortunate part was having every single one of our serving NCOs knocked out when the Battalion took the knock originally." One key to maintaining efficiency and morale was to keep active in the trenches, while being careful about snipers. The Scots Guards worked at dug-outs and shelters against grenades and shell fragments, constructed kitchen bays and made other improvements. The lesson had been firmly taken on board that the harder the work done the better the chances of being comfortable. It also occupied the time and helped to keep everyone warm. However, do what one would, the mud stuck to everything and everyone. Rubber boots appeared for the first time and also goatskin waistcoats for use chiefly by sentries at night. Both were trench stores and so handed over to the incoming battalion on relief. Lieutenant Swinton described the waistcoats, worn with the fleece outside, as being "very nice and warm, but if taken into the confined and warm space in a dug-out they were found to be very smelly." These arrived in this part of the line on 24 November and were nicknamed "Teddy Bear" coats. Sometimes they had sleeves as well. Later on in the War leather jerkins were issued instead.

On 30 November Lieutenant Saumarez wrote next to Gunhild "The Germans have been busier than usual today and might be preparing new defences. Heaps of thanks for your letters and parcels which I read over and over again in our culvert here after dinner while the rest are sleeping soundly on the straw. The wedding cake arrived yesterday all right. You did time it well and I had quite a merry party for my birthday dinner the cake was greatly appreciated, you couldn't have made a better choice." In Captain Paynter's absence, sick with bronchitis, Captain Dick Coke was commanding the Battalion. Lieutenant Saumarez continued that he "was shot through the back this afternoon at my side. I was just telling him that it was getting rather hot and that he had better come down into a ditch under cover when he gave a cry and fell at my feet. I got him under cover with difficulty as his back hurt him so poor fellow. However it may turn out all right. We have no captains left again and Loder commands." He told her that there was a very strong possibility of his getting a few days leave very soon.

On 1 December Major Cator, recently awarded the DSO, wished his mother many happy returns of her birthday on the 10th, hoping "when the next one comes round this war will be over after the Germans have been reduced to pulp and well thrashed for their disgusting barbarity. We have had quite an excitement here today. Last night we were told confidentially that the King was coming to see the troops, he didn't see many I am afraid as the majority were in the trenches. We got here at 3pm, while we were all waiting for him, two of our aeroplanes were patrolling to prevent any German ones coming near. The Germans began shelling our two aeroplanes, and the General got a bit fussed for fear of their shells coming near the King, however they were quite half a mile off and none came at the critical moment. He was accompanied by President Poincaré and General Joffre and the Prince of Wales; Purtan Singh, the Indian Prince also came, a marvellous old man of seventy six [Sir Pertab Singh]. Four of us were given the DSO. We filed past the King who pinned them on our jackets. I am sending mine home as it will only get lost and we don't wear medals out here." The King also presented a number of DCMs. He told her that the Brigade were "still very short of men, so they have to do seven days in and three out. The two Guards Battalions have been filled up, but the other two Batts, the Borders and Gordon Highlanders, have only 450 men apiece, the Gordons did have one draft of fifty men sent out, but they are so old, decrepit and infirm, the General is sending them home again." As it was understood that the Germans had moved a lot of troops across to face the Russians "I daresay we shall be advancing again soon." He recorded the testing of steel loopholes on 28 November at Brigade Headquarters and the finding that at fifty and one hundred yards the plates were not even dented. That might have been the case with ordinary ammunition, but when on 2 December the Germans sniped at these loopholes, apparently with armour piercing rounds, there were casualties. This came as a shock and a surprise. Also in his letter on 1 December he told his mother that a German sniper had killed a Scots Guardsman through one of the new holes and "it looks as if they have expert shots with telescopic sights on their rifles, as the hole in the plate is only 3 × 4"." Private James Carruthers died on 1 December. He had been a millworker when he joined up in 1905 in Glasgow. After three years he went to the Reserve and in April 1914 emigrated to the Transvaal, correctly giving Regimental Headquarters notice. Therefore, when general mobilization began in South Africa on 15 August he reported there. He came to France early in November, missing Ypres. His parents James and Elizabeth Carruthers were in Kilmarnock and an identity disc and some letters and postcards reached them there.

Between 1 and 6 December a number of letters passed between Lieutenant Saumarez and Gunhild. His on the 4th included "Have just got back to billets again for 2 days and am looking though all my kit. I find that I have too many sock and underwear etc so please tell people not to send any more for the present at any rate. Our mess box is also now quite full so you might tell Fortnum and Masons to hold fire for a bit. I wrote to Margaret yesterday to thank her for her beautiful scarf it really is a very nice one. I am afraid this will be a very short letter and uninteresting as I got out of bed this morning with a terrible head. The result of last evening repast!! as the old song goes – We were fortunate to find 2 bottles of Benedictine which unfortunately did not agree very well with our rum and milk punch sad to relate and immediate disaster came upon some but I was in excellent spirits till the following morn!" In a postscript "Thank you ever so much for the fur coat which arrived last night, it is a real beauty and quite light. It is the envy of all who behold it – By the way what our men want at the moment are boots 43 prs in my company are urgently required and I have put in for them to Head Quarters but the boot supply seems very bad." Company Sergeant Major Charles Lilley was on leave in England and was going to take back a letter and other things from Gunhild to Lieutenant Saumarez. Separately, two days later, she wrote on 6 December "We have been doing quite a lot since I last wrote to you. Yesterday there was a big recruiting meeting in Ipswich to which we attended. First we lunched with Lady Evelyn Cobbold and then we took our part in the procession going round the town which was that of representing Belgium. You see they had a lot of motor cars representing England the Colonies and the allies. Also there was troops, Boy Scouts, fire brigade, cartloads with mothers who had three sons and more at the front etc. We had hired a car which was decorated with flags and flowers in the Belgium colours and there was a wounded Belgium soldier on the front seat. First came the Salvation Army band, which played in a somewhat shrill way, and then came Evelyn and I in state! After the procession had gone all through Town the crowd and the troops assembled in front of the Town hall, and the mayor, Johnnie Cobbold in his robes and brown shoes held a speech. A major and a Colonel also held speeches, and then all was over. Tomorrow there is going to be a recruiting play, called "Sword and Fire" to which possible recruits are admitted free and on Wednesday there is a patriotic concert for them. They are being made rather a lot of and in a way it seems a bit unnecessary, when it is nothing but their simple duty to go, and when in case of conscription they could only be taken. However, we must hope that the unwilling ones are a small minority." Then, date unrecorded, Lieutenant Saumarez did go on leave and Gunhild "was amazed to see how well he looked, literally blooming, in spite of desperate shortage of sleep and food, sometimes only living on biscuits, meat tablets and chocolates, and what he could carry in his pockets. Through constant digging of trenches or graves he had filled out so much that he could not get into his civilian suits. Our last couple of days were spent in great luxury at Claridges Hotel, where my birthday was celebrated and our rooms were filled with masses of roses sent by Vincent's mother. When the day of parting came, I accompanied Vincent to Victoria Station, and we said our farewell in the taxi, as he did not want me to get out and face the crowd. On my return to Grosvenor Place I made a terribly distressing discovery. Vincent's luggage was still sitting on the roof of the taxi, and the train had gone! He had told his new soldier servant, Sinclair, to take charge of the luggage, and he had misunderstood the order, and left it on the taxi. Vincent had now gone to the trenches with nothing but what he stood up in." She then tried quickly to order and obtain replacements, there being no immediate means of having the luggage itself sent on, as no one was going out who could take it. From Boulogne Lieutenant Saumarez sent her a short note, uncertain of the date, I got your wire on the boat, and am leaving Sinclair behind here, it was his fault for not looking after it. Awful crossing! Am just having a mouthful of tea as our bus leaves in 5 minutes i.e. 5.30".

On 3 December Lieutenant Cator had written from billets "I myself with Clive and fifty men are in a different farmhouse this time and most comfortable we are, with a great big sitting room where I am now writing, and two small bedrooms so we have each got a bed this time. I am devoutly glad of this as Clive was not a pleasant bed companion snoring like a grampus and not being over fond of a wash when he gets the chance of one. He has now gone sick poor chap with very bad feet. We are all troubled with our feet and some of the men are very bad with them." He thought that it was a combination of frostbite and not being able to take off boots while in the trenches. He told how Captain Paynter "who has been a perfect hero throughout" had gone home for two weeks rest. "I well know how ill he has been feeling and would never give in till the day we last went into the trenches his temperature rose to 104, so he was sent off to hospital." In his absence Captain Dick Coke was commanding the Battalion, but, as Lieutenant Saumarez had already written home, on the night of 30 November a sniper hit him. He had been putting up barbed wire at La Cordonnerie Farm and Lieutenant Cator told his mother that he "was shot through the right side of his back just below the shoulder blade and the bullet is still somewhere. We got him away in a stretcher in great pain, but I have since heard he is doing alright."

On the afternoon of the 2nd both Cators went by car to shop in Armentières. "The Germans have shelled it very heavily and several of the buildings are complete wrecks, but when they were there for eight days they did not seem to have looted it as much as some other places as there were several excellent shops left there and we bought lots of things. The two things we wanted most however, candles and paraffin, were not to be had for love or money." They were able to have dinner together that night and the following one. The younger brother continued his letter of the 3rd, reverting again to sniping. "I had a very near squeak one night when digging as it was moonlight and we were being sniped a good deal and a bullet just grazed the sleeve of my woollen waistcoat. It took a lot of fluff but never touched my skin." While he understood that the senior commanders' view was that things were "going well for us and I am sure they are, but I cannot help but thinking it will be a long business yet…The Germans are sure to fight to the last and I give them their due they are gallant fighters and do not fear death." Then he turned to the situation at home. "You must all keep your hearts up in England as all will end well, but we must have more men and it is maddening to see in the papers these photographs of huge crowds watching football matches and there must be thousands of agricultural labourers who should be doing their share. The old men and women do all the work on the farms here and constantly under fire poor things, with their homes often wrecked and all their belongings looted by the Germans, who never seem to have paid for anything. They are delightful people and cannot do enough for us. I held a little voluntary service in the trenches for my Company on Sunday afternoon and several of the men came to it and loved it I think." He asked the men to choose the hymns "and they simply yelled them." Finally he asked "Will you tell the girls that the men have been getting lots of shirts, drawers, etc. but they would like Balaclava Helmets, mitts and woollen gloves, and also if possible black twist tobacco. The latter they are always longing for, as cigarettes come out in thousands and light tobacco, but most of the pipe smokers like the strong black twist."

The same day Major Cator heard that a German had shouted across to the Scots Guards "Don't you wish you were in London doing Guards?" On the 4th he noted "The recent heavy rain is causing a lot of the trenches to fall in. One man in the Borders being buried and suffocated before he could be got out." That day General Capper had arranged demonstrations of trench mortars and three types of grenade at Bac-St Maur, to which all the Brigade and Artillery staffs went. This Major Cator found "Quite one of the most "Dangerous" mornings of the campaign. The Mortar Guns we tried experiments with were two French Guns dated 1848. The 1st shot proved quite successful being fired with a light charge & the round shot was not charged with guncotton. It went some 200 feet in the air & landed about 150 yards away. Encouraged by this a heavier charge was used & the gun given more elevation, what happened to the shell we don't know, the gun went off with a roar, there was a crash amongst the boughs of an apple tree above the heads of the spectators standing behind, & the gun was seen to be pointing the reverse way to which it had been aimed." Subsequent shots proved only to underline the unreliability of the mortar, no two having in any way the same effect, but the gunners assured the audience that they could make it function correctly once they had made "further experiments". Next came the grenades, all three types "home made". The Royal Engineers had designed the first two, the "jam pot with two primers inside lit by a fuse, timed for four seconds. The second "the hairbrush" so called because of its shape, also fired with a second fuse." Then came a French version in which "A leather thong is attached to the percussion fuse which jerks it out of the bomb when thrown, the explosion taking place in two seconds." The view was that "The "jam pot" kind were not much use but the "hairbrushes" were good, bursting with a tremendous explosion." The French ones, however, they thought the best. The problems were production and supply, as well as training infantry how to use them. None of these or any other species of grenade were any real use and the British were at a disadvantage until the Mills bomb started to become generally available in the autumn of 1915. Until then the Germans had the upper hand with grenades. It took some time also before the British realised that grenade throwing could not be a specialist skill and that every soldier needed to know how to use them. Men now began being selected for training with grenades as specialists and in the 20th Brigade the bombers were first drawn from the newly arrived 1/6th Gordons, but the jam pot version was the only one available, nicknamed "Ticklers Artillery" from the jam manufacturer. Empty jam tins were collected and half filled with guncotton, an explosive, before bits of steel, shoe nails and the like were added. A fuse was next inserted and a top soldered on. The fuse was ignited by being rubbed on a piece of cardboard treated with the same material used for striking safety matches, fixed on the bomber's wrist, which, if wet, would not work. On 6 December it was seen that the Germans had put out "chevaux de frise" in front of all their trenches. These were wooden frames strung with barbed wire, assembled under cover and then placed in position in the dark. The British quickly copied them.

On 5 December the 1/6th Gordon Highlanders, Territorials, from Banff and Donside, joined the Brigade. Though they had been in France for a few weeks, they had not prepared for this and found it particularly arduous, both from their own and others' accounts. Private Alexander Runcie from Banff wrote "I don't think any of us had a true picture of what the front line was like, but we were not to be left long in doubt as our company was to be the first to go in, and that was the following night. We paraded in full kit, everything we had we took with us, blankets and trousers included, an issue of biscuits, not the usual hard tack but small, and sweets were handed out so we crammed our pockets with them. We had a not inconsiderable march before we reached the start of the communication trench. It was very dark and we had to wait a while until a party of men on the way out got clear…This journey was a real nightmare the trench we were using was waist deep in thick gluey mud in most places. Every one of the men wanted to get out on top of the ground but no amount of grumbling made any difference the orders were to use the trench and we did. One simply horrible part we encountered was at a kind of tunnel where we had to bend double, in doing so one's chin was in the mud…We eventually got through this tunnel on our hands and knees only. I like a few others lost our shoes there, and couldn't recover them." The tunnel he referred to was a covered part of the communication trench, roofed and turfed to conceal movement from enemy observation. In spite of the experience of Highlanders on the Aisne and since, these Gordons Territorials were still wearing black brogues, stockings and spats. If mud got in at the top of the spats gradually its pressure could remove everything, leaving only bare feet. Private Runcie continued "Those of us who had lost our shoes got hold of some dry sandbags and used these to cover our feet, they did that all right, but after our four days turn of duty in the front line we all suffered from frostbite." Some apparently lost their kilts as well. On 6 March 1917 Sir Douglas Haig inspected the Highlanders of the 44th Brigade and remembered General Joffre's remark about the kilt "Pour l'amour oui, mais pour la Guerre non." Major Cator wrote on the 11th "Very heavy rain all night. The communications are so full of mud that three men of 6th Bn Gordon Highlanders had to be dragged out as they were unable to move. The Highlanders shoes are quite useless as the mud drags them off and they get lost in the dark. The Gordons lost fifteen pairs last night." Sir Edward Hulse told his mother that the Gordons "have not quite shaken down yet, in fact the other day, when occupying the trenches next to us, they had given up the ghost complete; it had been pouring, and mud lay deep in the trenches; they were caked from head to foot, and I have never seen anything like their rifles! Not one would work, and they were just lying about in the trenches getting stiff and cold. One fellow had got both his feet jammed in the clay, and when told to get up by an officer, had to get on all fours; he then got his hands stuck in too, and was caught like a fly on a fly paper; all he could do was to look round and say to his pals, "For Gawd's sake, shoot me!" I laughed till I cried. But they will shake down soon, directly they learn that the harder one works in the trenches, the drier and more comfortable one can keep them and oneself."

Their arrival did have the definite advantage for everyone else of not having to spend so long at a time in the front line. The Borders and the 2nd and 1/6th Gordons now rotated their companies to and from the left hand sub-section of the Brigade trenches and their billets. The Scots Guards occupied the right hand sub-section on a four days in, four days out rota with the

1. Officers Mess Staff 1st Battalion 1914, left to right, front to back, K King [untraced], Privates David Turner, Joseph McLoone, Lance Sergeant Alfred Burgess, Privates George Whitney, Richard Dennis, Hugo Kershaw [Courtesy of the Regimental Trustees Scots Guards]

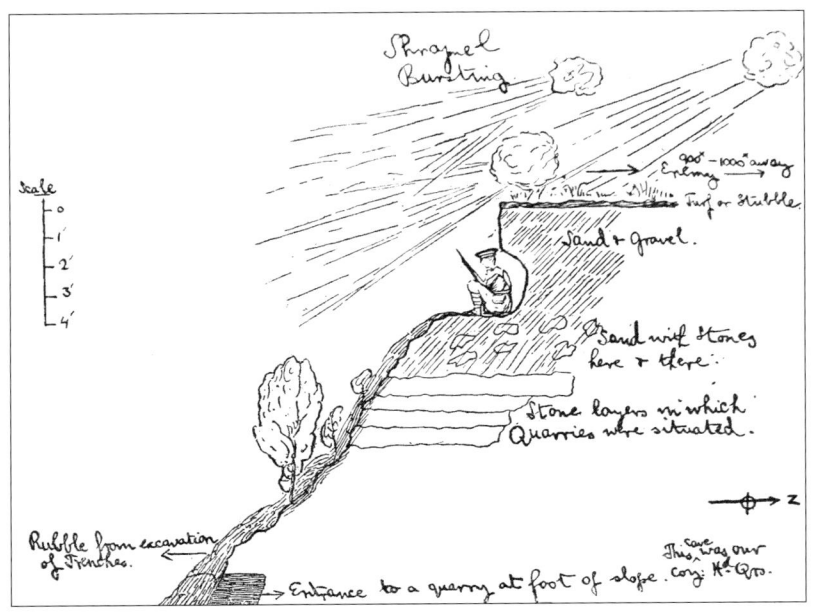

2. Drawing of front line on the Chemin des Dames, Battle of the Aisne
[Letters of Captain Sir Edward Hulse, Bt]

i

3. 2nd Battalion marching out of the Tower of London on 16 September 1914 [Courtesy of Lord de Saumarez]

4. F Company 2nd Battalion on SS *Lake Michigan* to Zeebrugge on 6 October 1914 [Courtesy of Lord de Saumarez]

5. 2nd Battalion train leaving Zeebrugge for Bruges on 7 October 1914 with wellwisher waving from top of railway signal [Courtesy of Lord de Saumarez]

6. 2nd Battalion Transport en route from Ostend to Ghent on 9 October 1914 [Courtesy of Lord de Saumarez]

7. Refugees near Ghent [Courtesy of Lord de Saumarez]

8. Lieutenant Edward Warner with G Company digging in among sugar beet near Ghent on 10 October 1914 [Courtesy of Lord de Saumarez]

9. 2nd Battalion halt on road from Thielt to Roulers on 13 October 1914
[Courtesy of Lord de Saumarez]

10. Lieutenant Colonel Pat Bolton with 2nd Battalion digging in at Zandvoorde on 16 October 1914
[Courtesy of Lord de Saumarez]

11. The 2nd Battalion advance towards Gheluwe on 20 October 1914 when Drummer Charles Steer was killed [Courtesy of Lord de Saumarez]

12. Sergeant William Young with men of the 2nd Oxfordshire and Buckinghamshire Light Infantry at west side of Polygon Wood on or just after 22 October 1914 [Courtesy of Lord de Saumarez]

13. Shrapnel exploding around Kruiseecke but far enough away from the men on left of picture [Courtesy of Lord de Saumarez]

14. Transport going west down the Menin Road through Hooge [Courtesy of Lord de Saumarez]

15. The Menin Road [Courtesy of Lord de Saumarez]

16. 2nd Battalion Roll Call at Hooge on 28 October 1914 with Sergeant Major Jimmy Moncur in the centre [Courtesy of Lord de Saumarez]

17. 2nd Battalion men breakfasting in woods at Hooge [Courtesy of Lord de Saumarez]

18. 2nd Battalion Transport on the Menin Road with shelling not far off
[Courtesy of Lord de Saumarez]

19. 2nd Battalion drafts at Méteren, November 1914 [Courtesy of Lord de Saumarez]

20. Clearing out a communication trench behind front line at Rouges Bancs, early Winter 1914 [Courtesy of Lord de Saumarez]

21. Breakfast in the front line opposite Rouges Bancs [Courtesy of Lord de Saumarez]

22. Cartoon by Major Alby Cator of a soldier coming out of the line [Courtesy of Christopher Cator]

23. Lieutenant Tom Ross, who, with Company Quartermaster Sergeant Horace Crabtree, second right, was in the 2nd Battalion throughout [Courtesy of Lord de Saumarez]

24. Regimental Aid Post at Rue Pétillon [Courtesy of Lord de Saumarez]

25. Captain The Honourable Dick Coke, Lieutenant Geoffrey Ottley and Captain George Paynter [Courtesy of Lord de Saumarez]

26. Cartoon by Major Alby Cator of himself and Brigadier General Frederick Heyworth setting off to visit the line [Courtesy of Christopher Cator]

27. Graves at Rue Pétillon [Courtesy of Lord de Saumarez]

28. Lieutenant Sir Edward Hulse and four of his raiding party on 26 November 1914, Private Leonard Dolley on left [Courtesy of Lord de Saumarez]

29. One German soldier [Courtesy of Lord de Saumarez]

30. Meerschaum pipe given by a German soldier to a Scots Guards sergeant during the Christmas Truce [Courtesy of the Regimental Trustees Scots Guards]

31. Lieutenant Alan Swinton in the Rouges Bancs trenches on Christmas Day 1914 [Courtesy of Major General Sir John Swinton]

32. 1st Battalion, one man wearing a Teddy Bear coat, with mountain gun in The Keep built from the brickstacks at Cuinchy, January 1915 [Courtesy of the Regimental Trustees Scots Guards]

33. 1st Battalion behind primitive breastworks probably near Festubert, early 1915 [Courtesy of the Regimental Trustees Scots Guards]

34. Lieutenant Neil Fergusson with Lieutenant Merton Beckwith Smith and Lieutenant Colonel John Ponsonby, both 1st Coldstream, and Captain Arthur "Nipper" Poynter and Lieutenant Lionel Norman, Spring 1915 [Courtesy of the Regimental Trustees Scots Guards]

35. 1st Battalion billets at Gonnehem, late April 1915
[Courtesy of the Regimental Trustees Scots Guards]

36. Lieutenant Arthur Mervyn Jones with 3 Platoon Right Flank 1st Battalion in the tannery, Richebourg-St Vaast, May 1915 [Courtesy of the Regimental Trustees Scots Guards]

37. Member of Right Flank 1st Battalion hit by shrapnel during Battle of Aubers on 9 May 1915 [Courtesy of the Regimental Trustees Scots Guards]

38. Waiting behind breastworks north of Rue du Bois during Battle of Aubers, Lieutenant Mervyn Jones at the back on right [Courtesy of the Regimental Trustees Scots Guards]

39. 1st Cameron Highlanders going into action on afternoon of 9 May 1915 [RT]

40. Company Sergeant Major Arthur Burrough, Right Flank 2nd Battalion, killed at Battle of Festubert on 16 May 1915 [Courtesy of the Regimental Trustees Scots Guards]

41. 1st Battalion trench at Le Rutoire just taken over from the French 296e Regiment, late May 1915 [Courtesy of the Regimental Trustees Scots Guards]

42. 1st Battalion rough front line trench at Le Rutoire soon after taking over [Courtesy of the Regimental Trustees Scots Guards]

43. Captain Harold Cuthbert outside Some Hut at Le Rutoire
[Courtesy of the Regimental Trustees Scots Guards]

44. 1st Battalion company cooker at Vermelles [Courtesy of the Regimental Trustees Scots Guards]

45. 1st Battalion billets at Sailly-Labourse where they were first in late May 1915
[Courtesy of the Regimental Trustees Scots Guards]

46. Captain Miles Barne
[Courtesy of Miles Barne]

47. 1st Battalion reading letters in the front line at Cuinchy, Summer 1915 [Courtesy of the Regimental Trustees Scots Guards]

48. 1st Battalion in front line at Cuinchy [Courtesy of the Regimental Trustees Scots Guards]

49. Corporal George Stewart, Right Flank 1st Battalion, firing a rifle grenade during a tour from 25-28 July 1915, days before his death on the 31st [Courtesy of the Regimental Trustees Scots Guards]

50. 1st Battalion sniperscope in front line at Cuinchy [Courtesy of the Regimental Trustees Scots Guards]

51. Lance Sergeant James Blair's cover for the July Spasm of the *Left Flank Magazine* [Courtesy of the Regimental Trustees Scots Guards]

52. Cartoon by Lance Corporal Paul Anderton of the Kaiser and Crown Prince and darkening cloud of Doom [Courtesy of the Regimental Trustees Scots Guards]

xxvi

WHY NOT HAVE "Smiling by Numbers!"

On the command "one"— Remove cigarette or chewing gum from the mouth, and adjust false teeth.

On the command "two"— Wipe off the sweat drops and think of "Blighty" or free beer.

On the command "three"— Make the mouth extend from the centre, corners turned up, and tickle yourself till a laugh is raised.

53. Cartoon by Lance Corporal Paul Anderton of Smiling by Numbers, following order when entering St Omer "When we march through the town I want you all to look happy, even if you don't feel that way." [Courtesy of the Regimental Trustees Scots Guards]

54. Cartoon by Lance Corporal Anderton of the march to St Omer
[Courtesy of the Regimental Trustees Scots Guards]

xxvii

55. 2nd Battalion sentry in sap beside trench block at Big Willie after 17 October 1915 [Courtesy of the Regimental Trustees Scots Guards]

56. Hole through Lieutenant Tom Ross' tent at the Transport Lines from shell 60 yards away, which caused no casualties, but others did that day in October 1915 [Courtesy of the Regimental Trustees Scots Guards]

57. A bombing post at the head of a sap in the Hohenzollern, October 1915 [Courtesy of the Regimental Trustees Scots Guards]

58. B Company 1st Battalion in Big Willie October 1915, grenade boxes on right [Courtesy of the Regimental Trustees Scots Guards]

59. After a relief at the Hohenzollern pipers playing the 2nd Battalion back to billets at Vermelles, October 1915 [Courtesy of the Regimental Trustees Scots Guards]

60. Left Flank 2nd Battalion in Big Willie before the bombing attack on 17 October 1915 [Courtesy of the Regimental Trustees Scots Guards]

61. Michael, the 2nd Battalion's illicit car, acquired by Lieutenant The Honourable Charlie Mills [Courtesy of the Regimental Trustees Scots Guards]

62. 2nd Battalion Lewis gunner, Neuve Chapelle area, December 1915 [Courtesy of the Regimental Trustees Scots Guards]

63. 2nd Battalion in front line breastworks, Neuve Chapelle area, late 1915, with Captain "Monty" Hill standing to the left of the duckboard [Courtesy of the Regimental Trustees Scots Guards]

64. The Reverend Alexander MacRae visiting men in the line, Neuve Chapelle area, December 1915 [Courtesy of the Regimental Trustees Scots Guards]

65. Member of 2nd Battalion pumping water from behind breastworks, Neuve Chapelle area, December 1915 [Courtesy of the Regimental Trustees Scots Guards]

66. Sergeants of Right Flank 2nd Battalion in front line breastworks, Neuve Chapelle area, late 1915 [Courtesy of the Regimental Trustees Scots Guards]

67. 2nd Battalion Lewis Gun team, Neuve Chapelle area, December 1915
[Courtesy of the Regimental Trustees Scots Guards]

68. 2nd Battalion water cart at front line, Neuve Chapelle area, December 1915
[Courtesy of the Regimental Trustees Scots Guards]

69. Lieutenant Colonel Alby Cator and Lieutenant Jimmy Lumsden with ratting pack at Laventie, December 1915 [Courtesy of the Regimental Trustees Scots Guards]

70. Miniature Fort Tickler, Neuve Chapelle area, December 1915 [Courtesy of the Regimental Trustees Scots Guards]

xxxv

71. Christmas tree given to a Scots Guards corporal by a German soldier during the brief truce on 25 December 1915 [Courtesy of the Regimental Trustees Scots Guards]

72. 2nd Battalion snowballing near Poperinghe, March 1916 [Courtesy of the Regimental Trustees Scots Guards]

73. The 2nd Battalion camp at Poperinghe, March 1916
[Courtesy of the Regimental Trustees Scots Guards]

74. The First Calais Spring Meeting on 12 March 1916, with two 2nd Irish Guards bookmakers in bowler hats prominent [Courtesy of the Regimental Trustees Scots Guards]

75. Lieutenant Calverley Bewicke winning a race [Courtesy of the Regimental Trustees Scots Guards]

76. The Snow Lady built by Captain Hugh Ross and Sir Iain Colquhoun [Courtesy of the Regimental Trustees Scots Guards]

77. 2nd Battalion in The Gully, Ypres Salient, looking towards an advanced bombing post, Spring 1916 [Courtesy of the Regimental Trustees Scots Guards]

78. 2nd Battalion in The Gully [Courtesy of the Regimental Trustees Scots Guards]

79. 2nd Battalion in front line on right of The Gully
[Courtesy of the Regimental Trustees Scots Guards]

80. 2nd Battalion in The Gully [Courtesy of the Regimental Trustees Scots Guards]

81. The Reverend Alexander MacRae at the Transport Lines near Poperinghe, Spring 1916 [Courtesy of the Regimental Trustees Scots Guards]

82. 2nd Battalion having a quiet game of nap along the Canal Bank, Ypres Salient, Spring 1916 [Courtesy of the Regimental Trustees Scots Guards]

87. 1st Battalion probably in reserve position, Ypres [Courtesy of the Regimental Trustees Scots Guards]

88. Sanctuary Wood in June 1916 [Courtesy of the Regimental Trustees Scots Guards]

81. The Reverend Alexander MacRae at the Transport Lines near Poperinghe, Spring 1916 [Courtesy of the Regimental Trustees Scots Guards]

82. 2nd Battalion having a quiet game of nap along the Canal Bank, Ypres Salient, Spring 1916 [Courtesy of the Regimental Trustees Scots Guards]

83. 2nd Battalion on the Canal Bank [Courtesy of the Regimental Trustees Scots Guards]

84. Mary of Ypres, born to one of the cows, near Poperinghe, Spring 1916 [Courtesy of the Regimental Trustees Scots Guards]

85. Company Sergeant Major John Shields, B Company 1st Battalion, Spring 1916 [Courtesy of the Regimental Trustees Scots Guards]

86. 1st Battalion in the line, Ypres Salient, early Summer 1916 [Courtesy of the Regimental Trustees Scots Guards]

87. 1st Battalion probably in reserve position, Ypres [Courtesy of the Regimental Trustees Scots Guards]

88. Sanctuary Wood in June 1916 [Courtesy of the Regimental Trustees Scots Guards]

89. Lieutenant Gordon Stirling, 2nd Guards Brigade Machine Gun Company, and his dog Wipers, late Spring 1916 [Courtesy of the Regimental Trustees Scots Guards]

90. 2nd Lieutenant Grey Leach, 1st Battalion, early Summer 1916 [Courtesy of the Regimental Trustees Scots Guards]

91. Blighty Bridge, Ypres Salient, early Summer 1916
[Courtesy of the Regimental Trustees Scots Guards]

92. Captain Jimmy Lumsden and Lieutenant David Chapman, 2nd Battalion, wading between platoon positions, Ypres Salient, early Summer 1916 [Courtesy of the Regimental Trustees Scots Guards]

93. Lieutenant Bobbie Abercromby, 1st Battalion, early Summer 1916 [Courtesy of the Regimental Trustees Scots Guards]

94. Drill Sergeant Charlie Kitchen, 1st Battalion, early Summer 1916 [Courtesy of the Regimental Trustees Scots Guards]

95. Lieutenants Eric Miller and Henry Dundas, 1st Battalion, in the support company line next to the French at Boesinghe, July 1916 [Courtesy of the Regimental Trustees Scots Guards]

96. Posed photograph of British, Russian and French prisoners at Schneidemühl, Lance Corporal Alexander Cairns standing in the middle at the back, Summer 1916, [Courtesy of the Regimental Trustees Scots Guards]

Grenadiers. This suited both as they were used to the same methods, most of all because neither of them needed to dig trenches deeper following a relief, which, because of their greater average height, was usually necessary when they took over from the line battalions. Conversely, if the relieving troops were not guardsmen, they might have to alter the firesteps in order to be able to see out. Lieutenant Swinton wrote of "the endless disputes" over this, in particular, from the varying needs of the different battalions. There was other niggle and irritation. Sir Edward Hulse complained to his mother about the failure of the line battalions to carry out reliefs timeously. "Every time we took over from the [Borders] or [Gordons] they were about two hours late relieving us, and never carried on the work we had been doing properly; result – a good deal of unpleasant bickering, which is very undesirable between battalions." Major Cator registered severe remarks about the 1/6th Gordons as "beginning to feel the strain of the trenches, all their men are very young and their discipline leaves much to be desired." Everyone had the challenge of trying to keep weapons functioning and, as Lieutenant Swinton put it, "despite the fact that every man had a canvas cover or a sock over the breech of his rifle, the bolt was often unworkable." Meanwhile each round of ammunition required regular checking and wiping to ensure that it was usable. Men had repeatedly to be warned and watched to prevent them being targets for snipers but on 9 December the much tattooed Private John Wells, who had got into trouble for not digging a trench when told to do so a few weeks before at Ypres, was in trouble again for "Breaking out of the trench", though exactly what he did was unclear. It cost him five days confined to barracks so he had to stay in his billet when out of the line.

On the 12th Lieutenant Cator wrote to his mother, like everyone else, about the rain. "The weather is awful now, perpetual rain and the inhabitants tell us it usually rains hard all December and January here. The weather is mild though, and one is not cold often, though perpetually wet." He was feeling very well himself although he had lost his voice sometime before, but regretted that Lieutenant Liddell Grainger "my best Subaltern went sick yesterday with terribly swollen feet and a high temperature." He went on that "at last thank goodness, I have been able to get new boots for the men. They were practically walking about bare footed poor chaps, and their feet ringing wet all the time. They are splendid chaps and always cheerful. The language is appalling, and so is my own I am afraid very often. Today we had a football match and my Company beat Left Flank by 4 goals. Tomorrow I have got to play with them, not having played football for 14 years! So I expect I shall be sick on the field."

The conditions increased the difficulties of bringing up all supplies. Sergeant Pilkington described what was supposed to happen and probably what he thought did, but had dire consequences when it did not. The Quartermaster's staff would cook food about a mile back from the front line, from where, Sergeant Pilkington stated, all that the companies had to do was collect it, take it up to the trenches, warm it up slightly and there it would be. He did not seem to know that it would take a ration party four hours to go back, collect the food and carry it forward. Warming it up was often impossible when bringing up fuel was so difficult. However, on top of that, the state of the communication trenches was such that just moving along them was laborious, while taking a chance by going in the open was a far greater hazard for a carrying party. The barely literate diary of an unknown Borders private painted the picture all too clearly.

Nov 24. Returned back to trenches found it took us 4½ hrs to go 2. miles owing to the Germans Snipers at work in the Communicatin Trench leading to the Firing Line 2 men killed and 4 wounded Fighting all night 7 men wounded.

Nov 25th Snipers at work shot 6 men getting walter killing 2 and wounded 4. 9.15 one mane shot in the eyes which blinded him was taken to hospital and died same night.

Nov 25th. Told off to go and draw rations with 11 men. We got Rations safe but coming back 5 men got shot 3 killed and 2 wounded so we lost half of the Rations So A and C Comp. had to go on half rations the next day.

Nov 26th. Relived out of trenches raining in torince wet through mud up to the knees 2 men of the Borders killed one officer of the Royal Engineers killed and 2 men of the Scotch Guards wounded.

Nov 27th. Had a bath rather a Luxury still raining. Never saw the sun for a week.

Private Runcie remembered "Cooking that first time in the trenches was quite a problem but we did succeed in getting tea warmed, corned beef was the main meal, there was no bread and the army biscuits we just couldn't soften however much we soaked them…Some pairs of boots had been sent up for us but our feet had swelled so we had a hard job getting a pair to fit even a size larger than our usual was painful." On getting back to billets after their first trench tour "A squad of RAMC men in charge of an officer, visited us that night and massaged those of us who had frostbitten feet, they used whale oil for this purpose, afterwards we did our own rubbing." Trench foot continued to be a challenge. It was thought that better insulation was a good protection, hence the whale oil. Gum boots and trench waders were supplied to help men to keep their legs dry and instructions were given that puttees were to be loosened when in the line. It was not the answer, though there may have been some improvement. Not until rather later did the medical authorities work out that blood circulation was the key factor and that it was not the cold, the wet and the tight fitting boots and puttees which caused trench foot, though they did exacerbate it. Rather, it was when it was impossible for men to move about enough in those conditions to keep their circulation going that trench foot took hold.

In billets, usually barns, the first requirements were rest and baths, proper meals and cleaning, checking and replacing clothing, equipment and weapons. The objective was for every man to get a bath once a fortnight, the Grenadiers War Diary recording that they had the use of the Divisional baths in a dye factory all day on 15 December. Initially, according to Lieutenant Swinton, the only parades were to ensure that clothing and equipment were serviceable, but there were also short route marches for exercise. Other activities included company concerts, inter company boxing and church parades. Sir Edward Hulse kept to fifteen minutes a church service that he had to take himself.

The variety of items which came by post was prodigious. Sir Edward Hulse wrote to his mother thanking her or asking her to pass on his thanks to others for cigarettes, chocolate, a plum pudding from Fortnum and Mason, a warm, woolly cap instead of his service issue stocking cap, socks, a balaclava helmet, caramels, cake, a warm waistcoat and a pair of puttees. He told her that they were pretty well set up, did not need anything else and requested her not to send him clothing for himself unless asked for. Seven pairs of gloves were sent out, knitted by his grandmother, for the soldiers. Among the parcels for his men were several simply addressed "OC G Company", very frequently anonymously, so it was impossible to write to thank the senders. Lieutenant Colonel Laurence Fisher Rowe, recently arrived to command the Grenadiers, so displacing Major Corkran, till after Ypres the Brigade Major of the 1st (Guards) Brigade, told his wife that the post was taking five days to arrive, but that outgoing post from the front line itself was less regular. The conditions in the trenches nearly always made letter writing impossible.

On the night of 9 December Lieutenant Ottley, now in G Company, and two men patrolled up to the German trenches and Lieutenant Cator told his mother on the 12th that "they crawled up a ditch in the dark 70 yards to see if a certain culvert was occupied by a German advance post. They found it wasn't, though it had been used for that purpose. They then crawled on and got within 5 yards of the German lines and then lay and listened to their conversation (Ottley understanding German). They heard their sentries challenging in <u>English</u> "Halt who comes there" and when some of them were making too much noise they heard a German NCO say in perfect English "Stop making that noise."" The patrol also established that these were German regulars, there having been apparently some idea that they were Austrians. Lieutenant Ottley "got a memo from General Capper complimenting him on his reconnaissance... He has only just left Sandhurst and is only 18." Sir Edward Hulse, writing home on the 11th, told how Lieutenant Ottley had "heard two officers talking about their dug-out, and saying that our machine gun had killed three of their men the night before while they were digging the dug-out for these two officers. We dig our own! He also found out that they have got good discipline in front of us, as just as he got near to their trenches, there were several Germans talking aloud in the trenches, and an officer told them to shut up, and they boxed up complete! (That's more than some of our bright little lot do; some of these old hairies who served in South Africa are the devil to deal with.)" Major Cator recorded how, when close to the German trenches, the enemy put up a star shell and Lieutenant Ottley discovered that he was lying on a dead German. He had the presence of mind to cut off shoulder straps and bring them back, so identifying the *121st Regiment*, who had been in a battle in the dark with the Royal Welsh Fusiliers on 29 October. Major Cator, with some knowledge of German, was very doubtful that the enemy had been speaking English and thought that Lieutenant Ottley must have misheard.

The Brigade line had just been extended for about half a mile from the Sailly-Fromelles road south towards Neuve Chapelle. Sir Edward Hulse told on the 11th how in the first tour they were here, he had had a man killed and two wounded. On the north side of the road the trenches were in places only about a hundred yards apart, but here between three hundred and fifty and five hundred and there was carelessness. "They had all three shown themselves, contrary to my orders, thinking that, as they were further off, they could put not only their heads but most of themselves outside the cover of the trenches." Then, after recounting shooting a German during the raid, he added that he had sniped a second one. "The other I bagged two days ago, a fair shot at 400 yards; he was carrying wood along his parapet, and he threw up both arms and went by the board completely." Most casualties were still from snipers, but shells caused some and minenwerfer were becoming a particular hazard.

Normally two officers at a time went home for a week's UK leave. On 12 December Lieutenant Cator told his mother that the next two should be leaving the next evening. After them it would be his turn, though leave could be suspended at any time. Then in a very short letter next day he had to tell her that all leave had been stopped and so he definitely would not be at home for Christmas. "I cannot say very much now about the reason for all this, but evidently some forward move is contemplated…I may have a great deal to say in my next letter, but am wondering where it will be written from." On the 17th Major Cator, who had just returned from leave himself, wrote to tell her that "Poor old Kit was wounded this morning, he was building a new parapet across a bit of exposed ground to give cover for the troops going in and out of the trenches. A sergeant of his was killed on the same spot a few minutes before Kit was hit. He was patting down a sandbag into position and a bullet came and fractured his left forearm just above the wrist, passed through the arm and grazed his forehead just in front of the temple, poor old chap he was in beastly pain, and never grumbled or groaned. I got on the pony as soon as I heard it, as they telephoned up to me that he wanted to see me, and galloped down there, to my intense relief I found it not too serious, though quite bad enough, and very painful. I took some antitetanus mixture with me, which the Doctor injected into him. The General was in the trenches and had advised the motor to meet him at the Dressing Station to take him home, so I put Kit and his servant Bailey, into the motor and sent him straight to the 23rd Field Ambulance Hospital." In the afternoon Major Cator went to see him at Sailly, but he had already been evacuated to Merville. This was his brother's first wound. From "the most delightful and comfortable hospital in Boulogne" Lieutenant Cator wrote home on the 19th to say "that I am going on splendidly…I was hit through my left arm, just above the wrist, then the same bullet just grazed my scalp, the luckiest thing you ever knew, as it has not damaged the scalp in the least. One or two bones are broken, I think, in the forearm, but I'll be alright today. I hope I shall get home for Christmas." Sergeant Ronald MacLennan from Lochboisdale, South Uist, where his mother Ann was a crofter, was killed the day that Lieutenant Cator was wounded. He had been serving for five and a half years and before that was a farm worker. He was in the Battalion from the beginning and was promoted three weeks before his death.

Private Wilfred Bailey, also spelt Baillie, Lieutenant Cator's servant, was a reenlisted former Scots Guardsman, a carriage smith in Sussex and a widower with a seven year old daughter. Almost immediately after this Private Bailey went down with influenza, the effects of which, bronchial catarrh, were so bad that he was sent home on 6 January with special leave for a week for specialist examination. When nothing more was heard of him the Battalion thought he had gone absent. He was, however, ill with respiratory problems, so much so that he was discharged with suspected TB five months later. His family either owned or were tenants of the Blacksmiths Arms, Adversane, and he was still there in the 1930s.

On 18 December Gunhild wrote to Lieutenant Saumarez "I am not quite sure, how long the letters take, but I hope this will reach you for Christmas, as I want to wish you as happy a Xmas, as is possible. It is a little hard we can't spend our first Christmas together! It will be rather a strange one for everybody! I am enclosing the only possible photograph of myself, I could find. As the birthday cake was a success, I have ordered another one like it and I hope it will reach you. I have heard that your battalion is now having 4 days in the trenches and 4 days off. I hope you are having the "off" days during Christmas!"

The night attack on 18 December

Sir Edward Hulse, his leave cancelled too, had also sensed that there was "some move in the air." Precisely what did not become clear until noon on 18 December. In dreadful weather with the ground a sodden mess and solely because of French pressure to do so the British were preparing diversionary attacks at staggered times all along their part of the line. Purely raiding the enemy trenches would have been less hazardous and might have caused more damage. Leaving aside the Aisne, this was the first time that the BEF as a whole attempted attacking enemy trenches, to distract the Germans from a larger French attack behind the Nôtre Dame de Lorette Ridge south of Loos and from an attempt to recapture the Messines Ridge, neither a success. That something was "in the wind" was apparent, but General Heyworth, who had been called to meet General Capper at seven o'clock on the 18th did not come back until nine with orders to make an attack at six that evening with two half battalions. Not until eleven could he give orders to his battalion commanders at Brigade Headquarters, by then at La Cordonnerie Farm. So the Scots Guards company commanders first got their orders face to face from Captain Paynter at noon. The attack frontage was about half a mile altogether, a company to each two hundred yards, with the right boundary on the Sailly-Fromelles road. The first requirement was to reorganise the troops in the trenches. General Heyworth had immediately decided that the 1/6th Gordons were too inexperienced to be involved, but some were in the line and had to be moved back. The Borders and the Scots Guards were each to attack with two companies, with their other two companies waiting in the front line to support them. Arranging this was as awkward as it could have been without also being at such short notice. Because of the Borders rota system their reserve companies had to come up from billets. Then they all had to move along the trenches to their right to link up with the Scots Guards. At the same time the reserve companies of the 2nd Gordons had to come up from billets to take over the Borders and some 1/6th Gordons trenches. The Grenadiers also had to come up from the rear to take over those Scots Guards trenches to the south of the Sailly-Fromelles road. Because of the shortage of time all this had to be done in daylight and the Grenadiers were fortunate in only losing five men in one company in the process. When they arrived the two Scots Guards companies they replaced moved north along the trenches to take their places behind the two attacking companies. Everyone in the line to the north and south of where the attacks were to go in was to fire on the enemy to prevent them interfering from the flanks. At half past four that afternoon a similarly ill prepared and unreconnoitred 22nd Brigade attack at Bois Grenier was repulsed with heavy casualties to the 2nd Queen's and 2nd Royal Warwicks. News reached Headquarters 20th Brigade half an hour later. It was inconceivable that the Germans opposite were not alert, but to some extent surprise was achieved.

Captain Henry Askew was to command the Borders attack and Captain Loder, recently promoted, the Scots Guards one. He reported afterwards that "I was ordered to meet Captain Askew and arrange details with him at 3.45pm… It was arranged that at 6pm the men should be posted over the parapet and to crawl out under the wire fence and lie down. When this was done, I was to blow my whistle and the line was then to move forward together, and walk as far as they could until the Germans opened fire, and then rush the front line trenches. Having reached the trench, I was to try to hold it if occupied, and if unoccupied to push on to the Second Line. The men carried spades and sandbags…At about three minutes to six pm the men were hoisted over the parapet and lay down. I blew my whistle as loud as I could, but owing to the noise of our gunfire, it appears that it was not generally heard. F Coy being on the right and LF on the left we began to move forward. After advancing about 60 yards I could see that in several places the line was not being maintained, some men moving forward faster than others. I could see this by the flash from the guns. I collected the men nearest to me, and I found myself practically on the parapet before the Germans opened fire. There was no wire entanglement at this point. We bayoneted and killed all the Germans we could see in the trench and then jumped down into it. There was a certain amount of shouting and confusion. I could not see far to my right or left or tell what was happening on either flank. The position of the trench in which I found myself was not traversed for a distance of at least 25 yards. I ordered the men to make firing positions in the rear face of the trench. I also told some men to watch the flanks, and if the enemy appeared to make traverses. I remained in the trench some time, about one hour, and then thought I had better try and see what had happened at other places in the line. I got out of the trench which I left in charge of Lieut Saumarez and told him to hang on. I found it impossible to get any information, but could see a good many dead bodies lying close to the German parapet. I decided to come back to report to Captain Paynter and explain what the situation was, and suggest that if the trench was to be held, reinforcements would have to be sent up. This he reported to the Brigadier." By this time it was apparent that reinforcing the attack would not help as only Left Flank had had any sort of success. F Company had had more trouble with German wire and Brigade Headquarters knew that the Borders companies had made little progress.

Amid the uncertainty, apart from evidence of heavy casualties, it became clear to those in the German fire trench that it would be impossible to hold on in daylight. They had to lie out on the back of it to shoot at all. Meanwhile, the companies in support had been trying to dig a communication trench one hundred and eighty yards out to them. This would have been very difficult to achieve under heavy fire even if the ground had been dry: it was an impossibility in the wet. Sir Edward Hulse, who had taken over G Company after Lieutenant Cator was wounded, described how they started digging as soon as the attack went in and they kept at it, "a dirty business". The main problem was the volume of fire coming from the German second line slightly higher up the Aubers Ridge, particularly from a well placed machine gun. The enemy moved it where it could be fired almost along the German front line. What also did not help, as Major Cator noted, was that "following wounding of RE officer that party failed to get up with grenades and block the trench captured with sandbags." Had they been there, it probably would not have made much difference. Also in his letter to his mother of 20 December Sir Edward Hulse reported that "five of our fellows literally lynched a German officer, and finally, when ordered to return to our trenches, came back with three candles, two boxes of sweets, three boxes of cigars, lots of papers belonging to him, two rings off his fingers, an iron cross, another medal, some very low and vulgar postcards and a photo of himself. He was a fat and very bourgeois vulgarian, and wore a 'eavy beard. They state that they caught him polishing off one of our officers (who was already wounded) with his revolver. They had completely gone through his "dug-out" and found it extremely "well appointed!"" He added "We took a young fellow prisoner whom two of our men found crouching, well out of the way, in a dug-out! He was a "*Jäger*.""

At the widest point the Borders only had about one hundred and fifty yards to cover, but started late, perhaps, possibly in part, because their Commanding Officer, Major George Warren, may have got the time of the attack wrong. There was initial confusion about which of his companies he wanted to make the attack before he returned from Brigade Headquarters, not till three in the afternoon, and then made changes to his subordinates' preparations. The Borders did not receive their orders until after Captain Loder had met Captain Askew. The main factor seemed to have been their not hearing Captain Loder's whistle. There was mention of the sound of guns contributing to the confusion over when to start, but when they did they immediately ran into very heavy fire from by then fully alert Germans. Only a very few, led by Captain Askew, got into the German trenches at all and were killed there. Others, close to the German trenches, were counterattacked in front of the parapet. Most, however, were trapped in the open between the lines. The unknown private recalled "It was about 4.45pm when the officer came down the Trench and told us that there was going to be charge that night. And it was to take place at 6pm. And then you could hear the men Praying to God to look after there wife and children should anythink happen to them the Orders came down the lne that we were to get through our own barbwire and then wait for the signal to make the Charge which as to be a Blast of a whistle which was to be blown by Capt Askew we waited till 6p.m.but never heard the Signal so A and C Company made the Companys for the Charge with B and D Companys as our supports the Scotch Guards on ur right and the 2nd Gordons on our left. Some how or the other our left was to soon with the charge and as soon as there voices when up so did the Germans lead and they let us have it we followed them but we were going down like rain drops as our trenches was only 70 yards apart so we retired an then made the 2nd charge but received the same. We retired again and stoped in midfield And it was like being in a Blacksmith shop watching him swing a hammer on a red hot shoe and the sparks flying all round you But instead of them being sparks they were Bullets. As the Germans had a inferlated Fire on us And we lieyed there it was a pitiful sight to see and hear our Comrades dyeing and could not get to help them as it ment serten death if we had moved. Then Orders came down the line for us to retire to the trenches. But we could not do so as the Fire was too heavy. After laying out there for 6½ Hrs most of them manage to get back while ourters got shot about 5 yards from our own trench I trying to get back. There was 18 men with me. We were so close that we dare not move if we we would not have live to tale the tail. So we had to lay there from 6.30 to 8.15a.m. the next morning. And as a Angle sent down from Heaven it came over verry misty and this being how only chance we made good of it. So we crawl halfway and then made a run for it. We could not see were we were going so fell over our Comrades who were dead. As we were making for our trenches as we were about to drop in the Trench we were challenged with our own men…And I must say I think it first time I said my Prayers in earness, which is nohing to my Credit for when I looked round and saw my Chums I thanked God he had spared me there fate."

This left the Scots Guards companies isolated on their left and with a machine gun enfilading their right, although the Grenadiers were doing what they could from the front line beyond, just as the 2nd Gordons were on the left of the Borders. Lieutenant Ottley led a platoon from G Company to try to deal with the machine gun. He was hit in the side of the neck near the German wire. Sir Edward Hulse described it in his next letter home. "I have heard all about him from a corporal who got him back under heavy fire, and whose name I am sending up to be "mentioned" for "good work under heavy fire". Although severely wounded Ottley got up and tried to get his men on and actually reached the German parapet, when he fell again and was carried back by the corporal I mentioned above. The doctor says he will get all right, but the nerves in his neck and shoulder are affected. He is a damned plucky fellow, and did very well indeed." Lance Corporal Andrew Mitchell carried him back and received the DCM. He enlisted in 1912 and came from Forfar, where his parents were living in the Station House. He was with the Battalion till injured accidentally by a grenade in late October 1916.

Lieutenant Saumarez told how, after the British guns had carried out a preliminary bombardment to cut the enemy wire, Left Flank "lined up on the parapet of our trench and lay down and waited for a whistle to be blown as a signal to start. At the sound of the whistle every man started forward at the double and immediately came in for very heavy rifle and machine gun fire from the opposite trenches. So many men were hit that the remaining men lay down but as many of the enemy's bullets were going low, many of our fellows were hit in the head instead of the ankle. Eventually I succeeded in lining some of the men in a depression close in front of the German wire and from there we charged the trench getting through the wire fairly successfully and jumped into the Boche trench. All we could see in the darkness was a line of points of fire, which were flashes from rifles which were being discharged all along the line. As it was so dark it was impossible to control a long line of men and I therefore only had eleven men with me at that time. On jumping into the trench they killed 22 Boches with their bayonets including an officer whom I shot with my revolver. I had been very particular to see that the safety catches of the men's rifles were back before we started so that there could be no firing. All the slaughter was with the bayonet. On jumping down into the enemy trench I landed more or less on top of this officer and shot him in the neck. He fell dead, after which there seemed to be a tremendous amount of pandemonium going on all around while the 22 Boches were being bayoneted by our eleven men. There was a great deal of shouting and cheering from our men mingled with groans and cries from the wounded Boches. The next clear thing that I remember was a Boche coming up to me and going down on his knees begging for mercy. Just at that moment one of our men coming up from behind ran a bayonet through his back which nearly knocked me over. I then told Corporal Jones to secure one end of our piece of captured trench and make a buttress of dead bodies while I went to secure the other end. I tried to extend our sector by going stealthily round the traverses. I shot a few Boches on the other side of the traverse. On reaching the other side of the next traverse I saw a figure in a cap outlined against the sky; I was not quite sure whether it was one of our men or not. Stooping down to ascertain this, I saw in an instant that the cap had no peak and it was therefore one of the enemy and as I raised my revolver to fire at him, I was fired at from a dug-out which I had not seen in the darkness on my right and the man was almost touching me with the point of his bayonet. The bullet struck my upraised revolver and ricocheted off the weapon, ripping off the top half of my wrist and entering my chest in two places. After that I remembered nothing for a time. I never knew whether I had actually discharged my revolver and killed the German in the cap or not. When I came to, I heard my name being called and found myself lying with my face to the ground and looking up on hearing my name being called, I realised my position. Some of the men then helped me to my feet and propped me up against the side of the trench and reformed a barrier of corpses immediately on my right to stop up our end of the trench. We then got to work posting sentries to keep a lookout on all sides and very soon the Boches began to wake up and having plenty of ammunition we opened fire wherever they made themselves heard. On hearing our approach they commenced shouting across to each other. They seemed to realize that we were only a small force in their midst. One of them climbed a willow tree nearby and we gave him a volley and he fell to the ground almost immediately. The Boches continued attacking from all sides all night long but not one of my eleven men, only myself, was touched. We had been told to expect support shortly after we had captured the position but as none arrived and as it was getting towards morning, I called for a volunteer to go back to our line and explain the position. A man volunteered and was never seen or heard of again. On the appearance of a little grey light in the east I called for another volunteer. A man named Clarkson immediately volunteered and succeeded in reaching our commanding officer Colonel [Captain] Paynter who dispatched a small relief party under Lieutenant Warner to our relief. His orders were to bring us back if he found the position untenable. This he did and ordered two stretcher bearers to carry me back and as I was being hoisted up on to the parapet the stretcher bearer at my head was shot dead. Another man took his place but he had not gone a few yards before he was hit in the leg whereupon I told them to discard the stretcher and I would crawl as best I could. Then two men, Corporal Jones and another man remained with me, one pushing my legs and the other pulling me until we reached our line when it was quite light. This tedious and painful operation must have taken quite an hour. They had hauled me down a shallow ditch filled with dead Boches which had set up a very bad poisoning in my lacerated arm. All the 11 men reached our trench in safety. The attack had been a failure and most of the rest of the line and my Company Sergeant Major James had penetrated a line a little further to the left for a few hours but found it impossible to hold and very heavy casualties had been incurred during the attack and when they were crossing No Man's Land. Our preliminary bombardment had given the enemy the tip that we were going to attack and they were all ready for us and the line was very strongly held, which was proved by the fact that in the small sector which we had held there were 22 Boches." Lieutenant Warner noted that Private Clarkson's message was that Lieutenant Saumarez' party were still holding part of the German trench at three in the morning. "I was sent off with a platoon to support them. Reached them with 6 men only owing to a mistake and had to expect position would become untenable at dawn as we could be practically surrounded. Sent back one prisoner and got the whole party back, including Saumarez and 2 wounded men, just before dawn."

On 6 January Lieutenant Warner replied to a letter from Lieutenant Saumarez, pleased to hear he was home and getting on all right, but "I am afraid I cannot get you the Iron X – Clarkson the man who had it was given permission to keep it and the other medal and they have gone to the Regimental Orderly Room [Regimental Headquarters] to be kept for him." He explained that all the papers taken had had to be sent to Brigade Headquarters but that he would try to get back a photograph of the German office. At some stage Lieutenant Saumarez either got the principal photograph or a copy. Private Lewis Clarkson was a farmworker when he enlisted in 1910 and was probably a reservist, because if he had been a serving soldier in a Battalion on the outbreak of war he would have found it difficult to marry his wife Jane on 5 August in Edinburgh. He was wounded in the left foot in April 1915 during a trench tour and transferred to the Royal Engineers the following year. Probably because of that and his therefore losing direct contact with the Scots Guards the Iron Cross ended up with Lieutenant Saumarez. When in 1919 Private Clarkson sent back the receipt for his 1914 Star from Bathgate he wrote on it "I should like to know what steps you are taking to return the Iron Cross which I got in 1914 to me." Company Sergeant Major Alfred James, first mentioned as a Sergeant at Ypres, and Corporal Richard Jones, who had been with Lieutenant Saumarez throughout and helped him back to the British line, both won the DCM. Corporal Jones was a miner at the Cwmdu Colliery at Maesteg, Glamorgan, and early October volunteer, who must have had some previous military service because he would not otherwise have arrived out in the BEF so quickly. He had also been swiftly promoted. He and Ellen Jones married in London in 1908 and had four children. In a letter on 23 January to Lieutenant Saumarez he wrote "I am pleased to say we got away without losing any of our men behind…I got one bullet through the sleeve of my coat & shirt & only burnt my arm and when we got to billets the next day I got a card from my wife wishing me many happy returns of the day the 18th was my birthday."

Lance Corporal Alexander Horne wrote to Lieutenant Saumarez on 6 January. Having started by saying how glad he was to hear that Lieutenant Saumarez was safely home he continued that "you must have suffered a great deal of pain while I was pulling you from the German trenches, when you counted every pull…I may draw your attention to the way the DCM was given I thought I was entitled to the credit which another receives because he happens to be an older Corpl you know I worked very hard that night & morning although it was only my Duty, I also left a lot of my personal property to get you to our tranches, I don't think it right that the DCM should be given for being in the German trench, I will leave it to you, to give me credit for bringing you back safely." Corporal Horne was a reenlisted Scots Guardsman, from Tranent originally, who had become a policeman in London. He and Emma Williamson married in Marylebone in October 1902 and had a son and a daughter. He rejoined the Army on 14 October and landed in France on 8 November, becoming a Lance Corporal on 13 December. Promoted to Sergeant at the beginning of October 1915 after the events at Hill 70, Loos, he was sent home in August 1916 suffering from contusion to his back and neurasthenia, consistent with having been blown up by a trench mortar explosion and buried, and given a medical discharge in October 1917.

From hospital in Blackpool Lance Corporal John Child wrote to Lieutenant Saumarez on the 11 January about his own experiences. He knew that there had been a lot of casualties and named Private John Worden in his section as being killed. He himself jumped into the enemy trench "almost on top of a German when he yelled in German & before I could recover my balance he shot me in the thigh at 2 paces. I kept my feet & found the next firing trench vacant [the next bay] so got well down in a corner & did some very serious thinking. Many Germans passed me but I kept very quiet & then commenced removing my kit & packed it in the right hand corner of the trench on top of a German kit & gave me sufficient height to jump over. I waited some time in hopes of our men taking the trenches & when next I looked up almost placed my nose against a bayonet & had to get down quickly as he belonged to us & took me for a German. I was watching my German friend all the time & he was working overtime firing & calling out in excellent English "Halt, who goes there, jump in here boys, We are British." I took a careful aim at him & fired for his body & pulled out of the trench & crawled back to ours. I've got a nasty wound & will be in bed 6 weeks yet. They found three pieces of lead in it." This suggested to him that the Germans were using explosive bullets. He was very keen to be discharged and to go back to his job, because he was considerably out of pocket in the Army. He had been on home leave from the Posts & Telegraphs Department in Pretoria when the War broke out, reenlisted as a former Scots Guardsman in London two weeks later and was soon promoted. Arriving in France in a September draft, he is likely to have joined the Battalion after Ypres. This wound kept him in hospital till the end of May 1915 and then, medically downgraded, he was in France from September 1915 to April 1917 attached to the Depot Company, Prisoners of War, Le Havre. Very shortly after that he was discharged medically unfit and went back to his old job in South Africa. He had an unmarried sister, Alice, in Lancaster. Private John Worden, also reenlisted, had just passed his forty fourth birthday when he died on 18 December. He had married Sarah Bowen at Chelsea in 1897 and they were living with their five children in Preston, where he was a carter. Sarah Worden was pregnant again when her husband left for the War and their youngest daughter was born on the day he was killed.

Private James Mackenzie, whose widowed mother Marion Mackenzie lived in Dumfries, was educated at Laurieknowe Public School, Maxwelltown, and was a groom before he enlisted nearly three years earlier. Though employed in the Battalion as a cook before the War, he was now a stretcher bearer. As it became more and more dangerous, the more so after daylight, the stretcher bearers were unable to get to the wounded in front of the German trenches but at some stage on 19 December Private Mackenzie went out on his own when others with a stretcher had had to give up. He brought in a badly wounded man from close to the German parapet. An unnamed fellow stretcher bearer described how Private Mackenzie was shot dead at two o'clock that afternoon. "He was returning to the trenches along with me and another stretcher bearer when it occurred. We had only two or three cases that morning, so the last one was taken by us three. After we took the wounded soldier to hospital we returned to see if there were any more. There was a very dangerous place to pass. I went first, followed by another, then James came behind, which caused his death. He was shot in the heart by a sniper, and only lived five minutes." Private Mackenzie was awarded the VC. Lance Corporal Jesse Stead, a fitter in Leeds when he joined up early in 1914, won the DCM for going forward from his trench under heavy machine gun fire and dragging two wounded men to safety. He was killed immediately afterwards. After the War when his 1914 Star was sent to his father Robert Stead, by then living at Attercliffe, Sheffield, he wrote on the receipt "Thanking you for the same wishing the Scots Guards every success." Lance Corporal Alexander Wilson, another former groom, from Edinburgh, with a tattoo of a woman's figure on his right forearm, also won the DCM for his leadership of stretcher bearers and especially for looking after the wounded that night and getting them back down the communication trenches. Captain Loder won the MC.

The casualties were severe. Of the eight officers directly involved in the attack and in supporting it only Captain Loder and Lieutenant Warner were unhit. Three, Captain Hugh Taylor, Lieutenant Dick Nugent and Lieutenant The Honourable Felix Hanbury Tracy were missing, Lieutenants Ottley and Saumarez badly wounded and Lieutenant Sir Frederick FitzWygram, Bt, lightly wounded with a graze to the head. On 4 January Sir Frederick FitzWygram wrote to Lieutenant Saumarez "I was extraordinarily lucky that night & am now none the worse except that my brain works very slow & my memory is awful; but both are improving rapidly…I was hit by a bullet on the top of my head when I was on the top of the German trench, & having a scrap with its occupants. If the bullet had gone more than ⅛ inch lower, it would have finished me. I struck an advanced post about a dozen yards in front of their line, so which really saved me, as I fell on to the left side of their parapet so that it covered me from their crossfire which came from the right, & on the left you & ½ my coy took the German trench. The next thing I remember was lying at the bottom of the parapet with the men lying on it & firing over it at the Germans below, who must have been close to the wall of the pit they were in, & fired up whenever anything appeared over the top. I could not move at first, but eventually managed to crawl up it to have another shoot, but I was immediately knocked over on to my back by the concussion of a shot that must have just missed my face. After a time I realised that every man that I could see had been killed with the exception of two who were wounded, so I thought we had better try & crawl back to our trenches before the Germans finished us off. This we managed to do, though I was so dazed, that when I struck a ditch that ran into our own trench, I started going the wrong way ! till I met a couple of men who I think must have belonged to the working party who were deepening it."

One hundred and eighty men were killed, wounded and missing. The most senior, who was killed, was Company Sergeant Major Charles Lilley, who shortly before had brought out to Lieutenant Saumarez a letter from Gunhild. Born in Ross-on-Wye, he was a groom in London when he enlisted in 1902. He married Hannah Thompson at Kensington on 12 September 1914, three weeks before the Battalion sailed for Belgium. One of the younger men killed was Private David Nelson, son of Major and Quartermaster David and Mary Nelson, who lived on the north side of Holyrood Park, Edinburgh. He gave his occupation as a clerk when he enlisted in April 1914, had come out as a reinforcement in September and been posted to the Battalion after Ypres. If his stated age was correct he died having only recently been nineteen. Of three serving soldiers who enlisted together on the same day, 26 October 1913, at Hamilton, one, Private William Purse, also just nineteen, was killed that night. A former coal miner, he was the son of John Purse of Hamilton. He had been out from the very start in August as a reinforcement, but probably because of his age, was not sent up the line till after Ypres.

   Much older men died, one of them, Private Reginald Ride, aged forty four. His wife Winifred lived in Stockwell, London, and they had six surviving children. Having served for twenty one years, he retired in March 1914 as an army pensioner and got a job as a commissionaire, but rejoined in September. The effects which reached his widow were a piece of boot and two coins. Private Denis Kelly was a labourer from Rutherglen, who volunteered in August 1914 in Glasgow, giving his age as thirty eight and two months. He had previous service as a Scots Guardsman and went out as a reinforcement within a month of reenlisting, but not joining till Méteren. After the War his widow Hannah gave his age when he died as forty six to the Imperial War Graves Commission. They had four children and a fifth, a daughter, was born at the end of January. Another older man killed was Private Thomas Robinson, who was forty two. Having settled in London after he originally left the Scots Guards in 1902 he trained as a furniture porter and was working for the Office of Works, Westminster. That was also where he and his wife Dora lived in Vincent Square. They had married at Westminster in April 1897, but had no children. Private Robinson reenlisted at Southwark in September 1914 and arrived in France under two months later. Private John Martin, a reenlisted former Scots Guardsman with Boer War service, was missing. He was a labourer in Glasgow where he lived with Margaret Boyd in Bridgton and their son, born in 1904. Before reenlisting on 14 September he and Margaret married three days earlier and this enabled her to get a war widow's pension. Private Richard Roscoe was a labourer in Preston where he and Harriett Fogg married in September 1914, already the parents of two daughters and a son. On 5 October he went to reenlist, his obligations as a Scots Guards reservist long expired. On 8 November he was in France and on 18 December dead at the age of forty four. Harriett Roscoe acknowledged receipt of his Princess Mary's Christmas Gift on 5 July 1915 "With deepest Gratitude" and was dead herself that October. Private William Beattie, also a time expired Scots Guardsman, reenlisted on 3 September. His parents William and Mary Beattie lived at Newcastle-under-Lyme and their son was a male nurse. Also on 8 November he was in France. On the night of 18 December Private Beattie was severely wounded in the left shoulder and died in hospital in Boulogne at twenty minutes before midnight on the 20th. In the same draft as him was Private William Shaw, who was killed. He had been a mounted policeman in Edinburgh, had no previous military service of any kind, enlisted in Edinburgh on 7 August 1914 and landed in France on 8 November. He was the youngest son of John and Isabella Shaw, who lived in Leith, and had been educated at Bonnington Academy and George Watson's, before moving on to Dollar Academy and then Edinburgh University. He was actively involved with the Newhaven Boy Scouts near his parents' home and with the Cowgate Mission in the Old Town. Sergeant John "Scrubber" McDonald was hit in the left hand and evacuated home, but would reappear later. He was from the Western Isles where his father was living on Scalpay, Harris. Regimental fable had it that when he joined the Army Sergeant McDonald had been living in a cave from which a recruiting sergeant tempted him with a bowl of porridge. More prosaically, he had been a labourer in Glasgow and by this time had nine years service. Privates Benjamin Bynoth and Joseph Deery were forty two year old forest keepers of Epping Forest, whose reserve commitments had expired in 1904. They reenlisted in the Scots Guards at the end of September and joined after Ypres. During the fighting on 18 December Private Bynoth was hit in the left shoulder and left the Army medically unfit in August 1915. His home was on the edge of the

Forest at Loughton, Essex, where his wife Elizabeth was with their daughter. Private Deery was hit in the head only four days later, but was back out in France early in 1915, serving for most of that year before being sent home with neurasthenia in November. After he recovered he trained as a Vickers machine gunner, went out to join the 2nd Guards Brigade Machine Gun Company in the autumn of 1916 and left what had become the 4th (Foot Guards) Battalion Guards Machine Gun Regiment to go home finally at the end of July 1918. He was discharged in February 1919 with war service induced rheumatism and went back to his wife Selina and their daughter in Epping Forest.

Lance Sergeant William Ross, having survived everything up till now since landing at Zeebrugge and was probably Lieutenant Cottrell Dormer's platoon sergeant at Kruiseecke, was missing and reported dead. Very soon after New Year a correspondence began when an acquaintance of Sergeant Ross' brother and sister in Glasgow wrote to ask on their behalf for more definite information. Colonel Fludyer tried to find out, without success. There was nothing to add and no identity discs had so far come to light. Then Jeannie Ross received a handwritten postcard dated 6 May 1915. It read "I AM AT: Wittenberg, Germany, a prisoner of war since December last and am keeping quite well. NOTICES: Hope you are well, and to see you soon. We may receive International Money Orders and you might send me a parcel weekly of eatables; Bread, Cake, Cheese, Butter, Jam, Chocolate and tinned stuff etc, Also tobacco and cigarettes "Glasgow Mixture" and thick black, and a tooth brush. Let, Peter, Jeanie, etc. know. Love to all Willie." This caused consternation as well as some doubt of authenticity, but after the handwriting was compared, both the postcard and an earlier sample being checked at Regimental Headquarters, there was no doubt but that Sergeant Ross was alive. Colonel Fludyer wrote to ask the Battalion that, if whoever had reported him dead was still alive himself, he should be interviewed and punished, if liable, because an enormous amount of worry and correspondence had been caused. Sergeant Ross was interned in Holland in 1918 and stayed on in the Army after the War. When he was posted to the Guards Depot in 1923 it was noted that he had a weak word of command, it being also recorded that when he had been a NCO there in 1912 he "broke his voice as a squad instructor."

A time expired former Scots Guardsman, Private Edward Jones, had gone back to being a collier. He was originally from Ruston in Derbyshire, but when he reenlisted he gave no details of any family or even friends and was not married. He came to the Battalion after Ypres. During the fighting in the dark he was hit by bullets in both legs and his left eye and the Germans found him first. "I lay on the field about 36 hours before I was picked up and taken to a dressing station. I was detained there a few hours and well treated, after which they took us to the railway station in a motor ambulance. We went by train to Lille and were taken on to Giessen, travelling for six days together, and the journey was very bad. I was badly wounded. The guards at the hospital treated us all right, but when the soldiers came back they treated us badly and called us swine and other objectionable names." In the military hospital there were only two other British soldiers, joined by two more later. "I was very ill here and had to have one leg off. I was unconscious when they took it off. I was looked after by a Belgian soldier, and if it had not been for him I should have died." Those in the hospital, whatever their nationality, helped each other and Private Jones particularly mentioned the Russians doing their best. The food "was all soup – potato soup, or potato water as we should call it – and bread." Because of his condition he was allowed more milk. While he could write home, he never received any parcels for some time and no mail came for him until Miss Cunningham of Clapham sent him a first letter.

After that letters came through regularly and parcels did likewise. "The food in the parcels arrived in good condition, with the exception of the bread which was generally mouldy, unless it was packed in tins." He was exchanged quite soon and spoke well of the journey "I had some experience of the German Red Cross which was very good. A lady met us at the station and gave us a splendid feed, and then drove us to the ambulance train. On the train coming back, the treatment could not have been better." Private Jones was repatriated in August 1915 and sent first to hospital in Wandsworth, then to the convalescent hospital at the Brighton Pavilion and then to Roehampton to be fitted with and learn to use an artificial leg. He had had his right foot amputated above the ankle and had also lost his left eye. He was discharged in October 1916.

Colonel Fisher Rowe told his wife that it had been "a foul wet night, blowing & raining like anything," that sixty wounded had come through his headquarters and that Captain Loder and Lieutenant Warner had come in there for breakfast at seven in the morning, not knowing much about the casualties in the dark. He got the impression that enemy losses were not many and remarked "I think personally the attack was a rotten idea as in my opinion it was much too small & that its no good taking a 100 yds or so of trench as you are bound to be boosted out of it very quickly & there weren't nearly enough men to support it properly." On the night of the 19th a party of thirty five men from the Borders had managed to get back under cover of darkness after lying out all through the day in a small ditch. Their casualties were four officers, two killed or died of wounds and two wounded, and one hundred and twenty three men. Captain Askew was killed. One who died of wounds on 29 December was Captain Cameron Lamb, who, as Major Cator then noted, had led their scouts early on at Ypres when they surprised and killed several German soldiers.

Major Cator wrote "The following was the description of the German trenches Depth 6 to 7 feet. Width about 5 feet. Two steps on the forward side for the fire positions. Loopholes very low down made by sinking a conical box narrow at one end and broadening out the narrow end nearest the enemy. Bullet proof plate placed in the broad end. All the loopholes set slightly obliquely to the line of fire. Wires were running along the inside of the trenches (telephone or mine). Traverses every ten yards. Floor and steps of the trench boarded. Dug-out in rear of the Fire Trench." He had some observations about the lessons learned from this abortive attack: "Activity amongst our troops was much too apparent when we moved troops down to reinforce the trenches. This together with the heavy shelling from our guns gave the Germans ample warning of something 'on'

The attacks were not simultaneous
The rifles got so clogged up with mud that only one in four could be used
The signal for the attack was not heard by all the troops
The men all lost their spades and sandbags
Arrangements must be made for the men to get through their own wire entanglements simultaneously before they start
Small isolated attacks are useless.

He also recorded that, though the Germans had behaved well in allowing the Scots Guards to bring in their wounded, they had shot Borders wounded in between the trenches the day after the attack. The reason could have been that a wounded or unwounded soldier, possibly from the group hiding in the ditch, fired at them or else they supposed that this had happened.

Also, seen from a distance it might not be easy to differentiate between a wounded man dragging himself over the ground and an unwounded one crawling carefully. All the same, Major Cator had heard that the Germans had waited before killing one man until, shot through both thighs, he had dragged himself right to the edge of the British trench. Sir Edward Hulse noted "The morning after our attack, there was almost a tacit understanding as to no firing, and about 6.15am I saw eight or nine German heads and shoulders appear, and then three of them crawled out a few feet in front of their parapet and began dragging in some of our fellows who were either dead or unconscious close to their parapet. I do not know what they intended to do with them, but I passed down the order that none of my men were to fire, and this seems to have been done all down the line. I helped one of our men in myself, and was not fired at, at all. I sincerely hope that their intentions were all that could be desired with regard to our wounded whom they fetched in. I also saw some of them, two cases, where the two Germans evidently were not quite sure about showing themselves, and pushed their rifles out to two of our wounded and got them to catch hold, and pulled them on to their parapet, and so into their trenches. Far the most ghastly part of this business is that the wounded have so little chance of being brought in, and if heavy fire is kept up, cannot even be sent for." They remained in the line on the 19th, the Grenadiers taking over in the evening, and spent the next day quietly in their billets. Lieutenant Warner went to dinner at Brigade Headquarters and heard "we were the only battalion who reached the enemy's trenches, also that our prisoner was the only result."

On the 20th the Borders noticed two men still lying wounded close to the German trenches. Not until after dark was it possible to do anything. Under fire from German machine guns and rifles discharged at random to catch real or imagined working parties and patrols Privates James Smith from Workington and Abraham Acton from Whitehaven crawled out. It took them an hour to bring in each man and both won the VC. Major Cator wrote that one wounded man was delirious, the other, whom he saw and talked to, quite sensible, but that in both cases their wounds had gone gangrenous. The second man had explained that they had simply played dead in order to try to survive and that he had drunk from a puddle at night. The anonymous private wrote "Dec 20th About 10.35am when the doctor saw 2 men out on the German Barbwire and said them too men are alive so get them so 2 men went out that night and got them in and when they got into our trench they said give me a smoke and a drink of water Now these too men had been out for 52 Hrs and how they live now one knows but thank God they are all right now and are doing well."

Lance Corporal Herbert Yates, a groom and the son of John and Mary Yates of Halewood, Liverpool, joined the Scots Guards in the first week of the War when just past his eighteenth birthday, the age he declared, arrived with the 12 November reinforcements and was appointed a Lance Corporal after only ten days. On 21 December he was brought into the field ambulance at Sailly, shot through both legs, at least one of which was broken and had to be amputated. Gangrene had set in. It had taken three days to find him. He died in hospital in Boulogne at half past five on Christmas morning. Lieutenant Ottley had been evacuated quickly to the Australian Volunteer Hospital at Wimereux, on the northern outskirts of Boulogne. Though he was said afterwards to have been positive and cheerful to begin with, he died at five o'clock in the morning on 21 December. He was a month short of his nineteenth birthday. Only a few hours later his parents arrived to visit him, but all they could do was take his body home. The first letter of condolence that Lady Ottley opened was from Lieutenant Swinton's mother. He had himself written on 20 December to tell Lady Ottley about her son's being wounded, without going into details for fear of frightening her. Very worried himself, he told his mother next day that the wound was where all the nerves were in the neck and that Lieutenant Ottley was in great pain. Apart from writing about the officer casualties and adding that had he left the trenches "I wouldn't be here now" he wrote "mince pies were excellent but plum puddings travel better…Don't send any more bulls eyes we have thousands." Then, ending the letter, "Do let me know at once how Geoff is, as soon as you can." Lady Ottley answered Elsie Swinton's letter at once, saying she prayed that she would not lose her son too and "We take our boy to Scotland tonight & lay him amongst the mountains he loved so, on Saturday."

Gunhild had a telegram from her husband "that shook me. "Slightly wounded. Please reserve a room for me at 17 Park Lane Hospital." Deeply distressed I started at once to try and obtain further news. On learning that a brother officer [Sir Frederick FitzWygram] was wounded and in a London hospital, my father-in-law went to see him He found [out] that Vincent was severely wounded, in hospital in Boulogne, and unable to be moved. My hope was now to be allowed to travel to Boulogne soonest possible and Lord de Saumarez kindly offered to escort me…we were on our way the following day. At Victoria Station I was carefully searched by a sympathetic woman detective, and our journey proved to be easy and comfortable. On arrival in Boulogne we were met by the handsome Sinclair, who took us straight to one of the many hotels in the town, now turned into hospitals. Vincent looked surprisingly well as his colour was high owing to fever, and he was very happy to see us. He had some difficulty in speaking and was short of breath, having been shot through the lung. His right hand was badly shattered, and many pieces of shrapnel were lodged in his inside. He was necessarily in serious pain, but his spirits remained surprisingly good. He shared a light pleasant room with a schoolfellow from Harrow, but his great desire was to be taken home, and this the overworked doctor refused to allow. He felt the risk was too great, and might prove fatal. Vincent used to ask me to go and see wounded brother officers in other hospitals, but I was deeply saddened by the invariable reply to my enquiry: "I am sorry to say, he has succumbed to his wounds." The wounded arrived by train straight from the trenches, and lay in the front hall on stretchers, in their muddy uniforms, until sorted out. My brother-in-law, Henrik, had handed over his yacht – the beautiful *Albion* – to the Red Cross, to serve as a hospital ship, and one day the good and strong minded doctor suddenly appeared in Vincent's room. After careful examination the doctor gave his verdict with comforting assurance. "We now have a chance of bringing him home comfortably. This chance may not occur again. I take full responsibility for his safety." Vincent was soon installed in Henrik's own cabin. He suffered great pain, but bore up with unfailing courage; happy to feel he was on his way home. It was Christmas Day – our first Christmas married. I was asked to join the Christmas party on board. Very soon the time came for me to take my leave, and I stood on the Boulogne quay watching the *Albion* glide silently out to sea in the black night – a large Red Cross painted on each side." On 29 December there was a telegram from the War Office "Beg to inform you that Lieut Hon J. St V. B. Saumarez Scots Guards in hospital 17 Park Lane wounded right arm and chest". What seemed to have happened was that the German bullet struck his revolver and shattered into several pieces, thus explaining the multiple wounds in his chest, though the main threat was infection. Though not immediately, it became apparent that his right hand was never going to recover and unless amputated would only be a constant source of pain. When Lieutenant Saumarez was fit enough to go to France again he went in 1917 as ADC to Major General Bertram Mitford of the 42nd (East Lancashire) Division, Territorial Force, and Private Orchard accompanied him. This continued till General Mitford was replaced in

October and they were posted home. In September 1918 he became ADC to Major General Sir Hugh Trenchard of the Independent Air Force, whose role was strategic bombing of Germany and Private Orchard again went with him.

Opposite Rouges Bancs the anonymous Borders private wrote "21st Dec This being my Birthday I spent resting the Trench with a good dinner of Corn Beef and a [indecipherable] and had a singsong with my chums." Meanwhile news came that the Indian Corps had lost some trenches further south and that I Corps were on their way there. This would involve the 1st Scots Guards.

Referring to the German cruisers shelling Hartlepool, Whitby and Scarborough on 16 December Colonel Fisher Rowe told his wife on the 22nd "Sitwell tells me his father had his house hit at Scarborough & was proud to have been under fire before his son. The son knows all about bullets now but has not been shelled." 2nd Lieutenant Osbert Sitwell had only arrived the day before. Lieutenant Swinton, his cousin, wrote home on the 22nd saying he was "More dejected and lost than it is possible to imagine, but he will soon get sorted and I hope soon get acclimatized." Sir Edward Hulse told his mother the same day "No sooner in billets and trying to get a well deserved rest, than I had to take my company out at short notice last night to dig. Four miles back to the dirty trenches – dig till midnight, and then relieved by another company, and four miles back in pouring rain and sleet. Our trenches are rapidly becoming young rivers, and one can do practically nothing to stop the water rising." General Heyworth wrote on the 23rd to Sir Robert Kindersley, on whose land near Oxford he had previously been training his London Territorials, that "here I live the same sort of life every day. Go into the trenches at 8.30am and get back about 1 to 2.30pm. Just now it is a very wet proceeding, as in some places in the communication trenches one goes in well over the knees in liquid mud and in others the mud is so sticky that it nearly pulls one's boots off; you would laugh at me if you could see me on my return from the trenches wet through to the waist, and the rest of me caked in yellow clay." The mud was no respecter of persons or types of footwear and Brigadier General The Honourable Francis Gordon of the 19th Brigade lost his boots completely while visiting the trenches a little further north on 4 January 1915. After touching on the events of 18 December General Heyworth, who with Major Cator, was assiduous in going round the line, continued his letter. "This is the most hideous country, absolutely flat, and nothing but deep plough, the ammunition column have started a pack of harriers and have had some fun I believe as there are lots of hares." Regretting that neither of the London Territorial battalions he knew were in his brigade, he then wrote "I only wish I had either of them instead of the Batt I have got the 6th Gordons, who are a very young lot with not much stamina." The Divisional Ammunition Column were gunners who brought up ammunition to the batteries, while "young" in military language also meant "inexperienced". Major Cator noted the same day that the Rivière des Layes had risen a foot, that water was rushing down the communication trenches and that parts of the fire trenches had a foot of water in them. Two and a half platoons of Grenadiers had had to be moved because the water in their fire trench was waist deep.

Sir Edward Hulse wrote that they were doing everything they could to brighten up Christmas Day for the men. This included a plum pudding from England for everyone in the Battalion. The officers had also put together "reserve sacks of food and warm things" to hand out to the men on the 25th. The contents were from their own parcels and from those for other officers who were casualties or sick. He was also preparing a concert party in G Company to sing carols, "Tipperary" and the like on Christmas evening in retaliation for the singing of German patriotic songs every night. This may have arisen, at least partly, because German sentries often sang to themselves while on duty. Meanwhile at Brigade Headquarters a parcel from the Army & Navy Stores arrived addressed to "Head Master, 20th Infantry Brigade, 7th Division, British Expeditionary Force." During the night of 23 December the cloud cleared and there was a hard frost, sufficient to harden the ground and very much reduce the mud. During the day the Brigade heard that after dark they were again to extend their sector a bit further southwards, because of the thinning out of troops in the 8th Division beyond. This meant that the Scots Guards, the right hand battalion, with only six fit officers, all had to move to their right, completed by half past seven. Lieutenant Warner and Right Flank had spent Christmas Eve "making trenches drier and arranged to dig urinal until got orders 2pm to move to my right at dark. Took over trenches, very bad and muddy, no dug-outs" from a London Territorial battalion. After the move Left Flank, under Lieutenant Swinton, were from immediately south of the Sailly-Fromelles road to "the tall poplar trees" with Right Flank from the trees to the divisional boundary with the 8th Division. F Company, very weak in numbers, were either in between or back in support. Going northwards from the road were G Company, next to them two companies of the Borders, beyond them two of the 1/6th Gordons and then two of the 2nd Gordons. The Grenadiers were in billets until the evening of 27 December. On Christmas Eve there was the usual sniping and two Scots Guardsmen died. One, Private Alexander Butters, serving under the alias of Kennedy, had a wife, Euphemia, and two sons in Leith. He was a forty three year old reenlisted Scots Guardsman and Boer War veteran, without a tooth in his upper jaw, who had been a cooper. The other, a serving soldier, was the knock-kneed Private Henry Teasdale, among the reinforcements on 12 November, formerly a miner and the son of Thomas and Mary Teasdale, then living in Bedale, Yorkshire.

The Christmas Truce

The following evening Lieutenant Swinton began writing home that on Christmas Eve "Ever since 5pm neither side had fired a shot, and about 7 they began shouting a merry Christmas to us; we answered and a regular concert took place. I had a very important bit of digging to do and this I started at 10.30. It was a deviation to avoid a bit of trench where a spring had appeared and the water was knee deep. We dug till 3am when I turned in, having previously had a good dinner at 9. During all this time the Germans were singing and shouting and showing lights, but not firing a shot." Captain Loder noted that the German trenches were lit up with lanterns and that there were sounds of singing. Lieutenant Swinton described later how "the German parapet, for miles to right and left, was lit up with numberless Christmas trees and similar decorations, and the singing was intensified." Private Peter Murker, was a battalion scout, previously in the 1st Battalion and wounded in the arm on the Aisne. He came to the 2nd Scots Guards at Méteren, with a record of getting into trouble and likely to have needed to be kept well occupied. It was he who went out between the lines and met a German patrol, who, Sir Edward Hulse heard, gave him a glass of whisky, more likely to have been schnapps, and some cigars with the message "that if we didn't fire at them, they would not fire at us." Apart from what came from their homes, at Christmas German soldiers received quantities of gifts collectively, notably from industrialists. Cheap cigars were easy to transport and hand out. Major Cator's account, slightly different but to the same effect, was "Pte Murker …heard a voice from the German Trenches shouting that the Germans would like a "parley". A man came out to him & said they wanted to have a quiet Xmas Day all their men were sick of the war. They had lost twenty two killed in last Friday's attack. On an officer approaching the man changed his conversation & began talking about Xmas. The officer gave our scout some cigars & sent a message to say that if we agreed not to shoot today they the Germans would do the same & Xmas Day might be passed in peace. The day passed off with not a shot being fired after 9am by either side." Sir Edward Hulse noticed that on Christmas morning there was a bit of firing early on but that it died down completely by eight except for a few shots over to the left. A Scots Guardsman was wounded and Private John Cameron of the 2nd Gordons from Keith, Banffshire, killed.

Captain Loder did not think that there had been any firing in the night but then "Early on Xmas morning a party of German *158 Regiment* came over to our wire fence, and a party from our trenches went out to meet them. They appeared to be most amicable and exchanged souvenirs, cap stars, badges, etc. Our men gave them plum puddings which they much appreciated." Lieutenant Swinton had been woken at seven and was breakfasting on porridge and scrambled eggs at eight after which "I then went out to find all my men walking about outside the trenches, which would have been absolute suicide yesterday. Finding it quite safe I did so myself." In his later, more detailed account he described how "At about 8.30 the lookout reported that a few of the enemy were leaving their trenches and coming towards us, unarmed. I should have said that at this particular part of the line my company was nearly 500 yards from the enemy. I told CSM James to send out an equal number of men, also unarmed, and to see that there were enough left in the front trench in case of any trouble, these to move up and down the trench to pretend that there were more men than we really had. I then went out myself, with my CSM, and we found an English speaking Hun who was full of Christmas cheer, wished us all a happy Christmas, and exchanged indifferent cigars for tinned plum pudding." In his letter that evening he went on that "At about 10 some of our people went over to the German lines and then the fun began… they were all very friendly and bore no ill will to us. One of them said that they believed France to be done and that they could hold Russia, but England they could not understand; they could not beat us and we were the only people keeping the war going. Some of them were quite fed up. I saw an officer and a man with Iron Crosses. We arranged an armistice for today officially till 4pm, but unofficially till tomorrow night. It is now 7 and they have not fired yet."

Dead from the week before lay out between the trenches to the north of the road as well as, possibly, others, British and German, caught at night during patrols or while putting up wire. More German dead were apparently from a counterattack in front of their own parapet on the Borders the week before, but most were from earlier German attacks, including that on the Royal Welsh Fusiliers beaten off in the dark on 29 October. Captain Bertrand Gordon of the 2nd Gordons was in command of the left sub-section of the Brigade trenches, including where the Borders had attacked a week earlier, while the Borders were now where Left Flank of the Scots Guards had attacked. He reported to Brigade Headquarters that "the Commandant of the German Forces immediately in front…came out of his trench about 10am. I met him halfway between the two lines of trenches. We agreed to bury the dead, any bodies of our men over the halfway line should be carried across by their men and vice versa, so that there was no possibility of viewing the trenches." He went on that all the dead were now buried and that they had found men from the Borders intermingled with Germans close to the enemy trenches, which indicated that the latter had made a counterattack. He commented that "the men are mostly young but of good physique. I noticed that the majority of them carried hand grenades at their sides. Several of them showed me the Iron Cross which they had received which would make it appear that they had been fighting in other parts before coming here." Lieutenant Colonel Gordon was killed commanding the 2nd Gordons on 20 July 1916 near High Wood during the Battle of the Somme.

Very instrumental in the arrangements was the Padre of the 1/6th Gordons, the Reverend Dr Esslemont Adams from Aberdeen. He was accompanying Lieutenant Colonel Colin McLean, from Bridge of Alford, Aberdeenshire, killed on 13 March 1915 at Neuve Chapelle. The Padre's first task was burying a man who had died of wounds on Christmas Eve. When he got to the forward trenches he saw an opportunity, described in an anonymous officer's published account, it being then common practice for families to forward letters from the front to newspapers. With soldiers of both sides standing outside "At last our Commanding Officer resolved to get out and see for himself. The Chaplain jumped up into the open at his heels, and crossing a ditch which runs down the middle of the field between the lines cried "Does anyone speak English?" As reply a private stepped forward, and then to our amazement we saw our Chaplain cross the ditch, salute the German commander and his staff, and begin to talk to them. Our Padre had seized his chance and found the German commanders very ready to agree that, after the dead had been buried, a short religious service should take place. We did not know all that was being said, but afterwards we asked the Padre two questions. The one was "Why did you and the German commander take off your hats to one another?" What happened, as we learned, was: The German took his cigar case out and offered the padre a cigar, which was accepted. The Padre said "May I be allowed not to smoke, but to keep this as a souvenir of Christmas here and of meeting you on Christmas Day?" The answer, with a laugh, was "Oh, yes, but can't you give me a souvenir? Then the hats came off. For the souvenir the padre gave was the copy of the "Soldier's prayer", which he had carried in the lining of his cap since the war commenced, and the German officer, in accepting it, took off his cap and put the slip in its lining, saying as he did it "I value this because I believe what it says, and when the war is over I shall take it out and give it as a keepsake to my youngest child."

On the card was:

Slip this inside your cap

A Soldier's Prayer
Almighty and most merciful Father,
Forgive me my sins:
Grant me Thy peace:
Give me Thy power:
Bless me in life and death,
For Jesus Christ's sake.
Amen

From the Chaplain-General Aug.1914
The Lord's Prayer was printed on the reverse.

The dead were then gathered together and both sides dug a grave into which they were laid in two lines. Captain Loder took a party to assist and collected the paybooks, personal effects and identity discs of all the Scots Guardsmen and the rifles on the British side of half way. The

Germans would not let them collect those on their side of it. While the grave was being dug Padre Adams prepared the service with the interpreter whom he had identified, as well as a German divinity student in the ranks. This included a short prayer which Padre Adams wrote out on a postcard and the interpreter then put into German.

Captain Loder learned from a German officer, whom he described as "a middle aged man, tall well set up and good looking" of the fate of two missing officers. One, Lieutenant Nugent, had been killed, the other, Lieutenant Hanbury Tracy, had died of wounds two days later in hospital and been buried in the German cemetery at Fromelles. Captain Loder gained the impression that they had treated their prisoners well and done everything they could for the wounded. Another German officer, who spoke neither French nor English, but appeared to want to express his feelings, kept on pointing to the dead Scots Guardsmen and reverently saying "Les Braves, c'est bien dommage." Lieutenant Hanbury Tracy had been at Harrow and Sandhurst and served for four years from 1903. He and his wife Madeleine had two sons and lived in Marylebone, London. She also got confirmation about her husband's death in German hands quite quickly through their reporting it. While there was still doubt about Lieutenant Nugent's fate until he had to be declared officially dead, his family still tried to hope for the best. Sometime in January Lieutenant Saumarez met Mary Nugent, his sister, in London, who wrote the same day "to thank you very much for all you told me today – it is a great help to being brave & hoping on, when one feels one knows all there is to be known." She excused herself for not sympathizing with all Lieutenant Saumarez had been through as "I am simply "living" now through this anxiety & had I spoken all I felt about that night attack I might have broken down,"

After filling in the grave British and Germans gathered on either side. Then Padre Adams said the 23rd Psalm with the German divinity student repeating each verse after him in German. Prayers were said sentence by sentence in each language. Captain Loder wrote "The whole of this was done in great solemnity and reverence. It was heartrending to see some of the chaps one knew so well and who had started out in such good spirits on December 18th lying there dead, some with terrible wounds." In this particular grave, there being others, there were twenty nine Scots Guardsmen, but though details were taken, they did not survive, any more than were recorded the numbers of men from the Borders, if there were any here, or the number of Germans. There was no more than temporary marking with wooden crosses. The Scots Guards carried back with them the body of Captain Taylor, found near the German parapet. They buried him in the little cemetery in the Rue Pétillon. He had been brought up at Chipchase Castle, Wark on Tyne, Northumberland, and, after Harrow and Balliol College, Oxford, was commissioned in 1907. He and Mary Taylor married in 1907 and had a son and a daughter.

The unknown soldier from the Borders also wrote about "Dec.25th X.mass day On Xmass morning about 5.30am a german officer show a wite flag on the trench and about 10 mts after came on top himself and walked half way across to our trench and asked to see one of our officers of the English Army So a officer of the Scots Guards went out to meet him they talked for a time and then returned to there trenches now sooner had the German officer returned when there voices shouted out a happy Christmas to all you English So we all wished them the same … about 8am we saw them get out of there trench and asked us not to Fire as they wanted to keep the Peace that day as it was Xmas so we did not Fire that day at 9.a.m. they came half way and we went out to meet them. And the first thing they asked us was when are you going to give in you are beat. So we asked them who had told them all this and they pointed to a paper they had in there hand. And they told me point blank that they had troop Reviewing in Hyde Park and also troops in Calais. Well me and my chum could not help laughing at them. And they looked at us and could not make it out. So I said to them, well I must admit that you have got troops in London But they are Prisoners of War they would not take that so my Chum gave them the New of the World and they thanked us and gave us a segar to smoke. At 11.15a.m. Orders came along that we were to fall in as the officer wished to speak to us so we all returned and found out that we were to Bury our Comrades that fell in the Charge on the 18th of Dec. so we all started digging and Burying them side by side and made them a Cross out of the wood of a Biscuit Box and layed them to rest on Xmas day when we had finished we all kneled and offered up a Pray to God above for our Comrades who fell in Honour."

Captain Loder found the Westphalian soldiers more communicative than the officers. "They appeared generally tired of fighting and wanted to get back to their various employments. Some lived in England. One man told me he had been seven years in England and was married last March. Another said he had a girl who lived in Suffolk and said that it had been impossible to communicate with her through Germany since war began. Their general opinion of the war was as follows. France is on her last legs and will soon have to give up. Russia has had a tremendous defeat in Poland and will soon be ready to make terms of peace. England is the nut which still has to be cracked, but with France and Russia out of the way She, Germany, would be too powerful. The war they thought might be over by the end of January." He went on "This shows what lies are circulated amongst the German troops and the hatred which exists between Germany and England." When Lieutenant Swinton got to Battalion Headquarters "It happened that the Brigadier, Pa Hayworth, was there, but after hearing my story, and saying it was all very irregular, he went away. George Paynter immediately turned to me and announced that he was also going to meet the Hun. So back we went, an unaccustomed journey, over the top of the fields in broad daylight and out into No Man's Land. This time we found a couple of very scruffy officers, and George arranged with them that there should be an official truce until 4.30 that evening so that we could bury the dead from our unfortunate affair of the 18th. I was detailed for that duty – a very unpleasant one for Christmas Day." Sir Edward Hulse wrote of Captain Paynter's meeting the local German commander and giving him a scarf. That evening a German orderly came to the halfway line bringing a reciprocal present of a pair of warm, woolly gloves.

Sir Edward Hulse, with G Company immediately to the north of the road, may not have personally seen everything that happened south of it and so have relied also on what he heard from Captains Paynter and Loder. He wrote to his mother as soon as he was back in billets on the 28th the most detailed account of the truce from anywhere along the whole British front. From where he was close to the road "At 8.30am I was looking out, and saw four Germans leave their trenches and come towards us; I told two of my men to go and meet them, unarmed (as the Germans were unarmed) and to see that they did not pass the halfway line. We were 350-400 yards apart at this point. My fellows were not very keen, not knowing what was up, so I went out alone, and met Barry, one of our ensigns, also coming out from another part of the line. By the time we got to them, they were ¾ of the way over, and much too near our barbed wire, so I moved them back. They were three private soldiers and a stretcher bearer. And their spokesman started off by saying that he thought it only right to come over and wish us a happy Christmas, and trusted us implicitly to keep the truce. He came from Suffolk, where he had left his best girl and a 3½ hp motorbike." Sir Edward Hulse, wearing an old stocking cap and a soldier's greatcoat, was taken by them for a corporal, which suited his purposes of obtaining information. "The little fellow I was talking to, was an undersized, pasty faced student type, talked four languages well, and had a business in England, so I mistrusted him at once. I asked them what orders they had from their officers as to coming over to us, and they said none; that they had just come over out of goodwill. They protested that they had no feeling of enmity at all towards us, but that everything lay with the authorities, and that being soldiers they had to obey. I believed that they were speaking the truth when they said this, and that they never wished to fire a shot again." There followed a discussion, heated but good natured, for half an hour, on various war matters, newspaper propaganda, atrocities and dum-dum bullets. He accompanied them back to their barbed wire and then went to Battalion Headquarters to report. The other officer, 2nd Lieutenant Ronald "Ronnie" Barry, a Harrovian, had served for a short time before the War and rejoined from the Reserve. He was trained as a machine gun officer and was now temporarily commanding F Company. After being wounded at Neuve Chapelle three months later his subsequent service in the BEF in 1916-17 was with the 3rd Guards Brigade Machine Gun Company.

When he got back at ten o'clock Sir Edward Hulse found the trenches unoccupied. "I heard strains of "Tipperary" floating down the breeze, swiftly followed by a burst of "Deutschland Über Alles", and…I saw, to my amazement, not only a crowd of about 150 British and Germans at the halfway house which I had appointed opposite my lines, but six or seven such crowds, all the way down our lines, extending towards the 8th Division on our right." By this time, wearing his own cap and rank badges, he went to find German officers in the crowd. Two appeared with whom he spoke through an interpreter. This encounter was somewhat distant but it was agreed "that strict orders must be maintained as to meeting halfway, and everyone unarmed; and we both agreed not to fire until the other did, thereby creating a complete deadlock and armistice (if strictly observed)."

"Meanwhile Scots and Huns were fraternizing in the most genuine possible manner. Every sort of souvenir was exchanged, addresses given and received, photos of families shown, etc…A German NCO with the Iron Cross, – gained, he told me, for conspicuous skill in sniping, started his fellows off on some marching tune. When they had done I set the note for "The Boys of Bonnie Scotland, where the heather and bluebells grow", and so we went on, singing everything from "Good King Wenceslaus" down to the ordinary Tommies' song, and ended up with "Auld Lang Syne", which we all, English, Scots, Irish, Prussian, Wurtembergers, etc., joined in. It was absolutely astounding, and if I had seen it on a cinematograph film I should have sworn that it was faked!" He went round talking to a lot of the Germans, many very young, but looking good, strong and pretty healthy. He wondered whether only the best of them had been allowed to leave their trenches. He identified *Jäger* from the *11th Battalion*, and the *158th*, *37th* and *15th Regiments*. He went on to describe how the weather had improved with the sharp frost and that "it was a perfect day, everything white, and the silence seemed extraordinary, after the usual din. From all sides birds seemed to arrive, and we hardly ever see a bird generally. Later in the day I fed about 50 sparrows outside my dug-out, which shows how complete the silence and quiet was."

Most unfortunately Sergeant Pilkington was on leave in England for several weeks and only returned on 2 January. Lieutenant Swinton made no further comment about the burial but afterwards, by which time fraternization was in full swing, he started taking photographs with his box camera. Most were of the Scots Guards in or out of their trenches during the day, but he took one of a large party of Germans. Sir Edward Hulse wrote "I hope to be able to send you shortly some small photos of self, Pip, servants, etc., in billets, and also, if they come out, a photo of us and the Germans together on Christmas day. Lieutenant Swinton took them with a little pocket camera, and the "padre" is taking the films home to get them developed. If the latter negative comes out, it will be a unique incident well recorded." This photograph did come out, indistinctly. He continued that "It was now 11.30am and at this moment George Paynter arrived on the scene with a hearty "Well, my lads, a Merry Christmas to you! This is damned comic, isn't it?" They were much amused with him, especially when he said it was damned cold; their spokesman immediately said, "Oh you feel the cold, do you? Of course, we don't, as we are used to harder winters in Germany than you are in England." George told them that he thought it only right that we should show that we could desist from hostilities on a day which was so important in both countries." He then handed over a bottle of non-ration rum which the Germans quickly polished off on the spot.

They went back to their trenches to eat. In his dug-out Sir Edward Hulse, the company cook, his servant and a gunner observation officer had steak, mashed potatoes, plum pudding, ginger biscuits, chocolate (hot), whisky and water and finished off drinking the health of everyone at home in Russian Kümmel. In the afternoon when British and Germans met up again he was told by one German "that he was longing to get back to London: I assured him that "So was I." He said that he was sick of the war, and I told him that when the truce was ended, any of his friends would be welcome in our trenches, and would be well received, fed, and given a free passage to the Isle of Man!" He asked a number of German soldiers how long they thought the War would last and most reckoned about three weeks. Only one, whom he identified as wiser and more thoughtful, said it could go on for a long time yet. At half past four in spite of British attempts to indicate that the truce was over the Germans would have none of it, insisting that they were not going to fire. Because the orders from Captain Paynter were not to fire unless the Germans did, they prepared for a quiet night. Sir Edward Hulse described how both sides had taken the opportunity of bringing up piles of wood, straw and other materials to improve dug-outs and make everything more secure and comfortable. Meanwhile he went on "Directly it was dark, I got the whole of my Coy on to improving and remaking our barbed wire entanglements, all along my front, and had my scouts out in front, and we finished off a real good obstacle unmolested."

An immediate source of new officers in the BEF was the Territorial Force and, in particular, those units with high calibre junior ranks, typically those who had joined before the War what was primarily a kind of good club, such as the Artists' Rifles. Four came to the 2nd Gordons, one of whom was 2nd Lieutenant Dougan Chater. They arrived as they stood, so that until Gordons uniforms could be found they wore their existing other ranks caps, jackets and trousers. Because of the hard weather he could start a letter to his mother from the trenches on the afternoon of Christmas Day, finished two days later in billets. "I am writing this in the trenches in my "dug-out" – with a wood fire going and plenty of straw it is rather cosy although it is freezing hard and real Christmas weather. I think I have seen one of the most extraordinary sights today that anyone has ever seen. Almost at 10 o'clock this morning I was peeping over the parapet when I saw a German, waving his arms, and presently two of them got out of their trenches and came towards us. We were just going to fire on them when we saw they had no rifles so one of our men went out to meet them and in about two minutes the ground between the two lines of trenches was swarming with men and officers of both sides, shaking hands and wishing each other a happy Christmas…Some of our officers were taking [photos of] groups of English and German soldiers…we have had our pipes playing all day and everyone has been wandering about in the open unmolested but not of course as far as the enemy's lines. The truce will probably go on until someone is foolish enough to let off his rifle – we nearly messed it up this afternoon, by one of our fellows letting off his rifle skywards by mistake but they did not seem to notice it so it did not matter." At the end of this letter he wrote "We are, at any rate having another truce on New Year's Day as the Germans want to see how the photos come out! Yesterday was lovely in the morning and I went for several quite long walks about the lines – It is difficult to realise what that means but of course in the ordinary way there is not a sign of life above ground and everyone who puts his head up gets shot at." Lieutenant Chater was the only one of these four Artists Rifles to survive the War and that at the price of having the right side of his lower jaw shattered by a bullet at Neuve Chapelle, the bullet hitting him from below when he must have been looking up. He was also hit twice in the left arm at the same time, though not badly. For several months afterwards he was in hospital at Wimereux while the American dental specialist Charles Valadier reconstructed his jaw, recognised at the time as a major pioneering achievement. Afterwards he remained in the Army but did not serve overseas again.

Colonel Fisher Rowe told his wife that the Germans had wanted to play football with the Scots Guards "but the Kiddies couldn't produce the ball." There was no other contemporary mention of football by anyone in the 20th Brigade trenches on Christmas Day. The unknown Borders private concluded his entry "We were having tea when the Germans started singing God save the King in as good English as they could. And then three Cheers went up from our trenches. So we all had a good singsong that night in our trenches. But we did not forget to have our look out as I do not think we became friends. And it was hear that we heard the fate of Capt. Askew a German officer gave one of the Officers of our Regt. the Cap and Collar Badges of our late officer and told us that they had buryed him behind there Firing Line and put these words on his Grave

> Hear lies a Brave British Officer
> Capt Askew"

The Germans were more likely to have been singing *"Heil Dir Im Siegerkranz"*, a Prussian anthem with the same tune as the British National Anthem, which British soldiers frequently thought that they were singing as a compliment. The diary petered out and then ceased in March 1915, its author perhaps a casualty of Neuve Chapelle, but whoever, British or German, had it six months later at Loos dropped it, because Captain Nowell Sievers of the 9th Essex Regiment, 12th (Eastern) Division, New Army, found it in a captured trench west of Hulluch. The 7th Division had been over the same ground earlier, having attacked there on 25 September.

Also on Christmas Day in the West Highlands a special train arrived at Fort William Station. A detachment of the Argyll and Sutherland Highlanders was drawn up on the platform. After unloading the coffin a bearer party carried Lieutenant Ottley's coffin, draped in the Union Jack and with his Scots Guards forage cap and belt on top, from the train and up the main street to St Andrew's Episcopal Church, led by a pipe band playing "The Flowers of the Forest". After the funeral service the bearer party carried the coffin out to the churchyard and once they had lowered it into the grave the detachment fired volleys, between each of which a piper played "Lochaber No More". Lieutenant Ottley's bravery was brought to Sir John French's attention and he was mentioned in despatches in the Commander-in-Chief's Despatch of 14 January 1915. A month later came the award of the DSO to then and to this day its youngest ever winner. He had been an only child. His father Rear Admiral Sir Charles Ottley was Secretary of the Committee of Imperial Defence till 1912, when Colonel Maurice Hankey of the Royal Marines succeeded him. His mother Kathleen Ottley had been a Stewart before her marriage. The family spent much of their time at Coruanan Lodge, on Loch Linnhe south of Fort William. By 1 January the Ottleys were back in London and Kathleen Ottley wrote again to Elsie Swinton expressing how "to feel our friends are with us in heart & sympathy does help, as much as anything can in this awful desolation…It seems so hard to know it is all for the best, & very very hard to say "Thy Will be done". I want too to thank you so much for the lovely flowers you sent, I hope someday you will see where we have laid him, he loved the mountains so, & they are all round him like the Everlasting Arms."

In the trenches Lieutenant Swinton still did not know about his friend's death and asked his family for news as he went on with his letter that evening. He told them that the hard frost had been the best Christmas present that they could have had and that "Amongst other presents every officer and man got a plum pudding from Selfridges, whether provided by that ancient institution or by the regiment, I don't know." He sent back with his letter the King's Christmas card. He also sent "a photo given me by a German as a souvenir; he is the 3rd from the left as you look at the photo in the top row. He didn't talk English but we got on well in French." On 20 December the Reverend Wilfred Abbot had arrived as Church of England Padre at Brigade Headquarters, and was based usually with the field ambulance at Sailly. He acquired from an unnamed Scots Guards sergeant a meerschaum pipe given by a German soldier during the truce. Lieutenant Warner had little to say about the truce, but recorded being out till three in the morning on Boxing Day "repairing wire in front." That day and the next small parties of Scots Guardsmen and Germans met at the halfway line and there was no rifle fire. Major Cator recorded "Most of the men reported missing on the night of 18-19 are now accounted for. The Germans say they only took ten prisoners. The remainder were all killed or died of wounds." He heard that the Germans stated that almost all their casualties were caused by bayonets which "is accounted for by the fact that our men's rifles were so clogged up with mud they were unable to fire with them. Means for avoiding this evil has now been adopted, each man is now being served out with a loose rough canvas bag to slip over the muzzle of his rifle & which is able to be pulled off instantly if required for use." He added that no harm was going to be done if the rifle had to be fired with the cover on. He went on to say that large parties of men had been busy cleaning out the Rivière des Layes in the hope of improving the flow and draining some of the water from the trenches. The next innovation was the first British version of chevaux de frise, much quicker than barbed wire to unroll and set up in front of trenches, so cutting down wiring parties' time in No Man's Land and reducing casualties. Once in position men still had to crawl out in order to peg them as firmly as possible in the ground.

During the afternoon of Boxing Day Lieutenant Swinton went on with his Christmas letter. "The truce continues; far to the right they have been gunning all day and I did hear a little rifle fire, but here all remains quiet. A slow thaw has also set in which is a nuisance, but we go back to billets tomorrow night." That evening, because of inaccurate information of an imminent night attack given by a German deserter to the 8th Division, the British guns plastered a place in the German rear where the deserter said two new regiments had just arrived to take part in that attack, while the British infantry stood to abortively in the front line. On the 27th Sir Edward

Hulse went out to meet the Germans and discussed this possible attack with them. They denied all knowledge of such a thing. They had done nothing to stop the British putting up more wire, unlikely if an attack was planned. He wrote that "here were these fellows still protesting that there was a truce, although I told them that it had ceased the evening before. So I kept to same arrangement, namely, that my NCO and two men should meet them halfway, and strict orders were given that no other man was to leave the lines." He felt that the Westphalians were "pretty sick of fighting, and found the truce a very welcome respite, and were therefore quite ready to prolong it; in fact made us prolong it by continually coming to talk." It thawed on the 27th and many trenches fell in and had to be repaired. Major Cator noted "The Germans tried to come over and enjoy another day's so called "armistice" but were informed they must keep in their trenches. They seemed to be quite indignant & said they wouldn't fire if we didn't, but if we had orders to fire to signal to them with three volleys first fired into the air." Lieutenant Warner noted that "4 of our men went to meet Germans in afternoon against orders and went into trenches with them. These men did not return." Once they were there they would have got useful information. The scout, Private Murker, was one of them. Another was Private Charles Oxley, a former Scots Guardsman outside his reserve commitment. In March 1910 he married Minnie Cook at Bermondsey, on the south bank of the Thames, their son being born three years later. In September 1914 he reenlisted at Westminster and was in the reinforcements who arrived at Méteren. It was there that Lance Corporal John McLean, with the butterfly tattoo on his wrist, was reduced to the ranks, reason unspecified. He was the third and sent a post card from Wittenberg to Margaret McLean to tell her, the first confirmed news of him. The fourth, a serving soldier, was Private William Kerr, from Dalswinton, near Dumfries, formerly a blacksmith, recorded as having been wounded in both legs and taken prisoner on 27 December, when there may have been a struggle as he realised what was happening. Private Kerr was the second of the three men who enlisted on 26 October 1913 at Hamilton. These four survived the War as prisoners.

Later on in the evening of the 27th the Grenadiers relieved the Scots Guards, coming over the open ground without having to use the communication trenches. Colonel Fisher Rowe told his wife that his right hand company were having to be careful because of firing from the south where the 8th Division had had no truce. Meanwhile the Westphalians opposite showed no wish to resume hostilities. He was wary nonetheless, writing on the 30th "it was a lovely morning very nice being able to walk on top, though I own that all the time I keep watching the Bosch trenches to see that some of them are out as I don't really quite trust them not to take the opportunity of a nice easy target. It makes a country walk distinctly exciting to feel that the other chap may start on you from about 200 yards at any moment." The following day there was no doubt about sniping from further south.

While Lieutenant Warner was involved in the formal inquiry into the four missing men he separately "Ascertained privately that one went to get Whisky." Sir Edward Hulse and Lieutenant Swinton were in billets together at a farm run by a farmer's wife and her niece, assisted by her two elder boys aged fourteen and fifteen. There were six more children. The farmer was in the French Army. Sir Edward Hulse wrote exultantly on the 28th that "I got six eggs from them this morning (at 6 sous each) – a rare luxury – and scrambled them extremely well myself. Milk, butter and eggs are not often to be had together, and we fairly gloated over the result!" On the 29th Lance Corporal John Kelliher, a reservist, got badly drunk. A court martial on New Year's Eve reduced him to the ranks and awarded him fifty six days FP No 1.

He was a clerk in Liverpool when he enlisted in 1904, served eight years and left the Colours at a recorded height of six foot two inches, one and three quarter inches taller than when he joined up. His mother Ellen lived in Rosborough, County Kerry, and his sister Julia was working nearby in an hotel at Parkansilla.

New Year's Eve

The Scots Guards came back into the line during the early evening on New Year's Eve, there having been heavy rain in the meantime. Sir Edward Hulse remarked that "we are rapidly becoming skilled drainage experts, and nearly all the work in the trenches now consists of draining, pumping, diverting channels, etc., and in one of our communication trenches which is deeper than most, 11ft 6in, the water has now attained the astounding and almost comic depth of nine feet!" As both sides were working at channelling water in each other's direction there came to be some formidable water obstacles in No Man's Land, quite apart from everything else. Still the lull continued with the *158th Regiment* not firing throughout the next four days. They could be clearly seen equally busy pumping water. Major Cator described the only practicable alternative "It has now become impossible to dig down any trench below a depth of two feet, water forming in the bottom at once if a greater depth is dug. In the very bad spots it has been necessary to retrench & build breastworks behind those parts of the trenches which have been made untenable by the floods."

On 1 January Lieutenant Spence Sanders of the 1/6th Gordons recorded that "we came in last night fairly easily. Of all extraordinary warfare this takes the biscuit. There was no firing until midnight or thereabouts when a few volleys were fired into the air to welcome in the New Year. We got a crowd together and sang "Auld Lang Syne" and "God Save the King". The Germans sang some songs and played "God Save The King" on the mouth organ and everyone shouted "Happy New Year". Then the Pipe Major came along and played; he had come down specially. We fortunately were able to give him a drop of rum. This morning the men are wandering about all over getting brown bread and other things from the Germans. It doesn't look as if they are short of food. Our artillery is going to start shooting soon. I believe the Germans have been warned." A little further along was Sir Edward Hulse. "We had another comic episode on New Year's Eve. Punctually at 11pm (German war time is an hour ahead of our's), the whole of the German trenches were illuminated at intervals of 15 or 20 yards. They all shouted, and then began singing their New Year and Patriotic songs. We watched them quietly, and they lit a few bonfires as well." Then "Just as they were settling down for the night again, our own midnight hour approached, and I had warned my company as to how I intended to receive the New Year. At midnight I fired a star shell, which was the signal, and the whole line fired a volley and then another star shell and three hearty cheers, yet another star shell, and the whole of us, led by myself and the Platoon Sergeant nearest to me, broke into "Auld Lang Syne". We sang it three times, and were materially assisted by the enemy, who also joined in. At the end, three more hearty cheers and then dead silence. It was extraordinary hearing "Auld Lang Syne" gradually dying away right down the line into the 8th Division. I fired three more star shells in different directions, to see that none of the enemy were crawling about near our wire, and finding all clear, I retired to my leaking bug hutch." He was about to be disturbed by an unexpected visitor. "I had warned all sentries as usual, and had succeeded in getting about ¾ of an hour's sleep, when the Platoon Sergeant of No 12…burst in and informed me, most laconically, "German to see you,

Sir!" I struck a light, tumbled out, and heard a voice outside saying, "Offizier? Hauptmann?" and found a little fellow, fairly clean and fairly superior to the average German private, being well hustled and pushed between two fixed bayonets. The minute he saw me he came up, saluted, covered in smiles, and awfully pleased with himself, said, "Nach London, Nach London?" I replied, "No, my lad, Nach the Isle of Man," on which the escort burst into loud guffaws! He could not talk a word of English, except "Happy New Year", which he kept on wishing us. He was a genuine deserter, and had come in absolutely unarmed. I went rapidly through his pockets, which were bulging on every side, and found no papers or anything of any value, but an incredible amount of food and comestibles. He had come in fully provided for the journey, and was annoyingly pleased with himself." He had the prisoner marched up to Battalion Headquarters and rang Captain Paynter to tell him he was sending him a New Year's present. The receipt for the prisoner read:

O.C. 2/Battalion Scots Guards. 7th Army Corps. 1.1. 15.

Herewith a German, *158th Regiment*, who came right into our trenches on my right, No. 12 Platoon. The Sentry saw him close to our barbed wire, and covered him and challenged. He continued to walk straight in, unarmed, and jumped into our trenches. Sergeant Macdonald (Platoon Sergt., No. 12 Platoon) brought him to me under escort.

E.HULSE, Lt
1.10a.m. Com. G. Coy.

I have taken nothing off the prisoner; his papers and effects are exactly as when he entered the trenches.

Received from Sir E. Hulse one prisoner at 1.32 a.m.
JAS. MONCUR, Serg.-Major,
2/Bn. Scots Guards.

Private William McDonald, the son of David and Margaret McDonald of Leith, was a clerk until he enlisted in March 1911. With the Battalion from the start, he was first promoted Lance Corporal on 12 October. A few days after they arrived at the Rouges Bancs trenches he was made Acting Sergeant and this could have been him. During leave in London at the end of April 1915 he married Clara Smith in Lambeth. At the end of May their son was born and she died the next day. Sergeant McDonald had a scalp wound on 16 May at Festubert and was sent back home to recover, but not till early June. He remained there for nearly three years during which in April 1917 he married Elsie Hall, who was living in Mossside, Manchester. He returned to the BEF in the large draft on 30 March 1918. Elsie McDonald had a son on 2 May that year, who lived for less than a fortnight. Sergeant McDonald was finally posted home in October. Two men were killed and two wounded on New Year's Day and one wounded the following day. One of those who died was Private William Everitt, a reservist, who had only left the previous January after serving seven years, and whose wife Annie, whom he married in 1908, was living in Lavender Hill, London, with their three small children. Annie Everitt was sent her husband's broken rosary and an education certificate. The other was Private Patrick Lowe, whose wife Jane, to whom he had been married for ten years, lived in St Rollox, Glasgow. He was a reenlisted Scots Guardsman and a moulder when he volunteered in September in Glasgow. He had arrived at Méteren. When he died he was the father of seven children, the youngest of whom, a daughter, was born on 9 November. He had several tattoos including a rose and KATE on the back of his right wrist.

Renewal of hostilities

Stern orders came down from above that hostilities were to resume while the Grenadiers were doing the next four day tour. Major Cator wrote to his sister Victoria Fellowes on 4 January "We are surely and slowly being flooded out, it never stops raining and every day the water is a little worse. The Germans are getting it too and we can hear them baling out all night. They are not at all a bad lot opposite us, this morning their men warned our's, their guns were going to fire, so as to let them get into their dug-outs, the latter have all got eighteen inches of water in them. I'm afraid the war is going to be a long job, it's a case of stalemate, neither side seems to make much headway, in spite of those rotten papers talking about the Allies progress, which is invariably lies." He told her of the death of Captain Stracey of the 1st Battalion that they had just heard about, who would be very much missed. Having been out of the trenches for four days the 2nd Scots Guards returned on the evening of the 8th when Lieutenant Warner found "Most of them full of water, including dug-outs. Grenadier Guards very fed up." He and his men worked till midnight putting out wire over flooded trenches. On the 9th they worked on, rain spoiling most of what they did. Around dawn next day he observed that General Heyworth "came round the water."

They had three clear days in billets from 13 January. Lieutenant Warner wrote of a concert that evening as "a great success and much enjoyed by the men. Baths in morning." Next day he thought Right Flank "in good form and smart on parade." On the 15th there was a nine mile route march and in the evening a boxing match, which both Sir William Pulteney and General Capper came to watch, the latter staying to dinner with the officers afterwards. On 14 January Lance Sergeant Harry Issott, with Lieutenant Saumarez at Kruiseecke and missing since 1 November at Ypres, reported back. His explanation was not recorded, but he was very lucky. A court martial found him guilty of Absence without Leave, sentencing him to forty two days FP No 1 and reduction to the ranks. There he stayed, being wounded two months later in the wrist at Neuve Chapelle, hit again in September 1916, wound unspecified, at Ginchy on the Somme and the third time on 31 July 1917, slightly, in the left arm, during the Battle of Pilckem Ridge, the opening of the Third Battle of Ypres. After that he was medically downgraded, classified PB (War Worn), "PB" standing for Permanent Base, sent to England permanently and discharged in May 1919.

Lieutenant Sitwell wrote to Elsie Swinton, his cousin, from the 1st Grenadiers on 15 January, giving his address as "This part of Armageddon". His letter was quite short. "As for myself, 'the rain, it raineth every day', and the unjust in mine own shape, is getting very wet, tired, and mudstained. I always expect to find that this part of France has been amalgamated with the North Sea (or German Ocean). Things have been quiet for the past week. This war is too big for me, especially if you visualize the whole thing. However my senses are now blunted, and in the roar of the cannon I hear music for Karsavina and in the desolate mud of this arid and unattractive country, can trace designs for new and wonderful brocades!! The scenery round here, or rather want of scenery, reminds one shockingly of Lincolnshire, a place I detest. Father has now left the Cellar at Wood End, and is in London, I believe." Tamara Karsavina was at the height of her career as a Russian ballerina, Wood End the Sitwells' house at Scarborough.

Lieutenant Swinton described starting to build breastworks, taking advantage of the continuing lull since Christmas to make what were quickly nicknamed "grouse butts". There was no firing of rifles again until 10 January. These "forts", as they were also called, initially consisted of crescent-shaped walls of earth held in place with sandbags and any available timber or metal or mesh and in time became a series of defensive posts. A great deal of building material was brought up from the rear in the open. Where it was impossible to do better, canvas screens were put up to conceal movement between forts. Gradually continuous breastworks were constructed. They needed constant attention to keep them bulletproof. As Lieutenant Swinton pointed out, loose earth would stop a bullet but, as it became compressed, it was less resistant and so more soil was needed. Major Cator described the posts as manned by a NCO and ten men "at intervals of about every fifty yards, the posts so held being dammed up at both ends & the water pumped out between the dams. Between these posts retrenchments are dug outside & just in rear of the trench." The basic breastwork constructed on the back of the former trenches consisted of the parados built up with sandbags to a height of three and a half feet and then dug down [retrenched] for a foot behind. Further back he described redoubts being made which were to be self contained, so being able to hold out if resupply was interrupted, and manned by between twenty and forty men. Existing buildings were also being fortified. Once there were lines of breastworks these redoubts and fortified buildings came to be known as "forts" or "keeps". January was generally fairly quiet, though Sir Edward Hulse watched a British trench mortar firing for the first time and making quite a mess of the German trenches. The German artillery retaliated and, while he remarked that their shells were less likely to be duds than previously, Major Cator wrote of their "using a new shell in their guns painted red & made of thick roughly smelted iron, very few of which burst." The Germans also tried night attacks on two consecutive nights, making no progress. During the last few days of January there were six days without rain, but with a keen frost and a little snow at night instead. Morale improved a lot and Sir Edward Hulse saw the men as they marched out of the trenches on the 27th "with mouth organs, penny whistles, etc., playing "Highland Laddie", as if they had only just landed in the country."

Major Cator wrote to his niece Anne Hawley on the 25th "I had two dogs here but have had to destroy one as he got eczema so badly, the other I only see at intervals as he is gun-shy and disappears whenever the guns fire." He told her about his horses, Cock Robin and Hopalong. The former "is always cross and Hopalong always nervous, he is very gun-shy. Cock Robin generally has a bite out of someone about once a week, but he doesn't mind the firing." Of his Belgian horse wounded at Ypres he had heard no more. He thought that there were different Germans opposite because they now never replied to shouts from the British. "We always let our papers blow across to them when the wind is right, as they then get some truth." He had heard that the French had not long before "shouted across "Does your Kaiser ever come and see you in the trenches?" "No" answered the Germans. "Oh but we are much luckier" said the Frenchmen "our President is coming tomorrow at 2.30." At 2.30 they mounted a top hat on a stick and walked it along the trench just showing above the parapet much to the Germans' delight, who riddled it with bullets thinking it was Poincaré, the French all running along shouting "Vive la France" "Vive Poincaré."" He wrote at much the same time to Anne's mother Georgina Baker Baker, another of his sisters, thanking her for a cake "which was an absolute topper, also the brace of pheasants…I hear the French say we are not doing enough and are grousing at us being inactive. They should come here themselves, devil take them for giving us this bit to hold in the winter…I tried to walk after a covey of partridges yesterday, and simply bogged on a plough. To attack over this ground is a physical impossibility. The men are all pretty fit, the wet doesn't hurt them half as much as frostbite." He told Victoria Fellowes in a letter in February that he had "found an old shot gun which I carry about when I go down to the trenches, and get a hare or a partridge occasionally, once a sight and lift at two very old cock pheasants. The best ground is nearest the trenches, the guns make too much noise for them back here. All the game is fearfully wild, the partridges are getting a little tamer as they are beginning to pair…A cat recently joined the establishment, but as it was of insanitary habits and thieved a box of sardines it got the sack." When it then returned through a window in the middle of the previous night and relieved itself on another officer's bed a piece of meat laced with strychnine was going to be waiting if it reappeared. The other officer was very angry.

Sir Edward Hulse and his Company Sergeant Major worked together as a sniper team, accounting in four days to 27 January for three of the enemy for certain, with two others probable. On 6 February he described one of their further operations in detail. "During the last few days in the trenches I have had grand sport with a telescopic sight on my rifle. It is giving the enemy a bit of their own, as a telescopic sight is a "Zeiss", made in Germany. We know that they use them a lot, and lately I have been worried with a swine who makes infernally good practice; he hits anything one puts up, and missed my CSM by not more than 2 inches. We put up several marks for him in the place that we generally snipe from, and which he had driven us out of, and watched carefully, and noticed that the bullets were coming at an angle; this meant that his position was right away to the flank, and that he was not opposite us, where we were looking for him. We found a convenient little spot which faced in the required direction, and was shielded from the front, and at once spotted him and two other swine, right away to the right at about 550 yards (the trenches are not more than about 350 yards apart at opposite points). My CSM and I had stocking caps on so as to draw less attention, and to assimilate easily with the background of the trench behind us. We had a man at the old place about 20 yards to our right, and we knew that the German had spotted us there, so we made the man hold up a big turnip, with a stocking cap on it, just above the loophole. I must explain that these rifles with telescopic sights cannot be used through loopholes, owing to the size of the fitting and rifle together. Well, sure enough, bullet after bullet plastered into and around the old turnip, and the German was so keen that he leaned well on to the parapet to make better practice. I could see his two pals with their caps just showing, but he showed half way down his chest, and I could make out his telescopic sight clearly on his rifle. The moment had arrived, and, with my CSM watching carefully with my glasses, I pulled! With these telescopic sights you can see everything, every little detail, and it was an extremely pretty moment for me – his arms went up and his head went back, his cap fell off and he disappeared backwards, heavily into the trench. He had let go his rifle, and one of his pals leant over quickly to get it, and I put another shot in, and just missed by the left. I was really pleased at getting the brute, as he had given us endless trouble."

Private John Peat was an early August 1914 volunteer in Glasgow, where he was an electrical engineer and where his father William Peat lived in Tollcross. He had arrived just after Ypres.

On 25 January he was hit in the right side of his face and sent home. In November a medical report stated that he had a "large gaping wound of right side of face extending into neck, lower jaw shattered 2½ inches of the right lower horizontal Taurus missing. Wound very septic the whole of the lower lip had been shot away & the tongue was hanging out of the gaping wound left." Plastic surgery created a new lower lip and his wounds healed, leaving "much scarring of the face. Lower lip much shortened, the lower jaw has united but contains no teeth. He is only able to take fluids & minced food – owing to the small size of the mouth & condition of the jaws it is impossible to fit artificial teeth." He was discharged on Christmas Eve 1915.

On 2 February Sir Edward Hulse wrote to his uncle Lord Burnham. He mentioned the improvised company bands with "Heilan' Laddie", the regimental quick march, being "not nearly as bad as you would think on a mouth organ." The shortage of officers was dire. "We are 4 Officers besides George and Giles Loder, and we are likely to remain so, as far as we can see. Needless to say we were not best pleased to hear that Viscount Clive, who went home with bad feet, is trying to get on General Haldane's staff;...or that Lisburne who went sick a short time before Xmas, has applied for a transfer to the "Blues". But the latter has been sat upon." He told his uncle that even they and the Grenadiers had been surprised by the order to all battalions in the 20th Brigade to do drill when in billets but they soon recognised its value. Then "Two officers from the 2nd Bn Rifle Brigade came over to see me the other day, and were absolutely astounded at the way our men, sentries, etc. saluted them, and when I told them we had Battalion drill, as on the Square, every morning in billets, they collapsed." Both Lord Clive and the Earl of Lisburne transferred to the Welsh Guards, who were raised at the end of the month. The former was badly wounded in September 1916 on the Somme and died later, the latter survived the War.

By the middle of February a lot of thought and practice was going into schemes for attacking enemy trenches by day and night. For one Brigade Headquarters exercise the 1/6th Gordons bombers, on reaching the barbed wire at the objective, were to throw live grenades into the trenches beyond. A grenade went off before the bomber threw it, badly injuring him and wounding another. The exercise then proceeded without grenades. Sir Edward Hulse observed "I have not yet heard what lessons the Brigadier learnt from our efforts, but I have formed several very well defined views on bombs and the shortage of wirecutters." In an undated letter to his mother Major Cator wrote that "The Government won't send out enough so we have to make them out of empty jam pots, beastly things and very dangerous. They are filled with guncotton and a fuse sticking out of the top, to explode them the fuse is lit by giving it a half turn and a sharp pull. Yesterday we had a nasty accident, one of the Gordon Highlanders was practising the attack with three jam pots in his haversack which suddenly went off and blew his leg off, at least it was only hanging by a small piece of flesh, I'm afraid the poor chap will die."

Immediately north of the Sailly-Fromelles road the British front line trench bulged out into a salient, still less than a hundred yards from the enemy in one place. A breastwork was built behind the front line trench and another trench dug straight south from La Cordonnerie Farm, now being formed into a strong point, almost to the road. Fresh wire was put out every night and the five defensive posts further back were built up further and enhanced with barbed wire. Major Cator described this process carried out by "two hundred and forty men...sent out nightly in four hour reliefs to effect all this work." These would have been working parties sent up from billets, but those in the line had to work hard too.

It was not possible for the Grenadiers and Scots Guards to have their tidy arrangement all the time. On the night of 17 February Right Flank had to take over trenches to the left from the Borders, which, since the reorganisation in early December, had been manned by other battalions. After an early afternoon briefing Captain Warner, promoted on 28 January, went to the Grenadiers Battalion Headquarters, changed into thigh waders belonging to Major Paynter, as he now was, and set off to look, for which he "waded through deep water to various posts, finding everything very bad, especially on left. No dug-outs for men and some of the posts knee deep in mud and water." When he got back he had to send his men straight off into it and then took Major Paynter round in the dark. He spent most of the night putting out wire. Next morning Major Paynter came round again and told him "to abandon the 2 worst posts and build forts. Our dug-out is a muddy cave which has to be bailed out every 2 hours and smells abominable." He was up most of that night laying out and building the forts and visiting everybody else in their posts and hard at work again through the next night during which he "had a working party from Borders and got a lot done by continually chasing them." By the end of the following night he was very pleased at the progress on seven forts. Two had had to be constructed from scratch, one of which was almost finished, the other well on, while a machine gun emplacement was complete. He mentioned that one man was killed on the 18th and another next day. Private William Southgate, a very young Liverpudlian printer, the son of Charles and Jane Southgate who lived at The Brook, was one of the very last men to enlist before the War. On 3 December he had been tried by court martial and convicted of insubordination and awarded forty two days FP No 1. The sentence was quashed. He was hit in the head on 18 February and died six days later in Merville. Private James Campbell, one of the nine children of John and Catherine Campbell of Kilchrenan, Argyll, was killed on the 19th. He had been a barman and waiter, probably in Edinburgh, because he enlisted there in June 1913, described as "Eager to join the Scots Guards". Apparently under age before September 1914, he was sent out in reinforcements and joined after Ypres. Some photographs and a pendant reached his family.

Sir Edward Hulse and G Company were next to Right Flank, who, he wrote, had found that "there was absolutely no cover at all, and the abovementioned Regiments must have simply sat still for two months and watched their parapets and defences fall in without doing one stitch of work." He undertook to help with the wiring in front of Right Flank and "kept my part of the bargain, – during the last four nights I have put up entanglements, including 43 coils of wire (¼ mile long each) and 870 posts and pegs! One night the enemy sent up a star shell, which dropped plum in the middle of my wiring party. The minute a star shell is sent up by either side, if one is out in front of one's trenches, one has to lie absolutely flat and still…It is always a ticklish job wiring in front, with occasional sniping, but I have some good NCOs who are absolutely expert on the job, and don't panic when shots come near in the middle of the night, as many do! We have been at it for eight days now (our last two spells in the trenches) and completed it just before we came out; we worked from 7pm to 1 and 2am every night, and have perpetrated such an entanglement as you never saw; it far exceeded General Pa's expectations, and he was awfully pleased, and talked for ten minutes on end about it. He asked me to compliment the wiring party, which I did, and incidentally gave them all a tot of neat whisky each on the quiet. It is highly skilled labour and a test on the nerves, so I thought a little whisky (a thing which they never get at all) would not come amiss! All ranks of my Coy are working awfully well, and by dint of constant organizing and drill when in billets, and heavy discipline, the whole machine is working really well now. It is a very different thing from two months ago, and makes it far easier, of course, for me."

In spite of poor health and eyesight 2nd Lieutenant Wilfrid "Bill" Ewart had succeeded in being accepted by the Scots Guards, possibly through the influence of his cousin, Lieutenant Colonel The Honourable Walter "Jerry" Hore Ruthven, now commanding the 1st Battalion. He arrived on the evening of 20 February at Merville from Le Havre in charge of a draft of officers and men for several regiments. Just before they left Merville on the 21st Lieutenant General Sir Henry Rawlinson, Corps Commander of IV Corps, appeared. "Next morning found us lined along a road leading out of the town – a variegated column fifteen hundred strong, for at nine o'clock we were to be inspected by the General. He spoke a few words, and the column moved off, through a dense grey mist that hid the fields on either hand, on a fifteen mile march to the Battalion. The highway was of pavé and trying to the feet. A Staff officer rode in front, and after an hour's trudging called a halt. The men were glad enough to fall out. It was their first march carrying packs and full weight of equipment. It was also my first march with full equipment, but I got through it better than I expected and found a friendly officer who took me into his billet and gave me food and drink. But what a desolate country, such squalid people, such squalid straggling towns and tenements! Opposite the halting place was a house with a gaping hole in the roof where, a few days before, a German shell had burst. This was our first taste of the war. Henceforward many of the houses by the roadside were similarly damaged, albeit they seemed to be occupied; for besides soldiers, women and children swarmed in the streets… We halted once again in a dirty street. By now our limbs were aching and tired. Then, turning off along a lane, we struck out into the open country. Presently we came upon a line of guns – 4.7's – cleverly concealed. The whole thing, the whole journey until we halted at about two o'clock in the afternoon before the farmhouse where the Staff of the Battalion was awaiting us, conveyed to the mind a sense of hopeless unreality. Surely this could not be a real war, I thought repeatedly."

The day after that the Battalion came out of the trenches and he wrote "I am writing this now in a farmhouse a mile from the German trenches. An occasional gun goes off, otherwise nothing comes out of the damp mist but the bark of a dog or the sound of our men chopping firewood outside… My Company Commander is a chap called Warner, who seems very decent. And besides Jarvis and myself, there is a very pleasant fellow named Teddy Hulse. Seymour, whom I know slightly, is with us here too, but he has just gone on leave. Our farmhouse is well within the range of the German guns, but I don't think they worry much about it. Warner has just been telling me of some things I shall want, and it appears I stand in need of gumboots, a periscope, carriage candles, matches, a bottle of port, a plum cake and a box of cigarettes. This afternoon we had an inspection by Heyworth, the Brigadier, who is a very efficient officer." Next he was to take out sixty men at six that evening to dig for four hours "within a hundred yards of the German trenches, so shall probably hear something of them." The day after "My brief visit to the trenches last night with my digging party was not very eventful. We started at 5 o'clock in the afternoon and got back at ten o'clock at night. Some of my men caught it from a Maxim gun, but no one was hit and only a few stray bullets came over, but it was quite exciting crawling down there and back. It seemed strange to be sitting within a hundred yards of the German lines and to hear them talking, shouting and singing and our people doing the same; big guns going intermittently all the time, with bursts of rifle fire and a machine gun tapping away at intervals. The Bosche snipers were also cracking off, and every now and then we would see a star rocket shoot off in the distance. For a mile or two in view of the trenches everything is laid waste – ruined farms and great shellpits in the ground. And very ghastly it all looks in the moonlight."

Lieutenant Ewart had brought with him 2nd Lieutenant Archibald Jarvis and two hundred and eight men. G Company got Lieutenant Jarvis and thirty four men and Sir Edward Hulse was promoted Captain. Since 18 December he had been on his own. Lieutenant Jarvis, who was a bit younger, had been at the same preparatory school and he was very pleased to have him, rather than Lieutenant Ewart. "They have sent us one very moderate young fellow, who is quite incapable, but luckily Pip has got the arduous task of training him, not I!" He was going to address his own newcomers on a few matters "including a few gentle hints on that highly scientific and necessary part of soldiering, the Art of Sanitation. What I don't know about latrine digging and "chloride of lime" is not worth the shovel which is so necessary an implement!" He told his mother that Captain Paynter "who has always dreaded being promoted "Major", has now got it; he says it makes him feel a hundred, and that it's a dirty old man's rank!" and added that he should have been promoted to Temporary Lieutenant Colonel, drawing Colonel's pay "as he has absolutely run the Battalion ever since Ypres, and pulled it together through very dirty and trying times."

On the evening of the 24th Lieutenant Ewart began his first full trench tour. "We marched off. Into a wintry sunset; the road yet muddy after recent rains; the dank fields lying cold and uninviting on either hand. Approaching the crossroads, we quickened step, for were they not marked by the German artillery? And of all the dreary places in all the dreary lands that I have seen I picture that group of wayside houses as the saddest. Always – except when the working parties hurried by – an unnatural stillness reigned. Roofless skeletons of houses and houses broken in a score of places; people creeping in and out, French peasants who cling pitifully to the relics of their homes; children peering out of the windows and doorways, too scared to play; heaps of ruins; and everywhere a great lonely emptiness. We turned off into the fields. Yet the sunset was still in the sky, and it was too light to cross the open lands. We had to wait. The men smoked cigarettes and fell to talking after their inconsequent fashion about the prospects of the night, also of professional football, and – their suppers. Then darkness crept up and the sun dipped beyond the rim of the Flanders plain. It was twilight. We moved across the ploughed fields. Not a sound, not a murmur of war. Until of a sudden we were in the road again, a road congested with troops. Battalion Headquarters lay before us, and many transport wagons were unloading by the wayside. Long files of men in hoods and capes and heavy equipment, the rifle slung over the shoulder, moved slowly along towards the trenches. There were orderlies on horseback, sitting their horses like statues silhouetted against the evening sky.

We crawled forward presently at a snail's pace until clear of the congested trench parties, then turned off to the left down a path, following a light ammunition railway. On the one hand were overhanging trees, on the other the ghastly wrecks of houses. Soon we came to the little cemetery where our comrades lie amid the shellpits and the ruined houses, under white wooden crosses. Nor could I pass by that spot, melancholy as it was, without recalling the company sergeant major's sly humour. Never would he bring the nervous newly-joined subaltern down that way, I had heard, but he showed him with unction, with emphasis – and a twinkle in his eye – that little cemetery of nameless graves. The occasional bullet pinging across our path told us how near we were to the trenches. Some desultory rifle fire in front gave additional warning. Soon we were in the machine gun zone and, stooping low, we hurried along the ditch beside the white strip of road, then across an open bit of ploughland towards the shelter of the parapet.

Suddenly a machine gun opened. We fell flat on our faces, and the bullets whistled overhead as the devilish thing swept round. But one man caught it and did not rise with us. Then we crept along behind the parapet which led rather steeply to a ruined barn. Here the troops in reserve were crouching over the fires they had kindled, cooking their supper. The fires cast a strange glare around. It was a place of shadows and passages and creeping armed men. The company whom we were to relieve filed out of the trenches and we filed in." The soldier killed was Private Wilfred Chilton, a former seaman, who had been serving for three years. His personal effects consisted of a mouth organ, a watch and chain, a medal, a pocket book, a strap, a charm, a notebook and some photographs, all of which reached his sister Mary in Liverpool. "I placed my sentries. I laid down my pack and equipment in my dug-out. Carrying only my revolver, I walked along the line of the breastwork, noting here an improvement that had been made since my former brief visit, and there a defect. Climbing the rear face of a little hill, I sat down behind the machine gun emplacement, which was safe and a vantage point. From there towards the enemy I could look across the plain.

And there you find me. I see a wide and shadowy country. The moon is rising out of the calm night. A little wind whines and whispers among the sandbags. I see dimly a land of poplars and small trees (dwarf oaks), orchards, and plentiful willows. I see flat fields and ditches and stagnant water, and red farms whose roofs are gone, stark skeletons in the moonlight. I see broad flat spaces and then a ridge – the ridge of Aubers. Only the German lines are hidden from sight. No sign of life. Silence and desolation reign. But here and there the faint glimmer of a fire indicates the presence of the enemy. Afar off, rockets, red and green and white, shoot up to the sky; star shells bursting above our trenches cast their baleful light around. Strange twisted figures of trees stand out against the horizon. There is no sound but an occasional homelike mating call of a pair of partridges in the fields and the peculiar laughing cry of the little speckled owl which here, as in England, dwells among the orchards. Creeping into the little den which I share with Warner, after a brief attempt at making things shipshape, I fall asleep.

I woke this morning – it was my first awakening in the trenches – to hear the sizzling of bacon in a pan. A ray of light came streaming in through the opening of the dug-out. It was nine o'clock. Warner was still asleep, breathing regularly. I turned over and, according to a lifelong habit, indulged in a little leisurely contemplation previous to waking up properly. I remembered how infernally cold my feet had been in the early hours of the morning when I had crept in to sleep. But now they were warm and comfortable, wrapped around with empty sandbags and covered over with a rug and greatcoat. The interior of the dug-out was moist and clammy. It was also exceedingly untidy. For the coverings and equipment of my companion and myself were strewn about the ground, grievously intermixed with straw, mud, newspapers, books, notebooks, and ration tins. The night before we had hastily rigged up little shelves, each in his corner, upon which we set those small things, such as matches and pencils, that are so apt to get lost, so that in parts there was a semblance of tidiness, but we had not been able to do much, for a candle stuck to a board by its own grease was the only illumination of our dug-out.

Then, while I was still contemplating, a face was pushed in through the dug-out opening, a hand prodded my lower extremities, and a voice said, "Breakfast is ready, sir." At the same moment le capitaine woke up. Smith, our faithful cook and my servant, began to pass in the food and the knives and the plates. First a plate of porridge, most welcome, and milk in a dark green bottle. This was followed by bread, and Belgian butter on a piece of paper, and marmalade from Piccadilly. Finally, steaming hot bacon and a poached egg on a plate. These we poised on our laps and ate voraciously. In fact, we didn't fare badly. Feeling like nothing on earth, we didn't talk, but Warner read the Westminster Gazette, while I had a copy of the Weekly Times. Presently our invaluable Smith produced some of Warner's port, after drinking which we felt better, and one of us swore down the telephone for about a quarter of an hour, finding the field telephone useful in more ways than one; letting it act as a kind of safety valve for our humours. Disentangling myself by degrees from the rugs and the coats and the sandbags, I then crawled outside. There is a narrow passageway under the front parapet between our own dug-out and that of the servants. Here Smith, and Warner's servant Walter [both untraced], had lighted their fire, over which they crouched, eating their own breakfast.

I climbed over this, and turned to the right into the fort, where a number of men were sitting around smoking, mending their clothes, and cleaning their rifles. It was a sunshiny morning with a sharp little wind, and the country behind looked quite attractive with its fields and farms. There was no shooting or sound of war, since the Germans, barely eighty yards away, were doubtless as leisurely engaged as we. I exchanged a few words with the artillery observation NCO and took a look through the periscope, which, however, disclosed nothing beyond the white facing of the enemy parapet showing here and there amid the irregularities of the ground. It was then about time to go down to the other end of the section held by the company, since in half an hour the Brigadier and CO were due to inspect it.

Being somewhat above six feet in height, I had to bend low as I passed down the line. In places, too, the breastwork is lower than in others, and there are often bits without any protection at all. The whole section, which is bordered at the further end by a road, is about five hundred yards long. At intervals of about one hundred and fifty yards there are "forts" – i.e. small walled in areas of ground containing a machine gun emplacement or observation post. I crept along rapidly from one to another of these, since it was not advisable to waste much time in between. At one point there has not been an opportunity of building up sandbags, so hurdles have been put up instead, with the earth banked up behind them and a shallow ditch dug on the inside. There was more than one plank bridge to cross. About halfway along, after emerging from a muddy pit, the path dips down into a veritable maze of deep narrow trenches, boarded at the bottom, with numerous communication trenches running out of them. Here and there are open spaces where the fires are lit, and around these are the dug-outs, which make the place look like nothing so much as the exposed section of a rabbit warren.

Through all these difficulties the Brigadier had to make his way – minus the gold lace, the red cap, and the Staff. For he, well known as a model of well groomed smartness, was just like the rest of us, clad in gumboots and an old uniform without a hat. At other times Heyworth has been known to ride horseback down the road to within a few hundred yards of the enemy, red cap, aide-de-camp, and all; and, as it happened, not a shot was fired. The inspection did not take long, and presently we were back in the dug-out, making arrangements for tonight's work. Reports and diaries had to be written up, and there was much telephoning to headquarters concerning the strength of the working parties to be detailed. Then it was luncheon time, which important event was preceded by an appetising whiff of cooking from the crackling fire outside. Luncheon was followed by a long and deep sleep, which, however, was disturbed by the conversation of the guns. I woke up with a start to find the ground quaking with the detonation, while boom after boom proclaimed that an artillery bombardment was in progress. In the midst of it from the recesses of the next dug-out I could hear the businesslike voice of the artillery NCO reporting the result of each shot to his battery as it was shouted across to him by the observation officer with the periscope. Going outside, I learned that this little affair had been in progress for an hour or more and that our own guns were just beginning to find the range of the enemy's fire trench. Almost yard by yard the observation officer brought them down to it, until presently a shell evidently landed right on the trench, for the explosion was followed by a great upheaval of earth and stones, in the midst of which there sailed upward a German's trousers."

The artillery fire from both sides continued through the afternoon, while a German sniper tried, persistently but unsuccessfully, to shoot down the telephone post above the dug-out. On the final day he wrote "Last night, it being Sunday, the Germans made a devil of a row with mouth organs. I could hear them singing too – the Austrian National Anthem – all along my front. It was very strange seeing right away down the German lines and watching the heavy fighting far to the right – the glare and flash of the big guns, the shooting of star rockets, and the fires lighted along the German lines. Other times it would be very quiet and I could see the Germans (like ourselves) creeping about in the moonlight, building up their barbed wire, digging and so forth. And, in a way I shall miss it, for today, it being the auspicious Monday, March 1st – as soon as it is dark – we move out of this mud into billets." Most had been able to sleep through a peaceful sunny morning but in the afternoon there was more gunfire, snipers and machine guns, and, to add to the noise, a thunderstorm. "Finally the setting sun peeped out upon a wet world, and we came swarming forth from our dug-outs and shelters like so many rabbits from their holes. It is packing up time. All the small litter that had accumulated during our days in the trenches we then threw upon the fires, the dug-outs were cleared of their contents, and the men began to get dressed. And what a collection of things some of them had – all their worldly goods! Some of them carried sandbags full of valued trifles, and others were decorated at every vantage so as greatly to resemble a Christmas tree. Once ready, they formed up in file along the support trench, only the sentries remaining on the watch, and awaited the arrival of the relieving party. Silence was enjoined – no smoking. Dusk had not long fallen when stealthy footsteps were heard approaching along the road. Presently the familiar muffled forms of soldiers appeared, each figure showing momentarily against the sky as it clambered into the trench. One by one they filed in and silently took their places alongside our men. When the sentries have been relieved and the incoming officer-in-charge has been shown the results of the work done on the trenches, wire entanglements, and parapets, we begin to move out in the same silent way. First along a deep ditch half full of water, then behind a stout sandbag breastwork which presently crosses the road. Much encumbered with mud and weeds, in places it is a mere pathway. Tonight we have the advantage of a deep blue gloaming, accompanied by a light veil of mist rising from the ground. Not a shot is fired, though everybody takes care to hurry along in small groups. The fields lie dark and uninviting on either hand. The white skeleton of some ruined building which may have been a cottage or farmhouse stares out of the gathering darkness. The ground rises slightly, and presently we are at the crossroads, where numerous bodies of troops, just relieved like ourselves from the trenches, are moving this way and that. Here the company is formed up and told off, while the remainder of the Battalion with the Transport takes its place in the rear. As soon as possible the column moves off in fours, the men light their cigarettes and talk. It is now pitch dark. Little can be seen on either hand but a foot or so of mud. But suddenly, as we emerge from the houses on to higher ground, a great glare in the sky ahead confronts our eyes. In the midst of it, though far away, one can discern through the various obstacles of distance a suggestion of bright flames leaping upward."

As they got closer to the burning village "we run into a great body of troops. Halted along the road they were in column of route, long lines of infantry, guns and transport. As may be supposed, the narrow country byway and the crossroads further on were terribly congested, and it was all we could do to make any headway. Mounted orderlies were constantly riding down the column shouting to "Make way! Make way!" while the Staff motorcars and transport wagons occupied a great deal of space. We pushed on by fits and starts." It was not the Grenadiers, but Canadians going up to the trenches for the first time. Gradually the Scots Guards got past them, also dazzled by the headlights of lorries. "Once beyond these, we swing along again, and the men break into their favourite marching songs "Who's Your Lady Friend?", the song about the high road and the low road, "On the Mississippi," and so forth, alternating with the eternal question, "Are we downhearted?" and the inevitable answer, "No". Always ahead of us, nearer and nearer, beckons the burning village, so close now that we seem to be walking into it, until presently we turn sharp to our right down a side road. We have come four miles. Half a dozen friendly pipers from a Highland regiment come out from their billets playing a complimentary air on their bagpipes; and so we march into supper – and bed." They were at Sailly, stayed for a further four days and, apart from very much a passing visit not long afterwards, had left Rouges Bancs for good. The 13th Canadian Brigade were taking over.

A bizarre feature of this last trench tour was their discovery, described by Sir Edward Hulse, that "the enemy 7 nights ago put up 5 little posts with dirty bits of rag, as flags, on top halfway between their trenches and mine. We investigated the matter the night after, having noticed them by day; we did so extremely carefully and gingerly, as I thought a wire might be attached, or explosive. However, we found each had a little bag tied on the post with…German proclamations to Indian troops, written in Hindustani, Urdu and a Punjabi dialect" which, in translation, read "Do not believe that the Germans are your enemies. On the contrary they are your friends. Those Sepoys who will be captured will be sent back to India and will not be put in gaol. Those who say that the Germans are your enemies are liars." The Indian Corps had not been in this area for over three months and were now south of Neuve Chapelle.

Lieutenant Ewart gave a sketch of Captain Warner at Sailly "He is my kennel companion – for only so can one describe it – and at the present moment he is washing himself in a little canvas pail. He is naked to the waist, his skin being very white, like a woman's, and he has a childish, pink face. His braces hang loose by his sides. He is swearing quietly to himself because it is very cold – and no one has a mightier vocabulary. A peculiarly urbane and agreeable young man, there is none more gallant or more capable. He does not "tell people off"; he does not fuss; but he gets things done. Which is the highest tribute one can pay a soldier." Then, following a morning of routine billet activities, there was a musketry parade "and afterwards we stroll down to a field to watch a football match. The battalion team is playing an artillery eleven. Everybody is there to watch the game: much excitement. No one notices the incessant boom of the German guns and the scream and the bang of their shells, which are exploding as regularly as clockwork around a farmstead not three hundred yards away, until attention is momentarily distracted by a shell bursting unmistakably in the very next field. Then someone bethinks himself of the threshing-machine, which, sending up a column of black smoke, offers an ideal target to the German artillery. At the same time our own guns take up the challenge, and the game of football goes calmly on beneath an unending procession of Jack Johnsons. So accustomed is everybody to this comparatively harmless demonstration that no one takes the smallest interest in it until a shell chances to crash the roof of the little inn which stands at the crossroads nearby."

The match was in General Capper's Divisional Football League, the gunners the 22nd Brigade RFA, the result unrecorded.

In the evening the officers were censoring letters when "presently the post arrives – the greatest event of this and every day – and it has to be answered. Writing letters home is a pleasure second only to that of receiving them. Also the English newspapers come to hand. And there is a bottle of port done up tantalisingly in straw, and a new cake, not to mention a beautiful boneless chicken in a glass case. Perhaps the thought is a little degrading – I mean one lives for one's stomach these days, and the invariable source of quarrel between man and his friend is that the latter has better food or more of it! After dinner the men have a concert in a big barn. There they all gather, serried masses of them, lying on the piles of straw and hay, ranged along the beams, and squatting in rows upon the floor." The turns, including Captain Warner telling "the most outrageous stories in the drollest manner possible," followed from one to the next "and everybody smokes and claps and jests and roars to their heart's content. So that for this brief hour we all forget the war – which, I verily believe, is the chief ambition of every honest soldier at the front."

They were told on 1 March that the Division were being relieved. There were baths on the afternoon of the 2nd, followed by the concert Lieutenant Ewart described. On the evening of the 3rd they left Sailly, marching eight miles, first downstream to Estaires, then across the Lys and on to Vieux-Berquin, in the Hazebrouck direction. Two sets of pipes had arrived, Captain Warner noting that they "cheered us up on the march." Lieutenant Ewart found "The march last night was rather trying, as none of us were in much condition for that sort of thing. We are in quite comfortable billets in a farmhouse by the road, and where we are there is something definitely in the wind, probably a big attack." Sir Edward Hulse wrote "We are hard at work cleaning up, drilling and lecturing, etc. We had a concert before we left the old place, and found some perfectly astounding talent in the new drafts. RF Coy has most of it, but I have the best of the whole lot, one Jamieson, a private, who has joined for the war. He is the nearest thing to a gentleman possible, and had one of the best tenor voices I have ever heard, and plays the piano the very best! The general tone and level of our concerts rises, as we get more fresh men, recruited from the higher circles, and the mixture of the better class song, with a few efforts of the very small minority of old serving soldiers and rough and tough nuts, whom we have left, is very curious. We were really sorry to leave the old trenches; they had become much as a home, and after all the work put into them, they had changed rapidly from a position of extreme and acute discomfort, into a very passably comfortable and clean line." Private Robert Jameson, a labourer who enlisted in September in Preston, came up with Lieutenant Ewart. Arthur and Maria Jameson were in Bradford.

Those who had lived through the three and a half months at Rouges Bancs were not to see such a stable pattern of trench operations for some time and, 18 December apart, they had been able to settle down thoroughly. The companies spent 4 March practising attacks individually and next day attacks by half battalion [in pairs]. The day after it was very wet and there was a full weapons inspection. Everyone wondered what was coming next. Sir Edward Hulse, avoiding any mention of a future offensive, had written to his mother that it seemed to be a matter of their either occupying trenches somewhere further south or else of their acting as a reserve at a threatened point, but commented that "our last place was neither strategical nor tactical, and the Huns would never make a big offensive there." They never did until the spring of 1918 and then only as part of a much bigger one. On the afternoon of 7 March Major Paynter and the company commanders were in the 8th Division trenches reconnoitring the ground towards Aubers from breastworks along the Rue Tilleloy south of Fauquissart. Though only a little south of Rouges Bancs, this was new to them. Meanwhile most of the Battalion were on their way back to Estaires, from where two companies were sent on to Pont-du-Hem, northwest of Neuve Chapelle, to dig what were probably assembly trenches. Lieutenant Ewart still did not know what was going to happen, expecting only to go into trenches in a different part of the line next day. He wrote from Vieux-Berquin before setting off "I wonder how much longer this war is going to last. Everyone who has been out here above a week or two is sick to death of it and praying for the end, and I am not surprised. Even if the billets are good, the country, the towns, and the people here in Artois are the most miserable I have ever struck."

On 8 March it was very cold and snowing. Captain Warner expected the 10th to be the day of the attack for which orders had come the day before. The companies again rehearsed attack drills. Then Major Paynter and the company commanders went over the plan. Captain Warner wrote "We are in Corps Reserve. Rode out to see dug-outs where we assemble and German position from an observation post." On returning he went through Right Flank's role with Lieutenants Ewart and Seymour. Lieutenant Conway "Con" Seymour, a Wykehamist, was commissioned on 15 August 1914, the same day as his cousin Lieutenant Kit Cator. He came out to France soon after New Year. His parents were The Reverend Lord Victor Seymour and Elizabeth Seymour, a Cator before she married. Sir Edward Hulse wrote very briefly to his mother that "Owing to possible hasty moves, do not expect regular correspondence; in fact, Field Service Postcard is the form it will probably take, and posts may be very irregular from here."

Notes on Chapter Sources

History of the Great War based on Official Documents by direction of the Historical Section of the Committee of Imperial Defence.
Brig Gen Sir JE Edmonds & Capt GC Wynne, *Military Operations France and Belgium, 1915: Volume I: Winter 1914–15: Battle of Neuve Chapelle: Battles of Ypres* (London: Macmillan and Co Ltd, 1927).
War Diary: 20th Infantry Brigade TNA/WO95/1650/2.
Pte Frank Richards, *Old Soldiers Never Die* (London: Faber & Faber 1933).
The Stock Exchange Memorial of those who fell in the Great War 1914-1919 (London: 1920) for short biographies of all and images of most, including Capt G Bagot Chester.
Diary of Sgt C Pilkington, IWM/Documents 14407.
Account of Bella and Bertha in Maj & QM T Ross, *The Fortune of War. Catalogue. Cameos of the Great War by an Eye Witness. Paintings depicted by Stewart Robertson, Official Artist – 2nd Army*, SGA.
Account of Pte A Runcie, IWM/Documents 25793.
Diary of unknown Border Regiment Private, IWM/MISC 30/ITEM 550.
Robert Blake (ed.), *The Private Papers of Douglas Haig* (London: Eyre & Spottiswoode 1952).
Maj Gen C Dunbar: 'Some Recollections and Reflections', SGM 1964, for his experience as a subaltern of RSM "Scrubber" Macdonald and reference to the bowl of porridge fable. Also the Sergeant Major's obituary, SGM 1954.

Letter of Brig Gen FJ Heyworth to Sir Robert Kindersley, Brig Lord Kindersley Papers, IWM/Documents 12174.

Brig AEJ Cavendish: *The 93rd Highlanders 1799-1927* (London: Privately 1928) for Brig Gen The Hon F Gordon losing his boots.

Diary of Capt S Sanders and letters, Liddle/WW1/GS/1422.

Papers of Lt Col L Fisher Rowe, IWM/Documents 16978.

Capt GH Loder statements in 2nd Scots Guards War Diary.

Interview with Pte E Jones, repatriated Prisoner of War, series TNA/WO161.

20th Brigade Calendar 1915, SGA.

Rev Dr J Esslemont Adams – quotes from newspaper cuttings, Liddle/WW1/GS/0527.

Letters of Capt D Chater, IWM/Documents 1697.

Letter of Sir Edward Hulse to Lord Burnham (not printed in his published letters and diary notes), IWM/Documents 2621.

Wilfrid Ewart, *Scots Guard* (London: Rich & Cowan 1934).

8

The La Bassée Canal and the Winter 1914-1915 – 1st Battalion

Reinforcing and retraining at Borre

Writing home on 16 November Captain Thorne told how "I am being rather inundated with pathetic letters from widows & mothers asking for details – it is almost impossible to know what to say as all my information is hearsay – anyhow the greater part is and I am so frightened of raising false hopes or killing off some comfort." About midday on 17 November Colonel Lowther came back after recovering from his wounds, found the small band of survivors at Westoutre and soon afterwards set off with them further west. After passing through Bailleul they were settled into longer term billets at Borre, just short of Hazebrouck. Now hearing at first hand about Ypres, he wrote "People at home do not realize what the troops go through in the trenches. I did not realize it. For days at a time they cannot even sit up in the trench by daylight; only by night can food, water and ammunition be brought up and wounded taken away. Shells actually in the trench are frequent and attacks are constant, even at night the shelling and sniping continue, but they are less accurate and one can take chances." He also learned that Captain Stracey had been wounded, presumably only slightly, and buried for two hours by a shell before being dug out, but had said nothing to anyone. There was a lot to do, including arranging for the sorting of three wagon loads of mail, for most of which there were by now no recipients. He sent Captain Stracey on four days leave, hearing "on all sides that he has commanded the Battalion splendidly. Kinlay – the quartermaster – had his boots off for the first time for 39 nights." Next day in Captain Thorne's letter "You can't imagine how absolutely caked with mud the troops are. When they are clean, we mean to try and instil self respect and refresh their discipline with some good old steady drill."

The Scots Guards stayed at Borre, being gradually, but not fully, reinforced, reequipped and reorganised. The shortage of officers was serious, whereas the 2nd Battalion did have a nucleus left from those with them throughout, as well as Sergeant Major Moncur. Also, because all the available men already in France as reinforcements or who arrived in time went to the 2nd Battalion immediately after Ypres, they received a disproportionate number of the remaining more experienced men, whether reservists or voluntarily reenlisted former soldiers. A lot of those who now came to the 1st Scots Guards were wartime volunteers and many very young at that. The first draft of five officers and eighty nine men arrived on 18 November. Lieutenant Balfour, fit again after his wound on the Aisne, was one and became Adjutant at once. The Battalion were put back onto a four company basis with forty men in each, pending the anticipated arrival of more. On the 19th Colonel Lowther was surprised to find the Prince of Wales "wandering down the road." He took him round the billets and Lieutenant Balfour thought "he looked awfully well and the men were very pleased to see him." Lieutenant Balfour spent much of his spare time trying to see his brother, worried because Private Duncan Balfour was not at all well. The London Scottish were now in the 1st (Guards) Brigade as part of the process whereby Territorial battalions joined Regular brigades, one per brigade, to boost the numbers.

For the rest of November they were required to do little, there was nothing significant, the training and route marching were limited and Captain Stewart, the Medical Officer, Lieutenant Kinlay, Sergeant Major Edward "Tiny" Cutler, who had replaced Sergeant Major Tate, and Regimental Quartermaster Sergeant Charles Woods all went home on leave. The Sergeant Major, with them till the end of November 1916, was born in Watford and a grocer's assistant before joining up in 1898. At the time it was noted that his eyebrows met and that his nose inclined to the left. He was mentioned in despatches in late December 1915, awarded the MC in January 1916 and commissioned as a Quartermaster in June 1919. Regimental Quartermaster Sergeant Woods came from Godalming, Surrey, and was a pupil [trainee] teacher when he enlisted in 1897. After serving in the Boer War he did a preliminary Arabic course while the 1st Scots Guards were in Cairo in 1912. At Ypres he was slightly wounded in the chest on 5 November. He transferred to the Welsh Guards in February 1915.

On 22 November Colonel Lowther rode into Hazebrouck where he met Brigadier General "Fatty" The Earl of Cavan on his way home on leave. "Most of his luggage consisted of half the base of a 13 inch shell which had hit his house one day and left little of it." Travelling on by train to St Omer he went, as arranged, to Headquarters BEF, where he heard officially from Sir Archibald Murray, what he privately knew already, that he was being promoted Brigadier General to command the 1st (Guards) Brigade. He then had lunch with Sir John French and returned to Borre to break the news. Lieutenant Balfour's reaction was "We shall be very sorry to lose him, but it is a comfort that he won't be far away." His departure as they were rebuilding was unfortunate and was felt right through the ranks. Private Stewart wrote that, while they were pleased by his promotion, "we were extremely sorry to lose such an excellent and kind hearted commanding officer." After he left on the 23rd General Lowther made his first visit to the 1st Coldstream, only now rejoining the Brigade. He found Colonel Ponsonby, also just returned, Lieutenant Boyd, the Quartermaster, and two ensigns as the only officers. Next he was summoned to Headquarters 1st Division to discuss the London Scottish. "They are in rather a sad state. Poorly commanded, everything horribly dirty and about 90 men being seen sick by the Doctor daily." The London Scottish had fought bravely at Messines, but, as occurred at this time with other Territorial battalions, they were not fit operationally. General Lowther set off the following morning and visited every London Scottish bivouac, aware that Lieutenant Colonel George Malcolm was too demoralised by his casualties and by the anxious letters he received asking about them to exercise command any longer. Very soon afterwards he was sent home sick. Captain James Sandilands, a Cameron Highlander, took his place and was soon promoted. Two days later General Lowther was haranguing their officers about the number of sick. It was cold, mostly freezing, but when it thawed the mud was very bad and throughout it was difficult to keep men warm. The London Scottish did not have a monopoly of the sick; the Coldstream had forty men with frozen feet. General Lowther described one bit of light relief on the 26th when some London Scottish "found a slop pail buried in their back garden with 200 gold louis and another 500 francs cash, besides papers. I hunted round the village and after a visit to the Mayor (a crippled old peasant with strawberry nose) found the owner who did not live where the money was found. He turned pale at the mention of digging in his mother's garden, and was much relieved to recover his property, buried when the Germans passed through." The day before Captain Thorne told his wife that Colonel Ponsonby was coming to dinner. "He is endeavouring to remake his Battn and is finding it rather a heartbreaking job, so Meat is hoping to cheer him up tonight."

On the 28th Sir John French, visiting the Brigade, inspected the 1st Scots Guards, drawn up in close column, and "spoke a few well chosen words". General Lowther noted the large number of senior officers with him, "lots of nuts" he called them. At the time someone described as a "nut" was considered to be excessively concerned with his personal appearance, which quickly fitted senior and staff officers. Captain Thorne had had a very tiresome time making arrangements with five fiercely competitive chaplains of different denominations who all wanted the same places at the same times for services. He regretted that he had annoyed them. "Still it is better to quarrel with the Chaplains than with the Doctors – the former only bury one, while the latter have great opportunities of revenge!" At the end of that letter he mentioned censoring a soldier's one which concluded "God bless you and save you from your loving husband." Next day General Lowther noted that he had apparently shocked his headquarters clerk by attending services of two different denominations that morning, Church of England Communion first and Church of Scotland later. From the 30th onwards, when the weather improved, the pace began to quicken and Lieutenant Balfour noted the new clothing issued comprising "Teddy Bear coats, great coats, cholera belts, scarfs, shirts, socks, drawers, mitts, handkerchiefs, etc just like Xmas." General Lowther recorded on 1 December that the Camerons had a man with scarlet fever. There were cases of measles everywhere.

From the beginning of that month the Brigade, although far from up to strength, were considered operational again and were told to be ready to move at once whenever they were warned off as "in waiting of General Reserve". On the afternoon of the 2nd Sir Douglas Haig rode through the Scots Guards billets at Borre and Lieutenant Balfour "had a few minutes talk to him". General Lowther went to Headquarters 1st Division that day where after lunch the new commander, Major General David Henderson, was particularly "talking about trench work. Warfare is moving backwards, as we are reverting to bombs, grenades, sapping, etc." That day a draft landed in France among whom was Private William McCulloch, a labourer with a thistle tattoo on his left forearm and smallpox marks on his nose, who lived with his wife Agnes and their son in Parkhead, Glasgow. He volunteered early in September 1914, at thirty four older than most, and left as a Sergeant in February 1919. By the end of the War he was in charge of the stretcher bearers and the citation for the DCM he received later recorded that during the fighting in 1918 he had been present at every battle in which the Battalion took part and that his skilful use of his men and the care he had given to the wounded had saved many lives. He also had the MM and was never wounded.

King George V inspected them on the 3rd, they, as Lieutenant Balfour described, having paraded at half past nine for the purpose "drawn up on both sides of the road in single rank shoulder to shoulder. Awful shower of rain, wet to the skin. The King walked up the middle of the road, accompanied by about 50 generals." Another hundred men arrived that day, led by Lieutenant Alastair Graham Menzies, returning after being sent back sick at Ypres. Among them was Private Henry Watson, the nineteen year old son of James and Mary Watson of Clapton, East London, who had trained as a fitter and turner in an engineering workshop at the Royal Albert Dock. He enlisted on 15 August at Stratford. When the War broke out he was surprised, because from his reading of journals he thought that the Germans were on the way to achieving what they wanted by economic and industrial power. Nevertheless he believed initially that the numerical strength of the Allies would mean that it could not last more than a year. After two months in the trenches he changed his mind on seeing the modern weapons and complex defences. He also said that "Whilst I expected to see bravery & courage & leadership those I experienced far exceeded my expectations but what I did not expect was the exhibitions of the baser passions by some which occurred in all armies, due I suppose to the precarious expectation of length of life." He was a good rifle shot before he joined up. The one element which was not covered in his training was trench warfare but "It was amazing how quickly one dug a trench… when under rifle, small arms or shellfire." Writing home Captain Thorne related a story doing the rounds "Two men are examining a belt they have each received on which is marked "A present from Mary R and the "Women of the Empire". Says one of them "I take it very kindly from the old polls at the "Empire" there was hardly one I didn't know, but who the hell is Mary R?"

On 4 December, "a bitter morning" General Lowther wrote, he and a number of officers and NCOs watched a demonstration of bomb throwing by the Royal Engineers "and also studying technical questions of trench work with the object of securing some similarity of principle." Meanwhile the Battalion went on a route march "carrying everything, Teddy Bear coats included." The training, including live firing, went on and the route marching went on, there being little affecting them up to the 20th. Lieutenant Colonel Hore Ruthven, an Etonian with a DSO from the Boer War, had arrived on the 5th as Commanding Officer, having been with the BEF throughout as Brigade Major of the 4th (Guards) Brigade. Private Stewart compared him unfavourably with his predecessor "Much less popular and certainly not so careful of his men." Every other officer he named he both liked and respected.

General Lowther was busy that day after "the most awful storm of wind, rain and snow all night" going to the Scots Guards billets in order "to fit in all the men now sleeping in the Church, latter being required for some special service tomorrow. The Cameron Highlanders sleeping there were badly caught out one day. Reveille was at 6.30, but at 6 most of the Parishioners came in for early mass. So the men could not move till it was over, most of them having taken off their kilt when they went to bed!!" On the 6th German planes bombed Hazebrouck, killing and wounding British soldiers and French civilians. Lieutenant Balfour went that afternoon to look, noting no material damage. Two days later General Lowther went to see the Coldstream practising digging trenches and, importantly, studying the drainage of them, while the following day he visited the Scots Guards who had been experimenting with various types of trenches, where he "suggested improvements." That evening the Scots Guards officers held a dinner party at which they ate a turkey, produced by Major Norman Orr Ewing. One of the guests was Captain Sir Thomas Erskine, Bt, now Adjutant of the Camerons, whom they would meet again much later. Major Orr Ewing had been with the 1st Irish Guards throughout the campaign to date and had commanded them, for which he was awarded the DSO, from after Lieutenant Colonel The Honourable George Morris was killed in the Forest of Retz during the Retreat.

Of General Lowther, writing on 7 December, Captain Thorne said that "there have been a great many saints in the past that have never been a quarter of the power for good that my General is with his great laugh and his big heart and his great enjoyment of everything, good & bad." There had been a mounted paper chase that day, though he was not there. In spite of the very heavy going "the "Kaiser" was hotly pursued in spite of it. They jumped a biggish brook twice & its water at one time contained a general & his two staff officers." General Lowther had a cold and a sore throat, while Major Bertram "Boy" Brooke, now Brigade Major, formerly Staff Captain of the 20th Brigade, was in bed with bronchitis. Major Corkran had gone to command the 1st Grenadiers, very temporarily as it turned out, but Captain Thorne was still Staff Captain. The weather was again "filthy". Sir Douglas Haig looked in during the afternoon of the 10th to outline probable future movements and General Lowther speculated whether the Germans really had that many men holding their line and so whether the British could break through, seeing as how the massed Germans had failed to break the British. He thought it would come down to the calibre of those doing the fighting. He was "busy all day making out recommendations for rewards and mentions in despatches from October 21st to present date. It is hard to get these things into line as different COs have very different ideas as to the merits of their respective battalions." It was particularly difficult when he had not been at Ypres himself. On the 11th there was a conference at Headquarters 1st Division, from which he deduced that an early move was likely, and went on to see another demonstration of bombs, this time of a French pattern consisting only of guncotton. "They say it is quite effectual in knocking out people and clearing a trench. Maybe the shock in a confined space is disagreeable. Then to various specimens of trenches. The bother is that all trenches are half full of water which makes permanent residence in them most uncomfortable. If on a hill they are all right, but the map tells me there are no hills between our advanced line and the Meuse." He had pheasant for dinner two nights running, shot some miles back by the supply officer. 12 December saw further experiments, this time with rifle grenades, fired by a blank round from an ordinary rifle, carrying for some two hundred yards and "very fairly successful". Then Sir Douglas Haig appeared again and told him more of what to expect, but he did not elaborate in his diary.

On the 13th General Lowther went to St Omer to lunch at the Intelligence Branch of GHQ with Colonel George McDonagh, the head of it, Lieutenant Colonel Ernest Swinton, under the nom de plume "Eyewitness" responsible for press statements, and others. There was much merriment about Colonel Jack Seely, formerly Secretary of State for War, now on the Staff at GHQ and viewed by those present with ridicule. Afterwards he got some "Camembert, foie gras, oranges and strawberry jam and chestnuts. Strawberry jam from the supplies does not get as far up as us. We get the apricot and plum, nearer the front one only gets plum and apple. Lower than that one cannot go." The next afternoon he walked round most of the battalions "and found them pretty well completed as regards ordnance stores, but a lot of the boots are of poor quality and many heels fall off after two or three days in the wet. I suppose few of our men have had dry feet for the past 3 weeks and it must be remembered that we are supposed to be under peace conditions." Two days later he went round again "interesting myself in such domestic matters as bacon, boots, tobacco, cookers, etc., quite dull but necessary. Two mails today to compensate for none yesterday, but nothing very exciting, dull papers…and no visitors from whom to glean misinformation." Over the next few days he remarked on the rapid deterioration of the roads, now with only a narrow strip of tarmac in the middle and mud six inches deep on either side, then on happening on a senior officer he knew and commenting how he "Little thought that I should ever find a Life Guards General with frozen toes travelling through Flanders in a "sidecar"" and next on the widespread disgust over the casualties caused by the German Navy shelling Scarborough and Whitby, as well as Hartlepool, the concept having only led to mirth when the first news came through.

What he did not include in his diary was what Captain Thorne told his wife on 15 December "Meat received a box marked "Glass with Care" and inside was a soldier doll about 8 inches long (evidently from Hamleys). Inside the box was written "After a horrible confinement it was all I could produce." It had come from a lady he had had lately & whom he had asked to keep the speckled ones for himself."

Givenchy-lez-La Bassée

Soon after three in the afternoon on 20 December the Brigade, on short notice, received the order to move and set off south an hour and a half later. General Lowther found it "Very cold all night sitting on a horse. Our first point was Merville which we reached about nine. There we got orders to march on to Béthune, a march for some of my Battalions of 19 miles. Very trying on bad roads and carrying big loads…it was evident that a heavy fight was in progress to the East of us. Guns going all the time and a lot of musketry fire. Also the constant flare of "Roman Candles" thrown up by the Germans whenever they are afraid of attacks. Gradually we ascertained that part of the Indian line (after a successful advance) had been driven in and that there is a bow in our line which we are required to flatten out again…It was past 3 when the last of my Battalions got to its billets at Béthune and I lay down for a while in a room of a huge girls' school where two whole battalions are billeted." The Scots Guards were one. Lieutenant Balfour, sent ahead from Merville at midnight with the billeting party, remarked of L'École des Jeunes Filles that the girls were not there and that the building was riddled with shells. Then the Battalion "arrives dead beat at 2am. Teas at 2.30am." Private Stewart, now in 8 Platoon of B Company, commanded by Sergeant Alexander McPherson, who had survived Ypres and been promoted on 10 December, sensed that there was an urgent need for reinforcements somewhere "for we performed that night what is known as a "forced march", only resting for several minutes on two occasions in a distance of approximately twenty miles." After Reveille at seven next morning, they waited to move at a moment's notice. What Lieutenant Balfour now heard in more detail about the Indian troops was that the Jullundur Brigade of the Lahore Division were holding the southern part of the line at Givenchy just north of the Aire-La Bassée Canal [generally known to the British as the La Bassée Canal] but, having successfully captured some German trenches, had been driven out by a counterattack. What was worse, the Germans then drove them out of their own forward trenches and through Givenchy almost as far as the canal bridge, the Pont Fixé, to the southwest. The 1st Manchester Regiment, the British battalion in the Jullundur Brigade, "made a brilliant counterattack and drove them back to Givenchy, but the Germans must be cleared out of the village and we await orders." The left of the French Army was on the south bank of the Canal, along which ran the embankment carrying the Béthune-La Bassée-Lille railway.

General Lowther, having had little to eat and, owing partly to the cold and partly to a painful elbow, little sleep either, but "luckily I got a sort of wash and shave which helps very much," was collected by car on the morning of the 21st to meet Major General Richard Haking, now commanding the 1st Division, because General Henderson was required by the RFC. General Haking had initially commanded the 5th Brigade, was wounded on the Aisne and returned after Ypres. As expected, the task was to retake the trenches on the east side of Givenchy lost on the 19th. It proved impossible to start this as planned at two that afternoon because neither the 1st (Guards) Brigade nor the 3rd Brigade, who were to attack on the right and on the left respectively, could be brought into position in time. The Scots Guards left Béthune at noon with their Brigade, the Canal being away to their left, and headed east down the La Bassée road through Beuvry and Annequin before turning off left at Cambrin towards Cuinchy. There they halted just south of the Canal, sheltering in some ruined buildings. Cuinchy was mostly on the south side of the Pont Fixé, but partly to the north. Private Stewart realised that "The German planes espied us and their artillery commenced shelling the road for more than two miles west of the scene of action. We suffered a few casualties from shrapnel, and were exceedingly lucky in escaping so lightly while proceeding up the road." At quarter to three the Brigade started to cross the Pont Fixé, losing some men to shelling, several of them Scots Guardsmen, as they did so, before deploying for the attack. Private Stewart described how "Night was fast approaching. We were told to prepare to rush across the bridge, when the order was given. A few minutes later…Number Eight Platoon rushed across the bridge in single file, and succeeded in crossing without mishap. Numerous dead bodies were lying at the north end of the bridge." The situation was inauspicious, the only favourable thing a heavy hailstorm in the Germans' faces. While it was understood that Givenchy was now clear of the enemy, the mauled Manchesters withdrew back through it in front of the Coldstream and Camerons as they were deploying to face east and the Germans did get back in. At quarter past four, in a very confused situation, the Scots Guards on the right, next to the canal bank, the Camerons in the centre and the Coldstream on the left tried to advance in the gathering darkness over ground they had never seen before. The Rue Ouverte outside the east of the village was their objective. Though it appeared when the attack went in as if most of the Germans had again left the village, snipers remained and there was heavy rifle fire in the dark, but no shelling. General Lowther commented "Most of the night I think we were shooting at one another a good deal, British bullets were cut out of our own men." Lieutenant Balfour was sure that the Scots Guards and the Camerons fired at each other, the Camerons having lost direction. The three forward Scots Guards companies got themselves into a line and awaited daylight, while Lieutenant Balfour and Left Flank, in reserve, busied themselves behind a bank further back excavating basic dug-outs. Lieutenant Balfour's sketch map suggested that the Scots Guards lined up south of the village facing north, with an undisturbed party of Indian troops on their right flank down to the Canal. So, with the Camerons advancing at right angles to them, if they fired on each other accidentally it was hardly surprising.

Private William Preston arrived at Borre with his friend Private Joe Richardson. They had enlisted at Kilmarnock on 21 August. Both were now in Right Flank. Private Preston came from Kilmaurs, Ayrshire, and had had a job as a fireman. He tended towards exaggeration, but his confusion was understandable. After they were across the Canal they "reached an old brewery and there awaited darkness. We now had our baptism of fire. Joe & I exchanged addresses and lay down to take some rest but I couldn't sleep and was glad a minute later a shell crashed through the roof…It burst a big water tank and we had to get. We moved on to a turnip field and it then commenced to rain steadily at first and then developed into a downpour. We were soon wet through." What he thought was a brewery was more likely the distillery just beyond the Pont Fixé. They were then lined out one man to every three yards and waited for dawn when "at daybreak we got the word that the Manchesters were falling back and we were to allow them to pass through our ranks which we did. At six o'clock a consternation arose whistles sounding on all sides and we were soon to learn the cause. Jerry was attacking in Block Column. There they were. Men in Grey marching ten abreast firing their rifles from the thigh. I bagged my first

Jerry soon after and many more before midday. The rain ceased and towards evening frost set in. I lost all feeling in my hands my legs cramp and my body like wood. Jerry attacked again but we warded him off. Darkness now began to settle down and we had to keep our ears open and eyes skinned expecting further attack. An order had come along ordering us to withdraw towards the bottom of the field. This order never reached us (we being on the extreme right of the Batt) with the result that we found ourselves isolated." He wrote of their having Sergeant Richard Westmacott with them, a well educated man who stood out not just because he was six foot six inches tall, but also because on 10 December he had been promoted Acting Sergeant almost immediately he arrived. Private Preston referred to him as "Lord Westmacott" and described him as now being feverish and unable to crawl. Private Preston crept about only to find that there were eleven of them out on their own, a diminishing number over the next four days. Eventually he found a Scots Guards stretcher bearer carrying a wounded man on his back, who told him where everyone else was. He saw Gurkhas on their way to capture and later dragging back a German prisoner.

Lieutenant Colonel Douglas MacEwen, commanding the Camerons, who had survived Ypres, was shot through the stomach and five more of his officers were hit. General Lowther estimated the total Brigade casualty list on 21 December up to midnight at between two hundred and fifty and three hundred. He wrote next day of "a bad night after a bad night and day, all our sleep was a few winks at intervals on a hard floor, with plenty of anxiety if one let oneself give way to it. By dawn we had arrived at some conception of where my line was, and it was not altogether satisfactory. Germans very busy indeed sapping and joining up trenches all along our front and seeming to show considerable force. 3rd Brigade on our left did not meet with any more success than I did. So all is very disappointing. A rotten patchy sort of war, more like fighting strikers in a London slum than one's conception of "glorious war". I feel for the German Officer who fell into one of our trenches one night and as a man sat on his chest ejaculated "this is a bloody war"…Coldstream pretty busy all day and had heavy losses. They took a machine gun emplacement and trench but had to quit again as their rifles jammed owing to dirt. The men get in an awful state, mud and water sometimes up to the waist. And some Gurkhas who were on the ground just N of Givenchy got their boots and putties sucked off by the clay!" The Coldstream had put in a dawn attack by three companies, captured the trench along the Rue Ouverte lost by the Indian Corps, but were then bombed out in a counterattack and had to withdraw. Not strong in numbers to start with, they lost a total of two hundred all ranks, killed, wounded and missing.

The Scots Guards had a quieter day on the 22nd. Lieutenant Balfour understood that Givenchy was at last clear of Germans. Left Flank were in reserve in their dug-outs two hundred yards back, the other three companies by now in a line of forward trenches, the original British support line, running from a hundred yards to the southeast of the village to the canal bank. There was some shelling. Over the two days Lieutenant Balfour noted that an officer and two men were killed, sixteen men wounded and seven missing. Lieutenant Hillyar Hill Trevor was definitely killed on the 21st, only child of The Honourable George and Ethel Hill Trevor of Brynkinalt, Chirk, North Wales. He was commissioned in August from an abbreviated course at Sandhurst, before which he was at Wellington, and arrived while they were at Borre. When he died he was still only eighteen and only three weeks older than Lieutenant Ottley of the 2nd Battalion, who died of wounds that same day. The recorded date of most of the other casualties was the 22nd, though the 21st was more likely. Private Robert Clark, the son of William and

Jane Clark, was a rope layer in Dundee, probably working with his father, a tenter. He volunteered in August and had been in France for a month. An identity disc was all that reached his family. Private William Smith, a Glasgow policeman who had joined up like many others on 1 September, was killed after being in France for less than three weeks. His parents James and Eliza Smith were on a farm near Pitlochry, Perthshire. Private Harry Miller, a labourer from Glasgow who volunteered three days after him, had also been in France for under three weeks. He was shot in the head and died on the 26th at Lillers. James and Mary Miller received a few of his belongings in Springburn. Another Glasgow policeman, Private Robert Mason, whose parents lived at Camelon, Stirlingshire, was wounded and evacuated two weeks later. Three weeks after that he married Winifred Greenland in Glasgow, where she lived from then on in Newlands Road. Not till November 1915 did he return to France, remaining in the BEF till early July 1917 when he was sent home sick, probably with trench foot, though there were no details. By late October 1917 he was on his way abroad once more and remained with the 1st Scots Guards till he went home in January 1919. Private John McAllister, also a Glasgow policeman, was from Argyll where his father Duncan McAllister lived at Carradale, Kintyre. Private McAllister was wounded in the arm and sent home to recover, but he never came out again. He became ill with TB, was discharged because of it in August 1916 and was dead by the time that his medals were sent out to him in 1921. Private Thomas Dick had been a railway engine fireman based in Glasgow, where his widowed father James Dick lived in Shettleston. On 1 August 1914 he had his nineteenth birthday, two days later he joined up and five days later reported to the Guards Depot at Caterham. After only five weeks there he was posted to the 3rd Battalion at Wellington Barracks. On 11 November he reached France and on 21 December he was mortally wounded, dying next day. An identity disc and a few cards reached his father.

On the afternoon of the 22nd General Lowther heard that the 6th Brigade of the 2nd Division were coming to relieve his men. In the event only the 1st Royal Berkshire Regiment appeared to relieve the Scots Guards, two of whose companies had to take over trenches from the French south of the Canal later in the evening. However, by juggling his battalions around, General Lowther was able to move back from Givenchy all three directly involved in the fighting there so far. The Brigade had lost four hundred men, only some of the trenches had been recaptured, there was an awkward bulge in the line at the north end of Givenchy, partly still in enemy hands, and the sniping was incessant and accurate. He heard of a London Scottish NCO, fired at and missed by two German snipers in the village itself, who pointed his wire cutters at them as if they were a pistol, charged and took them prisoner and also of Captain Geoffrey Stewart of the Coldstream being killed crawling out to reconnoitre. Sadly General Lowther wrote "That is not a Captain's job, they are too valuable." Everywhere trench foot, still identified as "frostbite", was now a major problem and many of all ranks were sick with it and from other complaints because of the conditions. Colonel Ponsonby was brought in very ill, suffering apparently from pleurisy, later amended to malaria, but then recovered quickly. Major Sandilands, commanding the London Scottish, had to go sick with rheumatism and Captain Arthur "Nipper" Poynter of the Scots Guards had "also cracked up with some trouble." He was forty three, had served in the 1890s and left before the Boer War. During that he was in the Imperial Yeomanry and won the DSO, as well as being very badly wounded. On the morning of the 23rd General Lowther was disappointed to be told that the Brigade were to stay where they were. "It is hard to write letters, diaries, or anything now. All day and all night messages drop in every few minutes so one gets little chance to sleep, and when there are no messages there are always cold feet and the noise of fire of all kinds to worry one and make one wonder what is going on. I have a very difficult place to hold in my section, the north side of the village of Givenchy is honeycombed with trenches up which it will be pretty easy for Germans to advance and be disagreeable if they feel like it. It is an important place too, so it makes one anxious." Two Scots Guards companies were in reserve, with their boots on at short notice to move, the other two still in the former French trenches. Those in reserve were in houses in Cuinchy, described in the War Diary as "in bits but habitable in places." Lieutenant Balfour noted "Our heavies start shooting like Hell behind us. Germans answer but they go about 200x short, may they stay there. 5pm shelling ceased." He had not had his boots off since leaving Borre.

They spent Christmas Eve at Cuinchy cleaning weapons and billets and their machine gunners came back having spent that day with the London Scottish in the front line. They had two opportunities to fire at the enemy, the first at a party of twenty at eight hundred yards, six of whom they reckoned they had hit, and the second in the early evening at a group round a brazier, knocking it over along with several men beside it. C Company buried two horses and the body of an Indian soldier found in an abandoned French dressing station. Lieutenant Balfour recorded "Heavy mail tonight; Get some v good shortbread from Mrs Macdonald." On receiving a congratulatory message from General Haking telling him that he had informed Sir Douglas Haig how well the Brigade had done in their attack, General Lowther remarked "very pleased I am at this, as I was not entirely satisfied with results myself. Got in fine mess going round the trenches, as they are so narrow that one rubs along each side, and comes upon frequent patches of mud nearly knee deep which almost pull off one's boots." Then "After dark an endless rattle of musketry and a lot of bombing. Some of them evidently big ones as the whole place shook. Nice sort of Xmas Eve and morning. In the night the London Scottish got in a wounded Munsters officer and 5 Coldstream from in front of their trench, these poor fellows must have been there 2 or 3 days." Following Gheluvelt the 1st Queen's were posted as GHQ troops and the 2nd Munsters, reconstituted after Etreux, took their place in the 3rd Brigade.

There was no Christmas truce in this part of the line, no singing by the Germans, no candlelit fir trees, no shouts across to the British. Instead General Lowther noted that Christmas Day "opened with ferocious firing east of us at 4am but we had a decent night's sleep. I got my feet warm for a short time. The Black Watch found a communication trench running forward from their trench and working along it brought in some more wounded Munster Fusiliers. We are rather in the line of sniping here. This morning when the servants were packing straw around the pump a bullet came just over their heads and the next one struck the pump itself. Just beside where this struck was another bullet embedded in the bricks. Xmas cards from the King and Queen arrived this morning as a surprise for everyone. Later. We hear now of some more Coldstream lying out wounded in front and inaccessible. In the flat ground north of Givenchy there must be many of the Munsters if they are not already dead. One cannot get at them and any attempt to do so only causes the loss of more lives. The enemy fires on any man trying to move wounded and I believe there never has been such a thing as an armistice for collecting casualties. This is certainly the most brutal war that has ever been known. We now hear that all the bombing and row that went on last night was nothing at all. The day passed fairly quietly and as decently as one could expect. Presents for every man from Princess Mary's fund came in the evening, together with a heavy and welcome mail from home." Two Scots Guards companies went to take over trenches at and beyond a farm on the north side of Givenchy, known as French Farm. This, according to Lieutenant Balfour, was "a bad place as some of the men have to be in the farm building, which is barely loopholed and not bullet proof in places and would be very nasty if the Germans started shelling. Horrible shamble of bodies in front of the trench, one can count 60. In Givenchy village there is not one house standing, even the church being a small pile of stones." Nothing happened but they found a Coldstreamer, wounded on the 21st, brought him in and Captain Stewart got him going by injecting strychnine into his heart.

On Boxing Day, after a very hard frost at night, they found and brought in a few more wounded, including a German who had been out between the lines, but crawling towards the British, for five days. Lieutenant Balfour heard that "on getting to the dressing station and being given OXO he became very cheerful. He was paralysed on the left side but could feel no pain, and his feet were frostbitten up to the ankles." General Lowther heard, by contrast, that he was thought unlikely to recover. The Scots Guards worked on the trenches and also buried eight men, two of them French, but Right Flank had a man killed and another wounded at French Farm by bullets through loopholes. The man who died was Private James Desmond, a slightly knock kneed painter, the son of Cornelius and Hannah Desmond of Hackney, London, who enlisted in August and sailed for France on 23 November. The only item which reached his family was an identity disc.

General Lowther went round the line on Boxing Day and found the Scots Guards, London Scottish and Coldstream "all very busy improving their positions. Far busier than the Black Watch, who seem to have been rather idle these days. It was very quiet up there, just a little sniping and machine gun fire, but later on one of our armoured trains turned up and as I write it seems to be livening things up. The AT usually draws a good deal of fire and is an unwholesome neighbour." The British armoured trains were mounted with naval guns manned by Royal Navy gunners. The two Scots Guards companies at French Farm were relieved by the other two in the evening without trouble. "The pack animals took up 16 boxes of ammunition and left them at the farm. 1 pack animal was hit in the stomach and had to be shot on reaching billets." Lieutenant Balfour was leading it and it was he who had to shoot it.

On the morning of 27 December General Lowther noted "quite a noise up north" which suggested another division was "at it pretty hard" while three hundred French guns then opened up to the south. He consulted General Haking about getting the Coldstream, Scots Guards and Camerons out of the line for a rest next day and organised the digging of a new trench to cut off a corner just north of Givenchy, done under Royal Engineers supervision after dark. "There was a lot of firing at the start and he had to wait 3 hours before beginning. When the Germans let off light balls all lay down flat. Unfortunately the Camerons occupying the trench in rear opened fire on their own digging party killing one and wounding two, otherwise no casualties in the line last night." On the 28th there were "A good many shells flying about, many of the Germans are "blind" i.e. do not explode. I think General Westmacott stirred up a hornets nest by shelling a sort of redoubt they have in a railway triangle between here and La Bassée." Brigadier General Claude Westmacott commanded the 2nd Brigade after General Bulfin was badly wounded on 1 November at Ypres. This railway triangle, south of the Canal, with its base along the main line, was a distinctive part of the embankment to the east of Cuinchy and immediately to the northwest of the mining village of Auchy-lez-La Bassée. At the western end of it one line coming from the Béthune direction branched off the main line to the southeast towards a number of pits and collieries, one of them called Fosse 8, and at the eastern end another line coming from the La Bassée direction branched off to the southwest towards Vermelles and more pits and collieries. Where these two branch lines crossed close to the Béthune-La Bassée road was the apex of the triangle, most of which the Germans already held. The British had now taken over from the French more of the line east of Cuinchy, including the western end of the triangle.

General Lowther continued on the 28th "Another wounded Coldstreamer (7 days lying out) was brought in this morning. His eyes looked dead but as he was not cold they brought him along. The Doctor injected Strychnine, in a short time he was taking notice and Bovril and half an hour later was asking for a square meal." While he would have had his emergency ration with him, General Lowther wrote that "even then nearly a week out in the cold and wet is a high trial. The man is expected to live." That afternoon the Black Watch and London Scottish replaced the others in the Givenchy trenches and were put temporarily under General Westmacott. Everyone else marched back to the tobacco factory and other buildings on the east of Béthune, accompanied on their way by a roaring southerly gale and some rain. They were still on call. "One battalion stands ready to move at ½ hour's notice. The remainder have a chance to get washed and decent and shake off some of the mud of the trenches. Got my clothes off for the first time for 8 days and had a bath before dinner." Very pleased that "the London Scottish have come on enormously in the past weeks and show plenty of energy and enterprise in the trenches. Internal administration and digging are their weak points" and he sent them a congratulatory order. "I am told that they appreciated it and have their tails well up." At Béthune the Scots Guards were "billeted in an orphanage and officers in a small chateau. Both very comfortable." Next day General Lowther went round the billets. "The men's clothes are caked in mud and the coats must weigh 14lbs or more. It is very hard, with no proper facilities, to get men or clothing dry or clean and warm, and ready to go up to the trenches again. Went into town (we are on the outskirts) and got my hair cut and visited the church. It has some good stained glass." He noted that "I complete 26 years' service yesterday." He heard of some Black Watch casualties and trenches blown in because of a German bombardment "by the minenwerfer, a devilish thing which throws a shell of over 100 lbs about 300 yards." Trench mortar bombs caused big explosions when they landed but, if seen in flight, as they often could be, and by night because of the sparks, were avoidable. Sentries also became alert to the sound of them being fired. There were different sizes of minenwerfer. Next a deserter from the *56th Regiment* came in "saying he did not like this war any more, that they were living in a foot of water and that the companies were commanded by NCOs." On 30 December some reinforcements came up, none Scots Guardsmen, and not enough to make up the casualties, but, as General Lowther remarked, "Even without casualties there's always a daily wastage of sick and injured dribbling away to the base."

On New Year's Eve at Béthune he "visited the bathing establishment arranged by the Division. We ought to get all the men washed before they go back to the trenches. Here they have an undressing place, a hot shower arrangement, and a supply of new underclothes. While in the bath their coats and trousers or kilts are taken to an ironing department and there ironed to kill possible lice!! And then they set forth cleaned and refreshed. The trouble is that the air is so damp that we cannot get the greatcoats dry and they are mostly still damp and mud-caked." While it was possible to do something about the lice in clothing, the process failed to have any effect on the eggs, so they quickly became as bad as before. In a brief lull General Lowther mentioned that he had "received a "Russian self-taught" that I had ordered from home, not that I think that it is likely we shall go there, but one needs something small in the way of literature to pass the idle hours. One cannot carry about a lot of books and they are soon read." Though otherwise the front line was quiet, at half past three that afternoon a message came that the

2nd KRRC in the western end of the railway triangle and nearby trenches were being heavily attacked and that the 1st (Guards) Brigade were to stand by. Everyone had to pack up in a hurry. At half past four orders came for the Scots Guards, whose turn it was since six the night before to be "in waiting" for twenty four hours, to march east to Beuvry and for General Lowther to report by car to Headquarters 1st Division there. He learned that the Germans had destroyed a forward observation post and machine gun emplacement on the triangle with two minenwerfer bombs and then rushed them.

The Railway Triangle

At five all three battalions left Béthune and halted at Beuvry, the Scots Guards having been in the lead but "the Battalion had been celebrating the near approach of New Year, and several men had to be left behind." At about six they received fresh orders to continue further east on their own, presumably to Annequin, under command of the 2nd Brigade. They waited for an hour on the road near there and Lieutenant Balfour was next "told to go on with billeting party to 2nd Bde to find a place for the night. Great difficulty in finding room but fix up Bn in some ruined houses close to Cambrin. Arrive in ruins at 10pm." Left Flank were detailed to go forward to Cuinchy with picks and shovels to be ready to dig in quickly once the 2nd KRRC recaptured their lost positions. Lieutenant Balfour heard about these at Headquarters 2nd Brigade and that if the counterattack failed the Scots Guards, who up till now knew little if anything, were to retake them. Meanwhile, General Lowther, whom no one kept up to date, found himself at Beuvry in a "very nice house, but occupied by the proprietors which is always a bore. One has to do a lot of politeness and they seem surprised and offended when one asks for a room in which to eat and work." With General Westmacott in command of operations, no new information and no reason to suppose that anything further untoward was afoot he went to bed.

At half past eleven the Scots Guards, totalling only two hundred and fifty men in the rifle companies, according to Lieutenant Balfour, were ordered to march at once to the KRRC Battalion Headquarters at Cuinchy. As they approached the village Private Preston's recollection was that they had gone cross country through a "quagmire, sometimes we were wading to our waist I was just thinking how the old folks would be seeing in the New Year when we halted." On arrival they were told to recapture the lost position "at all costs", the KRRC having failed. Hearing that they had tried straight along the railway embankment, Colonel Hore Ruthven decided to try something different. Whether or not it affected the outcome, one influence affecting any different line of approach was the canal dock for barges extending some way along the foot of the near side of the triangle. This forced him to attack from further to the right and because the object was to recover the lost posts the line of approach as they advanced would quickly put at their right rear the apex of the triangle where the colliery branch lines crossed each other.

They left their packs at Cuinchy and at quarter to two started forward past the Church at the east of the village and into the communication trenches to the new KRRC firing line. More would be heard of the packs later. Out in front of it they formed up in four lines twenty yards apart on open ground facing north, four hundred yards from the triangle. They were ready to start at twenty to three. Captain Stracey and C Company were in front, Major Orr Ewing and B Company next and 2nd Lieutenant Robert Dormer and Right Flank behind them. 2nd Lieutenant The Honourable Reggie "Dumps" Coke and Left Flank, still equipped, as previously, with entrenching tools, were the fourth line, in reserve, with orders to wait where they were. Private Preston found the communication trench "full of water and came to our armpits. We fixed bayonets and carried them above our heads. After we had gone about a hundred yards a fellow on the right of this trench was upping each man as he came along and assisting him out of the trench. Another further away was placing us a[t] six paces interval (our Coy was greatly under strength). Lieut Dormer one of the few remaining officers told each man as he crept past us that the enemy was less than a hundred yards away and that on the whistle blowing we would rise, shout like blazes, and show no mercy to any living thing we met."

The Germans had already held most of the triangle before capturing the two posts and lost no time in strengthening their hold. It was a moonlit but cloudy night and the objectives were clearly visible. The British guns opened fire at quarter to three and the counterattack started fifteen minutes later, supported by the KRRC machine guns firing from near the start line, by the 2nd Royal Sussex machine guns firing along the embankment and by fire from north of the Canal. To begin with there was little opposition but, when they were a hundred yards from the embankment, the Germans opened a heavy fire. All three companies were soon badly mixed up at the foot of it where there was a steep incline in front, but B Company on the right took the lost machine gun emplacement and C Company on the left the lost observation post. Very shortly, however, 2nd Lieutenant The Honourable Richard "Dick" Bethell was the only officer unhit. Colonel Hore Ruthven ordered Left Flank forward, without their tools, and went out to the embankment himself to help. There he found that his men were being shot at from the German trenches on the north side of the Canal, from down the line of the railway and, much the worst, from positions along the triangle behind their right rear. There was no cover. Everything had become very confused, the position was untenable and the men began to drift back. Lieutenant Coke, hit by a spent bullet, managed to get up again and continue, but, as Colonel Hore Ruthven reported, "It was a bitter disappointment to myself & the two remaining officers that we were unable to maintain our position after such a good start but I think the main reason for our failure was the fire from our right rear. Men will stand a great deal of fire from the front but reverse & enfilade fire seem to have a greater proportionate effect than a large volume of fire from the front. They advanced splendidly but the fire from the right rear was too much for them." After an hour there was no alternative but for those still on the embankment to pull back.

Private Stewart wrote that they all realised that a bayonet charge was likely, because that was what was to be expected when they were ordered to take off their packs. As they moved on "the enemy began shelling the communication trench, as well as the whole front. When near the end of that trench we followed [Major Orr Ewing] into the open and advanced in extended formation. The Germans, using bright flare lights, poured a hail of lead into us, sweeping our advance with machine gun fire. Our men were falling like flies." Then suddenly Major Orr Ewing "who was advancing close to me, fell. He did not get up. I lay down flat and rolled over to his side and enquired if he was wounded. He replied that he had been hit in the thigh, and could not move his leg, and feared he was seriously wounded. He asked me for a drink of water, which I gave him from my water bottle." A corporal came to help and the two of them carried him to the head of the communication trench. Private Stewart then went to find stretcher bearers, but while he was doing so the corporal and a sergeant from another regiment carried Major Orr Ewing back over the open. Private Stewart then went out again to where "the position had been taken but it was impossible to hold it." It was also impossible to recover most of the wounded. "We lost more than half our Battalion in this futile attack… The whole affair was a blunder which should never have taken place." He believed that the counterattack had been cancelled but that Colonel Hore Ruthven wanted to carry on, "wishing to have the honour of retaking the lost position." He added that just before going into action "many men in my own Company expressed the opinion that they would not live through the attack. One of these, a dear comrade of mine, named Gunn, bade his comrades goodbye before we went into the charge. He was one of those killed." Lance Corporal Hugh Gunn was a gardener, probably in or near Edinburgh, where he enlisted in the first week of the War. He had arrived at Borre and been promoted almost immediately. His parents Donald and Jean Gunn were crofters at Lairg, Sutherland.

Private Preston was waiting with Right Flank, his friend Private Richardson beside him. "Joe was wishing me a Happy New Year when off went the whistle and we started the course together. We reached this trench a short distance away to find it empty but immediately behind it we came on many shivering wretches. Our Scotch blood was up. At this spot much blood was shed. No quarter was given and none was expected. Our attack was checked at this point owing to hidden entanglements where Capt Stracey was killed." They got onto the railway embankment itself and started to dig in "and pandemonium reigned supreme." He saw Private Richardson bandaging Lieutenant Coke's head and then "we took our stand together on the far side of the metals, when an explosion on our right shook us off our feet." He believed that this was a mine activated by a trip wire, but it was more likely to have been a shell or minenwerfer bomb. He and others thought that the machine guns firing at them from the right were British ones. "About an hour later an opening came for further offence and we were led by Lieut Dormer but that officer became a casualty by being shot through the nose. A few minutes later I got my passport to Blighty. I had just crept round an old gun emplacement when something red hot seemed to catch me in the left thigh. I straightened and flopped for the count of ten. I shouted on Joe and he crept up to me but I got too weak and couldn't hear what he said."

Captain Stracey was killed on the railway embankment. His widowed mother Louisa Stracey was in London, though the family home was at Sprowston, Norfolk. When he started his diary the following autumn Sir Iain Colquhoun began that Captain Stracey "commanded my Company all through 1914. He was the finest officer I have ever known." Colonel Hore Ruthven wrote of "an irreparable loss to the Battn." Lieutenant Graham Menzies, who, after Wellington and Magdalen College, Oxford, had been serving for almost a year when the War began and had recently returned after being sent sick during First Ypres was also killed. William and Cecilia Graham Menzies lived at Hallyburton, Perthshire. Major Orr Ewing recovered from his leg wound and came out to command the 2nd Battalion in 1916. Lieutenant Dormer did not return to either Battalion, because he was never fit enough, though he remained in the Army, serving out of the line. He was thirty four when he was commissioned at the beginning of September 1914 and, though their mother was still alive, he named his younger brother Cecil Dormer in the Foreign Office as his next of kin. One hundred and nine men were killed, wounded and missing. They included Company Sergeant Major Thomas Holt, a Boer War veteran, promoted during the fighting at Gheluvelt, probably to replace Company Sergeant Major Dilworth of Right Flank. He was hit in the chest and died on 6 January at Béthune. His wife Ann and their two daughters were living near Windsor. Among the personal effects which reached her were a box of chocolate, three packets of tobacco and four boxes containing thirteen cigars. Anything of that type usually disappeared.

Private Preston came round lying in the wrecked vestry of Cuinchy Church. There was "a Fire in the middle of the floor with some bricks round it and some dixies boiling on the top. A very busy Doctor and quite as busy RAMC men. I had been carried there by a man with a bunch of cotton wool on his face [Lieut Dormer]. The place was full of Jerries & Tommies. The ambulances began to arrive. I went in the second, two Jerries, Private Owen, Private Brooker & myself were the occupants. The roads were being heavily shelled at the time. We got about half a kilo when we seemed to fall over a cliff. The car had plunged into a shellhole. The driver & a slightly wounded chap tore the cover off and lifted us out on to the side of the road. A car coming for its load picked us up." At Béthune he went straight onto a train to Boulogne, still in all his kit, still covered in mud. There "I was just beginning to feel my pain as up to now I had been a bit bewildered and felt dizzy." Next day his leg was operated on and a week later he was on his way to England. Private Wallace Owen had a slight scalp wound, but was sent to England too. He had been a labourer in Liverpool and joined up when the War was two weeks old, arriving in the Battalion at Borre. Private Richard Brooker, a London miller from Rotherhithe, enlisted a week earlier, but arrived at much the same time as Private Owen. He was not wounded but was sick with colic, which kept him in a field ambulance for four weeks. Private Joe Richardson was missing and there was never any trace. Like Private Preston he had been a fireman in Kilmarnock before the War, though he came from Dumfriesshire, where his widowed mother Margaret Richardson lived at Crocketford. Private James Sellar, born and brought up in South Queensferry, where his parents still lived, had an extended reserve commitment and was mobilised in August. After leaving the Colours in 1908 he returned to South Queensferry with his wife Kathleen, a Londoner. Their son was born the same year, followed by a daughter in 1912. Private Sellar arrived in the Battalion on 11 September and was slightly wounded two days later at the start of the Aisne. Now he was missing. So was Private Hugh Harris, a bachelor and sometime hotel boots, whose father Hugh Harris lived at Millom, Cumberland. He was nearing the end of the seventeenth year of a twenty one year engagement and had been in the BEF throughout. So was Private Thomas Crawford, wounded in the right shoulder at the Battle of Belmont during the Boer War. He had been living in Springburn, Glasgow, with his wife Sarah since he left the Colours after twelve years in 1911, but he too had a four year extended reserve commitment and so was mobilised. Private Daniel Sharkey, a forty two year old Fife coal miner, had enlisted on 23 October 1914 at Inverkeithing. Most unusually, in that he had been born in Liberton, Edinburgh, he had previous service in the Coldstream, but was well outside his reserve commitment. He was sent to France less than three weeks after joining up and was never seen again after this counterattack. His father George Sharkey was still living in Liberton. Private James Wills of Right Flank, a very early volunteer and previously a fitter, was also never seen again. His parents Ernest and Helen Wills lived in Leytonstone, Essex, and his younger brother Graham was in Left Flank, having joined up just before him in August. Private James MacKie, a Glasgow policeman, whose father James MacKie lived at Methil, Fife, was shot in the face near the right ear. Once he reached England on 4 January he was sent to the American Women's War Hospital at Paignton, Devon. He never fully recovered and was discharged medically unfit in 1917, there also being a complication with his chest. Private Alexander Macleod, a farm worker before he enlisted in 1908 and served for three years, had a tattoo of a girl's head and the name "Flora" in a scroll on his right forearm. He settled in Glasgow after leaving the Colours, married an Irish girl, Bridget Corrigan, in April 1912 and by this time they had two small daughters. Called up on mobilization, he went out to France in

September 1914. Not until 25 April 1915 was he reported missing on an unknown date, but 1 January was later determined as his presumed date of death.

Lieutenant Coke was awarded the DSO and Sergeant Alexander McPherson the DCM for taking command of B Company after all the officers became casualties and for his handling of "his men under very difficult circumstances with a gallantry and ability under a heavy close range fire." Colonel Hore Ruthven's third recommendation was for Corporal Robert Arnott who carried Major Orr Ewing out of action under very heavy fire, without which he would undoubtedly have been left in the hands of the Germans. Corporal Arnott, a reservist, could have been "the corporal" whom Private Stewart mentioned. He had been in the BEF since mid September and left on 18 January, invalided back to England with bronchitis, not serving abroad again. As he only held acting rank he reverted to Private on being sent home sick and, though a serving soldier, was sent in the autumn to work in the Munitions Department of Fairfields at Govan, in Glasgow. He was discharged in July 1917 at the end of sixteen years service. His and Maria Arnott's home was in Paisley, with a daughter born long before and a son born in 1916. He was mentioned in dispatches and in October 1916 received the MM. The fourth recommendation was for Lance Corporal William Bland who had volunteered to carry messages under very heavy fire. He, also a reservist, had been a seaman and arrived in the BEF after Ypres. He never received anything.

Meanwhile General Lowther had slept comfortably and when he first woke on New Year's Day all seemed to be quiet, only for him soon to find that it was anything but. At quarter to seven he was told to march his remaining two battalions east and report to General Haking at Cuinchy. Just as he was leaving a telegram arrived from General Westmacott saying that the Scots Guards had attacked at half past three, that he did not know where they were and that all the officers appeared to have been killed. "Thank God not quite true, but bad enough as poor Reggie Stracey, the only officer who has been out all the war, is dead. (One of our own shells I fear, but one don't say so here)."

While the rest went back to Cuinchy sixty of the survivors under Lieutenant Bethell had to stay on in a trench behind where the counterattack started. He had been at Eton and Magdalen College, Oxford, and, already in his thirties, was one of the many commissioned on 15 August 1914. He arrived at Borre. His wife Evelyn, whom he married in 1911, was in London. Lieutenant Balfour stayed out until nine in the morning collecting wounded and getting picks and shovels together for the men staying on in the trench. Then he came back at six in the evening with a relief for Lieutenant Bethell's party. From now on he was both Adjutant and also for the next three weeks commanding troops in the trenches. "The communication trench back to the church was about 1,000 yards and averaged about 1 foot deep in mud and in some places was 3 foot." The ground was very open to the east of Cuinchy and carrying out any relief in daylight was impossible. Conditions were very difficult and the trenches in a very bad state but officers and men built traverses and firmed up the bottom with bricks and straw. There was some German shelling in the afternoon, but the only subsequent Scots Guards casualties he mentioned were when a shell hit a billet behind the line and severely wounded ten men during a rifle inspection. Eventually on the evening of 2 January he "was relieved at 6pm and literally could hardly walk home owing to the weight of my clothes from mud. Have rather a swollen ankle too and a slight sprain caused from dragging one's feet out of the mire." Later on that night two officers, one of whom was Lieutenant Geoffrey Monckton, fit again after his wound on the Aisne, and two hundred men arrived. Because of the shortage of officers six Grenadiers came to be attached temporarily, as well as two commissioned from the Artists Rifles. A little after this General Westmacott sent Colonel Hore Ruthven an undated message, which Lieutenant Balfour kept with his diary. It began "I am most awfully sorry about the looting of your men's kits [packs] – it was a blackguardly thing to do – we are doing our best to trace the men who did it."

On 2 January General Lowther noted that aerial reconnaissance showed that the Germans were having the same problems with water and were consequently digging a fresh line a little further back. Their guns had been shooting accurately at the big chimney of the distillery slightly further north, hitting it four times in four minutes, but failing to knock it down and not causing any damage otherwise, but he had had "A bad night what with messages, and the rats just under my pillow in the straw." After breakfast on the 3rd he set off with Major Brooke to inspect the main trench at Givenchy, commenting that the Black Watch had not made it nearly deep enough, with the consequence that men would continue to be hit by stray bullets, irrespective of snipers. He added "It is most difficult to recognize one's own trenches from the distance and one runs the risk of either not shooting at the enemy, or else of shooting one's people. More bother with minenwerfer just before dark and some London Scottish wounded in French Farm." There was a scare in the small hours when Germans massed opposite it, possibly for an attack on what was the most prominent and vulnerable point in the Brigade line, but nothing happened and he suspected that "a number of Germans turned out to extinguish a burning haystack." In the evening on the 4th he finished off "So many people who come in are incapable of finishing their business and going away. They stay on wasting valuable time and being a nuisance and it is often difficult to continue being civil."

Trenches at Givenchy

On 3 January the Scots Guards came back under command of the 1st (Guards) Brigade and out of the trenches east of Cuinchy, only to have to go back north of the Canal after dark next day. While just under half of them stayed back around the distillery just beyond the Pont Fixé, the others, two hundred men, were in the front line. "Our section of trench runs from Canal bank N for 60 yards, gap (waterlogged) of 200 yds with detached post in centre on biscuit boxes, then 30 men, then about 60 men in trench 60 yds in advance, then 30 men level with the other 30. Trenches in an awful state, half falling in and communication trenches in places 3ft deep in mud." That meant some three hundred yards of mire. The main communication trench was one thousand five hundred yards long with endless disused trenches off it. There were great difficulties and consequent delays in carrying out this relief in the dark and it was not complete until two in the morning. Major Bernard "Romeo" Romilly, another officer with a strong family connection, his uncle having been a Colonel in the Scots Guards, came up that day on his own to join them, though almost immediately he went down with "a touch of fever". He was the son of Samuel and Lady Arabella Romilly of Huntington Park, Herefordshire, and had been at Charterhouse and Sandhurst before being commissioned in 1898. He had a DSO from the Boer War and had served almost entirely since then on secondment to the Egyptian Army, only leaving in the middle of December. While the relief on the evening of the 6th was a great improvement, there was still the mud in the communication trench. Two Scots Guardsmen got stuck and it took two hours to get them out. That day General Lowther was mainly concerned about snipers and "Went round the north and west trenches where sniping was very active indeed, and we had about 10 men wounded, 3 of them carrying up rations in rear. The Coldstream picked up a German about 3 days dead, evidently a sniper; they also found a quite warm rifle which must have belonged to another. While Brooke and I were looking out thro' two loopholes in French Farm a bullet came thro' the wall between our heads!" There was a lot of shelling by both sides, relative to that stage of the War, but particularly by the Germans with both HE and shrapnel, without any obvious purpose. The weather, rarely dry and more rarely sunny, was mostly very cold and very wet.

    He then noted that at a court martial "two of the Black Watch got 5 years each for "shamefully casting away their arms" on the night of the 21st when there was a hurroosh in Givenchy. Poor wretches, but such an offence has to be severely dropped on if one does get a chance to convict." General Haking set off to walk to see General Lowther but his GSO1 stopped him because "there were too many projectiles flying about in these parts. Not that Haking would mind that in the least, but Major Generals are too valuable." After dinner two 1st Division staff officers "brought aircraft photographs of our own and the German trenches. Very bewildering they are too, as the whole country for miles is a maze of trenches now." Captain Thorne spent the whole of the 7th and until half past two on the morning of the 8th, when the light gave out, transferring the air photograph details to the Brigade Headquarters maps, General Lowther commenting that "it looks a terrible tangle to the E and NE and a matter of about ten lines of trenches – old and new – lie across our path in that direction." Lieutenant Balfour was busy on the 7th. "About 9am saw the smoke of a German brazier in their trench: got the range and fire 5 shots at a loophole about 6" below parapet (range 550x): made the Germans put their fire out. Had several other shots at some inquisitive Germans: don't know if I hit them but anyhow silenced all sniping. Our artillery shelled the embankment very hard all the afternoon; saw one or two limbs and a whole German body blown up about 30 feet into the air. Relieved at 6pm by Romilly. I tried a short cut across the open (pitch dark so no risk entailed beyond stray bullets) in order to avoid the most muddy parts of the trench. Very successful as regards the mud but as I was ahead picking my way for the men following behind I fell into a stream I had forgotten and went up to my neck in water (damned cold), …but short cut good. It had never ceased raining all day but thanks to waders which had arrived only the night before I had kept dryish up to the time of my fatal plunge." On the 9th those going up to relieve the forward positions carried fascines and hurdles to line the bottom of the trenches. Until the full relief four days later most of the Battalion swapped over between the firing line and support every twenty four hours.

    General Lowther wrote that the enemy had gone quiet but were "letting off a lot of lights which is usually a proof of jumpiness." The conditions that they too were living in may have had something to do with it. On 8 January "Visited the Coldstream trenches, which were a quagmire and falling in everywhere with the rain, the Camerons are worse and the Scots Guards still worse. We can scarcely walk in the trenches and digging is most difficult, as the mud sticks to the spade and has to be shaken or scraped off, for each spadeful. Some early shelling of the distillery, evidently a new battery registering its zones, several of their shells fell in the canal. A German ration carrier wandered into the 2nd Brigade lines yesterday, he was distressingly clean, they say. An arm was also blown out of the German trenches into the 2nd Brigade trench by one of our big shells… Germans very busy baling water in their front trenches N of Givenchy this morning, so we hope they are not too comfortable. On returning from trenches had a change of underclothes and a complete wash out of doors at the pump. Pretty cold but very comforting, being the first full wash and change of the year. We are not losing more than about 6 men hit a day, very reasonable." The following day he noted, less favourably, that "we lose about 30 men sick a day in the Bde. And as time goes on will of course lose more as constitutions feel the strain. The London Scottish are the only [Battalion] who have next to no sick, and in November they were having 80 men seen by the surgeon daily."

Generally, but concentrating south of the Canal, the British artillery put down "a tremendous bombardment" on the enemy trenches for an hour at noon on the 8th, intended to make them think an attack imminent and disclose how strongly they were holding their trenches. The Germans retaliated by shelling the British infantry and for twenty minutes 120lb HE shells were raining down close to the wrecked house of the Scots Guards Battalion Headquarters. Two days later there was first a burst of rifle fire and ten minutes shelling from the British, starting just before noon. This was followed by an even heavier British bombardment of the railway embankment for an hour in the early afternoon. Lieutenant Balfour thought it the biggest of the War to date involving one hundred and fifty guns of all calibres, one battery firing 1005 rounds, with the infantry opening up as well with rifles and machine guns for half an hour and "the whole ground in front of us was like a big fire." The German guns replied, mainly shelling the Givenchy-Béthune road, but "20 coal boxes and a few woolly bears were aimed at us. One coal box fell into the Camerons' trench about 40x to my left, killing 2 and wounding 1. Three others pitched about 10x beyond my trench in the particular bit where I had chosen to sit and observe from…The shelling of the embankment was a most extraordinary sight for rails etc were being hurled about 60 feet into the air and bodies also could be seen whistling through space. Just as I was walking into one billet, I was struck by a spent bullet on the arm, nothing beyond a bruise; it did not even cut my coat." At the end of the bombardment the 2nd Royal Sussex attacked and recaptured the embankment posts at the west end of the railway triangle without opposition, the British guns having completely suppressed the German defences. A "woolly bear" was a shrapnel shell.

Matters did not rest there. The German guns started firing at eight in the morning on the 12th, aiming some two hundred yards behind the British trenches. Lieutenant Balfour could not understand why. "Can't think what they thought they were shooting at and I kept thinking of a remark a gunner made the other day when the Germans were missing his battery by about 50x "Some damned fool will go monkeying with the sights and then there will be an accident."" As two days earlier, there was a pause and then at two o'clock the firing started again, concentrating once more on the embankment. The British guns joined in and there was a fierce battle for much of the afternoon as the German infantry tried to drive the British out, which led to the loss, again, of the untenable observation post. General Lowther heard that a party of three hundred Germans had appeared from behind the embankment and stormed the post on a very narrow front. At the critical moment the British artillery observer's telephone line to his battery was cut by enemy fire. On the heavy shelling, General Lowther commented "About 90 shells were fired at a house a few hundred yards ahead of us, but no one was hurt. Two civilians selected the moment of the attack to go to this place to fetch some buried property, they were lucky to get away with whole skins." On the other side of the Canal Lieutenant Balfour watched as the Germans "hurled some minenwerfer bombs at our canal trench but missed it by some 50x and shook the whole country for miles…You can see it the whole of its flight and it comes sideways at you like a crab (not point foremost) looking like a large sausage, it goes wobbling to a great height and then comes down straight and blows everything near it to pieces. Its range is about 400x." He also remarked that "The German impudence is astounding. The other day a man stood on the parapet 500x away and one of our men missed him – so he signalled a miss with his spade and leisurely got back into the trench." There were casualties from apparently random shooting, quite apart from the sniping, and General Lowther noted the death of a Coldstreamer on the 12th from a bullet which came through a shutter and killed him where he was standing far back in a room, while a Cameron was shot through the heart while looking round the wall of the Brigade Headquarters house.

During this period Private Stewart "and three others were detailed for outpost duty at a very dangerous place in No Man's Land and only a few yards from the enemy's trenches. While proceeding to this outpost, which was in reality a round hole, one of our party fell across a low wire. A bunch of bells began to ring along the wire." The Germans immediately put up flares and swept the ground with machine guns. So far Private Stewart and his companions were safe while they lay low before continuing on their way. They stayed out for twenty four hours, but to little purpose, as they had to keep their heads down because of a sniper who fired at their parapet continuously "and finally succeeded in fatally wounding one of our party – a Welshman named Williams. He was struck in the neck by an explosive bullet, and died instantly. We buried him at that place when night arrived, and then fell back to our main firing line." Private James Williams, a Welshman working in the Scottish coalfields before the War, enlisted at the end of August in Falkirk and died on 10 January. His real name was William Gerald Lewis but, partly because he was serving under an assumed name and had given a false address for his sister, the first that his parents WP and Annie Lewis in Aberbran, Brecon, knew of his death was when they read his alias in a newspaper casualty list. He had been writing to them so they knew where he was, a field postcard sent on 5 January stating that he was well being the most recent.

On the 11th General Lowther had again gone round the trenches which were "in a sad condition of water and adhesive mud. I was several times thigh deep." He could not change his clothes any more than anyone else, in his case on account of "my other unders being in the wash at Béthune…Orders came in notifying probability of immediate relief, thank goodness. But I never pass these orders on till the change is imminent for fear of disappointment." Lieutenant Balfour wrote "It will be a great thing going down to Béthune if only for a few days for a rest is sadly needed for everybody has got the most awful colds and we lose about 8 men a day going sick with high temperatures. The new men although they have not quite got the discipline of the old lot are at heart wonderful and have still the spirit of the Bde of Guards and their cheerfulness in all the mud and slime is marvellous." Late on the 12th General Lowther was "disturbed by a visit from Nairne at midnight, with long orders about alleviating the lot of the men in the trenches." Lieutenant Colonel Edward Nairne was the new GSO1 of the 1st Division, only in the job ten days. When he turned up General Lowther was keeping an eye on the partial relief of his battalions, the Camerons finally getting back down the communication trenches past Brigade Headquarters at one in the morning. He himself got to sleep two hours later. Colonel Nairne reappeared the following morning to walk round the trenches and General Lowther remarked "We started in the first communication trench by wading knee deep through a cess pool." He heard that another division's bomb factory and explosive store had blown up accidentally near Béthune. While the casualties were light it was "Tiresome, as one needs to have a lot of bombs at hand tho' one don't often use them, and they deteriorate quickly in the wet trenches, where it is not easy to give them proper care." Lance Corporal Adam Kinloch, a policeman in Forfar until he enlisted in September, had arrived in France on 27 December, already promoted.

Soon he was on his way home for five months, a bullet having hit him in his left shoulder on the 13th. His father Robert Kinloch lived at Drumlithie, Kincardineshire.

As soon as night fell on 13 January the Scots Guards came out of the line and went to Beuvry. Battalion Headquarters and those in dug-outs around the distillery left first, but again there was delay when two men got stuck in the mud, one up to the armpits, and again it took two hours to get them out. The officers all slept on the floor of one large room at Beuvry. They marched back to Béthune the following afternoon to billets in the École Michelin. Lieutenant Balfour had "a very comfy billet with some very nice people, who provided me with a BIG bath, with 3 ft of water in it in which I soaked for an hour. What joy! Clean clothes and the sense and knowledge of cleanliness again." On the 16th he was told he could have four days leave from late that evening. So he had dinner with the officers and left afterwards. From London he took the overnight train to Berwick on the 17th, giving him two days and a night at home near Kelso, before returning to Béthune in time for dinner on the 20th. He travelled as far as Kelso with Captain The Honourable John Campbell and his eldest son Donald who were going on to their home at Hunthill, Jedburgh. Captain Campbell was forty eight and, without any obligation to do so, had insisted on rejoining to serve with the 1st Coldstream.

On 12 and 19 January two drafts arrived from the Base totalling three officers and two hundred and fifty eight men. Most had enlisted in late August and September and many were Glasgow policemen. When General Haking came down on 18 and 20 January visiting all his five battalions General Lowther noted that he made "a very complete tour, speaking to every single man. The men like it very much and even if they start with long faces soon cheer up…it is a very good thing the Divisional General speaking to every man in his command like that." On the evening of the 20th there was a "concert in the theatre organised by the Scottish regiments. Quite a good show. All lights went out and for a while the concert went on by the aid of hand electric torches. General Haking told him during dinner that there were some facetious Germans opposite Givenchy. One of them had shouted across to the 2nd Welsh "Is there anyone there from Swansea?" When several answered "Yes", he hurled a grenade across with the remark "Then you can divide that among you, you blighters."

Private Watson, formerly at the Royal Albert Dock, described life in the front line. "There was no lack of rifles, ammunition, food & water …We had to deal with circumstances as we found them when taking over trenches from others, & also as different circumstances arose. It is amazing how adaptable, & resilient, human beings can be under the threat of life or death; since bullet, bomb & shell were no respecter of persons, affluent or otherwise. We all endeavoured to help each other whether in section, platoon, company etc; comradeship was of a very high order…Boredom depended on the esprit de corps & the individual: as indeed it does in civilian life…During my early period in the war there was always something to do in the trenches; improving them; draining them; digging dug-outs, sometimes when off duty having a book to read or letter to write." He had with him eventually a complete pocket edition of Charles Dickens novels printed on rice paper and leather backed, as well as other books. When in the trenches he said that it was possible to wash one's hands and face and, if water was plentiful and a pail available, one's feet. He was most critical of the hard biscuits. "I could never understand why, if biscuits had to be supplied, why soft biscuits (plain) could not be supplied in tins, as they were then available, just like bully beef tins." These hard biscuits were issued initially instead of bread and were about three inches by two and half an inch thick and "as far as I can remember most of them were burnt as fuel." There was no fresh fruit at all other than any the soldiers bought for themselves. In the trenches the food was tinned and consisted of bully beef, various soups, pork and beans, some puddings and Ticklers jam initially, better jams coming later. All the food was cold, but they made hot tea by burning wood, biscuits or solid cubes of naphthalene. They ate when they could. He remarked that Ticklers jam had the viscosity of paraffin and penetrated everything through to the skin. There was never any shortage of food in the trenches owing partly to the amount supplied, but also to the oversupply resulting from casualties. Private Watson said that the communication trench known as the Old Kent Road at Cuinchy was paved with ration tins and if one was hungry it was simply a matter of picking one up. He mentioned that mine craters were a distinct help for drainage because they were often twenty feet deep or more and could take a lot of water out of nearby trenches. He also told of how six Scots Guardsmen saw a minenwerfer bomb coming straight at them, but calculated that it would fall behind. It did, exploding in a huge, flooded crater used for dead cats and dogs and as a trench cesspool. They were drenched and, though it was possible to clear the trench and do something to dry them out, the smell was beyond local attention. It caused great amusement. The only solution was to send them back down the line and so they missed the last two days of a trench tour. Of the men he said "Our soldiers seemed to have an inherent natural ability, & capacity to cope with unusual & unforeseen circumstances; plus the most valuable asset of a deep rooted sense of humour, which the Germans did not possess."

The Cuinchy brickstacks

On 21 January the Scots Guards paraded at half past eleven in pouring rain before lining the road east out of Béthune for Lieutenant General Sir Charles Monro, now commanding I Corps, past whom they then marched in fours. That day he had inspected all five battalions ahead of their going to the line south of the Canal. In the evening the Scots Guards went first to some roofless billets in Annequin and were told that over the next two weeks they would do three trench tours of forty eight hours, the first being from after dark on the 23rd until relief after dark two days later. Otherwise they would be in reserve and doing fatigues. Some three quarters of the men had been in the Battalion for less than a month and well over a third had never been in the line. Because of the recent heavy rain and snow General Lowther found the trenches very difficult to get round on the morning of the 22nd and he noted that those in them had to put in a lot of effort to rectify matters, adding at once "I don't much like our line." That afternoon he had visits from Sir Douglas Haig, General Haking, "the boss doctor" [unnamed], General Gaillot, commanding the French 183rd Brigade immediately to the right, and six others "the last disappearing about dinner time." He "found the French next to us most cheery and looking wide awake. They had an awful contraption called a "piège à Boches", so arranged that any German jumping in was impaled and caught in barbed wire."

The front line east of Cuinchy was now, because of the Germans on the railway triangle, a northeasterly bulge. The French were on the right from just south of the Béthune-La Bassée road. From there the British trenches ran north towards the lost posts at the western point of the railway triangle. As it approached these it bent back in almost a right angle to the west for about five hundred yards, called Barrossa Lines, and then went on northwest up to the railway embankment. The ground to the east of Cuinchy was open and exposed and there was no cover apart from the trenches themselves. There was also no formed support line, but among the brickstacks further back the British had constructed a strong point, The Keep, by building up the gaps between four stacks with more bricks so firmly and solidly that they were strong enough to keep out field gun shells. The only communication trench forward from Cuinchy Church to The Keep was the principal Old Kent Road. Behind The Keep, running south to north, was the Western Communication Trench, the part immediately behind The Keep being the Suez Canal. North of The Keep, linked by the Suez Canal to it was another communication trench running east, also called the Old Kent Road. A second communication trench, renamed High Street, but part of the original Old Kent Road, led directly east from The Keep. Further forward the Eastern Communication Trench ran broadly speaking from south to north halfway between The Keep and the front line.

After dark on the 23rd the Coldstream went up on the left to the railway embankment and Barrossa Lines where, on taking over, they found trenches that had not been completed, bad communication trenches and fire trenches full of water. It rained hard all night. It was impossible to do anything about this in daylight because of shelling. At the same time the Scots Guards took over the forward positions next to them, with the French brigade on the right. Two companies left Annequin in the early afternoon to go forward, their route taking them through Cuinchy and into the Old Kent Road, past The Keep and on along High Street to the front line. One went up behind them to occupy The Keep and the fourth stayed in reserve in Cuinchy in the cellars of wrecked houses. The one that Battalion Headquarters were in was, as Lieutenant Balfour noted, the only one "with some ground floor rooms intact but the top two storeys are knocked to pieces. The church is gutted both by shell and fire." Where the Coldstream and Scots Guards trenches met the enemy were "only 25 yards from our's so a bomb battle may rage there at any moment." There were telephones between the front line, The Keep, Battalion Headquarters and Brigade Headquarters and "owing to constant attention the main communication trench and the fire trenches are in excellent condition (very unlike what they were on New Year's Eve)." The other communication trenches were "awful". There was "very bad" sniping where the trenches were closest, which was opposite the Scots Guards, and the Germans were managing to put bullets through British loopholes, killing a Scots Guardsman on the morning of the 24th. Generally, however, that day was relatively quiet and such German shelling as there was seemed to General Lowther to be intended to smash the canal lock nearby. Lieutenant Balfour wrote that evening about the Royal Engineers Tunnelling Companies "There are some good dug-outs and listening galleries which are underground passages leading to within 10 yards from the German trenches from which they are supposed to hear if the Germans make any big movement or do much digging or mining. They have also charges in them so that if the Germans made a desperate attack we could blow them up." He admired "the wonderful underground passage leading under the main Béthune-La Bassée road towards the French, I had a chat with them: it is rather funny thinking that you could have a 350 mile walk along the trenches and get to Switzerland." After dark on the 24th the companies swapped over so that Left Flank were next to the French in the front line, with Right Flank next to the Coldstream, B Company in The Keep and C Company in reserve. The Keep's garrison included a machine gun team and a light artillery mountain gun.

At about six next morning a German deserter, Heinrich Schwarz, from Schwetzingen, to the southwest of Heidelberg, whose details General Lowther recorded, came into the Left Flank trench. He said that in half an hour there was going to be an attack by three battalions, preceded by an artillery bombardment and the explosion of mines dug under the trench. Everybody got ready for this, but there was little else they could do. Heinrich Schwarz was right in all respects except the precise timing, even allowing for German time being an hour ahead. At twenty past seven everything occurred as he had warned. The Germans blew a mine under the weakest point in the British front line, where Right Flank met No 4 Company of the Coldstream, and simultaneously fired a number of minenwerfer, with heavy shelling as well. Their infantry then moved in and, having initially thrown grenades, stormed the weak point, fanned out to left and right, clearing the trench both from behind and from the front. All the forward companies were completely overrun.

Major Clive "Cloche" Morrison Bell, educated at Eton and Sandhurst, had joined the Scots Guards in 1890 and left in 1908. Since 1910 he had been MP for Honiton and two years later he married The Honourable Lilah Wingfield, whose mother was a Coke. He was one of the few told so he could be on the platform at Farnborough when the Battalion stole away to France at the very beginning. Now he had rejoined, arriving on 19 January and taking command of Right Flank. To him "It all seemed very peaceful, and the war might have been a hundred miles away instead of thirty five yards, as it was opposite my platform." He got twenty minutes notice of the German attack, based on the information received, and, as instructed, passed the message to the Coldstream. "Here was a nice little bolt from the blue. I went back down the company, telling each man personally and told them to oil bolts and served out three extra boxes of ammunition…The men were in splendid spirits and soon got everything ready…A couple of heavy shells came whispering over from our guns and plumped into their lines and then all was still and suddenly an inferno began. A mine exploded a few yards from where I stood, but just round the bend in the trench. Tons of stuff seemed to come my way and I remember bending my back to try and support the weight I could see falling. It knocked me down, but I was not buried and still had hold of my revolver. Simultaneously with the mine their guns started shelling us, but chiefly the left end of the company, I think, and the Coldstream, but something worse happened. The explosion of the mine was the signal to the Germans, who were not a hundred yards off, to reach our trenches. They came across in hundreds and stopped on the edge of the trench shooting down on it. What could 130 men do against this? They did all they could, and not a man left the trench." He was very proud of the way that Right Flank fought it out for as long as they could. "The whole thing was over in a quarter of an hour. Looking to the left, where the trench went round a bit, you could see Germans kneeling on the edges, and just above I could hear them talking. They kept back as long as there was any firing, and I managed to get off nine shots with my revolver and emptied the contents of a rifle I picked up. At last there were only three men left on my left and one by one they were picked off. I realised suddenly I was alone, I slipped down into the trenches and squeezed against a little alcove and waited, feeling in a nice funk. Two men jumped down and covered me with revolvers and I said "Ich bin Offizier". They were both very decent and I felt I should not be killed. They crossed to the German trench, and as a shell burst over them one man gave me a frightful crack on the face. Otherwise they were all very decent." In captivity he found only Sergeant James Young and thirty two men and so deduced that at least a hundred had been killed, including his three other officers. Some other men, wounded, so he would not have seen them, were also captured. Only five men from Right Flank survived. Left Flank suffered in the same way but when, because of this assault, the French brigade on their right had to withdraw, eighteen managed to join them. Altogether forty from Left Flank got back. The only other survivor from the front trench was an unnamed machine gun sergeant who said that after he had "killed 3 officers and 150 men he was then shot at by 15 men at 10 yds but only got scratched on one of his fingers." He reached The Keep.

Heinrich Schwarz' warning lost the Germans surprise and so, in spite of the shock of the mine, they had to fight very hard. An anonymous account from a German engineer officer appeared soon afterwards in a Swiss newspaper and was picked up correctly as an accurate description. His own task was to set the charges for the mine. From what he wrote it would seem that there was only one and also that the fighting was very far from one sided. The mine went up and "Immediately after, there was a pandemonium of rifle fire and of machine gun discharges that bordered on the incredible. The hand to hand combat had begun almost instantly. The Scots fought like demons. Many of their comrades had been blown into the air with the earth of their trenches. The British artillery joined in, and fired with remarkable precision and a rapidity that gave us the shivers. Whilst I was busy withdrawing our mine installation, a British shell burst inside the trench in which our reserves were waiting. It killed every man within a radius of twenty feet, and I escaped as by a miracle. I immediately helped to attend to the wounded. Our troops continued the attack for two hours, and succeeded in pushing on to the second line of the British entrenchments. Our operations were considerably hampered by a number of brickstacks and sheds which the British had turned into fortifications... I had to make an inspection of one of the trenches. I had to do so crawling, as the enemy sniped us mercilessly. I have seen many horrors of the war, but I never saw any horror like this. The dead lay sometimes in twos and threes on each other, and I had to crawl over them."

The German infantry then headed towards the brickstacks, becoming very disorientated in the British communication trenches and also apparently wholly unaware of the existence of The Keep, manned by two B Company platoons under Major Romilly. Immediately north of it was Sergeant McPherson with the other two platoons in dug-outs among other brickstacks. Beyond were No 2 Company of the Coldstream with No 1 Company further left on and around the embankment. Major Romilly got a little warning from in front because survivors reached The Keep in some panic and almost immediately reports came that the enemy were approaching both from the north and the south. Because of the way that The Keep had been fortified it was difficult to fire out of it and initially, briefly, there was some confusion, but he quickly turned the mountain gun on the northern gate. This created two openings towards the north and northeast through which there were immediately good fields of fire. The unexpected presence of the gun alarmed the Germans and gave Major Romilly a brief space in which to deploy his men and organise a reserve. Some Coldstreamers had also joined him. Sergeant McPherson took charge outside The Keep from the west gate round across the whole of the north face of it, ably supported by No 2 Company who held their ground, as did No 1 Company. Major Romilly was then able to concentrate on the gap which had appeared between the south of The Keep and the French on the main road. Three platoons from C Company under Lieutenant Bethell came up to fill the left half of this and a message reached the French to fill the rest of it. By ten to eleven that morning Major Romilly was able to report that the situation was satisfactory and that the time was ripe for a counterattack. Lieutenant Balfour wrote of the fighting as "positively mediaeval. Men were sitting on the brickstacks dropping bombs on those below and a machine gun in the Keep was firing point blank range and the Germans were within 30 yards of the "Keep" before they realised its existence." With all the telephone wires cut he ran back to report to Brigade Headquarters, dodging Black Marias "for some way until at length I was knocked endways by the splash of clods from one which burst about 10x from me and had my wind knocked out for about 10 min and was violently sick." He reached Brigade Headquarters, told them what he knew and, feeling better after half an hour, set off back. As the few survivors from the front line came back to The Keep Private Stewart, with Sergeant McPherson, saw as "Without a moment's hesitation [Major] Romilly ordered the retiring men to halt, under threat of shooting the first man attempting to retire, and instructed Sergeant McPherson to place the men in fighting position and open rapid fire on the advancing masses of enemy who were now only a few yards away. We immediately commenced to fire at the advancing Germans as fast as each man could work the bolt of his rifle…we gave a good account of ourselves, and before midday, appeared to have the situation well in hand…by some good fortune, Sergeant McPherson arranged to provide rations for us, including rum, and the rum certainly helped us on that occasion."

Colonel Hore Ruthven was unhappy with the Battalion's performance and with how the front line had collapsed so quickly. His report began by stating that the men were nearly all very young soldiers, some with only a few weeks service, adding that the NCOs were likewise very young and that "we have Sergts with less than a year's service." He continued that "the "loud explosion" they all speak of shook them very much, & to put it plainly, a large number directly they saw the Germans, bolted." Though some of those few who first got back to The Keep did cause an initial scare, Major Romilly immediately contained it. At least one hundred and thirty of the Battalion lost their lives that day and others died of their wounds later, altogether about a quarter of the total fighting strength at the time. Only a few of the casualties were not in the forward two companies. The number of prisoners with Sergeant Young was not high and others captured were wounded, some mortally. In addition to Major Morrison Bell, 2nd Lieutenant Gerald Crutchley, a Harrovian who had arrived on 12 January, was also a prisoner, also unwounded. His father was Major General Sir Charles Crutchley, a Scots Guardsman, and his mother Sybil was a cousin of the Cokes. On his father's side he was a first cousin of Lieutenant Ronald Gibbs, killed two months before in the 2nd Battalion at Ypres. Batting in the Oxford first innings in the 1912 Varsity Match at Lord's he scored ninety nine runs not out by close of play on the first day, only to wake next morning with measles. He was unable to play again in the match.

Colonel Hore Ruthven did not identify the reasons for the Germans' initial success, their excellent timing in assaulting immediately after the mine went up and their use of overwhelming numbers, three battalions, to do so. He drew attention instead to what he considered the poor standard of his men's shooting, attributed to insufficient practice. That being the case, he felt that there should have been more men in the trenches to hold them. He then turned to the trenches themselves, only recently taken over from the French. These had been constructed with loopholes in the parapet, which made it very difficult to fight effectively at close range because there was no width of field of fire. Also the trenches were far too deep at ten feet and the firesteps or standing places onto which the men had to step up to shoot were unsteady for accurate shooting. There was no barbed wire at all in front. Finally, he remarked that there had been no formal second line. Much more constructively, though not acted upon in any way until much later, he recommended that there should be a lightly held front line with a second line as the main defence line about two hundred yards back, adding that there needed to be a large amount of barbed wire in between. Colonel Hore Ruthven credited the holding of the enemy attack directly to Major Romilly. "I should like to add that I consider Major Romilly's defence of The Keep deserving of the greatest praise. He had considerable difficulty with his men at first & it was only by standing at the gate revolver in hand & threatening to shoot the first man who attempted to leave that a panic was averted. The existence of The Keep & Major Romilly's defence of it undoubtedly saved the situation." He ended by commending Sergeant McPherson and passed on the Coldstream's recommendation of Private Johnstone Logan for volunteering for special duty, possibly taking a message. Major Romilly was mentioned in dispatches, Sergeant McPherson, who had played an outstanding part, was rewarded with a commission in the field into the 2nd Argylls, who were near Armentières, but Private Logan received nothing. He was one of the Glasgow policemen and the son of William Logan of Kilmarnock. Probably in the draft which arrived on New Year's Day, he fell seriously ill with pneumonia at the end of December 1915, was evacuated and died on 20 March 1916 of TB. Private Alexander Lamond had been serving since September 1907. Though born in Leith, he was in Glasgow working as a labourer when he enlisted under the alias of Alexander Grant. This was discovered and he admitted that Lamond was his real name, but there was a court martial. He had no relations and provided no names of next of kin. There were tattoos of the bust of a girl and a butterfly on his right forearm, others on his left. He first arrived in France in the New Year's Day draft and after 25 January was appointed Corporal for gallantry in the field. His rise from then on was fast and as a Lance Sergeant he became the Battalion Signal Sergeant. By June 1915 he was a Sergeant, was only ever very briefly sick with flu at the end of that month and was not wounded. On 6 November Sir Douglas Haig presented him with a French Croix de Guerre and on 12 January 1916 he left, commissioned into the 10th York and Lancaster Regiment.

At ten o'clock on the morning of the 25th the French counterattacked and recovered their trench. General Lowther brought up the Camerons and London Scottish to hold a second line at Cuinchy in case the support companies at the brickstacks were overwhelmed and ordered the Black Watch, back at Beuvry, to prepare a counterattack. The circumstances being similar to those on New Year's Eve, this did not start until one o'clock that afternoon and the Germans had had plenty of time to prepare. There were two hundred casualties and nothing was achieved, but separately the 2nd KRRC, on loan for the purpose, reached the line they were ordered to occupy without difficulty. The 2nd Royal Sussex, also on loan, counterattacked in the evening and succeeded in straightening out and digging in the new line from the railway embankment to The Keep, following which Royal Engineers came up at two in the morning and dug a new diagonal trench southeast to link up again with the French. There were some alarms in the night. Two German patrols were seen off, one as a result of Scots Guardsmen on a brickstack north of The Keep throwing grenades onto them as they tried to get into High Street, while the other fled when a sentry at the north gate shot their leader.

Lieutenant Balfour put the B Company losses as twelve "killed and buried" and twenty one wounded and the total losses of the two forward companies at two hundred and forty. Lieutenant Monckton, commanding Left Flank, was missing but several accounts arrived from prisoners in Germany confirming that he was dead. Of the attached Grenadier officers, one was killed and two missing, but dead, a fourth wounded, a fifth not involved, having probably been sent down sick, and the sixth, Captain Andrew Kingsmill, unscathed and remaining with the Battalion for some time. Both the Artists Rifles officers were missing, but dead. Two missing men were Private Percy Luck, originally an agricultural labourer from Eastbourne, who enlisted in 1905 and served seven years, and Lance Corporal Wallace Brookes, born in Parahaki, New Zealand, a seaman when he joined in Glasgow in 1907. On leaving the Army both went to Australia, having given undertakings to honour their reserve commitment. Both got married in the twelve months before the War. Percy and Edith Luck had a daughter at the end of September 1914. He probably never saw her. Wallace and Clarissa Brookes did not have children. Called up on mobilization, the two were likely to have travelled back to England at the same time. Both were posted abroad together, arriving in France on 27 December and coming up in one of the January drafts. Almost immediately on arrival Private Brookes was promoted Lance Corporal on 15 January. Several who died that day were recorded later by the IWGC as being eighteen or less. One of them, Private Charles Beal, who had won a schools shooting medal at Bisley and whose widowed mother Frances Beal was living in Holyhead, Anglesey, had given his age as nineteen and twenty days when he joined up. Another, Private James Pert, whose parents George and Margaret Pert were in Cowdenbeath, Fife, described himself as a fish merchant when he volunteered in early September, saying he was nineteen and seven months. He arrived in the Battalion only very shortly before he was killed. A third was Private Graham Wills of Left Flank, whose brother was missing after the counterattack on the Railway Triangle on New Year's morning. He had said he was nineteen on joining up. Their families told the IWGC that each was seventeen when he died. Helen Wills received a letter dated 28 January from Private Arthur Smith, one of the very many volunteers from Preston, in his case as early as 6 August, "Just a few lines as I am Jim and Graham's mate, and I am awfully sorry to break the news to you about Jim and Graham. Jim has been missing since New Year's morning, and Graham was killed doing his duty to his King and Country Monday 25th inst. Graham was a good and true soldier; before he died he told me he would fight to the last, and he did do it. I just managed to escape with three more chaps. If I live to return safely to England, I shall come and visit you and give you the full story as we are not allowed to say much about it. About Jim, we do not know exactly whether he is a prisoner or killed, but he is missing. All the Guards who knew them send their greatest sympathy, as they were two very nice young fellows."

Sergeant Samuel Penfold was a Boer War veteran who had been working for the Post Office in his home town of Gosport, Hampshire. He and his wife had eight children, the youngest born in 1912. He joined up again on 13 September and was promoted very soon to Sergeant. Though meant to go out with the draft which left Wellington Barracks on 27 December, he missed it by returning nearly twelve hours late from leave and was severely reprimanded. He went out with the next one, arriving in France on 4 January. Missing three weeks later, he was the second oldest Scots Guardsman in either Battalion to lose his life on the Western Front. He had completed twenty one years service in February 1906 and by now was forty nine. Amy Penfold was dead by late 1919 and their younger children were then all in a Dr Barnardo's Home. Two farm workers, with homes just west of Aberdeen, Private Alexander Beattie, whose parents Alex and Jane Beattie lived at Countesswells, and Private John Mathieson, whose father James Mathieson lived at Kinellar, joined up together on 12 August and were both missing. Private James Birss, a Glasgow policeman taken prisoner near Major Morrison Bell, sent Private Beattie's father a postcard from Germany to tell him of his son's death. Private Birss came from the same part of Aberdeenshire and James and Margaret Birss lived at the Police Station at Skene. Sergeant Richard Westmacott, mentioned deprecatingly by Private Preston at Givenchy, had given his occupation as a clerk when he enlisted on 28 August in London, the same day that his younger brother Lieutenant Eric Westmacott was killed on the light cruiser HMS *Arethusa* at the Battle of Heligoland Bight. He was the elder son of Edgell and Marion Westmacott, of Richmond, Surrey. Sergeant Westmacott was accepted as having been killed from a letter dated 14 July 1915 from Lance Corporal William Fraser, who was taken prisoner. He was the son of Jane Fraser, a widow who lived at Stratherrick, Invernessshire, and had been a farm worker before he enlisted in 1903, serving for a little over three years. When the War came he was in Western Australia and was mobilised there. He had been in France for a month.

Many of the dead were Glasgow policemen. Five who joined up on 1 September 1914 were Lance Corporal William Rettie, whose parents Robert and Annie Rettie lived at Burnhaven, just south of Peterhead, Private Farquhar Fraser, the son of Hugh and Helen Fraser, of Killen on the Black Isle, Easter Ross, Private Donald Steele, whose father Roderick Steele lived at North Boisdale, South Uist, Private Thomas Milroy, who was unusual for a Glasgow policeman in that he came from there, his home being in Govanhill, and Private James Watson, whose parents George and Susan Watson lived at Kirkton hill, Montrose. None were ever heard of again. Either immediately before or immediately after Private Milroy enlisted on 1 September Sheriff Fyfe married him and Janet Low the same day at the County Buildings, Glasgow. Private Watson's elder brother, Private George Watson, was one of the very first to join the Scots Guards in the War and survived. Their father had been in the Regiment and served in the Boer War. Two more Glasgow policemen who joined the Scots Guards on 1 September were alive at the Armistice. Private Donald McDonald from Dunvegan, Skye, was wounded twice later on, in the right thigh at Puits 14 Bis, Loos, at the end of September 1915 and in the head at St Léger in August 1918, just after the 1st Scots Guards began to move forward in the final advance which ended the War. Pipers led a generally protected existence. When on the same day another policeman joined up stating he played them, he was listed as a piper from the start. This was Piper William Craig, the son of Helen Craig of Glendye, Kincardineshire. He was not sent out to the BEF until January 1916 and survived the rest of the War unhit with the 2nd Battalion. Private Charles McEwan's sister, Johan McEwan, wrote on 12 February from Aberdeen after the report that her brother was missing arrived "I have been anxiously waiting for word of him and I shall be only too pleased to let you know if I hear any word of him. Trusting to hear Better news soon." Nothing more was heard. On 8 March men of the 2nd Division found the body of Private William Garven and buried him, the grave thereafter being permanently lost. His mother Agnes Garven lived in Garturk Street, Govanhill, and Private Milroy's widow, Janet, was a few doors away. On 16 November 1914, six weeks before he went to France, Private Garven had married Annie Morrison in London. She was living at Bonawe, Argyll. Lance Corporal Daniel Gallagher's mother, Anne Gallagher, wrote on 18 February from her home near Ballyshannon, County Donegal, "Would you kindly let me know anything concering the whereabouts of my son Dan Gallagher…As he is reported Missing since 25th Jany 1915. Such information I will kindly receive. Kindly oblidge." They were three more dead Glasgow policemen and there were several more.

Experienced soldiers were also killed. Company Sergeant Major John Lamb of Left Flank died near Lieutenant Monckton. He had served for twelve years in the 2nd Battalion and then got a job as a colliery fireman in West Lothian. On reenlisting on 19 August he was immediately promoted Sergeant. He joined after Ypres, becoming Company Sergeant Major after 1 January. His widow Mary lived at Faucheldean, near Winchburgh, with their daughter. Private Robert McArthur was missing. Listing his occupation as a contractor, he had reenlisted the previous September in Glasgow, where he was born and brought up. Agnes, his wife of ten years was in Falkirk. They did not have any children. He too joined after Ypres and was soon made a Lance Corporal which lasted until he was convicted of drunkenness on 5 January, sentenced to fifty six days FP No 1 and reduced to the ranks. Therefore he was under sentence when the Germans attacked on the 25th. It was they who reported that he was dead in a list received through the

American Embassy in Berlin in September 1915. Company Sergeant Major William Ellott, a Boer War veteran, born in Maidenhead, Berkshire, and a postman before he enlisted in London in 1897, had been in France for a month and was promoted two weeks after he arrived. He was never heard of again. His wife Elizabeth and their six children, all under ten, were living off Regent's Park, London. Drummer William Rowe, not yet eighteen and a half, was missing. He enlisted as a boy soldier just over three years before and had been in France for a month. William Rowe, his father, lived near the Elephant and Castle in London. Private Thomas Parker, a miner from Heath Hayes, Staffordshire, had sixteen years previous service in the Scots Guards including the Boer War. He reenlisted on 26 November 1914, arrived in France in that draft too and was now missing. He and Flower Parker had four daughters and a son, the youngest daughter born in 1914. After Flower Parker died about the end of the War, her mother Fanny Plumley became the children's guardian. Private Thomas Duck, son of Thomas and Caroline Duck of Old Ford, had been a carman in London until the previous September. When he lost his left eye on 25 January he had been in France for less than two weeks. He remained in England for the rest of the War and married Jessie Holland in London in March 1918. Only after the Armistice was he sent out briefly to the BEF. Private Hugh McCabe, the miner and reservist who was one of those who helped Lieutenant Eric Mackenzie back from above Vendresse after he was wounded on 14 September and was himself hit in the head the same day, had recovered. Back about a fortnight with the Battalion, he was now missing. In June 1912 he married Annie Cassidy in Kilmarnock and it was there that they lived. Annie McCabe had a daughter in 1913 and a son a month after her husband's death. Until 3 September 1914 Frank Brown, William Ironside and Andrew Irving were policemen in Paisley. That day they became Scots Guardsmen, with consecutive regimental numbers. Private Ironside was the eldest and an Aberdonian like his wife Margaret. They married in August 1908, settled in Paisley and had four children. He arrived in the Battalion at the beginning of December, was almost immediately made a Lance Corporal and on 15 January appointed Sergeant. Private Irving, the son of James and Ellen Irving of Mossdale, Kirkcudbrightshire, landed in France soon after New Year and Private Brown, the son of John Brown of Kirkmuirhill, Lanarkshire, in mid January. All three were missing and only Sergeant Ironside's body was ever found, long afterwards. The Coldstream losses were also very heavy. Ten officers and one hundred and ninety two men were killed, wounded and missing. Among the missing was Captain Campbell, Lieutenant Balfour's neighbour in the Borders. His son Lieutenant Donald Campbell of the 3rd Coldstream was twenty when he died on 19 July 1916 in the Ypres Salient.

Lieutenant Balfour wrote to his father "If we could have got reinforcements earlier and counterattacked at once we might have retaken our trenches and given the Germans more hell than they got." More would be heard of this. For General Lowther the 25th was "One of the worst days of my life." After dark "We spent a bad night dozing in chairs to be awakened now and again by news which was always bad. I had about 850 casualties in my Brigade and there were another 70 or so in the 2 borrowed Battalions and with all that loss we have been driven back 500 yards, imperilling the French on our right and inconveniencing the 3rd Brigade on our left. I search my conscience for cause of blame to myself and cannot find it tho' of course I have to take the responsibility. The worst of it is that in a certain circumstance the attack might have been stopped. This I put in to remind myself, and my friends need not worry their heads about it." What he meant he did not explain. From then on as the night progressed there was "a good deal of shooting at people digging. Visits from Staff Officers and others on and off, and at about 4am I sent Thorne off to see where our line really was. His report was not satisfactory." Captain Thorne had discovered that the Germans had got into some of the brickstacks north of The Keep and the 2nd KRRC had not managed to drive them out. Leaving them and the 2nd Royal Sussex in the front line, General Lowther withdrew most of his own companies, though C Company of the Scots Guards were still at The Keep. He went up himself at nine on the 26th to look at the situation at Cuinchy "and was not much pleased." Next came orders for relief that night by the 2nd Brigade and in the afternoon a visit from General Haking, who was "evidently not much pleased with me and no wonder." After dark General Lowther drove back to Béthune noting the recent shelling of the town and of Beuvry by the German heavy guns at a range of eleven thousand yards. They had "also put some shells round about the 1st Corps HQ whose personnel first of all took to the cellars and then left for Hinges further west."

At five that evening the Scots Guards went back "to Béthune for rest (how long?) Having had no sleep since arrival at Cuinchy owing to messages and running about am dead beat and have lovely bed and must sleep" wrote Lieutenant Balfour. They stayed until 2 February in Montmorency Barracks. Since they arrived in Béthune four and a half weeks before they had lost fourteen officers and three hundred and eighty two men, well over half of them missing, mostly dead. Recriminations persisted. General Lowther wrote on the 26th "Everyone who has been on that wretched ground where we were seems to have expected calamity." Sir Douglas Haig mentioned it in his private diary, the first information which reached him suggesting that the Coldstream and Scots Guards had not put up much of a fight. He wondered also about General Lowther's performance. He made further enquiries, from which he concluded that the 1st Division as a whole had not yet recovered from First Ypres, had had stiff fighting since around Givenchy and that the shortage of officers and NCOs in the Coldstream and Scots Guards was a major contributory factor. He recommended that the Division should be brought out of the line for preferably as long as three weeks training.

On the 27th General Lowther learned more when he visited the Coldstream, who now only had about a hundred and sixty men, and then the Scots Guards, who had seven officers and two hundred and ninety. What he heard indicated that there had been "a series of tremendous explosions in our lines at the time of the German attack…as the enemy only report about 120 prisoners I fear a very great number must have been buried or killed…I had hoped that many more were prisoners. It is very depressing." The Cuinchy area remained volatile. The 2nd Brigade were not disturbed much till the evening of the 28th when Lieutenant Balfour noted an "awful scare last night for there was terrific firing from our old spot and we were all ready to move at once." The firing died down at eleven and they were allowed to go to bed. The Germans had put in a heavy attack on The Keep and been driven off. They lost a lot of men, but there would be a lot more fighting around there in future. Through to the 31st the Scots Guards, still at a high state of alert at Béthune, were nevertheless hopeful of a chance of a more thorough rest. On the 29th Sir Victor Mackenzie, wounded at Gheluvelt, came back. On the 30th General Haking told General Lowther that "he was quite satisfied with everything I did on 25th. Very nice of him, glad somebody is pleased." His next remark was that Winston Churchill, accompanied by Lord Wimborne, had "turned up at Div HQ the former going to Cuinchy to have a look and (?) to give his advice. What would be said if the civilian responsible for naval affairs in Germany were to turn up at La Bassée[?]" On 1 February came the hoped for news of three to four weeks rest for the Brigade around Lillers, to the west of Béthune, and Lieutenant Balfour set off to find billets, good ones, in the mining village of Burbure. They marched there next day and the first two weeks were, in his words, "Very dull but peaceful." Two more officers and two hundred men arrived the same day. General Lowther noted that evening that two Coldstreamers were dead, asphyxiated in their sleep, and three others very ill from using a charcoal brazier in a room without ventilation. "A sad and foolish waste of lives." He spent most of the time over the next few days visiting his battalions, not apparently giving them any warning of his very early arrival in the mornings, so as to find out how active they were at Reveille. On the 5th General Haking came to see him and produced "more letters from on high about the 25th. He added that he had remarked "For goodness sake sack L[owther] or myself, or else tell us we are jolly good fellows, but don't go on teasing us and making us unhappy." He certainly takes everything in the best spirit and is an excellent man to work for." General Lowther was studying and preparing carefully for something else. On 6 February he was President of a Field General Court Martial trying Privates R Morgan and William Price of the 2nd Welsh for the murder of Company Sergeant Major Hughie Hayes, whom they shot and who died on 21 January. Both were found guilty and sentenced to death. On 15 February, after confirmation of the verdict and sentence, they died by firing squad.

In the evening of the 6th news came that the 4th (Guards) Brigade had recaptured all the brickstacks at Cuinchy after 9.2 inch howitzers had fired ninety five rounds or about ten tons of ammunition into the area first. After this battle Lieutenant Charles Cottrell Dormer of the 3rd Coldstream died of his wounds on the 8th, his Scots Guards elder brother having been killed at Kruiseecke. A message was passed on to General Lowther that day from Sir John French that he was pleased with the 1st Division's work over the past six weeks so "I suppose all is forgiven and forgotten." On the 10th there was a "Terrific row about Jamie Balfour who wrote something about operations on Jan 25th to his father, from whom by some mysterious means it got into the Daily Chronicle. The fat is in the fire with a vengeance. We've all done it to a greater or lesser extent, but have not been found out." Then he too was found out. Only the next day he heard that a section of his diary had been intercepted by the Censor and there was "a row about it for which I can see no justification. All the news was old when it left, and anyway, it was of the slightest and of this my friends frequently complain. You can't please everyone." He wrote also "Gradually we are getting the men washed at the colliery baths 5-6 miles away. There are 42 baths there." There were complaints from the men that they collected more lice there than they had on arrival, but he thought this wrong as clothes were boiled for twenty minutes at a temperature of two hundred and fifty degrees. Whatever the process, it was the men who were broadly right. General Haking spent the whole of the 10th visiting troops in billets, spending the afternoon with the 1st (Guards) Brigade and seeing all apart from the Black Watch. Next day General Lowther noted that it was hardly necessary to wake him at two in the morning to pass on a report that an airship had been seen passing over the previous afternoon. Then he went on leave for eight days. On return he remarked "Accidents in practice with bombs seem to be the general rule and we've lost some useful men thereby." Next day he was commenting on "Snowdrops coming up freely and a few primroses." There was heavy snow on the 24th, followed by a rapid thaw, which made the already very wet and muddy conditions that much worse.

As General Lowther had anticipated, it was confirmed on 25 February that their Division were to relieve part of the Indian Corps somewhere two days later, which turned out to be from Festubert north to near Neuve Chapelle. The 1st (Guards) Brigade took over from the Garhwal Brigade, whose commander, Brigadier General Cecil Blackader, had been a contemporary at Sandhurst. When he visited him on the 26th, General Lowther found "It is awfully wet and flat country and does not look promising on the map. But as a matter of fact it is very strong… Roads in rear are very bad, and the state of some of the billets so filthy that he [Blackader] was sick twice going round them a few days ago. (Before we got there he had made them quite presentable.)" When she heard that they were leaving General Lowther received "Long letter full of complaints from Mme Devys (our landlady) but she ended by saying that the condition of Château Philomel is far better now than when we took it over. I'll keep that letter, as one never knows what outrageous claims will be made later on." He had earlier referred to her as "a rapacious old girl, full of complaints, mostly unfounded." He went on to say that a man in Burbure had claimed four hundred francs compensation for damage to less than an acre of stubble caused by the Scots Guards drilling on it, alleging it had been sown with priceless clover. From Burbure both Colonel Hore Ruthven and Lieutenant Balfour went on leave and both then went down with severe attacks of flu requiring prolonged sick leave. Lieutenant Balfour came back on 11 March. General Haking was off sick for a while too and General Lowther woke up early on 1 March with vomiting and a very painful stomach, which for four days kept him in hospital in Béthune.

The Brigade took over their new line after dark on 28 February. Initially the Scots Guards were in billets in reserve in the Rue de l'Épinette, the road running up north from Festubert behind the front line to the Rue du Bois, and then did forty eight hours in the line, alternating from then on with the Camerons. More reinforcements arrived on 2 and 9 March. There were two officers, one being Lieutenant Eric Mackenzie, recovered from his wound on the Aisne, and two hundred and forty one men altogether. In the first draft was Private Herbert Johnes, his real surname, but owing to a clerical error when he enlisted he was recorded as being called "Jones" and that was what he served as. He came from Shifnal, Shropshire, where his widowed father was living. Private Johnes' mother had died when he was three. She, born Freda Feldmann, was a German from Celle, which her son was very careful not to say anything about. In August 1914 Herbert Johnes was a steward on the SS *Peleus*, a tramp steamer of the Blue Funnel Line, working out of Liverpool. The ship had left for the Far East in March with the expectation of at least a year in the Western Pacific. However, as it happened, they started back earlier than expected and were heading for Jeddah in the Red Sea to drop off Muslim pilgrims from Jakarta on their way to Mecca, with cargoes for Marseilles and Amsterdam. As they approached the Gulf of Aden on 8 August they met the SS *Ixion*, another ship of the Blue Funnel Line, and then heard of the outbreak of war. The reality struck them forcefully two days later when they saw HMS *Marlborough* order a German cargo ship to heave to and fire a shot across the bows when it did not do so at once. Continuing through the Suez Canal they docked at Marseilles and offloaded part of their cargo before continuing, as ordered by the Royal Navy, to Falmouth, still intending to go on to Amsterdam. From Falmouth there was no further traffic up the Channel and so the SS *Peleus* was sent to Liverpool, arriving there on 2 or 3 September. The crew were paid off and told to return a week later, but Herbert Johnes gravitated towards the recruiting office in the Haymarket. There, following advice from a tall policemen with whom he got into conversation, he volunteered on 10 September, having decided that his mother was Scots, and left next day for the Guards Depot. He found and thanked the policeman before he left. There were not enough uniforms for everyone at Caterham and some completed their basic training in civilian clothes before going on to Wellington Barracks. Those with any knowledge of Morse Code and other signalling were then selected for training as signallers and Private Johnes was one. Then in early February they were all called away to complete their live firing training on the ranges at Rainham, Essex, the reason being that still more men were urgently needed in France after the Cuinchy brickstacks. Not till a draft for overseas formed up were all of the men to go abroad fully kitted out. On the day they left they marched out to Waterloo Station. "There was some tear jerking on the part of parents and some of the fellows' wives, but it was a good send off from lots of wellwishers. The train trip from Waterloo station down to Southampton was a little grim, it gave a fellow time to think over the situation and wonder what was ahead of him. Some took advantage of the trip to write a last letter home. Some cheered things up with a sing song, old time songs in the main. Myself I tried to picture conditions at the front, what the trenches were like…The idea that from the time that one steps into the line at the front one's days may be numbered by mistakes occurred to me." They embarked on 24 February and crossed by night. On the train from Le Havre, which stopped frequently and unexpectedly, there were "no sanitary facilities…at every stop someone was wanting to go, with no place to go except at the side of the tracks, in full view of spectators, French, men, women, and children. To them it seemed an everyday occurrence." On the third morning in the train, 2 March, they arrived at Chocques, west of Béthune, and an officer from the Battalion met them. They marched east. "At first there were few signs of war going on, other than a few British soldiers of various supply units. The first actual sign was a plane up overhead with our insignia on it." To Private Johnes the countryside seemed peaceful and the French civilians waved as they went by. Then they started to hear gunfire, gradually more distinct, saw squads of French men and women preparing a new defence line of trenches and breastworks under French military direction, noticed more planes, mostly British, and later on sounds of machine gun fire. At Rue de l'Épinette the draft halted at Battalion Headquarters, where Major Romilly inspected them. Private Johnes looked around at the buildings, some destroyed, some damaged by shells, some fairly intact. A few French men were still about, but no women and children. The draft split up among the companies and Private Johnes joined 12 Platoon of C Company, "one of the rabbit companies", B Company being the other. 12 Platoon were in a barn, part of some farm buildings, built in a hollow square with the midden in the middle, reasonably weatherproof and comfortable for sleeping on straw, but offering no protection whatever against shells. Private Johnes found "The general spirit of the troops was good, both young and old fellows, serious, but they all could find some sense of humour." Already in this platoon was Lance Corporal Jock McAulay, the son of Isabella McAulay of Plean, Stirlingshire. He was a miner before joining the police in Glasgow where he won the police heavyweight boxing championship in 1912. Having volunteered early in September, he came out at the end of the year to France, but missed the events of January, because, while at the Base, he immediately had trouble with his knees. This would recur and he was sent home at the beginning of April, only returning in August.

That night, when the Battalion took over the forward positions, but C Company may have been in support, Private Johnes first encountered the rum ration and "without thinking took a good gulp and darn nearly ruined my tonsils" whereupon an old soldier offered to finish it for him and to give him two "pimp sticks" [cigarettes] in return for his whole ration the next night. Private Johnes did not fall for that. When they woke the next morning some of the draft found that they "had begun to get a little itchy, "Itchy Coo" it was tagged, or at a later date just plain bloody lousy. It was the first attack by the little bastards, an attack that never ceased." That day they came upon the Ticklers jam tin bomb. "Filled up with a mixture of explosive and junk metal when possible, sealed with a piece of fuse sticking out the end. It was passed from day to day to one another to take care of. You lit the fuse prayed to God and heaved it. It let off a terrific bang and a multitude of smoke but did little damage. Its place in billets was under the farm pump." The next night Private Johnes was sent out in a standing patrol of six men to a place he called Dead Cow Barn. "Being dark when we took over we could only go on sound, orders were no fires, no smoking and no talking… The weather was murky, damp and chilly, fellows off duty took a flop in the barn on a pile of straw. The barn was a small flimsy affair with the northeast corner knocked off by shellfire, it was exposed to God knows what. On sentry for the first time it was uncanny straining ears and eyes to try and detect any false movement, knowing that our chaps were working to the right and left of us, sloshing about in the mud trying to build breastworks. Occasionally a Jerry sentry would think he heard or saw something and pull the trigger, a bullet would thock into the mud or whine on by. As the dawn broke over to the east one could gradually detect on the horizon the ups and downs of Jerry's line, and also the reason why our post was called Dead Cow Barn, a couple of dead cows just to the north of it and several more with a horse and a pig lay scattered in between the lines." This place was generally known as Dead Cow Farm and had next to it Dead Cow Post.

There was a gap of about two hundred feet in the line of breastworks and the next night Private Johnes' section went up into the line just south of it. There was constant work on the breastwork in front of them, at this time about shoulder high. These consisted of revetments of branches, twisted and plaited by civilians further back and brought up to the line and fixed with stakes into the ground. "Earth was thrown over them onto the Jerries' side and built up with sandbags where possible. The ground was wet and soggy and we had to keep digging back from the breastwork to get spades full of earth, carry them back and throw over onto the Jerries' side…Sandbags were in short supply…The work was done whenever possible, but mostly at night." They also had to work their way out to the north building up a breastwork to close the gap. This started at night with the digging of a shallow zigzag trench, the earth being thrown up towards the enemy until gradually it was deep and high enough, very tedious, though the reason was clear enough. So as to watch No Man's Land and beyond peepholes were made in the breastworks, carefully concealed and masked with empty sandbags, and sentries had to make sure that at no time was there clear daylight behind them either. Private Johnes wrote of a man in his section making "a slight mistake and a Jerry sniper cut the plank holding the sandbags up in two, letting the top bags of sand down and sealing up the hole. A close call." Others were less fortunate. Private James Clark was a butcher in Hawick before the War. His parents were both dead and his next of kin was his married sister Mrs Dodds who also lived in the town. Private Clark arrived in France on 4 January 1915, was shot in the right leg a week later and came back in under a fortnight. On 7 March shrapnel struck him in the right thigh and fractured the bone. He was taken first to Rouen, then evacuated across the Channel and died at Netley on 1 June. He was one of five Scots Guardsmen who joined up on 11 September 1914 at Hawick.

Sniping was constant and the principal means here of establishing mastery over the other side and hence building up morale. Private Johnes remembered "From one of our peepholes we could see a short overlap bearing a little to the east about a couple of hundred yards away in Jerries' line. Once in a while a Jerry could be seen making a dash for it a little to the rear, it looked as if they had a latrine somewhere back of the gap. It was in a difficult position to get a sight on. In my trick on sentry I managed to squeeze the peephole a little north to cover the gap, and get a sight on it. Then it was wait for a Jerry to show up. Finally one did and passed to the rear, he was in his shirt sleeves. A few minutes later he showed up coming back, I pulled the trigger and he pitched forward and stayed put. No one else showed up. I could not count a definite hit but no further trips were made at that point." He spent three nights in the line of breastworks, then went out to billets, "and duty on road block again." For the next tour Corporal McAulay was commanding 12 Platoon in breastworks running through an orchard. Private Johnes was on sentry one night, completely exhausted. "We had a patrol out in front stringing barbed wire…I was all in…kept awake by scratching coolies, lice. However I did drop off, leaning up against the parapet, and a burst of machine gun fire brought me to. I in turn took a crack at the MG post occupied by Jerry. A few minutes later McAulay came along and bawled me out, our patrol still out…it had rained and the ground was soggy and difficult to walk about on without slipping. Very lights shot into the air by both sides made the situation uncanny. If out in the open a guy had to freeze otherwise his movement would be spotted, the best way was to drop to mother earth and stay dogo."

General Lowther had set off from his Headquarters at Le Touret in heavy rain on 6 March to see the southern half of his breastworks "not so intolerably wet and dirty as trenches. Going round one has to do a good deal of walking, quite out in the open, but in all the 2½ hours I was out I heard only one bullet instead of the hundreds one would have heard in our old trenches elsewhere…Stopping fell out of a front tooth, so I got Corporal Meeks of the London Scottish to come and fix it. He is a Harley Street practitioner of 11 years' standing." Corporal William Meeke was twenty eight when he enlisted in the London Scottish on 3 September 1914 and was one of the very last to do so who then fought at Messines on 31 October. A few weeks after he dealt with General Lowther's tooth he left France and was commissioned into the RAMC.

In view of the relative peace the Coldstream attempted to work in daylight on the 7th on a second line breastwork, but that led to shelling from what General Lowther variously described as a "pipsqueak" or "squirt" gun, the German 77mm field gun, so they had to stop, though no one was hit. There was also the following up of reports, initially by the Black Watch, of enemy tunnelling. The Royal Engineers were sceptical and proved correct when General Lowther ordered four counter mines to be dug at different locations, one of which struck quicksand only a few feet below the surface. On the evening of the 8th he sent out patrols to assess the possibilities of an "attack in certain eventualities. Not very healthy as the Germans are wired in in a veritable birdcage all along their lines." Meanwhile the weather alternated between heavy rain and snow or clear skies and hard frosts. There was a lot of adverse comment from everyone, except from General Haking, about the intercepted part of his diary. This led General Lowther to observe "I wonder what the Adjutant-General would say if he saw Smith-Dorrien's diary which goes the rounds so freely." Of what was imminent he made no mention and throughout was careful not to give the slightest hint of future operations.

Notes on Chapter Sources

War Diaries: 1st Division TNA/WO95/1228, including Lt Col The Hon WR Hore Ruthven's reports on Railway Triangle and Cuinchy brickstacks, and 1st Cameron Highlanders TNA/WO95/1264/2.
Interview transcript of Sgt H Watson, IWM Documents 7659.
Diary of LCpl W Preston, SGA.
Diary of Lt Col Sir Iain Colquhoun of Luss, Bt, Private Collection.
Account of Maj C Morrison Bell, IWM/91/12/1.

Translated account by German engineer officer, Wilfrid Ewart, F Loraine Petre, Cecil Lowther (Eds), *The Scots Guards in the Great War 1914-1918* (London: John Murray 1925).
Detail of 1912 Varsity Match from a press cutting in the author's possession.
LSgt H Johnes, *Old Soldiers Never Die, They Simply Fade Away: Memoirs Reflections*, SGA.

9

The Battles of Neuve Chapelle and Festubert and the Summer 1916 – 2nd Battalion

The Battle of Neuve Chapelle

The Battle of Neuve Chapelle began on 10 March from a repeat of French pressure on the BEF to attack in concert with the next French offensive north of Arras to include another attempt to drive the enemy off the Nôtre Dame de Lorette Ridge. There was sound operational logic for Neuve Chapelle because by the end of the autumn the Germans held an awkward salient jutting into the British line, including the ruins of the village. Provided that there was initial success and the momentum was then kept up, the intention was to carry on eastwards to capture the village of Aubers. This would gain a foothold on the southern end of the Aubers Ridge from which to develop operations towards Lille. There was every incentive to try to advance out of the sodden ground where they were. Critical, however, was the very limited amount of artillery ammunition, though it was believed that careful husbanding recently had ensured that there was sufficient to deal with the enemy wire and badly damage their other defences. Immediately prior to the infantry assault and without any other preliminary shelling every gun in the 7th, 8th and Meerut Divisions, formed in a horseshoe round the village, fired a thirty minute barrage, augmented by four siege batteries and two 9.2 inch and one 15 inch howitzers, some three hundred guns altogether, with ammunition carefully assembled. There were almost no reserves afterwards.

The attack was to be in three stages. First, the Meerut Division of the Indian Corps were to take the southern half of Neuve Chapelle and the 8th Division the northern half, so squeezing out the salient. The second stage required both to press on. Then the 7th Division, having already moved up to the original British front line, were to advance behind the 8th and in the third stage extend the attack beyond their left to capture Aubers and the top of the Ridge. The 20th Brigade's task was Aubers. Before the battle began Lieutenant Ewart watched and listened as they left Estaires at five in the morning on the 10th. Snow lay on the ground and snowflakes fell on the wind from the northeast. "Men's feet were silent as they moved about. There were no lights but the occasional flash of an electric torch and the beam which shot out from the half open door of some emptying billet. There were no sounds but the muffled thump of gloved hands sharply brought together, an occasional low exclamation, an occasional query in the darkness. Lines of men stretched dimly along the side of the road. Mysterious shapes they were in the dim light of dawn, mysterious, indefinite. Many wore hoods and all wore greatcoats with full weight of equipment – the pack bulking upon the back, the rifle slung over the shoulder. Here and there a mounted orderly sat like a statue, his figure and horse outlined against the gradually lightening sky. Now and then a motorcyclist, crouching low and heavily burdened, rattled past over the pavé. Further down the road long lines of transport could be discerned – tarpaulin-covered wagons, a machine gun section, numerous artillery limbers." As they moved off he noticed "the workmen and market-women…creeping along pavements even at this hour…going to their work in peaked caps and blue blouses, the women's heads covered with coloured shawls. Many who would otherwise be in bed are at their windows or doors, curious and rather frightened at the tramping of so many feet." Marching out of Estaires "the long column winds away to the right along a rough track, inches deep in mud, which leads across waste land in the rear of a factory." Beyond, among slag heaps and rubbish dumps the Brigade formed up on an open expanse of waste land where General Heyworth trotted past to inspect them. Then "Orders rattle out in quick succession. "Stand easy! Pile Arms! Packs off!" The men take off their equipment, lay it down, and sit upon their packs. The first refuge of the Tommy is his packet of cigarettes, the second his rations. Everywhere the rank and file lie about smoking and eating. The officers, meanwhile grouped around their Battalion Commanders, are deeply engaged in studying and comparing maps. Here one observes an animated discussion, there a silent, painstaking inquisition, whilst yonder a lively group of subalterns is laughing and joking." This continued until, suddenly, everybody stopped talking at the same moment. "All heads are turned the same way. Everybody listens. A low thunderous roll can be heard, punctured distantly by the bang-boom, boom-bang of innumerable guns." The bombardment at Neuve Chapelle started at half past seven, followed quickly by the appearance of aeroplanes and, shortly afterwards, by a German heavy shell which crashed into the waste land behind the factory and exploded harmlessly. While there was some apprehension of this heralding more none followed so the battalions continued to wait where they were. "Sitting and waiting is the hardest thing of all in anxious times." There was no news.

About two hours later they did move on and heard from a staff officer at a crossroads on the Armentières road that "the first two lines of German trenches have been taken with slight loss." Shortly after that another staff officer on a bicycle raised morale further with news that the first three lines had been captured, which Lieutenant Ewart remarked, led to the soldiers anticipating comfortable accommodation in Berlin and an early end to the War. By now more fully within range of the German guns, with evidence to prove it, the Brigade moved through fields well spread out before getting back onto the side road known as Cameron Lane, near Pont du Hem and northwest of Neuve Chapelle, and turning into a sheltered meadow. Nearby "howitzer batteries can be seen firing furiously: a flash, a boom, a recoil, and the little gunners – looking at a distance like so many insects – rush forward to recharge their guns. There they are, with their shirtsleeves rolled up and braces hanging loose, working like demons at the smoking breeches." In the meadow the infantry waited and relaxed. Lieutenant Ewart described what was "now a mild, sunny morning, and the chill wind has gone down. With all the sounds of war and death at hand, the countryside looks peaceful enough. Two fields away a peasant is ploughing stolidly, heedless of the shells which now and again scream over his head." He also saw and heard skylarks before the first real evidence of the battle as wounded "came trickling along the road. Bloody heads and hands roughly bandaged for the most part; albeit, now and then a still figure on a stretcher with chalky, quiet face tells a sadder story. And they are not in the least cheerful or boastful, as London newspapers delight to depict the wounded Tommy; but rather woebegone and very subdued."

Next came prisoners, escorted by French Territorials, as Lieutenant Ewart saw them "fine great men of the Prussian Guard, very stolid and expressionless (although a few looked scared), with coarse, typically Teuton faces. There are smaller fry, too, Saxons and Alsatians, rather untidy and unsoldierlike, and looking with no great favour upon their comrades, the Prussians…One and all admit the completeness of the surprise, to which, indeed, their lack of accoutrements and general disorder bear testimony. Nor would it be far wrong to say that every man jack of them is delighted to be a prisoner." French and British planes wheeled and circled above, observing what was happening on the ground, observed in their turn by the waiting infantry. This was interrupted by "a whistling shriek" which the Scots Guardsmen took to be a large calibre German shell coming straight for them. It was not, but rather the fatal descent of a buckled and crumpling British plane, falling like a stone, hit by British guns. Just afterwards another British plane just managed to land safely, having got back from above La Bassée, leaking fuel badly from a hole in the petrol tank the size of a man's arm caused by German shrapnel. "The two flying men, looking particularly cheerful in their leathern garments and headgear, seemed to treat the whole matter as a joke." Lieutenant Swinton wrote home on 18 March describing the battle. Of the first crashed plane he said "it suddenly collapsed in mid air & came down like a cock pheasant hit in the head."

In the absence either of any further news or of more wounded or of more prisoners the wait went on. They ate their chocolate rations and some sandwiches, watched the gunners as they continued to fire and registered mild interest when a German shell set fire to the thatch of a farmhouse roof. It was coming up to two o'clock. Then the order came to move forward into newly dug reserve trenches from where they watched German HE and shrapnel landing harmlessly every few minutes in the next field. Lieutenant Ewart remarked "It is generally considered the greatest artillery show of the war, and I almost pity the wretched Germans. We are snugly ensconced in our trenches. Lying down at the bottom to escape the chilly wind, we get some sleep." The men went and gathered firewood in an orchard close by and warmed themselves round their fires. As it got dark everything quietened down but the Battalion stood to arms "most of the night expecting to attack or be attacked at any moment. But no order comes… Apart from the star rockets and searchlights and flares which light up the sky everything is quite quiet."

A distinctive feature was the success of the surprise, but that was not enough. As soon as the bombardment stopped the infantry assaulted at eight o'clock. The Meerut Division managed to take the southern part of the Neuve Chapelle salient but never got any further, in particular failing to make any headway into the Bois de Biez, a large wood to the southeast. In the 8th Division the right hand leading brigade made very good progress from the start, but the left hand one suffered very heavily from an undamaged section of German trench and it was not till five hours later that they came up level, so causing delay in keeping the attack going. In the middle of the afternoon the 21st Brigade of the 7th Division then moved through the left brigade of the 8th Division and fought their way a bit further forward, but already the plan was unwinding. Nothing significant was possible after dark, so the British reorganised and prepared to repel a counterattack which did not materialise. However, the Germans reacted very rapidly, bringing up reserves and strengthening their new line. The British attack plans for 11 March, the delayed second two stages, were adjusted to the current situation on the ground as they knew it. Nothing went smoothly from the very start. The 20th Brigade moved forward to behind breastworks along the Rue Tilleloy which Major Cator described as the former British support line, where "Much to our disgust we found every available fire shelter occupied by the 8th Div Reserve on arrival, but after a deal of pushing & shoving we managed to squeeze the Brigade into trenches & breastworks already occupied, making the men lie down three deep. The only place we could find for Brigade Headquarters was a small sandbag breastwork up against a shrine, the latter had to be used as a telephone box." He added "Reports came in to say the Germans had brought up a reinforcement of 1 Division." The information they received also indicated that the 21st Brigade were much further forward than they were, the corrected information only arriving at half past six in the morning with the day's attack due to start half an hour later.

Starting from the Rue Tilleloy breastworks at seven the 2nd Scots Guards were to advance in support of the 1st Grenadiers on the right of the Brigade, heading almost due east in the direction of the Moulin de Pietre, from there to the hamlet of Pietre three hundred yards beyond it and then on to Aubers. The breastworks they were behind were those from which a few days earlier Major Paynter and others had examined the enemy positions. The 2nd Gordons, followed by the 2nd Borders, were to advance on their left. Captain Warner noted that they "left at 4am and went up to the breastworks in Rue Tilleloy with orders to attack behind Grenadiers. Heavily shelled in breastwork, lost some men. Moved out for attack about 7am and advanced some distance under fire, held up about 10am and remained all day." The Grenadiers had led off in eight lines of half companies, or two platoons in each line, and at ten past seven they followed in the same formation. Sir Frederick FitzWygram, recovered from his head wound at Rouges Bancs on 18 December, returned early in February and took over F Company again, but twisted his ankle during this battle and was away till 15 March. Then, temporarily in command of the Battalion, the battle report he then signed, drafted by Captain Warner, stated "After advancing for about 1000 yards under fire over several lines of trenches, and some wide and deep ditches rather difficult to negotiate, the attack was held up, and the Battn halted with the first line close up to and intermingled with the last line of the Grenadier Guards. The Battn remained in this position for the rest of the day, the men digging themselves in as well as they were able to, under a fairly heavy shellfire. Some men were also lost owing to rifle fire, i.e. overs fired at the Grenadier Guards, and an intermittent enfilade fire from the right."

Left Flank under Lieutenant Swinton were the rearmost company and he was at the back with the eighth line. Before they could move at all "we sat under our breastwork & waited, then the Huns seemed to realize that we must be there & started shelling the place with small shell. They chose the place where I was sitting & killed 3 & wounded 10 all round me. I was in a devil of a fright. At last the order came to advance & we moved to the right & over the breastworks to the first German trench which had been captured the previous day. There I stayed all day as the lines in front of me could not get on, the trench was not much better than our own and was full of German dead. Father would have revelled in it for it was full of rifles & kit, beautiful stuff for wall decoration. The dug-outs were excellent much better than our's but dirty."

There was serious confusion. The attack by the 20th and 21st Brigades had slowed and stalled, neither brigade headquarters knew where their battalions were and the battalions had little idea themselves. What was stopping the British infantry was not German guns so much as machine guns and rifles and, at close quarters, their better and more plentiful grenades. There was also accidental shelling from British artillery, notably by the worn out and erratic 4.7" guns. The

Grenadiers, whose leading companies were stuck in the open a hundred yards behind, so they thought, the 2nd Northamptons of the 8th Division, with the Germans between a hundred and fifty and two hundred yards beyond that, had lost a lot of officers and men and were at a small stream several hundred yards short of the Rivière des Layes, where they wrongly thought they were. None of the 20th Brigade managed to advance beyond the forward troops of the 8th Division and they lost heavily trying to do so without making any direct contact with the enemy. The 21st Brigade beyond them on the left were a little further on than anyone else, but had to stop where they were, facing, as they thought, northeast, but ending up facing southeast, with the 20th Brigade on their right facing northeast, but neither in contact with the other. Both were looking towards a bend in the Mauquissart-Piètre road, but some way back from it.

Lieutenant Ewart's day had begun with quite a prolonged halt at Brigade Headquarters while Major Paynter and Captain Loder conferred with staff officers. Then the Battalion moved on down a road, before following a light railway across the fields. "Eastward, the dawn breaks in streaks of ashy grey, shedding upon the countryside a cold and cheerless light… Not a word was spoken. It was all a man could do to pick his way along the narrow track on either side of which was liquid mud. Now and again we would meet parties of weary Highlanders trudging back from the firing line for a well earned rest. Presently in the distance a gun boomed. Close at hand another answered. Then one by one they took it up along the line behind…As the light grew, bullets began to whiz and hum above our heads. First occasionally, then increasingly, until the air sang with them." They crossed another field and found themselves in a road protected by a solid breastwork, but heavily congested with troops, so that it was difficult to get everyone into cover. This was eventually achieved "by splitting up the companies on either side of a gap in the line of sandbags through which bullets constantly whistled…It was a ticklish business crossing, and we began to lose men." This was the breastwork along the Rue Tilleloy. It was six o'clock and no one had had any breakfast before leaving. "So the men lie about eating their rations and smoking. Some take off their greatcoats and equipment, folding the former away in the pack; some clean their rifles and bayonets; some talk and laugh together over breakfast." Then the German guns started firing at the line of the breastwork, the shells landing in front and behind. "Men walking along the road sink down beside it suddenly, whimpering like children, holding the head or clasping the limbs with their hands. Splinters and shrapnel bullets fly in all directions. The closer to the breastwork one is, so much the safer. Seven o'clock approaches. Word comes that the attack on the right has been launched. Word is passed down to get ready. Officers load their revolvers and button their tunics across the throat. Platoons are marshalled together and told off. "Fix bayonets!" A cold, rasping sound, and six hundred blades flash in the morning sunlight." They then formed up on the road, turned to their right and headed off down it, Right Flank leading, to where a lane branched off to the east. Along the lane Major Paynter and Captain Loder were standing encouraging the men as they filed past them off it into a tangle of disused trenches up to the knees in mud and water, with planks laid here and there for better footing. The companies had to make their way along this series of trenches to the original British front line breastwork from which to start their attack. There they stopped and waited for the final order. When it came "Company officers blow their whistles and the whole front line swarms through the gaps in the sandbag breastwork and rushes pell-mell across a hundred yards of open ground, pitted with holes, and obstructed with loose strands of barbed wire." There was immediately very heavy rifle and shrapnel fire as they crossed the open to the previous German front line, which they found full of other troops. "Men cannot obtain shelter from the ceaseless stream of bullets. Some even have to crouch down on the top of the ground. A strapping fellow topples forward groaning into the trench, his hands clasped to his forehead, from which the blood pours. Another rolls quietly over on his side – stone dead. The lad next to me, virile and strong a moment ago, now lies feebly moaning, shot through the body. Two or three others, variously wounded, sit, half conscious, with their backs against the parapet. And we have seen out only five minutes!" Lieutenants Ewart and Seymour were in the leading platoons of Right Flank in another rush forward, but now having lost formation. Lieutenant Ewart's platoon reached a more substantial breastwork, also crowded with British infantry, protected in front by a large mound of earth thrown up by a British heavy shell. In the shellhole lay many German dead and "the body of a British soldier, stark and stiff, the face covered, doubtless by some comrade's hand, with a piece of white tarpaulin; the trivial things of life are there – biscuit tins, scraps of food, hand mirrors, the trivial things men carry in their pockets. And everywhere litter of equipment – German helmets, with the golden eagle emblazoned on the front, German caps and accoutrements, rifles, clips of cartridges, pistols, and weapons of all kinds."

He clambered with his men through the shellhole, up the mound beyond and then hurried "along a kind of ridge. A small river or large ditch of stagnant water is bridged at one place by a plank which has broken down. It is no time to hesitate. The only thing to do is to plunge in and somehow stagger across with the filthy, brackish, greenish water lapping one's chin. Rifle and bayonet, already clogged with mud, are rendered useless. On the further bank lies a wounded Grenadier officer attended by his sergeant. The country is now dead flat and open, the enemy cannot be more than three hundred yards distant. A broad stretch of ploughed field, heavy with recent rains, has to be crossed. Men fall right and left, prostrate khaki figures dot the ground in all directions. The crackle of rifle fire freshens, the whole air hums with bullets. Burdened with our packs and weight of equipment, we can only muster a jog trot in such heavy going. Many prefer to crawl over the ground on all fours, though this little advantages them; some pause for breath in the shellholes, others lie down in the open. On the far side of the ploughed field is a shallow depression in the ground. Here, the only available cover, are disposed a number of troops of various companies and regiments. Immediately in front, not one hundred and fifty yards away, is a group of buildings surmounted by a tall, redbrick chimney – a landmark in all that countryside – known as the Moulin du Piètre. It looks more like a mine in one of our own colliery districts than a mill. It fairly bristles with rifles and machine guns. The hail of bullets above our heads increases. We flatten our faces in the muddy ground and lie there for three solid hours under a hell fire that seems to come from every side but one. Shrapnel bursts as regularly as clockwork within twenty or thirty yards and scatters earth over one every time. Behind us the rear companies of the Battalion are still advancing. They come on in groups and batches in widely extended order. Meanwhile, we lie down in a long, irregular line which grows thicker, thus affording a better mark for the enemy's riflemen and artillery. So, presently, the order comes for two platoons to advance about a hundred yards to a line of temporary breastworks and rejoin the Grenadiers who are ahead. We show our heads and the bullets begin to fly as thick as hail. I had hardly got to my feet and was jumping over a ditch when I was hit in the left leg and took an unceremonious toss down the bank."

From then on he was on his own and unable to see what was happening. He had got a classic "Blighty" wound from the bullet through his calf muscle, but he was stranded, because of the pain and because of the enemy in the mill buildings. "So I lay on my face motionless, listening to the sounds of the battle. They were so numerous that I cannot enumerate them all. It was the shrapnel which caused the greatest dread. How narrowly it whizzed overhead, to burst about thirty yards behind with a deafening bang and a flash of fire followed by the sing-sing of many bullets which buried themselves in the ground." He could hear too "the faint shouting of men, the clink-clink of the entrenching tools as soldiers dug themselves in, the great hollow explosions which resounded afar off amid the ruins of Aubers and Neuve Chapelle. And the groans, the moans, the crying of those who lay around! I started to crawl back. The dressing station was at least a mile away, but things seemed quieter. I crawled over the ground ever so slowly, for those riflemen in the mill were doubtless watching. The ploughed field seemed interminable – I could not see the breastwork on the other side, and the only landmarks were dead and wounded men who lay at intervals along the direction of advance." However, the battle flared up again and "for half an hour I lay there, in company with a dead man, thinking the end of all things had come." When everything quietened down again "I, leaving my Burberry, crawled on among the shell pits and the relics of the soldiery…Past many an upturned waxen face and shreds of men where shells had done their work – and blood. A head showed itself above the rim of a shellhole. "Stop, sir," it said; "give me your pack. I'll keep it for you. You'll never carry it all the way." I did not like the face or the voice."

Next he came across a soldier he knew lying with a bullet through the chest and in great pain and saw close by the Medical Officer of the 2nd Royal Scots Fusiliers, "who, without summons, had doubled across the shell swept field to tend our wounded only himself to be shot through the body as he knelt beside them. At last the friendly wall of sandbags is in sight." First, however, he had to negotiate a filthy stream in front of it, presumably the same as on the way out, crossed in the one place which he could see by a single slippery plank, but with the body of an English soldier blocking it. He tried more than once to get over and was eventually rescued when a man behind the breastwork reached out to pull him in. Moving slowly on, pausing frequently for breath, he crossed the open field behind into an orchard where the birds were singing. Down the middle of the orchard was a long straight trench. A chaplain and two helpers were beginning to bury the dead, mostly British, some German, lying in rows nearby. In a dry ditch bordering the orchard Lieutenant Ewart "found two Scots Guards stretcher bearers apparently none too keen to enter the fray." Since the side road which led to the dressing station, now quarter of a mile away, was just beyond the ditch, he told them to carry him there, after they had put a couple of field dressings on his leg. "I could not have presented a very elegant appearance on this occasion – soaked to the skin with the brackish water of the foul ditches, clothes caked with mud and stained yellow up one side, and putties torn to shreds." He had discarded some of his equipment, the rest was caked in mud. The side road to the dressing station had been captured the day before. "Ammunition wagons, rushing up the road, had been caught by artillery fire and overturned or smashed. There they lay, half on the road, half off it. Dead horses blocked the ditch alongside, their legs protruding stiffly erect, their bodies half buried in mud and water, and all around a great litter of tackle and equipment. The road itself was pitted and furrowed, and upon its surface were little drops and trails of blood where the wounded had been carried. The milestones along this *via dolorosa* were the bodies of men who had fallen and died – some in the middle of the fairway and others beside it, resting on the grass." There was a constant procession of other wounded. At the dressing station Lieutenant Ewart noticed that three quarters seemed to have head wounds. He was fortunate to be quickly evacuated in a motor ambulance with "a sergeant, who moans restlessly, and a bucolic, bloodthirsty fellow, who loudly proclaims that he has been hit three times and has "done in" as many Germans." This man kept up a steady, unhelpful banter throughout the journey, although the sergeant asked him to stop. Unlike Lieutenant Ewart, both were probably unaware that the fourth stretcher in the ambulance held a silent, dying subaltern of the 1st Royal Irish Rifles of the 8th Division. At Estaires the field hospital was in a seminary for priests. Here Lieutenant Ewart received a new dressing, a tetanus injection and a label for England before being put into a large, cool room. There were two wounded officers already there. One was a colonel in a Scottish regiment with two shrapnel wounds, the other the young Royal Scots Fusiliers doctor, moaning quietly to himself in a darkened corner. His name was Lieutenant William Ingram RAMC and he had brought in personally many of the wounded of his own battalion on the opening day of the battle. Later that night Lieutenant Ewart started his journey back, but not at first to England, as he hoped and expected, but to Rouen. By the time he got there all he had were the clothes he had been wearing when he was hit. His breeches had been, of necessity, slit up the side. He counted himself very lucky.

The battle report afterwards stated that the losses during 11 March had been Lieutenant Seymour, wounded by shrapnel in the head, which kept him away for three months, Lieutenant Ewart and about fifty men. Captain Warner wrote to his mother on the 15th in more detail than in his diary. While they were held up behind the Grenadiers and being heavily shelled there "Seymour was hit lying next to me. I tied up his head with bandages as best I could and while I was doing it Ewart was hit by a bullet in the leg, just the other side of me. When the shelling got better they both got away. Seymour could walk and Ewart crawl, and we dug ourselves in and so remained till nightfall. We started digging proper trenches at dusk but soon got orders to stop as we were to move. FitzWygram and I had to go up into the front line to see some trenches with a view to relieving another Battalion." What this was about was in his diary "FitzWygram arrived and said RF and F were to relieve Northamptons and we were to go up and see their trenches. Went with him and found them with some difficulty in the dark. Some sniping and few shells. They knew nothing of being relieved." While they were doing this the Grenadiers were relieved and moved back and then the Scots Guards were told to go back to a support position, but the Borders and Gordons stayed. When the two officers returned they found a message to report to Major Paynter. Orders had arrived for an attack the following morning, the 12th, in which the Borders, on the left, were to assault a fort, a square shaped fortified German trench known as the Quadrilateral, and the Scots Guards, on the right, a house. This was not one house but a group of buildings at Mauquissart three hundred yards behind the fort and not far from the Moulin de Piètre, whose mill wheel was driven by the Rivière des Layes. The attack was to go in following a half hour's bombardment starting at seven, but, if mist made the bombardment impracticable then and it was delayed, the attack was to start half an hour after it did begin. Earlier that evening Major Cator had noticed a significant increase in the number of enemy batteries. Their guns fired intermittently through the night.

For three hours from five in the morning the German shelling was heavier while their newly arrived reserves counterattacked all along the line where it had been taken from them. They were beaten off. Soon after this began the Scots Guards moved off north along the Rue Tilleloy towards Fauquissart. Captain Warner soon found he had only a few men left with him after shells hit several of Right Flank, causing confusion and scattering, so most got lost in the dark. Without them the Battalion moved on "with lots of shells bursting near, about half a mile and got into some shallow trenches beside the road where we remained for some time." Captain Loder had fallen into a trench, tearing his hand badly on the barbed wire in it, and had to be evacuated. No one knew where F Company were. Lieutenant Swinton, to whom Major Paynter had given his orders during the night, was in the lead with Left Flank. "We fell in at 4.30am & started marching round to a point given to me the night before. We had to go along a typical French road straight with trees on each side, you know them. Several trees had fallen across the road, shrapnel was bursting over it, it ran parallel to our lines so there was a cross fire over it also the Huns were using trench mortar & chucking bombs by then over the road, how we got along I don't know but no one was hit." At the planned rendezvous he met Major Paynter and they lay down and waited. Then the German guns began firing very heavily on just that place. "The only thing we could do was to try to get the Btn into the trenches from which we were to make an attack so George & I led on hoping that the men would follow on, the distance was some 500 yards. The company got terribly strung out several were hit & shells were bursting like the devil. You can't imagine anything worse than being shelled in the dark, it is much worse than in daylight." They arrived at the trench "with about 6 men the remainder being strung out behind." There they waited till daylight which did come with thick mist, postponements of the bombardment and alterations to the fire plan, details of which had to be sent forward to the attacking battalions by orderlies. The idea of timing the assault for half an hour after the guns started firing was dropped. The last message that arrived told them of postponement of the attack till half past ten, extra time they needed to get into position. Not till half past eight did they move up a captured communication trench leading off the Rue Tilleloy. Then they occupied some shallow trenches others had dug across it at right angles the previous night. In places the communication trench was waist deep in water. Lieutenant Swinton continued his letter "So at 9 we managed to collect LF & G, F Company was lost & RF had scattered when the shelling first began & was also lost except for Pip & a dozen men. We crawled out into the open alongside the trench ready to start off." Shortly after hearing of the postponement Major Paynter and Captain Warner went back to find all the missing men, but failed. These apparently went back to and then remained all day where they started off from earlier in the night. The two officers then split up and soon afterwards Major Paynter was shot through the right lung, a serious wound but from which it was possible to recover, which he did. Sir Edward Hulse crawled across to him and was killed on the way back.

 The basic plan had not changed. The Borders, out in front in similar trenches, were to take the Quadrilateral and its surrounding trenches and the Scots Guards were to move up onto their right and capture the buildings at Mauquissart at the same time, the direction of attack being roughly northeast. Both battalions had to pass through the 21st Brigade's front line in order to reach the objectives, but then a fresh difficulty arose when, as the Scots Guards War Diary noted, "It subsequently became apparent that the two assaults could not be made simultaneous, as the house was 300 yards beyond the fort, and the latter had first to be reduced." Then, to make matters worse "A message from the Brigade postponing the attack until 12.30pm was not received owing to the orderlies who carried it being killed, and the attack was launched at 10.30am without artillery preparation. The Battn got up on the right of the Border Rgt, after some difficulty had been caused by a deep ditch, which had to be crossed, and after advancing about 150 yds was compelled to stop by a very heavy machine gun and rifle fire." The initial attempt to advance at half past ten without artillery had not gone well. Trying again himself, Captain Warner and six men, all of whom were hit on the way, had managed to reach Lieutenant Jarvis, who was out in front in a shallow trench. "We had a trying time when held up in the shallow trench as we could not put a finger out owing to the machine gun and rifle fire and it was very wet. I lay on a sort of hump and cut it away from under me with my bayonet putting the dry earth into the water and so gradually got a dry place to lie on. Jarvis and I then had lunch, duck sandwich and chocolate cake. We were lying side by side rather nose to heel." He was very impressed by the accuracy of the British guns when they did start firing. "Our guns were splendid and dropped shell after shell into the German trench, the noise being terrific. They stood it for a bit and then put up white flags and came out holding up their hands. Swinton and I went forward shouting to the men to come on and arrived in the fort mixed up with the Borders." While the British guns were shelling the Quadrilateral men of both battalions had crept right up to it and when the shelling stopped at about half past one they stormed in immediately, the defenders having been thoroughly shaken and demoralised.

Lieutenant Swinton continued his letter "At 10.30 we got up and advanced we were greeted at once by rapid fire & machine gun fire. I honestly wouldn't have believed it possible that anything could have lived through that fire. Lots were hit…but I ran on until I found a trench or rather ditch 2ft deep & 2ft wide into this I dropped & started to dig myself in with my bayonet here I stayed till 1.30. In the meantime we learnt that we had attacked too early that orderlies had been sent to George & to the Col of the Borders postponing the attack till 12.30 because the artillery could not see to bombard. Both these orderlies had been killed so we had never got the message & we had attacked too early so hence the fire against us. Anyway at noon the bombardment began, we of course were all lying flat in our scrapes as the Huns were shooting all the time. I have never heard such a noise as this bombardment in my life one continuous roar the whole time. Soon it was passed along that the Huns were putting up white flags. I looked up & saw that they were coming out of their trenches on the left, at that moment Pip got up & shouted to me to come on so I followed him with about 4 men & we assisted taking in the prisoners some 500 & 600 we then went on and formed a firing line in the old German trench firing at the retreating Huns." He was then sent to find and send up reinforcements. Having done that, however, he was unable to go forward again owing to the enemy fire now coming from the right, so he waited in a trench until dark. Major Cator put the length of the bombardment at forty minutes starting at ten to twelve. Whatever its duration it had the desired effect. "The bombardment had been appalling and had completely reduced the Germans to a state of abject terror, a captured German officer remarking "it isn't war, it's carnage." His figure for the prisoners brought in from this position was four hundred, the Scots Guards having also taken a machine gun. A lot of German shells of all types had been falling further back all day, mostly causing little damage, but Major Cator saw the consequences when "One Jack Johnson…burst on four men cooking their breakfast ten yards from Brigade Headquarters, two men were blown to atoms and could not be found, one cut in half and one blown up a tree, his clothing and portions of him hanging on the boughs 30 feet up."

Captain Warner found some Scots Guardsmen in a trench beyond the Quadrilateral, but not many others. He "returned to fort and could find very few of the Battn so helped a Border officer to organize defence of fort. We pushed our way up communication trench to our right front, but eventually got stopped." Enfilade fire from the right and machine guns in the buildings at Mauquissart were too much. The Grenadiers tried to come up level with them to continue the attack, became disorientated and lost almost as many men as the day before in front of the by now very strongly reinforced German position along the road south from Mauquissart. Colonel Fisher Rowe was mortally wounded and their total casualties at Neuve Chapelle were fourteen officers and three hundred and twenty five men. When the attack along the communication trench towards Mauquissart could go no further Captain Warner left the Borders holding it and returned to the Quadrilateral for the rest of the afternoon. After dark he went back to Brigade Headquarters where he heard of Major Paynter's being wounded and was told to find and collect the Battalion. First he took General Heyworth up to the Quadrilateral "and then spent all night hunting for various parts of the Battalion. Collected about 350 at HQ at 3.30 and told to send them back under Swinton which I did."

The scene for that night's events was set from General Capper's arrival at Headquarters 20th Brigade at eight for a conference which then lasted three hours. Major Cator recorded how in spite of its being "pointed out that it would be difficult to re-sort the line as the night was very dark and the country was closely intersected by numerous trenches and barbed wire and extremely heavy and wet" because General Capper was "anxious to continue the advance and capture Aubers" he ordered the redeployment of battalions of the 20th and 22nd Brigades there and then. The Scots Guardsmen collected through the night at Brigade Headquarters had much the best of what happened next as Lieutenant Swinton led them back to Cameron Lane before daylight on the 13th. Captain Warner's "very trying night" continued when at four in the morning he had to lead the 1/6th Gordons up to the new front line trenches "as no on else knew the way. Unfortunately we did not reach the trenches till after daylight and were shot at a good deal but they got in somehow and I managed to get back to the Battn about 8am." There at Cameron Lane "Found we had collected over 400 men, having lost about 200, only 50 missing."

The night was otherwise difficult for everyone. General Heyworth knew that carrying out front line reliefs in these conditions would take up most of it. Major Cator saw him setting off himself with a staff officer to take an officer from each battalion and show him precisely where he wanted them to go. It took them two hours across the damaged country in pitch dark just to find the Grenadiers, who by three in the morning had orders to move forward about a thousand yards. By dawn they had one company in the front line trenches and the rest scattered in the open behind. A daylight relief being impossible, the 2nd Royal Scots Fusiliers of the 21st Brigade, whom the Grenadiers were relieving, and the 2nd Gordons, whom the 1/6th Gordons were relieving, had to stay put. Nothing material affected the 2nd Scots Guards on the 13th, a troublesome and unpleasant one for most of the Division as it gradually became clear that nothing else was achievable. On the right the 8th Division tried to capture some more buildings during the night, but failed. Had they succeeded Major Cator thought that there was a fair chance that the 20th Brigade's subsequent attack on the Mauquissart buildings would have worked as there would have been no enfilade machine gun fire from the right, the heavy enemy shelling and British howitzer shells falling short notwithstanding. Owing to yet more confusion after dark on the 13th, though the Grenadiers and 1/6th Gordons were successfully withdrawn, the battalion from another brigade now to relieve the 2nd Gordons got lost, so they had another twenty four hours in the front line. There was no further attempt to attack and, apart from shelling, the Germans did nothing either.

After Neuve Chapelle the British identified the current most obvious issues and fundamental restrictions as being the shortage of all artillery ammunition and the lack of heavy calibre guns. The amount of 18 pounder field gun ammunition used on 10 March alone would take ten days' production to replenish. Another challenge, now fully apparent and never adequately solved in the War, was having reserves, in good order and well rested, in the right places, as well as the means of rapidly applying them as and when there was an opportunity to exploit. But just as problems were identified and solutions sought by the British, so the Germans learned from their errors too and made adjustments. The principal lesson that they took from Neuve Chapelle was that the BEF were capable of a major organised attack and planned accordingly. On a local tactical level Major Cator noted how effective the brigade grenade companies had been and the importance of keeping them up to their strength of one hundred and fifty men, plus officers. Under their direction an additional twenty men per battalion were to be similarly trained.

Twenty two Scots Guardsmen were killed, one hundred and thirty two wounded and thirty five missing, the lowest total in the Brigade, who had almost half of the 7th Division's casualties. Sir Edward Hulse was the only officer killed, four were wounded, two injured, another had had to go sick and only four were left. Captain Loder did not return to either of the Battalions but later on in the War was an ADC to Sir William Pulteney in III Corps. Among the men Private Henry Fricker died at three in the morning on 12 March from a gun shot wound to the head. He was forty one. He had served previously, leaving as a Lance Sergeant in 1898, only to return to the Colours throughout the Boer War. By 1914 he and Caroline his wife whom he had married at Walton, Somerset, in 1898, were living in Cardiff, where he was a wireman for the GPO. By now well clear of his reserve commitment, he reenlisted as a Private at the beginning of September 1914 and arrived in France on 9 November. His personal effects consisted of four pocket knives, a comb, a purse, a razor, a notebook, a testament [Bible], photographs and coins. Lance Corporal Alexander Sharpe enlisted at Perth in November 1903 when he was a parcel porter at the railway station. He had been out of the Army for eight years when he reported as a reservist. He and his wife Amelia married at Perth in August 1909, just under two months before their first daughter was born. Two more children followed before the War. The family were living in Cowdenbeath. Corporal Sharpe had already been wounded once on 11 January, probably only slightly because no details were given, before he was killed on 12 March. Another man who died, also a reservist, already wounded previously, was Private Frederick Hughes from Wellington, Shropshire. He had gone out originally with the 1st Battalion and been hit in the side by a bullet on the Aisne. He recovered in England and was then sent to the 2nd Scots Guards. Wounded a second time very severely at Neuve Chapelle, he died on 14 March at Merville. John and Sarah Hughes were sent some photographs, a notebook and a bag. Also dying of his wounds on the same day and at the same place was Private Henry Cuthbertson, a Glasgow warehouseman who volunteered early in September. His mother Barbara Cuthbertson received his letter case, pocket book, some cards and photographs and a pay-in-slip at her home in Pollokshaws Road. Private James MacGregor, another September volunteer, died at Merville the day before of a head wound, having been in France for less than three weeks. He had been a grocer in Glasgow and his mother Janet MacGregor, in acknowledging receipt of his Bible, a notebook, photos and a bag added "Pocket Book, Watch Chain * Trinkets still awaiting." Private Robert Herriott, in France for eleven weeks, was killed outright. He was one of the Fife miners who enlisted early on and had a tattoo of Buffalo Bill on his right forearm. His sister Christina Cairns in Larbert, Stirlingshire, was sent some photos and letters. Drummer Archie Clark, a former boy soldier, now with more than ten years service, was missing. He had gone out at the start, been hit in the right leg early on at Ypres, but not sent home, and returned soon after New Year from hospital in Rouen. In 1925 his body was found and a damaged identity disc sent to Donald and Isabella Clark in Southwick, Sussex.

Private Samuel Saunders had a bullet wound in his left forearm on 12 March. He was a groom before he joined the Army in 1905 in Poole, Dorset, and served continuously from then on with the Battalion, going to Zeebrugge in October 1914. He recovered from this wound in England and, having returned to the BEF at the beginning of August 1915, remained with them for the rest of the War. He and his wife Ethel married in 1913, had a daughter late in 1914 and a son in the spring of 1916. Lance Corporal George Fairbank, now one of the very few men still in F Company throughout, was shot in the right leg on 12 March. It was he who just before Christmas had written to Lord Kinnaird "on behalf of the remainder of the rank and file of the Company" about his son's death at Polygon Wood. Returning to France in October 1915 he joined the 1st Battalion, but a few months later was medically downgraded and spent the remainder of the War as Ration Sergeant at the Guards Division Base Depot at Harfleur. Private Michael Quinn, a labourer at a tube works, whose mother Annie Ward lived in Coatbridge, Lanarkshire, volunteered very early on and arrived just after First Ypres. He was badly wounded in the left thigh and evacuated home. His leg did not recover from damage to the sciatic nerve and he was discharged in June 1916. Private Thomas Rawstron, the son of John and Harriett Rawstron of Nelson, Lancashire, enlisted in September 1914. He had already been in the Scots Guards before the War but bought himself out and worked making surgical appliances. He had been in the BEF for a month and was wounded in the left shoulder and right hand and sent home to hospital, the first time he was a casualty. Private Robert Jameson, the man with the fine tenor voice whom Sir Edward Hulse mentioned at a concert just after the new draft arrived a few days earlier, was hit in the left thigh on the 12th and sent home immediately to hospital, also a casualty for the first time.

Company Sergeant Major James wrote on 6 April to thank Lieutenant Saumarez for a very good parcel which he shared with Private Sinclair. He mentioned that Lance Sergeant Jones was wounded in the leg at Neuve Chapelle while going for rations, also that Lance Sergeant John Davidson was killed. Lieutenant Saumarez' mother had sent a parcel of "woollens" to Private Sinclair and he added that he had distributed these among those who needed them most. His letter ended by saying that he and Private Sinclair were the only survivors of the original 13 Platoon. Private Sinclair, who had some mechanical skills, was sent home with rheumatism two months afterwards and later in 1915 released for munitions work with Messrs Waller & Co, Ltd in Vauxhall. He was discharged from the Army in May 1917. It would be a while yet before there was a break in Company Sergeant Major James' time with the Battalion. Sergeant Jones did not serve abroad again, but became a Company Sergeant Major at home. Lance Sergeant Davidson came from Hawick and was a clerk when he enlisted in Edinburgh in August 1903 and left three years later as a Corporal. After that he went to Canada, married Mabel Jarvis, a midwife, in Norwood Grove, Winnipeg, in January 1910 and they had a daughter in February 1914. Called up in Canada, he arrived in England on 4 September and was in a draft that reached the Battalion after Ypres. Mabel Davidson came with him from Canada and originally lived with his family in Hawick, though after her husband's death moved wherever she could find work. On 6 May 1915 James Davidson, his brother, wrote to Regimental Headquarters, still hoping for more and better news as "according to his comrades he was dangerously wounded in the thigh by a hand grenade. They however expected that he would be picked up as they were advancing. They have heard nothing of him since then and all our letters have been returned."

At the end of the battle report was the name of Lance Corporal John McVean, an early wartime volunteer, who had been a chemist in or near Dumbarton, for having shown great gallantry when he went out from the cover of a trench under heavy machine gun and rifle fire to take water to a wounded man on 12 March. Corporal McVean was mentioned in despatches and in February 1916 commissioned into the 9th Argylls. The other two soldiers named in the report were both stretcher bearers, one of whom, Corporal Samuel Lemon, got a bayonet wound in the right thigh during the battle and was evacuated home. Afterwards he remained in England, was awarded the DCM for Neuve Chapelle, news of which reached the Battalion on 8 April, and became a Sergeant in November 1915. He enlisted in 1894 at Shaftesbury, Dorset, served in the Boer War and went up and down the ranks a bit before 1914, coming good thereafter. He and Priscilla Plowman married in London in 1903 and she was in Battersea. On completing twenty two years service in May 1916 Sergeant Lemon left the Army and they settled in Shaftesbury. Private James Litster was a gardener in Dunbar before he enlisted in 1906. Called up as a reservist, he had first been wounded, hit, presumably only slightly, through the mouth, during Ypres. Eventually, on 11 January 1916 he too was awarded the DCM, cumulatively for several engagements as the citation read "For conspicuous gallantry and devotion as a stretcher bearer. On one occasion he worked continuously under a heavy fire when the enemy were only 60 yards away." He was wounded a second time in September 1916 at Ginchy on the Somme, with a gun shot wound to his left hand, but rejoined just over three weeks later. His third wound in January 1917 was in the head. He had married Margaret Marshall at Innerwick Manse just after New Year 1913 and their son arrived seven weeks later. What may have held back earlier recognition of him at Neuve Chapelle was his being extremely fortunate on 9 April 1915 only to get six days Field Punishment No 2 for being drunk on active service and sleeping when on sentry in the trenches, his recent bravery likely to have mitigated what could have been very much more severe. Later, having been promoted to Lance Sergeant, he was reduced to the ranks on 4 September 1916 for drunkenness, shortly before he was wounded for the second time. Sergeant William Young, photographed during First Ypres with men of the 2nd Oxford and Bucks LI near Polygon Wood, was awarded the DCM for his excellent work as Signal Sergeant of the Battalion "under very difficult circumstances."

The British carefully obtained and scrutinised the German press and translated extracts appeared in military bulletins. One of these issued on 15 March by Captain HW Stenhouse of Headquarters IV Corps was from a Magdeburg newspaper cutting published on 28 February. "Several battalions of suffragettes have landed at Havre. There are 500 women in each battalion. I want to warn you to be very careful when you meet them. – Don't let them scratch out your eyes, and above all, don't let them capture you. That would shame you before the whole world." Captain Stenhouse added the footnote "Several prisoners asked when the British Suffragette Corps would arrive at the front."

From the evening of 14 March the Scots Guards were at Laventie for four days. They were within range of German shells and Captain Warner, briefly the senior officer, noted that one narrowly missed the Transport and so he arranged to move them all to other billets next day. Sir Henry Rawlinson came to see them and told him that "the men looked well." General Heyworth also came on the morning of the 15th to talk to the men. On his return Sir Frederick FitzWygram stood in as Commanding Officer while Captain Warner became Adjutant. Over the next few weeks there were usually between three and five day intervals completely out of the line, but typical of these till the beginning of May was the entry in the War Diary on the 16th that three hundred and twenty five men had been away from five in the evening until ten that night digging. There were several other references to digging parties, some specifically for the 173rd Tunnelling Company Royal Engineers on twenty four hour details. The main activities were frequent drill parades by companies, route marches and field training. On Sundays there was church parade with separate services for the Church of England, Presbyterians collectively and Roman Catholics. The first tour in the breastworks began on the 18th. The 7th Division were now responsible for where the 8th Division had previously been from just north of Neuve Chapelle, near where the Rue Tilleloy met the road which headed southeast to the Quadrilateral and beyond, to a bit south of Rouges Bancs. Trench conditions were very much the same as previously but, because the 20th Brigade were now so weak, every battalion had to go into the line together except the 1/6th Gordons who were in reserve. Reinforcement drafts and gradually more officers arrived and Lieutenant Colonel Charles Corkran took command of the 1st Grenadiers. Sir Frederick FitzWygram wrote on 20 March to Lieutenant Saumarez to give him the news, among others of Major Paynter "doing well & is now practically out of danger" and of how Sir Edward Hulse had been killed. He continued that they now had about four hundred and twenty men for the line, but that another hundred were due that day. "I wish we could get some more officers as it is a desperate job running a battalion on our present number." There was still no definite news of what had happened to Lieutenant Nugent at Rouges Bancs, nor would there ever be. "We have had 2 great concerts lately & 1 boxing entertainment. There is quite a lot of talent among the last drafts, though our star performer, Jamieson, was wounded last week." About the battle he thought that "a little more push on the first day & I think we should have walked clean through them."

There was one more Scots Guards casualty of Neuve Chapelle. On 26 March at La Gorgue, just west of Estaires, a Field General Court Martial convened with Major John Hacket of the 2nd Royal Warwicks as President and Captains William "Monty" Hill of the 2nd Scots Guards and William Reid, a Seaforth Highlander attached to the 2nd Gordons, with whom he would be mortally wounded soon afterwards, as Members. Captain Hill had served for five years from January 1899, including being severely wounded at the Battle of Modder River during the Boer War. He rejoined in 1914, arrived in the 2nd Scots Guards on 17 March and moved on in March 1916 to command the 7th Loyals in the 19th Division and later other battalions. For a few weeks that spring he had as his Second in Command the frequently wounded, already one eyed and one armed Major Adrian Carton de Wiart, 4th Dragoon Guards, who would win the VC on the Somme commanding the 8th Gloucesters in the same Division. As was usual practice, Captain Warner, as Adjutant, was Prosecuting Officer, but all he put in his diary was that there was a court martial all afternoon. Considering the nature of the evidence that was inevitable, the charge being "when on active service desertion". The accused was Private Isaac Reid of F Company, who pleaded Not Guilty. Private Reid, general labourer from East Kilbride, was the third man who enlisted on 26 October 1913 at Hamilton. He had been out since Zeebrugge, was missing at the roll call on 28 October at Hooge and rejoined on 20 November, there being no recorded explanation of the circumstances, but he was neither charged with absence, nor with anything else, so there was nothing on his conduct sheets. First Ypres rapidly became chaotic and it was neither difficult for a soldier to become genuinely lost nor to give such an explanation, perhaps less genuine, for his having disappeared.

The prosecution had four witnesses. The first was Lance Corporal John McKechnie, who stated that at seven on 11 March Private Reid had advanced with his company and that he had last seen him taking cover with his section after they had gone two hundred yards. The next was Sergeant Major Moncur, in charge of the ammunition carts on the Estaires-La Bassée road when he saw Private Reid coming down it at about half past eleven. Knowing that this was not where Private Reid should have been, he asked what he was doing. The reply was that Sir Frederick FitzWygram had sent him back to his billet to get something.

The Sergeant Major detailed Corporal William Shearing, the third witness, to go with him to collect it. Private Reid then admitted to Corporal Shearing that he had gone to get some "cognac" for himself and a comrade. At that Corporal Shearing marched Private Reid at once to the Sergeant Major, who told him to return Private Reid to F Company under escort. The fourth witness was Company Sergeant Major James Lawton of F Company, who said that Corporal Shearing handed Private Reid over to him at about half past two in the area of the reserve trenches, when he came back with a party to collect more ammunition. He ordered Private Reid to fall in and remain with his ammunition party. He last saw him at about half past six but half an hour later, when the party were ready to go forward, there was no sign. The Company Sergeant Major came back to look for him again five hours later, without success, and next saw Private Reid at one o'clock in the afternoon on 16 March at Laventie. Nothing in any of the evidence of these four witnesses in any way suggested that Private Reid was incoherent, irrational or other than in control of his faculties. A note was produced to the Court from a Captain Walker of the Royal Horse Artillery that Private Reid had presented himself to him at quarter past six on the morning of the 16th and "stated that he had lost himself and spent the night in my men's billets."

Private Reid, who had been informed previously by Captain Warner that he could either address the Court or make a written plea [in mitigation], chose to do the latter. He wrote "I seemed to have lost my head…sincerely regret what has happened I lost my Company and not knowing what to do I took the course which has led to the charge." He continued that he had formerly done his duty, shared hardships and trusted to the leniency of the Court. Further, he claimed that he had met a military policeman on the 13th and asked him where to find the Battalion, but the Assistant Provost Marshal's enquiries failed to find anyone to corroborate this. There is no record of an "accused's friend" or defending officer at the trial, but Private Reid could have declined to have one. He was found Guilty and sentenced to death. The Court recommended mercy on the grounds of his former services and good character. The members had also seen the man and had time to evaluate him.

Danger always lurked out of the line whenever German guns were in range and that same day, 26 March, shells wounded three men at La Gorgue. Private James Dickson, from Penicuik, Midlothian, a gardener until he enlisted in 1903, married Annie Strachan in Brechin in October 1905. He left the Colours the following year. Both went to Canada in 1913 and were living in Lambton Mills, Ontario, when he was mobilised. He arrived in England on 4 September and went with the Battalion to Zeebrugge. Hit in the stomach, Private Dickson died at Laventie.

By the evening of 1 April they were in a salient in the line where the parapets were not bullet proof, only discovering this in daylight when seven men were hit. Captain Warner "Found trenches very unsafe…Brigadier came round in afternoon and was excited about enemy sniping. Companies hard at work at night, making things safer and putting in loop holes." One of those hit was Private Benjamin Newbury who died of wounds. A collier till he enlisted in August 1911, he left for the Reserve on 3 August 1914, only to be called up two days later. In the BEF since Zeebrugge, he had been wounded once before in the left arm in the Rouges Bancs attack and sent home. While there he married Millicent Tate at the end of February and she was living with their son in Cambridge. He had been back in France for less than a week when he died.

Captain Warner heard on 29 March who might come to command them. This was confirmed on 1 April and four days later Lieutenant Colonel Cator duly arrived. Next day a Sniping Section of twelve men was formed, equipped with six rifles with telescopic sights that had been presented to the Battalion. At the end of his brief diary entry on the 8th back at Laventie Captain Warner put "Had to see Reid." This was to tell him that he was going to be shot next morning because confirmation of the sentence had arrived. After the court martial General Heyworth reported to General Capper and recommended clemency because of the excellent state of discipline in the Battalion and because he said that this was just about their only instance of desertion. He was required to report on discipline in case it was felt necessary to make an example. On 29 March General Capper wrote to Headquarters IV Corps reporting these views, adding that the Commanding Officer, by whom he meant Sir Frederick FirzWygram, who had to say so, considered that Private Reid had acted deliberately and that while his general character was recorded as "Very Good" he did "not have a good character as a fighting man." That proved fatal, in particular given General Capper's own capacity for physical courage and his constantly near reckless example of it. Sir Frederick FitzWygram had been out with the Battalion since Zeebrugge, but only in F Company after Ypres. There had then been the interval after he was wounded at Rouges Bancs. Sergeant Major Moncur, with whom he would have discussed Private Reid, had not been away at all. General Capper emphasised Major Paynter's role in instilling good discipline, but what he took exception to was Private Reid's abandoning his comrades in action. "I fear it is a bad case, and I do not see any extenuating circumstances." He also picked out that Private Reid had not only left his section during the battle, but also left a second time after being ordered to stay with the ammunition party. Sir Henry Rawlinson agreed "that the sentence be carried out, not because it is necessary to make an example but because there is no excuse for the man." The file went on to Sir Douglas Haig, commanding First Army, who agreed with Generals Rawlinson and Capper, also noting Private Reid's not having "a good character as a fighting man," and confirmed the sentence. There was no record of this having gone on to Sir John French, as Commander in Chief, but he could have been away and so delegated his authority.

While there is no known first hand account, Private Stephen Graham put together the events of the morning of 9 April at Laventie from what he heard after he joined the Battalion in the spring of 1918. Reveille was an hour earlier than usual and the men dressed in the dark before putting on full fighting order for a route march. Private Reid, with a Military Police escort, was said to have been "calm, even cheerful" and to have talked with several men he knew while the Battalion formed three sides of a square. Private Graham was told that there was an attempt to find volunteers to shoot Private Reid, but that it came down to ordering the Battalion snipers to do it. Private Reid asked for a cigarette, lit it and walked across the field to the tree against which he was going to be shot. He did not want his eyes bandaged, but was overruled, and his feet and hands were tied. The Battalion stood to attention with sloped arms. The snipers were ready and loaded and, when the sentence had been read out, they took aim and shortly afterwards there were ten shots. Private Graham conveyed the disbelief, dread and sorrow among the watchers, but the Battalion then moved off sharply on a long route march "leaving the limp fallen body at the foot of the tree." Captain Bagot Chester, recently returned as Second in Command, would appear to have commanded that parade because it was he, as Acting Commanding Officer, who signed the certificate that the sentence had been carried out, though the War Diary noted that it was not till the next day that Colonel Cator went on leave for a week. Captain Warner's diary entry was "Parade 7.15. Deserter shot, went for a route march directly after." As required by the current regulations Colonel Fludyer signed a letter from Regimental Headquarters to Private Reid's mother Elizabeth Reid "No.8752, Private I. Reid, 2nd Bn. Scots Guards, was sentenced after trial by court martial to be shot for Desertion and the sentence was duly executed on 9th April, 1915." Because of his conviction Private Reid also forfeited any medals he was entitled to and any official recognition after the War that he had died in the service of his country. So there was neither memorial plaque nor scroll from the War Office.

Private Graham got the impression that, as seen by the men, particularly F Company, Company Sergeant Major Lawton was to blame, it being inferred that there was quite a bit of sympathy for Private Reid. The sense of shame and anger about it, most intense in F Company, perhaps influenced events in the next battle, as some subsequently believed. By April 1915 hardly anyone then in F Company could have known Private Reid's full history. Very few were left after First Ypres, the losses, in the dark, in the attack at Rouges Bancs were very heavy and there had been Neuve Chapelle itself as well, irrespective of those otherwise killed, badly wounded or sick. No one could have known details either of the court martial proceedings or of the subsequent reports. Company Sergeant Major Lawton's evidence on its own did not convict Private Reid and it had nothing to do with the sentence or its confirmation. Since he took over after Company Sergeant Major Lilley was killed at Rouges Bancs Company Sergeant Major Lawton could have given or been construed as having been giving Private Reid a hard time. So the Company Sergeant Major, if what Private Graham was told was accurate, was ostracised by F Company. Perhaps Private Reid was completely incapable of controlling his actions in the face of danger. If in the confusion of First Ypres he slipped away at Polygon Wood or elsewhere, an explanation on his return that he had simply got lost would have been unchallengeable, if in the dark at Rouges Bancs he had just lain low, no one else would have known, but at Neuve Chapelle all was out in the open.

The Breastworks at Neuve Chapelle

On 18 April General Capper had to be invalided because, while watching a demonstration of different ways of using the newly arrived trench mortars on the 1st, he had been injured by an accidental explosion, more seriously than first thought. For the Scots Guards there was much disappointment because "In him we have lost a friend and a fine leader." Sir John French visited the Brigade the day after and praised the Battalion particularly for Neuve Chapelle, alluding also to the fine leadership of Generals Capper and Heyworth. He spoke individually to each battalion and may well have said much the same every time. On the 19th in another letter to Sir Robert Kindersley, General Heyworth stated, referring to the Germans, "I am quite sure in my own mind that want of men on their side will finish the war and nothing else." That morning the 2nd Scots Guards "marched out 700 strong to meet the 1st Bn in a meadow just east of Vieux Chapelle. It is believed to have been the first occasion when the two Bns of the Regiment have met together on active service." Later Major General Hubert Gough, now commanding the 7th Division, "came round to see the Bn but only saw the CO and two other officers."

Writing from a German military hospital on 11 August Sir Frederick FitzWygram told Lieutenant Saumarez about the April drafts. "Moncur (the men call him 'dogface') was in great form with the drafts…Most of them arrived with red handkerchiefs round their necks & as you know that is like a red rag to a bull with him. I drew him on the subject one morning after a draft had arrived the previous afternoon while we were in the trenches, & he told me "I made one rush at them, Sir. I had 5 minutes of the best sport I ever had in my life etc." Can't you imagine him?"

One lesson had been learned. During the Scots Guards three days in the line, beginning on the 21st, initially fifty officers and NCOs from the West Riding Division, later the 49th (West Riding) Division, Territorial Force, were attached to them and then immediately afterwards four of their platoons. It was much more constructive than putting new battalions straight into the trenches, as happened to the 1/6th Gordons before Christmas. The state of the line was much the same as three weeks earlier. "Bad trenches and dangerous the Germans being in a position to enfilade them." There were casualties next day, but on the 23rd they got their own back when "2Lt Clark enfiladed German lines with machine gun at night firing 3,000 rounds." Also, during the night Left Flank opened fire on a German working party and "groans of wounded men were distinctly audible." On the 24th, during their last afternoon before that night's relief, the German guns fired very heavily, but the only damage was a single shell hitting and demolishing the orderlies room at Battalion Headquarters. Everybody had had to take to their dug-outs and stay there. Lieutenant Edmund "Eddie" Clarke had been at Eton and Trinity College, Cambridge, and was the son of Colonel Stephenson Clarke of Cuckfield, Sussex. He transferred in January 1915 from the 4th Royal Sussex and trained as a machine gun officer before he left England at the end of March. He joined the 3rd Guards Brigade Machine Gun Company from when it formed in September and was hit in the head on 17 October during the fighting in the Hohenzollern trenches at Loos. After that he was sent home to recover, which he never fully did, being classified as permanently unfit in August 1918.

Apart from the 20th Brigade, the whole Division were shortly put on call in case needed to help further north, where on the 22nd the Germans' first gas attack, chlorine, on the French around Langemarck initiated the Second Battle of Ypres and they started to capture ground. It quickly became a joint French and British battle. Accordingly, after three days in reserve in the Rue du Bacquerot, the next breastworks tour on the 27th was a long one. For this the Brigade had moved a bit further south, roughly to what the 8th Division captured on 10 March at Neuve Chapelle, the outgoing troops being the Bareilly Brigade of the Meerut Division. Colonel Cator told his mother on 30 April that they had not been involved up at Ypres but "The cannonade which we could hear quite plainly was terrific…it is a bit quieter now, but still goes on. Everyone says the Canadians fought like Demons." Reports about the French were less flattering. On the chlorine "the asphyxiating gas is not much good they say and can be counteracted by holding a damp flannel over the nose and mouth. We relieved the Indians here, their trenches were beautifully kept and they appear to have splendid discipline. The 4th Battn Black Watch's trenches which we also took over were too disgustingly filthy for words and I should think their discipline must be a very low standard; it has taken many days cleaning up after them and burying their refuse and paper." The War Diary remarked "their sanitary arrangements NIL." The 2nd Black Watch were the British Regular battalion in that Brigade, the 1/4th Black Watch the Territorial battalion who joined during the winter.

It was fairly quiet apart from some shelling but Colonel Cator was "not sure though they are not making a mine here, as they are doing a lot of sawing up wood, and there is a suspicious looking heap of earth in their lines which daily looks bigger. I am just off to go and make a close examination of the earth through a glass, as they cannot mine without getting blue clay here which is easily detected by its colour." On the 27th Captain Ivor Rivers Bulkeley had arrived to command Left Flank and be described in Lieutenant Swinton's letter of the 28th as "a tall dark square faced man & might be pleasant on closer inspection." His parents Colonel Charles and Constance Rivers Bulkeley lived in London and he was the younger brother of Captain Tommy

Rivers Bulkeley, killed at Polygon Wood during First Ypres. Lieutenant Swinton was writing home on the 30th "Weather still glorious. Please send a cake, some more sherbet, some of those small boxes of candles, & some cherry brandy & a Brunswick sausage from Fortnum & Mason."

Second Ypres notwithstanding, it was apparent that something else was in the offing, not least because their relief, of which they were told on the morning of 2 May, was soon cancelled and that afternoon Sir Henry Rawlinson visited them in the trenches. Captain Warner spent the following afternoon in the front line when "Germans were firing at our aeroplanes, we fired rifle grenades which they returned." He then had a disturbed evening because "Berkshires on our right said their trenches were ruined so I was kept up on the phone till midnight." Separately the battalion on the left had reported an enemy mine ready to be fired, so Sir Frederick FitzWygram went to investigate, only to find all quiet. Two hours more heavy shelling around Battalion Headquarters late on the 5th hit nothing but a haystack, but on his way back from Brigade Headquarters Captain Warner had to take cover in a fort after he was "Nearly hit by a shell which landed a few yards away but did not burst." All the same, after eight days in the line four men had been killed and eighteen wounded before they left that evening, replaced by West Riding Territorials, and marched back again to Laventie, arriving about midnight. Lance Corporal William Stones, a serving soldier since 1904 when he gave up being a telegraphist in Bradford, was killed on the 2nd. He had already been slightly wounded by shrapnel in his right thigh with the 1st Battalion on the Aisne. Clarissa Stones, whom he married in 1913, was in Bradford, where she received her husband's wristlet watch, a whistle, six photographs, some post cards, a cap star, a knife and a notebook. He was promoted in December in England and had been back in the BEF for less than three weeks. Private David Grant, the son of James Grant of Partick, had been a coal trimmer at the Queen's Dock on the Clyde until August 1914. Having been in the BEF for only six weeks, on 2 May he was badly hurt in the left arm, which was amputated. On 20 September 1916 he was at Roehampton, being fitted with an artificial limb, and two months later he was out of the Army by medical discharge. A medical board which decided this awarded him twenty five shillings weekly for two months and then thirteen shillings per week for life. A permanent disability pension was only granted where there was no prospect of recovery. On 3 May Private David Turner landed in France on his way to the 2nd Scots Guards. Formerly an ironworker in Edinburgh, he was in the 1st Battalion from enlistment in 1904 until war broke out when he was posted to the 3rd Battalion at Wellington Barracks. In December 1914 he married Jessie Markham in London, who was living at Salford, Oxfordshire. From now on he was in the BEF, went to the 3rd Guards Brigade Machine Gun Company in January 1916 and transferred eventually to the 4th (Foot Guards) Battalion Guards Machine Gun Regiment. He was only wounded once, by a gas shell on 19 September 1918, and sent home for good. He was one of the 1st Battalion's Officers Mess Staff photographed in 1914.

The Battle of Aubers

When nearly hit by the shell that did not burst Captain Warner had been to the first briefing for a two pronged attack, at the time planned for 8 May. On the left IV Corps, starting from opposite Rouges Bancs, were to thrust southeast towards Fromelles and up Aubers Ridge behind it, while, on the right, I Corps were to make a second thrust northeast towards Aubers and from there up the Ridge, starting from further down the line beyond Neuve Chapelle. This became known as the Battle of Aubers. On the 6th Lieutenant Swinton wrote home injudiciously and optimistically from Laventie "Just a line to let you know that we propose dining in Lille on <u>Saturday 8th</u> having previously lunched at Aubers. We are starting from our old trenches where we were all the winter." To begin with the 8th Division were to break into the German line at Rouges Bancs and exploit the breach. Not until they had done this were the 7th Division to follow through them to Fromelles and on beyond. There were thorough reconnaissance and briefings down to platoon commander level during the next two days, but on the evening of the 7th they heard of twenty four hours postponement. Not till after midnight on the 8th did they move out of Laventie, taking two and a half hours to reach dug-outs behind the line at Rouges Bancs. Lieutenant Swinton made notes on this, his and other people's timings varying a little, "We left Laventie at 12.40am & marched to dug-outs north of Rue du Bois & west of Sailly-Fromelles road. Got into these about 2am." Then "4am soup issued thanks to the ingenuity of Ross." From five the following morning the British guns bombarded the German defences for forty five minutes before the 8th Division attacked. He continued "5am to 5.15 wire cutting by forward guns. 5.10 – 5.40 bombardment. 5.40 mines exploded & 8th Div advance. It was some bombardment a battery just behind us was firing 40 rounds per minute for half an hour & others were the same. The 7th Div was supposed to have started at 6.25 22nd Brigade leading, then 20th & then 21st." The Germans had learned and implemented much since Neuve Chapelle, having their guns much better prepared to support their now more numerous infantry, as well as adding more and better sited machine guns and other means of putting down flanking fire on attackers, wherever they might come forward. The 8th Division achieved little at great cost and ultimately had to give up what little they had taken. The 7th Division did not move forward at all and the Scots Guards stayed in their dug-outs all day.

Later, Captain Warner putting the time at seven in the evening, the 7th Division were told to take over the 8th Division trenches and get ready for a fresh attack on Rouges Bancs at dawn the following morning. Lieutenant Swinton, detailed to reconnoitre, found that "at about 7pm I was sent up to Rue Pétillon with an officer from each btn to find the way to some starting off trenches into which we were to move that night & attack from next morning." They got as far as a fort but the Germans "started shelling like the devil, also rapid rifle fire, we could not get out of the fort for an hour & we then ran like hares. We got back to Brigade dug-out & reported that it was impossible to get up there. We hadn't been there long when Gough turned up & we repeated our report to him. We then had dinner in the Brigade mess…& I then returned to my trench having stolen some straw." Another factor was the state of the original British front line, badly disorganised because of the repulse of the 8th Division and their very heavy casualties. As everybody in the 7th Division was facing exactly the same difficulties of getting into position, their attack was cancelled. Instead, having been woken up in their dug-outs at one thirty in the morning, the Scots Guards, their sole casualty one man wounded, headed back towards Laventie. They bivouacked in a field at half past three for what remained of the night, only returning in the morning to their original billets. The wounded man was Private William Johnson, a reservist from Brighton, where he had first enlisted in 1904. Soon afterwards he was trained in military transport duties. He had an agricultural background, was therefore familiar with handling horses and went back to being a farm worker in 1906. He arrived out from England just as First Ypres was starting and probably did not join the Battalion until afterwards. On 9 May he was slightly wounded in the head by a shell, but was only away for five days being treated. He and Elizabeth Johnson had two sons and a daughter, all under five. Another daughter was born in 1915. Lance Sergeant William

Creelman, a reservist and boiler fireman, whose father John Creelman lived at Broxburn, West Lothian, came out late in October 1914 and did not join till after First Ypres. He was made a Lance Sergeant after Neuve Chapelle. Now he was evacuated with shell shock, never to return to the BEF. After hospital treatment, while remaining in the Army, he was released to munitions work in Glasgow.

On the 10th there were orders for another attack on Rouges Bancs at dawn next morning, also soon cancelled. Lieutenant Swinton wrote "Another fright. We were all told that we were going to move from here at 7.30 pm & attack… tomorrow morning but have just heard that it is all off so we are going to dine with the rest at the Hotel de France tonight to celebrate the occasion."

The Battle of Festubert

Instead, another plan started to develop, in effect a continuation of Neuve Chapelle and Aubers, but with altered artillery preparations and for the 7th Division over new ground. First they all had to move south, Béthune being the 20th Brigade's destination. So, Lieutenant Swinton having been sent on ahead to find billets, the Battalion paraded on the evening of the 10th to march there. It took six hours, with only one man falling out. The Division were temporarily under the command of Sir Charles Monro in I Corps and would attack from southwest of where the right hand thrust towards Aubers by the 1st Division had failed on 9 May. On their left the 2nd Division would attack over the same ground, either side of the Cinder Track, where the 1st Division had suffered and part of the Indian Corps would attack again close to Neuve Chapelle. The 7th Division attack had the 22nd Brigade on the right and the 20th on the left. The 21st, in reserve, were first to take over the front line breastworks from which the other two brigades would attack, keep the enemy occupied and prevent them from repairing the damage done to their wire, breastworks and trenches by the British guns. Though this area was unfamiliar to the 7th Division, its characteristics were very familiar. The ditches were particularly plentiful, obstacles to those trying to press forward under heavy fire, but refuges when further movement was impossible. The ruins of Festubert were close by and gave this battle its name. In contrast to the "hurricane" bombardment at the start on the 9th, which had not worked, the artillery plan was quite different. There was deliberate shelling of the German wire and front line breastworks with the aim of providing more opportunity for observing the results and putting down fresh fire where needed. Interspersed with this deliberate artillery fire, feint "hurricane" bombardments were fired to lure the Germans out from cover afterwards, only for them then to be deluged almost immediately by another burst of shells. It was hoped that this would inflict casualties and spread demoralisation and uncertainty.

On the 11th Colonel Cator had taken the company commanders to look at the front line from Festubert as far along as Richebourg-L'Avoué ahead of an attack the following morning, only for that to be cancelled. That caused congestion in the billeting plan, so that next day their Brigade, due to move out of Béthune to make the attack, instead had the disruption of going four miles northwest to Hinges. It was very wet on the 13th when General Heyworth and Colonel Cator had a further look at the ground. Then, when Headquarters First Army ordered the commanding officers of the assaulting battalions to satisfy themselves on the 14th that the German wire in front of them was cut sufficiently "to justify the launching of a successful attack," Colonel Cator was not satisfied. Six hours more shelling followed.

At six on the evening of the 15th the Brigade left Hinges. The Scots Guards were in the lead and, at twenty to nine, at the junction where the Rue de L'Épinette went to the right off the Rue du Bois, they found that because of "a somewhat heavy fire sweeping the ground" they had to go along a communication trench via Indian Village to their assault position. This they reached by eleven, with the 2nd Gordons ready in support behind them. Their left boundary was Princes Road, running south from its junction with the Rue du Bois at Chocolat Menier Corner. The Borders, the other assaulting battalion, who had moved separately, took their place in the front line the other side of the road, with the Grenadiers ready in support. The attack was due to start at quarter past three on the 16th after half an hour's further bombardment. Just to their north the 2nd Division had already attacked before midnight and their right hand brigade took the German front line, but that was all they took and that had consequences. The Borders, after capturing the enemy front line, were to clear to their left along the German position once they entered it, while the next Scots Guards objective was an orchard with some ruined houses, formed into a strong point, close to the junction of the Princes Road and the Rue des Cailloux, for which they would not have to change direction so much to their left. The Rue des Cailloux ran from its junction with the Rue de L'Épinette north of Festubert roughly eastwards to its junction, immediately south of the major German strong point at Cour L'Avoué Farm, with the much longer road from Festubert northeast to the main Estaires-La Bassée road at La Tourelle Farm. The Scots Guards were starting some three hundred yards north of the 1st Royal Welsh Fusiliers, on the 22nd Brigade's left, but it was anticipated that they would converge and move forward alongside.

Colonel Cator could see that, in spite of the additional shelling, there was only one gap a hundred yards wide in the German wire on the left near the Princes Road and he decided only to attack through it. He had the Battalion in two ranks behind the breastworks, fortuitously with the leading companies, Right Flank on the left and F Company on the right, nearest the gap. So, because of the narrow space and the need for the attack to have depth, it had to be by platoons, starting with 4 Platoon of Right Flank and 8 Platoon of F Company. The other platoons were to move to their left along the breastworks as the preceding platoons headed out to the gap. There were now far more officers in the Battalion, of whom several were left out of battle, and only three per company took part. During the night the British wire, cut previously, had been removed and ladders put up to make it easier for the assaulting troops to get over the breastwork. It was a warm night and all the men got some rest until quarter to three. Then the half hour bombardment began and, leaving their packs behind, they got ready and had a tot of rum.

Three minutes before the end of the bombardment the first two platoons lined up by the ladders and climbed over to cross No Man's Land while the Germans' heads were still kept down. Unfortunately, some of Right Flank were too quick, suffered casualties from British shells landing on the German breastwork and were held up in front of it. Captain Bagot Chester rushed across to lead them on and on they went. All the platoons followed in pairs at fifty yard intervals, the final two Left Flank ones under Lieutenant Swinton having orders to halt in the German front line and consolidate it. All surviving Germans were bayoneted and a minenwerfer captured. At 3.22 the Scots Guards report of having taken a hundred and fifty yards of the enemy line reached Brigade Headquarters, followed by another at 4.05 that they were in the German third line [as they found and described it]. They continued on and then took the orchard strong point, their first main objective, where, similarly, there was little resistance, a report being made at 5.25 of this and also that they were further on from it. However, as they were approaching the orchard strong point and continuously afterwards, heavy machine gun fire from the left caused a lot of casualties. Word of this reached Brigade Headquarters, who sent up some of the 2nd Gordons to help protect their left flank as well as linking up with the Borders. These German machine guns, firing from a series of strong points further up towards Cour d'Avoué Farm, along with a minenwerfer, had already contributed to stopping the Borders from making any progress on their way up the German front line. Initially they did succeed in clearing some two hundred yards, but were then driven back because they did not have enough grenades. They lost very heavily, stuck just inside the German front line facing east, with the Princes Road behind them. Among their dead was Private Abraham Acton, who had won the VC before Christmas. Beyond the Borders, who made further unsuccessful attacks after more British shelling, the 2nd Division were still no closer towards Cour d'Avoué Farm either. All this exposed the Scots Guards as they moved on. A message from them, timed 7.55, reached Brigade Headquarters just over an hour later that they were much disorganised but holding the orchard strong point and had dug themselves in south of it. There was little news thereafter and growing apprehension at Brigade Headquarters that their leading companies had got too far forward.

Their next task, according to the plan, was to swing further to their left and capture the ground up to La Quinque Rue from, on the left, a strong point just north of the German communication trench called Adalbert Alley to, on the right, La Quinque Rue Crossroads. From there a road headed southeast past a large orchard, also with ruined houses, the bottom corner of that orchard being the left objective of the Royal Welsh Fusiliers. Running from that corner towards Festubert was a German fortification and communication route called the North Breastwork, the principal objective of the 22nd Brigade. In the noise and confusion of the fighting some of F Company did not swing as far to their left as the rest and lost contact, but, conversely, some of the Royal Welsh Fusiliers, under Captain Herbert Coles, who was mortally wounded, did join up with a Scots Guards company at some stage and stayed with them. Captain Clifton "Cliff" Stockwell, commanding A Company of the Royal Welsh Fusiliers described the start of the battle. "We are nearing the smoke. Can't say I feel excited. There is a breach in the parapet in front of me. I decide to go through there. No Germans were apparent. Got through breach. Just as I got through a German comes round the corner of a traverse at me with a bayonet. I lift my pistol quickly and let drive – three times, quickly (one awful moment – will it work?). The Hun crumples up, and can see two more further on being bayoneted by our men. Went on through the German trench and met a crowd of Scots Guards coming from the left yelling. Am now in the German second line. One can hardly see from smoke of our lyddite shells, which is hanging all round the place. A Hun comes out of a dug-out and holds up his hands – a Scots Guard sticks him – pretty beastly. Then they all go mad, and all stick him, and stand round in a bunch yelling. I walk up to a man and say "What in the name of Hell are you doing?" He answers "Who the devil are you? And what's it got to do with you?" – so I hit him as hard as I can in the face and knock him down. I've cut my knuckle and jarred my wrist. I yell out, "Come on, boys," and they all come along, about thirty of our men, the Company Sergeant Major, Warner, Bridgeman, my servant and about thirty Scots Guards." Company Sergeant Major William Warner was killed at Loos. His servant was either Private WH Bridgeman, who survived the War, or Private Clifford Bridgeman who died at home in 1918. Captain Stockwell led his party on and, though they were losing men to more and more enfilade fire from the left, reached the southwest corner of the orchard at 6am. There they managed to take one house and captured and operated a German machine gun, but the number of enemy in the orchard and the other houses was such that they could not do more. They were joined through the day by little groups of officers and men from their own battalion, a platoon of 2nd Royal Warwicks, eight men from the Borders and a few more Scots Guardsmen. Captain Stockwell could see no one to his left or right, nor for five hundred yards back. At half past ten when a gunner officer and one from the 2nd Queen's reached him with a telephone he could send back accurate information. Reinforcements arrived at one o'clock and German counterattacks from the orchard all failed.

As most of F Company moved on from the captured orchard strong point they swung too far to their left, crossed the Rue des Cailloux and, not as far as La Quinque Rue, were being drawn towards the machine guns on their left. Many of these, quite undisturbed behind the German front line, had been swung round to fire south. At the same time German infantry, apparently from the local reserve, a half battalion of the *57th Infantry Regiment*, counterattacked, some appearing from the orchard beside Cour d'Avoué Farm and some from the communication trenches southwest of it, where the machine gun posts were. F Company were surrounded and cut off. Only Sir Frederick FitzWygram, unconscious from a head wound and with his right arm broken, and three other wounded men were taken prisoner there. Everyone else who had reached there, about eighty altogether, were killed. German dead in similar numbers lay in and around the rough circle in which they had fallen. Several days later, by which time this ground was in British hands after further attacks, Colonel Cator wrote of "A subsequent visit to the ground being a true testimony as to the gallant manner in which they fought, the German and Scots Guards dead being mingled together, and from appearances they must all have fought the battle out there to the finish." He noted that "some forty men fought their way out and joined the Royal Welsh Fusiliers." Later, as Private Graham heard in 1918, there would be talk of there having been a pact made by F Company after Private Reid's execution.

The German counterattackers, delayed and disrupted by F Company, then tried to work down the south side of the Rue des Cailloux. The Scots Guards around the former German orchard strong point, mainly G Company, with the Battalion machine gunners, were ready for them, destroyed the counterattack and drove them back. Soon after nine o'clock two Grenadier companies arrived, having followed their route from the British front line on finding that it was shielded from the enemy on their left, unlike that which the Borders had used. By now there was more confusion and so more disorganisation, added to by small groups of men from several regiments making their way back. The Scots Guards gathered them all up into a strong defensive position south of the junction of the Princes Road with the Rue des Cailloux, in the neighbourhood of the captured orchard strong point. It was for his part in this that Corporal Joseph Wilkinson, the son of Amelia Wilkinson of Preston, won the DCM. Previously a printer, he had been serving for five years and started to go quickly up the ranks after First Ypres, though reduced from Lance Sergeant to Corporal for drunkenness at the end of March at Laventie. Any further forward movement was still at the mercy of the strongly reinforced German defenders of the trenches just to the north and their attendant machine gun posts, whom the Borders had been unable to dislodge at the outset. Without having any idea of what had happened, Captain Warner started out on a patrol with a few men in the general direction of where F Company had succumbed, but found that it was impossible to go anywhere above ground because of the volume of fire. Only by getting into the long ditch running up the middle of the space between the Rue des Cailloux and La Quinque Rue, in which the water came up to their chests, were they able to get back safely.

Further south the 22nd Brigade had had more success, while confronted by the same problems. The Royal Welsh Fusiliers lost very heavily but Captain Stockwell's party had reached their objective at the orchard and had also occupied part of the North Breastwork. The Queen's, starting alongside them, endured heavy flanking machine gun and rifle fire from their right, in just the same way as the Borders had from their left, but still managed to keep up their momentum towards the North Breastwork, which some of them eventually reached. Unlike the Borders, whose immediate task on entering the German front line was to clear it northwards, in the case of the 22nd Brigade the task of clearing the front line to the south was given specifically to parties of bombers from the Royal Welsh Fusiliers and the 1st South Staffords, who did very well, capturing five hundred yards of the line as well as three German officers and nearly a hundred men. This made it easier for the right hand supporting battalion, the South Staffords, to move on and secure the ground of the former German second and third lines. However, the losses of both the Queen's and the Royal Welsh Fusiliers were so severe that at half past seven that evening they all had to pull back from the orchard and the North Breastwork, found to be not solid enough to stop bullets. Across to the left it was clear by five o'clock that there was nothing more that the 20th Brigade could do except reorganise and dig in, after all efforts by the Borders had come to nothing, after the Grenadiers had taken their place and made a small amount of progress up the German front line and after the 1/8th Royal Scots, Territorials, had attacked unsuccessfully beyond them. Just to the north the right of the 2nd Division had not achieved the capture of the Cour d'Avoué and du Bois Farms, the main strong points in front of them, nor had they linked up with the 20th Brigade, while further up the line the left of the 2nd Division and the Indian Corps had simply been checked.

When darkness fell Colonel Cator and Captain Warner started to gather the Battalion together, managing to assemble about three hundred men near the captured orchard strong point. Then the Grenadiers and 1/6th Gordons took over the new front line along the Princes Road and roughly south from its junction with the Rue des Cailloux while the Scots Guards, as well as the 2nd Gordons, occupied the old German front line taken that morning. The Scots Guardsmen turned it to face the opposite way and reversed the parapet. Rations arrived and everyone had a meal. It was impossible to find out the number of casualties. The whole of F Company and one Left Flank platoon were missing and Right Flank, who had been advancing further left than F Company and therefore closer to the machine guns on their flank, could only muster thirty men, though their company commander, Captain Hill, had not been hit. Throughout the night parties went out looking for the dead and wounded and bringing them in. Thirty seven men rejoined, mostly from F Company, with a glowing report from Captain Stockwell on how well they had fought and nothing about when he first saw them. The Royal Welsh Fusiliers started that day with twenty five officers, including their Medical Officer, and eight hundred and six men, and lost nineteen and five hundred and fifty nine. As it got light on the 17th there was "a tremendous Bombardment" of the German front line and its strong points, which had caused the Borders such trouble the day before, and "before long white flags could be seen going up and being waved all along their front line in this neighbourhood, many rushing across unarmed & holding up their hands to the British lines, to surrender." These surrendering Germans continued to be on the receiving end of the British guns and, it was believed at the time that German guns, machine guns and rifles had fired on them as well to try to stop them surrendering. Captain Warner heard that these were new troops who had been moved down in a hurry during the night from Armentières and, being Saxons, were none too happy about it. He also heard that it had been Prussians who shot at them, "the scum of Europe" he called them. Since the Germans had issued orders for a tactical withdrawal to a new front line prepared at short notice further back, they may not have realised that they still had men in their old front line and so fired on them by mistake. During 17 May, because it was felt that enough had been achieved the day before to justify continuing the battle, the 21st Brigade successfully attacked across the ground where the Saxons had surrendered and then took a major strong point on the Rue des Cailloux about five hundred yards from Cour d'Avoué Farm. There the British front line then moved forward.

The Scots Guards spent the whole of the 17th in the former German front line under heavy shellfire, but it all fell about fifty yards or so behind them and only one man was wounded. They went on looking for and bringing in more wounded and buried the dead whom they could find. Otherwise there was nothing to report except their losses. The fate of all of the missing would not become clear or beyond reasonable doubt for some time, but they established that ten officers were casualties, two killed, three wounded and five missing. Only six were now present out of sixteen who had started, of whom only two were among the twelve with the companies, Captain Hill and Lieutenant Swinton. He wrote home on the 20th and told his family what he knew about others, also that he "was in the rear line of the btn & when I got to the 1st German line I was told to stay there & put it in a state of defence. The rest of the btn went on, & I was left there all day. I went up to the front line that evening and sprained my ankle & on the way back did it again so not being any use I went to the Transport." Many who could not be found the day before did turn up but there were forty seven killed, one hundred and eighty two wounded and one hundred and seventy two missing among the rank and file, as at the 17th. The battle continued for some days and included an attack by the Canadians, who finally secured the large orchard, thereafter known as Canadian Orchard, at the east end of the North Breastwork, while the 4th (Guards) Brigade extended the front line beyond where F Company had made their last stand.

2nd Lieutenant Willie Garforth, educated at Charterhouse, had been the land agent at Waddesdon Manor, Buckinghamshire, before he was commissioned as a wartime volunteer, arriving in France just before Neuve Chapelle. He was the son of William Garforth and The Honourable Mrs Hylda Garforth of Westow, Yorkshire. Sir Frederick FitzWygram wrote from Germany that Lieutenant Garforth was badly wounded when he was and that the Germans told him of his death. In unspecified circumstances his identity disc was recovered. Also found and returned was his waterproof pouch, containing two white handkerchiefs and a khaki one. Attempts to learn more got nowhere. His mother wrote to The Secretary, The War Office, saying how much she would like to know how the identity disc had been recovered "if through a German Hospital or if he died on the battlefield? killed by a bomb or shell? or if, as supposed by some, that he was killed by our own guns? – at Festubert 16 May – any details wd be so gratefully recd, as probably the War Office has rec? them from France. Also if they happen to know, if his body was buried & where?" Private William Veitch was wounded in the German second line and saw Lieutenant Garforth advancing from there. They were in the same platoon and Private Veitch said that Lieutenant Garforth was a fine keen officer, who had told them all the day before that "they were never to stop but to go straight through the first enemy trenches." He added that he was afraid that Lieutenant Garforth was killed as he was so keen. Private Veitch was a serving soldier in 1914 and previously an assistant joiner's storekeeper in Bootle, the son of William and Mary Veitch. He had already been slightly wounded in the neck on 1 November during First Ypres and recovered at a Base hospital. This time he was hit in the left forearm and evacuated across the Channel, though the wound was not a serious one and he was soon back at Wellington Barracks. There he had a week's leave from which he was due back by midnight on 7 August 1915, but he deserted and disappeared completely. The third officer in F Company, 2nd Lieutenant Ferdinand "Ferdie" Marsham Townshend, was found dead on the battlefield. Another Etonian who had been to Christ Church, Oxford, he was commissioned in February and was less than two months with the Battalion. His father was dead and his mother Clara Marsham Townshend was living in Mayfair, London. His own home had been at Wroughton, Wiltshire, and he was unmarried. Five more officers were killed or missing. Lieutenant Archibald Jarvis was confirmed dead. He had been at Harrow, worked in London as a bill broker, and had previously been a member of the Royal Naval Volunteer Reserve before transferring in December. His father Major Louis Jarvis was serving with the County of London Yeomanry in the BEF, while his mother Adeline Jarvis was staying temporarily near Norwich. Their home was in Manchester Square, London. 2nd Lieutenant Alec Hepburne Scott, wounded and missing, was never seen again. After Repton he had gone to Balliol College, Oxford, and, still an undergraduate, had enlisted in the London Scottish as soon as war was declared, serving in the ranks in Belgium and France from 15 September 1914 until evacuated to England with jaundice in January. He was commissioned into the Scots Guards in March. His parents were The Master of Polwarth and Edith Hepburne Scott who lived at Humbie, East Lothian. Few men with no previous military experience could have gone on active service more quickly in 1914. Of the other three officers who were missing, Captain Ivor Rivers Bulkeley was never found, but on the 26th the bodies of Lieutenants Denys Stephenson and James Mackenzie were identified and recovered. Lieutenant Stephenson had been at Wellington and Trinity College, Cambridge, and started in the ranks of the Honourable Artillery Company before being commissioned into the Scots Guards in November 1914. He had strong family connections. His parents Russell and Gwendolen Stephenson lived in Mayfair. Lieutenant Mackenzie was the twenty year old son of James and Alice Mackenzie of Kansas City, Missouri, and had been educated at the Upper Canada College, Toronto. He was studying at London University and was commissioned from the Officers Training Corps in December 1914.

Private Alfred Millican, a gardener from Walton on Thames, where Esther, his mother, had a bakery, was wounded in the stomach by a shrapnel bullet and captured. He described being well treated medically at a German dressing station and fairly well attended to otherwise. He was in hospital at Koblenz, on the Rhine, till January 1916 and thereafter at Giessen. He thought his treatment as a prisoner was fair throughout and had neither experienced nor seen any cruelty. In December 1916 he was accepted for internment in Switzerland at Château D'Oeux, was there for nine months before being repatriated and then in January 1918 discharged, permanently disabled. His younger brother, Private Herbert Millican, a fitter, joined up with him in London in the middle of November 1914, but only lasted five weeks in the BEF before being sent home at the end of May because of neurasthenia. Later, when he was mentally stable enough, he went, though still a soldier, as a munitions worker to the Motor Omnibus Department of Eastbourne Corporation and there spent the rest of the War. Private John Robertson, the ship's carpenter from Glasgow, who was on patrol with Privates Ferguson and Rae at Rouges Bancs, for which he was mentioned in dispatches, when Private Rae was killed on 28 November 1914, was slightly wounded in both legs by shrapnel. This kept him away until July 1916. Privates John Pinnington and Edward Pinnington were brothers in their mid twenties, both of them clerks, who volunteered in October 1914 at Hamilton, though Edward and Margaret Pinnington lived in Motherwell. Both were badly wounded on 16 May. Private John Pinnington, the elder one, had multiple shrapnel wounds in his right arm, in his left side, affecting both abdomen and back, and in his right thigh and knee, these being the worst. At Boulogne he had a tetanus injection, contracted peritonitis and was evacuated across the Channel, where he remained five months and recovered, fit to return to the BEF. Private Edward Pinnington had shrapnel wounds in his back and was similarly evacuated. He was commissioned at the end of December, becoming an officer in the 12th Cavalry (Reserve) Regiment. Private William Hardie, whose family lived in Hawick, was a baker until he enlisted in Cowdenbeath in September 1914. In France for exactly three months before Festubert, he was hit in the stomach, slightly, and left knee, badly, and lost his leg. On 18 October he was discharged disabled when still in hospital at Chelmsford. Private John Robertson was a Glaswegian with some former military service as he stated when he enlisted at Liverpool in October 1914 that he had served for eighteen months with Bethune's Mounted Infantry in the Boer War. More recently he had been in Boston, Massachusetts, where he was a bookkeeper and married Margaret Stevenson in April 1914. When he sailed from there she came with him, stayed for a while in Paisley, then went back to South Boston, before returning once more. Their son was born in August 1915. Private Robertson arrived in France on 15 April and at Festubert was wounded in the arm and leg and evacuated. The wound in his arm caused permanent damage, his hand being described as "useless", and he was discharged disabled on 4 August 1916. Private Andrew Turner, a miner, whose father, also Andrew Turner, lived at Cousland, Midlothian, had volunteered the previous November and came out to France in late April. He was very badly hurt in the right arm at Festubert, so much so that he was classified as "Dangerously Ill" a few days later in hospital at Le Tréport, but he weathered that, though his arm had to be amputated below the elbow and not until 2 July was he stable enough to be evacuated. He was discharged disabled on 5 August 1916, the day after Private Robertson.

Privates David Duthie from Brechin and George Durward from St Cyrus had both been ploughmen, both enlisted in Forfar the same day, both came out in the same draft that landed in France on 16 March and both were wounded at Festubert, in the right leg and left ankle respectively. Private Duthie did not return until the spring of 1917 when he joined the 1st Battalion, serving with them for the rest of the War, being slightly wounded once more in July 1917 shortly before the Battle of Pilckem Ridge. While in England after his first wound he married Alice Murrell in 1916 in London. They had known each other for some time, already had a son and would soon have another. A daughter followed in 1918. Private Durward was back in France in October 1915 in the 1st Battalion, remaining with them till he was hit in the right shoulder at Ginchy on the Somme eleven months later. The wound was not a bad one and he only spent two weeks in a Base hospital before going back up the line. He was wounded a third time, this time badly in both legs on 30 July 1917, the day before Pilckem Ridge, and evacuated across the Channel. Sent out to the 2nd Scots Guards after the Armistice, he spent two more months with them until he finally went home. Also in that draft on 16 March 1915 was another volunteer, Private Charles Beattie, the son of John and Mary Beattie of Montrose and previously a commercial traveller. From the day he arrived in the Battalion he served with them till they went home from Cologne, by which time he was a Lance Sergeant. He was never wounded.

Private William Baxter, a carpenter, had by this time been in the Army for slightly more than seven months and in France for slightly more than one. He was very severely wounded in the thigh, stomach and left arm and died three days later at Chocques. When his father William Baxter and his mother, identified only by the initials C A, received his few effects, among them a piece of shrapnel, his mother wrote on the receipt "excuse me for taking liberty but I would like a small badge of the Regiment in memory of my dear boy." They lived at the Coast Guard Station, Felpham, on the Sussex coast. Private Herbert Beck, born in Windermere and a farm worker before enlisting in 1913, was killed. He had gone out with the Battalion at the beginning. Slightly wounded in the right knee later on during First Ypres, he next went down with scarlet fever and spent several weeks in hospital as a result, only returning in February. Frank and Mary Jane Beck lived at Roeburndale, near Lancaster. Also killed was Sergeant George Bell, born in Kirriemuir, who served for seven years before leaving in 1909 and becoming a policeman in Hamilton. Called up in August 1914, he was promoted Sergeant after Neuve Chapelle. Almost immediately he went down with influenza and was away for a month. He and his wife Alice, a Londoner, but now living in Springburn, Glasgow, had three children. She received his identity disc, postcards, photographs and letters. Private William Bellas, originally from Penrith, was a labourer in Liverpool who volunteered early the previous September and, at forty one, one of the oldest to die. He joined the Battalion after First Ypres. He and his wife Margaret had been living in Bootle with their two sons. Private Fred Buck and his younger brother, Private George Buck, both of them weavers, joined up in September 1914 in their home town of Preston. George and Elizabeth Buck lived at Lostock Hall. The elder brother was sent to the 2nd Scots Guards, arriving in France at the end of March, the younger to the 1st Scots Guards, arriving three weeks later. After Festubert Private Fred Buck was missing, but, though his body was never recovered, there was confirmation that he was dead after the 9th Royal Welsh Fusiliers found him in No Man's Land in December 1915.

Private Harry Corfield had left for the Reserve after three years in 1908. Born in Ballyhaunis, County Mayo, he had no contact with any family in Ireland and was a miner in Yorkshire prior to his enlistment in Leeds. After being mobilised he was sent out in September 1914 as a reinforcement and went to the 2nd Scots Guards after First Ypres. He was definitely killed, but there was no one to tell about it. His name was published in newspaper casualty lists on 14 June and that day John McConville wrote to Regimental Headquarters on behalf of his wife Bridget and himself for confirmation as he had lived with them for several years at Liscard, Cheshire, and they were looking after all his belongings. Private Corfield's letters, there being no other effects, were given officially to the McConvilles' young son. Private Ronald Smart's family lived at Broughty Ferry, just east of Dundee, and he had been a hotel boots before he joined up in 1905. Soon after he went onto the Reserve he emigrated in 1911 to Canada, providing the undertaking to keep his contact details up to date with the Officer Paying Pensions in Ottawa and to report if called up. He sailed from Dundee in March 1911 and went to Lumsden, Saskatchewan. When the War began he reported and by 8 September was back in London. Though he went out to France two months later he was sent back to England sick almost immediately. He only returned to France in the draft on 1 April. He was known to have been wounded and was missing. Sergeant William Ferrett, who had served in the Boer War and stayed on in the Army until 1906 when he went back to the family watchmaking business in Shrewsbury, was another who died. Because he had voluntarily extended his reserve duty when it expired in 1911, he was called up and was promoted Sergeant after First Ypres. His wife Florence who was living with their son in Willesden, London, wrote back on receiving by way of effects only some letters and a notebook "My husbands watch is not among the effects may I expect to get that." Private Thomas Hothersall, the son of David and Elizabeth Hothersall of Preston, had served in the Scots Guards previously and then emigrated to the USA, where he was working as a fireman. He was outside his reserve commitment, but came back to rejoin and was killed in action, aged thirty two.

Company Sergeant Major Arthur Burrough, a regular soldier, who worked on his family's dairy farm at Okeford Fitzpaine, Dorset, before he joined in 1905, was killed. A Sergeant before the War, he became Company Sergeant Major of Right Flank after First Ypres. His wife Ellen and their son, not quite ten months old, were living in Lambeth, London. Company Sergeant Major George Johnson of G Company was missing initially. He was a miner from Garforth when he enlisted twelve years before in Leeds, at which time a tattoo on his left forearm was noted consisting of crossed swords with "Love G&J" underneath. He and Beatrice his wife were married in 1906 and had two daughters. Afterwards he was found killed by a shot in the head, but still with a firm hold of his rifle with the bayonet stuck through a German soldier's skull. Company Sergeant Major Lawton of F Company was hit in the head by shell splinters on 16 May and died the day after. His parents were George and Elizabeth Lawton, of Newport, Shropshire, and it was there that he had been born and brought up and worked as a moulder, before joining up in the new year of 1900. He served in the Boer War, soon afterwards married Annie Robinson at Prittlewell, Essex, and they had two sons. Lieutenant Ross, the Quartermaster, rated Company Sergeant Major Lawton very highly and felt his death a great loss to the Battalion. Lance Corporal John McKechnie was a baker who volunteered early in September in Glasgow. He was killed outright and the photographs and letters he had with him, as well as his Bible and identity disc, reached Walter and Christine McKechnie in Chapelhall, Lanarkshire. He had been another witness at Private Reid's court martial. Private Hugh McCall, a Glasgow policeman, had only been in France for six weeks before he lost his life. His home was at Bargrennan, Kirkcudbrightshire, where his father James McCall was a farmer. Private John McDermott deserted in 1912 after a year as a soldier, but at the beginning of September 1914 he reappeared deliberately to serve with the Scots Guards in the War and was immediately pardoned. His mother Sarah McDermott lived at Glenties, County Donegal. There was some confusion about what had happened to him and he was posted as "missing and wounded", the War Office informing his mother on 10 June that he was in a convalescent hospital. It was a mistake. She wrote on 14 August to Regimental Headquarters asking for more information as she had not heard from him. There was no further news. Private William Purves came from Musselburgh, but after serving for a bit over three years from 1903, during which he received a reprimand for "Laughing at the Drill Sergeant", he emigrated to Australia. There he was called up the previous August, reporting at Melbourne and leaving behind his wife Maud and their child in Pakenham East, Victoria. He was dead at Festubert. Privates Joseph Morrison, Robert Innes and Donald Nicholson became Scots Guardsmen at Perth on 28 September 1914. The first two were gardeners, the third a hotel boots. James and Margaret Morrison, Private Morrison's parents, lived in Enniskillen, County Fermanagh, Mary Innes, Private Innes' mother, near Bridge of Earn, south of Perth, and Murdoch and Helen Nicholson, Private Nicholson's parents, at St Fillans on Loch Earn. All arrived in France in April 1915, but not all together, and all joined the 2nd Scots Guards. Soon after he got there Private Innes had to go sick with an infected ear and was sent home to recover. The other two were missing after

16 May and no more was ever heard of either. Private Innes came back to the Battalion later in the summer. He was in trouble in the trenches on 17 November and got an aggregate of nine days FP No 2 for being in an officers' dug-out contrary to orders, stealing rations from there and urinating in the trench, also specifically forbidden. Then on 25 September 1916 he was killed in the capture of Lesboeufs on the Somme.

On 21 May Private T Barton of the 2nd Grenadiers wrote to Miss Reid, the sister of Private Charles Reid of the 2nd Scots Guards, "Just a line to let you know that I found your Brother on the field of Battle and I am sorry to impart such news to you but I thought it my duty to do so. I searched his body to try to find out who he was and that is how I came to know your address. He died a Soldier's death (fighting) he was killed in a charge and please accept my deepest sympathy in your distress. I am glad to tell you that he was killed instantly as he was shot through the heart. He was buried as decently as we could do so and laid side by side with some of his comrades of the same regiment. There was nothing found on his body, only a few addresses and his equipment." Private Charles Reid, a clerk in Glasgow and another young volunteer the previous September, came from Rutherglen, where Isabella Reid, his mother, lived. Some postcards that Private Barton found were sent to her. This was probably Private Thomas Barton who won the DCM in August 1915 for rescuing wounded men from a trench blown up by a German mine at Givenchy. He was himself wounded, but survived the War. Awarded his second DCM for this at Givenchy and also wounded was Lance Corporal John Rhodes. As a Lance Sergeant he won the VC at the Battle of Poelcapelle, towards the end of Third Ypres, and was killed at Fontaine-Nôtre-Dame during the Battle of Cambrai.

Corporal James Western came from Bristol and had been serving since 1908, becoming a Corporal after Neuve Chapelle. With shell wounds to his right side and forearm he died on the way to an advanced dressing station on 16 May. He and his wife Ivy had been married in January 1913 and their son was born at the beginning of March 1915. His father probably never saw him. Significantly for something much later Corporal Western had a brother in the Battalion. Lance Corporal Alexander Wilson, who won the DCM when in charge of stretcher bearers on the night of 18 December 1914, died from multiple wounds on 17 May not far from Aire, while being evacuated along the La Bassée Canal on Barge A, No 2 Ambulance Flotilla. He was a former groom from Edinburgh and unmarried, with for four and a half years service, a string of disciplinary records and a tattoo of "a woman's figure" on his right forearm. He was described before the War as "hardworking, but unsteady in his habits". His next of kin was Mrs Catherine Ballantyne at an address near Edinburgh University, but notification of his death was returned as she had moved. Lance Sergeant Alfred Willey was a Londoner who had been serving for two and a half years when the War began. He was an orphan and the Vicar of St Mary's, Westminster, included on his enlistment reference "A quiet, gentle little fellow, who had rather a hard life, without parents, living with his brother." Private Willey went out with the 1st Battalion at the beginning, but was sent, probably from the Aisne, to a hospital at St Nazaire with diarrhoea and next posted to the 2nd Scots Guards after First Ypres. Soon after he left in August his girlfriend Alice Smith found that she was pregnant. They were unable to marry until 8 March at Wandsworth and it was just afterwards that he was promoted Lance Sergeant. He was very badly wounded and died on 25 May at Rouen of the gunshot wounds in his right hip, which was fractured. His and Alice's daughter had been born the day before. His personal effects were a bag, a knife, a cigarette case, a watch and a hymn book. Two men, whose paths had crossed before in the 1st Battalion when they were both wounded on 1 January 1915, had arrived in different drafts in the 2nd Scots Guards after recovering in England. These were Privates Wallace Owen and William Preston, who had been together in the ambulance on its way from Cuinchy to Béthune when it fell into a shellhole. Private Owen, who had been back in France for three weeks, was hit for the second time at Festubert, with wounds in his left foot and thigh, and was soon in hospital in England again. He would reappear in the BEF. Private Preston was not hit, wrote nothing useful about what he saw, only recording that afterwards "I got promoted Corporal and made the acquaintance of a Cpl Lawrie...We struck up a friendship and are Pals today." Private William Lawrie, a September 1914 volunteer, had had a job as a draper and lived with his mother Mary Ann Lawrie in Cathcart, Glasgow. He had been in the Battalion since before Neuve Chapelle and was very slightly wounded in the knee by shrapnel at Festubert, but did not need to be treated further back than at the field ambulance. Private Ralph Woods died at Festubert. Another September 1914 volunteer, a printer's assistant in Liverpool, he gave his age on enlistment as nineteen and seven months, but he may have been only eighteen when he was killed. Samuel and Elizabeth Woods lived in Everton. Private Samuel Webster, a turner in Liverpool, the son of William and Sarah Webster, enlisted there in September 1914 and arrived in France after Neuve Chapelle. At Festubert he was hit in the buttock and sent back to England, though he was not long in hospital in Chichester before being discharged and then having a week's sick leave. Next, however, a letter from Sarah Webster, dated 29 June and addressed to Lord Kitchener arrived at the War Office, explaining that her son was now in a local hospital at Seaforth and asking for his discharge from the Army "as think it his asking to mutch of a boy of sixteen to go through." She sent his birth certificate. The correct official response to this was to discharge Private Webster for having misstated his age on enlistment and so he left the Army. Without further explanation, however, in 1917, by which time he would have been approaching eighteen and liable for conscription, instructions came from the War Office to Regimental Headquarters to recover Samuel Webster's discharge documents and issue him instead with a medical discharge. Lance Corporal Edwin Hawkins, recovered from his sprain and flat feet with the 1st Battalion during the Retreat from Mons and posted to the 2nd Scots Guards after First Ypres, had been promoted Lance Corporal in March. He was one of six winners of the DCM after Festubert, his being for extricating and successfully leading back a party of men who were stranded behind a German counterattack. He was promptly promoted to Lance Sergeant and two months after that was he was further promoted to Sergeant. He went on leave immediately after the battle and married Cissie Young at Rochford Registry Office on 25 May before returning. Private John Kelly was hit in a testicle and evacuated and then in Glasgow Royal Infirmary and on sick leave for four months. He had been born in Turnham Green, Middlesex, but his mother had settled in Glasgow and he was working there as an accountant. In early September 1914 he volunteered and went out to France the following February. In January 1916 he was commissioned into the Royal Fusiliers.

About nine in the evening on the 17th the Scots Guards left the old German front line and went first into dug-outs at a fort on the Rue du Bois, bivouacked briefly around midday on the 18th in a field half a mile down the Rue de l'Épinette towards Festubert and set off back to Hinges late in the afternoon. On the 19th they marched on to Busnes, also close to the La Bassée Canal, but further west, where they were to have "a rest". That meant in practice trying to find out what had happened to the missing, but first sorting out and cleaning up their billets and then uniform and equipment checks. It also meant drill. There were early morning parades for arms drill, followed either by a short route march or physical training and then the men had the afternoons to themselves. The arms drill was a means to an end. "When men come out of action weary and unstrung, there is no better way of restoring alertness. As the war went on other methods were introduced, plans for teaching and "stiffening" were tried, but nothing ever was invented to improve on the old steady drill." Private Graham was told in 1918 as a popular story in the Battalion that Captain Bagot Chester had shot dead two captured German officers because of an argument on the battlefield. The men viewed him as a hero for it and the story delighted those who listened to it. That he himself was upset by what he had done and went out of his way afterwards to try to look after and be kind to German prisoners was not so popular a tale. Lieutenant Swinton sent home on 24 May a postcard taken from a German prisoner. It was an etching of the Kaiser's head sent by a lady called Else from Hagen, Saxony, on 5 April to Gefreiter Heinz Fürgens of the *1st Battalion, Infantry Regiment 57.*

One of the Festubert lessons was further emphasis on the absolute requirement for more bombers and Brigade Headquarters issued fresh instructions that three NCOs and twenty one men per company were to be trained as bomb throwers, with not less than two sergeants so trained in each battalion, together with a designated bombing officer. A proportion of these trained bombers were to be available at all times to the Brigade Grenade Company. Just after the battle two new company commanders arrived, one of whom, Captain Jack Stirling, took command of G Company and was with the Battalion, with only brief interruptions, till after the end of the War. His home was at Kippendavie, Perthshire, and after Eton he was commissioned in 1901, but left in 1905 to become a stockbroker and soon also a yeomanry officer in the Scottish Horse. By 1914 he was their Second in Command, but transferred back to the Scots Guards in May 1915. The previous December he had married Olive Guthrie, a widow, as his second wife, his first marriage having ended in a highly publicised and flamboyantly described divorce in his favour.

On 27 May General Joffre inspected the Division, walking down the front rank of each brigade, the battalions being drawn up one behind the other. They gave him three cheers and marched past him, with the 1st Grenadiers in the lead, to the massed pipes and drums. Lieutenant Swinton commented to his family when he wrote that evening that it was "rather a silly show but it's war or rather it isn't." The next day Lieutenant Ross, the Quartermaster, taking a letter for Lieutenant Swinton's family with him, went on special leave to London with the captured minenwerfer. Lieutenant Swinton added "I am sending home two parcels one contains two shell cartridges 13 pdr & the other a helmet, the latter belongs to my cook please send it on to the address you will find inside. I wish it was mine but I lost the two I had." General Gough came to Busnes to inspect them next day and that evening there was a Sergeants Mess Dinner at the Left Flank billets and also a battalion concert. On the 29th Colonel Cator wrote to his mother from Busnes as "such a jolly little place. I live in a cottage owned by an old couple, who have been married fifty five years; the old lady is 82 and as active as a cat. She cooks for us and washes the floor and makes the beds, get up at 5am always. We have had two Drafts to fill up our losses, 370 men, so we are nearly up to strength again. We lost 10 Officers and 399 men. The Battn fought magnificently and all the Generals were very pleased with them, but I fear the pick of them have gone, including 46 NCOs which one cannot ever replace." General Gough he thought "perfectly charming…a most awfully good soldier and we all have tremendous confidence in him." He went on, quoting the monthly national figures for losses which he heard "I think the war will become a war of exhaustion in men…I suppose the Germans will simply have to give in for lack of men. The trenches have become so strong it is impossible to make any big advance; every line of trench is now a fortress, and when one line is taken there are others to fall back on. General Joffre inspected our Division the day before yesterday as a compliment for our victory…the price of victory is too awful and it isn't till we get back here away from the din of the guns that we notice all the absent faces, and here in this peaceful spot it hits one harder. The Spring has been so lovely out here and it is only man that makes this world hideous in misery and cruelly. Up in the firing line everyone is rapidly becoming savages, goaded by German cruelty and barbarism. The Germans have made this war more hideous than our ancestors of 200 years ago ever dreamt of; for the sake of Christianity and civilization they must never be allowed to win. The men take very few prisoners now, unless they are Saxons who are decent soldiers. A splendid ham has arrived from Mrs Baker. I believe it is one you sent me through her. Everyone talks of the headquarters ham and its excellence…The horses are very well and my one remaining dog, Bimbo, never leaves me night or day; Joffy the other one got run over by a supply wagon."

On 9 June Lieutenant Swinton told his mother that when the next person went on leave he would send her a rifle saw bayonet. Bayonets adapted or made so that, instead of having normal blades, they had serrated edges, were detested weapons and any enemy found with them could expect no mercy. He then asked for cigarettes, tobacco and matches, which he was out of, also a packet of razor blades, adding that he would like Edinburgh Rock occasionally. After he went down with jaundice on the 12th he told her not to write to him again until he contacted her because it was difficult for mail to follow wounded and sick men as they moved back through the medical system. By the 15th he was in hospital in Rouen but soon on his way to England and to Lady Ridley's Hospital, 10 Carlton House Terrace, overlooking The Mall in London. On the 22nd came the announcement of his MC and many letters and messages followed to him and his parents. Colonel Ernest Swinton, not a near relation, but close to the family, wrote on the 25th both to him and separately to his parents from GHQ at St Omer. In the first of these, after congratulating him on his medal he added "Don't talk about it, but I have butted my "Caterpillar" idea right through here up to the War Office and shall probably have to run home about it. Anything that can be done to save you poor devils in the infantry from the Bosche's machine guns should be run for all it's worth. At present its my "hobby"." The "Caterpillar", a name which still stuck into 1916, was a tank. Many officers, knowing exactly what was going on, thought Colonel Swinton's composing anonymous GHQ statements for the press ridiculous. The press did not take kindly to it either, the more so once they identified "Eyewitness". By this time he had lost his principal assistant, been led to believe that "Eyewitness" was about to be closed down, which suited him, but was still "slinging slosh single handed". In his other letter to Lieutenant Swinton's father he added that "a decoration gained by anyone in the trenches is of a different calibre to one gained on the staff!"

Breastworks and Trenches at Festubert and Givenchy

The Scots Guards, out of the line at Mont Bernanchon, east of Busnes, put the Canal to use for bathing and water sports, including a water polo match on 9 June against the 2nd Gordons, whom they beat 3-2, and, more formally on the 11th, Battalion Swimming Sports and "Tea on Canal Bank for officers". Sir Henry Rawlinson and General Gough came to watch this and, later, the Prince of Wales. On the 13th they went into the line at Givenchy, new to them. Battalion Headquarters, with Left Flank in reserve, were at Windy Corner. The 14th was thoroughly unpleasant. Another attack was in the offing. Captain Warner, who had had "a night interrupted by messages, had a busy morning on the phone as our guns bombarding enemy's front line were firing short. Enemy began violent bombardment of our front line at 1.30pm and kept on till dark. F Company had a bad time and about 4pm Wynne Finch reported that enemy had broken Borders line on our left. Sent up some of LF to support line and sent for reserve bombers of 6th Gordons who did not arrive for two hours. Borders reported all well and we discovered that the report was a mistake. Yorkshires and Wiltshires relieved us in the evening, both having orders to attack German trenches in morning. Wiltshires very jumpy and did not relieve F Company till 12 midnight." During this he turned his ankle over and it "was rather painful to walk on" as he went back with Colonel Cator and Captain Houston, the Medical Officer, to Essars. Lieutenant Wynne Finch, an Etonian commissioned in 1913, had come back out after Festubert, recovered from his wound during First Ypres. His widowed mother Maud Wynne Finch was living in London and his elder brother was in the Coldstream. The family had extensive estates in North Wales. As a result of the efforts of both the British and German guns eight Scots Guardsmen died and fifteen were wounded.

Private Thomas Jess was one of the dead. A riveter in Glasgow till he enlisted in 1902, he had been a reservist for eight years. In March 1906, shortly before he completed four years with the Colours, he married Kate Holman at Battersea just before the birth of their first son, who was followed by five more children. They lived in Townhead, Glasgow, and he worked for Brownlie & Co, City Saw Mills, Port Dundas. Private Jess went to Zeebrugge at the start. His effects were a photograph, some letters and his watch. Kate Jess was dead herself by the autumn of 1919 and the children were with a Mrs Holman, probably their grandmother, in Halstead, Kent. Another reservist killed was Sergeant William McLean, whose family home was at Bonnyrigg, Midlothian, until 1909 when he married Alice Jenkins in London. After eight years with the Colours he went to the Reserve and was called up on mobilization, going out with the 1st Battalion at once. During the battle on 14 September 1914 on the Aisne he was hit in the back of the head and evacuated home. Six weeks before he died he returned to France, posted to the 2nd Scots Guards, and was promoted on 28 May to Sergeant. Pregnant with another boy who was born in November, Alice McLean and their two young sons and daughter were living with her family at Bromley, Kent. Her husband's watch and chain and some letters were sent to her. Lance Corporal Leo Foulds, promoted some three weeks before his death on the 14th, had enlisted as a boy soldier in July 1911 and went out in September 1914. He joined the 2nd Scots Guards after First Ypres and lasted for a month in the Rouges Bancs trenches before being sent home with "frostbite". He came back towards the end of March 1915. When he enlisted his father was Colour Sergeant Harry Foulds of the Sherwood Foresters and he and Martha Foulds were living in Derby. Private Andrew Marshall, a miner in Denny, Stirlingshire, volunteered there early in December 1914 at the age of thirty six and a half. He and Agnes Marshall married in January 1901 and had six children. Hit by shrapnel on 13 June and, wounded in both his arms, both his legs and his stomach, he died in a field ambulance next day. Only an identity disc reached Agnes Marshall. Later that year the Reverend Macara, the Minister of Denny, wrote on Agnes Marshall's behalf to ask whether any more of her husband's belongings had been recovered, in particular his watch and chain, but there was nothing.

The attack which the Yorkshires and Wiltshires made on 15 June failed, though Captain Warner heard that the Yorkshires had got into the German trenches. General Lowther and others in the 1st (Guards) Brigade were watching this from south of the Canal. That afternoon the Scots Guards were sent up to bivouac in Gorre Wood behind Givenchy in case there was anything to exploit next day when the Yorkshires and Wiltshires were to try again. There was nothing to exploit and once darkness fell a large Scots Guards fatigue party carried tools up to the front line, without interruption. However, when two companies were sent up after dark on the 17th for digging, the shelling was so bad that all they could do was lie low with the 2nd Gordons in the trenches, but no one was hurt. These failed attacks, later designated the 2nd Battle of Givenchy, ended the series which Neuve Chapelle began.

The Battalion next went on the 18th into the second "very insanitary owing to unburied dead" and third line trenches at Le Plantin, a hamlet between Festubert and Givenchy, part of the German front line until Festubert. When dawn broke next morning the British field guns fired shrapnel on the enemy trenches, leading to intermittent German shelling and so to the deaths of four Scots Guardsmen and the wounding of others. "Some difficulty was experienced owing to the number of corpses exhumed" in the course of the digging of a new trench in the second line to join up two company positions. This was, by now, an almost inevitable occurrence everywhere and at its worst where there had been heavy fighting. Captain Warner noted "Very unpleasant work as we kept digging up corpses." However, the digging had to go on and continued at night throughout an otherwise quiet time in the line till after dark on the 22nd. Going out of the line was not straightforward, Captain Warner remarking on "Very bad staff arrangements. Part of 3 different Battns relieved us." In the small hours of the 23rd they arrived near Hinges, rested and cleaned up before leaving next morning for Le Quesnoy, a hamlet next to the Canal, just east of Béthune. There they found Canadians in the billets and instead had to bivouac in a field for a wet night, though Captain Warner and Battalion Headquarters were "in a small chateau. Very comfortable." Next day they moved one company into a farm and the rest into railway carriages in a siding at Beuvry, which "made very good billets" in his opinion.

In a letter on the 26th Colonel Cator thanked his unmarried sister Diana for "a splendid ham…quite the most useful food you could have sent me." He told her that Violet sent him out "potted things every now and again which come in useful when we are in the trenches." He thought little of a recently published interview with the Pope which "made the latter out a bit of a swine and an unworthy representative of the Romans." He then went on to say that "the little Prince often comes to see us, and is awfully stiff mannered. The other day we had some swimming sports and we gave away about £15 in prizes which the Prince gave away, the men were so pleased, some of them sent their money notes home to be framed as they had been presented by their future King." Then he went on "The war is going on all right but it's a slow job…I believe the Germans will crack sooner than we think…There are rumours of our being sent back for a rest. I hope so we are all three parts worn out officers & men, the young ones want it most they are getting very over strung some of them." He was very pleased by General Heyworth's being made a Commander of the Bath "as he is a real hard worker & never spares himself any trouble or personal risk, many of them never go near the trenches, the latter are too indescribably beastly for words now, corpses are lying about literally in thousands some who have been buried others have been unburied by the shells, the stench & flies are indescribable but one gets used to it & they never keep us in more than four days at a time if they can help it, but for some of the more delicate stomachs it means four days vomiting."

On the afternoon of the 27th they began to go back into the line at Givenchy. During the evening next day, while Colonel Cator and Captain Warner were with F Company, the Germans set off a mine in No Man's Land opposite them and then started shelling, but no one was hurt.

On their calling up the British guns for support, there was retaliation and both of them "were shelled on the road near Windy Corner and had to get into the ditch." Next there were orders to occupy the mine crater, only for a patrol to report that it was too close to the German line. So, to stop them taking it over and creating a strong point, 2nd Lieutenant Richard "Dick" Warde and a party of bombers threw grenades into the crater all through the night and kept the enemy out of it. He, a very new arrival, came from Kent, where his widowed but remarried mother Mrs Charles Cruddas was living in Sevenoaks. He had been to school at Tonbridge and transferred from the Scottish Horse in May 1915, being sent out very shortly after Festubert. The 30th was very wet and the trenches became very uncomfortable, but General Gough came round them before they left in the evening. There followed a very long and trying march through the night for tired men in wet clothes and equipment, broken for an hour with a hot meal, all the way to the west of Busnes. The companies arrived between three and six in the morning but a "considerable" number fell out on the way. While Captain Warner recorded that all rejoined during the day, the last arrivals were "3 men not turning up till 6pm." One never arrived because Private Horace Perry, died of his wounds on 30 June, just behind the line, after being in France five weeks. When he enlisted in Manchester the previous November he gave his occupation as a traveller. Gertrude Perry and their two daughters were living there in Fallowfield.

A lull followed and for three weeks they were out of the line. Colonel Cator and Captain Bagot Chester went on leave and Captain Warner commanded. There were drill parades most mornings and training, including practising march discipline, a bombing class of thirty two men, a machine gun class and a lecture to everyone by a Royal Engineers officer on wire entanglements and the construction of dug-outs. Sir Douglas Haig visited Battalion Headquarters on 7 July and next day everyone was drawn up in close order on both sides of the road a mile west of Lillers as the Division lined the streets for Lord Kitchener's visit. Captain Warner observed that "He passed fairly quick in a motor, so did not see much of him." There were joint Church of England services with the Grenadiers on the 4th and 11th, the Grenadiers Corps of Drums providing the music for the second one. Meanwhile Church of Scotland services took place on the parade ground and the Roman Catholics went to Busnes Church. Other diversions were inter company cricket and a concert on the 10th by the Army Service Corps Concert Party. From the 11th Lieutenant Wynne Finch was Adjutant for fourteen months. Captain Warner had heard that Colonel Cator was unlikely to be back for some time and was beginning to be apprehensive about Captain Bagot Chester reappearing first and taking over command temporarily. He was reassured to hear on the 12th that while Colonel Cator would be away till the end of the month, Captain Bagot Chester was not expected back until 2 August. On the afternoon of the 13th they set off on a two hour march northeast, first crossing the Canal and then going on for four days to very good billets at Calonne-sur-la-Lys, near Merville.

Their next task was to man eight redoubts and smaller posts in the Rue de Chavatte, between Richebourg-St Vaast and Le Touret. This required two companies, everyone else being in billets and able to continue usual activities out of the line, such as the boxing competition on the evening of the 19th. All the redoubts and posts needed upgrading and rewiring, while Dead Cow, one of the larger ones, was missing any parados when they got there. Occupying the redoubts and posts was straightforward but when they arrived at the supporting billets they found the Borders in them. Captain Warner "After some trouble, got two farms from them and the rest of the Battalion into dug-outs." On the 21st they went forward to the front line northeast of Festubert from where it now crossed La Quinque Rue to opposite Cour d'Avoué Farm.

The farm buildings were completely ruined, abandoned by the Germans and in No Man's Land. General Capper, having come back that night after his bomb wound and resumed command of the Division, was by eight the following morning up in their trenches, where it was generally quiet. However, while most shells fired at random did little damage, occasionally one would land with fatal consequences. Battalion Headquarters were on the left side of the Princes Road in the pre-Festubert front line from where the Borders attacked on 16 May. Nearby was Tube Station, the end of the light railway bringing up supplies, including containers of hot food. A shrapnel shell landed there on 22 July and because the nine casualties were from all four companies they were probably members of ration parties. Six were killed outright and three wounded. Lance Corporal Charles Chisholm, a serving soldier when the War began and before that a warehouseman in his home town of Northampton, was killed outright. His parents were Colin and Emily Chisholm, his father being a Conductor in the Indian Ordnance. He went out to the BEF first in September 1914 in reinforcements and was posted to the 2nd Scots Guards after First Ypres. An early sufferer from trench foot in the Rouges Bancs trenches he was sent back to England in December, but in February 1915 returned to France and was sent to the 1st Battalion, only to be evacuated with a suspected "Tubercle lung". After that he reappeared in the 2nd Scots Guards immediately after Festubert and was made a Lance Corporal ten days before his death. Private William Cadogan, one of the Fife miners among the first to volunteer, also died. He was sent out to the 1st Battalion after First Ypres, went down with trench foot soon after New Year and was very soon sent back to England. On recovering he arrived again in the BEF at the end of May. He had tattoos of Buffalo Bill and of a rose with initials in the centre on his right arm and of a Union Jack, clasped hands and a lady's head on his left arm. His father was William Cadogan, but his effects, two photographs and some letters, went to his brother John Cadogan in Crossgates. The third man killed was Private George Castle, the son of Ann Castle, a widow whose home was at Tayport, Fife, and a ploughman until he volunteered in September 1914. His mother received his wallet with some letters and photographs. The fourth was Private Frank McMahon, a labourer and the son of Mrs Sarah Bagan of Calton, Glasgow, who had joined up in mid August 1914. He arrived in France after Neuve Chapelle and both before he got there and after he joined the 2nd Scots Guards was frequently in trouble. Most recently he had been awarded ten days FP No 1 on 9 July. The fifth was Private James Davidson, a Lanarkshire miner, an older man, married with four children, the youngest born at the end of September 1914. He enlisted at the start of that month and then deserted from Wellington Barracks on New Year's Eve, not rejoining till the beginning of February. The punishment was forty two days detention, seven of which were remitted for time in arrest before court martial, and another five for good behaviour in detention. Early in April he landed in France. Up to the time of his death he had been sending half of his pay to his wife Mary Davidson in Blantyre. The sixth who died was a Londoner, Private Edward Richardson, a polisher and the son of George and Alice Richardson of Walthamstow. Another September 1914 volunteer, he came out in a draft in mid February 1915. He and Florence Davey married at Walthamstow in October 1914 and she was living in Hendon. Captain Warner "Buried 6 men killed in evening and read Lord's Prayer." One of the wounded, hit in the head and left arm, died three days later in a Base hospital at Abbeville. He was Private Fred Strachan, another Fife miner, whose regimental number was that before Private Richardson's, with whom he had arrived in the same draft. Just over four years earlier he had married Jessie Grandison in Beath and she was living with their adopted daughter in Cowdenbeath. Someone later told Jessie Strachan that her husband was a prisoner of war and she wrote to the hospital where he had died about it, but there was no doubt. Private Peter McCracken, originally from Drumore, Wigtownshire, but a plater's helper when he enlisted at Whiteinch, Glasgow, in September 1914, was wounded so badly that he was discharged in June 1917. Private Patrick Docherty, evacuated from the 1st Battalion with shell shock during First Ypres in the trenches near Veldhoek, was hit in the arm, chest and thigh. He would return later to the BEF.

Captain Warner had spent that morning showing round the Commanding Officer of the 1st Royal Welsh Fusiliers, who were relieving them next day. "Went round with Brigadier in afternoon. Went up to front line after dinner and visited listening posts, also waited for patrol which had gone out to look for Germans to return." Afterwards they had a long march back again to Calonne. Captain Warner left the line at one in the morning, walked to Vieille Chapelle and rode from there to Calonne, taking four hours. The usual post trench tour activities followed, interspersed on 30 July with a route march to the Canal, where everybody bathed, and with a longer march back. They knew now that they were leaving the 7th Division to join the Guards Division. So the next week was one of preparing for farewell, though the drill and training went on as usual. Each evening a military band, corps of drums or pipes and drums beat Retreat at Brigade Headquarters at Robecq, their own Pipes and Drums playing on 3 and 5 August. Most of the boxing tournaments were company ones but on the 4th they held one for the whole Battalion at which Lieutenant Colonel John Stansfeld of the 2nd Gordons was the Referee. He died on 28 September of wounds three days earlier on the north side of the Hulluch-Vermelles road on the opening day of the Battle of Loos. On the afternoon of the 6th the officers of the 2nd Gordons staged a gymkhana for the Grenadier and Scots Guards officers. The day after a notice appeared in Brigade Orders "Lost at Gymkhana one Crooked Ash Stock (New). Anyone bringing the same to the Brigade Major, 20th Infantry Brigade, will be rewarded." Below it was a notice of the finding after the gymkhana of an oblong-shaped reindeer skin tobacco pouch. On the evening of the 6th the Scots Guards Sergeants held a farewell dinner and concert for the whole Division. At two o'clock on Sunday 8 August they paraded at Robecq in full marching order for General Capper's final inspection, after which he made "a delightful farewell speech on our leaving the 7th Division, praising the troops for all they had done since the outbreak of the war. Everybody, I think, was rather touched by his speech, for all ranks regretted very much leaving the Division." They marched away to the music of the Divisional Band, of the Band of the 9th Devonshire Regiment, just joining the Division, and of the Pipes and Drums of the 2nd Gordons, as officers and men of the Borders and Gordons and others lined the road and applauded.

Notes on Chapter Sources

History of the Great War based on Official Documents by direction of the Historical Section of the Committee of Imperial Defence.

Brig Gen Sir JE Edmonds, *Military Operations France and Belgium, 1915: Volume II: Battles of Aubers Ridge, Festubert, and Loos* (London: Macmillan and Co Ltd 1928).

2nd Scots Guards Report on Operations 10-12 March signed by Sir Frederick FitzWygram TNA/WO95/1657/3.

Copy letter from Capt ECT Warner to his mother on 15 March 1915, Swinton Papers, Private Collection.

John Buchan, *The History of the Royal Scots Fusiliers (1678-1918)* (Edinburgh: T Nelson and Sons, Limited, 1925).

Bulletin from HQ IV Corps of translated German newspaper cutting on suffragettes, Cator Papers, Private Collection.

Pte I Reid court martial papers and sentence, TNA/WO71/407 and TNA/WO93/409.

War Diary: 20th Infantry Brigade TNA/WO95/1651, 1st Royal Welsh Fusiliers TNA/WO95/1665.

Narrative of the 1st Royal Welsh Fusiliers at Festubert, Maj CH Dudley Ward, *Historical Records of The Royal Welch Fusiliers, Volume III* (London: Foster Groom & Co Ltd 1928). Capt Stockwell quotation printed in that history and his diary, "Cliff's Diary", held by Trustees of the Royal Welch Fusiliers Museum.

Photograph album of Maj and QM T Ross for captions of photograph of CSM W Lawton's grave referring to his qualities and of photograph of Tube Station listing all killed and wounded by a shell, SGA

Notices from 20th Infantry Brigade Orders on 7 August 1915, TNA/WO95/1651.

10

The Battles of Neuve Chapelle and Aubers and the Summer 1915 – 1st Battalion

The Battle of Neuve Chapelle

When the Battle of Neuve Chapelle started on 10 March the 1st (Guards) Brigade were holding their same breastworks to the southwest of the Meerut Division on the right of the attack. The 1st Scots Guards, in reserve in the village of Rue de l'Épinette, were ready to move at once. From the road junction at the north end of the village the Rue du Bois headed northeast to the junction with the Estaires-La Bassée road at Neuve Chapelle. The breastworks were roughly parallel to and southeast of the Rue du Bois. Private Johnes had "to stand to in fighting order, which meant to move at a moment's notice. It was cold and murky and we wore our greatcoats. Large tins of hard tack, not the flat big biscuit variety, but small oval ones, were opened up, and we filled our pockets with them, they were much easier than the usual flat ones to munch on. We also crammed in a tin of "Bully Beef" Fray Bentos…each section of four or five men had a tin of Ticklers Plum & Apple jam, some tea and sugar, and each soldier had his regular ration of cheese, a piece about three inches long, one inch wide and one deep." They could hear heavy gunfire a mile or two north. Then some German shells fell in front, one landing among their billets and wounding Major Romilly, Captain Kingsmill, the Grenadier with them since early January, and five men. Shrapnel went into the back of Major Romilly's head and out below the cheek bone. He was away for some time, but appeared to recover fully and returned to the Western Front in 1917. The German infantry opposite were mainly firing rifles at British aircraft having to fly beneath the low cloud. Otherwise there was nothing all day.

General Lowther listened as "At 7.30am an unholy bombardment began and continued for a good deal of the morning. Far the worst bombardment I've heard yet. Worse than what we got at Vendresse. Rumour says nearly 500 of our guns were at it. All sizes up to "Mother" and "Grandmother"." These were the British 9.2 inch and 15 inch howitzers. For Lance Corporal Stewart, promoted a fortnight earlier, "It was music to us to hear our own artillery thus retaliating for what we had suffered in the past, but with a vengeance which even surpassed, on the limited front chosen, anything the enemy had yet attempted." At five that afternoon they were told to march at quarter to six towards Richebourg-L'Avoué in support of the Bareilly Brigade of the Meerut Division. Having started, however, they were first halted on the roadside a kilometre short of Richebourg and then at eleven at night sent back to billets. It was sometime after dark, Private Johnes remembered, that C Company were told to move. "We wheeled in a northerly direction along a road which appeared to have a multiple of turns and twists in it, but which took us towards the rumpus, shell and machine gun fire, and Very lights. As we got closer in we started to get tangled up with GS wagons going and coming, wounded men trying to head back to a clearing station, and Jerry's fire trying to catch the roads leading up. Here and there he had made a hit. As far as I could see we were lucky. It was difficult to see your buddy ahead of you, the only thing to do was to push on into what appeared to be a general mix up." From where they still saw transport about they walked on. "The mud had become a hell of a problem…Rifle and machine gun fire was getting closer… It was the Battle of Neuve Chapelle, but we did not know it…Our attack had been heavy and had made some progress but seemed to be bogging down, shellfire had dropped off considerably on both sides, rifle and machine gun fire was tailing off, but Very lights kept a constant glimmer over the whole scene…The ground was a quagmire and the movement of troops and making way for the wounded was a bloody mess." He was well aware that the enemy had the pick of the positions on Aubers Ridge. At the time he thought that C Company had lost many men, though perhaps several got lost, because casualties were very few in the Battalion, but "the individual soldier knows only of what is going on immediately around him, in broad daylight, in the dark his buddy only six feet away could be killed without his knowing it." Then they heard that they were to go back to their billets where "we had a pleasant surprise. The company cook had his open air kitchen going full blast, with lots of good hot stew, and we also got a good big shot of rum, which really warmed up the cockles of our blood pumps. After that there was a lot of talking about the so called battle, but most of us fell asleep. Whoever led the way back made no mistake. We were home James."

Late at night General Lowther had to go see Brigadier General Henry Davies of the Bareilly Brigade, but could not make his way through in the car sent to collect him because "the road was choked with troops and transport." He got out and walked in what was very bad going, getting back to his own headquarters at one in the morning on the 11th. He soon had a visit from General Haking, by when the news was that quite a lot of ground and eleven hundred prisoners had been taken, but overall what had been achieved was not clear to him. Then his headquarters were "shelled in the morning for a change, but nothing landed really very near us. A few bits dropping on the roof and that's all." He heard of lots of German dead having been found in the captured trenches "and that their obvious counterattack of this morning was swept away before it had really begun." On the 12th "a thick and foggy morning" he did not learn to begin with how much shelling there had been, but heard "of German attacks being driven off and of the capture of further batches of prisoners…Some of the rumours (of capture of a lot of guns etc.) were not founded on fact, but taken all round the news is OK." There matters and both sides rested, for the 13th was very quiet. He received that day a letter sent from Madrid only four days before and noted that letters from London were now arriving in two days. His correspondent in Madrid and the recipient of his diary instalments was Mary, his eldest sister.

On 11 March Lieutenant Balfour had returned, recovered from his wound on the Aisne. Arriving at Béthune at midday he managed to get a message sent on from Headquarters 2nd Division so that his pony "Teddy Bear" was brought for him to ride to Rue de l'Épinette. That evening they took over from the Camerons in the front line for forty eight hours. Heavy shelling began at five next morning and two hours later a shell went through the Battalion Headquarters house, wounding four signallers. This went on till two in the afternoon and "misses our house by inches every time." All that Lieutenant Balfour heard about Neuve Chapelle was that the 8th Division had captured part of the Bois de Biez, that the Germans had lost two thousand killed and that five guns, seven machine guns and over two thousand prisoners had been captured. He wrote "If they push on much further the Germans in front of us will be cut off, and La Bassée must capitulate." They pushed on no further.

So as to find out whether the reported progress at Neuve Chapelle had destabilised the enemy defences between there and La Bassée the Scots Guards were told on the 13th to investigate the German front line opposite. Two NCOs volunteered and were within twenty yards of the enemy breastworks when they were fired at, but got back safely. The German lines were strongly held, one of several lessons that the enemy had learned from three days before, when they were caught napping. One volunteer was most likely to have been Lance Corporal Edward Collins who joined in 1907, having previously been a farm labourer in Otley, Yorkshire, and had completed seven years service in April 1914, only to be called up on mobilization. He was wounded in his right ankle by a bayonet, probably at Gheluvelt, as he reached hospital at Le Havre on 3 November. He qualified as a cold shoer at the beginning of April 1915 and eventually as a shoeing smith in the spring of 1918, by which time he was with the 2nd Battalion. He finally went home to England on 10 October 1918, rejoining his wife Isabella at an address off Aldgate in the City of London and leaving the Army the following year. The other is most likely to have been Lance Sergeant Randolph Churchill Spencer, a storekeeper who had enlisted the previous September in Liverpool and been in France since the beginning of January. He was wounded slightly early in April and then more seriously at Puits 14 Bis at Loos and evacuated quickly at the beginning of October 1915 to England. Then in June 1916 Sergeant Spencer married Gladys Dumbleton at Willesden and before the end of the year had been commissioned into the Heavy Branch, Machine Gun Corps, which meant tanks. From the Scots Guards he had two mentions in dispatches and a MM.

One of the very few casualties was Private Patrick Warren, an Irish labourer who enlisted in September in Inverkeithing. He arrived in France on 7 March, joined the Battalion on the 11th and was killed two days later. Patrick and Elizabeth Warren, whose home had been at Annaghmore, County Kerry, were dead and his next of kin was his brother John Warren in the Royal Irish Constabulary at Rathdowney, Queen's County. Much of the enemy gunfire, though often heavy, caused little damage. German field guns were those commonly targeted on the front line, but the heavier guns tried to hit billets, batteries and headquarters further back. Individual buildings were often systematically fired at, wherever they were. For an hour in the late afternoon of 14 March there was very heavy shelling of a ruined house just behind the front line breastworks and as a result Private James McKinlay, an iron moulder who enlisted in Liverpool at the beginning of September, was killed. John and Agnes McKinlay of Bainsford, Stirlingshire, received their son's pocket book, the letters he had on him and some photographs. Two other men were wounded. Lieutenant Balfour knew it could have been far worse. "The shells were plastering the house, one which went through passed within 3 feet of a stack of bombs." As they were coming out of the line that night Colonel Hore Ruthven returned after about a month's sick leave. He was known to Private Johnes as "Spud", a nickname perhaps unknown to the officers.

Breastworks south of Neuve Chapelle

As twelve officers were having lunch on 15 March at Battalion Headquarters in Rue de l'Épinette near the Rue du Bois junction Lieutenant Balfour was carving a turkey. At that moment a howitzer shell hit the house and exploded in the room above them. Bruised, shocked and covered with about six inches of dust and rubble they began to get up, finding that none had been hurt at all. Lying across Lieutenant Balfour, however, was the body of Private George Locke, with half his head taken off by the one fragment which had come through the ceiling. He was a printer before he enlisted on 31 October 1884 when he was nineteen. He and his wife Esther Maisey married at Fulham in 1902 and had two sons and a daughter. He was mentioned in dispatches following Ypres. For almost twenty of his thirty years in the Scots Guards he had been servant to Colonel Hore Ruthven, who, as General Lowther saw, was "very cut up about the loss of his faithful old friend." Private Locke, aged forty nine and seven months, was the oldest man of any rank to lose his life in the War while serving in either Battalion. Some photographs, a card and his identity disc were all that there were for his family. The shelling of the house then went on till after two o'clock, so the officers sheltered in its lee and then began a second lunch. That was not the end of it because, Lieutenant Balfour wrote, "At 5.30pm they started again and kept us outside showering us with bricks and mud until 8pm. They fired a shot every 3 minutes with the utmost regularity. This is a new enemy battery firing from somewhere near La Bassée. Dinner in peace but are rather jumpy. At 9.30pm I am damned if they did not start again and did not finish until 2.30am. This time with 10 min interval between each shell. We went into the house after each shell and retired again, when 9min were up the shell caught us napping and one piece of it knocked at the door but did not come in." No further damage was done but they moved three hundred yards south through the village to a less exposed building.

Currently the battalions were doing forty eight hours in the front line and forty eight hours out, with a company from one of those out of it constantly ready to move at a moment's notice at Danger Corner. This was the road junction of the Rue de l'Épinette, south of the village in the direction of Festubert, with the Rue des Cailloux. On the 17th General Lowther remarked "The newly arrived draft of the London Scottish seemed quite delighted at being shelled, standing about in the road watching the "crumps" fall round them and shouting with glee. Glad they like it, but it is a joy that soon palls on most people." A "crump" was another name for a German 150mm howitzer HE shell. Brigade Headquarters was in a farm where a source of diversion for General Lowther and his staff was the persistent fighting on the farm midden between various competitive cocks. "The oldest and most pugnacious of the cocks was caught in mid fight today and taken off by the patronne to the soup pot. This will sadly curtail our amusements and simple pleasures."

Next day Lieutenant Balfour recorded that when "A captured German officer was asked where the War would finish he replied "Where I am standing" meaning "We shall not be able to drive you back nor you us" I wonder." General Lowther went on a long walk round the line on the 18th with Captain Francis "Frankie" Chalmer of the Black Watch, acting as Staff Captain following Captain Thorne's departure to Headquarters 1st Division. He remarked on the accuracy of a German sniper who had a gap in a hedge well covered and fired every time they passed it, so that the Brigadier chose the safety of a wet ditch with water up to his knees, while the younger officer made a run for it. Significantly for later events he noted "The Germans seem in greater numbers than last week I think." That night it snowed, but thawed quickly.

After a few weeks Private Johnes was coming out of the line at the end of a trench tour when Lance Sergeant Lamond, the Signal Sergeant, intercepted him. He tested Private Johnes' knowledge of signalling and accepted him as a Battalion Signaller, so from then on, while he lived, trained and worked with Battalion Headquarters, he and the other signallers were allocated to the companies as and when necessary. A great deal of time out of the line was spent practising and improving skills with Morse Code. Here he got to know another signaller Private Ernest Evans, whom he called "George", once a hairdresser from near Whitchurch, Shropshire and a serving soldier for two years, who had been with the Battalion the whole time, unwounded. He said "The Lord wanted him for a sunbeam." Stephen Evans, his father, lived at Grindley Brook, Shropshire, and his younger brother Private Thomas Evans was in the 2nd Battalion.

The signallers' role was communications between Battalion Headquarters and the companies, their basic equipment the field telephone and the telegraph for Morse messages. The wire came up to the Battalion "in spools, eighteen feet to two feet in diameter, and required two linemen to handle the spool when laying it, and one or two other linemen to lay it." Behind the breastworks there were no communication trenches, but where the front line system was trenches with communication trenches, the signals lines were laid along the communication trenches. The signallers' principal problem was the breaking of the wires that they themselves had laid or checked on taking over at a relief. If the wires went, either because an enemy shell or minenwerfer bomb had broken them or else because a friendly foot, weapon or shovel had dislodged them, much more likely in communication trenches, signallers had to check along them until they came to the breaks and then mend or replace them. Though they trained in visual signalling, using this was hardly ever practicable. Many messages still went to and fro by runner. As, correctly, it was supposed that the Germans could pick up telephone and Morse messages, codes were used. They were also used for any important matter sent by runner.

While out of the line the Scots Guards spent 19 March constructing dug-outs around their billets for cover if there was more shelling. On the 20th they went back to the breastworks. Here they took part twice in deception plans by firing at the German lines along with the British guns in support of some French operation elsewhere. The only effect that they were aware of was that two Scots Guardsmen were wounded by British shells falling short, while the Brigadier wrote "Some bursts of fire by us last night only caused the Germans to start playing mouth organs with much noise." Colonel Ponsonby told him that some of his men dug up two HE shells which had landed nearby and did not burst. They had put them on a wall and thrown stones at them to see if that would set them off. Fortunately it did not. The following day a Coldstream sniper shot a German on a redoubt over a thousand yards behind their front line, while the Germans used a heavy howitzer to demolish the church spire at Richebourg "and made big craters in the cemetery where harmless folk had lain long years undisturbed." Private Johnes also noticed how "Many of the corpses in the graveyard were exposed, badly smashed. The Church from appearances of what was left had been a Beaut with a tall spire like tower."

Sometime during the 22nd Private John McSevney, until the previous September a ship's plater on the Clyde, was killed. He had been in France for a fortnight. In July 1908 he and Isabella Docherty married in Whiteinch and she was there with their two young sons. That evening, after a clear, warm day, the 2nd Brigade arrived to take over and they marched back to Béthune. The main event, recorded by Lieutenant Balfour, was a feast the next day consisting of soup, eight dozen oysters divided among the six officers who liked them, sole for those who did not, chicken pudding and sardines on toast. These were washed down with whisky and soda, four different liqueurs, port and some 1830 brandy produced by Lieutenant Bethell. After two more days in L'École des Jeunes Filles they moved on to near Locon, due north from Béthune over the Canal. They then had five clear days rest, but there were arms drill and route marches as well.

While there Private Johnes, whose reach was very short and whose right wrist, broken at school, had not healed sufficiently well for him to risk ever hitting anything hard, found himself put forward in a boxing contest. His first opponent complacently opened by punching him in the face, little expecting that Private Johnes would go for his stomach and knock him out. The next opponent was much taller and had his shorts hitched up so high that when Private Johnes went for him at waist level there was an appeal to the referee for a foul. This was overruled and the shorts were tied lower down the man's body, but not far enough, so when the fight resumed Private Johnes was quickly disqualified for hitting low. He heard the Quartermaster call him "a brute". He and some other signallers were allocated a small shed which had "a good looking layer of straw. The first night we slept well but it seemed to be hot. We dug into the straw and found it covered a good amount of manure. We decamped and built ourselves a bivouac in an open field nearby with our groundsheets." Meanwhile one of his principal friends, Private Charles Osborne Green, hence "Cog", was detailed to go out on fatigue near Richebourg-St Vaast helping the Royal Engineers to lay telephone line. There they slept in a stable next to an abandoned estaminet and one of them dislodged a stone in the floor. This made an opening into the cellar where there was still some wine. Private Green's share of this haul was three or four bottles which he brought back to the bivouac at Locon. He, Private Johnes and another man shared a tent and as Private Johnes was lying in the middle he had two swigs to the other men's one as each bottle was passed across from one to another and "I didn't last out." Private Green, a leatherworker from Liverpool and August 1914 volunteer, left in June on being commissioned into the 4th King's.

On the 30th the people he was billeted with told General Lowther that they had listened to the sound of guns and rifles every single day since mid October. "How sick they must be of it." He moved out that afternoon as they went to relieve the 2nd Brigade in the same place as previously, a lengthy and interrupted business on a very clear night, which meant more firing from the Germans. So he did not get to bed till half past one in the morning. Next day he wrote "Much disgusted to hear of the recruitment of the Welsh Guards and Irish Guards being forced up by raising the standard of height for the real guards' regiments to 5' 11" and lowering that of the "warts" to 5' 7". So much for political soldiering." Starting at quarter past five that evening he set off round the Coldstream and Camerons in the front line, "not entirely satisfactory yet, but improving." This took him and the new Staff Captain, Captain Guy Rasch of the Grenadiers, three and a quarter hours of steady walking. On the left of the Coldstream there was a lot of firing as the Germans machine gunned the parapet, so they did not go there. He found the men looking "very comfortable behind their breastworks with tidy shelters, lots of braziers and a good many minor comforts. Came in with two blistered heels from walking in top boots and thin cotton socks – a fools' trick!" He heard next day that the night before "the Germans were calling out "Hullo! Blackwatch, is Sergeant MacVea there?" He is their transport Sergt, but says he knows no Germans. Then they tried some Harry Lauder songs, but sung very badly indeed." [Sergeant MacVea untraced] On 2nd April the Brigadier was out and about again visiting and noting that everything was much better than previously and that Captain William Kedie of the Black Watch was upset by having had a box of tinned preserved pea soup successfully handed over to him as hand grenades by the outgoing 2nd KRRC. He had been wounded once, would be hit again a week later and killed in August.

Even with the Brigade in the line much of General Lowther's time was taken up with visitors, some with good reason, such as General Haking, who came very frequently, others with much less. He spent almost five hours on the afternoon of the 2nd dealing with them. There was also heavy routine paper work, among which he mentioned the next day "Long and tiresome things about seniority of officers in the London Scottish to write." About noon the weather broke, it started to rain and continued for nearly three whole days. General Lowther considered the "Germans tame on most of my line", there being few casualties, though that could change in an instant and views of what was quiet were relative. He wrote how he was "Much annoyed to hear that at home, people are inclined to run down the French and minimize all they do. This is the habit of allies, but in this case is not only unjust, but the worst of policies."

In this period the Scots Guards were initially in reserve, split between Le Touret, where Brigade Headquarters also were, and Richebourg-St Vaast, where they remained till the 3rd, mostly occupied every night helping the Royal Engineers to build new breastworks. On going into the line itself, this time for eight days, they rotated the companies. The 4th was Easter Day and Lieutenant Balfour wrote "Beastly wet just our luck it has been lovely for the last 10 days. 1 man killed and 1 wounded. The wounded man who had been with the Bn since 13 August 1914 on being hit exclaimed "Thank God at last". Very vicious Germans in front of us, they keep up perpetual sniping and are very good shots. The breastworks of the front line are very poor. Being but recently constructed and are hardly bullet proof within 8" of the top, and in some places the parapet is so low that one has to go on all fours." The man who died was Private George Bain, a policeman, who had joined up early in September in Motherwell and been in France for a little over three months. His mother, known both as Ellen and Helen Bain, lived at Lhanbryde, Morayshire.

Lieutenant Balfour recorded that the defence plan required holding the front line "at all costs" and the support line ready to counterattack "at once" if the front line was pierced. In an orchard there was also a "keep" defensible on all sides, to be held whatever happened and equipped with a water supply and bully beef in case it was cut off. It rained and went on raining and that there was only one communication trench did not help. It led into the orchard and from the east side of that forward to the front line and could be used in daylight provided that one stooped. "We are working very hard improving the breastwork using about 1500 sandbags a day. Perpetual work day and night on the trenches keeping them clean if work was stopped for an hour during this rain we should very soon be ankle deep in mud and water." They had a company of the 1/21st London Regiment, First Surrey Rifles, Territorials, with them under instruction, a platoon to each Scots Guards company to begin with, later with the whole company together "wedged" between two Scots Guards ones. Their visitors did not yet understand the point about keeping the trenches clear and so when they were rotated the Scots Guards went in and cleared up behind them. "Result in the morning one could walk down it in patent leather shoes."

When General Lowther went round the left section of the line on the 6th he "found it very muddy even behind the breastworks, and in front trench there was 18 inches of mud and water." The Prince of Wales came to lunch but "never eats any, or tea, only looks on. He looks much better and stronger than when he came to see us in November." Next day Sir Douglas Haig came in the afternoon "we'd not seen him for a long time." About this time Private Johnes and his fellow signallers found a large bowl in a wrecked bakery at Richebourg-St Vaast, which they filled with water. While some were having a bath, Private Evans the hairdresser, was cutting the hair of others. He had mischievously left two tufts of Private "Cog" Green's uncut, so he soaped them up like horns, which increased his resemblance to the German Crown Prince. Others were busy delousing. Suddenly Sergeant Lamond called them all to attention. "Who should hove into sight but the Prince of Wales." Accompanied by others "they were coming towards us…looked toward our game and gave a grin or two, and left us standing easy."

Lieutenant Lionel Norman, a thirty five year old Harrovian stockbroker, was commissioned in December 1914 and arrived in France on 6 February with the first large draft to replace the casualties of 25 January. He was not married and his father Henry Norman lived at Hayes, Kent. During this trench tour he was commanding Left Flank. He sent a message on 4 April at five past eight. "Work done. Laying bricks along trench. Strengthening parapet. Work was almost impossible owing to rain & strangeness of men to trenches. Please send stretcher to communication trench on Route de Bois for 9150 Pte Thompson suffering from Dysentery." Private John Thomson was a London hammerman and a very early recruit after the War began, already wounded in the left elbow just before Christmas at Givenchy and sent home to recover. Now he had been back out for a month, but because of the dysentery he was on his way home again and would remain in England till January 1917. His father was also called John Thomson and they lived in Battersea.

Just before midday the next message went "Work done. Rifle inspection. Bricking floor of trenches. Will require 500 sandbags for tonight. Have handed two of my periscopes to C Coy." In the evening he followed that with "C Coy have taken my 500 sandbags. Must have bags tonight or cannot do any work." Next he warned Battalion Headquarters that his ration party would be bringing back with them seven sandbags full of dirty ammunition picked up off the floor of the trenches and one sandbag containing cartridge cases from Very lights, a broken rifle and a haversack. On the 7th he reported the arrival of fifty sheets of corrugated iron, for which he had signed. That afternoon he reported again. "Delivering 12 loopholes for B Company and have carried up bridge but cannot get it up communication trench in daylight."

At twenty past seven on 9 April "killed No 7103 Pte George Bruce. Equipment sent to dressing station." Just over an hour later he reported "Work done. Placed bridge across stream in trench … Finished hurdling & carried on with earthing." but almost immediately afterwards "No 9864 Pte W Paul wounded in thigh, now proceeding to dressing station." Private Bruce from Lauder, a serving soldier in 1914, joined up in 1908 a few months after his younger brother. Before that he had been a baker. On his left forearm he had a tattoo of clasped hands, ivy leaves and "Auld Lang Syne". Among some distinctive entries on his conduct sheet from just before the War were being found with beer in his water bottle on parade and a few weeks later deliberately breaking four pots in the canteen. When he died he had just finished forty two days FP No 1 for breaking out of billets at Burbure. Richard and Janet Bruce's other son in the Scots Guards, Private Thomas Bruce, died of wounds in London after Ypres. Private William Paul was a London labourer and September 1914 volunteer. His wound was in his left thigh and he had two more during the War, in his lip in November 1916 and his head in July 1918, both in the trenches, not major battles. He left the Army in February 1919.

Corporal Arthur Tooley from South London, whose real name was James Bullard, though that did not come out till after the War, enlisted within a week of the start and arrived after Ypres. He was wounded in the right buttock on 7 April and evacuated, spending two months in hospital in London and then, just afterwards, marrying Ann Jordan in East Dulwich. In August 1915 he was on his way back to France and was with the Battalion from then on continuously till they went home from Cologne. On 10 August 1914 he was a boot maker in Camberwell, but by 1 September 1916 a Company Quartermaster Sergeant. The same day that he was wounded so was Private William Mahon, a sniper, who claimed to have shot fifteen Germans in the past four days. In the Army since 1901 when he stopped being a ship's steward and enlisted in his home town of Liverpool, he had already been wounded at Ypres, apparently superficially, but this time he had a sniper's bullet through his left elbow. After several operations he was left unable to move it and, though he had some movement in his wrist, his hand was wasted. On his discharge he managed to get a caretaking job in Liverpool. There had been steady casualties during this trench tour including nine dead, one of whom, Private Robert Elder, a policeman, killed on the 6th, was the second of the five men who volunteered on 11 September 1914 at Hawick. When he was hit Private Johnes, who had been in the same draft, was nearby and went to try to help, but Private Elder had been shot in the jugular vein through a gap in the sandbags. Andrew and Helen Elder, his parents, lived in Hawick, where his father was a gardener. Another who died, on the 8th, was Lance Corporal Robert Miller, a Glasgow policeman promoted immediately after the Cuinchy brickstacks battle. Five photographs were all that reached his father Thomas Miller at Whithorn, Wigtownshire. Altogether twenty eight men were wounded and that in spite of only one mention of shelling by German field guns. On the 9th Lieutenant Balfour retaliated "I fired 2 rifle grenades into German trench and saw several bits fly. I also knocked out several German periscopes with a rifle." They went back to Le Touret and Richebourg-St Vaast on the 11th for four days of further fatigues, digging and carrying parties until the Brigade left the line on the 15th.

If they had a suitable target, like the Black Watch working party who showed themselves on the 8th while General Lowther was on his way up with more visitors, then the German guns would open up. The Brigadier was intrigued by Lieutenant John Haldane of the Black Watch, the Brigade Trench Mortar Officer, who had chosen to go out between the lines on his own. He did this in his shirt tails, having taken off his coat and kilt for greater manoeuvrability, crawling along muddy ditches, often filled with dead bodies, to see more clearly the results of firing his mortars. General Lowther was not concerned about this for its own sake, but thought that if captured he would be in for a very uncomfortable journey to a prison camp. Lieutenant Haldane then appeared "with a prize under his arm in the shape of a German trench mortar bomb. He proposed this morning to take it to pieces in my office, but he was given a chair outside and told to get on with it there! It is about 16 inches long and 3 in diameter." During the 10th Lieutenant Haldane's mortars fired forty four bombs. What might have been a German fighting patrol, but was more likely to have been minenwerfer bombs in retaliation on the 11th, led to the death from wounds of 2nd Lieutenant Roderick Mackenzie of the Black Watch, the first officer in the Brigade killed since 25 January. As soon as a shoot was finished the trench mortar crew went on their way so firing a trench mortar was unpopular with the infantry who then had to take the enemy response. After about thirty bombs were fired from the London Scottish trenches on the 13th the Brigadier heard next day that an officer had told Lieutenant Haldane before he started that he strongly objected and that if he went ahead "he would write to the papers about it." General Lowther remarked that "He seems to be under the erroneous impression that (a) this is a health resort and (b) that he is not a soldier, both of which impressions will have to be removed."

Generally it had gone very quiet locally, so much so on the night of the 11th that the Royal Engineer working parties reported that it almost broke their nerve, albeit that "A big explosion (it did not wake me) disturbed things at 3am, it was a German mine making a bad shot at blowing up French trenches south of the La Bassée road." While General Lowther was out from early on the 13th visiting and then at Chocolat Menier Corner spying out the land it was "Phenomenally quiet, did not hear a shell fired or have a bullet pass within earshot all the time I was out." At Headquarters 1st Division on the afternoon of the 14th to discuss "general matters", about which he did not elaborate, he met Major General Joseph "Joey" Davies, a Grenadier then commanding the 8th Division, "who travels about with a large black cat and a small white terrier in his car."

15 April was a "Lovely sunny day and fairly warm. Some shelling at the dummy battery ¼ mile away, many shells did not burst! I stood and watched them for a while, and it gave a curious impression to see the silent Sunday-like country with absolutely no movement. Then a distant explosion followed by the rush of the shell (like rubbing a piece of wood over ribbed silk) and then the plump of the "blind" shell into the ground or the puff of the burst, and not a soul within ¼ mile of it." He commented on two means being used to identify where enemy snipers were. "The cardboard heads, to draw the enemy's fire, with which we have been supplied would not deceive a child. The Germans treated them with contempt, and shouted over "We thought Kitchener's army was all paper and now we know it." An umbrella is much the most effectual way of seeing where snipers are posted, we get two holes and thus the line of fire. The Germans always shoot as it is a tempting object and too big to miss. Hitherto the L Scottish have used one a good deal, but only when the "pipsqueak" was firing, to show contempt!"

The strain had told on Corporal Stewart, who was "about the only survivor of my original Company, and I found myself on the verge of a complete breakdown. I accordingly reported sick, but unless a man was seriously wounded there was not much chance of receiving consideration from the army doctors in those days. Our Battalion doctor, however, was an exception to the majority." Identified as having slight nervous debility on the 6th, Corporal Stewart was sent to hospital at Boulogne for two weeks prior to evacuation to Netley, where he was for five months. Subsequently he became a squad instructor at the Guards Depot, met and married Elizabeth Houston, who had sent him the first parcel of tobacco at Borre after Ypres, was discharged in August 1917 and returned to Canada. Major Romilly got married on 4 December 1915 in London "and invited all the men who fought with him at the battle of the Keep…to his wedding. We had a most enjoyable time and greatly appreciated [his] kindness, about a dozen of us spending a very happy evening at a hotel in the West End of London." The bride was Nellie Hozier, younger sister of Winston Churchill's wife Clementine.

They were out of the line for more than a fortnight during which General Lowther had an unexpected appointment on the 19th interviewing a Scots Guardsman, who told him he was a conscientious objector to inoculation. Next day Colonel Hore Ruthven reported that he had twenty three of them. Lieutenant Balfour recorded an unusual opportunity. "On the 20th we marched out towards Laventie and the 2nd Bn towards us and we met half way in an orchard when we piled arms and had an hour's break and chat…It was rather sad looking round and seeing how few old faces there were." He counted seven, mentioning the two Quartermasters and Captain Warner. There was a period of vigorous training and reequipping and altogether six officers and three hundred and three men arrived. A novel fatigue merited an entry in the War Diary when one evening they left their billets as it was getting dark and marched for two hours to the Rue du Bois south of Le Touret. There they dug for three and a half hours to make a trench two and a half feet deep into which they laid telephone cable before filling it in again, an activity very quickly repetitively commonplace to a depth of six feet. On the evening of the 24th they marched from Locon to Gonnehem, a small village to the northwest of Béthune and just south of the La Bassée Canal, remaining there a week. Gradually Lieutenant Balfour began to sense something. "There is some big attack brewing? We are now over strength and are practising the attack and the bomb throwers…had bombs about all day. Lovely place here apple blossoms all out and very peaceful. There is an aeroplane park about 1000 yards off where we go in the evening and see them coming in with their reports, etc." On 1 May there was a fighting strength of Commanding Officer and Adjutant, sixteen company officers and eight hundred and sixty two other ranks with, in addition, twenty one signallers and orderlies, thirteen pioneers, five snipers and four trench mortarmen.

General Lowther's first mention of Second Ypres, which had begun two days before, was on the 24th after he read of the Germans using poison gas for the first time. He commented "It must be a dreadful thing to be a German and to realize how many of one's countrymen have entirely lost all sense of decency, humanity and honour." Lieutenant Haldane, nicknamed "The Rajah of Bomb", left temporarily to help his father, the scientist John Scott Haldane, whom the Government had sent out to St Omer to identify the gases that the Germans were using. Lieutenant Haldane came back over to tea on 1 May and told the Brigadier that "the Professor usually experiments on him, but now that he has a military value he supposes that things are tried on his sister!" General Lowther spent the morning of Sunday 25 April visiting the Scots Guards and then the Coldstream on foot. "There was no Church of England service, as the parson has gone sick. Nice and sunny but not very warm. Heard of heavy fighting up north of Ypres on the French line, but information on it is conflicting. Called on Cameron Highlanders in pm. The surroundings struck me as a queer mixture as I walked over there. A peaceful landscape, children in their Première Communion dress on the roads. In the far distance the sound of guns, up over one the roar of aeroplanes, some of our maxims crackling at practice in a neighbouring claypit. In a house close by the busy tap of hammers in the regimental shoemakers' shop and behind the houses the bump of a football and the shouts of spectators at an inter-Company Match." He had been going round watching the battalions in training, often finding several other more senior officers when he arrived. On the 26th when he went to watch the Coldstream and some experiment with a field gun "Most of the generals in the district seemed to have collected… and several small fry such as myself. Sir D Haig came to see me in the afternoon. Plovers' eggs from Harrods for luncheon. And very nice too. There seemed to be a lot of shooting going on everywhere, but nothing of interest was reported."

On 2 May the Brigade went to the familiar line of breastworks adjoining the Rue du Bois, the relief being completed quietly by eleven that night, though there was a lot of what General Lowther called "gunning" further north from late afternoon onwards, local sniping through the night and some machine gun fire to the left. The Scots Guards paraded at half past four and marched east for three and a half hours to the line, where they found that much had been done while they had been away. There were now good breastworks and parados and many more of them, as well as two new communication trenches. Their right boundary was the Cinder Track leading south to La Quinque Rue and their left just short of the orchard keep which they had held before. On the 3rd General Lowther "Walked round the whole of my front line of trenches, which is very good. It took me 2½ hours. Very quiet indeed up there, but a few shells were flying just after we left. My headquarters is very decent considering it has been unoccupied by the owner for months and has always been within the fire zone since October. Shells have spared it, but the church, 100 yards away, is a wreck, the tower gone and roof, and not a whole pane of glass in it. My Headquarters belongs to a notaire and has quite a tidy garden, with lot of shrubs and some topiary work. But from lack of attention it will soon be a wilderness." He was soon less pleased by Richebourg-St Vaast for the following day he wrote "My house smells like a monkeys' or "small cats" ' house at the Zoo from the tannery opposite." Shelling and minenwerfer bombs did affect the Scots Guards both on the 3rd and more so on the afternoon of the 4th, causing fortunately very few casualties. One of them was Lance Sergeant John Shields, wounded this time slightly in the left arm, his first having been in the face early on 29 October at Gheluvelt. He was on his way across Channel for treatment shortly afterwards but would be back.

The Coldstream arrived to start to take over the line after dark on 4 May and the Scots Guards went into billets at Richebourg-St Vaast to prepare for the coming attack that they now knew about, due to begin at five in the morning four days later. Early on the 6th General Lowther had gone up with the battalion commanders to an observing station to look over the ground, but they were unable to see much because of mist. He then went on "It is queer to feel that there is quite a good chance of not being alive in 48 hours and to see how little it affects one; as one sleeps, eats and does everything just as usual…But the maintenance of correspondence, with the knowledge of big things coming on in a few days, is not easy. And I've known of the coming show, all but the date, for a month. Everyone very keen and pleased at the idea of making a push at last, after it has been in the air for so long." General Haking came to see him in the afternoon, then the Prince of Wales. Finally Captain Poynter, now returned after being sent home sick before Christmas, arrived for tea with Captain Harold Cuthbert, another former Scots Guards officer with a DSO from the Boer War, out of the Army for some time and also rejoined. Then "Nightingales very cheerful."

The Battle of Aubers

On the 7th early on there was again thick mist before it became hot and muggy for the third day running. After a conference of battalion commanders "making final arrangements for rather complicated movements" General Lowther's next visitor was Brigadier General George Thesiger, now commanding the 2nd Brigade, killed in September commanding the 9th (Scottish) Division, New Army, at Loos. General Haking came soon afterwards and "Just as he was leaving we heard belts of machine gun fire evidently at one of our aeroplanes. Some of the bullets fell in our courtyard. Two of the Scots Guards just across the street were wounded by them. Did not think that shots fired as high would do more than scratch or bruise on the way down." Shortly after five came news of a postponement for twenty four hours because the French attack north of Arras, the Nôtre Dame de Lorette again, with half a million men and two thousand four hundred guns was not ready. This had to start twelve hours before the British one. General Lowther marvelled at how the old men and the women and children had cultivated the fields round about as if there was nothing amiss. He wondered whether they would manage the harvest. "Please God the men will be attending to their business instead of fighting before harvest time comes along." He had to wrap himself up in the sitting room tablecloth for the night as all his kit was back with the Transport and was then kept awake by quite a bit of rifle fire. Away to the north, a long way off, there was very heavy and continuous gunfire. There was little to do but wait. After dark on the 8th the Black Watch and Coldstream in the front line were relieved respectively by battalions from the 2nd and 3rd Brigades and all those of the 1st (Guards) Brigade moved to their various assembly positions, some nearer than others to Windy Corner, but all starting from some way north of the Rue du Bois. This Windy Corner was a minor crossroads near to Richebourg-St Vaast on the southeast, from where Edward Road went south to the Rue du Bois, meeting it close to the start of the Cinder Track. General Lowther noted "A final shave concluded arrangements, there's no telling when we will get another."

Lieutenant Balfour recorded what the 1st Division were to do on the right in the battle. The 2nd and 3rd Brigades were each to attack in four waves on a frontage of five hundred yards to the right and left of the Cinder Track. As each wave moved forward the one behind would move up to take its place. The 1st (Guards) Brigade were ready to follow up. Everyone was to be in position by half past ten the evening before and they were. The start of the attack was a wire cutting bombardment of the German wire at five in the morning on 9 May for half an hour, followed at once by a ten minute intense artillery bombardment onto their front line. Two minutes before the end of that the leading battalions would climb over their own breastworks and creep forward, ready to pounce on the German ones seventy yards away as soon as the British guns lifted. The following battalions would then start moving forward.

Lieutenant Balfour thought "The wire cutting bombardment was terrific especially to us who were sitting about 200 yards in front of the guns. The intensity at 5.30 did not seem as intense as it ought to be." At twenty to six the Battalion moved forward a half mile from Windy Corner to the nearest line of breastworks, behind some houses on the north side of the Rue du Bois. "When we got there, and we were lucky to get there across the open with no casualties, we found the Camerons still there. This looked bad as we could not be getting forward in front. What happened was that the attackers got out in front and at 5.40 when the guns lifted and nothing ought to have been alive in the German trenches the Germans stood up shoulder to shoulder and with machine guns shot the attackers down to a man. Then they tried another intense bombardment and another attack with the same result." The German guns had started to fire back heavily too and the Scots Guards began to lose men killed and wounded. They were still behind the same breastwork at half past eight. Later in the morning orders came for the 2nd and 3rd Brigades to be extricated and for the 1st (Guards) Brigade to take over the front line, the Camerons left of the Cinder Track and the Black Watch right of it. Two Scots Guards companies were to occupy the second line of breastworks on the left with a Camerons company and two from the Coldstream were to occupy the second line of breastworks on the right with a Black Watch one.

At half past nine a shrapnel bullet struck Lieutenant Balfour through the biceps and so he walked off west down the Rue du Bois towards Le Touret. As he went along "we heard a roar coming our way and flattened ourselves on the road and an enormous old fashioned Maria burst within 10 to 15 yds of us. If we had not been flat we should never have moved again. The whole road is a trail of wounded and blood all over the road. I reached Le Touret and go down in an ambulance to Béthune. Have my bullet cut out and have lunch and proceed to Lillers by ambulance reaching Lillers at 3pm. I went to bed and slept until 7pm when I have some dinner. Chicken and champagne. Get on the train 11pm and arrive Boulogne (having breakfast on the train) at 8am." He went to a hospital there, then got cigarettes and whisky and soda, sent some telegrams, including to the families of the two other Scots Guards officers wounded, crossed the Channel by the two o'clock boat, arrived in London five hours later and was lying in bed in Wandsworth Hospital an hour after that.

Because of censorship General Lowther could only put an outline in his diary. In the end it had been too cold for anyone in Brigade Headquarters to sleep. They had breakfast at half past one before moving off soon after three to "a position of readiness at a very dirty school about a mile in rear of the firing line." The guns were bombarding the enemy wire and forward positions. "We sat the while very cold, and cracking foolish jokes, which were, for the most part, inaudible in the noise, and wondering how much the Germans were shelling. At 5.40 we moved forward and my Brigade started to get to its place of assembly. I expected a quiet walk up, but was wrong. There was quite a mass of bullets flying about and a gentleman with a machine gun, shooting down our road, made the walk unpleasant. Luckily there was such a row that one was only conscious of shots that passed close by or else struck the ground in front of one." As a result of their experiences at Neuve Chapelle the Germans had three rather than the previous two divisions in this area and had worked hard at stiffening their defences, bringing up more artillery and minenwerfer, as well as strengthening their breastworks. Most significantly they had developed their machine gun plan so that there were interlocking arcs of fire. The guns were positioned low down behind breastworks with slits through which to fire. The British bombardment had had some limited effect on their wire but almost none on their breastworks. The leading British battalions were mown down and then heavily shelled in No Man's Land and in their own front line.

Sometime after one o'clock General Lowther was told to make a fresh attack at four to the right of the Cinder Track. He chose the Black Watch, who were already there, and the Camerons, the next closest. However, there were still many men from other regiments, fit, wounded and dead, in the Camerons' way and they realised after a bit that they were only going to be able to get two of their companies into position in time. The Brigadier, informed of this, said that the attack had to go ahead as best it could and so it did. While the Camerons achieved little, the Black Watch fought their way into the German breastworks, but, by then, in too small numbers to hold on to them. Corporal John Ripley was awarded the VC. The losses were very heavy, the results nil. In the dark afterwards to the right of the Cinder Track Lieutenant Robert Stewart of the Camerons led a party of volunteers out into No Man's Land to find and carry back the wounded. They were using torches and the Germans largely held their fire, letting them get on with their task. Two of his volunteers were killed nevertheless. They managed to bring in thirty five wounded men. Lieutenant Stewart was given the MC. The story was the same right along the attack frontage, the 8th Division at the north end of it having made very limited progress at Rouges Bancs, lost very large numbers of men and ended up having to withdraw to where they started.

The Scots Guards casualties were caused mainly by gunfire. Apart from Lieutenant Balfour, the two officers wounded were Captain John Egerton Warburton, with a shrapnel wound in his right hip, and 2nd Lieutenant The Honourable Anthony Paul Methuen, the Field Marshal's second son. Both were among the most recently arrived. Captain Egerton Warburton had been at Eton and Christ Church, Oxford, and was a serving officer in 1914, having transferred from the Cheshire Yeomanry soon after university. His family home was at Arley Hall, Cheshire, and he and Lettice Egerton Warburton had one daughter. He died of his wounds on 30 August. Lieutenant Methuen, who had been at Wellington and New College, Oxford, was one of those commissioned on 15 August 1914. He was never fit enough to return to the War and spent the rest of it as a staff officer for his father, the Governor of Malta. Six men were killed and forty five wounded. Of those killed Sergeant Alexander Garroway, a reservist promoted to Sergeant only ten days before his death, the son of John and Margaret Garroway of Biggar, Lanarkshire, had first joined over ten years earlier. Called up as a Lance Sergeant on mobilization, he was sent to hospital because of the state of his feet during the Retreat from Mons and then evacuated, so missing everything till he came out again in the draft that Private Johnes was in. He and Ellen Garroway had been married for seven years, had a son and a daughter and were in London, living in Pimlico. The second, Private Charles Gaiger, a Londoner by birth and a serving soldier, had almost completed three years when the War began. He was the son of Albert and Lydia Gaiger of Battersea and had been a butcher. Already once slightly wounded in the leg at Gheluvelt during First Ypres, he recovered in England and was also in the draft with Lance Sergeant Garroway and Private Johnes. The other four were all wartime volunteers, the first being Private Harry Alston, the son of William and Dora Alston of Cadley, Preston. He joined up in September, before which he was a stoker on a motor wagon, and had been in France since the beginning of February. In August 1915 Regimental Headquarters received a letter from Clara Holme of Fulwood, Preston, asking for more details of his death. There was nothing they could add. The second was Private Francis McKernan, the son of Thomas and Catherine McKernan of Edge Hill, Liverpool, by now in France for five months. He was a parcel porter with the London & North Western Railway in Liverpool and joined up there in early September 1914. The third was Private John Ross, the son of Robert and Mary Ross of Alexandria, Dunbartonshire, in the Army three days less and in France three weeks less than Private McKernan. He was a plater before he enlisted at Dumbarton. The fourth was Lance Corporal George Thompson, a miner, the youngest of a large family, but by now with no parents, his eldest brother William in Gorebridge, Midlothian, being his next of kin. He enlisted on 6 August 1914 in Edinburgh and came out in the same draft as Private McKernan. After five weeks in the BEF he was made up to Lance Corporal and was with the Battalion until he died, except for three weeks hospital in March and April with eye problems and an abscess in his right gum. The only personal effects recovered for any of them were identity discs.

Next General Lowther heard that the other two Brigades were to hold the line after all, while his and any other battalions not needed on the spot marched off to billets. They were left undisturbed to do so. "The Germans must have had about enough of it, as they never shot at us at all as we went along our rear breastworks, exposed from the waist up, nor did they shell us down the Rue du Bois as we marched off in formed bodies over ground where it is the regular thing for a shell to greet every congregation of more than 5 or 6 people. We had a longish walk back to Hinges where a kind lady gave us an omelette and coffee and I got to bed at about 1, by which time most of the Brigade was in, some of the Coldstream having stayed on to help the 2nd Brigade. The Black Watch certainly distinguished themselves very much, and it was real bad luck that their work did not lead to a success on our part." The route took them through Le Touret, past Locon and just over the Canal to Hinges, northwest of Béthune.

Private Johnes had not been able to see much during the day. Then they were told to move off southwards before coming out at Chocolat Menier Corner. "Along the line we had to pick our way between dead and wounded lying out from the breastworks, six to seven deep. It was a bloody heart breaker." It was clear to them that the attacks near them had been a disaster and, though they did not know what had happened further north, they soon heard. Although writing long afterwards Private Johnes put his finger on the practical difficulties of assaulting well trained troops in well prepared positions, namely the impossible ground conditions caused very quickly by both sides' artillery prior to an attack, the generally very wet conditions all along the front from Festubert north to Rouges Bancs and the certainty that all communication requiring wires would cease as soon as the enemy guns began to retaliate and cut them when "the only means of getting a message through would be by runner. A damn long shot." He reflected on the dead who "just lay there, to at first be used as stepping stones, or to take cover behind until such time that they could be got at to be moved, or rotted in the mud, or should I say it? Until the rats moved in."

General Lowther heard that Lieutenant Haldane had come back that morning after helping his father at St Omer "studying noxious gases". Then, while possibly or possibly not an exaggeration, as Lieutenant Haldane was on his way on to rejoin the Black Watch for the battle "an enormous shell fell close to him and he tumbled into the crater. He emerged from it a gibbering lunatic, saluting all the officers, shaking hands with the men, trying to lecture about gases, and wounded in the shoulder. I believe it was a very painful sight." In the event not badly hurt, Lieutenant Haldane recovered, was wounded again in 1917 and after the War became a very eminent biochemist and biologist, Marxist and sometime Communist Party member, later rejecting it, and eventually an Indian citizen.

10 May was spent quietly at Hinges. General Lowther felt pretty tired and tried to sleep after lunch "but there were so many callers it was hopeless. Amongst others Haking came in and said that notwithstanding the disappointment, the Corps and Army Commanders were pleased with the performances of the troops of the Division. And if Sir DH says so, he must really be satisfied as he does not throw praise about broadcast. Moved, in afternoon, to a better house across the road inhabited by a nice old couple, ardent admirers of Napoleon, and my room is full of prints and engravings of him. About 10 hours good sleep in a nice bed." However, by contrast, the Scots Guards were initially in "Very bad billets" and so pleased to move that afternoon, only to find instead "Billets scarce". Lieutenant Arnold "Tommy" Thompson, a third officer commissioned from the Artists Rifles in January, became Adjutant. Now nearly thirty, he had been at Kent College and London University and so close to his home in Wandsworth.

Trench tours in familiar and unfamiliar places

What was due next General Lowther only learned on the morning of the 11th when called in a hurry to Headquarters 1st Division. The destination was familiar to him. That afternoon he took Major Brooke to call on Lord Cavan at Headquarters 4th (Guards) Brigade in a lockkeeper's house beside the La Bassée Canal at Givenchy, where "he has amused himself gardening and has the asparagus bed in working order." So, after Sir Charles Monro came on the afternoon of the 12th to speak to the Black Watch and commend them, the Brigade headed for Givenchy. There General Lowther noted "For the first time in my experience, the relief was effected in daylight and in perfect quiet" and that "Huge cases of ready prepared respirators reached us in the evening to counter the effect of the German stinks." These were probably the simple form of cotton wool inside gauze pads with tapes to tie them on with. There was a liquid issued with which to soak the pads, but everyone was told that if it was not there when needed they were to use urine instead. In the event they did not have to use them. The Scots Guards took over from the 1st Irish Guards in front of the village where they found themselves in "Very fine and elaborate trenches." General Lowther walked round most of the system the following morning and found complete communication trenches dug between six and eight feet deep and running back between half and three quarters of a mile from the front line.

The 1st Coldstream were south of the Canal and it was on the 13th that Captain Rowland "Snowball" Feilding arrived with them, an older officer who had rejoined and been briefly with the 3rd Coldstream, including at the Cuinchy brickstacks. In his letters to his wife, with the proper names added afterwards, he illustrated with great clarity and observation much that was common to the experiences of his Battalion and of the Scots Guards. He noticed that all the trenches around Cuinchy had London street names and that, bricks being readily available from ruined houses and from the brickstacks, in most places the floors of the trenches had been paved with them, more likely than the ration tins which Private Watson had described. The dug-outs in the sides of trenches or behind brickstacks were improvised, some almost strong enough to withstand a direct hit from a light shell, some anything but. Occasionally there was a grave in the trench with a rough penciled inscription. It struck him as odd how some religious statues still stood intact in the shattered churches, but strangest of all was the survival of the cemetery crucifix at Cuinchy. "I shall never forget the first time I saw it. I had plodded along many hundreds of yards of the communication trench, seeing nothing but the bricked floor and the clay walls – for there was nothing else to see. Then something above me caught my eye and I looked up, and saw this great crucifix towering above the trench, and facing me."

Suddenly word came to the Scots Guards at about five in the afternoon on the 13th that they were to leave Givenchy that evening. It took all night to complete the relief and it was not till early morning that they were clear and on their way to occupy the theatre and skating rink at Béthune. The Germans had been shelling the town, continued it during the night and there were civilian casualties. What was behind this sudden change was an agreement with the French to take over more of the line south from the Béthune-La Bassée road. So on 15 May in the rain the Brigade headed further south than they, or anyone else, had been before. The southern limit of the British line became the main Béthune-Lens road near which the trenches faced east up the long, slight Grenay Ridge. Behind that was the large mining village of Loos, invisible except for a large double slagheap to the south, the Double Crassier, and the distinctive double gantry pit winding gear soon known as Tower Bridge. The by now very well dug in German front line was just in front of the crest of this ridge, Grenay being a village at the southern end of it, near the Béthune-Lens road. Where it suited their purposes the Germans had dug saps out for observation posts. No Man's Land was between five and six hundred yards wide. The ground was chalk, harder to work but, once worked, providing good cover and requiring direct heavy artillery hits to do any real damage. The pattern of activity was relatively quiet over the next four weeks and much more time was spent out of the line than in it. To get there for the first time the Brigade marched southeast from Béthune through the villages of Sailly-Labourse and Noyelles. From there the Scots Guards went on until they reached the front line, taking over from the French 296e Regiment in front of Le Rutoire, a large farm east of Vermelles, itself a large village behind another slight rise in the ground and so sheltered from observation. Vermelles had been the scene of savage fighting the previous autumn and the French had driven the Germans back from there. Rather more than a mile to the north, beyond the Vermelles-Hulluch road, and jutting out from the German front line was a formidable defence work on slightly higher ground overlooking the British trenches. Behind this, the Hohenzollern Redoubt, was a large slagheap known as The Dump, north of which was the mine, Fosse 8.

The next four days were mainly wet, so there was a lot of water in the trenches by the morning of the 18th, sometimes cold and often under shellfire aimed at the trenches. The Brigadier remarked that his Headquarters were "in a decent house, quite filthy, full of mice, and smells of rabbits. All the outhouses, garden, and shrubbery full of French artillery horses which never seem to have their harness off them." He went to Vermelles to talk to the neighbouring French commanders during the quiet night of the 15th. Away to the north and to the south he could hear the battles raging. News came through of British successes at Richebourg, the Battle of

Festubert. He went out for over four hours and saw almost every yard of the Brigade line. "A working party of the Scots Guards attracted some shelling with HE Shrapnel. We could hear them coming and kept low every 20 seconds or so as they came. They did no damage…A good line, but not very sanitary. There must be a fly to every square inch." Then "A little way to one side of us, within eye and earshot, is raging a week old battle far larger than anything Napoleon ever dreamt of; a short way off on the other side is another in full blast, also bigger than any of Napoleon's. And all the attention one pays is to remark occasionally "They are shooting like the devil to the North! (or to the South)." One's sense of proportion has had an awful upset, and it will be hard to reestablish a proper conception of values. A shell poked its nose into a Scots Guards machine gun emplacement this afternoon, damaging the gun and killing one man and wounding 3. The gun had no business to be mounted and only one man should have been with the equipment." There was heavy firing to the north on the afternoon of the 18th "so we suppose that our attack is still being pushed on." It was. Nearer at hand Private Alex McPherson had been hit in the head on 16 May and later died in hospital at Wimereux. He was a labourer and had been in France for just over two months after joining up the previous September in Glasgow. His widowed mother Mary McKinnon had remarried and lived at Bernisdale, Skye.

The Coldstream relieved the Scots Guards on the night of the 19th and Captain Feilding and No 4 Company were in the reserve trench. His headquarters was a French dug-out of flimsy construction, but distinct charm in that "much care has been given to its interior decoration, which resembles a cottage parlour. The French are much more thorough in these matters than we are. It has a door, two windows with muslin curtains, a little fireplace with wax flowers on the mantelpiece, papered walls and ceiling, a boarded floor, a little crucifix, a big looking glass, and a sketch and poem by a former occupant nailed upon the wall. The former depicts an angel, flying, and blowing the trump of victory." He went on that the Scots Guards had christened this dug-out "Some Hut" and that it was also known as "Buck House". Out in front to the right lay the French dead from attacks simultaneous with the Battle of Aubers and a follow up two days later, "a saddening sight to look upon, the ground between the trenches being thickly strewn with dead." When they could they brought the dead in at night for burial, a revolting job. Several had been lying out for weeks or even months.

General Lowther found the 21st "A quiet day, some shelling of the trenches as usual, but nothing much. In 4 days the Camerons in the trenches had no casualties at all. Rode to Sailly-Labourse to see the troops in billets. From 6pm onwards a tremendous cannonade and battle raging to the N. In the midst of it Brooke and I rode off to dine with 1st Division to meet GOC I Corps. But the latter did not turn up, having had to move his quarters in a hurry: so we had the benefit of a great spread in his honour, excellent food and drink, and pipers round the table after dinner, just to remind one that one was mortal and liable to suffering." The gunfire to the north continued all through the night and all through the following day. General Lowther also recorded "Received strawberries from a kind friend at home, which arrived in about 2½ days and were perfectly excellent." On the 23rd "Last night as I went to bed at 11.30 a continuous roar of artillery from the French which, for continuity and steadiness, beat anything I've yet heard. This lasted for half an hour, and then, just to show the futility of human noises came a violent thunderstorm close over our heads." Most nights there was shelling, often heavy, in the neighbourhood, rifle and machine gun fire, and, by day, bombing from aeroplanes. When fine it had started to be very hot and, while there was often a breeze, it had no effect at all in the trenches, as he and Major Brooke noticed when visiting the Scots Guards on the 26th. That night the Camerons "caught a man of a German patrol of *113th (Baden) Regt*. A measly looking little beast who said he was 20 (looked 17) and had been seven months in the same trenches. He had not much information of any value." On three days out of the sixteen that the Brigade were in the line at Le Rutoire during the second half of May there were no casualties at all and it was unusually quiet, though there was a lot going on elsewhere. The battalions in reserve had to produce large fatigue parties every night for digging, during the course of which on the 22nd Private Thomas Pomfret of the Scots Guards was hit by shrapnel in the thigh, his first wound of the War, not a severe one. Before volunteering the previous October he was a labourer, living with his wife Bridget and their daughter in Preston.

On the 30th Captain Feilding was in the support trench at Le Rutoire. "Out in No man's land, close to the German line, grows a tree, which, though small and insignificant considered as such, is the only object in the broad and desolate and otherwise treeless space intervening here between the German Trenches and our own. This tree, therefore, has achieved a notoriety which it most certainly would not have achieved otherwise. It is known as "Lone Tree", and, I daresay, is as famous among the Germans and our own troops." A Coldstream patrol reconnoitering the enemy wire near the tree the night before bumped into a German post and lost two men killed. A third was wounded but carried back successfully.

Colonel Hore Ruthven wrote on the 30th to Lieutenant Colonel Sherard Godman, then commanding the 3rd Battalion, starting off "Are sandbags unknown in England?" Explaining that in the line the Battalion used on average two thousand sandbags a day he pointed out that officers and men arriving in drafts did not know how to use them to construct trenches, including breastworks, and traverses and spelled out precisely what they needed to know and be able to do it "in the dark". He suggested that it would only require setting aside a small part of the square at Wellington Barracks to train everyone. On 1 June, at two days notice, he left to become GSO1 of the 47th (2nd London) Division, Territorial Force, replaced temporarily by Sir Victor Mackenzie. The same day the Brigade left Le Rutoire and marched back up the main road to Béthune. There the Scots Guards were once again in L'École des Jeunes Filles. As he did from time to time General Lowther stayed on to have dinner with the incoming brigadier and was the last to leave Le Rutoire at eleven that night. He eventually got to bed in Béthune at one. Later next afternoon he walked with Major Brooke into the town and "got some champagne for our insides and Eau de Lubin for our outsides." Eau de Lubin was an aftershave. He was very impressed by the spirit of the large numbers of troops in the area. "All looked splendid, full of go – all singing and most cheerful." Next day, having first gone to have a tooth stopped at Lillers, he went to a conference at Divisional Headquarters, about which he could write nothing. There he heard that Henry Asquith, the Prime Minister, had been out. "A year ago one would not have expected him to be in Flanders, the guest of Sir JF and having tea with Hubert Gough, while Seely commanded a Brigade." This referred to the Curragh Incident and its repercussions. Just over a year earlier, following the introduction of the Liberal Government's Irish Home Rule Bill, there was apprehension of armed insurrection by Loyalists in Ulster. Colonel Seely, Secretary of State for War, had had plenty of warning that Army officers serving in Ireland were likely to object to taking action against Loyalists. This led to an offer from him to excuse those whose homes were in Ulster from being present to carry out their orders, but stating that all others who felt the same way would be dismissed from the Army. While otherwise this situation was generally well contained among officers in Ireland, the centre of attention quickly became the 3rd Cavalry Brigade at The Curragh, County Kildare. Almost all the officers, including their commander, Brigadier General Hubert Gough, resigned their commissions. The Government backed down and reinstated them, but these events and their subsequent handling led to resignations, including those of Colonel Seely and of Sir John French as Chief of the Imperial General Staff. This did nothing to help the relationship between the Government and the Army when the War broke out and later.

The Brigadier went on "Hear Joffre is most optimistic and looks hopefully for an end of hostilities in August." He expressed no opinion himself. After lunch with the Camerons on 4 June he went "to take part in some gas demonstration… It certainly is nasty smelling stuff and gives one a head and mouth with quite a small whiff. A few shells into town this evening and yesterday. The dirty dogs! But this wild shelling is quite futile and of no military value." On the 6th he had a visit from Captain Bagot Chester "who told us a lot about their fight near Richebourg, but his involved account left us little wiser." Colonel Cator would have made more sense of Festubert when he came to tea two days later. On the 7th it was blazing hot and, after attending while more senior commanders inspected some of his battalions, General Lowther went "to the open air swimming bath where about 300 men can bathe at a time. Nice and cool under the trees round it and very well arranged with the shallow parts penned off." He was not there when Private Edward Hamill "drowned at the bath this morning, and very nearly drowned one of the bathing piquet who tried to save him." Private Hamill enlisted in the Scots Guards in Liverpool, where James and Mary Hamill lived in Everton, at the end of August 1914 and arrived in France early in January. A former labourer, he had a tombstone tattoo on his left forearm. General Lowther recorded what he saw and, when he did not see it, what he heard, but Private Watson was nearer to this accident and described it differently. He remembered the water being far from translucent so that it was impossible to see the bottom of the pool. "About 60 soldiers used the pool at a time & after about 600 troops had used the pool the colour of the water was muddy-pea green. Nobody noticed Private Hamill disappear & it was when the Company lined up to return to billets that his absence was noticed." Following a futile search the unnamed company commander ordered the pool to be drained and they found the body.

This lull came to an end on the 10th when the Brigade were to return to the trenches immediately south of the Canal at Cuinchy with its brickstacks, where they had not been since the end of January. It had developed into a particularly vigorous area for mining by both sides, the trench lines being close. Captain Feilding, familiar with this from his time with the 3rd Coldstream, found that the enemy had set off two mines under the British front line killing a number of British miners as well as twenty or more infantrymen. "The external visible result of the explosion is the total extinction of the trench for a length of about 50 yards, and its substitution by an enormous crater. The incident took place about five days before we took over, since when all endeavours to repair the damage by digging round the lip of the crater have been frustrated, with considerable loss of life, owing to the bombing activity of the enemy, who is not more than 30 yards away." The situation was dire and Captain Feilding pitied the under strength and dejected battalions they found, who had suffered very severely and over whom, he observed, the Germans had gained the upper hand. It was here at this time that Lieutenant Robert Graves of the Royal Welsh Fusiliers, author of *Goodbye To All That*, had his first experiences of trench warfare when attached temporarily to the 2nd Welsh.

Colonel Godman, holder of a DSO from the Boer War who left the Army in 1908, arrived on the 10th to take command of the 1st Scots Guards. He had been at Eton and Christ Church, Oxford, and was a widower in his late forties. After further bathing parades and washing and cleaning of kit that day they marched east in the evening. In the course of the relief of the 1st South Wales Borderers of the 3rd Brigade three men were killed, Privates James Young, John Cunningham and Alexander Nicol, all wartime volunteers. Private Young, a miner and son of Thomas Young of Cowdenbeath, had enlisted the previous August, been in France since the end of December and with the Battalion except for six weeks at the beginning of 1915 in hospital with interconnective tissue disorder ("ICT"), a very common medical condition throughout the War. Private Cunningham was a ploughman from the Rhins of Galloway who joined up in October, leaving behind Grace, his wife of six months, at Port Logan, Wigtownshire. He had been with the BEF for just over two months. Private Nicol, also an October recruit, had been out for just under two months. He came from Kirkcaldy where Margaret Nicol, his mother, lived, but had been working as a postman near Fort William.

German shells and minenwerfer bombs killed a further four men and wounded seventeen more over the next three days. It had rained hard on the night of the 10th and when General Lowther went round the trenches in the morning they were "very wet and muddy. Chose the early hours as there are not so many things being thrown about at that hour." By that he meant rifle grenades, minenwerfer bombs, hand grenades "and other beastly fowl. Very different from the peaceful line of a couple of weeks ago." He went on about this next day when there was a lot more shelling and remarked "The Bosches are probably annoyed at some shell being put in some of their mine works yesterday. It is difficult to decide what to do with the beasts; if one leaves them alone they become impertinent, and if one hammers them they become quite offensive." On the 13th "A considerable bombardment (by us) began at 6am and very noisy it is, we are reduced to wearing cotton wool to save our ears. A damned noisy day." That evening the Scots Guards came out of the front line to the immediate support positions around Cambrin for three more days with fewer casualties. When it was not raining Private Johnes preferred the areas either side of the La Bassée Canal because they were higher above the water level and better drained. "The trenches we took over were well built and they were trenches, not breastworks and mud holes. The brickfields near La Bassée and the country around was red with poppies toward the end of May. It caused a little cheerfulness on sunny days, to sit on the firestep and see the larks flying and singing in the sky, and to keep a tab across No Man's Land to Jerry's line by looking through a bayonet periscope, a small looking glass in a metal frame, fixed by an adjustable arrangement onto the rifle bayonet. A sentry sitting on the firestep with his back to the parapet, and his rifle resting between his knees, could look up into the glass, and see everything going on between the lines by turning the rifle slowly around. Sitting on the firestep was also the favourite place to do a little delousing."

Because he described it as near the brickstacks it was probably during this trench tour that "all of a sudden an oldish chap, a little way along the line, took off his harness, equipment with ammunition pouches and bayonet scabbard, threw them onto the fire step, climbed over the parapet, and made off toward Jerry's line, he made a few steps before being nailed by a sniper." The man, unidentifiable, had been out for a few weeks, there was no warning that this might happen and they concluded that "he had suddenly snapped under tension."

What was developing nearby on the north side of the Canal was further continuation of the Battles of Aubers and Festubert as the 21st Brigade of the 7th Division attacked the German front line to the northeast of Givenchy and the 51st (Highland) Division, Territorial Force, simultaneously attacked from slightly further north. The purpose was to capture the higher ground around Violaines. All day on the 15th the British guns fired on the enemy trenches and wire. As had happened before, the wire was largely unaffected, while the depth and strength of the German defences could sustain everything but a direct hit from a heavy shell. At six that evening, after the day's bombardment had been intensified for half an hour, the 21st Brigade's attack by the Yorkshires and Wiltshires failed with heavy casualties, the enemy having had ample time to emerge to man the parapets long before the attackers were anywhere near. The attack achieved nothing useful. After it had been going on for an hour General Lowther "Went out just behind the house at 7pm a curious sight! All along the wall a crowd of 50 or 60 men idly watching a tremendous battle not much over a mile away. A few yards away a reverend little party assembled round the grave of a sapper who was killed yesterday and now being buried. In the middle distance green cornfields and hedges with the smoke of cooking fires curling peacefully heavenwards. In the distance the village which forms the battle centre, almost obscured by a cloud of dust in which the flashes of shrapnel from time to time appear, to the right of it huge puffs of smoke and dust, red, yellow, white and black form a slowly drifting pall, from the middle of which comes the endless rattle of musketry and machine gun." Next day "After all the row of the last days the result does not appear to be satisfactory. In the pm we are relieved, quite peacefully, by the 2nd Brigade, while Armageddon raged half a mile to the north of us, and we wandered off westward down the road, unshelled and unnoticed." On the 17th another attempt on Violaines failed.

Had an attack there succeeded the 1st (Guards) Brigade were to attack south of the Canal, which included Captain Feilding's company assaulting the Railway Triangle. The implications of this were all too apparent. On the 16th he wrote "The more you look at this Cuinchy Triangle the worse it looks. The problem is anything but a joke, but so hopeless is it universally regarded by those who know the Triangle, that it is treated as a sort of joke, and there is considerable chaff about it." When the orders first came out Captain Poynter of the Scots Guards told him "The only chance you have is that the attack on the left of the canal may fail."

After the Brigade relief on the 17th the Scots Guards went back through Béthune and on due west to Labeuvrière for a week in billets, with company training, a voluntary church parade on the Sunday and inter company cricket. Private Johnes remembered the Béthune-La Bassée road as "a beautiful stretch in places, lined with huge trees. But Napoleon Bonaparte…had laid the surface with stones "cobble" about six inches square, horrible for marching, we preferred the roadside under the trees, out of the sun and out of sight" of German planes or observation balloons and that main road ran east-west. The weather, as for some time, varied between fine, rainy and thunderstorms. On the 24th they moved further west to Burbure with "bad" billets which took much of the next day to clean up. There was also a football match with the Camerons, a 1-1 draw. Another voluntary church parade the next Sunday was followed on the 28th by practising grenade attacks on the training ground and by a boxing competition in the afternoon. The day after, very hot, they were on their way to Verquin, due south of Béthune, during which "a large number of men fell out." The billets were very sparse and so very crowded. There were fatigues and more company training, including more attacks with grenades, during which Lieutenant David Brand was injured, his first wound, and another match against the Camerons on a very hot afternoon, the Scots Guards winning 1-0. On 4 July, yet another very hot day, three German shells landed in the village and wounded four men of Right Flank. Of more interest to them 16 Platoon of Left Flank acquired a mongrel called Rabbie.

The next two weeks when the Brigade were back at Le Rutoire were mostly very quiet with only very occasional shelling. Captain Feilding was in Some Hut again. In the interval it had been "alas, plundered of its crucifix and other furnishings by some souvenir-hunting vandal." Colonel Godman wrote almost every day to his stepdaughter Marjorie Clarke Jervoise at their home in Esher, Surrey. Much was taken up with extensive requests to her of things to send out, news of family and friends. His style was illustrated by his letter on 5 July "I don't understand how my letters arrive uncensored as I censor them myself and put a beautiful red triangle stamp No 358 on them." However, he was circumspect and avoided naming places anywhere near the line. His letter the following day was from Le Rutoire itself, where they had arrived after dark the night before. "We are living in the ruins of what must have been a charming place either a château or a very large farm with a large garden most of which is now a cemetery of Germans. They made I believe a very fine stand here and the French shelled them to pieces. We are reduced to living in the cellar of what was probably the Stables partly because the Huns occasionally favour us with an odd shell but equally because the flies are such a nuisance in the brighter light. The German trenches are a little further off than usual here. The French built this line and some of the dug-outs are somewhat characteristic. Some one has stolen the contents of Harold's [Cuthbert] dug-out but last time he was here it had a very nice bronze statuette of a danceuse and other pictures from French papers and a well carved crucifix. My own dug-out is a very safely built arrangement with about 6 foot of earth & timber over it and looks rather like a section of the tube railway with iron walls, boarded floor & a door. Quite a show place & called St Cloud. No post arrived today. Possible they won't be able to get up in daylight. I should like to put the neighbouring village up in Hyde Park for people to see. It has been smashed literally to atoms. I don't think one house remains untouched and would give some of the people at home an idea of what invasion wd mean." Early on the morning of 14 July he was in bed in his dug-out when "I heard what I thought must be a Zep[pelin] and so nipped out to see. It was a covey of 14 of our aeroplanes who took a 20 minutes flight over the Huns lines. I don't know what they did but I suppose they were up to some mischief bombing some railway station or something unless it was an aerial regatta for the Quatorze Juillet." It was widely believed that a German attack was imminent but in his view "they have taken so much trouble to advertise their coming that I rather doubt its happening."

General Lowther heard that during the night of the 16th "the Camerons shot a German who was trying to bomb one of their saps. His correspondence showed him to be a bright boy. It included letters from parents whose daughters he had wronged and deserted, a variety of affectionate letters from young women and about fifteen addresses of Frauleins." Nowhere within range of German guns was safe, however, and when on the morning of 17 July the Scots Guards were in reserve back at Vermelles a shell mortally wounded Private Murray Hunter, who died in the evening. He had farmed with his father William Hunter near Stranraer, joined up in November and been in the Battalion for just over three weeks. Both sides used the colliery gantries but because of the lie of the land the German artillery observers could see further. While shelling was frequently speculative, in daylight it was often carelessness and indiscipline by working parties behind the line, spotted by the enemy, which brought down targeted fire.

Digging went on and on and they were getting fed up with it. Captain Feilding wrote on the 14th of his men singing on the march "Digging, digging, digging: always b----- well digging" to the hymn tune of Holy, Holy, Holy, Lord God Almighty. "They write about it in their letters home: they talk about it. Yesterday I saw, worked out on the parapet, in pieces of chalk…the following simple inscription – "1st C. Gds – Navvies".

It was now that the *Left Flank Magazine* first came out. Sir Victor Mackenzie, the company commander, quickly agreed when asked for permission. The impetus came from two wartime volunteers, the Editor, Private George Morris of 16 Platoon, and the principal cartoonist, Lance Sergeant James Blair of 15 Platoon. Private Morris was a seedsman near Dundee, aged twenty two when he enlisted there at the end of August 1914. Sergeant Blair, an engineer in Glasgow, joined up a few days later when he was just past his twentieth birthday. He was first promoted before he left London and became a Lance Sergeant at the beginning of July. Both were in the large draft that landed in France on 6 February and their homes were both in Edinburgh, Private Morris' father William living south of The Meadows and Sergeant Blair's parents Alexander and Maggie Blair in Murrayfield.

Private Morris did not refer to "editions" of the *Left Flank Magazine*, but instead to "spasms", then and later a word used in the Battalion for trench tours and other more direct contacts with the enemy or simply bursts of any activity. So the First Spasm appeared in July. It was written, edited and illustrated entirely by NCOs and men of Left Flank. Private Morris wrote much of the First Spasm himself, as well as much of those that followed, but he gave lively encouragement to one and all to produce contributions. Stories could be "of the blood and thunder variety, or the sloppiest of love yarns, providing the author gives his name and runs the risk of assassination." Then, "Poetry is permissible, but don't let us have such stuff as "An ode to Spring", or "To Anthea", etc. Any such poet will be severely dealt with." He went on to suggest forming "some sort of debating society. Some very heated discussions are held now and again as to which is the better man, a Scotsman or an Englishman. Being a Scotsman himself, the Editor does not need to be told the answer to this question, but invites his readers to send in their opinions. Please do not call personally, however, with sleeves rolled up and five rounds in the magazine, or the Editor may not be found at home." At the foot of this page was Sergeant Blair's drawing of "The Editor's Heavy Boot". The opposing trenches south of the La Bassée Canal having been very close to each other, a little further on in the First Spasm came "Tommy (shouting over to German lines): " 'Ave you any lices there?" Fritz: "No, ve vas all clean men here." Tommy: "I don't mean lousy lices, you chump, I mean lices wot yer puts in yer boots." Referring to the recent rest period at Burbure, which they knew from their earlier visit, Private Morris reflected "A little disappointment may have been felt in Left Flank that our billet was not the old brewery…Old favourite estaminets, coffee shops, etc., have been revisited, and Corporals wax fat on "oeufs", "pain de beurre", and "café au lait", though it must be admitted that the humble private is not so far behind in that line." Private Morris then ridiculed the rumour mongers who always "had it on good authority" about where they were all going next or that they were all getting a week's leave. The Company Sports had been much enjoyed mainly because so many of the events, such as sack races, were not serious ones and because the local females came out in their Sunday best to watch. He concluded "The open air concert was a fine finish up to the day's fun. It might have been well for their own sakes had some of the artistes brought written words, but so far as the audience was concerned, any lapse of memory was only additional cause for amusement."

His next effort was a parody entitled Burns' Address to a Tin of Bully.

> Deil tak yer muckle ugly face
> Great Chieftan o' the tinned meat race.
> Weel are ye worthy o' a grace –
> Gott strafe the maker.

Ye lie there noo sae quiet an' still,
Oor empty stammicks sune to fill;
Ma Certes I'm fear't ye'll mak me ill,
Then ----- "Number tens."

His knife, see starving Tammas dicht,
An' cut ye up wi' ready slight,
Chuckin' the tin wi' a' his micht
In tae the ditch.

Then, bite by bite, they stretch and strive,
Oh, what a hope on which to thrive,
I wunner hoo we're still alive
On sic a denner.

Puir devils, see them ower sic trash,
As feckless as a withered rash,
Their spindle shanks a guid whip lash,
Or guid for pull-throughs.

Oh, ye wha for oor sodjers care,
An' deal him oot his bill of fare,
Oor Tammas wants nae skinkin ware that comes frae Libby's,
But if ye wish his gratefu' prayer,
Gie him a ----- change.

Private William Taylor, another talent in 16 Platoon, described his efforts as a cook when in early April they were billeted in a tannery at Richebourg-St Vaast. "Along with some chums I made a reliable fireplace, and on the first day alone cooked no less than five potfuls of bully stew. Being an improvement on the *common* bully stew in that it contained carrots, beans and onions, my chums were highly delighted (? Editor) and placed me in the position of Head Cook and mess tin washer." Quickly they got bored and sacked him. Next "the discovery of a sack of flour resulted in ovens being made, on which were baked scones, marmalade tarts, hot cross buns, etc. As you may guess, they required a strong appetite and a good digester." Someone then appeared with a "mysterious football shaped thing in a cloth…We gazed on it with something like awe on our faces while he placed it in the pot to boil. The mystery was solved a few hours later when the cloth was unrolled and a marmalade pudding made its appearance. In a few seconds it had disappeared." His own attempt at rice pudding "brought me everlasting fame." He started off with rice and milk in one mess tin and put it on to boil. As it swelled he had to use first a second mess tin, then a third as well. Then "I fell asleep, and awoke to find the fire out, pudding overflowing and burnt, while the sleeve of my tunic also was burnt when I had rolled in my sleep too near the fire. Did that cure me? Oh, no!" He had been a gardener in Bradford until September 1914 and was in the draft with Private Morris and Sergeant Blair. Henry and Mary Taylor lived in Roundhay, Leeds.

A frequent contributor was Private James "Jimmy" Jones, also of 16 Platoon, another September 1914 volunteer and a former warehouseman from the London Docks, where Jessie

Jones, his mother, lived in Shadwell. He arrived later than the others. The main part of his first article read "It was my first time in the trenches, and not unnaturally I was "bobbing" a bit. Anyway, after the order to "Stand Down" I began to get worse, and my restlessness gradually affected the rest of the fellows in my traverse. I must have had a presentiment of what was coming, for away on our right was heard presently a heavy burst of rifle fire. Hastily getting close to the parapet we got "stuck into it" for all we were worth. The enemy, who had evidently been stoutly reinforced during the night, tried to seek what little cover there was available, but our fellows were merciless and picked them calmly off as if practising at the butts. There was very little talking. Now and then a muttered curse could be heard as one of our foes went down in a welter of blood, but for the most part we went at it with a calmness and steadiness that was the despair of our enemies. Presently, there was a commotion away back near the communication trench. Ah! a message was being passed up. Anxiously we awaited it, and then clearly on the morning air came the cry, "Look out boys! Here comes the Chaplain" and hastily donning our shirts we left the killing of our "companions" for a more favourable opportunity." Private Jones also carved a very fine Scots Guards star out of a piece of chalk from near Vermelles.

On the morning of 18 July Major Brooke returned from leave, during which he had married Prudence Sergison and added her name to his, so becoming Sergison Brooke. General Lowther, who had recently been in hospital with lumbago, went with him round a newly dug "very chalky second line of defence and communication trenches." In the afternoon they searched for a suitable place to use to train men on trench mortars. The main problem was identifying an instructor "as all the TM officers had been taught 4 kinds of TM, and the one we have for practice is a 5th sort." Eventually 2nd Lieutenant George Mitchell of the Black Watch, amateur heavyweight boxing champion of the North of England, was persuaded to take on the job, but on the 22nd a trench mortar exploded, killing him and killing and wounding several others. The Brigadier went to his funeral the next day.

Late on the 19th the Scots Guards returned to Verquin. They practised their shooting on the range, bathed at Béthune, played football again against the Camerons, who this time won 4-1, and participated in the Brigade Horse Show at the Champ des Sports at Annezin, the next village west of Béthune, winning first prizes for the competitions for the best machine gun limber, for the best light draft horse and for the best water cart. The officers won second prize in the jumping competition. General Lowther thought the horse show "A really great success. About a dozen events and 160 entries. I rode one of my horses in the jumping, but he refused the last fence once. Prizes pretty evenly distributed among the battalions, Haking gave them away. All horses in quite wonderful condition." On the 22nd Colonel Godman, commenting on the German advance into Poland, thought that if they captured Warsaw, which appeared likely, it would "prolong the war. I am beginning to think… 1919 is almost a possibility unless Lloyd George ruins us first. Strafe the politician says I. They are a nuisance even in peacetime and in war they are an absolute danger." There was much in his letters on the likely long duration and much in the same vein about politicians. On the 24th he wrote that the Guards Division, the possibility of which he had first heard of two days earlier from General Lowther, "is almost a certainty. Nobody out here really likes it but I hear K[itchener] means to have it so there is not much more to say."

Privates Johnes and Evans were very interested in a 15 inch howitzer near Verquigneul and went to look. "When this monster was fired it shook the ground for a mile around, and was bad medicine for eardrums. If lucky enough to be standing in the right place, well back from the gun and looking up toward the direction in which it was firing, the shell could be seen for a second or two, travelling upward after leaving the gun barrel until it was out of sight…Later we experienced, in the line, Jerry's retaliation…the sound of Jerry's gun being fired could be heard in the distance, after a few seconds had elapsed, a sound like an express train could be heard coming down out of the sky, but there was no way of knowing where it was going to land…We were in the Cambrin position and the shell landed two or three hundred yards away to the south. It made a terrific explosion and threw up a lot of earth, the ground shook like a jelly, but did very little damage other than making a big hole in the ground and perhaps scaring the daylights out of any of the fellows close to where it landed." He realised that he was "instinctively beginning to detect some kinds of shellfire, perhaps from the firing of the gun in the distance, to the shell coming over, and its probable proximity in landing. Private Evans had the same sensation that "one instinctively ducked in the right direction, at the same time giving a quick look for cover." Later they were not even thinking of what they were doing and "reflexes were more abrupt you were moving before you realized it. I know that on two occasions, one in Trones Wood in 1916, and one at Berles in 1918, I ducked just in time. It's a soldier's job to kill, and stay alive, to be of future use. You are no good dead, there is no cowardice in ducking or taking cover, you are either dumb or a bloody fool, to stand and offer yourself as a target. The one with your number will get you sooner or later."

On 24 July Private Thomas Beckett was posted back to England without any stated reason, but someone must have realised that he was not quite what he seemed. Like many others he enlisted the previous September at Preston, where he was a clerk. Unlike others and unusually, though quite permissibly, because by then the normal term of service had become three years or the duration of the War, Private Beckett signed on as a Regular for twelve years, stating that he was eighteen and seven months. This meant that he should not go abroad until after 1 February, once he was nineteen. He arrived in France on 1 June 1915 and joined the Battalion three weeks later. Eighteen months later a correspondence began about his true age concluding with his mother writing on 31 January 1917 from their home at Walton-le-Dale and sending his birth certificate to Regimental Headquarters. This proved that the next day would be Private Beckett's eighteenth birthday. The 3rd Battalion were told to make sure he was not selected for an overseas draft until he really was nineteen. He had understated his age by precisely three years.

Coming the other way on 25 July two officers arrived from England. The younger one, Lieutenant Donald "Wiejo" Ellis, educated at Repton and Clare College, Cambridge, was twenty four at the time and married. He had joined from the 6th East Surrey Regiment, Territorials, in February 1915. The elder one was forty one year old Captain Miles Barne, who, after Eton and Sandhurst, was commissioned in 1893, served in the Boer War and left in 1904 to return to his family home at Sotterley, Suffolk. His wife Violet was the sister of Major Orr Ewing, who in 1903 had been a subaltern in Captain Barne's company. For the time being there was no company for him to command, but as Sir Victor Mackenzie was on leave he was given Left Flank temporarily. It was to be a rude and immediate initiation as he found that they were "due to go into trenches at Cambrin this evening, so we parade at 5pm & march 7 miles there – the last part along a wide road Béthune–La Bassée, pick up some picks & shovels, dive into a communication trench & so on like so many moles, not having much idea of what the ground is like above ground. LF is to be the Reserve Coy held in readiness to make the "counterstroke" in case anything goes wrong in the front line. I share a very damp & smelly dug-out with Fergusson, who sleeps like a hog. Rather an anxious time taking over from the Gloucester Regt, making arrangements for the night in the dark – & all such new work to me – had quite a lively night – & have to "stand to" once or twice – not much sleep till after the regular dawn stand to, 2.30 – 3.30am, but am bound to say it is not an enjoyable time exactly." Lieutenant Neil Fergusson, who had been at Eton and Cambridge, was commissioned in September 1914 and had been in France for nearly four months. Already in his thirties, he had no previous military experience. His parents lived in South Kensington.

They were now immediately to the south of the Béthune-La-Bassée road, with the Cuinchy brickstacks to the north. On the morning of the 26th Captain Barne "Had a good look round our trenches, which are very near the Germans, varying from 25 to 60 yards, but there are several mine craters between us held by the Germans, 2 or 3 of which are quite close up to our parapets, the edge of crater & our parapet touching each other. The days are fairly peaceful in the trenches, broken by very noisy & angry periods called "Hates" locally – generally on in the morning about 9 – 10, then another about 4 and again about 6 to 7 which usually is continued on & off during the night. At these periods the air gets full of projectiles of all sorts & it is extraordinary how few casualties we have. A good many beetles & earwigs about, & the trenches are made additionally smelly by having dead Frenchmen & some Munster Fusiliers buried in the parapets – the latter inexcusable." Afterwards he added that on about that day "after a deal of firing the Germans began shouting & chaffing & calling out "Turn out the Scots Guards" etc. and eventually put up hundreds of helmeted heads – all close together – our men then put up their heads (about 1 to every German's 5). After more chaff a shot was fired when down went all the heads again."

In this tour two men were killed. One was Private John Gamble, with various tattoos, including "Girl's Head Edith" on his right arm, whose father James Gamble lived in Springburn, Glasgow. He was a machinist with the North British Railway Company before becoming a soldier in June 1913. Although with the 2nd Battalion in London at the start of the War, he was soon sent out to the 1st Scots Guards and was slightly wounded in the back on 29 October at Gheluvelt and evacuated home. He came back in February. Apart from his father as his next of kin he had asked that Miss N Toddy in Maida Vale, London, should be notified. The other was Private Alexander Whyte, another Glasgow policeman who joined the previous September, but he caught cowpox at the Guards Depot and so had only been in France since April. George and Jane Whyte lived at Strichen, Aberdeenshire, and were sent two wallets, some photographs, a notebook and a letter. Six more men were wounded, but it could have been much worse had it not been for the quick thinking and pluck of Private William Kilkenny, former labourer and former Scots Guardsman. Leaving his wife Elizabeth in Bridgeton, he reenlisted in Glasgow when the War had been going for a month and came to France in early January. On 26 July he was coming out of his dug-out to relieve a sentry when a minenwerfer bomb landed right at the entrance. He immediately picked it up and threw it over the parapet, where it exploded. His DCM citation concluded "His prompt action undoubtedly saved the life of the sentry, and probably also those of the men inside the dug-out." From September onwards Private Kilkenny had trouble with synovitis in his right knee, which led to his discharge two years later, though, presumably conscripted, he rejoined in the Army Service Corps in the spring of 1918. Captain Barne wrote of a less fortunate incident on the 27th with "a trench mortar bomb – horrible things trench mortars – going off just outside our dug-out & wounding Trafford's servant who was stirring the soup for dinner. I came in a few moments later & found all the food smothered in dust – such a mess, & the servant very unhappy – his arm badly damaged & another cut in his leg." Lieutenant Cecil Trafford had transferred in May 1915 from the Royal Garrison Artillery Reserve and arrived in the Battalion soon afterwards. He was the Transport Officer from late 1915 till the end of 1917. Then he went to headquarters work and eventually in the summer of 1918 to be a staff officer with the RAF. His wife Monica was at their home at Geldeston, Norfolk. Lieutenant Edward Trafford of the 2nd Battalion, a prisoner since First Ypres, was his younger brother.

After dark two days later they came out of the trenches once the Coldstream had taken their place and marched three miles to Sailly-Labourse. Captain Barne was "Very glad to get to a more peaceful spot, but can hear all the firing going on – hardly sleep a wink – & see glare of the Very lights and the guns etc constantly passing my window – ground floor – is also very disturbing. Have quite a nice cleanish room brick floor, electric light." General Lowther accompanied Sir Henry Rawlinson on 29 July going round the Coldstream trenches for four hours. They started at five in the morning. On 1 August he wrote "A year since Germany mobilized; are they pleased with what they've effected, and does it in any way agree with what they expected to do in the time?" There was another problem closer to hand. "The flies are almost intolerable, though the place is full of wire traps and flypapers, and we have saucers of formaldehyde everywhere, which makes our noses run and our eyes sore." Throughout these weeks he referred to endless visitors, many completely social in character. Two who came on 2 August "were going on to see the country from the Lorette Ridge, but from the look of that place later in the day, it appears to be an unhealthy spot for a picnic. The constant storms of rain are rather against the harvest which the poor inhabitants are trying to get in everywhere. Things are further complicated for them by the network of telephone wires which traverses the whole country. So I have an arrangement with the Mayor to be informed whenever a field is being cut and send out line men to move each telegraph post as the machine comes to it." The Nôtre Dame de Lorette Ridge was by this time back in French hands after extremely heavy fighting, which had, however, not so far extended to success on the next major feature southeast of it, Vimy Ridge.

At Sailly-Labourse the Scots Guards were mainly occupied in large working parties digging reserve trenches at Vermelles, but in order to go there and back they had to march through Philosophe, which was being thoroughly shelled. Then Sir Victor Mackenzie returned, so Captain Barne moved across as second in command to Captain John Thorpe in B Company, who, when they all went back on 31 July to the same trenches south of the La Bassée road, were "in the most unpleasant part – so we have plenty more anxiety." Captain Thorpe was a contemporary of his, having also joined in 1893 and served for ten years. He had been with the Battalion before, arriving after Christmas 1914 and lasting two weeks before he was sick with influenza and sent back to England. Early in May he came back in time for the Battle of Aubers. He and Cecilia Thorpe had one daughter and two homes, one at Coddington, Nottinghamshire, the other at Ardbrecknish, Argyll. That night "Harold Cuthbert chose to go out with a Corpl, most bravely but unnecessarily, to see whether a certain crater was occupied or not – it was. The Corp was killed & had to be left out there, HC wounded in head but not badly." Corporal George Stewart, a former drapery traveller from Glasgow, was hit by German grenades at very close range. His body was clearly visible and Captain Cuthbert, described by Captain Feilding in a letter on 7 August, when just back from leave, as "a very gallant fellow", crawled out himself again, probably the next night, to try to collect his personal belongings, without success. By the time the Coldstream were back in the line the Germans had recovered Corporal Stewart's body and Captain Feilding wrote that they called out to ask whether they had lost a Corporal born in Glasgow. On 14 August Corporal Stewart's father James Stewart wrote to Colonel Fludyer at Regimental Headquarters acknowledging receipt that day of formal notification of his son's death and asking if he might be given his proper rank of Corporal since "it may seem a small matter (seeing he is dead) to ask you to rectify but to the ordinary non army man it seems but right that what was hardly won in life should still designate him in death." He had already heard from Captain Cuthbert, who wrote immediately on 1 August, that he had intended to have his son, in charge of the company bombers, promoted to Sergeant. Colonel Godman was not pleased about Captain Cuthbert's patrol, though he did not know exactly what he had been doing, but he went further. So on 22 September Kathleen Cuthbert was writing to her husband's uncle, General Cuthbert, that "Colonel Godman to my mind is most extraordinary & rather nasty. Would you believe it he told Harold he could not have company captains taking foolish risks like that & then actually wrote to me & told me the same thing. I was & am furious. Surely the man ought to & must realize it is not a great pleasure to risk your life to try to find out where Germans are throwing bombs from."

The Germans fired more minenwerfer bombs on 1 August, but the British guns silenced that, and did so again through the next night, during which 2nd Lieutenant Arthur Boyd Rochfort was in charge of a small C Company party working on a communication trench. At two in the morning when he was safely in a bay nearby he saw a minenwerfer bomb land on the parapet six yards from an NCO and two men. He rushed out shouting a warning to them, seized the bomb and threw it away just before it went off. Colonel Godman came to tell the Brigadier about this the following evening after they were relieved, the latter observing "This is quite a different case from the man who picks up a bomb which has fallen near him and chucks it away, that is only self defence." Lieutenant Boyd Rochfort's wife Olivia was at their home, Middleton Park, County Westmeath. He had been at Eton and Trinity College, Cambridge, and was another officer well into his thirties. Commissioned in April 1915, he arrived in France in June.

Captain Barne noted "Every night there is a wiring party – putting up wire entanglements in front of a trench, in this case impossible in front of front trench as too near the enemy, there are usually some casualties – one poor Coldstream was killed, this the first dead man I saw, being carried down about July 27th. The trenches here are mined & countermined in every direction – very jumpy work for the miners I expect – listening posts etc, and if we hear the Germans mining before they hear us, up has to go the mine (or vice versa) & begin all over again. Hence all these craters. "Vesuvius" is just outside our parapet – several have names." He added later that on 2 August "the Germans had put up a notice on their parapet "*Hier werden Kriegserklärungen angenommen*" – meaning literally, "Here will declarations of war be received" – & colloquially "Let's hear when you want to have a fight". I was studying this with Thorpe's periscope, when – crash – & they broke the periscope to smithereens – it made me jump pretty well…first shot, probably 40 yards off the periscope measuring about 4in x 3in."

Back out of the line next day they returned to Sailly-Labourse at about five in the afternoon. That night Captain Barne "Slept like a log & feel much better for it." There was more digging in Vermelles the next two days. To Private Johnes "It had suffered a lot of punishment, there were no buildings standing whole, but there was a lot of broken up material and rubble with which fairly substantial shelters were built. There were still a few corpses to be found in various corners. The German advance in the early days of the war had apparently gone through

Vermelles and there had been hand to hand fighting in the town itself. There were slits in the gardens amongst the houses, where both sides had dug in and where some of the killed had been covered up. A few pickelhaubes… and other pieces of equipment, were to be found amongst the ruins." Captain Barne found the village "an absolute ruin hardly a roof left up – it was held by Germans last November for about 6 weeks against the French – the Chateau in particular being an objective, & defended to the last. The French mined up to it thinking they were under it, but were short – & then stormed it, losing very heavily. The whole place is a pitiful sight, no civilian inhabitants left now of course. A beautiful old Church is in ruins."

From General Lowther's perspective relations with the local inhabitants continued mixed. On 4 August "Our proprietor came to see if he could find any more damage to his house. He sends in a bill to British and French Governments about once a month." The day after that he heard about something much more original. "Last night Tommy Robartes got his "Company Band" playing in the trenches. (It consists, I think, of a fife, tin pan, ocarina and Jew's harp.) The Germans cheering and applauding. When plenty of them were out of their dug-outs listening, a lot of guns, howitzers, trench mortars, etc., were turned on to them with great success." Captain The Honourable Thomas Agar-Robartes commanded No 2 Company of the 1st Coldstream. He was MP for St Austell and Mid-Cornwall. The Brigadier was told that on the 5th, their last night in the trenches, they had "put up a notice in German to say their band would play at a certain time "no danger"…They could hear the officers, in evident mistrust, ordering the men back under cover whenever they put their noses out to listen to the music. And such music."

By now Captain Barne had been able to look properly at his surroundings. "This is a flat sort of country, with coalpits every here & there (fosses), apparently fertile, by the look of the crops – mostly oats, wheat & roots – but I should think in winter must be dreary beyond description there are clumps of trees here & there – mostly poplar, & a few walnuts." To the south he mentioned Nôtre Dame de Lorette and Souchez, the village at the foot of it on the southeast, around which "desperate fighting has been taking place for many months." He added "At times one can hear the guns there, sometimes for an hour or more – day or night – an incessant rumble." During the afternoon of the 6th the Brigade handed over both the line at Cambrin and the reserve billets at Sailly-Labourse and all went again to Verquin for six days rest. Captain Barne had a room "in a very primitive & quaint old farm house in a side street. The farmer & his sister live there together. Two cows live in the room next to mine, a horse, a heifer, some pigs all close by in a sort of very compact courtyard, with the inevitable kind of cesspool in the middle, but actually the house is pretty clean. The men are scattered about in various outhouses & buildings. There is quite a nice little garden at the back & a good view over Lorette, so one still sees the flares & "verylights" by night."

Private Johnes and the other signallers liked Verquin. "The civilians had not left the village, and we were able once in a while to buy ourselves a meal of French fried potatoes and eggs, and a bottle of wine. But the main thing was the chance to get cleaned up. We were kept busy training, marching, playing football or any game that would keep fellows busy and their minds off front line tension…We got along well with most of the villagers, we were a source of income to them." There was a lot of route marching. In C Company Captain Poynter "always rode at the head of the company on a dapple grey horse, he took us on one route march and miscued on the route, which called for a song from the troops "And a little child shall lead them", he saw no humour in it and kept us going for two hours without the usual break of ten minutes each hour. For that he lost a lot of marks in the thoughts of the troops."

On 8 August Captain Barne had finished inspecting B Company's rifles and each man's emergency rations to check for deficiencies, which, without good reason, would lead to a disciplinary charge when, to his great surprise, his younger brother, Lieutenant Seymour Barne, 20th Hussars, appeared "on a bike…come over about 16 miles to see me from Wittes. He lunched with us, and about 4pm we walked into Béthune, where I left him biking back." The day after, a very hot one, General Lowther walked over to the Scots Guards and in his turn received a visit from, among others, the Prince of Wales who came by bicycle. "He wears masses of clothes and never seems to turn a hair, when the rest of the world is dripping." No enthusiast for the forthcoming formation of the Guards Division and still hoping to be left where he was, General Lowther wrote "Prospects regarding Formation of Guards Division very gloomy for us; it looks like our happy home being broken up." Captain Barne recorded that the morning had been occupied with a boot fitting and repairing parade nearby, followed by a route march. "In the afternoon a Doctor's feet Inspection, when some men lost their names for having dirty feet – they certainly were so!" Washing was not a problem and there was plenty of water available from taps, as well as electric light in all the houses.

The August Spasm of the *Left Flank Magazine* opened with a cartoon by Sergeant Blair of Private Morris hard at work with pen and paper sitting outside a dug-out in a support or reserve trench. Private Morris had been very pleased at the response to the July Spasm and commented "If things go on at this rate, a typewriter will be needed, and of course a pretty typist. Then, who wouldn't be an editor?" Referring to the unfortunate march during which many fell out on the way from Burbure to Verquin, where their first stay had been "shorter than we anticipated or desired", he remarked that "perhaps our *hearts* were heavy as well as our *packs* when we set out… Of that march perhaps the less said the better…Left Flank, feeling the shame, has since sought to make amends, for the marching has been better of late. Now that the pipes have arrived we should do better still." However, no piper could play for ever and he exhorted the readership to do what they could with mouth organs, by whistling or singing for "then we will break forth into joyous melody, "Here we are, here we are, here we are again."" He expressed the appreciation of the whole Company to Sir Victor Mackenzie "for the frequent gifts of cigarettes."

There was ribald merriment about the recruiting campaign, not only in Ireland, which involved Sergeant Michael O'Leary of the 1st Irish Guards. As a Lance Corporal he had won the VC by single handedly knocking out two enemy positions during the 4th (Guards) Brigade's battle a few days later to recover the ground lost at the Cuinchy brickstacks on 25 January. An anonymous author, "Mike" of 13 Platoon, wrote on "How to Win a VC". His various suggestions included "Why not try and capture a battery of howitzers. To be able to present six 15" guns to your CO would be rather pleasing, but perhaps you would find a little difficulty in pulling the guns by yourself. If six are too many, try three at a time." Another cartoonist had appeared, Lance Corporal Percy Anderton of 14 Platoon, until last October a shop assistant in Liverpool. There was no mention of parents when he enlisted, but his next of kin, Mrs Helena Hurley in Birkenhead, could have been a relative.

"Diet" – The Army Variety" was Private Jones' contribution this time. "Soon after I joined the battalion we left for the trenches, and for the period of two or three weeks lived on all sorts of curious things. Chief among these was some funny red stuff with white streaks in it which we got out of tins, and some hard, white and brown oblong things, with little holes in them." The first was bully beef. "I had heard of this curious stuff before, but I must say I was very disappointed over the word "Bully". I had always thought it was an Americanism for good, extra, or "thumbs up", but, alas, when I came to taste the contents of a tin, I became wiser – much wiser." The other things, hard tack, "after closer examination proved to be biscuits; but what biscuits! Biscuits I had imagined to be crisp, delicious things, coated with cream and sugar, but these things! Ugh!" He supposed that the manufacturer could never have intended them to be biscuits, but that if he did his factory must be next to a cement works from which any shortage of flour was made up. So, looking on the positive side, it must mean good business for the makers of false teeth. Then, "I have nearly reached the limit of my allotted space, but before finishing I thought that I had better mention that "Tickler" has got a lot to answer for."

The notes from the four platoons included remarks both about those in them and about others who for various reasons were away or had gone home. From 13 Platoon there was much regret that Sergeant Jock Lamont, a Glasgow policeman and one of the few Left Flank survivors on 25 January, had gone "down the line" because of his teeth, while one of their bombers, Private Clarence Harry Kiff, had written from the enteric [typhoid] department of a Base hospital to say that he was slowly improving. Either Sergeant Lamont's teeth were very bad or else he went home soon afterwards on leave because he married Hannah Ikin on 4 September in Glasgow. He was very badly wounded in the back on 9 October 1917 in the Battle of Poelcapelle during Third Ypres and discharged eight months later. Private Kiff knew nothing of his family but had a guardian, William Kiff, living in Leyland. He worked as a labourer until a year before and had been in France since February. Because of the enteric he was sent home, not reappearing until August 1917, when he was struck down with dysentery at Le Havre and again sent home without leaving the Base Depot. When he came out again at the end of March 1918 he lasted six weeks before being evacuated with inflammation of the abdomen. A gastric ulcer attributable to war service led to his discharge. The author of the 13 Platoon notes was probably Lance Corporal Willie Moore, a London footman, whose parents Heber and Alice Moore lived in Bath. He joined up the previous September, arrived in France in April and was promoted in the middle of June.

In 14 Platoon, whose notes were written by Corporal Anderton, there was mention that Private Robert McLuckie, "our "gallous" bomber, has asked for his discharge." A miner from Kirkintilloch, Dunbartonshire, where his wife Jemima and their young daughter and son were, he had been on the Reserve since 1905. If mobilization occurred a soldier on a twelve year engagement had to serve thirteen years, which in his case would be up at the end of October 1915. He arrived in France in September 1914, missing the Retreat from Mons, but was slightly wounded in the head during First Ypres and was away for a month. While away he got into serious trouble for drunkenness at Le Havre, was absent soon afterwards and not long after that in trouble because of drink again, collecting a total of ninety eight days FP No 1. However, that was the last of it.

Of Private Fitzsimmons "better known as the "Irish Hun"", Corporal Anderton wrote that he had "become more pro-British lately." Private James Fitzsimmons was born in Edenderry, County Dublin, but in 1914 was working as an iron moulder in Falkirk, where a foster mother had brought him up. He knew his mother was called Susan, but had no idea where she was. Of his father there was no mention. He volunteered within a week of war being declared and, apart from a short period recovering from bronchitis in late January 1915, which meant that he missed 25 January, he had been in Left Flank since early December 1914. Of Private Henry McFadden it was asked what he was "trying for at Vermelles? Was it a VC, DCM, RIP, or an SO (soft one)?" A serving soldier in 1914 and beforehand also an iron moulder in Falkirk,

Private McFadden had always been with the 2nd Battalion until hit for the first time in October 1914 near Kruiseecke and slightly wounded, but enough for evacuation to England. He had come to the 1st Scots Guards at the end of April.

Sergeant Blair, writing the 15 Platoon notes, speculated whether those now back across the Channel, including Davy Peters, were pining away there and longing to return to the Western Front. Private David Peters was the eldest of three brothers from Leyland who joined up at the beginning of September 1914, giving their occupations respectively as a labourer, a dyer's labourer and a drayer. They were orphans and James Peters, their eldest brother, had brought them up. Private David Peters, also in the 6 February draft, was hit in the leg by shrapnel at Aubers and sent home to hospital. He returned to France at the end of 1916 and served with the 2nd Battalion till they came home from Cologne. Private Ralph Peters was also in that draft and in the 1st Scots Guards until wounded in September 1916 on the Somme and sent home. He came back at the end of October 1917, became a Lance Corporal the following February, missed the Armistice because he was on leave for the first two weeks of November 1918, and was posted home two months later. Both were married. Ellen Peters, married to Private David Peters, was living with their son at a house in Lostock Vale, Leyland, and Elizabeth Peters, married to Private Ralph Peters, was living in another house in the same street, with their four children, the youngest born four days after his father volunteered. The third and youngest brother, having been trained as a machine gunner, was already a Lance Corporal before he left England and went straight to the 2nd Guards Brigade Machine Gun Company on arrival in France at the end of September 1916 after the Guards Division battles on the Somme. He, Corporal Thomas Peters, continued as a machine gunner until badly affected by mustard gas in the trenches east of Arras in March 1918, just before the German offensives started. He did not serve abroad again. He married Sarah Haydock in October 1915 at St James' Parish Church, Leyland, where Ralph and Elizabeth Peters had married in February 1911. Before the War Thomas Peters was solo cornet player in the Leyland Prize Band. A fourth brother, Gunner John Peters RFA, also survived.

16 Platoon's notes, written by Private Morris, named more men who had left than any of the others. One of them was Lance Corporal Angus Adair whom they had heard from and who was "now in Lady Hamilton's Convalescent Home at Motherwell and getting on well." He was a clerk in Glasgow, where his parents Angus and Elizabeth Adair lived in Dennistoun. Already a Lance Corporal and in the 6 February draft, he had been with Left Flank until hit in the shoulder and side in mid June during the trench tour at the Cuinchy brickstacks. At the end of September 1915 he was commissioned into the 9th King's Own Scottish Borderers [KOSB] and later transferred to the Machine Gun Corps. "The platoon has been reinforced, however, by the advent of Sgt Muir and two others, nor must we forget the important member of the canine species who joined us during our first visit to Verquin. "Rabbie" stuck it well in the trenches, and even the bursting of a shell too near for human nerves, left him undismayed." Lance Sergeant John Muir, promoted on 24 July, was a miner until he enlisted in October 1913 and had been in France and Belgium since the start, so far unhit. He was probably posted to 16 Platoon from another one or from another company. His father, also John Muir, lived at Dreghorn, Ayrshire.

On 10 August General Lowther was "Busy all am working out the list of recommendations for honours and rewards. Always a long job, as some battalions recommend everyone for VCs and what not; others won't recommend anyone at all." It was a very hot day. Captain Barne was a member of a court martial on "one of our Sergts for drunkenness at Folkestone when returning from leave, one of our Corporals, a similar offence at Sailly-Labourse, and a man of the 1st Black Watch for disobedience of orders." At noon he walked into Béthune for a hired car to take him to lunch at Wittes with his brother whom he found with only his squadron leader. One man in four had been left "to look after the horses, which look very fit & well, & not too fat." The 20th Hussars were up digging trenches near Ypres. Lieutenant Seymour Barne's mess "is in a very nice farm & his room in another close by, surrounded by meadows & poplar trees, etc, but low down and will be very damp in winter. He says our 2nd Bn passed through the previous day on the way to St Omer & Con Seymour called at the Regtl HQ to see him." There had been much to look at and take in but "Got back about 7 – running over a poor little dog in the last ¼ mile."

B Company were busy on the 11th moving barbed wire out of a Royal Engineers store at a coal mine, loading it onto lorries and taking it to some back trenches. Later Major Orr Ewing and Captain Barne rode over to Château Labeuvrière to visit General Cuthbert, "looking somewhat greyer & fatter than when last I saw him, over a year ago, but very cheery and optimistic." Next morning he "Had my hair cut by Sgt (Piper) Martin, an old soldier of 20 years service – fearful talker – but I am told an extremely gallant man. He is one of the few who have been out with the Battn all the time." Sergeant Piper Alexander Martin had many years service, including the Boer War. Originally from Barrhead, Renfrewshire, he and Frances Martin had five children.

They paraded at half past six that evening to go to the trenches at Le Rutoire, about six miles. At Vermelles the guides from the 1st Gloucesters met them and on they went into the dark. B Company were in the reserve trenches, very scattered and it took till quarter past midnight to get everyone properly settled down. Then Captain Barne and Lieutenant Hammersley went to their dug-out where they found that their servants had got "an excellent meal of cold tongue etc ready – very welcome – stand to arms 2.55am to 3.55am rather a short night & disturbed by rats with which the ceiling of dug-out is infested, one can see their eyes gleaming through the straw, and they send down a shower bath of chips of straw onto one – personally I find the best plan is to put a newspaper over one's head." Lieutenant Hugh Hammersley was another commissioned on 15 August 1914 and another Etonian, in the BEF since mid January 1915. His parents were dead and his nearest relative was a sister, Mrs Post, living in Belgravia. He was with the Battalion till April 1916 when he was sent home sick and did not return.

General Lowther's Headquarters were at Noyelles, where they were greeted on arrival at seven o'clock with a salvo of 150mm shells, which he presumed was an attempt by the Germans to draw retaliatory fire in the dusk in order to help them to locate the British guns from the muzzle flashes. Then "Heard, to my infinite disgust, that I was to leave this Brigade and move over to one in the new so-called "Guards" Division, and am very sad at leaving the battalions I have been associated with for so long (nine months)." On 13 August he got up at five in the morning and set off "round the trenches for 4¼ hours, a walk of eleven miles before breakfast. At 2.50am a tremendous explosion in the German lines, don't know what. Noises at night, guns, rifles and beastly things. Fog when we started on our walk, with a maxim pipping away in the middle of it. Stupid! Found everything very peaceful indeed and enjoyed the walk, except in some of the new, half-dug trenches which are so narrow one can scarcely squeeze through." To Captain Barne these were "quite peaceful trenches, but horrible going round at night, long solitary walks along deserted old German trenches, broken-in dug-outs & goodness only knows how many corpses ½ buried in the various parapets."

The next day General Lowther was out looking at the "Keeps" in the second line and seeing new work under construction in various places. On this he remarked "As soon as (or sooner than) one piece of work is finished there is always other new work invented for us to tackle." He was told that he was to move to his new brigade on the 23rd. "All very depressed at being broken up after our long and happy association." In the trenches the Scots Guards had several visitors from higher headquarters, the main topic of conversation being the Guards Division. Captain Barne noted that "opinions vary as to its desirability – of two things I am certain, (1) that it would be a formidable force for attacking the Germans (2) that if it "takes the knock" there is no 2nd Guards Division to take its place."

On 15 August General Lowther was very much impressed when he went to look at the Vermelles Club, "a coffee bar for soldiers started by one of our chaplains… in the cellars of what was once a big brewery. A fine room with arched roof and red tiled floor. They sell about 40 dozen buns a day there and everything else in proportion. A great success and particularly useful to the Sappers and Gunners, who are hardly ever out of the line and at rest." That night the Scots Guards left the line and the Coldstream came in, but no sooner were B Company back in Vermelles than Lieutenant Hammersley and a hundred men had to go all the way back again to dig trenches. Captain Barne found waiting for him "a beautiful parcel from Violet – containing a cake & other food, cigarettes & writing paper for the men – an air cushion & other useful & welcome things." Meanwhile "The unfortunate Hammersley & party get drenched through & through, return about 2am. Our billet is quite fairly comfortable – all 3 in a small room – my sleep somewhat disturbed because the mice found the contents of my pillow & mattress, consisting of unthrashed barley, very good to eat, so were scuttling about all night – also our peace was disturbed by a battery of howitzers about 200 yds off firing intermittently throughout the night." That day he managed to have "a capital bath in another roofless house." General Lowther met General Haking the next afternoon in Béthune, who told him that he was about to command a corps "so I don't mind leaving the Division quite so much as I did." Throughout the next two days most Scots Guardsmen were on fatigues, sometimes with the Royal Engineers, sometimes digging, and most of the time there was shelling, almost all of it from the British guns, with little retaliation. Some officers went out with fatigue parties, but others had spare time. On the afternoon of the 17th Captain Barne went for a walk with two subalterns and, on returning to Vermelles, met Major Gilbert Popham RFA who invited them to look round his 18 pounder guns and emplacements and "gave us a lecture on the subject of Arty, & fired off a gun for us while we were in an emplacement, which will make me deaf for a week."

Before dinner that day the last three of the original officers of the Brigade Headquarters retired to the Brigadier's room "like naughty schoolboys and drunk our mutual healths on the disruption of the Staff in our only bottle of champagne, as there was not enough to go round at dinner with all the strangers there." It had been raining hard for two days and on the 18th General Lowther went up to the front line, taking with him the senior officers of the 8th Royal Berkshires, who were coming into the Brigade and needed trench instruction. He came back alone and found one communication trench "often nearly up to the knees in water." He got thoroughly soaked. General Haking was going on leave that day and came to say goodbye, handing him a farewell letter when he did so, as well as letters to be passed on to Colonels Ponsonby and Godman. The wording of all three was quite distinct and most appreciative. That to General Lowther began "I am afraid I cannot express my regret at the departure of your two Guards battalions and of yourself and the greater part of your Staff without using many stereotyped terms which sometimes do and sometimes do not convey any real meaning. I know, however, that you will believe me when I say that I am very sorry, and that you will fill in the rest. We have all fought together for many months and your cheery attitude and good fellowship has been of the greatest assistance to me on many occasions when the situation was difficult and the trenches and the weather were worse."

On the 18th Captain Barne recorded "A German shell hit a house, the bag was one horse & 7 rats. In evening back to the trenches, relieving 1st Bn Coldstream, B Coy is right front company this time. A fairly quiet night without incident." The next day "Have a good look round, can see the Germans occasionally looking over their parapets about 600x to 700x away. A certain amount of shelling on both sides – a Corp and 3 men of C Coy are hit by shrapnel – the Corp in 15 places, but not killed. Can hear every night a tremendous racket going on …where we were a fortnight ago; there is perpetual "hate" there. Heard we had 2 poor men blown up or blown in & buried in a mine – they were attached to the RE for mining work. One of them belonged to B Coy." This was near Cambrin. Privates Wilson McLean of Left Flank, just mentioned in the Magazine as having left 16 Platoon, and Patrick McCrae of B Company had been nearly three weeks with the 173rd Tunnelling Company, both of them miners before the War. Private McLean was nearly thirty three at the time he died and Private McCrae just twenty. Both joined up early in September, one in Uphall, West Lothian, the other in Glasgow, and they came to France in the same draft in mid March. Private McLean's family were in Broxburn, where, though his mother Lilian McLean was alive, his married sister Margaret Gibson was his next of kin, and Private McCrae's parents John and Frances McCrae in Shettleston, Glasgow.

On the morning of the 20th while Captain Barne was inspecting the men's rifles "a German shell burst just over the front of our parapet where I was, covering us all, & the clean rifles, with dirt and dust – about the nearest shave I have had so far, as had it come another yard would have been in the middle of us, in the trench." The next day a "good deal of shelling" killed two in Left Flank and wounded two more, as well as two of the 10th Gloucesters, another battalion joining the Brigade, some of whom were in the line "for instruction". One of the dead was Sergeant Blair, the writer and cartoonist, the other Private Frank Hodkinson, a Liverpool policeman before the War, whose parents Frank and Mary Hodkinson lived at Ewloe, Chester. He had arrived first with the large draft at the end of December, been hit on New Year's Day in the right side at the Railway Triangle at Cuinchy and had only just come back. His total time with the Battalion was a fortnight.

That day Captain Cuthbert wrote to his uncle. He started with an assessment of what the Germans were trying to do on the Eastern Front, which he judged to be the destruction of all Russian munition factories within their reach, as well as resupplying themselves from whatever and wherever they could. Then he turned to the Western Front. "We may drive the Germans back to Lille but on the map of Europe that is the thickness of a pencil line. Of course it is a coal district of immense importance to both sides, but when Germany is not pushing she doesn't use much ammunition. I mean by all this that complete success must take a long time in spite of cotton & copper shortage. Therefore such a big war prolonged must cripple all concerned to neutrals' gradual but probably lasting benefit. I can see heavy taxation ahead, very serious hardships for our lower classes out of work, and many companies going bust." Later in the letter he referred to the shelling that morning which had killed Sergeant Blair and Private Hodkinson. "This was to pay us out for a strafe the night before last on the Hulluch Road. We had heard carts coming up every night after dark & we shelled & fired 8 maxims at 9.30pm as hard as we could."

Private Johnes described how the communication trench from Vermelles up to the support and front line trenches at Le Rutoire "started from a point on the SW side of Vermelles, about one hundred yards west of the brow of the ridge and zigzagged in, over the ridge, and down the east slope in the same manner, across the valley and up the west side of Jerries ridge, into the support line at a point dubbed "The Triangle."" One of the front line company headquarters was there and the support trenches ran north and south of it. Most of the time when in the line Privates Johnes and Evans were together with C Company, but once he was sent to B Company with another signaller. They had the job of manning the telephone in a dug-out which "consisted of a slit in the communication trench wall, with poles laid across the top and a couple of groundsheets thrown over to keep out the rain, if any." Then one sunny afternoon when nothing else was going on and Private Johnes was on his own "Jerry decided to obliterate The Triangle and came down with a mixture of heavy ground stuff and shrapnel, mixed with salvos of "Pipsqueaks". I sat alone by the telephone as long as I could. It put me in mind of that ditty "I sat alone in the YMCA singing just like a lark"…In a few minutes enough debris and earth had landed on the dug-out roof to bust it down, leaving me with a dis phone and a shirt full of s---. But my hide was still whole, for which I was truly thankful. I scrambled from under the mess and managed to get hold of the phone which had not been damaged, but the line was shot." He used the word "dis" of signalling or other equipment which was out of order. Very soon after the shelling stopped, while B Company were clearing up in the badly blown in trenches and taking out the casualties, Sergeant Lamond and Private Gammack appeared from Battalion Headquarters in the ruined farm buildings at Le Rutoire, having run the line from there up the communication trench, now quickly back in working order, though it took longer to reconnect the others. Private James "Jimmy" Gammack was from Ellon, Aberdeenshire, where his mother Jane Gammack was still living, and first became a Glasgow policeman but gave that up in 1904 for three years as a soldier. Then he emigrated to Canada and settled in Toronto, where he married May Tew in 1911. On mobilization he returned across the Atlantic, reported on 4 September 1914 and came to France at the end of December.

Precisely when it happened he did not record but it could have been during these trench tours at Le Rutoire that Corporal Watson, of the Royal Albert Dock, promoted in mid June, went out into No Man's Land on patrol. He had no water bottle with him and, when they got back to their trench, a few bays away from where the patrol had started, he was very tensed up, his throat was very tight and he was very thirsty. He grabbed the first petrol can he saw and took a gulp. It was not water. The Royal Engineers had left behind a can of creosote. After this he described himself as "completely mentally & physically exhausted, & frequently collapsed on parades; on marches; and in the trenches." He was invalided home in September. Once fully fit again he returned in April 1916.

On 21 August Major John Hamilton, temporarily commanding the Black Watch, sent General Lowther a red hackle as a memento just before he left, not to take command of the new 2nd Guards Brigade as planned, but instead to become Military Secretary to Sir John French, responsible for the sensitive task of officers' appointments and promotions. He held that post until the end of the year and Sir John French's replacement as Commander in Chief by Sir Douglas Haig, who did invite him to continue, but soon it did not work out. For the rest of the War General Lowther was in England on the Staff of Sir John French, then Commander in Chief Home Forces, and became a Major General.

During the afternoon of the 21st when the Black Watch came to relieve them at Le Rutoire Captain Barne noted that a subaltern in the company taking over from B Company was 2nd Lieutenant Charles Lamb, commissioned in March 1915 and formerly a Company Sergeant Major in the 2nd Battalion. Afterwards they went back to Noyelles, in reserve. There "Hammersley & self share a room, or rather garret, over an estaminet – all the officers mess together, for the first time since I have been out, which is very nice." The next afternoon as they marched to Béthune "the men remarkably cheerful & songful. My Coy is billeted in a Maltings – which we reach at 9.30pm." Then, with the rest of the Brigade still in the line at Le Rutoire, early on the 23rd, a very hot day, they marched away northwest to join the Guards Division around St Omer. As they left Béthune Private Johnes remembered the pipers of the Black Watch and the Camerons playing them out of the town. "It was a bloody heartbreaker to leave the old Brigade, especially the older fellows who had made many pals." Captain Barne noted that they marched past Sir Henry Rawlinson "to the tune of "Auld Lang Syne". Pass through Lillers & have an outspan of 2 hrs for dinners. A beautiful view all round the country from our village (Dollinghem) – have a moonlight walk with Godman after dinner. A beautiful cake, some grapes and cigarettes arrive from home." On the 24th "An early start for a very hot march to Campagne." Their route took them through Wittes and "Quite by chance we put in at Seymour's squadron for an hour's halt, found him… just going out for a ride…so very soon we should have missed him altogether. During the afternoon had a visit from Cavan who commands our Divn & gave us a certain amount of news." As they were marching through another village that day the soldiers billeted there, a squadron of the Greys, turned out and cheered them.

Once they got to Campagne-lez-Wardreques, a little southeast of St Omer, on the evening of the 24th and were settled in Captain Barne went for a walk with Major Orr Ewing and watched B Company bathing in the canal. On the 25th it was again very hot for the "luckily not very long march through St Omer to Tatinghem – a long straggly village. St Omer is a very nice old fashioned Flemish town & fortress." It was still not known who was going to command the 2nd Guards Brigade but on arrival at Tatinghem General Heyworth, now commanding the 3rd Guards Brigade, was there to greet them, with his Brigade Major, Major Roger "Stormy Weather" Tempest. After school at Stonyhurst he joined from the Militia in 1898, serving with the Scots Guards in the Boer War to begin with and then commanding Tempest's Scouts. He had come out in the spring as brigade major of a Territorial brigade and then been sent home sick in early June. His home was at Broughton Hall, Skipton, and he and his wife Valerie had married in 1912.

The Guards Division, commanded by Major General Lord Cavan, consisted of the 1st Guards Brigade, the renamed 4th (Guards) Brigade, formerly in the 2nd Division, comprising the 2nd Grenadiers, 2nd and 3rd Coldstream and 1st Irish Guards, the 2nd Guards Brigade, comprising the 1st Coldstream and 1st Scots Guards, with the 3rd Grenadiers and 2nd Irish Guards joining from England and the 3rd Guards Brigade, comprising the 1st Grenadiers and 2nd Scots Guards, with the 4th Grenadiers and 1st Welsh Guards joining from England. There was an additional pioneer battalion, the 4th Coldstream, with the main task of construction and maintenance work on trenches, forts, headquarters, camps and roads. Every division had a pioneer battalion of infantrymen, who worked with and under the direction of the Royal Engineers and were occupied more as navvies than as soldiers, though they had to be able and ready to fight if needed. Except in emergencies they did not man the trenches. The supporting units mainly came from elsewhere but the 55th Field Company Royal Engineers moved across from the 7th Division and were with the Guards Division continuously.

Notes on Chapter Sources

In Wilfrid Ewart, F Loraine Petre, Cecil Lowther (Eds), *The Scots Guards in the Great War 1914-1918* (London: John Murray 1925) the two corporals are named as Collins and Spence. This Corporal Collins was in the Battalion at the time as was this Corporal Spencer, but there was no "Corporal Spence".

R Clark, *J.B.S.:The Life of J.B.S. Haldane* (London: Hodder and Stoughton Ltd 1968).

Lt L Norman Field Message Pads 1915-16, SGA.

Rowland Feilding, *War letters to a Wife 1915-1919* (London: The Medici Society Ltd 1929).

Only the first two pages of the letter dated 30 May 1915 to Lt Col S Godman about teaching trench construction have survived, the tone and style being as between officers of equal status, so, as it is not Lt Col ABE Cator's handwriting, it must be from Lt Col The Hon WR Hore Ruthven, Godman Papers, SGA.

Diary of Maj M Barne, Private Collection.

Copy letters of Maj Gen R Haking on 18 August 1915 to Lt Col J Ponsonby and Lt Col S Godman in Copy Diary of Brig Gen HC Lowther, IWM/Documents 6388.

The Left Flank Magazine, SGA.

Cuthbert Headlam, *History of the Guards Division in the Great War 1915-1918 Volume I* (London: John Murray 1924).

11

The Battle of Loos – 1st Battalion

The formation of the Guards Division at St Omer

As the 2nd Guards Brigade began to form the 1st Scots Guards were marching into Tatinghem on 25 August and the 1st Coldstream arriving nearby at Lumbres. The 3rd Grenadiers and 2nd Irish Guards had travelled from England shortly before. Next day Captain Barne recorded "Parade at 9.30am and do some drill and a short route march to Wisques, where is a fine old chateau & convent, the latter now a machine gun school." While they were there two 3rd Grenadiers rode up. One was Lieutenant Colonel Noel Lowry Corry, the Commanding Officer, the other Major George Molineux Montgomerie "riding the black mare Annie, or Geraldine which he lent us for so long. In the afternoon, a visit from Alby Cator who commands our 2nd Bn, and Ross the Qmr. We hear that John Ponsonby is to be our new Brigadier… A Company concert in the evening, without a piano; quite a success." Major Molineux Montgomerie's home at Garboldisham, Norfolk, where his wife Sybil and their two daughters were living, was just over the county boundary.

After a day of routine, on the evening of the 27th Captain Barne was at a "3rd Guards Dinner" at the former convent at Wisques, the Third Guards Club being the Scots Guards officers dining club. Thirty eight were there, the most senior being Sir William Pulteney. "After dinner the table was cleared and a reel was danced by those who knew how, as well as by several who didn't." The following morning he marched with B Company to visit the 2nd Battalion at Wizernes. "Took over "cooker", or kitchen on wheels with us, the men – or some of them – bathed, had dinners, saw their friends, the officers had lunch in different messes, and we got back to Tatinghem about 4.30pm." He went for a walk on the 31st with Captain Cuthbert and commented "The threshing & dressing of corn etc in these parts is done by making a horse do "treadmill" – which seems a very simple & economical, if old fashioned method. There is a shoeing smith just outside my billet – their methods are somewhat barbarous – the horse is placed in a small "pen" just his size & the foot to be shod is fixed up and lashed onto a bar – the spare horn & wall of foot underneath is pared off with a hammer & chisel, & apparently too much is taken off & pain evidently caused by the blows of the hammer."

On 1 September there was what was billed as a major divisional training exercise around Wismes, some distance further west. Privately he was scathing. "Called at 3.30am, parade 5am & marched to Wismes…where the whole division we were told was to assemble, some said for inspection by Joffre, some even assured us the King was coming over! We hid (we imagined from Aeroplanes) under fences round an orchard for an hour." Then they moved east as part of a battlefield scenario, passing enroute a number of senior officers, including Lord Cavan, and stopped in a village for two hours for dinners. However "no General Joffre or King tho' we looked behind every bush for them. It rained during the halt & on way home…arriving back at 6.20pm having covered 26 miles, only 1 man of my Compy & 5 of the Battn did not walk in with us, which – considering the men were carrying their packs – was not bad. The boots are getting very bad and a new supply must arrive before we move far. We never saw the rest of the Divn, only our Brigade, though we knew they were also out. Quite pretty country, hilly & in places woods and high fences." By contrast, next day there was more to enjoy at the 2nd Battalion Sports and "Horse Show" at which his brother in the 20th Hussars was particularly successful. Though the 1st Scots Guards won only the Tug of War, the 2nd Battalion managed to come third in the Regimental Jumping Teams [four horses] behind only Headquarters 5th Cavalry Brigade and the 20th Hussars. They beat the Greys and many others. To Captain Barne all this paled into insignificance when "Hear with infinite pleasure that A Boyd Rochfort has been awarded the VC." He recorded on 6 September "Played cricket with Newspaper Correspondents." The day after in a football match for the Regimental Cup the 2nd Battalion won 1-0 and then in a boxing match won every bout except the heavyweight, in which Lance Corporal Charles "The Tiger" Finch, in the 1st Scots Guards for a month, beat a "Corporal Leach" on points. This could have been Private Spiers Leitch, who arrived in France after Festubert. He was a labourer from Greenock who enlisted the previous December as a Regular. By January 1917 he was a Corporal but reverted to Private at his own request in May. On leave in the first fortnight of October 1918 he married Jeanie Lawrie in Glasgow. He survived the War unwounded. Corporal Finch, a town carman from South London, had joined up on 10 August 1914. He was married, but there were no details of his wife. He had been in France since early May.

The signallers were training too and Private Johnes and his colleagues "did a lot of visual signalling practice, and received instruction on the use of the heliograph, which used mirrors as a means of reflecting the sun, to create the necessary flashes. We had several old timers who had served in Egypt, who were experts on the heliograph." This was effective for transmitting messages provided that there were both line of sight and sunshine. On the ranges they "tried out different makes of ammunition and found that some, manufactured in the USA, .303 at three hundred yards, was falling short, it had little killing power." Hitherto no one knew anything about what was in the offing but on the evening of 7 September Major Orr Ewing and Captain Barne were asked to dinner at GHQ at St Omer by Lieutenant Colonel George Paynter, who, having recovered from being shot at Neuve Chapelle, was waiting to command a brigade. "Afterwards was shown some very interesting maps, marked with little flags in every direction." On the 8th there was a brigade exercise. Captain Barne felt that it had more to it than the previous divisional one "rather an interesting day ending up with taking a village at the point of the bayonet. The Prince of Wales… was out, riding about on a bicycle. He looked very young and rather unhappy, and am told he is very shy indeed." The next morning he and B Company did "Company Drill when I learned a good lot. Had not done any for 11 years." In the afternoon he went to see a boxing match between the 1st Coldstream and 2nd Irish Guards. This included an exhibition bout between Corporal Finch "and an Irish Guardsman Harris, who knocked out "The Tiger" in the 1st Round. Our Tug of War Team also pulled [against] the 2nd Irish, who won entirely owing to the unfair ground. We have challenged them again." Private Thomas

Harris, a former ship's steward, volunteered in December 1914 in Leith and joined the Irish Guards. He survived the War.

On the 10th Captain Barne took B Company "on extended order drill, when I think the men are rather astonished by some of my movements, which are original to say nothing else about them. A Presbyterian parson – Capt Gillieson – has arrived & is to be attached to us." The Reverend William Phin Gillieson, recently appointed a chaplain, had been Minister at Ayr. He and his wife Margaret had a one year old daughter. Captain Barne, with Colonel Godman and Major Orr Ewing, rode out on the 11th and visited "the remains of the old Abbey of St Bernard – an old woman told us her house was 900 years old – she looked about the same age – we rode round the farm buildings where found about 40 young women on top of a straw stack, very much hindering the work apparently of the farm men – and much surprised – some amused and some scared – at our sudden appearance." When they got back Captain Barne found that his and Lieutenant Ellis' applications for leave had been granted so they got ready to go early in the morning. The only thing he regretted very much was that his brother was due to come to lunch and "will find me flown."

Private Edward McCann was a butcher in Preston before volunteering the previous November. He landed in France in July 1915 and by this time had already been in hospital once, but rejoined on 5 September, only again to be admitted to a casualty clearing station on the 13th with an undiagnosed mental condition. He was sent to Boulogne, where, on light duties in a mental ward on the morning of the 26th, he was scrubbing the scullery floor. There were two other soldiers in the room, but when one of them moved away Private McCann dived through the open window and fell four floors, dying soon afterwards. Nothing suggested that he might do this and he was classed as "non-dangerous". He married Caroline Pinnington in January 1915 at Ribbleston, Lancashire, and their son was born in April.

Private Morris, having had a dig at Company Quartermaster Sergeant Bertie Lemon in the August Spasm of the *Left Flank Magazine* by asking when they were going to have the long promised currant duff, explained in the Editor's Chat at the start of the September Spasm that it was he who ran the risks for what was published, not the contributors, whose numbers he wished to increase. He illustrated this by alleging that "Our last number was not long published when – Behold! A voice, crying in the wilderness, "What's all this about Currant Duff? Where is that Editor?" Now, the Editor, when he heard, did tremble and was sore afraid, but his friends did conceal him with some overcoats, and he hid himself till such time as the big man, with the big voice, departed, breathing out threatenings and slaughter." Company Quartermaster Sergeant Lemon completed twelve years with the Colours and left as a Sergeant at the end of 1911, but he volunteered for four years on the Reserve and so was called up in 1914. Elizabeth Lemon was living in West Croydon, Surrey, with their three daughters and a son.

In his Company Notes Private Morris reviewed recent events. "Cambrin, as usual, was pretty lively. What with trench mortar bombs and pipsqueaks coming over every now and again, we had to take cover pretty often. "Bobbing" has now become a fine art with us." The days at Le Rutoire and Vermelles had been "just much as usual. With good dug-outs for a sleep by daytime, not too many fatigues, and the "Allemand" pretty quiet, we had rather a good time of it…We were much cut up about losing Sergeant Blair…and that on our last day too. He was a general favourite with us all, very keen on his work, and a thorough sport. We will miss his excellent drawings for the magazine too." They had all been pleased to set off for St Omer "but the last glimpse of Vermelles district would perhaps leave a lasting impression on us. The old places, grown so familiar, looked very pretty in the setting sun, and made a scene not likely to be forgotten in a hurry. Once past the danger zone, and permission given to smoke, etc, our pent up feelings found relief in – we will call it making a noise. "I canna hear the bagpipes" was hardly an excuse for not letting others hear though. By the noise we made going into Béthune, the French must have thought peace had been declared. It was rather an enjoyable march for the next three days, being fresh country, and a nice easy pace. "Auld Lang Syne" was a fitting tune for the band to play as we bid farewell to the First Division, and it was a hearty welcome to the Guards Division which the pipe band of the 2nd Battalion gave us on arrival at St Omer." As they approached the town Corporal Anderton picked up on the instructions "When we march through the town I want you to look happy, even if you don't feel that way" and drew a cartoon entitled "Smiling by Numbers."

Corporal Anderton's notes on 14 Platoon mentioned that Piper James Coventry, after two months off with influenza, had "returned to his old job of "piper". What a great attraction these kilts have." Piper Coventry, a September volunteer, had been a policeman in Lochee, Dundee, and that was what he went back to afterwards, unwounded and posted home in January 1919. Andrew and Mary Coventry lived in Cardenden, Fife. Another who had recently rejoined was Private Arthur Reynolds, a Londoner, who described himself as an indoor servant when he enlisted in late August 1914. He was in France soon after First Ypres but went down with "frost-bite feet" in January and was evacuated home. In the interval he married Effie Scott in May and she was living just off Wandsworth Common. Private Reynolds wrote a poem at the expense of the Army Service Corps, the last two verses being

> To others we leave all the fight,
> We don't like the mud and the fray,
> 'Twould upset us chaps to do such a thing
> For One and a penny a day.
>
> But who will get the praise and cheers
> Whene'er this war is o'er.
> Why, there's no doubt about it,
> The *Army Service Corps*

A clerk in Edinburgh until November 1914, with a sister Mary in Helensburgh, Dunbartonshire, Private Robert Hattle now wrote the notes for 15 Platoon. Remarking on a recent birth "The new arrival is not a prospective Scots Guardsman, but will, we hope, prove in time to be one of those bewitching Scottish demoiselles of whom most of us have tender recollections." He went on with great sadness about the death of Sergeant Blair, whom they had all known much better than Private Hodkinson "his comrade in death, but our sincere sympathy is also extended to all who mourn for him." He continued "It is gratifying to report that Templeton, who was wounded by the same shell, has already returned to duty." Private John Templeton, a mill worker and the son of John Templeton of Galashiels, joined up in September 1914. This wound was the first of three.

In 16 Platoon they were pleased to have back Sergeant Donald Thomson as their Platoon Sergeant. From a crofting family on Flotta, Orkney, he had been a soldier for nearly five years. Although in France from the start, he had tonsillitis during the Retreat from Mons and was sent home. He returned in February, became a Sergeant in June and had another, less serious, attack of tonsillitis only days afterwards. Private Morris remarked that Private Taylor, also of 16 Platoon and contributor to the Magazine, "has turned over a new leaf lately, and surprises us some mornings by being first out of bed."

Private Morris wrote on their local language in France which he called "Soldieranto" and the experiences of two Left Flankers in an estaminet. They had slowly learned that if they wanted sausages with their meal they would first have to go out and buy some from a butcher. Having been to get them, they were handing them to the patronne for cooking when one of them says "Better order some eggs, too, Jock. I could scoff that lot myself." "You order it yersel' then, ye're better at the parley than me. Nae wunner ye're fat, though." "Katter oofs, madame, pan dey berr and café au lait. " Oui, monsieur. Oeufs fri?" "Wee." "That sounds a'richt, onywey, if we're getting the oofs free. "Idiot! Fri is French for fry." "Oh! is it? A didna ken."

The September Spasm ended with another Private Morris poem, "Our Mascot" about Rabbie, first taken on by 16 Platoon in Verquin.

    LOST ------ and ------ FOUND

    Left Flank had a little dog,
    What breed I do not know,
    And everywhere that LF went
    That dog was sure to go.

    It followed to the trenches,
    Though 'twas against the rule,
    When from the shells our chaps were "bobbin",
    The dog remained quite cool.

    When "digging" was the order,
    Our "Rab" was always there,
    Of work, as well as rations
    He always had his share.

    Alas! One day we lost him,
    And searched without avail,
    No more we'll hear his cheery bark
    Or see him wag his tail.

    Unless he turns up smiling
    And takes us by surprise,
    But that is hardly likely,
    At least so I surmise.

    Somewhere in France he's roaming,
    All friendless and alone,
    Following the scent of some cooker

In hopes of a meaty bone.

All tales should end quite happy,
So something I've to add;
This sequel puts the finish
On a story rather sad.

Rab wasn't a deserter,
He'd only changed his corps,
And been with the Northamptons
For quite twelve days or more.

Dramatic was the meeting,
Rab knew his former pals,
And quickly he responded
To the whistles and the calls.

Then, great were the rejoicings,
And frequent were the cheers,
Though others, touched more deeply,
Could scarce restrain their tears.

O'er scenes like these, the poet
Is wont to draw a veil,
So, to be in the fashion,
I'll hereby end the tale.

"Bow-wow!"

At the foot of the page was Corporal Anderton's drawing of Rabbie.

The Battle of Loos

The Battle of Loos was imminent. The British had examined the whole area between Loos and the La Bassée Canal carefully some time before and concluded that it was unsuitable for a major assault. This was partly because it was a built up area of mines, shafts, coalmining villages and other buildings and partly because the Germans were in occupation of naturally formidable features, such as slagheaps. Another factor was artillery observation in that, while the British could see the German front line on the forward edge of the Grenay Ridge and also across northwards towards the La Bassée Canal, they could not see beyond. What was beyond was also outside field artillery range without taking the guns and ammunition forward and so first required at least the capture of the German front line. Sir Douglas Haig continued to believe that more was achievable around Fromelles in order to threaten Lille and its communications. However, because, as initially proposed, this was to be a joint operation with the French, who did not care for the Fromelles idea, it was dropped. The French intended to attack and capture

Vimy Ridge and also at this planning stage to contribute a major effort to the immediate south of Loos itself alongside the BEF. Their purpose was to break into the Douai Plain beyond and force a German withdrawal. Gradually the French composition of the overall operation eroded, particularly the projected effort beside the British, so the British began to question whether they should do anything. Though the French would not have been pleased, it might have been called off were it not for another factor, the pressure that the Germans were then putting on the Russians on the Eastern Front. It was because of this and the protests that the Russians were making about how small the British effort was so far in the War that Lord Kitchener ordered Sir John French to proceed at Loos.

Once that order was given the BEF and, in particular, the First Army, concentrated on making the attack work. One point that had been noted from that year's earlier battles was that when an attack was by only two divisions, as at Neuve Chapelle, the enemy troops and artillery on the flanks had been well placed to intervene. So it was thought that if an attack was on a much wider front it would be harder for the enemy to disrupt it. Hence the plan now was for the First Army's six divisions to attack together from just to the south of Loos up to Givenchy in the north. Much would rest on the first British use of gas to disrupt the enemy defences. Sir John French retained control of the new XI Corps, the reserve formation, under Lieutenant General Haking, consisting of the 21st and 24th Divisions, both New Army, and the Guards Division, to exploit the anticipated breakthrough and overcome any German opposition behind their identified defence lines. At a certain stage command of this reserve would pass to Sir Douglas Haig, but when and how was not determined and Headquarters First Army had no control over how XI Corps approached the battlefield.

On 15 September General Haking had briefed officers and some NCOs of the 2nd Guards Brigade. Captain Feilding was listening as "He spoke very confidently, comparing the German line to the crust of a pie, behind which, once broken, he said, there is not much resistance to be expected. He ended up by saying, "I don't tell you this to cheer you up. I tell you because I really believe it." As he spoke of "pie crust" I looked at the faces around me, and noticed a significant smile on those of some of the older campaigners who have already "been through it."" Captain Barne started back from London on the 20th or tried to, only to learn in the early evening at Victoria Station that all traffic was suspended, so he was told, because of German submarines. That gave him an extra twenty four hours and then "A calm crossing but having to zigzag took 2½ hours over arriving Boulogne 12 midnight." He travelled with Lieutenant Ellis and Lieutenant Guy Armstrong, very briefly in France in the spring before being sent home sick, but back out since May. He went to school at Bradfield and was the son of Charles and Angelina Armstrong of West Byfleet, Surrey. When the Boulogne train reached Wizernes they walked on and learned that the Battalion were to move after dark that day, the 22nd, orders having only just arrived. Marching at night was to avoid being seen by enemy aircraft. Colonel Godman told his stepdaughter that "I expect we are in for a pretty heavy time for some time to come…There is a good deal of news but not much that I can tell you."

The approach to the Loos battlefield

That night they marched five hours to billets at Herbelles, not far south of St Omer. To Captain Barne it was "a pleasant moonlight march," but he was still "pretty glad to get to bed." To Private Johnes "Like the Arabs, we packed our dunnage and silently stole away in the night. We pulled out of Tatinghem in full marching order and headed south. During the night we changed direction east, and towards dawn pulled into an orchard and bivouacked under cover with orders "To stay put and not to move around." Shellfire to the east was heavy." Private Johnes used the maritime word "dunnage" for personal kit and equipment. They stayed all day in billets and set off again at half past six on a longer march for destinations in and near Auchy-au-Bois, west of Lillers, again taking five hours. Private Johnes remembered "Shellfire up front had become very heavy and we knew we were in for something. The weather had not been bad but now it started to rain a bit." Brigade Headquarters noted that soon after the march began there was "Considerable delay at Thérouanne owing to horse falling, and drivers not clearing road at once" and that it was also "Very wet." Captain Barne wrote of "a long slow march (in pouring rain) most of the way to Ligny-lez-Aire, where I turned naked into quite a comfortable bed, window opening onto the bed. In the night a rat entered by the window and woke me up by sitting on and playing with my feet. He soon disappeared out of the window!" It "rained all night but cleared about 9am. To get to my room I have to go through the room occupied by Grandpère and Grandmère. They look so comical tucked up together in bed, with only their funny old weather beaten noses showing. Heard that my brother Seymour is appointed Staff Capt to Gen Pitman, 4th Cav[alry] Brigade. Am very glad as he richly deserves something of the sort, and one hopes he is slightly safer in the event of any big move. In the pm received interesting instructions from CO as to scheme for a general "push" commencing tomorrow and arrange to march 12 midnight, so to bed 4.30 – 7.30 and again at 9.30 making every preparation for long marches with no food etc., then orders come to march 6am and about 11pm an orderly brings me a note saying I am detailed to be a Liaison Officer with XI Army Corps and a motor car will pick me up at Ligny-lez-Aire at 4.45. I therefore have to arrange to be called at 3.20am."

Soon after four on the afternoon of the 24th a message had come of the postponement of the 2nd Guards Brigade's next move because of the congestion in front. At quarter past six on the 25th they set off for Lozinghem, not far away east and due south of Lillers. This took three and a half hours. By then the main battle had started, so there was less need for security from aerial observation and it was now impossible to wait till dark. Private Johnes realised that they were "headed into country that seemed familiar. At one point on the march, Field Marshal French sat on horseback, inspecting the troops as we passed by." Both man and horse were perfectly still and Private Johnes heard someone ahead say quietly but distinctly " "It's Alive" and got the answer "Aye it Moves." The tramp of feet cut the voices." At noon they were on their way again, stopped for dinners at two and got into Houchin, south of Béthune, at half past nine, not having had far to go. The reason it took so long was the congestion. "Great delay on the road as 21st and 24th Divisions were on same road ahead of us and 9th Cavalry Brigade passed through just outside Marles-les-Mines. Very wet and men got little sleep that night." Private Johnes described how "in the rain we had got within range of Jerries batteries and he was trying for the back area roads, once in a while a salvo found its mark. We were climbing a slight hill on the road when the ten minute halt was called, just ahead of us a shell had hit an artillery limber, the crew, horses, and limber were piled on the road, steaming, it was a gory mess. While we were taking our rest, the Prince of Wales and his equerry, heading the same way as us, came up pushing their bicycles, they had to pick their way around the debris. They turned their heads away and plodded on." At Houchin Privates Johnes and Evans and another signaller "found a dry spot in one of the smashed buildings and bedded down together. We generated enough heat in our wet clothes to cook spuds."

On the opening day of the battle the effect of the gas on the enemy was limited and in places it hindered the attackers, while the artillery bombardment, though partially successful, had sufficed neither completely to suppress the enemy infantry and machine guns nor completely to cut their wire. On the southern side of Loos the 47th Division succeeded in taking the large slagheap, the Double Crassier, in front of them and established a firm base on the southern flank. Their neighbours on the left, the 15th (Scottish) Division, New Army, were equally successful in clearing the German front line on the Grenay Ridge, captured a defensive complex called the Loos Road Redoubt and were fortunate to find the well constructed German second line on the reverse slope behind it unoccupied. Beyond the Grenay Ridge the ground fell away into another shallow valley in which lay Loos, with more open ground to the north. Beyond Loos the ground sloped up again onto a ridge higher than the Grenay Ridge with the Lens-La Bassée road running along it. Hill 70, due east of Loos, was the highest point. A short distance to the north downhill along the road were a mine shaft and accompanying buildings and chimney called Puits 14 Bis [Pit 14A], on the near side of the road and two woods, Bois Hugo behind the pit and Chalet Wood southeast of it, both on the far side of the road. Both woods were out of sight at ground level. Further on still on the near side of the road were a quarry and a small thin wood, the Chalk Pit and Chalk Pit Wood. After they crossed the German front line and took the Loos Road Redoubt the 15th Division, beginning to lose direction and having suffered severely, headed to their right for Loos, by now coming under enemy shellfire, still with some Germans and some French civilians in it. Instead of taking on the objectives on the next ridge line and the Lens-La Bassée road, those still standing all made for Hill 70. They took it, did not stop to consolidate, but streamed on, veering further to their right, by then very disorganised. The Germans stopped them beyond and drove them back. So it was that the enemy soon re-established themselves on the east side of Hill 70 in the redoubt and trenches they had constructed there, well placed to give enfilade support to north and south and with weapons sited so as to make it impossible for any attacker to get over the skyline to their front. By darkness on the 25th the situation on the slopes west of Hill 70 was very unstable, but the Germans did not press it.

South of the Vermelles-Hulluch road the 1st Division, suffering very heavy casualties, cleared the German front line on the Grenay Ridge and finished up level with the 7th Division on their left, short of the Lens-La Bassée road, somewhat spread out and very weak in numbers. North of the Vermelles-Hulluch road the 7th Division, also suffering very heavy casualties, captured The Quarries and their right hand brigade reached the Lens-La Bassée road but had to pull back. Next to the north, however, the 9th (Scottish) Division, New Army, though they lost heavily, took the Hohenzollern Redoubt and most of the trenches beyond it and got into the mining village, Corons de Pekin, and the mine buildings there, Fosse 8. Insufficient support came up and they were partly forced back by counterattacks, but still held much that they had captured to begin with. At the very northern end of the attack the 2nd Division, advancing from south of the Béthune–La Bassée road and from either side of the La Bassée Canal around Cuinchy and Givenchy, had made no useful progress at all, returning to their front line after heavy losses.

That was the broad picture at the end of 25 September. The Germans had fought well, many of their defences, machine gun posts and entanglements were largely unaffected by the British guns and their own guns had been little interrupted. Now they reacted quickly, reinforcing and consolidating their line. From then on in the southern half of the battlefield they concentrated on preventing any loss of ground to the east of the Lens-La Bassée road, thus obstructing

British observation over what lay beyond and maintaining their own observation westwards, only marginally impaired by the loss of the Grenay Ridge. However, in the northern half, beyond the Vermelles-Hulluch road, they began to make every effort to recapture what they had lost and during the night recaptured The Quarries.

The Château Philomel, which General Lowther had had as his Headquarters earlier in the year, became Sir John French's Headquarters at short notice just before the battle and when he moved in he had no telephone link to Headquarters First Army. Given cumulatively the very poor communications, the lack of awareness at all levels of what was going on and the much larger than anticipated problems for the divisions already on the battlefield of relieving exhausted battalions, sending up fresh ones, ammunition, food and water and evacuating very large numbers of wounded, had it been possible to put XI Corps or even the leading division onto the battlefield on the afternoon of 25 September, it might have made no difference. If Sir Douglas Haig was to be able to use these divisions as an exploitation force they needed to be available to him, but they were not in the battle plan in such terms. They remained under Sir John French's control until he decided to release them. There were also the problems that had arisen from moving the three divisions by one route, compounded by the heavy rain.

The 21st and 24th Divisions, their men exhausted, hungry and soaked, were not physically in the right place to take part until the 26th. Some of their brigades were then either put to work with the 7th Division in the area of The Quarries or to shore up the area nearer Hill 70, another attack on which failed. At 11am the remaining brigades of both Divisions went into action for the first time against the line of the Lens-La Bassée road and across it, respectively broadly in front of where the 1st Division had reached the day before and where the 15th Division should have cleared up to instead of all converging on Hill 70 and beyond. On the right the two brigades of the 21st Division were stopped short of the road by machine guns in and around the woods on the far side near Puits 14 Bis. On the left one and a half brigades of the 24th Division crossed the road and were mown down on the flat ground beyond from German positions which ran in a semi circle and also from the two woods, Chalet Wood and Bois Hugo. If there had been an exploitable opportunity, even quite limited, on the 25th in the southern half of the battlefield there no longer was next day.

As arranged, early in the morning on the 25th Captain Barne got "a large mug of coffee from my landlady and walk off to Ligny-lez-Aire with my "little-all" on my back, feeling very sore at leaving the Coy and the Battn. Some breakfast with the CO and Norman Orr Ewing, who are good enough to express their surprise and regret at my going, then a car arrives and am confronted with no less a person than HRH Prince of Wales which sets me wondering what I am in for, two other officers with him. We reach Noeux-les-Mines about 6am, the Headquarters of the XI Corps, where I find Gen Haking and his Staff. Bid Adieu to HRH, who is very shy and was terrified of going into Haking's room, and am sent off to the IV Corps under Rawlinson at Vaudricourt." There he reported to Brigadier General Archibald Montgomery, the GSO1. "It is rather alarming, nothing but Generals including one Buckland who is quite original and amusing… My job is practically nil, only to see that information and reports are sent on to the XI Corps. The working of the Staff is very interesting, but it is no place for me and I long to be back with the Battalion. The details of the day are better taken out of the Papers and Official Reports – a day let us hope which will mark the turning point in the war. I walk down to see a big batch of German prisoners, some look very young, all very tired and hungry and dirty." He began to find his role pointless as all information of importance was passing to XI Corps by telephone or telegraph, though it was interesting to hear first hand news and see interesting people, including Sir Douglas Haig. He saw some friends when the 3rd Cavalry Division went through and more when the 9th Cavalry Brigade turned up, who "bivouac close by and make free use of Sir H Rawlinson's Huts and Tents and any food or drink they can lay their hands on. It is a dreadful night for those fighting and the Divn which is digging itself into Hill 70 must be suffering many discomforts. So far the Guards Divn is still in "general reserve" under Sir J French. This is the one point which gave me comforting thoughts." Captain Barne woke on the 27th resolved to try to get back to the Battalion and was "confirmed in that when "the New Army" not being as successful as one hoped in the attack, I hear that the Gds Div is to be brought up, so I beg Gen Montgomery to get me sent back and he does so. At 1.30pm off I go in a motor car and am lucky in hitting off the Battn not far off."

The 2nd Guards Brigade had stayed put to begin with on the 26th and only moved forward at two through Sailly-Labourse and Vermelles towards Le Rutoire with the rest of the Division. That took five hours. After Vermelles and its ridge Private Johnes found they were "heading across old familiar ground but what a difference." In the dip where the east slope from Vermelles met the west slope of the Grenay Ridge were "crowded" British six and eight inch guns, while further forward were the eighteen pounders and field howitzers of the RFA. All were in action. There were a lot of troops about as well. At Le Rutoire Captain Feilding of the Coldstream found "The road and ruined courtyard of the farm were crammed with wounded and dead men. No one seemed to know what was happening in front. Some people were optimistic. Others, the reverse." Sent forward to reconnoitre with another officer he "crossed our old front line and No Man's Land – here about 500 yards wide – past the Lone Tree to the German trenches. The ground was strewn with our dead, and in all directions were wounded men crawling on their hands and knees. It was piteous, and it is a dreadful thought that there are occasions when one must resist the entreaties of men in such condition, and leave them out in the cold and wet, without food, and under fire, as they often have to do for days and nights together." The Brigade waited in the open for most of the night near Le Rutoire and then had to take over the old German front line on the near side of the Grenay Ridge, but not till the small hours of the 27th. Digging had to be done at once to adapt the German trenches to face the other way. The 1st Scots and 2nd Irish Guards were respectively on the right and left, the 1st Guards Brigade beyond them to the north and the 3rd Guards Brigade in reserve along the Vermelles-Auchy railway line. Captain Feilding found the German trenches "very like our own. The barbed wire entanglements in front of them were, however, far more formidable than our's. These formed a regular maze, and how our men got past them is a mystery. The ground was littered with German rifles, and bayonets, and bombs, and equipment of every sort. The air still reeked of gas, which clung to the ground and made our eyes smart; and every now and then a shell came crashing over from the other side, or a flight of machine gun bullets made us bob."

Privates Johnes and Evans were together and had seen a few German prisoners, but nothing else of the enemy so far. "George and I had tagged onto Left Flank…up the ridge… Jerries old defences…had taken a terrific pounding and were almost obliterated, they were mostly shell-holes. There was an immense number of dead Jerries and some of our's, scattered around. We appeared to be lining up along the top of the ridge and came to a halt in that position facing east. We stayed that way for some time and George and I selected a dry hole and flopped into it. We must have gone to sleep as we woke up hearing somebody talking, one said to the other "Look here at these two isn't it a shame." I guess they thought we were dead."

The attack on Puits 14 Bis and The Keep

By the 27th the enemy were thoroughly established at Hill 70 and had fortified the pit buildings at Puits 14 Bis. They may not have been occupying the Chalk Pit and Chalk Pit Wood but had these well covered. Any British idea of a conclusive breakthrough had disappeared, but tactically the capture and holding of the line of the Lens-La Bassée road would secure an advantage, not the least of which would be eliminating German artillery observation from it and perhaps making it possible to bring forward the British field guns to the neighbourhood of Loos. By now the only uncommitted British infantry were the Guards Division, to whom could be added dismounted cavalry brigades, but only to hold trenches. The Guards Division's unreconnoitred and unrehearsed task that day was to take and hold the line of the road, but without crossing it. Over to the left the 1st Guards Brigade were to advance up to where the 1st Division had reached on 25 September and secure it by digging in thoroughly and ensuring that there was a continuous trench system. The task of the 2nd Guards Brigade was to capture the Chalk Pit, Chalk Pit Wood and Puits 14 Bis. On 3 October General Ponsonby wrote his report. Following a heavy artillery bombardment the Irish Guards, supported by the Coldstream, were to take the Chalk Pit and Chalk Pit Wood, after which they were to support the Scots Guards when they attacked Puits 14 Bis. The Grenadiers were to be ready to move up behind the Scots Guards. "From where I issued my orders to Battalion Commanders one could plainly see on the other side of the valley, the Chalk Pit and two ruined houses. A small narrow Wood runs South West from the Pit, and further South stands the Puits, a prominent looking building with a high chimney. Close to the Puits and nearer to the Wood stands a smaller red house known as the Keep. To the right is Hill 70 which is practically on the sky line as one looks at it from Loos. A road passes along the top of the hill which is lined with trees, with a few houses scattered about." Hill 70 was not one of their objectives.

Privates Johnes and Evans, waking on the 27th, found that they had lost Left Flank, but went on, locating them in a German trench that ran northeast at the northwest edge of Loos "all of which was a shambles." This was probably the old German second line, unoccupied on the 25th. The two of them had no idea what was going on and, having been told to stay put, did so. "The question was "Where in Hell is Jerry?" Answer "Who in Hell knows." George and I scooped out a comfortable position in the bottom of a trench, with the belly of a nice bloated Jerry for a pillow." Sir Victor Mackenzie found them and told them to remove it at once. Except for some firing further away to the north and southeast "There was no rifle or machine gun fire, no Jerries in sight." But off to the east they could see Hill 70 and some buildings including one which Private Johnes thought might be an estaminet, possibly with a machine gun post in it. Nearby in Loos were buildings which "apparently had been a German Headquarters. They were all well tunnelled and reinforced with cement, below ground, above they were blown to bits." Overlooking everything was Tower Bridge though Private Johnes had another name for it. "The Twin Towers rose in the town from the bottom of the valley."

In theory there was a lot of artillery support available to the Guards Division, but there was no concentration of fire on the enemy positions to be attacked. The 2nd Guards Brigade attack began at four in the afternoon, with artillery fire lifting at that time from the Chalk Pit area, lifting from the Puits twenty minutes later and lifting from Hill 70 half an hour after that. So the Irish Guards began their attack as the artillery lifted from their objective, thus exposing them to the enemy at once as they approached. The Scots Guards were to begin their attack on the Puits as the Irish Guards captured Chalk Pit Wood, not at a set time. They started therefore at half past four, ten minutes after the guns had ceased firing onto the Puits, thus also exposing them to the enemy at once as they approached. While taking the Chalk Pit area ahead of attacking the Puits had a tactical logic, the attacks on the Puits and Hill 70 were not simultaneous.

The Irish Guards succeeded in taking the Chalk Pit and Chalk Pit Wood in a hard fight. Private Johnes and Left Flank were told at three in the afternoon "to prepare for attack and to sight our rifles for 1000 yards." When the Scots Guards went forward to assault the Puits at half past four in the afternoon they had to cover about fifteen hundred yards to reach their objective, advancing in extended order and doubling down the slope on the east side of the Grenay Ridge, with Loos over to their right. Although heavily shelled with shrapnel they reached the minor Loos-Hulluch road at the bottom of the slope with few casualties. Once they had linked up with the Irish Guards on their left at the Chalk Pit Wood they went on towards the Puits. General Ponsonby continued "At this moment, the Companies emerging from the Wood and up the slopes of the Hill came under a terrific fire from the enemy's Maxim Guns which were in concealed positions in Bois Hugo and in the Keep and Puits." The German machine gunners had waited until they were within four hundred yards, though because of the lie of the ground many would probably not have been able to see anything earlier. A lot of Scots Guardsmen were hit but "The Puits had been practically won and a small party under Captain JH Cuthbert DSO were fighting hand to hand with the Germans round the houses." The Brigadier sent up two 3rd Grenadier companies to help but most were unable to reach the Puits because of the machine guns. One platoon did get there and, using grenades, put a machine gun on the second floor of the Keep out of action. Between them they held on for some time "until practically no one was left, and no support could be pushed forward owing to the enfilade Maxim fire."

Private William Scott, in France since April, was a carter and the son of Alexander and Margaret Scott of Milnathort, Kinrossshire. At his first medical examination when he enlisted in Lochgelly in August 1914 it was noted that the little toes of both his feet curled over the toes next to them. He was hit early on. "It wasn't a hill as we call hills. It was simply a piece of rising ground and it was sufficient for the Germans to be looking down on us…We were crossing a sunken road just before the start of the rise. I got a bullet in the chest." He did not know whether he had been unconscious but "I was spitting blood for a while after this bullet hit me but there was no sign of a bullet. Just a little hole in the chest…I think it had been a spent bullet. After all it would be 1000 yards from where the Germans were, I think." There was still no sign of a bullet when he was X-rayed at a casualty clearing station, but next he developed trench fever in a Base hospital and remained there till he recovered. Back in the Battalion after that, in the middle of May 1916 he had a shell wound in his left arm in the Ypres Salient and was sent to England. In August 1917 he returned again, became a signaller because he knew Morse Code, but never had to use it, and remained with them till they went home from Cologne.

Privates Johnes and Evans followed when "The Bayonet men went over and we went with them in open order. When stretched out on the slope it was a thin line. The going was easy and we took it on the walk looking for any possible traps, Jerries, hidden amongst the dead or in shellholes. At first there was no shell or machine gun fire from Jerry, but it soon started and picked up, we got laced with shrapnel and some ground stuff, fellows began to drop, machine gun fire traversed the line with bullets chugging into fellows and whining past and into the ground. My side kick and I started to go ahead in short runs and dropping to the ground to try and get the location of Jerries machine guns. Our line was getting thinner." The building he had been able to see earlier and had thought was probably an estaminet, but was almost certainly The Keep, contained, as he had anticipated, a German machine gun post. "We were losing a lot of men getting close to the brow of the hill and we veered off towards the copse on our left front, it looked like it was good for cover. Jerries machine guns were cutting the ridge from the east side, traversing backwards and forwards along it, out of our sight, we could not get a shot at them. Some of our fellows were already starting to dig in just below the ridge and we joined in with them. It was dusk beginning to get dark, Jerries shelling had zeroed in on the ridge, together with the machine gun fire, to try for the ridge we would be sitting ducks in the sunset…There were still a few wounded chaps lying out from the previous two or three days fighting." There was no sign of any support and they knew that there were very few officers left, having heard also that Captain Poynter had been wounded early on.

"Our field telephone was useless without a line connection, and visual signalling was out of the question." Then a little after dark two signallers arrived from Battalion Headquarters. They had been trying to lay a line but had run out about half way down the Grenay Ridge. However, they could pass on orders to Privates Johnes and Evans to return as there was no point in their staying out until there was more line. At Battalion Headquarters Sergeant Lamond told them "to get our rations and try for some sleep. We decided to try for an upstairs apartment in a not too busted up house, and after eating and getting a rum ration we located a bed with a straw mattress in the second floor of a building. It was full of fresh air and we managed to get to sleep. About half an hour later the wall on the southeast corner of our bedroom got trimmed off by a Jerry shell and the floor above started to crumble away. We landed down below in what had been the front garden or something."

Captain Barne recorded "At 3pm, after much trouble about men's tea, rum and water, we advance to the attack over ground on which others had failed, passing and finding many gruesome if natural and typical battlefield sights. Are in support of the 1st Gds Bde who advance and we sit in another trench (in support) getting pretty well shelled, though, as a Gunner Col remarked "the German Gunners are losing their nerve and making very poor practice." We bury several dead and at 4.30 the attack proper begins, over a horribly open and bare space onto Hill 70 Loos, which Sir Douglas Haig says is of such immense importance. It is a redoubt heavily entrenched and surrounded by masses of barbed wire. A tremendous cannonade precedes the attack, an awful din. The Battn is in support and my Coy a nominal sort of reserve, anyhow, luckily for us, we go in last, getting heavily shelled as we go. All appears to go well at first, practically the whole Guards Div is launched, but the leading portions come suddenly under tremendous machine gun fire at close range, the Officers in our Brigade begin to disappear, the men, finding themselves without leaders, are at a loss to know what to do and turn. My Coy meet them and do what we can to bring them round. The Irish Guards have some offrs left and recover, also many of our Battn and some Grenadiers (I know not about Coldstream). We then under Col Butler, advance to a certain wood and entrench, which we do after dark." Later he remembered and added that early on in the day "two Germans were found in a small dug-out where we were halted, old German line, busy telephoning back to their own HQ, brave men, they were hauled out and shot which I thought unnecessary." Lieutenant Colonel The Honourable Lesley Butler commanded the 2nd Irish Guards. Captain Barne was wrong, but very understandably, about Hill 70 being a 2nd Guards Brigade objective.

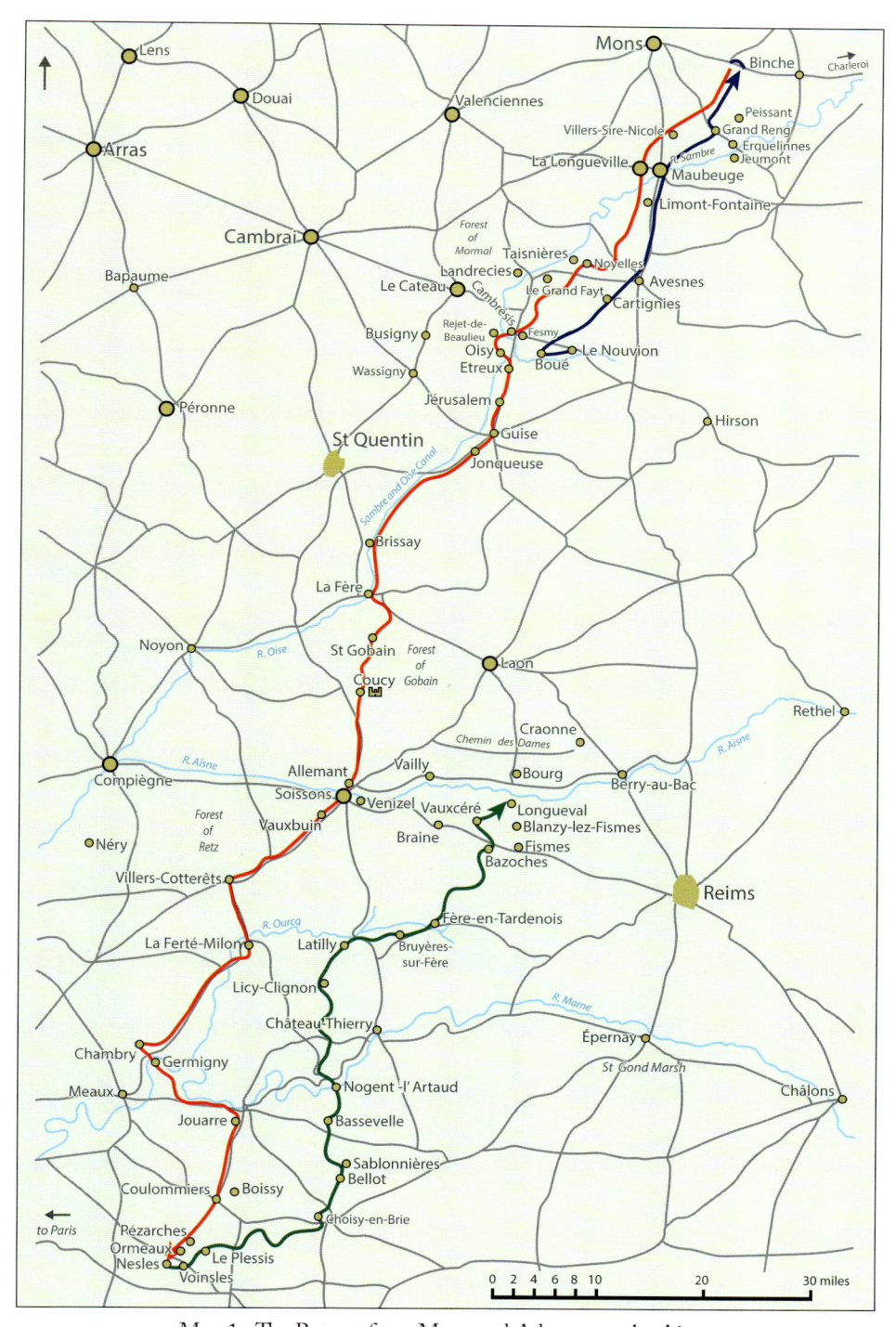

Map 1. The Retreat from Mons and Advance to the Aisne

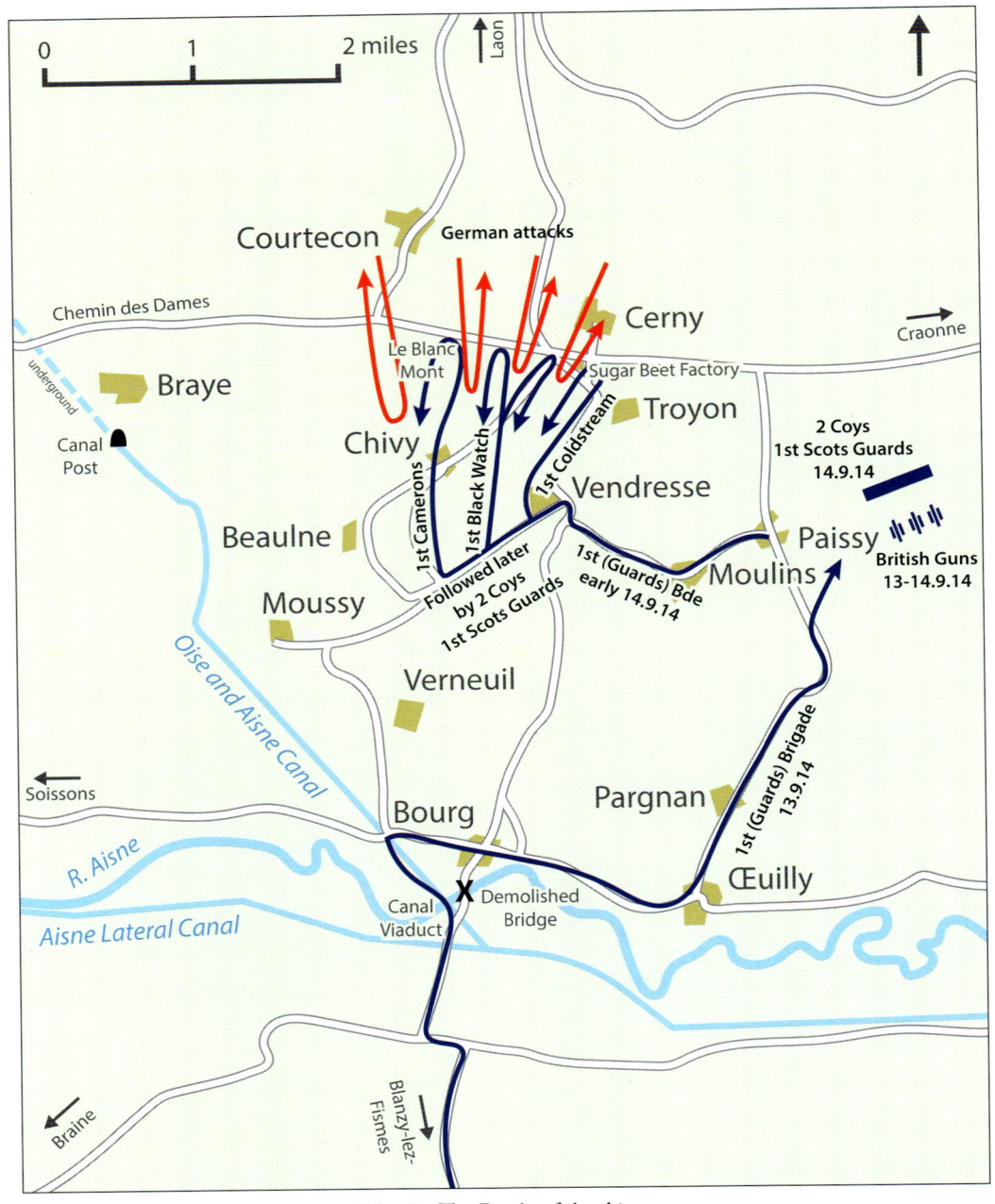

Map 2. The Battle of the Aisne

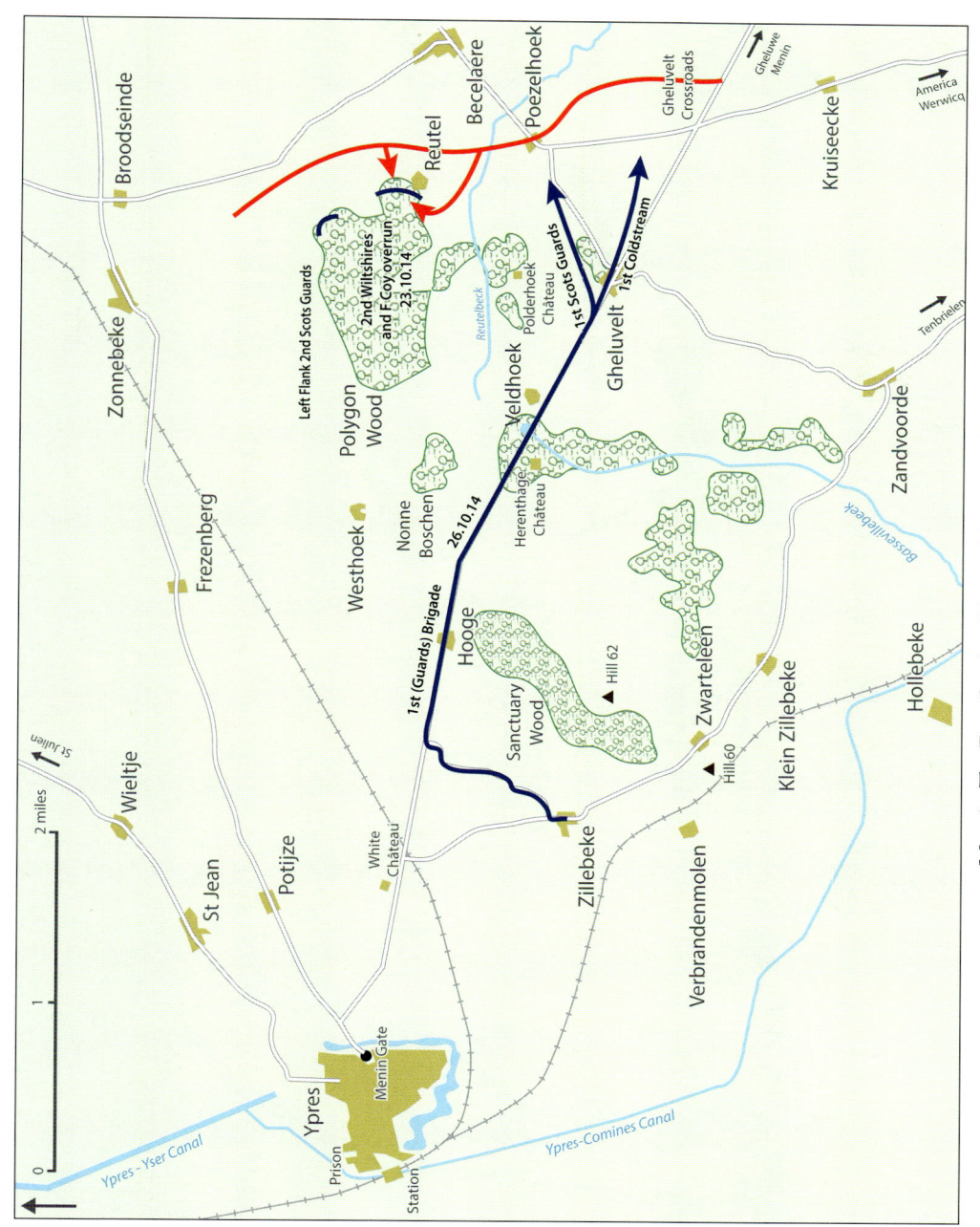

Map 3. The First Battle of Ypres – The Menin Road

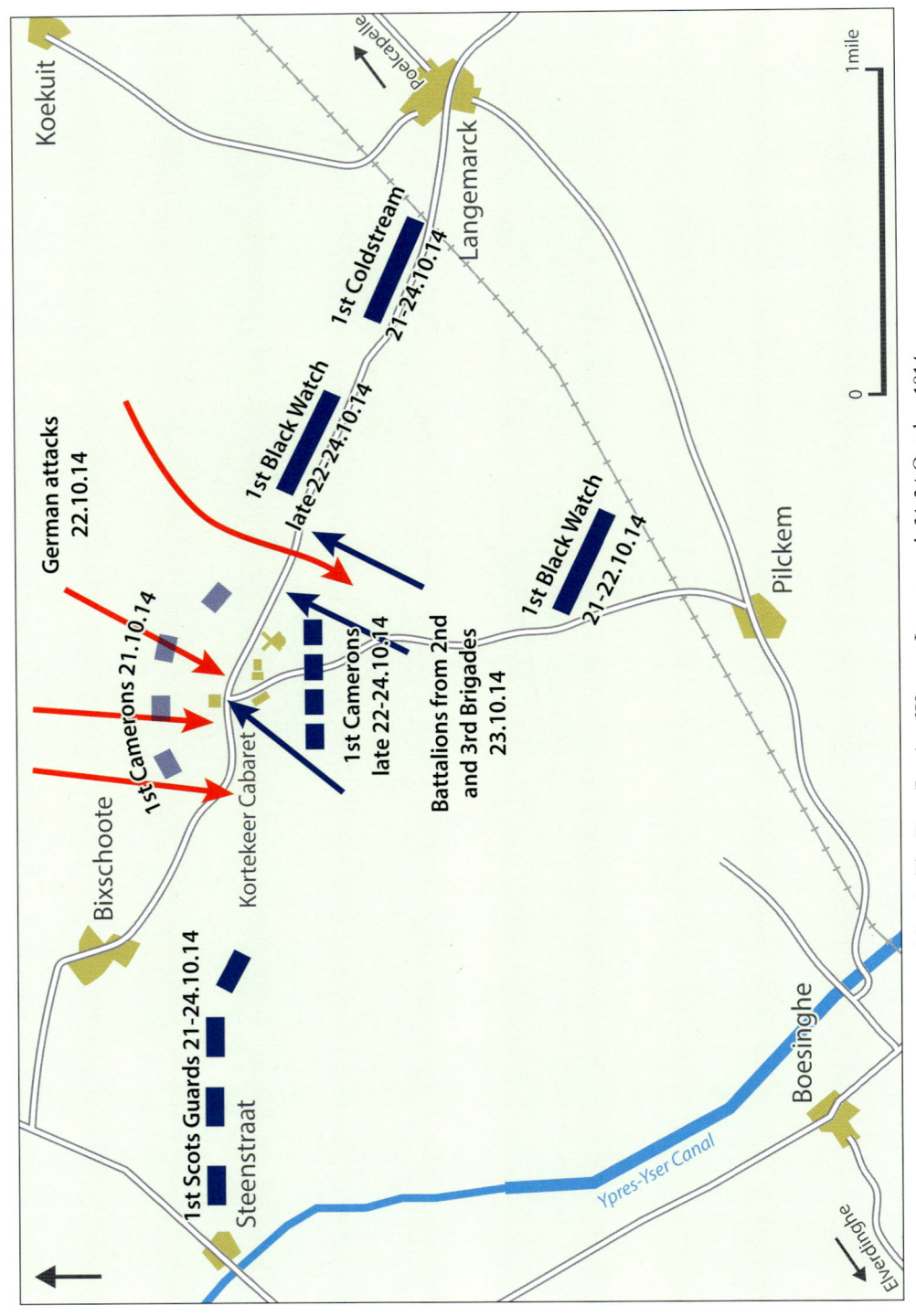

Map 4. The First Battle of Ypres – Langemarck 21-24 October 1914

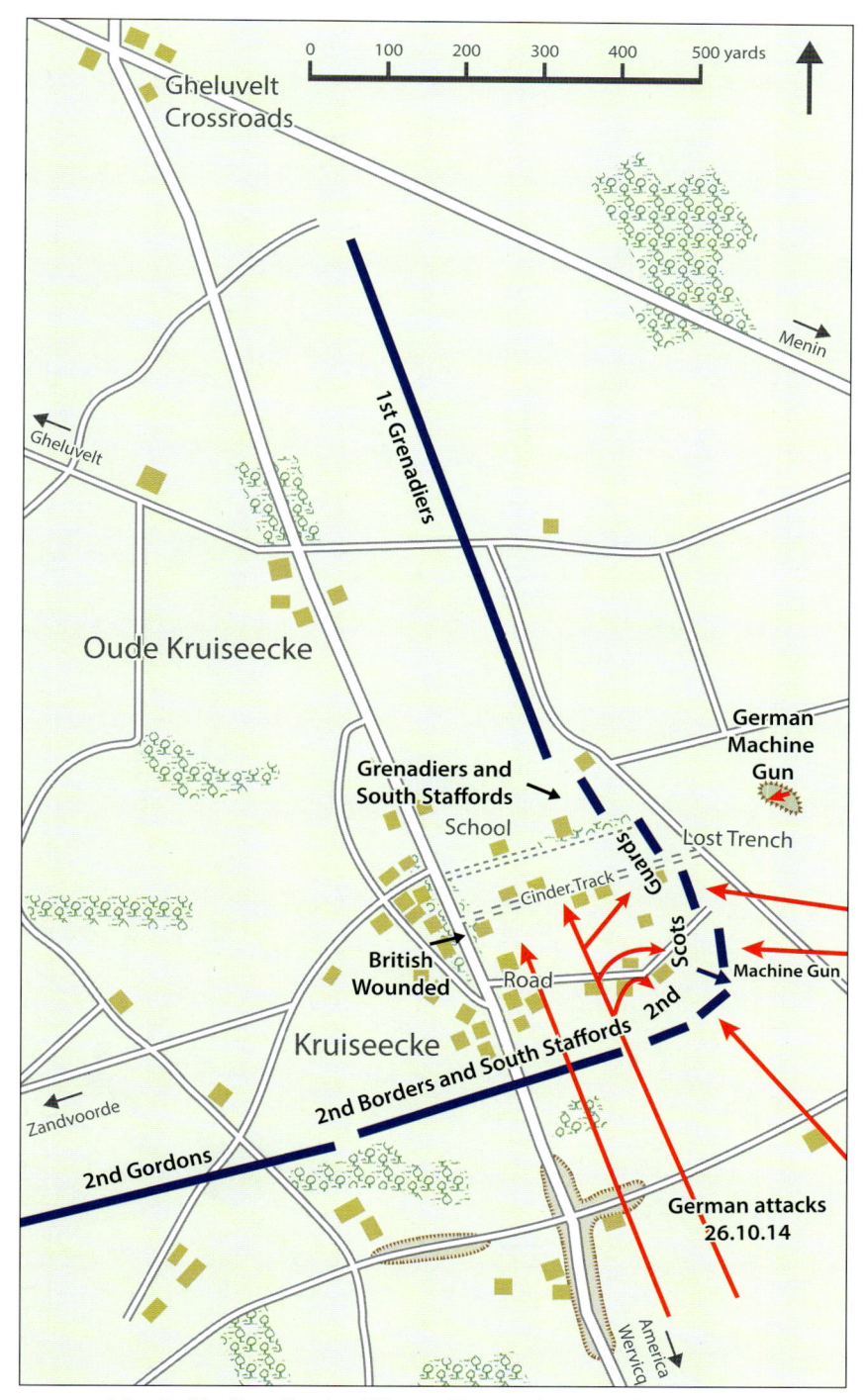

Map 5. The First Battle of Ypres – Kruiseecke 25-26 October 1914

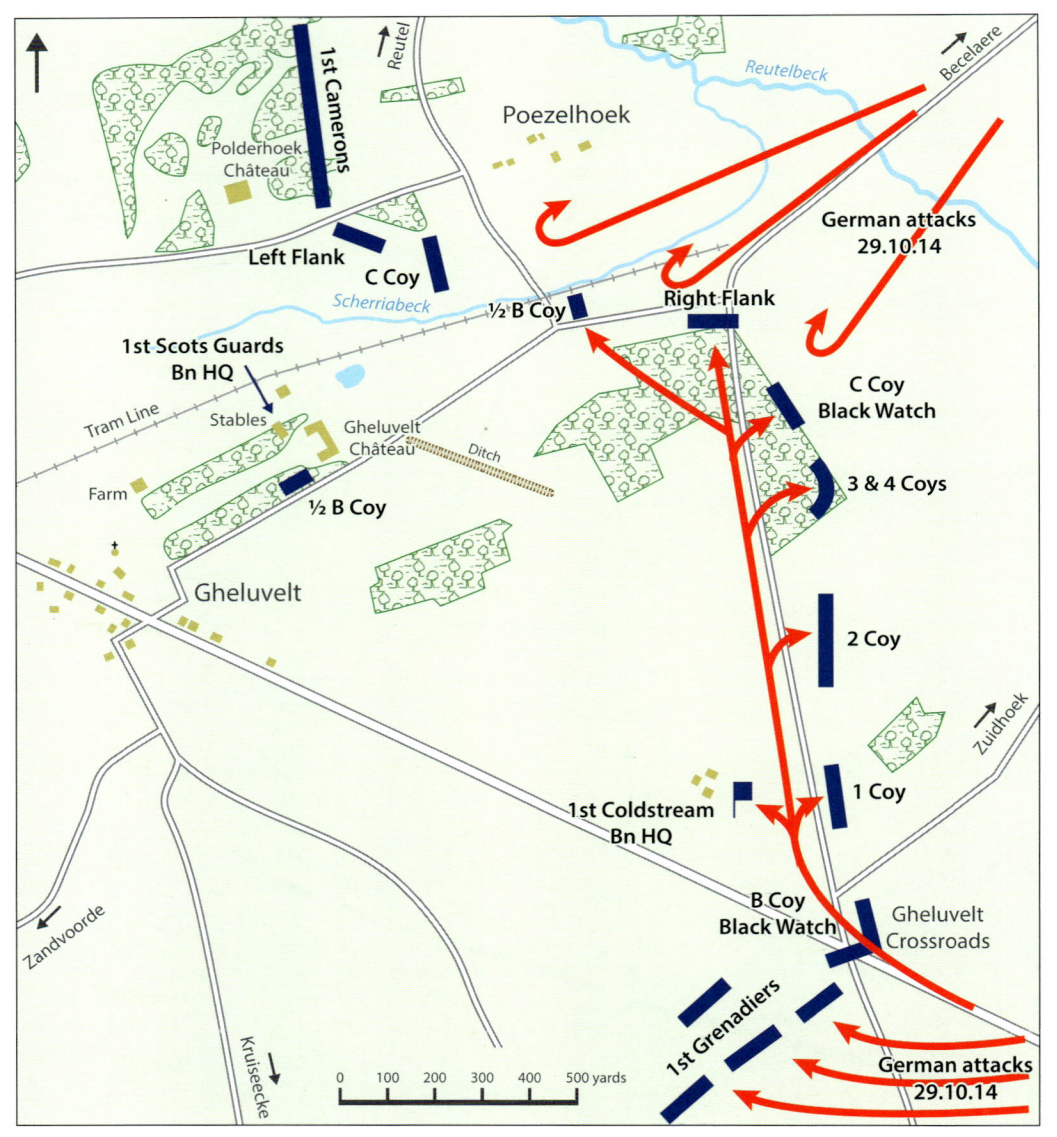

Map 6. The First Battle of Ypres – Gheluvelt 29 October 1914

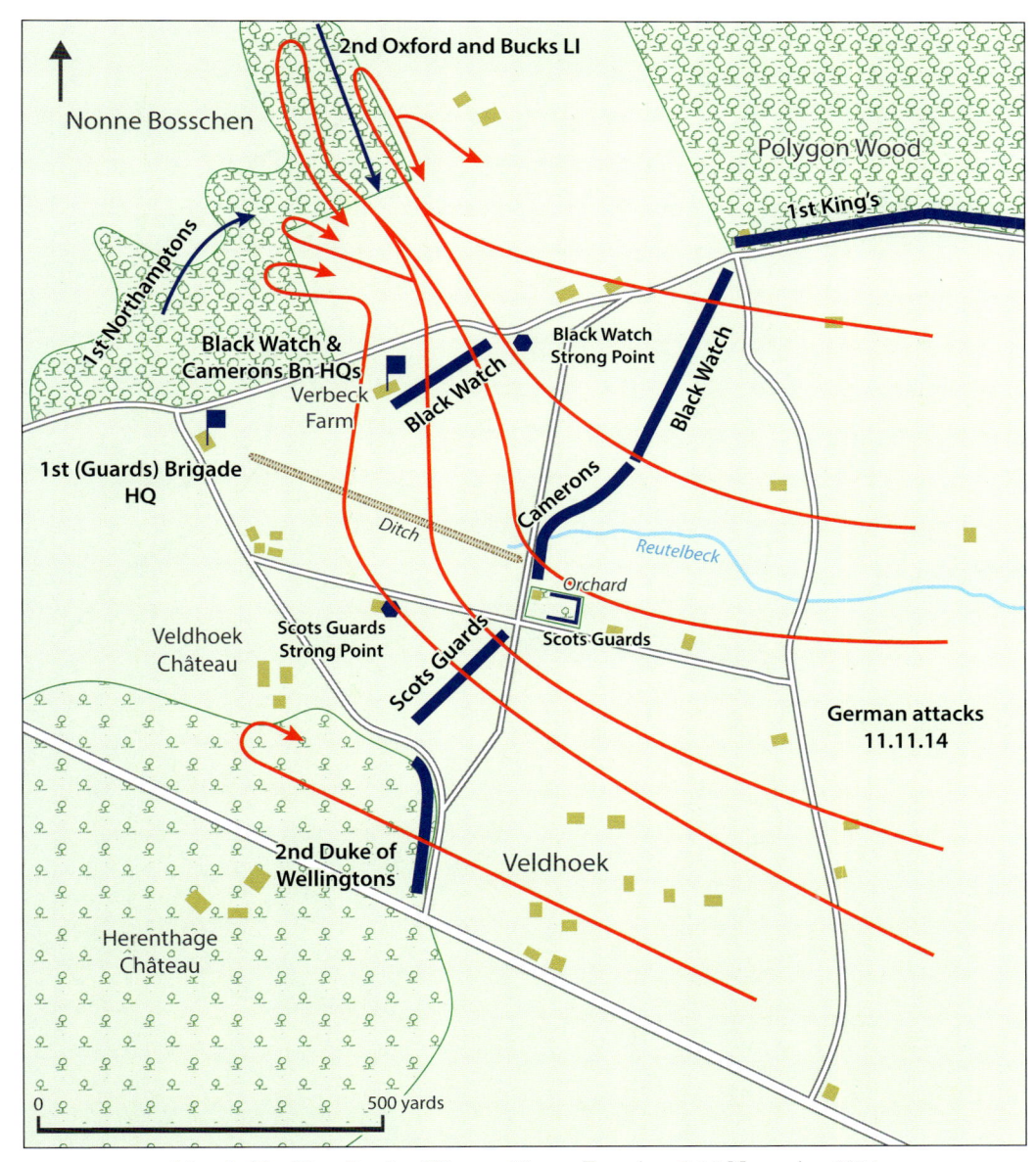

Map 7. The First Battle of Ypres – Nonne Bosschen 3-11 November 1914

Map 8. The Rouges Bancs Trenches – Winter 1914-15

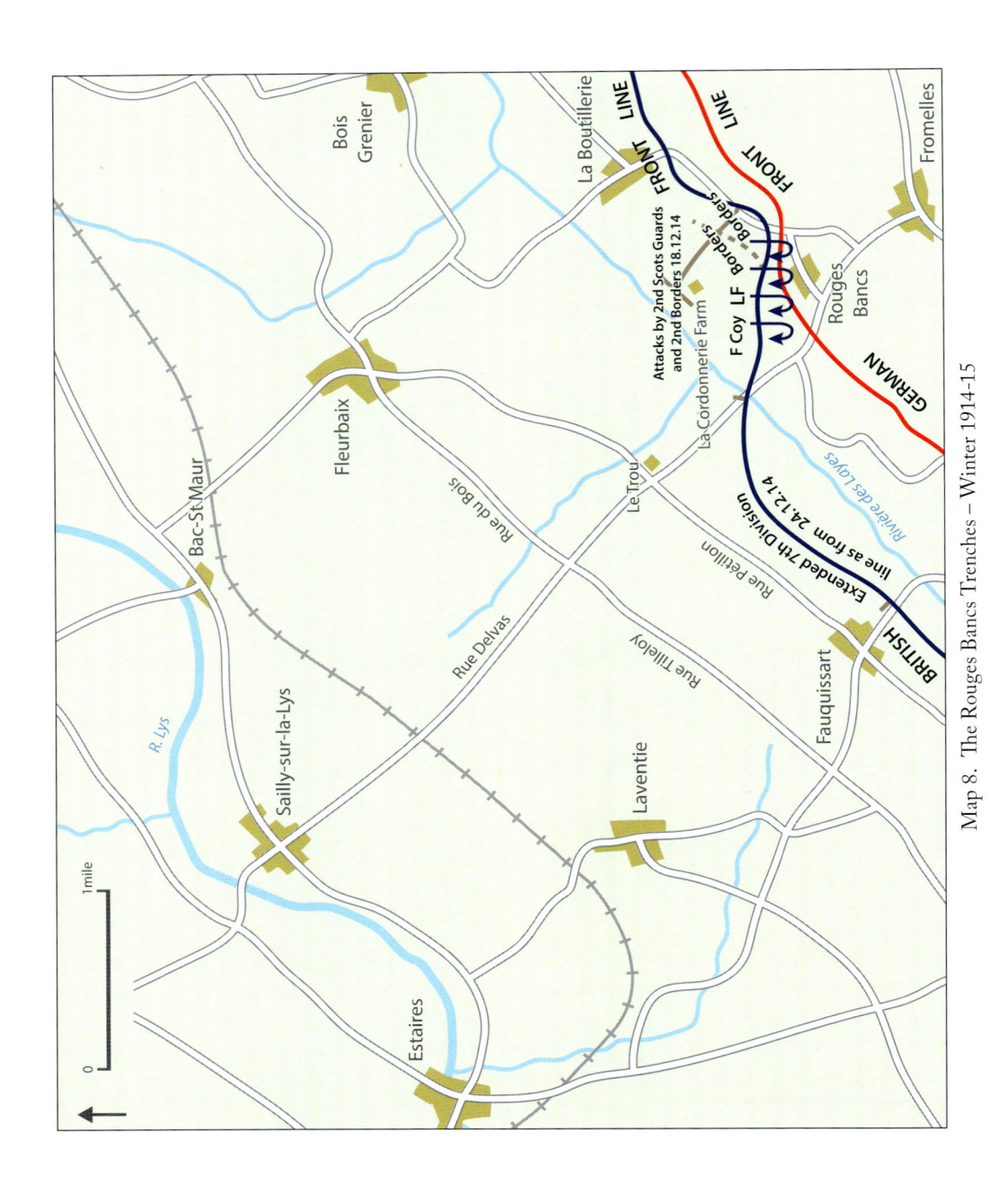

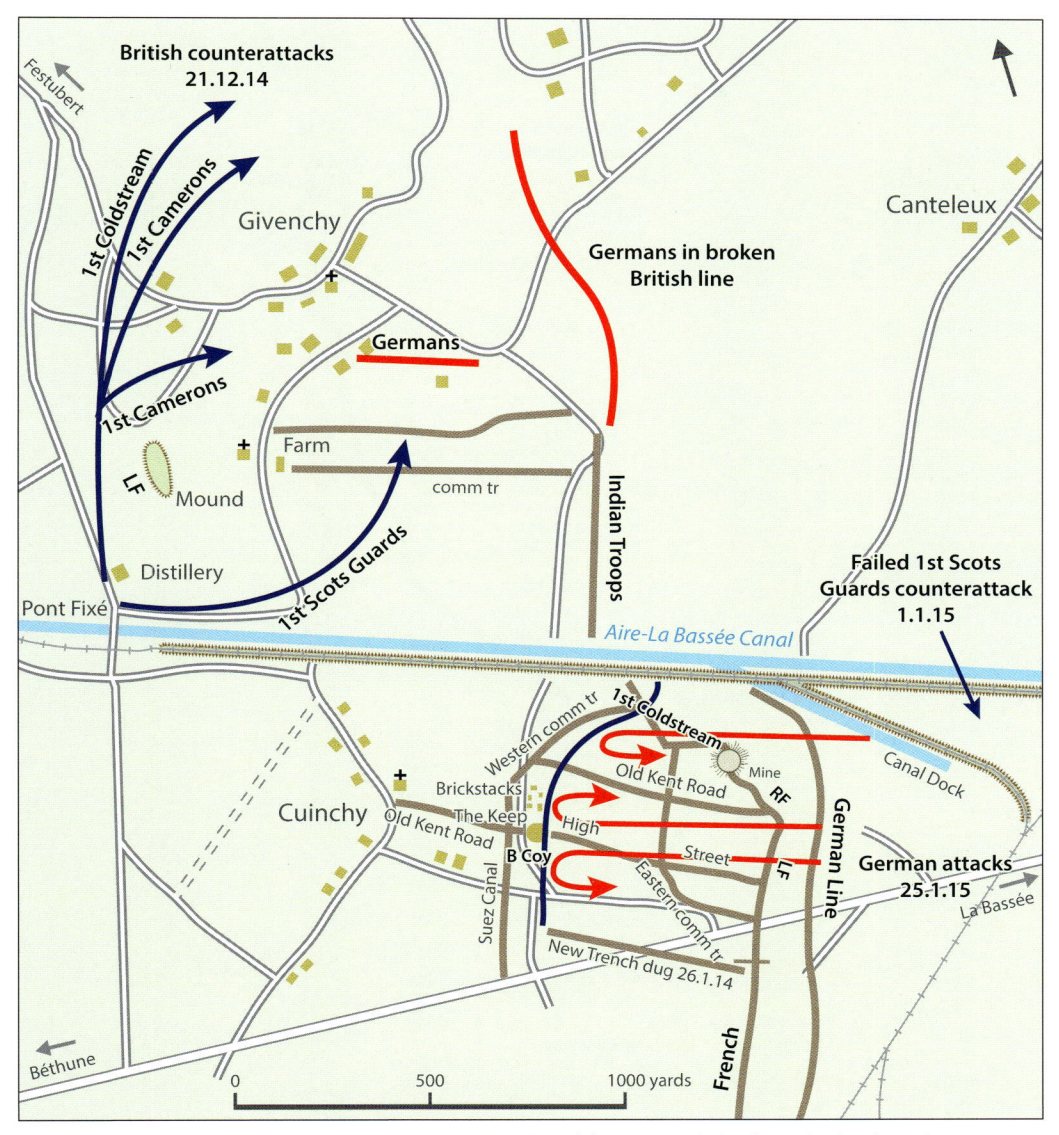

Map 9. The Actions at Givenchy, the Railway Triangle and the Cuinchy brickstacks

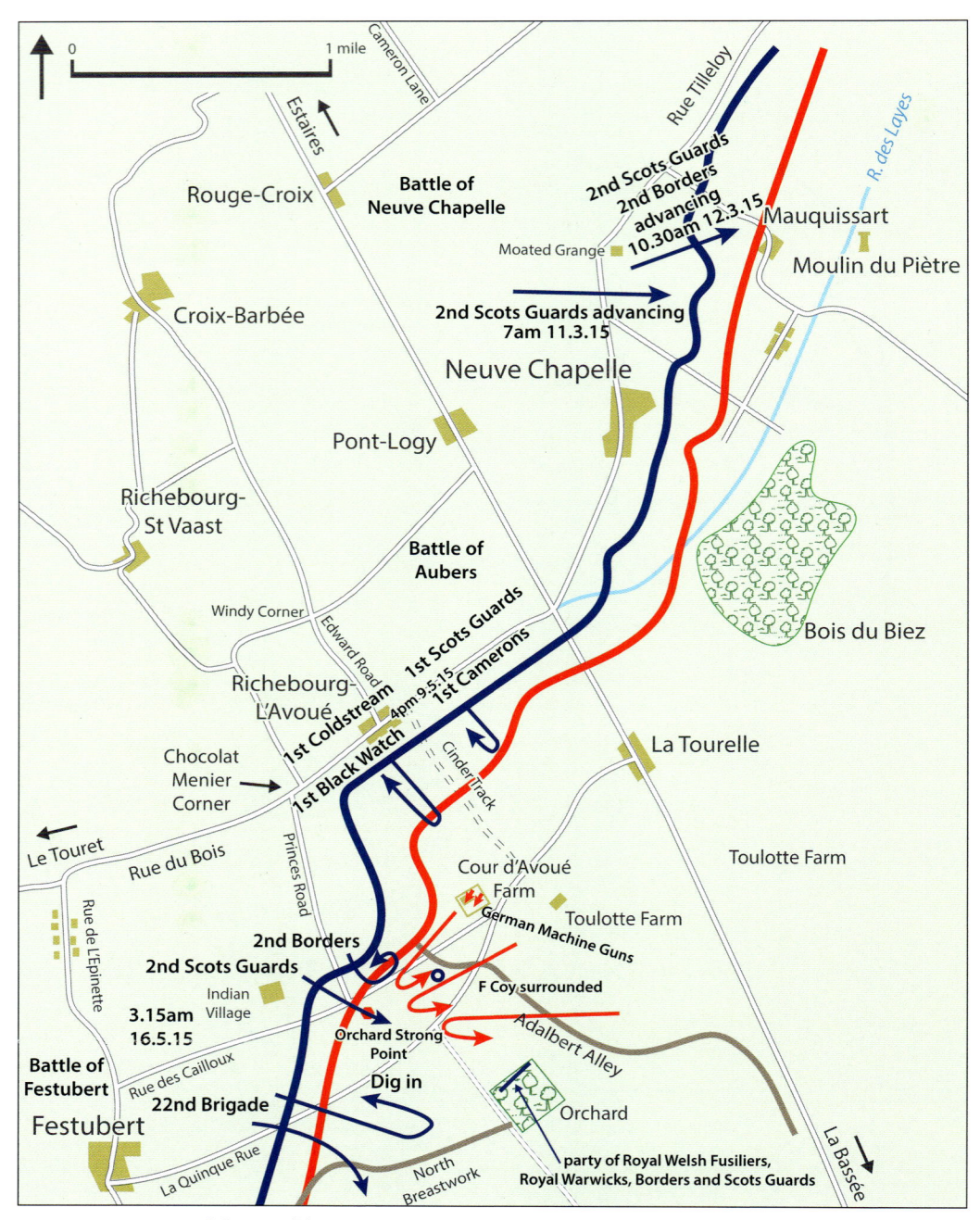

Map 10. The Battles of Neuve Chapelle, Aubers and Festubert

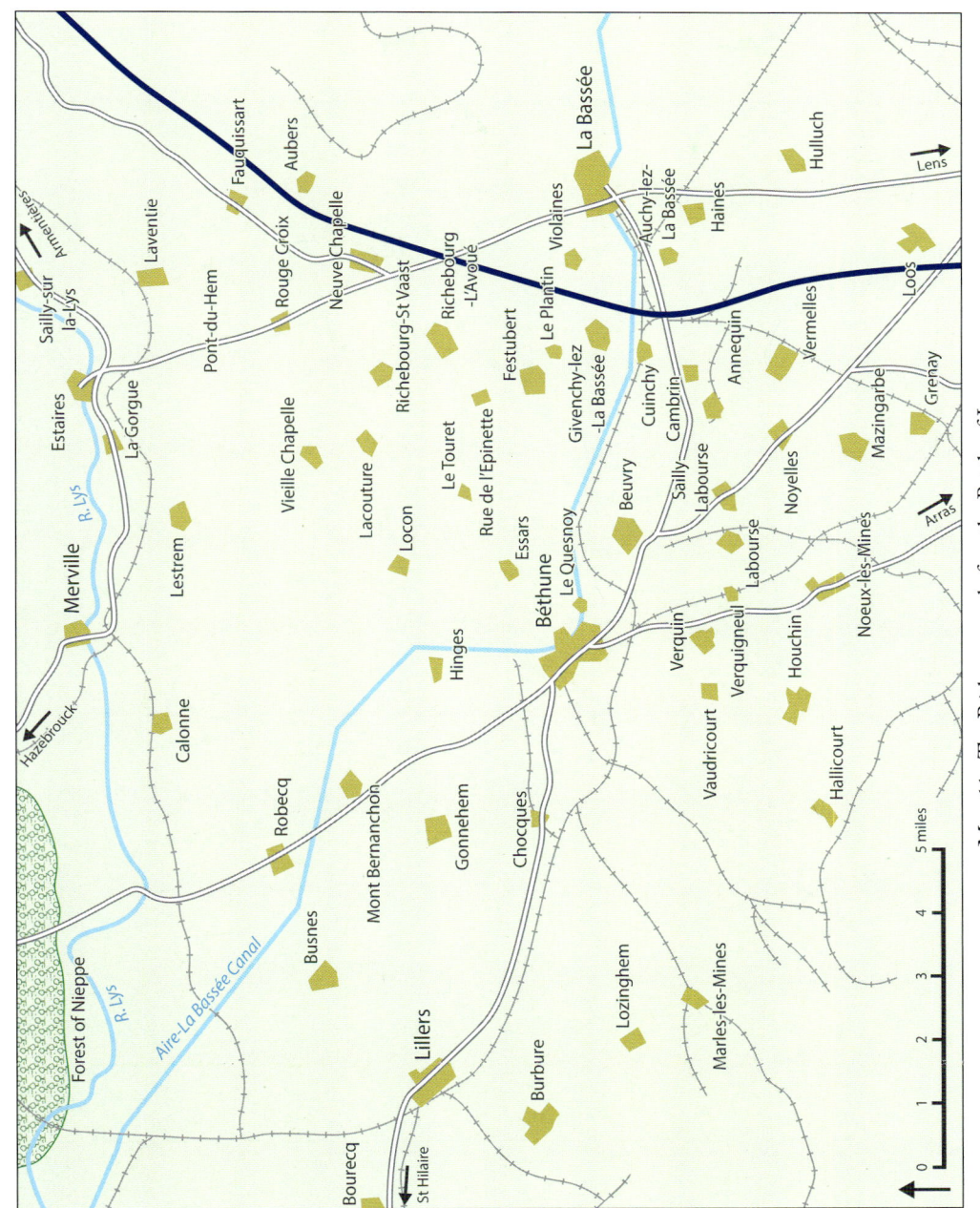

Map 11. The Béthune area before the Battle of Loos

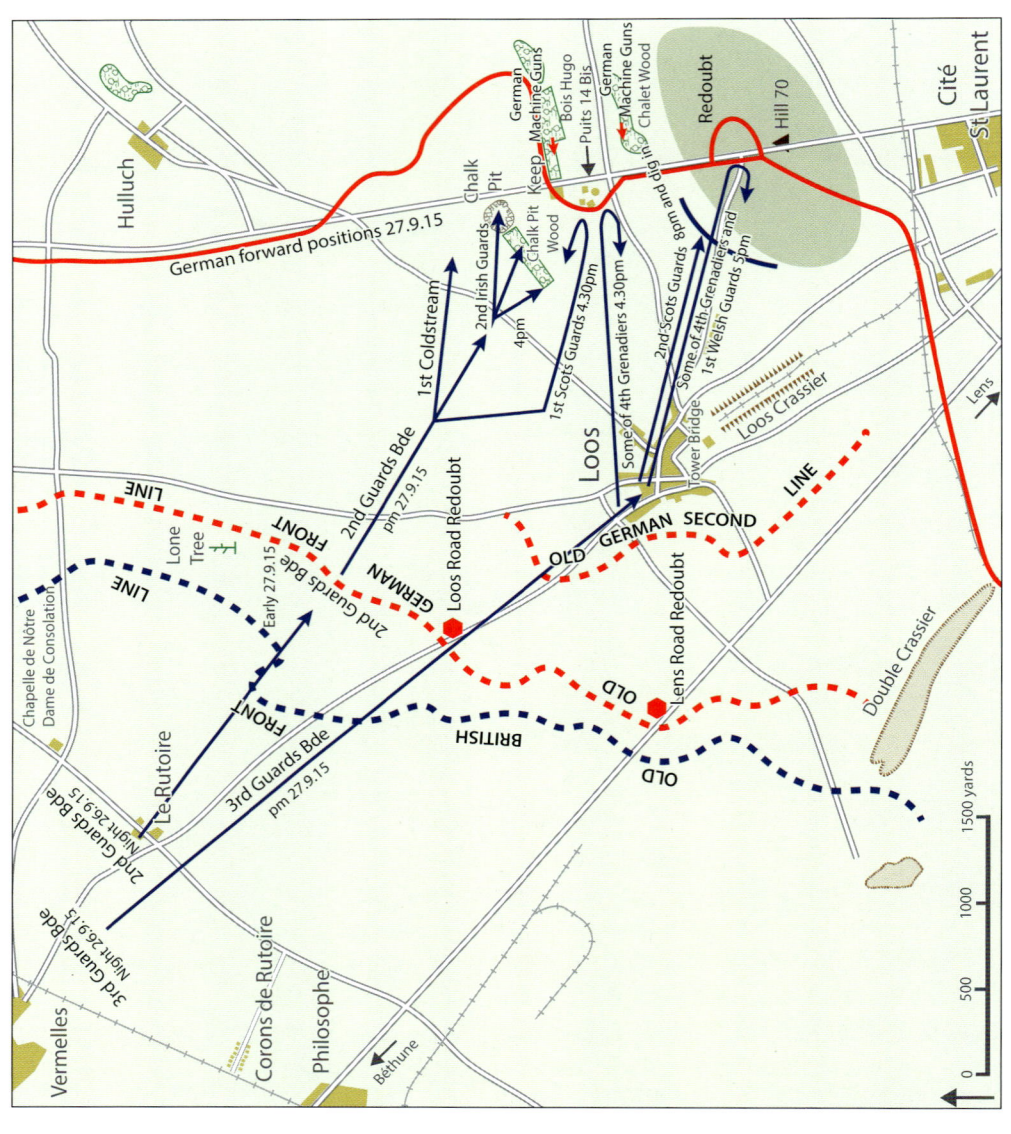

Map 12. The Battle of Loos – Puits 14 Bis and Hill 70 27 September 1915

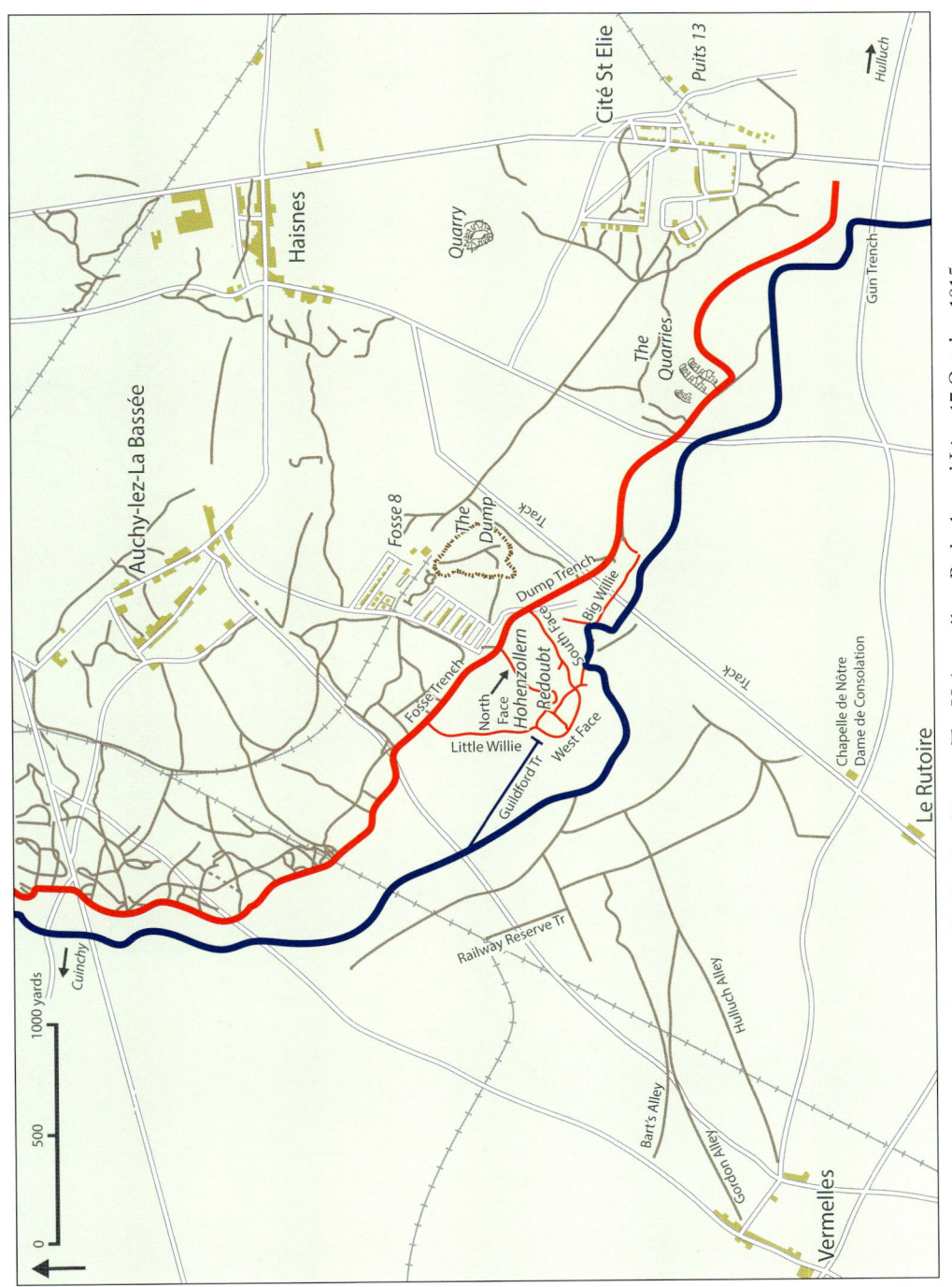

Map 13. The Battle of Loos – The Hohenzollern Redoubt and Line 17 October 1915

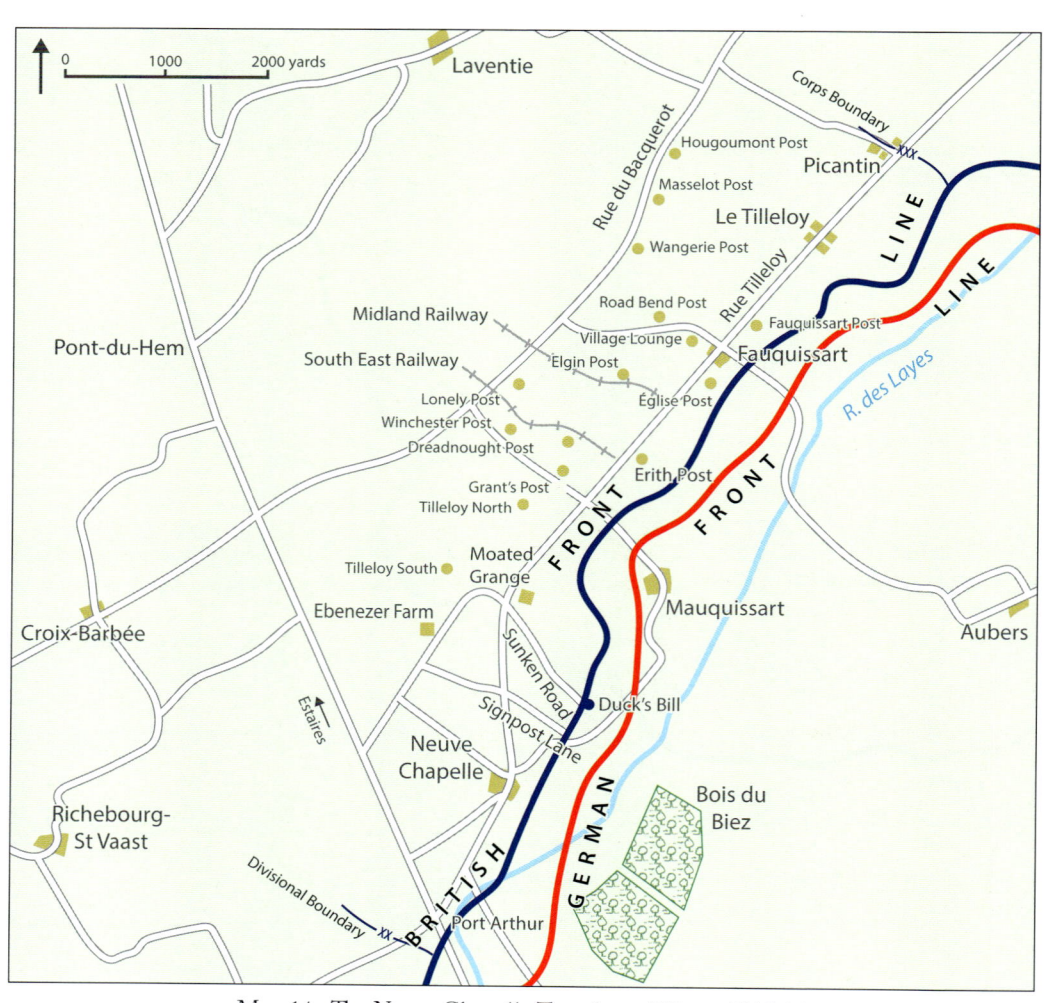

Map 14. The Neuve Chapelle Trenches – Winter 1915-16

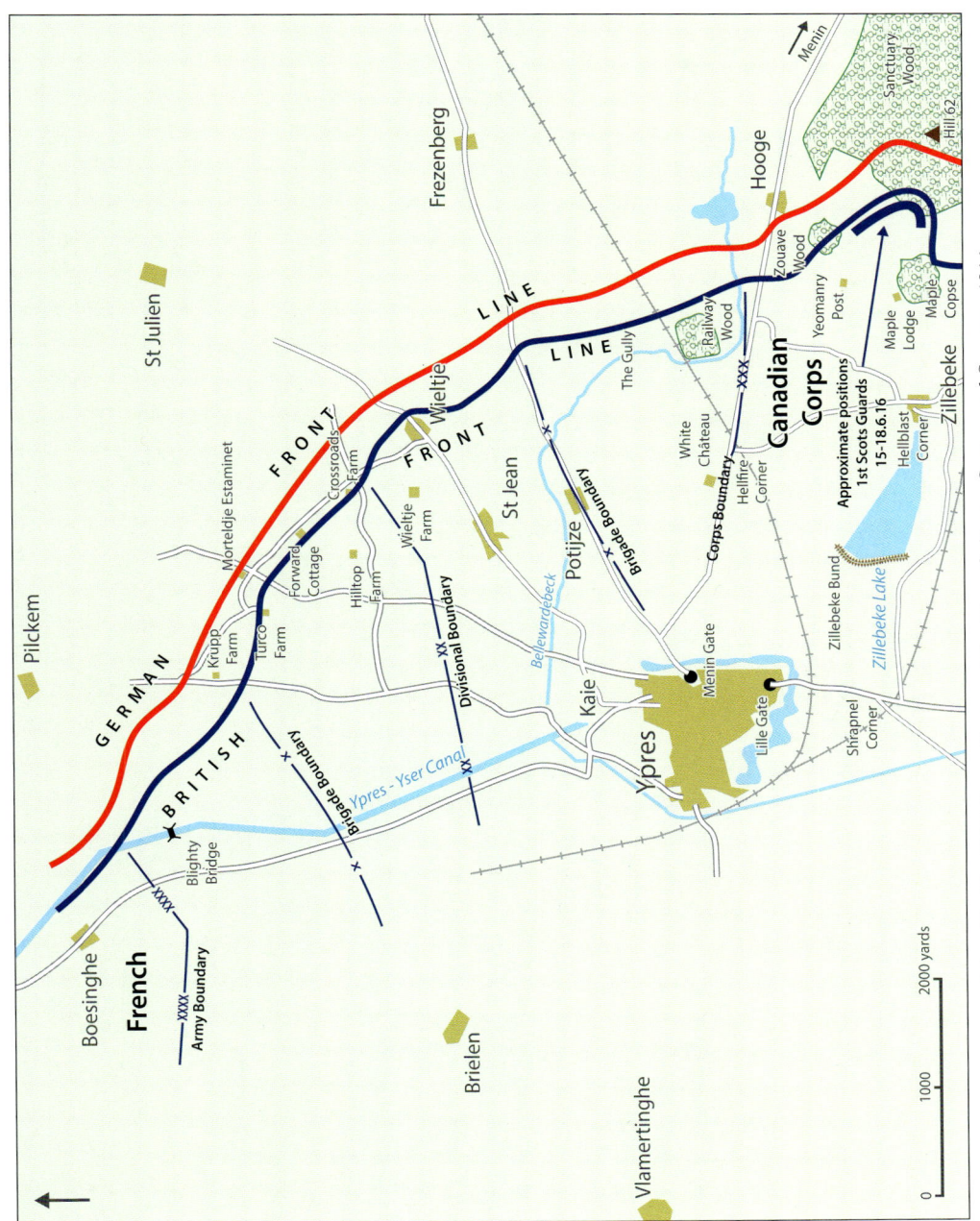

Map 15. The XIV Corps Sector of the Ypres Salient – Spring and Summer 1916

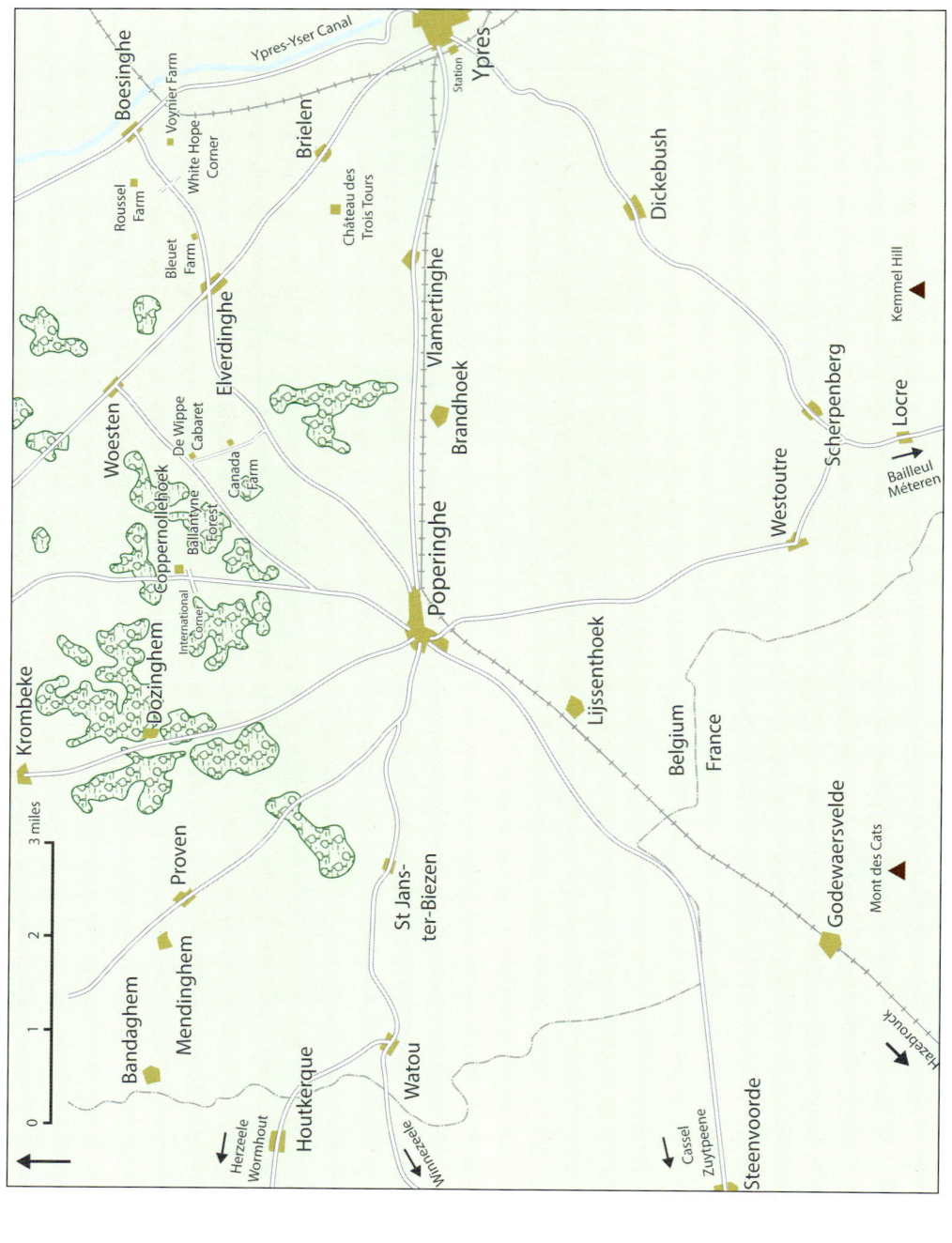

Map 16. The Poperinghe area behind the Ypres Salient

Captain Feilding's company were waiting behind when the rest of the Coldstream went forward. Then, as it was getting dark he walked ahead to try to find the others. "As I did so I met a stream of battle stragglers. Many were wounded, but with them there was also a liberal accompaniment of unwounded "friends" and others who obviously should not have been there." He tried to turn them, but they were not in the mood for that and, as he had his own job to do, he left them to Lieutenant The Honourable Dermot Browne, the Adjutant, who turned up at that moment and set about them "with a heavy hunting crop which he carried." When he led his men on it was dark and raining and, having failed to find any more of the Coldstream, he halted them behind Chalk Pit Wood. There was heavy firing from in front. Accompanied by an orderly, he made his way, stumbling past shellholes and sometimes into them, into and through the Wood. Beyond they could hear the sound of digging and the cries of the wounded whom they passed. Next he was very relieved to be hailed by Lieutenant Trafford of the Scots Guards, who recognised him in the murk. Here were Grenadier, Scots and Irish Guardsmen all mixed up "digging in for dear life."

He went back, having been away for about an hour, and collected his company, now aware of where the rest of the Coldstream were on the left of the Brigade. His company were to be out on the left flank, but there was no sign of the 1st Guards Brigade beyond and when he himself went to look he could not find them either. The 1st Guards Brigade had, with little interference, reached the line of the road and not only dug themselves in there but also, working very hard in the dark, successfully dug further north to link up with the 1st Division. As it ran north from Hill 70 the road to La Bassée ran gradually downhill and it was the high ground that the Germans were interested in.

The Scots Guards started to dig in further back down the slope in front of Puits 14 Bis and on through the night while the Coldstream and Irish Guards dug in around the Chalk Pit and Wood. Captain Barne noted "Irish Guards just beyond the wood, Scots Guards, consisting principally of our Coy, a few of R Flank, fewer of L Flank and one or two of C Coy, remainder I know not where. Thorpe takes charge of the Battn. It is all too ghastly to write about… We spend a horrible night entrenching where we are, looking for and bringing in wounded and trying to reorganise. Nobody seems to be able to say anything of anybody, the men dead beat, hungry and thirsty and sleepless. The night a soaking one." There were six officers left including him.

The night was "A very busy time, have made a capital start at the trench in the night, the men's rations and water were obtained, the RE supplied a few more entrenching tools and we collected a few more men, I think bringing the Battn up to 400 (250?). The stretcher parties were conspicuous by their absence and on all hands were they wanted, the wounded were lying about in heaps unattended, cold and miserable. We sent in what we could in mackintosh sheets, but a long way to the dressing station and there they seemed unable to deal with them quickly enough – all so different from what one had been led to believe by the newspapers." They were still hard at it next day. Then, later on the 28th "In the afternoon we are badly shelled with some losses, and the Coldstream on left have to give way. Things get very uncomfortable but by nightfall the shelling stops and all is well. To my horror about 4pm I hear Thorpe is hit and gone to dressing station and so I take over the Battn. Luckily for all concerned he returns about 6 with his hand bandaged up. Grainger, one of my subalterns, had a bullet in and out of his leg, but very pluckily took no notice (I think only through fat) and so we are still intact as a Coy. What is so horrible is knowing there must be many wounded between us and the Germans and being unable to get them, though we do bring in several and get shot at for our pains for doing so. On these occasions one always goes up to a body… and sees if alive or not, such ghastly sights does one see sometimes, for instance one poor creature whom Hammersley and two men and self brought in raving, was lying shot through the head and his teeth lying alongside him almost intact. Found the body of Lt Col ET Logan, the Cheshire Regt, amongst others. Had a man hit through the knee bringing in one wounded man." Colonel Edward Logan had commanded the 15th Durham Light Infantry [DLI], a New Army battalion in the 21st Division, and been killed on the 26th. Lieutenant Liddell Grainger had not lasted long with the 2nd Battalion in the trenches at Rouges Bancs before being evacuated home sick and also with "frostbite" the previous December. He had returned to France, this time to the 1st Scots Guards, two weeks before Loos, after which he was sent down the line because of his wound. Back on 7th November, he was sent home five weeks afterwards with trench foot for the second time and did not serve with either Battalion again.

On the 28th there were orders for a fresh attack on the Puits in the afternoon. General Ponsonby, with deep misgivings, recorded that it was impossible to consult Lord Cavan because the communications were constantly cut by shellfire. His own preference was to wait till after dark. By way of fire support the best he could do was concentrate his Brigade machine guns on the Grenay Ridge to fire on the Bois Hugo. The Coldstream, not involved like the Scots and Irish Guards the day before, then attacked the Puits from Chalk Pit Wood. General Ponsonby called off the attack himself when he saw it fail, with losses of nine officers and two hundred and fifty men. Captain Feilding's company were in support and were to rush forward from where they were to occupy the front line trench dug the night before from which Nos 1 and 2 Companies now attacked. The enemy quickly spotted what was happening "and a storm of fire burst out." He led his men forward as "Immediately we showed ourselves we were met by a terrific hurricane of machine gun and rifle fire from Bois Hugo – a wood on our left front – and by shellfire of every description. All was howling Inferno." When he himself reached the forward trench he found himself on his own, so he went back, gathered up the company and led them on. By this time the survivors of the attacking companies were making their way back. They went on working through the night in driving rain, soaked and sleepless. "We never lay down: there was nowhere to lie but the watery trench. Of course we had no hot food or drink, but mercifully a rum ration was got up which was a Godsend to us all. Occasionally, the moon shone out, lighting up the chalk like snow, and showing up the bodies of the dead that lay in the great pit. I was visited the first night by the Brigadier, who is always there when he is wanted, and glad I was to see him."

For Captain Barne, the day of the 29th "Passes full of incident though nothing very definite occurring. Were heavily shelled in trenches at which we work busily, the Coldstream very much worse shelled, and poor Arthur Egerton is blown sky high out of his dug-out. I suppose it was him we saw – about 140 yards off – as I don't think many were blown right up." Lieutenant Colonel Arthur Egerton, commanding the Coldstream, and Lieutenant Browne, the Adjutant, were killed by the same shell just outside their headquarters dug-out at the Chalk Pit. "Towards evening Thorpe and HQ and the remains of the other 3 companies are relieved out of their trenches, and my Company takes over a new piece of trench." Captain Thorpe's party totalled about one hundred and fifty and for the time being went back to occupy the old German front line which looked towards Le Rutoire. Some seventy Household Cavalrymen of the Divisional Cyclist Company took their places alongside B Company, who as night fell were "warned that the Germans are massing for an attack, so every preparation is made, but nothing much unusual occurs during the night." Captain Barne was very pleased that Lieutenant Ellis, missing till then, had been found and brought in, hit by a shell in the face, chest and the back of the neck. He was away ten months. A large number of officers had been wounded and Lieutenant Boyd Rochfort had badly wrenched his back muscles, but by this time only Captain Cuthbert and Lieutenant Armstrong were unaccounted for. Of the former Captain Barne wrote, referring to the period before the attack on the Puits, "Harold has been out since 24 hours previously without any sleep and was pretty well done up even he admitted. I saw a lot of him that morning and wondered if he had forebodings! He seemed rather different to usual, however he may yet be found all right."

30 September was another difficult day. "First thing when it is only just light it is reported to me that more wounded are seen in front, so we make another expedition to rescue and 3 are obtained, 2 of them drew fire but no casualty. One is a Corp in C Coy, one a private soldier of the Suffolk Regt, one of the DLI, who had been lying out there six days and tried to cut his throat but failed. Nothing can picture the appalling situation of these poor creatures, lying out in wind and rain (the former cold, the latter copious), no food or water and a broken leg or something and occasionally being heavily shelled by the German guns or shot at by those in the trenches getting a scare and blazing off their ammunition into the dark. There is always at same time their anguish of mind at feeling they have to die of exposure and hunger. One gallant man, who had been out for 5 or 6 days, when I asked him how he felt, said "Very well, Sir, but I should be better if I had been found sooner." When able they are always so grateful to their rescuers." Later in the morning the Commanding Officer and Adjutant of the 7th Norfolk Regiment came up on a reconnaissance ahead of the relief that night and, whether true or not, morale was improved by a report that the French had taken 35,000 prisoners and 100 guns. Where B Company were "There is much shelling of our trench during the day and 6 men get buried but are got out alive. It is an anxious time for all concerned. The relief is supposed to be at 7pm but, partly owing to a limber catching fire and lighting up the whole country, it was delayed and my Coy did not get away till past midnight, very tired and hungry, the men having no water or food or anything till arriving back at Verquigneul." The rest of the Brigade came out of the line too.

Private James Tonner's injuries were characteristic of someone dug out in time after being buried in a trench by shellfire. "The back & left side was strained." The treatment in hospital in the UK was "massage & movement." He had already been wounded once, bruising his shoulder in March, while the Battalion were on the periphery of Neuve Chapelle. Before September 1914 he was a rubber worker in Glasgow and lived in Anderston with Maggie Tonner and their two sons and two daughters, the last born the month after he enlisted. He would reappear.

The aftermath

By five in the morning on 1 October most of the Battalion were back at Verquigneul, with only Captain Barne and B Company an hour later. "About 6am after a long weary muddy wet march over the back part of the battlefield, seeing more ghastly sights, they are bundled into billets, Hammersley and self in a room and we sleep till noon. I never saw such a sleepy crowd. We had been out and about with hardly any sleep for five days and nights. A ration of rum was given out before the men turned in." Private Johnes "found billets and rations waiting for us, including a double ration of rum, which really was a blessing in disguise. It not only was a great pick-me-up, it helped to lessen the blow of seeing our empty ranks. The following day was roll call, and distributing of mail, which had caught up from leaving Tatinghem…Many of the parcels were addressed to buddies who did not answer to roll call, these were distributed amongst us…we were in clover as it almost amounted to one or two for each of us. Although it was a heartache when opening up their convoys, we knew that if they had answered roll, they would have shared with us." "Convoy" was a word soldiers used for a parcel.

When Captain Thorpe was sent home with his wounded hand on 2 October Captain Barne found himself in command. General Haking came to thank the Guards Division for their attack on the 27th and for their subsequent digging. Captain Barne saw him but "Gen Sir John French also came round and addressed the men quite unceremoniously in the street. I was sorry to miss him." He went to meet Colonel Cator to discuss borrowing officers temporarily until more arrived to fill up the gaps. Then at short notice they moved "to our old friend Vermelles" on 3 October where they were in reserve for the next two days and sorted themselves out. Suitable men were chosen as new NCOs and reinforcement drafts started to arrive. Five officers came over that day from the 2nd Battalion, including another of Captain Barne's brothers in law, Lieutenant Ernest "Tim" Orr Ewing, and his cousin, Lieutenant Seymour. Another, Lieutenant Arthur Purvis, saw the announcement of his brother's death in the paper that evening. Captain John Purvis of the 9th Rifle Brigade was killed on 25 September in a diversionary attack near Ypres which the 14th (Light) Division, New Army, made at Bellewarde Farm, north of the Menin Road, intended to distract the Germans from Loos. Their parents were Captain Herbert and Mabel Purvis from near Leuchars, Fife. Lieutenant Purvis had been born in Hawaii, went to school at Rugby before going to the École Nationale et Speciale des Beaux Arts, Paris, and was training to become an architect. He spoke fluent French. He started the War in the ranks of the Cameron Highlanders, but not in the BEF, and was commissioned into the Scots Guards in March 1915. He came out first in April and, apart from this brief attachment, was with the 2nd Battalion until he had appendicitis a year later. After that he trained as a Vickers Gun officer and went to the 3rd Guards Brigade Machine Gun Company with whom he was wounded on 8 July 1917 near Ypres in the lead up to the Battle of Pilckem Ridge.

Between 27 and 30 September the Scots Guards had two officers missing and twelve wounded, nine of them, including Colonel Godman, for the first time and, three, Major Orr Ewing, Sir Victor Mackenzie, shot in both thighs, and Lieutenant Eric Mackenzie, for the second. Captain Poynter, found and carried in, had had his thigh broken and later spent most of the remainder of the War as another of Sir William Pulteney's ADCs. Because of a bullet through the knee, though he did not lose the leg, Lieutenant Fergusson was permanently too badly hurt to do anything more and left the Army eighteen months later. His servant, Private William Watson, was dead, currently posted missing. A general labourer, he enlisted over a year earlier in Edinburgh, though James and Janet (or Annie) Watson were living at the time in Maryhill, Glasgow. Private Watson was in the large draft at the beginning of February and had been with the Battalion since then, apart from two brief periods off sick. Altogether twenty seven men were definitely known to have been killed, three hundred and twenty four had been wounded and ninety three were missing.

Private Samuel Falls, a wartime volunteer, was a Glasgow labourer until a year earlier and until now, when he was missing, had survived seven months in France. Five weeks later men of the 1/20th London Regiment, Blackheath and Woolwich, Territorials, found his body and buried him, but the grave was lost. John and Margaret Falls lived at Killymoon,

County Armagh. Lance Sergeant Thomas Rickman, with the DCM from First Ypres, where he was shot in the right leg, was killed. He had been serving since 1906 after joining up in Winchester, his home town. Brigid, his Irish wife of six years, was living in Westminster with their daughter and son. Sergeant Richard Brooker, Rotherhithe miller and the son of George and Emily Brooker, who had been in the ambulance on New Year's Day with Privates Owen and Preston when it fell into a shellhole on the way from Cuinchy to Béthune, was also killed. He was not married and, if his stated age on enlisting was correct, he was only twenty when he died. Born in Chicago, Illinois, Private John McTavish was with his mother Mary McTavish in Edinburgh before the War, employed as a gardener's assistant. Having volunteered in September 1914, he arrived in France in March 1915 and was wounded for the first time at the Puits with a bullet wound to his right foot. After recovering at home Private McTavish was sent to the 2nd Battalion in April 1916 and was hit a second time that September, in the head, at the start of the fighting at Ginchy on the Somme. Again sent home for treatment he returned to the 1st Scots Guards in June 1917 and, though very slightly wounded in October that year during Third Ypres, otherwise remained with them until they returned home from Cologne. On leaving the Army he sailed for the USA and went to live in North Bergen, New Jersey. Private Willie Anderson was a painter and when he volunteered in October 1914 in Hamilton he stated that he wanted to join the cavalry, but quickly found himself in the Scots Guards. Though in France since April, he had not joined the Battalion till mid August, partly because of being sick with myalgia in July. On 29 September he was hit in the head and died at St Omer on 8 October. His nearest relative was his eldest brother Robert Anderson in Chicago.

Private Allan Laing, a gardener, was the son of Walter and Annie Laing of Broughty Ferry. In November 1914 he gave his age as eighteen years and four months at the recruiting office in Edinburgh, but that he was therefore known to be under nineteen did not stop him being sent out at the beginning of May 1915. On 27 September he was hit for the first time in the War in the right thigh, but not seriously, and came back after two weeks in hospital at Étretat. Private Charles Hendrick, recovered long before from his head wound the previous November at Nonne Boschen, was wounded again, this time in the right buttock. Again it was not a serious wound, but he was evacuated to England. Discharged from hospital on 22 October he then went absent for forty four days, was punished with forty two days' detention, remitted to thirty. He remained in England through the winter.

Private Arthur Smith, the Preston soldier who wrote to Mrs Wills at the end of January about her two sons missing after the fighting at the Railway Triangle and the Cuinchy brickstacks, had a bullet wound in his left forearm and a bomb wound in his right arm. He recovered from these and, though gassed on 13 October 1917 in the First Battle of Passchendaele and twice wounded accidentally, all subsequently with the 2nd Battalion, survived the War. Private John Sutherland, a miner, joined up in Glasgow in early September 1914. He had been in France since February and got into trouble the following month for using his emergency ration contrary to orders, for which the punishment was seven days confined to barracks. He was missing after the fighting on 27 September and was never heard of again. Sutherland was also his home where Alexander and Elizabeth Sutherland lived at Brora. Private William Gilchrist was six foot five inches tall. He joined up in November 1914, arrived in France towards the end of April 1915 and, apart from a week in July having his teeth dealt with, was with the Battalion until reported wounded and missing after the attack on the Puits. He too was never heard of again. Before the War he was a farmer and his parents George and Jessie Gilchrist lived at Coldingham, Berwickshire.

Three men, all called William Wilson, were missing. Chronologically in order of enlistment, Private William Wilson, whose mother, Mrs MS Wilson, lived at Burntisland, Fife, was a clerk before he joined up in Edinburgh in January 1912. He was never heard of again. Sergeant William Wilson, a Yorkshireman, former Scots Guardsman and Boer War veteran, had been working as an engineman. He rejoined on 5 September 1914 at York and was immediately made a Lance Sergeant. Arriving in France towards the end of November, he was promoted Sergeant about a fortnight after he reached the Battalion at Borre. Almost six months after his death men of the 12th HLI found his body and buried him on 13 March 1916, but the grave was lost. An identity disc and some letters were forwarded to Walter Wilson, his father, in Tadcaster. Private William Wilson enlisted at Earlston, Berwickshire, in November 1914. He worked in the area both as a shepherd and as a road surfaceman. At the time he joined up his parents were not at the same address. His father James Wilson was at Fans, near Earlston, while his mother Isabella Wilson was at Yetholm, near Kelso. Private Wilson had been in France for nearly four months and he was another never heard of again.

Private William Dobbie volunteered just over a year before in Glasgow, where he was a fitter. He was hit in the leg, but not badly, on the 27th, and sent to Rouen to recover. Private David Gallacher, a carter, joined up the same day and had the next consecutive regimental number. He was killed. Both Private Dobbie's parents, Robert and Catherine Dobbie, and Private Gallacher's, James and Annie Gallacher, lived in Auchentoshan Terrace, Springburn. Privates David Naysmith and John Swan were both Fife miners, both had been born in Auchterderran, both had homes nearby in Lochgelly, both enlisted in Cowdenbeath on 1 September 1914, both were only five foot six and a half inches tall, both arrived in France on 6 February 1915 and both were slightly wounded in their left hands, one on 27, one on 28 September. Here their paths diverged and they went back by different medical routes to England. Much later on, in 1918, both came back out separately to the 2nd Battalion. Private Alexander Thomson, a blacksmith who joined up in Stranraer in early November 1914, was missing. His Bible, letters, postcards and photographs arrived at his home in Creetown, Kirkcudbrightshire, where his father was a police sergeant. He and Maggie Thomson had memorial cards printed with their son's photograph in uniform. It had a verse inside "In a distant blood-stained battlefield, With many of his comrades brave, Lies our dear boy sleeping In a cold and silent grave." Private Joseph Robinson, painter's labourer and the son of Hannah Robinson of Stranraer, enlisted the same day and he too was missing. Private John Smith, who also enlisted with them at Stranraer, was sent to the 2nd Battalion and survived all the 1915 events unhurt.

Privates Jim and Tom Duckett joined up in September 1914 in Preston, where Jim was a draughtsman and Tom worked with his father, also Thomas Duckett, a mineral water manufacturer. Jim was six years the elder. Both arrived in France on 9 April. Of Private Jim Duckett, posted wounded and missing, there was never any more news. Private Tom Duckett was also missing, but he had been wounded in the left thigh and captured. In November 1916 Louise Duckett, their mother, died in Preston. Just as there was the arrangement which took effect in March 1918 that long serving officer and NCO prisoners of both sides could be sent for internment in a neutral country, there were negotiations for a similar scheme for all private soldiers who had been in captivity for more than three years to be similarly interned and this was widely known about. In September 1918 Annie Duckett, his sister, wrote to Regimental Headquarters asking about this and when he might be released from Germany, adding how much he wanted to come home. Colonel Smith Neill had to reply that until the German Government ratified this internment agreement there was no hope of its being implemented. It never did.

Private John Hadden's home was in Banff, but he was a painter in Glasgow when he enlisted in September 1914. By this time he had been in France for seven months. He was hit by a shell on 28 September which broke his left leg and he died next day in Béthune. William and Isabella Hadden received a knife, two razors in cases, a wallet, letters, photos, a card, a religious book, a broken mirror, a handkerchief and a spray of heather. Private Archibald McLeaver, the son of Robert and Hannah McLeaver of Airdrie, had a single tattoo dot on his right wrist, which suggested a very brief experiment or a quick change of mind. He joined up in Glasgow at the end of August 1914, describing himself as a student. He was shot in the stomach, took two days to reach a casualty clearing station and died at Lillers on the 30th. Also dying of wounds was Private William Webster, a Glasgow policeman, whose mother Helen Webster lived in Oldmeldrum, Aberdeenshire. Having enlisted in September 1914 Private Webster arrived at Le Havre at the beginning of December where he was found to have gonorrhoea. That delayed his joining the Battalion, but after he did, because it was not fully treated, there was a recurrence in January and he was away for three weeks till it was. He had a bayonet wound in the left shoulder and a bullet in the right thigh, affecting the bladder, pelvis and the thigh itself. On 2 October he reached Rouen, by when the bladder wound was going septic. On the 5th a telegram was sent to his mother that he was "Dangerously Ill", but he lived till half past three on the afternoon of 21 October. She heard of his death by telegram sent the next day. His effects were a writing pad, a Bible, a mirror, a metal knife and some letters. Lance Corporal John Anderson, another Glasgow policeman, volunteered in October 1914 and arrived in France early in April 1915. Though he had been born in Clatt, Aberdeenshire, his mother, who had remarried, was in Broughty Ferry. Corporal Anderson was hit badly in the chest and evacuated, not to return again, remaining stationed in London until medically discharged in November 1917. In August 1916 he married Elsie Burgoyne in Barking and they had a son the next year. He went back to Glasgow and became a police sergeant. Six men became Scots Guardsmen on 5 January 1915 at Galashiels, two of whom did not complete training at the Guards Depot. Of the four who did, Private Adam Blaikie, a woodman, whose father John Blaikie lived at Newmill, the next village up the River Teviot from Hawick, was posted wounded and missing after 27 September. Nothing more was seen or heard of him.

Captain Thompson, the Adjutant, replied on 4 October to Colonel Godman who had written that he was not too badly hurt. There was still no news of either Captain Cuthbert or Lieutenant Armstrong, though they knew that Captain Cuthbert had managed to get further forward than anyone else and there was a possibility that he was still lying out wounded. He added that "Several of the 21st Division who had been wounded on Sunday and were subsequently rescued by our troops had been dressed and treated well by the Germans, so there is still hope." Of Lieutenant Armstrong he understood that he had been wounded fairly early on near Chalk Pit Wood so he could have been carried back by others. Captain Barne wrote the same day to Colonel Godman explaining how he came to be commanding the Battalion and that "everyone is very kind to me and I think we shall knock along all right until Esmé or some other competent person arrives, so I hope you won't feel anxious about us. Tommy has been all along A1, I must say." He mentioned the names of other officers who had done very well "unravelling the scrimmage during the action and during the subsequent few days which were rather trying ones, but as far as the Battalion went, nothing could have been finer than the way the men stood it, working day and night, digging, collecting dead and wounded, besides the difficulties they had to go through as regards rations and water etc., which could only be got up at night into Loos which was being heavily shelled all the time. Kinlay has played up well and a great help and of course the Doctor (all say) worked wonders and is as cheerful as ever." Further "The situation is satisfactory in one sense but casualties are awful and it seems a pity to try and go on pushing now that the Germans have fortified themselves so well again." At the head of the list of those recommended for bravery was Lance Corporal James Aitken, a machineman who enlisted in Paisley in September, came out at the beginning of February and was promoted in June. He carried Sir Victor Mackenzie back four hundred yards under fire and in the process wrenched his knee so badly that he was never fit again. He was evacuated home, very rapidly awarded the DCM, subsequently awarded a French Croix de Guerre and discharged in September 1917. His father Alexander Aitken lived at Cluny, Aberdeenshire.

All Kathleen Cuthbert heard was the official communication that her husband was missing as at 30 September. When last seen at the pit buildings he had not been hit. She began exploring every possible way of finding definite information, clinging to the hope that he was a prisoner. In a letter on 24 October to General Cuthbert, one of very many, she told him that she had heard that morning from Lady FitzWygram that when her son was badly wounded and captured at Festubert he had been allowed to write a postcard three days afterwards. The card then sat unsent until he left the German field hospital and so she had no definite news until 28 June, six weeks later. Kathleen Cuthbert had also heard from Major Morrison Bell's wife that she had known her husband was alive and well as a prisoner only seventeen days after the battle at the Cuinchy brickstacks, because he had chanced to meet a pre-war German friend, Prince Löwenstein, who arranged for a telegram to be sent to her through Holland. Then she continued "You know I simply cannot believe he is not alive, but oh how I long & long to know this suspense is terribly hard to bear." Two days later she was writing again having heard that "Young Kipling (of the Irish Guards) I supposed to have gone in there too & nothing has been heard of or from him. I expect how you have heard how an officer of the Munsters found Mr Armstrong's body somewhere quite near the German lines." Lieutenant Armstrong was posted and remained missing. Lieutenant John Kipling, 2nd Irish Guards, son of the writer and poet Rudyard Kipling and his wife Carrie, was missing too. Meanwhile she saw her husband's servant Alfred when he came home on leave, but he had no information. This was Private Alfred Triggs, a valet whose father Harry Triggs lived at Crawshawbooth, Lancashire. He enlisted at St Paul's Churchyard, London, after Christmas 1914, landed in France early in April 1915 and was in the Battalion for the rest of the War, never sick and never wounded.

Kathleen Cuthbert had no fresh news in 1915 or 1916. Writing to General Cuthbert on 10 May 1916 she mentioned that Mary Pollen was now engaged to Captain James Macindoe, another Scots Guards officer, who had been serving since 1909 and whose overseas war service was, apart from a short period in 1915, entirely in the Middle East attached to the Imperial Camel Corps. Almost a year earlier she had told him about Mary Pollen, the friend she had staying with her "poor girl she is still very miserable," who had lost her fiancé, Lieutenant Compton Thornhill, killed in September 1914 on the Aisne. Still Kathleen Cuthbert went on hoping. Then in a letter on 6 May 1917 to Major General Cuthbert, since July 1916 commanding the 39th Division, New Army, "After all these months & months of waiting & hoping & praying the worst has come." What she had received was a War Office document which read

"A report has been received on an official German List headed "List of Dead", forwarded by the Netherlands Legation, on the 1st April which states that "Captain J H Cuthbert, DSO 1st Battalion Scots Guards,…died on the 27 September,1915, on or near Trench 14."" There was no mention of when this was reported up the German chain of command. Kathleen Cuthbert went on "Until I got this I did not realize how absolutely I believed he was alive & coming home to me. It has been a bitter bitter blow. I can only hope he died at once without realizing he was going."

Private Peter Ennis, a Glasgow labourer, had volunteered the previous September and been in France for six months, interrupted with treatment for myalgia, for boils and to his teeth. He was hit in the left hand on 29 September and sent back to recover across the Channel. While on leave with his family he was shot in the chest and killed on 25 April 1916, the second day of the Easter Rising in Dublin. Recovered from his body and passed to his mother Catherine Ennis at her home not far from Grand Canal Dock were his cigarette case, a cigarette holder and a match box.

The Hohenzollern Redoubt

Though it did not directly affect the 2nd Guards Brigade to begin with because they were in reserve, by the time that the other two Guards Brigades were ordered into the line again on 3 October it was stable on the right from Hill 70, but back from the Lens-La Bassée road, northwards towards the Vermelles-Hulluch road. Short of where these roads met the British trenches turned west along the line of the Vermelles-Hulluch road until they curled round towards the north again at the Hohenzollern Redoubt. By this time the Germans had recovered almost everything that the 7th and 9th Divisions had captured on 25 September. Principal British attention for the next three weeks centred on this area and the 1st and 3rd Guards Brigades, taking over from the 2nd Division, were to occupy Gun Trench, facing north towards The Quarries and The Dump, the Hohenzollern being over to their left. The Germans had fortified The Dump, a level slag heap twenty foot high, from which a series of trenches fed into and supported the Hohenzollern. The Quarries, between The Dump and Hulluch and closer than The Dump to Gun Trench, had lent themselves naturally to further fortifications.

Around the Hohenzollern neither side, but particularly not the British, could make any move at all above ground in daylight and in the dark it was hazardous. Not surprisingly, those in the trenches had very little idea of what was in front of them. Both sides held parts of this trench system, but then on 4 October the Germans drove the 28th Division, Regular Army, out of almost the whole Redoubt itself. This put an end to the plans forming for an attack by the Guards Division on The Quarries and led to reorganisation in the front line at short notice, partly because the 28th Division had to be relieved. So, while on the left the 1st Guards Brigade stayed put in their part of Gun Trench, the 3rd Guards Brigade on their right left it and went back into reserve at Vermelles. Instead, the 2nd Guards Brigade were to come up on the 1st Guards Brigade's left and occupy the line to where the Vermelles-Auchy road crossed over No Man's Land.

Everything was rushed on 5 October and Captain Barne and the company commanders first had to meet General Ponsonby in the trenches that they were about to take over. It was pouring with rain. "The Battn parades at 5pm, being heavily shelled at Vermelles just before we start, one shell (heavy) falling almost on the doorstep of Officers Mess, only one man wounded. We go through the most dreadfully slow relief and are not eventually fixed up and taken over till 4am." They were now, mostly, opposite the Hohenzollern. "We are told to work very hard and be very busy for the next few days, are in some very muddy and neglected trenches, full of equipment, old gas plant, evidently used on Sept 25th, dead bodies, etc, etc…We get thoroughly shelled and are having several men wounded, personally I have had one or two narrow escapes, but I suppose this occurs every day…Our ration party goes down at 6pm, but gets lost on the return journey and does not eventually turn up till about 2am. Quite a lively night with incessant firing. I feel a little anxious at being weakened by the ration party's long absence." The next day he had "A long walk round with the Brigadier who showed me the work to be done. He…is certainly a very pleasant man to deal with." Private Johnes found the Hohenzollern "a labyrinth of trenches eight to ten feet deep in places, well fortified with machine gun posts, and with deep dug-outs for officers and men. Jerry had been driven out of part of the system, but he was hanging onto a large part of it. Many trenches were plugged off and held by bomb throwers, fire steps were cut into the east side of trenches, and many fellows scooped a long narrow hole in the side near the bottom of the parapet for cover from the weather and a place to get forty winks in. It was a bombers war. Shellfire was only heavy a little back from the front line." One company and two platoons of another were in the front line with everyone else in support. Apart from the heavy shelling and the wounding of several men, there was nothing else significant to begin with.

When he was hit was not recorded but on 7 October Private David Robertson was admitted to hospital in Le Havre with a wound to his nose, but only for four days. A September 1914 recruit, he was a Lanarkshire policeman before the War whose parents John and Jean Robertson lived near New Luce, Wigtownshire. He arrived in France in mid January 1915 in a draft, many soon casualties at the Cuinchy brickstacks. Apart from this minor wound he was with the Battalion right through to the end of the War, going back to London with them in March 1919. He was awarded the MM in July 1918. Afterwards he went back to the police in New Stevenston, Lanarkshire. Private Robert Cunningham was a Fife miner. He and Isabella Simpson married in Lochgelly in 1911 when he was only twenty and had an adopted daughter as well as a daughter and a son of their own. He joined up in mid October 1914 and came out to the BEF at the beginning of April 1915, being hit for the first time, in the left thigh, four weeks later while in the 2nd Battalion. After being evacuated across the Channel, where he stayed for a little over two months, he returned to France in July and was sent to the 1st Scots Guards. On 6 October he was wounded in the ear opposite the Hohenzollern Redoubt and sent to hospital in Boulogne. He was discharged from there on the 20th and was in a party of seven men from the Guards Division going to the Base Depot at Le Havre. As their train approached Rue, not far from Abbeville, it stopped a few hundred yards outside the station. Corporal Christopher Hughes, 2nd Irish Guards, was in charge of the party and subsequently stated "At Rue Pte Cunningham got out of the carriage to pump ship. While doing so another train came along the line – our train also started to move – Pte Cunningham jumped on the footboard – the draught from the train closing the door, the other train caught the door and broke it off its hinges, hitting Pte Cunningham and knocking him on the four foot way." Still alive, Private Cunningham was carried at quarter past five to the local hospice and died at half past seven of a fractured skull.

On the evening of 7 October there arrived in the trenches a very large draft of two hundred and sixty eight men. The two officers with them were 2nd Lieutenant The Honourable Paul Ayshford Methuen, the Field Marshal's eldest son, yet another commissioned in August 1914 and Captain Sir Iain Colquhoun, recovered from his wounds during First Ypres and now married to Dinah Tennant. Shortly before he left London Sir Iain Colquhoun met a very recently commissioned officer. This was 2nd Lieutenant Henry Dundas, son of Nevill and Cecil Dundas of Slateford, Edinburgh, who had just left Eton with an Open History Scholarship to Christ Church, Oxford. Two years before, on 17 September 1913, Henry Dundas, then sixteen, wrote:

> Saw little fairy one night at a ball,
> Sought little fairy the length of the hall;
> Then, when I'd found her: 'Pray, grant me this boon;
> Dance No 12 with me, Maimie Colquhoun?'

> 'Alas! I must go, though I'm dying to stay.
> My hostess is calling, & I must obey.'
> 'What!' said I anxiously 'Going so soon?
> Dance just this one with me, Maimie Colquhoun?'

> Rapture! She yields to my eloquent pleading;
> She dances, nor hostess, nor chaperone heeding:
> Then, sitting out, by the light of the moon,
> 'Dance this through life with me, Maimie Colquhoun?'

Lieutenant Dundas told his parents that Sir Iain Colquhoun's voice was just like his sister's.

In this draft was Private George Cumming, a wartime cavalry volunteer who transferred in March. They knew before they left London that they were "to replace the heavy casualties the regiment had sustained during that famous victory, the battle of Loos, or so the papers said." Formed up at Wellington Barracks they marched behind the 3rd Battalion's Pipes and Drums, accompanied and seen off from Waterloo Station by Sergeant Major Frederick "Bumps" Wadham, originally from Portsmouth, with eighteen years service and before that a groom. He and his wife Frances had married in Reading in 1902 and did not have children. Private Cumming told of the Sergeant Major that it was alleged "that two young ladies at the barrack gate were overheard to say: "Ooh, what a lot of times that man has been to the Front!" After a night journey across channel in which every light was blacked out we found ourselves gazing in the early morning at the scruffiest waterfront imaginable, the Port of Boulogne. So this was La Belle France of tradition! Small boys, as we disembarked, asked for bully beef and biscuits and offered to introduce us to their sisters." Like all other drafts they were soon in horse boxes on the railway to Béthune "stopping sometimes to scrounge hot water from the engine driver or perhaps raid an orchard. At Béthune we heard the sound of the guns for the first time and I do not think we were really happy as we marched up the long, cobbled road flanked by tall trees." They spent the very wet night of 6 October in an open field behind Vermelles. It was impossible to lie down and so impossible to sleep. All they could do was move about and wait for dawn and hot tea from the cookers which was "never more welcome." Another man in the draft was Private William Morse, a carpenter, who joined up in March in East London, was with the Battalion unwounded until they went home from Cologne, first becoming a Lance Corporal in October 1917 and winning the MM the following year. Ellen Morse, his mother, lived at St Margaret's Bay, Kent.

From now on much, but not all, at Loos centred on close quarter bombing battles along trenches, success in which required constant brute strength, constant stamina, constant grenade resupply and constant luck. Before there was any chance of capturing an enemy trench or part of it the attackers first had to demolish their own trench block, constructed as a barrier to the other side's bombers, covered by fire and located just outside bomb throwing range, so if an enemy crept up to it he was still not close enough to throw one effectively. Then they had to get through or past the enemy trench block. The Germans had had grenades as part of their normal equipment from the outset of the War and were well used to using them, the two commonest types being the "potato-masher", so called on account of the shape of its charge and its wooden handle, and the "egg" grenade. At Loos the British had for the first time the Number 5 Grenade, better known as the Mills Bomb, oval and about the size of an average avocado pear. A spring powered striker set off the percussion cap in the base which fired the time fuse. When that set off the grenade's explosive the grooved metal casing disintegrated, showering the vicinity with fragments. The striker handle was secured by a double pin, which the bomber first had to pull out, but still holding onto the handle with his other hand. Not until he threw the grenade would the handle spring up and the striker set off the percussion cap. Views varied about the correct length of the time fuse, which could be set differently, but five seconds became normal. Bombing was then still a specialist, not a universal, skill and so, if the trained bombers were casualties, other men often did not know what to do. Once a bombing attack started the machine gunners of both sides sprayed everywhere above ground, while, because of the proximity of the front trenches, each side's artillery concentrated on the other's support and communication trenches. Everything directly affecting the Guards Division over the next three weeks was against that background. There was one other factor, not by any means peculiar to the Loos battlefield, and that was ignorance about the enemy trench layout, quite apart from the variable of the enemy's own changes to it. Various forms of observation, particularly aerial, were gradually enhancing the information available to the mapmakers of the Royal Engineers Survey Companies. However, while a bombing attack was going on it was very difficult to know precisely where it had got to. That applied not only to the attackers themselves, but to those further back. It was also only too easy to get into what turned out to be a cul de sac with an enemy machine gun pointing down it. Because of the slight rise in the ground on which it was situated the Hohenzollern was tactically very important to both sides.

As Private Cumming went up from Vermelles "We entered the long communication trench, built originally by the French, in broad daylight. Today I can still visualise the board bearing the name "Hulluch Alley" which marked the way. The Germans had noted our arrival and marked it with an intense barrage and I was glad to note it was more sound and fury than actual destruction. One lives and learns. My company was B Company and the feeling that the enemy were expending a great deal of effort for little result vanished when we had joined the survivors in the reserve line. CSM "Nobby" Clarke…came round a bay with three blood-stained identity discs." Company Sergeant Major Cecil Clarke, born in Swansea, was a clerk in York when he enlisted in 1900. For much of the time before August 1914 he was on attachment in West Africa, but was soon back in London and went out to join the Battalion at the end of April 1915. His wife Annie was living in Long Ditton, Surrey.

Private Cumming found in the front line "The bottom of the trench… paved, if that is the right word, with dead Prussian Guards, and it was some time before the stretcher bearers could get a chance to remove the bodies. Burst bags containing German potato-masher bombs were strewn everywhere. The place was a shambles." The enemy were only thirty to forty yards away and the flanks along the trenches called Little Willie, running to the north, and Big Willie, running to the southeast, were "somewhat precarious…and our bombers…were kept busy. Some of them came back as if they had just been having a really high old time. Dusk brought a general "wind up" and rifle and machine gun fire blazed across No Man's Land. We had several casualties in the platoon, with NCOs and men shot through the head, but gradually the "hate" died down and we were able to take stock." Then came the fatigues. "Parties were needed, as they always were, to go back to an assembly point and bring up water and rations, to carry the most unwieldy things imaginable for the Royal Engineers or the trench mortar men. Not only were we fighting soldiers, but we were general labourers, navvies and dogsbodies to anyone who wanted something for nothing." The "most unwieldy things" were gas projectors being brought into the front line for a future attack, a hundred and twenty of them for each attacking brigade. In spite of the rain it was unexpectedly warm and Private Cumming thought that it might be the chalky soil which made everyone so thirsty.

When Sir Iain Colquhoun arrived he went up Barts Alley communication trench, there being another further north called Guys Alley, after the London teaching hospitals, to take command of C Company in the front line from 2nd Lieutenant Frank Ward, on loan from the 2nd Battalion. His first reaction, recorded in the diary that he now began, was "The trenches are very badly made, and much knocked about in parts, with quantities of every sort of equipment." After sorting out the large draft and settling them all down in their companies next day everyone spent what Captain Barne called "a very strenuous morning arranging as to installing the gas plant, making recesses, etc., and about 2pm a severe shelling contest begins." Captain Barne recognised Sir Iain Colquhoun as "a very useful and dependable officer." Lieutenant Ward, only slightly wounded, was one of the casualties of 8 October. He had been to school at Christ's Hospital and his mother was living in Kensington. When the War started he was an officer in the London Rifle Brigade, was wounded with them a month after they landed in France and evacuated. He transferred in May 1915 and came to the BEF again at the end of July.

Both Privates Robert Wilson, formerly a clerk, and Robert McDonald, a carter, were January 1915 volunteers and in the same draft as Private Cumming. The two of them landed in France on 4 October, joined the Battalion on the 7th and died next day. Private Wilson's mother Mary Wilson was in Leeds, Private McDonald's father Hugh McDonald in Dalry, Ayrshire. Private James Cockshott, a September 1914 volunteer, another man who lost his life that day, had been in the BEF for longer, but for much of the time since his arrival in February 1915 he was sick, with varicose veins and then debility, so it was not till July that he joined the Battalion. He was a textile factory worker before the War and the son of Dennis and Jane Cockshott of Nelson, Lancashire. He left his belongings, only an identity disc, to Bertha Garrett, also of Nelson. A fourth man killed was an old soldier, a signaller of over seven years service, Private John Wright. Once upon a time he had been a clerk. While the 1st Scots Guards were in Egypt he was sent on a course at the Camel Corps School and on 9 February 1911 they were on a march when his camel shied and threw him, breaking his wrist. An inquiry attributed no blame to him. He went to France in August 1914, was slightly wounded in the left forearm in October at Gheluvelt and only in hospital for a short time, but in March 1915 he went sick with influenza, sufficiently badly to be sent home. He returned in this draft that had just arrived. An identity disc and a photograph were all that there were to be sent to his married sister Ethel Bowman in Cheetham Hill, Manchester.

Unknown to Captain Barne it had become apparent to the British that the Germans were going to attack somewhere along the line because they had made various preparations, such as cutting their own wire around Hill 70. Where they had in mind was not clear, however. They did make an attack near Hill 70, but they also assaulted the point in, but south, of the main part of the Hohenzollern where the 3rd Grenadiers were in most of the trench called Big Willie, a salient into the German line. "About 3.30pm an attack is made on the 3rd Bn Gren Guards who are advanced to our right front. They repel the infantry attack but suffer severely by being taken in reverse by a heavy bomb attack out of an old German trench." The Germans drove back the Grenadiers from their front trench by outbombing them. On his own initiative Lance Sergeant Oliver Brooks of the 3rd Coldstream, on the right of the Grenadiers, organised his own battalion's bombers for a counterattack and completely defeated the Germans, recapturing the lost trench. There was further help from the 1st Irish Guards and from B Company and Left Flank of the 1st Scots Guards, sent up to assist if needed. This fight went on for three hours. Sergeant Brooks was awarded the VC. Captain Barne had no way of knowing what was going on. The two companies he had sent off "spend an exciting and unpleasant evening and night. There is more bombing during the night…by morning all is quiet. It was a most disturbed and anxious night for me, or rather for the two Coys out." In case he needed them two companies were sent up from the 2nd Scots Guards. While he mentioned the enemy attack, Sir Iain Colquhoun was much more interested in sorting out his own company position, building proper fire steps and deepening the trenches. They also "blocked old German communication trench leading straight into Hohenzollern, and put trench mortar and bombers at one end."

They were then told to relieve the 3rd Grenadiers as right forward battalion. So on the 9th Captain Barne had "All the morning taken up with going round the Grenadier trenches and learning the lie of the land, a terrible sight, the trench being scattered with mangled corpses and many more on the parapets. Am getting perfectly filthy not having had a bath, shaved or even washed my hands since we came into the trenches on the 5th. Goodness only knows when we shall get out. Our mode of living has been very primitive and our diet and cooking of the simplest. Nights are disturbed by (amongst other things) rats scratching and dropping bits of straw, earth etc. on our faces…In afternoon we carry out relief…in the forward trenches, with one trench practically ending in Hohenzollern Redoubt." They moved up and to their right towards the Grenadiers with whom "the double relief goes off quite smoothly barring a bit of a fracas between Col Corry and Con Seymour. A bombing attack is made on the 1st Guards Bde on our right, but ends in smoke. A peaceful night after about 7pm, very close quarters in a tiny dug-out, the Adjutant, a signaller, an Artillery Observation Officer and myself. The Adjutant sleeps on the floor and I in a niche just above him. The night is rather a worrying one as we are at work all the time and have a difficulty in keeping up the supply of sandbags."

The 10th was a Sunday and Captain Barne wrote of a "Quiet morning, but a lot of shelling in the afternoon, can hear a terrific bombardment by the French away to the South." That evening the 2nd Grenadiers, now on their right, prepared a bombing attack which would have been, at least partly, in front of them and invited Captain Barne "to cooperate, which I decline not having many bombers and of them eight are borrowed and inexperienced Grenadiers, we having lost so many on Sept 27th. However we undertake to help in a passive sort of way for mutual protection. The result is a terrific bombing contest which lasts most of the night, and our B Coy under Hammersley do a great deal of firing to help. The Grenadiers find the job a harder one than they anticipated and do not make as much headway as they hoped. However, in spite of counterattacks, they hold what they get." Next day he went on "The French at it again away on our right. We are getting a good many casualties in the Battalion, several caused by shelling, in one case six men were killed and buried all in a lump together, and some are being shot by snipers through the head…After being told we are to be relieved today, again deferred till tomorrow." Headquarters Guards Division recorded that nine thousand Mills bombs were used up on 8 October, of which six thousand were obtained from the 46th (North Midland) Division, Territorial Force. Five thousand more were received on the 9th and on the 13th "82 Steel splinter proof helmets issued to Guards Division for trial," the first British steel helmets.

Meanwhile plans were developing for an attack by the 12th (Eastern) Division, New Army, on The Quarries and by the 46th Division on the Hohenzollern and The Dump, and, all being well, on the colliery, Fosse 8, beyond. This was what the Scots Guards work bringing up chlorine gas dischargers and making recesses was for, so too the 1st Coldstream. Captain Feilding wrote afterwards that they had put in four hundred and twenty cylinders in their part of the trench. These each required two men to carry them with a relief team of another two. During 12 October the Scots Guards were busy fitting up scaling ladders and cutting steps in the parapet. Sir Iain Colquhoun noted "Lost a few men from splinters from our own guns, which were shelling short." That evening things did not go smoothly. The Germans, possibly alerted by their aircraft to a significant relief, attacked the 1st Guards Brigade as they were preparing to move, but were driven off, and meanwhile shelled everyone else. Inevitably the relief by the incoming 46th Division was disrupted. Sir Iain Colquhoun recorded very heavy enemy shelling and how he was himself twice partly buried, but C Company's casualties were few. He then complained that the incoming company "did not arrive until 2am. The communication trenches were hopelessly blocked, and we had to cross the open all the way to Vermelles. It was very misty, and we were not fired on or shelled. Very thankful to get back." Private Cumming echoed him in that the incoming battalion "jammed the communication trench from end to end [and we] staggered more or less from the maw of Hulluch Alley with empty water bottles and a feeling of sympathy for the French Foreign Legion." The march back to billets "was not exactly like a stroll in Hyde Park, but we made it by morning. A spell in the trenches was not conducive to that kind of physical fitness…The meagre attractions of the village speedily contributed to a remarkable recovery of spirits and stamina and the local red and white wines were sampled, although with not too great enthusiasm. French beer also lacked that inspiration which was characteristic of home brews in that day and age. Far from elevating the spirits, these beverages usually succeeded in upsetting that portion of the anatomy which my old gym instructor used to call "the abandom"." After assembling beside the brewery in Vermelles they marched on to Vaudricourt, just south of Béthune, taking four and a half hours. Captain Barne mirrored what the others said. "The relief, a most complicated business, is ordered to begin at 4.45pm and by the orders should be over by 11pm, but, owing to the enormous number of troops in the communication trenches, everything got delayed and the whole Battalion was not clear till 6am, and we did not reach our billets at Vaudricourt till 9am, the men very weary and exhausted, about an 8 miles march. For me it was a very anxious night, and I found the only thing to do was to get out of the trenches altogether and down to Vermelles on the top of the ground. The last 2 Coys to get away were LF and C, and this was a race against the daylight, it was just touch and go, as it was we were only spotted at the last minute, though I never know why not sooner, and fired on, but no casualties. We dived into the first empty trench we came to which was not for some time and were then safe. During the night while relieving some heavy shellfire was turned onto us and we had some casualties including one poor signaller buried. One shell lit on parapet a few feet from where the Adjt and myself were, it ½ stunned me and buried the Adjt all but his face, when I recovered I realized he was under a heap of earth and began scraping with the handle of my stick (it was too dark to see his face) and heard a squeak, and found I hooked his eye! We were not long getting him out. When his head was sticking out he remarked "I'm all right" and all through has been of the utmost value and shown great pluck…In afternoon received a visit from Alby Cator, commanding our 2nd Battn, who wants back some of the officers he lent us, but we found we were level so I could not let any go. He is splendid and just as keen about our efficiency as his own."

Altogether they had nine men killed, forty two wounded and six, all buried alive on the 10th, missing. One of the dead was Private Donald McKay, the son of Donald and Jessie McKay from near Kilmartin, Argyll. He was a footman, probably in Edinburgh, where he volunteered in early December 1914, and came to France in May 1915. To begin with he was in the 2nd Battalion but transferred to the 1st Scots Guards with the loan of officers on 3 October because he was Lieutenant Orr Ewing's servant. Private Sydney Snowball was admitted to a field ambulance with shell shock on the 7th. By this time he had been a soldier for eighteen months, after enlisting in Leeds. Till then he was a grocer's assistant, presumably in nearby Otley, where his home was. In 1914 he first came to France as a reinforcement and was sent to the 2nd Battalion after First Ypres, but went down with severe diarrhoea just before Christmas at Rouges Bancs and was evacuated to England. He returned to France in August and came to the 1st Scots Guards as the Guards Division was forming. After he had shell shock he was evacuated again to England, stayed there till October 1917 and then suffered neurasthenia as soon as he landed back in France. This continued for two months and, when then passed fit, only a week later he suffered from loss of memory. He remained in France for another seven months, kept away from the fighting, until he contracted bronchial pneumonia in July 1918 and went home for good. Private Henry Malone, a labourer in Glasgow until September 1914, had been in the BEF for six months, was hit in the face and head on or about 8 October and died on the 9th at Lillers. Among the belongings sent to Henry and Mary Malone in Ranelagh, Dublin, were a prayer book, a London Scottish cap badge and a jack knife. Private Thomas Pomfret was wounded for his second time, in both legs by a grenade, and sent to England. He remained there for a year and in 1916 he and Bridget Pomfret had their second daughter. Private Robert Davie, a hoistman in Govan, enlisted in September 1914. He arrived in France in February and had already been wounded in the back once in June, only slightly, and was away for a week recovering. Then on 15 July he was hit in the hand accidentally by another soldier's pick and sent home for treatment. He was back in France again in the 4 October draft and was killed on the 10th. His stepmother was his nearest relative and she, Annie Davie, was living in the South Side, Glasgow. Private James Rennie was mobilised from the Reserve in August 1914 and went out with a draft later that month, missing the Retreat from Mons. He was shot in the mouth on 11 November 1914 at Nonne Boschen and evacuated, returning to France at the beginning of May, though he did not rejoin the Battalion till 3 October. He was missing on the 10th and later confirmed as having been killed that day. Mrs H Rennie, his mother, lived at Glencarse, Perthshire. Private Thomas Robson was five days past his twentieth birthday when he enlisted in Keighley, Yorkshire, on 29 October 1914. He was an apprentice spinning overlooker with John Clough & Sons and his five year apprenticeship would be up on his twenty first birthday. He arrived in France at the beginning of May 1915 and missed the first part of Loos because he was in hospital in St Omer with dyspepsia. He was discharged on 1 October and sent back to the Battalion. On the 6th he was badly wounded in the back, presumably by a shell, and died next day at Chocques. Ebenezer and Maggie Robson received his wallet, a tin of cigarettes and some letters and photographs. But for the War his apprenticeship would have been complete on 24 October.

Private Johnes referred to the British trenches close to the Hohenzollern as a "jungle". While he and Private Evans were with C Company during one "trip in" they found themselves "dis of communication, and George started to run the line back…at the second bay he found the trench plugged, a shell had blown it in." From there they set off back checking and mending the line as they went until they met two signallers from Battalion Headquarters working in the opposite direction. "Two other linemen had set out…and had been caught in a section of the trench and blown up, buried." One was dug out alive but Private Jimmy Gammack, the reservist from Toronto, died on the 12th. Private Johnes wrote that he "had a premonition that he was going to be killed the next time in and he was."

When they got to Vaudricourt on the morning of the 13th Captain Barne had some breakfast and went straight to sleep till one o'clock. Then he "tubbed and shaved off my long grey beard and got things a bit square." While they might then have expected time to rest, they did not get it. Captain Barne went to Brigade Headquarters in the afternoon with the other commanding officers "to hear instructions…on many points." One of these led to bombing training for the whole Battalion which took up the whole morning of the 15th. Two men were accidentally injured. He observed that bombing was "now the most up to date form of warfare." That afternoon the Brigade were on their way back to the trenches because the attacks by the other two divisions had been disastrous, the 46th Division's particularly so, both of their attacking brigades having been badly mauled to no useful effect. Though gas and smoke were used and the British heavy artillery pounded the German positions, the enemy machine gun fire was still so effective that the right hand brigade never reached the German front line in Big Willie. The left hand brigade, having taken the Hohenzollern completely and Fosse Trench beyond it, were then driven back to where they started from and only just managed to hold onto the West Face Trench of the Redoubt.

The Coldstream took over again in the one part of trench in the Hohenzollern still in British hands and part of the line where they had previously placed gas cylinders. Captain Feilding described "The communication trenches – and in many places the fire trenches also – had been blown in by the enemy's shells. Both were littered with the sweepings of war – gas pipes and cylinders, discarded rifles and equipment, bombs, small arm ammunition boxes, and the dead. On the ground in front lay hundreds of our dead." That was not all. "The congestion in the trenches at night, during this time of battle, must be seen to be appreciated. The communication trenches, except where blown in by shells, are generally just wide enough for two men with packs to squeeze past one another with difficulty." If a company or battalion took a wrong turning on the way in or out and met another going the other way it was not easy to sort out. There was also the factor that some of the communication trenches were tunnels, known as Russian saps, and very claustrophobic unless men could keep moving through. The state of the front line was that of wide ditches, so much destruction had taken place and "It would, I suppose, be an exaggeration to say that the parapets at this place are built up with dead bodies, but it is true to say that they are dovetailed with them, and everywhere arms and legs and heads protrude." He continued "On all sides lie the dead. It is a war picture of the most frightful description; and the fact that the dead are, practically speaking, all our dead, arouses in me a wild craving for revenge. Where are the enemy's dead? We do not see them."

In what Captain Barne called "some safe trenches well back" they were initially in reserve in Sussex Trench behind the Vermelles-Auchy railway. The 16th was "A day of fatigue parties, cleaning up and repairing many communication trenches. Frogs and mice." They were there for two days. On the 17th, while others held the front line, the 1st Grenadiers and 2nd Scots Guards tried to bomb their way into the Hohenzollern. Captain Barne heard "They found they could not make much progress owing to the Germans having filled up some trenches, so that our men came under heavy machine gun fire from the Dump. We spent the night carrying up bombs and ammunition and the men are very weary." He knew that there had been heavy casualties. After dark the 1st Scots Guards swapped over with the 3rd Grenadiers in the front line, "the relief not being over till 2am, owing to the guides not turning up."

Privates Johnes, who went with B Company, and Evans were split up this time, each being allocated a new signaller fresh from England, with "the job of breaking them into the tricks of the trade, on their first spasm in the line. Which also proved to be our last trip into the Hohenzollern Redoubt. A hell of a place to break in new fellows…The rains had started to make things a little sloppy and some of the trenches had started to cave in, especially where the fellows had undercut the walls to make themselves sleeping quarters, they were dangerous, and more so when Jerry threw over heavy stuff, trench mortar bombs." On the second night he received a message from Battalion Headquarters for B Company to send down a party to collect grenades. An hour later another message stated that the party had not arrived. Another one went down and arrived, but all six men in the first had been buried when, after heavy shelling along the line of the main communication trench, parts caved in. Private Johnes may have confused this trench tour with the preceding one when describing the six men being buried. That was recorded as having occurred on the 10th, the second night in the line.

Captain Barne noted on the 18th "My little Elizabeth's birthday and I never wrote to her." They were digging a new front trench closer to the Germans, the plan being that, as they dug from one direction, the 4th Grenadiers would dig from the other "so there may be a lively time." Meanwhile the 1st Coldstream were in the only part of the Hohenzollern in British hands and Captain Barne went up there because of the proposed new trench, which Right Flank were to work on that night. Next day he noted that they had "made a good start with the new trench." He met a staff officer from Headquarters Guards Division "and we have quite a business to get the right line to meet the new trench being dug from the other end, put up two scarlet petrol tins as marks which the Germans amuse themselves by sniping at. It is pitiful to see the huge number of British dead lying around Hohenzollern, many had got right bang up to the barbed wire and were forcing their way through, which of course many must have done as the Redoubt was taken. About 4pm a tremendous fusillade was started, which turned out to be a German attack on a piece of trench which they recently lost, but while it lasted such a din as is not often heard. It died away about 8pm, result not known, but very disquieting while it lasted. We had 2 killed and 7 wounded, but were very lucky, and several men buried were dug out again." This attack on the neighbouring 12th Division was easily driven off by the 7th Norfolks and

9th Essex. Sir Iain Colquhoun noted "At 11pm the last shell of the evening partly blew in my dug-out killed 3 and wounded 3 Irish Guards, also burying two telephone operators whom we got out. I slept in the open for rest of the night." During the dark the digging of the new trench continued. Captain Barne remarked of one officer loaned by the 2nd Battalion that "Jack Stirling is a most useful officer and full of enterprise, of unceasing energy. We are now in a very deep dug-out in the chalk, very safe from shells (though in one case the concussion blew out our candle)…We breakfast and lunch in daylight and sup below. Are relieved by 3rd Grenadiers in evening and return back to Sussex Trench near Vermelles, well and safely away from bombs, but not for long."

They went into the front line on 21 October to the immediate north of where they had become accustomed in front of the Hohenzollern. They had the 1st Coldstream on their right and their left was on the Vermelles-Auchy railway. They took over in Guildford Trench from the 9th HLI, Glasgow Highlanders, Territorials, and 2nd Worcesters, both of the 5th Brigade, now commanded by General Corkran, a close friend of Captain Barne's. Sir Iain Colquhoun found the trenches taken over from the Glasgow Highlanders in good order and Captain Barne echoed him. He added "We seem to be in the only active bit of the line, judging by the English newspapers." Sir Iain Colquhoun noted that soon afterwards at "About 7pm the Germans fired rifle grenades at us one landed in trench, killing one man and wounding another. I telephoned the Gunners who shelled with 18 pounders and stopped all grenade firing for that night." The 22nd was a "Lovely morning. Arranged 2 sniping posts and fired 5 shots and probably got 2 Germans who show themselves very openly unless fired at. The lines are a short 100 yards apart here." He commented that the British guns were active all day with rare response from the Germans, who, however, had the range very accurately. That apart, the day held for Captain Barne "No special excitements till about 7.30pm when a message arrives saying the GOC has reason to believe the Germans contemplate making an attack within the next three days etc., so we go to bed (a granite like board covered with sandbags and crawling with mice) feeling rather jumpy." That day he heard that his friend Major Molineux Montgomerie of the 3rd Grenadiers, the owner of the bay mare Geraldine, had been shot through the eye by a sniper and killed, having left the trench to help two wounded men.

From the front line on the 22nd Captain Feilding wrote of the attitude of everyone. "There are no heroics. In fact, it is rather etiquette to grumble and pretend to be frightened. It is, I imagine, a sort of protective bravado. A short time ago I was listening to one of our young regular officers and a good one too, talking with another officer who is serving for the period of the war, and who came from China specially for the purpose. The latter was letting fly about things in general and got the reply "What have you got to grouse about? I joined the army to enjoy myself, and I find myself plunged into this ------ war. I have some right to complain. You joined the army to fight, and you've got what you came for. You have nothing to grouse about."" He also overheard two men of the Scots Guards talking about the War, one of whom said "If you gets wounded and it's a cushy one, you gets sent 'ome; and if you gets killed, well it's ------ all!"

There was no German attack during the night of the 22nd either and once darkness fell the next night the Brigade left the line and the Scots Guards marched back to Annequin. In this last week there had been only the one fatal casualty described by Sir Iain Colquhoun and eighteen men wounded. The man killed by a rifle grenade was probably Private Gilbert Ryan, a carter from Newmilns, Ayr, with no known grave. Volunteering late in 1914, he had been in France since July 1915, leaving behind his wife Jessie, to whom he had been married nearly five years, and their daughter, who was about to be three. By 1916 Jessie Ryan was an "asylum inmate" and Mary Ryan, her mother in law, was looking after the girl, described as "destitute". Though recorded as killed in action Lance Corporal Neville Clarkson may have died of wounds on 18 October once in the medical system. On enlisting after Christmas 1914 at Shoreditch, East London, he stated that he was nineteen and an agricultural student. Already a Lance Corporal, he was probably in the 4 October draft and was dead on the 18th. Kenneth and Harriet Clarkson lived in Stamford Hill. Private Thomas Rawstron, the surgical appliance maker from Nelson, was also in the 4 October draft, apparently fully recovered from his shoulder and hand wounds with the 2nd Battalion at Neuve Chapelle. However, he strained his shoulder, the wound reopened, he was sent down the line on the 22nd and was soon in England again. There was mention too of some lung infection which may or may not have been related. He would reappear before long.

Rest out of the line

Lieutenant Colonel Lord Esmé Gordon Lennox, badly wounded in October 1914 with the 2nd Battalion at Kruiseecke, arrived without warning on 24 October to take command. Captain Barne knew he had been appointed and was certain that it would be good for them, but "so I am deposed…I am to be second in command for a bit, which means nothing to do." On the 25th they marched to the station at Béthune, went to Lillers and marched on west to the villages of Bourecq and St Hilaire, half of them at each. It had poured hard all day and everyone was drenched. Sir Iain Colquhoun found his billet at Bourecq "Very comfortable… electric light, beds, etc." He told Dinah Colquhoun that on the 27th "I went into Lillers today and judged some boxing for the Black Watch and London Scottish – quite like old times… There are a few shops here which sell anything one wants and altogether it is very cheerful… We have a good portable gramophone here. Will you send me 6 or 8 records 4 Harry Lauder and anything else you like but none of your high art things as I doubt if the others would appreciate them." Captain Barne walked over to Hamm with Lord Esmé Gordon Lennox to visit the 4th Coldstream, who were "living in the very interesting remains of an old monastery with some beautiful old carvings and panelling in oak. In the garden is reposing the remains of a statue of an old Knight in Armour of 14th Century, with his shield hung on his left arm showing he had been killed in action. I dine at Brigade HQ where the Brigadier is in great form and full of fun and talk."

It was the start of a more relaxed period of nearly two weeks, but there were other interludes, one of them very irritating. On the 28th, a very wet day, the whole Guards Division were making their way towards Lillers for King George V to inspect them. Everyone was already soaked through on the march when a message came telling them to stop and return to where they had come from. At the time they all thought that the reason for the cancellation was the rain, in which case it was too late as everybody was already wet through. Private Johnes described "A beastly morning, raining "Cats and Dogs." Our groundsheet capes were not of much use, and we soon got wet through…we were turned about and back to our billets. We were a miserable outfit marching back…However, we were darn glad to get back to billets and changed into a dry shift of clothes." They had not had their packs with them. Private Cumming recalled how they marched in the rain "with our equipment hidden under groundsheets. As these simply diverted the water on to our nether regions, and allowed a considerable quantity to insinuate itself icily down our necks, the progress was not exactly jubilant." A few days later they "were considerably bucked by a newspaper caption under one of the pictures, "The King Chatting With His Troops". As "Chatting" had become the universal Army slang for delousing this went down well for many a day." Sir Iain Colquhoun then spent the whole afternoon playing bridge.

Captain Barne learned next day that the reason for the cancellation was that the King's horse had reared, thrown him and then fallen itself, landing on and injuring him badly. The next few days were all generally both cold and wet. Whenever he could he went for walks either on his own or with others. On the evening of 29 October he was by himself when he found "Paul Methuen sketching and take him on, a curious creature." Next there was "Bombing practice nearly all day. Jerry Ruthven comes over in the morning and tells us we are going to "nibble" by bombing attacks all the winter – a pleasing prospect!" When the Guards Division formed at St Omer Colonel Hore Ruthven became GSO1. On the 31st Captain Thorpe came back, his hand having healed, and took over as Second in Command, so Captain Barne became company commander of Left Flank, with his cousin, who was on leave, and his brother in law as his officers. He recorded the activities of 1 November. "Kit inspection and bombing and inspection of billets by CO. My new billet is a very nice room in a Brewery. It looked, I thought, a dear old building, well coloured and picturesquely matured by age, however I am rather startled to find a stone in wall with date – 1873! Wet all day."

There were bombing training and practice bombing attacks day after day, instruction on building the latest type of barbed wire entanglements, route marches and other training, but it was not intense and there was little pressure. The rest of the time was filled with lots of football, with several concerts and with boxing matches, at which Sir Iain Colquhoun was a judge. When on the afternoon of 3 November the Battalion met the 1st Coldstream at football, a 2-2 draw, the Regimental Band of the Grenadiers played to entertain the spectators. From this time on there was almost continuously one of the Regimental Bands out from London with the Guards Division. Lieutenant Seymour came back from leave on the 4th and announced his engagement to Kathleen Butler. A very recent arrival in the 3rd Grenadiers was 2nd Lieutenant Raymond Asquith, the Prime Minister's eldest son. After Eton and Balliol College, Oxford, he became a barrister and was now thirty six. Just after his arrival he was censoring his men's letters and reported to Katherine, his wife, what one of them had written about him. "He seems a very decent officer as yet. If his military style is as good as his classics he will do well." On 5 November he told her that the day before he had marched his company to the baths in the brewery vats at La Gorgue and that "while I was waiting for them in a garden behind the brewery a sergeant of the Scots Guards came up and asked me to umpire a drill competition. A corporal had bet a sergeant 5 francs that he – the corporal – had a better word of command. So I went into a field and heard them shout at a squad in turn; I awarded the apple to the corporal, because I thought that would be the popular thing to do; and so it was." On the 8th Private Johnes left for a week's leave. He described how not until that August was a proper leave system started for the men, who went home two at a time in the order of their arrival in the Battalion. Private Evans had gone not long before and he had been out since August 1914. It said much for the pattern of casualties that Private Johnes with eight months service in the BEF was not long behind him.

After the battle at Puits 14 Bis and the following days Lance Corporal Percy Anderton, the cartoonist and author of the 14 Platoon notes in the *Left Flank Magazine*, was missing and never heard of again. Sergeant Donald Thomson, the Platoon Sergeant of 16 Platoon, was also missing. Afterwards it became known that he had been shot in the head on 27 September and died on 2 October in a German field hospital. His brother James on Flotta, one of his large family of brothers and sisters, was his next of kin. Private George Morris, the Editor, hit in the hand, Private Jimmy Jones also of 16 Platoon, with flesh wounds in both thighs, and Private James "Irish Hun" Fitzsimmons of 14 Platoon, hit in the right leg, were all sent home to recover. All came out again later. Lance Corporal Willie Moore, the London footman who probably wrote the 13 Platoon notes was also sent home, hit in the right thigh. On 30 January 1917 he became an officer in the Tank Corps. Private Robert Hattle, the contributor who also wrote the 15 Platoon notes after Sergeant Blair's death, was only slightly wounded at Puits 14 Bis and treated in France, while Private William Taylor of 16 Platoon survived that, but was hit in the right shoulder on 17 October at the Hohenzollern Redoubt. He remained in England for some time after that.

Private Robert McLuckie, who survived everything, left France on 23 October and was discharged four days later on completing thirteen years service. Afterwards came the announcement of his DCM, not for any particular act of gallantry but for "marked bravery and coolness on many occasions. He is a most fearless bomb thrower, and is always volunteering for any dangerous work." Someone like him who had been a soldier and served his time could later on be called up after conscription was introduced, but if that happened he never returned to the Scots Guards and his trade as a miner could have kept him away from the Army thereafter. Private Arthur Reynolds, the contributor from 14 Platoon, was not hit either. However, there was never another Spasm of the *Left Flank Magazine*, never mention again of Rabbie.

Private Morris continued to write verse and by the end of the year was again at Wellington Barracks, where "Scots Wha Hae – a Christmas Dinner" appeared:

> Scots Guards wha at Loos hae bled
> Scots wha hae on bully fed.
> Welcome tae a glorious spread
> Turkey an' plum duff.
> Though oppressed by aches an' pains
> We'll eat a' that there remains
> Deil a thing we'll leave but banes,
> Scotsmen, follow me!

Notes on Chapter Sources

War Diaries: Guards Division A and Q Branch TNA/WO95/1197, 2nd Guards Brigade TNA/WO95/1217 (Series), 1st Scots Guards TNA/WO95/1219/3 (Series).
Capt TB Trappes Lomax, 'Artillery Support at Loos', Spring Number 1930, *Household Brigade Magazine*.
Report of Brig Gen J Ponsonby dated 3 October in 2nd Guards Brigade War Diary.
Account of Pte W Scott, Liddle Tape 394.
Articles by Pte G Cumming, SGM 1969, 1970, 1972, 1977 and 1978 not chronological in content, but what is drawn from them is.

Diary of Lt Col Sir Iain Colquhoun of Luss, Bt, Private Collection. Quotations from letters to his wife are identified as such.

John Jolliffe, *Raymond Asquith, Life and Letters* (London: Collins 1980).

LCpl G Morris, 'Extracts from a Notebook of World War I', SGM 1959, for the last verse above and those verses elsewhere in the text not published in the *Left Flank Magazine*. He wrote another article in SGM 1966.

Lt Col J Stewart and John Buchan, *The Fifteenth (Scottish) Division 1914-1919* (Edinburgh: William Blackwood and Sons 1926).

12

The Battle of Loos – 2nd Battalion

The formation of the Guards Division at St Omer

After a hot, trying march the 2nd Scots Guards arrived in the early evening of 9 August at Wizernes, where they were for six weeks, with one short interruption. Sergeant Walter Bold returned from home leave that day not knowing about the move north. On a full train from Boulogne he intended to go to Merville. There were eight other men in his compartment when he went to sleep. On waking at Chocques, west of Béthune, there was no one else left and his rifle, cap and most of his equipment had gone. He reported to the military police, who arranged for him to go to Wizernes. He had been serving for nearly two years when the War started and worked before that as an engine cleaner, apparently in Berwick, where he enlisted, though his home was in Portobello. He went out in October 1914 and was first promoted to Lance Corporal immediately after First Ypres, becoming a Lance Sergeant after Neuve Chapelle and a Sergeant four months later.

On Sundays there were church parades, Colonel Cator having to take a short one himself on the 15th when the Church of England padre failed to turn up. Later that day two men off duty were bathing in the nearby canal. One either got cramp or was out of his depth as a non-swimmer. Four others on the bank all leapt in at the cry for help, but too late. Private James Duncan drowned. He had only arrived the day before. A machinist and iron driller before he enlisted in September 1914 at Clydebank, he had been in the 1st Battalion for two months earlier in 1915 before being evacuated with a poisoned foot. He and Lizzie Crombie married in 1910 in Aberdeen, their elder son being born the same year. A younger son, born in 1914, died the year after.

From 15 August, but with only the 1st Grenadiers and 2nd Scots Guards there by then, the 3rd Guards Brigade began to form. Captain Warner, unhurt throughout since Zeebrugge, was appointed Staff Captain. He did not want to do this but on the 16th he "Saw the General and had to take staff job." This was presumably General Heyworth. Lord Kitchener, accompanied by M. Alexandre Millerand, the French Minister of War, inspected both battalions on the 16th at the Flying Ground on the Wizernes-St Omer road. Captain Warner was immediately taken up with billeting. On the 17th he was dealing with that for the Brigade Staff "Very tiresome." Soon afterwards the 4th Grenadiers and 1st Welsh Guards arrived from England and getting them settled in was also his responsibility. On the 24th Major Tempest arrived as Brigade Major, Captain Warner having been doing that as well as his own job.

Two recently joined Scots Guards officers were 2nd Lieutenants The Honourable Charles "Charlie" Mills and Esmé Arkwright, who both transferred in May from the West Kent Yeomanry, and landed next month in France. Lieutenant Mills had been at Magdalen College, Oxford, was MP for Uxbridge, the youngest elected in the 1910 General Election, a partner in the family bank, Glyn, Mills & Co, and eldest son of Lord and Lady Hillingdon, of Waltham Cross, Hertfordshire. Lieutenant Arkwright, an older man, was an Etonian and had been an officer in the 5th Lancers in the Boer War. He and his wife lived at Sharnbrook, Bedfordshire, and he was Master of the Oakley Hunt. Sometime in 1914 a Life Guards officer brought over his own car which was subsequently seized by the military police at Boulogne, where it stayed as there was no transport available to send it back. Now, in August 1915, Lieutenant Mills "acquired" it and brought it to the Battalion, where it was christened "Michael" and led a most useful if unauthorised career. It resembled and was disguised as an ambulance. On one occasion, taking officers to the leave boat, it was pursued by a RAMC colonel in a staff car, incensed that an ambulance was going so fast. The fat was then almost in the fire, but the successful solution was replacing the number plates with those of an Army Headquarters car known to be undergoing long term repairs in St Omer. Later, a calf of either Bella or Bertha was bartered on the military black market for a new set of tyres for "Michael" and two hundred gallons of petrol and Captain Ross, the Quartermaster, subsequently saw the same calf being carried onto a steamer at Boulogne on its way to England.

For the rest of August at Wizernes there was training at company and battalion level, which included not only drill on Helfaut common, firing on the ranges and route marching, but also skirmishing, use of cover and practising attacks in open country. All this was in line with what they might have to do next, about which they knew nothing. Later on in August and into September companies were sent out one at a time to a forest to cut timber. Like the 1st Battalion they were out for the Divisional Field Day on 1 September which appeared, since little took place except route marching, to be for staff instruction on movement procedures and timings. However, on the 6th the Brigade practised attacking over open country for which the 4th Grenadiers and Welsh Guards led on the left and right, with the 1st Grenadiers and 2nd Scots Guards in support. There was a similar exercise on the 21st, but also frequent mention of training of various sorts having to be cancelled because of the wet weather. A major problem then and later was drying out clothes and equipment, the men having only the one full set of uniform.

On 15 September Private Johnny Callachan, the son of John Callachan of Govan, was sentenced by court martial to three years penal servitude for hitting a corporal five days before. The sentence was confirmed but before he went to prison orders came that he was not to go until further notice. The sentence was suspended on 8 October. A soldier under suspended sentence could have it lifted and the sentence erased if he performed well later. Otherwise it stood and could be applied at any time subsequently, again depending on conduct. Private Callachan gave his occupation as a holder up when volunteering in Glasgow late in September 1914. While at the Guards Depot he incurred several punishments, one for hitting a fellow soldier. He arrived in France at the beginning of April.

The approach to the Loos battlefield

Just as he briefed officers and NCOs of the 2nd Guards Brigade on 15 September General Haking also explained to the 3rd Guards Brigade "in outline the operations they might be called upon to undertake in the open." On the 21st orders came to start to move, though no one knew where to. Great care was taken to ensure that the routes had been properly reconnoitred in advance and arrangements put in place for men from the divisional cyclist company to act as guides at doubtful intersections. Lieutenant Kit Cator was back in G Company, under Captain Stirling. He wrote on the 22nd to tell his mother that they were leaving for the front that day "by successive marches. You will probably have heard that a big move is on and there has been a continuous bombardment by our own and French artillery for some time. All the staff and everyone here feel very confident… it will be the biggest thing in the War, and if successful should go a long way towards ending it." The Division began to march south, but that evening the Battalion only went the short distance to Clarques. It then started raining hard. They marched the following evening in the rain to Norrent-Fontes, a few miles short of Lillers on the main road from St Omer. They stayed put the next day, the 24th, when "The situation for the forthcoming attack was given out. All ranks showed great eagerness for the coming fray. A heavy bombardment could be heard throughout the day." Lieutenant Cator had written what was partly a "farewell" letter to his mother on the 23rd, very pleased to have his brother as Commanding Officer and unable to say much, but "If we can only get these beastly Germans on the run my next letter may be from the banks of the Rhine!"

Because of the postponement of the Division's start time till six in the morning on the 25th, caused by the congestion and delays ahead, it was daylight when they set off again. This was initially only the two miles to Erquedecques, as it turned out little more than a protracted halt for the men's dinners. The first news they heard of the battle was that Givenchy and most of the German first line had been captured, both misleading. At two in the afternoon they were on the move again through Burbure, Lozinghem and Marles-les-Mines, swinging round to the southeast of Béthune, marching on well into the night in heavy rain. This was not helped by the 2nd Cavalry Brigade moving forward at Marles-les-Mines and cutting through their Brigade on the line of march, splitting them in half. Worst, all of them were already two miles past Haillicourt, due south of Béthune, when orders arrived that they had to go back there, which meant turning round on a very narrow road. The Scots Guards were more fortunate than some. "The battalion got into billets at 11.30 pm after a very tiring & wet march. The roads were in a terrible state of mud from the traffic." Others were much later.

Captain Warner had left Brigade Headquarters at eight on the morning of the 25th on a motorbike. First he arranged new billets for his Headquarters and the Scots Guards at Erquedecques. Then he went round the other three battalions with instructions and was back at Brigade Headquarters at half past eleven. New orders arrived to move on at two o'clock, he having left an hour before to go to Headquarters Cavalry Corps to ask what was going on. Next he came upon the bivouacs of the 21st Division and found a new place for Brigade Headquarters. He went back to meet all the Brigade billeting parties and then returned to the billets identified for Brigade Headquarters. Next at six in the evening an order came for the whole Brigade to go Haillicourt, but soon he heard that they were to move on to Houchin. He went there, found billets for Brigade Headquarters and bivouac sites for everyone else. Then at nine he was told to return to Haillicourt after all. So, consistent with what the battalions were experiencing and what he had to prepare for, amid whatever confusion and at whatever notice, half of the Brigade started arriving there from ten o'clock onwards. The other half were currently missing. He settled down those who had arrived and had dinner. The rest, through no fault of their own, turned up at half past one in the morning on the 26th. Captain Warner "Got them billeted and slept on mattress in Roger's room." Then he "Got up at 7am. No orders to move. Orders received about 12 to go to Vermelles. Left at 1.30pm, went on with guides from Sailly-Labourse, and after some difficulty found fields with trenches for Battalions. Brigade arrived at 8pm and were all in bivouacs by 9. Bde HQ in house built up with sandbags. No orders for tomorrow. Got some sleep after midnight." At Vermelles, though others were billeted in dug-outs, the 2nd Scots Guards were lined up bivouacking in the open behind the former British trenches at Corons de Rutoire. A cold wind blew all night.

The attack on Hill 70

The Battalion stood to at half past five on the morning of the 27th. They had been told during the night of the plan for the 2nd Guards Brigade's attack on the Chalk Pit, Chalk Pit Wood and Puits 14 Bis and that, if it succeeded, the 3rd Guards Brigade were to capture the western side of Hill 70. As it went on to do all day and on into the night, it rained hard as they waited that morning. There was also a certain amount of enemy shelling, aimed principally at the field artillery batteries in front of them, but one shell landed in a trench and killed an unnamed Scots Guards corporal. Captain Warner noted "Orders received at 11.30am to move to Loos and attack Hill 70, 2nd Brigade to attack Chalk Pit and Puits 14 Bis at 4pm. Our attack to follow. Brigadier and Bde Major went on to find places for Battns. I remained to guide Bde. Went with leading Battn 4 Gren Gds. Had to cross very exposed ground and were heavily shelled crossing the hill NW of Loos." The Brigade had started at two o'clock to move towards Loos along the line of the road from Vermelles, in the order 4th Grenadiers (left forward), Welsh Guards (right forward), Scots Guards (in support) and 1st Grenadiers (in reserve), so replicating the brigade field day at Wizernes. The battalion commanders were warned that as soon as they crossed the old German front line, just on the near side of the Grenay Ridge as they looked at it, they would be under direct observation by the enemy and were likely to come under shellfire. So it proved. Therefore as they came up to the Ridge they put their battalions into artillery formation and, as soon as they came to the former German second line trenches on the far side they used them to move into Loos, now being shelled itself, both with shrapnel and gas. The consequences of not taking all possible precautions when in view of enemy observers was illustrated by the remains of 21st Division Transport, destroyed by shellfire the day before.

Rifleman Reginald Prew, a soldier for two and a half years in the 1/8th London Regiment, Post Office Rifles, Territorials, was on the Double Crassier, captured by the 47th Division two days before. "During the morning we shifted our quarters to a dug-out underneath one of the crassiers, having twenty feet of chalk and forty feet of slag above us. About dinner time we went out on top of the trenches and looking towards Vermelles, we saw one of the best sights we had ever seen, that of the Guards Division coming up to reinforce the line where the supports had failed. In extended order, equal space between each man and with lines as straight as a rifle barrel. Anyone looking at them could imagine that they were watching military evolutions on the Barrack Square. They going on as if there was nothing amiss in the world, although the shrapnel was bursting above their heads and the number of casualties must have been heavy, but still no wavering." The casualties from shelling were very light. Captain Warner "Got Battn into trenches near town where I met Brigadier. He went on with leading Coys, I remained to send others on. When most of them had gone was heavily shelled with gas shells, so went into town which was also being shelled heavily. Found Brigadier and Roger collecting some of 4GG and Welsh Guards. Great confusion. Eventually most of Bde collected in position to attack."

General Heyworth's plan was for the 4th Grenadiers to attack Hill 70, but about a third of them skirted Loos to the north instead of going through it and then became drawn towards the 2nd Guards Brigade's neighbouring attack on Puits 14 Bis. Consequently he had to add the Welsh Guards to the attack on Hill 70. He was not to launch this unless the 2nd Guards Brigade's attack succeeded. However, he could see British soldiers on and around the Puits and therefore concluded that they had. He could not know that the few who had got into the Puits could not be reinforced and were about to be overwhelmed or forced to withdraw. A later message from Lord Cavan that he should proceed in any event did not arrive in time to make any difference and once he knew the true position at the Puits he had no means of stopping his attack on Hill 70. Although he had told both battalions not to go beyond the ridgeline, they did so because they were looking for the redoubt and trenches which their maps showed as on the north side of Hill 70. That it was on the east side was the cause of most of their casualties. Captain Warner understood that the 2nd Guards Brigade had reached their objectives but had had to retire. Then "Welsh Guards and some of 4GG attacked hill and reached but could not cross top. Both Battalions lost about 400 men."

When the 2nd Irish Guards attack on the Chalk Pit area began at four o'clock the enemy redoubt at Hill 70 had been under British bombardment for an hour, but the cut-off time was ten to five. Here, as at the Chalk Pit and at the Puits, the 3rd Guards Brigade attack went in unsupported by shelling to keep the enemy machine gunners under cover. The 2nd Guards Brigade could not have made more progress than they did, but had they achieved all they were required to do and been able to do so quickly, the 3rd Guards Brigade might have been able to attack Hill 70 while it was still being shelled. Just as infantry communications were very difficult and uncertain, so too were those of the artillery, which led to the inflexibility of fixed times.

The 2nd Scots Guards were moving into Loos at quarter to five as the leading battalions went on towards Hill 70. There then followed a very trying few hours. They had to wait in their gas helmets as German HE shells landed, knocking down buildings in the village. There were also gas shells. These "gas helmets", the first pattern, were of flannel soaked in glycerine with glass eye pieces and covered the head and neck. Trying to move quickly in them was difficult and became more so when intermingled condensation, glycerine and sweat fogged the eye pieces. About eight o'clock a message came from the Welsh Guards that they had taken the western face of Hill 70, whereupon General Heyworth ordered the Scots Guards to go forward to relieve them and dig in there. They soon found that, while some Welsh Guardsmen had reached the far slope on the eastern side of the "hog-backed ridge", but short of the German redoubt, it was apparent that the crest itself was untenable, because anybody who showed themselves against the skyline was certain to be shot. The only practical solution arrived at between Colonel Cator and Major Alan Brough, Commander Royal Engineers, Guards Division, was for three companies to dig in slightly back from the crest while the Royal Engineers put out wire in front of them. The fourth company remained in reserve to deal with emergencies. It proved very difficult to communicate with those Grenadiers and Welsh Guardsmen still on the far side of the crest because patrols sent forward were immediately shot down. Similarly, in spite of great courage by the stretcher bearers during the night and in daylight the following morning, recovering the wounded was often impossible. Captain Warner had heard that the 2nd Guards Brigade had established themselves around the Chalk Pit. He himself "Went through town to their HQ and later went again to guide Lord Cavan. A few shells and many bullets flying about. Got a little intermittent sleep. Brigade HQ in cellar NE of town."

By the following morning, when it was still raining hard, with the Germans well established in their redoubt some sixty yards away from them on the far side of Hill 70, the Scots Guards were well dug in on the near side. Over to the right they had bent their trench back to link up with that of the dismounted 8th Cavalry Brigade manning trenches next to them. However, on the left there was a gap because of the failure to take the Puits and so Colonel Cator decided that that end of his line had to be fortified into a redoubt and the gap beyond covered with two machine guns. It was impossible to do anything about this in daylight. After the 1st Coldstream attack on the Puits failed on the afternoon of the 28th, the 2nd Scots Guards, who had watched helplessly from the west slope of Hill 70, built their redoubt after dark with help from the Royal Engineers. They also dug communication trenches back towards the second line of trenches on the edge of Loos, where the Welsh Guards now were.

Captain Wynne Finch wrote in the War Diary for the 29th "The rain which had been coming down in sheets for the last three days showed no signs of stopping. The troops were very cold & wet & had had no sleep for three nights. In spite of all they were cheery & worked well. Orders arrived at 6.30pm to say we were to be relieved by the 22nd London Regiment. The relief did not take place till 1.30am 30th." They still had to get back through the shell trap of Loos but were lucky and lost no one on the way to Vermelles. There they paused till two on the afternoon of the 30th before moving back further to billets at Labourse. Nevertheless, it was on the 29th that Lieutenant Reginald Macdonald was recorded as having been hit on the head by a flying brick and soon sent home. He was educated at Loretto and Brasenose College, Oxford, was commissioned at the end of March and came out to join them in June 1915. After this wound he remained in England until August 1917 when he returned to France. His home was near Quirindi, New South Wales.

Captain Warner spent most of 28 September in the Brigade Headquarters cellar while "Enemy shelled Loos very heavily and twice blew out candles in dug-out with exploding shells." Next day was much the same until the relief started after dark. He was not on his way back till two in the morning on the 30th to Vermelles "a wonderful sight, practically flat, with many broken wagons, dead horses etc. on road. Dined at 3am and went to sleep." In the early afternoon he went on ahead to Verquigneul where the Brigade were to billet, but found the 2nd Guards Brigade already installed, though many were not yet back from the front line. He went to get fresh orders from Headquarters Guards Division. The first ones had been wrong and the 3rd Guards Brigade were to go to billets in Labourse, not Verquigneul. He continued "Billeting till 8pm. A good deal of trouble but got everyone under cover except 300 men." Next day he got shelters built for those without billets. The day after that he "Borrowed tubs for men's baths." For much of these two days he had been working on details of casualties and establishing accurate numbers of the officers and men fit to fight. Headquarters Guards Division recorded the delivery at Labourse on the 30th of twelve tons of coal at thirty eight francs per ton for the 3rd Guards Brigade.

Comparatively, the Scots Guards casualties had been fairly light. Sixteen men were killed, fifty one wounded and forty missing. One man only was recorded as having been gassed, without another wound. This was Private James Rands, erstwhile bamboo table maker and the son of James and Annie Rands of Hoxton, North London, a serving soldier in 1914, who first came to France very shortly after First Ypres. After being gassed now he was out in France again six months later. Lance Sergeant William Dougal, who would shortly be awarded the DCM, had gun shot wounds in both feet as well as being gassed. He had been slightly wounded once before, in the left arm at Neuve Chapelle. Originally from Dundee, where he was a waiter, he served for three years from 1909 and then became a reservist. He came out at the start to Zeebrugge but after Loos remained in England for the rest of the War, rising to Sergeant in the 3rd Battalion. He married Mary Scott, a widow from Glasgow, in 1917 and they had a daughter the year after. Private John Laurence, the serving soldier from Beeston Hill, Leeds, caught smoking while on outpost duty just before the main fighting started at First Ypres, had been through everything since then unhurt. On 28 September he was wounded in the left thigh and right groin and evacuated and it was a year before he was fit to return. Lance Corporal William Lawrie, who had made friends with Lance Corporal William Preston in the aftermath of Festubert, was shot in the shoulder and evacuated. Where the wounded were sent to hospital on getting back across the Channel often bore little relationship to where their homes were and Corporal Lawrie arrived a week later at the Ulster Volunteer Hospital, Belfast. He returned to the Battalion in September 1916 soon after the battle at Lesboeufs on the Somme, stayed with them from then on and became a Lance Sergeant a fortnight before the Armistice.

Private James Horsburgh and Lance Corporal John McDowall, who both joined up on 14 December 1910, respectively in Edinburgh and Girvan, Ayrshire, and had consecutive regimental numbers, were dead. Both were serving soldiers at the start of the War, but Private Horsburgh did not arrive until after First Ypres, later qualifying as a battalion signaller. Corporal McDowall had been in at the start at Zeebrugge. Alexander and Annie Horsburgh, lived at Miller Hill, Dalkeith, and William and Isabella McDowall, at Girvan, though she moved across Ayrshire to Maybole after she was widowed. Richard and Margaret Ibison were tenant farmers of the Earl of Derby near Woodplumpton in North Lancashire. Their two sons, Richard and George, the younger by a year, volunteered at Preston on 25 November 1914, giving their occupations as farmers. Private George Ibison was discharged medically unfit on 31 July 1915 without leaving England and issued with a khaki armlet to indicate that this was the case. His elder brother, who was missing the top joints of the first two fingers of his right hand, left for France on 1 June, was promoted to Lance Corporal on 24 September and was killed at or near Hill 70 three days later. An identity disc and an item described as "an emblem" were recovered.

Private Christopher Hay, a turner working in Glasgow, had volunteered a year earlier and been in France for six months. A shell blew off his right leg and he died in a casualty clearing station on 28 September. His home was in Newcastle where Christopher and Sarah Hay received his belongings, a tobacco tin, a wallet, a pocket knife, a metal chain, part of a cigarette lighter, letters and photos, some Scots Guards insignia and a "souvenir." A "souvenir" was usually either a piece of expended ammunition of some sort or else something a German had once owned. Private Lewis Alexander, previously a grocer in Glasgow and a serving soldier since the end of 1909, died on 1 October at a casualty clearing station with shrapnel wounds in both hips. James and Isabella Alexander lived at Urquhart, Morayshire. Lance Corporal James Warden was shot in the left shoulder and lung and died in a field ambulance at Noeux-les-Mines next day. Until the War he had been employed looking after horses for the City of Glasgow Police. He had already been badly wounded once when he was hit in the chest with the 1st Scots Guards at the Railway Triangle on New Year's Morning, after which he was evacuated to England. He came back in August and joined the Battalion on 3 September. James Warden, his father, lived near

Montrose and was sent a whistle, a corkscrew, badges, a button, an ID disc, a broken clay pipe and a notebook. Private Samuel Tyrrell, a leather finisher by trade and no longer a reservist, reenlisted in September 1914. Less than two months later he was in France. After Neuve Chapelle he was sick with neuralgia and defective vision for nearly six weeks and did not return till the end of July. He was wounded on the 28th, his foot blown away, and died the same day in a field ambulance at Mazingarbe. He had married Jeanie Crawford in Glasgow in December 1903 and she and their six sons were living in Bridgeton. Sergeant Gilbert Partridge, a carpenter in Bromyard, Herefordshire, when he became a soldier in 1906, was a Lance Sergeant when war broke out and was immediately promoted to Sergeant. He sailed to Zeebrugge and was wounded on 28 October during First Ypres, with a cut in his scalp. He recovered in England, came back in May 1915, rejoining after Festubert, and was killed on 29 September. Charles and Catherine (or Kathleen) Partridge lived in Bromyard, but he left his belongings to Miss EM Bull, then living in Bloomsbury, London. Later she received his medals.

During the digging in on the night of the 27th Lieutenant Kit Cator was slightly wounded when someone struck and set off a dud shell, his second wound. The same explosion mortally wounded Captain Lord Petre of the 4th Coldstream. At her home in Kinning Park, Glasgow, Martha McMillan was formally notified that her husband Private George McMillan had died of wounds on 3 October, but she was able to refute this, declaring that she was not a widow and that her husband, from whom she heard almost every day, was alive and well with the Transport of the 3rd Guards Brigade. Private McMillan had served for three years till 1912 and been mobilised as a reservist. He did not join the Battalion till after First Ypres, but was with them for only just over three weeks before a bullet hit him in the right calf on 8 December 1914 at Rouges Bancs. Once recovered he came back to France in March.

1 October was spent trying to find out about casualties and checking deficiencies of equipment and so was the day after, the highlight a visit from Sir John French, as elsewhere characteristically going round talking to the men. The 3rd, a Sunday, was a quiet day with voluntary church services.

Gun Trench in front of The Quarries

That night the forward battalions of the 1st and 3rd Guards Brigades, respectively on the left and right, were to occupy Gun Trench where it faced The Dump and the Quarries, the Hohenzollern Redoubt being over to the left. The 3rd Guards Brigade's plan on 3 October for the relief after dark of the 5th Brigade of the 2nd Division illustrated what was supposed to happen during a relief, but for a variety of reasons might not. To begin with the Welsh Guards were to be at Vermelles Church at four o'clock to take over as the reserve battalion from the Glasgow Highlanders. Then, starting from Vermelles Church, the Scots Guards were to leave at eight to take over from the 2nd HLI as the left hand battalion in the front line, the 1st Grenadiers at nine to take over from the 2nd Oxford and Bucks LI as the right hand battalion and the 4th Grenadiers at ten to relieve the 2nd Worcesters in support. The Brigade Machine Gun Company were to follow the Scots Guards. As each battalion reached Headquarters 5th Brigade at the Chapelle de Nôtre Dame de Consolation guides from the outgoing battalions were to meet each incoming platoon. The route for the relief followed the Vermelles-Hulluch road as far as the Vermelles-Auchy railway and then went into the communication trench, Chapel Alley, though they could use the road itself after dark. The outgoing battalions would hand over trench stores, bombs and Very lights, as well as the former petrol tins used to carry water, with their harnesses.

It took the Scots Guards about an hour and a half to go from Labourse to Vermelles, which they reached at eight, as ordered, and where they "found the roads blocked with traffic, nobody being there to direct." At Vermelles Church they collected tools and sandbags and then went on along the Vermelles-Hulluch road to the Chapelle. The guides sent to meet them there then lost their way, further delaying the relief of the 2nd HLI, which was not complete till a quarter to four in the morning. A problem and an inconvenience in Gun Trench was that while the 5th Brigade were there the Germans had captured fifty yards of it at a point now in between the two forward Scots Guards companies. Recovering this was to be a task for their Brigade, while the larger plan was forming for a Guards Division attack on The Quarries. In order to keep the enemy quiet a lot of grenades were thrown at them through the night with the desired effect. Then, while General Heyworth was going round next morning the German guns shelled the G Company trenches, blowing in the parapet in a number of places and burying several men. Most, but not all, were dug out unhurt.

Private Robert Baillie, on the Reserve for two years following eight years with the Colours, was killed. He was a grocer in Edinburgh before that and when he enlisted was provided with a set of artificial teeth and required to sign an undertaking to pay not more than three pounds for them or have stoppages deducted from his pay for the same amount. The undertaking continued that he was required "to maintain them in serviceable condition at my own expense during my period of service." While Isabella Baillie, his mother, was believed to be in Edinburgh, the address he had given for her was untraceable and it was impossible to notify her of her son's death, though later her whereabouts did become known. Then a letter dated 9 November arrived at Regimental Headquarters from Agnes Scott in Glasgow asking for details of Private Baillie's death, which she had seen in a casualty list published in The Citizen on 30 October. In reply she was asked to explain what her relationship was to him and whether she knew his mother's address. She wrote back "I am in no way related to deceased soldier. His name & address was sent to me by a friend, & I sent him a parcel every month from March last. I usually received a letter from him about ten days after same was sent off, and as I received no letter regarding last parcel I sent him, I wrote to you to know when he had been killed. I am sorry I cannot inform you of the address of his mother or any other relative." Private James Tait, a coachman who enlisted at Dumfries a year and a day before this and had been in the BEF for five months, had multiple shell wounds in his right hip, knee and leg and in his left hand and was sent home, permanently. Afterwards he had limited powers of grasp in his left hand and his right leg was very weak. He was discharged medically unfit in the spring of 1918. His stepmother Annie Johnston lived at Burnhead, Dumfriesshire.

There was still confusion about the fate of some at Hill 70. Private William Scott, in the Army since just before Christmas 1914 and in the BEF since the beginning of June, was recorded as wounded on 28 September and then either killed or died of wounds between that date and 4 October. He was a farmworker and married Jessie Chappel in July 1912 at Cockenzie. She was living with her family in Haddington and some letters and photographs were sent to her. The possible dates for the death of Private David Bryden, who had joined up shortly before Private Scott and been in the same draft, were the same. He too had been a farm worker, specifically a stockman looking after animals. David and Rose Bryden lived in Inverness and were sent a number of his belongings. That in both cases effects had been recovered pointed more towards 4 October.

There was more shelling of the G Company trenches, but worse, on the morning of 5 October and Lieutenant Mills was killed by a direct hit. That afternoon the British heavy artillery did the same to the German trenches after which everything quietened down. It was because of the events on the 4th across to the left at the Hohenzollern that there was the change of plan, which, while leaving the 1st Guards Brigade where they were, took the 3rd Guards Brigade out into reserve, so that the 2nd Guards Brigade could take over in front of the Hohenzollern. That night there was another slow relief for the Scots Guards, not complete till two in the morning, and not for another hour and a half were they in their billets at Corons de Rutoire. All the Brigade's billets, Captain Warner wrote, were "in shelled out houses."

Nine men were killed and twenty two wounded in Gun Trench, as well as Lieutenant Mills. One of the dead on the 5th was Sergeant Joseph Wilkinson, promoted again at the beginning of July, the DCM winner at Festubert. Slightly wounded at the beginning of June, he was back in twenty four hours. Amelia Wilkinson, his mother, wrote a little later to ask if she might be sent the medal that her son had not lived to receive. This was very promptly done. Private James Hamilton, an electrical engineer who volunteered in Glasgow in September 1914, in France since mid February, also died that day. John and Mary Hamilton lived in Kelvinbridge. Private William Fowler, the son of Archibald and Sarah Fowler of Dunfermline, had been a grocer until the War. He came out towards the end of May and was killed on the 5th, exactly a year and a day after he volunteered at Perth. Private Robert Donaldson, in the same draft, but a much older man, thirty four when he joined up, was also killed. Before the War he was a riveter and lived with his wife Isabella and their two sons and two daughters in Dalmarnock Road, Glasgow. A third man from the same draft killed that day in Gun Trench was Private David Robertson, a railway ticket collector, but since December a soldier, whose widowed mother Ann Robertson lived at Pitlochry. Private Thomas Cornes, however, was a reservist, a Glaswegian who had served eight years to 1912, been called up on mobilization and been out with the Battalion since the very start. He too was dead. His sister Margaret Jackson was in Hamilton.

The Hohenzollern Redoubt

The Battalion were not directly involved around the Hohenzollern until they went into the line there on the 15th. A great deal had happened during the previous ten days. Captain Warner recorded that on the 8th the "Germans started heavy bombardment 11am and attacked "Big Willie" about 4pm." This was the attack on the 3rd Grenadiers which led to Sergeant Brooks' VC, when, as a precaution, two 2nd Scots Guards companies were sent up to Barts Alley to be ready if needed. Captain Warner noted that the 4th Grenadiers had carried up fifty boxes of grenades to the front line. Colonel Cator, in his letter on the 9th, told his sister Gertrude Talbot about the other German attack the day before across the line of the Lens-La Bassée road near Hill 70 and the Chalk Pit. The French, now in the trenches at Hill 70 dug on the night of 27 September, had "mowed the Germans down like corn stalks as they topped the crest to attack them, we thought it rather a dream of a place when we dug it & hoped they would attack us there." British troops were holding the line at the Chalk Pit and they too held their ground successfully. Colonel Cator continued "Yesterday was the noisiest day I ever remember, we were in support all amongst our own batteries. The Germans started an intense bombardment at 11am & kept it up all day, there are crowds of guns here & each battery fired 1200 rounds so [you] can imagine how our ears buzzed, we are all as deaf as posts today. I got a slight bang on the leg yesterday, but except for it being a bit stiff am none the worse." Bulgaria, following the successful Turkish defence of Gallipoli, had come into the War on the German side. "What a bore it is the Bulgars coming in, I suppose it will prolong this beastly war. The troops are all in excellent spirits but they are awfully tired poor chaps. This battle began a fortnight ago today & looks like going on another fortnight, after that I suppose both sides will lie down & pant for a bit, our wretched little Army never seem to have enough troops & have to keep using the same ones over & over again. I pray God they bring in conscription & rope in all the funkers at the street corners from all classes."

The day after, the 10th, he wrote again to his mother "I shall never cease to thank God that I belong to the Guards Division, their splendid example the last fortnight had made everyone cease to "shy bricks at them". Discipline is everything out here, and our rigid Discipline has carried all before it. Please don't repeat this to outsiders as it sounds like "bucking" – but oh I <u>have</u> been proud of my lads the last five weeks, I can't tell you how I simply worship them." Lieutenant Mills was "a great loss, a real champion." The main activity over the next three days was large fatigue parties carrying gas dischargers up to the front line for the 46th Division's attack on the Hohenzollern on the 13th. On the 10th it was mysteriously reported that "a suspicious person had tried to get information from the men as to what they were doing but he was not arrested." Several German planes flew across that afternoon undisturbed, but next day four British ones immediately attacked one that came right over them, forcing it down near Annequin, the pilot and observer being captured unhurt. There were a lot of other fatigues taking up a lot of men and time. The Scots Guards then moved back to Annequin, only for two days as it turned out.

The 46th Division's attack was their first, though they had been in the BEF for some months. Their commander was Major General The Honourable Edward Montagu Stuart Wortley. On the afternoon of the 13th news reached the Scots Guards "that the gas attack on the Hohenzollern Redoubt was going well." It was not and the 4th Grenadiers and Welsh Guards had already been moved up just behind in order to help. The Scots Guards, already at an hour's notice, were told to move to Sailly-Labourse at eight on the 14th. There they went into billets, now at only half an hour's notice. That afternoon they were on their way back up to Vermelles, stopping again at the Church to collect sandbags, tools and bombs and then heading on towards and then down the communication trenches, Gordon Alley for most of the way to where it joined Hulluch Alley and then along that to the front line, approaching Big Willie from the south. Barts Alley was the next communication trench north of Gordon Alley.

When the 46th Division went up before their attack there were four main communication trenches. One brigade used the most northerly one and one the most southerly one, that which the Scots Guards had now gone up. One of the other ones was only for the troops whom the 46th Division relieved to go back by and the fourth was only to be used by stretcher bearers. After a failed attack when there had been many casualties that system was unlikely to hold steady, so that there was almost certain to be congestion, the walking wounded, among others, tending to use the first way out that they came across. The Scots Guards War Diary was an understatement "There was some difficulty about taking over the line as units & Brigades were very mixed up from the attack the previous day." The relief was complete by half past two in the morning. It was a very cold night with a thick mist, which, when dawn broke, helped getting round to examine the positions. Their first shock was finding that they only held about five yards of Big Willie, the second the state of the trenches, the third the human evidence of the

46th Division's failure. Dead were lying unburied in large numbers and they came upon some wounded of the 1/6th South Staffords in a communication trench whom they carried down to the nearest dressing station. By day it was difficult to do much about the trenches, but they began to repair them. That night they buried about eighty British dead, collected from out in the open.

The 46th Division's attack had been disastrous. Colonel Cator, not differentiating between Territorials and New Army, told his elder brother in Norfolk "I cannot tell you what some of K's Army Generals & Staff have been like, we have been through their battlefields after them. Stuart Wortley seems to us all to have been the worst offender. Hundreds of his dead were lying <u>behind</u> our first line, because he said he must attack from a line parallel to his front." His second line started "500 yards further off over exposed ground, it made us all simply gnash our teeth with anger at such a fool being allowed to wear a British Uniform, let alone command a Division. We took over from him & had to retake some trenches which he had lost. His men must have been splendid. Near our own lines lay masses of them and as they got nearer the German lines they got fewer & fewer till at last all down the German parapet one could see individual corpses here & there, every man lying with his face towards the enemy & all trying to do their bit, it was a sickening sight to see such good material wasted in incompetent hands." He went on "we have lost seven of our best officers the last fortnight including Charlie Mills who from all accounts is not only a loss to us but a great loss to the country. He was a perfectly charming chap…We have had some rather strenuous times lately, but are more than holding our own, gaining some ground & beating the swine back every time they try to attack."

There was next to be a Guards Division two phase attack, with the same purpose as the 46th Division's. The first, planned for early on the 17th, involved the 2nd Guards Brigade attacking Little Willie and the northern half of the Hohenzollern and Fosse Trench which ran behind it, while the 3rd Guards Brigade attacked Big Willie, the southern half of the Redoubt and Dump Trench which ran behind it, joining up with Fosse Trench there. The second phase, to capture Fosse 8 and The Dump could only take place when the first had succeeded. Unlike the 46th Division's attack, this was going to be fighting along trenches with grenades, the new Mills bombs. The Scots Guards were occupied throughout the 16th preparing to attack Big Willie, while the 1st Grenadiers were to attack on their right. General Heyworth came up to discuss the details as bomb stores and depots were set up throughout the trench system. The Welsh Guards carried up 3000 grenades for the 1st Grenadiers, 8000 for the Scots Guards, 500 for the 4th Grenadiers, 4000 for the Brigade Reserve and 1200 at a further reserve dump at Vermelles. In the evening there was an unsuccessful German gas attack, which went too high, and a bombing attack, also unsuccessful, followed later by shelling of the Scots Guards in the front line and a further bombing attack on Gun Trench over to the right. None of this had any material effect on the preparations. At four in the morning on the 17th three companies moved into position and G Company came up along the communication trench to be ready to occupy the front line as the attack progressed and to pass up more grenades and sandbags with which to make blocks in captured trenches. Behind them the 4th Grenadiers had formed a chain up the communication trenches to pass up still more grenades and sandbags, a process which worked very effectively throughout. In thick mist but reasonable light for the purpose the attack went in at five o'clock. Surprisingly the German guns did nothing while this went on. Apart from repeated calls from in front for more grenades there was no other information to begin with, but it became apparent that there was a very stiff fight going on. As the trained bombers became casualties other men, who did not know what to do, started throwing grenades, often without having pulled the pins out first. The Germans threw them back, without the pins. By the end of it F Company had captured and held about a hundred yards of Big Willie, while Right Flank had taken about fifty yards of a communication trench running back from it, but were unable to hold it. Left Flank, who were to attack along another communication trench, were stopped by machine gun fire after cutting the German wire. The 1st Grenadiers made no headway because they could not get through the enemy trench block and because of machine gun fire. At eight in the morning Headquarters Guards Division ordered consolidation of the ground gained, done without further interruption. When the attacks had only been going forty minutes Brigade Headquarters were told that there were no more grenades in the Brigade Reserve. Welsh Guardsmen managed to deliver the 1200 in the Vermelles dump to the trenches soon after nine in the morning and then spent six and a half hours putting fuses and detonators into 7200 more for the Brigade Reserve.

Captain Arthur "Daisy" Orr, whose widowed mother lived at Larbert, Stirlingshire, was killed commanding F Company when trying to speed up progress by attacking in the open. He had been quite badly wounded the previous October with F Company in Polygon Wood when under command of the 2nd Wiltshires. Lieutenant Nicholas Lechmere was also killed. He had been to Westminster and Sandhurst, but had left the Army. When the War began he joined the 10th Duke of Wellington's and transferred in June 1915, coming out very soon afterwards to France. When he died he had been in the Battalion for two and a half months. His parents were dead and he was himself a widower, but he had a brother living at Pershore, Worcestershire. He was a member of the Russian Orthodox Church. Right Flank's relative failure was ascribed to the loss of control when Lieutenant Cecil Shelley, commanding their attack, was killed. He, aged forty two and closely related to the poet Percy Bysshe Shelley, transferred from the 2nd Life Guards in August, travelling out to France at the beginning of October. He had been in the Battalion nine days. Two other officers were wounded, one, Lieutenant Dick Warde, hit in the leg, came in to have his wound dressed at about half past six and then went out again to continue directing his bombers before being wounded a second time in the shoulder and being brought in on a stretcher.

The total losses of men were eventually found to be one hundred and thirty six killed, wounded and missing. Private Patrick Tague, a miner, originally from Linlithgow, West Lothian, was very badly wounded in the chest and had a shell fragment behind his right rib cage. An early September 1914 volunteer, he had been out since February and very recently, while on leave on 20 September, he and Margaret Tague had got married in Kelty, Fife, where she was living. Private Tague had led a bombing attack, been wounded, gone on throwing grenades, kept the men with him together and refused to leave until ordered to do so. He won the DCM and would have known about it before he died of pneumonia on 13 February 1916 in a London hospital. Corporal Roderick MacLean, not a trained bomber, volunteered to help the attack, was wounded once in the head, but went on fighting until hit again. He was thirty one, older than most who enlisted early in the War, and was a marine engineer on the Clyde. In France since late March 1915, he became a Corporal after the events at Hill 70. He too won the DCM and he returned later.

Sergeant Alexander McHardy, a Glasgow policeman, was missing. His mother Louisa McHardy lived at Strathdon, Aberdeenshire. He arrived in France on 2 December 1914 to join the 1st Battalion at Borre. There he made an immediate impression and was promoted to

Corporal on 10 December. During the counterattack on New Year's Day 1915 on the Railway Triangle he was hit in the left knee and evacuated, spending three months in hospital and not coming back till the beginning of May, when he was sent to the 2nd Scots Guards. After surviving the early stages of Loos he was made up to Sergeant on 6 October. Sergeant Robert Leppington was another who died. When he enlisted in York in 1907 the recruiting officer described him as "A smart superior sort of man" and added that he refused to join the Army except in the Scots Guards. By trade a carpenter, he served as a pioneer in the 1st Battalion until he went onto the Reserve in April 1914. From August he was in the 2nd Scots Guards and went abroad in October, surviving everything unscathed and first being promoted to Lance Corporal after Neuve Chapelle, then to Lance Sergeant after Festubert. From 6 October he too was a Sergeant. Tom and Eliza Leppington received an identity disc and some letters and photographs at their home in Scarborough.

Private George McKenzie, a furnaceman until September 1914, arrived in France at the beginning of April 1915, but missed Festubert and most of the summer in the trenches because of tonsillitis and did not rejoin till the beginning of August. He was recorded as killed. His sister Mary McKenzie lived at Winchburgh, West Lothian. Also recorded killed was Private James Millar, a carter and the son of William and Catherine Millar of Dundee, who was in the same draft. On 15 June he had been caught "Sleeping in the Reserve Trenches with his boots and puttees off" for which he received seven days FP No 2. Private James Christie, an engineer in Glasgow who joined up later on in October 1914, arrived out in June 1915. He was missing. The instructions about his next of kin were unusual. First, Mrs Scott, living in Fulham, London, was to be told in the event of his being a casualty and she would then tell his father, only contactable at the South Pier, Oban. Private Christie had been born at Glassary, south of there. Private George Flather, a serving soldier in 1914 and former wool sorter from Halifax, went out first as a reinforcement and was sent to the 2nd Scots Guards after First Ypres. He had survived until Neuve Chapelle and then been slightly wounded and also had a bout of what was probably trench fever. In the Hohenzollern attack he was hit in the head and died two days later at Lillers. James and Mary Flather were sent his tobacco pouch, a pipe, a match box, a cap badge and a coin. Privates William Ewing and George Hunter had consecutive regimental numbers. Private Ewing had enlisted two days earlier in December 1914. Educated at Dollar Institution, he was a clerk with Gray & Harrower, Grain Merchants and Millers, Alloa Mills, and the son of William and Jeanie Ewing of Tullibody, Clackmannanshire. Private Hunter, a hall boy in the Aberdeen area where he enlisted, had an uncle George Hunter in Worksop, Nottinghamshire. Private Ewing stated that he was exactly nineteen when he joined up, Private Hunter that he was nineteen and ten days. Both were in the same draft late in May 1915 and both died on 17 October.

Corporal Preston described the Hohenzollern as "a spacious underground cellar capable of sheltering one thousand men provisions and ammunition. This [we] were destined to attack on the following morning. Forty bombers were detailed for the assault, myself included." He referred to the chain of Grenadier and Welsh Guardsmen passing bombs up the trenches. "Bayonet men and bombers played the chief parts. Twenty of us got into an old hole forty yards behind Jerry's parapet by three in the morning. We divested ourselves of tunic and equipment and at five the game started. We took them off their guard but they quickly returned and gave us bomb for bomb." He rated the Mills bomb as more effective than the German grenades and "by midday we had taken the outer wall of this fort. We consolidated our ground and during the night we were relieved and glad we were to smell good air after that stench of Ammonal & Lyddite. We got back to Vermelles but was shelled out so lay in a field more or less scattered."

There was thick mist after dawn and they gathered in and buried the dead. The rest of the day was quiet until after dark when the German guns started to fire and one shell hit their parapet burying seven men, only four of whom were dug out alive. The British guns retaliated on the German front line and soon all was quiet again. That night there was a full moon and they started sapping a new trench parallel to Big Willie, it being impossible to dig in the open. Sapping was not easy either as the Germans had a machine gun trained on the sap head. Private Robert Docherty was recorded as having died in a field ambulance at quarter past four in the morning on the 18th with shell wounds to his legs and mouth. He was a miner until just under a year before. Thomas and Janet Docherty at Crossgates, Lanarkshire, received a few of his belongings. Private Irvine Hughes, a shop manager from Liverpool, enlisted shortly after Private Docherty and arrived in France three weeks later in May 1915. He died at half past four in the morning of the 19th in a different field ambulance as the result of being buried. In Liverpool Janet Hughes, his mother, was sent a few of his belongings. Private Jesse Dowland joined up at the beginning of September, leaving his job as a verger and his parents Joseph and Martha Dowland at North Ripley, Hampshire. He had been in France since late February and died at quarter to two on the afternoon of the 19th as the result of being buried. He had with him a metal watch and strap, an ID disc, a pipe, two religious books, two photographs, a metal match box, a wallet, a piece of shrapnel, a locket and some letters.

The next day was uneventful until the 1st Coldstream came up to start a relief at four o'clock, interrupted by German shelling but completed four hours later. The Scots Guards marched back to Sailly-Labourse. On the afternoon of the 20th Lord Cavan spoke to all of them and congratulated them on what they had done in the bombing attack. He wrote to Colonel Cator two days before that "I have just seen the 1st Army Commander and he asked me to convey to you and your grand men his sincere appreciation of the great effort you made yesterday. I told him no battalion had fought with greater tenacity and courage than your's did yesterday, and I very deeply deplore your losses. It is, however, our very bounden duty to get a good line for further efforts, and your task, which was intensely difficult, gave us a good start. Please tell the men how much their work was appreciated by me and all above me." On the 21st there was drill on the transport field and Captain Wynne Finch noted in the War Diary that "The Battalion had not done any drill for 6 weeks, and were fairly steady." They were back out for more the day after.

Colonel Cator wrote to his sister Mary Fellowes on the 21st about her son, whom he said that he did not want to see out in France "for a long while, we had a wretched boy of eighteen only last week who had just joined us & completely broke down in our attack on the 17th & I had to send him back "sick" I suppose poor little chap he hadn't a very large heart on him to start with, but oh I do hate to have the boys who are mere children harassed, some stand it & are too brave, others don't seem to have their nerves fully developed, it's no shame to them it's just physical disability, crowds of them go off their heads under a heavy shell fire, most of them though are absolute marvels." He continued to be confident of beating the Germans because "at the back of our minds we always have the feeling we are "top dog" & can always more than hold our own with them. They are a wonderful nation and their science is simply extraordinary, but man for man they are children compared to our men, they will never beat us even if the war lasts a dozen years." He went on to say "I was so pleased with my NCOs the last action they carried on the fight after the Officers were knocked out & did extraordinarily well, I think that is the bedrock of our system of training. Making the NCOs responsible for a very great deal, it certainly seems to pay, I believe we do it to a very much greater extent than the rest of the Army." 2nd Lieutenant Guy Oliver, who was twenty three, was sent home, leaving France on 20 October "sick". Though commissioned at the end of March he had only landed in France for the first time on 3 October. Later he would come out again. His parents Charles and Sabina Oliver lived at Sunninghill, Berkshire.

The Battalion had one last trench tour in support in Railway Reserve Trench, for three days from the evening of 23 October. It was very cold and rained and rained on the men in the trenches, in a bad state of repair when taken over from 2nd Irish Guards. They worked at them in increasing mud, unable to drain off the water, while also having to provide many fatigue parties, in particular carrying trench stores for the Royal Engineers.

As Corporal Preston was walking along a trench about midday on 24 October a German field gun shell exploded on the parapet nearby. On "a piece of shrapnel catching me on the right side… I remembered no more. I woke up in Sailly-Labourse when I began to realize that I had been dished with a good packet." He was injected against tetanus and seven days later, during which he had been bleeding from the mouth, he was operated on at Le Tréport to remove a four ounce piece of shrapnel from his right lung. Back in England he made good progress until New Year's Eve, when gangrene set in, but he overcame that and once fit again transferred to the Royal Engineers. He survived the War.

The relief on the evening of the 26th was two hours late arriving, mainly because the 6th Buffs, East Kent Regiment, of the 12th Division had got all their companies muddled up before they got into the trenches. All was finally complete at eight, but it was not till half past three in the morning that the Scots Guards reached Cantraine, close to Lillers, primarily because the divisional cavalry traffic guides at the road junctions put the companies and everyone else onto the wrong routes.

Notes on Chapter Sources

War Diaries: Guards Division A&Q Branch TNA/WO95/1197 re coal delivery on 30 September and issue of grenades for attack on 17 October, 3rd Guards Brigade TNA/WO95/1221 (Series), 2nd Scots Guards TNA/WO95/1223/4 (Series).

For account of "Michael" Maj & QM T Ross, *The Fortune of War. Catalogue. Cameos of the Great War by an Eye Witness. Paintings depicted by Stewart Robertson, Official Artist – 2nd Army*, SGA.

Account of Rfn R Prew, IWM/88/46/1.

13

The Laventie and Neuve Chapelle Trenches and the Winter 1915-16 – 1st Battalion

---

Rest and breastworks

Commissioned from Sandhurst a year before but held back because of his age, Lieutenant Bobbie Abercromby arrived at Le Havre at the beginning of November and wrote to his mother Lady Northbrook shortly afterwards "The tunic has arrived all right, but there is no sign of the pyjamas. Pheasants will always be thankfully received. There are about 10 of us in the Mess here… I don't know how much longer I am going to stay here. The 1st Btn is full up and they always like keeping one officer in each Btn at the Base to look after any slightly wounded men who have been sent back. I have got about 70 here at present. I went down to Havre docks yesterday with a fatigue party to unload stores. The whole place is covered with barbed wire, ordinary wire, field kitchens, carts, guns, limbers, etc. and on one quai there were over 60 18pr and hundreds of limbers. In one storehouse there are 9 million sandbags…It is funny how the civil population hate us here. They hate us quite as much as the Germans if not more. Our men despise them, and call them "a nation of beggars"…that is about what they are, all the children run after you begging for food or money and our men cannot understand it. I have to read several hundred letters a day and this is the impression they give you. We have built enormous camps here, and the inhabitants think that we like fighting and have come over and settled down here for a change, and intend to stop. When they are asked why they think we like the war, they say that the trains that come back from the front are full of wounded, cheering and laughing and evidently enjoying themselves. Of course they don't see the bad cases. They would soon change their minds if they saw some of the letters I have opened. I must say I like this place much better than London, I feel much better, and eat about four times as much. I cannot think of anything more to say." By first postscript he asked "for more cascaras there are not many in the medicine case." These were laxatives. Then came a second postscript. "The pyjamas and food has just arrived. Please don't send me any more tongues as I cannot eat it by myself in my hut and I only get about half a slice if I put it in the mess. Please send me some chocolate biscuits."

The effects and the experiences of the previous winter were such that the Indian Corps were not to spend another in France. They left the BEF for the Middle East, though Indian cavalry stayed on. XI Corps were to take their place in the line. The Guards Division's part in this was from the junction of the Estaires-La Bassée road with the Rue du Bois at Port Arthur, just south of Neuve Chapelle, on the right, up to Picantin, to the east of Laventie, on the left. Here there was a front line of breastworks just east of the Rue du Bois, which became the Rue Tilleloy as it went north. This was backed by a series of forts as a support or second line. Further back still, as the third line, was a chain of fortified posts, known as the Croix Barbée System, running generally along the line of the Rue Bacquerot, itself roughly parallel to and west of the Rue du Bois/Rue Tilleloy. Winchester Post was one of the most important. The orders to those holding these lines were to do so at all costs, though it was thought unlikely that the Germans would launch an attack in winter over this terrain, their having no incentive to do so. A reserve line still further back could be manned quickly if needed. Croix Barbée itself was on a road junction with the Rue Bacquerot, a bit north of Festubert and outside the divisional southern boundary.

Considering all the trouble that there had been the previous winter over draining water from the front line and all the improvised efforts to do something about it, surprisingly it was not until the Guards Division took over here that anyone set out to learn exactly how the water normally drained north to the River Lys. Major Brough now put this in hand. After his survey and after an enormous amount of work over an extended period clearing out and improving drainage channels, making some new ones in the right places, and installing a large pump close to the line, the situation improved materially, but not necessarily as seen through the eyes of those at the breastworks. The Guards Division expanded the existing baths at La Gorgue to take a company at a time and made smaller ones at Pont-du-Hem. Though little could be done closer to the line, at La Gorgue they also set up facilities for drying out wet clothes and equipment and, connected to this, Headquarters Guards Division recorded a coal barge arriving on 2 December. At La Gorgue and Laventie soldiers clubs with reading and recreation rooms opened on 3 December. By January there were several forms of entertainment and that month saw performances by the 19th Division's "Follies," by No 1 Motor Ambulance Pantomime Company, by the Coldstream Guards Regimental Band and by the "Merville Macs." There was a "cinematograph entertainment" at La Gorgue on 20 January.

On the clear morning of 8 November the 1st Scots Guards left their villages at quarter to seven and marched northeast to take over billets near La Gorgue from Indian troops at what Captain Barne described as a "dirty big farm…Quite the dirtiest billets I have ever been in." Sir Iain Colquhoun was annoyed when many fell out on the march, fifteen miles altogether spread over seven and a half hours, remarking that it would "have only been a stroll to the old Batt." Captain Barne commented that "Their feet have got soft partly, and at Bourecq no doubt they lived very well, and had all the beer they wanted." Private Cumming's recollection was "of a painfully exhausting march" to billets where "we found a good deal of crude tobacco leaves lying around for which we could find no use. Their other legacy was what we claimed to be a specially voracious breed of lice – "with Bengali whiskers on" said someone."

Next day Captain Barne was with Left Flank who "Dug a trench to practise bombing which we did in the afternoon when I was hit on the temple by a splinter of a bomb, quite a narrow shave for my eye, in reality rather a good thing as it will teach us all to be more careful." Among the more newly arrived officers he found Lieutenant Methuen "a curious tall delicate looking creature, pleasant when not too cynical, of artistic taste, is a Professor of Pretoria Museum when in private life, and was an officer of the Wiltshire Yeomanry." In his own company he now had 2nd Lieutenant Warine "Warrie" Martindale "who has lived in Canada for three years studying the Law." He, commissioned two months earlier, had been born in Ferozepore in the Punjaub, where his father was a soldier, and went to school at Winchester, near his current home at Itchen Abbas. While training to be a barrister in Lethbridge, Alberta, he also had some interest in prospecting for minerals in the Rocky Mountains. Someone just returned after being invalided sick in the summer was Captain Sir John Swinnerton Dyer, Bt, usually referred to as either John or Jack Dyer, a regular officer commissioned from Sandhurst in 1910. He had come out to the Battalion during First Ypres and been wounded almost immediately on 8 November at Nonne Boschen. He was the only one of the six officers hit that day to survive and return to the BEF, which he did four months later. Captain Barne thought him "an exceptionally nice little man." He became Staff Captain of their Brigade the following summer. Almost every day there was a route march first, after which on 12 November, a new type of gas mask having been issued, Left Flank "practised putting on the new P pattern smoke helmets, which caused a good deal of merriment. The Padre dined last night and we played nap – at which I lost 5 francs. We are now in a very low lying flat country, every ditch full to the brim and quite the most dismal country I have ever seen…We are only about three miles behind the firing line and can hear much gun firing and see the old "verrilights" going all night." He was watching on the 14th, a Sunday, when a British aeroplane ran out of petrol and "came down by accident in a ploughed field near our farm, this is at 8.30am so rather interrupted our Padre's voluntary service at 9am. It had to be taken away in pieces." No one was hurt. Later that morning they paraded and moved again the short distance to Bout-Delville, south of Estaires, to Sir Iain Colquhoun "small, dirty, and billets not good." Captain Barne, however, thought them "not bad." Later Lord Esmé Gordon Lennox and the company commanders went to look at the trenches that they were to take over at Neuve Chapelle, recorded by Captain Barne as "better than I expected, quite wet and muddy, but we were able to avoid the communication trenches and keep above ground. These would have been above our knees in places."

The next day Private Johnes returned off leave having "managed to get back with a bottle of Scotch without busting it. It was a welcome sight for my buddies, we licked it round the old camp fire so to speak. One thing about the Army and the war, it produced wonderful comradeship, and reliance on one another, and of course sharing of the good things with the bad." He described the lie of the British line "with our favourite mole hill "Aubers Ridge"…with Jerry still in possession on it. The same ruddy creek which had us hog tied in front of the Richebourgs and Neuve Chapelle showed up here again… the line was simply a continuation of the old positions described previously, March through May, "a bloody swamp mate" with us wallowing in it." This was the Rivière des Layes. He mentioned the new facilities for the troops at La Gorgue, adding that the "Billets in the villages were practically clear of rats, but the farms and barns around them, where we were mostly billeted, swarmed with them."

On the 16th they were on their way to the line, marching down the Estaires-La Bassée road, collecting trench stores en route and in their positions in the Duck's Bill and to the north of it by half past seven that evening, each platoon being guided into place along the Sunken Road. The Duck's Bill at Neuve Chapelle, there was another at Givenchy, was beyond the end of the Sunken Road and stuck out from the British line, at its nearest point only about seventy yards from the Germans. Captain Barne wrote of "a beautiful moonlight night, but the men are very heavily laden and have a long walk and arrive rather weary, but have to work most of the night, revetting and rebuilding." He had not come across breastworks before. "These are not really trenches at all, but are paths with parapets and parados built a wall each side, the ground is so wet and boggy that anything you build below ground is quickly full of water." With Left Flank he was in "a very odd place which I have to hold…viz the "Duck's Neck" and "Duck's Bill," a very awkward shaped place, which is sniped from all round. However by morning we do a lot to improve it, and have no casualties there. There are the most enormous rats, and such a number of them, in these trenches, huge brutes which are extremely tame; Colquhoun says if you try to hit or frighten them they turn round, sit up and growl at you. They are very black and look like large kittens in the moonlight. Our dug-out is full of them and mice too, a perfect plague." It was a cold night with a hard frost. Wherever there was a trench it was full of half frozen mud. Just as trenches required continuous work, so did breastworks. If left unattended the weather quickly wore them down, no longer bullet proof and that much more likely simply to collapse. Captain Barne's impression was that the Indian Corps had "sadly neglected" the line "so there is endless work to be done." So they worked away, it being possible to hide activity from view behind the breastworks if one was careful. However, he continued, "The Germans seem to be just as uncomfortable as we are, and we can see them throwing water over their breastworks. They also explode mines to form some place in which to drain. There is an old mine crater just in front of the Duck's Bill which we occupy by night as a "listening post", it is often a question as to which side gets there first, the crater being nearer the German than our line." Private Cumming observed that "the Germans appeared to be well supplied with rifle grenades and both sides exchanged shouted insults. The regiment opposite were supposed to be Saxons, regarded as a nicer specimen of the Hun. They did not sound like it."

On the 17th Sir Iain Colquhoun noted "a good deal of sniping during the day, but only one man hit…Fired at German patrol at 6pm. The Germans exploded a mine near the Coldstream on our left, but did no damage. Worked at machine gun emplacements and shelters for front line." Captain Barne was more specific. "A big mine is exploded at 8.30am between the German and our line, I happen to be looking in that direction at the time; those inside dug-outs etc. said they were shaken about for several seconds, although the mine was ½ mile away. One of our men, Watson, the Company "sanitary man" is smothered to death by his (so called) dug-out, really above ground, collapsing, the soil here is all so wet. He has been out since the beginning of the war and has been wounded twice. A lot of rain during the day which makes things very horrid, very cold at night which was clear and a thick fog and white frost by sunrise." Private Hugh Watson was a steelworker in Motherwell before enlisting in 1905 and was a reservist for only eighteen months. He first landed in France in mid September 1914 and was slightly wounded in the middle finger of his right hand during the later stages of First Ypres and evacuated to England. He came out again at the end of February 1915 and was wounded a second time, in the face, again only slightly, on 10 March, the day when five men were also wounded by the shell that badly injured Major Romilly and Captain Kingsmill. That kept him away for a month at a Base hospital. He and Edith Grant married in London in 1910, a month before the birth of their first daughter, a son following and another daughter in January 1915.

On the 18th Captain Barne had a succession of visitors, including "the writer of the Daily Summary of Information, better known as the "Daily Liar" and several other outsiders…and I take them to see the Duck's Bill which seems to be quite a famous place; it is very amusing to see their manner when going there as they all think it dangerous and expect to be sniped at, and some are. We have no casualties, but this more by good fortune than anything else, some 100 shots were fired by snipers, one man got hit through his cap." During the afternoon the company were ordered to evacuate the Duck's Bill and Neck "while the gunners shell a ruined house said to contain a sniper who was making himself very objectionable; this just before dusk, so I feel a little nervous till we again occupy the place." Later all of them were relieved. Three platoons of C Company got out without difficulty, but the fourth had to stay put under cover for an extra hour because the Brigade machine gunners were firing at the

German lines. They got back to Bout-Delville at half past eight and had a meal after which Sir Iain Colquhoun "went to bed very tired, all of us covered in mud from head to foot." One of Captain Barne's platoons also had to wait behind and did not reach Bout-Delville until after midnight. The other three left the line at seven and arrived at their billets two hours later "after a very weary five or six mile march, the men wet and tired and carrying amongst other things their long thigh rubber boots, now served out to them. When I return I am handed, to my delight, my warrant for returning home on leave. I shave and dress overnight and am called at 2.45am and walk into La Gorgue to catch the 4am train which does not start till 6.30am. Rather a long wait, which is made amusing in a small degree by the men marking time to keep their feet warm, and whistling or singing various popular songs…Some amusement is caused by the difficulty in finding an officer to command the train, someone says he has seen a "pot bellied major" on the platform, so the word goes all down the train for the said p-b-m, there is no competition! Arrive London about 5pm."

In the line, Private Johnes remembered, "most of the time was spent in improving the trenches as much as possible and building shelters from the weather. As usual we got Jerries drainage and all the crap from his lines floating down into our "front yard". The situation was crummy but much better than it had been earlier… The trenches although flimsy were continuous, partly laid with duckboards. The troops had built shelters with what material there was to hand. We continued on with the work of laying duckboards and strengthening the parapets and firesteps. Rifle fire and burst of machine gun fire were sporadic. Shellfire was light from field artillery, pipsqueaks and whizz-bangs mostly. Jerry gunners giving us a belting once in a while to "clean their guns and sight in." We did have casualties, but not too heavy. Patrols went out at night to keep tab on Jerry, and trying to locate any of our dead, to get their identification discs, "Dog Tags". One day after a heavy rain, a dead fellow's arm flopped out of the side of a trench and hung there. It could not be moved that day, the body was too far in and to pull it out would have made the side of the trench collapse. One of the fellows shook hands with whoever it was and pushed the arm back in, tagging the spot to be attended to later. It was not a recent death, so was unknown to us. Our RFA batteries, covering our positions, had observation posts in our front line sighting in their guns. At night when Jerry was bringing up supplies, if it was a little quiet, our sentries could hear the clatter of their horse drawn limbers, bouncing over some of the cobblestone roads in the rear." Messages were then passed to the gunners who tried to work out where the German wagons were likely to be from the direction which the sentries reported and then opened fire on the most likely points, usually roads. "If they scored a hit, which they often did, our sentries could at times hear the racket, men, horses and wagon wheels, giving vent, squeals, howls, and perhaps horses bolting away with their loads. Sometimes it brought retaliation from Jerry. This section of the line had turned into a veritable rat warren. The bastards would argue their right to use the duckboards to run on. The artillery boys brought us in some small sacks of cordite, gun charges, when they could manage to. We would select a section of the trench with an abundance of rat holes, push a good charge into a centre hole, and plug up most of the others, leaving a few open for the rats to come or be blown out of. Two or three fellows would stand at the open holes with their entrenching tool handles at the ready to conk the ruddy varmints as they popped out. The charge was set off making a subdued noise but creating lots of smoke which chased or blew rats out by the score. It was fun for the troops while it lasted but later on after the smoke had cleared away, it didn't seem to have reduced their numbers overly much." Another pastime involved putting a small piece of bully beef onto the bayonet of a loaded rifle rested on the top of the parapet and pulling the trigger when a rat went for the meat.

On 15 November Captain Feilding and other officers had ridden up on bicycles to look at the line that the 1st Coldstream were to take over two days later. When remounting to ride back he missed his footing on a pedal, the bicycle lurched and slipped in some mud and he fell hard, landing on his knee. He was in England till April. On 22 November Sir Iain Colquhoun went out to have a fresh look at the routes to the front line, selected the best one and then came back through Neuve Chapelle. "Walking through the village I found a broken foot off the famous crucifix, which stood in the middle of the main street. Brought it home." He then went on home leave and returned to the Battalion, now in the line at the northern end, east of Laventie, on 4 December with Captain Barne, whose leave was extended when his mother died. They walked from La Gorgue, calling on various people as they went and reporting to Battalion Headquarters at teatime. Back with his company Captain Barne wrote "Every time anybody woke up and turned over in the night one saw a rat dash out of the window. The previous morning the servant opened the food box and found five mice inside having the time of their lives."

Over these weeks there were several forty eight hour tours up and down the Division's part of the line and a considerable amount of movement from one village to another. On a rotating basis one brigade were clear of the front line altogether for six days in reserve in and around Merville and the other two held the line, two battalions from each brigade being in the breastworks and forward forts, the other two close behind. Militarily everything was pretty quiet, but there were still casualties. On 28 November Private James Donaldson died in a field ambulance from the bullet wound to his back the day before. Having been a ploughman near St Andrews, he joined up in April and came to France in early October. His younger brother Private John Donaldson enlisted a month later, arrived in the same draft and was now in the Battalion. David and Jane Donaldson were then living at Wormit, Fife. Of the breastworks Sir Iain Colquhoun wrote that "by night one can walk straight up to them by road. The fire trenches are fairly dry, but the communication trenches are often over knee deep in mud and water." They went on 6 December to Laventie which Captain Barne noticed did "not seem to be nearly so much knocked about as many villages so near the firing line. We are in reserve here at 20 minutes notice." Lieutenant Norman, away because of his injured knee since July, rejoined from England, Captain Barne remarking that "He was out for six months previously and a very useful officer."

By the 9th, when they were in Merville, Captain Barne "Woke up in the night at 3am to hear a tearing torrent just outside my window, I thought it was coming in, sheets of floods everywhere and rising." Later, as he and Sir Iain Colquhoun went riding, they "were rather amused watching 2 six inch guns being brought through the town and over one of the canal bridges. It was too wide for the bridge in the ordinary way, so the roadway of the bridge had to be raised by building up with great baulks, thus allowing the guns to go between, or rather above the railings at the sides. There was a man in C Coy drowned last night, he seems just to have walked into a canal in the dark. Squalls and gale all day… The guns were being hauled along by motor engines with "caterpillar" wheels, the first I have ever seen." Private William Sharp, a miner in the Fife coalfield when he enlisted in February 1915, had been in France for just over two months when he died. He and Margaret Hynds married in July 1914 at Kilmaurs, Ayrshire, and she was living at Crosshouse, Kilmarnock. Lance Sergeant Frank Blessington was the only witness. He was on his way from the town to his billets when he saw a C Company man and told him to hurry up or he would be late back. The man replied "half a minute" and went to the urinal close by. Sergeant Blessington went on and crossed the canal bridge over the River Lys. "When I had just got across the bridge I heard a shout of "Sergeant." I answered "Come on, hurry up!" The next second I heard a splash in the water I ran back when I heard the splash but could see nothing." He raised the alarm but nothing could be done in the dark. He did not know who was missing until roll call next morning. Lord Esmé Gordon Lennox went to look and noted that "from the urinal there is a pathway which leads right to the edge of the lock. On such a dark night as this was I am perfectly certain that Private Sharp, on hearing Sergt Blessington reply, would have run down the path, thinking he was going straight to him, instead of which he must have fallen right into the lock. The downstream lock gates were open at the time and although search parties were out with lanterns for some considerable time, no trace of the man has since been seen. The river was in high flood…no one…could have lived in that heavy current." Private Sharp was recorded as Accidentally Drowned and his body later recovered. Sergeant Blessington, a waiter and from Haddington originally, enlisted in Edinburgh three weeks after the War began. His wife Fanny came from Burton-on-Trent, and was there with their son. He had been in the Battalion for almost a year, missed Loos because of illness, and was sent across the Channel with severe influenza in March 1916. He returned in the autumn of 1917 after Third Ypres and stayed with the Battalion till June 1918, when tonsillitis led to his second and final evacuation.

Sir Iain Colquhoun, who usually went to the Church of Scotland, attended the Sunday service on 12 December in the morning. "Spent the afternoon in throwing Mills bombs in the Merville Canal and killed about 150 small fish. Had them for dinner." Winston Churchill, having resigned as First Lord of the Admiralty and joined the Army, was about to take command of the 6th Royal Scots Fusiliers. On the 14th Captain Barne "Met Winston Churchill in the street yesterday, a terrible looking person, never saw anything so unlike a soldier, flabby face, more like an "unemployable" from the East End. Marched at 1pm to billets at Riez Bailleul, a fearful spot of desolation, billets in real squalor, my own room in a cottage where there is a woman and 7 children, can't imagine where they all live, eldest 11, as there are 3 officers, and the kitchen is permanently full of soldiers buying coffee." Then the 38th (Welsh) Division, New Army, recently landed in France, started arriving in the neighbourhood. Though causing crowding in the billets and in the line itself, D Company 13th Royal Welsh Fusiliers arrived through the night of the 14th for instruction as part of their trench warfare preparation. One platoon was attached to each Scots Guards company, initially at Riez Bailleul. This process continued till after New Year. Lieutenant Asquith described to Katherine Asquith those with his Grenadier company in the trenches as "little black spectacled dwarfs with no knowledge, no discipline, no experience, no digestion, and a surplus of nerves and vocabulary…they moaned and coughed and whined and vomited through the long night hours in a way that was truly distressing."

The redeeming feature of Riez Bailleul for the officers was the Guards Division Bombing School where they could go for tea and read the newspapers. Major Baden Powell ran it. Captain Barne noted on the 15th that "Baden did his best to blow up the Prince of Wales yesterday by handing him a detonated bomb to play with, and letting him pull out the pin, by extraordinary good luck the fuse was a bad one, so it did not explode, really a dispensation of Providence. Baden dined with us in the evening." The Mills bombs arrived in boxes inert and the infantry then had to insert the detonators and fuses, a process called detonating. So a detonated bomb was a live one. Next day "The little Prince of Wales biked through in the morning, the road being 3" deep in mud. I hope and suppose he does it because he likes to." That night they went into the front line taking the Royal Welsh Fusiliers with them, but leaving Lord Esmé Gordon Lennox behind with a "very bad throat". So bad was it that he went on sick leave. Captain Barne with Left Flank were in support "and divided into 4, at separate posts, and I live in comparative comfort at Battn HQ. Poor Tim and a Royal Welsh Fusilier attached have a perfectly horrible place, wet and muddy, and "draughty"." In this sense "draughty" meant exposed to more than the elements. 17 December was typical. "In the afternoon there is a heavy artillery duel to the south, just beyond Neuve Chapelle. We have 1 man killed and 2 wounded, by snipers at dawn. The trench boots issued to the men are capital things, I have been wallowing about in them all day and kept quite dry." He went round all four of his posts, some distance apart where he found it was so wet in places that "some of the men were quite unable to sit down all night, much less lie down." Private William Dingwall was shot dead. He was a young farm worker who enlisted in May, came out at the beginning of October and soon afterwards was slightly wounded in the head in front of the Hohenzollern. He was originally buried at Ebenezer Farm and that information was passed to Helen Dingwall, who lived near Kinross. After the War she wrote to ask for more details, but her son's body was never found again.

Captain Barne wrote of "A very quiet night with one or two exceptional moments, a big artillery duel early, and a batch of minenwerfer about 11pm. I walk round with Lionel Norman… We had a man wounded this morning, also a German bullet came through the magazine of one of our Lewis Guns, but did no further damage. A story: Tim Orr Ewing (when a bunch of bullets were falling pretty fast and near by) "It's all right, they are not likely to hit us, they don't even know we are here." Pte "They are damned good guessers then, that is all I can say." Another: Some men of C Coy were having some conversation across to the Germans, one of whom called out "We can't hear, tell somebody with a good voice to try," when up spoke a braw Highland Laddie, and said in stentorian tones "Hoo's the Crown Prince?" but he rolled his r's to such an extent that all that could be heard was a loud burring noise, to everyone's amusement! We are relieved… in the evening without adventure." They went back to the same billets, where different Welshmen arrived for the next trench tour, A Company 15th Royal Welsh Fusiliers. There was only one complete day out of the line this time and during the afternoon of 20 December they went back into the same place. There was a lot of machine gun fire during the relief and Right Flank "had two or three casualties." This time B Company were in the Duck's Bill and Left Flank in the front line breastworks to the north.

Thereafter Captain Barne had "a quiet night but such a beastly wet day, the mud and water simply unspeakable. Mice simply swarm in our dug-out, and Lionel Norman was amused to see them running over my lap while sitting asleep last night. A rat has his hole just behind where Tim sits at meals, so has to crawl there under Tim's arm. We do a lot of work during the day, building up parapets, draining and pumping. A certain amount also at night, especially by moonlight." The next day it was "Fine early, but wet as usual by midday. Thorpe…is hit by a rifle grenade, in the Duck's Bill about 11am, so…I again become CO of the Battalion for a few days." Captain Thorpe, though not seriously wounded in the shoulder, was sent to England. There had been rather more shelling than usual and seven men were wounded. One, Private John Stewart, a thirty two year old cattleman from Dumfriesshire, hit in the head, died on the 22nd in a casualty clearing station, after being in the Army for ten months and in the BEF for two and a half. His wife Joseann and their four children, the youngest of whom had just had her first birthday, were in Annan. On the night of the 22nd they left the line and went again to Riez Bailleul.

It had just been announced that Lord Cavan was being promoted to command XIV Corps, but he did not leave till after New Year. At Christmastime Private Alex Fleming of Right Flank, received a parcel from Duncan and Grace Fleming and the rest of his family in Dundee with a note which read "From Mother Dear Alex The school send you this parcel and when we were down town we bought this. Duncan." Duncan was his younger brother and what they bought was a Letts "The Soldier's Own Note Book And Pocket Diary." Until he enlisted in March he was a law clerk and had been in the Battalion since early October. During 1916 Private Fleming intermittently made brief matter of fact entries in the diary, recording his activities.

The other Christmas Truce

On Christmas Eve, as they prepared to go into the line once more at Neuve Chapelle, Private Johnes and a fellow signaller packed their rations, their telephones, which were not trench stores handed over at a relief, a bag of charcoal and a brazier, a bucket with holes knocked in it. They had been warned not to fraternise with the enemy. As they were moving in after dark the British gunners were busy shelling the German positions to discourage fraternization and the enemy retaliated, notably onto the Sunken Road. Private Johnes was told by those they relieved that everything was quiet and so it turned out. "We hooked up our telephone and checked through …and made ourselves as comfortable as possible…The weather was miserable, however, damp, cold, lots of rats and we were lousy." Later he remembered the lighting of braziers and men gathering round them to keep warm. "A few fellows started to sing Christmas Carols, which appeared to wake Jerry up over in his cabbage patch, as he joined in with his songs. The trenches were within bombing distance of one another in some places." The singing went on. Then "Some one up in Duck's Bill placed a brazier up on the parapet, it was followed by others in both ours and Jerries lines. Some Jerries could speak good English, one of them called across and asked how Soho was getting along. He had been a waiter in one of the restaurants in Soho Square in the "Smoke", London. There were some good singers on both sides, and the singing went sporadically through the night. No one left the trenches. As the dawn was breaking in the east behind Jerries line, which was a little higher than our's, one of our sentries reported seeing the head and shoulders of a Jerry up above their parapet, showing against the skyline. Gradually as it became brighter more Jerries showed up, heads and shoulders above the ground." The Scots Guardsmen were told to stay down out of sight "but it was a difficult order to enforce, it was a long line with turreted bays. Most of our men were standing on the parapet watching Jerry." To begin with there was some apprehension and reluctance, even among the bolder spirits, but when no shots were fired both sides became more confident. Then, as he recollected it, men got out of the trenches on both sides and mingled in the centre of No Man's Land. Because his telephone was out of order Private Johnes followed its line about one hundred and fifty yards along to the communication trench and then went part of the way back down it, checking line as he went, until he met a runner from Battalion Headquarters with a message ordering everyone back into cover as the British guns were about to open fire again in ten minutes. He asked the runner to check the line on his way back and returned above ground to his own company, passing as he did so two or three small groups of Scots Guardsmen and enemy soldiers, whom he identified as Württembergers "trying to chew the fat with one another. The fellows of both sides seemed to trust one another not to pull any dirty work. Some of the Germans were quite young, fair complexion, fair haired, looked at us with a degree of wonder, as though they expected us to be a gang of cutthroats, we must have passed muster as some of them cracked a smile and seemed happy about the whole thing, cigarettes were offered them by our chaps and in return they offered some kind of cigars, they sure liked our cigarettes." Both sides were trying to identify any of their dead. Then Private Johnes went back to his post where he found the line working again and took over to let the other signaller go outside to look at the Germans. "A short while afterwards the artillery sent over a warning shot of shrapnel, high up. The fellows got back into line and the bloody war continued." He added that any subsequent shots from the trenches must have been fired high as no one was hurt. "Talk amongst the troops afterwards was that it was a pity that some of the politicians and brass hats could not be invited to come out and spend a few days living with us under the conditions we were living under, in the mud, blood and corruption, with rats and lice for companions."

On Christmas morning C Company were in the front line from Signpost Lane up to just south of the Duck's Bill. Sir Iain Colquhoun recorded "Stand to at 6.30am. Germans very quiet. Remained in firing trenches. 8.30am no sign of anything unusual. When having breakfast about 9am a sentry reported to me that the Germans were standing up on their parapets, and walking towards our barbed wire. I ran out to our firing trenches and saw our men looking over the parapet, and the Germans outside our barbed wire. A German officer came forward and asked me for a truce for Xmas. I replied that this was impossible. He then asked for ¾ hr to bury his dead. I agreed. The Germans then started burying their dead and we did the same. This was finished in ½ hr our men and the Germans then talked and exchanged cigars, cigarettes, etc., for ¼ of an hour, and when the time was up, I blew a whistle and both sides returned to their trenches. For the rest of the day the Germans walked about and sat on their parapets, and their trenches were outlined for miles on either side." Captain Barne heard about it and added "Some of the companies on the left saw this and also came out and there was some handshaking and exchange of cigarettes and "souvenirs". He "went down about 10am with the Brigadier, and we agreed that we could not have ordered our men to fire on the defenceless Germans who came over trusting us. They put up white flags and a Xmas tree on the parapet (no candles, dolls, etc.). In one case I hear there was a full rigged tree put up, candles and all." He soon heard that this incident was not going to stop there as "the Divisional Commander is much annoyed at the whole thing and no difference should have been made, all should have been "as usual". There is anxiety in higher quarters at night, and the Adjutant has to go all round the trenches about midnight...the most tiresome Xmas I ever spent."

Lieutenant Norman sent in a report from Left Flank at twenty past three in the afternoon "<u>Operations</u> Bombardments at intervals by our Artillery, responded to by the enemy without effect on Front Line Trenches. <u>Intelligence</u> An unofficial semi-truce obtained during most of the morning. None of LF Coy were allowed beyond their own parapet. The amount of Germans seen suggest that enemy line is not lightly held. Their extremely clean kit free from mud suggests some extra good trench kit or adequate pumping arrangements. <u>Work</u> Owing to the extraordinary circumstances existing – little except pumping & draining of trenches was accomplished." Two hours later he sent a further one when more explanations were demanded from up the chain of command "(I) Only a very few men in this Coy left their parapet. Orders were given to the contrary, but on seeing men out on their right, it was impossible to restrict them. It was somehow understood that they could go out & bury the dead. (II) Exchange of tobacco & souvenirs Time out about 10 minutes." Another two and a half hours had passed when he sent a much more mundane, but pressing, request "We have only half a sack of coke tonight – two ration loafs & salt – no cocoa tea or milk. Is there any chance of getting these later on. Coke especially needed." In order that there should be no further unconventional happenings after dark the British guns were ordered to shell the German trenches, which were also machine gunned. Back came the retaliation and during the night Sir Iain Colquhoun had to leave his dug-out five times.

Consequences

On Boxing Day Captain Barne heard that "a neighbouring Division has spread the report that we were all deserting!" A Court of Inquiry to establish the facts met that morning at Winchester House. Though the 1st Scots Guards were at the centre of it, the 1st Coldstream and 2nd Scots Guards were also implicated, so "The fat is in the fire and the higher authorities are in a great state of mind about it all." Sir Iain Colquhoun noted that General Ponsonby, who came round about ten minutes after everyone was back in their trenches, "doesn't mind a bit, but the Major General [Cavan] is furious about it." Later in the afternoon General Ponsonby told Captain Barne that Lord Esmé Gordon Lennox was being invalided home and that Major Tempest was coming to take command. "I am evidently in disgrace and not allowed to command the Battalion any more!" That night they went to billets in La Gorgue for a whole week. The following morning Major Tempest arrived "and throws some light on the whole subject. Apparently he had seen Cavan, who was very much annoyed because I did not issue orders to shoot the Germans showing themselves. As the Brigadier, Ponsonby, was with me, and he never said anything was wrong, nor gave orders to shoot the unarmed Germans, but he stood himself on the firestep taking immense interest in everything, I concluded that nothing very wrong was being done. No hint was ever given me that a great point was made of "no truce" in high quarters or of course I would have issued very special orders on 24th. I issued order all was to be as usual. The only orders I issued on 25th were not to shoot Germans walking about unarmed, not to leave our trenches and on no account to allow Germans into our own except to surrender. This after hearing they were out. I issued these orders off my own bat, and not because I received any special orders. I did not dare say I had received no orders in giving my evidence before the Court of Inquiry, as it might have carted General Ponsonby, who they say ought to have given orders himself on the subject." When on the 27th Sir Iain Colquhoun wrote to his wife he did not mention any of this. She was just about to give birth and was very anxious to have him with her. He merely said that Christmas Day in the line had been quiet apart from the guns and went on "We are having our Christmas dinner tonight champagne and everything I shall make a beast of myself and get very tight. I had a real bath this morning. They have rigged one here for officers so I feel clean and very well." The gramophone records had arrived, also a pipe and tobacco.

Captain Hesketh Hesketh Pritchard had become the principal sniping instructor in the BEF after a career of travelling and big game shooting. On the morning of 28 December Captain Barne attended "a sniping lecture by Pritchard, who is a newspaper correspondent and big game shooter…Nothing very new or wonderful is told us." Later "The men have their Xmas dinner in their various billets, Roger [Tempest] makes a speech to each Company. Billet sing songs afterwards and a Battalion Concert in the evening at 5.30pm, when the Grenadier Band gives much satisfaction." Then "A bombshell falls in the shape of Esmé returning! Perhaps "bombshell" is the wrong word, as most people are delighted to see him back; so few knowing Roger and mistaking his character from the little they see of him. Personally one suits me as well as the other, both being very good pals to me." Sir Iain Colquhoun went to have a "very good dinner" that evening with the officers of the 1st Coldstream, after which they played poker and he lost a hundred and ten francs to Captain Gilbert "Gillie" Follett, known as "Mary" in the Coldstream, a relatively rare event for him as he usually won in games of chance. He admitted "Bad head next morning."

There were more demands for more detailed explanations about Christmas Day and on the 29th Captain Barne, accompanied by Lord Esmé Gordon Lennox, had to report to General Ponsonby. "The Brigadier treats the whole matter rather lightly, makes out a statement himself which he tries to read over, but fails to read his own handwriting, then we all have to criticise it, jokes fly about, during which Guy Baring comes in with his statement, for the Coldstream were worse off, if anything, than ourselves. The point which in high places they seem to dislike is my having told the company commanders not to shoot the unarmed Germans in the open who might be confidingly coming over," i.e. to surrender. So he understood that matters lay. Lieutenant Colonel The Honourable Guy Baring, MP for Winchester, had commanded the Coldstream since the end of September.

Meanwhile Sir Iain Colquhoun had to write out and rewrite his own account "about 8 times," but on the 31st he gave C Company "a New Year's Eve supper and concert. Great success. Everything very well done." Private Johnes remembered "a turkey dinner with all the trimmings available at that time and place. It was greatly appreciated by the troops and he was rated "Tops"." After all the officers dined together that evening Lord Esmé Gordon Lennox and Captain Barne went to bed. Sir Iain Colquhoun and the rest "kept it up till 12 midnight. Sang "Auld Lang Syne", then all went across to the Coldstream. We joined up and went to Divisional HQ & sang till Cavan came down in his pyjamas. Went on to the Prince of Wales, but either he wasn't in or wouldn't come out." Next they turned out General Ponsonby and his staff officers and "wished them a happy New Year. Got to bed about 1.30." Captain Barne heard that General Ponsonby thoroughly enjoyed it.

On a stormy New Year's Day they went into the line near Fauquissart. For Captain Barne, from this time on informally, and later formally, Second in Command of the Battalion, the timing of the relief "was arranged rather early, so, as many of us expected, we were spotted by the enemy and spent an unpleasant half hour at a corner, where we had to wait to get the gum boots, etc., being shelled, luckily no casualties." Battalion Headquarters were now at a new place called Wangerie, "a tumbledown and picturesque little farmhouse, several cats about and not many rats in consequence. I sleep in a sort of loft, quite comfortable. A gale blowing from the SW and an old house close by is blown down during the night, thereby the more exposing us to view." Next day he went round the front line in the afternoon with Captain Stewart, the Medical Officer, "who I am very keen should go into the water question; there are too many men with high temperatures and we find undoubtedly men are drinking trench water, much of which comes over from the German lines." Here these were on slightly higher ground.

That night Lieutenants Norman and Orr Ewing with two corporals went out successfully to examine the enemy wire, Lieutenant Norman and one of the corporals going close up to it right in front of the German parapet. A Very light went up very near and they kept very still. There was also a shot from a German sentry, whom they thought heard some noise, but it was very dark and he could not see anything. They came back with a lot of useful information. A lot of patrolling of various sorts went on, much of it aggressive. In connection with this the British gunners made gaps in the German wire in various selected places. This required five hundred rounds each time, followed up by forty rounds from time to time to keep the gaps open. It was essential that the British prevented the enemy from repairing the gaps and fighting patrols were part of this. The machine gun companies also frequently sprayed the gaps. Having several gaps open made it harder for the Germans to guard against a raid.

C Company were involved in something else. There were gas dischargers set up in the front line and on the 2nd "the RE hope to let it off tonight, but it is not to be followed by a raid." However, Sir Iain Colquhoun wrote on the 3rd "The wind has been unfavourable for two weeks, and the gas is to be removed tonight…at 10am a stray bullet came through the top of my dug-out (corrugated iron) grazed the tip of my finger and went through Cecil Boyd Rochfort's clothes in two places." Later the two of them with the men from the two platoons in the front line "carried gas cylinders from fire trenches to Elgin Fort trolley line. Took 3 hours, 2 men to each cylinder. Finished about 8.30pm and marched back to billets." Lieutenant Cecil Boyd Rochfort, Lieutenant Arthur Boyd Rochfort's youngest brother, had very recently rejoined after breaking a bone in his leg with the Battalion the previous spring. He too had been to Eton and was in the group of officers commissioned on 15 August 1914. Their widowed mother was living at Redditch, Worcestershire.

At eight in the morning on 4 January Lord Esmé Gordon Lennox walked into Captain Barne's room at Laventie and placed him under arrest, pending trial by General Court Martial. Sir Iain Colquhoun, billeted elsewhere, heard he was under arrest by written message half an hour later, that he was not allowed to leave his billet and that there were not going to be proceedings against anybody except Captain Barne and himself. By this time Major General Geoffrey Feilding had taken command of the Guards Division and he and everybody else were not only highly sympathetic, but also doing all that they could to have the matter dropped. Things had, however, gone too far and the word was that Sir Douglas Haig was insisting on the court martial. Captain Barne wrote to his London solicitor, Arthur Farrer, asking him to arrange with Sir Iain Colquhoun's solicitors to employ the best Counsel they could get, as well as requesting military permission to use a barrister. Meanwhile, he remarked that General Ponsonby was being very amusing and said that he would like to see the higher command " "cutting German wire" and me doing the Court Martials." More seriously, General Ponsonby said that he thought that the application to employ Counsel would "choke them off a bit." Apparently the Judge Advocate General's reaction to the evidence was that there was no case to answer, so changes were made in its presentation "which seems a curious proceeding. The Brigadier and everyone else who is qualified to judge thinks the people at the top have got hold of the wrong end of the stick altogether. Certainly if they expect me or any other officer to give an order to shoot down unarmed Germans in cold blood, they are very much mistaken, and, as Luss says, the men would not obey, adding "if they want it done let them do it themselves." I am released from arrest."

Sir Iain Colquhoun first mentioned to Dinah that there was "rather a row over the truce at Christmas time" on the 4th, because he would not get even special leave until the initial inquiry was over, which he thought would take a week. "Special leave" was compassionate leave in most circumstances. He was released from close arrest into open arrest the following afternoon and very soon afterwards had a message from his wife that the baby was starting and to come home quickly. He asked General Ponsonby whether there was any chance as she had had a difficult pregnancy and General Ponsonby said that he would speak to General Feilding. The next afternoon he heard that he had got five days leave and so saw his new son, born safely before he reached London. He also talked to others there about the imminent court martial. There was shelling in the line and on the 6th Private Fleming recorded "Sandy Lennox hit in the head. He afterwards died." Private Alexander Lennox, who had been with them three months, was very badly hurt, but able to be moved two days later to hospital in Calais. Laurence and Jessie Lennox lived in Galashiels. In her telegram on the 12th to Regimental Headquarters she asked "May he be visited by father Very anxious to go at once." The reply had to be that this could not happen until the War Office issued instructions. Private Lennox died at half past eight in the morning on the 16th, the Battalion's only battle casualty all month. When in the line the pattern of activity remained exactly the same each time and there was always work to be done. Private Fleming noted being on sandbag fatigue at night on the 10th and on water fatigue the day after, as well as spraining his foot. For several weeks after the Division took over this part of the line they were laying forty thousand filled sandbags every day in the three lines of defence.

General Ponsonby came to breakfast on 6 January at Battalion Headquarters with the warning that, if Counsel appeared for the defence, the military authorities would do likewise for the prosecution. Instead, he suggested that Captain Barne should have a "prisoner's friend", a serving officer, to defend him, much the best available being Lieutenant Asquith, currently on home leave. Coincidentally, Dinah Colquhoun was the niece of the Prime Minister's second wife, Margot Asquith. Captain Barne visited an artillery observation post that day and had a good look with a telescope at the enemy lines and at Aubers Ridge beyond. The Germans started shelling it while he was there. Everyone bolted to a dug-out and took cover. The third German shot was a direct hit, exploding in the house but injuring no one. "Either the Germans have discovered the OP by someone showing himself there, or it has been given away by a spy." They were back in Laventie after dark on the 11th. That night General Ponsonby "was arrested by the Military Police who took him for a spy. He gave a very comical description of it all. This place, Laventie, seems to be full of spies, I think one reason why the Germans do not shell it more."

Describing to Katherine Asquith how he was washing virtually naked in his billet when just back from leave on the morning of the 10th Lieutenant Asquith "was conscious of unintelligible but unmistakable brouhaha...of John Ponsonby." Though his servant did his best to keep the Brigadier out "the gallant fellow was not to be denied and burst into my room in a paroxysm of inarticulate enthusiasm." This was the first that Lieutenant Asquith had heard of Christmas Day's events. "There is a great to-do about it all, both on personal and regimental grounds." He set off soon afterwards to see Captain Barne, who "was pretty mopy." Sir Iain Colquhoun was not due back till the 12th and until then nothing definite could happen. Lieutenant Asquith wrote again on the 12th "There is a good deal of excitement about it here, and I am regarded as such an important life now that yesterday morning the Brigadier issued a special order that I was not to accompany my battalion into the trenches for this last turn of 48 hours, but to remain here in billets. I am accordingly living in comfort (though not in gaiety) at the HQ of the 1st Scots Guards, who kindly offered me bed and board."

On the 13th the Scots Guards left Laventie and marched north to different billets at Neuf-Berquin, close to Merville. After a fair amount of coming and going about court martial proceedings and preparations Captain Barne was dismayed that "on arrival at our new billets we hear that Luss and I are to be court martialed on 17th instant." Meanwhile Lieutenant Asquith had been very diligent and thorough. He met Sir Iain Colquhoun for the first time, describing him to his wife that day as "rather a sweet man of his type – arrogant, independent and brave."

He is quite indifferent about his case and hardly interested enough to talk about it." Lieutenant Asquith had been very bored staying with the Scots Guards in "a dreary mess. Lord Esmé Gordon Lennox commands them; he was kind and hospitable to me but piano to a fault, quite without vitality or interest: the others were a very Scotch doctor, a very Scotch adjutant, and a still more Scotch minister." For Captain Barne next day there was "Nothing of importance. Buy towel etc. in Merville, mine having been stolen at the last billet. Am now in a tiny room in a tiny cottage. Carter, my poor old servant, is ill, and being looked after by Madame and Mademoiselle… There is a small yellow dog here called "Milord". The Brigadier comes over to luncheon – he and the CO (Esmé) and in fact everybody I meet are most kind and sympathetic." Private George Carter was a shepherd in Dorset before enlisting in 1898 at Blandford. He served in the Boer War and by 1914 had signed on for twenty one years. When Captain Barne arrived the previous July Private Carter had been back for more than six months after being hit in the thigh on the Aisne. He had a brother, apparently living in Dover, but uncontactable, and an aunt in Balham, South London.

On the 15th Right Flank were paid after a big battalion route march in the morning and that afternoon Private Fleming and others "Went into Merville and had our group photo taken." Later the same day after mention of a "spread out", a regular enjoyment of his, he "went round cemetery and saw graves of two BW lads Allen & Fitzpatrick." Privates James Allen and John Fitzpatrick were both in the 1/4th Black Watch and from Dundee. Private Fleming may or may not have known them personally. Both had lost their lives a few months earlier. The Scots Guards officers, including Captain Barne, beat the Coldstream officers 1-0 at football that afternoon. "Great fun but I get the ball full in the eye at close range which causes me not to see anything with that eye for the rest of the game." Lieutenant Asquith wrote home that "on Monday there is this idiotic Court Martial, which has now begun to get rather on my nerves, because John Ponsonby is so excited about it and one of my 2 clients so terribly depressed." Sir Iain Colquhoun "on the other hand, is perfectly haughty and indifferent, and impresses me more and more as being a man of great individuality and charm, so far as one can have those things without a brain."

On the Sunday Private Fleming recorded "a nice church parade in YMCA Hut in Merville. Played in by pipe band. Had a good time in chip shop at night." The day after, the 17th, he was again in Merville in the afternoon. "Had photos taken by myself. Went into concert at night. It wasn't bad." That morning the court martial started at Headquarters Guards Division at La Gorgue. The President was Major General Arthur Holland of the 1st Division and there were four other Members, one of them General Cuthbert. The Prosecuting Officer was Captain R P Hills, KOSB, a well known barrister. Captain Barne's case came first. "There is great excitement about it all. At 10.45 we start with much pomp." However, to his and Lieutenant Asquith's astonishment the charge brought before the Court was a new one, of which they had had no notice. Instead of what they were ready for relating to his having issued orders that unarmed Germans showing themselves on or near their trenches were not to be shot at, contrary to the alleged instructions he had received that everything was to be done "as usual on Christmas Day", what they saw for the first time was a charge that he had given orders that Germans coming towards the British lines were not to be shot at with a view to getting them to surrender. "So that now we had to prove that the order that I practically admitted issuing was a right and proper order to give." Captain Hills made what he could of a very weak case before Lieutenant Asquith spoke very well and very clearly for fourteen minutes. He did not cross examine the prosecution witnesses because the facts were not in dispute, but he did call General Ponsonby and Lord Esmé Gordon Lennox as character witnesses. Once General Ponsonby had stated that he would himself have given the identical orders to those which Captain Barne had done and so would every commanding officer in his Brigade there was nothing left to be said. Captain Barne was found "Not Guilty, honourably acquitted, prisoner to be released." He left the court at three o'clock, had a rough lunch at La Gorgue and walked back to his billet.

Sir Iain Colquhoun's trial followed and went on five hours. Apart from the same two character witnesses, there were other witnesses called as to the facts, including Lieutenant Norman and three C Company NCOs, one of whom was Lance Sergeant McAulay, the Glasgow policeman. Everyone hoped that this case would end similarly, but he was found guilty of agreeing to the short truce for burial of the dead and the very modest fraternizing which followed. Lieutenant Asquith told his wife that "there was no doubt that he committed a technical offence, but in reality he showed a good deal of decision and common sense, and his military character is so first rate that they ought to take a lenient view of the case. I became much attached to Colquhoun in the course of the case. His deportment was quite faultless, both before and during the proceedings." He wrote very highly too of General Ponsonby "A very jolly fellow, quite my favourite soldier among those in high places."

Sir Iain Colquhoun was unable to write to Dinah until the 18th. "There was every sort of general and St Omer touts there and I was vastly entertained with the whole thing. I thought I would have been angry but the prosecutors were so obviously not gentlemen that it at once explained their attitude and no one expected them to behave otherwise than the way they did. They all went back to their armchairs and their port at the base and the air is all the sweeter for their departure. I expect they will all get DSOs for having scored off a fellow who prefers to do his duty in the trenches to sitting on his bottom at base." He had to wait three days for his sentence, the lightest it could have been, a reprimand. When the file reached Sir Douglas Haig he struck out the sentence because of Sir Iain Colquhoun's distinguished conduct in the field, though he left the court martial proceedings to stand at the time. The news reached the Battalion on the 22nd and Sir Iain Colquhoun, in telling Dinah about it, commented "Fancy all that fuss and now to end in nothing it's too childish." Captain Barne's observed "This is the least that they can do." On 12 December 1916 Sir Douglas Haig noted in his diary that he had directed that because of Sir Iain Colquhoun's record the case and all reference to it was to be expunged.

The last weeks near the Lys

On the afternoon of 19 January the officers played the sergeants at football with Captain Barne in the team. "We were 2 all for a long time and then I had the honour of kicking the winning goal (horrid fluke) just before time." The War Diary recorded a 3-3 draw. Sir Iain Colquhoun told Dinah on the 20th that he was apprehensive about Captain Jamie Balfour's imminent return because "I hope he isn't in this mess as it is such a splendid one at present and he will spoil everything." Then and very often in his letters to her he speculated about when he might next get leave, no matter how recently he had been away. Captain Barne "In the evening attended a Left Flank concert when to my surprise and in some ways pleasure my health was drunk or rather three cheers for me given with great enthusiasm. I don't know why particularly but I did wonder whether they knew the result of the GCM."

At Merville both on the 22nd and 24th there were bathing parades at the first of which Private Fleming "Got a good change. Paid at 12. Got more photos. Tres bon Pommes de terre." Next time he "Got a new towel" and then went to watch B Company beating his at football. For the last few days of January they were again in the forts and trenches east of Laventie, starting in the reserve position there and moving on to the breastworks on the 29th. Before they went forward Captain Barne recorded "The Brigadier calls in and says we are moving up to Ypres next week, which causes much talking and despondency! Some think it is a blind and so on." In the front trenches Sir Iain Colquhoun found "The line has been much improved since we were here last, and our dug-out has tables and chairs. Stood to at 6am. Started work at 10am built new traverses and firing steps, etc. The mist was so thick we could not see the enemy trench all day, enabling us to work on our own parapet." He told his wife that he had had a letter from someone on the estate at Luss on 28 January addressed simply "Sir Iain Colquhoun of Luss The Army" which arrived after two days in the post.

Lieutenant Dick Bethell sprained his ankle nine months before and was sent home. He now rejoined on the 27th, travelling with Lieutenant Calverley Bewicke, a Harrovian, previously in the Scots Guards for two years a decade earlier. On the outbreak of war Lieutenant Bewicke joined the 5th Royal Irish Regiment and was with them in the Mediterranean in the early stages of the Gallipoli landings before rejoining the Scots Guards in the summer. One evening Private Johnes was watching a film in the recreation hall, probably at La Gorgue, when the Prince of Wales and others "came in and sat down among the troops…They were recognised and given a hearty cheer. They stuck around for a while before leaving the show, as they left, the troops gave them a verse of that lovely little ditty "Oh Oh Oh it's a lovely war, what do we want with eggs and ham? When we have plum and apple jam? Form fours, right turn, what do we do with the money we earn? Oh Oh Oh it's a lovely war."

During the morning of the 30th Captain Barne went round all the trenches and posts "and on way back get some shells dropped unpleasantly near. There is a thickish fog, so I amuse myself getting over the parapet and looking at our loopholes from that side, a very interesting thing to do, one sees which sort show up and which sort are invisible etc." Next day there was "A beautiful east wind suitable for the Germans to gas us! A big bombardment is to take place." They were going to have to move out of their front trenches, because the German ones were so close "that the artillery might make mistakes and have accidents. At 10am I have to meet General Heyworth and show him certain places in the line selected for inserting "Bangalore Torpedoes" into the German wire. These we have chosen by means of patrols. They have to be dragged over by night – are 15' long and have to be exploded by an electric fuse from our own line. Heyworth is not in a good temper and I do not improve it by pointing out that his Bde had spoilt many of our loopholes. Methuen has been our Sniping Officer and is very keen and has taken a great deal of trouble, is much hurt about the matter and wrote a long report of his injuries, which I gave to the Brigadier this morning so we may hear more about this." General Heyworth was temporarily commanding the Guards Division. Later that morning Sir Iain Colquhoun was told to move his forward two platoons across to the right. The British guns then promptly shelled the German front line for some three hours to cut the wire "with apparently great effect. The Germans retaliated…blowing up houses, trees, etc. The duel was most interesting to watch as the Germans seldom retaliate on our front line and we could stand up and watch it all." Most of the retaliation had, however, been directed on Fort Elgin, held by a C Company platoon and Captain Barne was worried. "At the end about 2.30 I go down with Luss expecting to find many casualties, instead of which we find none, only one shell having landed in the post, – just showing how deceptive it is. From the front line it looked as if about 50 must have gone right into it." During the bombardment Private Fleming was one of a small party left behind in an observation post in the line and then immediately found himself on water fatigue.

On 1 February Captain Barne went "round the trenches early taking the Padre with me, he has never been into any front trenches before, swears he is "on duty" and is much excited. We go round and see all there is to be seen – Methuen the Battalion Sniping Officer, has stories of having accounted for several Germans including an officer, patrols had been out during the night and had found more of the Torpedo positions. We met General Feilding, Ponsonby and Anderson (Corps Staff) all very nice and agreeable." Then, with a similar bombardment planned for two in the afternoon, he arranged to clear the front part of the line in the same way as the day before. The bombardment resulted in "a very heavy retaliation by enemy on Rue Tilleloy and most of our cleared part of front line and posts. I then order a short sharp and sweet reply by our "heavies" which effectually brings them to their senses." There were two dead, both Grenadiers in the 2nd Guards Brigade Machine Gun Company, "killed in a dug-out – several dug-outs so called but really more weatherproof shelters get blown in including the C Company Sergeant Major's." Company Sergeant Major William Pyper had been a soldier for ten years and before that a joiner in Edinburgh, where his father Alexander Pyper was living in the east of the New Town. Since landing at Le Havre on 13 August 1914 he had been through everything up to the trenches at the Hohenzollern, when he was slightly shell shocked and sent home, but not for long. He had just been awarded the DCM. Private Fleming found everything "Fairly quiet up to dinner. Then the British guns to fire, but…Fritz did it instead. What a burst up. Two GG machine gunners blown to bits." C Company too had had to clear their front trenches and once everything seemed to have settled down Sir Iain Colquhoun took his men back at quarter to four when suddenly the German guns "opened on us, blew in my dug-out, did a lot of damage to trench stores… but did comparatively little damage." Private Johnes recalled that "Just about this time, a Padre who had not visited us in the line, decided he should put in an appearance before we took over new pastures, wherever they might be. He visited our company on the edge of the cleared space." When the German guns fired back "they overlapped the cleared space, catching the Padre in the shellfire, pipsqueaks. The Padre like every newcomer hit the boards and squirmed. Fortunately he was unharmed, but he learned what fear was in a small way and looked kind of sheepish about it."

Captain Barne met Colonel Cator with a visitor as the 2nd Battalion arrived to take over the line from them that night. This was "Admiral Colville, who is on a "holiday", visiting trenches and wants to see a relief – what he can see in pitch dark I don't know." Admiral Sir Stanley Colville, Flag Officer Orkney and therefore responsible for the Fleet anchorage at Scapa Flow, was about to take over as Commander-in-Chief Portsmouth. Captain Barne set off down the road to La Gorgue with two other officers "starting off in an atmosphere apparently full of bullets, luckily mostly over our heads. I think the Germans must have known there was a relief going on. We get in about 10pm and very glad of a good meal, the men too have soup and rum." He added that Lieutenant Bewicke, speaking during this, his first trench tour, and referring to Gallipoli, "says the shelling there is child's play to this." On the 2nd Captain Barne had to deal with a serious number of men on disciplinary charges and "when I have to send an unfortunate man to a court martial I feel inclined to tell him I hope he fares as well as I did – he will probably get five years for sleeping on his post." Rumours were frequent about moves "to Ypres, to Calais and every sort of place, no more leave etc."

He was lying in bed on the 4th. "A gale from SW my old landlady comes into my bedroom early in the morning to shut my window! I think they dislike open air as much as I dislike froust." That afternoon he rode into Merville on a horse he knew well, now his but previously that of his friend Major Molineux Montgomerie, and noted that "the pony Geraldine is very fit and quite a nice ride along the canal." That day there was an accident during grenade training and Private Robert "Rab" Wilson was injured in the right ear and face, not seriously. He was an unmarried labourer, whose father John Wilson lived in Irvine, Ayrshire, had been in the Army for just over a year and in the BEF since October. Sergeant "The Tiger" Finch, promoted that month, reported that "Pte R Wilson was one of a party practising bomb throwing. The party was in a trench and a bomb was thrown but it did not burst immediately. A second bomb was then thrown but before it touched the ground the first bomb exploded, and the concussion caused the second bomb to explode prematurely. Pte Wilson was at the end of the trench and was struck in the face by two or three small pieces of metal."

The next afternoon, a Saturday, the Coldstream officers got their own back, thrashing the Scots Guards officers 7-1 at football. Sir Iain Colquhoun told Dinah that "the team simply went to pieces I was furious." That evening the Coldstream Guards Band played at a concert, at which there was also some Scots Guards input, Private Fleming being disappointed at being unable to get in. They next played for the church parade in the concert hall. On the 7th Lord Esmé Gordon Lennox told Captain Barne that he was putting him up for promotion to Major "which is satisfactory, as it means the Court Martial is not meant to stand in my way, and that I haven't altogether made too great a muddle of things." That night they went back into the line at Neuve Chapelle. Battalion Headquarters were again at Ebenezer Farm, C Company in the Duck's Bill. On the 8th after "A quiet but cold night in our sepulchres" Captain Barne went round the line with Lord Esmé Gordon Lennox. They heard that they were about to get "an influx of "Bantams" 1 officer and 2 NCOs per company under instruction who will arrive about 4pm – Gloucesters and Cheshires." The minimum height for an Army recruit was five foot three inches and fit volunteers who were not tall enough were not accepted. As the result of pressure from some MPs the regulation was relaxed, but these men had to join specially formed Bantam Battalions.

It had been a quiet day, but Private Fleming was in a ration party after dark when machine guns just "about got us on Sunken Road & Railway." On the 9th he was "Filling Sand bags. Went out at 6.30. Machine guns turned on us in Sunken Road. Sandy Martin killed at Ebenezer Farm." This was just as the relief was finishing. Captain Barne wrote that "just as HQ were moving off to go into billets at Riez Bailleul Sgt Martin, Piper and Head Stretcher Bearer was hit through the head by a stray bullet. He was a great character – had been out the whole war, never missing one day's duty, he had received a DCM. A most amusing though conceited man – many stories are told about him. When congratulated on his DCM, he replied: "It was a long time coming"… He used to cut my hair and was going to do so tomorrow. Nobody has a better or finer reputation for bravery, in fact he knew no fear." Private Cumming heard that Sergeant Piper Martin had "walked along the duckboard towards the road when a sniper's bullet, probably fired from a fixed rifle, hit him in the head. There was just the one shot and the circumstances seemed to all of us indeed tragic." This was to be his last trench tour before he went home permanently. Not killed outright, he died at quarter past nine that evening at Estaires.

Sir Iain Colquhoun had little comment on that spell in the Duck's Bill other than his snipers claiming two Germans on the 8th and five on the 9th, similar claims being a feature subsequently, while Lieutenant Boyd Rochfort went out at night with a patrol to select where best to put a Bangalore torpedo under the enemy wire. From after dark on the 9th they were at Riez Bailleul for two days. Often there was little rest for those out of the line and when on the 10th Private Fleming went up to the trenches on fatigue, he was "Just about hit coming down communication trench." It rained throughout the 11th and they did nothing till the evening when they went back up to the front line "via Signpost Road. Very quiet on right of Dux Bill. No dug-out. Mine went up. Hell for 5 minutes." He meant Signpost Lane, south of the Sunken Road and roughly parallel to it.

For Sir Iain Colquhoun and everyone else this mine was something novel at close quarters. "At 7.30 an engineer officer warned me that they intended setting off a mine which they had worked under the German mine shaft. It was set off about 7.45pm and made a low rumbling sound and shook the earth. The Germans opened rapid fire, also machine gun fire and sent up numerous Very lights, but did not retaliate with artillery. Our gunners were meant to cooperate with the mine by firing at the German communication trenches, but owing to the mine being set off prematurely, I was unable to let the gunners know in time." Lord Esmé Gordon Lennox and Captain Barne looked at the crater next morning through periscopes. "Not a very big one." Sir Iain Colquhoun took a patrol out that night, but because it was very bright not till half past four in the morning, when "We crawled through our own barbed wire and right round the mine crater examining it very carefully. We were not seen and only a few stray shots came near. The crater is about 30 yds from our barbed wire and about 40 from the German. It is 12 ft deep and 40 ft across." Captain Barne noted in addition that they had "found no trace of German saps blown in which if the case is rather a sell. A light German trench gun in their front line has blown in one of our loopholes (double) which is annoying." On 13th February Sir Iain Colquhoun used the strong wind from behind him to let off six rifle grenades in the morning and another six in the afternoon, which led to precisely placed German field gun shelling and then the firing of single shots up and down the British line, but without doing any damage. Private Fleming described that day as very quiet, adding that during the trench tour he had "Slept all 3 nights on firing platform…Got a good sleep." The day after was a bit drier. He saw a lot of aeroplanes, including as many as seven German ones and "Got hit by piece of shell in arm" without being hurt. When he went back in a ration party they had a "rotten time" in the communication trench.

On the 14th after what Captain Barne described as "A quiet night. Methuen, Sniping Officer, has made some very obvious dummy loopholes to draw the fire of German trench gun which it did most successfully, upon which our guns were turned on it, and are said to have knocked it out." Sir Iain Colquhoun noted the firing of British trench mortars, little retaliation and then "At 3pm our 9.2s opened fire on the German front line, but a large percentage were duds." Captain Barne met "Orford, now an officer of SW Borderers, lately a Sgt of the Regt and City policeman often to be seen outside Liverpool St station. His Bn is in the line just on the right of us." Lance Sergeant Edgar Orford left in 1910 after twelve years in the 2nd Battalion and a DCM from the Boer War. Having reenlisted in the Army in 1914 he was at about the turn of the year appointed Regimental Sergeant Major of the 10th South Wales Borderers and had since been commissioned. The relief that night "went like clockwork" for Sir Iain Colquhoun, though "What a bally long march" was Private Fleming's comment on the road all the way to near La Gorgue. Captain Barne "walked back…with Paul Methuen who was pretty well done up after being up 3 days and nights sniping, with practically no rest or sleep. Luckily I was able to help him, with a drop of brandy and carrying his rifle, he was very glad to get in. I hear the Irish Guards have manufactured 2 corpses, put them out in No Man's Land with an oil drum, so arranged that on touching the corpses a bomb explodes. It is hoped to catch out some Bosches like this! There are already so many corpses lying out that personally I doubt their sending out a special night patrol to look at them! The corpses were so realistic that some women seeing them lying by the roadside in billets crossed themselves as they passed."

As usual the next morning was occupied with the inspection of rifles, equipment, billets and feet, but in the afternoon Sir Iain Colquhoun and Lieutenant Boyd Rochfort rode into La Gorgue and had a hot bath. They met and talked to a number of people they knew, including the Prince of Wales and Captain Andrew "Bulgy" Thorne, and came back to find that Captain Hugh Ross had arrived, recovered from his wound during First Ypres. Lieutenant Methuen left for good, sent to England sick, and was medically downgraded. Another departure, forced on him much against his own will and much against that of the Battalion, was that of Captain Stewart, the doctor who had been with them ever since First Ypres. Every ruse had been tried to retain him and every one had failed. From his billet Private Fleming went into Merville on the evening of 15 February where he saw "Bantams stationed there, Royal Scots, W Yorks & Berks." Private Johnes wrote of having men from the Bantams in the line with them too, whom he described as "a sturdy well trained bunch, in good physical condition…They had a few casualties before we pulled out and took them well. It's impossible to say what they thought about the trench pals (rats and lice), which we left for them. We introduced to them our way of getting rid of the lice (by turning the shirt inside out and one taking hold of the tail end and another taking hold of the arms, drawing it taut and passing it backward and forward over the flames of a hot fire, you could hear the darn things crack)." Reflecting on the line here Private Johnes described it as "a cushy position for the winter. Casualties had been light from actual combat, but there were cases of sickness, colds brought on through the climate, trench foot was appearing from the continual sloshing about in rubber boots full of muddy water, cold and hot, depending on the weather and how long a period of time they were worn. The feet swelled up and in some cases the rubbers had to be cut off the feet. Nerves, hypertension, depression showed up, but little attention was shown to shell shock and fatigue. However from time to time you would miss a face and wonder what had become of the owner." They paraded at eleven on the 16th, handed over their billets and marched off towards Le Sart, west of Merville, their first stage towards the Ypres Salient hinterland. This time Sir Iain Colquhoun remarked "The men marched very well & the last part of the march was in bright sunshine." It had been rougher to begin with and Major Barne described "Again a wind from west, squalls of rain, etc. which made the march though only about 6 miles seem like 10." They stayed at Le Sart for three nights, never again to return to between Armentières and Loos. Among the men the name of Ypres had gloomy implications, Private Cumming recording how they "felt that our prospects of survival had been considerably diminished, although we did not exactly say so."

On 17 February they were still at Le Sart and still the wind blew hard. In his recent letters Sir Iain Colquhoun had mentioned more than once to Dinah that a German attack was expected at any time and that they were ready for it. "It's the best thing that could possibly happen." The Germans did not do this anywhere near Neuve Chapelle but on the 14th they did attack The Bluff, a large spoil heap beside the Ypres-Comines Canal. Major Barne heard that the enemy had "taken about 600 yds of our trenches near Ypres. Bad." The British recovered it soon afterwards. He then spent the afternoon of the 17th going for a "walk with the Padre through a bit of the Forêt de Nieppe. Find an unexploded shell – (British) buried in an oak tree. There are some magnificent oaks here tall & clean. Saw a roe deer also some cowslips – but not any great variety of flora." On the 19th their Brigade marched fourteen miles north towards Godewaersvelde, northeast of Hazebrouck and about half way between there and Poperinghe, Major Barne noting that only one Scots Guardsman fell out "and this only when pressed by the doctor." Left behind in the field ambulance with a high temperature was Captain Hugh Ross. Sir Iain Colquhoun told his wife that he was looking very ill, but that it was probably very temporary. It had not prevented Captain Ross from having dinner with them on the 17th and being "very funny". Battalion Headquarters went to Godewaersvelde as the companies all halted elsewhere in scattered and rough accommodation. Major Barne went round each that night and found "the men very squashed up" and Private Fleming had "Got rotten billet." On the 20th Sir Iain Colquhoun was one of several officers who at different times rode up to the top of the Mont des Cats nearby. "There is a large monastery on the top, and one can see the country for miles around, Ypres, Poperinghe, Bailleul, etc." The next day he marched C Company up there. "Cold frosty morning, enjoyed march very much." Major Barne described being "in a large farm, & I have a funny little room looking West. To get to it – ditto Esmé to his – we have to go through Madame's room. She has 6 daughters, and one son who is serving in the French Army at Salonika." Soon after Festubert Private Ernest "Eric" Miller, just returned to France after being slightly wounded at the Cuinchy brickstacks with the 1st Scots Guards, was posted to the 2nd Battalion and made a Lance Sergeant on arrival, becoming a Sergeant less than two months later. By this time his mother lived in Tunbridge Wells, but previously their home was at Marple, Cheshire, and he went to Maxwells School, Manchester. He enlisted in London at the end of August 1914, aged thirty four, when home on leave from Karachi where he was a merchant. On 6 February he was commissioned, joining the 1st Scots Guards a fortnight later.

After three days, in now very wintry weather, they were on the road again to Herzeele, twelve miles north. Sir Iain Colquhoun wrote home that "we marched all the way yesterday in a howling blizzard of snow and sleet I rather enjoyed it. We reached these billets about 3pm they are quite good ones. This morning the snow is lying thick on the ground and more falling it's lucky we're not in the trenches… My uniform is getting very ragged and I have written for some more but it won't be out for some time I'm afraid." Private Fleming recorded "It snowed all the time. Wet through and cold. Got good billets but too crowded." To Major Barne the march was unnecessarily more unpleasant because they "took wrong turning which made it 2 miles further and we missed our billeting party who were waiting on the proper road, thus causing a long delay. Men's billets quite fair, officers very moderate. I am in the coldest of little rooms by myself facing North so that the icy wind blows right in & I have one of the coldest nights I ever remember – & find the floor very hard." Herzeele was a main training area, but, the weather being what it was, nothing was possible. Major Barne and Padre Gillieson set off on ten days leave on the evening of the 24th. At Hazebrouck they happened on a train just leaving for Boulogne, slept when they got there, crossed the Channel soon after midday and "arriving at Victoria at 4.50pm where find my Violet waiting for me." Just before leaving Hazebrouck Major Barne heard "Great rumours of the French having had some very successful operations, but am not sure the Germans don't seem to have got the best of it so far." The Battle of Verdun had started.

At half past five on the morning of the 25th the Battalion set off towards Ypres, crossed the Belgian border two hours later and stopped at St Jans-ter-Biezen, the last hamlet before Poperinghe, where they stayed in huts. Sir Iain Colquhoun commented "Hard frost and very cold wait at end of march as we were not expected till 12.30pm. Arrived 9.30am. Went into billets, little wooden huts and a few tents, everything frozen stiff. Bitterly cold." He explained to Dinah that "as coal is hard to get, it's pretty cold at times. The inhabitants all say this is the coldest weather they have had for 9 years. If it freezes tonight I will be able to use my skates tomorrow which will be topping…All leave has been stopped at present on account of German attacks on Verdun. The French seem quite pleased about the whole thing and say they don't care if Verdun does fall as everything has been removed from it, they must have killed a tremendous lot of Germans. General Feilding told us today that the big Russian offensive will come off sometime in June; we will probably cooperate by making some sort of attack here." In the same letter he told her how Captain Ross and he had "built a huge snow woman today and modelled it very carefully, we spent so much time and care over the breast part that they were lumps of ice instead of snow in the end."

The 27th was a Sunday and Private Fleming was "On parade at 9.30 up to neck in mud. Showed rifles. On parade at 2.20 again but dismissed as parson didn't show up." This would have been a visiting chaplain. Amid signs of a thaw that night four hundred men, with officers, had their first experience of the Ypres Salient. They went in lorries to dig trenches for a reserve position near Elverdinghe, a large village on the road northeast from Poperinghe towards Boesinghe, itself two miles further on and close behind the front line at the Canal. Private Fleming found it "Awful up behind front line from 6 – 8am digging reserve trench. Mud." Those not required for this concentrated on bomb throwing and tactics, which featured largely over the next few days. There was also instruction for snipers and Lewis gunners and on the effective revetting of trenches, a quite different matter from the maintenance of breastworks which they had become used to. The bad weather made any drill parades impossible. General Feilding gave a lecture on "Defences of the Ypres Salient" for all officers. Because he was on guard duty on 1 March Private Fleming missed the next fatigue party, but four hundred went up, many for a second time, with Sir Iain Colquhoun in command. When they got there, this time in buses, he "Divided party into 4 lots of 100 each, and sent them off under RE officers to dig 2nd Line defence scheme. Dug till 2am met again at Elverdinghe chateau, boarded the motor buses, and reached camp by 4.15am." They then had a big breakfast and slept all day. There were no casualties either time. Though Elverdinghe had been shelled a good deal its Château was almost untouched, because the owner was an Austrian nobleman, so it was believed. On 3 March Private Fleming's "Father came up to camp at 2.30pm. Had a good time with him in Poperinghe…Father looking well. Burnett came with him. It rained something awful." He did not say what his father was doing in the BEF, but they were able to meet a number of times. Private William Burnett, a friend in the Battalion, was also from Dundee.

Calais

On 5 March their Brigade went to Calais. The train carrying the Scots Guards from Poperinghe took five and a half hours, after which they had a two hour march to a rest camp at Beau Marais, on the road towards Dunkirk and about a mile from the sea. There were nineteen officers, nine hundred and fifty men, sixty nine horses, twenty three vehicles of all types and ten bicycles.

They lived in tents and it was wet and cold, with snow and sleet. Training continued, punctuated with route marches, but also there was time off. So, on the 6th Private Fleming noted that they were "Allowed into Calais" though Private Johnes remembered that they had to be back in camp by ten o'clock for a roll call. "The red light district was strictly taboo, out of bounds. Our Regimental Police, together with the regular military police, saw to it that it was. It was known as The Garden of Eden."

That evening Sir Iain Colquhoun and others started with a hot bath in the Hotel Maritime before drinks and dinner elsewhere. Following a route march next morning he wrote to his wife after lunch "There is 6 inches of snow everywhere but a hot sun. We had a very good dinner last night at a small restaurant but there is nothing to do afterwards, not even a cinematograph…I am dining quietly here tonight with about 8 others. Nearly everyone dines here as the mess tent gets a bit chilly at night as there are no fires or anything…Tomorrow our brigade is being inspected by Sir Douglas Haig; I hope he won't take long…The Belgian Army is near here; they hold about 10 miles of front and are pretty fair riff-raff. Their aerodrome is a huge place we use it for parading on." On the evening of the 7th sixteen officers went out to dinner at the Continental and afterwards all except Lord Esmé Gordon Lennox and Sir Iain Colquhoun, who went back to camp, "went round the town." Major Barne had returned and on reaching Calais "I first deliver a bed which I have brought out with care & trouble & expense & anxiety for the Brigadier, who rather sniffs at it as it is such a big package." He then joined the party at the Continental "having a very scrambly & expensive dinner. After dinner I try to find my way back to the Hotel Sauvage where I have leave to sleep, but have great difficulty as I never remember seeing such a dark or deserted town. I am lucky to find a vacant room – the last." The Hotel Sauvage was also Brigade Headquarters.

On the afternoon of the 9th Sir Douglas Haig inspected them and a detachment of Belgian gunners. Sir Iain Colquhoun reported to Dinah that as this "started at 2 and ended at 3.30 it was very cold hanging about. He is a very fine looking man and was very pleased with the Brigade." He went on "Leave will not reopen until the Verdun business is settled one way or the other. The Germans seem to be determined to have it. Haig said he is very pleased with everything and thinks Verdun will not fall." It was freezing. "The floor boards of the tents are very hard and as I can't lie on my wounded side it wakes me up whenever I turn on it in my sleep. It is funny how much more I feel the cold since being hit I suppose it is loss of blood." He was feeling better next day and told her that "Last night I dined at Brigade HQ and a lot of sort of nurses turned up and we all danced afterwards it was awful fun. They are what are called FANY. I don't know what it means but they drive motors etc and do awfully well I believe. They were all ladies; it seemed very funny talking to one again." He added that Sir Douglas Haig had told Major Rasch, the Brigade Major, "that we would be taking over a bit of the French line shortly and that we would not attack this year. I think it is a great pity if we don't." On the 10th Major Barne and several others went on a visit "to the Ordnance & Supply Depots, repairing shops, Bakery, etc. such a wonderful sight… The CO is ill so I get the Brigadier to order him to go & sleep in the town which he does without great difficulty, owing to our having engaged a room and a fly to take him down." Then he mentioned that the 3rd Grenadiers had had a bad accident with grenades, two men killed and twenty one wounded, "and these unfortunately are all the best bombers." The day's events for Private Fleming were "Bathing parade. No good. Btn paid out. Went into Calais again…many drunks." Next day he noted "Passes stopped." Major Barne wrote "Yesterday was "pay day", when there were 23 men absent, so at CO's orders this morning I have a big lot of criminals to settle – and all passes into the town have to be stopped." Instead, that night there was a battalion concert in the YMCA hut."

After church parades on the 12th they then played the Coldstream in the first round of the Brigade Football Cup presented by General Ponsonby, which ended in a scoreless draw, even after extra time, but next day won the replay 2-1. The pitch was on the Belgian Air Force aerodrome "which makes a wonderful field for football." A very great deal of football was played at Calais. Several officers were sick, apparently with heavy colds or flu, but Lieutenant Hammersley had measles. Next month he was invalided, possibly with some form of shell shock, and went home permanently in June. Then there was something completely different.

The Calais First Spring Meeting, another brainchild of General Ponsonby's, who acted as Judge, consisted of four flat races on the beach and one steeplechase. There was some apprehension that the incoming tide would demolish the very easy gorse fences before that could be run, but all was well. Every possible horse or pony was entered. Major Barne won the lightweight race for The Ponsonby Plate over five furlongs. It was, he wrote, "an easy win – The Tetrarch must be a very fast pony." This, a grey belonging to Sir Iain Colquhoun, but originally Captain Stracey's, had been with them all along, having arrived on 13 August 1914 at Le Havre. Other Scots Guards runners during the afternoon were Captain Ross' Fifinella, Captain Norman's Pretty Polly, Captain Thompson's Silver Tag and Lieutenant Boyd Rochfort's Synford. The champion jockey was Lieutenant Bewicke. Having won The Surrey Plate on his own horse, Old Fairyhouse, named after the racecourse in County Meath, he won the extra race at the end of the afternoon between the five best horses. In each race the entry money was five francs and the winner took all. The oldest competitor was Father Simon Knapp, Padre of the 2nd Irish Guards, aged fifty eight. Colonel Butler of the Irish Guards won the steeplechase very easily, in which Captain Kinlay's Ally Sloper, with Lieutenant Orr Ewing up, came fourth. The race crowd was large, enthusiastic and bet ferociously. Major Barne recorded that "2 officers of IG dressed up complete in fur collars brown billycocks and button holes were bookies, & made about £20 on the meeting." Sir Iain Colquhoun told his wife about it, adding that he "made quite a lot of money by bets and stake money…I rode my grey in the last race but John Dyer's pony kicked her, and I never got off at all to everyone's disgust as they had made her favourite (slightly stupid)… The last 4 days everyone has talked about nothing else but racing and football and the war is never mentioned. It is a very good thing as one gets very tired of war shop. The Belgians must think us off our nuts…6 of our officers have gone sick lately and are going home I believe. The cold knocked them out…I shall be very sorry to leave this place as we have had a topping time and many merry dinners in the town."

On the afternoon of the 14th the Scots Guards beat the Grenadiers by a goal to nil to win the Brigade Football Cup in what the War Diary called "another keen and exciting game" and Sir Iain Colquhoun "a good game, but very foul." The prize was a bronze mounted French cavalryman. Major Barne described "Great rejoicing in the Battn." Lord Esmé Gordon Lennox was back, though Major Barne thought him "very seedy still," and explained to them "the Ypres defence scheme – we don't look forward to going there." Then Sir Iain Colquhoun recorded that they could not play football "as Belgians were flying and kept flying over our heads to drive us off the ground." This delayed the officers football final between the Coldstream and Scots Guards, which, after negotiations with a Belgian captain, eventually started at five o'clock and went on well after dark. The Coldstream finally won 5-2 by scoring three goals in extra time,

Major Barne attributing it "I think partly owing to their having white jerseys on & so able to see and pass to one other." He went to dinner at the Continental on this, his forty second birthday.

Then the Brigade left Calais to be in divisional reserve at Poperinghe as the Guards Division replaced the 6th Division in the line.

Notes on Chapter Sources

History of the Great War based on Official Documents by direction of the Historical Section of the Committee of Imperial Defence.
Brig Gen Sir JE Edmonds, *Military Operations France and Belgium, 1916: Volume I: Sir Douglas Haig's Command to the 1st July: Battle of the Somme* (London: Macmillan and Co Ltd 1932).
Abercromby Papers, Private Collection.
LSgt A Fleming, 1916 Letts *"The Soldier's Own Note Book And Pocket Diary"*, IWM MISC11 Item 246.

14

The Laventie and Neuve Chapelle Trenches and the Winter 1915-16 – 2nd Battalion

Rest and breastworks

On 31 October the 2nd Scots Guards were still at Cantraine when Lieutenant Ewart returned in charge of a draft from the Base Depot. There were route marching, training in bombing, in wiring and in the Lewis Gun, the light machine gun now coming into service for the first time, and a very substantial amount of drill. Captain Wynne Finch took a firm view of officers' drill. He was not satisfied at all and there was repeated mention of their parading under the Sergeant Major. He believed that many thought that, since they were only there for the War, drill was not something that they needed much knowledge of "as they had not realized that without good drill and proper discipline one was not at one's maximum usefulness. Provided one had the proper grounding of these two, one could be fairly certain of oneself in the crisis of a battle or at any other time." Captain Warner's activities in the week beginning 12 November included checking near Laventie where Brigade Headquarters would be up in the line two days later, inspecting the billets of the two reserve battalions, identifying a suitable barn for gas mask testing and training, billeting everyone when they arrived on the 14th, dealing with "Many visitors, principally Chaplains," looking for bath arrangements and suitable sites for boot stores and drying rooms and "Plenty of correspondence". Generally, it was his job to make sure that there was sufficient accommodation for everyone when required out of the front line itself and when there were mix-ups over arrangements, as there frequently were, sorting them out. As he found most of these before any troops arrived they would never know. His most common means of transport was the sidecar of a motorbike.

On 6 November Colonel Cator wrote to Brigade Headquarters about Private Callachan's three year prison sentence, drawing attention to his conduct during the attack on Big Willie. After most of the bombers had been killed and wounded Private Callachan volunteered "to bomb up the trench & showed conspicuous gallantry & good work throughout the day." He asked if in the light of this "his case could be forwarded to higher authority with a view to remitting a portion of the sentence." General Heyworth replied two weeks later that he could not see a reason to do so for the time being but told Colonel Cator that, provided Private Callachan's behaviour was satisfactory over the next three months, he should request a review again. Meanwhile a letter on Private Callachan's behalf had arrived at the War Office, a typed copy of which was sent to Regimental Headquarters with directions to make enquiries. The writer was Bella Parker of Govan. "I am writing to you to see if you could do nothing for him

– its hard to think of him lying in prison 3 years if you could only pardon him and let him out to do his bit with the rest I am sure he has tried to do his best for his king and country for 10 months and oh sir wouldn't he be far happier fighting than lying in a prison cell – Dear Sir if you only knew all his troubles since he has been fighting you would be sorry for him. His mother had shamed them since he went away and a happy home was broke up and then his poor father was well nigh burnt to death and is disabled for life and in a very poor state of health and this has nearly broke his poor heart and he has 2 poor we sisters and a we brother and dear sir could you not try and get him off so that he can do his bit out in France and God is good maybe he will spare him to come home and work for his poor father and the young children whom there mother has left to fight there battle alone I am only a girl of 18 myself and have had to fight my way along without father or mother this 10 years and my sweetheart Johnny is about the only true friend I have in this wide world and I know him to be a true Hearted upright young man – Dear Sir I hope you won't scorn my appeal for it comes from a broken Heart and if you can help him anyway no matter how little it is you will be blessed by me day and night."

Little caught Lieutenant Ewart's attention until the 11th by which time they had been at Merville for two days. Then "Our visit to the trenches is set for three days hence, for Sunday, and we are likely to be under fire for the next month or six weeks at least. I cannot say that I look forward to it, but I hope that the trenches are respectable. JA Stirling has succeeded Arkwright as my Company Commander, and at present we have a very strong Battalion, but I expect they will soon start going sick. Arkwright has gone home with a nervous breakdown. He was a nice chap and a good soldier." When Lieutenant Arkwright had the breakdown was not recorded, but while on sick leave in December at home he was invalided. On Colonel Cator's recommendation he was given the MC in January 1916, but never came back to either Battalion and did staff jobs elsewhere from then on. Both men's marriages broke down and soon after the end of the War Captain Arkwright married Violet Cator.

On the 13th the much tattooed Private John Wells was in trouble again, charged with gambling, a military offence in the ranks, and awarded five days FP No 2. A Military Mounted Police patrol had caught him in an estaminet in Merville. Gambling was pervasive, though usually very well concealed, with Crown and Anchor, depending on the fall of its dice, particularly popular.

They marched out at quarter to two on 14 November for the first time to the new Guards Division sector, which for them meant on the right close to Mauquissart and on the left just outside Fauquissart on the road that then crossed the German front line and wound its way up the slope beyond to Aubers. Mauquissart was where they had made their second attack at Neuve Chapelle, Fauquissart only a short way south of Rouges Bancs. Three companies were in front with Right Flank in support occupying four forts, Erith, Église, Elgin and Road Bend. When they could first see properly after dawn on the 15th they found that all was not as they would want it to be. Work started at once on repairing and building up the parapets of the breastworks. Bringing up flooring for the dug-outs was another priority. There was quite a bit of sniping which wounded one man and killed Private William Hendry, erstwhile Edinburgh labourer, a soldier for nearly a year, in the BEF for six months, and son of William and Annie Hendry of Colinton. The Welsh Guards, with whom they usually alternated, took over that evening and they went back to billets in Laventie. Lieutenant Ewart was sent to hospital in Merville with suspected jaundice "having been taken queer on coming out of the trenches. I quite enjoyed myself there, having a heart-to-heart with the Germans. But on leaving felt very ill indeed."

After a few days he was much better and went out with an Irish Guards officer in the same hospital "to luncheon in the local inn, which is reckoned a great dissipation."

The settled pattern of normal activity, with slight variations, over a period of twelve days in the front and support lines, followed by six days in reserve around Merville, applied to the 2nd Scots Guards as to everyone else. Unusually the slightly prolonged next front line tour finished well after daylight on the morning of the 24th and they went to Laventie. That night a fatigue party of two hundred men, plus officers, left for four hours work under the Royal Engineers on the Central Railway, also known as the Midland Railway, Rue Tilleloy, repeated the following night with another party of the same size drawn from the other two companies. This light railway stopped at Église Station just west of the Rue Tilleloy and some five hundred yards down it from Fauquissart. Another, the South East Railway, was a little further south.

After lunch on the 26th they left for six days in reserve and marched just over two hours in the falling snow to Merville. Their Brigade moved into the billets as the 2nd Guards Brigade moved out for the line. On the 28th there was an unusual entry, very welcome to those chosen "Four men sent for a permanent woodcutting fatigue to the Forest of Nieppe." Recovered and back in the Battalion, Lieutenant Ewart wrote of a "great battalion concert" on the 30th, St Andrew's Day, followed by a dinner party. The Brigadier came and the Grenadier Guards Band played during the evening. "Several people got tight." Captain Warner went to this "returning 11.30pm. At work with papers when Roger returned 12.30am. To bed about 1.15am. Tiring day." On 3 December he went round in the afternoon with their French interpreter "to arrange Baths and drying rooms etc. French people very tiresome and not much result. Got very wet."

On 2 December the Scots Guards were packing up at Merville for the next twelve days in and out of the line, further south than they had been the time before. F Company were in the forts, Erith again, Dreadnought, North Tilleloy and Winchester House. This was quiet as far as fighting went, but the Germans shelled the breastworks a few times and the British guns retaliated. It was very, very wet and as the pouring rain fell the water rose. Therefore the worst part of this tour was the discomfort, made worse still because all the dug-outs had been condemned as unfit after one had fallen in a week earlier, killing, so they heard, a Welsh Guardsman and injuring three. They worked hard at repairing the parapets, pumping water out of the trenches and constructing new dug-outs. On the 4th they spotted a German machine gun emplacement in a mine crater in No Man's Land opposite. A British 4.5 inch howitzer fired at it and "considerable damage was done." They came out that night, but two days later again swapped over with the Welsh Guards in the course of which Private William Marshall was hit by a shell in the right leg and buttock. He was twenty three when he enlisted in September 1914 and had already been a miner for nine years with Young's Paraffin Light & Mineral Oil Company in West Lothian. This was his second time in France as he was in the 1st Battalion for a matter of days in January before being wounded in the ear at the Cuinchy brickstacks. He had been out again since the end of May. This wound was much more serious, the leg was amputated, and after his discharge in March 1917 he went back disabled to West Calder. He had no recorded family.

For a time, without a new dug-out, Lieutenant Ewart "rested – for sleep was impossible – under a bit of corrugated iron in the fire trench which I shared with a sergeant and a private. In fact, I have had a fairly hard time; what between Lonely Post, the trenches with their rats and mice worse than ever, and a five hour patrol at night. Lonely Post was a beastly place and a responsible one, as I was there all by myself. It was in a depressing part of the line on the borders of the battlefield of Neuve Chapelle. Some of the dead men of the Rifle Brigade still lay out in front, while behind, to cheer me up, there was a perfect forest of little mud graves and crosses, mostly very rough, and marked "In Memory of a British Soldier, RIP". In the distance I could see approximately the place where Seymour and I got wounded and poor Teddy Hulse was killed." He was unlikely to have been in Lonely Post, a fort back on the Rue Bacquerot half a mile away, for which the support battalion were responsible.

During a subsequent tour a party of 4th Grenadiers, on their right, raided the enemy line on the night of the 11th. "We were all on the *qui vive*, not knowing what might happen. Under cover of darkness they crept across No Man's Land, through the German wire, and up to the parapet. At a given time our guns opened fire and the Grenadiers rushed the German trench, scuppered the machine gunners and spiked their gun. At the same time another lot ran along the German trench bombing every dug-out and bayoneting every German they met. On the blowing of a whistle they all jumped back over the parapet and raced back to our lines, having had one officer slightly wounded. It was a smart job. I watched from our parapet, and it was like a play, although of course I could not see all that was actually happening. The sky behind was lit up by the flashes of the guns, and presently there was a furious burst of rifle fire from the German trenches, followed by the flash and boom of their guns from Aubers Ridge and the flickering glare of innumerable star lights and rockets which the Bosches sent up. Then all was dead still and dark, as if the curtain had been rung down." This was a highly successful operation lasting about a quarter of an hour, surprise was complete and the few Grenadier casualties, an officer and four men wounded, all got back safely. They had killed several Germans and destroyed a machine gun.

That day, half way through their tour, the Scots Guards had the 13th Royal Welsh Fusiliers battalion headquarters and one company attached for instruction, a platoon with each host company. Lieutenant Ewart found "it was *très drôle* when they came into the trenches for the first time. They ducked and jumped about, apparently oblivious of the fact that there was a four-foot breastwork between them and the Germans." On the 13th Captain Warner noted that Lord Cavan had come to see the Grenadiers who had taken part in the raid and later that he "Saw Winston going into trenches". Three days later he read of the removal of Sir John French as Commander-in-Chief and the appointment of Sir Douglas Haig. On the 19th he "Attended meeting of QrMasters re Xmas dinners".

The other Christmas Truce

After another six days at Merville they were in the line again on the 20th, G Company in the forts and the other three manning the breastworks, with them the 14th Royal Welsh Fusiliers second in command and a company. That night they sent out patrols to examine how much enemy wire there was and in what condition. This may have had something to do with the change in German behaviour the following night, the enemy having been very quiet till then. After dark on the 21st German machine guns were very active all night. All the same Lieutenant Ewart found there was not much going on apart from "the usual strafing. I have just received an early Christmas parcel of food and a packet containing tobacco, pipes, chocolate, a pound cake, bedroom slippers, and a knitted scarf." He gave the pipes and tobacco to his NCOs. Meanwhile everyone went on working away at the breastworks and the forts and draining away the water before leaving for Laventie the next evening.

On the 20th a plan began to form at Brigade Headquarters for a Welsh Guards raid on the German trenches "in connection with a gas attack." The next day Captain Warner "ordered bridges, bludgeons, lamps etc. from RE." When he went to the line in the afternoon to see the Welsh Guards he found Lieutenant Colonel William Murray Threipland and his officers "not very keen. Message after dinner postponing raid. Gas is to be let off at first opportunity but only patrols are to go out." The wind was "unfavourable" on the 22nd and again "unfavourable" early on the 24th but the Welsh Guards asked to do the raid when conditions were right. Because of these postponements there had been till then a possibility of the Scots Guards raiding later on the 24th or the day after. However, as the Welsh Guards wished to do it later, when the Scots Guards went into the front line after dark on Christmas Eve they did not need to think about it. Both British and Germans shouted to each other through the night.

Early on Christmas Day a German sniper killed Company Sergeant Major James Oliver of Right Flank as he was peering over the parapet. Reservists like him who had previously been NCOs were essential for the training of volunteers and he had only been six months in France. He was a groom till January 1906 when he joined up in Preston, serving eight years. He and Alice Hutchings were married at the end of 1912 at Kilburn, London, a month before he went to the Reserve. She and their son, born in August 1914, were living in Lee, also in London. His death, he being the "British sergeant" referred to below, did not deter anyone else. Some Scots Guardsmen got out of their trenches and mingled with the Germans very briefly, possibly stimulated to do so by what they could see of the 1st Coldstream and 1st Scots Guards across to the right. Lieutenant Ewart watched it all "So soon as it grows light this morning, we start peeping at each other over the top of the parapet…calling across to each other. And presently, at about 7.50, a German stands up openly on the parapet and waves his arms. He is followed by two in field grey overcoats and pill box caps. Then they come out all down the line, stand on the parapet, wave, shout, and finally swarm forth from their trenches on either side. A British sergeant is shot dead almost at the outset, as he stands on the parapet. But this makes no difference. It must be an accident. The supreme craving of humanity, the irresistible, spontaneous impulse born of a common faith and a common fear, fully triumph. And so the grey and khaki figures surge towards each other as one man. The movement has started on the right. It spreads like contagion. Only we officers, the sentries, and a few non commissioned officers remain in our trench. The men meet at the willow lined stream; they even cross it and mingle together in a haphazard throng. They talk and gesticulate, and shake hands over and over again. They pat each other on the shoulder and laugh like schoolboys, and leap across the stream for fun. And when an Englishman falls in and a Bosche helps him out there is a shout of laughter that echoes back to the trenches. The Germans exchange cigars and pieces of sausages, and *sauerkraut* and concentrated coffee for cigarettes, and bully beef and ration biscuits and tobacco. They express mutual admiration by pointing and signs. It is our leather waistcoats and trench coats that attract their attention; it is their trench overalls, made of coarse canvas, that attract our's. We shout "Hullo, Fritz!" "Good morning, Fritz!" "Merry Christmas!" "Happy Christmas!" "How's your father?" "Come over and call!" "Come and have breakfast," and the like, amid roars of laughter…So for ten brief – all too brief – minutes there is peace and goodwill among the trenches on Christmas Day. Then from the trenches of the *Ninety fifth Bavarian Reserve Infantry Regiment* two officers in black accoutrements and shiny field boots come out, wishing to take photographs of our Tommies, and offering them cigars. Their request is refused, and presently they say "You will have five minutes to get back to your trenches before our artillery will open fire." And it does. And two or three men are wounded almost at once. But for twenty four hours not a shot is fired on either side. A common brotherhood of suffering – or is it an act of God, or just human curiosity? – has united Englishman and Bavarian in fraternity on the battlefield this grey Christmas morning which no one on either side who has taken part in this quaint scene will ever forget."

The first that was heard of this at Battalion Headquarters came down from Headquarters XI Corps. Colonel Cator immediately went up to the front line to put a stop to it, but, by the time he arrived everything was back to normal and the men of both sides were again under cover. There were no repercussions for any of the 2nd Scots Guards. The German guns fired some twenty shells at Road Bend fort near the Rue Bacquerot after midday, without damage. After night fell the Germans started shouting across again. Captain Warner went on Christmas Day "To church in Railway shed with Brigadier. Some of the Scots Guards went out to meet Germans, but were quickly got back. Many of the 2nd Bde with Officers went out. Court of Enquiry is to be held."

On Boxing Day the German guns fired at Road Bend and also at the front line, again without effect. Back at Laventie that evening there were further guests, a 17th Royal Welsh Fusiliers company. The wind that night was yet again wrong for gas and Captain Warner made no further mention of it. Meanwhile there was upheaval at Brigade Headquarters when Major Tempest was sent to take command of the 1st Scots Guards on the 27th, only to ring up the following evening to say he was coming back as "The whole thing was a mistake."

Colonel Cator's sister Mary Fellowes had sent him a Christmas cake and some apples and he wrote on the 27th, telling her of "rather a rotten Xmas day...I had my best sergeant killed early in the morning, then in the afternoon I had my Headquarters shelled & we had to clear out. We waited till they got a direct hit after that I cleared everyone & we went off to one side & watched the Hun shelling our poor little trench home. The Presbyterian Parson who is an awfully good chap came up into the trenches & had a communion service." There had been two services at Battalion Headquarters and a few officers and men were sent from each company at a time. "I have never been to a Presbyterian service before it is quite different to our's in the ritual part, however he is an awfully sincere manly chap & he said some awfully nice prayers. Our Church of England padre is a prig & doesn't go down with the men. He didn't come into the trenches which I thought slack of him." Mary Fellowes' son, Charles, was old enough for his future in the Army to be under discussion and Colonel Cator recommended Sandhurst in the first instance as "it is no good boys coming out here under 19. The work is too hard whilst they are still growing but I hope for yr sake the war will be over before he joins." The Reverend Alexander MacRae was the Church of Scotland padre. He came from Kingussie, Invernessshire, and was educated there and at St Andrews University before being ordained. In June 1915 he became an army chaplain after being chaplain for several years to the Royal Scottish Corporation and Royal Scottish Asylum in London. He was fifty two years old at this time and was with the Battalion for two years.

The last weeks near the Lys

During their last forty eight hours in the line in 1915 they saw three enemy planes over them on the 29th and there was more of this next day. At night, after reports that the Germans were working on their wire the Brigade Vickers Gun and Battalion Lewis Gun teams fired heavily over No Man's Land. There was nothing else to report and on the evening of the 30th they were all soon back in Laventie, going on to Merville after lunch on the 31st, where they could relax. However, at some stage on the 30th 2nd Lieutenant Erskine Knollys was going round the line with a NCO and found Private Charles Brown asleep on sentry. Private Brown, the seaman son of William and Mary Brown of Douglas, Isle of Man, enlisted there late in August 1914 and had been in France since April. Injured accidentally in the knee on 11 September when G Company were employed cutting timber near St Omer he was in hospital for ten days afterwards. Now he was in close arrest. Lieutenant Knollys, from a family with a long regimental association, was commissioned on 29 August 1915 after starting the War as a Private in the Canadian Mounted Rifles.

Lieutenant Ewart next wrote "We celebrated the New Year last night in a simple way. Stirling went out to dinner, but Knollys and I had a Grenadier and a stray artillery officer in for a meal. The servants and orderlies made a sing song and we made some whiskey punch. Tomorrow night the men are going to have a great New Year's dinner in rest billets at Merville, and so are some officers with, I believe, a lot of generals – the "blokes", as the men call them. The Germans have livened up here lately and have shelled us mildly several times without doing any damage. My company has been garrisoning the forts just behind the line – a rotten job, as we don't get to our reserve billets when the others do. As for companionship we are reduced to only three officers."

2 January was a Sunday. It was current practice out of the line to parade for church services on Sunday mornings, separate ones for the Church of England and Church of Scotland, while the Roman Catholics went to Merville Parish Church. Christmas Dinner for the men started at half past four to which Captain Warner went with General Heyworth. The focus of attention up to the 12th for almost everyone was on drill, with route marches a poor second, but there was also grenade training and Company Sergeant Major Thomas Wilkinson was very badly hurt on the 4th. He was the son of Watson and Jane Wilkinson of Easingwold, Yorkshire, and had served with the Imperial Yeomanry in the Boer War before joining the Scots Guards in March 1903, giving his occupation as a farmer. A Sergeant in the 1st Battalion from the start of the War, he was wounded in the hand during the Prussian Guards attack at Nonne Boschen. He returned to the BEF, but to the 2nd Scots Guards in June 1915. From hospital in Calais he was reported initially "Dangerously Ill", but a little later he was removed from that list. At an unspecified date his left leg was amputated and, either before or after that, he was sent home, to begin with to hospital at Sandgate, Kent, and then in the autumn to Roehampton. A few weeks later he was out of the Army with a weekly pension of twenty two shillings and three pence for life.

On the 5th a court martial found Private Brown guilty of "Sleeping on his post" and sentenced him to death. Sir Henry Rawlinson commuted this to three years penal servitude and suspended it. So Private Brown returned to his place in the Battalion with the sentence hanging over him from then on. On the 6th they were back in the line east of Laventie with, on their right, the 38th Division, whose arrival in the area had made possible the recent much longer than usual rest period at Merville. For the rest of January the routine in the line continued, shared with the Welsh Guards. Whenever the weather was fine and clear and so visibility good, the shelling increased. There was much more mention of German shelling than previously. What the German gunners intended to fire at with varying intensity was usually obvious as soon as they started. Most was at the further back forts, the light railways, possible headquarters and the British guns, a field gun being hit on 7 February. Almost always it failed to cause any damage that mattered. At night there tended to be more machine gun fire, but that too was very variable. However, real harm was done by a 5.9 inch shell which hit Hougoumont Fort at one o'clock on 23 January. Four men died and five more were wounded.

One of the dead, in the Battalion just over six months, was Private Hugh McDonald, before the War a carriage driver in Glasgow, where he lived with his widowed mother Jessie McDonald in Maryhill. He had a heart with a dagger tattooed on his left arm and "HMD" with a horse-shoe and a whip on the right. A few belongings, including his rosary, were sent home. A month later a letter reached Regimental Headquarters. "Sir I take the liberty of writing to [you] on behalf of Mrs J McDonald 44 Murano St Maryhill Glasgow. You see her son 13154 Pte Hugh McDonald 2nd Scots Guards was killed in France on the 23rd Jan 1916. You will wonder why I write to you. He was my Chum since boyhood up to he enlisted. And I know that his mother has had a sore time of it. She lost her husband three years ago. Her other son was taken to a Institution. And she freely gave Hugh for to fight for our Country's cause. He was a good son to her and she has taken a terrible sore to heart about his death. She is very poor and could you Sir try and help her in her trials and grief." He mentioned back pay and then continued "She is all alone in the world but a daughter who is in service. And it takes her to help herself. Sir if its not to much trouble try and take up her case as early as possible if you can. I expect to be called up and I would like to see her provided for Sir I am your obedient servant E J McVey" Colonel Fludyer did investigate and established that twelve shillings and sixpence per week would continue to be paid to Jessie McDonald until a decision was taken on whether she would receive a pension or a gratuity as a dependant.

Also killed there and then was Private Archibald McLaren, a miner and the son of James McLaren of Shettleston, Glasgow. He joined up at the end of November 1914 and arrived in France the following June, but next spent seven weeks being treated for gonorrhoea, so did not arrive in the Battalion until after the bombing attack at the Hohenzollern. Lance Corporal John Deeney, promoted six weeks earlier, was mortally wounded and died the same day at a field ambulance. The son of Denis and Margaret Jane Deeney of Glenvar, County Donegal, he was a seaman who enlisted in September 1914 in Glasgow and arrived in France in March 1915. Lance Sergeant George Campbell, hit in the head, reached a casualty clearing station and died there next day, an older man, in his early thirties, originally from the Aberdeen area, but working as a butler before he enlisted in October 1914 in Chichester, Sussex. He and Maggie Mitchell married in February 1915 and two months later he went to France, already a Lance Corporal. She was living in Forest Hill, Southeast London, when she gave birth to their son at the end of September 1915, a few days before her husband was made a Lance Sergeant. Recovered and sent to her were his clasp knife, whistle, pipe, pouch, platoon book, photographs, a Christmas card, a cigarette lighter and a pair of scissors.

It was the evening of 1 February as they were taking over from the 1st Battalion in the line that Admiral Colville came on a visit and stayed the night at Battalion Headquarters. In the morning it was very quiet when Captain Warner, having had orders the day before for the Bangalore torpedoes, "Went round trenches and saw places where torpedoes are to be put in." Later, however, the German gunners were accurate and busy, completely destroying an observation post called Village Lounge, near Fauquissart. After nightfall a patrol of two Welsh Guardsmen and two sappers came up from the rear and went into No Man's Land to check for obstructions at a possible site for firing a torpedo under the German wire. The patrol was successful, but a sapper was missing and two Scots Guards patrols could find no trace of him.

The project was put into abeyance in case he had been captured and told the Germans what he was doing. Not until a week later did a Scots Guards patrol next go out to identify a suitable route to carry a torpedo across No Mans Land.

A new scheme was afoot for a Welsh Guards raid, not apparently involving gas. In connection with this a Scots Guards patrol of two officers and four men went out on the night of the 6th "to put up sandbags under cover of which the Welsh Guards could lie in wait for a German patrol." Captain Warner had been writing orders that day for a practice gas alarm. Because initially gas was discharged from canisters in clouds it was regarded as an area weapon and therefore if gas was detected it was believed necessary to alert everyone. This made for inconvenience and military ineffectiveness while large numbers of men put on gas helmets when there might not be any gas anywhere near most of them. The following night "1GG exploded their torpedo successfully at midnight (7/8th). Practice gas alarm took place at 5.45am. All went well except the rockets, which were bad." He completed a report on the times by which each unit had turned out at the alert wearing gas helmets. On the 9th he went to see where the Bangalore torpedo had exploded and found "Enemy wire seemed much damaged." The Scots Guards were back in the line again that night and a patrol went out to look for another place to explode a torpedo. Then, very early on the 10th while it was still dark a German howitzer shell happened to hit a G Company dug-out. Five of those in it were killed.

Private John Dickinson, the only pre-war soldier, was a gardener before that, by now had over two years service and had been in the BEF since the beginning of October 1914. His mother Margaret Dickinson lived in West Derby, Liverpool, and on receiving her son's pocket book with some photographs and postcards she wrote "many thanks to all Officers & Men" on the receipt before sending it back. The other four were all wartime volunteers. Private Tobias Murphy, a miner, was an older man in his early thirties and a September 1914 volunteer. He and Catherine Murphy, who married in Blantyre, Lanarkshire, in 1904, had five children, the youngest born in 1914 before the War began. He had been sending half his pay home to her in Blantyre. Private John Ross was a labourer in Dundee and enlisted two months later. He did not have any parents, but his sister Mary Ann Smith was living in Dundee, though she proved hard to contact when he was killed. Before the War he had an affiliation order against him for a child born in November 1913 to Annie Knight. He arrived in France at the start of June 1915 and was in trouble twice in July before getting twenty one days FP No 1 in August for drunkenness. Private James Forrester, a bricklayer, gave his age as thirty five when he enlisted in November 1914 in Glasgow. He and Mary McKiel married in Dennistoun at the very end of 1898 and had three children. Their home was in Mile End, Glasgow. The fifth was Private Johnny Callachan, still under the suspended three year sentence of penal servitude.

10 February was bright and clear and the Germans had another successful strike. It caused no casualties, but hit a house filled with trench materials and stores, including 18,000 rounds of rifle ammunition. All were destroyed. A British plane flew up and down along the British front line that afternoon, fortunately not being hit. So vigorous was the enemy fire that it suggested that their line was more strongly held than thought. As it was dull and rainy next day there was much less firing, but after British field guns enfiladed their communication trenches and roads the Germans reacted, including landing a shell in one of the forts. It hurt no one and caused little damage. On the 12th the British heavy guns shelled the German breastworks, very little came back and after dark most of the Battalion went out of the line here for the last time, Right Flank staying behind to occupy four forts. At Laventie Lieutenant Kit Cator returned and

Lieutenant Ewart was sent to command a Scots Guards company in the Entrenching Battalion at Chipilly on the Somme. He stayed down there till early May 1916 when "In some ways I shall be very sorry to leave here; in others not. The country is very pleasant, but the hours of work are very, very long and terribly monotonous. The Bosche keeps quiet, but on our side there is evidently something impending before long."

On the 13th, in anticipation of more marching than for some weeks, there was a thorough inspection of every soldier's boots. Soon after midday two days later they moved off to billets north of Merville. Right Flank rejoined them from the forts at ten that evening. Next morning they marched the short distance to the station at Lestrem, just south of La Gorgue. The train was loaded at quarter past twelve and half an hour later they left for Calais.

With only two days notice Colonel Cator had gone on the 13th to command the 37th Brigade, 12th Division. One of his battalions were the 6th Buffs, who had caused so much disorder during a trench relief in October at the Hohenzollern. Brigadier General Cator wrote to his mother on the 14th "It makes me feel very old before my time but they have made me a General, and I left my beloved Batt'n last night to take over here. This is a K's New Army Brigade, and they have been out here since last May…I haven't had much time to more than look round, but judging from a casual glance when I went round them all this morning, they look a fine lot of men, the Officers are the weak point." He was optimistic, however, "I am sure we will soon have a good show, at any rate I am going to go at them all, for all I am worth, if only I could feel fresher myself, but I daresay there won't be such hard physical work, some times I have been feeling I must have a rest…It was a bad wrench leaving my Batt'n, they were all so splendid and no worries, everything was going on oiled wheels, I feel like a Stranger in a strange land, friends and comrades mean so much out here. Kit turned up the day before I left. I was so sorry to leave him." He did not know who would succeed him "but whoever it is is lucky just as I was to command such men, they <u>made me</u>, not I them." He then went on about Lieutenant Seymour. "You have no idea how Con has come on as a soldier, he has quite the best Company in the Scots Guards and works like a black, poor little lad he is fearfully lovesick and such a perfect hero, he never spares himself an ounce – his men adore him." He left a recommendation that his brother should be given command of a company "which I hope my successor will follow up."

Three weeks later, on 6 March, the 12th Division captured the Hohenzollern Redoubt. There had already been a steady tunnelling and mining war through the winter and the whole area was a mass of craters. Then, after careful work and preparation by the 170th Tunnelling Company and very thorough planning, the British blew their mines under the Redoubt. The 36th Brigade stormed in at once before the Germans could react and the rest of the Division successfully held it afterwards. In an undated letter just afterwards General Cator told his sister Edith Cator "I landed into a hot corner taking over this line with my new Brigade, but they have fought splendidly. We have taken over the worst bit of line I have ever seen since I left Ypres. Have been in ten days, and lost 800 men and 30 Officers, all of which are my best, the best are always the ones that suffer…Its all very close fighting, mostly with hand grenades. Some nights they fire as many as ten thousand. The Germans are furious at our having blown up their Hohenzollern Redoubt, we blew it up and rushed in and occupied the craters, joining them up with trenches, making a new line, the craters are a wonderful sight 80 to 100 yards across and 40 to 50 ft down…We beat off our 10th German attack on them last night, but lost another 67 men. I dislike mining warfare more than anything I know. Our miners are streets ahead of the German ones, and work much quicker and more silently, the German uses a pick, and our men use a bayonet to mine with, they hammer their props in, and our men knock them in with the heel of their hand. The whole thing is done by listening on an instrument called a geophone. There are two methods in mining. No 1 Offensive which blows in the enemy's parapet. No 2 Defensive which are shafts put out all along our front & as soon as they hear the enemy mining towards our parapet they lay a charge & blow in his shaft, all this is done fifty feet below the level of the ground. It is very jumpy work & the mining Officer told me that none of his men last more than nine months. Our last show we had seven big shafts out right under the Hohenzollern Redoubt, some of them had 12,000lbs of gunpowder and ammonal mixed, and we blew the whole redoubt to kingdom come, by a lucky mistake the whole of our Artillery opened a quarter of an hour too early, the Germans immediately manned their parapets very strongly, (according to a prisoner) so many more "went up" or were buried than would have been the case normally, as they thought we were going to attack. We are now into some of their shafts which we are using. In one of their shafts the miners found a German Srg't and a private both dead, rolled up in their blankets, on the former they found a plan of the whole of the German mining system, which has proved most useful. The only living thing they found in the shaft was [a] little brown fluffy dog, who was delighted to meet them. I met him coming back down the trenches, with a string round his neck, very pleased with himself & quite ready to swop sides. Since we have been putting the craters in a state of defence, we have dug up crowds of Germans. I imagine we must have done in 7 or 8 hundred. I have recommended one of our men, a Corporal Cotter, of the 6th Buffs for a VC, I do hope he will get it. He had a leg blown off & continued directing and encouraging his men for two hours, he would not be carried away till they had beaten off the German attacks. Glorious chap. I hope it will be all right, I got Gen'l Gough to take an interest in it. The latter has lent me his "elephant gun", yesterday we smashed in four German Plates with it, the snipers had been worrying us a lot from them, they are now silent, I hope it smashed in their ugly faces too. This dirty war how I hate it all." Corporal William Cotter, from Sandgate, just west of Folkestone, did win the VC but did not live to know it, dying of his wounds at Lillers on 14 March. Lieutenant General Sir Hubert Gough was just about to hand over command of I Corps at the end of the month. General Cator described the area to his sister Diana Cator on 29 March as "a dirty beastly bit of the country, so black really not worth the holding, of no strategic importance and very expensive to hold. I wish I was Commander in Chief, I wouldn't hold any unimportant ground, which was expensive to us. Ypres and Loos would be the first two to straighten out. I think if we had straightened out the Ypres salient a year ago we should have saved 50,000 men. I may be wrong and probably am but it is lodged very tight in the back of my brain…I am writing this in a funk hole where I live 30 feet below ground level, a very good dug-out, but simply crowded out with rats who as far as I can gather, hold a meeting most nights on my bed. Bimbo my dog is quite busy smelling them out and doing a strategic retirement, he is an awful coward."

Where the original document came from was not recorded, but Headquarters First Army circulated the translation, a copy of which is in the Cator Papers. A *Deckoffizier* was a German naval non-commissioned rank, but *decken* means to cover.

TRANSLATION OF A GERMAN DOCUMENT DATED 20/2/16, FOUND ON A GERMAN PRISONER RECENTLY CAPTURED

Committee for the increase of the Population.

Notice No.13875.

Sir,
On account of all the able bodied men having been called to the Colours, it remains the duty of all those left behind, for the sake of the Fatherland, to interest themselves in the happiness of the married women and maidens by doubling or even trebling the number of births.

Your name had been given to us as a capable man, and you are herewith requested to take on this office of honour and to do your duty in right German style. It must here be pointed out that your wife or fiancée will not be able to claim a divorce; it is in fact to be hoped that the women will bear this discomfort heroically for the sake of the War.

You will be given the district of .... Should you not feel capable of coping with the situation, you will be given three days in which to name someone in your place.

On the other hand, if you are prepared to take on a second district as well, you will become a "*Deckoffizier*" and receive a pension.

An exhibition of women and maidens as well as a collection of photographs is to be found at our office. You are requested to bring this letter with you.

Your good work should commence immediately and it is in your interests to submit to us a full report of results after 9 months.

1st Army. W.L.O.TWISS, Major.
General Staff.
22-3-16

Calais and Wormhout

Captain Warner had left for Calais on the afternoon of 14 February and after staying the night at the Grand Hotel "Quite comfortable" went to look at the camp next morning where he "found most of the tents had been blown down by gale." He put the fifteen men he had with him to work to start rectifying matters and found another twenty for the afternoon. Then he checked the train arrival times for the 16th. Back at the camp after lunch "Arranged for fatigue party of 100 men tomorrow, also saw Chaplain and arranged for all the men to be fed on arrival. Returned to town and got stables and billets for signals." When he went to the camp the next morning he "found half the tents blown down. Tried to arrange for other accommodation but none available. Met Brigadier about 12.30pm....and took him to see camp. Arranged for each unit to pitch camp for next arrivals. Met trains at 3pm, 6pm, 9pm, 12 mn and 4am. Detraining worked smoothly. Got back to Hotel at 6am. Told I was to be Brigade Major." Major Tempest was to command the 2nd Scots Guards.

They arrived in the second train, marched the three miles to camp, most of it flattened by the gale roaring round. They put all the tents back up and settled down for a very cold night. It was impossible to clear up until the following morning. Once that had been done their next task was to prepare a training area with practice trenches. To begin with it went on raining very hard, obstructing the digging as well as the proposed route marching and drill. There had been a lot of thought about how best to carry out bombing attacks since Loos and the Hohenzollern. The 2nd Scots Guards were introduced to the new methods and started practising in their dummy trenches. Then a bombing range had to be prepared. Now that they were completely away from the line what Calais illustrated clearly was how difficult it was to carry out effective training for anything other than trench routine when doing trench tours at the same time, quite apart from the unavoidable fatigues. Lieutenant Colonel Tempest arrived on the 19th. As and when the weather cleared so the digging intensified and the companies practised bombing attacks and trained with bombs, but not live ones for the time being. Drill occupied much of the rest of the time. On the 22nd, when there was hail most of the day, two companies had two hours on a rifle range, before moving to the beach for drill. Lunch was brought out to them and then they marched back to camp. By the 23rd training with live grenades was practicable and each company did so for an hour in the afternoon. There was snow for much of the day. On the 24th Left Flank went to the baths in the morning and had an hour's drill in the afternoon while everyone else went for a route march.

Private Alexander McIver reenlisted on 24 April 1915, having arrived at Plymouth from Argentina. He came originally from New Valley, Lewis, the son of Dugald and Kate McIver. From 1903 onwards his service as a Scots Guardsman was erratic and included an instance of fraudulent enlistment into the Cameron Highlanders. However, in 1909, by which time he was on the Reserve, he applied to extend his commitment for four years, only to disappear in 1911, failing to report in as required. Two months after rejoining in Plymouth Private McIver was sent to France. On 20 February he disappeared at Calais. Somehow he managed to cross the Channel. Where and when he was apprehended or gave himself up was not recorded but at the end of April he was absent again in England and consequently missed the draft he was due to travel with. Not till 17 May was he back on French soil in close arrest. There he remained for six weeks pending a court martial on 11 July which sentenced him to fifty six days FP No 1.

On 20 February two visitors came to Brigade Headquarters at Calais, Lord Cavan, who came to lunch, and shortly afterwards General Sir Herbert Plumer, commanding Second Army, responsible for the Salient, who looked in briefly. Later Captain Warner, now Brigade Major, was "making notes of Cavan's conversation." After training of various kinds in falling snow, the late evening of the 25th was set for departure from Calais. Over roads with two and a half inches of snow the Scots Guards marched from camp to the station, where they had hot soup. All then sat on the train with all the Transport and equipment for an hour before it moved, taking over six hours to Cassel and arriving three and a half hours later than if it had left and travelled on time. There was another hour's wait before disembarking, taking another hour, before they formed up in a nearby field, breakfasted and at nine marched north to billets at Wormhout, nearly another three hours. Because of the slipperiness of Cassel Hill the Transport had to go by a different route, not arriving till mid afternoon. The next few days were similar to those at Calais. Much effort went into constructing another bombing range and trenches, but there were also careful fitting of equipment, training in describing targets and fire control, along with emphasis on saluting, route marching and drill. There were tactical discussions and talks on various quite different subjects, including "open fighting", how to disable a field gun, and on 2 March by General Feilding to all the officers on the Ypres situation. Headquarters Guards Division were currently nearby and so were most of the other troops.

Mills bombs were the most dangerous things the infantry had to train with and a major cause of accidental injuries and deaths. On the afternoon of the 4th, while everyone else was on a route march, there was instruction for those not yet trained on them. One went off prematurely and Major Baden Powell, briefly Second in Command of the Battalion, and five men were wounded. One, Private Robert Rossiter, a September 1914 volunteer, died next day. A Glasgow civil engineering student, he was the son of Robert and Eva Rossiter who were at Murree in the Punjaub. Three other similar incidents occurred at the time elsewhere in the Guards Division and another seven officers and twenty men were killed or wounded. Confidence began to slip and General Feilding pointed out to Headquarters XIV Corps that it would improve if the fuses were set at five seconds, as done originally, and not at three, as had become the practice. That was done.

Notes on Chapter Sources

Personal details of Chaplains from Museum of Army Chaplaincy, Amport House, Andover.
Headquarters First Army translation of German document dated 20 February 1916 found on a prisoner, Cator Papers.

15

The Ypres Salient 1916 – 2nd Battalion

Ypres in 1916

After First Ypres died down in November 1914 the British and French were left still holding sufficient of the Gheluvelt Plateau to give them a sound platform. In particular, the Germans had no direct observation over the immediate approaches to Ypres itself and the plain around it. All that changed after Second Ypres in April and May 1915. There were smaller local attacks subsequently, which in late July at Hooge included the first use of flamethrowers against the British. The consequence of this fighting and several costly and largely unproductive counterattacks was that the British held the entirely exposed slopes east and southeast of Ypres over which the Germans now had complete observation in most places, less so to the southeast, while the French were left holding the line of the Ypres-Yser Canal from Boesinghe northwards, with the Belgians beyond them. This, the Ypres Salient, was the most disliked part, though run close by where the Guards Division had just been, and the most feared part of the whole British line then and throughout the War. Its shape resembled nearly half of a shallow saucer with an unevenly shaped rim, Ypres at the centre and the German positions mostly forward a bit from the rim. Neatly bisecting the two halves of the Salient for the purpose of British operational boundaries was the Menin Road and each had a corps of three divisions responsible for it.

In the right hand half the front line went from St Eloi past or through, on the ridges east of Zillebeke, among others, Hill 60, beside a railway cutting, The Bluff, a spoil heap next to the uncompleted Ypres-Comines Canal, Hill 61, Hill 62 and Sanctuary Wood. The struggle for visual domination was remorseless and there were a series of German attacks through the first half of 1916. Those in February started just ahead of their assault on the French at Verdun, those later, particularly in June, anticipated the British and French opening of the Battle of the Somme. The enemy did not need to make attacks to capture ground north of the Menin Road because of their already clear observation over the longer, shallower slopes to their front, on which they fired shells and minenwerfer, sniped and from time to time made raids.

XIV Corps under Lord Cavan were responsible for the left hand half of the Salient from just north of the Menin Road at Hooge across in a slightly curving northwards arc which ended just short of Boesinghe at the boundary with the French. At any time two divisions held the front line and its support and reserve positions, while the third stayed well back, resting and training, but available if needed. At this point the 6th Division, on the right, and 20th (Light) Division, New Army, were in the line, the 14th Division having only just gone into reserve, where they were to stay for the time being. The Guards Division were to replace the 14th Division but, as they were not immediately required, they had a quiet period away from Ypres to begin with. This was why each brigade next spent time at Calais, where the 3rd Guards Brigade went first, and on training areas.

Poperinghe became the Guards Division base for the next six months. When it was their turn to take over in the Salient one brigade remained in divisional reserve at Poperinghe, while the other two took over a sector of the line, each with two battalions in the front and support line positions and two not far back behind them in the brigade reserve, billeted in Ypres. In principle, the battalions within each brigade would swap over every four days, just as, in principle, each brigade spent two weeks in one sector, two weeks in the other sector and two in divisional reserve away from the immediate line. There was mud awaiting them everywhere, the communication trenches were awash and the front line trenches were in need of a lot of work, including being made deeper. Unlike in the Neuve Chapelle area, building breastworks instead was not practicable. There both sides needed to use them, but here the Germans on the higher ground had no such need and could quickly knock down any structure they saw which appeared above ground level. Though not exclusive to it, this provided another notable and very unpleasant feature of the Salient, the German selection of some part of the British line and then submitting it and its communication trenches to a solid and prolonged "hate" on a particular day. This might or might not be the prelude to an infantry raid. The British gunners increasingly did the same to the German infantry.

Almost no matter what those who had been in the front and support line previously had done, if the weather was wet, which it was, whether or not there was any significant enemy shelling, which there usually was, continuous renovation and draining work on all trenches was needed by the current occupants. That said, it appeared to the Guards Division that the 6th Division had let the Germans get the better of them. As in daylight the Germans could spot any movement and could often, indeed, look into the back of the trenches, it was impossible to do anything then and shells could come from anywhere in a one hundred and eighty degree angle. Work therefore had to be done entirely in the dark and concealed as far as possible. If the Germans noticed anything different they would shell that place immediately. All stores and all types of materials had to be brought up from behind Ypres. If it was wet at night, making it darker still, it would be practically impossible to do any constructive work.

Final preparations

On 6 March the 2nd Scots Guards marched in snow storms along the route through Herzeele, Houtkerque, Watou and St Jans-ter-Biezen, which would become very well known, to a camp two miles west of Poperinghe. The snow was so bad next day that nothing could be done outside, but they had a visit in the morning from Lord Cavan. Conditions were a bit better over the following days. There were physical training, bayonet exercise, route marching, Lewis Gun training and firing and, importantly, instruction for a group of officers and NCOs on revetting trenches. There was also detailed instruction about gas from a RAMC officer and rehearsal and fitting of gas helmets. The other main feature of infantry life in or near the Ypres Salient began on the evening of the 8th when two whole companies went up on a digging fatigue. They did not come back until half past eight at night three days later and Private Stewart Robertson did not come back at all. He was killed on the 10th, the first Scots Guardsman to die in the Salient.

Charles and Isabella Robertson lived in Carnoustie, while his wife Elizabeth was nearby in Dundee. When mobilised in 1914 he had been a reservist for seven years. After being slightly wounded in the knee with the 1st Battalion during First Ypres and evacuated to England he continued to have trouble with it after he came back out in April 1915 to the 2nd Scots Guards.

Captain Warner went for his first look at the Ypres and Poperinghe area on 1 March, visiting posts with General Heyworth and the four commanding officers. After General Feilding's lecture the next day he was "Writing notes on Ypres Salient all afternoon to send to Battalions." He saw Lord Cavan over meals twice that week and was writing operation and other orders almost every day, these frequently having to be altered. On the 6th he had lunch with Brigadier General Mansel Shewen, who commanded the 71st Brigade in the 6th Division. "He was very gloomy about the Salient." It was they whom the Guards Division were going to take over from to the north of the Menin Road. It snowed hard outside as Captain Warner was working on orders on the morning of the 7th when the "Ceiling fell and just missed my head. At work rather late." On the 9th he arranged a move to a better house and spent some time asking staff officers of the 6th Division about several issues, "especially mining in the trenches to be taken over." On the 10th he and General Heyworth had their first look at the line, going to Potijze on the left first, having lunch in the Ramparts, the old city walls, and then looking at the right along the Menin Road, but without having time to go into the front line trenches. There were meetings repeatedly with staff officers of the 6th Division and of their Brigades. On the 15th he, General Heyworth and Colonel Tempest went to see the left of the line at Potijze "finding it in a very bad state." As it did not directly concern Colonel Tempest, he did not go when they went to look at the right of the line next morning, about which Captain Warner did not comment. That night Brigade Headquarters moved into the Canal Bank as the Brigade became the first from the Guards Division into the Salient, immediately north of the corps boundary along the Menin Road.

On the 17th and 19th Captain Warner and General Heyworth found that the defences at the Ramparts "nearly all want digging afresh" and those at the Kaie [Quay] Salient, between Ypres and the Canal, were "in a very bad state." General Feilding came to see them on the 17th "and explained the mining situation in Railway Wood which is not very pleasant." However, when they went round the right of the front line before dawn on the 18th they found that the 4th Grenadiers had already done a lot of work. The Grenadiers had their right on the Menin Road, were facing Bellewarde Lake, Railway Wood being just behind their left forward positions, and had the line of the Ypres-Roulers railway as their left boundary. After heavy 5.9 inch howitzer shelling of the Canal Bank on the morning of the 20th, which blew in and destroyed three dug-outs and caused twenty casualties, Brigade Headquarters moved into the Ramparts.

At half past seven on the evening of the 15th the 2nd Scots Guards paraded on the road outside camp and marched to Poperinghe Station, the Transport having left that afternoon by road for Ypres. While they were getting onto their train another ran into the back of it. An unnamed sergeant was badly concussed and everyone else shaken, but not otherwise hurt. After an hour they arrived at Asylum Station, Ypres, and set off to their billets for twenty four hours in the cellars of five different buildings. After a bright sunny day on the 16th, but one with a good deal of shelling, at half past ten that night their first company marched out of the Menin Gate, a gap in the Ramparts on the east side, the others following at half hour intervals. By half past two next morning the 1st West Yorkshire Regiment had handed over to them the section of the line north of the 4th Grenadiers, from the Ypres-Roulers railway up to just short of the

Ypres-Potijze-Zonnebeke road. There were three lines of defence. Right Flank and G Company were in the front line trenches, but with two G Company platoons in the immediate support line behind. Left Flank and F Company were in the X Line, a little further back. It was not that much further back to Ypres itself and it was there that the other two battalions in the Brigade lay up in the cellars, ready to come to help if needed. Battalion Headquarters were in the remains of Potijze Château.

Through the remainder of the night the German machine gunners fired frequently over the lines, making awkward any work that they tried to do on the trenches "which were in a bad state of repair, the parapets not being bullet proof & parados almost non-existent & no drainage attempted." They did what they could before daylight. A shell landed in the X Line that afternoon and four men were hit. One who was wounded was Private Robert Wilson, an engine driver who volunteered in Jedburgh in November 1914. He was hit in both legs and it was not till two years later that he came back out, serving for the last few months of the War. His father James Wilson lived at Fans, Berwickshire. Another was the rapidly promoted Sergeant John Fulton, a professional footballer before the War with Morton, Everton and Rangers, out since March 1915 and hit now for the only time, slightly in the hip. He volunteered early in September 1914 in Glasgow. Apart from this minor wound he served continuously till they went home from Cologne, for much of 1917 and the first half of 1918 as a Company Sergeant Major, being awarded the Meritorious Service Medal in June 1918. His father William Fulton lived in Paisley. Lance Corporal Ernest Kelly was killed. Until October 1914 he was a carpenter, six months after that he went to France and a month before he died he became a Lance Corporal. A few of his possessions reached James and Margaret Kelly at West Kirby, Cheshire. The other man who died there was Private Victor Vandermotten, serving under his middle name O'Neil, a December 1914 volunteer. For much of the previous five months he had been detached to Headquarters XI Corps and later Headquarters III Corps, the explanation lying in his profession, a mason. He was an older man and gave his age as thirty five and a half when he enlisted. He had been back for just over a month. Hugh and Frances Vandermotten lived in the South Side, Glasgow.

When darkness fell on the 18th they were ready for a busy night. Two of the most pressing trench requirements in the X Line were to heighten the parapets so men could walk along without being seen and to drain them properly. In the front line the main need was for revetting and, next, constructing better shelter. There was some shelling in the evening, none significant. Early on the 19th, a very bright night, as the 2nd Grenadiers of the 1st Guards Brigade replaced the 11th Essex of the 6th Division to their left, the 2nd Scots Guards were swapping over their companies between the front line and the X Line. This limited the amount of work done. Then a German heavy minenwerfer fired several 60lb rounds towards the front line. All dropped in No Man's Land with neither injuries nor damage. The 20th was quiet in the line itself, the most distinctive event being very heavy German shelling along the Canal. That night most went to the Ypres cellars once the Welsh Guards came up, but two platoons had to stay on in the Potijze defences. Other than digging fatigues there was nothing significant before they went into the line again after dark on the 24th, only for forty eight hours, but with snow on the ground. Captain Warner had discussed with both the Scots Guards and the 4th Grenadiers the possibilities of raids to identify the Germans opposite but that night's "Attempts to capture a prisoner were made without success, though the Scots Guards got a revolver from a patrol which escaped." Meanwhile everyone else worked away with pick and shovel. They had particularly good reason to leave everything in the best possible state because on the 26th the 1st Scots Guards were to relieve them. This process was not as smooth as it could have been, because the new arrivals, whose first tour it was in the Salient, had organised themselves to man the trench lines differently from how the 2nd Scots Guards had been doing. This took till half past two to sort out.

They went straight to the Asylum Station and left at three for Poperinghe and billets east of the square. In the afternoon there were baths for everyone. The next few days were ones of kit inspections, including one which Colonel Tempest personally did of each company, and the usual training and route marching. By the evening of 3 April they were on their way back to the Ypres cellars, this time on foot, for four days. Mist limited the German shelling, but the inevitable parties went out to dig in various places and help carry stores to the line for the Royal Engineers. There were one or two casualties in Ypres itself, one of whom, killed, was Private Frank Schuard, who by August 1914 had nearly completed a year as a soldier. After travelling to Zeebrugge at the beginning he was hit on the right side of the head at or near Kruiseecke during First Ypres and sent home, returning just at the start of the Hohenzollern fighting. He was a Londoner, born in Holborn, and his sister Amelia received a few of his belongings there. His elder brother Private Frederick Schuard had been serving for two and a half years when the War started. He did not go out at the start, only joining the 1st Battalion later on. He was hit during First Ypres in the right arm, left buttocks and hip and discharged disabled in August 1915. Sergeant Sydney Spencer, son of John and Mary Spencer, was a railway porter working for the Midland Railway Company at the Goods Depot, St Pancras Station, near his home in London until he enlisted in May 1911. He went with the 2nd Scots Guards to Zeebrugge and was sent sick to Rouen during First Ypres, but not for long, before again being sent sick from the Rouges Bancs trenches in January 1915, again not away long. At Neuve Chapelle he was very slightly wounded in the nose and missed Festubert because he was in hospital for nearly two weeks with myalgia. Now, on either 3 or 4 April he was slightly wounded in the right knee and very badly wounded in the post tibial artery in his left leg, which was amputated through the thigh. He was discharged disabled in November 1916. Private Robert Dundas had eighteen months service as a soldier when the War began, having been a farmworker before that. He was in the 1st Battalion to begin with and was slightly wounded in the right arm on 11 November 1914 at Nonne Boschen, though it was not that but sickness, including heart trouble, which led him to be sent home six weeks later. When he came back to the BEF in November 1915 it was to the 2nd Scots Guards and he had now been with them for three months. Hit in the head by a shell on the 6th, he died three days later. David and Betsy Dundas lived in the Kincardineshire fishing village of Johnshaven and were sent their son's possessions, mainly letters and photographs.

Because their next spell was going to be in a different place Colonel Tempest and the company commanders went on the 6th to look at the trenches of the left front battalion in the left sector at Wieltje. Initially the 2nd Coldstream of the 1st Guards Brigade were their neighbours on the south and the 20th Division, the left hand division at the time, on the north. The route from Ypres was the road through St Jean and Wieltje which then crossed No Man's Land and went on to St Julien and Poelcapelle. The front line, here running roughly northwest, was two hundred yards or so east of Wieltje before bending back short of a minor crossroads, itself just outside their left boundary. During the relief on the 7th shrapnel hit and wounded two officers and five men on the road. One of the officers, Captain Jack Astley Corbett, had gone out with the 1st Battalion at the start of the War and went through the Retreat from Mons and the Aisne until evacuated with diarrhoea. He had only arrived on 1 April. He reappeared for much of the final winter and was then posted as an ADC in April 1918. Private William Hall, a reservist, who went to Zeebrugge in October 1914, was fatally wounded in the stomach by a shell and died next day. Though born in Pittsburgh, Pennsylvania, his family had been back in Scotland for some time when in October 1903 he enlisted in Edinburgh. Before his three years were up his father died in 1906 and Private Hall successfully applied to be released early to the Reserve "to continue the business lately carried out by his father (now deceased) of Boot & Shoemaker, High St, Loanhead." He married Edith Williamson in 1907 at Lasswade and they had two sons. During the War his family were living in Abbeyhill, Edinburgh, and there his widow received an identity disc, some letters and photographs, his purse and a language manual.

The relief was complete by eleven and the next four days were typical. The trenches taken over from the Welsh Guards had been knocked about by enemy shelling just before and, though much was done on the 8th to remedy matters, further shelling of the ruins of Wieltje, about fifty 5.9 inch shells next day, quickly made the trenches much the same as they had been previously. In spite of all this there were very few casualties. On the 9th one man was killed, Private Alfred Richardson, a reservist from Leeds, who had started as a 1st Battalion reinforcement in September 1914 and then been sent home sick at Christmas. He came back three months later, to the 2nd Scots Guards, was in hospital for several weeks with measles soon afterwards and did not reappear till late August. He married Edith Hanson in June 1911 in Leeds and she was living in Driffield. They could hear on the 9th a very heavy bombardment, they thought around St Eloi, away at the south of the Salient. Nearer at hand on the 11th it had been very quiet all day because it was wet and dull until suddenly at half past four that afternoon the enemy began shelling the 61st Brigade on their left very heavily indeed. This went on for ninety minutes at the end of which a SOS message came from their neighbours that the Germans were attacking them. They stood to arms, nothing happened affecting them and they heard no more before they went out of the line that evening.

After four days in Ypres they returned to the line at Wieltje on the evening of the 15th, to be disappointed next day that the anti-aircraft gunners did nothing about a large number of enemy planes flying over them. General Feilding, who had visited their front line trenches not long before, came up to Battalion Headquarters at St Jean in the evening and across to their left the 6th Division took over the northern half of the XIV Corps area from the 20th Division. On the 17th Private James Keenan, the son of James and Isobel Keenan of Langbank, Renfrewshire, a fitter's helper who enlisted at Port Glasgow early in September 1914, was hit in the arm by a shell. Although he had been in France for most of the previous year he had been sick for much of the time and had therefore been at Le Havre. He had also needed to be equipped with false teeth. On 4 April 1916 he arrived back in the Battalion and on 1 May he died of wounds in hospital at Boulogne.

The deficiencies of the Canal Bank were one of Captain Warner's concerns. Now that the Brigade were on the Guards Division's left in the line it was not practicable to have Brigade Headquarters anywhere else. Fatigue parties and Royal Engineers dug, burrowed, excavated and then fortified. Captain Warner drafted, adjusted and perfected a defence scheme for the area if there was a major German assault, though it required regular updating. On 8 April General Feilding came to see them and "explained that there is a shortage of ammunition due to difficulty of freightage." On the 11th Captain Warner was out siting positions for Stokes trench mortars on the left of the line. When the SOS came in from the 61st Brigade that evening, though it was all quiet elsewhere, he ordered the Welsh Guards to stand to arms in Ypres and warned the 1st Grenadiers to concentrate behind the town. He also warned the Vickers Gun teams in reserve to be ready to move. Everything settled down after half past nine and he heard that the 61st Brigade had driven off two small attacks. He was habitually out and about going round the trenches.

The Wieltje Trench Raid on 19 April

Captain Jamie Balfour, fit again after his second wound, had been waiting for three weeks at Le Havre in quarantine after the officer with whom he was sharing a hut got measles. He arrived at ten on the evening of 18 April at Battalion Headquarters at St Jean, shown the way, the two miles from the Cloth Hall in Ypres, by a Welsh Guards guide. He went straight up into the trenches with a ration party to take command of Right Flank, who spent a quiet night working on the traverses and making fire steps. From six next morning the German field guns opened up. Though most shells fell short, several landed in the trenches. A comparative lull at eleven gave the Scots Guards an opportunity to have breakfast, but at noon the enemy howitzers started an intermittent bombardment, continuing till half past four. Then the British heavy artillery put down six rounds in retaliation, whereupon at quarter to five two howitzer shells suddenly pitched at the mouth of the company headquarters dug-out. The officers in it scattered, Captain Balfour and Lieutenant Swinton, back in France since January [he would leave again at the end of May], going north beyond John Street, a communication trench, and Lieutenant Sandy Scott going south. Captain Balfour wrote "Then hell broke loose. Never before have I seen such a bombardment and it is the worst anybody in this Battn has seen. Those who saw our bombardment at Neuve Chapelle say it was similar to that. At 6pm shelling still raging and the trench a mere shamble. I crawled about and found we had 40 men as far as about 40 yards south of John Street, where one could get no further owing to a barrage fire. Among these 40 odd men I found we had only 3 rifles and 12 bombs so decided the only thing was to try and get away up John Street, and get back to the next line and as soon as the fire lifted to get hold of another platoon and with my 40 men with bombs reoccupy the remains of the trench." At the base of John Street, a communication trench, he got another platoon ready. Then he heard that Lieutenant Scott and twenty remaining men with him, as well as Lieutenant Frank Thewlis of the 1st Coldstream, up ahead of that night's relief, were holding a fifty yard length of the front trench in detached groups and that there was so far no sign of German infantry. Unknown to him at the time, between eight and nine that evening German patrols approached and entered part of the front line, not completely without profit. Reconnaissance now showed that from about fifty yards north of the John Street junction with the front line the trenches were demolished and more men were going to be needed to reoccupy and restore them, as well as bombing out any Germans who had come forward. Two platoons were assembled at eleven, one equipped with shovels. Lieutenant David Bethell then went up the front line bombing as he went, but without finding any trace of German occupation. Just prior to this Captain Balfour fired forty eight trench mortar bombs into the German line at Wieltje. Lieutenant Bethell had previously been in the 9th KOYLI, including being in the 21st Division. He transferred in mid October 1915. He had been at Eton and Trinity College, Cambridge, and was the son of Colonel EH Bethell of London. His brother, Brigadier General HK Bethell, was a gunner.

On recovering the front trenches, Right Flank dug out several dead men and also some still alive after being buried. The wounded were carried away. There were ten killed, twenty one wounded and fourteen missing, as well as five more casualties in the rest of the Battalion. Lance Sergeant David Boyle, a reservist whose sister Agnes Boyle was in Glasgow, became a Great Northern Railway policeman in London in 1913. He did not go out immediately with the 1st Battalion, joined them later and was wounded in the stomach at Gheluvelt in October 1914. On recovering he returned, joined the 2nd Scots Guards after Loos and was promoted in February. He was definitely killed. The precise location of his grave near the front trench was carefully recorded by grid reference and "marked by a very rough wooden cross", but could not be found after the War. The same was the case with Lance Sergeant Joe Thomson, an Orcadian, formerly a railwayman in Edinburgh and by this time with almost nine years in the Army. Stationed at the Guards Depot at the start of the War, he did not join the Battalion till after Loos. He was slightly wounded in the head accidentally at the beginning of March and away for a month recovering. The letter telling Robert and Isabella Thomson of St Mary Hope, Orkney, of their son's death went out on 1 May from Regimental Headquarters, much quicker than many. Robert Thomson replied on 5 May "Sir, Your letter of 1st May just to hand announcing the death of 6747 Lance Sergeant J Thomson 2nd Battalion Scots Guards. I was not aware that my son was in the Army as I have had no word from him for some time but I am afraid it refers to my son Joe Thomson as my other son John is in the Seaforths presently near Cromarty. Will you kindly let me know name in full and the place where he enlisted I will then be sure about the matter. Thanking you in anticipation. Yours respectfully Robert Thomson." There was no doubt about who it was.

Private Kenneth Murdoch was a reenlisted former Scots Guardsman, settled in Edinburgh as a brewery labourer and living near Holyrood with Margaret Murdoch and their small daughter and son. Another son was born in 1915. Private Murdoch was nearly six feet three inches tall and arrived in France in mid November 1914, two months after joining up for the second time, but was evacuated home with trench foot immediately after New Year 1915 and away for a year. He was dead at Wieltje. So was Private William Flight, a Lanarkshire policeman, in the Army for eleven months, in France for five and in the Battalion for three and a half. He was definitely buried in a recorded place, but that grave was lost afterwards. William and Mary Flight lived at Broughty Ferry and they received a few effects. There was an enquiry about him from Miss Aggas from Kennington, South London, who wrote on 15 May to say she had heard nothing from him for five weeks. Sergeant Walter Bold, who went to sleep in the train from Boulogne on his way back from leave in August 1915 to find that others had stolen almost everything he owned, had another three weeks leave in January. He was missing initially and then confirmed dead and buried by the 1st Coldstream, who recorded where the grave was and that it was "marked by a very rough wooden cross". An identity disc, letters, photographs and a prayer book were recovered and sent to John and Alice Bold in Portobello. Their son's body was found in 1923. Private Nicholas Marino, a violinist, volunteered in December 1914 stating that he was just past his nineteenth birthday, and arrived after Festubert. He had been with them since, apart from some time sick with influenza in July 1915 and ten days home leave in February 1916. He and Nellie O'Neill married in Edinburgh in January 1914 and had a daughter in June 1915. He died on 19 April. Private Norman Cobbold, a clerk, volunteered in May 1915 and came to the BEF after Loos. He was killed and buried that night near the front trench and the location of his grave recorded. A few letters were recovered and sent to Walter and Margaret Cobbold in Buenos Aires, from where their son had sailed to Liverpool to join up. Arrangements were in place for Regimental Headquarters also to notify the Manager of the Anglo-South American Bank in the City of London and that was done. Private John Laing died four days afterwards of shell wounds to his leg and stomach in Poperinghe. A September 1914 volunteer, he was before that a government clerk in Cowdenbeath, probably in the labour exchange, because it was recorded that in the event of his being a casualty the Ministry of Labour required to be told. James and Mary Laing received several of his belongings at their home in Cowdenbeath.

Captain Balfour heard that at some stage before he led the platoons forward to reoccupy the front line a German patrol got into the trench and called on a Scots Guardsman they came upon to surrender. He shouted "Damn all hands up!" and threw a bomb at them, at which they fled and he shot five of them himself within twenty five yards as they did so. A Grenadier patrol caught a sixth German shortly afterwards. Also, just before his platoons got forward, about fifty Germans approached but withdrew quickly when fired at, though Captain Balfour wrote that about half of them were hit a hundred yards back by the British guns and were found later by a Scots Guards patrol in the dark who "finished off the wounded. The Huns living said "Mercy Comrades" and our patrol replied "**** mercy you gave us this afternoon" and killed them." Private James Venters, a miner from Leven and October 1914 volunteer, was wounded in his left leg at Hill 70. Now he was missing. He described how "on the day that I was captured I saw a sergeant of the Coldstream (he had come up to see the position with a view to relieving our company the same night). He was wounded and was captured when I was. After his capture he asked for mercy, but the Germans shot and killed him. There were others wounded who held up their hands in token of surrender and they were also killed. I believe that I was the only Englishman captured at this place who escaped with his life, and I did not hold up my hands. We were surrounded and had no chance of escape and held out to the last." Some others were taken prisoner. Private Venters, captured unwounded, had trouble with his spine in captivity, was exchanged in January 1918 and discharged medically unfit two months later.

The relief went ahead at half past one in the morning, long after it was due to start, but completed without interruption, though the Coldstream had little time before dawn in which to remedy matters any further. Most Scots Guardsmen reached Asylum Station in time for the train to take them to Poperinghe. Captain Balfour and some others, plus Battalion Headquarters, were delayed. "We got back to Ypres at 4am and found the train which runs from Ypres (in the dark only of course) had gone owing to daylight. We walked back to Vlamertinghe in small parties, as they shell the road which is overlooked by them all the way. About a four miles walk and got the train to come there and reached Poperinghe at 5.45am (21st). I have never been so wet, tired, bruised and forlorn in my life." His servant, who had gone back ahead, had his valise out ready for him, so he had a sponge down all over and then slept till half past one. After a bath he had lunch at three, which was, apart from a slice of bread and a cup of tea soon after dawn the day before, his first food for over forty eight hours. He heard that there had been a series of five probing attacks by the Germans the day before, all ultimately unsuccessful. He added "The Huns if they really wanted to could not help taking the entire Ypres salient – for they can enfilade every single bit of it and our guns – owing to the salient – cannot reach anything hardly beyond the enemy's front trench – and run a considerable danger of being knocked out as they can be enfiladed anywhere. It is not the Huns game to take the salient – for they can give us an enormous wastage there every day – and suffer very little themselves."

Then he collapsed with shell shock. His father described how "intense vomiting was the first symptom – and then incoherence of speech and inability to control one's actions afterwards. When I first saw him about four days after, he could not string his sentences together properly, and had to stop and ask what he was saying. The effect of it lasted a long time." When he returned to duty later on, having also had appendicitis, Captain Balfour spent the rest of the War in command of a NCOs training school in Edinburgh. Lieutenant Scott was a Harrovian, who had transferred from the 7th King's Shropshire Light Infantry [KSLI] in February 1915. He had been in France since before Christmas but only reached the Battalion five days before this. Four days later he went down with tonsillitis, which was bad enough for him to be evacuated home. He returned to the BEF later. His parents lived at Branksome, Dorset, where his father Edward Scott was a clergyman.

Talbot House, Poperinghe

One of his most loyal supporters, Captain Leonard Browne RAMC, wrote of the Reverend "Tubby" Clayton, that "Talbot House presented a most perfect illustration of "a round peg in a round hole"…But rotundity was no bar to activity: while activity was no bar to rotundity." The Reverend "Tubby" Clayton himself observed "Some humorist on GHQ had arranged at the time – April 1916 – that the Guards and the Canadians should occupy the town together, and the result was as instructive as it was amusing. In the Guards' area, to a civilian encountering them for the first time, the feeling was one of dismay. NCOs and privates were unable to share the same rooms, and when one returned from shopping in their quarter of the town, the problem of returning salutes while leading home a primus stove, however lawfully purchased, was harassing to the last degree. Ultimately I became so nervous of these ordeals that I walked only by night in the Guards' area, and then said "Friend" hurriedly in the dark to the buttresses of the church. In the Canadian area there was no such shyness, though in their later days saluting became, I believe, quite in vogue with them as well." He went on to tell how "One April day a popular Canadian major burst in upon "a bunch of boys" in their billet with "Boys! Get a move on; the Guards are drilling in the Square. It's a sight worth coming over the water to see."

Major Henry Beckles Willson, a Canadian officer, professional journalist and special correspondent for *The Daily Express* wrote an article that he dated 25 June 1916 which included an account of watching a Guards inter company drill competition. "The drill sergeants were superhuman, immense. You expect a drill sergeant to speak a strange and esoteric language, to be vociferous, explosive, but the burly NCO deputy high priest of the Guards at these functions suggests a combination of a City toastmaster and the bursting high explosive shell popularly known as a "whizz-bang"." In the article he stated that a number of Guards sergeants had been lent to the Canadians to instruct them in drill.

Whatever his reaction to the initial outward appearances the Reverend "Tubby" Clayton was deeply impressed by how much the officers' absolutely supreme concern was the comfort and welfare of their men. He added "Yet the Guards were not only admirable; they were lovable. In no division that came our way was there so strong a family feeling. There was rivalry, but it was a rivalry towards a common ideal. There was hard and minute discipline, but the task was hard before them…one of our best friends was Lieutenant Guy Dawkins, of 2nd Scots Guards…It was he who discovered to me the fact so hard for the civilian mind to grasp – that in the very fixity of the gulf between each grade of command lay the scope for an intimacy and mutual understanding impossible otherwise."

Lieutenant Dawkins, very tall at six foot five inches, enlisted in the London Scottish in the first week of the War and went to France with them on 14 September 1914. He fought at Messines on 30 October and at Zillebeke on 9 November during First Ypres. After the London Scottish joined the 1st (Guards) Brigade he was involved at Givenchy before Christmas, around the Cuinchy brickstacks in January 1915, at Neuve Chapelle and Aubers, as well as the trench warfare in between. On 19 September he was commissioned direct from the ranks into the 1st Battalion and wounded with shrapnel in the right thigh ten days later at Puits 14 Bis. On recovering in England he came out again in the spring and on 20 April joined the 2nd Scots Guards at Poperinghe. Another Scots Guardsman active at Toc H was Private Arthur Smith, who had written in January 1915 to Mrs Wills in Leytonstone about her two sons, one missing after the counterattack on the Railway Triangle at Cuinchy on New Year's morning and the other killed in the German attack on the Cuinchy brickstacks on the 25th. A third was Lance Corporal Jacob Bennett, a dairyman in Great Crosby, Liverpool, before the War, who first came out in May 1915 and gained his first promotion after Hill 70. The Reverend "Tubby" Clayton particularly mentioned Company Quartermaster Sergeant Selwyn Rendell of the Welsh Guards. A tinplate worker in Swansea, he enlisted in the Grenadiers on 8 August 1914, transferring to the Welsh Guards six months later. He arrived in France with them, already a Sergeant, and was promoted again very soon after Hill 70. What he was up to at Toc H was leading the Welsh Guards Choir.

Some officers and men found religious faith important and helpful, a quite separate matter from the compulsory church parades for all denominations most Sundays when out of the line. However, the number of Bibles, prayer and hymn books, as well as rosaries for Roman Catholics, among the effects of dead soldiers sent to their families, suggested that these meant something, even if only sentimentally in some cases, as no one was going to carry with them anything that was not useful or important. Very few would make any kind of public profession of their beliefs.

The Last Weeks in the Salient

The 2nd Scots Guards spent the first ten days between 20 April and 9 May at Poperinghe and Vlamertinghe. They had the use of the Guards Division baths on the 20th and in the course of the next few days everybody was inoculated against paratyphoid. Nothing unusual took place. German heavy guns shelled the road to Ypres twice near Vlamertinghe and German planes dropped bombs near Poperinghe in the dark early on the 25th, "without doing much damage" so Captain Warner noted. Also they could hear a major bombardment from the St Eloi direction on the 30th. They went up to the Salient in front of Potijze for five days on the night of 1 May, the same place as their first two trench tours. Activity was routine with a lot of ineffective shelling, the main irritant a heavy thunderstorm on the afternoon of the 2nd making a mess of the trenches and the main event the apparently very satisfactory blowing by the Royal Engineers of a defensive mine at Railway Wood on the 3rd. However, patrols that went to inspect came back with nothing significant to report. In the afternoon on the 6th there was a little shelling of the Potijze crossroads, where the Menin Road met that from Ypres to Potijze and Zonnebeke, only a foretaste of what was coming next. At half past seven the Germans began shelling all the roads east of Ypres, apparently with field guns and howitzers. From eight this became very systematic with five shells a minute hitting the Potijze road. The Welsh Guards still persevered and began relieving them at quarter past eleven. The shelling went on, prolonging completion for two and a half hours, and suddenly stopped at two in the morning. It was supposed that the Germans had been told "by their spies" that a relief was going to take place and kept on shelling until they assumed either that it was over or that they had prevented it. Five Scots Guardsmen were wounded, none seriously. Those who got there early enough caught the train to Vlamertinghe, the remainder went on foot and everyone had the rest of the day off.

A quiet trench tour was merely relative and did not always mean one free of casualties. James and Janet Ross lived in Leith and their son Corporal Robert Ross was a labourer there until eighteen months before. By this time he had been abroad for nearly a year, having become a Lance Corporal a month after he arrived. More importantly, as soon as the Battalion came out of the Hohenzollern trenches the previous October he was promoted to paid Corporal "for conduct in the field". There were tattoos of a cross, a heart, his initials and flags on his left arm. Corporal Ross had had ten days leave in February. On 2 May he was shot in the head and immediately classified "Dangerously Ill". A week later a telegram went from No 24 General Hospital at Étaples to Regimental Headquarters asking for his first name and his religion, which was Church of Scotland. On 24 May he died. Among his effects were two "English-French books". Without the enemy doing anything there could still be quite bad injuries. As he came out of the line on the night of the 13th after a two day trench tour Lance Corporal Thomas Wilkie, a former shop porter from Edinburgh, unscathed for almost fourteen months, fell and broke his shin bone. He was evacuated to England at the end of June and was there till October 1917.

During the morning of the 9th news arrived that a German sniper had shot General Heyworth, temporarily commanding the Guards Division, while he was going round the front line trenches. Sir Iain Colquhoun heard that he was on his way to inspect a mine that the Germans had blown the afternoon before at Railway Wood and was "climbing over a blown in part of muddy lane" when he was killed. For his funeral the next afternoon there was a guard of honour from the 2nd Scots Guards and the Corps of Drums and Pipes and Drums of both Battalions led the procession to Brandhoek Cemetery. The Reverend Pat McCormick, Senior Chaplain of the Guards Division, took the service. Brigadier General Charles Corkran arrived in his place to command the 3rd Guards Brigade.

Lieutenant Ewart returned on the 15th from the Entrenching Battalion on the Somme. His first four days back were very lively by his standards and "quite long enough to see what sort of place this is. The first night the Bosches made an aeroplane raid and dropped bombs all round the camp. The second night they repeated the performance. The third night there was a gas alarm from the front line and we all stood to arms. Shelling all day and Bosche aeroplanes constantly over; ours have no chance. At the present moment the Germans are shelling heavily a road about three hundred yards away. This camp is in the middle of a beautiful wood and the weather is lovely and one can sit out of doors and read." On the 19th, however, when the Guards Division were supposed to be coming completely out of the Salient for a month, each brigade had to find a battalion to do extra work digging communication trenches behind the front line of the 6th Division south of Boesinghe. The 2nd Scots Guards drew one of the short straws so they moved to a camp near Elverdinghe, closer to where they were needed. The digging was at Machine Gun Farm, two companies initially for forty eight hours at a time. Lieutenant Ewart described the scene as "When this slow summer dusk begins to deepen, we can begin to stir in the trenches. We have been here now nearly a week, and the procedure is always the same.

All day long the men have slept or dozed in the warm sunshine, lain in their dug-outs – little holes in the parados – or nodded on the firestep in a sultry atmosphere of buzzing bluebottles and occasional shots from snipers' rifles. For here one cannot move or walk about by day, the sniping (from dominating positions) is too keen. But when the dusk deepens into that pearly-blue light which for a man moving is the most invisible, long files of men start off to join us and the sound of tramping feet is heard on the roads. Night by night – and all night long – those files of ghostly figures move along the roads towards us. Ration parties, carrying parties, parties with working material, engineers, generals and officers of inspection rank, parties with pick and shovel, and many other sorts of workers move along these roads. A little later, and we see them, patiently bending under their loads, silhouetted against the rising moon. Some of the carriers are so strangely silent they seem like ghosts of men tramping across the plain, only their feet go pit-patter, pit-patter, when they are quite near; these are wearing long thigh boots with rubber soles. And they have to hurry. For the midsummer night is short, and between the grey twilight and the rosy dawn there is but a space of four hours. God help him who is caught by the sunshine in an open place!

And with the deepening dusk a new life begins with us in the trenches. The buzz of bluebottles and the crack of the sniper's rifle give place to the chatter of machine guns and the slow glare of the star lights. Shadow and mystery creep in where was the stark nakedness of shellholes, broken trees, and lines of battered sandbags.

To take one instance of this life, that of my working-party. Slowly, with many exclamations, pauses, and much hard swearing, it now moves along the crowded trench, then out into the sap. There is a little narrow ridge between the parapet of the sap and a chain of enormous shellholes. In these the water glistens. The men are silent now that they are in the middle of No Man's Land scarcely seventy yards from the Germans. Only when one of them trips over the frequent loose strands of wire or stumbles into a shellhole do I hear a scuffle, followed by a muttered curse. It is a question of digging a new trench. Get them lined out quickly, quietly, three yards apart; let each man work his hardest to dig himself in. They know it too and put their backs into the task. It is surprising how quickly they get into the ground considering the heavy, spongy state of all this waterlogged country. Quickly they throw up the earth in front, which gives a feeling of protection, even if a somewhat illusory one. Nor can the task be considered in any way pleasant. A peculiar and horrible stench clings to the ground, thicker and more foetid in some places than in others, but all pervading. It is the sickly stench of dead bodies. Strange and sometimes fearsome things are dug out of the ground. All drab and muddy, yielding and soft, so that you could not recognise it as a human thing, was a body of a German. There was no head, only the trunk. Someone cuts off two of his buttons as a memento, another finds his rifle, completely rusted and caked in mud. Then they dig up a machine gun, rusted too, and mud-caked, which must have been buried in the last battle. The curious thing about this is that it is evidently a British gun converted by the Germans, for the lock is German, so is the barrel. Once cleaned it will be serviceable again and will be reconverted to fire British ammunition.

The night is a fairly quiet one. Yet apart from the stertorous breathing of the men labouring at their trench, the darkness is full of sounds. Now it is the dismal wail of a stray bullet hungrily seeking a billet. Now it is the clack-clack-clack of the machine guns chattering to each other, like demons in Hell. One of these sweeps round – traverses, the gunners call it – regularly every few minutes, and the terrifying rush of bullets causes every man to lie flat on his stomach. A machine gun, when traversing, nearly always sweeps back again, so it is not safe to get up at once.

Every now and then a succession of explosions, sharp, yet heavy and dull, unlike that of a shell, proclaims that bombs are being thrown not far off – probably from adjacent saps. Occasionally through the night a terrific explosion causes the atmosphere to reverberate and everyone to start. It is a minenwerfer bomb bursting somewhere away on the right, and it is followed by a succession of sharp reports and heavy explosions from one of our own trench guns retaliating. In the silent pauses between these sounds may be heard the harsh cry of some bird – I know not its name – which haunts the coarse grass and secret places of the Salient. Occasionally a distant rattle and a harsh grating sound become audible – the German transport on the roads beyond the ridge. A lighter and more continuous grating sound is made by the trolleys rolling along one of the numerous light railways which run just behind the enemy's front line. Every now and again, too, in silent pauses, the barking of dogs may be distinguished – these are the German pets which they keep in their trenches.

Two or three times in the night the whole horizon is of a sudden lit up by the vivid flashes of our own guns, so vivid that one may distinguish trees and other objects against their background; then one hears a distant rumble followed by the roar of the shells, and observes the quick glare as they burst on the enemy's second line.

Strange figures come prowling through the darkness – one cannot tell for certain whether friend or foe. Ever and anon the star lights go up, and in their cold radiance one may see those figures standing still as statues. Yet they would be better advised to throw themselves down. They are the covering parties and the engineers moving out in front. Once the man who fires the Very pistol can be plainly seen, and then one knows that the Germans, too, are out in No Man's Land. Once three lights go up in succession, and simultaneously two shots ring out. These are followed immediately by a loud outcry close at hand, which shows that at least one of the bullets has done its work – "Oh! oh! oh!" Gradually the loud cries sink into a pitiful murmur as a child in pain, and presently this lapses into silence. "Pass the word down for the stretcher bearer!" They lay him down in a shellhole – it is an officer of engineers, shot through both thighs. They do not think he is bad, but the moon shines down upon a face unnaturally still and pallid, and when the doctor comes he is dead.

A fresh feeling in the air and a faint lightening in the sky beyond the German lines suggest that daybreak is not far off. The men have dug their trench, many are resting on their spades, perspiring profusely. They prepare to move off. Suddenly a machine gun opens and one of them sits down quickly, clasping his ankle with both hands. "Oo-er," he mutters, "I'm hit. It don't 'arf hurt." A comrade takes off his puttees and unlaces his boot. "Is it a Blighty one, d'ye think?" inquires this victim anxiously, and upon being told that it probably is, since he has been shot through the ankle, he becomes quite cheerful despite the pain. Soon the word is passed down to lead back, and so the men file once more along the sap into the main trench. From the woods afar off comes the call of a cuckoo, and gradually the various points of the landscape appear. Everybody makes tea, and before long is enjoying a hearty breakfast, followed by a long sleep."

It was during this that Corporal Hector McPherson died on the 28th. He was a labourer from Leyton, Essex, joined up in November 1914 and arrived in France the following April. He was sick with what was described as rheumatism or myalgia for nearly three months just before Loos but thereafter began to be promoted. In the middle of May 1916, less than a fortnight before his death, something unrecorded occurred which led to his being reduced from Lance Sergeant to Corporal. 2 June would have been his second wedding anniversary. Emma McPherson received some of his effects including a locket with a photo.

There was then a lull of three weeks out of the Salient. To begin with they went briefly to the training area at Herzeele just over the French border, about ten miles west of Poperinghe. There were firing ranges and a distinctive element was the amount of time spent training the snipers, not only in accurate shooting but also in observation and concealment, including building a "crow's nest". On 1 June they marched back to Poperinghe, taking three hours on a very hot morning, and the Medical Officer, Captain Gideon Walker, spent the afternoon inspecting all the men's feet. On the 6th the Director Medical Services of the Second Army inspected all NCOs and men, but since most were on fatigues that afternoon, the commonest current activity being burying telephone cable, this was limited.

On the 8th they marched on the usual route to Wormhout, to Lieutenant Ewart "the hell of a march", while the recently arrived Scots Guards Band and the Pipes and Drums of the Battalion "played alternately all the way. They bucked the French people by playing the Marseillaise and other patriotic airs going through the towns, and the First Grenadiers with their band came behind. So it was a great show." The Regimental Band went separately to Watou and waited for them to arrive. The march took four and a half hours this time. Lieutenant Gifford "Giffy" Tyringham, the Assistant Adjutant, remarked in the War Diary "The marching was very slow owing to the presence of the band." Lieutenant Tyringham, from Lelant, near St Ives, Cornwall, had recently left Eton when he was another commissioned on 15 August 1914. He first came to France at the beginning of April 1915, was not involved at Festubert, but was sent to England at the beginning of August. No reason was recorded. He returned after Loos. Life was not easy; Colonel Tempest worked everyone very hard. The next week was one of training in bombing, range firing, PT, drill, bayonet fighting, fire control and practising getting everyone out onto the line of march in the correct order in the dark. One day was taken up with the Battalion Sports. On the 16th, having first had a complete inspection in full marching order, they were on their way back again towards Ypres, but stopping for three days at St Jans-ter-Biezen amid frequent alarms. They were turned out at half past one in the morning on the 17th "but nothing came of it." The reason, though they did not know, was the Canadian battle south of the Menin Road. Lieutenant Ewart remarked that the atmosphere was electric with everyone expecting to go up to the trenches. They did leave on the evening of the 18th by train to Asylum Station, Ypres, most then being billeted at Château des Trois Tours and the rest in the Canal Bank dug-outs. Later that evening he had to go up to the Salient with an engineer officer to inspect the construction of a deep dug-out. Setting off from his own dug-out on the edge of Ypres he found it looked "curiously seductive and homelike. There lie the remains of a late supper; there are the two beds and the two sets of pyjamas; there is the book left open at the page half read; and there are the gramophone records lying in an untidy heap beside the gramophone. The atmosphere is pungent with tobacco smoke, but warm and comfortable. The servants are just going to sleep. Darkness has long since fallen." Everyone was very dissatisfied with the state of the billets at the Château des Trois Tours and worked hard on them while every night large fatigue parties set off to work under the Royal Engineers in the front line and carry up stores. During the afternoon of the 20th, having located it, the Germans shelled a British battery about three hundred yards away from the Château, scoring a direct hit on one gun. The following afternoon, on a much warmer day, some of the men played water polo in the Château moat. Next day one of three British planes shot down crashed nearby and Lieutenant Ewart went over with others to look at the wreckage and at the dead pilot, shot through the face.

By this time the 20th Division were on the right down to the Menin Road and the 6th Division, on the left up to Boesinghe, having come out, the Guards Division replaced them. To begin with the 3rd Guards Brigade were between the 20th Division and the 1st Guards Brigade on the extreme left next to the French. On the night of the 22nd the Scots Guards took over as the left forward battalion of their Brigade. This was new territory. Krupp Farm was just outside their left boundary at a point where there was a slight German salient into the British line and Turco Farm was just behind them. Roughly half way along their trenches the Ypres-Langemarck road crossed into No Man's Land and out on the far edge of it were the remains of a crossroads with the ruins of the Morteldje Estaminet. There was only one functioning communication trench to the front line, unsatisfactory for every reason, and there was a lot of water about, but work had to be done and done it was. The close proximity of the enemy machine guns made this very tricky and, in addition, feeding the forward companies during the short summer nights the more difficult because ration parties had to be completely clear before dawn. Throughout the 24th the British guns were shelling the Morteldje Estaminet to cut the German wire and, related to this, in the afternoon General Corkran came up to the support line to discuss possible offensive operations. This meant an attack to take Pilckem Ridge, at this time definitely being considered and prepared. There was an increase in the tempo everywhere because of what was imminent on the Somme. He returned after dark and went round all the front line trenches to inspect improvements. There was one abandoned trench which, if "reclaimed" was going to be useful, but it was very slow progress to reopen it, far worse than digging a completely new one. More digging went on in reopening fallen in saps and opening new ones out into No Man's Land.

Soon after stand down on the morning of the 26th Private Charlie Ross was making his breakfast. There was a shot and he fell dead with a sniper's bullet through the back of his head. A young serving soldier at the start of the War, he enlisted in the late autumn of 1913 in Edinburgh, having been working as a gardener at Mid Calder. At the beginning of August 1914 he was still a few weeks under nineteen so he only went to France in September and was sent to the Battalion after First Ypres. He was the youngest of a family of three brothers and six sisters, whose home was at Port Charlotte, Islay. Someone who saw was Private James Hardie, an August 1914 volunteer at Cowdenbeath, of whom more would be heard. Generally the 26th had been a quiet day. That changed after dark when, over to the right, raiders from the 20th Division went out from Wieltje and came back with sixteen prisoners. Meanwhile, the Scots Guards went on digging, repairing and improving in spite of the heavy rain, which as usual made a mess of the trenches. Then a minenwerfer bomb fell in the front line near where Lieutenant Ewart was and an officer with him he did not name was knocked clean over and concussed "so he has gone down to GHQ on a course." That explosion also killed four men. There were more heavy rain showers the next day and it became clear that, although they had managed to connect up the new trench line, it was currently untenable except in the form of bombing posts. The German machine guns, very close and very active, caused a number of casualties, but in the evening they watched British planes shoot down three German observation balloons in flames. Twenty four hours later, in spite of yet more showers, they had made the new trench line practicable and General Corkran was impressed when he came to see. The last day, the 28th, was quiet, and after the relief they filed away in the darkness to the reserve billets at the Château and the Canal Bank. During the six days in the line nine men had been killed, three had died of wounds and twenty had been wounded. "The men's clothing had got into a filthy condition."

Private Leonard Moore, the son of Harry and Flora Moore of Littlehampton, Sussex, was hit in the head on the 26th. Before he became a soldier in 1904 he was a postman, but he had been serving ever since and, having come out to Zeebrugge at the start, had been with them almost all the time, with two short periods away sick in 1915. When he reached hospital in Boulogne Private Moore was "Dangerously Ill", but then improved, was removed from that list and evacuated to hospital in Orpington, Kent. There he died on 19 July. Private Alexander Paterson, born and brought up in Cork, where Alexander and Agnes Paterson were living at Lee Mills House, was mortally wounded on the 26th and died the same day. He had previous military experience, having purchased his discharge from the Cameron Highlanders, and was a seaman when he enlisted in Liverpool in November 1914. Listed to go to France in a draft at the beginning of May 1915, he went absent for a week and missed it. Later in the month he was on his way. While on leave in London in April 1916 he married Dorothy Baker, who received several of his possessions including a Bible, a card case, a tobacco pouch and a trinket. Private David Pryce, a fitter, who enlisted there two days after Private Paterson and was in the draft that he missed, was killed. John and Alice Price lived in Dingle, Liverpool. Private Thomas Johnson, Leeds labourer and December 1914 volunteer, was killed on the 27th. He had been in France since the beginning of June 1915 and apart from being sick with influenza and myalgia over New Year and ten days leave in April, was with them all the time. Gertrude Johnson and their son William were living in Normanton, where she was sent one letter, his wallet and a small case. Private William Anderson was also killed on the 27th. He, a traveller, volunteered in April 1915, when he was described as "A smart well educated man, and a suitable recruit for the Guards. A superior type." He went out to France at the end of October. Some belongings reached his father, William Anderson, who lived off the top of Leith Walk in Edinburgh.

Apart from the 30th, when over four hundred men were required for fatigues, the next few days were quiet, enabling them to clean up and refit in their own time. However, Private Gordon Smith, formerly of the Metropolitan Police, was very severely wounded that day and died two days later. He had been in the BEF for fourteen months, got into trouble on 27 July the year before and been given three days FP No 2 for "Quitting the ranks without permission", presumably during a route march as they were at Calonne at the time, and at Hill 70 sprained his ankle sufficiently badly to be away for over three months. When he died his father, also Gordon Smith, was living in Dufftown, Banffshire, where he received a very large number of personal effects including twenty one letters, seventeen photographs, a prayer book, a Bible and a Soldiers Friend.

Up in the line it was now far from quiet. The Welsh Guards raided the Morteldje Estaminet on 1 July. This began well with few casualties and they brought back two prisoners, but then the German guns retaliated while they were trying to dig in two new bombing posts. This left them eventually with four officers and seventy six men killed, wounded and missing. Instead, they next tried to sap out to the proposed bombing posts. The Germans seem to have detected this, because there was very heavy shelling all afternoon on the 3rd. This complicated that night's relief, because the Scots Guards, expecting to go back to everything as they left it, found that much that they had known and worked on no longer existed. Some platoons had to be redeployed. There was nothing for it but to start digging again at once to repair the front line, but almost immediately a minenwerfer bomb landed in a G Company platoon hitting six men. This minenwerfer went on damaging the trenches. Again it was very wet, which added to the slow progress of restoring them. There were more showers, intermittent shelling and, to their right, a cancelled raid early on the 7th. The 4th Grenadiers had been about to raid a place called Canadian Dug-outs, but they became aware, fortunately in time, that the Germans were expecting them. After the relief during the night of the 8th the Scots Guards marched away to Vlamertinghe, halting on the way for hot soup.

Private Frank Johnston, a clerk, volunteered in January 1915 in Edinburgh, though his home, where his father John Johnston worked, was the Kennels at Ayton Castle, Berwickshire. He arrived in early November and was wounded for the only time on 5 July, very slightly in the left arm, requiring only five days in hospital, before he was discharged fully fit again to the Guards Division Base Depot. Thereafter he was with the Battalion till they left Cologne, having missed the Armistice because he went on a fortnight's leave that day. Lance Corporal James White left on the 8th for England. He was a Glasgow policeman, joined up in November 1914 and arrived in France early in May 1915. He was first promoted Lance Corporal in August, but missed Loos because suffering from neurasthenia. He recovered, returned and was promoted Lance Corporal in April 1916, but when the neurasthenia recurred in July he had to go home and was discharged a year later, disabled. Margaret White, his mother, lived in Lossiemouth, Morayshire.

Distinctive after Colonel Tempest became Commanding Officer was the frequency of his inspections, whether of companies, billets, the Transport or reinforcement drafts. The current period out of the line was no exception and he was consistently exacting. On the evening of the 8th he inspected all NCOs, the 9th was a Sunday, on the 10th he inspected the Flank Companies and the day after the others. That day orders came to provide the Headquarters of a Detachment representing the BEF to take part in the Bastille Day parades in Paris. Colonel Tempest was to command it, with Captain Wynne Finch as Adjutant and Captain Ross as Quartermaster. The Battalion were to provide their Sergeant Major, an orderly, a clerk from the Orderly Room, two cooks and nine other selected men. Quite what notice was given of this unexpected diversion was not recorded, but that evening the party left by train for Abbeville, where the Detachment assembled. Apart from a substantial number from the Brigade of Guards, there were officers and men from Australia, Canada, The Rifle Brigade, the Indian Cavalry, dismounted, the 16th (Irish) and 36th (Ulster) Divisions, both New Army, Newfoundland, New Zealand, The Gordon Highlanders, South Africa and The Royal Welsh Fusiliers.

In Paris on the morning of the 14th they paraded at ten to seven at their barracks in the Rue St Lazare and marched to the Place des Invalides, where they were drawn up with the Belgian Detachment on their left and the Russian Detachment on their right. On the opposite side of the road were French Colonial troops from Algeria. It started raining at half past seven and went on raining for over two hours. President Poincaré walked down the lines of troops at quarter to nine by way of inspection. Having formed up at ten, as they stepped off they marched past the President before crossing the Pont d'Alexandre III and reaching the end of the Champs Elysée. They marched the length of it, over the Place de la Concorde, down La Rue Royale, along the Boulevard Madeleine, on by the Grands Boulevards to the Port St Denis and finally to the Place de la République. It was half past twelve. After they dismissed lorries took them back to the Rue St Lazare. The Scots Guards party were back in Poperinghe late on the afternoon of the 18th.

For everyone else there was nothing so colourful. On the 10th General Corkran inspected them in full marching order and came back to inspect the Transport the day after. In camp the usual businesslike training took up the days until they went up to the reserve position on the Canal Bank on the 15th, where generally little happened to disturb them, but British heavy artillery shells were hammering away into the German wire in front of the Welsh Guards. The exception was a burst of shrapnel on the 17th, causing eight casualties to Left Flank.

Initial reports reaching them about the Battle of the Somme were good and that was the impression they continued to have for the time being. Lord Cavan had spoken to the 4th Grenadiers and they read into what he said that the Allies were not in any hurry to win the War, but would let "things take their course for another twelve months, by which time, military opinion says, the Bosches will be in a bad way." Lieutenant Ewart concluded that the War was unlikely to end before December 1917 and, knowing the Somme from his time there with the Entrenching Battalion, thought that Sir Douglas Haig was unlikely to push much further "as he has all the best of the ground." In reserve at the Canal Bank they were "lazing through this dreamy, hot afternoon of 17th July among the leafy surroundings of the Château des Trois Tours, about a couple of miles behind the front line. Some sleep, some bathe in the artificial lake; and some read books or write letters, half lying, half sitting in the shade of the trees. It is a modern château such as the bourgeois love, turreted, jerry built, and doll's house like, but luxurious withal in its greenery and silence." However all afternoon reports from the front line were of the trenches being pounded to nothing as the Germans retaliated for a successful raid against them the night before. "Tonight there is to be a relief. None look forward to it, and the ceaseless roo-coo-roocoo-coo of the wood pigeons in their leafy fastnesses makes one long for the infinite peace of an English summer."

On the evening of the 18th they went to the front line for four days, this time on the very left only a short distance in front of the Canal and next to the French, with whom they had communications. In the French sector the Canal itself was No Man's Land. Apart from the digging and the general process of trench improvements, on every night that the Scots Guards were there they worked at adding to the wire out in front. In spite of the usual practice of having a covering party out as protection it was still very dangerous and in the course of it 2nd Lieutenant Percy Gold was killed and Captain The Honourable Arthur Howard wounded. Lieutenant Ewart heard of Lieutenant Gold that "A star light went up and, instead of throwing himself down, he stood still and got shot through the head." Separately, two other officers were wounded, Lieutenants Lumsden and Maynard. "Lumsden was hit in the foot by a piece of shell, Howard was out wiring when the Germans crept up and threw some bombs and he got a few pieces in him; while Maynard was wounded in the head by a ricochet bullet. They have all gone to Blighty, lucky devils – I find it is terribly tantalising to see people going off like that, but they had certainly earned it." Not just officers were hit.

Lieutenant Gold's father, W H Gold, had a business and contact address in Gracechurch Street in the City of London. His son had been to school at Churcher's College, Petersfield, Hampshire. After training with the Inns of Court OTC he was commissioned in February 1916, arrived in France towards the end of May and joined the Battalion on 11 June. Writing later in his barely started chronicle Captain Henry Dundas of the 1st Scots Guards, who knew him in England and at the Guards Division Base Depot remembered how "Old "Perce" the soul of generosity, was a successful businessman from Singapore & just very nice & much older than me." He was thirty three. Captain Howard, just past his twentieth birthday and just promoted temporarily, had been at Eton and, briefly, at Magdalen College, Oxford, before being commissioned in March 1915. When he first tried to join the Army at the start of the War, he was rejected for defective eyesight. His father was dead and his mother, Lady Strathcona in her own right, lived in Mayfair. He arrived the previous October, a week before they first went into the Hohenzollern trenches. His wounds were in a buttock, thigh and elbow, but once recovered at home he came back. Lieutenant Anthony "Tony" Maynard, another Etonian, started the War in the 10th Hussars, transferring in April 1915. By this time he had been in the BEF for a year but only in the Battalion since after the bombing attack at the Hohenzollern in October. After he recovered from a heavy bruise on his right foot, a wound to his forehead and concussion, he too came back again. His home was at Hoon Ridge, Derbyshire. Lieutenant James "Jimmy" Lumsden was forty, had been educated in the Royal Navy and began the War in the Intelligence Corps at Headquarters BEF from August 1914. He transferred in September 1915, joining just before Loos, and by this time was commanding Left Flank. The shell fragment which hit him severely bruised his right foot and he took no further part in the War with the Scots Guards. He was the son of Colonel Henry Lumsden of Pitcaple Castle, Aberdeenshire.

Private William Barry, who arrived soon after Festubert, died on the 18th. Originally a Londoner, he gave his occupation as a hawker when enlisting in Leeds in November 1914. His sister Ellen Barry lived in Shoreditch, but he left his belongings to Mrs Charles Reynolds in Bradford. Private David Adamson, a miner, was killed on the 20th. James and Kate Adamson lived in Motherwell. He first arrived shortly before Festubert, when he was hit in the thigh by shrapnel and sent home to hospital, though in France just over two months later and back with the Battalion for eleven months before his death. At the end of May he had ten days home leave. Private Thomas Reid was a reservist called up on mobilization and went at the start to Zeebrugge. His original occupation was as a porter in Edinburgh, but his home was at Loth, Sutherland, and he married Margaret McKay there in July 1914. Their son was born three weeks later. Soon after First Ypres Private Reid was sent home because of his teeth and did not leave again for the BEF until July 1915. His first son died in March 1915, aged five months, but Margaret Reid was pregnant again and their second son was born at the end of September, but only survived a month. Not long before that Private Reid was admitted to a military VD hospital and what with treatment there and a prolonged period with the Entrenching Battalion he was not back with the 2nd Scots Guards until after New Year. He too was killed on the 20th. The same day Private David Galloway, the son of James Galloway, who lived near Meigle, Perthshire, was also killed, a ship's steward who enlisted in London in December 1914. Not long before he left for the BEF at the end of May 1915 he married Margaret Ramsay at Kinnoull, Perthshire. They already had a son born in 1913 and another was born at Christmas 1915. Shortly before then Private Galloway was promoted Lance Corporal, but was reduced to the ranks for drunkenness two months later and given twenty eight days FP No 1. On the 25th Margaret Galloway wrote to Regimental Headquarters asking for news of her husband "It is past his usual time of writing me as he always did so very regularly up till now thus my cause for deep anxiety." She received some letters, photographs, cards and a single coin. Private Percy Avery, son of Robert and Mary Avery of Birkenhead, was an engine driver till he joined up in January 1915. It was not till May 1916 that he went abroad and he arrived in the Battalion six weeks before his death, also on the 20th. On the evening of the 22nd, as they were waiting for the Welsh Guards to arrive, a 5.9 inch shell landed in a trench hitting seven men. Private Alexander Gibb, with the Battalion for eight weeks, died. He was a shepherd, the son of Agnes McClumpher of Whithorn, Wigtownshire, and volunteered in November 1914. Compared with Private Avery there was an even longer period between his enlistment and his going to the BEF, not till April 1916. Less than two weeks before leaving for France he married Ruth Rank in Chelsea and she received some letters, a ring, his wallet, some photographs and postcards, a tobacco pouch and his purse at her home near Waterloo Station.

They went back for two days of fatigues and Colonel Tempest's inspections into the reserve position in the dug-outs along the Canal Bank, to Lieutenant Ewart "a very sepulchral spot". Then there were two days more in the front line as the result of which Private Ralph Lawson, hit by a shell in the stomach on the 25th, his right leg also broken, died in a casualty clearing station early the next morning. He was a September 1914 volunteer, who had worked as a driller. Already wounded once, hit in the thumb just after Easter 1915 during the long 1st Battalion trench tour south of Neuve Chapelle, he was sent home to recover and had now been back in the BEF for nearly four months. His home was in South Queensferry and James and Emma Lawson were sent an identity disc, some letters, his pocket book, cigarette case, some photographs, a match box and lighter, a knife, a pair of scissors, a cap badge and two charms.

Leaving the Salient

Next, on the evening of the 27th the 1st Somerset Light Infantry and two platoons of the 1st Rifle Brigade arrived to take over, a process which went slowly "because the relieving battalion had nothing but new officers." They were in the 4th Division, just come from the Somme, where they had been fighting from 1 July onwards between Beaumont-Hamel and Serre, near the left of the British attack on the opening day. Meanwhile, in Lieutenant Ewart's words "The news has just come direct from Divisional Headquarters. The groups standing and lying about on the Canal Bank get it first; then like lightning, it flashes down the Yperlee and reaches the innermost recesses of every dug-out, and is even conveyed to the newly brought in wounded who are lying at the dressing station dug-outs. Near Bridge Four it collects a crowd; at Blighty Bridge quite a number are discussing it half an hour after the first whisper has got abroad. By nightfall it has crept uncannily along the three quarters of a mile of communication trenches to the front line: it travels faster than any gas wave. The only people who know nothing of it are the three canvas-shrouded figures lying side by side on stretchers in a cul-de-sac. And they will never know it. "The Division is moving south!" The news flies from mouth to mouth, and everybody congratulates everybody else. Everybody's heart leaps for joy because the dead weight of doom is lifted from their souls. The Salient is to be left behind, with its brown ditches, its impotence for the defenders, and – its implacable Fate. No more sitting still and suffering. There is to be a pause, at any rate, in the slow procession of the maimed, the dying, and the dead. There is to be a change of country, of scenery, of air, of habits. There is to be a long journey, long marching, gorgeous rests in remote places, quiet nights and still, lazy days, and a breath of Peace – and of Life. And at the end – who knows? Nothing worse than a battlefield on which one fights and lives or dies as men should, not lies in a ditch and waits for the inevitable end like dogs. Give us the first a thousand times! Make no mistake – Ypres gets on the nerves."

Afterwards they marched back through the night to a field near Vlamertinghe for hot soup and then on for a very short time. They arrived in a camp at four in the morning on the 28th and paraded to leave at quarter to eight for Poperinghe Station. Two narrow gauge trains took them to Bollezeele and nearby they went into billets. Lieutenant Ewart wrote of "A still, misty morning at the end of July resolves itself into brilliant sunshine and great heat. And as the first train leaves the railway siding near the old Poperinghe road, cheer upon cheer goes up to the blue sky…there is nothing but singing, laughter, and shouting today." About Bollezeele he went on that "The detraining point has an unpronounceable name; it is also insignificant, being a mere sun-baked, sleepy railway yard without a square inch of shade. But here for the first time there is no sign of war." They marched on what was, by now, a very hot day, for about an hour and a half to billets in a village called Millain. There was a halt en route "in a shady oak wood, and the men, recklessly happy, throw themselves down amid the long grass, the convolvuli, the straying honeysuckle. Yes, we are happy now, we who have suffered much! And so at two of the afternoon, smoking, singing and dust covered, we march into billets. Everybody's thought is, God grant we stay here a while! For it is a lovely little village." Later on "In the afternoon the Company are paid in the farmyard in front of our billets, and later, towards evening, we take books and a deck chair – hero of many vicissitudes this, and survivor of all! – out into the box arbour and abandon ourselves to the dreamy stillness which steals over country places towards evening. We doze." The next day, all NCOs with Lewis Guns and Number 2s on the guns themselves having been issued with revolvers, they were trained to use them in lieu of the rifles they had carried before. Also "The Battalion bathed." Otherwise, as Lieutenant Ewart watched, it "had been spent practically in idleness and resting, for the troops dozed away the hot middle hours, and only in the evening walked out into the country, watched the peasants working in the field, strolled about, and looked at the gay, village gardens."

Extracting the Brigade from the Salient and moving elsewhere was not straightforward. On the 24th Captain Warner was up in the line inspecting drainage and work done on communication trenches. Then orders arrived for the relief by the 4th Division and he was up till two in the morning writing the Brigade orders for this and the subsequent moves. The whole process was "Very complicated". So far as he then knew they were not going further than by train to Bollezeele and then on foot to villages not far further west. First there was the relief, then the move back to camps, then the move to Bollezeele. By the morning of the 27th the relief was complete and everyone was in camps. That afternoon new orders arrived for another move from the Bollezeele area to Frévent, west of Arras. Captain Warner wrote more orders. By the next day his patience was becoming tested. Having arrived by car at one of the villages west of Bollezeele "Various unnecessary orders about move received from Div. and destroyed."

Soon after dawn on the 30th in the early morning mists the Scots Guards were on their way again for thirteen miles towards Cassel. As they went Lieutenant Ewart saw that "people appeared at the gates of their cottages, at the crossroads, and in groups and little family parties on their way to early church; which latter was the first intimation we had that it was Sunday, for in our vagrant stirring life of movement the days passed by almost uncounted." When close to Cassel most of them halted in some fields at Zuytpeene not far from the railway station, while one company and the Transport went on to load up. "There was to be a three hours' rest in the heat of the day before entraining. The men ate their dinners – which had been cooking on the march – under the shade of some majestic elms, and a fine spread awaited us officers (previously arranged by a thoughtful quartermaster) at the farmhouse nearby. This was followed by a smoke and sleep, after which, the hour being about one o'clock, it was time to entrain. Cassel shimmered in the heat-haze; the sun scorched down upon a station yard ankle deep in dust." The train left Bavinchove, outside Cassel, went through Hazebrouck, past the western edge of the coalfields of Béthune and Loos and then through St Pol in the much more appealing rolling and wooded countryside west of Arras. For Lieutenant Ewart "what a perspiring, jolting, stifling journey it was! It rather reminded me of going home from school for the summer holidays."

Notes on Chapter Sources

Interview of Pte J Venters among Interviews of former Prisoners of War, either repatriated for reasons of sickness or injury or escapers, back in the UK before the end of the War, series TNA/WO161.
Reverend PB Clayton, *Tales of Talbot House in Poperinghe & Ypres* (London: Chatto & Windus 1919).
Individual named supporters of Toc H, Records of Talbot House Museum, Poperinghe.
Copy of Maj H Beckles Willson's *Daily Express* article in Lt N Fergusson photograph album, SGA.
Composition of Bastille Day Detachment, RSM GA Scarff document, SGA.
Capt H Dundas chronicle, Dundas Papers, Private Collection.

16

The Ypres Salient 1916 – 1st Battalion

Final preparations

From Calais the 1st Scots Guards went by train as far as Cassel on 16 March, billeted nearby and three days later marched to Poperinghe, arriving at noon. Major Barne found that Battalion Headquarters and the Officers Mess, for meals, was "at a big villa without much glass in windows (none in my room)", but to Sir Iain Colquhoun they had the "Best billets we have ever had for everyone. Big houses and heaps of room. Had my hair cut and wandered about the town…Leave reopens today. I ought to go…but gave my leave to Lionel [Norman] as he isn't well." His and others' main diversion in Poperinghe was going to shows by the 6th Division's concert party, The Fancies, who did music hall acts and consisted of soldiers struck off all trench duties, but liable for daytime fatigues. However, as the Reverend "Tubby" Clayton recalled, they, unusually, had "two Belgian ladies known respectively as Lanoline and Vaseline, who could neither sing nor dance, but at least added a touch of femininity." While Lord Esmé Gordon Lennox, Captain Thompson, and some company commanders were making a first visit to Ypres Major Barne went round the company billets next morning. He too was impressed when he saw them "all in houses and a convent in the town. They are in very good order though filthy when taken over yesterday…About 7am two German aeroplanes come over and drop 4 bombs quite close to Battn HQ. Weather much warmer. Baden appears to tea, he is looking for a suitable place for a new bombing school."

The seriousness of what was coming next was underlined by the attention given to checking that everyone's gas helmets fitted and functioned properly and that everyone knew precisely how to put them on, but Major Barne thought the briefing by an unnamed medical officer in the Cinema Hall at Poperinghe on the 21st for all officers, company sergeant majors and platoon sergeants on what to do if there was a gas attack "very poor and badly delivered." Meanwhile amid the other preparations and training the Lewis Gun teams practised with their weapons, there were bathing parades, the companies did drill and inevitably there were demands for large fatigue parties. Major Barne walked "with Luss to get the key (from an old woman about three kilometres away) of a room to be Sergts Mess. She was most ungracious in spite of our promises to pay for all damage, & would not hear of such a thing. I think the Belgians are a very 2nd rate people, a French woman would not have refused in all probability, or would have done so politely." The Coldstream Guards Band played, somewhat dampened by rain, in the Scots Guards Officers Mess garden and everyone went to see The Fancies that evening. Major Barne also thought them excellent, but ended that day's entry with "There is not much sign of spring here, but the woods are carpeted with periwinkles." Next morning he and Lord Esmé Gordon Lennox met Captain Tom Ross, the 2nd Battalion Quartermaster, "who said his transport had been properly shelled last night going down to Ypres, & some stampeded, several casualties to men & horses. He was looking for it at the time. The Bn had suffered in consequence. Oh! we have got our heads into a Hornet's nest here."

On the 23rd Sir Iain Colquhoun went to the Salient for the first time to see the trenches manned by the 3rd Guards Brigade. He "Got up at 3am and motored up to Ypres, with the Colonel and Hugh Ross. Got out at Menin Gate about 4.30 and went… up the Potijze road to Welsh Guards HQ. Had breakfast and went up communication trench to Front Line. All trenches are in a very bad state, only waist high in parts and ankle deep in mud. The communication trench is only 2 ft deep and is overlooked by the Germans from high ground all round." Next they looked at the support trenches which C Company were going to be in and then returned the way they had come. From Ypres they walked to Vlamertinghe, picked up their horses waiting there "and rode back to Poperinghe about 11.30 covered in mud." Major Barne saw them when they got back, heard what they had to say and hoped "I don't suppose they are as bad as made out." There was more snow. Sir Iain Colquhoun told his wife "The Division we relieved had completely lost heart and done nothing but sit there consequently there will be a great deal to do… My new suit came out yesterday I am swaggering about in it today…The snow has cleared away now and the birds are singing…I am the 3rd oldest inhabitant in this Batt. Now all the others have gone home with nerves and one thing and another." By this he meant officers of whom only Lieutenant Kinlay, the Quartermaster, and Major Barne had been there longer. Major Barne drew "a beautiful pair of gum boots from the Quartermaster & a blanket" on the morning of the 24th. Then Lord Esmé Gordon Lennox "gives us a talk about the part of the line we are going to hold. There is no doubt it is not to be all beer & skittles."

Into the Salient

At half past eight on the evening of the 25th, a day of heavy showers, they left Poperinghe by train for Asylum Station. Initially they went to take over from the Welsh Guards the left forward reserve role in Ypres for the right hand brigade sector and so were temporarily under command of the 3rd Guards Brigade. It was reasonably safe in cellars at the Prison and the Convent and less so in dug-outs in the Canal Bank at the southern end of the Ypres-Yser Canal on the east side of Ypres, where was the quay for barges. This was just for twenty four hours.

Hitherto Major Barne had not been forward of Poperinghe. The train took "only about fifteen minutes, glided in there without a single light or sound, the engine driver seems to have made a study of this. Schiff…who is our billeting officer, having gone ahead as usual, was waiting for us and on the lookout, but even then he never heard or saw us arrive though not 200 yards from the train. We made a slow & solemn march through this wretched deserted tumbledown ruined town – with the ghostly remains of its once very picturesque houses, streets and public buildings watching us – to our various dug-outs. The Battn HQ ones being in the Canal Bank quite good so far as comfort goes, but very far from being shellproof. The night is disturbed only by the banging of our own guns all round us, some very close." Lieutenant Marcus Schiff was born in Cincinnati, Ohio, though at school at Uppingham, and his widowed mother was now living in London. He had been in the BEF with the Honourable Artillery Company, Territorials, since

20 September 1914 and was wounded nine months later commanding a company. He transferred at the end of September 1915 and joined the Battalion a few weeks later. Sir Iain Colquhoun remarked of the Canal Bank "Quite good dug-outs, but wet and unhealthy and the canal is full of every sort of filth." One company went on to Potijze where they were needed in part of the support line. The following morning, the 26th, Lord Esmé Gordon Lennox inspected the billets, which, more importantly, enabled him to see and speak to the men. Sir Iain Colquhoun told his wife "The Canadians are just next door to us and are a very fine Division, we are lucky to have them." He continued that Captain Jamie Balfour "has gone to the 2nd Batt. I am glad as he gets on my nerves at times…A man called Tom Evans rode 20 miles to see me the other day. He is a sergeant in the Royal Scots and I used to box with him in Edinburgh." Sergeant Evans was an Army Boxing Champion at featherweight. The Canadian Corps were in the course of taking over the right half of the Salient from the Menin Road south from Hooge.

Next day Lord Esmé Gordon Lennox and Major Barne went round to visit the companies and then to report to Headquarters 3rd Guards Brigade "for we are under Genl Pa Heyworth for a few hours…Find him very affable. Have a good look round the town – the Cathedral and Cloth Hall, etc or rather what is left of them, still very beautiful. Quite a lot of gunning on both sides." The 2nd Guards Brigade took over the right hand brigade sector completely once darkness had fallen on the 26th and at ten the 1st Scots Guards paraded and passed through the old town defences by the Menin Gate to go into the line at Potijze, relieving their 2nd Battalion. It was pitch dark, raining hard and very difficult to see anything, this being when the 2nd Battalion subsequently commented that they were holding their part of the line in a different way from that which the newcomers had prepared for. Major Barne described the relief as "a very slow one – the trenches being awkwardly sited and arranged…not over till 2am." The Coldstream were on their right from Railway Wood to the near side of the Menin Road, with Bellewarde Lake in front of them. The Ypres-Roulers railway was the inter-battalion boundary, but there were no linked trench lines and C Company held the gap on the right between the battalions with one Lewis Gun and two bombing posts.

As Private Cumming moved through Ypres "The Salient itself was outlined by constantly rising and falling flares and there was a feeling that the tension could give way at any moment to merry hell…it was a characteristic we would come to recognise. Our way lay through the cobbled square fronted by the partially destroyed Cloth Hall. The limbers and the guns passing over the cobbles created a racket that could be heard for miles and invited enemy shelling. Through a narrow street we came to the ramparts…The Menin Gate was simply a couple of pillars that had been rather battered about and the moat was green with slime. The moat was the start of the really tricky part. Hellfire Corner had the reputation but the crossroads beyond the ramparts were just as dangerous and a sudden salvo could cause death and destruction in a few moments. To add to the unpleasantness, a cemetery on the left had been ploughed up so thoroughly by the enemy missiles that on a warm night the smell was ghastly."

Private Johnes had not yet had the chance to look round Ypres properly. As C Company headed for the Menin Gate he remembered "we had to cross the cobbled stone square in small groups on the double, Jerry was sending over salvoes of shrapnel mixed with ground chats, the sparks were flying off the cobbles." Further along the Menin Road they also had to move fast at Hellfire Corner for the same reason. When they got up the communication trench to Potijze Wood, which he spelt and pronounced "Pottagee", he found "the ground was much more solid here than in the swamps in France where we had spent the winter." Then "at daylight when we could get a look around, it was the same old type of battle ground, trenches, firesteps, and dug-outs, but more substantial." Then Sir Iain Colquhoun recorded that on the 27th "About 4.30am 2 of our mines were set off by St Eloi, about 7 miles east of my position. From then till 7am there was an intense bombardment by both sides, but no shelling near my position." A complete lull followed for about four hours and during this General Ponsonby came round the front line, but "At 11.30am the Germans started shelling the Coldstream in Railway Wood (just on my right). They shelled them for 3 hours with guns of all calibres – our guns replied – and until 2pm there was a continual uproar. It was so close to my trench that I could watch the whole thing through a periscope and enemy splinters came in. The Coldstream got shelled right out of one part, and about 20 of them ran across the open to an old disused trench. Afraid they must have lost heavily. Pitch black night. Sheets of rain and continual bombardment all round. Stretcher bearers came up to remove 2 of my company who had been sniped in the afternoon, missed the road in the dark, and went right out into the open with both bodies. Luckily they ran into one of our bombing posts who sent them back. Our ration party did the same thing slightly later. Our Lewis Gun very nearly fired on a Coldstream listening post. I fell into a mud hole, and got soaked from head to foot (no change for 3 days). A horrible night altogether."

Further south a British attack had started the Battle of the St Eloi Craters. Major Barne was at Battalion Headquarters when General Ponsonby first arrived at about six o'clock with Lieutenant Colonel Cecil "Guffin" Heywood of the Coldstream, recently appointed GSO1 of the Guards Division. "They say the 3rd Divn has blown up 3 mines at St Eloi, which accounts for the noise and bombardment, evidently an attack is being made at same time. At 8am the Brigr came running breathlessly into our dug-out, asking for shelter, for indeed the Bosch is shelling our neighbourhood. We had turned in 6-8am for another nap. At 10am I went round our trenches alone, such a fearful mess, in some places hardly a "line" at all, merely heaps of mud. These trenches, like those at Laventie, seem to have been utterly neglected till our Divn took them over 10 days ago and will require a lot of work on them before they are fit for anything. Hardly any dug-outs or firesteps or drainage or traverses or parados, and we are warned that as soon as any are put up, unless well disguised, the Bosch will have them down again at once. There are several very "draughty" corners and I got sniped a bit. The Battn HQ is fairly good in a sort of 2d tube iron lining, almost *in* a cemetery. While I am out, there is a heavy bombardment of Railway Wood on our right, held by the 1st Coldm the key of our position. I hear this often happens and there are good deep dug-outs there. Ypres is plainly visible about three kilometres behind us. Heavy gunning continues to South and over us all day. We have several casualties… In afternoon I go and visit RF Coy which I had not time to do this morning – found them very restless, their line being briskly shelled, 1 killed 3 wounded so far. I did not loiter much in the dangerous area, which they had cleared altogether, quite wisely as they are a sort of third line. The Battn's casualties for the day 3 killed and 5 wounded, a bad start." Private James Tully, the son of William and Agnes Tully from Colfin, Wigtownshire, had been a bank clerk. He died on the 27th after nearly six months in the BEF, having arrived in the large October 1915 draft who went straight into the Hohenzollern trenches. Private Murray Hunter, whose home was nearby, enlisted on the same day at the end of November 1914 at Ayr and was killed on 17 July 1915. The second man killed on the 27th was a former clerk, Private Henry Flavell, a widower whose father Henry Flavell lived in Airdrie. He joined in January 1915 and arrived in the BEF the day after Private Tully. Corporal George McKellar, in the BEF for just over a year and a Corporal for just over a month, was the third. He was a joiner, originally from Greenock, probably working in

Whiteinch on the other side of the Clyde, where he enlisted early in September 1914 at the age of thirty five, leaving behind his wife Sarah and their two small boys. They married in Greenock in 1902, but her home was in Ballymoney, County Antrim, where she went with her sons when he joined the Army. Private John Morrison in the 2nd Battalion had enlisted at Whiteinch on the same day, having been an apprentice joiner for three years.

The 28th was not so bad but enemy field guns fired intermittently from ten in the morning till three during which, as Sir Iain Colquhoun described, "The parapet was blown in in 3 places, but otherwise little damage was done. It keeps everyone in the parapets and makes sleep impossible…The men are very tired as no one has slept for 48 hrs. I have rheumatism for the first time in my life, I suppose owing to being wet for 2 days. My trench waders are full of water." One morning while Private Johnes and others were sitting outside the signal dug-out after brewing up tea Sir Iain Colquhoun stopped to talk to them when "just at that moment the Jerry gunners decided to disturb the peace with a little battery fire of ground stuff, and the jokers in his front line joined in with trench mortar fire. They were off target but close enough to throw up a lot of corruption, muck and shell splinters, which covered our party, a chunk hit me on the left breast, the captain saw it and took a look asking if it had gone through, it had not, but my paybook in my left breast pocket had a hole punched in it and a lump later rose on the top rib." That night the companies swapped over but Sir Iain Colquhoun was disappointed that Left Flank were very late in arriving in the front line. "The relief ought to have arrived at 10.30 but the ration party had been shelled and the night was pitch dark. Reached X3 about 4.45am, snowing and very cold. Everyone crawled into their dug-outs, tired and wet, and went to sleep." X3, part of the third line of defence, was just east of Potijze. There the trenches were dry and the dug-outs good. On the morning of the 29th there was more shelling, including some which fell in their trenches, doing no harm, and once it stopped it became possible to sleep that afternoon. After dark they worked on the traverses and Sir Iain Colquhoun took a working and carrying party up to Left Flank where they "worked a communication trench…for 2½ hrs up to our knees in mud and water." There were no casualties on either the 28th or 29th.

There had been two doctors with the Battalion since Captain Stewart left but now there was a third who remained for some months, who, Major Barne wrote, was "a little Yankee, Alexander, who was attached to the Canadians, rather a tiresome though clever and amusing little man." As they were sharing a dug-out it was "a little trying at times, tonight he would read out to me a long letter from "The New Moses" whom he had once already put in a lunatic asylum."

The Potijze trench bombardment on 30 March

Sir Iain Colquhoun had more to write about on the 30th. "Cold, frosty night, but lovely clear morning. Germans started shelling at 7.30am and kept it up all morning. They also shelled Potijze Wood and road, and kept us up in the parapet all morning. Several field gun and small howitzer shells fell in the trench. As the day was so fine there were many aeroplanes up, and the air was full of anti-aircraft shells. This position is like the firing line, completely enfiladed, and shells can come from any angle. At 1.30pm the Germans started a very heavy bombardment all along the reserve trenches and firing line. The parapet was blown to pieces in many places all along the line, the dug-outs knocked flat, and many men killed, buried and wounded. It stopped at 3 o'clock, and for an hour we dressed the wounded men, and got the rifles ready. At 4.30pm the bombardment started again with even greater severity, and until 7pm there was one continual roar, shells bursting in, above and all round the trench every second. 4.5s 5.2s and field guns firing HE into the trench and HE Shrapnel over it. Everyone was smothered in earth and deafened by the noise, and many men were quite dazed at the end. At 7pm the bombardment stopped, and we were able to look about and see the damage done. The trench has been fearfully knocked about in most places, but is still capable of putting up a big defence."

Major Barne "went round line early again taking a Grenadier Coy Sgt Major and Platoon Sgt who will relieve us tonight. Got sniped at badly again the bullet seemed to go close by my ear in one place and struck a traverse about a yard off. The line has been improved during the night, but only a start made, anyhow one can now get along the trench without going on "all fours" till it is next blown in! Such a glorious morning, even a wood pigeon cooing near our Battn HQ but guns and howitzers and anti-aircraft weapons etc etc going off in all directions such a continuous fire as we never heard in the Laventie line – but at 12.45 there commences such an intense bombardment as I have never had against me before, at 3pm they knock off we get telephone communication with Luss, C Coy, who says in his usual drawly way "wretched shooting" and he has had no casualties tho' all his dug-outs burst in, but B Coy has 4 killed and 1 wounded, RF 1 wounded, LF we can't hear from, but the front line do not seem to have had much at them." Another visitor, Lieutenant Colonel Claude Raul "Crawley" Champion de Crespigny, commanding the 2nd Grenadiers, "dropped in about 12.30pm to see Esmé, and had to stay with us right up till 3pm because he could not get away. It is a marvel anybody is left but luckily Luss was right and the shooting very poor. At 4pm the intense bombardment continues till 5.15pm then breaks off, (while we have tea) till 5.45pm and continues till 7pm, after which at intermittent periods of ½ hr or so through the night. The Relief by 3rd GG takes place commencing at 8pm but owing to the "straffing" is a very slow business, casualties keep happening – dead & wounded have to be found in the wrecked trenches – rifles equipment packs etc etc have to be looked for and distributed – a very dark night – the Bn HQ does not get away till 2.30am when by a cross country route we are able to get to our new billets in Ypres Canal dug-outs safely – about 3.30am after which I go round the Coys with the Adjt – hearing dismal tales – and finally get to bed at 4.30am nearly the round of the clock, after one of the worst…days I ever remember. LF & RF trenches have after all been almost annihilated and flattened out – and the men much rattled and disorganized – sitting being bombarded without being able to do anything in reply is very weary and trying work – making an attack – even though casualties might be higher – would be preferable in many ways." He heard two days later of a Scots Guardsman "left for dead with his forehead and most of his body buried with two Grenadiers in a bombing post, both Grenadiers were killed and our man only found by chance and found to be alive."

Private Johnes wrote "The ground shook, trenches were blown in. We were forced to stay low, expecting to see shells coming through the parapets, some did, there were many casualties in all our lines and the communication trenches were almost obliterated…The Good Lord still wanted my sidekick Evans and me for sunbeams, we came through with only a few bumps from falling debris and the "shakes". As the straff eased off I know my teeth were chattering. It was our relief night and as soon as we could get at it we made what repairs we could to the telephone line…Our relief came in about eight or nine o'clock and George and I hooked up and handed over to, I think, the Grenadiers. We made it out to the road at Pottagee Wood and headed back towards Ypres. Jerry was still keeping it up with shelling but had eased off considerably, a few gas shells were dropping near the road and sparks were flying from shrap bursts. About half a mile up the road toward Ypres George and I took shelter behind the wall of a wrecked building on the north side of the road for a blow and a cigarette. While there, part of one of our companies coming out passed by stepping in Indian file, heading for Ypres. Our eyes had become used to the semi darkness and the gun and shell flashes. It was uncanny to see the troops high tailing it along, sometimes going down or ducking for cover. Flashes of gunfire and exploding shells were almost continuous…Our artillery had not been idle during the bombardment, they were giving as good as we got. We finished our fags and joined in with the fellows on the road to "Wipers". When we finally got back to billets amongst the ruins, teeth were chattering and we were shivering…and got something to eat and a double ration of rum, then laid us down to sleep amongst the rats and lice, thanking the Lord we were still whole instead of in pieces. Don't let anyone tell you that after several hours of continued straffing, knowing that the next second may be your last, as it was for many, that they "did not have the shakes." Shell shock is a terrible feeling, I may tell you."

During the previous night Private Cumming's section had been detailed to occupy a small post in No Man's Land. They were assured that the Germans did not know about it and all that they were to do was lie still and keep quiet but "at the crack of dawn next morning it was obvious that the enemy was very well aware of every tiny crack and crevice in that well pulverised landscape." The shelling was almost ceaseless "and our particular share was one nasty weapon of small calibre that sniped all the time and a more leisurely and larger gun with a terrific burst." Crouching at the bottom of their trench they could hear the larger gun being fired, not that they could do much about it. At one stage "A Sergeant and several men from the Grenadier Guards came flying over the top from a nearby farmhouse where they had been so badly shocked that they were dripping wet, having taken a dive into a flooded cellar. One…had a shrapnel bullet in the lower part of the abdomen but we could not get him away until after dusk. He displayed an admirable calm and I hope he survived." His section's post was not hit but after dark they learned about the havoc in the main trenches where men had been buried alive or simply obliterated.

The unavoidable delays in the relief were such that long after dawn had broken Scots Guardsmen were still struggling back into Ypres. Sir Iain Colquhoun added "We were unable to remove all our wounded before leaving as the communication trenches were blown flat, but the Grenadiers removed most of them…during the night. After such an intense bombardment I expected an attack, but the Germans never showed up. If they had, they would have got hell, as the men were by no means done." Private Fleming's diary entries became less frequent and less often significant, but he wrote of the 30th in the trenches that they were "Shelled continually for 7 hours. Btn lost heavily. About 2.00 Burnett…blown to bits in 1st Line." His Dundee friend, Private Burnett, the son of William and Annie Burnett, described himself as a calendar worker when he joined up in January 1915. He came to France in November and joined the Battalion on Christmas Eve.

Two officers were slightly wounded, twenty four men killed, forty seven wounded, eight missing and twenty sent back with shell shock. Of C Company Sir Iain Colquhoun could write "By great good luck I only lost 3 killed and 7 wounded." Private James Duff was a miner in the Fife coalfield who joined up early on. He had been in trouble three times the previous autumn, namely "Falling out on the line of march without a cause", "Wilfully damaging public property viz greatcoat value 24/-" and "Talking after Lights Out & Making a highly improper remark to a NCO." Respectively the punishments were "12 days FP No 2 & forfeit pay", "3 days FP No 1" and "6 days FP No 1." He was one of the many who fell out on 8 November on the way to La Gorgue, which annoyed Sir Iain Colquhoun so much. Private Duff was killed and buried at Potijze and the site recorded. A few belongings reached his mother Margaret Duff in Perth. It was there that on 9 February 1915 four men joined the Scots Guards, all from Dunning, of whom only one survived the War. Private James Winton, a joiner and the son of Thomas Winton, was the first to die. He arrived in the Battalion early in October 1915 just when they were starting at the Hohenzollern and was killed on 30 March. Lance Corporal John MacRae was a foreman furnaceman, living at Foyers on Loch Ness, and a widower, his wife having died in 1912, with three sons and a daughter. His mother Charlotte Ross in Inverness was his nearest other relative. In January 1915 he joined the Army, aged thirty three, arrived ten days after Private Winton and now lost his life. His daughter Jessie died twelve days later. Sergeant Walter Bird from the East End of London and a clerk before the War, was killed. He and Maud White married in Stepney on 2 August 1914, he enlisted a month later and arrived in France the following February. He was first promoted to Lance Corporal and Acting Sergeant immediately after Puits 14 Bis and became a Lance Sergeant two weeks later. Sergeant Thomas O'May, a Glaswegian from Dennistoun, rose up the ranks even faster and was a Sergeant by the beginning of August 1915. He too was a clerk, enlisted the day after Sergeant Bird and, already a Lance Corporal, came to France the day after him in February 1915. Sergeant O'May had shell wounds in his thigh and left patella and left ankle, had his left foot amputated and was discharged in 1917. He was awarded the MM in 1916 and the Bar to it in 1919. Three days after Sergeant O'May joined up in Glasgow so did Private William Rodgers, a granary hand from Partick, now dead. He first landed in France very soon after Sergeant O'May and was then hit in the thigh by shellfire in May 1915 at the Battle of Aubers. After recovering the other side of the Channel he returned five months later but did not rejoin the Battalion till just after New Year. All there was to be sent on to his father Robert Rodgers were some photographs.

Lance Corporal William Petrie was a country labourer before he enlisted late in October 1914 in Edinburgh. He came to France in May 1915, was promoted in December and until now had not been hit. First he was reported missing, but then the 3rd Grenadiers reported that there was a grave marked by a cross for an unknown Scots Guards Corporal. It was Corporal Petrie. There was nothing to send to Alexander and Catherine Petrie at Hoxa Head, South Ronaldshay, Orkney. Private David Leighton joined the Army in January 1915 and arrived in the Battalion after Loos. He had been sick, each time for a week, first with "chilled feet" just before Christmas and then influenza soon after New Year. His widowed mother Margaret Leighton was in Dundee, where he was a clerk in the jute trade, but he had been born on the Aegean island of Chios and educated at George Watson's in Edinburgh. He was known to be dead. A damaged identity disc of his was found in 1923. One of those with shell shock, as well as laryngitis, was Sergeant Frank Inglis, from both of which he recovered. Originally from Gateshead, where his wife Margaret's home also was, he was a sandblaster in Glasgow for a while before the War. The family lived in Cathcart and there were a daughter and two sons. He volunteered in early September 1914, arrived in the BEF in early December and was made a Lance Corporal almost as soon as he arrived in the Battalion.

Two men with consecutive regimental numbers, Private George Davies, a bricklayer, and Private Robert Howlett, a labourer, both Liverpudlians, joined up on 26 September 1914 and both came out, but separately, in the spring of 1915. Private Davies had ten days leave over Christmas, Private Howlett at the end of January, but he had been in trouble on 4 December for wilfully damaging a greatcoat worth twenty four shillings on the evidence of Company Sergeant Major Clarke of B Company and received three days FP No 1 and forfeiture of pay.

Though no details of the greatcoat damage were recorded it was a fairly common offence and the consequence of men, in despair as their greatcoats dragged in the mud, cutting off the bottoms. Next Private Howlett was twenty four hours late returning from leave and that led to another five days FP No 1. He was now dead. His mother Anne Howlett lived in Everton. On 2 April, presumably in Ypres, Private Davies was hit by a shell in the back and face and died two days later from the consequent stomach injuries. His married sister Mary Bolton lived in Edge Hill and she received quite a lot of his belongings, including a writing case, a French book, a religious book, his pipe and tobacco pouch. Private John Farquharson had shell wounds in his right thigh and also in his left leg, which had to be amputated. He died at Boulogne on 9 April. He was a gamekeeper and his father Tom Farquharson, himself dead by this time, had lived at Killiecrankie, Perthshire. Private Farquharson volunteered in October 1914 and had been in France since April 1915. He was awarded three days FP No 1 for being asleep when his company were standing to arms on 27 July 1915 in the trenches at Cambrin, but from before Loos till soon before the Battalion moved north he was away in a fatigue party at Headquarters XI Corps. Thomas Farquharson in Dundee received his brother's effects, consisting of letters and photographs, a pipe, a pouch, a cigarette lighter, a metal mirror, a wallet and a Bible.

The bombardment had apparently been of such novel scale and duration to both Lord Cavan and General Feilding that they came to see Lord Esmé Gordon Lennox early next morning. Sir Iain Colquhoun heard that "they don't understand it, and are worried about the whole thing." Shells landed frequently in Ypres and around their billets and dug-outs over the next four days. Major Barne had already been woken once around midnight on the 31st by the sound of heavy rifle and shell fire, apparently further south. "Later, about 4am, I am awakened by the sentry prodding me in the stomach, I find he has lit my candle & tells me there is more firing, however all is quiet on our front. I was wondering whether he was making an April fool of me or not – but the firing was being continued to the south." As it went on he noted "All this activity is difficult to account for, those who have been here some time agree that it is more than for some months past. On 30th, the gunners estimate with curious though usual diversity of opinion that the number of enemy shells vary from 4000 to 10000! In any case considering the number sent over, it is extraordinary how few casualties we had in the Divn." Though others thought that the Germans might have been contemplating an attack, to him it was improbable because the wind had been in the wrong direction for gas. As a footnote he remarked that "young Martindale, LF, was twice over buried & dug out on 30th & then this evening he was going off on a night fatigue near the front – happy as possible – I shall do all I can to get the CO to send his name in – as an example like that in a much shaken Coy is invaluable and all the more creditable when the (acting) Coy Commander is in such a shaky state." He had already commented that "Poor old Dick Bethell seems much aged and rattled since Thursday I hope he will be sent off for a change." Sir Iain Colquhoun was critical of the RFC's inability to drive off enemy planes and of the British anti-aircraft gunners' inability to hit any. On 1 April he "Sat in the ruins of the Cathedral, and wrote letters all morning. The sun was so hot, it was like summer. Had luncheon in the garden… This billet is just beside the Cloth Hall and Cathedral and there are still a few hyacinths blooming in the little shattered garden." On the 2nd he went up after dark with a working party of eighty to build a machine gun emplacement at Potijze and they all got back safely at midnight. Writing to Dinah on the 3rd he said "The last 4 days have been simply marvellous, I have had breakfast luncheon and tea out of doors each day and it is really almost too hot…Dick Bethell has gone home with nerves!! He's a rotter…I have got a very good souvenir I found it in the ruined cathedral here it is a 1700 bible or rather Missa (the Roman Catholic service) with the name of the place on it and some entries by the priests. It is very large and I will have some difficulty bringing it home…It is hard to get any letters away from here but this one goes by the Transport." Lieutenant Bethell did not serve with either Battalion again during the War. He had been shell shocked, tried to continue, but had to be sent down the line on the 2nd. He had also been wounded in the back. Major Barne wrote that "Several men still going away from "shell shock" – this generally continues for another 10 days. Dick Bethell I am glad to hear is to be sent away – his nerves seem completely gone."

In and out of the front line, Ypres and Poperinghe

Major Barne now had the, admittedly obvious, explanation for such shelling of Ypres at night as there was "owing to the transport which comes up, & right through as far as Potijze etc. The rattle on a still night can be heard for miles. Esmé has proposed that it should come up in motor lorries, but these apparently are not allowed beyond the town. It would be far less risky." They were very soon back in the line, from 3 to 7 April, in the same places as last time. As he always did beforehand, Sir Iain Colquhoun lectured all his NCOs that afternoon. The relief took four hours and from half past ten Major Barne and other officers from Battalion Headquarters "waited at the Menin Gate (which is really just a hole in the ramparts) for an hour or so to see the Coys pass before we went off – a very unpleasant wait there as a good deal of shelling going on in neighbourhood and one never quite knew when it would come our way." Two men were wounded by shrapnel on the way in and Sir Iain Colquhoun recorded "Machine guns and snipers very active all night." Major Barne and an orderly set off at half past four in the morning to visit the front line "which I found in an appalling state after a bombardment on the 30th, though meanwhile the Grenadiers had done their best. I slipped about & stuck in mud, caught in broken trench boards etc.; it was wonderful that the relief went as well as it did. A cold grey morning, such a change from yesterday which was grilling hot."

On the 4th the British heavy guns were to fire a major bombardment starting at half past ten in the morning and did so, but haze intervened and then the mist thickened in the evening and, as the artillery observers could no longer see, it was not as systematic as intended, but still enough to make life very uncomfortable above ground level and not much better below it, particularly since the German heavy gun at Pilckem started to shoot back at them in enfilade, as Major Barne noted, but "Luckily no damage was done to anybody, but more havoc to the trenches!" Sir Iain Colquhoun and C Company were in the front line. "The whole day everyone had to crouch under the parapet expecting them to retaliate, and there was not 20 seconds during which a shell of some kind was not whistling over one. If one moves about at all, their snipers are on to one, and it means sitting with one's ankles under water the whole day. We feel like rats in traps here…It is very bad for the men's moral." After dark he took Major Barne right along his front line, the latter seeing "all the bombing posts etc. of course having to keep very quiet, as the Germans have their listening posts close by. It is impossible to get along in the trench, so part of the way we go over ground, which personally I never very much care about." There was more of the same on the 5th, with four Scots Guardsmen losing their lives and sixteen wounded. To Major Barne "There were the usual many stories and narrow squeaks and altogether the Bn has been lucky considering the number of shells." Sir Iain Colquhoun estimated that 40% of all the heavy artillery shells fired by both sides were duds, but that the British fired more rounds altogether. As all the telephone wires were cut he could not communicate with anyone until after dark. When they were reconnected a handwritten message reached Battalion Headquarters in the early evening that German listening apparatus could pick up any telephone conversation within 1500 yards. This led to changes to the planned swapping over of companies and so Major Barne went off to brief Captain Ross verbally "and there is a general stir up, in consequence of the hasty alteration." As Sir Iain Colquhoun went back later from the front line he found the communication trench "Duke Street had been completely blown in, and we had to go across the open most of the way." Then at the support line he found that most of the dug-outs had also been blown in. However, during the next day "Practically no shelling near us all morning, and the relief is beyond all description. Hugh Ross & I sat in our own dug-out all day and enjoyed the rest."

Major Barne left at two in the morning on the 6th to visit the companies and was out for nearly three hours in which he found "the going is much worse than y'day, the night much darker, the line very thinly held – partly owing to the bombardments there is less room for them, and partly owing to our many casualties and sick our numbers have very seriously dwindled. The men are somewhat rattled and their nerves have not recovered… and until we get a new draft or a longish rest they won't appreciate the honour of being in the trenches. I found Ross & Luss both very cheerful – in fact all the officers are – but they say the men have temporarily deteriorated." General Feilding came to visit them and with him General Ponsonby, always an active and frequent visitor to the line, whatever was going on. "Sure enough a prisoner had a notebook containing everything sent on the telephone by one of our Battns near St Eloi. A comparatively quiet day. No shelling of front trenches, though a good bit round Bn HQ, luckily nothing big on the dug-outs – or I should probably not be here to write this. In evening the 4 men killed on 5th are buried just outside our dug-outs – in the dark – 2 RCs by Father Knapp – & 2 others by Rogers, the C of E chaplain to the Bde, Gillieson being unable to get up here. The RC service usually takes 20 minutes on active service but in the dark barely 5! Whether there was too much machine gun fire going on at the time, or whether the Priest had forgotten the words of the service I don't know." He was then surprised when Lord Esmé Gordon Lennox "forbade me to go round the line during the night – why I can't think – which was a real disappointment as I particularly wanted to see the Left Flank Coy and Tim O E, and the other officers who I believe really like to see a visitor up there, even though such a dull one as myself." He was in for another quite different surprise. "Who should suddenly appear out of a hole in my dug-out but a stoat, quite tame. I amuse myself now every evening by sawing firewood – there are heaps of broken trees and branches about everywhere ready for sawing up. This old Chateau and its surroundings must have been formerly very charming."

The Reverend Guy Rogers, a Church of England padre, was posted to the Brigade the previous autumn, but was disconcerted to find himself based with a field ambulance and not nearer the centre of things. Then he realised that he was under careful scrutiny. In order to do his job and be available to help where he felt he could contribute most, once others were persuaded that this was desirable, he was settled at Brigade Headquarters. There, under General Ponsonby's wing, he was completely accepted. This did not mean that he did not get into embarrassing situations. He made the mistake of saying in the presence of the Earl of Clanwilliam, the Assistant Provost Marshal, that the Orangemen in Northern Ireland had caused as much difficulty and trouble as the Sinn Feiners. A serious row followed. This led to his being told off by the Senior Chaplain of the Guards Division and warned to keep clear of politics. General Ponsonby's view was predictable, given his approach to life, "Is it true that one was a Sinn Feiner and the other an Orangeman? In that case, you can believe neither of them. The case is dismissed." Padre Rogers had some difficulty in understanding the different regimental idiosyncrasies of the Foot Guards and in what he thought was harmless conversation would make faux pas about which General Ponsonby, who had chosen his nickname, gently chided him "Rogerum, it is your duty as a good Guardsman to know these things and to know them accurately." The Reverend "Tubby" Williams stated that "Rogerum" was a song version of the parable of Dives and Lazarus, part of the repertoire of "The Fancies," and that the 6th Division also sang it on the march.

Padre Rogers could have been referring to these burials when he wrote "The Guards expected their padres, once they had taken them to their bosom (the metaphor seems singularly inapt), to share their dangers with them. If they disliked their padre, they left him with the baggage. I remember once being summoned to take a funeral at an unpleasant place called Hellfire Corner. The padre, not one of our's, whose duty it was to take it, had been left behind with the baggage, and it never occurred to them that their likes and dislikes might have particular consequences for other people. I argued the matter on ethical grounds on my return, much to their amusement, needless to say." He was a great admirer of Father Knapp. A stray kitten, which General Ponsonby had adopted and named Pop-it, thereafter had to play its part in the life of the mess. In 1917, having been approached to do so, Padre Rogers left the Army to take over the Parish of West Ham and it was not long before Pop-it was living at the vicarage.

One of the four who died on the 5th was a reservist called up in August 1914. Private John McKenna was born in Clogher, County Tyrone, and, once a country labourer, joined up in Edinburgh in 1905 and served for three years. He missed the Retreat from Mons and arrived in a draft before the Aisne, where he was wounded in the left foot on 19 September and eventually evacuated to England, reappearing in the winter of 1915. He and Alice McKenna married in London in 1908 and she was living in Haringey. They did not have any children. The second was Private James Gorman, a miner and September 1914 volunteer in Edinburgh, in France since March 1915. Only his identity disc and a belt reached his wife Helen in Forth, Lanarkshire. They had married nearly seven years before in Fauldhouse and had a daughter in 1910. The third was Private James White who was thirty five. He volunteered in March 1915 in Chester and was a draper. His parents were dead and his nearest relative was his sister Margaret, living at Mere, Cheshire. Some of his belongings reached her, but not his cigarette case, which she pointed out. She also wrote to ask the Regiment to keep the diary he was writing up till "this dreadful war is over." It never came to light. She added that he never mentioned the War in his letters. The fourth, Private Christopher Jones, was almost thirty seven when he died, a commercial traveller who enlisted in April 1915. His wife Isabella came from Falkirk, but they had been in Edinburgh since they married in 1907. They had a daughter and a son. Some of his possessions reached her. When he was hit was not recorded but Private Peter McCarthy, a Liverpudlian coal heaver, died of wounds on the 7th in a casualty clearing station. He volunteered in January 1915, when it was noted that he had a full set of upper false teeth. He and Margaret McCarthy, of Bootle, married in 1912 and had two very young sons. His belongings, sent to her at the end of June, consisted of his identity disc, a prayer book, letters, a photo case, five photos, a steel mirror, a razor, a lighter, a fountain pen, a metal ring, a crucifix, a packet of Roman Catholic emblems and his false teeth. Privates White, Jones and McCarthy all arrived at the Hohenzollern early in October 1915. Company Sergeant Major Cecil "Nobby" Clarke was badly wounded in the right knee and thigh on the 5th and died on the 24th at Étaples. During the fighting at the Hohenzollern he became Company Sergeant Major of B Company where Private Cumming first saw him coming round a corner with three bloodstained identity discs. Private John Maxwell, a gamekeeper, enlisted after Christmas 1914 in Dumfries, near where his parents lived at Auldgirth, though his wife Williamina and their two very young daughters were in Gretna Green. Private Maxwell arrived in the Battalion on 14 October 1915 at the Hohenzollern. Evacuated now with wounds to both his arms, his right leg, his face and around his eyes, he recovered and would return.

Generally the enemy guns did not fire much at night, although they were well aware that it was then that all British reliefs, trench and route improvement work went on, just as their own did. So, strange as it seemed, the immediate area of Ypres itself was often relatively safe then and on their way back from the trenches in the dark on the 7th the Battalion marched through the Menin Gate, across the Square past the wrecked Cloth Hall and on to the train to Vlamertinghe. Major Barne had gone on ahead to wait for them "but by 2.30 when the train has to go only 2½ coys have arrived. Another train goes at 3.30am, without any warning, leaving about 6 officers and 40 men behind. The CO is dragged on by unknown hands at last moment – those left – including myself – start walking, but soon meet a train which is lucky, about 4.15am when getting light and we get into our Camp A without further adventure. The train could not have gone any later, & had we had to walk all the way, would very likely have been shelled. The camp is quite a good one, just wooden huts dotted about irregularly to avoid being spotted by Aeroplanes – & surrounded by trees and so unseen from German lines." That evening he "Saw a Zeppelin sailing over the German line at dusk." Late the next day Sir Iain Colquhoun eventually went home on leave to Rossdhu. Letter after letter he had sent his wife had raised his and her hopes and then dashed them because of local circumstances and changes. Travelling with him as far as London was Captain Norman who was going over briefly in order to receive his MC at Buckingham Palace. It was still at that time standard practice for officers from the BEF to go back specially to receive their gallantry medals from the King.

Major Barne heard that on the 10th Private Montague Dade of the 2nd Grenadiers had accosted Company Quartermaster Sergeant Lemon of Left Flank to ask after him. Private Dade, from Yoxford, Suffolk, had worked as a gamekeeper for Major Barne before joining the Grenadiers in 1913. He survived the first two years of the War unscathed but was hit in both feet six months later on the Somme and thereafter remained in England. Major Barne had "tried to find him several times but always just miss him." After being fine for several days it poured on the 11th and that night while the officers were having dinner the SOS message arrived "signifying that the Germans "have popped their parapet", so for a while there is preparation to move out, but after an hour or so all the excitement is over & we turn in. Apparently somebody in the 20th Div on our left had "got the wind up" which is the popular expression for being jumpy – I hear some funny conversation amongst the signallers on the subject. When all the episode is over they said "the wind is away"." Two days later they heard that the Germans did make three small raids on the 20th Division, getting into their trenches in one place, but leaving some twenty five dead lying out in the open in another. More rain followed on the 12th and leave was suddenly stopped, so abruptly that Lieutenant Schiff was called back before even leaving Poperinghe. On the 14th Sir Herbert Plumer visited them and Major Barne watched as he "struggled about in the mud" on his way to watch training. "He looks 70, tho' the papers call him only 59! He has the most comical face, wears an eye glass, & is just like the typical

General depicted in Punch. I hope he learned something by coming here." That evening there was a battalion concert in the Church Army Hut. On the 15th Major Barne was "Woken up at 6.30am by sounds of apparent rapid fire, which lasted ¾ hr. This turned out to be some Coldstream Ammunn Supply on fire about 500 yds away – a great many thousand rounds must have been destroyed." Lieutenant David Brand returned. "The last time I saw him was crawling back on all fours after being wounded at Loos." That was his second wound, the first having been in a grenade accident. The enemy were never to be underestimated. On the 10th German aircraft dropped bombs nearby and were very busy early on the 16th, which may have been connected to a German heavy battery soon afterwards shelling a point in the woods about half a mile north where there were more camps.

On 17 April a novel piece of captured equipment was put on display at Headquarters Guards Division, a "German instrument for picking up signals". The Battalion Sports took place that afternoon, which included a race in full marching order with gas helmets on. In the officers handicap, half a yard for each year of age, Lord Esmé Gordon Lennox came third, 2nd Lieutenant Ronnie Powell, a very recent arrival, second, while the winner, as effective on his own feet as on a horse, was Lieutenant Bewicke. The son of the Reverend Robert Powell and his wife Mary, Lieutenant Powell had been at Eton and Trinity College, Cambridge, and rowed for the University in the 1904, 1905 and 1906 Boat Races. With another oarsman he won the Silver Goblets at Henley in both 1906 and 1907 and then went to farm in Australia. That day 2nd Lieutenant Grey "Guy" Leach arrived. He went to Uppingham, enlisted in the first week of the War in the 1/5th East Surrey Regiment, Territorials, and soon afterwards sailed with them to India. As the British Regular battalions in India were sent on active service Territorial ones replaced them in the garrisons. In December 1915 he was commissioned into the Scots Guards. Sir Iain Colquhoun was meant to return on the 21st but was summoned back early by telegram on the 17th, without explanation, only learning later why those then on leave were all called back, just to reduce the traffic pressure at Easter. The night train from Glasgow did not reach London early enough for him to get on the leave train next day and on the 19th he was very sick on a very rough crossing to Boulogne. He then had a six hour wait and so went to a hospital to have lunch with Lieutenants Frank Ward, originally loaned from the 2nd Battalion after Puits 14 Bis, and Frank Mann, a more recent arrival, the two officers wounded on 30 March. Lieutenant Mann had been at Malvern and played cricket for Cambridge University and Middlesex. Later he would captain England.

The first thing that Major Barne did on the 18th was "by request of the Padre, to witness a very odd little show; namely about 7 men of the Battn being admitted into the Church of Scotland & receiving the Sacraments for the first time." Then he went to Poperinghe to be president of a court martial which convicted and sentenced a Grenadier to 42 days FP No 1 for overstaying his leave in England and found a NCO of the 20th Hussars, attached to the Guards Division as a military policeman, Not Guilty of drunkenness. Later, during a walk, he discovered that the shelling to the north two days before had landed mainly on sham gun positions. He saw "a dummy gun in a wood, dreadful havoc among the trees." They were preparing again for the line and a party of officers and sergeants went up to familiarise themselves with the left hand brigade sector, the front line just east of Wieltje on the Ypres-Poelcapelle road. The 6th Division, now replacing the Guards Division in reserve, had battalions moving into the Vlamertinghe camps. Lieutenant Colonel Ernest Stracey, commanding the 9th Norfolks, was the elder brother of Captain Reggie Stracey, killed on New Year's Day 1915 at the Railway

Triangle at Cuinchy. The 9th Suffolk Regiment were also now nearby. In both Major Barne looked for and found people whom he knew from home.

In the evening on the 19th he went up with the Battalion in the train to Ypres, "but after 5 minutes the train pulled up, a shell having bust up the rails, & we walked along the line. There was considerable shelling in the countryside from about 6pm onwards, and it soon became evident that something unusual was up." As they approached Ypres a Welsh Guards officer met them to say that, instead of relieving the 4th Grenadiers in the line as planned, they were to go into the reserve positions in the Prison and neighbouring cellars and wait there. He said that the Germans were attacking the British trenches and so the Welsh Guards had been called forward. Major Barne heard "various rumours, including one that our 2nd Battn had been badly handled." They had been, at Wieltje. About midnight word came that the shelling had died down and none of the enemy were left in the front trenches. The relief then went ahead, the 1st Coldstream taking over from the badly shelled 2nd Battalion and the 1st Scots Guards taking over in two hours, very quick, from the 4th Grenadiers, immediately to the left of where they had been the first two times in the Salient. The Grenadiers had lost men in the German shelling, but had not been attacked. They had, however, caught a German prisoner from the *236th Regiment*, two of whose fingers the 1st Scots Guards Medical Officer had to amputate. Next day Major Barne "Saw swallow over front line." This tour was much quieter and only two men were wounded over four days. Good Friday was on the 21st and in the small hours Major Barne set off round the front trenches with one of the battalion orderlies, Private William Moss, "who sounds very different to what he really is (the best) and I think we may have been spotted from the German lines when against the moon, now very low down. Anyhow a bouquet of bullets splattered on the ground and buildings (we were going up "overland") all round us. Found the Coys in front line had done quite a lot of work, clearing wreckage, draining & wiring front, tho' owing to bright night they had to knock off this, having had a machine gun switched onto them. Got back at 5am, a glorious morning, wood pigeon cooing in the Potijze wood." Private Moss was a plasterer in Leeds, served eight years and then went to the Reserve just before Christmas 1912, he and Clare Moss having married in Fulham a few days earlier. Their daughter was born not long before the War and he was mobilised, going out at once, but first joining the Battalion on 20 September 1914 on the Aisne.

The artillery duels, though noisy, went on elsewhere by day and night, but there was much more aerial activity with the brighter, clearer weather. The British anti-aircraft guns, "our "Archibald"…or "Coughing Kate" (there are also other names) being kept pretty busy," but wholly without results to show for it, as Major Barne could see. He was soon again in command. Lord Esmé Gordon Lennox was sick again with flu or something similar, tried to cope in the Battalion Headquarters dug-out, failed and was sent down the line. About half past five on Good Friday a German plane flew very low over them and they fired vigorously at it with rifles and Lewis Guns "at which he laughed heartily." Bad weather, the 22nd being very wet, had the disadvantage of added discomfort, but also an advantage, as Sir Iain Colquhoun noted, "Pouring rain, and scarcely a shell fired all day." He had returned from his cut short leave the afternoon before and managed to write to his wife, from whom five letters had arrived. "The bunch of primroses in one of them is hanging up in the dug-out now." They both frequently sent one another flowers with their letters. "I shan't get the parcel you sent me till Monday as they can't come up here but it will keep all right. The others never opened the other parcel with the haggis etc it might be in great condition now."

At three on Easter Morning Major Barne set off again with Private Moss to the line "having an unpleasant but exciting journey thither as enemy machine guns very active. I found afterwards the reason was that the RF "Listening Post" had been spotted going out and the enemy wanted to try and make sure of getting them coming in at dawn. However they got in without adventure – or casualty. Heard the cuckoo." He then went on to describe the trees coming out wherever there were still branches "some very fine specimens, clean tall stems." After he had got into his bunk that night he had a visitor. On the right the 2nd Coldstream had come into the line and Lieutenant Colonel Gilbert "Gillie" Follett, now commanding, appeared and disturbed him. He "asked every sort of question about our line, which his Bn is to have next time, and made me draw a map. It was rather tiresome, the night being short as it is, and I told him I was available all the following day. He was very solemn and pompous." Lieutenant Miller had to go sick with a poisoned foot, 2nd Lieutenant Robert Smith Cunningham was seriously wounded in the ankle on the 23rd, accidentally, by a bayonet, and two other officers were unwell, Lieutenant Powell sticking it out better than the other. Lieutenant Smith Cunningham, a Scot by birth though his home was at Godstone, Surrey, had been to Harrow and was already in his late twenties when the War came. In October 1915 he was commissioned from the Inns of Court Officers Training Corps and after a few weeks in France arrived in the Battalion in January 1916. Because of this injury he was at home for five months, not returning until October.

The German planes were very active on the 24th. Three British anti-aircraft shells came down on the parapet of one of Sir Iain Colquhoun's platoons without going off, but a fourth exploded on landing on another platoon's parapet, hurting no one. "The men got the nose cap etc." That night they went back into reserve at Ypres, staying there for the next four days. Lord Esmé Gordon Lennox was now in hospital and sent up the plovers eggs that someone had given him. Major Barne sent "our thanks by pigeon post." From time to time there was German shelling in Ypres but they lived in those buildings with good cellars and others, such as the Prison, robustly enough built to withstand most of what might hit them. There was no incentive to venture out unless one had to and if one had to it was to go out on the incessant fatigue parties. Major Barne met the Town Major, Captain George Wigram of the KRRC, "a huge rifleman, who also lives in the prison…who complains that the shelling of the town has recently increased owing to troops' carelessness walking about and showing themselves in the streets, so I issue a long winded Battn order on the subject." When he came to dinner the next night Captain Wigram objected to the Scots Guards Lewis Gun set up on the roof to shoot at aircraft on the grounds that he was "more or less permanent here, & we are only visitors and he will get the benefit, not us, of anything rash that might be done! I don't blame him." They had orders to have Lewis Guns manned night and day for this purpose. Town majors were the military equivalent of civilian mayors, but responsible only for local military administration and liaison with the civil authorities. There was very heavy firing, apparently German, towards St Eloi so they thought, through the evening of 25 April and on till two in the morning. Later they heard that the Canadians had been attacked there and lost four hundred yards of their front and support trenches before retaking them.

Major Barne went to see C Company in the Canal Bank dug-outs on the evening of the 26th. "I find them amusing themselves trying to cross the canal in a tub – shooting with a small rook rifle at bottles etc, & Luss tries some fishing with my hooks, but I don't think does much good." In his letter home next day Sir Iain Colquhoun wrote "I have been shooting bottles and sparrows with my revolver I also tried to fish in the canal but got nothing as it is all choked up with weeds, etc." There had been another attack on the Canadians and another successful counterattack. "I got my disk and the gold earring the day after I arrived…The electric torch also turned up and is very useful…Send me one or two mealy puddings when you have time and some scones, they would carry quite well. I heard the cuckoo for the first time the day before yesterday." Dinah Colquhoun sent him quantities of food, including game, cooked and uncooked, haggis, white or mealy puddings, kippers and sometimes fresh fruit and arranged for Fortnum & Mason to send out delicacies such as the "sweets, quails, (tinned) dates and pullets." He told her these had arrived recently. They had failed to include some other things which had been ordered. He wore the gold earring.

By the 28th, while Major Barne was "Getting rather tired of being in prison", Sir Iain Colquhoun was completely relaxed at the Canal Bank with Captain Ross. "The transport brought up the gramophone and a set of pipes last night. Hugh and I played them all morning. Sat in the sun all afternoon, and watched aeroplanes." Next day they were due to go back to the line after dark. Major Barne and Lieutenant Brand went for a walk "to look at some little gardens with lilies of the valley & other spring flowers coming out apace, then poked about near Ramparts on S side of town – very picturesque – and Railway Station. In afternoon am sent for by Brigadier who tells me several points concerning work to be done in line during our 3 days." Sir Iain Colquhoun had problems in C Company because Lieutenant Powell had now been sent on a sniping officer's course, Lieutenant Bewicke was on leave, 2nd Lieutenant Malcolm Menzies, a new arrival who had only been through one trench tour, had gone down with nerves, but not away long, and Company Sergeant Major Pyper had flu. He borrowed another newly arrived officer, 2nd Lieutenant Francis Fenner. The relief went quickly, without incident, and all was quiet until about an hour past midnight. Then, in Major Barne's words, "there begins & continues till nearly 3am the most intense bombardment ever heard away to the South. Presently a message arrives from Bde saying the Germans are making a gas attack at Messines." In the early morning he went round the line. "The enemy the previous night had made a bombing attack in a small way so we are doing all the wiring we can to prevent them getting right in." That was why throughout the hours of darkness on 30 April and 1 May Sir Iain Colquhoun worked with half his men repairing their parapet in the front line, standing up in front to do so, while Lieutenant Fenner and the other half worked on the barbed wire out in front. Lieutenant Menzies transferred in August 1915 from the 3rd Royal Scots and was the younger brother of Lieutenant Alastair Graham Menzies, killed on New Year's Day 1915 at the Railway Triangle at Cuinchy. Lieutenant Fenner, educated at Felsted and now thirty eight, joined the Scots Guards within days of Lieutenant Menzies. His parents Dr Robert and Mary Fenner lived in Marylebone.

There was shelling through the afternoon of the 30th, the only casualty in the front line being a man who had a rib broken by a bit of shell but Company Quartermaster Sergeant Stewart Davidson of Right Flank and two men with him were wounded walking across the square in Ypres. He, formerly a railway clerk in Glasgow, had been serving for fifteen years, starting with the later stages of the Boer War. He was wounded three times, all of them at Ypres, first by a bullet in the thigh near Nonne Boschen during First Ypres, then by this shell in the neck and lastly by a bullet in the right shoulder in September 1917 during Third Ypres. The third wound put him out of the War, but he returned after the Armistice. His home was at Ardvorlich, Perthshire. As dawn was approaching on 1 May Major Barne and Private Moss were still out visiting the front line. There was a shower of bullets as they walked in the open and he resolved that "the Bosch always starts this sort of thing just before dawn, so I vow tomorrow either to go up earlier or else up a communication trench, the worst of which however is that it takes a long time." Most of that day's shelling was long range and went over their heads but Lance Sergeant Frederick Bassett was wounded for the second time. A London draper's packer from Hoxton until he enlisted in 1912, he was in the 2nd Battalion to begin with and survived First Ypres and everything else that followed in 1914 and 1915 until as a Lance Sergeant he was hit in the left arm at Hill 70. Sent to England to recover, he was only there for six weeks, but enough time for him to do something unrecorded for which he was reduced to Corporal. Not long after he returned to the BEF, this time to the 1st Scots Guards, he was promoted again. Now he was evacuated home once more, hit in the right knee and buttocks by shell fragments, but returned three months later. He finally left in November when he became an officer in the 2nd Essex. Later Major Barne remarked that "A notice board is put up on the German parapet saying "Kut has fallen, Rule Britannia!" this the same day as the bad news appears in the London Papers." Since the beginning of December 1915 Major General Sir Charles Townshend and the Poona Division of the Indian Army had been besieged by the Turks at Kut el Amara on the River Tigris. When they might still have been able to break out they were ordered not to and all subsequent relief operations failed.

After dark "A listening post – consisting of a hole not far outside our wire which is nightly occupied by us & has been for a long time, is approached about 9.30 by our listening patrol – on arriving there they receive a volley – 2 of them Cpl Miller & Wishart fall dead into the post: the 3rd runs back through the gap in our wire & falls wounded by six bullets into our trench – Ashton – feared by the Dr to be fatal. The Germans had evidently crept along an old bank right up to the place, the mystery is how they knew exactly where it was, and it shows how carefully they watch & study our actions, no doubt for many nights they had laid out watching the arrival of this patrol. It is easy to be wise after the event, but now one sees the folly of these fixed listening posts. It is far better to be out anywhere in the open. Our men have no cunning about them, I have noticed it both in this war and in S Africa, they shrink from doing anything which is not quite straightforward, and are quite content walking bolt upright straight ahead rather than crouch or take any of the natural precautions, when they do take precautions it is only being made to do so by an officer who they invariably put down as "having the wind up"." Lance Corporal Hugh Miller was the youngest of the three, aged twenty two. Born and brought up in San Fernando, Trinidad, his next of kin was his aunt Jean Miller at Mauchline, Ayrshire. Before enlisting in January 1915 he was an agricultural student and arrived in the BEF in October, being promoted to Lance Corporal two months later. Private George Wishart was a watchmaker, apparently working in Crieff, Perthshire, where he volunteered in October 1914. He had been in the Battalion for a little over three months. George and Jessie Wishart lived at Kemnay, Aberdeenshire. Private John Ashton was the first of the three to join up, at the end of August 1914 in Liverpool, where William and Elizabeth Ashton lived in West Derby. To begin with he was in the 2nd Battalion in the early spring of 1915 until hit in the right shoulder at Neuve Chapelle and sent home. When he next came out four months later he never joined either Battalion in the field because he was sent home with piles. His third arrival in France was on New Year's Day 1916 when he was sent to the 1st Scots Guards. He was carried in after the ambush, shot in the right shoulder, left arm, bladder and right leg. Unable to survive these wounds, he died at quarter past five in the evening on 3 May in a casualty clearing station. He had directed that his belongings should go to his sister Ellen and that was done.

At half past nine on the morning of the 2nd the German guns opened up and Major Barne regretted "Another instance of our lack of cunning…some new work we have recently done has been blown in…because we have failed to disguise our new work." These were the repairs that C Company and others had been doing two nights before. "Luckily only one man was slightly wounded tho' ½ buried and much "shaken"." During the night their 2nd Battalion had come into the line on the right and for twenty four hours the two were side by side for the first time in the trenches at Ypres. Major Barne went to dinner with Colonel Tempest shortly before their undisturbed relief later on, but "2 of our pioneers are badly wounded in Vlamertinghe, having got a lift in a RE wagon & an unlucky shell catching them, one driver being killed & one losing a leg." Through April and May Private Fleming wrote mostly about fatigues at Ypres. For these they were billeted in the Prison if the work, such as helping the Royal Engineers on the Ramparts, was in Ypres itself, but if it was for the troops in the front line, such as taking up rations or wiring, the most usual billet was in one of the many dug-outs in the Canal Bank. These met with his approval for on 29 April he "went into dug-outs on Canal Bank. Very good too." Later he would remark on their electric lighting. Whenever he could Major Barne was out walking, looking at the country, the ruins, the cemeteries, the flowers and the trees. On 10 May, when they were at Poperinghe, he "sat in a wood listening to a nightingale." After being released from hospital Lord Esmé Gordon Lennox went on home leave but was now back.

There was a distinct pattern into which they were settled and there was, for some time, little that was distinctive that occurred in or out of the line. The casualties were usually few and almost less likely in the front line than from shelling further back. New and returning officers arrived by ones and twos, some of them accompanying smaller or larger drafts of men. Among the new ones was 2nd Lieutenant Dudley Shortt, educated at Charterhouse, the son of Edward and Isabella Shortt. Edward Shortt was a Liberal MP from the Northeast of England and a supporter of David Lloyd George, then Minister of Munitions. Another was Lieutenant Mark Tennant, Dinah Colquhoun's brother, who had transferred from the 1/4th Seaforths, Territorials. On 3 May her husband told her that her brother "looks very well". He was deliberately sent to another company. In the same letter was the news that four of his men had been struck by lightning the day before, not apparently seriously.

They had been at Poperinghe since 4 May and as soon as it was dark on the 11th went up by train to Ypres, where Major Barne found Battalion Headquarters "billeted this time in a cellar, the Companies being divided up in barracks – a Convent & the Ramparts. Some shelling of the town (Pop) in morning, one shell catching the 1st Coldm billets, killing 9 men & wounding 9 more, besides some RE & civilians." The War Diary referred to "casualties also including women." Major Barne had "Quite a comfortable night in the cellar, though a bit stuffy & smelly. Walked round some of the billets in morning with Luss and Tim O E – saw where they lived, both in cellars, quite safe ones to all appearances." He excepted from this a direct hit by one of the heaviest German guns, frequent enough around here in the past, but now, he supposed, all at Verdun. On the evening of the 12th they took over from the 2nd Battalion again in front of Potijze, with the 1st Coldstream again on their right as far as the Menin Road. Company Sergeant Major Pyper was slightly wounded in the right leg by shellfire as he and Sir Iain Colquhoun marched side by side just beyond the Menin Gate. He was only away for ten days. This was his only wound, though he had been slightly shell shocked previously. Later he became a Drill Sergeant in the 2nd Battalion. In December 1916 he and Barbara Black married at Newton, West Lothian. Just after the relief was over Major Barne saw "an inferno of shrapnel" landing behind them just where the outgoing 2nd Battalion Headquarters might be on the way out "to say nothing of Ration Parties and out going relief etc. It is quite marvellous how few casualties there are at times like this." Next day there was bad news. "We had our poor mess cart driver killed by a shell at the Menin Gate last night and the officers' trench kit limber driver wounded rather badly." Private Robert Fullerton, who was killed, was a former Scots Guardsman and a gas stoker until he rejoined in February 1915, aged thirty three. In view of his previous service it was a matter of only three months before he came to France, joining the Battalion straight away. His mother Grace Fullerton was in Glasgow. Private William Dobbie, from Auchentoshan Terrace, Glasgow, had only been back with the Battalion five weeks after being wounded in the left leg at Puits 14 Bis. There his neighbour in the same street in Springburn, Private David Gallacher, was killed. A shell hit him in the thigh on the 12th and he was sent home a second time to hospital, but would return. Private Frank Hudson's job before, aged just nineteen, he enlisted in February 1915 at Preston was as flag man for a steam roller. He was in the large October draft that arrived at the Hohenzollern. Hit in the head on the 12th by a shell, he died three days later. To begin with all that was sent to Robert and Margaret Hudson at their home off New Hall Lane, Preston, were their son's identity disc and two metal rings. On 9 August Margaret Hudson acknowledged receipt of these but wrote to Regimental Headquarters that "I am not at all satisfied there are other articles that I know he had on him when he was shot he had a watch I only sent him at the beginning of March I want to know what as become of that I think that ought to have come back by all means unless some mean contemptible fellow as pinched it from him after he was shot & if a fellow will rob a poor lad of what he as after he as been killed he ought to be shot to[o]." Enquiries revealed that Private Hudson had only had with him the disc and rings when he was brought into the casualty clearing station where he died. However, fortunately and unusually, his pack must then have been found because a month later more possessions of his were sent to his home, a wallet and letters, a belt with a badge, a pipe, a knife, two coins, a chain and medallion, a metal watch (broken), a note book and a piece of shell. Margaret Hudson wrote that she had "received all with thanks quite safe."

In the small hours of the 13th Lord Esmé Gordon Lennox and Major Barne went round the line, taking an hour and a half. On went the shelling and then at about two in the morning the rain started. Major Barne was grateful that the rain was "luckily warm. The Chateau grounds are getting more & more like a wilderness & less & less like a garden." In the evening he went to see Lieutenant Orr Ewing and B Company in the support position known as the Potijze defences "and inspected the graveyard where many of our men killed on Mar 30th are buried. It has been much knocked about & is full of shellholes." As a result of all that the other two brigades had done the trenches and dug-outs were in much better condition than when they had known them previously, but there was still work to do. As he always did every night, Major Barne went round the line, this time starting late on the 14th and visiting "every part of it including the bombing posts between us & Coldstream. Got horribly scared when going through the watery derelict trench near the Gulley by a machine gun from near Railway Wood, the bullets seemed to rake down the trench & hit the sides close to me, so I sat right down in the water, my dignity had to suffer, but there was no one to see & only a born fool would have remained standing up. As it is there is a scrape on my helmet, whether from a bullet or no I cannot say a bullet we all think it must be! Found L Norman anything but happy, he is in quite an isolated bit & nobody can blame him for not enjoying it. The men are pretty damp too – raining all night – steady drizzle, but warm. Got back to Bn HQ at 3.30am slept till 9am found that they had been shelled steadily all night, everybody had narrow squeaks including the Dr who was very eloquent on the subject." The Gully or Gulley was a part of the trench close to the railway on the right of their front line.

A Lieutenant French of the Royal Engineers, nicknamed "Slinks", was the Brigade Signal Officer. That night Major Barne described him having "an apparatus for listening to German telephones" and how he "had to crawl out to lay a wire as near as possible to the German lines, if possible right up to their wire. He gets about ¾ of the way over, is covered by a party from C Coy, then returns. Time will show how much German conversation we shall hear. A C Coy man gets sniped through the head, otherwise no casualties today." Also during the night Right Flank had changed places with Left Flank and were in the most awkward part of the front line trenches, including the Gully. Private Fleming commented "The Gulley very wet and no dug-out. Rigged my oil sheet. Went on digging all night. Not bad." Fatigue parties were building up and strengthening fortified posts within the trench system. While Major Barne and the other officers at Battalion Headquarters were having lunch on the 15th "a shell burst outside the CO's dug-out wounding a RE there – he would have been killed had it not been for his steel helmet – breaking in the window & shattering the CO's shaving soap, iron jug and mug." Late in the evening he set off on his own going round slowly to see the men working and again visiting the two isolated bombing posts to the right of the Battalion's trenches, the link with the Coldstream. Meanwhile, Lord Esmé Gordon Lennox, going round separately, "found a man in Duke Street hammering in a stake and singing at the top of his voice – between the two making a horrible noise. When asked if this was quite necessary he replied he thought he would try & drown the noise of the hammering, so that the Germans should not hear!"

From early on the 16th they were in Ypres for four days of fatigues, working on defence works, and a lot of shelling, believed to be trying to hit concealed British batteries. Because of the fine weather both sides' planes were very evident and the connection between aerial reconnaissance and subsequent shelling was becoming very well coordinated. Private Fleming had some spare time on the 18th and "Had a walk round old Ypres. She has had an awful bashing." Padre Rogers saw Randall Davidson, the Archbishop of Canterbury, in his clerical garb and steel helmet in Ypres that day and remarked that "though his legs were rooted in tradition, his head was moving with the times." He thought this "one of the sights of the war." Major Barne "met him in a street in the town, long black coat, black buskins and – a steel helmet on his head! He looked rather out of place and very hot! He had been going to lunch with the Brigadier, who was much disappointed, as he wanted to make him stand on a chair as he always does anybody who commits any mistake at a meal. Spent most of the day in our little back garden writing reading & gardening – in evening walked round some of the billets and to Rly Stn with Tim, where found some rly tickets etc for the children."

Ypres still had novelties. Major Barne and Captain Thompson went on the 20th "to look at the Horn Works a sort of outwork, E of the town, had to go through the "Sallyport" under the Ramparts & across a temporary wooden bridge over the moat or canal, & there found the most interesting subterranean vaults & passages at which our men are constantly at work, under the RE, improving & developing for use in case we have to hold this line at any time. These vaults etc were only recently discovered by somebody at the British Museum. We are rather amused to see in the "Daily Liar" just what we had anticipated – namely that some patrol has been brilliant enough to discover – & cut – the wire which runs over to the German wire, laid with much trouble & care & risk by the RE officer some nights ago – for the purpose of listening to German telephones." Then, "This afternoon up in the line a garrison gunner was wounded out in an isolated trench, so far as I can make out, he was the sentry & by himself looking after a trench mortar. One of our men, a machine gunner went out to help him and got killed whereupon Stirling – of this Battn – machine gun officer – went out in broad daylight and carried both in to safety – one after the other tho' unfortunately one was past all help. Stirling himself had his haversack riddled, but was unwounded. I know him to be a very cool person having seen him wandering up to the line overland one morning, just after daylight, when all shooting usually stops, though of course had he been spotted he would have received a very warm welcome. I hear he has been recommended by the Brigadier for reward. Since writing above I find he has been awarded a Military Cross tho' in any former war he would have received a VC." Lieutenant Gordon Stirling's parents lived in Salmon Arm, British Columbia. On the outbreak of war he enlisted in the ranks of Lord Strathcona's Horse and was among the first Canadian troops to arrive in England, in time to take part in the 1914 Lord Mayor's Show in London. Fairly soon after that he joined the Royal Horse Guards and served in France as a remount officer on a temporary commission before receiving a Special Reserve commission when he transferred to the Scots Guards. Though a member of the Battalion, he was detached to the 2nd Guards Brigade Machine Gun Company. At Ypres he found a small abandoned dog in the ruins, very weak from starvation and very frightened, but won her trust and took her on. Her name was Wipers. They became well known and inseparable and he took her with him on leave to England.

On the 20th Major Barne continued "An unfortunate shell landed just outside a LF dug-out in the Ramparts, killing one man & wounding another. This was a very bad piece of luck – the shell landing between the dug-out and the parados, in the trench as it were. A very quiet day and evening, when we march down to the Asylum Siding to catch the 9pm train – allowing 20 mins for entraining. We had no sooner got there than the Germans began putting shrapnel very near, but this only lasted a few minutes, so we made up our minds it was intended for some Battery. All was then quiet for a while, when they began again this time just over our heads, between the Rly line & the road, but with some heavy stuff. At last the train came in at 9.30 and we were off by 9.40pm there was not much time wasted in entraining …the last shot was uncomfortably close to the Battn crowded along the line." Private Robert Martin was killed, a gardener who joined up in December 1914 and arrived in France ten months later. Unusually, two, rather than one, identity discs reached Robert and Elsie Martin at Inchture to the west of Dundee, with a number of other possessions, including three clasp knives, a ring and a cap badge, his wallet and his purse.

When they got out of the train from Ypres they were to go into Camp L at Poperinghe, but found the 1st Coldstream in it and had to go to Camp K instead. That evening the Division became the reserve division and so everyone was around Poperinghe. Lieutenant Mann returned next day recovered from his wound on 30 March. Major Barne's morning activities over the next few days consisted of "a sort of variety entertainment – viz Lewis Guns, Snipers, bombers, signallers, pipers, bayonet exercise, transport etc., making myself generally objectionable & interfering" or visiting fatigue parties and in the afternoons riding, usually with other officers, or playing games, often football, but as on the 23rd, "cricket against the Coldstream whom we beat – followed by rounders when they beat us." The weather was mainly bright sunshine, but the War was always present as German planes came over at night to drop bombs and there was the sound by day and night of the shelling in the Salient and beyond "mostly to the south towards Armentières." Training went on as much as fatigues would allow. This often meant parties of five hundred and fifty, plus officers, being repeatedly required, one task being railway construction. Up till now trench warfare training had been all that most of those then in the Battalion had ever known. Now, right away, there was to be instruction for officers and NCOs in map reading, signalling, using visual means of Morse code by lamps and of semaphore code by flags, and reconnaissance patrols, all in preparation for a general advance. Further, as they had "a competent instructor" from the Royal Engineers with them, he started a course in "Defence, by means of wire entanglements." By this time the sophistication of these was considerable and fundamental when consolidating captured ground. There were also lectures on "Bombing during an advance from a line of trenches." There was very good, but unmentioned, reason for this, the proposed attack on Pilckem Ridge. On the 24th the Scots Guards Band had arrived to take their turn with the Division and on some evenings played for up to two hours in the camp. Sir Iain Colquhoun practised throwing the hammer and there was quite a lot of rough cricket. On the 25th the officers played the servants and others at cricket and football and won both, but lost the return football match next day. Next day he told Dinah "Mark has applied to go to the Machine Gun Company. He ought to get it all right as there is no great run on it… we always see quite a lot of them. They don't go into the front line at all in this sector…That ass Dundas has just been posted to the 1st Batt. I shall kick his bottom if he talks as much as he used to." On the 27th no one was up to much in C Company as they were all "inoculated at 11am, felt very rotten for rest of day." The injections were against paratyphoid. Major Barne went on two weeks leave.

Lieutenant Asquith wrote to his wife on the 28th "We have a parson attached to us now – a Cambridge don – who wanted to hold a service in our battalion mess room, but the walls have been so thickly papered with French pictures of naked women that he had to confess the site inappropriate for any holy purpose." This was the Reverend Frederick "Tail" Head, Fellow of Emmanuel College, Cambridge, just appointed as a Church of England chaplain with the Guards Division. He did very well. Padre Rogers liked and admired him, one of his considerable talents being his easy way of engaging the attention of anybody of any rank. To start with he was with the 3rd Grenadiers, was later Senior Chaplain of the Guards Division, twice won the MC and after the War became Archbishop of Melbourne.

On the 30th the Scots Guards heard that they were to move two days later, in the first instance to Herzeele for a night. The Regimental Band played as they left on the morning of 1 June, joining the rest of the Brigade on the line of march. From Herzeele, where the B and C Company officers dined very satisfactorily in an estaminet, they went next day to meet up with the other battalions at Wormhout, but Right Flank, in Sir Iain Colquhoun's words, "were late, and got left behind." On the road west Sir Herbert Plumer was waiting at Esquelbecq to watch them march past on the way to Bollezeele. That night Lieutenant Asquith complained to Katherine "The French – what is left of them – are really too beastly. The population consists entirely of invalid old women who are incredibly timid, inhospitable, prejudiced, audacious and obstinate…There are many of these rheumatic old bitches I would gladly throw to the Bosches." At Bollezeele there was no prepared training area and almost all the Scots Guards spent almost all three of the next four days digging a series of practice trenches, including German replicas, the day off being a Sunday. The other battalions were doing exactly the same thing and on the 7th practice assaults started. By the 12th there was a joint exercise with the Coldstream. The intention was that this training, with clear offensive purpose, would continue to develop.

Sir Iain Colquhoun liked Bollezeele. "These are the best billets we've ever had, very clean and nice, my bedroom has got real sheets and lace curtains and the mess is also very nice. We start about 7am and dig trenches till 12 then we have luncheon and dig from 2 to 4, I love it as it is very good exercise…The orderly room has been open all night to get messages about the big sea fight but so far we haven't heard much and all the rumours are contradictory. The Canadians are doing much better now and have got back some of their trenches; they hope to get them all back soon." So he told Dinah on the 4th, going on in another letter three days later that the Canadians were still fighting "but I think it is all right now. I wish we could get some definite news of this naval battle, it is impossible to find out what really happened…We have just heard that K has been drowned. Poor old K he was a fine man and did very well up to a point. I'm afraid it will have a big morale effect." The big sea fight was the Battle of Jutland. What he wrote about the Canadians was the local battle that started on 2 June when the Germans attacked and took parts of the Canadian trenches in the right hand half of the Salient from Hooge to St Eloi. The Canadians, with some other support, fought back until in a skilful counterattack on the 14th they recaptured almost all the lost ground along the ridges. This was later designated the Battle of Mount Sorrel. Field Marshal Lord Kitchener was drowned on the 5th on his way to Archangel in Russia when HMS *Hampshire* hit a German mine in a storm west of Orkney and quickly sank. Owing to the storm and the cliffs of Marwick Head there were very few survivors.

Major Barne returned on the 9th. In his absence Lieutenant Eric Mackenzie, wounded first on the Aisne and again at Puits 14 Bis, had arrived to take over as Adjutant. Captain Thompson left for good and did staff jobs for the rest of the War, being awarded the DSO and MC. By the 10th the open warfare training had reached the stage of a practice attack by the Scots Guards on the left and the Coldstream on the right over ground with trenches dug, as Major Barne found, as "an exact replica of what we are destined to attack and many details well thought out, to get us really familiar with the ground which however is sure to be quite different when the time comes." They heard about the Russian attacks against the Austrians, the Brusilov Offensive, which began on the 4th, part of a series of preconcerted Allied operations agreed the previous December at the Chantilly Conference. In both his letters on the 11th and 12th Sir Iain Colquhoun commented on the Russian successes, initially spectacular, and included veiled indications that the British would shortly be doing something themselves. He had a real prospect of leave again in a few days. On the 12th Major Barne wrote of how they "Practised the attack by day in a downpour – started at 7.15pm to do it by night but …a messenger arrived to say all was cancelled, tho' fine at the time it turned very wet later & the men who have now no blankets, would have suffered much…To my astonishment this morning about 5am my old landlady came into my room and shut my window because she said the rain was driving in." In the afternoon next day he went by train to Dunkirk to try unsuccessfully, not for the first time, to see his naval brother, Lieutenant Commander Mike Barne, who commanded a monitor, in effect a floating heavy gun platform. This alternated between there and Dover and that day was at Dover. Having listened "to a number of yarns and anecdotes in a very short space of time" on another monitor where the officers were playing roulette, Major Barne caught a train to Bollezeele, where his pony was waiting, and rode back. Then he watched the 2nd Irish Guards and 3rd Grenadiers "do a night attack in the rain, amidst rockets, Very lights etc, etc our own attack was again deferred owing to the wet. Then I met Esmé who gave me the astounding news that during the day that orders had come for us to be at one hour's notice but now we were to move at midday tomorrow to go up to the line at Ypres to help the Canadians. What would my feelings have been had I returned from D to find the Battn gone!"

Sanctuary Wood

At Sanctuary Wood, south of Hooge, east of Zillebeke and near Hill 62, the Canadians, although about to restore and stabilise the wider situation in the continuing battle on the ridges, were very hard pressed. The 2nd Guards Brigade left Bollezeele mid morning. Thirty eight buses were used to move each battalion and some lorries as well, but they stopped every kilometre, either because a bus broke down or in order to close up. The first seven kilometres took two and a half hours and the whole thirty kilometre journey ten hours to Brandhoek. From there the Scots Guards then had to march the last stage to Camp B at Vlamertinghe, usually a Canadian base, but found the residents still there and had to wait for them to move out. The camp was "very dirty", but they had got themselves sorted out and were settling in. Major Barne put the time then as seven o'clock. Next, however, "When at last the men get their dinners about 7.30pm on the arrival of the cookers we are told to turn out and occupy Camp C less than a mile away, so off we go at 8.30pm luckily a bright moon is behind thick clouds, mud & wet everywhere, and cold as March. Bn HQ in a filthy farm house, the kitchen of which is used as a sort of estaminet by the Canadians. Dirt everywhere." Camp C was in much the same state as they had first found its predecessor. Lord Esmé Gordon Lennox and the company commanders went up to Sanctuary Wood to see the lie of the land. There was all too much evidence of the recent fighting, all too little means of reaching or communicating with the front line trenches except over the open and not one telephone line left. Major Barne heard that they had "found the line in such a state that none of the officers knew exactly where it was." They never got beyond Battalion Headquarters of the Canadian 60th Battalion, Victoria Rifles of Canada, in consequence.

After a late breakfast on the 15th the officers inspected rifles, ammunition and equipment and met for Lord Esmé Gordon Lennox's briefing that afternoon. B and C Companies with half of Left Flank were to be in the front line, Right Flank and the other half of Left Flank in reserve. The two forward platoons of Left Flank would not be in the front trenches, but in strong points just behind, SP14 and SP16, the first of which was to cause a lot of trouble. From what they were told Lieutenant Abercromby noted "The trenches faced every sort of direction. Had dinner about 8. After we had sat down Schiff noticed that there were 13 at the table and 3 candles." Lieutenant Schiff was commanding B Company. Lieutenant Abercromby continued "We moved off from the camp at 9.10, got into the train at Brandhoek and arrived at the Asylum about 10.10. We marched to the Lille Gate where we found our guides & after waiting some time went on by platoons. We took about 1½ hours to get up. Very quiet, no rifle fire except on the left & no gun fire. My two platoons 1 & 2 were supposed to take over a trench behind Maple Copse, but the guide told us that it had been blown flat so we took over from a party of 35 Canadians who were in a shallow communication trench in front of Maple Lodge. My two platoons were about 80 strong. The trench we took over was about 3ft deep & 7 broad with about a foot of mud at the bottom & a few shelters hollowed out of the sides, & in full view of the enemy from both flanks. We spent the night in deepening the trench and making more dug-outs." Private Fleming and 2 Platoon "Went into trenches at night. Very long walk up. Canadians very glad they were being relieved. In a sort of communication trench. Dug in." The relief itself went through quietly and without interruption, but was not complete till about half past one in the morning. Major Barne took with him "a pack & everything on me that am likely to want during the 3 days, even food." Near Zillebeke "is the Battn HQ in a cellar, officers, signallers, orderlies & all in the same room, not the height of comfort – no water except what we brought with us and unable to light fires day or night. However we sleep well though the atmosphere is horrible."

Private Johnes, detailed to go with Left Flank, had with him the reservist and former Edinburgh telegraph messenger Private George "Jimmy" Plant, "who had been wounded earlier on and come back out as a signaller." Private Johnes described him as slightly built and did not then know that his wound in October 1914 with the 2nd Battalion during First Ypres was a stomach one and so likely to have affected his stamina. Private Plant had now been back in the BEF for two months and was with them until part of a shell hit him in the right arm just over a year later in the lead up to the Battle of Pilckem Ridge. He recovered and came out once more at the end of March 1918, was back with the 2nd Battalion till mid August and then with the 1st Scots Guards till they left Cologne. As they made their way forward now he was carrying their rations and Private Johnes the telephone and signalling equipment. As he put it "the Canadians had taken a thumping. The position was unknown to me nor apparently to anyone else in the Battalion. We frogged it in to beyond Zillebeke bund, a water reservoir for Ypres, and then the fun began. The guide had lost his way and the company became broken up…It seemed we were just heading for where some fighting was going on, Very lights were going up, some rifle fire was taking place, and shellfire was from both ways, but not heavy. We finally got into what once had been a wood and were told it was Sanctuary Wood. The trees were blown to smithereens, and trenches were where you found them. My partner was sagging a bit, but we were still with our regiment but not Left Flank. The moon had come up and we judged where the east and north should be from its position, and tried to find our company. We got into an open space and headed east, rounding a shellhole, a voice called for help from it. A fellow was in it up to his armpits in mud and trying to keep his rifle above water. He was a Canadian, lost from his company and he could not get out of the hole. We reached out to him but could not get him out. We finally persuaded him to lay his rifle down in front of him and try to get his feet on it so that he would have a little footing to help. He was afraid of losing his rifle, a Ross, and no good in mud anyhow. We dared not venture into the mud hole to him, but somehow managed to wiggle him out with our rifles. He had no idea of where he was or how long he had been in the hole. We could hear men working with shovels on a ridge towards the east. I left my partner with the Canadian and got as close as I could to the gang working, but could hear no soldier language as I knew it, so I backed down to my buddy. My mess tin fastened onto my haversack on my back, would have shone in the moonlight like a boil on a black's rear end, so I did not dare turn it toward the work party, I would have been duck soup for a sniper. The Canadian had got himself organized a bit and we headed back into Sanctuary Wood, or whatever it was. We were in luck, we had not gone far when two or three chaps came at us out of a trench, for a moment it looked like shutters for us, but when we spoke it was Captain Colquhoun and fellows of C Coy who were manning a trench facing in the direction from which we were coming." They recognised each other and Sir Iain Colquhoun told Private Johnes, who was now so out of breath that he found it difficult to speak, where to find Left Flank. Private Plant and the Canadian were "finding it difficult to get along." They left the Canadian with C Company and went on till they found Left Flank "linking up shellholes to line up a trench. The remainder of the night we spent cleaning out a bit of trench and rigging up cover." There was no line connection with anyone to begin with but "Two linemen got through to us with a line in the early morning, and we were in communication for a few hours."

At half past two in the morning on the 16th Captain Norman sent his first message from Left Flank to Battalion Headquarters reporting that they had completed the relief of the strong points. He went on "Not very clear of my exact position yet. Am holding SP 14 and a trench not marked on any map, running in front of SP 16. Am going out to get in touch on my flanks." While it was still dark Major Barne went out "round part of the line, tho' not all as I have to get back before it is light." He realised that the stories of the fighting during the past two weeks that the Canadian officers had told them "cannot have been much exaggerated, for I never saw anything like the state of the ground & trenches as well as Maple Copse etc. A RE dump near the line was an amazing sight – wire, sandbags, mauls etc. etc being chopped up & hurled in very direction – all mixed up with dead bodies or bits of them." Lieutenant Abercromby continued "The other platoons were in holes in the ground about 200 yds in front. RF & LF headquarters were in the only dug-out in Maple Copse which had not been blown in. It was about 200 yds from where we were. In the dug-out were 7 officers, 2 CSM & servants, orderlies, signallers & about 2 foot of water, rotten meat, equipment, coats, etc., German & Canadian. The whole wood had been blown flat, about 250,000 shells were supposed to have been put in in 5 hours?? It is still shelled very heavily every day. The place is full of dead, some fresh, some have been here for a long time but were stirred up in bombardments. And the smell! The dug-out is fairly good but not shellproof. The Grenadiers who took over from us refused to use it because of the smell." Right Flank did everything they could while it was still dark and then got everyone and their equipment under cover before dawn. "The men who had no shelters had to lie at the bottom of the trench." He and 2nd Lieutenant Reginald "Pardon" Champion "had a dug-out which we had room to lie in side by side with our feet sticking out into the trench." Lieutenant Champion began the War in the 1/18th London Regiment, London Irish Rifles, and served with them in the BEF from June 1915 till wounded at the end of August. He was commissioned into the Scots Guards in November 1915 and arrived in France the following spring, joining the Battalion at the beginning of May. He had been at the Royal Grammar School Guildford and Jesus College, Oxford. Sir Iain Colquhoun found "The trenches are fearfully blown about and the men have to get in anywhere they can. They also face every way, and is altogether a very difficult position. Neither side holds the old British front line and we are not quite sure where the Germans are."

German shelling went on all day, starting at about half past eight on a dull and cold morning and at its worst for a couple of hours in the afternoon. However, because the two Right Flank platoons in their communication trench kept so still, Lieutenant Abercromby formed the impression that the Germans thought that there was nobody there. They were firing right down the line of it, the whizz-bangs landing a hundred and fifty yards away, "and if they had put up their range 150 yds they would have had every one of us in 5 minutes. As it was we got plenty of splinters." The worst of it, he thought, was hitting B and C Companies in the front line, as well as Maple Copse, but, all things considered, the casualties were fairly light up till dark at about ten o'clock. Sir Iain Colquhoun ascribed the little damage to most of the shells falling well back from them.

Private Fleming noted "Very heavy bombardments now and then throughout the day. Thought two or three times that he [the enemy] was coming over but nothing doing. Went up to C Coy in front line with rations in broad daylight. Bombarded during day. Very quiet at night time not a sound heard." Captain Norman sent two messages back at quarter past nine, the first with a map showing where Left Flank were and explaining that this was a new trench, only just begun. They had done what they could about deepening it before dawn, but after that could do nothing and the men simply sat at the bottom out of sight of the enemy throughout the hours of daylight. Meanwhile they had managed to drain the officers' dug-out. He also mentioned heavy German shelling with HE shrapnel on Sanctuary Wood, Maple Copse and the two communication trenches, Border Lane and Lovers Walk, from five in the afternoon to the time of his message. His second message reported the burying soon after they arrived of four Canadians, continued that when he took over the night before there were no trench stores to take over at all and no trench logbook either and finished by saying that they would dig latrines that night and continue deepening the new trench. This was not to be.

Soon afterwards, when it got dark, Captain Ross came round and told Lieutenant Abercromby that 3 Platoon had had one man killed and one wounded and Left Flank had had seven men hit, while there were more in the front line companies. Just before eleven Captain Norman sent his next message "MATCHES BENT 2 in Main Line. 7 in SP14. Two seriously. Suggest withdrawing men from SP14 which I consider foolish to hold." The code meant that nine men had been wounded. Then, though it may have started earlier, Private Fleming thought that "About 11.30 the real shelling began. I don't know what started it, the Canadians on our right were going to make a small bombing attack, whether that started it or not I don't know." Every calibre of gun opened fire and the British guns replied, including the heaviest ones. As the Germans shelled the same places as they had during the day Lieutenant Abercromby noted that not a man in 1 and 2 Platoons was hit. "But the front line had absolute hell. They had about 50 casualties. Schiff…was killed. He was standing next to Mann outside a dug-out. A shell came through the dug-out, carried away Schiff's legs and broke Mann's arm. Another shell went into the signallers dug-out and killed 2 signallers & 4 servants. Then the SOS went up and started the guns off worse than ever. Both sides thinking that they were about to be attacked. About one o'clock somebody shouted out that they could smell gas. So we all put on our helmets. We left them on for about half an hour and then took them off finding that nothing happened. About this time Gifford the RF orderly jumped into the trench & ran a bayonet through his leg." In 1914 Private George Gifford had been a shepherd in Patagonia, but volunteered in Argentina under the auspices of the British Patriotic Committee of Buenos Aires and sailed for Liverpool. Arriving there on 2 February 1915 he enlisted formally and joined the Battalion in the autumn, probably not till after Loos. There was no aftermath of his self inflicted wound, which could have led to a serious charge. He came back to France early in 1917, was badly wounded in the thigh early in August just after the main fighting of the Battle of Pilckem Ridge, and reappeared again in September 1918. After the War he was repatriated to Port San Julian in Patagonia. The casualties in the two forward companies were not quite as bad as Lieutenant Abercromby thought.

For five hours there had been very heavy firing and bombardment of the British trenches which for Sir Iain Colquhoun "was one continual roar, shells of all calibres bursting everywhere. My dug-out was blown in and Langley killed." He referred to Lieutenant Schiff's death, but did not mention that later on he had personally buried him behind the front line trench, only for the grave to be blown up by a direct hit later in the bombardment. Lieutenant Mann's wound was his second in three months. Sir Iain Colquhoun counted his casualties as "roughly 6 killed and 8 wounded. Everyone thought that the bombardment would be followed by an attack. But it never came off. The Germans were firing very wildly otherwise they must have done far more damage. All my equipment, papers, coat, rations, etc were buried in my dug-out. No ration parties or water parties could be sent down as the shelling was too severe." Private John Langley, just back from leave, came from North Yorkshire, where John and Caroline Langley, lived at Langthorpe, just outside Boroughbridge. He was a farm worker but since 1906 served continuously after enlisting in Ripon. He arrived in the Battalion at the very end of First Ypres, but not apparently in time to take part in it. He was properly buried in Sanctuary Wood and reported as killed in action, with as precise details of the map reference of his grave as possible. In addition, some small sticks were put round it and a bottle left in the ground nearby with full particulars. Photographs, letters and an Army 3rd Class Education Certificate reached his family. He had been Sir Iain Colquhoun's servant since just before Christmas 1915, before that Colonel Godman's and before that Captain Jamie Balfour's.

The German bombardment may have been another instance of their guns picking on a specific part of the British trenches and the communications. However, with this place's recent history it was natural to think that a German night attack was starting. Major Barne found it "difficult to remember the exact sequence of events. There were some very intense bombardments – particularly one about 11pm, mostly on the Coldstream on our left – we saw some green rockets go up which we took to be "SOS" signal so put on our equipment & got ready – with all the signallers etc. etc, – for any emergency – a bit later a gas gong or horn was heard so we all donned our gas helmets, and sat awaiting events. However the gas, if any, never came our way & I believe the green lights were really some German Art[illery] signal." In consequence the British guns opened up very heavily indeed and the whole process was prolonged. Afterwards they heard that there had been a German gas attack some distance south. Next Lieutenant Trafford and a party from the Transport arrived at Battalion Headquarters with the rations and Lieutenant Mann "appeared with his arm broken by a shell, reporting that Schiff had been killed and also several others wounded. The next arrival was General Ponsonby, accompanied by almost all the Brigade Headquarters staff officers, including Padre Rogers. Major Barne was disappointed. "The only wonder was the Vet & interpreter were absent! He seemed in good spirits as usual, & thought it a capital joke that he had been caught in the Coldm lines while they were being bombarded." While this was going on an orderly reached Left Flank with a message for Captain Norman to which he replied just after midnight "Re <u>Buried Canadians</u> Quite impossible to state exactly where buried. The bodies were buried as soon as we took over fire trench. On second thoughts cannot even swear they were Canadians; may have been Germans. Will interview platoon sergeant as soon as it is possible to reach him & let you know."

Private Johnes continued "Then Jerry started to get dirty. It had been quiet through the night seeming as though neither side knew just where or what to fire at…Jerry kept up with his straf all day and as night came on increased it. At one point in daylight he was sending over some very heavy stuff into B Coy. As the big ones came in…looking towards B Coy from our position and watching the area in which they were landing, they could plainly be seen like big stones landing at a low trajectory. At first sight we thought someone was throwing Mills bombs, but the result proved otherwise." Two of our B Coy signallers were killed, Baxter, an old signaller, and a new one, whom I did not know." Private James Baxter joined two weeks after the outbreak of war, enlisting in London where he had worked as a salesman. As with Private Langley, his grave was detailed by grid reference and "Marked by small sticks & a bottle containing full particulars placed within a few feet of the grave". Nothing was recovered to send to Archibald and Nellie Baxter in Abbeyhill, Edinburgh. "Toward evening and dusk Jerry started to move his target up in our direction. He had had planes over during the day, I guess taking a stock of the situation." Privates Johnes and Plant had their signalling post in the northern end of a bay off the main Left Flank trench and the officers and their servants had a dug-out at the south end of the bay. "Jerries shelling was creeping up and getting closer all the time, the next thing I knew I was trying to clear a bunch of junk off my chest and face and someone said "This fellow is still alive" someone started to claw at the junk on me, my mouth felt muddy and I tried to wipe it free, my tin hat was gone and the top of my head hurt, back to the right hand side. My sidekick Jimmy came along and he was sure glad to see me, he told me I had been missing for nearly two hours, kept asking if I was alright, I was except for a headache and a lump on the top. I apparently had been KOd, a shell had obliterated the officers dug-out and part of the trench where the fellows had been. I was blown into the next bay and Jimmy was blown round the corner, he was OK. Part of the carnage from the officers dug-out and trench covered me. I found my tin hat later, it had a gash in it about an inch and a half long, pear shaped from front over to the back on the right side, covering the spot where the lump was on my noggin." Not until daylight could he see that what had covered him was "mud, blood and human flesh." He did not go sick then or later.

Private Frederick Allen came from Bournemouth, had been in the Battalion since 1912 and went out to France in August 1914. He was either at the Base or at some stage could have been sent back sick, though nothing was recorded, because he was posted to the 2nd Battalion with all available reinforcements after First Ypres. Later he returned to the 1st Scots Guards, serving as an orderly, carrying messages, throughout the War and never being wounded. At two in the morning Major Barne "went off with the orderly Allen, to see what was happening in the front line B & C Coys all communication being cut off. Got as far as the edge of Sanctuary Wood where they were when a terrific bombardment was opened on it, a sight I shall never forget. The shells seemed to be bursting by the score at a time all round us, we three (I had also a guide from B Coy Pte Casey, who had brought Mann down) squatted in a bit of old communication trench expecting every moment to be our last – and thinking it quite impossible anyone should be alive in the wood where B & C Coys were: after what seemed like an hour the fire slackened so I determined to try and get back to LF Coy which we did successfully – about 400 yds, found no officer so took command & got ready thinking the Germans might very likely be coming over. After further search I found all the officers together and presently Brand came in with a few others, wounded in 2 places shoulder and back. He could not give much information about B & C Coys but Sgt Jacobs of LF appeared, apparently about the sole survivor of his post, saying he did not think the front line (C and part of B) had caught it very badly so I settled to try again, this time taking about 6 men carrying water & rations for these two companies – all volunteers for the job I believe. There was a fortunate lull in the firing just when we had to go, but dawn was appearing & so I expected to have to stay there the day. We had some difficulty in finding our way to any part of the line – all trenches blown in & shellholes about a foot apart everywhere, fallen trees, bits of wire etc etc etc, but soon came on a party – now HQ of B Coy, under Lt Leach where we dumped the water etc. I sent back the men to their companies & told Leach to try & send water on to C Coy & remainder to B. I then went forward cautiously to look for more men, almost expecting to meet Germans. The place for a while seemed deserted – not a sound – only dead & remains of human beings – not a sign of a trench. Was on point of giving up owing to approaching daylight when suddenly came on a bit of trench full of men of B Coy huddled together, followed this along till we came on another batch, then another, then to C Coy where I found Luss, as usual quite happy, but not knowing how many men he had left or where they were, & would not probably know till tonight. I saw a certain number of dead bodies & pieces – including poor Schiff – but could not judge numbers as I had only seen a small part of the line. I then came away in almost broad daylight feeling very sorry for the poor things, and rather a brute to leave them, but thought it just as well to report what I had seen to Esmé, & he was glad to hear what I could tell him. Some signallers & officers of B Coy had been killed and I expect we shall find they have suffered worst being in the middle of the wood. The whole thing appears such a jumble up in some ways, that it may be difficult to relieve the front coys and bring away their wounded, & hardly possible to bring out the dead." Long afterwards Private Cumming remembered "the heroic Major Barne who carried up a sack of rations on his back on a memorable night in Sanctuary Wood where we were hard pressed."

Private Patrick Casey, with family connections in Ballycastle, County Antrim, and previously a cabinetmaker in Glasgow, enlisted early in September 1914, arriving in France six months later. When they were in the trenches they dug short of Puits 14 Bis after the failure of the attack on the pit buildings Private Casey was slightly wounded in the finger the next day, but was back five weeks later. Lieutenant Brand was hit slightly in the arm by a shell while walking from the Left Flank dug-out in Maple Copse to the front line, his third wound. Captain Norman reported him "BOX BENT", which meant wounded officer, when sending down next morning the names of his casualties. The shelling had gone on all through the night and it was impossible to work on the trenches while it continued. If a thing or place was described as "bent" that could mean that it was damaged. Sergeant Albert Jacobs' home was in Plumstead, Kent, and he had been a valet in London before volunteering in August 1914. Since first landing in France in January 1915 he had been wounded twice, first by shrapnel in the left leg in May 1915 at Aubers, after which he recovered in England, and then in the neck during the shelling on 30 March at Potijze, a minor wound in that he was back three weeks afterwards. In addition to the three officers the recorded casualties on the 17th were sixteen men killed and twenty six wounded, the carrying back of the wounded being very awkward. There continued to be no telephone links to the front line.

Lieutenant Abercromby heard of a man who said to a friend when he was hit "John MacDonald is wounded. Let the war proceed. Good bye lads. I will see ye again." Private Johnes remembered this too in very similar words, describing him as "an old Highlander". Private John MacDonald volunteered in Glasgow at the end of September 1914, describing himself as a seaman. He spent seven months in France in 1915 until hit at Puits 14 Bis. Then, wounded in the penis and severely in the left thigh, he was evacuated home but in spite of these wounds was back three months later. In Sanctuary Wood part of a shell struck him in the stomach and he died two days later in a casualty clearing station. On enlistment he said that he had a brother called Frederick but did not know where he was and so his stated next of kin was a friend called Roderick Mathieson in Glasgow, who was sent a razor, a jack knife, a pipe, a photograph and an identity disc. If anybody recognised Private MacDonald nothing was recorded officially if for no other reason than that he had changed his name, broken contact with his family and said nothing about previous military service when he joined up. He was a reenlisted former Scots Guardsman called Piper Norman Martin, a Boer War veteran and once a fisherman in the Western Isles. A letter came in 1924 to ask about his belongings from Mrs Murdina Martin of Stornoway. Lieutenant Abercromby also heard that Sergeant David Cowie "had one leg blown off and the other shattered & stayed in the trench till night smoking cigarettes. He also died at the dressing station." The dressing station was from the 1st Canadian Field Ambulance.

Sergeant Cowie came from Dunoon where his mother Elizabeth Cowie was living, and had been a carpenter before he enlisted in 1913. Having been out with the BEF from the start as a Private, he was wounded on 14 September 1914 during the heavy fighting above Vendresse on the Aisne, with severe bruising to his left knee, and did not return until October 1915. By then a Lance Corporal, he was instantly promoted to Sergeant on arrival at the Hohenzollern. A large number of his belongings reached his mother.

Private Alexander McFarlane was killed outright and the location of his grave in Sanctuary Wood carefully recorded at the time. He was a Glasgow policeman, volunteered in August 1914 and came to France early in January 1915. He was slightly wounded in the head in the shelling in May 1915 at Aubers. James and Catherine McFarlane lived at Cambuslang, Lanarkshire. Private James Morris was dead, recorded as having been buried in an unmarked grave, a Yorkshireman who joined up in January 1915 in London. He was a ship's fireman and had elaborate tattoos comprising a chain of flowers round his neck, a butterfly on each shoulder, a basket of flowers on his left forearm, clasped hands, a cross and embellishments on his right forearm and a star on each foot. He arrived in a draft at the Hohenzollern, since when he had only twice had any event recorded, both in April 1916, the first being when he was awarded ten days FP No 1 for refusing to obey an order from a NCO, the second going sick with boils, which kept him away for two weeks. Boils were a common problem. Private Morris' father was dead and his mother Mrs Sarah Breeze lived in Luddenham. Private John MacLean was hit in both his arms and both his legs and was quickly evacuated home. He could not walk afterwards without pain and was discharged in March 1917. He and Bella Maclean and their young son and daughter lived in Bathgate, where he was a miner in the Balbardie Mine, Linlithgow. When he was wounded he had been out in the BEF since April 1915, having enlisted six months earlier. Private Thomas Shepherd, a dyer's labourer and the son of Thomas Shepherd of Perth, was also very badly hurt with wounds to his back, right arm and right knee, of which the third was the worst at the time, though the wound in his arm was noted as severe. He joined up three weeks after Private MacLean but both were in the same draft in April 1915. Then Private Shepherd was a casualty at Puits 14 Bis, hit in the left thigh, and sent home. Now he had been back for two months. He recovered sufficiently to return to the BEF once more in the spring of 1917 and was posted to the 2nd Battalion until finally sent home that autumn. The wound to his arm had not healed properly and he had wasting to his hand resulting in paralysis. Private William Dick was a former Scots Guardsman and Boer War soldier who reenlisted in Edinburgh on New Year's Day 1915. He gave his occupation as stationer/broker. A shell broke his left leg and he died at quarter past three in the afternoon on 20 June at a casualty clearing station. He and Margaret Reilly married at Dunbar in 1911 and she was living in Haddington with their three young daughters. Private Tom Stevenson, a Yorkshireman and the son of Tom and Bessie Stevenson of Spofforth, was a railwayman until he enlisted after Christmas 1914 in Keighley as a regular. At Sanctuary Wood he was hit in the neck and back and sent home to recover. When he returned to the BEF in March 1917 he remained with the Battalion thereafter till posted home from Cologne in January 1919.

Around dawn on the 17th the shelling quietened down, restarted again at six for a couple of hours, but much less than earlier, and then reverted to the pattern of the day before. The afternoon was fairly quiet, dusk a bit noisier and then after dark nothing but occasional rifle shots. Right Flank managed to do some work on their positions during the night and everyone got about three hours sleep. The main danger to the two platoons with Lieutenant Abercromby still came from shell splinters and three men were hit in the legs. Sir Iain Colquhoun managed to sleep for most of the morning and as soon as it was dark sent off ration and water parties from C Company. He mentioned random shelling through the night. He observed that it had been a "Lovely day". Apart from a heavy bombardment about ten o'clock on the Canadians over to the right it was generally quieter still on the 18th. At half past six that evening Lieutenant Abercromby got orders to send two guides down for the relief by the 3rd Grenadiers after dark. Three hours later the Germans spotted two men, whom he thought were from another company, crossing the end of his trench, and fired five rounds of shrapnel at them. "They missed the men but hit my bombing sergeant, Sgt Macdonald, through the back and stomach. I sent him off at once on a stretcher. But he died as soon as he reached the dressing station." Private Fleming heard about a shell hitting a dug-out, but he was himself right on the spot to see "Sgt McDonald hit very badly while speaking to me." Lance Sergeant Allan Macdonald came from Rhu, on the east side of the Gareloch beyond Helensburgh, where he had worked both as a sailor and as a groom, and enlisted at the end of August 1914. Arriving in France in February 1915, he soon worked his way up to Lance Sergeant and trained as a specialist with grenades, being detached as an instructor for a month early in 1916. He was carried back to a Canadian dressing station and died there. A lot of his belongings reached his father, Malcolm Macdonald, including his rosary and a number of other Roman Catholic emblems and pendants, his Bible, his metal watch, compass and whistle and, lastly, a lock of hair.

Captain Norman gave written instructions to Company Sergeant Major Hubert Butler for the relief of Left Flank which began with a guide from each platoon leaving after dark to be at the west end of the Zillebeke Bund at quarter past ten to meet the incoming Grenadier company. Once relieved, the platoons were to make their way back individually to the Cavalry Barracks at the first turning on the left past the Lille Gate in Ypres. At nine forty he sent his last report to Battalion Headquarters, including details of the wind direction and strength and mention of a German plane having apparently been hit in the early morning, because it descended very abruptly behind their lines. Company Sergeant Major Butler had a lot of service, including the Boer War. He then bought himself out of the Army, but rejoined in 1904 and by 1913 was on a twenty one year engagement. Detached for some time as an Army Physical Training and Swimming Instructor, in November 1915 he returned at his own request and came out to the 1st Scots Guards almost immediately. There he took over as Company Sergeant Major of Left Flank. His wife Ethel and their two children were living in Borough on the south side of the Thames in London. On 25 August he left the Battalion, commissioned into the 6th Dorsetshire Regiment, appropriately because he had been born in Gillingham.

Both sides had shelled each other for most of the 18th, the enemy shelling of Maple Copse for nearly three hours from seven that morning being particularly severe. Left Flank had managed to deepen their trench a bit more. The Grenadiers had been in the reserve line in the dug-outs behind the Zillebeke Bund for the last three days and Major Barne went down there just after dark to take over from them. Shortly afterwards he met Lieutenant Trafford, who had brought up rations and water, ready for everyone as they came in.

After sending off his guides Sir Iain Colquhoun went up to have a thorough look at the front line trenches. There he noticed a German machine gun, which he had dug out, with its fittings and equipment, and carried back. The Grenadiers arrived around half past ten and C Company reached the Bund at about half past three, all without any interruption or difficulty. About half past eleven those relieving Right Flank arrived and Lieutenant Abercromby "handed over the trench & got away as soon as possible." Most of the Battalion went into the dug-outs behind the Bund and remained there till the 21st, shelled a certain amount, without damage. They had to send parties of fifty men at night to help dig communication trenches, but otherwise were comfortable, more or less out of danger short of a direct hit and able to rest properly. Captain Norman sent a report to Battalion Headquarters on the morning of the 19th that "LF was present & in billets at 1.45 this morning. Brought down eleven Canadian rifles & handed them to Canadian dump at Lille Gate on entering." The Canadians were still using their own Ross rifle. Not long after this they took up the British .303 Lee Enfield. Sir Iain Colquhoun, after a sound sleep and having arranged for the machine gunners to clean his trophy, went to look round the wreckage of Zillebeke with two other officers in the afternoon and spent the evening hunting rats with Lord Esmé Gordon Lennox and Lieutenant Mackenzie. Private Cumming reflected that "As my birthday was on the 17th June, I felt the occasion had been celebrated somewhat unusually."

Meanwhile Lieutenant Abercromby with two platoons of Right Flank "had to stay in the ruined village of Zillebeke. Zillebeke is absolutely flat. We lived in a dug-out in a ruined house. There were a lot of dead men lying all round & the smell was awful. Also the dug-out would not have kept out a shell of any kind. We got all the men into cellars and dug-outs somehow or other. Then I went down to Btn HQ with a message. I got back about 3am, got into the dug-out and went to sleep. They put a few crumps near us but we hardly noticed them. We had had hardly any sleep and nothing to eat for three days. So we slept most of that day. About 9.30pm a message arrived saying that I was to take my two platoons to join the rest of the Btn in the Bund, which I did about 11pm. We were all very glad to leave Zillebeke as apart from the shelling the smell was terrible." Major Barne elaborated on the trenches the Canadians had lost and retaken, knocked about still more by the shelling while the Scots Guards were there "The ground in consequence shows every sign of severe fighting having taken place – dead everywhere, tho' we have buried many... The trenches themselves could hardly be called trenches, no wire in front... Some guns were lost and retaken by Canadians in Sanctuary Wood – 3 field guns – our gunners were to go and get them out last night. They were fought to the last, close by were found the bodies of a Canadian Scottish & a German gripping each other's throats. The amount of equipment and ammunition lying about almost rivalled Loos!"

On 20 June Captain Norman sent a message to Lord Esmé Gordon Lennox "I beg to bring before your notice the following names for gallantry in the field:-

No 8255 L/Corpl McFadden H
No 8054 Pte Jackson J

On the night of June 16th 1916 whilst under very heavy fire the above mentioned L/Corpl & Private whilst the Coy stretcher bearers were away with a wounded man, picked up a Canadian stretcher lying beside them & went & brought away Pte Ross from a detached post SP14 in Sanctuary Wood. I consider this a case for immediate reward for bravery."

Corporal Henry McFadden was the same man mentioned in the 14 Platoon notes of the August 1915 Spasm of the *Left Flank Magazine* and was first promoted during Loos. While clearly a reliable and capable NCO he was twice reprimanded for insubordination, which could have cost him his rank. He was wounded very slightly two weeks before this, but not evacuated. Private James Jackson from Dundee had nearly completed three years service when the War began. He was wounded in the shoulder, but not seriously, in November 1914 on the day before the Prussian Guards battle at Nonne Boschen and after that remained for a year in England before he came out again. Private Thomas Ross, whose mother Sarah Ross lived in Motherwell, was a miner until February 1915 and had been out since that October. The shell that hit him smashed his thigh and he was discharged from the Army in February 1917. Nothing happened to recognise his rescuers' courage.

When Left Flank returned to Ypres Private Johnes went with Private Plant to join the other signallers at the Zillebeke Bund. Two days later he and his friend Private Evans "were sitting in the sun in front of the shelters, delousing. The English Church Padre Rev Head, a fine fellow, came along and mucked in chewing the fat. He recited his experience of the night of the "Fireworks". He had been right where we were at the moment. He said he climbed up the bank and was looking across the Lake at our lines. "The lights were going up on both the German and our sides, some Green, some Red, and many of the ordinary lights to see by, Guns were flashing on both sides, shells were bursting all over, the noise was terrific, the moon was shining, and the reflection of it all, in the water of the Lake, was "the most beautiful sight" he had ever seen." His listeners knew that the coloured lights were SOS signals by both sides, put up in the erroneous belief that attacks were imminent or taking place, even that the front line had been lost, to which both sides' gunners responded. There was no means for those who knew better in the front line to pass back accurate situation reports, other than by runner, difficult, dangerous and never quick. "The Reverend was so enthusiastic about his story we hated to enlighten him with the truth. We agreed with him that it must have been a great sight. He wished us well and departed. If we had told him in soldier language what we had thought of it he would probably have called for Prayer." When the Grenadiers went up to Sanctuary Wood they left Padre Head with the Scots Guards, who were now getting to know him well.

Major Barne wrote of "A lot of shelling all day, some big stuff into Ypres & several very near our dug-outs – so much so that we took refuge in a deep hole made underneath. After emerging after all was over a ½ dead rat was found sitting on the trench boards – expect several others were killed. There seem to be more here than anywhere with many young ones – the place seems to swarm with them at night, & stinks accordingly. There were great jokes when the Brigadier came round, about our first having watched the Bde HQ in Ypres being shelled and thought it quite a good joke, and then in the afternoon we were being shelled the Bde staff is supposed to have been much amused. The Brigadier orders Hugh Ross to draw a series of pictures to suit. At night the two padres, Head and Rogers, had to go up to the line and bury Canadians & Germans who were being collected by the Gren[adiers] all over the place. They returned just before daylight." The 21st was quiet all morning, then there was an hour and a half of shelling landing unpleasantly close, but Major Barne heard that the Grenadiers had had a quiet time. Later there was some shelling in daylight while they waited for the Canadian 49th Battalion, Edmonton Regiment, to take over at the Bund. This, Major Barne noted, they did "at dusk, by driblets. They come in no special formation, and do things quite differently to other people. Their discipline is conspicuous by its absence, or rather by its uniqueness, for there must be some form of discipline. But they bring trouble on themselves and get many unnecessary casualties, everyone of our Battn has some story of the odd way they do things & their disregard of conventionality, which however does not pay. At night we go out joining our motor buses & lorries at the Asylum, thence to Camp E, a very pleasant spot. A bombshell arrives in the shape of an order to Esmé to report himself to 4th Army HQ on 23rd, which I suppose means getting a Bde."

Back out of the line

They rested on the 22nd, a quiet day, at Vlamertinghe. Not so the day after when several German aircraft were up and their heavy guns fired shrapnel over the camp, hitting no one. The Battalion paraded and the companies then did drill. Major Barne went riding in the afternoon with Lieutenant Orr Ewing to try to find his brother Captain Seymour Barne, but heard that the cavalry had moved further south. "On return watch some Canadians playing Baseball, then ourselves play rounders – after which L Norman, Trafford and I sow some mustard & cress etc. seed." Lord Esmé Gordon Lennox left on the 23rd for the Somme, travelling in the Prince of Wales' car. He soon took command of the 95th Brigade in the 56th (London) Division, Territorial Force, to Lieutenant Mackenzie "a great loss to us". Major Barne had spent the morning as president of a FGCM hearing five cases, "one of which is for desertion – to whom we give 10 years penal servitude, owing to him having a pretty good character." All the companies went to the baths and in the evening the Regimental Band played inside a large recreation hut in the camp. It had been a pretty wet day, with thunder and lightening. The next few days were uneventful. Sir Iain Colquhoun's leave at last came through and home he went.

Lieutenant Miller, his poisoned foot better, returned and 2nd Lieutenants Leslie Childers and Henry Dundas, who had both come from England a month before, arrived the same day. Lieutenant Childers had been to school at Haileybury and began the War in the Royal Naval Air Service before transferring in December 1915. His father was a Colonel in the Royal Engineers, stationed at Salisbury. Early in 1918 Lieutenant Dundas began a chronicle though he did not get very far with it. Of the officers he had trained with in England and travelled out with he took to Lieutenant Childers as "much the most likely to be a congenial spirit". When they reached the Base Depot at Harfleur they did not know which Battalion they were to go to, but "Roger Tempest at that time commanded the 2nd Bn & this excellent soldier's reputation for ferocity had penetrated even to Wellington Barracks" so both of them favoured the less defined prospect of Lord Esmé Gordon Lennox. Lieutenant Dundas had an additional reason for hoping for the 1st Scots Guards because of Lieutenant Mackenzie, whom he liked and respected. Very soon they did know where they were going and very soon they were initially on their way to Chipilly on the Somme. Lieutenant Dundas did not take to the Entrenching Battalion, commanded by a Grenadier, Major Edward "Kerby" Ellice, who, he told his parents on 9 June, was "a kindly old ass but the worst type of dug-out – one of those old men who think a certain number of years service in the Grenadiers makes a man an expert in every branch of science, commerce, art or anything, whereas it really only gives him a nodding acquaintance with the duties of a chucker out at the Empire." He put in his later embryonic chronicle that "The men did the most absurd & useless fatigues all day, & then shivered in soaking tents at night – all blankets had been called in, & the weather was quite appalling. No wonder they all loathed it." There were a lot of officers there, underoccupied and only rarely called upon to go with fatigue parties. Lieutenant Dundas was unlikely to know that Major Ellice, born in 1858, was a competent amateur watercolour painter. Captain Feilding of the 1st Coldstream, his knee recovered, was in charge of the Coldstreamers here at the time. He found Major Ellice friendly and helpful, but life was dull. Not till 25 August was he on his way back to the Coldstream.

After the officer casualties at Sanctuary Wood replacements were needed and Lieutenants Dundas and Childers were first in line. So "the summons was sent out and Leslie and I were "for it" in earnest. How pleased I was! Just to make the picture complete we left the Entrenching

Battalion at 4am but what matter? The usual day's journey supervened…we stopped most of the night at Abbeville – whenever I hear an engine whistle at night now I think of Abbeville and I remember dining with one Chapman bound for the 2nd Battalion." This was Lieutenant Arthur Chapman, a Marlburian and rubber planter, the son of Arthur and Estelle Chapman of Iver, Buckinghamshire. The elder Arthur Chapman had rejoined the Army and was now Lieutenant Arthur Chapman of the 29th Middlesex, contactable at The Naval and Military Club, Piccadilly. The younger Arthur Chapman transferred in March 1916 from the 3/1st Buckinghamshire Battalion, a home Territorial battalion of the Oxford and Bucks LI. It was late the following afternoon when they got to Poperinghe and headed off on foot "along what is now probably the most famous road in the world – the Vlamertinghe road. After asking the way about a dozen times more from nervousness than anything else – we at last took the proper turn off to the left, and there, in Ack Thirty Forest, we found our camp." In some trepidation they approached the Officers Mess where they were greeted "By an immaculate young man in lavender breeches & faultless field boots with gold spurs attached. He welcomed us with a cordiality which was all the more creditable as it was on the whole alien to his nature…This was Cecil Trafford the Transport Officer…a most extraordinary character. A pleasant & sociable man in ordinary intercourse…he becomes, officially, a curmudgeon of the most oppressive type." What was more he feuded incessantly with Captain Kinlay, the Quartermaster, to whom Lieutenant Dundas attached very little of the blame, and this discord "was a constant source of weakness to the Battalion…His manner with the men was so bad as to preclude all chance of his getting a company." Next they met Major Barne "a tiny figure emerging from a hut."

It was not until the 1918 chronicle that he mentioned that at Bollezeele the Guards Division had been "practising for an attack on the Pilckem Ridge – which fronted the position – billed to take place about August 14." The way that the Battle of the Somme developed put paid to that. Meanwhile "The weather was perfect and the camp good, and there was a good deal of cricket and football – the latter played by the private soldier, especially the Scot, the whole year round, irrespective of the weather. Of Militarism there was none – for the Gordon Lennox theory of doing nothing when out of the line was then in force and was clearly reflected in the appalling caps and general slovenliness of the men's appearances which by this time had earned for the Battalion the reputation of being the worst turned out in the Division." He added that it had taken till early 1918 before this changed. "The theory of doing nothing when out of the line seems to me to be absolutely fatal." According to him this would continue and though Lieutenant Mackenzie tried to get a grip he was thwarted. "Of course I was far too incompetent and ignorant myself at the time to appreciate the situation. Indeed I had got into the absurd habit of rather looking down on smartness as being "Grenadier" and offensive. This was due a good deal to association with the officers of the 1st Bn Coldstream – who as a matter of principle loathed the 3rd Bn Grenadiers, both on general grounds & especially on account of their certainly rather moderate performances at Loos…At this time – June 1916 – they had not had an opportunity of really wiping out the stigma by an actual performance in a battle but as far as efficiency went they were… as good, if not better, than any battalion in the Division. This was due almost entirely to two men, and especially the first – BN Sergison Brooke, their Commanding Officer, and Oliver Lyttleton, their Adjutant." Captain Lyttleton was Dinah Colquhoun's cousin.

Now in B Company, Lieutenant Dundas wrote home again on 25 June. It was a Sunday and they were resting "not so the wretched Grenadiers, who seem to have been church-parading for about 2 hours (our men had a service at 10 quite quietly without any fuss or drill)…There is no news, at least none that I can reveal without incurring a charge of treason…Very pleasant just now sitting in one's hut, with the sun streaming in, listening to the Grenadiers drums and the hum of aeroplanes overhead. Everything is peaceful & yet seven miles up are the trenches. What fun…There was a Sergeants concert last night at which Shields the Company Sergeant Major of B Company and a really wonderful man sang "I'm for the noo" so brilliantly that he must have had personal experience. A wonderful performance:- but what an example!!… Apparently the mails are going to be stopped for a fortnight on the 27th – or thereabouts – for about a fortnight." So he warned them that they would have to put up with field postcards for the time being, but did not say that if the mail was stopped it was likely to mean that a battle was about to start and would apply to the whole BEF indiscriminately. Lieutenant Dundas much preferred frequent letters and often sent his family more than one a day. "This day-to-day correspondence is a thing that makes the War much more bearable."

The line near Boesinghe

The move to Sanctuary Wood had been an emergency. In the meantime the Division had done a routine switch to the northern end of the Salient, new to them and with the French on their left, "a rather careless lot who brought down enemy shellfire by smoke from their fires" according to Private Cumming, while "Our own cooking or "brewing up" in mess tins was more cautionary. We cut pieces of wood into fine splinters to avoid smoke and found this to be both economical and effective." In advance of their going up there Major Barne and the company commanders had been to visit the 2nd Coldstream where he "was shown round the line by Col Follett…, not a very pleasant bit of line, some of it only 40 yds across from the Germans…Downpour of very heavy rain tonight. What conditions will the trenches be in!" Leaving camp at half past nine on the rainy evening of the 27th they went into the reserve position dug-outs on the Canal Bank. Lieutenant Dundas found "Going into the line for the first time is rather thrilling and, I think, essentially the *new* sensation produced by the War. For a long time I had been imagining what the line would be like." Major Barne sent him across as liaison officer with the French. The next night they crossed over the Canal to the front line trenches and Private Fleming went "Up to Bombing Post in front of front line." Here he had a "very quiet first day. Can't be shelled here as we are only 30 yards from Fritz." Major Barne started off round the trenches for the first time at one in the morning on the 29th and was out for three hours. He found them "rather complicated & wander about almost lost." In daylight he showed round Colonel Sergison Brooke "a long business, as we did a lot of prospecting through periscopes." Lieutenant Mackenzie had "a quiet night in the line. B Coy had 4 wounded by pipsqueak…Doctor and I started to go round the trenches in the afternoon. Got as far as Lionel when they started pipsqueaking us, landing one finally against our dug-out, so we retired & the Doctor and I considering we had had enough returned home."

Very early on the 30th Major Barne was going round with Lieutenant Allan "Sloper" Mackenzie of the 3rd Grenadiers, Lieutenant Asquith's company commander and the middle brother of the two Scots Guards Mackenzies. However, "when we got as far as the right of RF (Left of our front) a tremendous bombing was heard – we hastened on and found a little bombing show going on the extreme left of our line by the Canal, where we join the French. I found Hugh Ross in the bombing posts – quite exciting while it lasted – very confusing bit of trenches, wherever I went a voice warned me "Mind that corner" etc. The German machine guns were very busy & seemed to come in every direction. There were 4 men wounded and Ross had quite a business to get them away. It all died off by about 2.30am & I eventually got to bed by 3.30am." Private Fleming "Started bombing had quite a good scrap. 4 wounded." One of the wounded was Private Arthur Hedges, until October 1914 a shunter [railwayman]. His parents William and Francis Hedges lived in Walthamstow, as did Emma, his wife, and their two young children. They would have another son in 1917. Private Hedges was hit in two places, the left buttock and high up on his back, where there was a bullet lodged under the skin over his right shoulder blade. It was the fourth time he had been hit in a period of just over a year. The first time, in June 1915, was in the face during a trench tour south of the La Bassée Canal, next he had a badly bruised back and suffered shock, probably from being buried by a shell, at the Hohenzollern and most recently, six weeks earlier, he was hit in both hands by shell particles. Not until this fourth wound was he sent to England to recover. Illustrative of the rehabilitation process in the BEF was where he was after his second wound, three months in Base hospitals and convalescing and then three months in the Entrenching Battalion before coming back to the Battalion at the beginning of April. Private William Brown, a Midlothian miner until November 1914, was hit in the stomach, his injuries including ones to his bladder and a buttock from which he did not recover. He died next day, having been out for fourteen months though he was away for much of the summer of 1915 after going sick, initially with influenza. He was wounded once before, a slight head wound at the Hohenzollern, on the same day that Private Hedges was wounded there. Private Brown had ten days home leave in January 1916. Hugh and Helen Brown in Arniston received a number of his effects, including a "devotional book".

During the day Major Barne watched the French shelling the Germans but the 30th was otherwise quiet and after the Grenadiers arrived once it was dark they went back to the Canal Bank and spent "all night thickening our roofs [as] tomorrow we are to do a big bombardment, expecting retaliation from the enemy. Trafford brings up rations and water (none is here procurable so all has to be brought up in petrol tins) not meaning to come again till night of 3rd." From now on over a fortnight they alternated with the Grenadiers, following the four day system between the front trenches and the Canal Bank. On 1 July, as the Fourth Army began the Battle of the Somme, at Ypres the British gunners shelled the German lines vigorously in the morning, starting up again in the afternoon. There was some initial retaliation and Major Barne recorded "direct hits on our dug-outs or very close to them – up to lunch time we have only 2 men wounded. During the morning we hear for the first time openly of the beginning of the great advance namely that "the 4th Army and the French have reached their first objectives everywhere." Very good news – what will the next step be I wonder…During the day various telegrams arrive about "the push" but leave us rather hazy as to the net result." By the end of the day he was describing the German shelling as "pretty severe". Lieutenant Mackenzie was particularly doubtful about the news from the south. "Heard that 4th Army and French had been successful everywhere in gaining their first objective … which cheered us up. We had no visitors during the morning! …During the day we got given reports concerning the 4th Army attack – after the 1st report we did not think so very much of it. The taking of Serre seems to be doubtful they seem to have 2 Bns there who are cut off from the rest. Three corps are held: too much of our just holding the west edges of ridges and redoubts which looks as if we had hardly moved at all in places. They say we have 2,000 prisoners & French have 3,000 but the whole thing does not seem to have gone smoothly."

Next day he went on "Had a long night's sleep and a quiet morning during which we played the gramophone most of the time. Fine warm morning. Had one man buried (shell shock) and Sgt Bannister slightly wounded by a pipsqueak." He played poker with other officers in the afternoon and chemin de fer with Captain Ross in the evening. Later he went to Brigade Headquarters to check time, which had to be precisely the same for everyone, and there General Ponsonby told him that he had written to Headquarters Guards Division requesting that Major Norman Orr Ewing be sent out from England to take command of the Battalion and that they had supported him by sending on his letter. Major Barne had been learning to play chess and his "spare moments are now occupied with dominoes and chess." Lance Sergeant Percy Bannister was a pre-war soldier and probably a reservist in 1914. He married Edith Bushman at Southwark early in September and a month later went to Zeebrugge with the 2nd Battalion and was shot in the right hip during First Ypres. He left hospital in England in mid January 1915 and was subsequently posted to the 1st Scots Guards, with whom he remained till January 1917 when transferred to tanks in the Heavy Branch, Machine Gun Corps.

Currently the main British activity in the Salient, other than shelling the Germans, was raids on their trenches. The tempo increased to precede and then continued after the start on the Somme. These were to cause damage and casualties quickly, ideally capture a prisoner or two for interrogation and identification and sometimes to achieve a local tactical advantage. The 3rd Guards Brigade had raided twice the previous week and the Germans were thoroughly on the alert. On 2 July Lieutenant Dundas wrote "Another day of rest – in every sense. The guns, which were well on the job all last night, have ceased momentarily & there is peace. Some din last night – a field gun battery just behind us spitting out its 25 shells a minute, then the whine of the heavy howitzer shells going over from behind, and of course every now and then a heavy dunck as of J Braid playing a push shot at Walton Heath, and the dug-out quivers. German retaliation: as a matter of fact there wasn't very much. I suppose they've got some hell up their sleeves." James Braid was a leading Scottish golfer before the War and since 1912, when he retired from championship competitions, had been the professional at Walton Heath Golf Club. "We have raids almost nightly – 50 men and a couple of officers. Artillery preparation on a fairly wide front so as to keep the Germans in the dark as to where the actual entry is going to be made into the trenches, then they ring off for 5 minutes; the raiders rush across, and the Artillery lengthens the range a bit and forms a barrage behind the sector which is being raided. The raiders are generally over for about half an hour, and at a given signal are supposed to leap out of the trench and return with as much plunder, human and otherwise, as they can get. That is the programme, which of course is subject to alterations according to the preparedness of the Germans. If the latter has been properly ragged by the bombardment they generally get back intact. If not – that is, if he remains – is ready – well, you see all about successful raids in the papers, but the other night a raiding party from the ---- went over & not one came back." He wrote that Lieutenant Orr Ewing, his company commander, whom he liked and admired, "foams at the ludicrous optimism of people at home over nothing at all. How right – why be anything till there is a reason. Quite good news today from the south but it'll be a fortnight's show & there was too much of the "we took the western edge…we are holding the northern boundary of this village" etc. sort of thing…I must confess that I am not in the least imbued with "that cheery optimism which characterises our lads in the trenches", nor have I seen much of it out here. No one is in the least gloomy, but most are quite unable to see any signs of the end."

After dark on the 2nd the British guns, having spent the previous day putting down a long, steady bombardment on the German trench lines, shelled those nearby very heavily for twenty minutes from twenty past nine. What was coming next was a 2nd Irish Guards bombing raid over to the right near Krupp Farm. They captured two prisoners and stayed to do as much damage as they could for ten minutes, but were soon being shelled by the Germans, firing fiercely onto the lost piece of trench and beyond. Lieutenant Mackenzie only heard of a single prisoner being taken, whose name was Joseph. "Joseph was suffering from shell shock which is not surprising! A trench mortar officer who had been operating during the attack looked in for about 4 drinks afterwards! News from the south seems better – we have got 3,500 prisoners, 2 or 3 villages, but they state that our attack is held up in several places which is bad." The Irish Guards lost an officer and fifty two men in this raid. On the 3rd Lieutenant Mackenzie was "Woken up by one large gun which persisted in firing every two minutes at a battery (I suppose) about 400 yards behind us making a hideous noise and keeping it up all morning." Then after dark and more shelling "we had a gas alert and everyone stuck on their helmets in the new way i.e. pinned to the front of the shirt ready to slip on…Saw 4 herons in the evening flying about." Private James Naylor was sent back with shell shock that day, but not away long. A joiner by trade, he volunteered in Hamilton in January 1915 and arrived just after Puits 14 Bis. Apart from this he was with the Battalion throughout until they left Cologne. His sister Isobel Naylor was in Coatbridge.

From near Boesinghe northwards the French and the Germans faced each other across the Ypres-Yser Canal, which the front line then crossed into the Salient. Private Johnes described how "About a quarter of a mile south of where our line crossed the canal…the REs had built a cable bridge across it…It was a footbridge only, cable and plank foot-walk with a cable handrail on each side. The north handrail was draped with gunny sacking to keep Jerry from seeing anyone crossing…He could not get a good decko at it in daylight because of the angle from his line, but at night he could take a chance and give it an occasional sweep of machine gun fire." He and Private Evans were manning a signals dug-out in the Canal Bank south of the bridge one morning when a battalion orderly looked in to borrow a gas mask. General Ponsonby had come up to look at the trenches "and had come along without his. George pointed to several masks hanging in their satchels by the entrance. The orderly grabbed one and went. George went to wash out a pair of his dirty socks, but could not find the satchel that they were in. An hour or so later the General's party returned and the borrowed satchel was returned with thanks. George washed his socks which the General had taken on a tour of the line. In the same spot a couple of evenings later, several of us were sitting outside chewing the fat, Jerry was taking pot shots with shrapnel, bursting about twenty feet up. One exploded just at the back of us and the splintered butt end of the shell buried itself in the trunk of a tree above our heads, the shrap had gone on by, a near miss, from Heaven, for some of us. General Ponsonby…was well thought of by the troops." Two of Private Evans' brothers were in a KSLI battalion, often nearby when out of the line, and Private Johnes accompanied him on visits to them. Typically "We stayed with them for a couple of hours and indulged in a little (21 or bust) Black Jack…we returned "home" with sufficient funds to finance us till next pay day."

Sir Iain Colquhoun came back off leave on the 3rd to find them at the Canal Bank before they went up to the front line in the dark on the 4th, where, next morning "At 10am, the Germans bombed my left hand listening post, but whether they were hand grenades or thrown from a catapult it is difficult to tell." They had stood to at three in the morning for an hour when he "had breakfast. Cloudy dull morning, & no shelling. Slept till 9.30am. Saw rifles at 10am. The doctor came round with the mail in the afternoon. These trenches are the extreme left of the British line, and we join up with the French although as they are on the other side of the Yser Canal we cannot talk to them. The trenches are good but very confused and difficult to follow. In places my Company is over 250 yds from the Germans, & in others, they come to about 40 yds. I have 5 bombing posts and 2 listening posts, which is rather a strain on the men at night. We have a good dug-out and the line is pretty dry, but snipers are very troublesome, as in many places the parapet is not bullet proof. Quiet afternoon and evening. At 1.15am the Germans again bombed my left hand listening post but did no damage. We threw double the number back." He had a number of visitors. Then "At 2am some green and one red rocket went up from the German line, and a light bombardment of our line started. The parapet was blown in in one place, but no one hurt. Left Flank had trouble with trench mortars and bombs, and the noise went on till daylight." That day General Feilding was touring their trenches when suddenly he was required urgently and no one knew where he was, except that he was last seen passing Battalion Headquarters. Orderlies were sent all over the trench system trying to find him. Lieutenant Mackenzie could not refer to him as "the Major General" over the telephone and instead used his first name, Geoffrey, as a code word, hoping that he would not be thought impertinent for doing so and subsequently writing to General Feilding to make his apologies, which the General acknowledged. Lieutenant Dundas, in a dug-out in the support line, again liaising with the French, had been "furthering the Entente by convincing the little French signaller up here of the earnestness of Great Britain in the war. He seemed to think we had done nothing & of course they feel Verdun frightfully. He almost wept when he spoke of it. And after all, the French have borne the brunt of the land warfare, which is all the ordinary Frenchman can be expected to understand. However, he was loud in his praises of "la Flotte" and was specially delighted at my being in "La garde Écossaise." It's a very real thing, the Franco-Scottish alliance, which, after all, – tell it not in Gath – is the result of a centuries old mutual antipathy to the Sassenach." Charles "Chick" Evans, an amateur golfer, had just won the US Open with a score of 286, which Lieutenant Dundas described as "a pretty stout performance", adding that the previous year another amateur had won it "but of course the American pros aren't very bright."

Private Fleming noted that the 5th was "very quiet all day owing to mist hanging about" but the 6th "Very lively last night. Trench mortars flying in all directions…and lights." Lieutenant Mackenzie remarked "About 2am tremendous windiness on part of the Germans who trench mortared right & left about 7.30 – the whole place ablaze with Very lights." Major Barne slept right through it. Normally a sentry would have woken him when this started, but this had not happened. Lieutenant Dundas was writing home again, having noticed that the Marquess of Lansdowne's daughter in law was about to remarry, "Isn't it curious to see how many of the broken hearted war widows of yesterday become the blushing brides of today? I suppose it's a sort of craze for record breaking. If the 2nd husband is a soldier too, as generally happens, to see how many husbands you can get through during the war. This is the only extenuating circumstance I can find for the almost indecent haste with which some women rush to exchange the weeds for the blossom (orange). I shrewdly suspect that the idea "He may never come back is responsible for enormous numbers of "war weddings". Very often of course it pans out all right – and he doesn't. But there will be a lot of work for Sir Samuel Evans & Co after the war, arising out of the consequences of the omissions of fate – in the shape of war husbands who have survived." There was speculation in the Battalion, but nothing definite, that they were about to move, which could only be to the Somme. Lieutenant Dundas understood that the British advance had halted to consolidate, which he thought sensible, but that the French were still attacking there. "Marvellous people to be able to go on taking the offensive with Verdun still on their hands."

Very early on the 7th a bombardment began ahead of a Grenadier raid. Then, after twenty minutes, Lieutenant Dundas heard the German guns give the British front line "absolute hell. They had about 60 casualties…This shelling isn't much fun. You're absolutely helpless – as to go into a dug-out is merely to exchange burial alive for disintegration – buried alive "It's such a stuffy death" as Yum Yum [Gilbert and Sullivan's *The Mikado*] said on a celebrated occasion." Of the raid Major Barne noted "not a great success, we hear. There have been far too many, and the enemy are far too watchful & knows how to act." Later he added, referring opaquely to the attack planned on Pilckem Ridge, "Many rumours going about that our "biff" is not coming off just yet…News from the advance in the South is tailing off, but they have done well. Some shelling of our line in the afternoon – no casualties though many squeaks, a Sgt got a bullet right through his steel helmet, (head piece, not brim) & never touched him." Sir Iain Colquhoun observed that "At 4pm, the Germans in the sap head opposite my left hand listening post, threw a lot of bombs between the lines obviously with the intention of making our men look up in order to snipe them. Through my periscope I could see the sniper quite distinctly."

Next day Lieutenant Dundas wrote "Gloom has fallen over us again – or rather resignation – as the result of the communiqué from the South. So that little dream has been effectively dissipated. The old story, Professional v Amateur – with the inevitable result. By the way how ludicrous the papers are. Photographs of men wounded in this show, beaming with joy, to illustrate our excellent "morale". It merely gives true expression to the unspoken wish of every man I've met out here whose sole idea is to get a nice soft wound & return. "The Heroes of the Somme" are objects of universal envy." It was pretty muddy but on the whole, expecting the worst and prepared for it, he found being in the trenches better than he expected. "Of course it is irritating to think of the Germans with beautiful concrete trenches 10 feet deep, dug-outs down stairs, & electric light etc but then we are we & they are they. Amateurs v Pros again." One night in the front line, so he told his parents on the 11th, he had had "to take 18 men to hold some outposts in front of the line where there was a gap in it – from 10.30 or as soon as we could with safety walk over the top and 2 in the morning. I first took them out & then had to come back. But I was out there about an hour and throughout the entire time discussed heatedly the respective merits of the Hearts and the Celtic."

As Sir Iain Colquhoun and C Company left the line that night they "came through Right Flank down Barnsley Road across bridge 6D to the dug-outs in Canal Bank. Had a bad mix up there which took ¾ hr to settle…we all got to bed very tired, cross and dirty about 2am." Barnsley Road was the main communication trench and Bridge 6D, also known as "Blighty Bridge", the one Private Johnes described with a German machine gun placed to shoot straight down the line of the Canal. There was more than one bridge, but that made no difference to the danger and, in particular, the sacking used on the sides to disguise movement did not screen anything when the sun in the west silhouetted men's shadows. Writing home on the 9th Sir Iain Colquhoun complained that it was very quiet in the Salient. "I wish they would take us down South and let us have a go there instead of keeping us sitting here; I am getting very tired of trench warfare. Dundas has just come out he is much improved." When he returned off leave "I found my parcel from Fortnum & Mason waiting for me also two month old haggis, green with age, the smell was awful!" Meanwhile Lieutenant Dundas was telling his family that "There is a youth here named Martindale – essentially Wykehamist…who is going to get on my nerves unless I am very careful. But I must control myself. Like Pooh-Bah [also *The Mikado*] "At all costs I must set bounds to my insatiable capacity for being irritated!!" Lieutenant Mackenzie spent the afternoons of the 10th and 11th helping Sir Iain Colquhoun and his men lay down trench grids and make bridges so it would be easier to get about when it was wet and "got quite a lot of exercise." The news from the Somme was better, there was also a good report of what the Russians were achieving in the east and word of a number of senior commanders in the Fourth Army being sacked, including General Stuart Wortley of the 46th Division.

On the 10th after dark C Company had to send forward three large fatigue parties, each under an officer. Meanwhile there were visitors to dinner and afterwards Sir Iain Colquhoun won three hundred and seventy francs at baccarat. Later the enemy shelled the communication trenches heavily for three hours in the dark. "The working parties had rather a bad time, 2 hit." Private John Kerr died of wounds the following day after being in the BEF since the previous November. From Kirkcudbrightshire originally, he was a farm worker when he volunteered in January 1915. In December 1908 he married Alice Black at Kelton and she, their three sons and one daughter were now living in Plantation, Glasgow. Also on the 11th, Private Cumming was hit in the left arm by a bullet at Blighty Bridge. "The sweetest words I have ever heard was when I woke up in a hospital bed in St Omer and the doctor said, "Yes, you can go to England."

It had been quiet for the last two days at the Canal Bank. That changed on the 12th when Right Flank and B were "crumped a bit in the morning" with their cook the only casualty initially. Lieutenant Mackenzie continued "At 2 o'clock our gunners elected to try out some new heavy guns just over from home – this brought retaliation on to the Canal Bank – then counter retaliation and so on ad inf: which quietened down at 8pm. Heard from Norman Orr Ewing saying Sherard Godman has got command of this Bn. Poor Norman very upset about it. News from the south not good today. We have lost Mametz Wood & Bois des Trones. Shelling again bad between 8.15 and 9pm. Then it stopped; a lot of big stuff down the Canal Bank. 9 men in Right Flank and B were wounded…Two men killed Hislop and Biggar. Reliefs went off quietly and were completed by midnight." Private Fleming wrote "Fritz shelled bridge. Big ones dropping all round. Tom Hislop killed." Private Thomas Hislop, a Glasgow postman, enlisted in September 1914, but did not reach the Battalion as soon as intended because in May 1915 he was absent for nearly five days, the penalty twenty eight days detention at Wellington Barracks. Crucially, however, he had missed his draft. When he did go out at the beginning of October he was sent up the line very quickly to the Hohenzollern. His mother Margaret Hislop in Glasgow received his cigarette lighter, letters, photographs, cards, a handkerchief, a metal wrist watch, a razor, a tooth brush and a pocket book. The other killed, Private Charles Biggar, was a car conductor and motorman on the Glasgow Tramways between 1908 and 1910, when he enlisted for three years. Though mobilised in 1914, he did not reach France until April 1916, the reasons being medical, persistent gonorrhoea and persistent rheumatism in both feet, between them keeping him on light duties and home service. His mother Ellen Biggar lived in Maryhill, Glasgow. Private Robert Dunlop, Captain Ross' servant, was hit in the right arm and cheek and sent home. He was a serving soldier of nearly ten years service and previously a riveter in Glasgow, though his mother Jessie Dunlop lived in Bathgate. He had been in the BEF at the very start and was wounded severely for the first time on the Aisne, following which he was away for eighteen months. In August 1917 he returned, was with the 1st Scots Guards till August 1918 and then went to the 2nd Battalion where Major Ross was by then Second in Command. While on leave in September 1918 he married Hilda Lund in London.

On the evening of the 12th they were going forward into the front line again. Lieutenant Dundas told his parents about the Germans' intermittent machine gunning of the Canal bridge so that "going across is always fraught with a certain interest…Curiously enough – or perhaps naturally – as we have had a very easy time my feelings have not been those of fear. But, after all, a certain degree of personal courage is a sine qua non, or rather a power of concealing terror, that every one possesses. The merit lies in how much fear there is to conceal. So far I have been fortunate in escaping its paralysing influence. But wait till you get a bad bombardment ("said I to myself, said I") [Gilbert and Sullivan's *Iolanthe*]. Then we shall see. Of course the longer one stays out here the worse one's nerves become." He knew that the fighting on the Somme had renewed, thought the casualties as listed not " "utterly bad"…but we've restarted in earnest now & I expect the losses will continue, as the advance will continue. We've got our continental-sized army now, so we must use it on the continental system. Brutal – but so is war altogether." He was very impressed by the French progress in the southern part of the Somme battlefield. "But it is all dreadfully slow – very costly." From the trenches he wrote on the 13th "We have got rather a dreadful old clergyman – a Presb. I'm sorry to say he plays poker & then runs along to people who don't play & says "Isn't it awful those people playing poker there – shocking." He never comes up into the trenches which the English men do, also the RC Irish Guards man & altogether is I'm afraid no advertisement for Scotland or the Church thereof. Doubtless he is an exception." By contrast there was a new subaltern, Lieutenant Vernon Daniell, "a nice lad typically English & was originally at Uppingham. Frightfully hearty & willing – a satisfactory person to do any work with. As a matter of fact in this sort of stunt there is nothing for the officers to do – or for anyone as far as that goes. We go round the line every now & then. Otherwise – nil. The Brigade have designed a new hell which requires the presence of an officer always at the telephone in Coy HQ because the signallers talk such a lot." This was intended to reduce the use of the telephone and so make it more difficult for the enemy to listen in. "We've got a great code book, which only the army could have evolved. There are code numbers for such things as "Enemy advancing in close order", "Enemy in the trench" and can't you see the conscientious officer wildly running over the pages of the code book of the latter emergency."

Sir Iain Colquhoun, writing the same day, told Dinah, now they knew, "that Godman had got the Batt for certain and would be out in a day or two. I am awfully sick about it as Norman was such a friend of mine and a much better man." That day Lieutenant Mackenzie heard that the two woods on the Somme had been taken again and on the 14th "Very good news from the South. We have Bazentin Le Grand and Le Petit also Longueval and our cavalry has moved in. In fact good news continued to pour in all day."

There having been heavy machine gunning of the bridges on the 14th Major Barne did "not waste time in crossing. These bridges are a permanent source of danger, discomfort and anxiety to us and one is always glad to be safely over." He was well aware that if there was an attack by either side the Germans would put down a barrage on them and they would be very vulnerable. Then there was something quite different. After a working party had finished in No Man's Land the night before six Germans tried to rush the covering party, who were ready for them. Five Germans ran away, leaving a sixth behind, but, owing to a misunderstanding between the NCO in charge of the covering party and the RE officer directing the working party, he was not brought in. Major Barne was up inspecting the line in the afternoon with a gunner officer equipped with a particularly good periscope when he received an urgent message to go to see the Brigadier. There was then discussion on "some interesting things about our future" and orders for a reconnaissance of a particular part of No Man's Land. Major Barne already had in mind to recover the German left the night before but General Ponsonby wanted "a trap laid for any Germans who might come back to look." Major Barne had already detailed Lieutenant Dundas for the original task. Now he went through careful and detailed plans for the additional ambush. Further, there had been a warning given out generally in the Salient about a possible large German raid and everybody was therefore at a higher level of alertness. In the event all went well and no one was hit, the only disappointment being that there was no German to be found in No Man's Land and therefore no Germans to be ambushed either. Major Barne supposed that "he was only wounded, and crawled away."

In moonlight the Brigade returned to Vlamertinghe after the relief on the 15th. On reaching camp Major Barne had "a good meal, & to bed at 2am, when I slept soundly till 9am." They had had to march about five and a half miles after a four day trench tour and Sir Iain Colquhoun found the "Men very tired when they got in." That evening Lieutenant Asquith wrote to Katherine "The night before we went out we had a game of trench baccarat. Sloper and I got in 3 officers of the Scots Guards and we made ourselves rather drunk and gambled and argued about Germany and St Paul's and the things that drunken Scotchmen talk about – including Scotland – from dinner till dawn. I won quite a lot of money, but I don't suppose I shall ever get paid as there was a good deal of confusion and in the end the score blew away into a wet shellhole." The Scots Guards remained at Vlamertinghe for ten days of routine activity, including working parties near the front line, occasional long range enemy shelling and performances by the Regimental Band. Sir Iain Colquhoun was playing cricket or rounders most afternoons, the cricket always being lost except when he was playing for C Company against another Scots Guards company. At night, however, he was winning at baccarat, roulette and poker. The Pipes and Drums having been at the Bastille Day parades in Paris, he wrote home on the 17th that "Our pipers have just come back from Paris where they had a hell of a time. They say the French wouldn't listen to any of the bands at all but kept shouting for the pipes, thus showing their sense." Next day Major Barne noted the "Great excitement caused by Captains & upwards being asked to volunteer to command New Army Bns, to replace casualties on the Somme. Luss & Lionel Norman apply. I hate having to send in their names. Even if I wanted to I am not allowed to apply, which I suppose I ought to regard as a compliment, tho' a distinct grievance – not having any chance of promotion here." On the 19th the Prince of Wales lent his car to Lieutenant Mackenzie and four Grenadiers, one of them his brother Allan. After also borrowing a second car they went to Boulogne. "Delightful day. Lunched at Mony's excellent food. Sloper bathed in the sea, we looked on. Bought fish at the market. Went to the cinema and saw Charlie Chaplin! Lovely drive back by night." Two days later, after judging the 2nd Irish Guards drill competition in the morning, he "Played cricket for the Eton team v the World – we won – got my eye cut open." Meanwhile the Battalion football team beat the Belgians 5-0. Earlier Major Barne was with General Ponsonby as he inspected the Battalion Transport "and expressed the greatest satisfaction. He is a very charming man, having his little jokes all the time, & even if he had to criticize he has the knack of doing it in a very charming way." He then had a pleasant surprise when Captain Seymour Barne turned up unannounced.

Private Johnes noticed how the RFC were becoming much more skilful during the summer. "They were continually on reconnaissance over Jerries lines, and there were many "Dog Fights" up in the sky which provided us with great entertainment, especially if it was a Jerry shot down. There were many experts at fighting on both sides. Our "Sausages" Observation Balloons, used to get Hell from the Jerry pilots. They would come in from the north, having evaded the Belgians or French up there, and make a sweep down the line of sausage OBs and put tracer bullets into them, setting them on fire. We saw as many as four or five downed in one sweep by Jerry. In one Dog Fight over our lines a Jerry took fire well up, and he jumped from it. If he had a parachute, it did not open and he came down spread eagled, one almost felt sorry for him, he was a gone goose anyway. No doubt our fellows were doing the same to Jerry sausages behind his lines."

Lieutenant Dundas regretted that there were only five Scots among the officers of by now a predominantly Scottish battalion. He named Sir Iain Colquhoun and Captain Ross, Lieutenants Orr Ewing and Abercromby and himself, forgetting Lieutenant Mackenzie. He felt that they made up for it on the evening of the 21st when "Last night we had a great stunt at Brigade Headquarters. The band was playing, so the Brigadier sent round an invitation to anybody to roll up, which we did. They cleared out the room, and we danced till about midnight. We had a great foursome – "Sloper" Mackenzie, Eric's brother in the Grenadiers, Luss Colquhoun, Wolrige Gordon, and self – Hugh Ross supplying the melody on the pipes – a crowd of admiring Sassenachs standing round." They had been totally absorbed by it in spite of the sound of the guns, of the flares going up in the Salient and of the sense, of which all were aware, that they must become involved on the Somme. Lieutenant Robert Wolrige Gordon of the 3rd Grenadiers came from Esslemont, Aberdeenshire. Sir Iain Colquhoun wrote home how "Yesterday was lovely, we played cricket in the afternoon and in the evening after dinner we all went round to the Brigadier's. He has a hut in the wood with a garden and had it all lit up. Our band played and we all danced. Hugh and I played the pipes and danced reels, it was the best evening I have ever had out here. I danced twice with the Prince of Wales!!!...We have all had a very good rest with no alarms, but I think within the next month or two we will be out of this fighting somewhere. Everyone still thinks that things are going well in the South and apparently the thing is going on for months as there are heaps of troops still who haven't been in yet."

After going to dinner with the 9th Suffolks Major Barne went on to General Ponsonby's "Garden Party, a weird scene band, & Pipers, dancing, easy chairs, electric light – small tables, champagne cup, peaches & foie gras sandwiches – at Bde HQ in the wood, not far off the inevitable circle of Very lights, & the usual chorus of machine guns, rifles, bombs & Artillery...Nobody enjoyed the entertainment more than the old Brigadier. The little Prince of Wales was there, & I had a short chat with him, when he startled me by reminding me he took me down to Loos last September, I never thought he knew at the time who I was, & even if he did thought he must have forgotten, but suppose he has the usual Royal memory for people & faces – even my ugly one." On the 23rd Captain Seymour Barne arrived in a car and they went to Dunkirk only to find that their naval brother was again at Dover. After lunch they drove to look at the wreckage of a large ammunition store successfully bombed by one German airman a few days before. "A very deplorable sight, acres and acres of shells scattered in every direction...Whoever designed the store must feel rather foolish, for it had proved the greatest failure." Then they came back, stopping at Cassel, where they had tea and admired the view, but back at camp "most strange of all during my absence orders had arrived altering everything." They had been expecting to go back to the line, but now were to go on the 26th to Bollezeele. Sir Iain Colquhoun noted that "At 12.30pm news came in that we were leaving the salient, and not going back to the trenches. Everyone delighted." In a letter on the 24th he told Dinah "We have had a splendid rest and the men are very fit. Last night at 5.30pm on the parade square there was going on at the same time, a cricket match, finals of a boxing competition, 2 church services and a tug of war all within 20 yds of each other. It was very funny…I'm afraid the chances of this war being over this winter are very remote, everyone hoped it would at one time, but it can't be helped." With leave currently closed for everyone, when it reopened he would be at the bottom of the list "so it won't take me for another 2 months after it reopens I'm afraid, unless we go to the Somme, when I shall be head of the list in no time I expect." Dinah Colquhoun sent him a piece of heather in one of the two letters he had just had from her.

On the 25th Major Barne noted that the 1st Hampshire Regiment had gone into a camp nearby "fresh from the Somme, but only very few of the officers and men were there." They were in the same brigade of the 4th Division as the 1st Somerset LI and 1st Rifle Brigade. That day Sir Iain Colquhoun told Dinah that "I am so pleased at getting away from this blasted Salient, I always loathed it and I don't care where we go now." After midday on the 26th they marched to Poperinghe and went for three hours in four trains for twenty miles to Bollezeele. Major Barne saw the Prince of Wales again just before they left when he came round showing great interest, telling them that on the Somme British troops had captured Pozières, on the road from Albert to Bapaume. "We steamed out of the station – or rather the siding – at 2.55pm wondering much whether we have seen the last of "the Salient". It seems impossible to believe that we have." He reflected that all in all the Division in general and the two Scots Guards Battalions in particular had been very lucky.

Next day Sir Iain Colquhoun was writing home about "a long day yesterday getting here but the place is worth it as it is very clean and quiet, the billets are good, and you can't even hear the guns." They were back in the billets they had been in before. "I have my old bedroom with the lace curtains and very pretty wall paper, sweet peas on a light brown background. We shall be here for another 2 or 3 days I hope, and then I don't know where we go to." He warned her that because of what some people were still writing in letters censorship was becoming stricter and stricter and "so when there is any movement on they may only allow us field postcards…We have still no Colonel but I am afraid that Godman is a certainty…The haggis and white puddings still go on. Didn't you stop them? Send me some scones (potato) if you have time." He had a losing streak at poker while at Bollezeele, the worst evening being on the 28th when it cost him two thousand three hundred francs. That day Lieutenant Ellis returned, ten months after his multiple wounds at Puits 14 Bis.

Major Barne recorded on the 22nd that "Our Doctor, Alexander, has gone sick & left us." Captain Hugh Bayly RAMC, his replacement, was forty two, had served in the Boer War and become a specialist in venereal disease. When he went to offer his services at the War Office only days before the start of the War an official rejected him on the grounds that nothing of the sort was imminent. Instead the Admiralty took him on with alacrity. He therefore began as a naval doctor, served for a year on board HMS *Princess Royal* and was at the Battles of the Heligoland Bight on 28 August 1914 and of the Dogger Bank on 24 January 1915. After a year with the Navy he went ashore and transferred to the Army, remaining in

England for the time being. Hitherto he had not been a Regimental Medical Officer, but he liked the idea of serving with a Foot Guards Battalion so he applied for the vacancy with the 1st Scots Guards. On the 27th he arrived "in glorious summer weather and beautiful peaceful country surroundings, untouched by war." He mentioned four officers of Battalion Headquarters at the start of his time with them. He found Major Barne "a delightful man about forty, equally popular with officers and men", but Lieutenant Mackenzie, the Adjutant, "of the martial rather than the intellectual type." Lieutenant Powell, the Sniping Officer, very much interested him in that "He had a genuinely good heart and seemed to be one of those rare individuals born without any sense of fear…somewhat of a braggart and yet, contrary to one's expectations, his boastings usually came true." He heard that when Lieutenant Powell first arrived he had made quite a bit of money on wagers that he could beat almost anybody at almost any athletic feat and almost always did. What was more Lieutenant Powell told him himself "that he *liked* No Man's Land, where he wandered off when favourable opportunities arose for a bit of sniping. Altogether a fine and simple man, who would always be there, or thereabouts, in any situation requiring pluck or athleticism." The fourth officer he wrote of was Lieutenant Leach, now the Bombing Officer, "who possessed nerves and imagination and was of the intellectual type. A charming boy."

At Bollezeele, with its training area complete with trenches, they started to practise attacking and then consolidating captured positions. Though Sergeant Henry Watson did not say when and where it happened, since he was a Sergeant by this time the circumstances suggested a training area behind the Salient in the summer of 1916. He told how when he and another sergeant were billeted at a farm, both of them smelling strongly after three weeks, they tried out the farm pond after dark in the nude, only to find that the smell, once they were in it, was terrible. "We promptly retreated & still nude found some old sacking & went to the farm pump, wetted the sacking & washed ourselves down in the dark. The farmer's wife, hearing the pump noise, to our consternation, came out & to her surprise, found two nude men with sacking round their loins; in halting & broken French I explained what had happened. To our relief she roared with laughter, told us to wait, & in a short while, returned with some hot coffee & cognac which was very gratefully received. She told us not to mention what she had done because her coffee & cognac supplies were very limited. We dressed, when she had gone, & returned to our billets."

When on the 29th the Brigade were told to move next day to the Somme, initially only for a billeting move it was said, the training stopped at once. Major Barne and Sir Iain Colquhoun went by train in the afternoon to try once more to find his brother at Dunkirk. This time his monitor was there, but he was not, because "He is out fishing. A signalman & I go onto the pier to look for him and we hail a boat which looks like his, but is not…so miss the last chance of seeing him. Bad luck." The Battalion quickly packed up and prepared for a lengthy journey and Lieutenant Bewicke left permanently for Headquarters 3rd Guards Brigade. Reveille was at four on the morning of the 30th and at half past five Major Barne and others were breakfasting in the Lion d'Or. The Transport with one company needed to help loading had left earlier, but everyone else paraded at quarter to seven and marched five miles to Esquelbecq. They had an hour's wait, but were all on the train at quarter to ten, leaving soon afterwards on what had become a very hot day. Their route, sweeping round to the west of Arras, went by Hazebrouck and St Pol to Petit Houvin, near Doullens. At half past two they "detrained and found weather intensely hot."

Notes on Chapter Sources

Rev G Rogers, *A Rebel at Heart* (London: Longmans Green & Co 1956).
Copy Diary of Capt ED Mackenzie, SGA.
The National Canine Defence League, Leaflet No 387, *The Dog of Ypres*, NAM/2004-03-27.
N Dundas, *Henry Dundas, Scots Guards: A Memoir* (Edinburgh: William Blackwood & Sons 1921).
Dundas Papers, Private Collection.
Dr HW Bayly: *Triple Challenge: Or, War, Whirligigs and Windmills* (London: Hutchinson & Co 1933).

Alphabetical List of Other Ranks Showing Their Ranks, Substantive or Acting, When First Mentioned in the Text

(† indicates deaths from all causes at any date and * indicates prisoners of war. All are Scots Guards unless otherwise specified and information about others is as complete as available)

16647 Private John Abel †
10694 Private Abraham Acton, 2nd Border Regiment †
10059 Lance Corporal Angus Adair
12468 Sergeant James Adam
16380 Private James Angus Adam
9318 Private John Adams
10246 Private David Adamson †
9744 Lance Corporal Arthur Charles Adlam
10437 Lance Corporal James Aitken
15254 Private George Alexander †
7530 Private Lewis Alexander †
12855 Lance Sergeant James Alker
12884 Sergeant Thomas Alker
12883 Guardsman William Alker
10060 Private Alexander Allan*
2670 Private James Allan, 1/4th Black Watch †
12156 Private James Allardyce
12155 Sergeant William Allardyce
8476 Private Frederick Albert Allen
7538 Private Samuel James Allen †
7280 Private Dan Walter Allison †
10071 Private Harry Alston †
11634 Lance Corporal John Paul Anderson
10729 Private Thomas Anderson †
12190 Private William "Willie" Anderson †
13831 Private William Anderson †
11505 Lance Corporal Percy Ronald Anderton †
6576 Lance Corporal Thomas Malcolm Archibald †
11932 Private Samuel Armstrong
11480 Private Thomas Hunter Armstrong †
11317 Private William Armstrong
10679 Private Charles Arnold †
3973 Corporal Robert Arnott

7251 Sergeant Henry Arrowsmith (also Smith)
9882 Private John Ashton †
8884 Private Arthur Aslett †
14909 Private Henry Aspinall †
8270 Private Albert Auger
13087 Private Percy Avery †
3172 Regimental Sergeant Major Sydney Axten, 1st Cameron Highlanders
8321 Private James Badams, 1st Royal Welsh Fusiliers*
9428 Private George Bailey †
9631 Private Wilfred Charles Bailey (also Baillie)
5768 Private Robert Baillie †
10259 Private George Bain †
10428 Private John Bain
6946 Private Peter Baird
10778 Private Albert Baker †
4787 Company Sergeant Major George Ernest Baker †
8100 Lance Corporal Joseph Balch †
1639 Private Duncan Balfour, 1/14th London Regiment, London Scottish
16867 Private James Banks †
6471 Lance Sergeant Percy Bannister
16291 Lance Corporal William Barclay
5147 Private Harry Barker, 1st Coldstream Guards*
5243 Company Sergeant Major Albert John "Jack" Barker
5383 Private Evan Barnett*†
8194 Private George Benjamin Barrett
8929 Private Joseph Barry*†
10323 Sergeant Robert Barry †
12014 Private William Barry †
9819 Private Herbert Bartlett, 1st Coldstream Guards †

15529 Private Thomas Barton, 2nd Grenadier Guards
3218 Company Sergeant Major Joseph Barwick
8297 Lance Sergeant Frederick Arthur Bassett
13152 Private Thomas Batchelor †
9134 Lance Corporal William Edgar Batten
9381 Private James Robertson Baxter †
11485 Private William Charles Baxter †
9329 Private Henry Charles Arthur Beal †
6683 Private Alexander Beattie*
9216 Private Alexander Beattie †
11324 Private Charles Beattie
9141 Private William Beattie †
8780 Private Herbert Harvey Beck †
10710 Private Thomas Ewart Beckett †
17012 Private William Bedford †
12021 Private William Beeby*
9346 Private James Begg †
10847 Lance Corporal Thomas Belger †
4734 Sergeant George Bell †
6628 Private George Bell*
14544 Private George Bell †
11031 Private James Bell †
6570 Sergeant John Bell
10551 Private William Bellas †
11299 Lance Corporal Jacob Bennett
14666 Private Arthur Bergenroth †
11115 Private James Beveridge (also Bergenroth) †
7755 Private Charles Biggar †
17007 Private Charles George Sam "Bigsey" or "Mrs Wiggs" Biggs
11352 Private James Binnie †
7959 Private Lenord Bird*†
9726 Sergeant Walter Henry Bird †
10525 Private Alexander Birnie †
10288 Private James Birss*
15524 Private Robert Thomson Bisset †
6400 Lance Sergeant Alexander Black †
11997 Lance Corporal William Black †
6487 Private William Blackburn*
6027 Sergeant Sidney Blackman*
8037 Private Charles Worsley Blackshaw †
12794 Private Adam Blaikie †
10268 Lance Sergeant James McLay Blair †
14822 Private James Charles Blair
8815 Lance Corporal Oliver Blaze*
7387 Lance Corporal William Bland*
9450 Lance Sergeant Frank Joseph Blessington
7843 Private Alfred Blucher †
10188 Private Victor Blundell †
[Number unknown] Private Frederick Bodsworth, KOYLI*
9232 Private Henry Bolam, 1st Coldstream Guards*†

8386 Sergeant Walter Bold †
8456 Private Thomas Bolwell, 2nd Wiltshire Regiment*
17126 Private William Boot †
8428 Private Alex Borland*
8958 Private David Bowles
15722 Private Ernest Alfred Bowles †
6302 Lance Sergeant David Boyle †
14817 Private William Boyle
7496 Drummer Frederick Bradford †
5426 Private Thomas Bradshaw*
9474 Private James Brand †
15533 Private William Brechin
13438 Private Isaiah Breckenridge
14516 Private John Henry Breckenridge
13608 Lance Corporal John Duncan Bremner †
10363 Private WH Bridgeman, 1st Royal Welsh Fusiliers
10696 Private Clifford Bridgeman, 1st Royal Welsh Fusiliers †
11651 Company Sergeant Major Henry Brightmore †
9221 Private Richard Alfred Brooker †
6862 Lance Corporal Wallace Abercrombie Brookes †
6738 Lance Sergeant Oliver Brooks, 3rd Coldstream Guards
9827 Private Charles Brown †
16626 Private Edward Brown
9890 Private Frank Brown †
7609 Lance Sergeant Frederick Brown
10142 Private George Walker Brown
4410 Private John Brown †
12517 Private Reuben Brown †
6938 Private Robert Brown †
11913 Private William George Brown †
7414 Private George Browne †
6115 Company Sergeant Major Thomas Brownlow
7103 Private George Bruce †
7798 Lance Corporal Gilbert Bruce*†
7021 Private Thomas Redpath Bruce †
12196 Private Andrew Bryce
10641 Private David Bryce †
17008 Private Wilson James Bryce
12454 Private David Bryden †
5156 Corporal John Weir Buchan †
16834 Private Alexander Buchanan †
10646 Private Fred Buck †
10647 Private George Buck †
7846 Lance Corporal John William Bucknell †
13081 Lance Corporal Donald Budge †
7080 Sergeant John George Burke
7194 Lance Sergeant Alfred Burgess

7842 Private Arthur Burgess, 1st Cameron Highlanders*
11777 Private John Burn †
9763 Private Arthur Burns
12971 Private William Burnett †
7629 Private Peter Burns †
6289 Company Sergeant Major Arthur George Burrough
6552 Lance Corporal Charles Burtenshaw*
16594 Private Harold Bury †
5620 Private Henry Butler*
5327 Company Sergeant Major Hubert Butler
5927 Lance Corporal Robert Butters †
11222 Private Benjamin Bynoth
9252 Private William Cadogan †
8730 Private Alexander Cairns*
5064 Private Thomas Cairns
11946 Private Thomas Cairns †
9037 Company Quartermaster Sergeant Robert Calder †
11296 Private John "Johnny" Callachan †
14377 Private David Robert Cameron †
16322 Private John Cameron
528 Private John Cameron, 2nd Gordon Highlanders †
13435 Private Alexander Campbell †
15636 Private Andrew Campbell †
11486 Lance Sergeant George Strachan Campbell †
12279 Guardsman Hugh Campbell
12280 Guardsman Hugh Campbell
8642 Private James Campbell †
12281 Sergeant John Campbell
9440 Private Peter Campbell †
13976 Lance Corporal Robert Campbell †
16218 Private Thomas Campbell †
54550 Gunner George Canton, 117th Battery RFA †
9451 Private Walter Capstick †
84 Lance Corporal George Carlé, 1/5th London Regiment, London Rifle Brigade*
5754 Lance Sergeant James Carnighan †
16085 Private Arthur Carr †
7015 Private David Carrie †
16898 Private William Carrol †
6088 Private James Carruthers †
1867 Private George Carter
10495 Private Patrick Casey †
11215 Private George Richard Castle †
16796 Guardsman Frank Cavers
5302 Sergeant Jonathan Bertie Chaddock †
7824 Private Clifford Chapman †
5833 Sergeant William Chapman*
6336 Corporal Ralph Charman*

7953 Sergeant Alfred Chase
13174 Lance Sergeant Ralph Cheetham †
6249 Sergeant James Cherry
6864 Private James Cheyne
9267 Lance Corporal John Henry Child
8157 Private Wilfred Chilton
8745 Lance Corporal Charles Chisholm †
11724 Private James Christie †
5359 Private Joseph Clancy †
4790 Private Alexander Andrew Clark
5409 Drummer Archie Ferguson Clark †
16678 Private George Murray Clark*†
8593 Private Harry Clark †
24048 Lance Corporal Hugh Cuthbert Clark, 7th Suffolk Regiment †
10748 Private James Clark †
9283 Private Robert Fyfe Clark †
15606 Private Peter Clark †
17015 Private Sidney Charles Clark †
4577 Private William Clark
3289 Company Sergeant Major Cecil George "Nobby" Clarke †
6652 Private Harry Clarke
7905 Private Harry Clarke
7767 Private Lewis Clarkson
12743 Lance Corporal Neville Francis Watts Clarkson †
15452 Private John McIntosh Clyde †
7157 Lance Corporal Arthur Richard Coates
13882 Private Norman Cobbold †
16893 Private Thomas Cochrane
5453 Private Jesse Cockerton
9867 Private James Cockshott †
6715 Lance Corporal Edward Collins
7146 Lance Sergeant John Combe †
16328 Private Frederick Connelly †
3924 Sergeant Angus Connor †
50662 Corporal VG Cook, 16th Battery RFA †
2568 Private Percy Cooke, 15th Battalion Australian Imperial Force*
5437 Private Patrick Corcoran †
6063 Private Harry Corfield †
17004 Private James Corker
13823 Private Ernest Corkhill †
7852 Lance Corporal Robert Corlett
16224 Private John David Cormack †
5585 Private Thomas Glen Cornes †
9485 Sergeant Frederick Robert Corney †
4513 Private George Edward Cossey
7214 Sergeant Patrick Costello †
6707 Corporal William Richard Cotter, 1/6th Buffs †
9357 Private Isaac Coulter †
11156 Piper James Coventry

7873 Private Thomas Cowan*†
12798 Private William James Cowan †
14056 Lance Sergeant David James Cowie †
8661 Sergeant David Sutherland Cowie †
13780 Private Charles Coyne
5559 Company Sergeant Major Horace Crabtree
6736 Private Thomas Craig*†
13027 Private Thomas Craig †
10025 Piper William Dinnes Craig
7534 Private William Craine*
15421 Private Alexander Crawford †
2690 Private Thomas Crawford †
7869 Lance Sergeant William Creelman
3769 Private John Cripps †
7321 Private Wilfred Crossfield †
8532 Private William Crowe*
9247 Sergeant William Crowe †
16897 Private Adam Cruickshank †
13597 Private George Cumming
15898 Private John Cunliffe †
11512 Private John Cunningham †
11633 Private Robert Cunningham †
15130 Private James Currie †
7129 Private Sidney Francis Curtis †
10090 Private Henry Cuthbertson †
8567 Private David Cuthill*†
1931 Sergeant Major Edward Thomas "Tiny" Cutler
13330 Private Stanley Dack
16519 Private Montague G Dade, 2nd Grenadier Guards
9398 Private Robert Daisley
16782 Private Francis Dallas †
8461 Private Herbert Charles "Phyllis" Dare †
5636 Private Herbert Garnet Wolseley Dash †
8985 Private Daniel Davidson †
9720 Private James Davidson †
4969 Lance Sergeant John Davidson †
3759 Company Quartermaster Stewart Davidson
10373 Private Robert Davie †
11799 Private George Davies †
7131 Private William Henry Davies
15957 Private George Edward Davis †
9710 Private WM "Napper" Davis, 1st Gloucestershire Regiment*†
16057 Lance Corporal Thomas Dawson †
10510 Lance Corporal John James Deeney †
11224 Private Joseph Deery
7292 Private Patrick Deignan*†
7045 Private Richard Dennis †
9106 Private James Jeremiah Desmond †
6032 Private John Devan †
8728 Private Mandy Devir (also Diver) †
6528 Private James Devlin*

4295 Drill Sergeant George Dewar †
13865 Private Albert Dews †
15935 Private Harry Dey †
9028 Private Thomas Dick †
12779 Private William Dick †
3089 Private George Dickinson †
8772 Private John Edward Dickinson †
4865 Private James Dickson †
2395 Company Sergeant Major William Dilworth †
13912 Private William Dingwall †
11542 Private Horace William Dixcey †
10383 Private William Dobbie †
7012 Private James Dobson †
9018 Private Patrick Docherty †
12142 Private Robert Wyper Docherty †
6807 Lance Corporal Frank Dodd*
5471 Private Martin Dohney †
7863 Private Leonard Ernest Dolley †
17431 Private George Donaldson †
13861 Private James Donaldson †
10745 Private James R Donaldson
13909 Private John Donaldson †
11545 Private Robert Donaldson †
7338 Private Albert Doody †
13270 Lance Corporal William Dorans †
7351 Private George Dorrins †
7406 Lance Sergeant William Dougal
13350 Sergeant James Dougall
[Other details unknown] Lance Corporal Douglas, 1st Cameron Highlanders
15587 Private Andrew Douglas †
6386 Private James Douglas †
15682 Private William Douglas †
8659 Private Matthew Dowd*
9637 Private Jesse Dowland †
9155 Private Charles Doyle †
9323 Private Edward George Drew
16615 Lance Corporal William J Drummond
9636 Private Thomas Reuben Duck
10766 Private John James "Jim" Duckett †
10768 Private Thomas "Tom" H Duckett*
9298 Private James Duff †
7121 Private John Duffy*
9913 Private James Dumbreck †
8289 Private David Duncan
10239 Private James Duncan †
13108 Private William Duncan †
8493 Private Robert Scott Dundas †
6666 Private Robert Stewart Dunlop
14566 Private William Durran †
11323 Private George Durward
11322 Private David Duthie
13566 Private Francis Eadie †

8367 Private Fredrick Eccles*†
10516 Lance Sergeant George Edge
6567 Sergeant James Edmond †
11640 Private Robert Duthie Edmond †
13904 Private John Law Ednie †
15078 Lance Corporal George Edward †
3025 Company Sergeant Major William Edwards*
13709 Private Edward Eggie †
6573 Private John Sinclair Elder †
10746 Private Robert Elder †
18066 Private Harry Barnard Eldridge, 1st Grenadier Guards †
8755 Private Albert Ellender †
10684 Lance Corporal Benjamin Elliott †
1517 Company Sergeant Major William Joshua Ellott †
10404 Private Peter Ennis †
11126 Private Alexander Erskine †
8600 Lance Sergeant Ernest Arthur "George" Evans
8717 Sergeant Thomas "Tom" Evans, Royal Scots
8525 Private Thomas Richard Evans
4258 Private William Everitt †
12496 Private William Whitehead Ewing †
1898 Lance Corporal George Fairbank
11097 Private Samuel Falls †
11804 Private John Farquharson †
5447 Private James Farrell †
5139 Private George Farries*
16478 Private Bernard Saville Faulder †
6255 Private Frank William Fay †
6124 Private Edward Fegan*†
16863 Private Alexander Black Ferguson
8914 Private John Ferguson
2925 Sergeant William Henry John Ferrett †
9159 Lance Corporal Charles Edward "The Tiger" Finch †
15310 Private Adam Finlayson †
5912 Private James Finlayson
12482 Private James Finnie †
8705 Private William Finnie, 1st Cameron Highlanders †
17006 Private Paul Fitzell
1736 Private John Fitzpatrick, 1/4th Black Watch †
9082 Private James Fitzsimmons
8499 Private George Norris Flather †
13304 Private Henry Flavell †
10800 Private Alexander Mitchell Fleming †
13835 Private Alexander "Alex" Munro Fleming
11370 Private John Cairns Fleming †
14863 Lance Corporal William Fleming †
13958 Private William Flight †
8746 Private Alexander Forbes*

13007 Private Peter Forbes †
10913 Private William Forbes*†
10747 Private William Ford
5285 Lance Corporal William Forster, 1st Coldstream Guards*
12492 Private James Forrester †
9732 Private John Foster
12015 Lance Sergeant James Fotheringham †
7955 Lance Corporal Leo Sydney John Foulds †
3617 Company Sergeant Major William Fowler †
5192 Lance Corporal John Howard "Jack" Frampton †
9704 Private Farquhar Fraser †
16899 Private Ian Fraser †
11652 Private John Fraser †
5159 Lance Corporal William Fraser*
13153 Private Thomas Freeman
6396 Private James Freemantle †
7764 Private Percy William Freemantle
6268 Private Thomas Freemantle †
8678 Private John Friars †
10084 Private Henry Fricker †
10083 Private Walter Fudge †
10251 Sergeant Harry Fuller †
13529 Private Robert Fullerton †
10286 Sergeant John Connell Fulton
8044 Private Charles Gaiger †
5022 Lance Corporal John Gall*
10384 Private David Gallacher †
9397 Lance Corporal Daniel Gallagher †
14027 Private Edward Gallagher
12513 Private David Hunter Galloway †
4952 Lance Corporal William Galloway, 1st Coldstream Guards
8633 Private John Gamble †
6248 Private William James Gamble †
5550 Private James "Jimmy" Gammack †
13434 Private James Gardiner †
11920 Private David Gardyne †
6838 Private John Gargan
5632 Sergeant Alexander Garroway †
10029 Private William Garven †
8704 Lance Corporal Harry Gaunt †
7894 Lance Sergeant George Geddes, 1st Cameron Highlanders †
12009 Private Alexander Gibb †
16947 Private Norman Gibb †
6998 Private John Edward Gibson †
12501 Private William Gibson
13408 Private George Patrick Gifford
11990 Private William Gilchrist †
9567 Private Denis Gildea †
6247 Lance Corporal John "Jack" Gill*
15293 Private Charles Gilmour †

11518 Private David Gilmour †
14695 Private David Gilmour
4560 Company Quartermaster Sergeant William Goddard*†
16503 Private George Frederick Godfrey †
13477 Sergeant James Hutchison Goldie
7152 Private Benjamin Good (true name Kenneth Cook Whistler)*
5545 Private John Goodread †
15161 Private Charles Gordon †
4967 Company Sergeant Major W Gordon, 1st Cameron Highlanders
11194 Private James Gorman †
8444 Private Herbert Frank Gosling †
3158 Sergeant Owen Percy Gosling
12175 Private James Henry Govan
13552 Private Angus Graham †
6532 Sergeant Harry Graham*
12193 Private James Graham †
17021 Private Stephen Graham
15790 Lance Corporal William Graham †
9393 Private David Grant
7338 Company Sergeant Major Donald Grant, 1st Cameron Highlanders †
13932 Lance Corporal George Henry Grant †
13643 Private James Grant
7940 Private John Grant, 1st Cameron Highlanders †
7558 Private Peter Grant
12488 Lance Corporal Richard Grant †
16741 Private John C Gray*
11079 Lance Corporal Thomas Gray †
9466 Private Charles Osborne "Cog" Green
7721 Lance Corporal Charles Edward Green*
12115 Sergeant Herbert William Green †
6127 Private Denis Greenwood †
10783 Private William Greig †
16487 Private William Groundwater
9384 Private Harry Groves †
9046 Lance Corporal Hugh Gunn †
17009 Private Edward Gurton †
12214 Corporal Benjamin Guy, 1st Coldstream Guards*
9926 Private John Hacking †
10878 Private John Hadden †
16729 Private James Hair †
15858 Private William Haldenby †
16450 Private Charles Henry Hall †
16050 Guardsman William Parbery Hall
5076 Private William Hall †
5053 Private William John Hall †
9879 Private Edward Hamill †
10366 Private James Hamilton †
16713 Private James Robertson Hamilton

5645 Private Thomas Hampton †
15739 Private Alexander Handyside †
12257 Private Owen Edward Hanson †
11259 Private James Hardie †
11329 Private William Currie Hardie
15607 Private Edward William Harper †
17069 Private William Arthur Harper †
7095 Sergeant Frederick Harris*
1920 Private Hugh Harris †
6135 Private Thomas Harris, 2nd Irish Guards
2670 Private John Robert Cameron Harrison †
4398 Private Neil Harrison †
5460 Private John Edward Hartland †
14304 Private Glen Haslam †
10322 Private Adam Hyslop Hastings †
16102 Private Alexander Gordon Hastings
7958 Private Patrick Michael Hastings †
12050 Private Robert Gordon Hattle
7153 Private Edwin Hawkins
15703 Lance Corporal Ernest Alfred Hawkins
16655 Private Alexander Hay †
11037 Private Christopher Hay †
5019 Company Sergeant Major Hughie Job Hayes, 2nd Welsh Regiment †
11788 Private John Healey
17010 Private Sydney Heard
12388 Lance Sergeant Ernest A Heaton
11889 Private Arthur Hedges †
3363 Quartermaster Sergeant Herbert Edward Heffer
8381 Private Herbert Helstrip*
17220 Private Andrew Henderson †
11579 Lance Corporal Douglas Gilruth Henderson †
16298 Private James Henderson †
16555 Private James Henderson †
10400 Lance Corporal James MacDowall Henderson †
15844 Private Thomas Henderson †
8602 Private Charles Adophus Hendrick
12559 Private William Hendry †
15377 Private Peter Henry
9673 Private Robert Herriott †
11935 Private Charles Heverley †
7250 Company Sergeant Major Harry Heyes †
6762 Private Arthur Hill
14240 Lance Corporal David Hill †
10530 Private John Hipkin*
11397 Private Thomas "Tom" Hislop †
15911 Private Arthur Hodgson †
11992 Private Peter Hodgson †
11018 Private Frank Hodkinson †
8111 Drill Sergeant William Hogan, 1st Grenadier Guards*

Alphabetical List of Other Ranks 575

5342 Private Adam Hogg †
7220 Lance Corporal John Henry "Harry" Holden
15312 Private Fred Holdsworth
4965 Private George "Joe" Holroyd*
1315 Company Sergeant Major Thomas Holt †
12366 Private Allan Hook
1384 Company Sergeant Major William Hopkins
11599 Lance Corporal Alexander Horne
12208 Lance Sergeant Alexander "Sandy" Horne †
15303 Private William Horne †
14315 Lance Corporal James Horrocks †
7774 Private James Horsburgh †
13464 Private Thomas Hothersall †
8857 Sergeant Francis Thomas House †
7358 Private Vincent Howard*
11800 Private Robert Howlett †
5665 Sergeant Frank Howson
13463 Private Frank Hudson †
7631 Private George Hudson, 1st Coldstream Guards*
[Number unknown] Private Hudson, Yorkshire Regiment*
3353 Lance Corporal Albert Huggins*†
6776 Corporal Christopher Hughes, 2nd Irish Guards
7932 Private Douglas Hughes (true name John McRae)*†
7562 Private Frederick John Hughes †
12560 Private Irvine Hughes †
14009 Lance Sergeant Thomas Lister Hughes
9328 Private John Hull †
11009 Private Frederick William Hunt
12497 Private George Hunter †
12383 Private Murray Hunter †
5406 Sergeant James Huston*
14095 Private Robert Hutchinson
7523 Private Thomas Hutchison
12362 Lance Corporal Richard Ibison †
12361 Private George Ibison
14814 Private Harry James Imrie †
7088 Private Albert Ingham*
3463 Drill Sergeant David Ingham*
14527 Lance Corporal Thomas Bennett Ingleson †
10482 Sergeant Frank Inglis
11544 Lance Sergeant Alexander Ian Ingram
9685 Lance Corporal James Innes
11331 Private Robert Innes †
10529 Private Adam Ion †
2215 Sergeant Clement Irons*
9889 Sergeant William George Ironside †
9888 Private Andrew Irving †

10636 Private John Hamilton Irwin †
13221 Lance Corporal Arthur Isaac
5948 Lance Sergeant Harry Issott
5099 Private Gilbert Ivall †
5794 Lance Corporal Alexander Jack †
13269 Private Alexander Jack †
13838 Private James Jack †
10015 Private Robert Jack †
8054 Private James Jackson †
14716 Lance Corporal William Jackson (true name Thomas Percival Sutton)
9604 Sergeant Albert Edward Jacobs
8038 Sergeant Alfred James
11247 Private Robert William Jameson †
16311 Private James Lawrence Jamieson
15993 Private James Slater Jamieson †
6295 Private Samuel William Jarman †
6948 Private James Jarvis †
7793 Sergeant Leonard James Jeffrey
10415 Private Thomas Jeffrey
4642 Private Thomas Jess †
11046 Private Herbert Sydney Johnes (also Jones)
5450 Private Frank Johnson*†
4866 Company Sergeant Major George Johnson †
12618 Private Thomas Johnson †
5307 Private William Johnson †
8766 Sergeant William Edward Johnson †
[Other details unknown] Sergeant Johnson 1st Coldstream Guards
15196 Private Alexander Johnston †
12941 Private Frank Johnston
15415 Lance Corporal Daniel J Jolly
27910 Lance Corporal Andrew Jones, 48th Canadian Battalion, Highlanders*
13870 Private Christopher Jones †
10557 Private Edward Jones*
11353 Private James "Jimmy" Jones †
11535 Corporal Richard Jones
8132 Private William Henry Jones
6625 Private William Thomas "Paddy" Kane
7848 Private Clifford Keay*†
6374 Private Walter Keeler, 1st Coldstream Guards*
10880 Private James Keenan †
11966 Sergeant Bernard Keeney †
14644 Private John Patterson Keillor †
5266 Lance Corporal John William Kelliher †
6784 Corporal Bernard Kelly †
9437 Private Denis Kelly †
11744 Lance Corporal Ernest James Kelly †
8355 Lance Sergeant John Kelly †
10376 Private John Edney Tindall Kelly
15340 Lance Corporal Patrick Kelly †
16788 Private Bertram Henry Kendall †

7555 Private James Lionel Kendall †
9841 Private Alexander Kennedy (true name Butters) †
7632 Private Cecil Kennedy*
7490 Private Harold "Ginger" Kennedy †
5335 Private William Claude Kennett †
15509 Lance Corporal Wilfred Henry George Kerley †
12922 Private John Kerr †
13975 Private Robert Kerr
8753 Private William Kerr*
10109 Lance Sergeant Henry Holland Kershaw
7930 Private Hugo James Kershaw †
4732 Private Frederick Kewell*
10681 Private Clarence Harry Kiff (later Scaife)
10494 Private William Kilkenny
14765 Private Thomas Kilpatrick †
12599 Private William "Billy" King †
10535 Lance Corporal Alexander Adam Kinloch †
8908 Private James Kinniburgh †
13525 Private John Blain Kirk †
9023 Private Henry Thomas Kirkaldie †
2128 Drill Sergeant Charles Kitchen
13755 Private Charles Kneale
12448 Private Alexander Knox †
9790 Private James Lacey †
11872 Private Allan Laing
11040 Private John Laing †
15398 Lance Corporal William Laird
13850 Private James Christie Lamb
9231 Company Sergeant Major John Lamb †
8923 Sergeant William Lamb
8078 Private Peter Lambe †
6832 Private Alexander W Lamond (enlisted in 1907 as Alexander Grant)
10454 Sergeant John "Jock" Lamont
14488 Private John Duncan MacFarlane Lamont †
8325 Lance Corporal Cecil Langdale
6379 Private John Langley †
10197 Private Thomas Latto †
8313 Private John Laurence †
5579 Lance Corporal Richard Law, 1st Cameron Highlanders*
14347 Lance Sergeant William Robert Lawrence †
14637 Private Alexander Lawrie †
10897 Private William Lawrie
6610 Private Peter Lawson*
9738 Private Ralph Lawson †
12796 Private Walter Lawson
3187 Company Sergeant Major James Lawton †
3853 Private Thomas Carlyle Laxton

15225 Private Jacob Lazarus
7883 Lance Corporal Eric Leary †
6811 Sergeant Robert Leary
17965 Private John Leckie
13125 Private David Ferrier Leighton †
9075 Lance Sergeant George Leitch
12591 Private Spiers Leitch
14606 Private William Leitch †
3024 Company Quartermaster Sergeant Henry Bertie Lemon
414 Corporal Samuel Lemon
12801 Private Alexander "Sandy" Lennox †
6723 Sergeant Robert Leppington †
13715 Private Thomas W Lett
12859 Private James Libberton †
4769 Company Sergeant Major Charles Edward Lilley †
14426 Lance Corporal Harold Lindekvist †
16627 Lance Corporal Francis Thomas Lindsay †
7987 Lance Corporal Albert Lintott, 1st Coldstream Guards †
6892 Private William Linthwaite †
6608 Private James Litster
15382 Private William Loader †
6640 Private George Locke †
9917 Private Johnstone Logan †
8162 Private John Long*
8859 Private John Hargreaves Lord
15304 Private George Low †
9300 Private Robert Low †
10965 Private Patrick Lowe †
6320 Private Percy Luck †
5440 Private William Alfred Luck
8221 Private William Lucy †
7889 Private Fred Lumb †
7772 Private Richard Valentine Lumb †
11522 Private Laurence Lupton †
15749 Lance Corporal James Lyall †
9251 Private Peter Lyon*
7581 Private Archibald McAffer †
10281 Private John McAllister †
12284 Private John McArthur
10568 Private Robert McArthur †
10053 Lance Corporal Jock McAulay
7425 Private Hugh McCabe †
11036 Private Hugh McCall †
15551 Private Charles McCalley †
12242 Private Edward McCann †
12950 Private Peter McCarthy †
16199 Private Lachlan McCoag †
7761 Sergeant Robert Mitchell McConnell †
10449 Private Peter McCracken
11083 Private Patrick McCrae †
10218 Private William McCulloch

12792 Private Peter McDermott
8125 Private John McDermott †
15724 Private Alan Macdonald
10443 Lance Sergeant Allan John Macdonald †
9301 Private Angus McDonald †
9703 Private Donald McDonald
14412 Private Donald Macdonald †
13154 Private Hugh McDonald †
244 Gunner J Macdonald, Clyde Battery, attached 110th Siege Battery, RGA †
4749 Sergeant John Macdonald
6040 Sergeant John "Scrubber" McDonald
11333 Private John MacDonald (formerly Norman Martin) †
15154 Private Joseph McDonald †
12963 Private Robert McDonald †
5000 Private Roderick McDonald †
7845 Private William Cameron Smith McDonald
9506 Private William Macdonald †
14049 Private Andrew McDougall †
14267 Private Angus Joseph MacDougall
12813 Lance Corporal James McDougall
7775 Lance Corporal John McDowall †
8934 Private Charles McEwan*†
10028 Private Charles McEwan †
8255 Private Henry McFadden †
18278 Private William "Billy" Frederick McFadzean, 14th Royal Irish Rifles †
9399 Private Alexander McFarlane †
15870 Private Robert McGarrity
14954 Private Patrick McGarry †
4661 Private Robert McGill †
14920 Private John MacGillivray †
6981 Private James McGinlay*
11074 Private James MacGregor †
14440 Private Robert Chapman McGregor †
5277 Private Edward McGowan †
11066 Sergeant Alexander McHardy †
3356 Private William McHugh (also William Boal)*†
10853 Private Owen McIlarney †
16228 Private Angus MacInnes †
7743 Sergeant Piper Andrew McIntosh
9653 Private Duncan "Skull" McIntosh
16334 Private James MacIntosh †
13406 Private John Muir Macintosh
16392 Private George Alexander McIntyre *†
11922 Lance Corporal John McIntyre
10753 Lance Corporal Malcolm McIntyre †
13854 Private Alexander McIver
6432 Private William McIver †
14578 Lance Corporal David McKay
16321 Private Donald MacKay
12481 Private Donald G McKay †

10143 Lance Corporal John McKay
15103 Private William Pringle Mackay †
15378 Private William George MacKay †
11094 Lance Corporal John McKechnie †
12293 Private John McKeith
10455 Corporal George Ledingham McKellar †
6260 Private John McKenna †
5997 Lance Corporal Alexander MacKenzie †
5128 Company Sergeant Major Donald McKenzie
13740 Private George MacKenzie
10923 Private George Peat McKenzie †
8549 Piper James Mackenzie †
8185 Private James Mackenzie †
14774 Private James McKenzie
12935 Private James Gordon McKenzie †
15384 Private John Mackenzie †
13741 Private John Angus MacKenzie †
10798 Lance Sergeant Stewart McKenzie †
5743 Sergeant Thomas Mackenzie †
10068 Private Francis Christopher McKernan †
13539 Lance Corporal Charles Mackie
9389 Private James MacKie
14235 Private Robert McKie †
4739 Lance Corporal Thomas Alex McKim †
10596 Private James McKinlay †
6225 [probable] Private Robert McLagan, 1st Cameron Highlanders
7972 Lance Corporal David McLanachan
12391 Private Archibald McLaren
14312 Private Donald McLaren
10295 Private Thomas McLaren †
16742 Private Thomas MacLaren*
3355 Lance Corporal William McLarnon †
10485 Private Donald Maclean
6883 Private Duncan McLean †
9073 Lance Corporal John McLean*
11557 Private John MacLean
11024 Corporal Roderick MacLean †
5023 Sergeant William McLean †
10692 Private Wilson McLean †
10039 Private Archibald McLeaver †
16832 Private Donald MacLellan †
13224 Private Peter McLellan †
6657 Lance Corporal David Bain MacLennan †
7408 Sergeant Ronald MacLennan †
7387 Private William McLennan †
7107 Private Alexander Macleod †
10154 Private John McLeod †
4665 Private John McLinden †
8036 Private Joseph McLoone
4641 Private Robert McLuckie
9178 Private Frank McMahon †
5988 Private James McMahon †

7434 Private George McMillan †
7559 Private James McNab*
10939 Private Archibald McNair †
5829 Private Bernard McNally †
8769 Private John McNeil †
12768 Private Archibald Alexander McNeill †
13957 Private David McNeill
15472 Private Donald McNeill †
13301 Lance Sergeant Fred McNess
10749 Private John McPhail †
13981 Lance Sergeant Hugh McPhee,
10915 Private Alex McPherson †
6786 Private Alexander McPherson
12093 Corporal Hector James Heath McPherson †
4759 Private William McPherson †
15632 Private William McQuillan †
285283 Private Patrick McQuillan, 1/6th Seaforth Highlanders †
13373 Lance Corporal John Charles MacRae †
17231 Private Roderick MacRae †
10459 Private John McSevney †
11244 Private John McTavish
9522 Lance Corporal John McVean
9285 Private Frederick Macey, 1st Coldstream Guards †
8081 Piper Charles Scott Maguire †
7122 Private William Mahon
16792 Private Francis Thomas Maine
8969 Private John Malarkie †
14367 Private Robert Mallett †
10273 Private Henry Malone †
13070 Sergeant Robert Manzie †
12530 Private Nicholas Marino †
12502 Private Andrew Marshall †
11274 Private William Marshall
12994 Private Samuel Marston †
991 Sergeant Piper Alexander "Sandy" Martin †
10818 Private John Martin †
12397 Private Robert Martin †
13965 Lance Corporal William Martin †
9061 Lance Corporal William Muir Martin*
10062 Private John J Mason
9909 Private Robert Mason
14371 Lance Sergeant Benjamin Matthews
9215 Private John Mathieson †
7188 Private George William Maudsley †
7424 Lance Corporal Alexander Law Mavor
12750 Private John Maxwell †
15332 Private David Melville Mechan †
3189 Corporal William Meeke, 1/14th London Regiment, London Scottish
6118 Private Ernest Mellor*†
8433 Private John Menzies

10922 Lance Corporal Samuel Menzies †
13978 Private George Mercer
13229 Lance Sergeant Ellis F Merryweather †
15659 Private Robson Messer †
11499 Corporal Sydney Frank Miles †
7966 Private Stephen Miles †
11255 Private James Pyatt Millar †
12500 Private Arthur John Millard
9666 Private Ernest "Eric" Miller
12799 Private George Miller
10394 Private Harry Miller †
13302 Lance Corporal Hugh Hay Miller †
10031 Lance Corporal Robert Miller †
5169 Private William Miller †
9432 Private William Miller*
12113 Private Alfred Millican*
12114 Private Herbert Millican
8416 Lance Corporal John Milligan*
13421 Private James Milliken
5160 Private Frank Mills*
5422 Private David Milne*
15534 Private James Milne
11153 Private William Milne †
10024 Private Thomas Mills Milroy †
5628 Company Sergeant Major Alfred Mitchell
8127 Lance Corporal Andrew Mitchell
9803 Private Charles Alexander Mitchell †
6039 Sergeant Thomas Mitchell †
11091 Private William Mitchell †
8966 Sergeant Major James "Jimmy" Moncur
5751 Private Leonard George Moore †
10063 Lance Corporal Willie Moore
14489 Private Harold Morant
8050 Sergeant Norman Morant
14303 Private John Mordue
11967 Private R Morgan, 2nd Welsh Regiment †
9762 Private George Shadforth Morris
8663 Private Harry Morris*
13029 Private James Morris †
9212 Private David Morrison
10409 Private John Morrison †
11330 Private Joseph Morrison †
16829 Private Neil Morrison †
13809 Private Philip Morrison
13646 Private William Henry Morse
5716 Private William Moss †
15921 Private Alfred Mountjoy †
7708 Lance Sergeant John Moyney, 2nd Irish Guards
8747 Lance Sergeant John Muir
8747 Sergeant John Muir
11912 Private David Grieve Munro
225 Lance Sergeant Hector Hugh Munro ("Saki"), 22nd Royal Fusiliers †

10571 Private Kenneth Murdoch †
8497 Private Peter Murker*
9943 Private Tobias Murphy †
8727 Private James Murray †
5459 Company Sergeant Major William "Dooley" Murray
13083 Private James McGregor Naylor
9832 Private David Naysmith
15952 Private Alfred Edward Neale †
13516 Lance Corporal Andrew Neil †
8932 Private David Anderson Nelson †
13604 Lance Corporal Thomas William Nelson †
5306 Private William Ness †
7981 Private Benjamin Newbury †
6788 Private James Newlands †
7885 Corporal Theophilus Newman †
7868 Private William Newton Newton †
11332 Private Donald Nicholson †
11780 Private Alexander Nicol †
15709 Lance Sergeant John A Nicol
16733 Private Andrew James Nicoll
14823 Private John Maltman Wilson Nisbet
15563 Private James Nockles †
6909 Company Quartermaster Sergeant Patrick Nolan, 2nd South Lancashire Regiment*
12437 Private Peter Nolan
10159 Private Wilfred Norman, 1st Coldstream Guards †
16299 Private William George Bruce Norrie
15483 Lance Corporal Henry Norrington †
6347 Private Edward Nye
6282 Company Sergeant Major Edmund O'Connor †
8880 Private Joseph Bradburn Ogden †
6632 Private James O'Halloran
3556 Sergeant Michael O'Leary, 1st Irish Guards
6406 Company Sergeant Major James Archibald Leslie Oliver †
10369 Sergeant Thomas O'May
12100 Private Leonard Henry Victor Oram †
1941 Private Arthur William Orchard
12446 Lance Corporal William David O'Reilly*
2363 Lance Sergeant Edgar Francis Orford
5860 Private John Osborne*
13698 Private James Outram †
9359 Private Wallace Harwood Owen
10230 Private Charles Oxley*
13393 Sergeant William Richard Pace
7816 Private Edward Page †
826 [probable] Private Walter Palmer, 2nd Royal Warwickshire Regiment*
11165 Private Alexander Park †
10458 Private Richard Park
16807 Private Thomas Park †

12339 Private Thomas Parker †
13614 Private John Parlett
16004 Private Raymond John "Jack" Parsons †
6427 Sergeant Gilbert Partridge †
8760 Private William Pasfield †
12206 Private Alexander Paterson †
7113 Sergeant Robert Paterson
13537 Private Henry Paton †
14794 Private John Paton †
2429 Private Peter Paton*†
15867 Private James N Paul
9864 Private William M G Paul
10374 Private Robert Chapman Pauley (also Polley)
8889 Private William George Pearson †
9396 Private John Peat
6113 Private James Peebles †
5654 Private Wallace Peel †
16500 Private James Mitchell Pendrigh †
11267 Sergeant Samuel Penfold †
11903 Private Horace Perry †
10638 Private James Pert †
9989 Private David "Davy" Peters
[Number unknown] Gunner John Peters RFA
9988 Private Ralph Peters
9981 Lance Corporal Thomas Abbott Peters
14086 Private Samuel Petrie †
11856 Lance Corporal William Laird Petrie †
1310 Company Sergeant Major Albert Edward Pettit
8720 Private Walter Edward Pickard †
15331 Private Robert Pickett †
[Number unknown] Sergeant Christopher Pilkington, 1/28th London Regiment, Artists Rifles
11840 Private John Noel Pinnington †
11841 Private Edward Forbes Pinnington
952 Lance Corporal Thomas Pitt, 2nd KRRC*
7840 Private George Stirling "Jimmy" Plant
8430 Private George Pollock*
11679 Private Thomas Pomfret
9961 Sergeant Alfred Edgar Herbert Portlock
16447 Private Clayton Poulter †
10825 Private Alexander Prain †
13005 Private Andrew Pratt
13006 Private John Pratt
15390 Private John Prentice
4970 Sergeant William Preston †
9276 Private William H Preston
10272 Private William Ranken Preston †
6695 Private John Pretswell †
1606 Rifleman Reginald Prew, 1/8th London Regiment, Post Office Rifles
5343 Private Oscar Price †

12942 Private William Price, 2nd Welsh Regiment †
15766 Private George Frederick Prout †
7541 Sergeant William Proven
12226 Private David Pryce †
8751 Private William Purse †
4763 Private Walter Purver †
6363 Private Alfred Purver*†
4763 Private William Purves †
6018 Company Sergeant Major William Pyper
14335 Private Hugh Quigley †
6619 Private Hugh Quinn*
9143 Private Michael Quinn
9027 Private John Rae †
6024 Private Robert Foreman Raeburn †
12026 Private Matthew Ramage
8905 Private James Edward Rands
9868 Private Thomas Rawstron †
6152 Sergeant Charles Fordham Read †
3398 Private George Reed, 54th Battalion, Australian Imperial Force*
12186 Private William Reeder †
13972 Lance Corporal Benjamin Reid †
10500 Private Charles Reid †
8752 Private Isaac Reid †
11125 Lance Sergeant John Reid*
9694 Private John Fairley Reid †
12176 Private John Elliot Reid †
7498 Private Thomas Gordon Reid †
5821 Private John Reilly †
13665 Private Alexander Rendell †
14245 Private John Rendell †
53 Company Quartermaster Sergeant Selwyn Rendell, 1st Welsh Guards
14685 Private Thomas Rendell †
6841 Private James Rennie †
13987 Private James Renwick †
9702 Lance Corporal William John Rettie †
9556 Private Arthur Reynolds
16541 Private William Reynolds †
15122 Lance Corporal John Harold Rhodes, 2nd Grenadier Guards †
[Number unknown] Private Frank Richards, 2nd Royal Welsh Fusiliers
6768 Private Alfred Richardson †
10699 Private Edward William George Richardson †
9275 Private Joseph "Joe" Richardson †
[Number unknown] Corporal Thomas Richardson, 16th Battery RFA †
6484 Private Thomas Rickman †
15376 Private Hugh Smith Riddell
5496 Private Peter Riddle
11537 Private Reginald William Ride †
12484 Private Robert Marsden Rigby †
12945 Private Thomas Riley †
11387 Private Peter Ritchie
16403 Private Thomas Roberts †
12739 Lance Corporal Alexander Robertson
11406 Lance Sergeant Alexander Robertson
12198 Corporal Daniel Robertson †
10727 Private David Robertson
10940 Private David Robertson †
12601 Private David B Robertson †
9071 Private David Robertson
8696 Private John Robertson †
16727 Private John Robertson †
11743 Private John Robertson
16727 Private John Robertson †
9891 Lance Corporal Robert Robertson
15615 Lance Corporal Robert Robertson
9891 Lance Corporal Robert Robertson †
5569 Private Stewart Robertson †
11976 Private Joseph Robinson †
10771 Private Thomas Robinson †
11827 Private Thomas Neil Robson †
10392 Private William Rodgers †
8688 Private William Charles Roff*
11577 Private Richard Roscoe †
9426 Lance Corporal Charles William Rose †
9009 Lance Corporal Medwell Rose †
7605 Private William Moore Rose †
7880 Corporal Carl Rosenthal
8638 Private Alexander "Donald" Ross*†
8762 Private Charles "Charlie" Hugh Ross †
13819 Sergeant Hugh Ross †
9850 Private John Ross †
11918 Private John Ross †
11911 Corporal Robert R Ross †
13579 Private Thomas Ross
7526 Lance Sergeant William Ross*
11552 Company Sergeant Major William John Ross †
10219 Private Robert Francis Rossiter †
12487 Guardsman Duncan Campbell Rough †
8082 Drummer William Terence Rowe †
7391 Private Herbert Rowlands
1623 Sergeant Robert John Royall †
1171 Private Alexander Runcie, 1/6th Gordon Highlanders
10581 Lance Sergeant John Rush †
13223 Private Arthur Russell †
4810 Private Hugh Russell
15482 Private Maxwell Russell
16927 Private Thomas Russell †
13974 Private Walter Rutherford †
12397 Private Gilbert Ryan †
16046 Private Robert Samuel

Alphabetical List of Other Ranks 581

10126 Private Thomas Sanderson †
7684 Private Henry Thomas Walter Sargent
8500 Lance Sergeant D'Arcy Sargent †
6121 Private Samuel Saunders
4001 Sergeant Major George Arthur Scarff
7674 Private William Schmidt (later Smith)
8717 Private Frank Schuard †
8238 Private Frederick Schuard
15793 Private George Scott †
16379 Private James Scott
14050 Lance Corporal John William Scott †
16226 Private Leonard Scott
13362 Private Robert Scott †
9313 Private William Scott
12666 Private William Scott †
8068 Private James Scoular*
8479 Private Michael Screeney †
3544 Private James Sellar †
13037 Private Charles Alexander Shand †
14322 Sergeant David Millar Shannon
11730 Private Daniel Sharkey †
13397 Private William Sharp †
5093 Lance Corporal Alexander Sharpe †
4574 Private Reginald Hoffrock Sharpe †
12378 Private Edward Sharples †
12379 Private Frederick Sharples
13449 Private Evan Sharrock †
14796 Private John Shaw †
8189 Private John William Shaw †
9033 Private William Vaughan Shaw †
6264 Private William Henry Shaw*†
14962 Private Peter Shearer †
4014 Corporal William Shearing
13935 Private John Sheed
16425 Lance Corporal David Fair Shepherd †
14619 Private George Shepherd †
11855 Private Thomas Shepherd
6894 Sergeant William "Bill" Shepherd*
7407 Lance Sergeant John "Sam" or "Sammy" Shields
[Number and details unknown] Private Sillence, Hampshire Regiment*
11344 Private Dundas Simpson †
15644 Private Peter Simpson †
8456 Private Thomas Simpson
17283 Private William Robertson Simpson †
6043 Private Temple Frederick Sinclair
14729 Guardsman John Slidders
12829 Private John Smart †
9036 Lance Corporal Peter Smart †
6062 Private Ronald Smart †
15294 Private Andrew Smith †
9040 Private Arthur Smith
6423 Private James Smith, 2nd Border Regiment

9483 Private Frederick Smith (also Frederick Packman)*†
12360 Private Gordon Smith †
7841 Sergeant Hugh Fowler Smith †
16212 Lance Corporal Jesse Gordon Smith
11975 Private John Smith †
10072 Private William Smith †
14399 Private William Smith*†
5345 Lance Corporal Solo Snow †
8920 Private Sydney Snowball
11757 Private Andrew Somerville
9750 Sergeant Thomas Henry Sorrell †
9011 Private William Henry Southgate †
12123 Private Charles Speight †
14011 Lance Corporal James Dewar Spence †
11050 Lance Sergeant Randolph Churchill Spencer
8588 Private Reginald Spencer*†
7901 Sergeant Sydney Reginald Spencer
12135 Sergeant Hamilton McKee Spiers
10245 Private William Spiers †
16939 Private James Ernest Standing
8874 Lance Corporal Jesse Stead†
5970 Sergeant Francis Stedman*
12902 Private Robert Steel
10027 Private Donald Steele †
7734 Drummer Charles Henry Steer †
17238 Private Robert Stenhouse †
7607 Private Peter Stenson, 1st Coldstream Guards †
16389 Private Andrew Stephen
12757 Private Tom Stevenson
6007 Private Donald M Stewart
13849 Private Donald Stewart †
10372 Corporal George Thomson Robertson Stewart †
15375 Private James Stewart †
13487 Private John James Stewart †
16362 Private Peter Stewart †
5507 Private William Stimpson, 1st Coldstream Guards *†
9846 Lance Corporal George Stirling
9761 Private Andrew Stiven †
5607 Lance Corporal Cornelius William Stones †
15674 Lance Corporal Alfred John Strachan †
10668 Private Frederick "Fred" Strachan
12924 Lance Sergeant William Strang †
16045 Private Henry Lumsden Strathearn †
7830 Private William Henry Stride †
12881 Private Henry Strong †
7298 Sergeant Arthur Stuart †
13574 Private Edward Henry Sullivan
7744 Private William Summers †
11489 Private Alexander Sutherland †

10833 Lance Corporal George Stanley Sutherland †
10049 Private John Mathieson Sutherland †
11583 Private Thomas Sutherland
5360 Private William Sutherland †
9833 Private John Swan †
11921 Lance Corporal William Swan †
7310 Private Sidney Christopher Swanson †
12800 Private James V F Swanston †
7652 Private Brian Sweeney
9424 Lance Corporal Willis Swithenbank, 1st Cameron Highlanders
6957 Private Thomas Taggart
9894 Private Patrick Tague †
11484 Private James Tait
3497 Private John Tait
10861 Private Robert Tannahill †
1345 Sergeant Major Thomas S Tate*
6782 Guardsman Benjamin Tattershall
4947 Private John Tattershall*
10619 Lance Corporal Alexander Taylor*
15831 Lance Corporal Edward George Taylor †
14342 Private Thomas Taylor †
10611 Private William "Willie" Taylor †
13603 Private Frank Teal †
4735 Private Walter Teale
8327 Private Henry Cecil Lunn Teasdale †
10185 Private John Davidson Templeton
12044 Private Thomas Tewkesbury
12781 Private Charles W Thane
15671 Lance Corporal Albert Robert Thom †
4807 Private George Thomas
17070 Private Joseph Benjamin James Thomas †
245 Private W Thomas, 13th Middlesex Regiment †
16531 Private Edward William (also William Edward) Thompson †
9041 Lance Corporal George Younger Thompson †
14059 Private Joseph James Thompson †
5764 Private Richard Thompson, 1/14th London Regiment, London Scottish*
8706 Private Robert Thompson
6378 Lance Corporal Alexander Thomson †
11974 Private Alexander Thomson †
8543 Lance Corporal David "Davy" Thomson †
7776 Sergeant Donald Thomson*†
7560 Private John Thomson*
9150 Private John William Thomson
6747 Lance Sergeant Joseph "Joe" Thomson †
17287 Private Norman Drummond Thomson †
13959 Lance Corporal Robert Thomson
5797 Private Robert Thomson †
137320 Gunner Robert "Bob" W Thurtle, RFA

8212 Private Leo Augustine Thwaites †
10979 Private John Todd
14169 Private Joseph Todhunter
7281 Private Ross Tollerton, 1st Cameron Highlanders
8928 Private Frank Tolley †
10386 Private James Tonner †
9161 Corporal Arthur James Tooley (true name James Bullard)
9448 Private Thomas Topping
14306 Private James Moir Ross Torrie
10744 Private George Townsend
15007 Private Harry Towse
11879 Private John Travers
12763 Private Alfred Triggs
14620 Private Alexander Trotter †
8938 Private William Truman
13664 Private Edward Tuffin
13663 Private Grantly Henry Tuffin †
12382 Private James Wither Tully †
[Other details unknown] Private Turner, 1st Cameron Highlanders
11991 Private Andrew Turner
13181 Private Andrew Turner †
5430 Private David Turner
2137 Sergeant John Turner*
13719 Private William Turner †
5100 Private Albert Turton †
10674 Private James Tweed †
10841 Private Samuel Tyrrell †
10731 Private Graham Drummond Tytler †
5344 Private Charlie Unsted*
6418 Private John Unwin †
6061 Private George Urquhart
12536 Private Victor Vandermotten (also O'Neil) †
16043 Private Basil Charles Gordon Vaughan †
8074 Private William George Vaughan
8004 Private William Robert Veitch
11676 Private James Venters*
7116 Private Sydney Venton, 1st Coldstream Guards*
2957 Private Richard Henry Vine †
12551 Lance Corporal John Waddell
10695 Sergeant Adolphus Harry Wade †
1542 Sergeant Major Frederick John "Bumps" Wadham
9016 Lance Corporal Francis Walker
14435 Private Ralph Walker †
15143 Lance Corporal Norman Wills McGlashan Wallace †
9180 Sergeant John Walsh †
2510 Sergeant David Walshe, 1st Irish Guards*
5384 Private Thomas Walmsley*

13351 Private James Todd Wann †
10165 Lance Corporal James Warden †
13648 Private David Wardrope †
8285 Company Sergeant Major William Walter Warner, 1st Royal Welsh Fusiliers †
11041 Private Patrick Warren †
11547 Private William Waterson †
9083 Private George Watson
9210 Private Henry Daniel Watson
5925 Private Hugh Shaw Watson †
9897 Private James Watson †
11725 Private Peter Watson †
9756 Private William Watson †
5202 Corporal William "Billie" Boyle Watson †
13933 Private George Watt †
15523 Private James Bryden Watt †
15721 Private Adam Waugh †
11122 Private David Waugh †
10925 Private James Webster †
11049 Private Samuel Webster
10451 Private William Webster †
7908 Private John Wells †
15941 Private Clarke Wooding Wesley †
13954 Private John Wessell
7249 Lance Sergeant James Western †
4478 Lance Sergeant Joseph Henry Western †
9621 Sergeant Richard Innes Edgell Westmacott †
7060 Sergeant Joseph Weston
8786 Private Archibald White †
11996 Lance Corporal James White
13704 Private James Henry White †
12177 Private Andrew Whitelaw
8383 Private Charles Edward Whitley †
8046 Private George Augustus Whitney*
9920 Private Alexander Whyte †
10799 Private George Whyte
14008 Private John "Jack" Whyte
11655 Private William Robertson Whyte †
3755 Company Sergeant Major Herbert Wilford †
10722 Lance Corporal Thomas Wilkie †
5353 Lance Sergeant Angus McMillan Wilkinson †
7709 Corporal Joseph Bertie Wilkinson †
4831 Company Sergeant Major Thomas Alfred Wilkinson
8168 Lance Sergeant Alfred Charles Willey †
12111 Private Henry "Harry" W Williams †
9822 Private James Williams (true name William Gerald Lewis) †

9182 Private Herbert Graham Wills †
9209 Private James "Jim" Cadenhead Wills †
7749 Lance Corporal Alexander Wilson †
14274 Private Charles Wilson †
14818 Private David Wilson †
13934 Private George Wilson †
5541 Private George Henry Wilson †
12603 Private Gilbert Wilson
8167 Lance Corporal Henry Wilson, 1st Coldstream Guards*
11304 Private James Wilson
14823 Private Norman Wilson
12283 Private Robert Wilson
12815 Private Robert Wilson †
13274 Private Robert "Rab" Wilson
3143 Company Sergeant Major Sidney Wilson †
8174 Private William Wilson †
10113 Sergeant William Wilson †
12164 Private William Wilson †
16326 Private William Wilson †
13433 Private Francis Winton
13432 Private James Winton †
11770 Private George Wishart †
8566 Private Henry Frederick Witt †
6179 Private Donald Wood
7695 Private Harold Wood †
16444 Private Harry Blanchard Wood
15521 Private James Wood †
8387 Private Thomas Woodcock, 2nd Irish Guards †
1378 Regimental Quartermaster Sergeant Charles Ernest Woods
10364 Private Ralph Woods
20562 Private S Woods, 7th Suffolk Regiment †
10785 Private John Worden †
15756 Private John Henry Worker
7969 Private William Henry Wrigglesworth
5372 Private Hugh Wright †
16728 Private James Clark Wright †
6988 Private John Edwin Leigh Wright †
8926 Lance Corporal Herbert James Yates †
15295 Private Roger Yates †
8219 Private Stephen Frank Yates †
8783 Private Alexander Young*†
14382 Private George Young †
3635 Sergeant James Young*
9470 Private James Young †
636 Sergeant William Young
10540 Private Frank Yoxall †

Select Bibliography

Maj AG Ainslie, *Hand Grenades* (London 1917)
Army and Navy Gazette, *Honours and Awards of the Old Contemptibles* (London 1915)
CT Atkinson, *The Seventh Division 1914-1918* (London: John Murray 1927)
Dr Hugh Wansey Bayly, *Triple Challenge: Or, War, Whirligigs and Windmills* (London: Hutchinson & Co 1933)
Ian Beckett, *Ypres The First Battle 1914* (Harlow: Pearson Education Ltd 2004)
Maj AF Becke, *History of the Great War Order of Battle of Divisions Parts 1, 2a, 2b, 3, 4 and Index* (London: HMSO 1945)
Robert Blake (Ed.), *The Private Papers of Douglas Haig* (London: Eyre & Spottiswoode 1952)
Walter Bloem, *The Advance From Mons 1914* (Solihull: Helion & Company Ltd 2004)
Brian Bond and Others, *"Look To Your Front" Studies in The First World War* (Staplehurst: Spellmount Ltd 1999)
Donald Boyd, *Salute of Guns* (London: Jonathan Cape Ltd 1930)
Lt Gen Sir Tom Bridges: *Alarms and Excursions: Reminiscences of a Soldier* (London: Longmans Green and Co 1938)
John Brophy and Alan Partridge: *Songs and Slang of the British Soldier 1914-1918* (London: Eric Partridge Ltd 1930)
Malcolm Brown and Shirley Seaton, *Christmas Truce* (London: Pan Macmillan Ltd 2001)
John Buchan, *The History of the Royal Scots Fusiliers (1678-1918)* (London: Thomas Nelson and Sons, Limited, 1925)
Burke's Landed Gentry 13th Edition 1921
Burke's Peerage Baronetage and Knightage, 96th Edition 1938
Lt Gen Sir Adrian Carton de Wiart, *Happy Odyssey: The Memoirs of Lieutenant General Sir Adrian Carton de Wiart* (London: Jonathan Cape 1950)
Brig AEJ Cavendish: *The 93rd Highlanders 1799-1927* (London: Published privately 1928)
Peter Chasseaud, *Topography of Armageddon* (London: Mapbooks 1991)
Winston Churchill, *Great Contemporaries* (London: Thornton Butterworth Ltd 1937)
R Clark, *J.B.S.:The Life of J.B.S. Haldane* (London: Hodder and Stoughton Ltd 1968)
Rev PB Clayton, *Tales of Talbot House in Poperinghe & Ypres* (London: Chatto & Windus 1919)
Colonel AL Clutterbuck and Others, *The Bond of Sacrifice, Volumes I August to December 1914 and II January to June 1915* (London: The Anglo-African Publishing Contractors 1916)
Maj Gordon Corrigan, *Mud, Blood and Poppycock* (London: Cassell 2003)
Douglas Cuddeford, *And All For What?* (London: Heath Cranton Ltd 1933)
Norman Dixon, *On the Psychology of Military Incompetence* (London: Jonathan Cape Ltd 1976)

Maj CH Dudley Ward, *The Welsh Regiment of Foot Guards 1915-1918* (London: John Murray 1920)
Maj CH Dudley Ward, *Historical Records of The Royal Welch Fusiliers, Volume III* (London: Foster Groom & Co Ltd 1928)
Christopher Duffy, *Through German eyes: the British & the Somme 1916* (London: Weidenfeld & Nicolson 2006)
N Dundas, *Henry Dundas, Scots Guards. A Memoir* (Edinburgh: William Blackwood & Sons 1921)
Capt JC Dunn, *The War the Infantry Knew 1914-1919* (London: Jane's Publishing Company Ltd 1987)
Max Egremont: *Under Two Flags The Life of Major General Sir Edward Spears* (London: Weidenfeld & Nicolson 1997)
David Erskine, *The Scots Guards 1919-1955* (London: William Clowes and Sons, Ltd 1956)
Wilfrid Ewart, *Scots Guard* (London: Rich & Cowan Ltd 1934)
Gen Erich von Falkenhayn, *General Headquarters 1914-1916 and its Critical Decisions* (London: Hutchinson and Co 1919)
Gen Sir Anthony Farrer-Hockley, *The Somme* (London: BT Batsford Ltd 1964)
Gen Sir Anthony Farrer-Hockley: *Ypres 1914 Death of an Army* (London: Arthur Barker Ltd London 1967)
Lt Col Rowland Feilding, *War Letters to a Wife 1915-1919* (London: The Medici Society Ltd 1929)
Niall Ferguson, *The Pity of War* (London: Penguin Books 1999)
General Staff: *Notes for Infantry Officers on Trench Warfare* (London: War Office 1916)
Capt Stair Gillon, *The Story of the 29th Division* (London: Thomas Nelson and Sons, Ltd 1925)
Gerald Gliddon, *Somme 1916 A Battlefield Companion* (Stroud: The History Press 2009)
Stephen Graham, *A Private in the Guards* (London: Macmillan and Co Ltd 1919)
Stephen Graham, *The Challenge of the Dead* (London: Cassell and Company, Ltd 1921)
Robert Graves, *Goodbye to All That* (London: Jonathan Cape 1929)
Bryn Hammond: *Cambrai 1917* (London: Weidenfeld & Nicolson 2008)
Simon Harris, *History of the 43rd and 52nd (Oxfordshire and Buckinghamshire) Light Infantry Volume II The 52nd Light Infantry in France and Belgium* (Clenchwarton: Rooke Publishing 2012)
Maj MCC Harrison and Capt HA Cartwright, *Within Four Walls* (London: Edward Arnold & Co 1930)
Peter Hart, *1918 A Very British Victory* (London: Weidenfeld & Nicolson 2008)
Cuthbert Headlam, *History of the Guards Division in the Great War 1915-1918* in two volumes (London: John Murray 1924)
AP Herbert, *The Secret Battle* (London: Methuen & Co Ltd 1919)
Historical Records of the Queen's Own Cameron Highlanders, Volume III (Edinburgh and London, William Blackwood & Sons, Ltd, 1931)
History of the Great War based on Official Documents by direction of the Historical Section of the Committee of Imperial Defence.
    Brig Gen Sir JE Edmonds, *Military Operations France and Belgium, 1914: Volume I: Mons, the Retreat to the Seine, the Marne and the Aisne, August – October 1914* (London: Macmillan and Co Ltd 1922)

Brig Gen Sir JE Edmonds, *Military Operations France and Belgium, 1914: Volume II: Antwerp, La Bassée, Armentières, Messines, and Ypres, October-November 1914* (London: Macmillan and Co Ltd 1925)

Brig Gen Sir JE Edmonds & Capt GC Wynne, *Military Operations France and Belgium, 1915: Volume I: Winter 1914–15: Battle of Neuve Chapelle: Battles of Ypres* (London: Macmillan and Co Ltd 1927)

Brig Gen Sir JE Edmonds, *Military Operations France and Belgium, 1915: Volume II: Battles of Aubers Ridge, Festubert, and Loos* (London: Macmillan and Co Ltd 1928)

Brig Gen Sir JE Edmonds, *Military Operations France and Belgium, 1916: Volume I: Sir Douglas Haig's Command to the 1st July: Battle of the Somme* (London: Macmillan and Co Ltd 1932)

Capt W Miles, *Military Operations France and Belgium, 1916: Volume II: 2 July 1916 to the end of the Battles of the Somme* ((London: Macmillan and Co Ltd 1938)

Capt C Falls, *Military Operations France and Belgium, 1917: Volume I: The German Retreat to the Hindenburg Line and the Battles of Arras* (London: Macmillan and Co Ltd, 1940)

Brig Gen Sir JE Edmonds, *Military Operations France and Belgium, 1917: Volume II: Messines and Third Ypres (Passchendaele)* (London: His Majesty's Stationery Office 1948)

Capt W Miles, *Military Operations France and Belgium, 1917: Volume III: The Battle of Cambrai* (London: His Majesty's Stationery Office 1940)

Brig Gen Sir JE Edmonds, *Military Operations France and Belgium, 1918: Volume I: The German March Offensive and its Preliminaries* (London: Macmillan and Co Ltd 1935)

Brig Gen Sir JE Edmonds, *Military Operations France and Belgium, 1918: Volume II: March–April: Continuation of the German Offensives* (London: Macmillan and Co Ltd 1937)

Brig Gen Sir JE Edmonds, *Military Operations France and Belgium, 1918: Volume III: May–July: The German Diversion Offensives and the First Allied Counter-Offensive* (London: Macmillan and Co Ltd 1939)

Brig Gen Sir JE Edmonds, *Military Operations France and Belgium, 1918: Volume IV: 8 August – 26 September: The Franco-British Offensive* (London: His Majesty's Stationery Office 1947)

Brig Gen Sir JE Edmonds & Lt Col R Maxwell-Hyslop, *Military Operations France and Belgium, 1918, Volume V: 26 September – 11 November: The Advance to Victory* (London: His Majesty's Stationery Office 1947)

Volumes with accompanying map cases and, as appropriate, volumes of appendices

Richard Holmes, *Riding The Retreat* (London: Jonathan Cape Ltd 1995)

Richard Holmes, *Tommy: The British Soldier on the Western Front* (London: HarperCollins 2004)

Capt Sir Edward Hamilton Westrow Hulse, Bt, *Letters Written from the English Front in France between September 1914 and March 1915* (Privately published, 1916)

Capt EA James, *A Record of the Battles and Engagements of the British Armies in France and Flanders, 1914-1918* (Aldershot: Gale & Polden Ltd 1924)

John Jolliffe, *Raymond Asquith, Life and Letters* (London: Collins 1980)

Ernst Jünger, *Storm of Steel* (London: Penguin Books Ltd 2004 in translation by Michael Hoffman 2003)

Lt Col A Kearsey: *1915 Campaign in France* (Aldershot: Gale & Polden Ltd 1929)

Lt Col A Kearsey: *The Battle of Amiens* (Aldershot: Gale & Polden Ltd 1950)

Col NCE Kenrick, *The Wiltshire Regiment* (Aldershot: Gale & Polden Ltd 1963)

Gen Alexander von Kluck, *The March on Paris and the Battle of the Marne 1914* (London: Edward Arnold 1920)
Maj Gen A de C L Leask, *Putty* (Solihull: Helion & Co Ltd 2015)
John Lewis-Stempel, *The War Behind The Wire* (London: Weidenfeld & Nicolson 2014)
Peter Liddle (ed.), *Passchendaele in Perspective The Third Battle of Ypres* (London: Leo Cooper Ltd 1997)
Lt Col JH Lindsay, *The London Scottish in the Great War* (London: Regimental Headquarters 1925)
Nick Lloyd, *Loos 1915* (Stroud: Tempus Publishing Ltd 2006)
Maj Gen Thomas Marden (Ed), *A Short History of the 6th Division 1914-1919* (London: Hugh Rees Ltd 1920)
Capt S McCance, *History of the Royal Munster Fusiliers, Volume II* (Aldershot: Gale & Polden Ltd 1927)
Charles Messenger, *Call to Arms: The British Army 1914-1918* (London: Weidenfeld & Nicolson 2005)
Lt Gen Sir Philip Neame: *Playing with Strife* (London: George G Harrap & Co. Ltd 1946)
Robin Neillands, *The Great War Generals on the Western Front 1914-1918* (London: Robinson Publishing Ltd 1999)
Nigel Nicolson, *Alex: The Life of Field Marshal Earl Alexander of Tunis* (London: Weidenfeld & Nicolson 1973)
Gen Sir O'Moore Creagh and EM Humphris (eds), *The V.C. and D.S.O* in three volumes (London: The Standard Art Book Co Ltd, undated)
Ian Passingham, *The German Offensives of 1918* (Barnsley: Pen & Sword 2008)
Ian Passingham, *All The Kaiser's Men* (Stroud: Sutton Publishing Ltd 2003)
Wilfrid Ewart, F Loraine Petre, Cecil Lowther (Eds), *The Scots Guards in the Great War 1914-1918* (London: John Murray 1925)
William Philpott, *Bloody Victory The Sacrifice On The Somme* (London: Brown, Little Book Group 2009)
Barrie Pitt, *1918 The Last Act* (London: Cassell & Co Ltd 1962)
Mrs Pope-Hennessy, *Map of the Main Prison Camps in Germany and Austria* (London: Nisbet & Co Ltd – undated)
Walter Reid, *Douglas Haig Architect of Victory* (Edinburgh: Birlinn Ltd 2006)
Lord Reith, *Wearing Spurs* (London: Hutchinson & Co Ltd 1966)
Irina Renz and Others, *Scorched Earth: The Germans on the Somme 1914-1918* (Barnsley: Pen & Sword 2009)
Pte Frank Richards, *Old Soldiers Never Die* (London: Faber & Faber 1933)
Gerhard Ritter, *The Schlieffen Plan* (London: Oscar Wolf (Publishers) Ltd 1958)
Duncan Rogers (Ed.), *Landrecies to Cambrai* (Solihull: Helion & Company Ltd 2011)
Rev Guy Rogers, *A Rebel at Heart* (London: Longmans Green & Co 1956)
Sidney Rogerson, *Twelve Days on the Somme* (London: Greenhill Books 2006)
Sir John Ross of Bladensburg, *The Coldstream Guards 1914-1918, Volumes I and II* (Oxford University Press, London: Humphrey Milford 1928)
Maj & QM T Ross, *The Fortune of War. Catalogue. Cameos of the Great War by an Eye Witness. Paintings depicted by Stewart Robertson, Official Artist – 2nd Army*, SGA
Gary Sheffield, *The Somme* (London: Cassell 2003)

Gary Sheffield, *Forgotten Victory The First World War: Myths and Realities* (London: Headline Book Publishing 2001)
Gary Sheffield: *The Chief Douglas Haig and the British Army* (London: Aurum Press Ltd 2011)
Gary Sheffield and Dan Todman (Eds), *Command and Control on the Western Front* (Stroud: Spellmount Ltd 2004)
Gary Sheffield and John Bourne (Eds), *Douglas Haig War Diaries and Letters 1914-1918* (London: Weidenfeld & Nicolson 2005)
Jack Sheldon, *The German Army at Cambrai* (Barnsley: Pen & Sword 2009)
Jack Sheldon, *The German Army at Ypres* (Barnsley: Pen & Sword 2010)
Capt H FitzM Stacke, *The Worcestershire Regiment in the Great War* (Kidderminster: GT Cheshire & Sons Ltd 1928)
David Stevenson, *Cataclysm: The First World War as Political Tragedy* (London: Allen Lane Ltd 2004)
David Stevenson, *With Our Backs To The Wall* (London: Penguin Books Ltd 2012)
Pte D Stewart, *With the "Old Contemptibles" in 1914 against Germany's formidable War Machine* (1938 New Westminster, British Columbia, SGA)
Lt Col J Stewart and John Buchan, *The Fifteenth (Scottish) Division 1914 -1919* (Edinburgh: William Blackwood and Sons 1926)
The Stock Exchange Memorial of those who fell in the Great War 1914-1919 (London: 1920)
Hew Strachan (Ed.), *The Oxford Illustrated History of the First World War New Edition* (Oxford: Oxford University Press 2014)
Hew Strachan, *The First World War* (London: Simon & Schuster UK Ltd 2003)
Hew Strachan, *The First World War: Volume I: To Arms* (Oxford: Oxford University Press (2001)
Hew Strachan, *Carl von Clausewitz's On War A Biography* (London: Atlantic Books 2007)
RB Talbot Kelly, *A Subaltern's Odyssey* (London: William Kimber & Co Ltd 1980)
John Terraine, *The Western Front 1914-1918* (London: Hutchinson 1964)
John Terraine, *The Smoke and the Fire*: *Myths and Anti-myths of War, 1861-1945* (London: Leo Cooper 1980)
John Terraine, *Douglas Haig The Educated Soldier* (London: Hutchinson 1963)
John Terraine, *Mons* (London: BT Batsford Ltd 1960)
John Terraine (Ed.), *General Jack's Diary 1914-1918* (London: Eyre & Spottiswoode 1964)
RR Thompson, *The Fifty-Second (Lowland) Division, 1914–1918* (Glasgow: Maclehose, Jackson, & Co 1923)
Lt Col LH Thornton & Pamela Fraser, *The Congreves* (London: John Murray 1930)
GM Trevelyan, *Grey of Falloden* (London: Longmans, Green and Co Ltd 1937)
Barbara W Tuchman, *August 1914* (London: Constable & Co Ltd 1962)
The War Office, *Battle of the Marne 8th-10th September, 1914 Tour of the Battlefield* (London: HMSO 1935)
The War Office, *Battle of the Aisne 13th-15th September, 1914 Tour of the Battlefield* (London: HMSO 1934)
Archibald Wavell, *Allenby* (London: George G Harrap & Co Ltd 1940)
Alan Wilkinson, *The Church of England and the First World War* (London: SCM Press Ltd 1996)
V Wheeler-Holohan, *Divisional and Other Signs* (London: John Murray 1924)
Ashby Williams, *Experiences of the Great War* (Roanoke, Press of The Stone Printing and Manufacturing Co 1919)

E Armine Wodehouse, *On Leave Poems and Sonnets* (London: Elkin Matthews 1917)
Col Harold Carmichael Wylly, *The Border Regiment in the Great War* (Aldershot: Gale & Polden Ltd 1924)
Everard Wyrall, *The Gloucestershire Regiment in the War 1914-1918* (London: Methuen & Co Ltd 1931)
The Wipers Times (London: Conway 2013)

Unpublished – Private Collections
Abercromby papers
Balfour Papers
Barne papers
Cator Papers
Colquhoun Papers
Cuthbert Papers
Dundas Papers
Kinnaird Papers
Ross Papers
Saumarez Papers
Warner Papers

Scots Guards Archives – Magazine Articles, Records, Photograph Albums and Printed Documents
Articles by Pte G Cumming, SGM 1969, 1970, 1972, 1977 and 1978
Article by Maj Gen C Dunbar, 'Some Recollections and Reflections', SGM 1964
The Left Flank Magazine
Diary-style account of Pte W Luck, SGM 1968
Copy Diary of Capt ED Mackenzie
Article by LCpl G Morris, 'Extracts from a Notebook of World War I', SGM 1959
Lt L Norman Field Message Pads 1915-16
Officers' Christmas Dinner Menu and Sets of Pipe Music 1917
Officers' Files
Order of Service Brigade of Guards Memorial Service
Regimental Medal Book First World War
Maj & QM T Ross, *The Fortune of War. Catalogue. Cameos of the Great War by an Eye Witness. Paintings depicted by Stewart Robertson, Official Artist – 2nd Army*, for account of the car, Michael
Sgt W Shepherd, 'Fifty, or more, years ago', SGM 1958
Soldiers' Personal Records and Enlistment Books
Articles by Brigadier AHC Swinton, SGM 1957, 1958 and 1970.
Articles by LCpl J Torrie, SGM 1959, 1960, 1961, 1962, 1963, 1964, 1965, 1966, 1968
Capt TB Trappes Lomax, 'Artillery Support at Loos', Spring Number 1930, *Household Brigade Magazine*
Articles by Pte JH Worker, SGM 1970 and 1973
Standing Orders of the Scots Guards 1901
20th Brigade Calendar 1915
Collected photograph albums and other photographs

Scots Guards Archives – Documents of Individuals
Diary of Capt CJ Balfour, SGA
Copy letter of Lt The Hon J Burns dated 10 December 1917 to LSgt H Kershaw
Papers of Lt Col SH Godman
Letter of Sgt J Goldie dated 28 November 1942
LSgt H Johnes, *Old Soldiers Never Die, They Simply Fade Away: Memoirs Reflections*
Account by LSgt D Jolly
Diary of Lt The Hon PC Kinnaird
Reprinted diary of Pte J Osborne, 1954 SGM
Letter from Maj Gen C Pereira to Col Smith Neill dated 17 February 1917
Diary of LCpl W Preston
Papers of Lt CAA Robertson
Diary of Capt J Stewart RAMC and papers, SGA
Papers of Lt Col JA Stirling
Statement by Lt CE Trafford about 17 September 1917 in Maj M Barne file

The Black Watch Museum
Details of officers of the 1st Black Watch,

The Highlanders Museum
Craig Brown Papers

Imperial War Museum
LSgt A Fleming, 1916 Letts *"The Soldier's Own Note Book And Pocket Diary"*, IWM MISC11 Item 246
Brig Lord Kindersley Papers, IWM/Documents 12174
Account by Pte W Nisbet, IWM 74/152/1
Diary-style account and diary of LCpl CE Green, IWM/Documents 4303
Copy Diary of Maj Gen Sir Cecil Lowther, IWM/Documents 6388
Letters of Capt AFAN Thorne and other papers, NAM/1987-03-31 and IWM/Documents 5583
Diary of Pte E Mellor, IWM/07/1/1
Papers of Gen Sir Ivor Maxse with reference to the 2nd Royal Munster Fusiliers, IWM/Documents 3255
Diary of Brig Gen C FitzClarence with Thorne Papers, NAM/1987-03-31
Papers of Brig Gen HC Rees, IWM/77/179/1
Diary of Capt KH Bruce, Gordon Highlanders, IWM/Documents 12125
Diary of Maj E Craig Brown, IWM/Documents 1862Diary of Sgt C Pilkington, IWM/Documents 14407
Account of Pte A Runcie, IWM/Documents 25793
Diary of unknown Border Regiment Private, IWM/MISC 30/ITEM 550
Papers of Lt Col L Fisher Rowe, IWM/Documents 16978
Letters of Capt D Chater, IWM/Documents 1697
Account of Maj C Morrison Bell, IWM/91/12/1
Account by Pte W Nisbet, IWM 74/152/1

Letter of Sir Edward Hulse to Lord Burnham, IWM/Documents 2621
Account of Rfn R Prew, IWM/88/46/1
Interview transcript of Sgt H Watson, IWM Documents 7659

National Army Museum
Letters of Capt AFAN Thorne and other papers, NAM/1987-03-31 and IWM/Documents 5583
Interviews of POWs at courts of enquiry from March to June 1918 at The Hague in eight files of sworn statements and other documents sent to the Government Committee on the Treatment by the Germans of British Prisoners of War, series NAM/2001-07-703
The National Canine Defence League, Leaflet No 387, *The Dog of Ypres*, NAM/2004-03-27

Liddle Collection, Brotherton Library, University of Leeds
Papers of Brig HL Graham, Liddle/WW1/GS/0650
Account of Pte N Wilson, Liddle Tape 507/Transcript
Diary-style account and diary of LCpl CE Green, Liddle/WW1/GS/0657 G and IWM/Documents 4303
Lt J StV B Saumarez accounts, Liddle/WW1/GS/0454
Diary of Capt S Sanders and letters, Liddle/WW1/GS/1422
Rev Dr J Esslemont Adams papers, Liddle/WW1/GS/0527
Account of LCpl H Wilson, 1st Coldstream, LIDDLE/WW1/POW/070
Account of Pte W Scott, Liddle Tape 394

University of Birmingham Special Collections
Letters of Lt F Pretyman to Lady Cynthia Curzon, OMN/A/4/2/7/10-14

George Watson's College
Watson's War Records on www.gwc.org.uk

Ipswich Record Office
Lt J StV B Saumarez letters to him and to his wife from Scots Guards officers and men, HA93/SA/3/1/27

The National Archives
Report by Lt Col W Murray Threipland dated 13 September 1916, TNA/CAB45/138
Account by Lt Col R Tempest, TNA/CAB45/138
Prisoner of War Interviews, TNA/WO161
Account of Capt StA Warde-Aldam, TNA/CAB45/141
Account of Lt RH FitzRoy, TNA/CAB45/140
Letter of Lt J Boyd, TNA/CAB45/140
Statement of Capt EG Christie Miller, TNA/CAB45/141
Maj Gen H Landon letter of 7 November to Maj Gen F Wing, TNA/WO154/18
Two accounts of Maj H Rochfort Boyd, TNA/CAB45/141 and 143
Account of Capt AFAN Thorne, TNA/CAB45/143

Reports and correspondence on POW camp conditions, escapes, reports on treatment of prisoners, including compulsion to work, subversion, deaths in captivity, the transfer of sick and badly injured to Switzerland and events there and the handling of captured German submariners in 1915 and consequences, series TNA/FO383

Pte I Reid court martial papers and sentence, TNA/WO71/407 and TNA/WO93/409

Report by Lt Col W Murray Threipland dated 13 September 1916, TNA/CAB45/138

Account by Lt Col R Tempest, TNA/CAB45/138

Headquarters Guards Division, Cambrai: Report on Operations TNA/WO158/385

Officers' files, mostly TNA/WO339, a few in TNA/WO374

War Diaries

1st Division TNA/WO95/1227, 1st (Guards) Brigade TNA/WO95/1261, 26th Brigade RFA TNA/WO95/1250, 1st Coldstream Guards TNA/WO95/ 1263/1, 1st Scots Guards TNA/WO95/1263/2, 1st Black Watch TNA/WO95/1263/3, 2nd Royal Munster Fusiliers TNA/WO95/1279/1, 1st Cameron Highlanders TNA/WO95/1264/1, 25th Brigade RFA, including 113th Battery, TNA/WO95/1248

20th Infantry Brigade TNA/WO95/1650, 1st Grenadier Guards TNA/WO95/1657/2, 2nd Scots Guards TNA/WO95/1657/3, 2nd Bedfordshire Regiment WO 95/1658/2, 2nd Yorkshire Regiment WO95/1659/4, 2nd Border Regiment TNA/WO95/1655/1, 2nd Worcestershire Regiment TNA/WO95/1351/1, 2nd Wiltshire Regiment TNA/WO 95/1659/3, 2nd Gordon Highlanders WO 95/1656/2, 41 Brigade RFA TNA/WO95/1326 and related material TNA/CAB45/141, 2nd Duke of Wellington's Regiment TNA/WO95/1552, 20th Infantry Brigade TNA/WO95/1650/2, 1st Division TNA/WO95/1228, 1st Cameron Highlanders TNA/WO95/1264/2

20th Infantry Brigade TNA/WO95/1651, 1st Royal Welsh Fusiliers TNA/WO95/1665, Guards Division A and Q Branch TNA/WO95/1197, 2nd Guards Brigade TNA/WO95/1217 (Series), 1st Scots Guards TNA/WO95/1219/3

(Series), 3rd Guards Brigade TNA/WO95/1221 (Series), 2nd Scots Guards TNA/WO95/1223/4 (Series), 2nd Guards Brigade TNA/WO95/1218 (Series), War Diary: 3rd Guards Brigade TNA/WO95/1222 (Series), 119th Brigade TNA/WO95/2606, 19th Royal Welsh Fusiliers TNA/WO95/2606

University of Birmingham Special Collections

Letters of Lt F Pretyman to Lady Cynthia Curzon, OMN/A/4/2/7/10-14

The Commonwealth War Graves Commission

website www.cwgc.org, with reliable regimental numbers

Index

PEOPLE

Notes: Individuals sharing the same surname are listed in alphabetical order of forename. Ranks shown are generally those which appear first in the book.

Abercromby, Lieutenant Bobbie 456, 543, 545-546, 549-552
Anderson, Lieutenant Francis 168, 175-176
Anderton, Lance Corporal Percy 394-395, 406, 408, 437
Armstrong, Lieutenant Guy 409, 419, 423-424
Askew, Captain Henry 245-247, 254, 265
Asquith, Katherine 437, 462, 469, 541, 564
Asquith, 2nd Lieutenant Raymond 437, 462, 469-471, 541, 556, 564

Baden Powell, Major Baden 23, 462, 495, 519
Bagot Chester, Captain Greville "Bubbles" 230, 282, 338, 344, 355, 359, 382
Balfour, Lieutenant James "Jamie" 37, 39, 41-44, 46-52, 55-60, 63-71, 75, 179, 284-287, 289-291, 293-294, 296, 300-305, 307, 309, 311, 314-317, 364-367, 369, 371-372, 375-376, 471, 502, 504-505, 521, 547
Balfour, Captain Robert "Jack" 60, 82, 149, 155-156
Barne, Captain Miles 389-394, 396-399, 401, 403-405, 409-410, 412-413, 416-420, 423, 425, 429-431, 433-437, 457-463, 465-477, 479-481, 519-524, 527-529, 531-545, 547-549, 551-558, 560-561, 563-567
Barne, Lieutenant Seymour 394, 397, 401, 410, 554, 565
Barwick, Company Sergeant Major Joseph 152, 159-160, 164-165, 178, 181
Beattie, Private Alexander 185, 198-200, 205, 208, 312

Bethell, 2nd Lieutenant The Honourable Richard "Dick" 297, 300, 309, 367, 502, 472, 527-528
Bewicke, Lieutenant Calverley 472-473, 480, 532, 535, 567
Blair, Lance Sergeant James 386-387, 394, 396, 399, 405-406, 438
Bolton, Lieutenant Colonel Richard "Pat" 91, 100, 107, 109, 111, 113, 116, 119, 125, 135, 139, 194-196
Borland, Private Alex 202-203, 210
Boyd Rochfort, 2nd Lieutenant Arthur 392, 404, 419, 468, 475-476, 480
Boyd, Lieutenant John 161, 166, 285
Brand, Lieutenant David "Brandy" 384, 532, 535, 548-549
Brooke, Captain Bertram "Boy" 122-123, 288, 301-302, 378, 380-381, 388, 555-556
Bruce, Captain Kenneth 96, 100-104, 111-112, 134
Bulfin, Brigadier General Edward 72, 160, 294

Callachan, Private Johnny 441, 482, 490
Campbell Krook, Major Axel 153-154, 157-158
Capper, Major General Thompson 93, 111, 116, 129-130, 132-134, 136, 228, 239, 243, 245, 270, 281, 332, 338-339, 360-361
Carpenter Garnier, Major Jack "Chips" 47, 58, 76, 79, 160
Cator, Major Albemarle "Alby" 96-98, 100-103, 111-112, 116, 122-124, 126, 128-130, 132, 134-137, 139, 225-228, 231,

593

235-236, 239-241, 243-244, 246, 254-255, 257-258, 266-268, 270-271, 273, 325, 329, 331-333, 337-338, 340, 343-344, 346-347, 355, 357-359, 382, 420, 440, 444-445, 449, 451, 454, 473, 482-483, 487, 491
Cator, Lieutenant Kit 132-133, 138, 228-230, 235, 238, 241, 243-244, 246, 282, 442, 447, 490
Cator, Violet 130, 136-137, 227, 358, 483
Cavan, Brigadier General "Fatty", The Earl of 285, 378, 401, 404, 418, 444-445, 454, 464, 466-467, 485, 494, 496-498, 514, 527
Champion, Lieutenant Reginald "Pardon" 545
Chapman, Sergeant William 193, 200-204
Churchill, Winston 20, 207, 315, 372, 462
Clancy, Private Joseph 78, 161, 164, 169, 178
Clarke, Company Sergeant Major Cecil "Nobby" 428, 526, 530
Clive, Lieutenant Viscount 229, 238, 273
Coke, Captain The Honourable John "Jack" 92-93, 194, 207, 231
Coke, 2nd Lieutenant The Honourable Reggie "Dumps" 296-298, 300
Coke, Captain The Honourable Richard "Dick" 231, 236, 238
Colquhoun (née Tennant), Dinah 38, 66, 87, 427, 436, 468-469, 471, 474, 476, 478-479, 527, 535, 537, 541-542, 555, 563, 566
Colquhoun of Luss, Lieutenant Sir Iain 38, 66, 85, 87, 91, 148, 152, 167, 298, 427, 429-431, 434-437, 457-462, 465-480, 507, 519-524, 525, 527-529, 531-535, 537, 541-542, 544-548, 551-552, 554, 559, 560-567
Corkran, Major Charles 37, 44, 175, 177, 242, 288, 336, 435, 507, 511, 513
Cottrell Dormer, 2nd Lieutenant Clement 116-118, 120, 135, 194, 253
Craig Brown, Major Ernest 168, 172, 174-178
Cumming, Private George 427-429, 431, 436, 457, 459, 474, 476, 521, 525, 531, 549, 552, 556, 562
Cuthbert, Brigadier General Gerald "Cupid" 25, 392, 397, 424, 470
Cuthbert, Captain Harold 374, 385, 391-392, 399, 403, 415, 419, 423, 425
Cuthbert, Kathleen 392, 424-425

Dalrymple, Major The Viscount "Jack" 92, 112-119, 139, 194

De La Pasture, Captain Charles "Pash" 84, 151, 155, 158-159, 190
Deignan, Private Patrick 161, 178, 189
Dormer, 2nd Lieutenant Robert 296-299
Drummond, Lieutenant David 101, 114, 127, 131, 135
Dundas, 2nd Lieutenant Henry 28, 427, 514, 541, 554-556, 558, 560-565

Earle, Lieutenant Colonel Maxwell 187, 193, 220
Ellis, Lieutenant Donald "Wiejo" 389, 405, 409, 419, 566
Evans, Private Ernest "George" 27, 367, 369, 389, 400, 410, 413-416, 433-434, 437, 524, 553, 559
Ewart, 2nd Lieutenant Wilfrid "Bill" 275-276, 280-282, 322-324, 326-329, 482-486, 488, 491, 507, 510-511, 514, 516-517

Fane Gladwin, Lieutenant Ralph 115, 117, 119, 171, 186, 194
Feilding, Major General Geoffrey 468, 473, 478, 495, 498, 501, 527, 529, 560
Feilding, Captain Rowland "Snowball" 378, 380-382, 384-385, 391-392, 409, 413, 417-418, 431, 433, 435, 461, 554
Fisher Rowe, Lieutenant Colonel Laurence 242, 254, 257, 265, 267, 331
FitzClarence, Brigadier General Charles 84, 86, 138, 142, 146-147, 151-154, 157, 161-162, 164-165, 167-168, 170, 176-178
FitzWygram, Lieutenant Sir Frederick 131, 251, 256, 325, 329, 335-336, 338-339, 341, 346, 348
Fleming, Private Alex 464, 469-470, 472-479, 525, 537, 539, 543, 545-546, 551, 556-557, 560, 562
Fludyer, Colonel Henry 21, 193, 207, 253, 338, 392, 489
Foch, General Ferdinand 54, 57, 62, 67
Fortune, Captain Victor 122, 170-171, 178
Fox, Captain Charles 99, 107, 114-115, 117, 119, 135, 139-140, 185-187, 194-195, 210-211
Fraser, Major The Honourable Hugh "Bosun" 91, 103, 107, 112-115, 135, 194
French, General Sir John 43-48, 53-55, 62-63, 71, 83, 102, 121, 132, 137, 139, 144, 146, 168, 265, 285-286, 316, 338-339, 381-382, 400, 409-410, 412-413, 420, 447, 485

Galloway, Lance Corporal William 215-217
King George V 82, 211, 236, 286, 436, 531
Gibbs, Lieutenant Ronald 108-109, 125, 131, 135, 310
Gillieson, Reverend William Phin 405, 477, 529
Gipps, Lieutenant Nigel 58, 66, 93, 171
Godman, Lieutenant Colonel Sherard 381-382, 385, 388, 392, 398, 401-402, 405, 409, 420, 423, 547, 562-563, 566
Gordon Lennox, Major Lord Esmé 106-107, 436, 458, 462-463, 466-468, 470-471, 474-475, 479-480, 519-521, 527, 529, 532-534, 537-539, 543, 552, 554-555
Gough, Major General Hubert 339, 342, 355-356, 359, 381-382, 492
Graham, Private Stephen 29, 338-339, 346, 355
Green, Lance Corporal Charles 40-45, 55-57, 67, 70, 73-74, 80-81, 83-86, 90, 141, 143, 146-147, 149, 151-154, 156, 162, 190, 192-193, 201-204, 212-219, 223-224
Grosvenor, Lieutenant Lord Gerald "Gerry" 118, 186, 194-195
Guy, Corporal Benjamin 190, 200, 203, 209

Haig, Lieutenant General Sir Douglas 37, 48, 53, 84, 123, 132, 146, 155, 160, 167, 240, 282, 286, 288, 293, 306, 311, 315, 338, 359, 369, 373, 378, 400, 408-409, 412-413, 416, 468, 471, 479, 481, 485, 514, 584, 586-588
Haking, Major General Richard 289, 293-294, 300, 302, 305-306, 315-317, 320, 364, 368, 374, 378, 388, 398, 409, 412, 420, 441
Haldane, Lieutenant John 371, 373, 378
Hamilton, Major The Honourable Leslie 145, 150-152, 157
Hammersley, Lieutenant Hugh 397-398, 401, 418-419, 431, 480
Hendrick, Private Charles 27, 168, 421
Heyworth, Brigadier General Frederick "Pa" 21, 137, 225, 229, 234, 245, 257, 270, 274-275, 278, 323, 332, 335, 338-339, 343, 358, 401, 440, 444, 448, 451, 472, 482, 488, 498, 507, 521
Hill, Captain William "Monty" 336, 347-348
Holbech, Lieutenant William "Willie" 111, 112-113, 115

Holroyd, Private George "Joe" 57, 86, 149, 192, 203
Hope, Lieutenant George 115-116, 122
Hore Ruthven, Lieutenant Colonel The Honourable Walter "Jerry" 275, 287, 296-298, 300-301, 310, 317, 365-366, 372, 381, 437
Howard, Private Vincent 184-185, 198-200, 205, 208
Hulse, Lieutenant Sir Edward 37-38, 41-43, 47, 57-58, 63-65, 68-69, 80-81, 93, 137, 143, 228, 231-232, 234-235, 240-244, 246-247, 255, 257-259, 262-264, 266-269, 271-276, 280-283, 330, 333-334, 336, 485

Issott, Lance Sergeant Harry 118, 130, 270

James, Sergeant Alfred 117-118, 127, 249, 259, 334
Jarvis, 2nd Lieutenant Archibald 275-276, 330-331, 349
Joffre, General Joseph 46, 48, 53-54, 57, 62, 102, 144, 236, 240, 355-356, 382, 403-404
Johnes, Private Herbert 317-320, 363, 365-369, 371, 376-377, 383-384, 388, 392-393, 400-401, 404, 409-410, 413-416, 419, 426, 433-434, 436-437, 458, 460, 464-465, 467, 472-473, 476, 479, 521, 523-524, 544, 547-549, 553, 559, 561, 565
Johnson, Private Frank 214-216
Jolliffe, Lieutenant Gerald 147, 158, 191, 207
Jones, Private James "Jimmy" 388, 394, 438
Jones, Corporal Richard 248-249, 334

Kemble, Captain Horace 94, 114, 125
Kingsmill, Captain Andrew 311, 363, 459
Kinlay, Lieutenant David 39, 284-285, 424, 480, 520, 555
Kinnaird, Captain The Honourable Douglas 91-94, 96, 101-105, 107-109, 135
Kitchener, Field Marshal Lord 25, 39-40, 43, 55, 85, 92, 144-145, 160, 213, 354, 359, 372, 409, 440, 542
Kluck, General Alexander von 40, 44, 46, 48, 53, 55, 57, 62
Knapp, Father Simon 480, 529-530

Lamond, Private Alexander 311, 366, 369, 400, 416

Lanrezac, General Charles 45-46, 48, 53-54, 57
Lawson, 2nd Lieutenant The Honourable William "Bill" 37, 93, 125, 143
Lawton, Company Sergeant Major James 337, 339, 352
Leach, Lieutenant Colonel Burleigh 163-166
Leach, 2nd Lieutenant Grey "Guy" 532, 548, 567
Liddell Grainger, Lieutenant Henry "Fat Boy" 234, 241, 417-418
Lilley, Company Sergeant Major Charles 33, 237, 251, 339
Loder, Lieutenant Giles 94, 113, 116, 123, 127, 131, 236, 245-246, 251, 254, 258-262, 273, 326, 329, 333
Lowther, Lieutenant Colonel Cecil "Meat" 38-50, 52-60, 63-69, 72-74, 77-79, 158, 160-161, 163, 191, 284-296, 300-307, 311, 314-317, 320, 357, 363-364, 366, 368-369, 371-378, 380-385, 388, 391, 393-394, 396-398, 400, 412
Luck, Private William 19, 39-47, 52-54, 59, 75, 79-80, 82, 141, 156, 161

Macdonald, Sergeant John 146, 148, 152, 155-156, 159, 163, 172, 181, 269
Mackenzie, 2nd Lieutenant Eric 39, 74, 76, 179, 314, 317, 420, 542, 552, 554-557, 559-560, 562-565, 567
Mackenzie, Private James 24, 250-251
Mackenzie, Captain Sir Victor 39, 74, 83, 85, 89, 148, 151, 156, 159-160, 181, 315, 381, 386, 389, 391, 394, 414, 420, 424
Mann, Lieutenant Frank 532, 540, 546-548
Martindale, 2nd Lieutenant Warine "Warrie" 457, 527, 562
Maxse, Brigadier General Ivor 37, 44-46, 50, 68, 80, 84
McAulay, Lance Corporal Jock 318, 320, 471
McFadden, Private Henry 395-396, 552
McGinlay, Private James 190, 193, 201, 210
McPherson, Private Alexander 86, 289, 300, 309-311
Meaden, Captain Alban 70, 78, 155-156, 165, 168, 178, 194
Mellor, Private Ernest "Bill" 43, 55, 57, 61, 79, 149, 192, 203
Methuen, 2nd Lieutenant The Honourable Anthony Paul 376
Methuen, 2nd Lieutenant The Honourable Paul Ayshford 426, 437, 457, 472-473, 475-476
Miller, Private Ernest "Eric" 477, 534, 554
Mills, 2nd Lieutenant The Honourable Charles "Charlie" 441, 449-451
Molineux Montgomerie, Major George 403, 435, 474
Monckton, Lieutenant Francis 64-65, 171
Monckton, Lieutenant Geoffrey 64, 71, 300, 311, 313
Moncur, Sergeant Major James "Jimmy" 147, 269, 284, 336, 338-339
Morris, Private George 29, 386-387, 394, 396, 405, 407, 438
Morrison Bell, Major Clive "Cloche" 308, 310, 312, 424
Moss, Private William 533-535
Murker, Private Peter 74, 258, 267

Norman, Lieutenant Lionel 370, 461, 463, 465, 467, 471, 480, 531, 545-547, 549, 551-552, 564
Northbrook, Lady 94, 109, 456
Nugent, Lieutenant Dick 234, 251, 261, 336

Orchard, Private Richard 95, 106, 121, 125, 256-257
Orr, Lieutenant Alastair "Daisy" 108, 125, 452
Orr Ewing, Lieutenant Ernest "Tim" 420, 463, 467, 480, 529, 537-538, 554, 558, 565
Orr Ewing, Major Norman 287, 296-298, 300, 389, 397, 401, 404-405, 412, 420, 558, 562
Osborne, Private John 38-40, 47, 51-53, 56, 58, 60, 63-64, 66, 70, 75, 79, 82-83, 88, 141, 143, 149, 209-210
Ottley, Lieutenant Geoffrey 23, 137, 231, 243, 247, 251, 255-256, 265-266, 291
Ottley, Lady Kathleen 255-256, 266
Owen, Private Wallace 299, 354, 421

Paynter, Captain George 113-115, 123, 125, 131, 133-134, 136-139, 236, 238, 245-246, 248, 262, 264, 269, 274, 276, 281-282, 325-326, 329-330, 332, 336, 338, 404
Pilkington, Sergeant Christopher 96, 109, 111, 114, 123, 160, 227, 234, 241, 263
Plant, Private George "Jimmy" 124, 544, 548, 553
Plumer, Lieutenant General Sir Herbert 43, 494, 531, 541

Ponsonby, Lieutenant Colonel John 75, 145, 285-286, 292, 367, 398, 403, 414-415, 418, 425, 466-471, 473, 480, 522, 529-530, 547, 558-559, 564-565
Powell, 2nd Lieutenant Ronnie 532, 534-535, 567
Poynter, Captain Arthur "Nipper" 292, 374, 384, 393, 416, 420
Preston, Private William 290-291, 296-299, 312, 354, 446, 453, 455
Pulteney, Lieutenant General Sir William "Putty" 134, 221, 270, 333, 403, 420
Pyper, Company Sergeant Major William 473, 535, 537

Rae, Private John 98, 112, 235, 349
Rawlinson, Lieutenant General Sir Henry 275, 335, 338, 341, 356, 391, 401, 412-413, 488
Rees, Captain Hubert 87, 163, 167
Reid, Private Isaac 336-339, 346, 352, 515
Rivers Bulkeley, Captain Ivor 340, 349
Rivers Bulkeley, Captain Thomas "Tommy" 103, 107, 109, 135, 340-341
Robertson, Private John 235, 349-350
Rochfort Boyd, Major Henry 172-173, 175
Rogers, Reverend Guy 529-530, 539, 541, 547
Romer, Captain Malcolm "Flossie" 93, 137-138, 171, 230
Romilly, Major Bernard "Romeo" 301-302, 309-311, 318, 363, 372, 459
Ross, Lieutenant Hugh 41, 83, 87, 167, 476-477, 480, 520, 529, 535, 546, 553, 556-558, 563, 565
Ross, Lieutenant Tom "Tam" 29, 93, 114, 135, 147, 227, 342, 352, 355, 403, 441, 513, 520
Ross, Lance Sergeant William 117-118, 127, 253
Ruggles Brise, Brigadier General Henry 93, 110-113, 116, 124, 128, 130

Saumarez, Gunhild 91, 93-97, 100, 102, 121, 124, 131, 135, 137, 230, 232, 236-237, 244, 251, 256
Saumarez, Lieutenant The Honourable Vincent 91-92, 95-97, 100-104, 106, 111, 113-118, 120-121, 124-125, 127-132, 134-135, 137, 194, 230, 232, 234, 236-238, 244, 246-247, 249-251, 256, 261, 270, 334, 336, 339
Schiff, Lieutenant Marcus 520, 531, 543, 546-547, 549

Scott, Private William 415, 448-449
Seely, Colonel Jack 288, 381-382
Sergison Brooke *see* Brooke
Seymour, Lieutenant Conway "Con" 275, 282, 327, 329, 397, 420, 430, 437, 491
Shaw, Private William (Bill) 57, 149, 192, 203, 252
Shaw, Private William Henry 192
Shepherd, Sergeant William "Bill" 68, 147, 151-152, 154-156, 158-161, 163-166
Shields, Lance Sergeant John 153-154, 156, 374, 556
Sinclair, Private Temple 106, 125, 137, 238, 256, 334
Smith Dorrien, Lieutenant General Sir Horace 43, 48, 320
Smith, Private Arthur 312, 421, 506
Sorel Cameron, Major George 142-143, 145, 156, 159, 161
Stephen, Captain Albert 41, 58, 67-68, 74, 79, 134, 152, 156, 158-161
Steuart Menzies, Lieutenant Ronald 94, 113, 131, 135, 194, 207
Stewart, Private Donald 169, 169-170, 172, 177, 285, 287, 289-290, 297, 300, 304, 310, 363, 372, 391-392
Stewart, Lieutenant James 154, 162, 168, 171, 177, 285, 294, 467, 476, 523
Stirling, Captain Jack 355, 435, 442, 483, 488
Stockwell, Captain Clifton "Cliff" 345-347
Stracey, Captain Reggie 77, 80, 127, 143, 151, 155, 159-161, 164-165, 167, 170-171, 173, 177, 181, 230, 270, 284, 296, 298, 300, 480, 532
Stride, Private William "Bill" 57, 149, 154, 162
Stuart Wortley, Major General The Honourable Edward Montagu 450-451, 562
Swinnerton Dyer, Lieutenant Sir John "Jack" 458
Swinton, Lieutenant Alan 66, 137-138, 226-227, 231-232, 236, 241-242, 255-259, 262-264, 266-267, 270-271, 324-325, 330-332, 340-344, 348, 355-356, 502
Swinton, Elsie 137, 255-256, 266, 270

Tate, Sergeant Major Thomas 164, 178, 181, 285
Taylor, Private William 387, 407, 438
Tempest, Major Roger "Stormy Weather" 401, 440, 466, 487, 493-494, 498, 500, 510, 513, 516, 537, 554

Tennant, Dinah *see* Colquhoun, Dinah
Thompson, Lieutenant Arnold "Tommy" 378, 423, 480, 519, 539, 542
Thorne, Captain Andrew "Bulgy" 37, 40-41, 57, 68, 80, 83, 85-89, 153, 155, 163-165, 167-168, 170, 172, 175, 177-178, 284, 286-289, 302, 315, 366, 476
Thorpe, Captain John 391-392, 417-418, 420, 437, 463
Trafford, Lieutenant Cecil 391, 417, 547, 551, 554-555, 557
Trafford, Lieutenant Edward 194, 207, 211, 391
Turner, Sergeant John 156, 194, 221

Wales, Prince of 22, 236, 285, 356, 369-370, 374, 394, 404, 410, 412, 462, 467, 472, 476, 554, 564-566
Walmsley, Private Thomas 214-215, 224
Warner, Lieutenant Edward 95-98, 101, 106-107, 110-112, 114, 121, 132, 248-249, 251, 254-255, 258, 266-267, 270, 274, 280-282, 325, 329-332, 335-338, 341-342, 346-348, 357-361, 372, 440, 442-445, 449, 482, 484-490, 493-494, 498-499, 501, 506, 517
Watson, Private Henry 286, 305-306, 379, 382, 400, 567
Wells, Private John 131, 241, 483
Westmacott, Brigadier General Claude 294-296, 300-301
Wickham, Captain William "Peckham" 63, 82, 165
Wynne Finch, 2nd Lieutenant Billy 103, 115-116, 357, 359, 445, 454, 482, 513

Young, Sergeant James 196, 308, 310

PLACES

Abbeville 360, 426, 513, 555
Abbeyhill 124, 501, 547
Aberdeen 59, 98, 135, 139, 154, 184, 260, 312-313, 440, 453, 489
Aire-La Bassée 89, 196, 289
Aisne Canal 69, 82
Aisne River iii-iv, ix, 39, 55, 60, 62, 67-69, 72, 76, 78, 82, 89, 94, 100, 108, 137, 142, 149, 155, 160-161, 163, 168-169, 171-172, 179, 192, 223, 240, 244, 258, 284, 289, 299-300, 317, 333, 341, 353, 357, 364, 424, 470, 501, 530, 533, 542, 550, 562, 585, 588
Aldershot 37, 39-40, 52-53, 61, 86, 121, 139, 147, 192, 196, 586-587, 589
Amiens 27, 53-55, 586
Annequin 290, 296, 306-307, 435, 450
Antwerp 35, 46, 87-88, 94, 96-99, 139, 163, 586
Armentières 31, 33, 35, 89, 132, 139, 225, 238, 311, 323, 348, 476, 541, 586
Arras 33, 41, 90, 173, 322, 374, 396, 517, 567, 586
Artois 89, 282
Asylum Station 498, 500, 504, 510, 520
Aubers (incl Aubers Ridge) iii, v-vi, ix, 89, 225, 231, 246, 277, 282, 322, 325, 328, 332, 341-343, 361, 363-364, 374, 380, 383, 391, 396, 458, 469, 483, 485, 506, 526, 549-550, 586
Ayrshire 71, 84, 89, 115, 220, 290, 396, 429, 446, 461, 474, 536

Bac-St Maur 225, 239
Bailleul 134, 136, 225, 284, 462-463, 474-475, 477
Banff 240, 423
Barts Alley 429, 449-450
Bassevelle 65-66
Bathgate 249, 550, 562
Beaulne 75, 83, 87
Beaumont-Hamel 516
Becelaere 102, 104, 147-148, 150-151, 153, 156, 191
Beienrode 205-206
Bellewarde Lake 498, 521
Bellot 64-65
Berwick 71, 305, 440
Berwickshire 37, 167, 234, 422, 499, 513
Béthune ix, 120, 289-290, 294-296, 298-299, 303-307, 315, 317-318, 343, 354, 358, 364, 367, 372, 375, 377, 379, 381, 384, 388-390, 394, 397-398, 401, 406, 410-411, 421, 423, 427, 431, 436, 440, 442, 517
Beuthen 212-213, 215-216
Beuvry 290, 296, 305, 311, 315, 358
Biggar 76, 376, 562, 570

Birkenhead 201, 223, 394, 515
Bixschoote 141-143
Blanzy-lez-Fismes 90, 172
Blighty Bridge viii, 516, 561-562
Boesinghe viii, 141, 145-146, 478, 496, 507, 511, 556, 559
Bois de Biez 324, 364
Bois Grenier 225, 245
Bollezeele 516-517, 541-543, 555, 566-567
Borre 284-286, 290-291, 293, 298-300, 372, 422, 452
Borsigwerk 212, 214
Boué 42-44, 49, 53, 58
Boulogne 33, 89-90, 120, 127, 142, 144, 149, 161, 163, 169-170, 238, 244, 252, 255-256, 299, 350, 372, 375, 405, 409, 426-427, 440-441, 477, 501, 503, 512, 527, 532, 564
Bourecq 436, 457
Bourlon Wood xv, 104
Braine 70, 86, 89
Brechin 337, 350, 570
Broodseinde 102, 107
Burbure 315, 317, 370, 384, 386, 394, 442
Busnes 354-356, 359

Calais vii, 40, 89, 262, 469, 474, 478-481, 488, 491, 493-494, 497, 519
Calonne 359, 361, 512
Cambrai xiv-xv, 27, 42, 104, 219, 353, 585-588, 592
Cambridge 22, 59, 91, 165, 169, 337, 340, 349, 389-390, 392, 502, 532, 541
Cambrin 290, 296, 383, 389, 393, 399, 405, 527
Caterham 25, 28, 76, 105, 120, 127, 139, 292, 317
Celle 198, 206, 317
Cerny 72-73, 75, 85
Chalet Wood 411-412
Chalk Pit Wood 411, 414-415, 417-418, 423, 443
Châlons 57, 67-68
Charleroi 37, 45, 53
Château D'Oex 197, 220-221
Château Wood 129, 133, 151-152, 154, 156, 162-165, 168-172, 174, 176
Château-Thierry 57, 66-67
Chemin des Dames iv, 69, 72-75, 79, 82, 85, 87, 89, 218

Chocolat Menier Corner 344, 371, 377
Chocques 318, 351, 433, 440
Coulommiers 57-59, 65, 86, 149, 192, 203
Cour d'Avoué Farm 345-346, 348, 359
Courtrai 180, 185-187, 191, 198, 220
Cowdenbeath 312, 333, 350, 360, 383, 422, 504, 511
Crefeld 186, 194-195, 207, 210-211
Cuinchy v-vi, ix, 30, 120, 196, 221-222, 293-296, 299-301, 306-307, 311, 315-316, 318, 320, 354, 371, 378-379, 382, 384, 390, 394, 396, 399, 411, 421, 424, 426, 477, 484, 506, 533, 535
Cuinchy brickstacks ix, 30, 120, 196, 221-222, 306, 318, 320, 371, 378, 390, 394, 396, 421, 424, 426, 477, 484, 506

Doullens 33, 567
Dublin 76, 163, 181, 185, 213, 395, 425, 432
Dumbarton 118, 149, 334, 377
Dumfries 250, 267, 448, 531
Dunbar 282, 335, 550, 589
Dunbartonshire 86, 218, 377, 395, 406
Dundee 42, 110, 119, 171, 180, 292, 351, 386, 406, 446, 453, 464, 470, 478, 490, 498, 525-527, 540, 552
Dunfermline 193, 207, 449
Dunkirk 96, 478, 542, 565, 567
Dunoon 197, 550

Ebenezer Farm 463, 474
Edinburgh 40, 76, 78, 89-90, 99, 124, 126, 138, 142, 148, 153, 170, 179, 185, 190, 192, 197-198, 208, 218, 223, 249, 251-252, 274, 298-299, 334, 341, 353, 356, 362, 377, 386, 406, 420-422, 427, 432, 439, 446, 448, 462, 473, 483, 501, 503, 505, 507, 511-513, 515, 521, 526, 530, 544, 547, 550, 568, 585, 587-588
Egypt 37, 91, 94, 179, 404, 429
Elgin 468, 472, 483
Elverdinghe 141, 478, 507
Esquelbec 541, 567
Esslemont 260, 283, 565, 591
Estaires 281-282, 322-323, 329, 336, 344, 363, 456, 458, 474
Étaples 507, 531
Etreux 42, 49-51, 84, 87, 293

Fauquissart 282, 329, 467, 483-484, 489
Fère-en-Tardenois 68, 71, 78
Festubert iii, v-vi, ix, 95, 269, 316-317, 322, 343-345, 348, 350-352, 354-362, 366, 377, 380, 382-383, 404, 424, 446-447, 449, 453, 457, 477, 500, 503, 510, 515, 586
Fife 25-26, 84, 127, 138, 180, 185, 207, 299, 312, 333, 360, 393, 406, 420, 422, 426, 452, 461, 525
Forfar 68, 146, 247, 304, 350
Fort William 85, 265-266, 383
French Farm 293-294, 301-302
Friedrichsfeld 185, 188, 197, 209, 222
Fromelles 209, 225, 231, 243, 245, 258, 261, 273, 341-342, 408

Galashiels 76, 406, 423, 469
Gallipoli 31, 450, 472-473
Gheluvelt ix, 102-103, 105-106, 111-113, 116, 118, 122-123, 125-129, 144, 146-148, 150, 152-160, 162-166, 173, 178-179, 181, 183, 187, 189, 192-193, 201-202, 204, 206, 209, 211-212, 214, 217-218, 220-221, 223, 293, 298, 315, 365, 374, 377, 390, 429, 496, 503
Gheluvelt Château 127, 147-148, 152, 154-155, 158, 162-163, 178-179, 183, 193, 221
Gheluvelt Château Wood 154, 162-163
Gheluvelt Crossroads 102-103, 106, 111-113, 123, 125, 147, 150, 152-156
Gheluvelt Plateau 144, 173, 496
Ginchy 27, 30-31, 126, 270, 335, 350, 421
Givenchy ix, 25, 289-295, 301-303, 305, 312, 315, 353, 356, 358, 370, 378-379, 383, 409, 411, 442, 458, 506
Glasgow 23, 25-26, 38, 70-71, 76, 78, 82, 85, 89, 93, 100, 111, 115, 118, 120-121, 123, 135, 142, 149, 154, 162-163, 167, 179, 190, 197, 202, 222-223, 227, 235, 237, 252-253, 270, 272, 286, 292, 299-300, 305, 311-313, 318, 333, 343, 349, 351-354, 357, 360-361, 371, 380, 386, 390-392, 395-396, 399-400, 404, 419-423, 425, 432, 435, 441, 446-449, 452-453, 471, 489-490, 495, 499, 501, 503, 513, 526, 532, 535, 538, 549-550, 562, 588
Glencorse Wood 168, 176-177
Göttingen 121, 144, 184, 188-189, 198-200, 205, 222
Govan 78, 300, 432, 441, 482, 574

Greenock 202, 404, 522-523
Grenay Ridge 379, 408, 411-413, 415-416, 418, 443
Guise 49-51, 53-54, 59

The Hague 121, 166, 204, 209, 217, 224, 591
Hanover 188, 196, 198
Harfleur 27, 40-41, 334, 554
Hawick 220, 319, 334, 350, 371, 423
Heidelberg 194, 196, 307
Hellfire Corner 521, 530
Herenthage Château 129-130, 133, 168, 170
Herzeele 477, 497, 510, 541
High Wood 33, 260
Hill 62 129, 496, 543
Hill 70 ix, 138, 250, 411-417, 425, 430, 443-446, 448-449, 452, 504, 506, 512, 536
Hinges 315, 343-344, 354, 358, 377-378, 426
Hohenzollern Redoubt ix, 379, 411, 425-426, 430, 434, 438, 447, 449-450, 491-492
Hooge iv-v, 121, 123, 171, 181, 336, 496, 521, 542-543
Hulluch 265, 361, 379, 399, 411-412, 415, 425, 428, 431, 447-448, 450
Hyde Park 262, 385, 431

Inverkeithing 138, 299, 365
Inverness 76, 89, 138, 147, 154, 162, 169, 176, 448, 526
Ireland 22-23, 25, 66, 189, 351, 381, 394, 529
Isle of Man 215, 264, 269, 488

Kilmarnock 76, 237, 290, 299, 311, 314, 461
Kincardineshire 25, 305, 313, 500
Kirkcudbrightshire 25, 314, 352, 422, 562
Krupp Farm 511, 559

La Bassée iii, 25, 30, 35, 89, 139, 171, 196, 284, 289-290, 294, 306-307, 315, 324, 336, 344, 353-354, 363, 365-366, 371-372, 378-379, 383-384, 386, 389, 391, 408, 411-412, 414, 417, 425, 449, 456, 458, 557, 586
La Bassée Canal iii, 30, 89, 196, 284, 289, 353-354, 372, 378, 383, 386, 408, 411, 557
La Cordonnerie Farm 226-227, 238, 245, 273
La Gorgue 336-337, 437, 457-458, 460-461, 466, 470-473, 476, 491, 525
La Quinque Rue 345-347, 359, 373

Labourse vi, 379-380, 391-393, 397, 413, 443, 445, 448, 450, 454-455
Lamsdorf 213, 215-216, 219, 223
Lanarkshire 30, 76, 110, 121, 171, 217, 314, 334, 352, 360, 376, 426, 454, 490, 503, 530, 550
Landrecies 47-49, 53, 56, 63, 587
Langemarck ix, 141-142, 144, 146, 340, 511
Laon 69, 72-73, 75
Lavender Hill 189, 270
Laventie iii, vii, 335, 337-338, 341-342, 346, 372, 456-457, 461, 468-469, 472, 482-485, 487-488, 490, 522, 524
Le Blanc Mont 73, 77
Le Cateau 42, 48-49, 52, 57, 63
Le Havre 27, 39-42, 89, 132, 137, 250, 275, 318, 365, 395, 423, 426, 456, 473, 480, 501-502
Le Mans 59, 149, 166
Le Rutoire vi, 379, 381, 384-385, 397, 400-401, 405, 413, 418
Le Touret 320, 359, 369, 371-372, 375, 377
Le Tréport 350, 455
Lechfeld 205-206
Leith 86, 120, 192, 224, 227, 252, 258, 269, 311, 405, 507, 512
Lens 89, 379, 411-412, 414, 425, 449
Lesboeufs 31, 126, 353, 446
Lille 197-198, 253, 289, 322, 342, 399, 408, 543, 551-552
Lillers 292, 315, 359, 375, 381, 401, 410, 423, 432, 436, 442, 453, 455, 492
Longueval 33, 69, 90, 563
Loos iii, ix, 27, 33, 126, 138, 244, 250, 265, 313, 340, 345, 361, 365, 374, 379, 403, 408-409, 411, 414-416, 418, 420, 424, 427-428, 433, 438, 440-441, 443-446, 453, 462, 476, 492, 494, 503, 509-510, 513, 515, 517, 526-527, 532, 546, 552, 555, 565, 586-587, 589
Lozinghem 410, 442
Lüneburg Heath 196, 211
Lys River 103, 225, 231, 457, 462

Magdeburg 197, 206, 221, 335
Maple Copse 543, 545-546, 549, 551
Marne River iii, x, 57, 60, 62, 65-66, 585, 587-588
Maubeuge 37, 44, 46-47, 69, 79
Mauquissart 326, 329-332, 483

Menin iv-v, ix, 102-104, 106-107, 110-112, 114, 118, 122-126, 128-130, 133, 136, 144, 146-148, 150-153, 155-159, 161-163, 165-168, 170-173, 181, 190, 193, 223, 420, 496, 498, 506, 510-511, 520-521, 528, 531, 537-538
Menin Gate 498, 520-521, 528, 531, 537-538
Menin Road iv-v, ix, 102-104, 106-107, 110-112, 114, 118, 122-126, 128-130, 133, 136, 144, 146, 148, 150-153, 156-157, 159, 161-163, 165-168, 170-173, 181, 190, 193, 223, 420, 496, 498, 506, 510-511, 521, 537
Merseburg 196-198, 220-223
Merville 244, 274-275, 289, 333, 359, 440, 457, 461-462, 469-470, 472, 474, 476, 483-485, 488, 491
Messines 35, 102, 139, 244, 285, 320, 506, 535, 586
Méteren v, 134-137, 231, 235, 252, 258, 267, 270
Midlothian 110, 119, 337, 350, 357, 377, 557
Miechowitz 212, 214-219
Minden 187, 219
Mons iii, ix, xiv, 25, 36-37, 44-47, 59-60, 68, 79, 84, 142, 158, 165, 194, 212, 354, 376, 395, 406, 432, 501, 530, 584-585, 588
Montrose 124, 313, 350, 447
Morayshire 369, 446, 513
Motherwell 350, 369, 396, 459, 515, 553
Münster 184, 200, 205
Mürren 196-197, 204, 220-221
Musselburgh 148, 229, 352

Netley 319, 372
Neuve Chapelle iii, vii, ix, xiii, 33, 95, 104, 226, 243, 260, 263, 265, 270, 280, 282, 316, 322-324, 328, 331-336, 339-343, 348, 351, 353-354, 358, 360, 363-365, 376, 404, 409, 419, 436, 440, 446-447, 453, 456, 458, 461, 463-464, 474, 476, 482-483, 485, 497, 500, 502, 506, 516, 536, 586
Noeux-les-Mines 412, 446
Nogent-l'Artaud 66
Nonne Boschen 166, 173, 176, 178, 181, 189, 421, 432, 458, 488, 500, 535, 553
Nôtre Dame de Lorette 244, 322, 374, 391, 393
Noyelles 47, 379, 397, 401

Oeuilly 69-71, 81-83
Oise River 53, 55, 69, 82

Oise Canal 42, 48-49
Orkney Islands 213, 406, 473, 503, 526, 542
Ostend iv, xiv, 66, 94, 96-98
Oxford 22, 37, 71, 76, 95, 171, 185, 192, 257, 261, 298, 300, 310, 349, 376, 382, 427, 437, 441, 445, 514, 545

Paisley 180, 204, 300, 314, 350, 424, 499
Paissy 70-73, 75
Paris 53-55, 59, 62, 66, 71, 78, 81, 90, 150, 420, 513, 564, 587
Perth 90, 198, 212, 333, 352, 449, 526, 550
Perthshire 40, 91, 292, 298, 355, 432, 515, 527, 535-536
Petersfield 166, 514
Piètre 325-327, 329
Pilckem 141, 146, 161, 270, 350, 420, 511, 528, 541, 544, 546, 555, 561
Pilckem Ridge 270, 350, 420, 511, 541, 544, 546, 555, 561
Pitlochry 292, 449
Pochhammer 213-214
Poelcapelle 27, 353, 395, 500, 532
Poezelhoek 107-108, 147-148, 150-156, 162, 178, 202
Poezelhoek Wood 148, 151-152, 154
Poland 219, 262, 388
Polderhoek (including Château and Wood) 147-148, 151-152, 154, 162, 165
Polygon Wood iv, 102, 106-108, 111, 113, 125, 136, 139, 146-148, 152, 165-168, 173, 175-177, 183-185, 198, 334-335, 339, 341, 452
Pont Fixé 289-290, 301
Pont-du-Hem 282, 457
Poperinghe vii-viii, xviii, 32, 34, 141, 172, 477-478, 481, 497-498, 500, 504-506, 510, 513, 516, 518-520, 528, 531-532, 537, 540, 555, 566, 584
Potijze 498-499, 506-507, 520-521, 523, 526-528, 533, 537-538, 549
Potijze Wood 521, 523, 533
Pozières 209, 566

Reims 69, 218
Renfrewshire 397, 501
Reutel 102, 106-108, 146, 152, 154, 183-184, 188, 208
Reutelbeck 168, 172, 174-176
Rhine River 194, 209, 349, 442

Richebourg-L'Avoué 343, 363
Richebourg-St Vaast v, 343, 359, 363, 367-369, 371, 374, 379, 382, 387
Riez Bailleul 462-463, 474-475
Rivière des Layes 231, 257, 266, 326, 329, 458
Rouen 41-42, 89, 95, 168, 319, 329, 333, 353, 356, 422-423, 500
Rouges Bancs iii, v, ix, 33, 222, 225, 231, 257, 269, 280-282, 325, 336-339, 341-343, 349, 357, 360, 376-377, 418, 432, 447, 483, 500
Roulers iv, 101, 193, 498, 521

Sailly vi, 225, 231-232, 243-245, 255, 258, 266, 273, 280-281, 342, 379-380, 391-393, 397, 413, 443, 450, 454-455
Sambre River 44-45, 47-49
Sanctuary Wood viii, 496, 543-544, 546-550, 552-554, 556
Sandhurst 22-23, 37-38, 66, 81, 123, 137, 171, 194, 229, 231, 234, 243, 261, 291, 301, 308, 316, 389, 452, 456, 458, 487
Saxony 121, 144, 188, 194-196, 210, 355
Scarborough 257, 271, 288, 453
Schneidemühl viii, xvii, 189-193, 198, 200-204, 209-210, 212, 215, 217-218, 220, 223
Silesia 190, 212-213, 215
Skye (Isle of) 313, 380
Soissons 54-55, 67-69, 72
Soltau 196, 198, 222
Southampton 39-40, 59, 66, 79, 85, 92-93, 95-96, 114, 154, 188, 234, 318
St Andrews xii, 137, 461, 487
St Eloi 496, 501, 506, 522, 529, 534, 542
St Jans-ter-Biezen 478, 497, 510
St Jean 146, 500-502
St Julien 141, 500
St Nazaire 59, 169, 180, 353
St Omer vi, 285, 288, 356, 373, 378, 397, 401, 403-406, 409, 421, 433, 437, 440-442, 471, 488, 562
St Pol 517, 567
St Quentin xvi, 28, 51-53
Stirling viii, xvii, 76, 171, 227, 355, 435, 442, 483, 488, 540, 579, 581, 590
Stirlingshire 74, 292, 318, 333, 357, 365, 452
Stranraer 385, 422
Switzerland 140, 184, 190, 194, 196-197, 204, 219-222, 224, 307, 349, 592

Thames River 91, 180, 267, 551
Thielt iv, 100-101
Trones Wood 562
Troyon 72, 74, 76, 85

Veldhoek 106-107, 123, 126, 128-129, 146-147, 151, 153-154, 157, 161, 167-172, 174, 176, 221, 361
Veldhoek Château 168-172, 174, 176
Vendresse 70, 72-78, 80, 85-86, 88, 90, 166, 179, 314, 363, 550
Verbeck Farm 168, 175-177
Verdun xv, 54, 477-479, 496, 537, 560-561
Vermelles vi-vii, 294, 361, 379, 385, 388, 391-393, 395, 397-398, 400, 405, 411-413, 420, 425, 427-428, 431, 434-435, 443, 445, 447-448, 450-452, 454
Verquigneul 388, 419, 445
Verquin 384, 388, 393-394, 396, 407
Vimy Ridge 391, 409
Violaines 383-384
Vlamertinghe 181, 504, 506-507, 513, 516, 520, 531-532, 537, 543, 554-555, 564

Wellington Barracks 20, 28, 100, 150, 209, 292, 312, 317, 341, 349, 360, 381, 427, 438, 554, 562
West Lothian 149, 313, 343, 399, 452-453, 484, 537
Wester Ross 89, 169
Western Isles 252, 549
Westoutre 181, 284
Westphalia 184, 189, 219
Wettringen 205, 208
Wieltje 500-503, 511, 532-533

Wigtownshire 25, 92, 194, 361, 371, 383, 426, 515, 522
Wimereux 255, 265, 380
Winchester 94, 120, 179, 181, 230, 421, 457, 467
Wizernes 403, 409, 440-441, 443
Wormhout 493-494, 510, 541

York 38, 71, 99, 120, 311, 422, 428, 453
Ypres iii, viii-ix, xi, xv-xviii, 21, 26-28, 31-32, 34-35, 39-40, 66, 90-91, 100-102, 106, 110, 114, 125, 128-130, 132, 134, 136-139, 144, 146-149, 151, 155, 158-160, 169, 171, 173, 181, 183, 196, 198, 205, 208, 222-223, 225-226, 229, 233, 235, 237, 241-242, 249-254, 270-272, 274, 276, 282, 284-286, 288-289, 291, 294, 298, 300, 310, 313-315, 333-336, 338-343, 346, 349, 351-354, 357, 360-361, 366, 370-373, 377, 391, 395, 397, 406, 415, 420-421, 426, 432, 440, 445-447, 453, 458-459, 462, 472, 474, 476-478, 480, 491-492, 495-502, 504, 506, 510-511, 515-516, 518-522, 524-525, 527-528, 531-537, 539-540, 543-544, 547-548, 551, 553, 557-558, 568, 584-588, 591
Ypres-Yser Canal 100, 141, 496, 520, 559

Zandvoorde iv, 102-107, 112, 123, 125-129
Zeebrugge iv, xiv, 95-96, 222, 253, 333, 336-338, 357, 440, 446-447, 500-501, 512, 515, 558
Zillebeke 101, 128-130, 146-147, 165, 172, 496, 506, 543-544, 551-553
Zonnebeke xv, 102, 106-107, 141, 144, 184, 499, 506

INDEX OF BRITISH MILITARY UNITS & FORMATIONS

Armies
First Army 454, 493
Fourth Army 54, 553, 557, 562

Corps
II Corps 43, 45-46, 48, 52, 171
III Corps 57, 89, 134, 333, 499
XI 409-410, 412, 456, 487, 499, 527
XIV Corps ix, 464, 495-496, 501
XV Corps 69, 72, 166
Cavalry Corps 48, 55, 72, 442
Indian Corps 171, 226, 257, 280, 291, 316, 322, 343, 347, 456, 459

Divisions
Guards Division 397
1st Division 37, 44, 46, 50-51, 61, 69, 72-74, 86, 89-90, 128-129, 136, 141, 144, 152, 154, 168, 170, 172-173, 181, 285-286, 288-289, 296, 302, 304, 315-316, 320, 343, 366, 372, 375, 378, 380, 411-412, 414, 417, 470, 592
2nd Division 37, 52, 82, 108, 111, 136, 141, 154, 173, 175-176, 292, 313, 343-345, 347, 364, 401, 411, 425, 447
3rd Cavalry Division 97, 100-101, 136, 413
3rd Division 41, 134, 170, 172, 174, 522
4th Division 56-57, 173, 516-517, 566
6th Division 81, 132, 139, 481, 496-499, 501, 507, 511, 519, 530, 532, 587
7th Division xv, 93, 95-98, 100, 106, 111, 123, 125-126, 128-129, 132, 136, 139, 141, 144, 146-147, 162-163, 165, 168, 172, 225, 232, 258, 265, 322, 324, 333, 336, 339, 342-343, 361, 383, 401, 411-412, 584
8th Division 226, 258, 263, 266-268, 282, 322, 324, 325-326, 329, 332, 336, 340, 342, 364, 372, 376
9th (Scottish) Division 374, 411
12th (Eastern) Division 265, 431, 434, 455, 491
14th (Light) Division 420, 496-497
15th (Scottish) Division 411-412
19th (Western) Division 336, 457
20th (Light) Division 496, 500-501, 511, 531
21st Division 412, 418, 423, 442-443, 502
38th (Welsh) Division 462, 488
46th (North Midland) Division xv, 431, 433, 450-451, 562
47th (2nd London) Division 381, 411, 443
51st (Highland) Division 178, 383
Meerut Division 322, 324, 340, 363

Brigades
1st (Guards) Brigade 37, 40, 61, 65, 69, 72, 90, 122-123, 125, 138, 141, 146-147, 152-153, 156, 167, 173, 176, 242, 285, 289, 296, 301, 316, 357, 363, 374-375, 384, 506, 592
1st Guards Brigade 401, 413-414, 417, 425, 431, 449, 499-500, 511
2nd Cavalry Brigade 66, 442
2nd Guards Brigade viii, 253, 396, 400-401, 403, 409-410, 413-414, 416, 425, 438, 441, 443-445, 449, 451, 473, 484, 521, 540, 543, 592
2nd Brigade 49, 67, 72-73, 129-130, 143, 162, 168, 294, 296, 302, 315, 367-368, 374, 377, 384, 443
3rd Cavalry Brigade 57, 105, 381
3rd Guards Brigade 161, 263, 340-341, 401, 413, 420, 425, 440-441, 443-445, 447, 449, 451, 455, 497, 507, 511, 520-521, 558, 567, 592
3rd Brigade 48, 59, 69, 73, 77, 126, 128-129, 141, 143, 153, 157, 159-160, 162, 164-165, 289, 291, 293, 314, 383
4th (Guards) Brigade 43, 48, 53, 55-56, 111, 129, 146-148, 166, 177, 287, 316, 348, 378, 394, 401
5th Cavalry Brigade 105, 404
5th Brigade 82, 108, 111, 165, 289, 435, 447-448
19th Brigade 139, 225, 257
20th Brigade xv, 93, 97, 102, 104-105, 107, 111, 123, 125-126, 128-129, 132, 134, 139, 146, 151, 153, 157, 225, 235, 239, 245, 258, 265, 273, 283, 288, 322, 325-326, 332, 336, 340, 343, 347, 361-362, 589, 592
21st Brigade 98, 102, 106-107, 111-112, 123, 128-129, 147, 324-326, 330, 332, 348, 383-384
22nd Brigade 98, 102, 104, 106-108, 112-113, 126, 128-129, 141, 146, 245, 281, 342-345, 347
61st Brigade 501-502

Index   605

Regiments & Corps
Bedfordshire Regiment 102, 139, 151, 592
Black Watch xvii, 49-51, 56, 58, 63-65, 71, 73-74, 80-81, 90, 94, 122, 131, 142-143, 151-154, 156-157, 168, 170-171, 173, 175-176, 181, 293-295, 301-302, 311, 316, 320, 366, 368, 371, 374-378, 388, 400-401, 436, 590
Border Regiment 19, 93, 101, 103-106, 110-111, 116-119, 122-123, 125-126, 128-131, 134, 139, 186, 212, 225, 233, 236, 239-242, 245-247, 254-255, 257-259, 261, 265, 274, 282, 314, 325, 329-332, 344-347, 357, 359-361, 484, 589-590, 592
Cameronians (Scottish Rifles) 195, 204
Duke of Wellington's Regiment 171, 174, 176
Gloucestershire Regiment xv, 127, 141-142, 145-146, 153, 157-158, 161, 166, 176, 211, 213, 336, 397, 399, 474
Gordon Highlanders 94, 96-97, 100-106, 110-112, 123, 125-130, 133-136, 235-236, 240
Hampshire Regiment 216, 566, 581
Irish Guards vii, 84, 177, 206, 287, 368, 378, 394, 401, 403-405, 413-418, 424, 426, 430, 435, 444, 455, 476, 480, 484, 542, 559, 563-564, 574-575, 578-579, 582-583
London Rifle Brigade 208, 429, 571
London Scottish xvii, 71, 209, 285, 292-295, 301, 303, 311, 320, 349, 366, 369, 371, 432, 436, 506, 569, 578, 582, 587
Queen's Own Cameron Highlanders 63-65, 73-75, 77, 83, 87-90, 141-146, 151-152, 154-156, 158, 161-162, 167-168, 170-178, 181, 286-287, 290-291, 294, 302-304, 311, 317, 364, 368, 375-376, 380-382, 384-385, 388, 401, 585
Royal Munster Fusiliers 37, 61, 293, 390, 587, 590, 592
Royal Fusiliers 84, 225, 354, 578
Royal Garrison Artillery 230, 391
Royal Marines 40, 98, 266
Royal Scots 120, 138, 347, 476, 521, 535
Royal Scots Greys 45
Royal Scots Fusiliers 107-108, 147, 328-329, 332, 362, 462, 584
Royal Welsh Fusiliers 107-108, 147, 328-329, 332, 462, 584

Sherwood Foresters 81, 159, 357
South Staffordshire Regiment 113, 117-119, 121-123, 148, 186, 347, 451
South Wales Borderers 153, 160-166, 383, 475
Rifle Brigade xv, 485, 513
Welsh Guards xvii, 22, 29, 273, 285, 368, 401, 440-441, 443-445, 447, 450-453, 483-484, 486, 488-489, 490, 499, 501-502, 506-507, 512, 514-515, 520, 533, 580
Wiltshire Regiment 107-109, 111
Worcestershire Regiment 108-109, 111, 133, 151, 165-166, 435, 447

RAMC 28, 41, 65, 83, 99, 123, 144, 154, 181, 242, 299, 320, 329, 441, 497, 505, 566, 590
RFC/RAF 38, 78, 87, 151, 289, 391, 527, 565
Royal Engineers 28, 58, 69, 83, 85, 130, 132, 162, 165, 167, 176, 232, 235, 239, 242, 249, 287, 294, 307, 311, 320, 335, 359, 368-369, 371, 397-398, 400-401, 428-429, 444-445, 455, 484, 500-501, 506, 510, 537, 539, 541, 554

Battalions & Miscellaneous Units
2nd Bedfordshire Regiment 102-103, 139, 147-148, 592
1st Black Watch 37, 61, 90, 122, 125, 397, 590, 592
1/4th Black Watch 340, 470, 569, 573
2nd Border Regiment 93, 139, 186, 225, 325, 569, 581, 592
48th (British Columbia) Battalion CEF 206, 575
6th Buffs 455, 491-492, 571
1st Cheshire Regiment 170, 195
1st Coldstream Guards v, 37, 43, 61, 118, 125-126, 190, 193, 200-201, 203-204, 209, 212, 215, 219, 224, 285, 305, 378, 393, 399, 401, 403-404, 431, 434-435, 437, 445, 454, 461, 466-467, 486, 502-503, 522, 533, 537, 540, 554-555, 569-570, 573-576, 578-579, 581-583, 591-592
2nd Coldstream Guards 500, 534, 556
3rd Coldstream Guards 43, 120, 166, 314, 316, 378, 382, 401, 430, 570
4th Coldstream Guards 401, 436, 447
4th Dragoon Guards 44, 66, 336
9th Essex Regiment 265, 435

1st Gloucestershire Regiment xv, 127, 141, 153, 211, 213, 397, 572
2nd Gordon Highlanders 93, 123, 139, 157, 245, 247, 258-260, 264, 325, 332, 336, 344-345, 347, 356, 358, 361, 571, 592
1/6th Gordon Highlanders 239-241, 245, 257-258, 260, 268, 273, 332, 336, 340, 347, 357, 580
1st Grenadier Guards 22, 93-94, 139, 151, 157, 163, 187, 193, 204, 220, 225, 270, 288, 325, 336, 355, 401, 434, 440-441, 443, 447, 451-452, 502, 572-574, 592
4th Grenadier Guards 401, 434, 440-441, 443-444, 447, 449-451, 485, 498-499, 513-514, 533
7th Guards Entrenching Battalion 27, 34
4th Guards Machine Gun Regiment 27, 253, 341
2nd Highland Light Infantry 447-448
20th Hussars 394, 397, 404, 532
1st Irish Guards 177, 206, 287, 378, 394, 401, 430, 579, 582
2nd Irish Guards vii, 401, 403-404, 413, 416, 424, 426, 444, 455, 480, 542, 559, 564, 574-575, 578, 583
2nd KRRC 72, 127, 162-163, 166, 217, 296, 311, 315, 368, 579
2nd Life Guards 84, 452
1/5th London Regiment 208, 571
1/8th London Regiment 443, 579
1/14th London Regiment 71, 569, 578, 582
1/28th London Regiment 93, 579
4th Middlesex 47, 100, 212
2nd Oxfordshire & Buckinghamshire Light Infantry iv, 111, 176, 335, 447

2nd Queen's Royal West Surrey Regiment 126, 245, 346
1st Rifle Brigade 516, 566
2nd Royal Munster Fusiliers 37, 61, 177, 293, 590, 592
2nd Royal Scots Fusiliers 107, 147, 328, 332
2nd Royal Sussex Regiment 67, 72-73, 297, 303, 311, 315
2nd Royal Warwickshire Regiment 108, 189, 245, 336, 346, 579
1st Royal Welsh Fusiliers 136, 205, 344, 361-362, 569-570, 583, 592
2nd Royal Welsh Fusiliers 225, 580
13th Royal Welsh Fusiliers 462, 485
1st Somerset Light Infantry 516, 566
2nd South Lancashire Regiment 189, 579
1st South Staffordshire Regiment 186, 347
1st South Wales Borderers 153, 162, 165, 383
1st Welsh Guards 22, 401, 440, 580
2nd Welsh Regiment 77, 87, 162, 181, 305, 316, 382, 574, 578, 580
2nd Wiltshire Regiment 183, 194, 199, 452
2nd Worcestershire Regiment 82, 108, 139, 151, 165, 435, 447, 592
2nd Yorkshire Regiment 102, 131, 139, 147, 153, 592

16th Battery RFA 173, 175, 571, 580
26th Brigade RFA 55, 61, 65, 146-147, 592
41st Brigade RFA 173, 178
55th Field Company RE 235, 401
2nd Guards Brigade Machine Gun Company viii, 253, 396, 473, 540
173rd Tunnelling Company 335, 399

GENERAL & MISCELLANEOUS TERMS

Absence without leave 93, 270
Aircraft 86, 133, 151, 302, 363, 409, 431, 501, 523-524, 527, 532-534, 554
Ambulances 59, 70-71, 77-78, 89, 115, 127, 142, 148, 154, 159-162, 178, 244, 253-255, 266, 299, 328-329, 353-354, 357, 375, 421, 432, 441, 446-447, 454, 457, 461, 477, 489, 529, 549
Anti-aircraft weapons 501, 523-524, 527, 533-534

Artillery xv, 33, 44-45, 49-50, 52, 55, 63-64, 67, 70, 73-75, 82, 85-86, 90, 98, 100, 103, 106-107, 109, 112, 117-118, 126, 133-134, 143-145, 147, 151-152, 154, 156-158, 169-170, 172-173, 175-176, 229-230, 239, 268, 271, 276, 278-280, 290, 302-303, 307, 309, 322-325, 327-328, 330-332, 337, 343, 349, 363, 375-377, 379-380, 385, 391, 408-411, 414, 428, 430, 433, 438, 442-444, 449, 460, 463, 465, 469, 472, 475, 486, 488,

492, 502, 514, 520, 525, 528, 533, 558, 565, 589

Bagpipes 280, 406
Balloons 384, 511, 565
Band 87, 143, 167, 216, 225, 237, 265, 284, 361, 393, 396, 406, 437, 457, 466, 470, 474, 484, 510, 519, 541, 554, 564-565
Bangalore torpedo 475, 489, 490
Barbed wire 28, 60, 84-85, 87, 166-167, 174, 191, 233, 238, 240, 262-264, 266, 269, 273, 279, 306, 310, 320, 326, 329, 332, 397, 413, 416, 434, 437, 456, 465, 475, 535
Barracks 20, 28, 37, 39, 91, 93, 100, 126, 131, 134, 147, 150, 188, 207, 209, 220, 241, 292, 312, 315, 317, 341, 349, 360, 381, 421, 427, 438, 513, 537, 551, 554, 562
Bayonets 53, 83, 106, 108, 115, 149, 167, 173, 177, 212, 248, 250, 297, 327, 331, 335, 345, 352, 356, 365, 383, 404, 415, 423, 453, 461, 492, 497, 510, 534, 540, 546
Billets v-vii, 42-44, 47, 49, 52, 56-57, 67-68, 94, 96-97, 100-101, 127, 134-135, 137, 141, 226, 229, 232, 237-238, 240, 242, 245, 249, 255, 257-258, 262, 264, 266-267, 270, 273-274, 279-282, 284-287, 289, 293-295, 305-306, 315-317, 319-320, 335, 337, 342-343, 354-355, 358-359, 363-365, 367, 370, 372, 374, 377-378, 380, 382, 384, 393, 409-410, 419, 431, 436-437, 442, 445, 449-450, 457-458, 460-463, 466, 468-469, 474, 476-478, 482-484, 488, 491, 493-494, 498, 500, 510-511, 513, 516-517, 519, 521, 524-525, 527, 537, 539, 542, 552, 566-567
Boer War xi, 23, 25, 38, 50, 65, 74, 76-77, 80, 84, 92-93, 107, 109, 111, 113-114, 120, 137, 149, 155, 158-159, 161, 178, 180, 186, 188, 194, 202, 220, 230-231, 252, 258, 285, 287, 292, 298-299, 301, 312-314, 333, 335-336, 350-352, 374, 382, 389, 397, 401, 422, 441, 470, 475, 488, 535, 549-551, 566
Boots 31, 43, 68, 86, 88, 100, 102, 131, 134-135, 168, 190, 196, 199, 201, 205, 209, 211-212, 215, 228-229, 231, 236-238, 241-242, 257, 283-284, 288, 291, 293, 299, 351-352, 368, 386, 404, 453, 460, 463, 467, 476, 486, 491, 508, 520, 555
Breastworks v-vii, 268, 271, 282, 318-320, 325, 327, 336, 339-340, 343-344, 356, 363, 365, 367-369, 373, 375-377, 381, 383, 456-459, 461, 463, 472, 478, 482-485, 490, 497
Bronchitis 197, 222, 236, 288, 300, 395

Canadians 66, 280, 340, 348, 358, 505, 521, 523, 534-535, 542-544, 546-547, 551-554
Casualty clearing stations 30, 70, 405, 415, 423, 446, 463, 489, 516, 530, 536, 538, 549-550
Cavalry 20, 40, 44-45, 47-52, 55-58, 60, 62-64, 66, 68-70, 72, 97-98, 100-101, 103, 105-106, 128-130, 136, 141, 155, 185, 215, 225, 350, 381, 404, 410, 413-414, 421, 427, 442, 445, 455-456, 513, 551, 554, 563
Church of England 71, 266, 286, 335, 359, 373, 440, 487-488, 529, 541, 588
Church of Scotland 286, 359, 462, 487-488, 507, 532
Church parade 229-230, 335, 384, 470, 474
Civilians xiv, 23, 187, 194, 196-198, 206, 212-215, 218, 287, 303, 318-319, 393, 411, 537
Commonwealth War Graves Commission xvii, 32, 35, 592
Communication trenches 28, 85, 112, 168, 173, 231, 241, 251, 257, 267-268, 278, 296, 301, 304, 307, 309, 346, 367, 373, 378, 388, 428, 431, 433-434, 445, 450-451, 458, 461, 475, 490, 497, 507, 516-517, 524-525, 546, 552, 562
Conscription xiv, 26, 136, 231, 237, 354, 438, 450
Corps of Drums 359, 361, 507
Court martials 30, 92, 137, 178, 210, 267, 270, 274, 302, 311, 316, 336, 338-339, 352, 360, 362, 396, 441, 468-471, 473-474, 488, 494, 532, 592

Desertion 92, 188, 203, 336, 338-339, 554
Discipline x, 22, 29, 38, 52, 183, 199-200, 204, 220, 232, 241, 243, 274, 284, 304, 338, 340, 359, 450, 462, 482, 505, 553
Dressing Stations 31, 70-71, 78-80, 85-86, 142, 159, 161, 168, 177-179, 197, 244, 253, 293-294, 328, 349, 353, 370, 417, 451, 516, 549, 551
Drill viii, x, 22, 28-29, 80, 136, 139, 178, 181, 204, 221, 273-274, 284, 335, 352, 354-355, 359, 361, 367, 403-405, 437, 441, 454, 478,

482, 488, 494, 505, 510, 519, 537, 554, 556, 564, 572, 574-576

Football 184, 195, 197, 199, 203, 239, 241, 265, 276, 280-281, 373, 384, 387-388, 393, 404, 437, 470-472, 474, 480, 540-541, 555, 564

Gangrene 31, 149, 231, 255, 455
Gas 27, 30, 39, 148, 180, 187, 219, 231, 340-341, 373, 382, 396, 409, 411, 413, 426, 429, 431, 433, 443-444, 450-451, 458, 468, 472, 482, 486-487, 490, 497, 507, 516, 519, 524, 527, 532, 535, 538, 546-547, 559
Gonorrhea 24, 142, 423, 489, 562
Grenades 86, 88, 232, 236, 239, 246, 259, 273, 286, 288, 308, 311, 325, 341, 345, 359, 368, 371, 383-384, 391, 415, 428, 434-435, 448-449, 451-453, 455, 459, 475, 479, 491, 494, 551, 559, 584

Jaundice 349, 356, 483

Machine guns viii, 22, 27, 30, 43, 52, 70, 74, 78-79, 106, 112, 115, 117, 119, 122, 136, 143, 145, 148, 151, 153, 161, 163-164, 169-171, 175, 185-186, 233, 243, 246-247, 251, 253, 263, 274-278, 291, 294, 296-297, 307-309, 318, 320, 323, 330-332, 334, 340-341, 345-347, 359, 364-365, 373-374, 376, 380, 384, 388, 396, 403, 411, 413-416, 418, 420, 426, 428-429, 433-434, 447, 452, 454, 459-460, 463, 468, 473, 475, 482, 484-485, 489, 507-509, 527, 529, 533, 538, 540-541, 551, 558-559, 561
Military Police 338, 440-441, 469, 479
Mines 28, 110, 183, 197, 199, 204-205, 212, 218, 224, 307, 320, 342, 382, 408, 410, 412, 442, 446, 459, 491, 522
Myalgia 421, 425, 500, 509, 512

Pipers/pipes and drums vii, 21, 80, 87, 191, 265, 280-281, 313, 355, 361, 380, 394, 401, 427, 433, 485, 507, 510, 535, 540, 564-565

Pneumonia 89, 186, 219, 311, 432, 452
Prisoners of war iii, viii, 32, 49, 58, 65, 67, 71, 73, 77, 80, 87, 90, 102, 114-116, 119, 121, 123-124, 135, 139, 143-144, 148, 158, 162-166, 178-179, 183-184, 186, 189-190, 193-207, 209-224, 250, 261-262, 266-267, 310-311, 315, 324, 331, 335, 355-356, 364, 412-413, 419, 422, 511-512, 518, 557, 559, 569, 591-592

Raids 33, 214, 244, 486, 496, 499, 531, 558
Railways iv, ix, xiv, 19, 28-29, 42, 49, 70, 85-86, 90, 97-98, 105-106, 111, 128, 146, 163, 169, 189, 191-192, 206, 208, 212, 222, 253, 276, 289, 292, 294, 296-298, 303, 306-307, 311-312, 320, 326, 333, 358, 360, 377, 384-385, 390, 399, 413, 421, 427, 434-435, 446-447, 449, 453, 455, 474, 484, 487, 496, 498, 500, 503, 506-507, 516-517, 521-522, 532, 535, 538-539, 541
Red Cross 75, 81, 187-188, 193-195, 206, 210, 214, 254, 256
Redoubts 271, 359, 557
Refugees iv, xiv, 46-47, 54, 58, 97-98, 103, 141
Rheumatism 68, 81, 235, 253, 292, 334, 509, 523, 562
Rockets 87, 277, 279, 324, 485, 490, 542, 547

Shell Shock 30-31, 39, 170, 219, 343, 361, 432, 476, 480, 505, 525-526, 528, 558-559
Snipers 87, 98, 103, 113, 115, 226-229, 232, 234, 236, 241-243, 275, 279, 290, 292, 301, 338, 372-373, 431, 459, 463, 475, 478, 492, 508, 510, 528, 540, 560
Spanish Flu 32, 139, 183, 219, 223
Stretcher Bearers 21, 64, 70, 83, 121, 134, 154-156, 168, 170, 178, 194, 204, 248, 250-251, 286, 297, 328, 335, 353, 428, 444, 450, 522, 552

Tanks 44, 290, 324, 356, 438